T0215710

Lecture Notes in Computer Science 11954

Tom Gedeon · Kok Wai Wong ·
Minho Lee (Eds.)

Neural
Information Processing

26th International Conference, ICONIP 2019
Sydney, NSW, Australia, December 12–15, 2019
Proceedings, Part II

 Springer

Editors
Tom Gedeon 🄳
Australian National University
Canberra, ACT, Australia

Kok Wai Wong 🄳
Murdoch University
Murdoch, WA, Australia

Minho Lee 🄳
Kyungpook National University
Daegu, Korea (Republic of)

ISSN 0302-9743   ISSN 1611-3349   (electronic)
Lecture Notes in Computer Science
ISBN 978-3-030-36710-7   ISBN 978-3-030-36711-4   (eBook)
https://doi.org/10.1007/978-3-030-36711-4

LNCS Sublibrary: SL1 – Theoretical Computer Science and General Issues

This Springer imprint is published by the registered company Springer Nature Switzerland AG
The registered company address is: Gewerbestrasse 11, 6330 Cham, Switzerland

Preface

Welcome to the proceedings of the 26th International Conference on Neural Information Processing of the Asia-Pacific Neural Network Society (APNNS 2019), held in Sydney during December 12–15, 2019.

The mission of the Asia-Pacific Neural Network Society is to promote active interactions among researchers, scientists, and industry professionals who are working in Neural Networks and related fields in the Asia-Pacific region. APNNS had Governing Board Members from 13 countries/regions – Australia, China, Hong Kong, India, Japan, Malaysia, New Zealand, Singapore, South Korea, Qatar, Taiwan, Thailand, and Turkey. The society's flagship annual conference is the International Conference of Neural Information Processing (ICONIP).

The three-volume set of LNCS 11953–11955 includes 177 papers from 645 submission, and represents an acceptance rate of 27.4%, reflecting the increasingly high quality of research in Neural Networks and related areas in the Asia-Pacific.

The conference had three main themes, "Theory and Algorithms," "Computational and Cognitive Neurosciences," and "Human Centred Computing and Applications." The three volumes are organized in topical sections which were also the names of the 20-minute presentation sessions at the conference. The topics were Adversarial Networks and Learning; Convolutional Neural Networks; Deep Neural Networks; Feature Learning and Representation; Human Centred Computing; Hybrid Models; Artificial Intelligence and Cybersecurity; Image Processing by Neural Techniques; Learning from Incomplete Data; Model Compression and Optimisation; Neural Learning Models; Neural Network Applications; Social Network Computing; Semantic and Graph Based Approaches; Spiking Neuron and Related Models; Text Computing Using Neural Techniques; Time-Series and Related Models; and Unsupervised Neural Models.

Thanks very much in particular to the reviewers who devoted their time to our rigorous peer-review process. Their insightful reviews and timely feedback ensured the high quality of the papers accepted for publication. Finally, thank you to all the authors of papers, presenters, and participants at the conference. Your support and engagement made it all worthwhile.

October 2019

Tom Gedeon
Kok Wai Wong
Minho Lee

Organization

Program Chairs

Tom Gedeon   The Australian National University, Australia
Kok Wai Wong   Murdoch University, Australia
Minho Lee   Kyungpook National University, South Korea

Program Committee

Hussein Abbass	UNSW Canberra, Australia
Hosni Adil Imad Eddine	Beijing Institute of Technology, China
Shotaro Akaho	AIST, Japan
Alaa Al-Kaysi	University of Technology, Iraq
Bradley Alexander	The University of Adelaide, Australia
Georgios Alexandridis	National Technical University of Athens, Greece
Usman Ali	Shanghai Jiao Tong University, China
Ahmad Ali	Shanghai Jiao Tong University, China
Abdulrahman Altahhan	Leeds Beckett University, UK
Muhamad Erza Aminanto	NICT, Japan
Ali Anaissi	The University of Sydney, Australia
Khairul Anam	University of Jember, Indonesia
Emel Arslan	Istanbul University, Turkey
Sunil Aryal	Deakin University, Australia
Arnulfo Azcarraga	De La Salle University, Philippines
Donglin Bai	Shanghai Jiao Tong University, China
Hongliang Bai	Beijing Faceall Technology Co., Ltd., China
Mehala Balamurali	The University of Sydney, Australia
Mohamad Hardyman Barawi	Universiti Malaysia Sarawak, Malaysia
Younès Bennani	Université Paris 13 and Université Sorbonne-Paris-Cité, France
Christoph Bergmeir	Monash University, Australia
Gui-Bin Bian	Chinese Academy of Sciences, China
Larbi Boubchir	University of Paris 8, France
Amel Bouzeghoub	Télécom SudParis, France
Congbo Cai	Xiamen University, China
Jian Cao	Shanghai Jiaotong University, China
Xiaocong Chen	University of New South Wales, Australia
Junsha Chen	UCAS, China
Junjie Chen	Inner Mongolia University, China
Qingcai Chen	Harbin Institute of Technology, Shenzhen, China

Gang Chen	Victoria University of Wellington, New Zealand
Junya Chen	Fudan University, USA
Dong Chen	Wuhan University, China
Weiyang Chen	Qilu University of Technology, China
Jianhui Chen	Institute of Neuroscience, Chinese Academy of Science, China
Girija Chetty	University of Canberra, Australia
Sung-Bae Cho	Yonsei University, South Korea
Chaikesh Chouragade	Indian Institute of Science, India
Tan Chuanqi	Tsinghua University, China
Yuk Chung	The University of Sydney, Australia
Younjin Chung	The Australian National University, Australia
Tao Dai	Tsinghua University, China
Yong Dai	Hunan University, China
Popescu Dan	UPB, Romania
V. Susheela Devi	Indian Institute of Science, India
Bettebghor Dimitri	Expleo Group, France
Hai Dong	RMIT University, Australia
Anan Du	University of Technology Sydney, Australia
Piotr Duda	Czestochowa University of Technology, Poland
Pratik Dutta	IIT Patna, India
Asif Ekbal	IIT Patna, India
Mounim El Yacoubi	Télécom SudParis, France
Haytham Elghazel	LIRIS Lab, France
Zhijie Fang	Chinese Academy of Sciences, China
Yuchun Fang	Shanghai University, China
Yong Feng	Chongqing University, China
Raul Fernandez Rojas	UNSW Canberra, Australia
Junjie Fu	Southeast University, China
Bogdan Gabrys	University of Technology Sydney, Australia
Junbin Gao	The University of Sydney, Australia
Guangwei Gao	Nanjing University of Posts and Telecommunications, China
Tom Gedeon	The Australian National University, Australia
Ashish Ghosh	Indian Statistical Institute, India
Heitor Murilo Gomes	The University of Waikato, New Zealand
Iqbal Gondal	Federation University, Australia
Yuri Gordienko	National Technical University of Ukraine, Ukraine
Raju Gottumukkala	University of Louisiana at Lafayette, USA
Jianping Gou	Jiangsu University, China
Xiaodong Gu	Fudan University, China
Joachim Gudmundsson	The University of Sydney, Australia
Xian Guo	Nankai University, China
Jun Guo	East China Normal University, China
Katsuyuki Hagiwara	Mie University, Japan
Sangchul Hahn	Handong Global University, South Korea

Ali Haidar	University of New South Wales, Australia
Rim Haidar	The University of Sydney, Australia
Fayçal Hamdi	CEDRIC-CNAM Paris, France
Maissa Hamouda	SETIT, Tunisia
Jiqing Han	Harbin Institute of Technology, China
Chansu Han	National Institute of Information and Communications Technology, Japan
Tao Han	Hubei Normal University, China
Jean Benoit Heroux	IBM Research - Tokyo, Japan
Hansika Hewamalage	Monash University, Australia
Md. Zakir Hossain	Murdoch University, Australia
Zexi Hu	The University of Sydney, Australia
Shaohan Hu	Tsinghua University, China
Xiyuan Hu	Chinese Academy of Sciences, China
Gang Hu	Ant Financial Services Group, China
Xinyi Hu	State Key Laboratory of Mathematical Engineering and Advanced Computing, China
Han Hu	Tsinghua University, China
Yue Huang	Xiamen University, China
Shudong Huang	University of Electronic Science and Technology of China, China
Kaizhu Huang	Xi'an Jiaotong-Liverpool University, China
Yanhong Huang	East China Normal University, China
Xiaolin Huang	Shanghai Jiao Tong University, China
Chaoran Huang	University of New South Wales, Australia
Shin-Ying Huang	Institute for Information Industry, Taiwan
Mohamed Ibm Khedher	IRT SystemX, France
Loretta Ichim	UPB, Romania
David Andrei Iclanzan	Sapientia University, Romania
Keiichiro Inagaki	Chubu University, Japan
Radu Ionescu	University of Bucharest, Romania
Masatoshi Ishii	IBM Research - Tokyo, Japan
Masumi Ishikawa	Kyushu Institute of Technology, Japan
Megumi Ito	IBM Research - Tokyo, Japan
Yi Ji	Soochow University, China
Sun Jinguang	Liaoning Technical University, China
Francois Jacquenet	University of Lyon, France
Seyed Mohammad Jafar Jalali	Deakin University, Australia
Zohaib Muhammad Jan	Central Queensland University, Australia
Yasir Jan	Murdoch University, Australia
Norbert Jankowski	Nicolaus Copernicus University, Poland
Sungmoon Jeong	Kyungpook National University, South Korea
Xiaoyan Jiang	Shanghai University of Engineering Science, China
Fei Jiang	Shanghai Jiao Tong University, China
Houda Jmila	Télécom SudParis, France

Mingyong Li	Donghua University, China
Chengcheng Li	Tianjin University, China
Xia Liang	University of Science and Technology, China
Alan Wee-Chung Liew	Griffith University, Australia
Chin-Teng Lin	UTS, Australia
Zheng Lin	Chinese Academy of Sciences, China
Yang Lin	The University of Sydney, Australia
Wei Liu	University of Technology Sydney, Australia
Jiayang Liu	Tsinghua University, China
Yunlong Liu	Xiamen University, China
Yi Liu	Zhejiang University of Technology, China
Ye Liu	Nanjing University of Posts and Telecommunications, China
Zhilei Liu	Tianjin University, China
Zheng Liu	Nanjing University of Posts and Telecommunications, China
Cheng Liu	City University of Hong Kong, Hong Kong, China
Linfeng Liu	Nanjing University of Posts and Telecommunications, China
Baoping Liu	IIE, China
Guiping Liu	Hetao College, China
Huan Liu	Xi'an Jiaotong University, China
Gongshen Liu	Shanghai Jiao Tong University, China
Zhi-Yong Liu	Institute of Automation, Chinese Academy of Science, China
Fan Liu	Beijing Ant Financial Services Information Service Co., Ltd., China
Zhi-Wei Liu	Huazhong University of Science and Technology, China
Chu Kiong Loo	University of Malaya, Malaysia
Xuequan Lu	Deakin University, Australia
Huimin Lu	Kyushu Institute of Technology, Japan
Biao Lu	Nankai University, China
Qun Lu	Yancheng Institute of Technology, China
Bao-Liang Lu	Shanghai Jiao Tong University, China
Shen Lu	The University of Sydney, Australia
Junyu Lu	University of Electronic Science and Technology of China, China
Zhengding Luo	Peking University, China
Yun Luo	Shanghai Jiao Tong University, China
Xiaoqing Lyu	Peking University, China
Kavitha MS	Hiroshima University, Japan
Wanli Ma	University of Canberra, Australia
Jinwen Ma	Peking University, China
Supriyo Mandal	Indian Institute of Technology Patna, India
Sukanya Manna	Santa Clara University, USA
Basarab Matei	University of Paris 13, France

Jimson Mathew	IIT Patna, India
Toshihiko Matsuka	Chiba University, Japan
Timothy McIntosh	La Trobe University, Australia
Philip Mehrgardt	The University of Sydney, Australia
Jingjie Mo	Chinese Academy of Sciences, China
Seyed Sahand Mohammadi Ziabari	Vrije Universiteit Amsterdam, The Netherlands
Rafiq Mohammed	Murdoch University, Australia
Bonaventure Molokwu	University of Windsor, Canada
Maram Monshi	The University of Sydney, Australia
Ajit Narayanan	Auckland University of Technology, New Zealand
Mehdi Neshat	The University of Adelaide, Australia
Aneta Neumann	The University of Adelaide, Australia
Frank Neumann	The University of Adelaide, Australia
Dang Nguyen	University of Canberra, Australia
Thanh Nguyen	Robert Gordon University, UK
Tien Dung Nguyen	University of Technology Sydney, Australia
Thi Thu Thuy Nguyen	Griffith University, Australia
Boda Ning	RMIT University, Australia
Roger Nkambou	UQAM, Canada
Akiyo Nomura	IBM Research - Tokyo, Japan
Anupiya Nugaliyadde	Murdoch University, Australia
Atsuya Okazaki	IBM Research, Japan
Jonathan Oliver	Trend Micro, Australia
Toshiaki Omori	Kobe University, Japan
Takashi Omori	Tamagawa University, Japan
Shih Yin Ooi	Multimedia University, Malaysia
Seiichi Ozawa	Kobe University, Japan
Huan Pan	Ningxia University, China
Paul Pang	Unitec Institute of Technology, New Zealand
Shuchao Pang	Macquarie University, Australia
Kitsuchart Pasupa	King Mongkut's Institute of Technology Ladkrabang, Thailand
Jagdish Patra	Swinburne University of Technology, Australia
Cuong Pham	Griffith University, Australia
Mukesh Prasad	University of Technology Sydney, Australia
Yu Qiao	Shanghai Jiao Tong University
Feno Heriniaina Rabevohitra	Chongqing University, China
Sutharshan Rajasegarar	Deakin University, Australia
Md Mashud Rana	CSIRO, Australia
Md Mamunur Rashid	Central Queensland University, Australia
Pengju Ren	Xi'an Jiaotong University, China
Rim Romdhane	Devoteam, France
Yi Rong	Wuhan University of Technology, China
Leszek Rutkowski	Częstochowa University of Technology, Poland

Fariza Sabrina	Central Queensland University, Australia
Naveen Saini	Indian Institute of Technology Patna, India
Toshimichi Saito	Hosei University, Japan
Michel Salomon	Université Bourgogne-Franche-Comté, France
Toshikazu Samura	Yamaguchi University, Japan
Naoyuki Sato	Future University Hakodate, Japan
Ravindra Savangouder	Swinburne University of Technology, Australia
Rafal Scherer	Częstochowa University of Technology, Poland
Erich Schikuta	University of Vienna, Austria
Fatima Seeme	Monash University, Australia
Feng Sha	The University of Sydney, Australia
Jie Shao	University of Electronic Science and Technology, China
Qi She	Intel Labs China, China
Michael Sheng	Macquarie University, Australia
Jinhua Sheng	Hangzhou Dianzi University, China
Iksoo Shin	Korea Institute of Science and Technology Information, South Korea
Mohd Fairuz Shiratuddin	Murdoch University, Australia
Hayaru Shouno	University of Electro-Communications, Japan
Sarah Ali Siddiqui	Macquarie University, Australia
Katherine Silversides	The University of Sydney, Australia
Jiri Sima	Czech Academy of Sciences, Czech Republic
Chiranjibi Sitaula	Deakin University, Australia
Marek Śmieja	Jagiellonian University, Poland
Ferdous Sohel	Murdoch University, Australia
Aneesh Srivallabh Chivukula	University of Technology Sydney, Australia
Xiangdong Su	Inner Mongolia University, China
Jérémie Sublime	ISEP, France
Liang Sun	University of Science and Technology Beijing, China
Laszlo Szilagyi	Óbuda University, Hungary
Takeshi Takahashi	National Institute of Information and Communications Technology, Japan
Hakaru Tamukoh	Kyushu Institute of Technology, Japan
Leonard Tan	University of Southern Queensland, Australia
Gouhei Tanaka	The University of Tokyo, Japan
Maolin Tang	Queensland University of Technology, Australia
Selvarajah Thuseethan	Deakin University, Australia
Dat Tran	University of Canberra, Australia
Oanh Tran	Vietnam National University, Vietnam
Enmei Tu	Shanghai Jiao Tong University, China
Hiroaki Uchida	Hosei University, Japan
Shinsuke Uda	Kyushu University, Japan
Brijesh Verma	Central Queensland University, Australia
Chaokun Wang	Tsinghua University, China

Xiaolian Wang	University of Chinese Academy of Sciences, China
Zeyuan Wang	The University of Sydney, Australia
Dong Wang	Hunan University, China
Qiufeng Wang	Xi'an Jiaotong-Liverpool University, China
Chen Wang	Institute of Automation, Chinese Academy of Sciences, China
Jue Wang	BIT, China
Xiaokang Wang	Beihang University, China
Zhenhua Wang	Zhejiang University of Technology, China
Zexian Wang	Shanghai Jiao Tong University, China
Lijie Wang	University of Macau, Macau, China
Ding Wang	Chinese Academy of Sciences, China
Peijun Wang	Anhui Normal University, China
Yaqing Wang	HKUST, China
Zheng Wang	Southwest University, China
Shuo Wang	Monash University and CSIRO, Australia
Shi-Lin Wang	Shanghai Jiaotong University, China
Yu-Kai Wang	University of Technology Sydney, Australia
Weiqun Wang	Institute of Automation, Chinese Academy of Sciences, China
Yoshikazu Washizawa	University of Electro-Communications, Japan
Chihiro Watanabe	NTT Communication Science Laboratories, Japan
Michael Watts	Auckland Institute of Studies, New Zealand
Yanling Wei	University of Leuven, Belgium
Hongxi Wei	Inner Mongolia University, China
Kok-Wai Wong	Murdoch University, Australia
Marcin Woüniak	Silesian University of Technology, Poland
Dongrui Wu	Huazhong University of Science and Technology, China
Huijun Wu	University of New South Wales, Australia
Fei Wu	Nanjing University of Posts and Telecommunications, China
Wei Wu	Inner Mongolia University, China
Weibin Wu	Chinese University of Hong Kong, Hong Kong, China
Guoqiang Xiao	Shanghai Jiao Tong University, China
Shi Xiaohua	Shanghai Jiao Tong University, China
Zhenchang Xing	The Australian National University, Australia
Jianhua Xu	Nanjing Normal University, China
Huali Xu	Inner Mongolia University, China
Peng Xu	Jiangnan University, China
Guoxia Xu	Hohai University, China
Jiaming Xu	Institute of Automation, Chinese Academy of Sciences, China
Qing Xu	Tianjin University, China
Li Xuewei	Tianjin University, China
Toshiyuki Yamane	IBM, Japan
Haiqin Yang	Hang Seng University of Hong Kong, Hong Kong, China

Bo Yang	University of Electronic Science and Technology of China, China
Wei Yang	University of Science and Technology of China, China
Xi Yang	Xi'an Jiaotong-Liverpool University, China
Chun Yang	University of Science and Technology Beijing, China
Deyin Yao	Guangdong University of Technology, China
Yinghua Yao	Southern University of Science and Technology, China
Yuan Yao	Tsinghua University, China
Lina Yao	University of New South Wales, Australia
Wenbin Yao	Beijing Key Laboratory of Intelligent Telecommunications Software and Multimedia, China
Xu-Cheng Yin	University of Science and Technology Beijing, China
Xiaohan Yu	Griffith University, Australia
Yong Yuan	Chinese Academy of Science, China
Ye Yuan	Southwest University, China
Yun-Hao Yuan	Yangzhou University, China
Xiaodong Yue	Shanghai University, China
Seid Miad Zandavi	The University of Sydney, Australia
Daren Zha	Chinese Academy of Sciences, China
Yan Zhang	Tianjin University, China
Xiao Zhang	Huazhong University of Science and Technology, China
Yifan Zhang	CSIRO, Australia
Wei Zhang	The University of Adelaide, Australia
Lin Zhang	Beijing Institute of Technology, China
Yifei Zhang	University of Chinese Academy of Sciences, China
Huisheng Zhang	Dalian Maritime University, China
Gaoyan Zhang	Tianjin University, China
Liming Zhang	University of Macau, Macau, China
Xiang Zhang	University of New South Wales, Australia
Yuren Zhang	ByteDance Ltd., China
Jianhua Zhang	Zhejiang University of Technology, China
Dalin Zhang	University of New South Wales, Australia
Bo Zhao	Beijing Normal University, China
Jing Zhao	East China Normal University, China
Baojiang Zhong	Soochow University, China
Guoqiang Zhong	Ocean University, China
Caiming Zhong	Ningbo University, China
Jinghui Zhong	South China University of Technology, China
Mingyang Zhong	Central Queensland University, Australia
Xinyu Zhou	Jiangxi Normal University, China
Jie Zhou	Shenzhen University, China
Yuanping Zhu	Tianjin Normal University, China
Lei Zhu	Lingnan Normal University, China
Chao Zhu	University of Science and Technology Beijing, China

Xiaobin Zhu   University of Science and Technology Beijing, China
Dengya Zhu   Curtin University, Australia
Yuan Zong   Southeast University, China
Futai Zou   Shanghai Jiao Tong University, China

Contents – Part II

Image Processing by Neural Techniques

Learning from Incomplete Data

Model Compression and Optimisation

Neural Learning Models

Neural Network Applications

Image Processing by Neural Techniques

STNet: A Style Transformation Network for Deep Image Steganography

Zihan Wang[1,2,3], Neng Gao[1,3], Xin Wang[3(✉)], Ji Xiang[3], and Guanqun Liu[2,3]

[1] State Key Laboratory of Information Security,
Institute of Information Engineering, CAS, Beijing, China
[2] School of Cyber Security, University of Chinese Academy of Sciences,
Beijing, China
[3] Institute of Information Engineering, Chinese Academy of Sciences, Beijing, China
{wangzihan,gaoneng,wangxin,xiangji,liuguanqun}@iie.ac.cn

Abstract. Image steganography is the technique of hiding information within images in plain sight. With the rapid development of deep learning in the field of steganalysis, it becomes a tremendous challenge to design a secure steganographic algorithm. To this end, we propose a novel steganographic network based on style transfer, named STNet. This network accepts the content and style images as input to synthesize art image with content from the former and style from the latter and embeds the secret information in style features. It can effectively resist most steganalysis tools. Steganalysis can identify stego images from cover images, but they cannot distinguish our stego images from other art images. Meanwhile, our method produces stego images of arbitrary size with 0.06 bit per pixel, improving over other deep steganographic models which only can embed fixed-length secret. Experiment results demonstrate that our STNet can achieve great visual effect, security, and reliability.

Keywords: Steganography · Style transfer · Deep learning

1 Introduction

Steganography and cryptography are both techniques used in secret communication. However, they have different goals that cryptography makes the secret data unreadable, while steganography hides the presence of secret communications. Image steganographic algorithm is designed to hide information into a static image. The carrier image for this purpose is called cover image, and the output image embedded with secret information is named stego image. On the contrary, steganalysis is the method to distinguish stego images from cover images.

In traditional image steganographic algorithms, the cover image embeds secret information by changing the values of some pixels, which are chosen by a suitably defined distortion function, such as HUGO [19] and WOW [7]. These methods design the distortion function with complex artificial rules. The secret information generally embeds into noisy regions or complex textures and avoids

© Springer Nature Switzerland AG 2019
T. Gedeon et al. (Eds.): ICONIP 2019, LNCS 11954, pp. 3–14, 2019.
https://doi.org/10.1007/978-3-030-36711-4_1

smooth regions of the cover image. They keep security by reducing the disturbances to the appearance and statistical features of the cover image. But they still face the risks of being detected, especially when the steganalysis algorithm is based on deep learning.

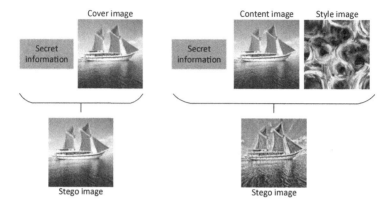

Fig. 1. The difference between the traditional steganographic method (left) and our STNet model (right). The traditional method generates the stego image by embedding secret information into the cover image. Our STNet accepts the content image and stego image as input and embed secret information into the style feature.

Nowadays, many researchers have attempted to introduce deep learning into the field of steganography, such as SteGAN [6] and HiDDeN [28]. These methods can automatically learn the steganographic strategy without any domain knowledge. They use neural networks instead of distortion functions to find pixels that are suitable for embedding secret information. However, they also face the security issue. Besides, one disadvantage of the deep learning steganographic algorithm is that it can only conceal fixed length of secret information. The size and capacity of stego images are fixed when the model has been trained.

To improve these situations, we attempt to find an innovative steganographic algorithm. CycleGAN [29] is a well-known image-to-image domain transformation model. However, recent research finds that CycleGAN is vulnerable to adversarial examples attacks [3]. It conceals information about source image into the target images imperceptibly, and can recover the source image from target images end-to-end. We explore whether it can be beneficial. We connect this phenomenon with steganography that neural networks can learn to encode a mass of secret information in the process of image domain transformation. In addition, nowadays makeup and art effect applications on images are widely used in our daily life, which makes it possible to transmit style transformation images unobtrusively in public media. So we propose a novel deep image steganographic model based on style transfer, which is called STNet (Fig. 1).

STNet is an end-to-end unsupervised training model without any domain knowledge. It accepts the content image and style image as input and recomposes content image in the feeling of style image. The secret information embeds in the style features of the stego image. We transmit the stego image in the public network, and the receiver will decode the secret information from the stego image successfully. Compared with previous steganographic methods, the main contributions of our work are as follows:

- To the best of our knowledge, STNet is the first steganographic method based on style transfer. It generates a new image that matches the content and style representation of two different source images. We design the model structure elaborately that secret information is embedded in style features of stego image.
- Our model has high security and can resist most existing steganalysis tools. The traditional steganographic algorithm has the cover and stego images pair so that the steganalysis tool can be trained to detect stego images. However, we generate the new art image as stego image directly. It is useless to detect out stego images from cover images because our style transformation images are indistinguishable from countless art images on the internet.
- Once the model has completed training, most deep learning steganographic algorithms can only output fixed size stego images with a fixed capacity. However, our model is a fully convolutional network and can accept arbitrary size content and style images as input. We introduce adaptive instance normalization (AdaIN) to perform style transfer, and the size of the stego image is the same as content image. Therefore, we can embed arbitrary bits of secret information.
- We conduct experiments on COCO and wikiart dataset. It produces visually pleasant style transformation results with high security and reliability.

The rest of the paper is organized as follows. Section 2 introduces the related work of steganography and style transfer. Section 3 describes our model architecture and learning objectives. Section 4 presents our experimental results and analysis. The conclusion and future works are presented in Sect. 5.

2 Related Work

2.1 Steganography

In the traditional steganographic algorithm, least significant bit (LSB) is a general steganographic algorithm that it hides the information by replacing the least significant bits of the cover image pixels. The changes of the image are imperceptible, but it does not preserve the statistical characteristic of the image and makes it vulnerable to the steganalysis. In order to solve this problem, most image steganographic methods use a distortion function that finds the pixel with the least disturbance to the image, thereby preserving image statistical characteristic. Highly Undetectable Steganography (HUGO) [19] defines the distortion function as the weighted difference of feature vectors, which already used in steganalysis algorithms. Wavelet Obtained Weights (WOW) [7] uses directional high-pass filters to force the embedding focus on highly textured or noisy regions. Universal wavelet relative distortion (UNIWARD) [8] can embed in an arbitrary domain, it computers the relative changes of directional filter bank decomposition of the image.

In recent years, a large number of steganographic algorithms try to combine with deep learning. ASDL-GAN [22] and VT-SCA-GAN [26] first propose to use generative adversarial network instead of distortion function to decide the embedding position. SGAN [24] and SSGAN [20] generate new cover images that are most suitable for embedding by the classical steganographic algorithm. For further performance, SteGAN and HiDDeN propose an end-to-end model that neural network directly outputs the final stego image. They achieve the best performance of current steganography with generative adversarial networks. SSteGAN [25] directly produces realistic and secure stego images with the noise and secret information as input instead of cover images. There also have some studies attempt to embed color or grayscale image in another color image of the same size [1,27]. Compared with other steganographic algorithms, they reduces the requirements for recovering secret data accurately, which does not interfere with image comprehension.

2.2   Style Transfer

Style transfer is an art of modifying the style of an image while preserving its content. Gatys et al. [5] first propose a way that iteratively updates the input image by minimizing the content loss and style loss based on features extracted from a pre-trained network. This method is computationally expensive since each iteration optimization requires both forward and backward propagation. [10,12, 23] proposes a variety of fast feed-forward network models to reduce the heavy computational cost. However, these networks are trained to transfer multiple content images to a fixed style. To address this problem, Dumolin et al. [4] introduce a single network with conditional instance normalization that can represent 32 styles at the same time. Huang et al. [9] propose arbitrary style transformation network by matching the mean and variance of content and style features. Li et al. [13] boost the style transformation performance by learning linear transformations between content feature and transformation matrix.

3   Model

As shown in Fig. 2, our model consists of three parts: style transformation network, reveal network, and loss network. The style transformation network is also the steganographic network. It embeds secret information in the high-frequency style features of the output image while the style is being converted. The reveal network accepts the stego image as input and accurately recovers secret information. The loss network is a pre-training model used to calculate the style and content loss of the stego image. Next, we will detail each part of the model.

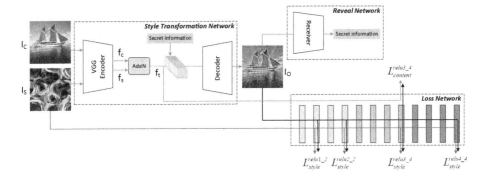

Fig. 2. Overview of the proposed method. Our model contains a style transformation network, a reveal network, and a loss network. We train the style transformation network to transform content and style image to stego image. The reveal network is used to decode secret information from the stego image. The loss network defines the loss function to train style transformation network.

3.1 Style Transformation Network

The VGG Encoder, Decoder, AdaIN layer, and secret information constitute the style transformation network. It takes an arbitrary content image I_c and style image I_s as inputs and produces the stego image I_o that simultaneously matches the content representation of the I_c and the style representation of the I_s. As we all know, convolutional neural networks are useful in image processing tasks. It uses multiple filters to extract specific features of the input image. In particular, when convolutional neural networks are trained for image classification, they convert the input image into a high-dimensional representation of the object information. That is to say, the output of a convolutional neural network contains the style or content characteristics of the input image. We use the Encoder to get the feature representation f_c and f_s of the content image and the style image. In our experiment, Encoder is the first fewer layers of VGG-19 [21] network pre-trained on the ImageNet dataset for image classification.

Then we use an adaptive instance normalization (AdaIN) layer [9] to perform style transformation in the feature space. It receives the feature map f_c and f_s as input and output target feature representation f_t. AdaIN has no learnable weight parameters, it aligns the mean μ and variance σ of content feature f_c to match those of style feature f_s in channel-wise.

$$AdaIN(f_C, f_S) = \sigma(f_S)\left(\frac{f_C - \mu(f_C)}{\sigma(f_C)}\right) + \mu(f_S) \tag{1}$$

Similar to the method of batch normalization (BN) and Instance Normalization(IN), we simply scale the normalized content input with $\sigma(f_s)$, and shift it with $\mu(f_s)$. Now, we get a new feature f_t which contains the high-level content feature of the I_c and the texture information of the I_s.

The Decoder is used to convert the feature map back to the image space. We first concat the secret information M with the output of AdaIN layer f_t as the input of the Decoder, and then the Decoder outputs the stego image I_o, which embeds the secret information into the image style feature. Its network structure is the opposite of Encoder. We use Nearest-Neighbor upsampling instead of fractionally-strided convolutions to replace all pooling layers because it can reduce checkerboard artifacts [18] effects. Meanwhile, we use reflection padding in both Encoder and Decoder to avoid border artifacts.

3.2 Reveal Network

The reveal network receives the stego image as input and recovers secret information $\hat{M}$ end-to-end. It uses a series of deep convolutional networks to extract secret information from the stego image. The reveal network is made up of six convolution layers with batch normalization, and Leaky ReLU activation function, except the final layer which uses Tanh and without batch normalization. The reveal network's goal is to recover secret information $\hat{M}$ accurately. Concretely, We use the squared Euclidean distance as secret information reconstruction loss. Note that L indicates the number of bits of the secret information.

$$L_m(M, \hat{M}) = \left\| M - \hat{M} \right\|_2^2 / L \qquad (2)$$

3.3 Loss Network

The loss network also is the pre-training VGG-19 network. The parameters of VGG encoder remain unchanged during the training process. Different from the traditional steganographic mode, which changes the pixel value of the cover image as little as possible, we pay more attention to the content and style of the image compared to specific pixel values. We attempts to measure perceptual differences in content and style of input and output images, and define the content loss L_c and style loss L_s for training the style transformation network.

Content Loss. Let $\phi_l(x)$ be the feature maps of the specific layer l for the VGG network when the x as input. The content loss is the squared Euclidean distance between the target features and the features of the output image. We hope that the secret information should be as unrelated as possible to content features of the stego image. We use the AdaIN output f_t as the target feature, rather than the feature of the content image.

$$L_c = \frac{1}{C \times H \times W} \|\phi(f_t) - \phi(f_c)\|_2^2 \qquad (3)$$

Style Loss. There are two general methods to compute style loss and produce similar results: perceptual loss [10] and BN Statistics Matching [14]. We use the BN Statistics Matching for the convenience of calculation. We construct style loss by aligning the mean and standard deviation of two feature maps between the style image and the stego image.

$$\mathcal{L}_s = \frac{1}{N}\sum_{i=1}^{N}(\|\mu\left(\phi_i(I_o)\right) - \mu\left(\phi_i(I_s)\right)\|_2^2 + \|\sigma\left(\phi_i(I_o)\right) - \sigma\left(\phi_i(I_s)\right)\|_2^2) \qquad (4)$$

Where $\mu(\phi_i(I_s))$ and $\sigma(\phi_i(I_s))$ is the mean and standard deviation of the loss network i-th layer. In our experiment, We adopt the $relu3\_4$ layer for the content loss, and $relu1\_2$, $relu2\_2$, $relu3\_4$, $relu4\_4$ for the style loss.

Total Loss. In total, we use the weighted sum of the content loss, style loss, and secret information reconstruction loss as the total loss function of STNet. α and β are weight factors that control the importance of each loss terms.

$$L_{total} = L_C + \alpha L_S + \beta L_m \qquad (5)$$

4   Experiments

In this section, we first briefly describe some experimental implementation details. Then we present results of STNet and compare with other style transfer methods. Furthermore, we analyze the capacity and accuracy of secret information recovery. In the following, we evaluate the security and reliability of our steganographic model.

Fig. 3. Comparison between results by our style steganographic method and other style transfer algorithms. All images are resized to 512×512 pixels to facilitate presentation.

We conduct our experiment using COCO dataset [16] as content images and a dataset of paintings obtain from wikiart.org [17] as style images, following the setting of [2,9]. Each dataset has approximately 80,000 natural images or paintings as training examples. We resize each image to 512×512 pixels, then randomly crop regions of size 256×256. All model is trained with a batch size of 8 with epochs 8. We use Adam optimizer [11] with the learning rate of 1×10^{-4} and default hyperparameters. At each batch, we train style transformation network and reveal network at the same time.

In Fig. 3, we show the output image of our model and compare with other comparative models. Our results are qualitatively similar to comparative models. Due to the difference in architecture, loss function, style weight, etc. The output images produced by different models are slightly different. Overall, the secret information is embedded in the style feature and does not affect the content of the output image. The change of the style result is imperceptible to humans.

In order to evaluate the accuracy of secret information recovery, we randomly select 10,000 content and style images to generate 10,000 stego images as test images. Note that all the test images never appear in the training set. Reveal network can successfully decode 99.8% of the secret information. In practical application, in order to achieve 100% accuracy, we can introduce error correction coding (ECC) to correct the error bits. Different from other deep steganographic algorithms, our model is a fully convolutional network. Thus, we can input content and style images of arbitrary size, and the output image has the same size as the content image with the capacity of 0.06 bpp. We can choose the appropriate size image according to the length of the secret information. In comparison, other deep learning steganographic models can only embed fixed-length secret information when the model has completed training. The maximum stego image size and capacity of different models are shown in Table 1.

Table 1. The maximum image size and capacity of different steganographic algorithms.

Model	Our model	SteGAN	HiDDeN
Stego image size (max)	Arbitrary size	32×32	16×16
Capacity (max)	0.06 bpp	0.4 bpp	0.2 bpp
Secret information (max)	Arbitrary length	409 bit	51 bit

4.1 Security

The traditional image steganographic algorithm hides secret information by modifying the value of some specific pixels and minimize the disturbance to image appearance and statistical properties. Most steganalysis assumes that it knows the steganographic algorithm and get a large number of cover and stego images pair for training. Then the model can detect whether the image contains secret information, when it receives an image as input. Different from the traditional steganographic algorithm, we directly generate a new art image with secret information embed in style feature. There exists an essential difference between our method and the traditional steganographic algorithm so that our method can resist most existing steganalysis tools. The task of steganalysis has become to distinguish our style transformation images from countless art images.

To evaluate the security of our model, we built a steganalysis model to distinguish our stego image from other style transformation images. We denote the combination of the convolutional neural network, batch normalization and Leaky ReLU as a Conv-BN-LReLU block. The steganalysis model consists of five Conv-BN-LReLU blocks, three maxpooling layers and a dense layer. For the training dataset, positive samples are the stego images generated by our STNet. The outputs of the other three style transformation models [9,13,15] are regarded as negative samples. After training, we test the classification accuracy of the steganalysis model.

There are four sets of different data for testing, generated according to the following experimental conditions: C1, We use the model used in training to generate positive and negative samples. C2, We train a new STNet with different random seed and weight factors (α and β) to generate images as positive samples. C3, We train a new STNet with different hyperparameter (whether to use BN or not) to generate images as positive samples. C4, We train a new STNet with different training dataset to generate images as positive samples. At the same time, we use another style transformation model [2] to generate the negative samples and used in C2, C3 and C4.

The experiment results are shown in Table 2. C1 achieves a detection accuracy of 0.993, which indicate that our steganalysis model performance well. The steganalysis model can precisely distinguish the stego image from the image generated by the model used in training. However, in case C2, C3, and C4, when we detect images generated by models that do not appear in training, the accuracy of detection has dropped rapidly. There are a variety of style transformation networks and countless art images on the internet. It is a great challenge to train a steganalysis model to distinguish our stego images from all art images. What is more, the steganalysis knows our algorithm but does not have access to the trained model itself (it does not know the hyperparameters and dataset). Experimental results demonstrate that our model has high security, and our stego images are indistinguishable from art images on the internet.

Table 2. The accuracy of the steganalysis algorithm according to experimental conditions C1-C4. C1: baseline. C2: different random seed and weight factor. C3: whether to use BN or not. C4: different training data.

Experimental conditions	$C1$	$C2$	$C3$	$C4$
Classification accuracy	0.993	0.786	0.592	0.753

4.2   Reliability

In particular, there has a threat scenario that the adversary knows STNet is being used and tries to decode the stego image. To test the reliability of our model, we assume that the adversary knows the network structure, hyperparameters, and dataset, but does not have the random seed (which is used to initialize the parameters and can affect the values of final model parameters).

We have two separately STNet. One model is used to embed secret information and produces the stego images. The other model attempts to predict secret information from these stego images. We first train two models with the same training conditions (hyperparameters and dataset). The accuracy of secret information recovery can reach 0.99. In the second experimental case, we use different random seed while other training conditions stay the same. It cannot get any useful information with the decoding accuracy of 0.39 (0.5 equivalent to random guess). This result demonstrates that our model has a high reliability. Even if the adversary masters the algorithm and the stego image, they still can not get the secret information. To further improve steganographic security, we can encrypt the secret information before concealing it into cover images (Table 3).

The neural network of our model can automatically learn the unique steganographic strategy, and the strategy is similar when we train the model with identical training conditions. In the actual application scenario, it is very danger and trouble to transmit the entire model parameters directly in the public channel. Therefore, the two communicating parties can share the training conditions instead of transmitting the entire model parameters. They train the model locally with the same training conditions. Then the sender uses its style transformation network generates a stego image, and the receiver uses its reveal network decode the secret information successfully. What is more, we can always get a new steganographic system by merely altering training conditions.

Table 3. The accuracy of secret information recovery on experimental conditions C5 and C6. C5: two models have the same training conditions. C6: two models have different random seed value.

Experimental conditions	$C5$	$C6$
Decoding accuracy	0.99	0.39

5   Conclusion

In this paper, we propose a novel image steganographic method based on the style transfer. It is an end-to-end unsupervised neural network without any steganographic domain knowledge. The secret information embeds in the style features of the stego image. Our STNet can resist the most existing steganalysis algorithm, and its stego images are indistinguishable from art images on the internet.

For capacity, STNet can produce stego images of arbitrary size with 0.06 bit per pixel. That is to say, we can conceal the arbitrary length of secret information. The experiment results demonstrate that our method is competitive with existing steganographic algorithms on visual effect, capacity, security, and reliability. However, our model has the same limitations as other deep steganographic models. Compared with the traditional steganographic method, it needs extra cost to train the whole neural network. In future work, we will explore to apply our proposed scheme to other domains, such as text and video.

Acknowledgement. This work is supported by the National Key Research and Development Program of China, and the National Natural Science Foundation of China (No. U163620068).

References

1. Baluja, S.: Hiding images in plain sight: deep steganography. In: Advances in Neural Information Processing Systems, pp. 2066–2076 (2017)
2. Chen, T.Q., Schmidt, M.: Fast patch-based style transfer of arbitrary style. arXiv preprint arXiv:1612.04337 (2016)
3. Chu, C., Zhmoginov, A., Sandler, M.: CycleGAN, a master of steganography. arXiv preprint arXiv:1712.02950 (2017)
4. Dumoulin, V., Shlens, J., Kudlur, M.: A learned representation for artisticstyle. In: Proceedings of ICLR, vol. 2 (2017)
5. Gatys, L.A., Ecker, A.S., Bethge, M.: Image style transfer using convolutional neural networks. In: Proceedings of the IEEE Conference on Computer Vision and Pattern Recognition, pp. 2414–2423 (2016)
6. Hayes, J., Danezis, G.: Generating steganographic images via adversarial training. In: Advances in Neural Information Processing Systems, pp. 1954–1963 (2017)
7. Holub, V., Fridrich, J.: Designing steganographic distortion using directional filters. In: 2012 IEEE International Workshop on Information Forensics and Security (WIFS), pp. 234–239. IEEE (2012)
8. Holub, V., Fridrich, J., Denemark, T.: Universal distortion function for steganography in an arbitrary domain. EURASIP J. Inform. Secur. **2014**(1), 1 (2014)
9. Huang, X., Belongie, S.: Arbitrary style transfer in real-time with adaptive instance normalization. In: Proceedings of the IEEE International Conference on Computer Vision, pp. 1501–1510 (2017)
10. Johnson, J., Alahi, A., Fei-Fei, L.: Perceptual losses for real-time style transfer and super-resolution. In: Leibe, B., Matas, J., Sebe, N., Welling, M. (eds.) ECCV 2016. LNCS, vol. 9906, pp. 694–711. Springer, Cham (2016). https://doi.org/10.1007/978-3-319-46475-6_43
11. Kingma, D.P., Ba, J.: Adam: a method for stochastic optimization. arXiv preprint arXiv:1412.6980 (2014)
12. Li, C., Wand, M.: Precomputed real-time texture synthesis with markovian generative adversarial networks. In: Leibe, B., Matas, J., Sebe, N., Welling, M. (eds.) ECCV 2016. LNCS, vol. 9907, pp. 702–716. Springer, Cham (2016). https://doi.org/10.1007/978-3-319-46487-9_43
13. Li, X., Liu, S., Kautz, J., Yang, M.H.: Learning linear transformations for fast arbitrary style transfer. arXiv preprint arXiv:1808.04537 (2018)

14. Li, Y., Wang, N., Liu, J., Hou, X.: Demystifying neural style transfer. arXiv preprint arXiv:1701.01036 (2017)
15. Li, Y., Fang, C., Yang, J., Wang, Z., Lu, X., Yang, M.H.: Universal style transfer via feature transforms. In: Advances in Neural Information Processing Systems, pp. 386–396 (2017)
16. Lin, T.-Y., et al.: Microsoft COCO: common objects in context. In: Fleet, D., Pajdla, T., Schiele, B., Tuytelaars, T. (eds.) ECCV 2014. LNCS, vol. 8693, pp. 740–755. Springer, Cham (2014). https://doi.org/10.1007/978-3-319-10602-1_48
17. Nichol, K.: Painter by numbers (2016). https://www.kaggle.com/c/painter-by-numbers
18. Odena, A., Dumoulin, V., Olah, C.: Deconvolution and checkerboard artifacts. Distill (2016). http://distill.pub/2016/deconv-checkerboard/
19. Pevný, T., Filler, T., Bas, P.: Using high-dimensional image models to perform highly undetectable steganography. In: Böhme, R., Fong, P.W.L., Safavi-Naini, R. (eds.) IH 2010. LNCS, vol. 6387, pp. 161–177. Springer, Heidelberg (2010). https://doi.org/10.1007/978-3-642-16435-4_13
20. Shi, H., Dong, J., Wang, W., Qian, Y., Zhang, X.: SSGAN: secure steganography based on generative adversarial networks. In: Zeng, B., Huang, Q., El Saddik, A., Li, H., Jiang, S., Fan, X. (eds.) PCM 2017. LNCS, vol. 10735, pp. 534–544. Springer, Cham (2018). https://doi.org/10.1007/978-3-319-77380-3_51
21. Simonyan, K., Zisserman, A.: Very deep convolutional networks for large-scale image recognition. arXiv preprint arXiv:1409.1556 (2014)
22. Tang, W., Tan, S., Li, B., Huang, J.: Automatic steganographic distortion learning using a generative adversarial network. IEEE Signal Process. Lett. 24(10), 1547–1551 (2017)
23. Ulyanov, D., Lebedev, V., Vedaldi, A., Lempitsky, V.S.: Texture networks: feedforward synthesis of textures and stylized images. In: ICML, p. 4 (2016)
24. Volkhonskiy, D., Nazarov, I., Borisenko, B., Burnaev, E.: Steganographic generative adversarial networks. arXiv preprint arXiv:1703.05502 (2017)
25. Wang, Z., Gao, N., Wang, X., Qu, X., Li, L.: SSteGAN: self-learning steganography based on generative adversarial networks. In: Cheng, L., Leung, A.C.S., Ozawa, S. (eds.) ICONIP 2018. LNCS, vol. 11302, pp. 253–264. Springer, Cham (2018). https://doi.org/10.1007/978-3-030-04179-3_22
26. Yang, J., Liu, K., Kang, X., Wong, E.K., Shi, Y.Q.: Spatial image steganography based on generative adversarial network. arXiv preprint arXiv:1804.07939 (2018)
27. Zhang, R., Dong, S., Liu, J.: Invisible steganography via generative adversarial networks. Multimed. Tools Appl. 78(7), 8559–8575 (2019)
28. Zhu, J., Kaplan, R., Johnson, J., Fei-Fei, L.: Hidden: hiding data with deep networks. In: Proceedings of the European Conference on Computer Vision (ECCV), pp. 657–672 (2018)
29. Zhu, J.Y., Park, T., Isola, P., Efros, A.A.: Unpaired image-to-image translation using cycle-consistent adversarial networks. In: Proceedings of the IEEE International Conference on Computer Vision, pp. 2223–2232 (2017)

Multi-person 3D Pose Estimation from Monocular Image Sequences

Ran Li, Nayun Xu, Xutong Lu, Yucheng Xing, Haohua Zhao, Li Niu, and Liqing Zhang[✉]

Department of Computer Science, Shanghai Jiao Tong University, Shanghai 200240, China
{liran920526,xunayun,luxutong,haoh.zhao,ustcnewly}@sjtu.edu.cn, ericxing0430@gmail.com, zhang-lq@cs.sjtu.edu.cn

Abstract. This article tackles the problem of multi-person 3D human pose estimation based on monocular image sequence in a three-step framework: (1) we detect 2D human skeletons in each frame across the image sequence; (2) we track each person through the image sequence and identify the sequence of 2D skeletons for each person; (3) we reconstruct the 3D human skeleton for each person from the detected 2D human joints, by using prelearned base poses and considering the temporal smoothness. We evaluate our framework on the Human3.6M dataset and the multi-person image sequence captured by ourselves. The quantitative results on the Human3.6M dataset and the qualitative results on our constructed test data demonstrate the effectiveness of our proposed method.

Keywords: 3D human pose estimation · 2D human pose estimation · Human tracking

1 Introduction

With the rapid development of visual action recognition, 3D human skeleton reconstruction in a single image and image sequences has attracted plenty of attention in recent years. Compared with 2D human skeleton, 3D human skeleton generally leads to better performance of action recognition, due to the rotation invariance of 3D human skeleton. Several works have been done for action recognition based on 3D human skeleton. For example, the work in [17] explored Lie group theory to represent dynamics of the 3D human skeletons. Following [17], Lie group theory is combined with a deep network architecture to learn more representative features in [6]. The work [8] and [9] proposed to use CNN and LSTM to extract the spatio-temporal feature from 3D human skeleton.

Although action recognition based on 3D human skeleton has achieved great success, collecting 3D human skeletons with wearable devices is very expensive and sometimes not accurate. An alternative way is to reconstruct 3D human skeleton from 2D human skeleton because 2D human skeletons are more accessible. However, the reconstruction of 3D human skeleton from 2D human skeleton

© Springer Nature Switzerland AG 2019
T. Gedeon et al. (Eds.): ICONIP 2019, LNCS 11954, pp. 15–24, 2019.
https://doi.org/10.1007/978-3-030-36711-4_2

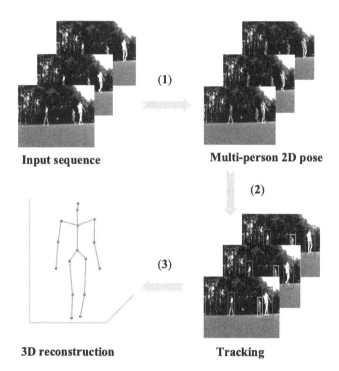

Fig. 1. Framework overview: (1) We first estimate the 2D pose in each frame using Regional Multi-person Pose Estimation (RMPE). (2) Then, we track each person using Discriminative Scale Space Tracker (DSST). (3) Finally, we reconstruct 3D human pose from estimated 2D human pose for each person in each frame.

is a very difficult task, because one 2D pose may correspond to multiple 3D poses with different camera parameters. To address this problem, some recent works [18, 21] alternately update the 3D pose and camera parameters, yielding the estimated camera parameters and the corresponding 3D pose.

Nevertheless, 2D human skeletons could also be unavailable in the real world. In this case, our goal is to reconstruct 3D human skeleton from monocular image sequence, in which we need to initially estimate the 2D human skeletons based on the image sequence. Moreover, multiple persons may appear simultaneously in one image sequence, so we need to separate the sequence of 2D human skeletons belonging to different persons. Therefore, the design of an integrated framework remains an open and challenging problem.

In this paper, we propose a multi-person 3D pose estimation framework based on monocular image sequences, which integrates a 2D human pose estimator, a human tracker, and a 3D reconstruction method based on the estimated 2D human pose. Specifically, we first detect 2D human skeletons by locating 2D human joints in each frame across the image sequence using Regional Multi-person Pose Estimation (RMPE) [5]. Then, we track each person through the image sequence and identify the sequence of 2D skeletons for each person by using Discriminative Scale Space Tracker (DSST) [4]. Finally, we reconstruct 3D human skeletons from detected 2D skeletons by using prelearned base poses and considering the temporal smoothness. Our framework is illustrated in Fig. 1.

Our experiments are conducted on the single-person Human3.6M dataset and multi-person image sequence collected by ourselves. The results on the Human3.6M dataset demonstrate that the proposed method outperforms the current state-of-art methods. Besides, the estimated 3D human pose in multi-person image sequence shows the advantage of our proposed framework in a qualitative fashion.

2   Related Work

In this section, we will discuss the related works on 3D human pose estimation based on single image or image sequence.

2.1   3D Human Pose Estimation Based on Single Image

Most papers on 3D pose estimation assume that 3D poses can be represented by a linear combination of a set of base poses, and learn the combination coefficients of bases poses. Some works [13, 15] require manually labeled 2D joint locations as input while other works [14, 19, 20] only require a single image as input. For the works only requiring a single image, they either jointly estimate the 2D pose and the 3D pose [14], or initially estimate the 2D pose followed by 3D pose reconstruction [20]. However, all the above works focus on a single image while our framework focuses on image sequence.

2.2   3D Human Pose Estimation Based on Image Sequence

There also exist some works [18, 21] using monocular image sequence as input. Compared with those works based on a single image, they exploit the relation between neighboring frames in the image sequence. For instance, Wandt *et al.* [18] make a strong periodic assumption on 3D human poses for periodic motion (*e.g.*, walking and running), and use the variances of all bone lengths as a regularizer for non-periodic motion. Zhou *et al.* [21] applied the discrete temporal derivative operator to make the 3D human poses across the sequences smoother. However, all these approaches only deal with single-person image sequence while our framework can handle the multi-person image sequence.

3   Our Framework

Our framework consists of three steps. In the first step, we adopt the Regional Multi-person Pose Estimation (RMPE) [5] to obtain the 2D joint locations in each frame across the image sequence, given the fact that RMPE has shown excellent performance for multi-person 2D pose estimation. In the second step, with the detected 2D human skeletons in each frame, we use the Discriminative Scale Space Tracker (DSST) [4] to identify the sequence of bounding boxes belonging to each person, leading to a sequence of 2D human skeletons belonging to each person. The reason of choosing DSST tracker can be explained as follows. In the real world, people may move towards different directions, closer to or farther from the camera, resulting in different scales of person in different frames. Thus, we adopt the DSST, which is robust with various scales, to track each person. In the third step, for 3D human pose estimation, we use a 3D human skeleton reconstruction algorithm, which takes a sequence of 2D poses of each person as input and output a sequence of 3D poses for each person.

3.1   Representation of 3D Poses Using Base Poses

We use $\mathbf{Y}_t \in \mathbb{R}^{3 \times a}$ to denote the 3D pose in t-th frame with a being the number of joints. Following [2,13], to regulate reconstructed 3D pose, we assume that 3D pose can be represented as a linear combination of the $\mathbf{K}$ base poses $\mathbf{Q}_k \in \mathbb{R}^{3 \times a}, k = 1, 2 ... K$:

$$\mathbf{Y}_t = \sum_{k=1}^{K} (\mathbf{w}_{kt} \times \mathbf{Q}_k), \tag{1}$$

where $\mathbf{w}_{kt}$ is the coefficient corresponding to the k-th base pose for the t-th frame. We learn K ($K = 64$ in our experiments) base poses from the motion capture dataset, following the method used in [2,13]. The learned base poses form an overcomplete dictionary, which means that the number of the base poses is large and the combination coefficients of a given 3D pose are sparse.

3.2   3D Pose Reconstruction Based on a Sequence of 2D Poses

Given a 3D pose of the t-th frame $\mathbf{Y}_t$ and camera parameters, we can obtain the corresponding 2D pose $\mathbf{X}_t \in \mathbb{R}^{2 \times a}$. In particular, with the camera parameters including the projection matrix $\mathbf{M}_t \in \mathbb{R}^{2 \times 3}$ and translation vector $\mathbf{T}_t \in \mathbb{R}^2$, the 3D pose $\mathbf{Y}_t$ can be projected to the 2D pose $\mathbf{X}_t$ as follows,

$$\mathbf{X}_t = \mathbf{M}_t \times \mathbf{Y}_t + \mathbf{T}_t \mathbf{1}^T, \tag{2}$$

where $\mathbf{1}$ is an a-dim column vector. However, the equation in (2) only holds in ideal cases. Considering the representation error of 3D poses $\mathbf{Y}_t$ based on the linear combination of based poses, we tolerate the projection error to a certain degree and aim to minimize the following projection error:

$$P(\mathbf{W}, \mathbf{M}, \mathbf{T}) = \frac{1}{2} \|\mathbf{X}_t - \mathbf{M}_t \times \mathbf{Y}_t - \mathbf{T}_t \mathbf{1}^T\|_F^2, \tag{3}$$

where Frobenius norm is used to calculate the projection error, $\mathbf{X}$ (resp., $\mathbf{W}$, $\mathbf{M}$, and $\mathbf{T}$) is the collection of $\mathbf{X}_t$ (resp., $\mathbf{W}_t$, $\mathbf{M}_t$, and $\mathbf{T}_t$).

Considering that for the neighboring frames in the sequence, their camera parameter $\mathbf{M}$ and representation coefficient of base poses $\mathbf{W}$ should vary smoothly.

Table 1. Quantitative comparison with state-of-the-art results on Human3.6M dataset. We report the mean per joint errors (mm) of the test subjects S9 and S11.

	3D (mm)
LinKDE [7]	162.14
Tekin et al. [16]	125.28
Ours	**119.76**

We impose first-order temporal smoothness regularizer $\|\nabla_t \mathbf{W}\|_F^2$ (*resp.*, $\mathbf{M}\|_F^2$) on $\mathbf{W}$ (*resp.*, $\mathbf{M}$), in which ∇_t stands for the derivative on temporal factor. Moreover, the representation coefficient of 3D poses $\mathbf{W}$ should be sparse according to the analysis in Sect. 3.1, so we add a L1 norm $\|\mathbf{W}\|_1$ to ensure the sparsity of $\mathbf{W}$. To this end, we collect the penalty terms as follows,

$$R(\mathbf{W}, \mathbf{M}) = \alpha\|\mathbf{W}\|_1 + \beta\|\nabla_t \mathbf{W}\|_F^2 + \gamma\|\nabla_t \mathbf{M}\|_F^2, \tag{4}$$

in which α, β, and γ are trade-off parameters and empirically fixed as 0.1, 5, and 0.5 respectively in our experiments.

By combining (3) and (4), we reach our final formulation:

$$\min_{\mathbf{W}, \mathbf{M}, \mathbf{T}} P(\mathbf{W}, \mathbf{M}, \mathbf{T}) + R(\mathbf{W}, \mathbf{M}). \tag{5}$$

By solving (5), we can obtain $\mathbf{W}_t$ and recover $\mathbf{Y}_t$ based on (2).

3.3 Optimization

The problem in (5) can be solved using block coordinate descent, which means alternatively updating one variable while fixing other variables.

Update the Representation Coefficients $\mathbf{W}$: The subproblem *w.r.t.* $\mathbf{W}$ can be written as

$$\min_{\mathbf{W}} P(\mathbf{W}, \mathbf{M}, \mathbf{T}) + \alpha\|\mathbf{W}\|_1 + \beta\|\nabla_t \mathbf{W}\|_F^2, \tag{6}$$

which can be solved via accelerated proximal gradient (APG) [11]. Since this problem is convex, the global minimum can be guaranteed.

Update the Rotation Matrix $\mathbf{M}$: The subproblem *w.r.t.* $\mathbf{M}$ can be written as

$$\min_{\mathbf{M}} P(\mathbf{W}, \mathbf{M}, \mathbf{T}) + \gamma\|\nabla_t \mathbf{M}\|_F^2, \tag{7}$$

which is a manifold optimization problem and can be solved via the matlab toolbox Manopt following [3].

Update the Translation Matrix $\mathbf{T}$: The subproblem *w.r.t.* $\mathbf{T}$ can be written as

$$\mathbf{T}_t = \mathbf{1}^T \left(\mathbf{X}_t - \mathbf{M}_t \sum_{k=1}^{K} (\mathbf{w}_{kt} \times \mathbf{Q}_k) \right), \tag{8}$$

which computes the average of rows in $\mathbf{X}_t - \mathbf{M}_t \sum_{k=1}^{K} (\mathbf{w}_{kt} \times \mathbf{Q}_k)$.

We alternatingly update three variables until the objective function in (5) converges. In each step, the objective function is non-increasing, so the convergence of this algorithm is ensured. Besides, considering the impact of initialization on our solution, we opt for the initialization method proposed in [1], which proves to be very effective.

4   Experimental Results

In this section, we first demonstrate the superiority of our framework on a recently published single-person dataset Human3.6M, because there is no available multi-person 3D pose estimation dataset based on image sequence as far as we are concerned. Then, we collect multi-person image sequences and compare our framework with the state-of-the-art methods in a qualitative fashion by showing the reconstructed 3D skeletons of two persons, which again verifies the effectiveness of our framework.

4.1   Implementation Details

In our framework, for 2D human pose estimation, we use Regional Multi-person Pose Estimation (RMPE) [5] as the 2D human pose estimator to locate 16 2D human joints for each person, in which the stacked hourglass network structure [12] is adopted. For human tracking, we use Discriminative Scale Space Tracker (DSST) [4] with two correlation filers composed of one 1-dim scale filer and one 2-dim translation filter, in which Fast Fourier Transform (FFT) is applied to significantly improve the tracking efficiency. To initiate the tracking process, we employ VGG-based Single Shot Detector (SSD) [10] to detect the persons in the first frame of each image sequence, and then increase the detected human proposals by 30% both at length and width to ensure the intactness of each detected person. For 3D human skeleton reconstruction from a sequence of 2D human skeletons, we impose the periodic assumption [18] to ensure the smooth transition between neighboring frames across the sequence.

4.2   Evaluation on the Human3.6M Dataset

The Human3.6M dataset contains 11 subjects performing 17 actions, such as walking, smoking, and eating. All the videos are captured by a MoCap system from 4 different viewpoints in a controlled environment, in which each video has only one person. Accurate 2D human skeletons are also provided for all videos. The frame rate is downsampled from 50 fps to 10 fps. We use two subjects (S9, S11) to evaluate different methods and other subjects to learn K base poses following previous work.

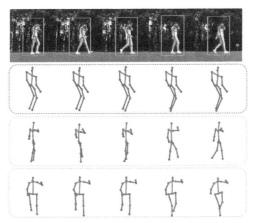

(a)The reconstruction result of walking person for the first five frames.

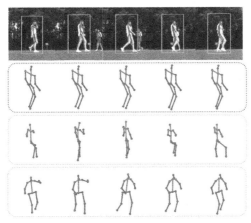

(b)The reconstruction result of walking person for the subsequent five frames.

Fig. 2. The comparison results of one running person within 10 frames.

In this experiment, we compare our framework with two state-of-the-art baselines on the evaluation set S9 and S11 of all the aspects. The first baseline [7] is based on the single frame regression. It is provided with the Hman3.6M dataset. The second baseline [16] explores motion information from consecutive frames in short image sequences. The results are summarized in Table 1, which demonstrates that our framework outperforms other methods on the large-scale Human3.6M dataset, which shows the effectiveness of integrating 2D human pose estimator and sequential 3D human skeleton reconstruction into our framework.

(a)The reconstruction result of running person for the first five frames.

(b)The reconstruction result of running person for the subsequent five frames.

Fig. 3. We select 10 frames of two persons in our captured multi-person image sequence to show the comparative results. In both Figs. 3 and 2, the first row is the original image sequences with 2D human pose estimator and human tracking. The second row is the reconstruction result of RMPE+DSST+[18]. The third row is the reconstruction result of RMPE+DSST+[13]. The fourth row is the reconstruction result of our proposed framework.

4.3   Evaluation on Multi-person Image Sequence

To the best of our knowledge, there is no available multi-person 3D pose estimation dataset based on image sequence. Hence, we sample 10 frames for each person from one captured video clip with two persons and 91 frames and evaluate our framework on this multi-person image sequence. We compare our framework with two baseline methods [13,18], in which the former method reconstructs the

3D human skeleton from monocular image sequences with the periodic assumption and the latter method estimates the 3D human poses from single images. By combining these two methods with our used 2D human pose estimator (*i.e.*, RMPE) and tracker (*i.e.*, DSST), we can also obtain the multi-person 3D human skeletons from the image sequence. The selected images with tracking and 2D pose detector and the comparative results are showed in Figs. 3 and 2.

The comparative results of one walking person are illustrated in Fig. 3. In the second row, we can observe that the results obtained by [18] fails to reconstruct the 3D skeletons corresponding to hand raising during walking, and the reconstructed skeletons rarely move. In the third row, we can see that the results obtained by [13] contain some strange poses like the 6th and the 9th frame. Our reconstruction results are shown in the last row, in which the 3D skeletons corresponding to hand raising bear a strong resemblance to the original image sequences and the transition between neighboring frames is smoother compared with the other two methods.

The comparative results of one running person are illustrated in Fig. 2. In the second row, we can observe that the results obtained by [18] always use the wrong legs and the motion is a little dramatic. In the third row, it can be seen that the results obtained by [13] contain sharp changes and strange poses. For example, the angle of the left knee is unrealistic in the 9th frame on the 3rd row. In contrast, as shown in the last row, our framework can achieve both smooth and realistic 3D human skeletons.

5   Conclusion

In this paper, we have proposed a multi-person 3D pose estimation framework based on monocular image sequences. Our proposed framework has integrated a 2D human pose estimator, a human tracker, and 3D human skeleton reconstruction in a coherent and effective manner. According to the quantitative comparison on the recently published large-scale dataset Human3.6M and the qualitative analyses on our captured multi-person image sequence, our framework achieve better results than state-of-the-art baseline methods, which clearly demonstrate the validness of our proposed framework.

Acknowledgements. The work was supported by the National Basic Research Program of China under Grant (No. 2015CB856004) and the Key Basic Research Program of Shanghai Science and Technology Commission, China under Grant (Nos. 15JC1400103, 16JC1402800).

References

1. 3D shape estimation from 2D landmarks: a convex relaxation approach (2015)
2. Akhter, I., Black, M.J.: Pose-conditioned joint angle limits for 3D human pose reconstruction. In: CVPR, pp. 1446–1455 (2015)
3. Boumal, N.: Manopt, a matlab toolbox for optimization on manifolds. JMLR **15**(1), 1455–1459 (2014)

4. Danelljan, M., Häger, G.: Accurate scale estimation for robust visual tracking. In: BMVC. BMVA Press (2014)
5. Fang, H.: RMPE: regional multi-person pose estimation. CoRR abs/1612.00137, 4321–4330 (2016)
6. Huang, Z., Wan, C., Probst, T., Van Gool, L.: Deep learning on lie groups for skeleton-based action recognition. In: CVPR, pp. 1243–1252 (2017)
7. Ionescu, C., Papava, D., Olaru, V., Sminchisescu, C.: Human3.6M: large scale datasets and predictive methods for 3D human sensing in natural environments. T-PAMI **36**(7), 1325–1339 (2014)
8. Ke, Q., Bennamoun, M., An, S., Sohel, F., Boussaid, F.: A new representation of skeleton sequences for 3D action recognition. In: CVPR, pp. 4570–4579 (2017)
9. Liu, J., Wang, G., Hu, P., Duan, L.Y., Kot, A.C.: Global context-aware attention LSTM networks for 3D action recognition. In: CVPR, vol. 7, p. 43 (2017)
10. Liu, W., et al.: SSD: single shot multibox detector. In: Leibe, B., Matas, J., Sebe, N., Welling, M. (eds.) ECCV 2016. LNCS, vol. 9905, pp. 21–37. Springer, Cham (2016). https://doi.org/10.1007/978-3-319-46448-0_2
11. Nesterov, Y., et al.: Gradient methods for minimizing composite objective function (2007)
12. Newell, A., Yang, K., Deng, J.: Stacked hourglass networks for human pose estimation. In: Leibe, B., Matas, J., Sebe, N., Welling, M. (eds.) ECCV 2016. LNCS, vol. 9912, pp. 483–499. Springer, Cham (2016). https://doi.org/10.1007/978-3-319-46484-8_29
13. Ramakrishna, V., Kanade, T., Sheikh, Y.: Reconstructing 3D human pose from 2D image landmarks. In: Fitzgibbon, A., Lazebnik, S., Perona, P., Sato, Y., Schmid, C. (eds.) ECCV 2012. LNCS, vol. 7575, pp. 573–586. Springer, Heidelberg (2012). https://doi.org/10.1007/978-3-642-33765-9_41
14. Simo-Serra, E., Quattoni, A.: A joint model for 2D and 3D pose estimation from a single image. In: CVPR, pp. 3634–3641 (2013)
15. Taylor, C.J.: Reconstruction of articulated objects from point correspondences in a single uncalibrated image. In: CVPR, pp. 1677–1684 (2000)
16. Tekin, B., Sun, X., Wang, X., Lepetit, V., Fua, P.: Predicting people's 3D poses from short sequences. CoRR abs/1504.08200 (2015)
17. Vemulapalli, R., Arrate, F.: Human action recognition by representing 3D skeletons as points in a lie group. In: CVPR, pp. 588–595 (2014)
18. Wandt, B.: 3D reconstruction of human motion from monocular image sequences. T-PAMI **38**, 1505–1516 (2016)
19. Wang, C., Wang, Y.: Robust estimation of 3D human poses from a single image. In: CVPR, pp. 2369–2376 (2014)
20. Yasin, H., Iqbal, U.: A dual-source approach for 3D pose estimation from a single image. In: CVPR, pp. 4948–4956 (2016)
21. Zhou, X., Zhu, M.: Sparseness meets deepness: 3d human pose estimation from monocular video. In: CVPR, pp. 4966–4975 (2016)

Super-Resolution Network for General Static Degradation Model

Yingjie Xu, Wenan Zhou$^{(\boxtimes)}$, and Ying Xing

Beijing University of Posts and Telecommunications, Beijing, China
{Yingjie,zhouwa}@bupt.edu.cn

Abstract. Recent research on single image super-resolution (SISR) has made some progress. However, most previous SISR methods simply assume that a low-resolution (LR) image is bicubicly downsampled from a high-resolution (HR) image. when the LR images don't follow this assumption, these previous methods will generate poor HR images that still retain the blur and noise information. To solve this problem, we propose the super-resolution network for general static degradation model (SR-GSD). Specifically, we propose degradation factors proposal Network (DFPN) which can automatically identify blur kernel and noise level, and furthermore, we utilize predicted degradation factors and the LR images to reconstruct the HR images in a high-resolution reconstruction network (HRN). Moreover, to simplify the training process, we unify the two-stages steps into a neural network and jointly optimize it through a multi-task loss function. Extensive experiments show that our SR-GSD can achieve satisfactory results on the general static degradation model.

Keywords: Super-resolution · Deep learning · Multi-task learning

1 Introduction

Single image super-resolution (SISR) aims to reconstruct a high-resolution (HR) image from a degraded low-resolution (LR) image, which is an ill-posed inverse problem [7]. As a classic computer vision problem, SISR is used in various applications, ranging from security and surveillance imaging [26], medical imaging [17], as well as satellite and aerial image [21]. In this paper, we consider the general static degradation model in order to increase the practicability of the model. Under this assumption, an LR image y can be modeled as:

$$y = (x \otimes k) \downarrow_s + n, \tag{1}$$

where x is the original HR image, k represents a non-motion blur kernel, $\otimes$ represents blurring operator, $\downarrow_s$ is a subsequent downsampling operation with scale factor s and n usually is additive white Gaussian noise (AWGN) with standard deviation (noise level) n.

© Springer Nature Switzerland AG 2019
T. Gedeon et al. (Eds.): ICONIP 2019, LNCS 11954, pp. 25–36, 2019.
https://doi.org/10.1007/978-3-030-36711-4_3

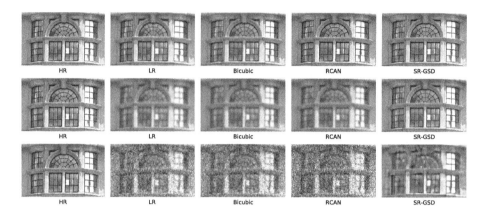

Fig. 1. Visual results with different degradations (2x) on "img 053" from Urban100 [10]. The LR image in first line is bicubicly downsampled from an HR image. The LR image of the second line is obtained by bicubic interpolation downsampling and Gaussian blur with a standard deviation of 2. The LR image of the last line adds a Gaussian white noise with a standard deviation of 50 on the LR image of the second line.

However, most of the recent convolutional neural network (CNN) based methods directly assume the LR image is downsampled by bicubic interpolation. Dong et al. [6] first proposed a CNN-based SR method, and in this paper, he synthesized low-resolution images via bicubic interpolation. This simplified degradation model is given by

$$y = x \downarrow_s, \tag{2}$$

where $\downarrow_s$ represents the bicubic downsampler with scale factor s. Due to its simplicity, the bicubic degradation model has become the benchmark-setting in the recent CNN-based method. Under this benchmark, SISR methods aim to improve performance in terms of peak signal-to-noise ratio (PSNR). The bicubic degradation model has achieved some success, but when the low-resolution images do not follow the bicubic degradation model, the most recent methods will get poor performance. As shown in the second and third lines of Fig. 1, the HR images reconstructed from previous methods still retain the blur and noise information.

To practically solve the problem, Zhang et al. proposed SRMD [23], which analyzes the general model-based SISR methods under the maximum a posteriori (MAP) framework. SRMD takes the degraded LR image and two degradation factors (blur kernel and noise level) as input, but in practice, the degradation factors of LR images are difficult to obtain.

Naturally, we would like to predict whether the degradation factors can be predicted from the existing LR images. In the field of image deblurring, Sun et al. [18] use CNN to estimate blur kernel. Chakrabarti [3] predicted deconvolution kernel in the frequency domain. Inspired by these image deblurring methods, we also try to predict the blur kernel using a convolutional neural network (CNN), but different from image deblurring, we also need to predict the noise level and then reconstruct HR images using the degraded LR images and the predicted degradation factors.

In this paper, we propose a two-stage Super-Resolution Network for General Static Degradation Model (SR-GSD), which can achieve better visual SR results compared with the previous CNN-based method as shown in Fig. 1. In the first stage, we use the Degradation Factors Proposal Network (DFPN) to estimate the blur kernel and noise level. Compared to the non-blind SR method, our method doesn't need to know the blur kernel and noise level in advance. In the second stage, we propose a High-Resolution Reconstruction Network (HRN) which uses degraded LR images and predicted degradation factors to reconstruct HR images. In the meanwhile, we unify the two-stages steps into a single neural network SR-GSD and jointly optimize network parameters through a multi-task loss function.

2   Related Work

To solve the super-resolution problem, early methods used fast interpolation techniques but achieve poor performance. Many methods aimed to learn a compact representation between LR and HR pairs. Those methods relied on techniques ranging from random forest, neighbor embedding and sparse coding.

With the development of the convolutional neural network, many CNN-based SISR methods have been proposed in the computer vision community. Dong et al. first presented SRCNN [6] which achieved dramatic improvements with a three-layers convolutional neural network. The SRCNN upscale the LR image via bicubic interpolation before feeding into the network. Kim et al. introduced residual learning for stable training in VDSR [11]. The VDSR achieved significant improvement with 20 layers. Tai et al. later proposed DRRN [19] which introduced recursive blocks to reduce the parameters of the model. Tai et al. also introduced memory block in MemNet [20]. However, these methods take the bicubicly interpolated LR images as input, which is computationally inefficient.

Shi et al. firstly introduced the sub-pixel convolution layer in ESPCNN [16], which used degraded LR image as input and upscaled the image at the end of the network. Lim et al. proposed EDSR [13] which removed the BN layer in conventional residual networks and achieved significant improvement. Zhang et al. presented a very deep residual channel attention networks (RCAN [24]) by proposing a channel attention mechanism to adaptively rescale channel-wise features. Dai et al. proposed SAN [5] for more powerful feature expression and feature correlation learning. Hu et al. presented Meta-SR [9] which firstly solve super-resolution of arbitrary scale factor with a single model. But these methods used the bicubic interpolation by adopting the Matlab function imresize to synthesize the LR images, which simplified the degradation process of high resolution images in practical applications.

In EDSR [13], the authors pointed out that other degrading factors such as blur kernel or noise level can be considered for practical applications, but he did not propose a practical solution. Zhang et al. firstly taken two degradation factors and degraded LR image as input in SRMD [23]. The SRMD can handle multiple degradations. However, the blur kernel and noise level are difficult to obtain in practical applications.

If our network can only take the LR image which is generated from a general static degradation model as input, it will greatly increase the usability of the model. To achieve this inspiration, we propose SR-GSD which we will detail in the next section.

3   Proposed Methods

As shown in Fig. 2, we introduce a novel super-resolution network for general static degradation model, called SR-GSD which is composed of two modules. The first module is the degradation factors proposal network (DFPN) that proposes a blur kernel and noise level from an LR image. The second module is a high-resolution reconstruction network (HRN) which uses the predicted degradation factors and a degraded LR image to reconstruct a HR image. The entire system is a single, unified network for super-resolution.

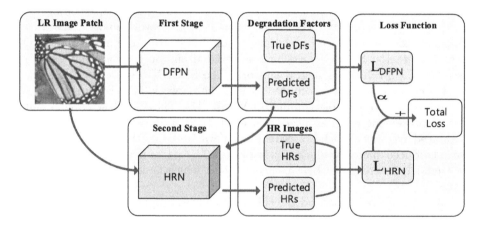

Fig. 2. Network architecture of our super-resolution network for general static degradation model (SR-GSD), DFs are abbreviations for degradation factors.

3.1   Degradation Factors Proposal Network (DFPN)

Figure 3 illustrates our DFPN method, our DFPN mainly consists of three parts: feature extraction, blur kernel proposal, noise level proposal. In this section, we take the degraded low-resolution image as input. Since the size of the input image is arbitrary, we use a fully convolutional network for super-resolution. In order to control the network parameters, we do not use a complex network structure

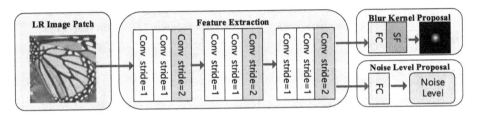

Fig. 3. Network architecture of our degradation factors proposal network (DFPN), each Conv layer is followed by a BN and ReLU layer, FC and SF represent the fully connected layer and the softmax layer, respectively

in the feature extraction part. we use three convolutional layers to extract the deep feature F from the LR image

$$F_1 = H_{DF}(I_{LR}), \tag{3}$$

where $H_{DF}(\cdot)$ includes two convolution layers with a stride of 1 and a convolution layer with a stride of 2, each conv layer is followed by a BN and ReLU layer. The number of channels in the first two layers is c, and the number of channels in the third layer is $2c$. After three $H_{DF}(\cdot)$ operations, the feature map F_3 size is $[h/8, w/8, 8c]$. At the end of feature extraction, we use global average pooling to extract the deep features in the LR image.

$$F_{DF} = H_{gap}(F_3), \tag{4}$$

where $H_{gap}(\cdot)$ denotes global average pooling operation. F_{DF} is then used to predict blur kernel and noise level.

$$Ker_p = \sigma(Fc_k(F_{DF})), Noise_p = Fc_n(F_{DF}) \tag{5}$$

where $Fc_k(\cdot)$ denotes convolution operation with a convolution kernel of 1×1 and t^2 filters, $\sigma(\cdot)$ represents the softmax function which aims to make the sum of the blur kernel is 1, $Fc_n(\cdot)$ denotes convolution operation with a convolution kernel of 1×1 and one filter, Ker_p and $Noise_p$ respectively represent the predicted blur kernel and noise level.

The DFPN module is optimized with L1 loss function. Given a training set $\{I_{LR}^i, \{K_t^i, N_t^i\}\}_{i=1}^N$, which contains N LR images and their true corresponding degradation factors in the process of synthesizing low-resolution images. The DFPN aims to minimize the $L1$ loss function

$$L_{DFPN}(\theta_d) = \frac{1}{N} \sum_{i=1}^N (\|Ker_p - K_t^i\|_1 + \|Noise_p - N_t^i\|_1) \tag{6}$$

where θ_d denotes the parameter set of our DFPN module. More detail of training would be shown in Sect. 4. All in all, The DFPN module can accurately extract the degradation factors from an LR image, and in the next subsection, we will introduce that how to reconstruct the HR image using the predicted degradation factors and the input LR image.

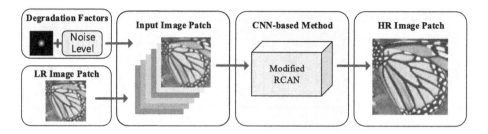

Fig. 4. Network architecture of our High-resolution Reconstruction Network (HRN)

3.2   High-Resolution Reconstruction Network(HRN)

We now give more details about our proposed HRN structure (see Fig. 4). Inspired by the SRMD [23] method, our HRN mainly consist of three parts: degradation factors reduction, dimensionality stretching strategy and super-resolution reconstruction. In this module we take the LR image and the degradation factors predicted from DFPN as inputs. we use one convolutional layer to project the predicted blur kernel onto a space of dimension t

$$K_r = C_{1 \times 1}(K_p), \tag{7}$$

where $C_{1 \times 1}(\cdot)$ is applied to feature dimension reduction and K_r is a blur kernel projection of dimension t.

After that, we connect K_r and noise level into features v with size of $1 \times 1 \times (t + 1)$, then v is stretched into degradation factor maps M_d of size $H \times W \times (t + 1)$, where H is the height of the LR image and W is the weight of the LR image. All the elements of i-th map are v_i. Through the dimensionality stretching strategy, we can contcat the LR image and the degradation factor map into a unified input M, which size is $H \times W \times (C + t + 1)$.

After getting the network input M, we can use the previous CNN-based method that only needs to change the first convolutional layer. Many CNN-based methods have been investigated, such as VDSR [11], EDSR [13], RDN [25], RCAN [24] and SAN [5]. In our experiment, we choose RCAN as our backbone network. The final SR image can be formulated as

$$I_{SR} = H_{RCAN}(M), \tag{8}$$

where $H_{RCAN}(\cdot)$ denotes the modified RCAN method. The RCAN proposed residual in residual structure and channel attention mechanism to adaptively extract the high-frequency information, then RCAN used the sub-piexl convolution layer to reconstruct the HR image. More details of RCAN is shown in [24]. At the same time, other CNN-based SR methods can be used instead of RCAN.

After the three modules of HRN, we finally get the reconstructed SR image I_{SR}. To show the effectiveness of our HRN, we choose the same loss function as previous works (e.g., L_1 loss function). Given a training set $\{I_{LR}^i, I_{HR}^i\}_{i=1}^N$, which contains N LR images and their original HR images. The loss function of the HRN module can be expressed as

$$L_{HRN}(\theta_h) = \frac{1}{N} \sum_{i=1}^{N} ||I_{SR}^i - I_{HR}^i||_1, \tag{9}$$

where θ_h denotes the parameter set of the HRN modules. More details of the training would be shown in Sect. 4. The cascade DFPN model and the HRN model can achieve acceptable performance, but in order to simplify the model, we use a multi-task loss function to combine the two modules into a unified network called SR-GSD.

3.3 Multi-task Loss Function

Multi-task learning has shown its unique advantages in the field of computer vision. In the Faster RCNN [15], the author chose to optimize the multi-task loss function to learn the parameters of RPN and Rast RCNN modules, which not only avoided the cumbersome steps of alternate training networks but further enhances the ease of use of the model. He et al. proposed Mask RCNN [8] which optimized the tasks of classification, object detection and instance segmentation with a multi-task loss function, which increased the generalization ability of the model.

In this section, we also borrowed the multi-task loss function and build a unified network. As shown in Fig. 2. Our SR-GSD chooses to optimize a multi-task loss which is formulated as

$$L_{SR-GSD} = \alpha L_{DFPN} + L_{HRN}, \tag{10}$$

where L_{DFPN} is the loss of the DFPN module and L_{HRN} is the loss of the HRN module. The two terms are weighted by a balancing parameter α. In our SR-GAN model, the degradation factors predicted from DFPN play a crucial role in the HRN, so we have to increase the value of the balancing parameter α. By default, we set $\alpha = 10$ and the total loss function is optimized by using stochastic gradient descent.

Based on the degradation factors proposal network (DFPN) and high-resolution reconstruction Network (HRN), we construct a blind super-resolution network SR-GSD and we can reconstruct an HR image from an LR image generated from general static degradation model. More experimental results will be shown in Sect. 4.

4   Experiments

4.1   Datasets Synthesis and Training Details

In our experiments, we use the DIV2K [1] dataset as the HR images of the training dataset. DIV2K dataset is a high-quality image dataset which is released in the NTIRE 2017 Challenge on SISR. There are 800 training images, 100 validation images and 100 test images in the DIV2K dataset. For testing, we compare the performance on four standard benchmark datasets: Set5 [2], Set14 [22], B100 [14] and Urban100 [10].

Different from previous methods based on a bicubic degradation model, we need to synthesize LR images according to Eq. 1. Before synthesizing low-resolution images, it is necessary to define the degradation factors. In Eq. 1, the degradation factors consist of blur kernels, noise level, and downsampling operation. For the downsampling operation, we choose the bicubic interpolation with a scale factor s to downsample the HR images. For the blur kernels, we use gaussian blur to simulate a general static degradation model same as [4]. Specifically, the ranges of standard deviation in the x-axis and y-axis are respectively set to $[0.2, 2]$, $[0.2, 3]$ and $[0.2, 4]$ for scale factors 2, 3 and 4. We sample it by a stride of 0.1 and the kernel size is fixed to 15×15. For scale factors 2, 3 and 4, there are 361, 841 and 1521 blur kernels, respectively. For the noise level range, we set the standard deviation of additive gaussian white noise from 0 to 70. Then, given an HR image, we synthesize LR image by blurring it with a blur kernel k, bicubic downsampling it with a scale factor s and followed by addition of AWGN with noise level n.

For training, we set the LR patch sizes to 48×48 which means the corresponding HR patch sizes for scale factors 2,3 and 4 are 96×96, 144×144 and 192×192, respectively. During the training process, we randomly select a blur kernel k and a noise level n to synthesize LR image patches. Furthermore, we argument the training dataset with random horizontal flips, random vertical flips, and 90 rotations. We set the mini-batch size to 16, and crop 16000 LR/HR patch pairs for each epoch. We train our SR-GSD model with ADAM optimizer by setting $\beta_1 = 0.9$, $\beta_2 = 0.999$ and $\epsilon = 10^{-8}$. The initial learning rate is set to 10^{-4} and then halved at every 200 epochs. We use PyTorch to implement our models with a GTX 1080 Ti GPU.

4.2   Experiments on General Static Degradations Model

In this subsection, we evaluate the performance of the SR-GSD on the general static degradations model. To show the advantages of our introduced method, we use three different degradation settings when synthesizing the LR test images. First, to compare with the previous method designed for the bicubic degradation model, the first degradation setting D_1 only consists of bicubic downsampler with scale factor s. The second degradation setting D_2 involves 15×15 Gaussian kernel with width 2 and bicubic downsampler with scale s, the third degradation setting D_3 adds Gaussian white noise with a standard deviation of 50 to the second set.

As shown in Table 1, we present the PSNR results of the CNN-based methods on different degradation settings, different test datasets, and different scale factors. As one can see, our proposed SR-GSD is superior to most methods with the bicubic degradation setting. Compared with RCAN or SAN, the performance of our method has a slight decline because of the additional blur and

Table 1. The PSNR results on different degradation settings, different test datasets, and different scale factors. D1, D2, and D3 represent the three degradation settings mentioned in Sect. 4.2. The best results are highlighted in bold.

Method	Scale	Set5	Set 14	B100	Urban100
		PSNR($D1/D2/D3$)			
Bicubic	×2	33.66/27.70/20.21	30.24/25.67/19.70	29.56/25.74/19.76	26.88/22.86/18.77
SRCNN	×2	36.66/27.71/20.25	32.45/25.75/19.80	31.36/25.98/19.87	29.50/23.18/18.99
DRCN	×2	37.53/27.83/16.91	33.06/25.79/16.60	31.80/25.83/16.50	30.70/22.98/16.05
RCAN	×2	38.27/27.88/16.61	**34.12**/25.82/16.31	32.41/25.86/16.19	**33.34**/23.03/15.82
SAN	×2	**38.31**/27.89/16.57	34.07/25.80/16.37	**32.42**/25.89/16.08	33.10/23.01/15.87
SR-GSD	×2	38.04/**33.84/25.31**	33.65/**29.70/23.96**	32.24/**29.38/23.61**	32.48/**27.19/22.27**
Bicubic	×3	30.39/27.23/20.13	27.55/25.32/19.65	27.21/25.42/19.62	24.46/22.54/18.59
SRCNN	×3	32.75/27.49/20.07	29.30/25.16/19.84	28.41/25.91/19.76	26.24/23.01/19.14
DRCN	×3	33.78/27.78/16.66	29.82/25.74/16.37	28.77/25.77/16.23	27.11/22.94/15.80
RCAN	×3	34.74/27.81/15.81	**30.64**/25.78/15.39	29.32/25.79/15.32	**29.08**/22.97/15.00
SAN	×2	**34.75**/27.81/15.79	30.59/25.81/15.42	**29.33**/25.80/15.17	28.98/22.97/15.30
SR-GSD	×3	34.56/**33.30/24.63**	30.46/**29.33/23.46**	29.18/**28.60/23.19**	28.61/**26.61/21.86**
Bicubic	×4	28.42/26.58/19.90	26.00/24.81/19.49	25.96/24.99/19.50	23.14/22.10/18.41
SRCNN	×4	30.48/26.79/20.10	27.50/25.23/19.53	26.90/25.14/19.64	24.52/22.94/19.00
DRCN	×4	31.51/27.64/16.37	28.08/25.64/16.13	27.22/25.61/16.03	25.11/22.82/15.58
RCAN	×4	32.62/27.70/16.41	28.86/25.64/16.16	27.76/25.61/16.03	**26.82**/22.88/15.60
SAN	×4	**32.64**/27.72/16.40	**28.92**/25.67/16.12	**27.78**/25.60/15.98	26.79/22.86/15.63
SR-GSD	×4	31.87/**30.22/24.34**	28.43/**26.80/23.28**	27.50/**26.42/23.40**	25.80/**24.12/21.57**

noise information, but in another two degraded settings our method is superior to the SAN. Besides, we observe that the previous method has a better effect on the bicubic degradation model, but the performance is worse when the LR image is synthesized from the general static degradation model. Therefore a reasonable degradation model is assumed to be critical for super-resolution.

Fig. 5. SISR performance comparison on image "Butterfly". The degradation involves 7 × 7 Gaussian kernel with width 1.5 and direct downsampler with scale factor 2.

To further show the scalability of our SR-GSD, we use 7 × 7 Gaussian kernel with width 1.5 and direct downsampler with scale factor 3 to synthesize the test image. we compare our SR-GSD with 4 state-of-the-art methods: DRCN [12], RCAN [24], SAN [5]. The visual comparison is given in Fig. 5. It can be seen that the proposed method produces more image texture details than the previous method.

4.3   Experiments on Real Images

In addition to experimenting on the synthetic LR images according to Eq. 1, we also do experiments on real LR images to demonstrate our proposed method. Since there are no ground-truth HR images, we only provide the visual comparison in Fig. 6.

Fig. 6. SISR performance comparison on real image "Chip" and "Frog" with scale factor 2

Figure 6 illustrates the SISR results on two real LR images "Chip" and "Frog", respectively. In this section, we also compare the proposed method with DRCN, RCAN and SAN. In contrast, our SR-GSD can alleviate the blurring artifacts better and recover more details. It can be observed from the SR images that our method is slightly better than the previous method for the restoration of the real blurred image, but for the real image with unknown noise, our method can obtain the SR image with better visual effect.

5   Conclusion

In this paper, we propose a super-resolution network for the general static degradation model (SR-GSD) for higher practicality image SISR. Different from existing CNN based methods for the bicubic degradation model, SR-GSD is designed for the general static degradation model and can achieve better visual SR results without any prior information. Specifically, we propose the degradation factors proposal network (DFPN) to estimate the blur kernel and noise level. Furthermore, the high-resolution reconstruction network is designed to utilize the predicted degradation factors to reconstruct HR images. The results on synthetic LR images demonstrated that the proposed method can produce better performance on the general static degradation model and the performance is slightly reduced on the bicubic degradation model. Moreover, the results on real LR images show that the proposed method can reconstruct visually plausible HR images. In summary, the proposed SR-GSD method offers a practical solution toward the SISR applications.

Acknowledgment. This work was supported by the National Natural Science Foundation of China (No. 61702044) and the Fundamental Research Funds for the Central Universities (No. 2019XD-A20).

References

1. Agustsson, E., Timofte, R.: Ntire 2017 challenge on single image super-resolution: dataset and study, pp. 1122–1131, July 2017. https://doi.org/10.1109/CVPRW. 2017.150
2. Bevilacqua, M., Roumy, A., Guillemot, C., Alberi-Morel, M.L.: Low-complexity single image super-resolution based on nonnegative neighbor embedding, September 2012. https://doi.org/10.5244/C.26.135
3. Chakrabarti, A.: A neural approach to blind motion deblurring. In: Leibe, B., Matas, J., Sebe, N., Welling, M. (eds.) ECCV 2016. LNCS, vol. 9907, pp. 221–235. Springer, Cham (2016). https://doi.org/10.1007/978-3-319-46487-9_14
4. Chetouani, A., Beghdadi, A., Deriche, M.: A new reference-free image quality index for blur estimation in the frequency domain. In: 2009 IEEE International Symposium on Signal Processing and Information Technology (ISSPIT), pp. 155–159. IEEE (2009)
5. Dai, T., Cai, J., Zhang, Y., Xia, S.T., Zhang, L.: Second-order attention network for single image super-resolution. In: Proceedings of the IEEE Conference on Computer Vision and Pattern Recognition, pp. 11065–11074 (2019)
6. Dong, C., Loy, C.C., He, K., Tang, X.: Image super-resolution using deep convolutional networks. CoRR abs/1501.00092 (2015)
7. Freeman, W.T., Pasztor, E.C., Carmichael, O.T.: Learning low-level vision. Int. J. Comput. Vision **40**(1), 25–47 (2000). https://doi.org/10.1023/A:1026501619075
8. He, K., Gkioxari, G., Dollár, P., Girshick, R.B.: Mask R-CNN. CoRR abs/17 03.06870 (2017). http://arxiv.org/abs/1703.06870
9. Hu, X., Mu, H., Zhang, X., Wang, Z., Tan, T., Sun, J.: Meta-SR: a magnification-arbitrary network for super-resolution. CoRR abs/1903.00875 (2019). http://arxiv.org/abs/1903.00875
10. Huang, J.B., Singh, A., Ahuja, N.: Single image super-resolution from transformed self-exemplars (2015). https://doi.org/10.1109/CVPR.2015.7299156
11. Kim, J., Lee, J.K., Lee, K.M.: Accurate image super-resolution using very deep convolutional networks. CoRR abs/1511.04587 (2015)
12. Kim, J., Lee, J.K., Lee, K.M.: Deeply-recursive convolutional network for image super-resolution. CoRR abs/1511.04491 (2015)
13. Lim, B., Son, S., Kim, H., Nah, S., Mu Lee, K.: Enhanced deep residual networks for single image super-resolution, July 2017
14. Martin, D., Fowlkes, C., Tal, D., Malik, J.: A database of human segmented natural images and its application to evaluating segmentation algorithms and measuring ecological statistics. In: Proceedings Eighth IEEE International Conference on Computer Vision, ICCV 2001, vol. 2, pp. 416–423, July 2001. https://doi.org/10. 1109/ICCV.2001.937655
15. Ren, S., He, K., Girshick, R.B., Sun, J.: Faster R-CNN: towards real-time object detection with region proposal networks. CoRR abs/1506.01497 (2015)
16. Shi, W., et al.: Real-time single image and video super-resolution using an efficient sub-pixel convolutional neural network, June 2016. https://doi.org/10.1109/ CVPR.2016.207

17. Shi, W., et al.: Cardiac image super-resolution with global correspondence using multi-atlas PatchMatch. In: Mori, K., Sakuma, I., Sato, Y., Barillot, C., Navab, N. (eds.) MICCAI 2013. LNCS, vol. 8151, pp. 9–16. Springer, Heidelberg (2013). https://doi.org/10.1007/978-3-642-40760-4_2

18. Sun, J., Cao, W., Xu, Z., Ponce, J.: Learning a convolutional neural network for non-uniform motion blur removal, March 2015

19. Tai, Y., Yang, J., Liu, X.: Image super-resolution via deep recursive residual network, July 2017. https://doi.org/10.1109/CVPR.2017.298

20. Tai, Y., Yang, J., Liu, X., Xu, C.: MemNet: a persistent memory network for image restoration. CoRR abs/1708.02209 (2017)

21. Yıldırım, D., Gungor, O.: A novel image fusion method using IKONOS satellite images. J. Geodesy Geoinform. **1**, 27–34 (2012). https://doi.org/10.9733/jgg.170512.1

22. Zeyde, R., Elad, M., Protter, M.: On single image scale-up using sparse-representations. In: Boissonnat, J.-D., et al. (eds.) Curves and Surfaces 2010. LNCS, vol. 6920, pp. 711–730. Springer, Heidelberg (2012). https://doi.org/10.1007/978-3-642-27413-8_47

23. Zhang, K., Zuo, W., Zhang, L.: Learning a single convolutional super-resolution network for multiple degradations. CoRR abs/1712.06116 (2017)

24. Zhang, Y., Li, K., Li, K., Wang, L., Zhong, B., Fu, Y.: Image super-resolution using very deep residual channel attention networks, July 2018

25. Zhang, Y., Tian, Y., Kong, Y., Zhong, B., Fu, Y.: Residual dense network for image super-resolution. CoRR abs/1802.08797 (2018)

26. Zou, W.W.W., Yuen, P.C.: Very low resolution face recognition problem. IEEE Trans. Image Process. **21**(1), 327–340 (2012). https://doi.org/10.1109/TIP.2011.2162423

Feature Combination Based on Receptive Fields and Cross-Fusion Feature Pyramid for Object Detection

Yongqiang Zhao, Yuan Rao$^{(\boxtimes)}$, Shipeng Dong, and Jiangnan Qi

Xi'an Jiaotong University, Xi'an 710049, China
yongqiang1210@stu.xjtu.edu.cn, yuanrao@163.com

Abstract. Currently, the state-of-the-art method about object detector in image mainly depends on deep backbones, such as ResNet-50, DarkNet-53, ResNet-101 and DenseNet-169, which benefits for their powerful capability of feature representations but suffers from high computational cost. On the basis of fast lightweight backbone network (i.e., VGG-16), this paper improves the capability of feature representations by combining features of different receptive fields and cross-fusing feature pyramids, and finally establishes a fast and accurate detector. The architecture of our model is designed to integrate FC-CF Net with two sub-modules: FC module and CF module. Inspired by the structure of receptive fields in visual systems of human, we propose a novel method about Feature Combination Based on Receptive Fields module (FC module), which takes the relationship between the size and eccentricity of receptive fields into account, and then combine them with original features for increasing the receptive field and information of the feature map. Furthermore, based on the structure of FPN (Feature Pyramid Network), we design a novel Cross-Fusion Feature Pyramid module (CF module), which combines top-down and bottom-up connections to fuse features across scales, and achieves high-level semantic feature map at all scales. Extensive experiments on PASCAL VOC 2007 and 2012 demonstrate that FC-CF Net achieves state-of-the-art detection accuracy (i.e. **82.4%** mAP, **80.5%** mAP) with high efficiency (i.e. **69 FPS**, **35 FPS**).

Keywords: Feature Combination · Receptive fields · Cross-fusion · Feature pyramid

1 Introduction

Object detection is no doubt one of the cutting edge applications in computer vision drawing attentions of researchers from various fields. In recent years, object detection has achieved significant advance with Hinton proposed to use deep neural network (DNN [1]) to automatic learn the high-level features of multimedia data. In general, the latest state-of-the-art detectors always can be divided into two categories: the two-stage approach [2–4] and the single-stage approach [5–7].

In the two-stage approach, a sparse set of category-agnostic object proposals within the given image is first generated, and then they are further classified and regressed according to CNN based deep features. It means that CNN representation plays a

© Springer Nature Switzerland AG 2019
T. Gedeon et al. (Eds.): ICONIP 2019, LNCS 11954, pp. 37–49, 2019.
https://doi.org/10.1007/978-3-030-36711-4_4

crucial role in the two-state methods, and the deeper of CNN backbone is, the powerful of feature representations is. A number of recent efforts have confirmed such a fact. For instance, Fu [8] and Zhou [9] extract feature from deeper CNN backbones, like ResNet-101 and DenseNet-169. All these methods adopt improved features to reach better results. However, such features basically come from deeper neural networks with heavy computational costs, making them suffer from a low inference speed.

In order to obtain high computational efficiency, a single-stage framework is investigated, where the phase of object proposal generation is discarded. In traditional single-stage approach, such as YOLO [5] and SSD [6], the capability of real-time processing has been illustrated, but the detection accuracy is usually behind that of the two-stage approach. Recently, YOLOv3 [7], DSSD [8] and STDN [9] substantially improve the detection accuracy, which are comparable to the top ones reported by the two-stage detectors, unfortunately, their performance are credited to deeper backbone (e.g., DarkNet-53, ResNet-101, DenseNet-169) as well, which limits the efficiency.

According to the advantages and disadvantages of single-stage and two-stage methods, to build a fast and accurate detector, an effective alternative method is proposed in this paper to enhance feature representation with the lightweight network by bringing in certain hand-crafted mechanisms rather than stubbornly deepening the

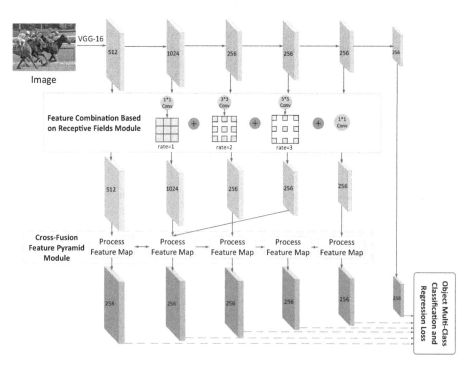

Fig. 1. Architecture of FC-CF Net. For better visualization, we only display the input and output layer corresponding to FC module and CF module. It can be seen from the architecture that the image in FC-CF network passes through the backbone network (VGG-16) first, then through FC module and CF module, finally carries on the classification and regression processing.

backbone. Therefore, a novel model, named FC-CF Net, merges two sub-modules (i.e. Feature Combination Based on Receptive Fields module (FC module) and Cross-Fusion Feature Pyramid module (CF module)) into the model of SSD. The detail structure is illustrated in Fig. 1.

FC module is inspired by the structure of receptive fields in the human visual system, which first processes the feature map obtained from VGG-16. Specifically, FC module uses the multi-branch pooling to process the feature map of different sizes with different rate dilated convolution layers to control their receptive field, and then reshapes them to generate representation. Finally, feature map is obtained by combining the dilated convolution feature map with the original feature map from VGG-16. FC module takes the relationship between the size and eccentricity of receptive fields into account for increasing the receptive field and information of the feature map. CF module is inspired by the structure of FPN [2]. CF module developed for building high-level semantic feature map at all scales, which processes the feature maps obtained by FC module and cross-fusing feature maps with different sizes. Furthermore, an advanced single-stage detector, named FC-CF Net, is constructed by assembling the FC module and CF module to the top of SSD, which is a real-time method with a lightweight backbone of VGG-16. Therefore, FC-CF Net delivers relatively decent scores that are comparable to the ones of up-to-date detectors [3, 4, 8, 9] with deeper backbone network and the faster speed than original lightweight detector.

The main contributions of our work are summarized as follows: (1) in order to enhance deep and overall features of lightweight CNN networks, we propose the FC module to simulate the configuration in terms of the size and eccentricity of receptive fields in human visual systems, and then combine the dilated convolution feature map with the original feature map. (2) a CF module is proposed to achieve high-level semantic feature map at all scales, which combines the cross connections to integrate all the features across different scales. (3) We construct a FC-CF Net based detector to replace the top convolution layers of SSD with FC module and CF module, which significantly upgrades the performance and still keeps the computational cost under control.

2 Related Work

Classical Object Detectors. Early object detection methods are mainly based on the sliding-window paradigm, which apply the hand-crafted features and classifiers on dense image grids to find objects. Firstly, Girshick et al. [10] designed deep learning in R-CNN, which is an end-to-end training method merging feature extraction, feature selection and feature classification into the same model. The overall of performance and efficiency have been optimized and the detection accuracy has been improved from 29.2% to 66%. Furthermore, the object detection task is quickly dominated by the CNN-based detectors with the deep convolutional network, which also can be roughly divided into two categories, i.e., the two-stage approach and single-stage approach.

Two-Stage Approach. The two-stage approach consists of two parts, the first one is to generate a set of candidate objects, and the second one is to determine the accurate object regions and the corresponding class labels based on convolutional network. R-CNN is the signature to start the new era of deep learning in the field of object detection, there are many optimized methods based on R-CNN, such as Faster R-CNN [11], FPN [2], to achieve dominant performance on several challenging datasets (e.g., PASCAL VOC [12], MS COCO [13] and ILSVRC [14]). Moreover, a series of effective algorithms are proposed to improve the accuracy of object detection, such as Mask R-CNN [3], Cascade R-CNN [4], RefineDet [15], and so on.

Single-Stage Approach. The single-stage approach only uses a single feedforward convolutional network to directly predict object classes and locations. The dominate detectors of single-stage are YOLO and SSD. Both of the two detectors adopt light-weight backbone for acceleration, while their accuracies apparently trail those methods about the top of two-stage. Considering the high efficiency, the single-stage approach attracts much more attention recently. DSSD [8] used deeper ResNet-101 and introduced additional context into SSD to improve the accuracy, STDN [9] directly utilized deeper DenseNet-169 network to detect the feature map and improved the detection accuracy from DSSD 78.6% to 79.3%, and this accuracy is even superior to the state-of-the-art methods of two-stage, however, such accuracy gains largely consume their advantage in speed.

Receptive Field. In order to increase the receptive field and semantic information in single-stage for mapping those features with higher-speed and lower computational burden, we design a novel mechanism about receptive fields instead of applying deeper backbone to integrate these features with original features. Actually, there exits several studies to discuss receptive fields in object detection, such as Inception-v4 [16] and ASPP [17]. While, Inception-v4 requires larger kernel size to reach the same sampling coverage and loses some crucial details. In addition, ASPP uses dilated convolution to change the sampling distance from center, but the features have the same resolution from the previous convolution layers with the same core size, in which process all clues are equal. However, this method can increase the confusion between objects and context. Therefore, FC module, similar to RFB Net [18], highlights the relationship between receptive field size and eccentricity in a combine-shape configuration, and increase the receptive field and semantic information of the feature map to enhance the feature discriminability and robustness.

Feature Pyramid. Feature pyramid is the basis of solutions for many computer vision applications in multi-scale processing. There are some methods exploiting lateral/ship connections or lateral-ship connections that maps the high-low-level feature into resolution and semantic levels. Some methods (e.g., Faster R-CNN [11], SSD [6]) adopts pyramidal architecture to predict the features in all levels, the others (FPN [2]) rely on the architecture for integrating those features with low-resolution, strong semantic information into high-resolution and weak semantic features by a top-down pathway and lateral connections. While, the semantic information of the image contained in these methods are insufficient. Based on these works, we propose a CF module to achieve the high-level semantic feature map at all scales by crossing connections for fusing the features in across scales.

3 Method

3.1 Feature Combination Based on Receptive Fields Module

In the past decades, researchers found there is a positive correlation between receptive field size and eccentricity. In this paper, we proposed a FC module by considering both of two factors to enhance the discriminability and robustness of features and build a more fast and accurate detection. Furthermore, FC module is a multi-branch convolution block which consist of five parts: the 1×1 convolution layer with different kernels; the dilated convolution layers with different rate (1, 2, 3), the combination layer of feature map after dilated convolution processing with different rates; the combination layer of combination feature map and the feature map from backbone (VGG-16). Figure 2 illustrates FC module along with specific operation method. We elaborate five parts and their detailed functions as following:

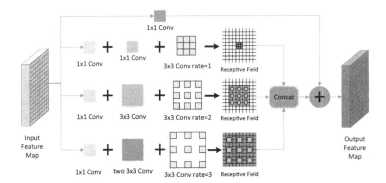

Fig. 2. The overview of the FC module. First, the first three branches use 1×1 convolution to change the number of channels in the feature map, then use multiple different kernels convolution and different rates dilated convolution to simulate the ratio between the size and eccentricity of the receptive fields, then concatenation the feature map. Finally, combination the feature map processed by 1×1 convolution with the concatenation feature map.

The first part is used to change the channels of input feature maps, which can reduce the computational complexity of the model. In order to capture more information like Inception, the second part utilizes two 3×3 convolution layer, which can also reduce the scale of parameters in this model. The third part utilizes the relation between the receptive field size and eccentricity in the human visual system. The fourth part is to produce the fusion features obtained from the convolution of each branch, which can capture more information in different receptive field. The last part is to merge the fusion features and the original features together, which can strength the influence about original feature and provide across-scale information of the feature map.

3.2   Cross-Fusion Feature Pyramid Module

In order to capture more feature and semantic information, a high-level semantic feature pyramid model should be proposed as object detection backbone, which is universal model described the cross-fusion feature based on the hierarchy pyramid in FC module. In this paper, we fix the size and scale-decreasing feature map obtained by FC module as input. The structure of cross-fusion feature pyramid model, including both of pathway about bottom-up and cross-fusion, shows in Fig. 3.

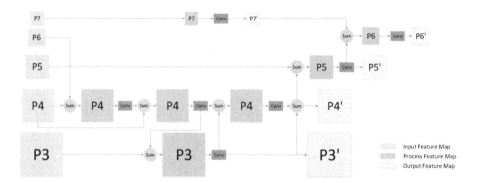

Fig. 3. The overview of the CF module. The CF module have 5 different size input layers (light blue) and 5 different size output feature maps (light yellow), Conv is stands for ReLU-Conv-BatchNorm, Sum is stands for changing the size of feature maps and then adding them. (Color figure online)

The bottom-up pathway is the feed forward computation of the FC module. It is a pyramid feature hierarchy composed of different size feature maps, and the scaling ratio is 2. Specifically, the output feature maps of FC module are {P2, P3, P4, P5, P6}, and their corresponding scales are {39, 19, 10, 5, 3}, the number of channels is {512, 1024, 256, 256}, respectively.

In cross-fusion pathway, the feature map is generated by the fusion of feature maps of different scales, so the resulting feature map has more image information and semantic information. Firstly, the channels of the input feature map which from bottom-up pathway is changed to 256 to facilitate cross-fusion. Then, some other processing inside the cross-fusion channel, include ReLU, Conv, BatchNorm and Sum. In the end, the output feature maps of CF module are {P2′, P3′, P4′, P5′, P6′}, which corresponding scale are {39, 19, 10, 5, 3} and the number of channels is 256. More specific fusion mode is shown in Fig. 3.

3.3   FC-CF Net Detection Architecture

Thanks to the FC module and CF module are satisfied to integrate into CNN network, we design a FC-CF Net detector to replace the top convolution layer by FC module and CF module on the basis of SSD. The FC-CF Net detector reuses the single-stage and multi-scale framework of SSD, where the FC module and CF module are embedded to ameliorate the feature extracted from the lightweight backbone, so that this kind of detector is more accurate and still fast enough.

Lightweight backbone: Although many lightweight networks have been proposed recently (e.g. ShuffleNet v1 [19], MobileNet v2 [20], ShuffleNet v2 [21]), We utilize original SSD as the backbone network to compare with VGG-16. Specifically, a VGG-16 architecture trained in advance on ILSVRC CLS-LOC datasets [14].

Feature Combination Based on Receptive Fields: In original SSD, there is a series of convolution layers to form different feature maps that continuously reduce spatial resolution and increase visual field. We only maintain the cascade structure of SSD, but the front convolution layers are replaced by FC module, which can increase the image information and visual field of feature map.

Cross-Fusion Feature Pyramid: In the traditional SSD model, a series of feature maps behind the basic network will be directly used for classification and regression operations. The different is that we use CF module to cross-fuse the feature maps output by FC module, so that feature maps can contains more image information and high-level semantic information. Finally, the feature maps obtained by CF module are classified and regressed using SSD architecture.

3.4   Training Settings

In order to maintain consistency, our training strategy is similar to SSD, including data augmentation, scale and aspect ratios for default boxes, smooth L1 loss for localization and softmax loss for classification. All the new conv-layers are initialized by MSRA method [22]. Meanwhile, in order to adapt to FC-CF network detector, we slightly adjust the learning rate. More details are given in the experimental section.

4   Experiments

We conducted experiments on three different datasets: PASCAL VOC 2007 and 2012 and MS COCO. There are 20 and 80 object classes in the VOC and COCO datasets, respectively. At the same time, the classes in VOC are the subset of that in COCO. We implement FC-CF Net detector based on Pytorch1.0.0 framework and utilize the mean Average Precision (mAP) as the metric to evaluate detection performance.

4.1   PASCAL VOC 2007 and PASCAL VOC 2012

All models are trained on the VOC 2007+2012 trainval set, and are tested on the VOC 2007 test set. In VOC 2007, a predicted bounding box is positive if its Intersection over Union (IoU) with the ground truth is higher than 0.5. In terms of learning rate setting, we use the warmup [23] strategy. In the first two epochs, the learning rate is gradually increased from 10^{-6} to 4×10^{-4}. The warmup strategy can keep the model running steadily during the initial training. After the warmup, the learning rate will be reduced to 10 times at 150 epoch and 200 epoch. The total number of training epochs is 250, the weight decay is 0.0005 and the momentum is 0.9. We use the default batch size 32 in training, and only use VGG-16 as the backbone network for all experiments on VOC dataset.

We compare FC-CF Net with the state-of-the-art detectors. With low dimension input size (300 × 300), FC-CF Net produces 80.8% mAP, compared with its base model (SSD [6]), its detection accuracy has improved by 3.6% mAP, which detection accuracy has reached the current highest level with such small input images, much better than several modern objectors (e.g., its detection accuracy is 2.2% higher than 78.6% of DSSD321 [8], 1.5% higher than 79.3% of STDN3221 [9], 0.8% higher than 80.0% of RefineDet320 [15]). By using larger input size 512 × 512, FC-CF Net achieves 82.9% mAP, surpassing many deep object detection methods (e.g., its detection accuracy is 9.7% higher than 73.2% of Faster R-CNN [11], 1.4% higher than 81.5% of DSSD512 [8], 2% higher than 80.9% of STDN512 [9]). From the experimental results, we can also find that FC-CF Net has fast detection speed (e.g., the detection speed of FC-CF Net300 is 76, FC-CF Net512 is 35) than many methods. In summary, FC-CF Net achieve the highest level between accuracy and speed. The specific information of the related algorithm is shown in Table 1, and the intuitive comparison information about the accuracy and speed of the algorithm is shown in Fig. 4.

We also tested our model on PASCAL VOC 2012. We use PASCAL VOC 2007 + 2012 trainval set for training, and test on PASCAL VOC 2012 test set, the other parts and relevant parameters of FC-CF Net remain unchanged. The results of correlation algorithm on VOC 2012 are shown in Table 1.

Table 1. Detection results on PASCAL VOC dataset.

Method	Backbone	Data	mAP (%) VOC2007	mAP (%) VOC2012	FPS
[A] Faster R-CNN [11]	VGG-16	07+12	73.2	70.4	7
[B] HyperNet [24]	VGG-16	07+12	76.3	71.4	0.88
[C] MR-CNN[25]	VGG-16	07+12	78.2	73.9	0.03
[d] RefineDet320 [15]	VGG-16	07+12	80.0	78.1	40.3
[D] RefineDet512 [15]	VGG-16	07+12	81.8	80.1	24.1
SSD321 [6]	VGG-16	07+12	77.2	75.8	120
[E] SSD512 [6]	VGG-16	07+12	79.8	78.5	50
[F] YOLOv2 [26]	Darknet-19	07+12	78.6	73.4	40
[g] DSSD321 [8]	ResNet-101	07+12	78.6	76.3	9.5
[G] DSSD513 [8]	ResNet-101	07+12	81.5	80.0	5.5
[h] STDN321 [9]	DenseNet-169	07+12	79.3	–	40.1
[H] STDN512 [9]	DarkNet-169	07+12	80.9	–	28.6
[i] FC-CF Net300	VGG-16	07+12	80.8	78.5	**69**
[I] FC-CF Net512	VGG-16	07+12	**82.4**	**80.5**	35
[j] FC-CF Net300*	ResNet-101	07+12	81.2	79.2	11
[J] FC-CF Net512*	ResNet-101	07+12	**82.9**	**81.1**	7

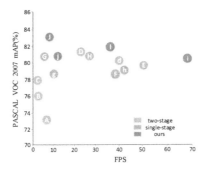

Fig. 4. Speed (FPS) vs. accuracy (mAP) on VOC 2007 test-dev. Enabled by the proposed FC-CF Net and FC-CF Net* our single-stage detector surpasses all existing high frame rate detectors.

4.2   Ablation Study

In order to demonstrate the effectiveness of different components in FC-CF Net, we select three kinds of algorithm (i.e., SSD [6], STDN321 [9], RefineDet320 [15]) as backbone framework and evaluate them on VOC 2007. In addition, the same parameters and input size have been set for a fair comparison during the process of evaluation. All models are trained on VOC 2007+2012 trainval set and tested on VOC 2007 test set. Table 2 and Fig. 5 shows the improvement effect of FC module and CF module on the basis of SSD, STDN, RefineDet, and also shows the improvement effect of the combination of FC module and CF module on the model. From the experimental results, it can be found that FC module and CF module can be used in other network models separately, thus improving the detection performance of the model. The improvement based on SSD is explained in detail below.

Table 2. Comparison of detection methods on the PASCAL VOC 2007 test set.

Method	Backbone	Data	mAP	Delta
SSD [6] (baseline)	VGG-16	07+12	77.2	0
SSD [6] + FC module	VGG-16	07+12	79.2	+2.0
SSD [6] + CF module	VGG-16	07+12	79.3	+2.1
SSD [6] + FC module + CF module	VGG-16	07+12	**80.8**	**+3.6**
STDN321 [9] (baseline)	DenseNet-169	07+12	79.3	0
STDN321 [9] + FC module	DenseNet-169	07+12	80.1	+0.8
STDN321 [9] + CF module	DenseNet-169	07+12	80.2	+0.9
STDN321 [9] + FC module + CF module	DenseNet-169	07+12	**80.8**	**+1.5**
RefineDet320 [15] (baseline)	VGG-16	07+12	80.0	0
RefineDet320 [15] + FC module	VGG-16	07+12	80.5	+0.5
RefineDet320 [15] + CF module	VGG-16	07+12	80.7	+0.7
RefineDet320 [15] + FC module + CF module	VGG-16	07+12	**81.1**	**+1.1**

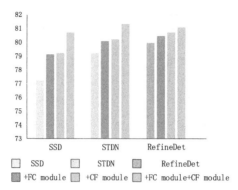

Fig. 5. Comparison of algorithms (i.e., SSD, STDN321, RefineDet320) and different methods (i.e., FC module, CF module, FC module + CF module) on the PASCAL VOC 2007 test set.

To demonstrate the effectiveness of FC module, we only remove FC module from the FC-CF Net and keep other part unchanged. In this case, VGG-16 is processed firstly, and then the results directly entered into the CF module for cross-feature fusion. When we remove FC module from FC-CF Net, the detection accuracy reduces in 1.6% (i.e., from 80.8% to 79.2%). At the same time, if we merge FC module into SSD model, the detection accuracy can immediately improve by 2% (i.e., from 77.2% to 79.2%). Maybe, there are two reasons can explain why FC module can improve the detection accuracy of the model. Firstly, the FC module can increase the receptive field of the feature without losing the feature information. Secondly, it can enhance the feature discriminability and robustness.

In addition,to validate the effectiveness of the CF module, we redesign the network structure by removing the CF module from the FC-CF Net and other parts remain unchanged. In this case, the image processed by VGG-16 first and then directly entered into the FC module for feature combination based on receptive field. After removing the CF module, the detection accuracy decreased by 1.5% (i.e., from 80.8% to 79.3%). At the same time, we add the CF module on the basis of SSD, the detection accuracy of the model is improved by 2.0% (i.e., from 77.2% to 79.2%). The reasons is that CF module can increase the low-level image information and high-level semantic information of features, thereby improving the detection accuracy of the model.

4.3   Ms Coco

In addition to PASCAL VOC 2007 and 2012, we also evaluate FC-CF Net on MS COCO [13]. Although, the detection methods using deep backbone always achieve better performance than those using VGG-16 on COCO, we use the FC-CF Net with VGG-16 backbone achieve the best detection accuracy. Following the protocol in COCO, we use the trainval35k set [27] for training and evaluate the results from test-dev evaluation server. Other parts and relevant parameters of FC-CF Net still remain unchanged.

The experiment results on COCO test-dev set are illustrated in Table 3. FC-CF Net300 with VGG16 can produce 30.3% AP that is better than all the two-stage methods based on VGG-16 (e.g., Faster R-CNN [11], OHEM [28], RefineDet320 [15]) and all the single-stage methods based on VGG-16 (e.g., SSD321 [6] and DSSD321 [8]). The accuracy of FC-CF Net can be improved to 33.5% by using larger input size (i.e., 512×512), which is much better than several modern object detectors, (e.g., SSD512 [6], DSSD512 [8], RefineDet512 [15]).

Table 3. Detection results on MS COCO test-dev set. Bold indicates the best performance.

Method	Data	Backbone	AP	AP50	AP75	APS	APM	APL
Faster R-CNN [11]	trainval	VGG-16	21.9	42.7	–	–	–	–
OHEM [28]	trainval	VGG-16	22.6	42.5	22.2	5.0	23.7	37.9
R-FCN [29]	trainval	ResNet-101	29.9	51.9	–	10.8	32.8	45.0
RefineDet320 [15]	traival35k	VGG-16	29.4	49.2	31.3	10.0	32.0	44.4
RefineDet512 [15]	traival35k	VGG-16	33.0	54.5	35.5	16.3	36.3	44.3
YOLOv2 [25]	traival35k	DarkNet-19	21.6	44.0	19.2	5.0	22.4	35.5
SSD321 [6]	trainval	ResNet-101	28.0	45.4	29.3	6.2	28.3	49.3
SSD513 [6]	trainval	ResNet-101	31.2	50.4	33.3	10.2	34.5	49.8
DSSD321 [8]	traival35k	ResNet-101	28.0	46.1	29.2	7.4	28.1	74.6
DSSD512 [8]	traival35k	ResNet-101	33.2	53.3	35.2	13.0	35.4	51.1
FC-CF Net300	traival35k	VGG-16	30.7	50.3	32.4	10.6	32.6	45.1
FC-CF Net512	traival35k	VGG-16	34.1	55.1	36.1	16.9	37.0	44.9
FC-CF Net300*	traival35k	ResNet-101	31.7	51.5	33.1	11.9	33.6	46.8
FC-CF Net512*	traival35k	ResNet-101	**34.6**	**56.4**	**37.2**	**18.3**	**38.2**	**45.7**

5 Conclusion and Feature Works

In general, the traditional object detect algorithm always depends on the deep backbone network to improve the capability of feature representations and the accuracy, but reduces the detection speed. In order to enhance the feature representation ability of fast lightweight network, we design a fast and powerful target detection network FC-CF Net based on FC module and CF module. Several experiments have done on PASCAL VOC 2007, 2012, and MS COCO to demonstrate that FC-CF Net achieves the state-of-the-art detection accuracy with high efficiency. In the future, we plan to use FC-CF Net to detect more other specific objects, such as faces, vehicles, traffic signs, and introduce the attention mechanics and reinforcement learning to enhance the whole performance.

References

1. Lecun, Y., Bengio, Y., Hinton, G.: Deep learning. Nature **521**(7553), 436 (2015)
2. Seferbekov, S.S., Iglovikov, V.I., Buslaev, A.V., et al.: Feature pyramid network for multi-class land segmentation. In: IEEE/CVF Conference on Computer Vision and Pattern Recognition, pp. 272–275 (2018)
3. He, K., Gkioxari, G., Dollár, P., Girshick, R.: Mask R-CNN. In: IEEE International Conference on Computer Vision, pp. 2980–2988 (2017)

4. Cai, Z., Vasconcelos, N.: Cascade R-CNN: delving into high quality object detection. In: IEEE/CVF Conference on Computer Vision and Pattern Recognition, pp. 6154–6162 (2018)
5. Redmon, J., Divvala, S., Girshick, R., Farhadi, A.: You only look once: Unified, real-time object detection. In: CVPR (2016)
6. Liu, W., et al.: SSD: single shot multibox detector. In: Leibe, B., Matas, J., Sebe, N., Welling, M. (eds.) ECCV 2016. LNCS, vol. 9905, pp. 21–37. Springer, Cham (2016). https://doi.org/10.1007/978-3-319-46448-0_2
7. Redmon, J., Farhadi, A.: YOLOv3: an incremental improvement. arXiv preprint arXiv:1804. 02767 (2018)
8. Fu, C.Y., et al.: DSSD: deconvolutional single shot detector. arXiv preprint arXiv:1701. 06659 (2017)
9. Zhou, P., Geng, C.: Transmission. Scale-transferrable object detection. In: IEEE/CVF Conference on Computer Vision and Pattern Recognition, pp. 528–537 (2018)
10. Girshick, R.B., Donahue, J., Darrell, T., Malik, J.: Rich featurehier archies for accurate object detection and semantic segmentation. In: CVPR, pp. 580–587 (2014)
11. Ren, S., He, K., Girshick, R., et al.: Faster R-CNN: towards real-time object detection with region proposal networks In: International Conference on Neural Information Processing Systems (2015)
12. Everingham, M., Van Gool, L., Williams, C.K., Winn, J., Zisserman, A.: The pascal visual object classes (VOC) challenge. IJCV **88**, 303–308 (2010)
13. Lin, T.-Y., et al.: Microsoft COCO: common objects in context. In: Fleet, D., Pajdla, T., Schiele, B., Tuytelaars, T. (eds.) ECCV 2014. LNCS, vol. 8693, pp. 740–755. Springer, Cham (2014). https://doi.org/10.1007/978-3-319-10602-1_48
14. Russakovsky, O., et al.: Imagenet large scale visual recognition challenge. IJCV **115**, 211–252 (2015)
15. Zhang, S., Wen, L., Bian, X., et al.: Single-shot refinement neural network for object detection. In: IEEE/CVF Conference on Computer Vision and Pattern Recognition, pp. 4203–4212 (2018)
16. Szegedy, C., Ioffe, S., Vanhoucke, V., Alemi, A.A.: Inception-v4, inception-resnet and the impact of residual connections on learning. In: AAAI (2017)
17. Chen, L.C., Papandreou, G., Schroff, F., Adam, H.: Rethinking atrous convolution for semantic image segmentation. arXiv preprint arXiv:1706.05587 (2017)
18. Liu, S., Huang, D., Wang, Y.: Receptive field block net for accurate and fast object detection (2018)
19. Zhang, X., Zhou, X., Lin, M., et al.: ShuffleNet: an extremely efficient convolutional neural network for mobile devices. arXiv preprint arXiv:1707.01083 (2017)
20. Sandler, M., Howard, A., Zhu, M., et al.: Inverted residuals and linear bottlenecks: mobile networks for classification, detection and segmentation. arXiv preprint arXiv:1801.04381 (2018)
21. Ma, N., Zhang, X., Zheng, H.T., et al.: ShuffleNet V2: practical guidelines for efficient CNN architecture design. In: European Conference on Computer Vision (2018)
22. He, K., Zhang, X., Ren, S., Sun, J.: Delving deep into rectifiers: surpassing human level performance on imagenet classification. In: ICCV (2015)
23. Gotmare, A., Keskar, N.S., Xiong, C., et al.: A closer look at deep learning heuristics: learning rate restarts, warmup and distillation (2018)
24. Lin, T., Goyal, P., Girshick, R.B., He, K., Dollár, P.: Focal loss for dense object detection. In: ICCV (2017)
25. Gidaris, S., Komodakis, N.: Object detection via a multi region and semantic segmentation-aware CNN model. In: ICCV, pp. 1134–1142 (2015)

26. Redmon, J., Farhadi, A.: YOLO9000: better, faster, stronger. In: IEEE/CVF Conference on Computer Vision and Pattern Recognition, pp. 6517–6525 (2017)
27. Bell, S., Zitnick, C.L., Bala, K., Girshick, R.B.: Inside-outside net: detecting objects in context with skip pooling and recurrent neural networks. In: CVPR, pp. 2874–2883 (2016)
28. Shrivastava, A., Gupta, A., Girshick, R.B.: Training region-based object detectors with online hard example mining. In: CVPR, pp. 761–769 (2016)
29. Dai, J., Li, Y., He, K., Sun, J.: R-FCN: object detection via region-based fully convolutional networks. In: NIPS, pp. 379–387 (2016)

Multi-scale Information Distillation Network for Image Super Resolution in NSCT Domain

Yu Sang$^{(\boxtimes)}$, Jinguang Sun, Simiao Wang, Yanfei Peng,
Xinjun Zhang, and Zhiyang Yang

School of Electronic and Information Engineering,
Liaoning Technical University, Huludao 125105, China
sangyu2008bj@sina.com

Abstract. Deep learning based methods have dominated super-resolution (SR) field due to their remarkable performance in terms of effectiveness and efficiency. In this paper, we propose a new multi-scale information distillation network (MSID-N) in the non-subsampled contourlet transform (NSCT) domain for single image super resolution (SISR). MSID-N mainly consists of a series of stacked multi-scale information distillation (MSID) blocks to fully exploit features from images and effectively restore the low resolution (LR) images to high-resolution (HR) images. In addition, most previous methods predict the HR images in the spatial domain, producing over-smoothed outputs while losing texture details. Thus, we integrate NSCT and demonstrate the superiority of NSCT over wavelet transform (WT), and formulate the SISR problem as the prediction of NSCT coefficients, which is able to further make MSID-N preserve richer structure details than that in spatial domain. The experimental results on three standard image datasets show that our proposed method is capable of obtaining higher PSNR/SSIM values and preserving complex edges and curves better than other state-of-the-art methods.

Keywords: Single Image Super Resolution (SISR) · Multi-scale information distillation network · Non-subsampled Contourlet Transform (NSCT) · Convolutional Neural Networks (CNNs)

1 Introduction

SISR is an important low-level vision task which has high practical value in many application fields such as remote sensing, medical imaging and object detecting. It aims at reconstructing a HR image from a single LR image, which is an ill-posed inverse problem.

In recent years, CNNs-based models [1–20] significantly improve the super resolution (SR) quality from the first SRCNN [1] to the latest RCAN [17], which are remarkably better than conventional SR methods. The performance of SRCNN was limited by its shallow structure. To achieve higher performance the networks are tend to be deeper and deeper, Kim et al. proposed the VDSR [3] model with a deeper structure. Recently, some very deep models have been proposed such as EDSR [4] and RCAN, which achieves very pleasing performance on super-resolution tasks. Moreover,

© Springer Nature Switzerland AG 2019
T. Gedeon et al. (Eds.): ICONIP 2019, LNCS 11954, pp. 50–59, 2019.
https://doi.org/10.1007/978-3-030-36711-4_5

super-resolution models integrated with dense connections have been proposed, such as SRDenseNet [8] and MemNet [9], which boosts the performance further more. In addition, some more effective CNN-based SR methods construct the entire network by connecting a series of identical feature extraction modules such as MSRN [14], RDN [15], IDN [16], indicating the capability of each block plays a crucial role.

The above SR methods are conducted in the spatial domain. By contrast, SR in the transform domain can preserve the image's context and texture information in different layers to produce better SR results. With that in mind, Guo et al. [18] designed a deep wavelet super-resolution (DWSR) network to acquire HR image by predicting "missing details" of wavelet coefficients of the LR image. Later, the same team [19] integrated discrete cosine transformation (DCT) into CNN and put forward an orthogonally regularized deep network. In addition, Huang et al. [20] applied WT to CNN-based face SR to validate that this method can accurately capture global topology information and local textural details of faces. The existing models received excellent performance in terms of peak signal-to-noise ratio (PSNR) and structural similarity index (SSIM) in the SISR problem.

In this paper, we present a novel CNN architecture in the NSCT domain for SISR. The main contributions are as follows:

(1) We propose multi-scale information distillation (MSID) block to fully exploit features from images; and MSID-N is mainly formed by multiple MSID blocks to effectively restore the LR images.
(2) We integrate NSCT and demonstrate the superiority of NSCT over WT, and formulate the SISR problem as the prediction of NSCT coefficients, which is able to make MSID-N preserve richer detail information than that in spatial domain.
(3) We evaluate the proposed method with three standard image datasets. The qualitative and quantitative results confirm that our method is capable of obtaining data with higher PSNR/SSIM values and preserving complex edges and curves better than other state-of-the-art methods.

2   Proposed Method

In this section, we will first describe the architecture of our proposed MSID-N. After that, we will provide a brief introduction to the proposed MSID block, followed by the description of NSCT domain.

2.1   Network Architecture

As shown in Fig. 1, our MSID-N consists of two parts, the shallow feature extraction (SFE) module and the deep feature extraction (DFE) module. Let's denote the I^{LR} and I^{HR} as the LR images and HR images respectively. Our ultimate goal is to learn an end-to-end mapping function F between I^{LR} and I^{HR}. So, we solve the following problem:

$$\hat{\theta} = \arg\min_{\theta} \frac{1}{N} \sum_{i=1}^{N} L^{SR}\left(F_\theta\left(I_i^{LR}\right), I_i^{HR}\right), \tag{1}$$

where $\theta = \{w^1, w^2, \cdots, w^p, b^1, b^2, \cdots, b^p\}$ denotes the weights and bias of our p convolutional layers. N is the number of training samples. L^{SR} is the loss function for minimizing the difference between the I^{LR} and I^{HR}.

The mean square error (MSE) function is the most widely-used objective optimization function in image super-resolution [2, 7, 9]. However, Lim et al. [14] have experimentally demonstrated that training with MSE loss is not a good choice. In order to avoid introducing unnecessary training tricks and reduce computations, we use the mean absolute error (MAE) function L^{SR} as a better alternative, as defined below

$$L^{SR}\left(F_\theta\left(I_i^{LR}\right), I_i^{HR}\right) = \frac{1}{N} \sum_{i=1}^{N} \left\| I_i^{LR} - I_i^{HR} \right\|_1. \tag{2}$$

Specially, we use two convolution layers to extract the shallow feature M_0 from the noisy seismic signals. So we can have

$$M_0 = H_{SFE1}\left(H_{SFE2}\left(I^{LR}\right)\right), \tag{3}$$

where H_{SFE1} and H_{SFE2} denote the convolution operation of the two layers in SFE module respectively. After shallow feature module, the shallow feature M_0 is used for DFE module, which contains a set of cascaded MSID blocks. Each MSID block can gather more information as much as possible and distill more useful information. After that we use a 1×1 convolutional layer to adaptively control the output information. We name this operation as feature fusion formulated as

$$M_{GF} = H_{GFF}\left([M_1, M_2, \cdots, M_D]\right), \tag{4}$$

where $[M_1, M_2, \cdots, M_D]$ denotes the concatenation of feature maps produced by MSID blocks 1, 2, ..., D. H_{GFF} is a composite function of 1×1 convolutional layer. Global residual learning is utilized after feature fusion to obtain the feature maps I_{Output}, which can be formulated as

$$I_{Output} = M_{GF} + M_0. \tag{5}$$

In our MSID-N, all convolutional layers have 64 filters, except that in feature fusion, whose has 128 filters.

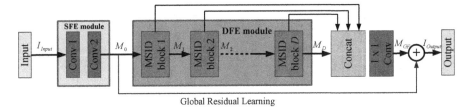

Fig. 1. The architecture of our proposed MSID-N.

2.2 MSID Block

The proposed MSID block is shown in Fig. 2. Each MSID block can be divided into two parts, which are used for exploiting short and long-path features. Different from the IDN model [19], we construct three-bypass network in each part and different bypass use different convolutional kernels. In this way, our model can adaptively detect the short and long-path features at different scales.

Supposing the input and output of the first part are M_{d-1} and O_{P1}, we have

$$O_{P1} = \sigma\big(Y_{1\times1}^1\big(\big[\sigma\big(Y_{3\times3}^2(M_{d-1})\big) + \sigma\big(Y_{5\times5}^3(M_{d-1})\big) + \sigma\big(Y_{7\times7}^4(M_{d-1})\big)\big]\big)\big), \quad (6)$$

where $Y_{1\times1}^1$, $Y_{3\times3}^2$, $Y_{5\times5}^3$ and $Y_{7\times7}^4$ refers to the function of 1×1, 3×3, 5×5 and 7×7 convolutional layers in the first part respectively. $[\cdot]$ indicates the concatenation of feature maps by different convolutional kernels. σ denotes the ReLU function [21]. After that, the feature maps with 64 dimensions of O_{P1} and the input M_{d-1} are concatenated in the channel dimension,

$$R = C(S(O_{P1}, 64), M_{d-1}), \quad (7)$$

where C and S indicate concatenation operation and slice operation respectively. Therefore, the 64 dimensional features are fetched from S. The purpose is to combine the current multi-scale information with the previous information. It can be regarded as retained short path information. And then, we take the rest of 64 dimensional feature maps as the input of the second part, which mainly further extracts long path information,

$$O_{P2} = \sigma\big(Y_{1\times1}^5\big(\big[\sigma\big(Y_{3\times3}^6(O_{P1}, 64)\big) + \sigma\big(Y_{5\times5}^7(O_{P1}, 64)\big) + \sigma\big(Y_{7\times7}^8(O_{P1}, 64)\big)\big]\big)\big), \quad (8)$$

where $Y_{1\times1}^5$, $Y_{3\times3}^6$, $Y_{5\times5}^7$ and $Y_{7\times7}^8$ refers to the function of 1×1, 3×3, 5×5 and 7×7 convolutional layers in the second part respectively. Finally, the input information, the short path information and the long path information are aggregated, which can be formulated as follows:

$$M_d = R + O_{P2}. \quad (9)$$

where M_d indicates the output of the MSID block.

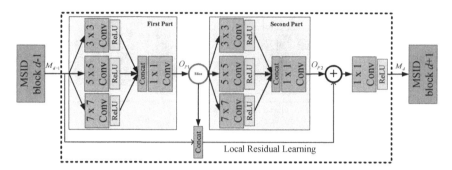

Fig. 2. The architecture of MSID block.

2.3 Non-subsampled Contourlet Transform (NSCT) Prediction

Wavelet analysis [22] cannot "optimally" represent image functions with straight lines and curves. The contourlet transform (CT) [23] improved WT. It is constructed by two filter-bank stages, a Laplacian Pyramid (LP) followed by a Directional Filter Bank (DFB). CT is a shift-variant transform, as it involves sampling at both the LP and the DFB stages. However, shift-variance is not a desirable property for various multimedia processing tasks. To overcome this problem, Cunha et al. [24] proposed NSCT, which is a translation-invariant version of the CT. This transform eliminates all sub-sampling operations, resulting in high redundancy.

NSCT mainly comprises non-subsampled pyramid filter bank (NSPFB) and non-subsampled direction filter bank (NSDFB) in cascade. Firstly, decomposition is made on the image by NSPFB and the resulting sub-bands is taken as input of NSDFB to get decomposition results of the original image in multiple dimensions and directions K-level decomposition is made on any image by NSCT to get one low-frequency sub-band and some high-frequency band-pass sub-bands, all of which have the same size as the original image. Both NSPFB and NSDFB are eligible for full reconstruction so NSCT is fully rebuilt as well.

As stated in the introduction, SR in the transform domain can achieve better results than spatial domain. In this paper, we formulate the SISR problem as the prediction of NSCT coefficients, which is able to make MSID-N further preserve richer structure details. In Fig. 3, we compare the high-frequency coefficients of NSCT and WT, where we can clearly see that NSCT represents the curvature more accurately. This demonstrates the superiority of NSCT over WT.

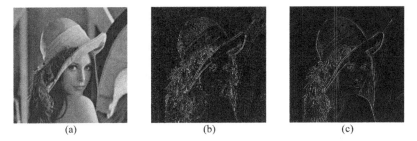

            (a)   (b)   (c)

Fig. 3. Comparison of NSCT and WT coefficients on the Lena image: (a) The original HR image Lena; (b) the fusion of NSCT high-frequency coefficients; (c) the fusion of discrete WT high-frequency coefficients.

In this paper, we formulate the SR problem as the prediction of NSCT coefficients as show in Fig. 4, which is able to make MSID-N further preserve richer structure details than that in spatial domain. It is worth mentioning that NSCT can be used in different SR networks, which is a simple and effective way to improve the performance. Speaking of the role of NSCT, it is to take further experiment in Sect. 3.3. The detailed process of NSCT implementation can be found in [24].

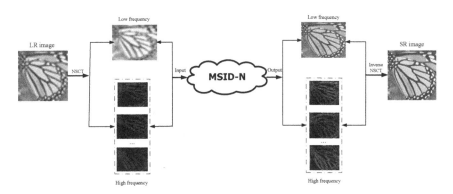

Fig. 4. NSCT domain coefficients prediction.

3 Experiments

In the experiments, the performance of the proposed method is evaluated on both qualitative and quantitative aspects. PSNR and SSIM [25] are used for quantitative evaluation.

3.1 Implementation Details

Recently, Timofte et al. [26] have released a high-quality dataset DIV2 K for image restoration applications. We train our model with 800 training images and use 5 validation images in the training process. For testing, we use the standard benchmark datasets: Set5, Set14, and BSD100. We use the RGB input patches of size 48 × 48 from the LR input for training. We sample the LR patches randomly and augment them by flipping horizontally or vertically and rotating 90. We implement our method with the Torch7 framework and update it with the ADAM optimizer. The mini-batch size is 64, and the learning rate begins with 0.0001 and decreases half for every 100 epochs. Training our model roughly takes 12 h with a NVIDIA Tesla P100 for 200 epochs.

3.2   Evaluation of Results

In this section, we evaluate the performance of our method on three standard image datasets. In order to evaluate the SISR performance, we use PSNR and SSIM as a quantitative evaluation metric to justify the reconstruction results. For fair comparison, we use the released codes of the above models and train all models with the same training set. The PSNR (dB) and SSIM values for comparison are shown in Tables 1 and 2. The tables show that our proposed method obtains higher PSNR/SSIM values than other methods; it is that our model constructs multi-bypass network to adaptively detect the short and long-path features and distill more useful information at different scales in transform domain (Fig. 5).

Table 1. Average PSNR values for scaling factor ×2, ×3, and ×4.

Datasets	Scale	Bicubic	VDSR	MemNet	DWSR	IDN	MSRN	Ours
Set5	×2	33.66	37.53	37.78	37.43	37.83	38.08	38.51
	×3	30.39	33.66	34.09	33.82	34.11	34.38	34.75
	×4	28.42	31.35	31.74	31.39	31.82	32.07	32.36
Set14	×2	30.24	33.03	33.28	33.07	33.30	33.74	34.21
	×3	27.55	29.77	30.00	29.83	29.99	30.34	30.68
	×4	26.00	28.01	28.26	28.04	28.25	28.60	28.88
BSD100	×2	29.56	31.90	32.08	31.80	32.08	32.23	32.59
	×3	27.21	28.82	28.96	–	28.95	29.08	29.44
	×4	25.96	27.29	27.40	27.25	27.41	27.52	27.84

Table 2. Average SSIM values for scaling factor ×2, ×3, and ×4.

Datasets	Scale	Bicubic	VDSR	MemNet	DWSR	IDN	MSRN	Ours
Set5	×2	0.9299	0.9587	0.9597	0.9568	0.9600	0.9605	0.9664
	×3	0.8682	0.9213	0.9248	0.9215	0.9253	0.9262	0.9289
	×4	0.8104	0.8838	0.8893	0.8833	0.8903	0.8903	0.8937
Set14	×2	0.8688	0.9124	0.9142	0.9106	0.9148	0.9170	0.9203
	×3	0.7742	0.8314	0.8350	0.8308	0.8354	0.8395	0.8412
	×4	0.7024	0.7674	0.7723	0.7669	0.7730	0.7751	0.7774
BSD100	×2	0.8431	0.8960	0.8978	0.8940	0.8985	0.9013	0.9061
	×3	0.7385	0.7976	0.8001	–	0.8013	0.8041	0.8064
	×4	0.6675	0.7251	0.7281	0.7240	0.7297	0.7273	0.7302

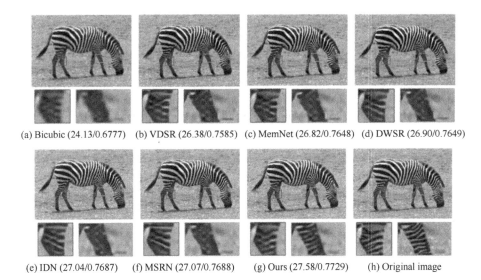

(a) Bicubic (24.13/0.6777)   (b) VDSR (26.38/0.7585)   (c) MemNet (26.82/0.7648)   (d) DWSR (26.90/0.7649)

(e) IDN (27.04/0.7687)   (f) MSRN (27.07/0.7688)   (g) Ours (27.58/0.7729)   (h) Original image

Fig. 5. Visual results (PSNR/SSIM) of our method and several state-of-the-art methods.

3.3 Ablation Investigation

Given that in this paper, we introduce to predict NSCT coefficients for SISR. We evaluate the effect of the contribution on scale $2\times$. We use three methods (MSRN, IDN and MSID-N) and integrate them with NSCT prediction. Figure 6(a) shows the comparison results of MSID-N across different image datasets. Figure 6(b) shows the comparison results of IDN and MSRN. From Fig. 6, we can see that three methods can be improved significantly when integrated with NSCT. Experimental results demonstrate that NSCT prediction is superior to spatial domain; the improvements are consistent across various networks and benchmarks.

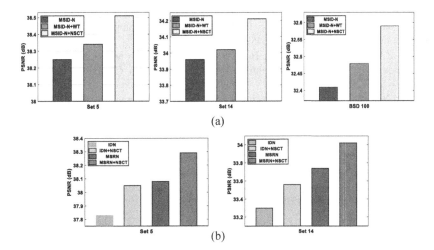

Fig. 6. Effectiveness of NSCT prediction. (a) Comparison for spatial domain, WT domain and NSCT domain. (b) NSCT prediction using different networks.

4 Conclusions

In this paper, a CNN-based SISR method is proposed. Our network MSID-N contains a set of cascaded MSID blocks, which effectively exploit features of image to improve the SISR performance. In addition, NSCT is applied to the network structure to effectively preserve richer detail information than spatial domain, which further improves the SISR performance. Qualitative and quantitative results show that the proposed method is much better than other state-of-the-art methods, boosting restoration ability of LR images.

Acknowledgements. This work was supported in part by the National Science Foundation of China under Grant Nos. 61602226; in part by the PhD Startup Foundation of Liaoning Technical University of China under Grant No. 18-1021; in part by the Basic Research Project of Colleges and Universities of Liaoning Provincial Department of Education under Grant No. LJ2017FBL004.

References

1. Dong, C., Loy, C.C., He, K., Tang, X.: Learning a deep convolutional network for image super-resolution. In: Fleet, D., Pajdla, T., Schiele, B., Tuytelaars, T. (eds.) ECCV 2014. LNCS, vol. 8692, pp. 184–199. Springer, Cham (2014). https://doi.org/10.1007/978-3-319-10593-2_13
2. Dong, C., Loy, C.C., Tang, X.: Accelerating the super-resolution convolutional neural network. In: Leibe, B., Matas, J., Sebe, N., Welling, M. (eds.) ECCV 2016. LNCS, vol. 9906, pp. 391–407. Springer, Cham (2016). https://doi.org/10.1007/978-3-319-46475-6_25
3. Kim, J., Lee, J.K., Lee, K.M.: Accurate image super-resolution using very deep convolutional networks. In: Proceedings of the IEEE Conference on Computer Vision and Pattern Recognition (CVPR), pp. 1646–1654 (2016)
4. Lim, B., Son, S., Kim, H., Nah, S., Lee, K.M.: Enhanced deep residual networks for single image super-resolution. In: Proceedings of the IEEE Conference on Computer Vision and Pattern Recognition Workshops (CVPRW) (2017)
5. Kim, J., Lee, J.K., Lee, K.M.: Deeply-recursive convolutional network for image super-resolution. In: Proceedings of the IEEE Conference on Computer Vision and Pattern Recognition (CVPR), pp. 1637–1645 (2016)
6. Wang, Z.W., Liu, D., Yang, J.C., Han, W., Huang, T.: Deep networks for image super-resolution with sparse prior. In: International Conference on Computer Vision (ICCV), pp. 370–378 (2016)
7. Tai, Y., Yang, J., Liu, X.M.: Image super-resolution via deep recursive residual network. In: Proceedings of the IEEE Conference on Computer Vision and Pattern Recognition (CVPR), pp. 3147–3155 (2017)
8. Tong, T., Li, G., Liu, X., Gao, Q.Q.: Image super-resolution using dense skip connections. In: International Conference on Computer Vision (ICCV), pp. 4809–4817 (2017)
9. Tai, Y., Yang, J., Liu, X.M., Xu, C.Y.: MemNet: a persistent memory network for image restoration. In: Proceedings of the IEEE Conference on Computer Vision and Pattern Recognition (CVPR), pp. 4539–4547 (2017)

10. Bricman, P.A., Ionescu, R.T.: CocoNet: a deep neural network for mapping pixel coordinates to color values. In: Cheng, L., Leung, A.C.S., Ozawa, S. (eds.) ICONIP 2018. LNCS, vol. 11302, pp. 64–76. Springer, Cham (2018). https://doi.org/10.1007/978-3-030-04179-3_6

11. Ahn, N., Kang, B., Sohn, K.A.: Fast, accurate, and lightweight super-resolution with cascading residual network. In: Proceedings of ECCV (2018)

12. Shocher, A., Cohen, N., Irani, M.: Zero-shot super-resolution using deep internal learning. In: Proceedings of CVPR (2018)

13. Zhang, K., Zuo, W., Zhang, L.: Learning a single convolutional super-resolution network for multiple degradations. In: Proceedings of CVPR (2018)

14. Li, J.C., Fang, F.M., Mei, K.F., Zhang, G.X.: Multi-scale residual network for image super-resolution. In: European Conference on Computer Vision (ECCV), pp. 527–542 (2018)

15. Zhang, Y.L., Tian, Y.P., Kong, Y., Zhong, B.N., Fu, Y.: Residual dense network for image super-resolution. In: The IEEE Conference on Computer Vision and Pattern Recognition (CVPR) (2018)

16. Hui, Z., Wang, X.M., Gao, X.B.: Fast and accurate single image super-resolution via information distillation network. In: Proceedings of the IEEE Conference on Computer Vision and Pattern Recognition (CVPR), pp. 723–731 (2018)

17. Zhang, Y., Li, K., Li, K., Wang, L., Zhong, B., Fu, Y.: Image super-resolution using very deep residual channel attention networks. In: Ferrari, V., Hebert, M., Sminchisescu, C., Weiss, Y. (eds.) ECCV 2018. LNCS, vol. 11211, pp. 294–310. Springer, Cham (2018). https://doi.org/10.1007/978-3-030-01234-2_18

18. Guo, T.T., Mousavi, H.S., Vu, T.H., Monga, V.: Deep wavelet prediction for image super-resolution. In: The IEEE Conference on Computer Vision and Pattern Recognition Workshops (CVPRW), pp. 104–113 (2017)

19. Guo, T.T., Mousavi, H.S., Monga, V.: Orthogonally regularized deep networks for image super-resolution. arXiv preprint arXiv:1802.02018 (2018)

20. Huang, H.B., He, R., Sun, Z.N., Tan, T.N.: Wavelet-srnet: a wavelet-based CNN for multi-scale face super resolution. In: Proceedings of the IEEE Conference on Computer Vision and Pattern Recognition (CVPR), pp. 1689–1697 (2017)

21. Glorot, X., Bordes, A., Bengio, Y.: Deep sparse rectifier neural networks. In: Proceedings of International Conference on Artificial Intelligence and Statistics (AISTATS), pp. 315–323 (2011)

22. Mallat, S.: A Wavelet Tour of Signal Processing: The Sparse Way. Academic Press, Cambridge (2008)

23. Do, M.N., Vetterli, M.: The contourlet transform: an efficient directional multiresolution image representation. IEEE Trans. Image Process. **14**(12), 2091–2160 (2005)

24. Cunha, A.L., Zhou, J., Do, M.N.: The nonsubsampled contourlet transform: theory, design, and applications. IEEE Trans. Image Process. **15**(10), 3089–3101 (2006)

25. Wang, Z., Bovik, A.C., Sheikh, H.R., Simoncelli, E.: Image quality assessment: from error visibility to structural similarity. IEEE Trans. Image Process. **13**(4), 600–612 (2004)

26. Agustsson, E., Timofte, R.: Ntire 2017 challenge on single image super-resolution: dataset and study. In: Proceedings of the IEEE Conference on Computer Vision and Pattern Recognition Workshops (CVPRW), pp. 126–135 (2017)

Image Denoising Networks with Residual Blocks and RReLUs

Sheng He[1,2] and Genke Yang[1,3(✉)]

[1] Department of Automation, Shanghai Jiao Tong University, Shanghai, China
{627064558,gkyang}@sjtu.edu.cn
[2] Key Laboratory of System Control and Information Processing,
Ministry of Education of China, Beijing, China
[3] Ningbo Artificial Intelligence Institute, Shanghai Jiao Tong University,
Shanghai, China

Abstract. Discriminative learning methods have been widely studied in image denoising due to their swift inference and favorable performance. Nonetheless, their application range is greatly restricted by the specialized task (i.e., a specific model is required for each considered noise level), which prompts us to train a single network to tackle the blind image denoising problem. To this end, we take the advantages of state-of-the-art progress in deep learning to construct our denoising networks. Particularly, residual learning is utilized in our deep CNNs (convolutional neural networks) with pre-activation strategy to accelerate the training process. Furthermore, we employ RReLU (randomized leaky rectified linear unit) as the activation rather than the conventional use of ReLU (rectified linear unit). Extensive experiments are conducted to demonstrate that our model enjoys two desirable properties, including: (1) the ability to yield competitive denoising quality in comparison to specifically trained denoisers in several predetermined noise level and (2) the ability to handle a wide scope of noise levels effectively with a single network. The experimental results reveal its efficiency and effectiveness for image denoising tasks.

Keywords: Image denoising · Residual learning · Pre-activation · RReLU

1 Introduction

Image denoising is a long-standing crucial problem in low-level vision for its indispensability in many practical applications. Traditionally, the thinking of image prior modeling has long been considered as the pillar in image denoising and assorted denoising models have been proposed based on it over the past few decades, including nonlocal self-similarity (NSS) models [1, 2], Markov random field (MRF) models [3, 4], gradient models [5], and sparse models [6]. Many state-of-the-art denoising methods are derived from these image prior models such as BM3D [2], LSSC [6], WNNM [7], etc. In particular, BM3D is currently the most widely-used one for its high denoising quality. Since their favorable denoising performance, there are typically two major limitations burdening most of the prior-based approaches. First, the models are generally non-convex and sometimes manually determined hyper-parameters are inevitable [2, 6],

© Springer Nature Switzerland AG 2019
T. Gedeon et al. (Eds.): ICONIP 2019, LNCS 11954, pp. 60–69, 2019.
https://doi.org/10.1007/978-3-030-36711-4_6

which provides extra room for improvements in denoising quality. Second and more significantly, these image prior-based methods are predominantly time-consuming [7] as complicated optimization problems are usually involved in the testing stage.

To overcome the restraint of image prior-based methods, several discriminative learning methods have been proposed in image denoising which simultaneously achieve satisfactory efficiency and high image restoration quality. Schmidt and Roth [8] proposed a cascade of shrinkage fields (CSF) approach that learns a separate filter bank and shrinkage function for each stage of their cascade using discriminative training. Chen et al. [9] proposed a trainable nonlinear reaction diffusion (TNRD) model which learns a modified Fields of Experts [4] image prior by unrolling a fixed number of gradient descent inference steps. Although their relatively outstanding results bridge the gap between denoising quality and computational efficiency, the priors learned in these methods are generally grounded on the analysis model. Such feature may lead to their lack in capturing full characteristics of the image input. In addition, it seems that the algorithms are not good at handling blind image denoising, so we usually need to train a specific model for a certain noise level.

Recently, deep neural networks (DNNs) have been successfully introduced in various low-level vision applications. Also, several historic attempts have been made in image denoising. Jain and Seung [10] applied CNNs in image denoising and stated that the representation power of CNNs are comparable or even better than that of MRF model. Burger et al. [11] used the multi-layer perceptron (MLP) and achieved competitive results. Xie et al. [12] adopted stacked sparse denoising auto-encoders method to tackle Gaussian noise removal and realized matching results to K-SVD. These networks have shown their excellent performance in image denoising. Their success is probably attributed to the appreciable representational ability and feed-forward nature of their inference (i.e. avoid solving an optimization problem during inference). However, just like other discriminative learning methods, these models may encounter some impediments in coping with blind image denoising. Therefore, to design an approach boasting the capability both to amalgamate exceptional denoising quality with computational efficiency and to handle blind image denoising is of considerable value.

In this paper, we aim to train an efficient network to well work across a range of noise levels. Rather than learn a discriminative model based on specific image prior, we instead treat image denoising as a plain discriminative learning problem and adopt plain CNNs to build the denoisers, so as to embrace the cutting-edge progress in very deep architecture, regularization methods, etc. We refer to the proposed denoising convolutional neural networks as DnRnets. Specifically, we employ residual learning strategy in our network with consecutive residual blocks [13, 14] to construct a deep residual network (ResNet) using pre-addition activation structure [14]. In addition, batch normalization (BN) [15] are introduced into the network to speed up the training process as well as lift the denoising performance. Different from previous works, randomized leaky rectified linear unit (RReLU) [16] is utilized as the activation function. Extensive experiments on noisy observations are conducted to evaluate our approach in comparison with state-of-the-art denoisers. The competitive results show that our approach methodically takes the advantages of the sophisticated techniques in deep learning. Furthermore, as opposed to many other existing deep networks which require the training of a specific model for each considered noise level, the proposed model achieves high performance in a wide range of noise levels through a single set of learned parameters, demonstrating its superiority in blind image denoising.

The contributions of this paper are summarized as follows:

- We propose an efficient end-to-end trainable deep network architecture for image denoising based on a deep ResNet and empirically verify the merits of RReLUs in our networks.
- We find that our DnRnet produces competitive results in comparison to the state-of-the-art image denoisers for Gaussian denoising with a certain noise level.
- We conduct extensive experiments to show that our DnRnet is capable of well handling blind image denoising, in contrast to the existing discriminative denoising methods that train a separate model for each individual noise level.

The remainder of the paper is organized as follows. A brief survey of related work is stated in Sect. 2. We describe our approach in Sect. 3. A quantitative evaluation on well-recognized benchmark datasets along with a discussion are arranged in Sect. 4 and the concluding remarks is provided in Sect. 5.

2   Related Work

2.1   Deep Neural Networks for Blind Image Denoising

The early discriminative denoising method which achieves performance on par with BM3D in blind image denoising is the plain MLP proposed by Burger et al. [11]. In [17], Zhang et al. trained a very deep CNN with residual learning [13] and batch normalization [15] algorithms and produced state-of-the-art results in Gaussian denoising. For blind Gaussian denoising, a single denoising convolutional neural network (DnCNN) was trained by using noisy images of different levels. They showed that residual learning and BN [15] are well-integrated and benefit from each other in the DnCNN, which may account for the success of denoising [17]. Recently, Chen et al. [18] proposed a GAN-CNN Based Blind Denoiser (GCBD) to tackle the lack of paired training data in the training.

These DNN-based methods have shown better performance in blind image denoising than the previous ones [2, 5] to some extent. Our work is partially related to the DnCNN of [17], which treated image denoising as a plain discriminative learning problem rather than learn a discriminative model with an explicit image prior [8, 9, 11]. Following are the main differences between DnCNN and this work: (1) While DnCNN chooses ReLU as the activation function, we introduce RReLU to construct our denoiser to take the advantage of the cutting-edge development in deep learning; and (2) While DnCNN uses conventional post-activation of the weight layers, we construct our ResNet with the structure of full pre-activation. As shown later in the experiments section, our network clearly outperforms the generatively trained one.

2.2 ResNet with Pre-activation and RReLU

ResNet with Pre-activation. In [14], He et al. proposed a new residual unit design to adopt pre-activation in contrast to the conventional wisdom of post-activation of the weight layer. Based on this unit, a novel ResNet was constructed and yielded competitive results. They claimed that such construction is much easier to train and generalizes better than the original ResNet [13].

RReLU. Xu et al. [15] investigated the performance of different types of rectified activation functions used in CNN: standard rectified linear unit (ReLU), leaky rectified linear unit (Leaky ReLU), parametric rectified linear unit (PReLU) and a new randomized leaky rectified linear units (RReLU). The results suggest that incorporating a non-zero slope for negative part in rectified activation units could consistently improve the results. Moreover, the finding also shows that using randomized negative slopes instead of their deterministic counterpart might have good impact in reduce overfitting. These findings give us inspiration to replace the ReLU with RReLU in the ResNet.

3 The Proposed Denoising Residual Networks

3.1 Problem Formulation

Generally, the purpose of image denoising is to recover the latent clean image x from its degraded noisy observation $y = x + v$. One common assumption is that v is additive white Gaussian noise (AWGN) with standard deviation σ. Discriminative learning models such as MLP [11] and CSF [8] aim to learn a mapping function $F(y) \Rightarrow x$ to predict the latent clean image. To this end, the prior parameters Θ is required to be learned through an optimization of a loss function on a training set containing degraded-clean image pairs [2, 7]. The objective is given by

$$\min_{\Theta_\sigma} \ell(x, \hat{x}) \quad s.t. \quad \hat{x} = \arg \min_x \frac{1}{2} \|y - x\|^2 + \lambda \Phi(x, \Theta_\sigma) \tag{1}$$

where the solution minimizes a fidelity term $\frac{1}{2} \| y - x \|^2$, a regularization term $\Phi(x, \Theta_\sigma)$ and a trade-off parameter λ. Formally, the averaged mean squared error (MSE) between the desired images x and estimated ones $\hat{x}$ from noisy input y is designed as loss function and given by

$$\ell(\Theta_\sigma) = \frac{1}{2N} \sum_{i=1}^{N} \| F(y_i, \Theta_\sigma) - x_i \|^2 \tag{2}$$

Here $\{(y_i, x_i)\}_{i=1}^{N}$ represents N noisy-clean training image pairs. The model parameters Θ_σ are trained for noisy observation corrupted by AWGN with a fixed noise level σ. From Eqs. (1) and (2), we can clearly find that since the trained parameters Θ_σ are highly related to the noise level σ, it is hard to be directly applied to images with other noise levels (i.e. lacks flexibility to deal with blind image denoising). In this paper, different from the previous ones, we want to train a single network with the model parameters Θ invariant to noise level σ. In the following, we explain the architecture of our image denoising network and its underlying rationale.

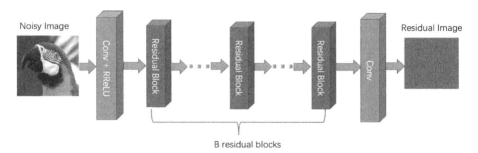

Fig. 1. The architecture of the proposed image denoising network. Note that "Conv" denotes convolutional layer; "BN" represents batch normalization [15]; "RReLU" is the randomized leaky rectified linear unit [16].

3.2 Network Architecture

Considering the speed and performance, deep CNN is chosen to learn the discriminative denoisers. The reasons of using CNN are two-fold. First, CNNs own the great capability of the network architecture to learn the latent noise model from the paired training dataset implicitly, which loosens the dependence on human knowledge of image priors. Second, substantial advancement in training and designing of CNNs have been made during the past few years, and we can take advantage of those progress to facilitate discriminative learning. Thus, a CNN is utilized in our framework for denoising.

The architecture of the DnRnet for learning $R(y)$ is illustrated in Fig. 1. The network can be regarded as a single residual unit to predict the residual image (i.e., the difference between the input noisy image and the latent clean image). The entire framework consists of three parts, including a "Conv+RReLU" block placed firstly to absorb the input noisy observation, B consecutive "Residual Blocks" stacked as the middle layers, and a "Conv" block in the last to produce the output residual image. Zero padding method is adopted to ensure the consistency between the dimension of the input and output. In the following, we will give some more important details.

3.3 Residual Learning Strategy Combined with Batch Normalization

As analyzed in Sect. 3.1, our network outputs a residual image $\hat{v}$ in contrast to the more intuitive method that outputs an estimated image $\hat{x}$. As pointed out in [13], when the original mapping is more similar to an identity mapping, the residual mapping will be much easier to be well-optimized to reduce the degradation problem in very deep networks. It is noteworthy that [17] the noisy observation y is usually much more like the latent clean image x than the residual image v, (i.e., the mapping $F(y) \Rightarrow x$ would be closer to an identity mapping than the residual mapping $R(y) \Rightarrow v$). Therefore, the residual learning formulation may be more suitable for image denoising.

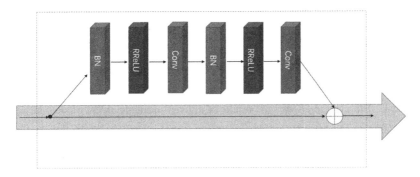

Fig. 2. The structure of a single residual block.

To this end, we adopt the residual learning strategy to in the construction of extremely deep CNN [13, 14]. As demonstrated in Fig. 1, this residual mapping produces an estimate of noise and then the estimated images can be derived through $\hat{x} = y - \hat{v}$. Specifically, the loss function is transferred from Eq. (2) to

$$\ell(\Theta) = \frac{1}{2N} \sum_{i=1}^{N} \| R(y_i, \Theta) - (y_i - x_i) \|^2 \tag{3}$$

To better exploit the performance of residual learning, we also employ the batch normalization to alleviate internal covariate shift problem [15]. Additionally, it has been claimed [17] that the combination of batch normalization and residual learning is practically effective for Gaussian denoising since they are beneficial to each other. In this paper, we adopt the strategy and empirically verify the synergy between them.

3.4 The Adoption of Pre-activation Design and RReLU

The inside structure of a single residual block in our networks is unfolded in Fig. 2. Different from widely-used conventional residual unit proposed in [13], we adopt the pre-activation structure as the basis unit. Extensive ablation experiments [14] have suggested that when using identity mappings as the skip connections and after-addition activation, the forward and backward signals can be straightforwardly propagated from one block to any other block. Thus, this construction facilitates the path for information propagation. Besides, the impact of pre-activation is also considerable [14]. First, the optimization is further eased because of the identity mapping. Second, using BN as pre-activation ameliorates the regularization quality of the ResNets.

Particularly, we take the advantage of RReLU to additionally promote the performance. After considering a broader class of the rectified unit family, significant superiority of RReLU is achieved [14] compared to the baseline ReLU, which inspires us to adopt this variant activation function in our network to further modify the original residual block.

Fig. 3. 12 widely-used testing images for image denoising.

Table 1. The average PSNR (dB) results of different methods on the BSD68 dataset.

Methods	BM3D [2]	MLP [11]	CSF [8]	TNRD [9]	DnCNN [17]	DnRnet-S	DnRnet-B
$\sigma = 15$	31.07	–	31.20	31.45	31.68	**31.70**	31.60
$\sigma = 25$	28.56	28.94	28.78	28.93	29.17	**29.20**	29.14
$\sigma = 50$	25.6	26.02	–	25.98	26.21	**26.22**	26.17

4   Experiment

4.1   Experimental Setting and Compared Methods

We follow [9] to use 400 images of size 180×180 for Gaussian denoising with either known or unknown noise level. To train DnRnet for Gaussian denoising with known noise level, three noise levels are taken into consideration (i.e., $\sigma = 15, 25, 50$). The patch size is set as 40×40 and 128×1600 patches are cropped to train the network. For convenience, our model for Gaussian denoising with known specific noise level as DnRnet-S.

For blind Gaussian denoising, we set the range of the noise levels as $\sigma \in [0, 55]$. The patch size is set as 50×50 and 128×3000 patches are cropped to train the blind image denoiser. The model for blind Gaussian denoising is referred to as DnRnet-B.

We evaluate our approach on benchmark datasets, one is Berkeley segmentation dataset (BSD68) [4] which contains 68 natural images and the other one containing 12 widely-used testing images shown in Fig. 3. The evaluation metric is based on the well-recognized peak signal-to-noise ratio (PSRN) of images.

15-stacked residual blocks are used to construct out DnRnet-S and DnRnet-B. The equivalent network depth is 32 after taking the input layer and output layer into consideration, effectively exploiting the ability of deep network to capture image information for denoising. The loss function in Eq. (3) is adopted and SGD is used with weight decay of 0.0001, a momentum of 0.9 and a mini-batch size of 128. We train 50 epochs for our DnRnets. The learning rate was decayed exponentially from $1 \times e^{-1}$ to $1 \times e^{-4}$. We utilize the PyTorch (0.4.1) to train the proposed models and all the experiments are conducted on a PC with Intel Core I7 and Nvidia GTX 1080Ti GPUs.

The proposed denoiser is compared with several state-of-the-art methods, including two non-local similarity based method (i.e., BM3D [2] and WNNM [7]), three discriminative training based methods (i.e., MLP [11], CSF [8] and TNRD [9]), one CNN-based methods (i.e., DnCNN [17]).

4.2   Results

The average PSNR results of different methods on the BSD68 dataset are shown in Table 1. As we can see, the proposed DnRnet-S achieve the best PSNR results than any other state-of-the-art methods in all given noise levels. Particularly, if trained with known specific noise level, our DnRnet-S can outperform BM3D by a substantial PSNR gain of more than 0.62 dB, while it is claimed that few methods can outperform. BM3D by more than 0.3 dB on average [19]. Furthermore, even with a single model without known noise level, our DnRnet-B can still yield competitive results in comparison to a DnCNN model trained with known specific noise level, which demonstrates the feasibility of our model to be applied in blind image denoising. It should be pointed out that both DnRnet-S and DnRnet-B outperform BM3D by about 0.6 dB, exceedingly close to the estimated PSNR bound over BM3D (0.7 dB) [20].

Table 2. The PSNR (dB) results of different methods on 12 widely used testing images.

Images	C. man	House	Peppers	Starfish	Moth	Airplane	Parrot	Lena	Barbara	Boat	Man	Couple	Average
Noise Level	$\sigma = 15$												
BM3D [2]	31.90	34.90	32.70	31.12	31.84	31.06	31.35	34.25	33.08	32.10	31.92	32.10	32.360
CSF [8]	31.95	34.38	32.84	31.52	32.30	32.33	31.36	34.05	31.90	32.00	32.07	31.96	32.388
TNRD [9]	32.19	34.54	33.01	31.76	32.55	31.47	31.64	34.25	32.15	32.14	32.24	32.10	32.503
DnCNN [17]	32.50	34.89	**33.30**	32.18	33.09	31.68	31.75	34.52	**32.57**	**32.39**	32.32	32.38	32.798
DnRnet-S	**32.55**	**34.97**	33.27	**32.21**	**33.10**	31.69	**31.88**	**34.54**	32.51	32.33	**32.37**	**32.40**	**32.818**
Noise Level	$\sigma = 25$												
BM3D [2]	29.45	32.84	30.13	28.58	29.27	28.43	28.94	32.08	30.72	29.92	29.62	29.76	29.978
MLP [11]	29.60	32.50	30.28	28.80	29.62	28.84	29.26	32.26	29.55	29.98	29.84	29.67	30.017
CSF [8]	29.48	32.37	30.33	28.79	29.58	28.69	28.92	31.80	29.06	29.77	29.72	29.54	29.838
TNRD [9]	29.73	32.49	30.53	29.01	29.83	28.79	29.17	32.00	29.40	29.89	29.86	29.69	30.033
DnCNN [17]	30.04	33.01	30.85	29.37	**30.38**	29.15	29.48	**32.34**	29.85	30.12	**30.03**	**30.00**	30.385
DnRnet-S	**30.14**	**33.11**	**30.90**	**29.45**	30.35	**29.17**	**29.52**	32.33	**29.86**	**30.19**	29.99	29.97	**30.415**
Noise Level	$\sigma = 50$												
BM3D [2]	26.12	29.68	26.67	25.04	25.82	25.09	25.86	29.08	27.12	26.75	26.80	26.45	26.707
MLP [11]	26.36	29.64	26.65	25.40	26.24	25.55	26.10	29.30	25.24	27.03	27.05	26.67	26.769
TNRD [10]	26.62	29.45	27.08	25.40	26.30	25.56	26.15	28.92	25.69	26.94	26.98	26.50	26.799
DnCNN [17]	26.99	30.00	27.20	25.61	26.80	25.87	**26.46**	29.30	**26.21**	27.06	27.18	**26.88**	27.130
DnRnet-S	27.01	**30.10**	**27.22**	**25.75**	**26.93**	25.88	26.38	**29.36**	26.20	**27.10**	**27.19**	26.87	**27.166**

Table 2 demonstrates the PSNR results of different methods on the 12 testing images in Fig. 3. It is remarkable that all the best results are produced by CNN-based methods, and our proposed DnRnet-S win the majority and top the average PSNR results. It is very likely that our proposed DnRnet further extend its capability through the application of residual blocks and RReLUs.

The visual results of different methods are demonstrated in Fig. 4. It can be seen that image prior-based methods tend to produce over-smooth edges and textures, while DnCNN may reduce the details in the edge regions which harms the wholeness of image information. Contrastingly, DnRnets own the capability both in the recovery of sharp edges and subtle textures and in the preservation of image details.

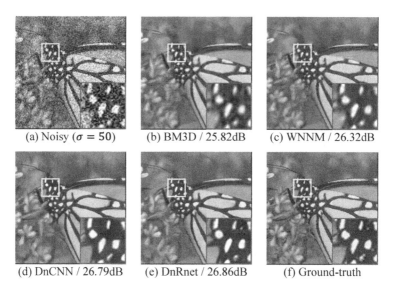

(a) Noisy ($\sigma = 50$)   (b) BM3D / 25.82dB   (c) WNNM / 26.32dB

(d) DnCNN / 26.79dB   (e) DnRnet / 26.86dB   (f) Ground-truth

Fig. 4. Denoising results of the image "moth" with noise level 50. Zoom in for better view.

5   Conclusion

In this paper, we have designed and trained a set of CNN-based residual networks for image denoising. Specially, on the foundation of deep CNN, we have introduced residual blocks with pre-activation strategy to accelerate the training process. Besides, we have employed RReLU to additionally promote the performance. Extensive experimental results have corroborated that the integration of ResNet with pre-activation and RReLU probably result in an efficient framework of denoiser, which demonstrates the effectiveness of our approach for image denoising tasks.

Acknowledgement. This research was partially funded by the China national R&D Key Research Program (2017YFA60700602).

References

1. Buades, A., Coll, B., Morel, J.-M.: A non-local algorithm for image denoising. In: IEEE Conference on Computer Vision and Pattern Recognition, vol. 2, pp. 60–65 (2005)
2. Dabov, K., Foi, A., Katkovnik, V., Egiazarian, K.: Image denoising by sparse 3-D transform-domain collaborative filtering. IEEE Trans. Image Process. **16**(8), 2080–2095 (2007)
3. Lan, X., Roth, S., Huttenlocher, D., Black, M.J.: Efficient belief propagation with learned higher-order Markov Random fields. In: Leonardis, A., Bischof, H., Pinz, A. (eds.) ECCV 2006. LNCS, vol. 3952, pp. 269–282. Springer, Heidelberg (2006). https://doi.org/10.1007/11744047_21
4. Roth, S., Black, M.J.: Fields of experts. Int. J. Comput. Vis. **82**(2), 205–229 (2009)

5. Rudin, L.I., Osher, S., Fatemi, E.: Nonlinear total variation based noise removal algorithms. Physica D: Nonlinear Phenom. **60**(1), 259–268 (1992)
6. Mairal, J., Bach, F., Ponce, J., Sapiro, G., Zisserman, A.: Non-local sparse models for image restoration. In: IEEE International Conference on Computer Vision, pp. 2272–2279 (2009)
7. Gu, S., Zhang, L., Zuo, W., Feng, X.: Weighted nuclear norm minimization with application to image denoising. In: IEEE Conference on Computer Vision and Pattern Recognition, pp. 2862–2869 (2014)
8. Schmidt, U., Roth, S.: Shrinkage fields for effective image restoration. In: IEEE Conference on Computer Vision and Pattern Recognition, pp. 2774–2781 (2014)
9. Chen, Y., Pock, T.: Trainable nonlinear reaction diffusion: a flexible framework for fast and effective image restoration. IEEE Trans. Pattern Anal. Mach. Intell. **39**(6), 1256–1272 (2016)
10. Jain, V., Seung, S.: Natural image denoising with convolutional networks. In: Advances in Neural Information Processing Systems, pp. 769–776 (2009)
11. Burger, H.C., Schuler, C.J., Harmeling, S.: Image denoising: can plain neural networks compete with BM3D? In: IEEE Conference on Computer Vision and Pattern Recognition, pp. 2392–2399 (2012)
12. Xie, J., Xu, L., Chen, E.: Image denoising and inpainting with deep neural networks. In: Advances in Neural Information Processing Systems, pp. 341–349 (2012)
13. He, K., Zhang, X., Ren, S., et al.: Deep residual learning for image recognition. In: IEEE Conference on Computer Vision and Pattern Recognition, pp. 770–778 (2016)
14. He, K., Zhang, X., Ren, S., Sun, J.: Identity mappings in deep residual networks. In: Leibe, B., Matas, J., Sebe, N., Welling, M. (eds.) ECCV 2016. LNCS, vol. 9908, pp. 630–645. Springer, Cham (2016). https://doi.org/10.1007/978-3-319-46493-0_38
15. Ioffe, S., Szegedy, C.: Batch normalization: accelerating deep network training by reducing internal covariate shift. In: International Conference on Machine Learning, pp. 448–456 (2015)
16. Xu, B., Wang, N., Chen, T., et al.: Empirical evaluation of rectified activations in convolutional network. arXiv preprint arXiv:1505.00853 (2015)
17. Zhang, K., Zuo, W., Chen, Y., Meng, D., Zhang, L.: Beyond a Gaussian denoiser: residual learning of deep CNN for image denoising. IEEE Trans. Image Process. **26**(7), 3142–3155 (2017)
18. Chen, J., Chao, H., et al.: Image blind denoising with generative adversarial network based noise modeling. In: IEEE Conference on Computer Vision and Pattern Recognition, pp 3155–3164 (2018)
19. Levin, A., Nadler, B.: Natural image denoising: optimality and inherent bounds. In: IEEE Conference on Computer Vision and Pattern Recognition, pp. 2833–2840 (2011)
20. Levin, A., Nadler, B., Durand, F., Freeman, W.T.: Patch complexity, finite pixel correlations and optimal denoising. In: Fitzgibbon, A., Lazebnik, S., Perona, P., Sato, Y., Schmid, C. (eds.) ECCV 2012. LNCS, vol. 7576, pp. 73–86. Springer, Heidelberg (2012). https://doi.org/10.1007/978-3-642-33715-4_6

Shape Description and Retrieval in a Fused Scale Space

Wen Zhou[1], Baojiang Zhong[1(✉)], and Jianyu Yang[2]

[1] School of Computer Science and Technology, Soochow University, Suzhou, China
20164227039@stu.suda.edu.cn, bjzhong@suda.edu.cn
[2] School of Rail Transportation, Soochow University, Suzhou, China
jyyang@suda.edu.cn

Abstract. In this work, a scale-space shape descriptor is proposed for shape retrieval, which is motivated by the multiscale mechanism of our human visual perception. First, morphological operations and the Gaussian smoothing are jointly used to produce a fused scale-space description of the input shape, which is able to handle strong noise, intra-class shape variation and irregular deformation simultaneously. Then, the height-function features of the shape are extracted across scales. Finally, shape retrieval is conducted by an integration of the retrieval results individually yielded at multiple scales. Experimental results on benchmark datasets validate the accuracy, efficiency and robustness of our proposed method.

Keywords: Shape retrieval · Fused scale space · Scale-space description · Scale-space retrieval · Height function

1 Introduction

Shape is considered as an important kind of visual features in image analysis and computer vision. Shape description is a key issue for shape retrieval, which has been successfully applied to solve many tasks such as image retrieval [1–4], face recognition [5] and 3D model reconstruction [6–8].

Existing shape descriptors can be roughly divided into two main categories as follows: the global descriptors and the local descriptors. Typical global descriptors (such as the *shape context* (SC) [9] and the *inner-distance shape context* (IDSC) [10]) describe the relative spatial distribution of the feature points by the information of other points. They are naturally robust to local deformation, but fail to capture local details. On the other hand, local descriptors are precise to represent local shape features. For that, an effective way is to decompose the input shape into parts via various strategies, such as the *hierarchical procrustes matching* (HPM) [11], the *shape tree* [12], and the *hierarchical string cut* (HSC) [1]. However, local descriptors suffer from strong noise and local deformation.

To overcome the shortcoming caused by noise and intra-class variations, the concept of multiple scale for shape description is proposed. The *curvature scale*

© Springer Nature Switzerland AG 2019
T. Gedeon et al. (Eds.): ICONIP 2019, LNCS 11954, pp. 70–82, 2019.
https://doi.org/10.1007/978-3-030-36711-4_7

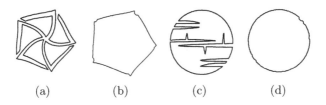

(a)   (b)   (c)   (d)

Fig. 1. Effect of using morphological operations to handle irregular shape deformations. (a, c): the input shapes; (b, d): the corresponding shapes of (a, c) after using morphological operations.

space (CSS) [13] exploits the Gaussian kernel to produce a multiscale shape representation for shape retrieval. Alajlan et al. [14] propose the *triangle area* (TAR) which describes convexity/concavity of each contour point using the signed areas of triangles formed by boundary points at different scales. Yang et al. [15] define three invariant multi-scale features to represent the shape. Zhang et al. [16] propose a *multiscale ellipse descriptor* (MED) method where both spatial location and topology structure are used to extract the coarse-to-fine shape details. A small scale has strong shape descriptive ability to local details while a large scale has stable shape features to overcome the drawbacks of noise and local deformation. The underlying idea of a multiscale shape descriptor is to obtain more shape information at different scales. Besides, some algorithms based on deep features have appeared for shape retrieval, e.g. CNN [26] and DeepGM [27]. Oliveira et al. [28] create a complex network with boundary points of 2D shapes, and the dynamic of the network is analyzed by means of the spectral graph theory. However, it is still a challenging problem to match shapes with strong noise, intra-class variation and irregular deformation simultaneously.

The intra-class variation indicates the varying geometric transformations of shapes, including rotation, scaling, affine transformation, etc. The shapes with noise or intra-class variations can be easily classified to the same class by human perception, while they are certainly difficult for shape retrieval algorithms. The irregular deformation refers to dramatic gap inside shapes like Fig. 1(a, c), which causes too many interference points and increases the shape dissimilarity of the same class. Therefore, it is critical to design an effective, discriminative and robust method for shape retrieval.

To satisfy all the challenges above, it is desirable to extract robust shape features to deal with strong noise. Besides, considering the advantages of global and local shape descriptors, a straightforward idea is to combine the global and local shape features for an exhaustive shape representation in different feature scales, which should be robust to intra-class variations and irregular deformation.

In this paper, a novel fused scale-space description is proposed for shape retrieval as shown in Fig. 2. Based on height function method [20], we extend the sequence feature derived from the shape. Then morphological operations and Gaussian smoothing are jointly used to produce a fused scale space, which obtains the multiscale shape information. The morphological scale space can well

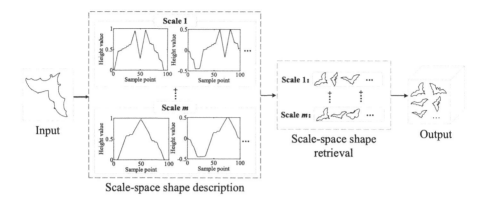

Scale-space shape description

Fig. 2. Pipeline of our proposed method: first, a multiscale description of the input shape is produced by extracting its height features in the fused scale-space; then, a multiscale integration strategy is used for shape retrieval.

deal with intra-class and irregular deformations in accord with human perception, while the Gaussian scale space is robust to noise. Finally, we propose a new integration strategy of the ultimate shape similarity in multiple scales to obtain a qualitative matching result.

The main contribution of this paper is two folds. First, the fused scale-space description is proposed to overcome the problems result from different transformations simultaneously in Sect. 2. The second is that a scale-space integration strategy for shape retrieval is proposed in Sect. 3, which combines the individual retrieval results produced in different scales to generate the final output. Extensive experiments are carried out to show the effectiveness and robustness of the proposed method.

2   Shape Description in a Fused Scale Space

When objects are retrieved based on shape features, the retrieval results would be easily influenced due to our perceptual customs. It is well known that the Gaussian smoothing can effectively remove noise along the contour, but it is not able to handle irregular deformations properly. Therefore, the Gaussian smoothing cannot be used alone to simulate human perception. Moreover, morphological operations can capture the main structure of shape well. Inspired by the work of Hu et al. [17], we combine the advantages of the two operations and jointly exploit them to produce a scale-space description of the input shape for getting more comprehensive features.

2.1   The Morphological Scale Space

Morphological operations include the *dilation* and the *erosion*, which are realized by using a *structuring element* (SE) to modify the shape according to two specific

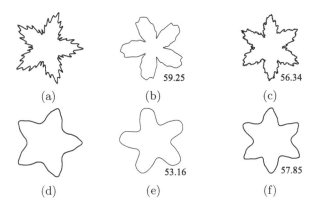

(a)   (b)   (c)

(d)   (e)   (f)

Fig. 3. Effect of using Gaussian smoothing to handle contour noise. The first row presents three shapes taken from the MPEG-7 database, where the first two belong to the same class, and the third one belongs to another shape class. The second row presents the smoothed versions of the input shapes correspondingly. In each row, the Euclidean distances between the last two shapes and the first shape (used as a reference) are computed and marked at their right bottom corners, respectively.

rules, respectively [18]. Especially, opening operation and closing operation are defined by different sequence with the same structuring element of dilation and erosion operators. In our method, *morphological scale space* (MSS) is obtained by closing (dilation+erosion) the binary shape with operators of increasing size (1). The closing operation is defined as:

$$M\left(\varsigma, x, y\right) = B\left(x, y\right) \bullet f\left(\varsigma, x, y\right),\tag{1}$$

where the $\bullet$ operator denotes the morphological closing operation applied to the binary shape $B\left(x, y\right)$. The structuring element $f\left(\cdot, \cdot\right)$ is parameterised by size ς. At each MSS level, ς is increased such that the closing operation affects a large region, which can be regarded as the scale parameter. In our experiments, ς is $m \cdot 5$ pixels, where m is the MSS level starting from 0.

From Fig. 1, we know that this operation can well handle shapes with irregular deformations and preserve the main structure to conform human visual perception by $\varsigma = 20$. In more detail, we first use the Matlab function 'strel' to create flat disk-shaped structuring elements by using different ς which are invariant to shape rotation. Then, a sequence of shapes are generated by adjusting different ς under different morphological scales.

2.2   The Gaussian Scale Space

The Gaussian is a conventional kernel for producing a multiscale shape representation [19], by which noise and insignificant shape features can be effectively suppressed along the shape contour. Denote the considered shape contour as:

$$C = \left(x\left(u\right), y\left(u\right)\right),\tag{2}$$

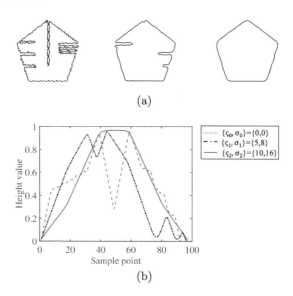

(a)

(b)

Fig. 4. The proposed scale-space shape description under different scale parameters: (a) the evolved versions of the input shape under the scale $\{\varsigma_0, \sigma_0\} = \{0, 0\}$, $\{\varsigma_1, \sigma_1\} = \{5, 8\}$ and $\{\varsigma_2, \sigma_2\} = \{10, 16\}$, respectively; (b) the height values of the three evolved versions.

where u is arc length parameter normalized by contour length. The one-dimensional Gaussian filter is expressed as:

$$g(u, \sigma) = \frac{1}{\sigma\sqrt{2\pi}} \exp\left(-\frac{u^2}{2\sigma^2}\right),\tag{3}$$

where σ is the width of Gaussian kernel and regarded as the scale parameter. Let $X(u, \sigma)$ and $Y(u, \sigma)$ be the coordinate functions of the contour curve at the scale σ, which are produced by the convolution operation as follows:

$$X(u, \sigma) = x(u) * g(u, \sigma),\tag{4}$$

$$Y(u, \sigma) = y(u) * g(u, \sigma).\tag{5}$$

Figure 3 shows the visual effect of Gaussian smoothing and similarity calculations with shapes of the same or different class. It is clear that Gaussian smoothing has good effect when facing shapes with strong noise along the shape contour. As shown in Fig. 3, the first row shows three shapes taken from the MPEG-7 dataset, where second shape is of the same class as the first one, while the third shape belongs to a different class. However, when referred with the first shape (a), the third shape (c) has a closer Euclidean distance than that of the second shape (b) (the distance values are marked on the right bottom corner of the two shapes, respectively). This will lead to an incorrect retrieval result. The second row shows the smoothed versions of the three shapes correspondingly, where the miss-retrieved problem has been solved as the second shape (e)

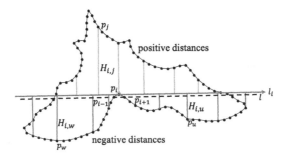

Fig. 5. Height function feature descriptor.

becomes more closer than the third shape (f) to the first one (d). It satisfies the basic principle of minimizing intra-class distance and maximizing distance between different classes in pattern recognition.

2.3   The Fused Scale Space

To jointly exploit the advantages of morphological operations and Gaussian smoothing, we propose the fused scale-space shape description which is generated by using the two operations together with different ς and σ, that is, $\{\varsigma, \sigma\}$. The effect of this description is demonstrated in Fig. 4.

From Fig. 4, it is seen that the device shape can preserve better structure at $\{\varsigma, \sigma\} = \{0, 0\}$, while $\{\varsigma, \sigma\} = \{10, 16\}$ are suitable for human perception. In Fig. 4(b), the height function in our paper for the same sample point shows scale-space shape description under different fused scale parameters. With more experiments, it can be concluded that shapes with small deformations need lower ς and σ, while irregular deformations should be handled with larger ς and σ. Hence, individual results yielded under different scales should be fused to handle different transformations simultaneously.

At each joint scale (consist of a ς and a σ), the height-function shape features [20] are extracted. Figure 5 shows the schematic diagram of the height function descriptor. More specific details can refer to [20]. The feature vector of the point p_i is an ordered sequence of the height function:

$$
\begin{aligned}
H_i &= \left(H_i^1, H_i^2, ..., H_i^{N-1}\right)^T \\
&= \left(H_{i,i+1}, ..., H_{i,N}, H_{i,1}, ..., H_{i,i-1}\right)^T,
\end{aligned}
\tag{6}
$$

where $H_{i,j}$ denotes the height value of the jth sample point p_j with regard to the point p_i, calculated by:

$$
H_{i,j} = \frac{\det \left(p_{i-1}, p_j, p_{i+1}\right)}{|p_{i-1}p_{i+1}|}.
\tag{7}
$$

3 Scale-Space Shape Retrieval

For shape retrieval, we first use the dynamic programming to find the optimal correspondence of contour points between the query and model shape. Then, the shapes in datasets are ranked according to their matching scores measured by the Euclidean distance of corresponding points. This produces the retrieval result at each scale individually.

To conduct a scale-space shape retrieval, a key step is to fuse the individual results of different scales properly. In this work, we select n scales to conduct such an integration. At each scale, the top m most similar shapes are considered. Note that the similarity scores are inconsistent across scales because the shapes have suffered different levels of morphological operations and Gaussian smoothing at different scales. Therefore, we reset the similarity scores of the returned shapes by using a uniform criterion. In more detail, we denote the set of retrieval shapes at the scale S_t as $\{r_1^t, r_2^t, ..., r_m^t\}$. For each shape in the S_t, a new similarity score is assigned based on its order in the return shapes. The new similarity score could be defined as a non-linear function of its order; that is,

$$\text{sim}_i^t = \exp\left(-2 \times L_i^t\right), \tag{8}$$

where L_i^t is the ranking order of the i-th shape at the scale S_t, $i \in \{1, 2, ..., m\}$. The function defined above is a descending one, which describes the score of similarity between the return shape and the query shape at the same fused scale.

The final retrieval result will be generated by using a union of the returned shape sets; that is, $U = \{S_0, S_1, .., S_n\}$, in which each shape has been assigned with the new similarity score. Since a database shape could have multiple response in U, the length of U might vary from m to $m \cdot n$. To calculate the final similarity score of each shape in U, if a shape C_j is not a returned one at a certain scale, we assume that $\text{sim}_j^t = 0$ $(j \in \{1, 2, ..., m\})$.

With the above preparation, the final similarity score of each database shape in U is produced as follows:

$$F_j = \sum_{k=0}^n w_k \cdot \text{sim}_j^k \tag{9}$$

where w_k is a weightage to determine the contribution of the retrieval result at individual scales. The retrieval results are finally obtained by ranking the shapes in U according to their similarity score F_j $(j \in \{1, 2, ..., m\})$ in a multiscale sense.

4 Experimental Results

4.1 MPEG-7 Shape Dataset

The MPEG-7 shape dataset [10,21] has been widely used for evaluating a shape retrieval algorithm. This dataset consists of 1400 shapes, belonging to 70 classes

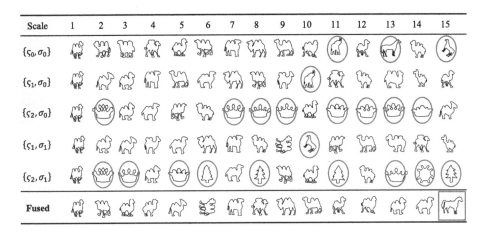

Fig. 6. Top 15 retrieved shapes of the query shape "camel" at different scales. The fused result is generated by the proposed multiscale retrieval.

Table 1. Performance comparison of different methods by using Bulls-eye score on MPEG-7 dataset

Method	IDSC [10]	HSC [1]	HF [20]	CNSS [28]	IMD [15]	SFR [22]	MFD [23]	**Ours**
BER (%)	85.40	87.31	89.66	89.47	91.25	92.70	83.94	**93.64**

with 20 shapes in each class. The retrieval accuracy is measured by the well-known *bulls-eye* score. The result of our method, comparing with other 8 state-of-the-art methods, is documented in Table 1, where our method achieves the highest accuracy.

To illustrate how the proposed multiscale retrieval method works, an exemplary experiment is shown in Fig. 6, where 5 joint scales are used; that is, $\{\varsigma_0, \sigma_0\}$, $\{\varsigma_1, \sigma_0\}$, $\{\varsigma_2, \sigma_0\}$, $\{\varsigma_0, \sigma_1\}$ and $\{\varsigma_0, \sigma_2\}$, with $\varsigma \in \{0, 5, 10\}$, $\sigma \in \{0, 8, 16\}$. The query shape is a "camel", and the top 15 retrieved shapes are presented at each used scale individually. The non-linear function defined in (9) is then used to compute a new similarity score for each shape. The default value is $m = 40$ and the weightages in (9) are taken to be $w_0 = 0.4, w_1 = 0.2, w_2 = 0.2, w_3 = 0.1$ and $w_4 = 0.1$. In Fig. 6, the shapes marked in ellipses or boxes represent false positive retrieved shapes. One can see that our multiscale retrieval (the fused result) is clearly superior over the conventional retrieval (the result at $\{\varsigma_0, \sigma_0\}$). It might be argued that the result at some fused scale is better than the multi-scale retrieval. However, in practice there is no prior about which scale performs best, and we observe that the multiscale retrieval can perform better than any single scale in average.

Table 2. Retrieval results on the Kimia-99 dataset

Method	1st	2nd	3rd	4th	5th	6th	7th	8th	9th	10th
IDSC [10]	99	99	99	98	98	97	97	98	94	79
TAR [14]	99	99	99	98	98	97	98	95	93	80
CDPH+EMD [25]	96	94	94	87	88	82	80	70	62	55
IMD [15]	99	99	99	99	98	97	95	94	90	83
Ours	**99**	**99**	**99**	**98**	**98**	**98**	**99**	**99**	**96**	**88**

Table 3. Retrieval results on the Kimia-216 dataset

Method	1st	2nd	3rd	4th	5th	6th	7th	8th	9th	10th	11th
SC [9]	214	209	205	197	191	178	161	144	131	101	78
CDPH+EMD [25]	215	215	213	205	203	204	190	180	168	154	123
IMD [15]	216	216	214	210	207	207	201	194	188	182	163
Ours	**216**	**215**	**215**	**213**	**215**	**211**	**211**	**209**	**195**	**190**	**185**

4.2 Kimia Shape Datasets

The Kimia database [24] is another widely used benchmark database for shape retrieval, including Kimia-99 and Kimia-216 datasets. The Kimia-99 dataset contains 99 shapes grouped into 9 classes. The retrieval rates are summarized as the number of shapes from the same class among the top 1 to 10 most similar shapes. The best possible result of the retrieval is 99. In experiments, we set 4 joint scales, where $\{\varsigma_0, \sigma_0\}$, $\{\varsigma_0, \sigma_1\}$, $\{\varsigma_0, \sigma_2\}$ and $\{\varsigma_0, \sigma_3\}$, with $\varsigma_0 = 0$, $\sigma \in \{0, 5, 8, 12\}$. The weightages in (9) are taken to be $w_0 = 0.4, w_1 = 0.3, w_2 = 0.2$ and $w_3 = 0.1$.

The Kimia-216 dataset consists of 18 classes with 12 shapes in each class. The top 11 closest matches are selected which are in the same class as the query shape and the best result is 216. In experiments, we set 4 joint scales, where $\{\varsigma_0, \sigma_0\}$, $\{\varsigma_1, \sigma_1\}$, $\{\varsigma_1, \sigma_2\}$ and $\{\varsigma_1, \sigma_3\}$, with $\varsigma \in \{0, 5\}$, $\sigma \in \{0, 5, 8, 10\}$. The weightages in (9) are $w_0 = w_1 = w_2 = w_3 = 0.25$. The overall retrieval results comparing with other methods are shown in Tables 2 and 3.

4.3 Robustness Against Noise, Intra-class, and Irregular Transformations

To evaluate our method in the presence of noise, the shape contours are perturbed by Gaussian noise with zero mean and varying deviation. The deviation value increases from 0.2 to 0.8, and the noisy effect is demonstrated in Fig. 7. Figure 8 shows the performance of different methods on the Kimia-99 dataset, and the average retrieval result of each method is plotted against noise. It can be seen that our proposed method performs stably well and produces the best results under various intensity of noise.

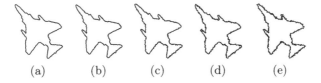

(a)　　　　(b)　　　　(c)　　　　(d)　　　　(e)

Fig. 7. Noisy shape contours. (a) The original shape contour; (b) to (e): The noise intensity increases from 0.2 to 0.8.

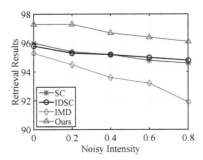

Fig. 8. Robustness against noise on the Kimia-99 dataset.

Table 4. Runtimes on the MPEG-7 dataset

Method	SC [9]	IDSC [10]	TAR [14]	ST [12]	IMD [15]	**Ours**
Time (ms)	200	310	70	500	65	**60**

Furthermore, in order to verify the effectiveness of our method, we compare the Euclidean distances of query shape and other shapes facing Gaussian noise, intra-class variation and irregular deformation simultaneously, as shown in Fig. 9. From the comparison results, we can see that the distance values are very similar even with 18 different types of transformations, which shows strong robustness of the proposed method.

4.4 Runtimes of Different Methods

To verify the computational efficiency of our proposed method, we conduct experimental tests on the MPEG-7 dataset comparing with some state-of-the-art methods. Each shape in the dataset is used for retrieval, and the average calculation time of each query shape is recorded. The comparison results are shown in Table 4. It can be seen that the calculation time required with the proposed algorithm is 60 ms. Compared with the other five representative shape retrieval algorithms, it has obvious computational efficiency superiority.

Query 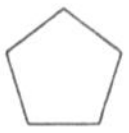	$\sigma_1 = 0.4$			$\sigma_2 = 0.8$		
	Rotated	Scaled	Rotated and scaled	Rotated	Scaled	Rotated and scaled
Irreg-1 	9.099	11.113	12.145	9.009	11.202	12.084
Irreg-2 	7.379	10.843	10.966	7.363	10.954	11.224
Irreg-3 	8.125	11.610	11.265	8.076	11.248	11.564

Fig. 9. The Euclidean distances comparison with different Gaussian noise, intra-class variation and irregular deformation simultaneously.

5   Conclusion

In this paper, a new scale-space method is proposed for shape description and retrieval. To overcome the difficulties caused by strong noise, intra-class shape variation and irregular deformation simultaneously, morphological operations and Gaussian smoothing are jointly used, so that a fused scale space of the input shape is generated. Based on height function, shape features are extracted across scales. The retrieval results under multiple scales are fused by using an integration strategy. The experimental results on benchmark datasets are presented to validate the effectiveness and robustness of the proposed method.

Acknowledgments. This work was supported by the National Natural Science Foundation of China (NSFC No. 61572341, No. 61773272), Six Talent Peaks Project of Jiangsu Province, China (No. XYDXX-053), Suzhou Research Project of Technical Innovation, Jiangsu, China (Grant No. SYG201711), and a Project Funded by the Priority Academic Program Development of Jiangsu Higher Education Institutions.

References

1. Wang, B., Gao, Y.: Hierarchical string cuts: a translation, rotation, scale, and mirror invariant descriptor for fast shape retrieval. IEEE Trans. Image Process. **23**(9), 4101–4111 (2014)
2. Leborgne, A., Mille, J., Tougne, L.: Hierarchical skeleton for shape matching. In: IEEE International Conference on Image Processing, pp. 3603–3607 (2016)
3. Demisse, G.G., Aouada, D., Ottersten, B.: Deformation based curved shape representation. IEEE Trans. Pattern Anal. Mach. Intell. **40**(6), 1338–1351 (2018)
4. Ni, F., Wang, B.: Integral contour angle: an invariant shape descriptor for classification and retrieval of leaf images. In: IEEE International Conference on Image Processing, pp. 1223–1227 (2018)
5. Lu, Z.G., Yang, J., Liu, Q.S.: Face image retrieval based on shape and texture feature fusion. Comput. Vis. Med. **3**(4), 359–368 (2017)
6. Xie, J., Dai, G., Fang, Y.: Deep multimetric learning for shape-based 3D model retrieval. IEEE Trans. Multimed. **19**(11), 2463–2474 (2017)

7. Xie, J., Fang, Y., Zhu, F., Edward, W.: DeepShape: deep learned shape descriptor for 3D shape matching and retrieval. In: IEEE Conference on Computer Vision and Pattern Recognition, pp. 1275–1283 (2015)

8. Su, H., Maji, S., Kalogerakis, E., Learned-Miller, E.: Multi-view convolutional neural networks for 3D shape recognition. In: IEEE International Conference on Computer Vision, pp. 945–953 (2015)

9. Belongie, S., Malik, J., Puzicha, J.: Shape matching and object recognition using shape contexts. IEEE Trans. Pattern Anal. Mach. Intell. **24**(4), 509–522 (2002)

10. Ling, H., Jacobs, D.W.: Shape classification using the inner-distance. IEEE Trans. Pattern Anal. Mach. Intell. **29**(2), 286–299 (2007)

11. McNeill, G., Vijayakumar, S.: Hierarchical procrustes matching for shape retrieval. In: IEEE Computer Society Conference on Computer Vision and Pattern Recognition, vol. 1, pp. 885–894 (2006)

12. Felzenszwalb, P.F., Schwartz, J.D.: Hierarchical matching of deformable shapes. In: IEEE Conference on Computer Vision and Pattern Recognition, pp. 1–8 (2007)

13. Jalba, A.C., Wilkinson, M.H., Roerdink, J.B.: Shape representation and recognition through morphological curvature scale spaces. IEEE Trans. Image Process. **15**(2), 331–341 (2006)

14. Alajlan, N., Rube, I.E., Kamel, M.S., Freeman, G.: Shape retrieval using triangle-area representation and dynamic space warping. Pattern Recogn. **40**(7), 1911–1920 (2007)

15. Yang, J.Y., Wang, H.X., Yuan, J.S., Li, Y.F., Liu, J.Y.: Invariant multi-scale descriptor for shape representation, matching and retrieval. Comput. Vis. Image Underst. **145**(C), 43–58 (2016)

16. Zhang, X., Xiang, J., Xiong, S.: Shape retrieval using multiscale ellipse descriptor. In: IEEE International Conference on Image Processing, pp. 1042–1046 (2017)

17. Hu, R.X., Jia, W., Zhao, Y., Gui, J.: Perceptually motivated morphological strategies for shape retrieval. Pattern Recogn. **45**(9), 3222–3230 (2012)

18. Akagndz, E.: Shape recognition using orientational and morphological scale-spaces of curvatures. IET Comput. Vis. **9**, 750–757 (2015)

19. Hong, B., Soatto, S.: Shape matching using multiscale integral invariants. IEEE Trans. Pattern Anal. Mach. Intell. **37**(1), 151–160 (2015)

20. Wang, J.W., Bai, X., You, X.G., Liu, W.Y., Latecki, L.J.: Shape matching and classification using height functions. Pattern Recogn. Lett. **33**(2), 134–143 (2012)

21. Yang, C., Christian, F., Oliver, T., Shirahama, K., Grzegorzek, M.: Shape-based object matching using interesting points and high-order graphs. Pattern Recogn. Lett. **83**(P3), 251–260 (2016)

22. Yahya, S., Demirci, M.F.: 2D and 3D shape retrieval using skeleton filling rate. Multimed. Tools Appl. **76**(6), 7823–7848 (2017)

23. Yang, C.Z., Yu, Q.: Multiscale fourier descriptor based on triangular features for shape retrieval. Signal Process. Image Commun. **71**, 110–119 (2019)

24. Jomma, H.D., Hussein, A.I.: Circle views signature: a novel shape representation for shape recognition and retrieval. Can. J. Electr. Comput. Eng. **39**(4), 274–282 (2016)

25. Shu, X., Wu, X.J.: A novel contour descriptor for 2D shape matching and its application to image retrieval. Image Vis. Comput. **29**(4), 286–294 (2011)

26. Zhu, Z.X., Rao, C., Bai, S., Latecki, L.J.: Training convolutional neural network from multi-domain contour images for 3D shape retrieval. Pattern Recogn. Lett. **119**, 41–48 (2019)
27. Luciano, L., Hamza, A.B.: A global geometric framework for 3D shape retrieval using deep learning. Comput. Graph. **79**, 14–23 (2019)
28. Oliveira, A.B., Silva, P.R., Barone, D.A.C.: A novel 2D shape signature method based on complex network spectrum. Pattern Recogn. Lett. **63**, 43–49 (2015)

Only Image Cosine Embedding
for Few-Shot Learning

Songyi Gao[1(✉)], Weijie Shen[1(✉)], Zelin Liu[1], An Zhu[2], and Yang Yu[1]

[1] National Key Laboratory for Novel Software Technology, Nanjing University,
Nanjing 210023, China
songyigao@gmail.com, weijieshen93@gmail.com, jalynnlau@outlook.com
[2] Nanjing Landingnext Information Technology Co., Ltd., Nanjing, China

Abstract. Few-shot learning in computer vision is a very challenging task. Many approaches have been proposed to tackle the few-shot learning problem. Meta learning, a method of learning to learn, is introduced into few-shot learning problem and has achieved pretty good results. But there is still a very big gap between the machine and our human in the few-shot learning tasks. We think it's because the existing methods do not make full use of global knowledge (similar to the priori knowledge of human understanding of images) thus lacking a world view of the task. In other words, they focus too much on local information and neglect the whole task. In this paper, we rethink about the few-shot learning problem, and propose that we should make full use of global knowledge. Seen data set is used to obtain a embedding function between images and feature vectors, the images are embedded onto a hypersphere in the manner of cosine embedding. By taking this embedding function as global knowledge, we train a classifier to classify the corresponding embedded vector of images. The experiment proved that our approach significantly outperforms both baseline models and previous state-of-the-art methods. It surpasses most existing methods in terms of flexibility, simplicity and accuracy. Codes are available at https://github.com/SongyiGao/OICEFFSL.

Keywords: Few-shot learning · Image classification · Global knowledge

1 Introduction

In recent years, deep learning has achieved great success in various visual tasks [5, 7,9,14]. In order to improve the effect of the model, more and more data is used for training, and the data set in ten thousand units seems to have become the standard of deep learning. However, data is expensive to obtain, and on some special tasks, data is not available. Therefore, it is very valuable and challenging to use deep learning to achieve better results in a small number of data set.

© Springer Nature Switzerland AG 2019
T. Gedeon et al. (Eds.): ICONIP 2019, LNCS 11954, pp. 83–94, 2019.
https://doi.org/10.1007/978-3-030-36711-4_8

Few shot learning is a magic challenge for machine learning. Human can rapidly learn the new categories from very few samples, because we can understand the images by the prior knowledge. Prior knowledge constitutes our knowledge of the world, it can also be seen as the overall cognition of the task in the learning task. So the premise of fast learning is the global understanding of the problem, that is, the global knowledge. Besides, our global knowledge is not going to change very dramatically when we learn new things. However, most of the existing few-shot learning methods always use the novel labeled samples to update the parameters for the entire model. Although this seems to make the model more adaptable to the new task, it only retains relatively little global knowledge in practice. Such approach is easy to be overfitting because it learns a lot of local knowledge rather than global knowledge.

One of the most popular developed few-shot learning strategies is to take a meta-learning perspective coupled with episodic trainings. Meta-learning is the science of systematically observing how different machine learning approaches perform on a wide range of learning tasks, and then learning from this experience, or meta-data, to solve new tasks much faster than otherwise possible. However, the existing meta learning approaches have one drawback. They are over-fitting on the task. Usually, the meta learner must have predefined task settings, for example, the model trained on the 5-way 1-shot tasks or the 5-way 5-shot tasks. Model weights trained from different settings cannot be shared, which is very inefficient compared to humans. By contrast, the human beings are capable of continuous learning, we have only one brain but we can handle all problems.

In practice, we're not sure how big our task-size (K-shot, N-way) is, K and N can be any positive integer, and even sample size of different classes may not be equal. The common approach of existing few-shot learning methods is to train a unique model for each set of tasks, it's a huge waste of resources. There are already some works focusing on the problem. SNAIL [11] trained a dynamic adaptive meta-learner by changing the k value in the train phase. And the AML [13] used the prior knowledge and the attention mechanism to solve the problem. But they still have some flaws.

Towards these, we propose a few-shot learning approach based on cosine embedding in this paper. Our approach trains a embedding network between images and feature vectors and use this embedding network as global knowledge. To classify samples belong to unseen classes, a classifier is generated by standard transfer learning. Experimental results show that our simple method has advantages over existing small sample learning in flexibility, simplicity and accuracy. We hope our work will bring new ideas to solve few-shot learning tasks.

The main contributions of our work are:

1. We rethink about the few-shot learning problems and propose that the retention of global knowledge is very important.
2. We exhibit our method which uses cosine distance embedding, the result surprisingly achieves state-of-the-art performance on several few-shot learning benchmarks.

3. Based on our approach, some tricks are discussed to further improve performance.

2   Background

Given sufficient training samples on seen classes (base set), few-shot learning aims to train a high-precision model using few training samples on the unseen classes (novel set). In the few-shot learning of image recognition, task is a base unit, which is represented as a N-way K-shot classification problem with N classes sampled from the novel set, and $K + Q$ non-repeating samples sampled for each class. The N*K samples (support set) are used to train the classifier, the remaining N*Q samples (query set) are used to test the accuracy of the classifier. The base set can also be used to assist training classifier.

Many important works on few-shot learning problems have been contributed. The successful methods of initialization of model parameters [3,12] aim to meta-learn an initial condition that can be effectively fine-tuned in a few gradient-descent update steps. Similar to our work, the MatchingNet [20] uses cosine similarity as distance metric to train the learner, and Euclidean distance metric is used by ProtoNet [17]. The RelationNet [19] approach by Sung et al. proposed a learnable similarity metric. The method in [4] learns a weight generator to predict the novel class classifier using an attention based mechanism. The work [1] proposed a distance-based method by reducing intra-class variation.

Our work draws on some existing ideas, the difference is that we consider the importance of global knowledge and make better use of global knowledge by improving embedding network. Details will be given in Sects. 3 and 4.

3   Methodology

Our method follows the standard transfer learning which consists of two steps: pre-training and fintune. In the pre-training phase, we first use base set to train a classifier, then remove the full connection layers, leaving only the convolution layers as images embedding function. In the fintune phase, we freeze the parameters of convolutional layers and initialize a new classifier by defining and initializing the full connection layer based on task setting. Here we consider freezed convolutional layers parameters as global knowledge. We use the support set to train the newly initialized classifier, and then test the classification accuracy on the query set.

3.1   Pre-training Phase

Different from many few-shot learning methods which generate tasks by sampling in the training phase, our method use a CNN network as a feature extractor, followed by a classifier C (removed the bias of the FC layer) from scratch by minimizing standard cross-entropy classification loss which use the training examples in the base set. What calls for special attention is that the classifier is only used in pre-training phase. Through the convolution layers, the image is embedded to a feature vector with dimension d. We hope to reduce intra-class variation of features and increase between-class variation of features, so the pre-training classifier is trained by a special method. Algorithm 1 summarizes the training process, Algorithm 2 presents how to train the specially classifier.

In the train phase, we randomly initialize parameters of the entire network, and then apply weight-normalization [16] to the fully connected layer (line 1 in Algorithm 1). Weight normalization is a reparameterization that decouples the magnitude of a weight tensor from its direction. This replaces the parameter specified with two parameters: one specifies the magnitude and the other specifies direction. Through the convolution layers, the input images are encoded into d-dimensional feature vectors (line 4–5 in Algorithm 1). Now, we can calculate the classification loss of the feature vectors by Algorithm 2. To limit the prediction to the unit hypersphere, the feature vectors are L2 normalized (line 3 in Algorithm 2). And we can write the weight matrix of the full connection layer W_b as $[w_1, w_2, ..., w_n]$, where each class has a corresponding d-dimension weight vector w_i. The cosine similarity scores is obtained by matrix multiplication of image feature vectors and weight vectors that represent categories. We can get the probability of prediction for each category by normalizing the similarity score with a softmax function.

$$w_i^{'} = \frac{\alpha w_c + w_i}{\|\alpha w_c + w_i\|}, (i \neq c) \tag{1}$$

To get a better embedding network which can reduce intra-class variation and increase inter-class separability, we use weights-biased softmax function [8] to take place of the oral softmax (line 4 in Algorithm 2) in the train phase, which encourages the probabilities of the negative classes as well as the increase of their loss thus making the feature distance smaller within the class and the margin larger between classes. For the feature vector of each sample, let c be the index of positive classifier weight vector and i be the index of negative classifier weight vector, the original weight matrix W ($[w_1, w_2, ..., w_n]$) is converted to $W^{'}$ ($[w_1^{'}, w_2^{'}, ..., w_n^{'}]$) through Eq. 1 where only the positive weight vector with true label w_c is not transformed.

Since the corresponding $W^{'}$ of each sample needs to be calculated separately, the cosine similarity scores of the entire batch samples have to be calculated iteratively. Obviously, this will increase training time. But fortunately, we can use the original softmax for inference.

After we get the similarity scores between the weights-biased weight vector and the image vector (line 5 in Algorithm 2), a softmax function is used to normalize the prediction probability for every class (line 6 in Algorithm 2). Finally, after the whole batch loss was obtained using the cross entropy loss function (line 7 in Algorithm 2), we update the weight of B and C with backpropagation algorithm (line 7 in Algorithm 1).

Algorithm 1. Training Process

Input: Train Dataset T; Batchsize B

Output: Feature extractor F, Classifier C

1 Randomly initialize F and C, apply weight-normalization to the fully connected layer;

2 **for** *epoch* **do**

3   **for** *batch* **do**

4   sample batch images data I($[I_1, I_2, ..., I_B]$) and labels Y($[y_1, y_2, ..., y_B]$);

5   Get feature vectors X=F(I) as X=$[X_1, X_2, ..., X_B]$;

6   Algorithm2;

7   update all parameters in B and C;

8   **end**

9 **end**

Algorithm 2. Train special classifier

Input: Batch Features vectors X and labels Y,Classifier C with weight matrix W = $[w_1, w_2, ..., w_C]$

Output: The total classification loss

1 Initialize total loss L ⟵ 0;

2 **for** X_i, y_i *in* X, Y **do**

3   Get the $X_n \leftarrow$ L2-normalization(X_i);

4   Transform classifier weight matrix W by Equation1, get new weight matrix W';

5   Calculate the similarity score $S_i \leftarrow W' * X_n$;

6   Get normalization the prediction probility with a softmax function;

7   Use cross entropy loss to calculate batch loss $L \leftarrow L + CrossEntropy(S_i, y_i)$;

8 **end**

3.2 Fintune Phase

Go through the pre-training phase, a model embedding images on unit hypersphere has been successfully constructed. We freeze the model as global knowledge and initialize a new classifier based on task setting (K-shot N-way), then train the new classifier using the fewer labeled samples (support set) by minimizing classification losses and test the trained classifier accuracy on the corresponding query set. Note when testing on query set, model uses the original Softmax in place of weights-biased softmax.

4   Experimental

4.1   Dataset

We conduct few-shot learning experiments on MiniImageNet [20], which is widely used in recent works [3,11,13,17,20]. It is a subset of the ImageNet [15] that includes 100 classes with 600 images for per class. Our work uses the follow-up setting provided by Chen and Li [1], which is composed of randomly selected 64 base, 16 validation, and 20 novel classes. In addition to this, we also use CUB-200 dataset [21] which contains 200 classes and 11,788 images in total. Following the related work, we randomly split the dataset into 100 base, 50 validation, and 50 novel classes.

4.2   Implementation Details

We consider three backbones: Conv-4, ResNet-10 and ResNet-18. Conv-4 consists of $3*3$ convolutions and 64 filters, followed by a batch normalization [6], a ReLU Nonlinear activation layer and a $2*2$ max-pooling. ResNet-10 and ResNet-18 are more popular in recent works [1,2,18]. It contains 4 residual blocks and each block has 3 convolution layers with $3*3$ kernels. At the end of each residual block [5], a $2*2$ max-pooling layer is applied. The number of filters starts from 64 and is doubled every next block. During the pre-training, the SGD optimizer is employed and the initial learning rate is set to be 0.1. Then we adjust the learning rate to 0.01 and 0.001 respectively at the begining of the 100th and 200th epoch. In the fintune phase, we fixed the learning rate at 0.01 to train newly initialized classifier for 100 epochs on the support set. Usually, we average the experimental results over 600 experiments.

4.3   Experiments on MiniImagenet and CUB-200 Dataset

Expermiments on Minimagent: Upon the MiniImagenet, we test the 3 backbone extractors, Conv-4, ResNet-10 and ResNet-18, and compare these with other methods (few-shot learning and meta learning). The comparison of the accuracy is reported in Table 1. Only when we choose Conv-4 as backbone in the 5-way 1-shot task setting, the result of our approach is not the best, with the accuracy less than the ProtoNet and RelationNet. Our method outperforms the other works in all the other sets of tasks, e.g. using the ResNet-18 as backbone in the 5-way 1-shot and 5-way 5-shot task setting, the accuracy of our approach is 3% higher than other works.

Expermiments on CUB-200 Dataset: In order to prove that the feature vectors obtained by our method are more representative for the input images, we conducted an experiment on CUB-200 dataset. This dataset includes 200 fine-grained categories of birds. Each image is again resized to $84*84$ pixels. We specifically chose the work of Cheny and Fuy [2] as the baseline for comparison.

Table 1. Few-shot classification accuracy on MiniImageNet dataset. We validate our approach on the MiniImageNet dataset using three backbones (Conv-4, ResNet-10 and ResNet-18). We use 84 * 84 input size when the backbone is Conv-4, and use 224 * 224 input size in ResNet backbone. To be fair, some experiments results come from [1], and we use the same image size training data with the same backbone. We use the approach proposed in [1] as a baseline approach. The superscript "*" indicates that we use base and validation data for model training with a total of 80 classes.

Methods	BackBone	1-shot	5-shot
Matching-net	Conv-4	44.42 ± 0.84	63.48 ± 0.66
ProtoNet	Conv-4	47.74 ± 0.84	64.24 ± 0.72
MAML	Conv-4	46.67 ± 0.82	62.71 ± 0.71
RelationNet	Conv-4	$\mathbf{49.31 \pm 0.85}$	66.60 ± 0.71
Basline	Conv-4	48.24 ± 0.75	66.43 ± 0.63
Ours	Conv-4	47.17 ± 0.71	$\mathbf{67.04 \pm 0.65}$
Matching-net	ResNet-10	54.49 ± 0.81	74.69 ± 0.64
ProtoNet	ResNet-10	51.98 ± 0.84	72.64 ± 0.64
MAML	ResNet-10	54.69 ± 0.89	66.62 ± 0.83
RelationNet	ResNet-10	52.19 ± 0.83	70.20 ± 0.66
Basline	ResNet-10	53.97 ± 0.79	75.90 ± 0.61
Ours	ResNet-10	$\mathbf{58.77 \pm 0.86}$	$\mathbf{78.39 \pm 0.62}$
Matching-net	ResNet-18	52.91 ± 0.77	68.88 ± 0.69
ProtoNet	ResNet-18	54.16 ± 0.82	73.68 ± 0.65
MAML	ResNet-18	49.61 ± 0.92	65.72 ± 0.77
RelationNet	ResNet-18	52.48 ± 0.86	69.83 ± 0.68
Basline	ResNet-18	51.87 ± 0.77	75.68 ± 0.63
Ours	ResNet-18	$\mathbf{57.95 \pm 0.82}$	79.10 ± 0.57
Ours*	ResNet-18	$\mathbf{61.94 \pm 0.79}$	$\mathbf{80.46 \pm 0.61}$

Table 2. Few-shot classification results on CUB-200 dataset. ResNet-18 dosen't have feature enhancement. As the name suggests, ResNet-18+Gaussian Noise uses Gaussian Noise for feature enhancement. Resnet-18+DualTriNet uses the semantic information contained in the class name for feature enhancement.

Methods	1-shot	5-shot
ResNet-18	66.54 ± 0.53	82.38 ± 0.43
ResNet-18+Gaussian Noise	65.02 ± 0.60	80.79 ± 0.49
ResNet-18+DualTriNet	$\mathbf{69.60 \pm 0.46}$	84.10 ± 0.35
ResNet-18+Ours	69.31 ± 0.88	$\mathbf{85.03 \pm 0.52}$

As in Table 2, even though the ResNet-18+DualTriNet approach applies additional semantic information for feature enhancement, the performance of our approach is still very competitive.

Experiment with Different K Values on MiniImageNet: To establish the impact of the sample size on our approach, we used ResNet-18 as the backbone for detailed experiments. As shown in Fig. 1, the precision rate increases rapidly with the increase of K value (where N = 5, 10, 15, 20, K = 1, 2, 3, 5, 8, 10, 15, 20, 30). When K exceeds 5, the increase speed of precision rate slows down. In the 5-way 30-shot task setting, our model achieved an accuracy of up to 88%.

Table 3. N-way 5-shot experiment. All methods use ResNet-18 as backbone. The MatchingNet, ProtoNet and RelationNet use the 5-way 5-shot task setting in train phase.

Methods	5-way	10-way	15-way	20-way
Matching-net	68.88 ± 0.69	52.27 ± 0.46	-	36.78 ± 0.25
ProtoNet	73.68 ± 0.65	59.22 ± 0.44	-	44.96 ± 0.26
RelationNet	69.83 ± 0.68	53.88 ± 0.48	-	39.17 ± 0.25
Ours	$\mathbf{79.10 \pm 0.57}$	$\mathbf{62.64 \pm 0.44}$	$\mathbf{58.22 \pm 0.34}$	$\mathbf{52.63 \pm 0.26}$
Ours*	$\mathbf{80.46 \pm 0.61}$	$\mathbf{66.80 \pm 0.43}$	$\mathbf{59.29 \pm 0.31}$	$\mathbf{54.15 \pm 0.25}$

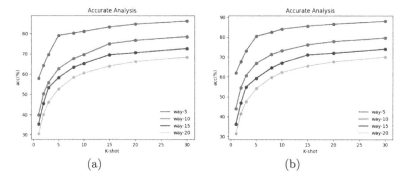

Fig. 1. (a) shows the model test results using only base set training data; (b) shows the result of using base and validation data for model training with a total of 80 classes.

Experiment with Different *N* Values on MiniImageNet: We also did experiments with a practical setting that handles different testing scenarios. Expermiments of N-way 5-shot are conducted to examine the effect of testing scenarios that are different from training, where $N \rightarrow \{5, 10, 15, 20\}$. The results are shown in Table 3. We compare our method with MathingNet, ProtoNet and

RelationNet. All the methods shown in the table used same data and backbone for training. In our method, the model was only trained when a backbone was selected. The result of our method is adaptable to all kinds of experimental settings. We hold the opinion that there are two reasons for this. Firstly, our method is trained on the train set which consists of all the classes, and can capture the most important features between the novel classes since it's informed. What's more, our method is not as sensitive to N values as other methods. In fact, our algorithm is the least affected by N value compared with other methods.

Feature Vectors Analysis: To understand how our method works, we reduce the feature vectors of novel class into a 2-dimension space with t-SNE [10] algorithm and visualize them on the Fig. 2. It is clear that our pre-trained embedding network has a strong generalization ability on unseen classes images. This generalization ability can also be understood as the ability to understand new images – global knowledge.

4.4   Extended Experiment

In this section, we introduce some tricks that can further improve the performance of our approach. As is shown before, our method has two parts, the first one is pre-train the image-feature embedding network on the base set and the second is train a classifier on the support set from scratch. As a result, there are two ways to continue to improve the accuracy of the classifier. The first is to improve the embedding network, and the second is to optimize the classifier. We will introduce three methods to improve the performance of the algorithm in the following part.

Use Mixup to Augment the Train Data: MixUp [22] is a recently proposed data augmentation scheme, which linearly interpolates a random pair of training examples and correspondingly the one-hot representations of their labels. We want to be able to embed the image into a good feature space, and by using mixup, the feature space gets smoother. We fix the hyperparameter λ to be 0.5 in MixUp algorithm. And in Eq. 1, w_i becomes $0.5 * (w_j + w_k)$. The result in Table 4 shows it has an improvement of about 0.45%.

Delete Some Features: Since we find the feature dimensions we used is far exceeding the sample size of the support set, which is easy to overfit, we tried to train the classifier with partial features. Like the Fig. 3 shows, the result is improved after we select some features and set them to zero. The feature selection mechanism is very simple. Firstly, train a new classfier on the support set and calculate the loss of support set. Then iteratively set one feature to zero and

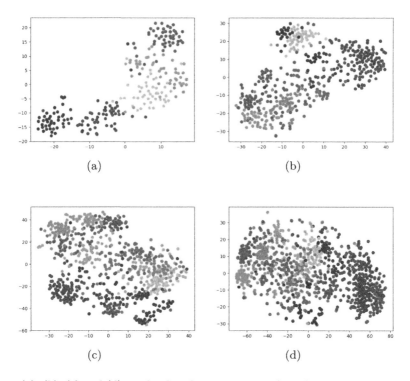

Fig. 2. (a), (b), (c) and (d) randomly select 5, 10, 15 and 20 classes on the novel set of MiniImageNet, and each class randomly sampled 50 samples for feature visualization and backone is ResNet-18.

calculate the difference between the new loss and loss in the first step. After traversing the features of all dimensions, we set the feature that cause the most loss reduce to zero and thus generate a new feature vector. Finally, repeat the process until a fixed number of features are zeroed.

Don't Use the Weights-Biased Softmax in the Fintune Phase: After several experiments, we found an interesting phenomenon which indicates that the accuracy is upper when we use oral softmax in the fintune phase. To testify this phenomenon, we sampled 10000 tasks for statistics, the result shows in the Table 4. We believe that the reason for this is that the supporting set samples are very few, thus the use of the weights-biased softmax becomes more likely to lead to model overfitting.

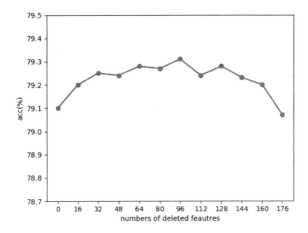

Fig. 3. Few-shot classification accuracy vs. remove the dimension of the feature. The task setting is 5-way 5-shot and backone is ResNet-18.

Table 4. Extended experiment. The task setting is 5-way 5-shot and backone is ResNet-18.

Methods	Accuracy
Ours	79.10 ± 0.57
Ours+mixup	79.55 ± 0.77
Ours+Delete some feature	79.31 ± 0.60
Ours+No weight-bias softmax	79.38 ± 0.15
Ours+all	79.91 ± 0.75

5   Conclusion

In this paper, we rethink about the few-shot learning problem and proposed the global knowledge which is crucial for solving few-shot learning task. We train a Image-Feature embedding network to imitate humans' understanding of images through prior knowledge. It turns out that our method is simple and effective. We hope our work will shed new light on the study of few-shot learning.

References

1. Chen, W.Y., Liu, Y.C., Kira, Z., Wang, Y.C.F., Huang, J.B.: A closer look at few-shot classification. arXiv preprint arXiv:1904.04232 (2019)
2. Cheny, Z., Fuy, Y., Zhang, Y., Jiang, Y.G., Xue, X., Sigal, L.: Multi-level semantic feature augmentation for one-shot learning. IEEE Trans. Image Process. **28**(9), 4594–4605 (2019)
3. Finn, C., Abbeel, P., Levine, S.: Model-agnostic meta-learning for fast adaptation of deep networks. In: Proceedings of the 34th International Conference on Machine Learning, vol. 70, pp. 1126–1135. JMLR. org (2017)

4. Gidaris, S., Komodakis, N.: Dynamic few-shot visual learning without forgetting. In: Proceedings of the IEEE Conference on Computer Vision and Pattern Recognition, pp. 4367–4375 (2018)
5. He, K., Zhang, X., Ren, S., Sun, J.: Deep residual learning for image recognition. In: Proceedings of the IEEE Conference on Computer Vision and Pattern Recognition, pp. 770–778 (2016)
6. Ioffe, S., Szegedy, C.: Batch normalization: accelerating deep network training by reducing internal covariate shift. arXiv preprint arXiv:1502.03167 (2015)
7. LeCun, Y., Bengio, Y., Hinton, G.: Deep learning. Nature **521**(7553), 436 (2015)
8. Li, X., Wang, W.: Learning discriminative features via weights-biased softmax loss. arXiv preprint arXiv:1904.11138 (2019)
9. Long, J., Shelhamer, E., Darrell, T.: Fully convolutional networks for semantic segmentation. In: Proceedings of the IEEE Conference on Computer Vision and Pattern Recognition, pp. 3431–3440 (2015)
10. Maaten, L.v.d., Hinton, G.: Visualizing data using T-SNE. J. Mach. Learn. Res. **9**(Nov), 2579–2605 (2008)
11. Mishra, N., Rohaninejad, M., Chen, X., Abbeel, P.: A simple neural attentive meta-learner. arXiv preprint arXiv:1707.03141 (2017)
12. Nichol, A., Achiam, J., Schulman, J.: On first-order meta-learning algorithms. arXiv preprint arXiv:1803.02999 (2018)
13. Qin, Y., et al.: Rethink and redesign meta learning. arXiv preprint arXiv:1812.04955 (2018)
14. Ronneberger, O., Fischer, P., Brox, T.: U-Net: convolutional networks for biomedical image segmentation. In: Navab, N., Hornegger, J., Wells, W.M., Frangi, A.F. (eds.) MICCAI 2015. LNCS, vol. 9351, pp. 234–241. Springer, Cham (2015). https://doi.org/10.1007/978-3-319-24574-4_28
15. Russakovsky, O., et al.: Imagenet large scale visual recognition challenge. Int. J. Comput. Vis. **115**(3), 211–252 (2015)
16. Salimans, T., Kingma, D.P.: Weight normalization: a simple reparameterization to accelerate training of deep neural networks. In: Advances in Neural Information Processing Systems, pp. 901–909 (2016)
17. Snell, J., Swersky, K., Zemel, R.: Prototypical networks for few-shot learning. In: Advances in Neural Information Processing Systems, pp. 4077–4087 (2017)
18. Sun, Q., Liu, Y., Chua, T.S., Schiele, B.: Meta-transfer learning for few-shot learning. arXiv preprint arXiv:1812.02391 (2018)
19. Sung, F., Yang, Y., Zhang, L., Xiang, T., Torr, P.H., Hospedales, T.M.: Learning to compare: relation network for few-shot learning. In: Proceedings of the IEEE Conference on Computer Vision and Pattern Recognition, pp. 1199–1208 (2018)
20. Vinyals, O., Blundell, C., Lillicrap, T., Wierstra, D., et al.: Matching networks for one shot learning. In: Advances in Neural Information Processing Systems, pp. 3630–3638 (2016)
21. Wah, C., Branson, S., Welinder, P., Perona, P., Belongie, S.: The Caltech-UCSD Birds-200-2011 dataset (2011)
22. Zhang, H., Cisse, M., Dauphin, Y.N., Lopez-Paz, D.: mixup: beyond empirical risk minimization. arXiv preprint arXiv:1710.09412 (2017)

Deep 3D Segmentation and Classification of Point Clouds for Identifying AusRAP Attributes

Mingyang Zhong[1(✉)], Brijesh Verma[1], and Joseph Affum[2]

[1] Centre for Intelligent Systems, Central Queensland University,
Brisbane, Australia
{m.zhong, b.verma}@cqu.edu.au
[2] Transport Safety, Australian Road Research Board (ARRB),
Brisbane, Australia
joseph.affum@arrb.com.au

Abstract. Identifying Australian Road Assessment Programme (AusRAP) attributes, such as speed signs, trees and electric poles, is the focus of road safety management. The major challenges are accurately segmenting and classifying AusRAP attributes. Researchers have focused on sematic segmentation and object classification to address the challenges mostly in 2D image setting, and few of them have recently extended techniques from 2D to 3D setting. However, most of them are designed for general objects and small scenes rather than large roadside scenes, and their performance on identifying AusRAP attributes, such as poles and trees, is limited. In this paper, we investigate segmentation and classification in roadside 3D setting, and propose an automatic 3D segmentation and classification framework for identifying AusRAP attributes. The proposed framework is able to directly take large raw 3D point cloud data collected by Light Detection and Ranging technique as input. We evaluate the proposed framework on real-world point cloud data provided by the Queensland Department of Transport and Main Roads.

Keywords: 3D segmentation and classification · Neural networks · Point cloud · AusRAP attributes

1 Introduction

Many lives are lost on our roads, according to Australian government and Queensland Department of Transport and Main Roads (DTMR) statistics [1, 2]. The road deaths for 2019 are 10.3% higher than the same period last year. AusRAP is a member of iRAP (the International Road Assessment Programme) and is dedicated to saving lives by providing safer roads. Various types of data that contain the status of road condition and safety information are regularly collected by DTMR [3, 4] and have been used for various operations such as road risk analysis and road maintenance. However, it is very challenging to have accurate data because of the changing conditions and the manual process. 2D Digital Video Recording (DVR) data and 3D Mobile Laser Scanning (MLS) data of state roads are collected periodically by vehicle mounted sensors. Thus,

© Springer Nature Switzerland AG 2019
T. Gedeon et al. (Eds.): ICONIP 2019, LNCS 11954, pp. 95–105, 2019.
https://doi.org/10.1007/978-3-030-36711-4_9

investigating the 2D DVR data and/or the 3D MLS data also known as LiDAR data (LiDAR, Light Detection and Ranging, a remote sensing technique, uses light in the form of a pulsed laser to measure ranges/distances to objects) has the potential to provide various value-added products consistently with low cost.

The focus of DTMR for reducing safety risks is on the road safety evaluation that assesses road condition and produces iRAP star rating for the road. The core of the evaluation is identifying AusRAP attributes such as speed signs, trees and poles. However, the current systems that produce the road safety assessment are insufficient, as the safety assessments that have been done by inspectors manually incur error and are time-consuming and costly. Therefore, research on systems that employ vehicle mounted sensors for road design, maintenance and management with promising precision are commercially valuable. Research based on 2D data [26–28] is a fundamental research area. Majority of the existing works are based on 2D image or video and focus on e.g. vehicle and number plate recognition [5, 6]. For example, Wang et al. proposed a method based on a cascade method with saliency test and neighboring scale awareness for traffic sign detection [5]. There are many methods that are designed for general object detection and segmentation tasks, such as [7, 8]. However, the performance of applying these methods designed for general objects to road scenarios is limited. For example, when applying CNN to road attributes segmentation, the accuracy of recognizing pole and tree is low [9]. By contrast, LiDAR data, also termed point cloud data, is collected by the remote-sensing technique that densely samples the surface of objects and produces highly accurate 3D geometric x, y, z and intensity measurements. It naturally provides two more dimensions compared with 2D image, including height and intensity that is based on the reflectivity of the object by the laser pulse. These two measures can be used as aids in classification and segmentation tasks.

In this paper, we investigate LiDAR data and propose deep learning techniques for automatic extraction of AusRAP attributes from roadside LiDAR data. Few works [10, 11] have been proposed for LiDAR data and roadside scenarios, which are surveyed in the following section. The key contributions of this paper are listed as follows:

- We propose an automatic 3D segmentation and classification framework on point cloud for identifying AusRAP attributes.
- The proposed framework is able to directly take LAS file that is an industry-standard binary format for storing LiDAR data of large roadside scene, as input. The pipeline process of our framework is able to produce per point classification of the whole roadside scene.
- We evaluate the proposed framework on real-world data collected for Queensland state roads.

In the following section, we review the most relevant state-of-the-art methods. Section 3 presents our proposed automatic 3D segmentation and classification framework for roadside point clouds. In Sect. 4, we detail the experiments and report the results. Finally, Sect. 5 concludes the paper.

2 Related Work

Object Recognition with Hand-Crafted Features. There are many works on object recognition using point cloud data collected by LiDAR sensors. Many of them extract various hand-crafted features and then use a classifier for classification [10, 12, 13], and have problems for identifying poles and trees. Thus, poles and trees are generally classified into a pole-like category [10]. Similarly, for semantic segmentation, structured output classifiers are used instead of the single output classifier [14, 15]. Unlike these approaches, our framework extracts features and performs point-wise classification from raw point cloud data, and our extracted features contain richer information than these hand-crafted features.

Deep Learning on Transformed Data. CNNs have been applied to RGBD data and considers the additional depth channel [16, 17]. However, these extended methods do not leverage the geometric information of the data. By transforming the 3D point cloud data into 2D images, some works [18, 19] apply 2D CNNs to classify them, such as [19]. However, it is not straightforward to map the 2D classification results back to 3D setting. Voxelization is another popular transformation and produces volumetric representations that are able to partially preserve the geometric information in the data. Using these volumetric representations, 3D CNNs can be applied [11]. However, this kind of transformation, such as voxelization, is limited by its resolution and also suffers from the computation cost of the transformation. To ease the resolution issue, space partition methods such as k-d trees [20] are proposed. Moreover, performing 3D CNNs on volumetric representations of large point clouds is also costly. By contrast, our framework extracts point-wise feature directly from raw data without losing information.

Deep Learning on Raw Data. Recently, Qi et al. [21, 22] design a deep neural network, PointNet, using series of Multi-Layer Perceptrons (MLPs) that can work with point cloud data, and follow-up approaches [23, 24] have been designed to investigate point features. Inspired by PointNet [21], we propose a 3D segmentation and classification framework that automatically identifies AusRAP attributes from point clouds using industrial standards.

3 Proposed Framework

3.1 Problem Statement

A point cloud of a roadside scene recorded in LAS format is represented as a set of points $P = \{p_i | i = 1, 2, ..., n\}$, where n is the number of points and each point p_i is a vector of its (x_i, y_i, z_i) coordinate and intensity feature channel $intensity_i$. Our framework directly takes raw point clouds from LAS files as input and outputs $n \times m$ scores for each of n points and the m semantic categories of AusRAP attributes. In following sections, we introduce our 3D segmentation and classification framework on point cloud.

3.2   Architecture

Most of the existing methods [11, 21, 22] are built based on input samples with small number of points. However, as for our real-world LiDAR data, the point cloud of kilometers highway contains multi-billion sensing points. There is no method that can directly take input in such scale. Furthermore, point-wise labelling on a point cloud with multi-billion points is even costly. Therefore, we adopt the idea of cutting a large scene into small blocks and integrate a gridding process to our framework. Figure 1 presents the architecture of our framework. The proposed framework performs in a pipeline fashion. Taking the raw LiDAR data as input, our framework first cuts the point cloud of a large scene into small grids. Then these grids are manually annotated and fed to our 3D Segmentation and Classification Network (3DSCN) for training and testing. As for testing, with a trained 3DSCN, our framework predicts point-wise classification for each point in a grid that can be finally aligned back to the original point cloud.

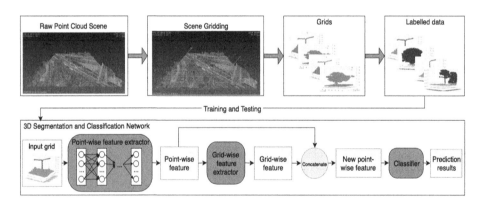

Fig. 1. 3D segmentation and classification framework on point cloud.

3.3   Gridding and Labelling

We split the large roadside scene into fix-sized grids along the x, y coordinate system to generate 3D grids, as shown in Fig. 2. After the gridding process, we manually annotate each point in a grid with one of the semantic labels from the defined categories (e.g. pole, tree and road) to prepare the training data.

Fig. 2. Gridding process.

3.4 3D Segmentation and Classification Network

Our 3DSCN directly takes raw point cloud of a $n \times d$ grid as an input, where n is the number of points in the grid and d is the dimension of each point (in our case, $d = 4$, [x, y, z, intensity] detailed in Sect. 4). The annotated grids are used for training and testing and new grids can be used for testing. Different to 2D pixel images or 3D volumetric grids, point clouds are sets of points without specific order. In other words, 3DSCN requires to be insensitive to the order of points in the point cloud. Qi et al. [21] have demonstrated that Multi-Layer Perceptron (MLP) is able to approximate a symmetric function R that transforms a point cloud to a point feature set:

$$f(x_1, x_2, \ldots, x_n) \approx L(h(x_1), h(x_2), \ldots, h(x_n)) \tag{1}$$

where $f : \underbrace{R^N, R^N, \ldots, R^N}_{n} \rightarrow R^K, h : R^N \rightarrow R^K$ and $\underbrace{R^K, R^K, \ldots, R^K}_{n} \rightarrow R^K$ is the symmetric function. We integrate this approximation and learn h by a series of MLPs and L by max pooling. As shown in Fig. 1, a $n \times d$ input grid is fed to the point-wise feature extractor that consists of a shared series of MLPs, and for each point, it extracts the k dimension point-wise feature vector $[f_1, f_2, \ldots, f_k]$. Then the gird-wise feature extractor pools the K dimension gird-wise feature vector from the $n \times k$ point-wise feature matrix. After that, we aggregate the point-wise and the grid-wise features by concatenating them. The concatenated new point-wise features of the n points with the dimension of $n \times (k + K)$ integrate both point-wise and grid-wise information. Finally, a classifier (a series of MLPs) is employed and trained to output the $n \times m$ point-wise prediction results, where m is the number of semantic categories.

Algorithm 1 depicts the training process of the proposed framework, using TensorFlow pseudocode. As for the testing process, after gridding, the grids are fed to 3DSCN that loads the trained weights, and then girds with point-wise predictions are outputted. Finally, the grids are aligned to generate the complete roadside scene with point-wise predictions.

Algorithm 1. Training process of the proposed framework.

Input: Raw point cloud data P and $p_i = (x_i, y_i, z_i, intensity_i)$, size of grid s, 3DSCN training parameters such as *epoch, learning rate* and *batch size*

Begin

Gridding:

1. for i_x in *range((max(x)-min(x))/s)*
2.   for i_y in *range((max(y)-min(y))/s)*
3.   generate grid g
            where g is a $n \times 4$ matrix of n points with 4 dimensions (*x, y, z, intensity*).

Labelling:

4. annotate the grids and output the annotated grids g's
    where g' is a $n \times 5$ matrix of n points with 5 dimensions (*x, y, z, intensity, label*).

3DSCN training:

5. initialize the weights of 3DSCN
6. *optimizer = AdamOptimizer(learning rate)*
7. *loss = sparse_softmax_cross_entropy_with_logits(prediction, label)*
8. for e in *range(epoch)*
9.   for *batch* in *range(batch size)*
10.   feed the $n \times 4$ point cloud of *batch* to the point-wise feature extractor (shared MLPs).
            Taking the last layer of the MLPs as an example, the k dimension point-wise feature
            f_{point} is computed: $f_{point} = \varnothing(w \cdot x + b)$,
            where $\varnothing$ is the activation function, x is the feature vector of each point
            w and b are the weights and the bias of this layer.
11.   feed f_{point}s of the n points to the grid-wise feature extractor and compute the K
            dimension grid-wise feature f_{grid} by *max pooling*.
12.   concatenate f_{point}s of the n points and f_{grid} into a new $n \times (k+K)$ feature matrix
13.   feed the $n \times (k+K)$ feature matrix to the classifier (shared MLPs similar to line 10)
            to predict the $n \times m$ output, where m is the number of semantic categories.
14. save the trained weights of 3DSCN

End

Output: The weights of 3DSCN

---

4   Experiments and Results

In this section, we compare the proposed framework with our own 3D CNN baseline that has a similar architecture as [11]. We report quantitative results for our framework and the compared methods on a challenging real-world dataset.

DTMR Roadside LiDAR Dataset. This dataset consists of Queensland state roads and it is collected by vehicle mounted LiDAR sensors. Each point p_i in the point clouds of the LiDAR data contains its 3D geometric x, y, z and intensity measurements, $p_i = [x_i, y_i, z_i, intensity_i]$.

AusRAP Attributes for LiDAR Dataset. Different from the 2D image data, our LiDAR dataset does not contain RGB channels. In this paper, we focus on the AusRAP attributes that are not effectively identified in 2D setting [9], such as poles and trees. Currently, we annotated 3 semantic categories, including Pole, Tree and Other. We annotated 104 grids of point clouds (52 for Pole and 52 for Tree) that contain over 50 million points. Note that all grids have annotated points of the category Other.

4.1 Metrics

We evaluate our framework on three commonly used metrics [21], including Intersection over Union (*IoU*), average per class accuracy and overall accuracy. *IoU* is computed as:

$$IoU = \frac{TP}{TP + FP + FN} \tag{2}$$

where *TP*, *FP* and *FN* are the numbers of true positives, false positives and false negatives, respectively. Average per Class Accuracy (*ApC*) is computed as:

$$ApC = \frac{\sum_{i=1}^{m} \left(\frac{n_{correct\_class_i}}{n_{all\_class_i}} \right)}{m} \tag{3}$$

where m is the number of semantic categories, $n_{correct\_class_i}$ is the number of correct predictions in category i and $n_{all\_class_i}$ is the total number of points in category i. Overall Accuracy (*OA*) is computed as:

$$OA = \frac{n_{correct}}{n_{all}} \tag{4}$$

where $n_{correct}$ is the number of correct predictions in add categories and n_{all} is the total number of points in all categories.

4.2 Results

Quantitative Results. We split our annotated dataset into training and testing sets with the percentage of 60% and 40%, respectively (32 samples for each category as training set in which 7 samples of each category are used in validation, and 20 samples for each category as testing set). We implement the proposed framework using Python and TensorFlow. As for 3DSCN, the point-wise feature extractor is composed of a shared three-layer MLP with output sizes 64, 128 and 1024 for each layer ($k = 1024$). We employ another three-layer MLP as the classifier with output sizes 512, 256 and 3 for

Table 1. Performance comparison on different metrics.

Method	IoU of pole	IoU of tree	Mean IoU	ApC	OA
3D CNN	10.52%	53.09%	45.96%	56.53%	81.20%
Our framework	48.20%	89.88%	77.17%	86.62%	90.01%

each layer ($m = 3$). The size of the max pooling layer is set to 1024 ($K = 1024$). Except the last one, ReLU and batch normalization are included in all other laters. With the similar evaluation setup as [21], the initial decay rate of batch normalization is 0.5 and is gradually increased to 0.99. We employ Adam optimizer with batch size 32 and initial learning rate 0.001 that is halved every 10 epochs. We are able to present the improved results over our 3D CNN baseline, as shown in Table 1.

As for the object-wise accuracy of AusRAP Attributes, we adopt a similar metric as [9]. For each 3D grid, the object type of each labelled ground truth point is compared with the prediction result of the same point, and the most common prediction among all points of each object class is considered as the overall prediction. As shown in Table 2, the proposed framework achieves the accuracy of 90% for Pole and 100% for Tree on testing set. 18 out of 20 Pole samples and 20 out of 20 Tree samples have been correctly identified. By contrast, the 3D CNN shows limited performance on identifying Pole in terms of object-wise accuracy. Rather than classifying poles and trees in the same pole-like category [10] or with limited accuracy in 2D setting [9], the proposed framework can identify them with good accuracy using point cloud data.

Table 2. Performance comparison on object-wise accuracy.

Predicted object class		3D CNN			Our framework		
		Pole	Tree	Object-wise accuracy	Pole	Tree	Object-wise accuracy
Actual object class	Pole	11	9	55%	18	2	90%
	Tree	0	20	100%	0	20	100%

Qualitative Results. We present qualitative results of our framework applied to our roadside data. Figure 3 shows the segmentation on three testing grids. Figure 4 is the visualization of an unlabeled roadside scene in which grids have been aligned back and Fig. 5 is the zoomed visualization of Fig. 4. We can see that our framework produces good segmentation and classification results.

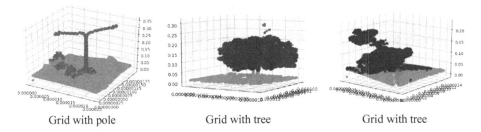

|Grid with pole|Grid with tree|Grid with tree|

Fig. 3. Segmentation on three grids. Note that, red: pole, blue: tree, gray: other. (Color figure online)

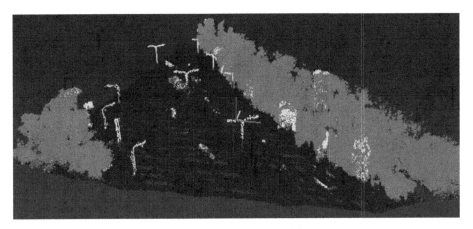

Fig. 4. Segmentation of a roadside scene. Note that, green: pole, red: tree, black: other. (Color figure online)

Fig. 5. Zoomed visualization of the segmentation of the roadside scene. Note that, green: Pole, red: tree, black: other. (Color figure online)

5   Conclusion

In this paper, we proposed an automatic 3D segmentation and classification framework for identifying AusRAP attributes from DTMR's roadside point cloud data. The proposed framework was able to directly take point cloud as an input and produce classified point cloud output. We demonstrate the effectiveness of the proposed framework on identifying AusRAP attributes that are difficult to classify in 2D setting, such as poles and trees. Although it is time-consuming to build the annotated dataset, we are continuing making progress and our framework and even at this early stage our framework performs well. It achieved quite impressive accuracy for poles and trees. In addition to high accuracy, it can automatically segment and classify large files with point cloud data into objects. In the future, more AusRAP attributes will be annotated and added to our dataset.

Acknowledgements. This research was supported under Australian Research Council's Linkage Projects funding scheme (project number LP170101255).

References

1. Australian Governments Road Safety Statistics. https://www.bitre.gov.au/statistics/safety/
2. Queensland Department of Transport and Main Roads (TMR) Road Safety Statistics. https://www.tmr.qld.gov.au/Safety/Transport-and-road-statistics/Road-safety-statistics.aspx
3. Turner, B., Tziotis, M., Cairney, P., Jurewicz, C.: Safe system infrastructure national roundtable report. No. Research Report ARR 370 (2009)
4. Verma, B., Zhang, L., Stockwell, D.: Roadside Video Data Analysis: Deep Learning. Springer, Heidelberg (2017)
5. Wang, D., Hou, X., Xu, J., Yue, S., Liu, C.L.: Traffic sign detection using a cascade method with fast feature extraction and saliency test. IEEE Trans. Intell. Transp. Syst. **18**(12), 3290–3302 (2017)
6. Tian, Y., Luo, P., Wang, X., Tang, X.: Deep learning strong parts for pedestrian detection. In: Proceedings of the IEEE International Conference on Computer Vision, pp. 1904–1912 (2015)
7. Long, J., Shelhamer, E., Darrell, T.: Fully convolutional networks for semantic segmentation. In: Proceedings of the IEEE Conference on Computer Vision and Pattern Recognition, pp. 3431–3440 (2015)
8. Ren, S., He, K., Girshick, R., Sun, J.: Faster R-CNN: towards real-time object detection with region proposal networks. In: Advances in Neural Information Processing Systems, pp. 91–99 (2015)
9. Jan, Z., Verma, B., Affum, J., Atabak, S., Moir, L.: A convolutional neural network based deep learning technique for identifying road attributes. In: IEEE International Conference on Image and Vision Computing New Zealand, pp. 1–6 (2018)
10. Fukano, K., Masuda, H.: Detection and classification of pole-like objects from mobile mapping data. ISPRS Ann. Photogram. Rem. Sens. Spat. Inf. Sci. **2** (2015)
11. Maturana, D., Scherer, S.: VoxNet: a 3D convolutional neural network for realtime object recognition. In: IEEE/RSJ International Conference on Intelligent Robots and Systems, pp. 922–928 (2015)
12. Frome, A., Huber, D., Kolluri, R., Bülow, T., Malik, J.: Recognizing objects in range data using regional point descriptors. In: Pajdla, T., Matas, J. (eds.) ECCV 2004. LNCS, vol. 3023, pp. 224–237. Springer, Heidelberg (2004). https://doi.org/10.1007/978-3-540-24672-5_18

13. Behley, J., Steinhage, V., Cremers, A.B.: Performance of histogram descriptors for the classification of 3D laser range data in urban environments. In: IEEE International Conference on Robotics and Automation, pp. 4391–4398 (2012)
14. Munoz, D., Vandapel, N., Hebert, M.: Onboard contextual classification of 3-D point clouds with learned high-order markov random fields. In: IEEE International Conference on Robotics and Automation (2009)
15. Koppula, H.S., Anand, A., Joachims, T., Saxena, A.: Semantic labeling of 3D point clouds for indoor scenes. In: Advances in Neural Information Processing Systems, pp. 244–252 (2011)
16. Socher, R., Huval, B., Bath, B., Manning, C.D., Ng, A.Y.: Convolutional-recursive deep learning for 3D object Classification. In: Advances in Neural Information Processing Systems, pp. 656–664 (2012)
17. Alexandre, L.A.: 3D object recognition using convolutional neural networks with transfer learning between input channels. In: Menegatti, E., Michael, N., Berns, K., Yamaguchi, H. (eds.) Intelligent Autonomous Systems 13. AISC, vol. 302, pp. 889–898. Springer, Cham (2016). https://doi.org/10.1007/978-3-319-08338-4_64
18. Su, H., Maji, S., Kalogerakis, E., Learned-Miller, E.: Multi-view convolutional neural networks for 3D shape recognition. In: Proceedings of the IEEE International Conference on Computer Vision, pp. 945–953 (2015)
19. Wu, B., Wan, A., Yue, X., Keutzer, K.: SqueezeSeg: convolutional neural nets with recurrent CRF for real-time road-object segmentation from 3D lidar point cloud. In: IEEE International Conference on Robotics and Automation, pp. 18871893 (2018)
20. Klokov, R., Lempitsky, V.: Escape from cells: deep Kd-networks for the recognition of 3D point cloud models. In: Proceedings of the IEEE International Conference on Computer Vision (2017)
21. Qi, C.R., Su, H., Mo, K., Guibas, L.J.: PointNet: deep learning on point sets for 3D Classification and Segmentation. In: Proceedings of the IEEE Conference on Computer Vision and Pattern Recognition, pp. 652–660 (2017)
22. Qi, C.R., Yi, L., Su, H., Guibas, L.J.: PointNet++: deep hierarchical feature learning on point sets in a metric space. In: Advances in Neural Information Processing Systems, pp. 5099–5108 (2017)
23. Shen, Y., Feng, C., Yang, Y., Tian, D.: Neighbors do help: deeply exploiting local structures of point clouds. arXiv preprint arXiv:1712.06760, 1(2) (2017)
24. Engelmann, F., Kontogianni, T., Hermans, A., Leibe, B.: Exploring spatial context for 3d semantic segmentation of point clouds. In: Proceedings of the IEEE International Conference on Computer Vision, pp. 716–724 (2017)
25. Huang, G., Liu, Z., Van Der Maaten, L., Weinberger, K.Q.: Densely connected convolutional networks. In: Proceedings of the IEEE Conference on Computer Vision and Pattern Recognition, pp. 4700–4708 (2017)
26. Li, M., Wang, D.: 2-D stochastic configuration networks for image data analytics. IEEE Trans. Cybern. (2019). https://doi.org/10.1109/tcyb.2019.2925883
27. Li, M., Huang, C., Wang, D.: Robust stochastic configuration networks with maximum correntropy criterion for uncertain data regression. Inform. Sci. **473**, 73–86 (2019)
28. Li, M., Wang, D.: Insights into randomized algorithms for neural networks: practical issues and common pitfalls. Inform. Sci. **382**, 170–178 (2017)

A Robustness and Low Bit-Rate Image Compression Network for Underwater Acoustic Communication

Mingyong Zhuang[1,2], Yan Luo[2,3], Xinghao Ding[2,3], Yue Huang[2,3], and Yinghao Liao[1(✉)]

[1] School of Electronic Science and Engineering, Xiamen University, Xiamen 361005, Fujian, China
myzhuang@stu.xmu.edu.cn, yhliao@xmu.edu.cn
[2] Key Laboratory of Underwater Acoustic Communication and Marine Information Technology, Ministry of Education, Xiamen 361005, Fujian, China
23320171153184@stu.xmu.edu.cn
[3] School of Informatics, Xiamen University, Xiamen 361005, Fujian, China
{yhuang2010,dxh}@xmu.edu.cn

Abstract. Image compression algorithm is an important technology in the process of image transmission. Algorithm faces more difficult challenges in underwater acoustic communication. Images are required to be transmitted at a low bit-rate due to the limited underwater bandwidth and the noisy underwater acoustic environment will cause errors like random bit flip or packet loss. Therefore, the performance of common compression algorithms (JPEG, BPG, etc.) will be greatly reduced. Based on deep neural network (DNN), we propose an image compression algorithm that compresses the image texture and color separately for reducing the bit-rate. Moreover, we simulate the underwater acoustic environment and add different types of errors to compressed bit codes in our training process. Extensive experiments show that this training method improves the robustness of decoder and reconstruction performance. Besides, the algorithm is better than common compression algorithms and DNN based algorithms for underwater acoustic communication.

Keywords: Image compression · Deep neural network · Underwater acoustic communication

1 Introduction

About 70% of the earth is ocean, and the deepest ocean is more than 10,000 m deep. Usually, humans use ROV (Remote Operated Vehicle) to explore underwater space and photograph underwater objects for research with cameras. Through

This work was supported in part by the National Natural Science Foundation of China under Grants 61971369, 61571382, 81671766, 61571005, 81671674, 61671309 and U1605252, in part by the Fundamental Research Funds for the Central Universities under Grants 20720160075 and 20720180059, in part by the CCF-Tencent open fund, and the Natural Science Foundation of Fujian Province of China (No. 2017J01126).

© Springer Nature Switzerland AG 2019
T. Gedeon et al. (Eds.): ICONIP 2019, LNCS 11954, pp. 106–116, 2019.
https://doi.org/10.1007/978-3-030-36711-4_10

underwater acoustic communication technology, ROV sends underwater images to overwater equipment. However, the main challenges of underwater image application [17] are the limited bandwidth (3–5 khz) and the strong noise of underwater space. In our underwater acoustic communication experiment, it took more than 20 min to transmit a 256×256 pixels underwater image to a receiver 1 km away. We took so long to transmit the image because of the high error rate of underwater acoustic communication and needing to retransmit the wrong part many times. At present, many methods can correct coding errors to reduce the error rate, but researchers pay less attention to the robustness of decoder. If the decoder is more robust and can tolerate more errors, the transmission time can be greatly reduced.

In underwater acoustic communication, there are two main error modes: (1) random bit flip error: random bits flip in a binary data packet, and (2) packet loss error: the entire binary data packet is lost during transmission. These two error modes occur randomly during transmission. The most serious error mode is packet loss error, which will lead to a large number of bits loss and have a great impact on the quality of image reconstruction. Random bit flip error will lead to the degradation of image reconstruction quality (Fig. 1).

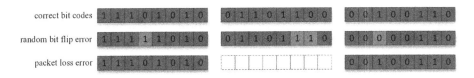

Fig. 1. Different types of errors. The blue parts are correct bits, the red parts are wrong bits, and the dashed parts indicate packet loss. (Color figure online)

Recent researches [10,12] show the image autoencoder based on deep neural network produces promising results. It achieves better reconstruction performance and robustness than many traditional image compression techniques (BPG [4], JPEG [15], JPEG2000 [6], etc.). We propose to use DNN as encoder and decoder of compression system. Meanwhile, during the training process, we simulated the errors in underwater acoustic communication, and added random bit flip errors and packet loss errors into the compressed bit codes. Experiments show the reconstruction performance and error tolerance of the proposed method are better than other methods, including the traditional image compression method and the deep learning compression method without adding error training.

In addition to considering errors, we also use neural networks to compress images at low bit-rate according to the characteristics of underwater images. Images taken in an underwater space are very different from natural images. There is little light in the underwater space. The light in the water has a longer wavelength. The sediment and microorganisms in the water will block and absorb some of the light. We observe the underwater images have dim color, low contrast and simple texture. The complex texture of the underwater image focuses on the targets (such as fish, coral, diver, robotic arm, and etc.), while the background part has smooth texture and low contrast. At the same time, humans are less sensitive to color differences than textures. Also humans are less likely to detect slight changes in color, especially in low-contrast underwater images. Based on the above observations, we found underwater images have a lot of visual redundancy, which provides the possibility for us to compress underwater images with low bit-rate.

The contributions of this article are as follows: in order to solve the problem of poor quality and long transmission time of underwater image compression under the condition of low bit-rate and high error rate, we simulate the random bit flip error and packet loss error during the training process to improve the robustness of the decoder. In order to compress the image at a low bit-rate, we design the network to compress the texture and color of the image and represent them with different numbers of binary bits.

2   Related Works

For decades, image compression has been a basic and important research topic in the field of image processing. Traditional image compression algorithms, such as JPEG [15], JPEG2000 [6] and BPG [4], rely on handcrafted encoder and decoder block diagrams. In recent years, the application of neural network in image compression [11,14] has made great progress. The works [3,13] proposed a differentiable approximation of the quantization and the entropy rate estimation for an end-to-end autoencoder. The work [2,3,14] used a recurrent network for compressing full-resolution images. Priming and spatially adaptive bit rate were further considered in [10]. GAN was used in the work [1] to reconstruct the full resolution picture from latent compressed vector and generate the discarded details. [13] demonstrated that CAEs achieve higher coding efficiency than JPEG [15] due to the property of compact representation of autoencoders. On large compression ratio, based GAN methods show potential advantages and high subjective quality reconstruction. The method based on super-resolution [5,7] cannot compress the images with complex texture and small resolution well.

3   Proposed Methods

The proposed network architecture is shown in Fig. 2 and we will give a detail description of it as follows.

The network architecture consists of encoder $E_{texture}$, E_{color}, quantizer Q and decoder D. Given the training image x, the encoder $E_{texture}$ extracts the texture information of image x and maps it to a latent representation vector $z_{texture}$. Encoder E_{color} extracts the color information of image x and maps it into a latent representation vector z_{color}. We concatenate latent representation vectors $z_{texture}$ and z_{color} to z. In each encoder, we use 4 residual blocks to extract the important features in the image. To solve vanishing gradient problem, we

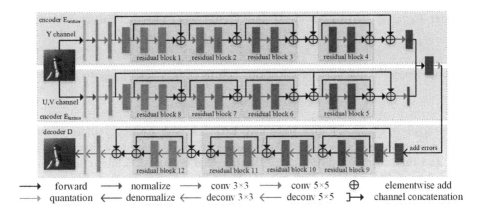

Fig. 2. The proposed image compression network architecture. (Color figure online)

design two skip connections. The second convolution layer output feature maps are element-wise added to input and output of the fourth residual block. We quantize z into binary vector $\hat{z}$ using the quantizer Q. In the training process, we model errors in underwater transmission and build an error mask M_{bit} or M_{byte}. We use $\hat{z}$ and M_{bit} or M_{byte} to get latent representation vector with error codes, $\hat{z}_{error}$. We design a decoder that is symmetric with the encoders for image restoration. We also used 4 residual blocks to restore important features from latent representation vector. Decoder D reconstructs the image $\hat{x}$ from $\hat{z}_{error}$. We use $d(x, \hat{x})$ to measure the reconstruction error. In training, we want $\hat{z}$ to be as compact as possible, with $d(x, \hat{x})$ as small as possible. Lossy image compression allows some distortion in the reconstructed image to reduce the number of bits stored. This leads to a rate-distortion trade-off, which is expressed in

$$L = \frac{1}{N} \sum_{i=1}^{N} d(x^{(i)}, \hat{x}^{(i)}) + \beta H(\tilde{z}^{(i)}), \qquad (1)$$

where $\beta > 0$ balances the two competing objectives. In Eq. 1, N represents the batch size and H denotes the entropy of latent representation vector $\tilde{z}_i$.

3.1 Encoder

We design two encoders $E_{texture}$ and E_{color} to extract the texture and color features of the image respectively. Common image compression algorithms use RGB format as input. However, YUV format is often used as input in underwater image compression, because YUV format realizes the separation of texture and color. Encoder $E_{texture}$ is used to encode the Y channel to extract the texture features of image:

$$E_{texture}(Y) = z_{texture}. \qquad (2)$$

Encoder E_{color} is used to encode U and V channels to extract image color features:

$$E_{color}(U,V) = z_{color}. \tag{3}$$

We concatenate compact representation vectors $z_{texture}$ and z_{color} to z:

$$z = Concatenate(z_{texture}, z_{color}). \tag{4}$$

As shown in Fig. 2, the first green area is the encoder $E_{texture}$, whose input is the Y channel layer of the image. Y channel is firstly processed by normalization layer, and then two convolution layers with kernel size of 5×5 and output channel number of 64 and 128, respectively. The orange areas in Fig. 2 are residual blocks, and the structure of each residual block is the same, which is composed of two convolution layers with kernel size 3×3 and 128 output channels. Four residual blocks are used in encoder $E_{texture}$, and their connection mode is shown in Fig. 2. After 4 residual blocks, we design a convolution layer with kernel size 5×5 and output channel number C_1 to control the compression rate. The second green area is the encoder E_{color}, whose input is the U and V channel layers of the image. The architecture of encoder E_{color} is the same as that of encoder $E_{texture}$, except that the number of output channels used to control the compression rate is C_2. In our experiments, we set $C_1{:}C_2 = 4{:}1$.

3.2 Quantitative

Quantization is an important step in compression, and the quantization methods used in [8] are not differentiable. This affects the network backpropagation, so we use the nearest neighbor quantization and differentiable soft quantization methods proposed in Mentzer *et al.* [12]. In the process of image compression, we use nearest neighbor quantization. Firstly, we define the quantitation centers $C = \{c_1, c_2, c_3, \cdots, c_L\}$. Then, the nearest neighbor allocation algorithm is used to quantize z:

$$\hat{z}_i = Q(z_i) := arg\ min_j \|z_i - c_i\|. \tag{5}$$

But in the process of training, we use differentiable soft quantization method to get the quantized latent representation vector $\tilde{z}$:

$$\tilde{z}_i = \sum_{j=1}^{L} \frac{exp(-\sigma\|z_i - c_j\|)}{\sum_{l=1}^{L} exp(-\sigma\|z_j - c_l\|)} c_j. \tag{6}$$

(5) is differentiable, and we use (6) to calculate the gradient in backpropagation.

3.3 Training with Errors

In the training process, we simulated packet loss error and random bit flip error in underwater acoustic communication, and added errors to the quantized bit coding $\hat{z}$ by masking.

In adding random bit flip errors, we set up an error mask M_{bit}. We set the binary compression bit codes

$$\hat{z}_{bit} = \{z_1, z_2, z_3, \cdots, z_i\}, \tag{7}$$

where $\hat{z}_i \in \{0,1\}$. During the training process, we simulated the random bit flip errors in underwater acoustic communication and randomly selected some elements in $\hat{z}$ to add bit flip errors. We use

$$N_{bit} = \{n_1, n_2, n_3, \cdots, n_j\} \tag{8}$$

to represent the subscript of the elements in $\hat{z}$ which need to add the errors, where $j < i$. We set up an error mask M_{bit}, which has the same size as $\hat{z}$.

$$M_{bit} = \{m_1, m_2, m_3, \cdots, m_i\}, \tag{9}$$

where $m_i \in \{0,1\}$. The values of each element in the M_{bit} are defined as follows

$$m_i = \begin{cases} 0 & i \in N_{bit}, \\ 1 & i \notin N_{bit}. \end{cases} \tag{10}$$

We use bit operations to add random bit flip errors to $\hat{z}_{bit}$:

$$\hat{z}_{error} = \hat{z}_{bit} \odot M_{bit}. \tag{11}$$

In Eq. 8 we get $\hat{z}_{error}$ from $\hat{z}$ and M_{bit}. The operator $\odot$ represents bitwise exclusive NOR operate between two binary bit codes.

In the training with packet loss error, we regard every 8 bit of $\hat{z}$ as a packet. We rewrite Eq. 7 as

$$\hat{z}_{byte} = \{z_1, z_2, z_3, \cdots, z_i\}. \tag{12}$$

We randomly selected some elements in $\hat{z}_{byte}$ to discard and use 0 to represent each bit in the discarded bytes. We use

$$N_{byte} = \{N_1, N_2, N_3, \cdots, N_i\} \tag{13}$$

to represent the subscript of the elements in $\hat{z}_{byte}$ which need to discard, where $j < i$. We set up an error mask M_{byte}, which has the same size as $\hat{z}_{byte}$.

$$M_{byte} = \{m_1, m_2, m_3, \cdots, m_i\}, \tag{14}$$

where $m_i \in 0, 1$. The values of each element in the M_{byte} are defined as follows:

$$m_i = \begin{cases} 0 & i \in N_{bit}, \\ 1 & i \notin N_{bit}. \end{cases} \tag{15}$$

We use bit operations to add packet loss errors to $\hat{z}_{byte}$:

$$\hat{z}_{error} = \hat{z}_{byte} \& M_{byte}. \tag{16}$$

In Eq. 16 we get $\hat{z}_{error}$ which adds packet loss errors from $\hat{z}_{byte}$ and M_{byte}. The operator $\&$ represents bitwise NOR operate between two binary bit codes.

3.4 Decoder

We use decoder D to restore the latent representation vector $\hat{z}_{error}$ to image:

$$\hat{x} = D(\hat{z}_{error}) \qquad (17)$$

In Fig. 2, the blue area is the decoder D. The input of decoder D is the compact representation vector $\hat{z}_{error}$ after adding errors. $\hat{z}_{error}$ firstly input a deconvolution layer with kernel size of 3×3 and output channel number of 128, and then input four residual blocks. The connection mode of the four residual blocks is shown in Fig. 2. After four residual blocks, we designed two deconvolution layers with kernel size of 5×5 and output channels number of 64 and 3, respectively, to restore the size of the feature layer to the same as the input image. Finally, we denormalize the feature map to output reconstructed image $\hat{x}$.

4   Experiment

4.1 Training

The experiments were implemented in a server with NIVDIA GeForce Xp GPU, 128G RAM and 56 Intel(R) Xeon(R) CPU E5-2683 V3 @ 2.00 GHz. We use the Adam optimizer [9] with a mini batch size of 40 to train our models. Each model is trained to maximize multiscale structural similarity index (MS-SSIM) [16]. Based on SSIM, MS-SSIM is a more reasonable and flexible method to measure the similarity between two images. The distance from the image to the observer affects the perception of the image details. MS-SSIM considers the influence of this factor on image quality through multi-scale down sampling, so we use MS-SSIM to calculate the reconstruction error of the network. The learning rate was set to 3×10^{-4}, and then was reduced to 10^{-5} after 10000 times training.

The dataset we use is composed of real underwater images collected by the underwater AUV. These images include different kinds of fish, coral reefs, divers and other targets. Our training dataset has 3,400 images of 256×256 pixels, and the test dataset has 400 images of 256×256 pixels. We chose MS-SSIM as the evaluation index of our experiment and it reportedly correlates better with human perception of distortion than mean squared error (MSE).

4.2 Experiment Results

In order to visually compare the effects of different types of errors on reconstructed images, we show a real underwater picture after adding packet loss errors and random bit flip errors in Fig. 3. In each row, we show the reconstruction images without adding error, with adding random bit flip error and with adding packet loss error. In the experiment with adding random bit flip errors, we added random bit flip errors to the compact representation bit codes as the error rate 10^{-4}. In the experiment with adding packet loss error, we added packet loss errors to the compact representation bit codes as the error rate 10^{-5}.

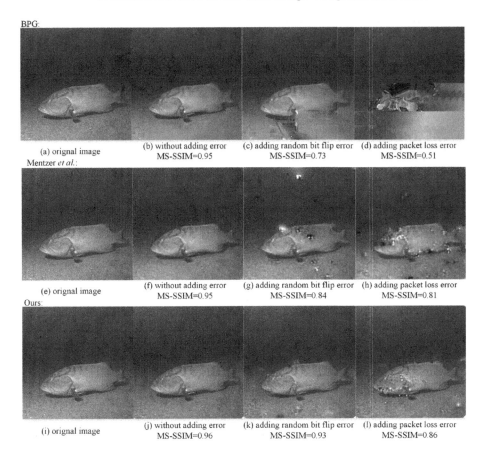

Fig. 3. Underwater images reconstructed using different methods. We visually compared the reconstruction performance of BPG, Mentzer *et al.* and the proposed method under the same bit-rate 0.1 bpp. We test without adding error, with adding random bit flip error and with adding packet loss error.

We find that the BPG [4] method has good reconstruction performance without error in compressed bit codes. However, when adding random bit flip errors or packet loss errors to compressed bit codes, image reconstruction quality drops seriously and the decoder products many image blocks by mistake. In our experiment, even the BPG [4] decoder could not decode the compressed bit coding. Comparing with BPG [4] and Mentzer *et al.* [12], the reconstruction performance of our proposed method is competitive without errors. When the random bit flip error or packet loss error is added to the compressed bit codes, the image reconstruction quality of our proposed method is not seriously degraded. Compared with Fig. 3(g), (h), (k) and (l), the proposed method has a better suppression effect on random bit flip errors and packet loss errors, and the reconstruction performance of decoded images with errors is better than that of Mentzer *et al.*

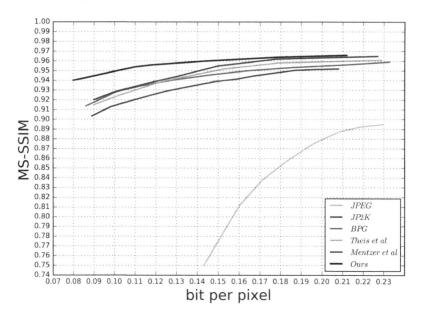

Fig. 4. We compared the reconstruction performance of different methods at low bit-rate.

In Fig. 4, we compare our proposed method with JPEG [15], JPEG2000 [6], BPG [4], Theis *et al.* [13] and Mentzer *et al.* [12] methods. Our proposed method performs better than other methods in the low bit-rate range of 0.08 bpp to 0.23 bpp. It is worth noting that the reconstruction performance of our proposed method is significantly better than that of the common compression methods and other based DNN methods at a lower bit-rate (less than 0.12 bpp).

In order to prove that our proposed method has good error tolerance, we compare our proposed method with common compression methods (JPEG [15], JPEG2000 [6] and BPG [4]) and DNN based methods (Mentzer *et al.* [12] and Theis *et al.* [13]) in Table 1. We set each method at the same 0.1 bpp (JPEG [15] at the lowest 0.14 bpp) and compared the reconstruction performance at different error rates. We used error rates of 0, 10^{-5}, 10^{-4} and 10^{-3} for the experiments. The experiments included packet loss error and random bit flip error and these two errors occurred randomly in binary bit coding. With the error rate 0, JPEG2000 [6], BPG [4], Theis *et al.* [13] and Mentzer *et al.* [12] method have good performance and our proposed method has the best reconstruction performance, achieving an average MS-SSIM of 0.951. However, when the error rate rises to 10^{-5}, the performance of BPG [4], JPEG [15] and JPEG2000 [6] methods declines significantly, and the error coding begins to affect the decoding. It is worth noting that the DNN based method has a high error tolerance. The MS-SSIM of reconstructed images using Mentzer *et al.* method decreased by only 0.01, while the MS-SSIM of reconstructed images using our proposed

Table 1. At different error rates, we compared the reconstruction performance of different methods in MS-SSIM.

Error rate	0	10^{-3}	10^{-4}	10^{-5}
BPG [4]	0.948	0.548	0.471	0.444
JPEG [15]	0.750	0.681	0.678	0.664
JPEG2000 [6]	0.913	0.569	0.567	0.455
Mentzer *et al.* [12]	0.928	0.918	0.909	0.857
Theis *et al.* [13]	0.922	0.903	0.889	0.836
Ours without error train	0.952	0.948	0.926	0.861
Ours with error train	0.952	0.950	0.937	0.910

method decreased by 0.002. Under the condition of 10^{-3} error rate, the reconstruction performance of Mentzer *et al.* [12] decreased significantly, reaching 0.857. Thanks to the training of adding errors, the reconstruction performance index of our proposed method can be maintained at 0.910 without significant decline. In Table 1, we also compared the reconstruction performance of our proposed method with error training and without error training. When the error rate is 0, the performance of the proposed method without error training is close to that with error training. However, when we add 10^{-5}, 10^{-4} and 10^{-3} errors rate respectively, the performance of our proposed method without error training will be worse than that with error training.

Experiments in Figs. 3, 4 and Table 1 show that, for underwater images, the reconstruction performance of our proposed method is better than that of BPG [4], JPEG [15], JPEG2000 [6], Theis *et al.* [13] and Mentzer *et al.* [12] Methods under the condition of low bit-rate. At the same time, our method has a higher tolerance for binary coding with high error rate, and still has good reconstruction performance under the high error rate of 10^{-3}.

5 Conclusion

Based on the characteristics of high bit error rate and limited bandwidth of underwater acoustic communication, a deep neural network suitable for underwater image compression is proposed. In the training process, we add random bit flip and packet loss error in the compressed representation bit codes, which improves the error tolerance of decoder and can shorten the transmission time of underwater image. At the same time, we compress the texture and color information separately to achieve a lower bit-rate compression.

References

1. Agustsson, E., Tschannen, M., Mentzer, F., Timofte, R., Van Gool, L.: Generative adversarial networks for extreme learned image compression. arXiv preprint arXiv:1804.02958 (2018)
2. Ballé, J., Laparra, V., Simoncelli, E.P.: End-to-end optimization of nonlinear transform codes for perceptual quality. In: 2016 Picture Coding Symposium (PCS), pp. 1–5. IEEE (2016)
3. Ballé, J., Laparra, V., Simoncelli, E.P.: End-to-end optimized image compression. arXiv preprint arXiv:1611.01704 (2016)
4. Bellard, F.: BPG image format (2014). http://bellard.org/bpg/
5. Bruna, J., Sprechmann, P., LeCun, Y.: Super-resolution with deep convolutional sufficient statistics. arXiv preprint arXiv:1511.05666 (2015)
6. Christopoulos, C., Skodras, A., Ebrahimi, T.: The JPEG2000 still image coding system: an overview. IEEE Trans. Consum. Electron. **46**(4), 1103–1127 (2000)
7. Dong, C., Deng, Y., Change Loy, C., Tang, X.: Compression artifacts reduction by a deep convolutional network. In: Proceedings of the IEEE International Conference on Computer Vision, pp. 576–584 (2015)
8. Jiang, F., Tao, W., Liu, S., Ren, J., Guo, X., Zhao, D.: An end-to-end compression framework based on convolutional neural networks. IEEE Trans. Circ. Syst. Video Technol. **28**(10), 3007–3018 (2017)
9. Kingma, D.P., Ba, J.: Adam: a method for stochastic optimization. arXiv preprint arXiv:1412.6980 (2014)
10. Li, M., Zuo, W., Gu, S., Zhao, D., Zhang, D.: Learning convolutional networks for content-weighted image compression. In: Proceedings of the IEEE Conference on Computer Vision and Pattern Recognition, pp. 3214–3223 (2018)
11. Maleki, D., Nadalian, S., Derakhshani, M.M., Sadeghi, M.A.: BlockCNN: a deep network for artifact removal and image compression. arXiv preprint arXiv:1805.11091 (2018)
12. Mentzer, F., Agustsson, E., Tschannen, M., Timofte, R., Van Gool, L.: Conditional probability models for deep image compression. In: Proceedings of the IEEE Conference on Computer Vision and Pattern Recognition, pp. 4394–4402 (2018)
13. Theis, L., Shi, W., Cunningham, A., Huszár, F.: Lossy image compression with compressive autoencoders. arXiv preprint arXiv:1703.00395 (2017)
14. Toderici, G., et al.: Full resolution image compression with recurrent neural networks. In: Proceedings of the IEEE Conference on Computer Vision and Pattern Recognition, pp. 5306–5314 (2017)
15. Wallace, G.K.: The JPEG still picture compression standard. IEEE Trans. Consum. Electron. **38**(1), xviii–xxxiv (1992)
16. Wang, Z., Simoncelli, E.P., Bovik, A.C.: Multiscale structural similarity for image quality assessment. In: Asilomar Conference on Signals, Systems and Computers, vol. 2, pp. 1398–1402 (2003)
17. Zhang, Y., Negahdaripour, S., Li, Q.: Low bit-rate compression of underwater imagery based on adaptive hybrid wavelets and directional filter banks. Sign. Process.: Image Commun. **47**, 96–114 (2016)

Gated Contiguous Memory U-Net for Single Image Dehazing

Lei Xiang[1,2(✉)], Hang Dong[1], Fei Wang[1], Yu Guo[2], and Kaisheng Ma[3]

[1] National Engineering Laboratory for Vision Information Processing and Application, Xi'an Jiaotong University, Xi'an 710049, Shaanxi, China
xianglei96@stu.xjtu.edu.cn, dhunter1230@gmail.com, wfx@mail.xjtu.edu.cn
[2] School of Software Engineering, Xi'an Jiaotong University, Xi'an 710049, Shaanxi, China
yu.guo@xjtu.edu.cn
[3] Tsinghua University, Beijing 100084, China
kaisheng@mail.tsinghua.edu.cn

Abstract. Single image dehazing is a challenging problem that aims to recover a high-quality haze-free image from a hazy image. In this paper, we propose an U-Net like deep network with contiguous memory residual blocks and gated fusion sub-network module to deal with the single image dehazing problem. The contiguous memory residual block is used to increase the flow of information by feature reusing and a gated fusion sub-network module is used to better combine the features of different levels. We evaluate our proposed method using two public image dehazing benchmarks. The experiments demonstrate that our network can achieve a state-of-the-art performance when compared with other popular methods.

Keywords: Single image dehazing · U-Net like deep network · Contiguous memory resblock · Gated fusion sub-network

1 Introduction

Hazy images are generated by scattering and absorption of the turbid medium (e.g., particles, water-droplets) in the atmosphere. As shown in Fig. 1, hazy images lose contrast and color fidelity, which will bring difficulties to many automated computer vision applications today. Image dehaze aims to recover clean images from hazy input, which has received significant attention as images need to be first enhanced before other high-level vision tasks.

Image quality degradation caused by haze can be roughly mathematically formulated [2, 19, 21, 29] as:

$$I(x) = J(x)t(x) + A(x)(1 - t(x)) \tag{1}$$

where I is the observed hazy image, x is the pixel coordinates, J is the true scene radiance or clear image, $t(x) = e^{-\rho d(x)}$ is the transmission map [6], A is

© Springer Nature Switzerland AG 2019
T. Gedeon et al. (Eds.): ICONIP 2019, LNCS 11954, pp. 117–127, 2019.
https://doi.org/10.1007/978-3-030-36711-4_11

Fig. 1. Examples of realistic hazy images.

the global atmospheric light which indicates the intensity of ambient light. As shown in the formula, only the observed image $I(x)$ is known, recovering the scene radiance $J(x)$ is an ill-posed inverse problem.

The traditional single image dehazing methods [3,7,8,15,18,22,23] have investigated various image prior to estimate transmission maps and atmospheric lights. However, the image prior assumptions may not be valid in all cases. For example, He et al. [8] assumes that value of the dark channel in clear images is close to zero and then use this assumption to estimate the transmission map. However, this assumption may not work well when the scene objects are similar to atmospheric light.

There are also some deep learning-based methods which have been proposed to estimate the transmissions instead of using image priors. However, inaccuracies in the estimation of transmission map lead to low quality dehazed result. To avoid the aforementioned problems, we adopt an end-to-end trainable neural network like [4,14,17,26] which directly restores hazy-free images without estimating the transmission and atmospheric light.

PFFNet [17] is the method that performs best on our datasets in existing methods, but it produces undesired artifacts on the planar region when applied on some images. In order to improve the performance of PFFNet [17], our proposed network adds extra contiguous memory resblocks and gated fusion sub-network based on PFFNet [17]. The encoder convolves input image into feature maps. The decoder then recovers image details from the encoded feature. We add contiguous memory residual blocks to each scale of the encoder and decoder in order to extract the features on each scale. Inspired by fact that fusing different levels of features are often beneficial for both low-level and high-level tasks [4,16,31], we use a gated fusion sub-network [4,26,33] to determine the importance of different levels and then fuse them based on their corresponding importance weights. To evaluate our proposed network, we test it on two public image dehazing benchmarks. Compared with several popular methods, the experimental results have shown that our proposed network outperforms all the previous methods.

To summarize, the contributions of this paper are three-fold:

– We propose a new trainable U-Net like end-to-end network for image dehazing, which can perform well on both indoor and outdoor images.

- The proposed architecture uses the contiguous memory resblocks to better extract the features on each scale, and a gated fusion sub-network is applied to fuse the features of different levels.
- Experiments show that our method is better than all previous single image dehazing methods. In addition, our proposed network can directly process ultra-high definition realistic haze images with up to 4K resolution at a reasonable speed and memory usage. To validate the importance and necessity of each module, we also provide comprehensive ablation studies.

2   Related Works

As image dehazing is not an easy problem, early methods [11,20,21,27,28,30] usually require multiple images to solve this problem. These methods make the same assumption that there are multiple images from the same scene. However, we can only get one image for a specific scene in most cases. So image priors based methods have been proposed to solve the problem of single image dehazing at early stages. Tan et al. [29] maximized the contrast to enhance the visibility of hazy images. He et al. [8] proposed a dark channel prior (DCP) based method to estimate transmission map, which is based on the observation that the local minimum of dark channels of haze-free images is close to zero. But sometimes these priors that mainly relies on human observations does not work well.

With the successful application of convolutional neural networks in the field of computer vision, recent algorithms [1,24,25,31,32] directly learn transmission map using a deep convolutional neural network. Ren et al. [25] propose a Multi-Scale CNN (MSCNN) to estimate the transmission map. DCPDN [31] and [32] joint transmission map estimation and dehazing using deep networks. However, inaccurate transmission map estimation often harms dehazing results [31]. Instead of estimating the transmission map, the AOD-Net [12] introduces a new intermediate variable to recover the final haze-free image, but it does not bring good results. Similar to the algorithms in [4,14,17,26], we use an end-to-end network to recover the haze-free image directly without estimating the transmission map.

Although the existing single image dehazing algorithm can remove the haze on the image to a certain extent, they all cannot get the expected high-quality hazy-free image. Compared with several existing single image dehazing methods, the PFFNet [17] shows the best performance on RESIDE [13] datasets. The PFFNet [17] can recover most of the outdoor hazy images as expected, but when applied to indoor hazy images, it produces undesired artifacts. In order to solve the problem that the PFFNet [17] does not perform well on indoor hazy images, we have made some improvements based on it to make our method work well both indoors and outdoors.

3   Proposed Method

3.1   Overview

In this part, we will introduce the main modules of our method in detail. The overall network architecture is shown in Fig. 2. The goal of our network is to restore the hazy-free image corresponding to the hazy image. Our network consists of four main parts: (1) an encoder with contiguous memory resblocks; (2) a base feature extraction module to extract structural and contour; (3) an extra gated fusion sub-network; (4) a decoder with contiguous memory resblocks.

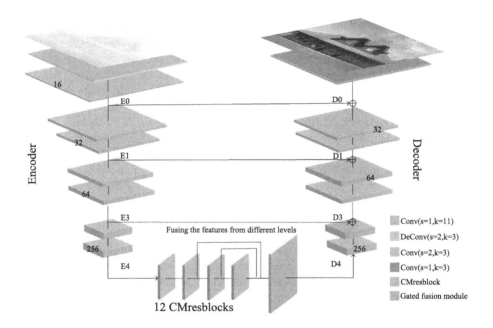

Fig. 2. The architecture of our proposed network for image dehazing.

3.2   Network Structure

The encoder-decoder network architecture which has been used for many tasks [4,5,9,17,26] is also applied in our network to recover the haze-free image. Unlike the encoder-decoder network used in PFFNet [17], we add a CMres behind the convolutional and deconvolution layers of each scale for better features extracting. If the size of the input hazy image is $w \times h \times 3$, then the size of the output of the encoder module is $\frac{1}{16}w \times \frac{1}{16}h \times 256$, where w and h are width and height respectively.

After the encoder module, we use 12 contiguous memory resblocks as the feature extraction module to learn features. Then we use the gated fusion sub-network to fuse the features extracted by the feature extraction module. Furthermore, we employ skip connections between corresponding layers of different level from encoder and decoder.

As shown in Fig. 2, the proposed network contains four strided convolutional layers and four strided deconvolutional layers. The contiguous memory resblock includes two residual blocks with the filter size set as 3×3 and the bottleneck convolutional layer with filter size set as 1×1. The filter size is set as 11×11 pixels in the first convolutional layer in the encoder module and 3×3 in all other convolutional and deconvolutional layers.

3.3 Contiguous Memory Resblock

Our contiguous memory resblock (CMres) consists of two common resblocks with kernel size 3×3 and a convolutional layer with kernel size 1×1. As shown in Fig. 3, contiguous memory mechanism [35] is realized by the operation similar to denseblock which increases the flow of information by feature reusing. In order to reduce memory usage and runtime, the concatenation is only used between each ordinary resblock rather than each convolution layer. Let F_{d-1} and F_d be the input and output of the d-th CMres respectively, the output of d-th CMres can be formulated as

$$F_d = H_d[F_{d-1}, F_{d,1}, F_{d,2}] \tag{2}$$

where H denotes the bottleneck layers. $F_{d,1}$ and $F_{d,2}$ are the feature-maps produced by the ordinary residual blocks 1 and 2 in the d-th scale.

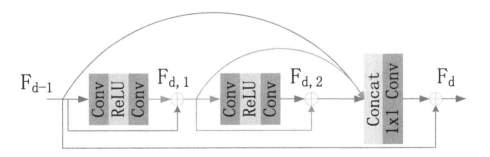

Fig. 3. Contiguous memory resblock architecture.

3.4 Gated Fusion Sub-network

Motivated by this idea [16,31] that fusing the features from different levels usually brings the improvement of experimental results, we adopt a gated fusion sub-network ∂. We feed the feature maps extracted from different levels (F_4, F_8, F_{12})

into the gated fusion sub-network. The output of the gated fusion sub-network are the weights (W_4, W_8, W_{12}) respectively corresponding to each feature level. Once the weights calculated, they multiplied by the three feature maps to get the final feature map.

$$(W_4, W_8, W_{12}) = \partial(F_4, F_8, F_{12}) \tag{3}$$

$$F_o = W_4 * F_4 + W_8 * F_8 + W_{12} * F_{12} \tag{4}$$

Then we feed the combined feature map F_o into the decoder to get the target hazy-free image.

4 Experiments

4.1 Implementation Details

In this section, we will describe the parameter settings of our proposed network in image dehazing. We use Parametric Rectified Linear Unit (PReLU) as the activation function. When training our network we use the mean square error (MSE) as the loss function to constrain the network output and ground truth. We use the ADAM solver [10] with $\beta_1 = 0.9$ and $\beta_2 = 0.999$ to optimize the network. We use an initial learning rate of 0.0001 with a decay rate of 0.1 every 50 epochs and the epoch is set to be 80. And we use a batch size of 16 and increase the training data by random rotation and horizontal flipping. All the training and evaluation processes are conducted on an NVIDIA GeForce GTX 1080Ti graphics card. The source code used in the paper are publicly available at the website: https://github.com/xianglei96/CRF-GFN.

4.2 Dataset

In order to train our network, we need to feed pairs of hazy and hazy-free images to the network. But the question is that it is difficult to get a large number of such pairs of images, so we use synthetic images based on formula 1 to train the network.

Recently, an image dehazing benchmark RESIDE [13] has been proposed, which contains a lot of synthetic training and testing hazy image pairs from depth and stereo datasets. In order to get the training dataset, we randomly select 5005 outdoor hazy image pairs in 35 different haze concentrations and 5000 indoor hazy image pairs in 10 different haze concentrations from RESIDE training sets. We then crop image pairs selected into 256×256 patches with a stride of 128 to obtain hazy-free patches I and hazy patches J.

We evaluate our methods on the RESIDE [13] and HazeRD [34] datasets. The test set of the RESIDE dataset [13] named as SOTS, consists of 500 indoor image pairs and 500 outdoor image pairs. HazeDR [34] consists of 75 hazy images produced by simulation in 15 different scenes and all these images are close to 4K resolution level. Due to resource constraints, most current dehazed algorithms cannot be tested on HazeDR [34]. For guarantee absolute fairness, we resize all the images in HazeDR [34] to the same size of 512 × 512.

4.3   Performance Evaluation

We compare our method with several single image dehazing methods, including methods based on hand-crafted features (DCP [8]) and deep convolutional neural networks (AOD [12], DcGAN [14], GFN [26], GCANet [4], and PFFNet [17]). We use the MSE, PSNR and SSIM metrics to evaluate the quality of each restored image. As most existing methods based on deep models are not trained on the datasets we used, we re-train the models of GFN [26], GCANet [4] and PFFNet [17] on our training dataset for fair comparisons.

Table 1. Quantitative evaluations on the benchmark dehazing datasets. Red texts and blue texts indicate the best and second-best performance respectively.

Methods		DCP [8]	AODNet [12]	DcGAN [14]	GFN* [26]	GCANet* [4]	PFFNet* [17]	Ours
SOTS	MSE	0.0178	0.0160	0.0038	0.0059	0.0048	0.0019	0.0013
	PSNR	17.01	18.84	25.46	23.51	26.39	27.76	29.82
	SSIM	0.8213	0.8330	0.9167	0.8935	0.9410	0.9045	0.9592
HazeRD	MSE	0.0377	0.0242	0.0332	0.0271	0.0355	0.0352	0.0183
	PSNR	14.83	16.54	16.20	16.94	15.63	16.11	19.23
	SSIM	0.7805	0.8085	0.8263	0.8173	0.8190	0.8050	0.8417
	CIEDE2000	14.83	13.23	12.02	11.59	14.45	12.89	9.625

As shown in Table 1, the methods based on hand-crafted features [8] or learning based method accompanied by intermediate estimates [12] do not perform well. The learning based methods [4,14,17,26] which direct estimation recover the haze-free image have better performance. And our method outperforms almost all the existing methods on the two datasets.

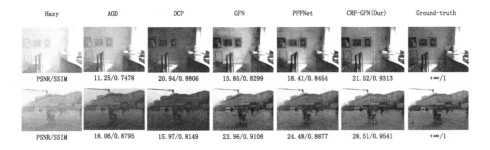

Fig. 4. Visual comparisons with state-of-the-art methods on SOTS.

Figure 4 shows two examples from the SOTS dataset. We can see that the AOD-Net [12] cannot remove the haze clearly as expected and the DCP [8] may lead to color distortion. The learning based methods GFN [26] and PFFNet [17] produce undesired artifacts on the planar region. However, the proposed method generates better results on both indoors and outdoors images.

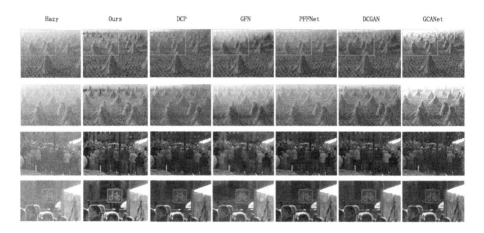

Fig. 5. Visual comparison on the real-world image. The second and fourth lines of images are the enlargement of the red box in the first and third lines of images, respectively. (Color figure online)

To further evaluate the performance of our algorithm, we also test on real images. Figure 5 shows a real hazy image and dehazed results from the state-of-the-art methods. We can see that other methods cannot remove haze clearly or have color distortion. However, the proposed method generates a much better dehazed image.

4.4   Ablation Study

We analyze how the proposed method performs and demonstrates its effectiveness for image dehazing with ablation studies. All the baseline methods mentioned above are trained using the same settings as the proposed algorithm for fair comparisons.

As shown in Fig. 6(a), replacing CMresblocks with denseblocks or resblocks will result in the final result getting worse. So we finally use a structure between denseblocks and resblocks which we call as CMresblocks.

For choosing the appropriate amount of CMresblocks for the base feature extraction module, we did some additional experiments. We can see from Fig. 6(b) that 6CMres and 9CMres are not good enough, and 12CMres can achieve almost the same effect as 15CMres under more resource-saving conditions.

In order to demonstrate the improvements obtained for each module introduced in the proposed network, we conducted an ablation study involving the

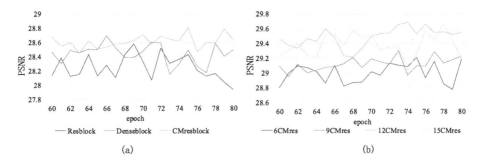

Fig. 6. (a): The testing performance comparisons on SOTS of the network using different blocks. (b): The testing performance comparisons on SOTS in different CMresblock size of the base feature extraction module.

Table 2. Analysis on key components in the proposed network. All the models are trained on the RESIDE dataset with the same hyper-parameters.

Modifications	Baseline	Model-1	Model-2	Model-3
resblock		✓		
CMresblock			✓	✓
gate fusion				✓
PSNR	27.76	28.58	29.68	29.82

following four experiments as shown in Table 2: (1) using ordinary resblocks without contiguous memory mechanism and omitting the gated fusion sub-network (Model-1), (2) using contiguous memory resblocks but omitting the gated fusion sub-network (Model-2), (3) the proposed network with contiguous memory resblocks and the gated fusion sub-network (Model-3).

As shown in Table 2, adding resblocks to Baseline (PFFNet [17]) has a nearly one point increase in PSNR. Based on Model-1, when the original resblocks replaced by CMresblocks, there will be some improvement in the result. Comparisons of Model-2 and Model-3 show that the gated fusion sub-network fusing the feature from different levels can also bring about an improvement in results.

5   Conclusion

In this paper, we propose an U-Net like deep network for single image dehazing which accompanied by contiguous memory residual blocks and gated fusion sub-network. The ablation study validates that the contiguous memory resblocks and the gated fusion sub-network module for feature level fusion can boost the performance of the proposed network. In addition, our dehazing network with U-Net like encoder-decoder architecture, has efficient memory usage and can directly recover the images close to 4K resolution level. Because it is difficult to get real-world pairs of hazy and hazy-free images, we will consider unsupervised learning in the future.

Acknowledgments. This work was supported in part by the National Major Science and Technology Projects of China grant under number 2018ZX01008103, National Natural Science Foundation of China (61603291), Natural Science Basic Research Plan in Shaanxi Province of China (Program No. 2018JM6057) and the Fundamental Research Funds for the Central Universities.

References

1. Cai, B., Xu, X., Jia, K., Qing, C., Tao, D.: DehazeNet: an end-to-end system for single image haze removal. IEEE Trans. Image Process. **25** (2016). https://doi.org/10.1109/TIP.2016.2598681
2. Cantor, A.: Optics of the atmosphere-scattering by molecules and particles. IEEE J. Quantum Electron. **14**(9), 698–699 (1978)
3. Chen, C., Do, M.N., Wang, J.: Robust image and video dehazing with visual artifact suppression via gradient residual minimization. In: Leibe, B., Matas, J., Sebe, N., Welling, M. (eds.) ECCV 2016. LNCS, vol. 9906, pp. 576–591. Springer, Cham (2016). https://doi.org/10.1007/978-3-319-46475-6_36
4. Chen, D., et al.: Gated context aggregation network for image dehazing and deraining. arXiv preprint arXiv:1811.08747 (2018)
5. Fan, Q., Yang, J., Hua, G., Chen, B., Wipf, D.: A generic deep architecture for single image reflection removal and image smoothing. In: Proceedings of the IEEE International Conference on Computer Vision, pp. 3238–3247 (2017)
6. Fattal, R.: Single image dehazing. ACM Trans. Graph. **27**(3), 1–9 (2008)
7. Hautière, N., Tarel, J.P., Aubert, D.: Towards fog-free in-vehicle vision systems through contrast restoration. In: IEEE Conference on Computer Vision & Pattern Recognition (2007)
8. He, K., Jian, S., Tang, X.: Single image haze removal using dark channel prior. In: IEEE Conference on Computer Vision & Pattern Recognition (2009)
9. Johnson, J., Alahi, A., Fei-Fei, L.: Perceptual losses for real-time style transfer and super-resolution. In: Leibe, B., Matas, J., Sebe, N., Welling, M. (eds.) ECCV 2016. LNCS, vol. 9906, pp. 694–711. Springer, Cham (2016). https://doi.org/10.1007/978-3-319-46475-6_43
10. Kingma, D.P., Ba, J.: Adam: a method for stochastic optimization. arXiv preprint arXiv:1412.6980 (2014)
11. Kopf, J., et al.: Deep photo:model-based photograph enhancement and viewing. ACM Trans. Graph. **27**(5), 1–10 (2008)
12. Li, B., Peng, X., Wang, Z., Xu, J., Dan, F.: AOD-Net: All-in-One dehazing network. In: IEEE International Conference on Computer Vision (2017)
13. Li, B., et al.: Benchmarking single image dehazing and beyond. IEEE Trans. Image Process. 1 (2018). https://doi.org/10.1109/TIP.2018.2867951
14. Li, R., Pan, J., Li, Z., Tang, J.: Single image dehazing via conditional generative adversarial network, pp. 8202–8211 (2018). https://doi.org/10.1109/CVPR.2018.00856
15. Li, Z., Ping, T., Tan, R.T., Zou, D., Zhou, S.Z., Cheong, L.F.: Simultaneous video defogging and stereo reconstruction. In: Computer Vision & Pattern Recognition (2015)
16. Lin, T.Y., Dollár, P., Girshick, R., He, K., Hariharan, B., Belongie, S.: Feature pyramid networks for object detection. In: Proceedings of the IEEE Conference on Computer Vision and Pattern Recognition, pp. 2117–2125 (2017)

17. Mei, K., Jiang, A., Li, J., Wang, M.: Progressive feature fusion network for realistic image dehazing. CoRR abs/1810.02283 (2018). http://arxiv.org/abs/1810.02283

18. Meng, G., Ying, W., Duan, J., Xiang, S., Pan, C.: Efficient image dehazing with boundary constraint and contextual regularization. In: IEEE International Conference on Computer Vision (2014)

19. Narasimhan, S.G., Nayar, S.K.: Vision and the atmosphere. Int. J. Comput. Vis. **48**(3), 233–254 (2002)

20. Narasimhan, S.G., Nayar, S.K.: Contrast restoration of weather degraded images. IEEE Trans. Pattern Anal. Mach. Intell. **25**(6), 713–724 (2003)

21. Narasimhan, S.G., Nayar, S.K.: Chromatic framework for vision in bad weather. In: IEEE Conference on Computer Vision & Pattern Recognition (2002)

22. Pei, S.C., Lee, T.Y.: Nighttime haze removal using color transfer pre-processing and dark channel prior. In: IEEE International Conference on Image Processing (2012)

23. Qingsong, Z., Jiaming, M., Ling, S.: A fast single image haze removal algorithm using color attenuation prior. IEEE Trans. Image Process. **24**(11), 3522–3533 (2015)

24. Ren, W., Cao, X.: Deep video dehazing. In: Zeng, B., Huang, Q., El Saddik, A., Li, H., Jiang, S., Fan, X. (eds.) PCM 2017. LNCS, vol. 10735, pp. 14–24. Springer, Cham (2018). https://doi.org/10.1007/978-3-319-77380-3_2

25. Ren, W., Liu, S., Zhang, H., Pan, J., Cao, X., Yang, M.-H.: Single image dehazing via multi-scale convolutional neural networks. In: Leibe, B., Matas, J., Sebe, N., Welling, M. (eds.) ECCV 2016. LNCS, vol. 9906, pp. 154–169. Springer, Cham (2016). https://doi.org/10.1007/978-3-319-46475-6_10

26. Ren, W., et al.: Gated fusion network for single image dehazing. In: Proceedings of the IEEE Conference on Computer Vision and Pattern Recognition, pp. 3253–3261 (2018)

27. Schechner, Y.Y., Narasimhan, S.G., Nayar, S.K.: Instant dehazing of images using polarization. In: Proceedings IEEE Conference Computer Vision & Pattern Recognition, vol. 1, p. 325 (2001)

28. Shwartz, S., Namer, E., Schechner, Y.Y.: Blind haze separation. In: IEEE Computer Society Conference on Computer Vision & Pattern Recognition (2006)

29. Tan, R.T.: Visibility in bad weather from a single image. In: IEEE Conference on Computer Vision & Pattern Recognition (2008)

30. Treibitz, T., Schechner, Y.Y.: Polarization: Beneficial for visibility enhancement? In: IEEE Conference on Computer Vision & Pattern Recognition (2009)

31. Zhang, H., Patel, V.M.: Densely connected pyramid dehazing network. In: Proceedings of the IEEE Conference on Computer Vision and Pattern Recognition, pp. 3194–3203 (2018)

32. Zhang, H., Sindagi, V., Patel, V.M.: Joint transmission map estimation and dehazing using deep networks. arXiv preprint arXiv:1708.00581 (2017)

33. Zhang, X., Dong, H., Hu, Z., Lai, W., Wang, F., Yang, M.: Gated fusion network for joint image deblurring and super-resolution. CoRR abs/1807.10806 (2018). http://arxiv.org/abs/1807.10806

34. Zhang, Y., Li, D., Sharma, G.: HazeRD: an outdoor scene dataset and benchmark for single image dehazing. In: IEEE International Conference on Image Processing (2018)

35. Zhang, Y., Tian, Y., Kong, Y., Zhong, B., Fu, Y.: Residual dense network for image super-resolution. In: Proceedings of the IEEE Conference on Computer Vision and Pattern Recognition, pp. 2472–2481 (2018)

Combined Correlation Filters with Siamese Region Proposal Network for Visual Tracking

Shugang Cui, Shu Tian[(✉)], and Xucheng Yin

School of Computer and Communication Engineering,
University of Science and Technology Beijing, Beijing 100083, China
csg_charles@foxmail.com, {shutian,xuchengyin}@ustb.edu.cn

Abstract. Siamese network based trackers have received extensive attention with their trade-off between accuracy and speed. In particular, Siamese Region Proposal Network (SiamRPN) tracker can get more accurate bounding box with proposal refinement, yet, most siamese trackers are lack of discrimination without target classification and robustness without online learning module. To tackle the problem, in this paper, we propose an ensemble tracking framework based on SiamRPN tracker, consisting of two components: (1) Correlation Filter module with hierarchical features fusion; and (2) SiamRPN module. The Correlation Filter module fully exploits both the semantic features for classification and the lower-level features for precise localization through online learning process. By cascading the Correlation Filter to SiamRPN tracker, which can equip with discrimination power. The entire network based on multitask learning strategy is trained in an end-to-end manner, which enhances both robustness and module adaptability effect. In extensive experiments evaluations on GOT-10K test dataset, OTB2015 and VOT2016 benchmarks, our tracking approach obtains better performance than other trackers, including SiamRPN tracker, by a notable margin.

Keywords: Correlation Filters · Siamese Region Proposal Network · Visual tracking

1 Introduction

Visual object tracking is one of the most challenging tasks in computer vision, which has been widely applied in areas such as video surveillance and intelligent transportation systems. Due to the object appearance changes and complex motion scene, it still suffer many challenges including occlusion, scale variation, etc.

Correlation Filter (CF) based trackers regard object tracking as a two-class problem between target and background information. With its efficient performing operations in frequency domain, it has been attracted wide attention and

ⓒ Springer Nature Switzerland AG 2019
T. Gedeon et al. (Eds.): ICONIP 2019, LNCS 11954, pp. 128–138, 2019.
https://doi.org/10.1007/978-3-030-36711-4_12

achieved rapid progress. Since deep neural network can extract image features more accurately, correlation filter based trackers started using deep features to improve the accuracy, however, these features are usually pre-trained and mainly from classification and detection tasks, which can not better applied to object tracking task.

Recently, siamese network based trackers have made significant progress. Most siamese trackers achieved remarkable tracking performance by reducing the heavy burden of online learning in offline learning way. However, they can't effectively distinguish object from background information in clutter scene, besides, since no online learning is performed, most siamese trackers are lack of good robustness. To learn the convolutional features and perform the correlation tracking process simultaneously, Wang et al. [1] treated CF as a differentiable network layer added in siamese network, which enable get a significant accuracy compared with traditional CF tracking algorithms. However, they proposed tracker only utilized low-level features representations which lacked rich high-level semantic information and can not effectively distinguish different types of objects. Additionally, with traditional multi-scale test, the DCFNet [1] tracker only can obtain the central position of the target, but not the specific target size.

In this paper, we propose a tracking method of hierarchical features fusion based on Siamese Region Proposal Network (SiamRPN) [2]. Our tracker consists of two components: (1) Correlation Filter module with hierarchical features fusion; and (2) SiamRPN module. The CF module of our tracker that utilize the characteristics of convolutional networks at different levels can learn strong semantic and localization information. The entire network based on multi-task learning strategy is trained in an end-to-end manner, which enhances both discrimination and generation effect.

2   Related Work

Visual object tracking has been extensively studied in recent decades, in this section, we discuss tracking methods closely related to this work.

Correlation Filter Based Trackers (CF). The basic idea of CF trackers is to learn a filter template and let the image of the next frame correlates with the filter template, where the greatest response is the target of prediction. These trackers regress the input circulant matrix features to a target Gaussian function by minimizing the mean square error. Since Henriques et al. [3] diagonalized circulant matrix with the discrete fourier transform to propose a kernelized correlation filter (KCF) tracker, many extensions has been proposed to improve the tracking accuracy. Besides handcrafted features, a series of CF trackers utilized deep convolutional features to train classifier, e.g. [4] exploited three convolutional layers features from pretrained VGG-19 net to learn three independent CF, and then the final target position is obtained by weighted fusion of the three score maps. However, the pretrained feature representations from other computer vision tasks cant't suit object tracking well. In this work, we combine the online learning CF with the off-line trained SiamRPN [2] tracker, improving the tracking performance.

Siamese Network Based Trackers. Siamese networks have drawn increasing interest in the tracking community because of its super tracking speed and higher accuracy. SiamFC [5] used siamese neural network to learn a kind of similarity measure function between target patch and a test patch, which designed an end-to-end network and exceeded the real-time requirement. Since then, many siamese network based trackers have emerged. The challenge of the siamFC-based approaches are lack of robustness and discrimination. He et al. [6] used complementary semantic features and appearance features to present two fold siamese network named SA-Siam with real-time tracking effect, and it's performance largely exceeded all other real-time trackers at the time. Another main challenges of siamFC-based trackers are how to handle target scale and shape changes, Li et al. [2] exploited Region Proposal Network (RPN) [7] to get more accurate bounding boxes by using box refinement process. Different from them, we enhance discriminability of SiamRPN tracker by exploiting CF trackers with hierarchical features fusion.

Ensemble Trackers. The ensemble framework usually contains multiple models rather than using a single one, which makes the ensemble tracker have stronger generalization ability. e.g. Qi [8] presented an typical ensemble tracking framework, which contained different convolution layers and used adaptive hedging method to hedge several CNN-based trackers into a stronger tracker. BranchOut [9] as an online ensemble tracker had multi-level target representation, which can learn robust target appearance models with diversity and handle various challenges effectively. Similarly, In our designed tracker, the adaptive Correlation Filter with hierarchical features fusion complement with the SiamRPN [2] module, and they are jointly trained in an end-to-end manner.

3   Proposed Method

3.1   Framework

Our proposed framework that is integrated in a unified multi-task network architecture is shown in Fig. 1. We cascade a differentiable Correlation Filter layer to SiamRPN [2] tracker. Our proposed tracker contains Correlation Filter and SiamRPN two parts, which can enable correlation filter tightly to couple to the deep features. More details refer to Sect. 3.4.

3.2   Hierarchical Features Fusion

In order to fully exploit the multi-level features, we learn the Correlation Filter by building hierarchical features at various scales in top-down pathway and lateral connections manner [10]. The top-down process enlarges higher resolution

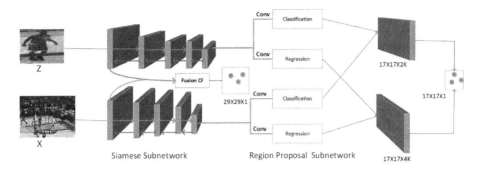

Fig. 1. The proposed ensemble tracking framework. The framework contains Correlation Filter module with hierarchical features fusion and SiamRPN [2] module. The network inputs target patch Z and search patch X, the extracted features are fused for correlation filter tracker and exploited by SiamRPN, respectively. Where $\rightarrow$ denotes features extraction, denotes features fusion in top-down pathway and lateral connections way, Conv denotes one convolutional operation and denotes predicted target location.

features to the same size as the former lower feature by up-sampling, to take advantage of the underlying location details, the lateral connection fuses the features of the high-level layer after the upsampling and the current layer by addition method. Therefore, the fused features contains the semantic features for classification and the lower-level for precise localization.

Figure 2 shows the detailed process of fusion. Conv1, Conv2, Conv3, Conv4, Conv5 denotes each layer of network, individually. The Conv5 layer undergoes a 1×1 convolutional layer to adjust channel dimensions and obtains feature map M5. After M5 feature is upsampled, it is then merged with the Conv4 layer (which also needs a 1×1 convolutional operation) in element-wise addition way to obtain feature map M4. This process is iterated until the finest resolution feature map M1 is generated. Finally, The merged feature map M1 is appended a 3×3 convolution to generate the final feature map P, which is to reduce the aliasing effect of upsampling. Different from detection task, visual tracking is more dependent on features that contain object location information, we only add a differentiable CF lay with extracting fusion features in lowest level feature map P, which can complement SiamRPN [2] discrimination effect.

3.3 Correlation Filters

Standard correlation filters learn a discriminative classifier by ridge regression, which can get a simple closed-form solution. By successfully utilizing the diagonalization property of cyclic matrix with fast fourier transforms, correlation filters greatly reduce the amount of operation and improves the speed of operation. The goal of training is to find a function f(Z) that minimizes the squared error over samples Z and response values y that is a 2D gaussian function:

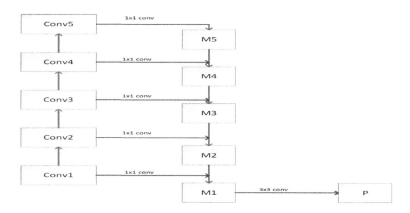

Fig. 2. The top-down pathway and lateral connections manner. Where ↑ denotes features extraction, denotes features fusion in top-down pathway and → denotes lateral connections.

$$\min_{w} \| Zw - y \|_2^2 + \lambda \| w \|_2^2 \tag{1}$$

where w refers to learned correlation filter, the features of target patch Z is extracted by certain circulant shift operation, and λ is a regularization parameter that controls overfitting. With diagonalization of fourier frequency domain of cyclic matrix, the closed-form solution can be obtained:

$$\hat{w} = \frac{\hat{Z}^* \odot \hat{y}}{\hat{Z}^* \odot \hat{Z} + \lambda} \tag{2}$$

where $\hat{Z}^*$ is the complex-conjugate of Z, $\hat{Z}$ denotes the Discrete Fourier Transform of the generating vector and $\odot$ denotes the Hadamard product.

In the tracking process, we extract features in the next search region X, and the response can be obtained according to the trained filter template w and the sample based on the target position of the previous frame Z.

3.4   Refined Siamese Region Proposal Network

In this section, we begin with an overview of the general Siamese Region Proposal Network (SiamRPN) [2] and discuss how to combine it with Correlation Filter module.

SiamRPN [2] consists of Siamese Subnetwork (left side of Fig. 1) for features extraction and Region Proposal Subnetwork (right side of Fig. 1) for classification and regression task. Siamese Subnetwork consists of target template branch and detection branch, the former branch takes cropped target patch Z as input, the latter branch takes cropped search region patch X in the next frame as input. To ensure classification and regression for each anchor, convolutional operation is needed to adjust the channels into suitable forms. Therefore, after Siamese

Subnetwork, the extracted feature $\varphi(z)$ of target template branch perform two convolutional operations individually, hence, $\varphi(z)$ is split into two parts $[\varphi(z)]_{cls}$ and $[\varphi(z)]_{reg}$. Similarly, the extracted features $\varphi(x)$ of detection branch also perform two convolutional operations individually, and then $\varphi(x)$ become $[\varphi(x)]_{cls}$ and $[\varphi(x)]_{reg}$ two parts. Therefore, the final classification scores cls_{2k} and regression offsets reg_{2k} of output can be obtained as follows:

$$\begin{aligned} \{cls_{2k}\} &= corr([\varphi(z)]_{cls}, [\varphi(x)]_{cls}) \\ \{reg_{2k}\} &= corr([\varphi(z)]_{reg}, [\varphi(x)]_{reg}) \end{aligned} \tag{3}$$

where corr(a, b) denotes convolution between a and b, the feature maps $[\varphi(z)]_{cls}$ and $[\varphi(z)]_{reg}$ are used as kernels, k denotes the number of anchors. The SiamRPN [2] is trained in end to end manner, which consists of cross-entropy loss for classification and smooth L1 loss for regression. The multi-task loss is as follows and detailed loss information refer to [2].

$$L_{SiamRPN} = L_{cls} + L_{reg} \tag{4}$$

where L_{cls} and L_{reg} denote classification loss and regression loss, respectively.

Compared with traditional SiamRPN [2], our proposed tracker is shown in Fig. 1, after Siamese Subnetwork extract features of target template Z and the search region X, we cascade a correlation filter module with multi-level fusion for discriminative tracking between Siamese Subnetwork and Region Proposal Subnetwork. After template branch feature $\varphi(z)$ is fused by the way described in Sect. 3.2, we obtain final fused features $z = P(z; \theta)$, likewise, the fused detection branch features denoted as $x = P(x; \theta)$. θ represent the parameters of these convolutional layers. The specific cascaded CF loss function is as follows:

$$L_{CF} = \parallel g(x) - y \parallel_2^2 + \gamma \parallel \theta \parallel^2 \tag{5}$$

$$g(x) = F^{-1}(\hat{\varphi}(x; \theta) \odot \hat{w}) \tag{6}$$

where $\hat{x}$ is the Discrete Fourier Transform of x and $\hat{w}$ is the learned CF based on fused target feature z, γ is a regularization parameter. The derivatives of L_{CF} can be obtained as follows:

$$\frac{\delta L_{CF}}{\delta \hat{g}^*} = 2(\hat{g}(x) - \hat{y}) \tag{7}$$

$$\frac{\delta L_{CF}}{\delta x} = F^{-1}(\frac{\delta L_{CF}}{\delta \hat{g}^*} \odot \hat{w}^*) \tag{8}$$

$$\frac{\delta L_{CF}}{\delta \hat{w}} = \frac{\delta L_{CF}}{\delta \hat{g}^*} \odot \hat{x}^* \tag{9}$$

$$\frac{\delta L_{CF}}{\delta z} = F^{-1}(\frac{\delta L_{CF}}{\delta \hat{w}} \odot \frac{\hat{y}^* - 2\text{Re}(\hat{z}^* \odot \hat{w})}{\hat{z}^* \odot \hat{z}}) \tag{10}$$

where $\text{Re}(\cdot)$ is the real part of a complex-valued matrix.

Due to the correlation filters and siamRPN [2] modules complement each other in multi-scale regression and recognition tracking based on multi-resolution representation. We adopt multi-task learning strategy to end-to-end train the network, the overall loss function can be written as:

$$L_{ALL} = L_{CF} + \mu L_{SiamRPN} \tag{11}$$

where L_{CF} denotes the correlation filters module loss and $L_{SiamRPN}$ denotes the SiameseRPN module loss, μ is hyper-parameter to balance the two parts.

In the tracking process, we feed target patch Z and search region X centered at the previous target position into the network, then we can get their corresponding feature representations of target template branch and detection branch through Siamese Subnetwork. On one hand, The two branch features with hierarchical features fusion are exploited by CF module, on the other hand, these features are further fed into Region Proposal Subnetwork (RPN) module for classification and localization. The target state is obtained in Eq. 12, which is estimated by finding the maximum of the fused CF module scores given in Eq. 6 and classification scores given in Eq. 3.

$$\arg\max_{m,n} = \{cls_{2k}\}_{m,n} + g_{m,n}(X) \tag{12}$$

Then the final target bounding box can be obtained with the max target state give in Eq. 12 and the regression offsets given in Eq. 3 by non-maximum-suppression (NMS). Note that in Eq. 12, we adopt the bilinear interpolation method to fuse $\{cls_{2k}\}$ and g(x) to have consistent resolution.

In order to make our tracker adaptive to continuous changes in the appearance of the object, we adopt incremental update strategy. The training goal in Eq. 1 is changed as follows:

$$\min_{w_p} = \sum_{t=1}^{p} \beta_t(\| Zw_p - y \|_2^2 + \lambda \| w_p \|_2^2) \tag{13}$$

where β_t is a hyper parameter, the advantage is that we do not have to maintain a large exemplar set and only need small memory footprint. The solution can be gained as:

$$\hat{w}_p = \frac{\sum_{t=1}^{p} \beta_t \hat{y} \odot \hat{Z}^*}{\sum_{t=1}^{p} \beta_t(\hat{Z}^* \odot \hat{Z} + \lambda)} \tag{14}$$

4   Experiments

4.1   Datasets

Our network is end-to-end trained on the GOT-10K train dataset. We evaluate tracking performance on GOT-10K [11] test dataset, OTB2015 [12], and VOT2016 [13] benchmarks. Notice that different from SiamRPN tracker [2], We need end-to-end train our proposed framework, therefore, for fair comparison, we also retrain SiamRPN [2] tracker on GOT-10K [11] train dataset as our baseline.

GOT-10K [11] is a large high-diversity database for generic object tracking, which owns more than 10 thousand video segments and 1.5 million bounding boxes. It is also a generic evaluating benchmark including three subsets:train, validation and test datasets. It uses average overlap (AO) and success rate (SR) as evaluation indicator. The AO denotes the average of overlaps between the tracked and groundtruth bounding boxes, while the SR measures the percentage of successfully tracked frames where the overlaps exceed 0.5.

OTB2015 [12] benchmark with 100 videos is a fair testbed. It adopts the precision and success for evaluation, the success plot shows the ratios of successful frames when the threshold varies from 0 to 1, the precision plots show the percentage of frames where the center location error is within a threshold 20. The area under curve (AUC) of success plot is used to rank tracking algorithm.

The VOT2016 [13] benchmark has 60 sequences to evaluate a tracker with applying a reset-based methodology. it exploited accuracy (A), robustness (R) and expected average overlap (EAO) to compare different trackers.

4.2   Implementation Details

Our experiment is implemented in python using Pytorch of deep learning framework on two Nvidia GTX 1080 with 20 GB memory. Following SiamRPN [2], we use first five layers of pre-trained classification model on ImageNet dataset as our backbone and train the network on GOT-10K train dataset. The target patch has a size of $127 \times 127 \times 3$, and search region patch has a size of $255 \times 255 \times 3$. After features extraction by Siamese Subnetwork, its output is fused with hierarchical features to train CF classifier, at the same time, the output features are directly fed to the RPN [7] layer for further classification and localization. During training process, We apply stochastic gradient descent (SGD) to train the network and the regularization parameters μ is set 0.8, the learning rate exponentially decays from 0.01 to 0.0005. The model is trained for 10 epoches with a mini-batch size of 20.

4.3   Results and Conclusions

GOT-10K Test Datasest. Table 1 shows the comparisons between on GOT-10K test datasest, by introducing a discriminative correlation filter with hierarchical features fusion, it proves that the AO, SR and speed metrics in our tracker perform better than baseline SiamRPN [2] tracker, Compared to the SRDCF tracker that is a general correlation filter, it also proves that our method is much more efficient with ensemble strategy.

OTB2015 Benchmark. We compare our tracker with KCF [3], ECO [14], SiamFC [5], Staple [15], SiamRPN [7], DCFNet [1] et al. trackers on OTB2015 benchmark. The precision plots and success plots of one path evaluation (OPE)

Table 1. Results on GOT-10K test dataset with average overlap (AO), success rate (SR) metrics at the threshold of 0.5 and Speed.

Tracker	AO	SR	Speed
SiamRPN	40.1	45.0	70
CF2	31.5	30.0	5.57
CCOT	32.5	32.8	0.68
MDNet	29.9	30.3	1.52
CFNetc2	29.3	26.5	35.62
ECOhc	28.6	27.6	34.5
Staple	24.6	23.9	28.87
SRDCF	23.6	22.3	5.58
KCF	20.3	17.7	94.66
Ours	40.5	45.9	55

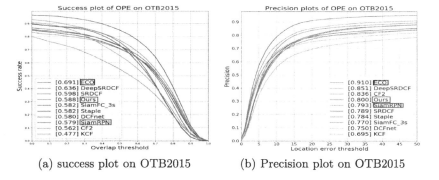

(a) success plot on OTB2015   (b) Precision plot on OTB2015

Fig. 3. Success and precision comparisons on OTB2015.

are shown in Fig. 3. We obtain the 0.588 AUC and 0.800 precision scores on success and precision metrics, respectively. Compared with the baseline SiamRPN [2] tracker, our ensemble method performs slightly better with online update strategy. Due to the ECO tracker [14] has more diversity data and its correlation filter method is optimized, there still is a gap between our tracker and ECO [14].

VOT2016 Benchmark. We compare our tracker with SiamRPN [2] and other trackers on VOT2016 benchmark. Table 2 shows our tracker ranks 3rd, 4th and 5th in the overall performance evaluations based on the accuracy (A), robustness (R) and expected average overlap (EAO) metrics, respectively. Compared with the baseline SiamRPN [2], Our tracker achieves gain of 2.9% on EAO, 2.8% on R and 1.1% on A. Even if our method adds CF, the speed (fps) still shows better performance. In addition, our tracker outperforms many correlation filter based

Table 2. Comparison with trackers on VOT2016 benchmark. A, R and EAO denote accuracy, robustness and expected average overlap, respectively. The larger values of ECO and A, they represent better performance, however, the larger value of R, it represents worse performance. The best results are highlighted in **black thick fonts** on the three metrics, respectively.

Tracker	A	R	EAO	Speed
SiamRPN	0.557	0.317	0.280	160
SiamFC	0.549	0.382	0.277	86
C-RPN	**0.594**	0.95	**0.363**	1
MDNet	0.54	0.34	0.257	1
ECO	0.55	0.20	0.375	8
C-COT	0.539	0.238	0.331	0.3
Staple	0.544	0.378	0.295	80
SPM	0.620	**0.210**	0.434	120
SSKCF	0.547	0.373	0.277	150
Ours	0.568	0.289	0.309	150

trackers. However, due to C-RPN [16] owns larger train dataset, therefore, it performs better than our tracker.

Conclusions. In this paper, we present an ensemble tracker with SiamRPN [2] module and Correlation Filter module. The Correlation Filter of our tracker is learned with hierarchical features fusion to localize and online update for adaptive tracking. Our tracker is evaluated on GOT-10K test dataset, OTB2015 and VOT2016 benchmarks, they show our method can achieve more significant performance than baseline SiamRPN [2] tracker and most correlation filter based trackers.

Acknowledgments. The research is partly supported by National Natural Science Foundation of China (61806017).

References

1. Wang, Q., Gao, J., Xing, J., et al.: DCFNet: discriminant correlation filters network for visual tracking. arXiv:1704.04057 (2017)
2. Li, B., Yan, J., Wu, W., et al.: High performance visual tracking with siamese region proposal network. In: 2018 31st IEEE/CVF Conference on Computer Vision and Pattern Recognition, CVPR 2018, Salt Lake City, UT, 18–23 June 2018, pp. 8971–8980 (2018)
3. Henriques, J.F., Caseiro, R., Martins, P., Batista, J.: High-speed tracking with kernelized correlation filters. 2015 IEEE Trans. Pattern Anal. Mach. Intell. J. **37**(3), 583–596 (2015)

4. Ma, C., Huang, J.-B., Yang, X., Yang, M.-H.: Hierarchical convolutional features for visual tracking. In: 2015 IEEE International Conference on Computer Vision, ICCV 2015, Santiago, Chile, 11–18 December 2015, pp. 3074–3082 (2015)
5. Bertinetto, L., Valmadre, J., Henriques, J.F., Vedaldi, A., Torr, P.H.S.: Fully-convolutional siamese networks for object tracking. In: Hua, G., Jégou, H. (eds.) ECCV 2016. LNCS, vol. 9914, pp. 850–865. Springer, Cham (2016). https://doi.org/10.1007/978-3-319-48881-3_56
6. He, A., Luo, C., Tian, X., Zeng, W.: A twofold Siamese network for real-time object tracking. In:2018 31st IEEE/CVF Conference on Computer Vision and Pattern Recognition, CVPR 2018, Salt Lake City, UT, 18–23 June 2018, pp. 4834–4843 (2018)
7. Ren, S., He, K., Girshick, R., Sun, J.: Faster R-CNN: towards real-time object detection with region proposal networks. In:2015 29th Annual Conference on Neural Information Processing Systems, NIPS 2015, Montreal, Canada, 07–12 December 2015, pp. 91–99 (2015)
8. Qi, Y., Zhang, S., Qin, L., Yao, H., et al.: Hedged deep tracking. In: 2016 IEEE Conference on Computer Vision and Pattern Recognition, CVPR 2016, Seattle, WA, 27–30 June 2016, pp. 4303–4311 (2016)
9. Han, B., Sim, J., Adam, H.: BranchOut: regularization for online ensemble tracking with convolutional neural networks. In: 2017 IEEE Conference on Computer Vision and Pattern Recognition, CVPR 2017, Honolulu, HI, 21–26 July 2017, pp. 521–530 (2017)
10. Lin, T.-Y., Dollar, P., Girshick, R.: Feature pyramid networks for object detection. In: 2017 30th IEEE/CVF Conference on Computer Vision and Pattern Recognition, CVPR 2017, Honolulu, HI, 21–26 July 2017, pp. 936–944 (2017)
11. Huang, L., Zhao, X., Huang, K.: GOT-10k: a large high-diversity benchmark for generic object tracking in the wild. IEEE Trans. Pattern Anal. Mach. Intell. J. **37**(9) (2018)
12. Wu, Y., Lim, J., Yang, M.-H.: Object tracking benchmark. 2015 IEEE Trans. Pattern Anal. Mach. Intell. J. **37**(9), 1834–1848 (2015)
13. Kristan, M., et al.: The visual object tracking VOT2016 challenge results. In: Hua, G., Jégou, H. (eds.) ECCV 2016. LNCS, vol. 9914, pp. 777–823. Springer, Cham (2016). https://doi.org/10.1007/978-3-319-48881-3_54
14. Danelljan, M., Bhat, G., Shahbaz Khan, F., et al.: ECO: efficient convolution operators for tracking. In: 2017 30th IEEE/CVF Conference on Computer Vision and Pattern Recognition, CVPR 2017, Honolulu, HI, 21–26 July (2017)
15. Bertinetto, L., Valmadre, J., Golodetz, S., et al.: Complementary learners for real-time tracking. In: IEEE Conference on Computer Vision and Pattern Recognition, CVPR 2016, Seattle, WA, 27–30 June 2016, pp. 1401–1409 (2016)
16. Fan, H., Ling, H.: Siamese cascaded region proposal networks for real-time visual tracking. In: 2019 32st IEEE/CVF Conference on Computer Vision and Pattern Recognition, CVPR 2019, Long Beach, CA, 16–20 June (2019)

RAUNet: Residual Attention U-Net for Semantic Segmentation of Cataract Surgical Instruments

Zhen-Liang Ni[1,2], Gui-Bin Bian[1,2(✉)], Xiao-Hu Zhou[2], Zeng-Guang Hou[1,2,3], Xiao-Liang Xie[2], Chen Wang[1,2], Yan-Jie Zhou[1,2], Rui-Qi Li[1,2], and Zhen Li[1,2]

[1] The School of Artificial Intelligence, University of Chinese Academy of Sciences, Beijing 100049, China
[2] State Key Laboratory of Management and Control for Complex Systems, Institute of Automation, Chinese Academy of Sciences, Beijing 100190, China
{nizhenliang2017,guibin.bian}@ia.ac.cn
[3] CAS Center for Excellence in Brain Science and Intelligence Technology, Beijing 100190, China

Abstract. Semantic segmentation of surgical instruments plays a crucial role in robot-assisted surgery. However, accurate segmentation of cataract surgical instruments is still a challenge due to specular reflection and class imbalance issues. In this paper, an attention-guided network is proposed to segment the cataract surgical instrument. A new attention module is designed to learn discriminative features and address the specular reflection issue. It captures global context and encodes semantic dependencies to emphasize key semantic features, boosting the feature representation. This attention module has very few parameters, which helps to save memory. Thus, it can be flexibly plugged into other networks. Besides, a hybrid loss is introduced to train our network for addressing the class imbalance issue, which merges cross entropy and logarithms of Dice loss. A new dataset named Cata7 is constructed to evaluate our network. To the best of our knowledge, this is the first cataract surgical instrument dataset for semantic segmentation. Based on this dataset, RAUNet achieves state-of-the-art performance 97.71% mean Dice and 95.62% mean IOU.

Keywords: Attention · Semantic segmentation · Cataract · Surgical instrument

1 Introduction

In recent years, semantic segmentation of surgical instruments has gained increasing popularity due to its promising applications in robot-assisted surgery. One of the crucial applications is the localization and pose estimation of surgical instruments, which contributes to surgical robot control. Potential applications of segmenting surgical instruments include objective surgical skills assessment,

© Springer Nature Switzerland AG 2019
T. Gedeon et al. (Eds.): ICONIP 2019, LNCS 11954, pp. 139–149, 2019.
https://doi.org/10.1007/978-3-030-36711-4_13

surgical workflow optimization, report generation, etc. [1]. These applications can reduce the workload of doctors and improve the safety of surgery.

Cataract surgery is the most common ophthalmic surgery in the world. It is performed approximately 19 million times a year [2]. Cataract surgery is highly demanding for doctors. Computer-assisted surgery can significantly reduce the probability of accidental operation. However, most of the research related to surgical instrument segmentation focuses on endoscopic surgeries. There are few studies on cataract surgeries. To the best of our knowledge, this is the first study to segment and classify cataract surgical instruments.

Recently, a serious of methods have been proposed to segment surgical instruments. García-Peraza-Herrera *et al.* [3] presented a network based on Fully Convolutional Networks (FCN) and optic flow to solve problems such as occlusion and deformation of surgical instruments. RASNet [4] adopted an attention module to emphasize the targets region and improve the feature representation. Laina *et al.* [5] proposed a novel U-shape network to provide segmentation and pose estimation of instruments simultaneously. A method combining both recurrent network and the convolutional network was employed by Attia *et al.* [6] to improve the segmentation accuracy. From mentioned above, it can be seen that the convolutional neural network has achieved excellent performance in segmentation of surgical instruments. However, the methods mentioned above are all based on endoscopic surgery. Semantic segmentation of surgical instruments for cataract surgery is quite different from that of endoscopic surgery.

Many challenges need to be faced for the semantic segmentation of cataract surgical instruments. Different from endoscopic surgery, cataract surgery requires strong lighting conditions, leading to serious specular reflection. Specular reflection changes the visual characteristics of surgical instruments. Also, cataract surgery instruments are small for micromanipulation. Hence it is very common that surgical instruments only occupy a small region of the image. The number of background pixels is much larger than that of foreground pixels, which cause serious class imbalance issue. As a result, the surgical instrument is more likely to be misidentified as a background. Occlusion caused by eye tissues and the limited view of the camera is also important issues, causing a part of the surgical instrument to be invisible. These issues make it difficult to identify and segment the surgical instrument.

To address these issues, a novel network, Residual Attention U-Net (RAUNet), is proposed. It introduces an attention module to improve feature representation. The contributions of this work are as follows.

1. An innovative attention module called augmented attention module (AAM) is designed to efficiently fuse multi-level features and improve feature representation, contributing to addressing the specular reflection issue. Also, it has very few parameters, which helps to save memory.
2. A hybrid loss is introduced to solve the class imbalance issue. It merges cross entropy and logarithm of Dice loss to take advantage of both their merit.

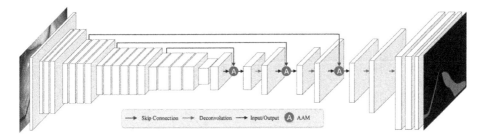

Fig. 1. The architecture of Residual Attention U-Net. ResNet34 pre-trained on the ImageNet is used as the encoder to capture deep semantic features. The decoder consists of augmented attention module and transposed convolution.

3. To evaluate the proposed network, we construct a cataract surgery instrument dataset named Cata7. As far as we know, this is the first cataract surgery instrument dataset that can be used for semantic segmentation.

2 Residual Attention U-Net

2.1 Overview

High-resolution images provide more detailed location information, helping doctors perform accurate operations. Thus, Residual Attention U-Net (RAUNet) adopts an encoder-decoder architecture to get high-resolution masks. The architecture of RAUNet is illustrated in Fig. 1. ResNet34 [7] pre-trained on the ImageNet is used as the encoder to extract semantic features. It helps reduce the model size and improve inference speed. In the decoder, a new attention module augmented attention module (AAM) is designed to fuse multi-level features and capture global context. Furthermore, transposed convolution is used to carry out upsampling for acquiring refined edges.

2.2 Augmented Attention Module

The decoder recovers the position details by upsampling. However, upsampling leads to blurring of edge and the loss of location details. Some existing work [8] adopts skip connections to concatenate the low-level features with the high-level features, which contributes to replenishing the position details. But this is a naive method. Due to the lack of semantic information in low-level features, it contains a lot of useless background information. This information may interfere with the segmentation of the target object. To address this problem, the augmented attention module is designed to capture high-level semantic information and emphasize target features.

Each channel corresponds to a specific semantic response. Surgical instruments and human tissues are often concerned with different channels. Thus, the

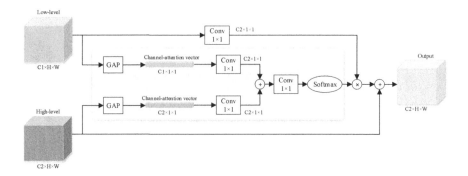

Fig. 2. The architecture of augmented attention module. $\otimes$ denotes element-wise multiplication. $\oplus$ denotes matrix addition.

augmented attention module model the semantic dependencies to emphasize target channels. It captures the semantic information in high-level feature maps and the global context in the low-level feature maps to encode semantic dependencies. High-level feature maps contain rich semantic information that can be used to guide low-level feature maps to select important location details. Furthermore, the global context of low-level feature maps encodes the semantic relationship between different channels, helping to filter interference information. By using this information efficiently, augmented attention module can emphasize target region and improve the feature representation. Augmented attention module is illustrated in Fig. 2.

Global average pooling is performed to extract global context and semantic information, which is described in Eq. (3). It squeezes global information into an attentive vector which encodes the semantic dependencies, contributing to emphasizing key features and filter background information. The generation of the attentive vector is described in the following:

$$F_a(x, y) = \delta_1 \left[W_\alpha g(x) + b_\alpha \right] + \delta_1 \left[W_\beta g(y) + b_\beta \right] \tag{1}$$

$$A_c = \delta_2 \left[W_\varphi F_a(x, y) + b_\varphi \right] \tag{2}$$

where x and y refer to the high-level and low-level feature maps, respectively. g denotes the global average pooling. δ_1 denotes ReLU function and δ_2 denotes Softmax function. $W_\alpha, W_\beta, W_\varphi$ refers to the parameter of the 1×1 convolution. $b_\alpha, b_\beta, b_\varphi$ refers to the bias.

$$g(x_k) = \frac{1}{W \times H} \sum_{i=1}^{H} \sum_{j=1}^{W} x_k(i, j) \tag{3}$$

where $k = 1, 2, ..., c$ and $x = [x_1, x_2, ..., x_c]$.

Then 1×1 convolution with batch normalization is performed on the vector to further captures semantic dependencies. The softmax function is adopted as the activation function to normalize the vector. The low-level feature maps are multiplied by the attentive vector to generate an attentive feature map. Finally, the attentive feature map is calibrated by adding with the high-level feature map. Addition can reduce parameters of convolution compared with concatenation, which contributes to reducing the computational cost. Also, since it only uses global average pooling and 1×1 convolution, this module does not add too many parameters. The global average pooling squeezes global information into a vector, which also greatly reduces computational costs.

2.3   Loss Function

Semantic segmentation of surgery instruments can be considered as classifying each pixel. Therefore, cross entropy loss can be used for classification of pixels. It is the most commonly used loss function for classification. And it is denoted as H in the Eq. (4).

$$H = -\frac{1}{w \times h} \sum_{k=1}^{c} \sum_{i=1}^{w} \sum_{j=1}^{h} y_{ijk} \log(\frac{e^{\widehat{y}_{ijk}}}{\sum_{k=1}^{c} e^{\widehat{y}_{ijk}}}) \tag{4}$$

where w, h represent the width and the height of the predictions. And c is the number of classes. y_{ijk} is the ground truth of a pixel and $\widehat{y}_{ijk}$ is the prediction of a pixel.

It is common that the surgical instrument only occupies a small area of the image, which leads to serious class imbalance issue. However, the performance of cross entropy is greatly affected by this issue. The prediction is more inclined to recognize pixels as background. Therefore the surgical instrument may be partially detected or ignored. The Dice loss defined in Eq. (5) can be used to solve this problem [9]. It evaluates the similarity between the prediction and the ground truth, which is not affected by the ratio of foreground pixels to background pixels.

$$D = \frac{2 \sum_{i}^{w} \sum_{j}^{h} p_{ij} g_{ij}}{\sum_{i}^{w} \sum_{j}^{h} p_{ij} + \sum_{i}^{w} \sum_{j}^{h} g_{ij}} \tag{5}$$

where w, h represent the width and the height of the predictions, p represents the prediction, g represents the ground truth.

To effectively utilize the excellent characteristics of these two losses, we merge the Dice loss with the cross entropy function in the following:

$$L = (1 - \alpha)H - \alpha \log(D) \tag{6}$$

where α is a weight used to balance cross entropy loss and Dice loss. D is between 0 and 1. $\log(D)$ extends the value range from 0 to negative infinity. When the prediction is greatly different from the ground truth, D is small and $\log(D)$

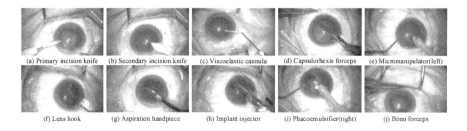

Fig. 3. Ten cataract surgical instruments used in Cata7.

is close to negative infinity. The loss will increase a lot to penalize this poor prediction. This method can not only use the characteristics of the Dice loss but also improve the sensitivity of loss.

This loss is named Cross Entropy Log Dice (CEL-Dice). It combines the stability of cross entropy and the property that Dice loss is not affected by class imbalance. Therefore, it solves class imbalance better than cross entropy and its stability is better than Dice loss.

Table 1. Details of Cata7 Dataset. The Cata7 dataset contains a total of 2500 images. It is split into the training set and the test set. Up to two surgical instruments in each image.

No.	Instrument	Number	Train	Test
1	Primary incision knife	62	39	23
2	Secondary incision knife	226	197	29
3	Viscoelastic cannula	535	420	115
4	Capsulorhexis forceps	119	34	85
5	Micromanipulator	507	366	141
6	Lens hook	475	405	70
7	Aspiration handpiece	515	364	151
8	Implant injector	303	277	26
9	Phacoemulsifier handpiece	677	526	151
10	Bonn forceps	222	101	121
-	Total	3641	2729	912
-	Number of Frames	2500	1800	700

3   Experiments

3.1   Datasets

A new dataset, Cata7, is constructed to evaluate our network, which is the first cataract surgical instrument dataset for semantic segmentation. The dataset consists of seven videos while each video records a complete cataract surgery. All videos are from Beijing Tongren Hospital. Each video is split into a sequence of images, where resolution is 1920 × 1080 pixels. To reduce redundancy, the videos are downsampled from 30 fps to 1 fps. Also, images without surgical instruments are manually removed. Each image is labeled with precise edges and types of surgical instruments.

This dataset contains 2,500 images, which is divided into training and test sets. The training set consists of five video sequences and test set consists of two video sequences. The number of surgical instruments in each category is illustrated in Table 1. There are ten surgical instruments used in the surgery, which are shown in Fig. 3.

3.2   Training

ResNet34 pre-trained on the ImageNet is utilized as the encoder. Pre-training can accelerate network convergence and improve network performance [10]. Due to limited computing resources, each image for training is resized to 960 × 544 pixels. The network is trained by using Adam with batch size 8. The learning rate is dynamically adjusted during training to prevent overfitting. The initial learning rate is 4×10^{-5}. For every 30 iterations, the learning rate is multiplied by 0.8. As for the α in the CEL-Dice, it is set to 0.2 after several experiments. Dice coefficient and Intersection-Over-Union (IOU) are selected as the evaluation metric.

Data augmentation is performed to prevent overfitting. The augmented samples are generated by random rotation, shifting and flipping. 800 images are obtained by data augmentation, increasing feature diversity to prevent overfitting effectively. Batch normalization is used for regularization. In the decoder, batch normalization is performed after each convolution.

3.3   Results

Ablation for Augmented Attention Module. Augmented attention module (AAM) is designed to aggregate multi-level features. It captures global context and semantic dependencies to emphasize key features and suppress background features. To verify its performance, we set up a series of experiments. The results are shown in the Table 2.

Table 2. Performance comparison of attention module (AM).

Method	AM	mDice (%)	mIOU (%)	Param
BaseNet	–	95.12	91.31	21.80M
BaseNet	AAM (Ours)	97.71	95.62	22.06M
BaseNet	GAU [11]	96.61	93.76	22.66M

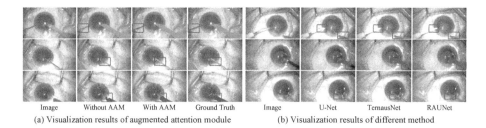

| Image | Without AAM | With AAM | Ground Truth | Image | U-Net | TernausNet | RAUNet |

(a) Visualization results of augmented attention module   (b) Visualization results of different method

Fig. 4. Visualization of segmentation results. (a) the visualization results of augmented attention module. (b) the visualization results of various method. (Color figure online)

RAUNet without AAM is used as the base network, which achieves 95.12% mean Dice and 91.31% mean IOU. The base network with AAM achieves 97.71% mean Dice and 95.62% mean IOU. By applying AAM, mean Dice increases by 2.59% and mean IOU increases by 4.31%. Furthermore, AAM is compared with GAU [11]. The base network with GAU achieves 96.61% mean Dice and 93.76% mean IOU. Compared to the base network with AAM, its mean Dice and mean IOU are reduced by 1.10% and 1.86%, respectively. Besides, by applying AAM, parameters only increase by 0.26M, which is 1.19% of the base network. By applying GAU, parameters increase by 0.60M, which is 2.31 times the amount of parameters increased by AAM. These results show that AAM can not only significantly increase the segmentation accuracy, but also does not add too many parameters.

To give an intuitive comparison, the segmentation results of the base network and RAUNet are visualized in Fig. 4(a). The red line marks the contrasted region. It can be found that there are classification errors in the results of the base network. Besides, surgical instruments are not entirely segmented in the third image. Meanwhile, RAUNet can accurately segment surgical instruments by applying AAM. The masks achieved by RAUNet are the same as the ground truth. This shows that AAM contributes to capturing high-level semantic features and improving feature representation.

Comparison with State-of-the-Art. To further verify the performance of RAUNet, it is compared with the U-Net [8], TernausNet [10] and LinkNet [12]. As shown in Table 3, RAUNet achieves state-of-the-art performance 97.71% mean Dice and 95.62% mean IOU, which outperforms other methods. U-Net [8] achieves 94.99% mean Dice and 91.11% mean IOU. TernausNet [10] and LinkNet [12] achieve 92.98% and 92.21% mean IOU respectively. The performance of these methods is much poor than our RAUNet.

Table 3. Performance comparison of various methods on Cata7.

Method	mDice (%)	mIOU (%)	Param
U-Net [8]	94.99	91.11	7.85M
LinkNet [10]	95.75	92.21	21.80M
TernausNet [12]	96.24	92.98	25.36M
RAUNet (Ours)	97.71	95.62	22.06M

Pixel accuracy achieved by various methods is visualized in Fig. 5. It can be found that the primary incision knife is often misclassified by U-Net, TernausNet, and LinkNet. Since the primary incision knife is used for a short time in surgery, its samples are few, leading to the underfitting of the network. Also, lens hook is often misclassified by U-Net. This result is since the lens hook is very thin and cause severe class imbalance. Furthermore, it is similar to other surgical instruments. U-Net cannot capture high-level semantic information, which causes the misclassification. Despite these difficulties, our method still achieves high pixel accuracy. The pixel accuracy of lens hook and primary incision knife are 90.23% and 100% respectively. These results show that RAUNet can capture discriminative semantic features and address the class imbalance issue.

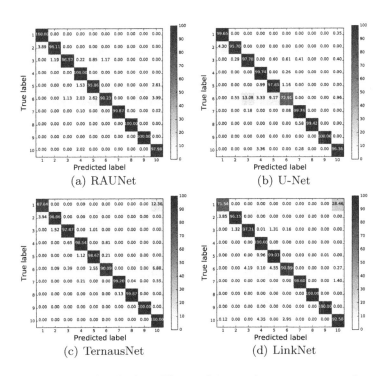

Fig. 5. Pixel accuracy of each class. The numbers on the axes represent the categories of surgical instruments.

To give an intuitive result, the segmentation results of the above method are visualized in Fig. 4(b). The segmentation results of RAUNet are the same as the ground truth, which is significantly better than other methods. Also, more results of RAUNet are shown in Fig. 6.

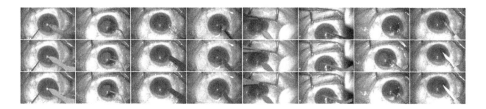

Fig. 6. Visualization results of ten cataract surgical instruments. From top to low: original image, ground truth and prediction of RAUNet.

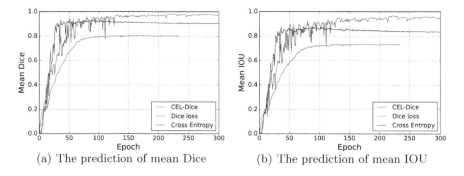

(a) The prediction of mean Dice   (b) The prediction of mean IOU

Fig. 7. Performance comparison of loss functions. (a) the prediction of mean dice and (b) the prediction of mean IOU.

Verify the Performance of CEL-Dice. CEL-Dice is utilized to solve the class balance issue. It combines the stability of cross entropy and the property that Dice loss is not affected by class imbalance. To verify its performance, it is compared with cross entropy and Dice loss. The mean Dice and mean IOU achieved by the network on the test set is illustrated in Fig. 7. They change with the training epoch. It can discover that CEL-Dice can significantly improve segmentation accuracy, which is better than Dice loss and cross entropy.

4   Conclusion

A novel network called RAUNet is proposed for semantic segmentation of surgical instruments. The augmented attention module is designed to emphasize key regions. Experimental results show that the augmented attention module can significantly improve segmentation accuracy while adds very few parameters. Also, a hybrid loss called Cross Entropy Log Dice is introduced, contributing to addressing the class imbalance issue. Proved by experiments, RAUNet achieves state-of-the-art performance on Cata7 dataset.

Acknowledgment. This research is supported by the National Key Research and Development Program of China (Grant 2017YFB1302704), the National Natural Science Foundation of China (Grants 61533016, U1713220), the Beijing Science and Technology Plan (Grant Z191100002019013) and the Strategic Priority Research Program of CAS (Grant XDBS01040100).

References

1. Sarikaya, D., Corso, J.J., Guru, K.A.: Detection and localization of robotic tools in robot-assisted surgery videos using deep neural networks for region proposal and detection. IEEE Trans. Med. Imaging **36**(7), 1542–1549 (2017)
2. Trikha, S., Turnbull, A., Morris, R., Anderson, D., Hossain, P.: The journey to femtosecond laser-assisted cataract surgery: new beginnings or a false dawn? Eye **27**(4), 461 (2013)
3. García-Peraza-Herrera, L.C., et al.: Real-time segmentation of non-rigid surgical tools based on deep learning and tracking. In: Peters, T., et al. (eds.) CARE 2016. LNCS, vol. 10170, pp. 84–95. Springer, Cham (2017). https://doi.org/10.1007/978-3-319-54057-3_8
4. Ni, Z.L., Bian, G.B., Xie, X.L., Hou, Z.G., Zhou, X.H., Zhou, Y.J.: RASNet: segmentation for tracking surgical instruments in surgical videos using refined attention segmentation network. arXiv preprint arXiv:1905.08663 (2019)
5. Laina, I., et al.: Concurrent segmentation and localization for tracking of surgical instruments. In: Descoteaux, M., Maier-Hein, L., Franz, A., Jannin, P., Collins, D.L., Duchesne, S. (eds.) MICCAI 2017. LNCS, vol. 10434, pp. 664–672. Springer, Cham (2017). https://doi.org/10.1007/978-3-319-66185-8_75
6. Attia, M., Hossny, M., Nahavandi, S., Asadi, H.: Surgical tool segmentation using a hybrid deep CNN-RNN auto encoder-decoder. In: 2017 IEEE International Conference on Systems, Man, and Cybernetics (SMC), pp. 3373–3378. IEEE (2017)
7. He, K., Zhang, X., Ren, S., Sun, J.: Deep residual learning for image recognition. In: 2016 IEEE Conference on Computer Vision and Pattern Recognition (CVPR), pp. 770–778, June 2016
8. Ronneberger, O., Fischer, P., Brox, T.: U-Net: convolutional networks for biomedical image segmentation. In: Navab, N., Hornegger, J., Wells, W.M., Frangi, A.F. (eds.) MICCAI 2015. LNCS, vol. 9351, pp. 234–241. Springer, Cham (2015). https://doi.org/10.1007/978-3-319-24574-4_28
9. Milletari, F., Navab, N., Ahmadi, S.: V-Net: fully convolutional neural networks for volumetric medical image segmentation. In: 2016 Fourth International Conference on 3D Vision (3DV), pp. 565–571, October 2016
10. Iglovikov, V., Shvets, A.: TernausNet: U-Net with VGG11 encoder pre-trained on ImageNet for image segmentation. arXiv preprint arXiv:1801.05746 (2018)
11. Li, H., Xiong, P., An, J., Wang, L.: Pyramid attention network for semantic segmentation. arXiv preprint arXiv:1805.10180 (2018)
12. Chaurasia, A., Culurciello, E.: LinkNet: exploiting encoder representations for efficient semantic segmentation. In: 2017 IEEE Visual Communications and Image Processing (VCIP), pp. 1–4. IEEE (2017)

A Novel Image-Based Malware Classification Model Using Deep Learning

Yongkang Jiang, Shenghong Li, Yue Wu$^{(\boxtimes)}$, and Futai Zou

School of Electronic, Information and Electrical Engineering,
Shanghai Jiao Tong University, Shanghai 200240, China
{jiangyongkang,shli,wuyue,zoufutai}@sjtu.edu.cn

Abstract. Nowadays, the vast volume of data which needs to be evaluated potentially malicious is becoming one of the major challenges of antivirus products. In this paper, we propose a novel image-based malware classification model using deep learning to counter large-scale malware analysis. The model includes a malware embedding method called YongImage which maps instruction-level information and disassembly metadata generated by IDA disassembler tool into an image vector, and a deep neural network named malVecNet which has simpler structure and faster convergence rate.

Our proposed YongImage converts malware analysis tasks into image classification problems, which do not rely on domain knowledge and complex feature extraction. Meanwhile, we use the thought of sentence-level classification in Natural Language Processing to establish and optimize our malVecNet. Compared to previous work, malVecNet has better theoretical interpretability and can be trained more effectively.

We use 10-fold cross-validation on Microsoft malware classification challenge dataset to evaluate our model. The results demonstrate that our model can achieve 99.49% accuracy with 0.022 log loss. Although our scheme is less precise than the winner's, it makes an orders-of-magnitude performance boost. Compared with other related work, our model also outperforms most of them.

Keywords: Malware · Embedding · Classification · Deep learning

1   Introduction

Malware is a term for all software that intend to cause harm or inflict damage on computer systems. Recently, with introducing of polymorphic and metamorphic techniques, malicious software gets explosive growth on both quality and quantity. Malware classification has always been a concerned field in recent decade, which is an issue of giving a malicious sample i, calculating a family label j from knowledge base. Hence, malware classification can associate a fresh variant to a known family, which is meaningful to malware detection.

The research of Microsoft [11] indicates that the vast volume of data which needs to be detected is becoming one of the major challenges of anti-malware

© Springer Nature Switzerland AG 2019
T. Gedeon et al. (Eds.): ICONIP 2019, LNCS 11954, pp. 150–161, 2019.
https://doi.org/10.1007/978-3-030-36711-4_14

companies. Traditional signature-based and behavior-based malware analysis techniques are difficult to meet the demand, a more effective method is needed [19]. Deep learning is a good choice, under the gpu acceleration, a model can be easily trained and the detection is even more efficient. In addition, inspired by the excellent performance of convolution neural network in image field, we decide to explore a simpler model, converting malware classification tasks into image classification problems.

In fact, recent research of malware analysis, both static and dynamic, is moving from traditional aspects to deep learning. Ronen et al. [15] make a comparison between research papers using Microsoft malware classification challenge dataset (BIG2015). The results suggest that none of 12 papers in 2016 introducing deep learning, but 5 of 17 papers in 2017. Although most of them still rely on solid domain knowledge, researchers are exploring an end-to-end model to extract and fuse malware features automatically.

Nataraj et al. [13] propose first malware embedding method called NatarajImage based on binary file in 2011. Although NatarajImage is believed vulnerable to obfuscation and packing techniques, their work has been followed by many others [1,7,8,18]. Andrew et al. [2] propose another malware embedding method named AndrewImage based on disassembly file at Black Hat conference 2015. As far as we know, AndrewImage has not been introduced in any research paper. Compared with NatarajImage, AndrewImage embeds instruction-level information, which has better robustness and interpretability. Unfortunately, AndrewImage uses so much zero padding that the accuracy still remains a challenge.

To summarize, this paper has the following contributions. 1. We propose a novel image-based malware classification model including a malware embedding method called YongImage and a simple deep neural network named malVec-Net. YongImage directly embeds hexadecimal instruction and other metadata into vector space. MalVecNet has better theoretical interpretability and can be trained more effectively. Our model converts malware analysis tasks into image classification problems that do not rely on domain knowledge and time-consuming feature extraction. 2. We successfully train the model on Microsoft malware classification challenge dataset, the results indicate that our model outperforms most of the related work. As far as we know, it is the state-of-the-art solution for large-scale malware classification tasks. 3. We make the code for malware embedding and training based on the model described in this paper, now is available in github.[1]

2   Malware Embedding

Formally, malware embedding maps malicious software into a vector space, helps learning algorithms to obtain better performance in malware analysis tasks. Similar to word embedding [12] in Natural Language Processing (NLP), this choice has several advantages—simplicity, effectiveness and the observation that

---

[1] https://github.com/jyker?tab=repositories.

some image-based models trained on huge malware dataset outperform most of traditional signature-based and behavior-based methods. Differently, malware embedding now focuses more on how to choose atomic units.

2.1   NatarajImage and AndrewImage

NatarajImage [13], as shown in Fig. 1, chooses 8-bit malware binary as atomic units, maps whole Portable Executable (PE) file or only .text section into a gray image vector.

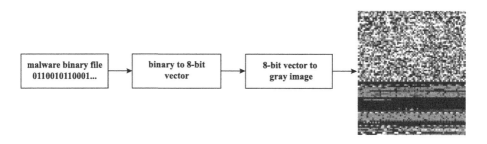

Fig. 1. NatarajImage embedding process

However, even without considering obfuscation and packing techniques, Ahmadi et al. [1] find that the texture pattern of NatarajImage in different malware families may be exactly similar. Therefore, models based on NatarajImage are vulnerable to attackers.

Differently, AndrewImage [2], as shown in Fig. 2, chooses hexadecimal instruction in disassembly file as atomic units, embeds malware instruction into a black-white image vector.

Fig. 2. AndrewImage embedding process

In fact, AndrewImage has excellent semantic features —one line instruction, one row vector. Unfortunately, it is also this excellent visual interpretability that uses a large percentage of invalid zero padding, which makes output image vector too large to train, and high accuracy still remains a challenge.

2.2 YongImage

Inspired by previous work, we propose YongImage. As Fig. 3 shows, a PE malware disassembly file generated by IDA Pro[2] contains two aspects of information—hexadecimal instruction, and corresponding metadata, *i.e.* section name, address of instruction, opcode and operand.

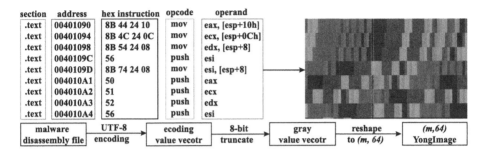

Fig. 3. YongImage embedding process

We embed these information as following steps: 1. Encode malware disassembly file with UTF-8 [20]. 2. Obtain gray vector by truncating each encoded value from a high order to 8-bit. 3. Reshape the gray vector to $(m, 64)$. Intuitively, the visual interpretability of YongImage is not as well as AndrewImage. In fact, YongImage retains instruction-level interpretability by reshaping the gray vector to $(m, 64)$.

Why (m, 64). Firstly, Let us prove the optimal padding length in AndrewImage is $L = 64$.

The Intel 64 and IA-32 architectures instruction encodings are subsets of the format shown in Fig. 4, which specifies the maximum length of an instruction is 15 *bytes*, in general, it does not exceed 11 *bytes* [5]. For example, the hexadecimal instruction {**8B 44 24 10**} in Fig. 2 is only 4 *bytes*.

Instruction Prefixes	Opcode	ModR/M	SIB	Displacement	Immediate
Prefixes of 1 byte each (optional)	1-, 2-, or 3-byte opcode	1 byte (if required)	1 byte (if required)	Address displacement of 1, 2, or 4 bytes or none	Immediate data of 1, 2, or 4 bytes or none

Fig. 4. Intel 64 and IA-32 architectures instruction format [5]

---

[2] https://www.hex-rays.com/products/ida/.

Therefore, the first idea is to pad binary digits to 120-bit to cover all instructions or just truncate binary digits to 88-bit vector to support most. However, in that case, the output vector is too large to train.

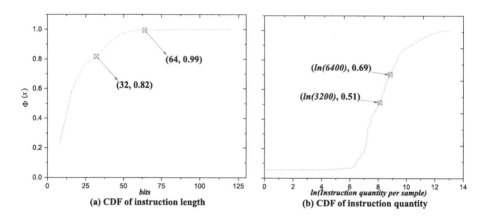

(a) CDF of instruction length

(b) CDF of instruction quantity

Fig. 5. The cumulative distribution function of instruction in BIG2015 dataset

By analyzing samples in Microsoft malware classification challenge dataset (BIG2015) [15], we obtain the cumulative distribution function (CDF) of instruction length in samples, as shown in Fig. 5(a), which indicates that 99% of instructions do not exceed 64 *bits* and 82% of instructions do not exceed 32 *bits*. Therefore, $L = 64$ is chosen to cover almost all instructions while maintaining smaller vector size. Differently, YongImage does not truncate each line vector to 64-bit, as an alternative, we reshape the vector to $(m, 64)$. Since 64-bit is almost sufficient for a line of disassembly file encoded by UTF-8, m can be approximated as number of instruction lines, *i.e.* instruction quantity.

Another problem of YongImage is how many lines of instructions should be embedded, *i.e.* how to choose m. Certainly, the larger m can lead to better accuracy without considering performance. However, when the model reaches a certain accuracy, m should be as small as possible. Figure 5(b) indicates that the instruction quantity in disassembly file varies greatly, 50% of files contain no more than 3200 instructions, and 69% of files contain no more than 6400. In our experiment, 3200 and 6400 are two candidate values of m.

3   Model Definition

Kim *et al.* [9] propose a simple novel convolution neural network (CNN) architecture with little hyperparameter tuning and static vectors, which achieves excellent results. Inspired by their work, we propose a variant architecture named malVectNet, as shown in Fig. 6.

Malware embedding outputs an image vector with size $(m, 64)$, where m represents the number of instructions. Channel transformation is designed to

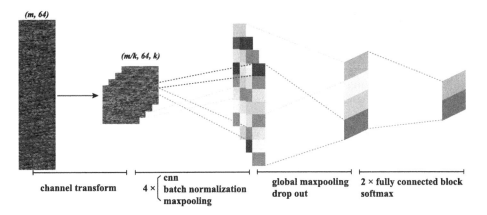

Fig. 6. Image-Based malware classification model architecture

turn vector into a new shape of $(\frac{m}{k}, 64, k)$, in which k represents the number of channels.

Next, we use a special value $k = 1$ to illustrate our malVecNet.

First, let $S_j \in \mathbb{R}^{64}$ be the 64-dimensional instruction vector corresponding to the j-th instruction in m. Then, a malware sample X_i is represented as:

$$X_i = [S_1, S_2, ..., S_j, ..., S_m]. \tag{1}$$

Each convolution layer includes several filters $w \in \mathbb{R}^{hc}$, which apply a window with size (h, c). For instance, $c_{i,t}$ is a vector generated from a window $X_{i:i+h}(t : t + c)$ by

$$c_{i,t} = w \cdot X_{i:i+h}(t : t + c) + b, \tag{2}$$

where $b \in \mathbb{R}$ is bias. When a row convolution is finished, we obtain a new row feature vector as follows:

$$c_i = [c_{i,1}, c_{i,2}, ..., c_{i,64}], \tag{3}$$

Similarly, when whole convolution is completed, a new abstract instruction vector is generated, *i.e.*

$$c = [c_1, c_2, ..., c_i, ..., c_m]. \tag{4}$$

Then, batch normalization (BN) [6] is applied on c. Details of BN on mini-batch are in Algorithm 1. Recent research has shown that BN can smooth the objective function [16], which is significant to accelerate deep neural network.

After that, we use a non-linear activation function f and max-pooling on e_i, which aims to reduce the dimension of the feature vector.

$$e = maxpooling(f([e_1, e_2, ..., e_i, ..., e_m])); e_i = BN_{\beta,\gamma}(c_i) \tag{5}$$

So far, we have described the process of one CNN block in malVecNet, which uses four similar CNN blocks. Therefore, the input of global max-pooling is a normalized, activated and pooled feature vector, *i.e.*

Algorithm 1. The algorithm of batch normalization on mini-batch

---

Input: c value on each mini-batch $\varphi = \{c_{1...n}\}$

1: parameters to learn γ, β

Output: $e_i = BN_{\beta,\gamma}(c_i)$

2: calculate mean of mini-batch $\mu \leftarrow \frac{1}{n}\sum_{i=1}^{n} c_i$

3: calculate variance of mini-batch $\sigma_\varphi^2 \leftarrow \frac{1}{n}\sum_{i=1}^{n}(c_i - \mu_\varphi)^2$

4: standardize $\hat{c}_i \leftarrow \frac{c_i - \mu_\varphi}{\sqrt{\sigma^2 + \varepsilon}}$

5: scale and shift $e_i \leftarrow \gamma\hat{c}_i + \beta \equiv BN_{\beta,\gamma}(c_i)$

$$e = [e_1, e_2, ..., e_g]. \tag{6}$$

where g is determined by the specific parameters of the before layers. In order to preserve the most important features (one with highest value) while reducing the dimension of the final feature vector, we apply global max-pooling on e and take $\hat{e} = max\{e\}$ as the final instruction-level features vector.

Finally, we use two fully-connected blocks and a softmax layer to get:

$$y = [y_1, y_2, ..., y_n]. \tag{7}$$

in which y_i is the probability of malware family i, n represents the number of malware families.

We use the idea of sentence-level classification to construct the entire model. In theory, it is more suitable for instruction-level malware embedding methods, such as AndrewImage and YongImage.

4   Experiments and Results

4.1   Dataset

BIG2015 [15] contains 21741 malware samples of 9 different families, *i.e.* Ramnit(F1), Lollipop(F2), Kelihos_ver3(F3), Vundo(F4), Simda(F5), Tracur(F6), Kelihos_ver1(F7), Obfuscator.ACY(F8) and Gatak(F9).

Since only 10868 training samples in BIG2015 is labeled, we choose this part as experimental dataset. As shown in Fig. 7(a), the dataset is extremely unbalanced. Therefore, we combine the following two methods to eliminate the impact of this unbalance on the model. Firstly, F4, F5 and F7 are randomly upsampled to 500. Secondly, a loss function weight that is inversely proportional to the class frequency is set in the input data [10].

4.2   Platform and Environment

We evaluate malVecNet on the platform environment presented in Table 1. More model details can be found in our github.[3]

---

[3] https://github.com/jyker/zklearn.

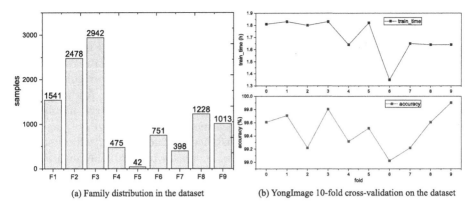

(a) Family distribution in the dataset   (b) YongImage 10-fold cross-validation on the dataset

Fig. 7. The distribution of dataset and cross-validation results

Table 1. The platform environment of experiment

Platform	Content
Hardware	2 × GeForce GTX 1080 @ 8 GB
	1 × E5-2630 v3 @ 2.40 GHz
	32 GB of memory
Software	CentOS 7.4
	python 3.6.5
	tensorflow-gpu 1.8.0
	Keras 2.2.0
	scikit-learn 0.19.1
	numpy 1.14.3
	Pillow 5.1.0

Loss function of the model is cross entropy, which is defined in Eq. (8),

$$loss = -\frac{1}{M}\sum_{i}^{M}\sum_{j}^{N} y_{ij}\log p_{ij}. \tag{8}$$

where M is the number of samples in min-batch, N is the number of malware classes, y_{ij} is 1 if sample i is in class j, otherwise, y_{ij} is 0, and p_{ij} is the predicated probability of sample i in class j.

At the same time, we choose accuracy, precision, recall and f1-score[4] to evaluate the performance of our model.

---

[4] https://scikit-learn.org/stable/modules/model_evaluation.html#precision-recall-f-measure-metrics.

4.3   Hyperparameter

In this section, we begin to discuss hyperparameters in our model. Firstly, it is the instruction quantity m. Experiment results shown in Table 2 indicate YongImage outperforms AndrewImage on all metrics regardless of m. In particular, when m reaches 6400, the accuracy of YongImage is increased, and AndrewImage decreased. One potential reason is that as m increases, the large number of invalid zero padding in AndrewImage causes more interference.

Intuitively, a larger m covers more instruction information, which should achieve a higher accuracy. In fact, when m increases to 6400, the accuracy of YongImage is only slightly improved, however the training time almost increases by half. Therefore, our model takes $m = 3200$.

Table 2. The impact of instruction quantity m

Method	m	Accuracy (%)	Precision (%)	Recall (%)	Train_time (h)
AndrewImage	3200	97.87	98.08	97.87	1.95
	6400	96.16	97.01	96.16	3.31
YongImage	3200	99.49	99.51	99.51	1.70
	6400	99.55	99.57	99.56	3.23

Note: BIG2015 tenfold cross-validation results; k = 1

Second hyperparameter is k, which represents the initial number of channels. In fact, the initial idea is to analyze the correlation between instructions by stacking k instructions in the channel direction to obtain higher model accuracy. However, the experimental results in Table 3 indicate that this design is only beneficial to accelerate model training. In order to achieve better accuracy, we finally choose $k = 1$.

Table 3. The impact of channel parameter k

Method	k	Accuracy (%)	Precision (%)	Recall (%)	Train_time (h)
YongImage	1	99.49	99.51	99.51	1.70
	4	98.87	98.89	98.87	1.01
	8	98.54	98.57	98.54	0.69

Note: BIG2015 10-fold cross-validation results; m = 3200

We use tenfold cross-validation on BIG2015 to evaluate the above hyperparameters. Particularly, the detail results of YongImage with $k = 1$ and $m = 3200$ is shown in Fig. 7(b), where the average accuracy is 99.49%, and the average training time is 1.70 h.

4.4 Comparison with Other Work

In this part, we compare malVecNet with several methods that have performed well on BIG2015 in recent years. Certainly, due to differences in experimental platforms, time metric is only a certain degree of reference.

The results in Table 4, suggest that only the solutions of Kaggle Winner [17] (BIG2015 winner) and Ahmadi [1] are slightly more accurate than our malVec-Net. However, they all rely on time and labor consuming feature engineering, which is inefficient during both training and detecting phases. Hence, compared with them, malVecNet makes an orders-of-magnitude performance boost.

Garcia et al. [4] introduce random forest based on NatarajImage to classify variant malware. Unfortunately, it is believed that NatarajImage is vulnerable to obfuscation and packing techniques, so their solution is less robust.

Raff et al. [14] propose a novel valid distance metric named Lempel-Ziv Jaccard Distance (LZJD) to classify malware in raw data, which obtains greater performance improvement than Normalized Compression Distance (NCD). However, models combining distance metrics with clustering algorithm are easy to train but time-consuming to detect.

Drew et al. [3] introduce strand gen sequence to malware classification, which achieves 98.89% accuracy and requires only 0.75h to train. Unfortunately, the detection time of strand gen sequence classifier is still too long for large-scale malware.

In fact, only the method of Yan et al. [18], which stacks VGG (based on NatarajImage), LSTM (based on opcode), achieves similar performance as our malVecNet. However, our model still has obvious advantages despite the differences in the experimental platform. Firstly, we use YongImage as the only input feature vector, model preprocessing and training are relatively simple, certainly, detection is faster. Secondly, benefit from instruction embedding and sentence-level modeling, our solution is more robust and interpretable.

Therefore, as far as we know, our malVecNet is the advanced solution for large-scale malware classification tasks.

Table 4. The comparison with other work

Methods	Accuracy (%)	Process (h)	Train (h)	Detect (s)
(2015) Kaggle Winner [17]	99.83	72	1	13649
(2016) Novel Features [1]	99.77	21.86	—	4096
(2016) Random Forest [4]	95.62	—	—	—
(2017) LZJD [14]	97.10	1.35	—	—
(2017) Strand Gene Sequence [3]	98.59	—	0.75	307.20
(2018) VGG LSTM [18]	99.36	—	2.91	30.72
malVecNet	99.49	0.22	1.70	4.79

Note: detection time is measured on 1024 samples.

5   Conclusion

This research aims to explore a simple and practical model to convert malware classification tasks into image classification problems.

We propose a novel image-based malware classification model including a malware embedding method called YongImage and a simple deep neural network named malVecNet. YongImage directly embeds hexadecimal instruction and other metadata into vector space. MalVecNet has better theoretical interpretability and can be trained more effectively. Our model does not rely on solid domain knowledge and time-consuming feature extraction.

We successfully train the model on Microsoft malware classification challenge dataset, the results indicate that our model outperforms most of the related work. To the best of our knowledge, it is the state-of-the-art solution for large-scale malware classification tasks.

Acknowledgment. This work is supported by the 2019 Science and Technology Project of SGCC "Security Protection Technology of Embedded Components and Control Units in Power System Terminal, No.2019GW-12", National Key Research and Development Program of China (No. 2017YFB0802300), NSFC-Zhejiang Joint Fund for the Integration of Industrialization and Informatization (No. U1509219), and National Key Research and Development Program of China (No. 2018YFB0803500).

References

1. Ahmadi, M., Ulyanov, D., Semenov, S., Trofimov, M., Giacinto, G.: Novel feature extraction, selection and fusion for effective Malware family classification. In: Proceedings of the Sixth ACM Conference on Data and Application Security and Privacy, pp. 183–194. ACM (2016)
2. Andrew Davis, M.W.: Deep learning on disassembly data. Internet (2015). https://www.blackhat.com/docs/us-15/materials/us-15-Davis-Deep-Learning-On-Disassembly.pdf
3. Drew, J., Hahsler, M., Moore, T.: Polymorphic Malware detection using sequence classification methods and ensembles. EURASIP J. Inf. Secur. **2017**(1), 2 (2017)
4. Garcia, F.C.C., Muga, F.P.: Random forest for malware classification. Cryptography and Security (2016). arXiv
5. Intel: Intel® 64 and ia-32 architectures software developer's manual, volume 2: Instruction set reference. Internet, September 2016. https://www.intel.com/content/dam/www/public/us/en/documents/manuals/64-ia-32-architectures-software-developer-instruction-set-reference-manual-325383.pdf
6. Ioffe, S., Szegedy, C.: Batch normalization: accelerating deep network training by reducing internal covariate shift. In: International Conference on Machine Learning, pp. 448–456 (2015)
7. Kebede, T.M., Djaneye-Boundjou, O., Narayanan, B.N., Ralescu, A., Kapp, D.: Classification of malware programs using autoencoders based deep learning architecture and its application to the Microsoft Malware classification challenge (big 2015) dataset. In: 2017 IEEE National Aerospace and Electronics Conference (NAECON), pp. 70–75. IEEE (2017)

8. Kim, H.-J.: Image-based Malware classification using convolutional neural network. In: Park, J.J., Loia, V., Yi, G., Sung, Y. (eds.) CUTE/CSA -2017. LNEE, vol. 474, pp. 1352–1357. Springer, Singapore (2018). https://doi.org/10.1007/978-981-10-7605-3_215

9. Kim, Y.: Convolutional neural networks for sentence classification. In: Empirical Methods in Natural Language Processing, pp. 1746–1751 (2014)

10. King, G., Zeng, L.: Logistic regression in rare events data. Polit. Anal. **9**(2), 137–163 (2001)

11. Microft: Sam cybersecurity engagement kit. Internet (2018). https://assets.microsoft.com/en-nz/cybersecurity-sam-engagement-kit.pdf

12. Mikolov, T., Sutskever, I., Chen, K., Corrado, G.S., Dean, J.: Distributed representations of words and phrases and their compositionality. In: Advances in Neural Information Processing Systems, pp. 3111–3119 (2013)

13. Nataraj, L., Karthikeyan, S., Jacob, G., Manjunath, B.: Malware images: visualization and automatic classification. In: Proceedings of the 8th International Symposium on Visualization for Cyber Security, p. 4. ACM (2011)

14. Raff, E., Nicholas, C.: An alternative to NCD for large sequences, Lempel-Ziv Jaccard distance. In: Proceedings of the 23rd ACM SIGKDD International Conference on Knowledge Discovery and Data Mining, pp. 1007–1015. ACM (2017)

15. Ronen, R., Radu, M., Feuerstein, C.E., Yomtov, E., Ahmadi, M.: Microsoft Malware classification challenge. Cryptography and Security (2018). arXiv

16. Santurkar, S., Tsipras, D., Ilyas, A., Madry, A.: How does batch normalization help optimization? In: Advances in Neural Information Processing Systems, pp. 2483–2493 (2018)

17. Xiaozhou Wang, J.L., Chen, X.: Microsoft Malware classification challenge (big2015): First place team: Say no to overfitting. Internet (2015). https://github.com/xiaozhouwang/kaggle_Microsoft_Malware/blob/master/Saynotooverfitting.pdf

18. Yan, J., Qi, Y., Rao, Q.: Detecting Malware with an ensemble method based on deep neural network. Secur. Commun. Netw. **2018**, 16 (2018)

19. Ye, Y., Li, T., Adjeroh, D.A., Iyengar, S.S.: A survey on Malware detection using data mining techniques. ACM Comput. Surv. **50**(3), 41 (2017)

20. Yergeau, F.: UTF-8, a transformation format of ISO 10646. Technical report (2003)

Visual Saliency Detection via Convolutional Gated Recurrent Units

Sayanti Bardhan[1,2]([✉]) [iD], Sukhendu Das[1] [iD], and Shibu Jacob[2]

[1] Indian Institute of Technology Madras, Chennai 600036, India
sayanti@smail.iitm.ac.in, sdas@iitm.ac.in
[2] National Institute of Ocean Technology, Chennai 600100, India
shibu@niot.res.in

Abstract. Context is an important aspect for accurate saliency detection. However, the question of how to formally model image context within saliency detection frameworks is still an open problem. Recent saliency detection models designed using complex Deep Neural Networks to extract robust features, however often fail to select the right contextual features. These methods generally utilize physical attributes of objects for generating final saliency maps, but ignores scene contextual information. In this paper, we overcome such limitation using (i) a proposed novel end-to-end framework with a Contextual Unit (CTU) module that models the scene contextual information to give efficient saliency maps with the help of Convolutional GRU (Conv-GRU). This is the first work reported so far that utilizes Conv-GRU to generate image saliency maps. In addition, (ii) we propose a novel way of using the Conv-GRU that helps to refine saliency maps based on input image context. The proposed model has been evaluated on challenging benchmark saliency datasets, where it outperforms prominent state-of-the-art methods.

Keywords: Visual saliency · Deep learning · Gated Recurrent Unit

1 Introduction

Saliency refers to computational process for identification of image regions that attract human attention. In the past few years, with advent of Deep Neural Networks (DNNs), more accurate saliency detection methods have been designed for complex scenarios. Effective deep structures for saliency detection include short connections [7], adaptive aggregation [32] etc. Till date, despite such improvement in accuracy, saliency models have performance constraints.

In this paper, we observe that such constraints are largely mitigated if saliency prediction model make use of scene contextual information. Context is defined as circumstances that form the setting of an environment or event. In human visual system, context of a scene determines the relative importance of objects in the scene, which in turn attracts our visual attention and determines its saliency [22]. To further support the importance of context in image

© Springer Nature Switzerland AG 2019
T. Gedeon et al. (Eds.): ICONIP 2019, LNCS 11954, pp. 162–174, 2019.
https://doi.org/10.1007/978-3-030-36711-4_15

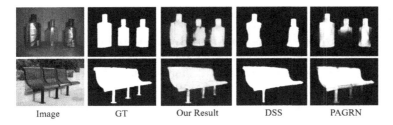

| Image | GT | Our Result | DSS | PAGRN |

Fig. 1. Results on challenging examples from saliency datasets. The state-of-the-art methods, DSS [7], PAGRN [35], fail to detect transparent objects (first row) and legs of the chair (second row) as salient. Our method overcomes such limitations.

saliency detection task, we take the help of an example in Fig. 1. First row of Fig. 1 demonstrates an image of three bottles, of which the middle one is transparent. It is observed that recent state of the art saliency detection methods like DSS [7] and PAGRN [35], fail to segment the middle bottle (whole or in part) because of its transparency. This is due to the fact that deep saliency networks extract features based on physical attributes and ignore the vital information of image context. Similarly, in the second row of Fig. 1, the image has three moulded chairs with colour of legs different than that of the seat of the chair. It is seen that prior methods [7,35] detect the three (chair) seats jointly but fail to detect all three legs of the chairs because of their colour. If scene context is taken into account, such failures will not occur, since it is quite common that chairs will have legs. We propose to overcome such limitations of saliency detection approaches by image context modeling. We define scene contextual information as the relationship between co-occurring objects or among their parts in a scene [22], which must be utilized for accurate saliency detection. Our results in Fig. 1 demonstrate that our model imitates human vision system better, as we approach saliency as a reasoning problem (i.e., chairs will have legs).

In this paper, we present a novel saliency detection framework with an explicit memory module that helps in context modelling. The paper proposes Convolutional GRU (Conv-GRU) [1] as a memory cell that accumulates scene context information from raw image to refine the network generated saliency map for incorporation of rich contextual information. The proposed architecture is based on VGGNet [21]. Here, short connections [7] to skip layer structure [28] are used to fuse multi-scale and multi-level features extracted from VGGNet. In addition, the side outputs [7] obtained from short connections are rich in features from both the deeper and shallower layers, but generally lack context information. To get context aware rich feature maps, the side outputs are refined using the Contextual Unit (CTU). CTU comprises of Conv-GRU modelled as a memory cell. The Conv-GRU module in CTU takes scene features as input and assigns short connection feature maps as initial state of Conv-GRU. This helps the Conv-GRU to refine saliency map based on scene context.

The key contributions of our work are summarized:

(1) The paper proposes a *novel end-to-end framework* utilizing rich scene context for accurate salient object detection. This work proposes *novel Contextual Unit* to model scene context information in an image.

(2) This paper proposes the use of Conv-GRU [1] as a memory cell. To the best of our knowledge, the proposed model is the first work reported so far that utilizes *Conv-GRU* to generate image saliency maps, helping it to make it context aware.

(3) In the prior published work, recurrent network based models usually initialize hidden state as empty or with random vectors. They iteratively refine the output based on the input state. Different from other recurrent network based models, our proposed Contextual Unit has image features fed as an input while the network generated saliency map is fed as an initial hidden state. This helps the Conv-GRU to refine the saliency map based on scene context information learnt from image features. Hence, our *implementation of Conv-GRU differs from other recurrent network based models*.

2   Related Work

Saliency and Deep Learning: Recently, saliency detection has achieved considerable performance improvement with DNNs [4,8,12,25,27,30,33,34] and conventional method [18]. Hou *et al.* [7] introduces short connections to skip-layer structures in a HED architecture [28]. Recurrent Fully Convolutional Networks was recently proposed by Wang *et al.* [24] to incorporate prior knowledge of saliency for accurate prediction. Liu *et al.* [15] propose a network that learns to attend to global and local contexts. While these methods achieve considerable accuracy, they fail to model contextual information of an image. Ignoring context information constraints the accuracy of the salient object detection methods. It may also be noted here that focus of this paper is on saliency, not attention.

Saliency Using Contextual Information: Contextual information is vital for saliency detection. Luo *et al.* [17], Zhao *et al.* [36] and Zhang *et al.* [32] utilize multi-level contexts for saliency prediction. Liu *et al.* [14] proposed deep hierarchical saliency network that further integrates local context information to refine details of saliency maps. Zhang *et al.* [31] develop a message passing model to integrate features from multi-level for salient object prediction. Zhang *et al.* [35] propose a progressive attention guided module to selectively fuse multiple contextual information of multi-level features. Wang *et al.* [26] exploit contextual information by the weighted response of feature maps in order to localize salient objects. While, these approaches mostly model context based on multi-scale feature concatenation and dilated convolutions, our proposed model of using Conv-GRU based CTU acting as a memory cell for context modelling increases the accuracy of our saliency predicting model. This is because it accounts for the saliency considering both spatial as well as semantic context of scene.

Difference from Other Recurrent Neural Networks: Recurrent Neural Network (RNN) maps history of previous inputs to the output. It has been used in various tasks like object detection [16], scene labelling [3,20] etc. For saliency prediction, Kuen *et al.* [10] propose the use of recurrent network and a spatial transformer to iteratively select image sub-regions for saliency refinement. Sun *et al.* [21] propose combining self-attention mechanism and recurrent convolutional layers to enhance global and local saliency information.

Our method differs from [10,21] in the following aspects: (i) This paper proposes utilization of Conv-GRU [1] as memory unit. Here, a novel CTU comprising of Conv-GRU is proposed to model scene context in an image. (ii) The scene is fed as an input to the Conv-GRU and network generated saliency map is used as an initial state of the Conv-GRU. Unlike, most of the recurrent based saliency detection methods, the initial state of the GRU is not any random or zero vectors. The purpose and implementation of Conv-GRU in our network is different from that proposed earlier in published literature. (iii) It may also be noted that proposed CTU module is generic in nature and can be adopted for other tasks like semantic segmentation of images, scene labelling etc.

3   Our Approach

Our prime objective is to model contextual information of images for saliency detection. We propose a saliency detection framework comprising novel Contextual Unit (CTU) to model scene level context.

3.1   Background

Convolutional GRU: Gated Recurrent Unit (GRU) [5] is an improved variant of Recurrent Neural Network (RNN). GRU is computationally less expensive and equally efficient as Long Short Term Memory (LSTM) [6]. In this paper we choose GRU to model scene context information. GRU had been however used earlier for mostly processing text and speech data. It uses fully connected units to model connections of input to hidden and hidden to hidden layers. However, while using GRU on images, we encounter the following issues [1]: (1) If GRU is directly applied on images, the number of parameters becomes very large. For instance, if GRU is applied on an image feature map of spatial size $h \times w \times c$, the input to hidden layer of GRU will require $h \times w \times c \times o$ parameters, where o is the dimensionality of the GRU hidden layer. Processing such huge set of parameters makes the model computationally inefficient, as a larger search space for the optimizer is harder to train. (2) Features extracted from images have strong local correlations over spatial locations. Application of GRUs directly on images ignore such spatial connectivity shared between pixels of image feature maps. Hence, this paper proposes the use of Conv-GRU [1] for image saliency prediction.

Conv-GRU replaces the dot products in GRU by the convolutional operations, from input to hidden and hidden to hidden layers. Formulation of Conv-GRU can be expressed as [1]:

$$z_t = \sigma \left(W_{xz} * x_t + U_{hz} * h_{t-1} \right) \tag{1}$$

$$r_t = \sigma \left(W_{xr} * x_t + U_{hr} * h_{t-1} \right) \tag{2}$$

$$\tilde{h}_t = tanh \left(U_h * \left(r_t \odot h_{t-1} \right) + W_x * x_t \right) \tag{3}$$

$$h_t = z_t \odot \tilde{h}_t + \left(1 - z_t \right) \odot h_{t-1} \tag{4}$$

where, W_{xz}, W_{xr}, W_x, U_{hz}, U_{hr} and U_h are 2-D convolutional kernels. At any time t, x_t is the input, h_t is the hidden state, r_t and z_t are reset and update gate respectively and $\tilde{h}_t$ is memory unit. The symbols *, $\odot$ and σ represent convolutional operator, element-wise multiplication and the sigmoid function respectively. Instead of learning individual weights for each pixel as in GRU, Conv-GRU learns an overall spatially invariant filter for the entire image. Thus, using filters with identical parameters preserve the spatial connectivity between image pixels and further enhances the accuracy of saliency prediction.

3.2   Overall Salient Object Detection Framework

Our proposed network is built upon DSS [7] architecture and uses VGG-16 [21] as its backbone. Figure 2 illustrates our proposed framework. As in [7], side outputs and short connections, are introduced to VGGNet. To each side output from VGGNet, a set of three convolutional layers [7] (indicated as blue box in Fig. 2) are added. The side outputs are further fused [7] (as indicated by blue dashed lines in Fig. 2) allowing concatenation of features of different scales, followed by a 1×1 convolutional layer giving output maps of dimension 256×256 [7]. It may be noted that our proposed model is built upon [7] because it allows us to take full advantage of the generated multi-scale features.

Further to incorporate scene level context, we utilize a set of novel Contextual Units (indicated as green box in Fig. 2) comprising Conv-GRU. Context learned from input image features (indicated by red arrows in Fig. 2) iteratively refine the saliency maps. The details of context modelling by Contextual Unit is discussed in Sect. 3.3. The output from each Contextual Unit is of dimension 256×256 and undergoes weighted fusion [7] (as indicated by black dashed lines in Fig. 2) followed by sigmoid activation function to give the saliency map. As a post processing tool, to further improve spatial coherence and preserve boundary information of saliency maps, we use the fully connected Conditional Random Field (CRF) [9] model to obtain the final saliency map.

3.3   Context Modelling by Contextual Unit

In this work, we propose a Contextual Unit (CTU) consisting of Conv-GRU as the core memory module to accumulate information from an input image to model its context. Figure 2 illustrates the layout of the Contextual Unit. It must

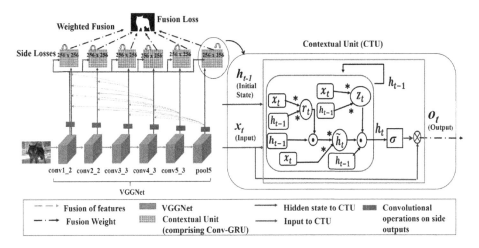

Fig. 2. Overview of proposed saliency detection (deep CNN-based) architecture, based on VGGNet [21]. It introduces six side outputs on VGGNet. Each side output undergoes three convolutional operations. Further, features from deeper layers are fused with that from shallow layers. The CTU module (green boxes) refines saliency maps by modelling input image context from input image features (red arrows). Output of CTU undergoes weighted fusion to give the final saliency map. A set of side loss and fusion loss functions make accurate saliency predictions. (Color figure online)

be noted here, that unlike most recurrent units, where initial state is usually fed as an empty or a random vector, our proposed CTU module uses the short connection generated feature map (blue arrows in Fig. 2) as the initial state. Here, image feature from the conv 1_2 layer (red arrows in Fig. 2) is used as CTU input. As illustrated in Fig. 2, the CTU module encodes context information from image feature (say x_t), and refines the short connection generated feature map (say h_{t-1}). Refinement of h_{t-1} is done in two ways: (i) forget non-essential parts of the initial state, h_{t-1}, that are not relevant with the learned image context; (ii) use context information learned from image features, x_t, to detect parts of objects that were not detected in the initial (or previous) state feature map, h_{t-1}. This refines h_{t-1} to give h_t at time step t. Due to recurrent nature of CTU, at the next time step h_t is fed as the updated state in place of h_{t-1}. However, the input to CTU, x_t, remains the same for all time steps of CTU. For every time step, the new initial state of CTU, h_{t-1}, gets iteratively refined by the image features, x_t. Here, t is empirically chosen as 2. After two time steps, h_t is fed to the sigmoid and then multiplied with x_t to generate the CTU output, o_t as:

$$o_t = \sigma\left(h_t\right) \odot x_t \tag{5}$$

Each side output of the proposed network has a CTU module (refer Fig. 2). Saliency maps obtained at the output of CTUs are combined by weighted fusion [7] followed by sigmoid activation function. It is observed that extracted saliency maps leverage the recurrent memory module in CTU to include contextual information in their maps. These are detailed using the results later. *Training the Network*: As in [28] and [7], deep supervision is applied to each side output. Popular Cross entropy loss is applied at both fusion and side output layers of the network. The overall loss function, $\tilde{L}_{final}$ is defined as:

$$\tilde{L}_{final}\left(\tilde{w}, W, f_w, s\right) = \tilde{L}_{fuse}\left(\tilde{w}, W, f_w, s\right) + \tilde{L}_{side}\left(\tilde{w}, W, s\right) \qquad (6)$$

where, $\tilde{L}_{fuse}$ is fusion loss and $\tilde{L}_{side}$ is side loss, as defined in [7]. W is the network layer parameters, $\tilde{w}$ are side output weights, f_w is the fusion weight and s is weight of the short connections within side outputs.

4   Experimental Results and Discussions

4.1   Experimental Setup

We train our network using DUTS-TR dataset (training set in DUTS) [23]. We use data augmentation of training set images by horizontal flipping that doubles the size of the set. The proposed network is trained end-to-end and optimized with Stochastic Gradient Descend. The initial learning rate is set to 0.01 and reduced by 10% every 10 epochs. Other hyperparameters used in this work are: batch size (8), momentum (0.9) and weight decay ($1e^{-4}$). The fusion layer weights are initialized to 0.1667. Our network is implemented using Pytorch library[1] and deployed on a NVIDIA GTX1080ti GPU with 11 GB RAM.

We evaluate our method on five representative saliency datasets, HKU-IS [11], ECSSD [19], PASCAL-S [13], DUT-OMORON [29] and DUTS-TE (test set of DUTS) [23]. We follow [7] and use the standard metrics: Precision Recall (PR) Curve, F measure ($\beta = 0.3$) and Mean Absolute Error (MAE), to evaluate the performance of our proposed and competing state-of-the-art methods. Further details regarding the evaluation metrics can be found in [2].

4.2   Comparison with State-of-the-Art Methods

To evaluate the performance of our method we compare with 13 deep-learning based state-of-the-art saliency models, DSS [7], BDMP [31], DGRL [26], PAGRN [35], LPSD [30], ASNet [27], LFR [34], CKT [12], RA [4], NLDF [17], AMU [32], UCF [33] and SRM [25]. For fair comparison only networks based on VGGNet are included. Saliency maps of these methods are produced by either executing source codes provided by authors or from results published by them.

Quantitative Evaluation: Quantitative evaluation of proposed framework with metrics, F_β and MAE, is given in Table 1. It can be seen that proposed model mostly outperforms all other state-of-the-art methods. The following are the observations from Table 1: (1) It can be seen that our method beats other

---

[1] https://pytorch.org.

Table 1. Quantitative comparison using 5 saliency datasets. Best three results are shown in RED, GREEN and BLUE respectively. F_β: higher the better and MAE: lower the better.

Methods		ECSSD		PASCAL-S		DUTS		HKU-IS		DUT-OMORON	
Name	Year	F_β	MAE	F_β	MAE	F_β	MAE	F_β	MAE	F_β	MAE
OURS	–	0.938	0.042	**0.859**	0.072	0.833	0.047	0.932	0.032	0.788	0.054
DSS [7]	PAMI-19	0.915	0.052	0.830	0.080	0.791	0.056	**0.913**	0.039	0.729	0.066
BDMP [31]	CVPR-18	0.928	**0.044**	0.862	0.074	0.850	0.049	0.920	0.038	0.692	0.064
DGRL [26]	CVPR-18	0.903	0.045	0.868	**0.079**	0.768	**0.051**	0.882	**0.037**	0.709	0.063
PAGRN [35]	CVPR-18	0.891	0.064	0.803	0.092	0.788	0.055	0.886	0.048	0.711	0.072
LPSD [30]	CVPR-18	0.908	0.049	0.811	0.091	0.787	0.059	0.899	0.039	**0.780**	0.066
ASNet [27]	CVPR-18	0.928	0.043	0.857	0.072	**0.831**	0.060	0.920	0.045	–	–
RA [4]	ECCV-18	**0.918**	0.059	0.834	0.104	**0.831**	0.058	**0.913**	0.045	0.780	**0.062**
CKT [12]	ECCV-18	0.910	0.054	0.846	0.081	0.807	0.062	0.896	0.048	0.757	0.071
LFR [34]	IJCAI-18	0.880	0.052	0.772	0.105	0.716	0.083	0.875	0.039	0.696	0.086
NDLF [17]	CVPR-17	0.878	0.063	0.779	0.099	0.743	0.065	0.872	0.048	0.684	0.079
SRM [25]	ICCV-17	0.892	0.054	0.801	0.085	0.757	0.058	0.873	0.046	0.707	0.069
AMU [32]	ICCV-17	0.868	0.059	0.768	0.098	0.682	0.085	0.843	0.050	0.647	0.098
UCF [33]	ICCV-17	0.844	0.069	0.735	0.115	0.635	0.112	0.823	0.061	0.621	0.120

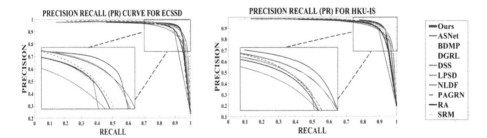

Fig. 3. Precision Recall Curve for two challenging datasets- ECSSD and HKU-IS. For higher recall (i.e., ≥ 0.8) our method beats the other state-of-the-art models.

competitive methods by a significant margin on challenging datasets like HKU-IS and ECSSD. It reduces the lowest MAE score by 8.5% and 2.3% and improves the F_β measure by 1.3% and 1% on HKU-IS and ECSSD dataset respectively. (2) In datasets like DUT-OMORON and DUTS, our method beats the other state-of-the-art in MAE metric by a substantial margin of 10% and 4% respectively. This indicates that proposed framework has significantly less wrong predictions. (3) For PASCAL-S dataset, the second best method, BDMP (marked in green), beats our method by a very less margin of 0.34% in F_β measure.

Figure 3 compares the performance of our method using PR curve for two challenging datasets, ECSSD and HKU-IS. It exhibits that for higher values of recall (≥ 0.8) our method beats the other state-of-the-art models. This demonstrates that proposed framework detects salient objects more accurately. It may be noted in Fig. 3 that the PR curves of our proposed model terminate earlier due to high confidence (contrast) expressed in our saliency maps.

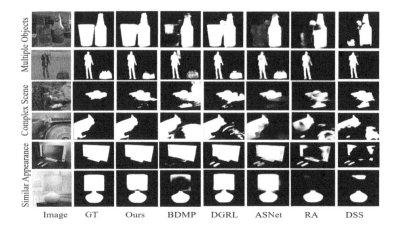

Fig. 4. Qualitative comparison of results with images from various saliency datasets. The complexity in each pair of images are mentioned in the left. Top two best performing methods are BDMP and DGRL. Our results give saliency maps closest to the Ground Truth (GT).

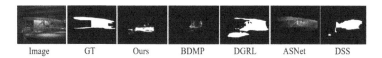

Fig. 5. A case of failure of our method, for a sample from PASCAL-S dataset

Qualitative Evaluation: Figure 4 illustrates the visual comparison of our results with the state-of-the-art methods. Here, we compare our results with only the top five best performing methods (i.e., BDMP, DGRL, ASNet, RA and DSS). We demonstrate images from multiple circumstances like complex scene, similar appearance of foreground and background and scenes with multiple objects. For multiple objects (first and second row), proposed method generate saliency maps closest to Ground Truth compared to the other state-of-the-art methods. In complex scenes (third and fourth row), competitive methods detect parts of foreground as well as background as salient. However, our method performs well is such circumstances. In situations like similar colour contrast (fifth row), all competing methods fail to segment the complete television set and/or identify the pair of remotes to be salient, as both the television frame and remotes have the same white colour. However, our method, best segments the television as the foreground and the pair of remotes in-front as the background (as given in GT). Compared to state-of-the-art methods, our method demonstrates capability of incorporating context and better distinguish foreground from background. Our method consistently performs the best on an average in all circumstances for examples as shown in Fig. 4. It must also be noted that in addition to this, our method also performs well in detection of transparent objects (first row in Fig. 4), as indicated earlier in Sect. 1. *Computation time:* We compare our average execution time with the top five best performing methods (i.e., BDMP, DGRL, ASNet, RA and DSS). As seen in Table 2, our average execution time is comparable with the other competitive methods.

4.3   Discussions

Our model proposes implementation of Conv-GRU that differs from other recurrent network based models. We further compare our results with a case where only the short connection generated feature map is used as CTU input for iterative refinement (initial hidden state is null). From Table 3 we observe that on ECSSD and HKU-IS dataset, our proposed Conv-GRU implementation reduces MAE by 12% and increased the F_β by 0.9% on average. Similar results are observed across PASCAL-S, DUTS and DUT-OMORON datasets as well.

We also analyse cases where our model fails to perform well. Figure 5 gives one such example where all models (our proposed, as well as competing ones published earlier) fail. It is observed that in most of such cases images have low contrast and complex background. Better modelling of foreground-background relationship and training dataset with more challenging examples will definitely mitigate such errors.

Table 2. Average execution time comparison with top five best performing methods

Methods	**Ours**	BDMP [31]	DGRL [26]	ASNet [27]	RA [4]	DSS [7]
Time (s)	**0.07**	0.04	0.20	0.08	0.02	0.05

Table 3. Comparison of performance to observe the effect of initial state on CTU module.

Dataset	Initial state of CTU: null vector		Initial state of CTU: image feature maps	
	F_β	MAE	F_β	MAE
ECSSD	0.927	0.050	**0.938**	**0.042**
HKU-IS	0.925	0.035	**0.932**	**0.032**

5   Conclusion

This work proposes a novel framework, that uses contextual information from an input image for generating efficient saliency maps. It is the first ever work that proposes utilization of Convolutional GRU for image saliency prediction. This work also proposes a novel Contextual Unit that utilizes Conv-GRU, in a solitary way, different than that used earlier, to model scene context to provide refined saliency maps. Experiments on five saliency datasets show that our model outperforms recent state-of-the-art saliency detection models.

References

1. Ballas, N., Yao, L., Pal, C.J., Courville, A.C.: Delving deeper into convolutional networks for learning video representations. CoRR abs/1511.06432 (2016)
2. Borji, A., Cheng, M., Jiang, H., Li, J.: Salient object detection: a benchmark. IEEE Trans. Image Process. **24**(12), 5706–5722 (2015). https://doi.org/10.1109/TIP.2015.2487833
3. Byeon, W., Breuel, T.M., Raue, F., Liwicki, M.: Scene labeling with LSTM recurrent neural networks. In: 2015 IEEE Conference on Computer Vision and Pattern Recognition (CVPR), pp. 3547–3555, June 2015. https://doi.org/10.1109/CVPR.2015.7298977
4. Chen, S., Tan, X., Wang, B., Hu, X.: Reverse attention for salient object detection. In: Ferrari, V., Hebert, M., Sminchisescu, C., Weiss, Y. (eds.) ECCV 2018. LNCS, vol. 11213, pp. 236–252. Springer, Cham (2018). https://doi.org/10.1007/978-3-030-01240-3_15
5. Cho, K., et al.: Learning phrase representations using RNN encoder-decoder for statistical machine translation. In: Proceedings of the 2014 Conference on Empirical Methods in Natural Language Processing (EMNLP), pp. 1724–1734. Association for Computational Linguistics, Doha, Qatar, October 2014. https://doi.org/10.3115/v1/D14-1179, https://www.aclweb.org/anthology/D14-1179
6. Chung, J., Gulcehre, C., Cho, K., Bengio, Y.: Empirical evaluation of gated recurrent neural networks on sequence modeling. In: NIPS 2014 Workshop on Deep Learning, December 2014 (2014)
7. Hou, Q., Cheng, M., Hu, X., Borji, A., Tu, Z., Torr, P.H.S.: Deeply supervised salient object detection with short connections. IEEE Trans. Pattern Anal. Mach. Intell. **41**(4), 815–828 (2019). https://doi.org/10.1109/TPAMI.2018.2815688
8. Hu, P., Shuai, B., Liu, J., Wang, G.: Deep level sets for salient object detection. In: 2017 IEEE Conference on Computer Vision and Pattern Recognition (CVPR), pp. 540–549, July 2017. https://doi.org/10.1109/CVPR.2017.65
9. Krähenbühl, P., Koltun, V.: Efficient inference in fully connected CRFs with Gaussian edge potentials. In: Shawe-Taylor, J., Zemel, R.S., Bartlett, P.L., Pereira, F., Weinberger, K.Q. (eds.) Advances in Neural Information Processing Systems 24, pp. 109–117. Curran Associates, Inc. (2011). http://papers.nips.cc/paper/4296-efficient-inference-in-fully-connected-crfs-with-gaussian-edge-potentials.pdf
10. Kuen, J., Wang, Z., Wang, G.: Recurrent attentional networks for saliency detection. In: The IEEE Conference on Computer Vision and Pattern Recognition (CVPR), June 2016
11. Li, G., Yu, Y.: Visual saliency detection based on multiscale deep CNN features. IEEE Trans. Image Process. **25**(11), 5012–5024 (2016). https://doi.org/10.1109/TIP.2016.2602079
12. Li, X., Yang, F., Cheng, H., Liu, W., Shen, D.: Contour knowledge transfer for salient object detection. In: Ferrari, V., Hebert, M., Sminchisescu, C., Weiss, Y. (eds.) ECCV 2018. LNCS, vol. 11219, pp. 370–385. Springer, Cham (2018). https://doi.org/10.1007/978-3-030-01267-0_22
13. Li, Y., Hou, X., Koch, C., Rehg, J.M., Yuille, A.L.: The secrets of salient object segmentation. In: 2014 IEEE Conference on Computer Vision and Pattern Recognition, pp. 280–287, June 2014. https://doi.org/10.1109/CVPR.2014.43
14. Liu, N., Han, J.: DHSNet: deep hierarchical saliency network for salient object detection. In: 2016 IEEE Conference on Computer Vision and Pattern Recognition (CVPR), pp. 678–686, June 2016. https://doi.org/10.1109/CVPR.2016.80

15. Liu, N., Han, J., Yang, M.: PiCANet: learning pixel-wise contextual attention for saliency detection. In: 2018 IEEE/CVF Conference on Computer Vision and Pattern Recognition, pp. 3089–3098, June 2018. https://doi.org/10.1109/CVPR.2018.00326
16. Liu, Y., Wang, R., Shan, S., Chen, X.: Structure inference net: object detection using scene-level context and instance-level relationships. In: The IEEE Conference on Computer Vision and Pattern Recognition (CVPR), June 2018
17. Luo, Z., Mishra, A., Achkar, A., Eichel, J., Li, S., Jodoin, P.: Non-local deep features for salient object detection. In: 2017 IEEE Conference on Computer Vision and Pattern Recognition (CVPR), pp. 6593–6601, July 2017. https://doi.org/10.1109/CVPR.2017.698
18. Roy, S., Das, S.: Multi-criteria energy minimization with boundedness, edge-density and rarity, for object saliency in natural images. In: The Ninth Indian Conference on Computer Vision, Graphics, Image Processing (ICVGIP), Bangalore, India, 14–17 December 2014 (2014)
19. Shi, J., Yan, Q., Xu, L., Jia, J.: Hierarchical image saliency detection on extended CSSD. IEEE Trans. Pattern Anal. Mach. Intell. **38**(4), 717–729 (2016). https://doi.org/10.1109/TPAMI.2015.2465960
20. Siam, M., Valipour, S., Jagersand, M., Ray, N.: Convolutional gated recurrent networks for video segmentation. In: 2017 IEEE International Conference on Image Processing (ICIP), pp. 3090–3094, September 2017. https://doi.org/10.1109/ICIP.2017.8296851
21. Simonyan, K., Zisserman, A.: Very deep convolutional networks for large-scale image recognition. arXiv:1409.1556, September 2014
22. Torralba, A., Castelhano, M.S., Oliva, A., Henderson, J.M.: Contextual guidance of eye movements and attention in real-world scenes: the role of global features in object search. Psychol. Rev. **113**, 2006 (2006)
23. Wang, L., et al.: Learning to detect salient objects with image-level supervision. In: 2017 IEEE Conference on Computer Vision and Pattern Recognition (CVPR), pp. 3796–3805, July 2017. https://doi.org/10.1109/CVPR.2017.404
24. Wang, L., Wang, L., Lu, H., Zhang, P., Ruan, X.: Salient object detection with recurrent fully convolutional networks. IEEE Trans. Pattern Anal. Mach. Intell. 1 (2018). https://doi.org/10.1109/TPAMI.2018.2846598
25. Wang, T., Borji, A., Zhang, L., Zhang, P., Lu, H.: A stagewise refinement model for detecting salient objects in images. In: 2017 IEEE International Conference on Computer Vision (ICCV), pp. 4039–4048, October 2017. https://doi.org/10.1109/ICCV.2017.433
26. Wang, T., et al.: Detect globally, refine locally: a novel approach to saliency detection. In: 2018 IEEE/CVF Conference on Computer Vision and Pattern Recognition, pp. 3127–3135, June 2018. https://doi.org/10.1109/CVPR.2018.00330
27. Wang, W., Shen, J., Dong, X., Borji, A.: Salient object detection driven by fixation prediction. In: The IEEE Conference on Computer Vision and Pattern Recognition (CVPR), June 2018
28. Xie, S., Tu, Z.: Holistically-nested edge detection. In: 2015 IEEE International Conference on Computer Vision (ICCV), pp. 1395–1403, December 2015. https://doi.org/10.1109/ICCV.2015.164
29. Yang, C., Zhang, L., Lu, H., Ruan, X., Yang, M.: Saliency detection via graph-based manifold ranking. In: 2013 IEEE Conference on Computer Vision and Pattern Recognition, pp. 3166–3173, June 2013. https://doi.org/10.1109/CVPR.2013.407

30. Zeng, Y., Lu, H., Zhang, L., Feng, M., Borji, A.: Learning to promote saliency detectors. In: 2018 IEEE/CVF Conference on Computer Vision and Pattern Recognition, pp. 1644–1653, June 2018. https://doi.org/10.1109/CVPR.2018.00177
31. Zhang, L., Dai, J., Lu, H., He, Y., Wang, G.: A bi-directional message passing model for salient object detection. In: 2018 IEEE/CVF Conference on Computer Vision and Pattern Recognition, pp. 1741–1750, June 2018. https://doi.org/10.1109/CVPR.2018.00187
32. Zhang, P., Wang, D., Lu, H., Wang, H., Ruan, X.: Amulet: aggregating multi-level convolutional features for salient object detection. In: 2017 IEEE International Conference on Computer Vision (ICCV), pp. 202–211, October 2017. https://doi.org/10.1109/ICCV.2017.31
33. Zhang, P., Wang, D., Lu, H., Wang, H., Yin, B.: Learning uncertain convolutional features for accurate saliency detection. In: 2017 IEEE International Conference on Computer Vision (ICCV), pp. 212–221, October 2017. https://doi.org/10.1109/ICCV.2017.32
34. Zhang, P., Liu, W., Lu, H., Shen, C.: Salient object detection by lossless feature reflection. In: Proceedings of the 27th International Joint Conference on Artificial Intelligence, IJCAI 2018, pp. 1149–1155. AAAI Press (2018). http://dl.acm.org/citation.cfm?id=3304415.3304578
35. Zhang, X., Wang, T., Qi, J., Lu, H., Wang, G.: Progressive attention guided recurrent network for salient object detection. In: The IEEE Conference on Computer Vision and Pattern Recognition (CVPR), June 2018
36. Zhao, R., Ouyang, W., Li, H., Wang, X.: Saliency detection by multi-context deep learning. In: 2015 IEEE Conference on Computer Vision and Pattern Recognition (CVPR), pp. 1265–1274, June 2015. https://doi.org/10.1109/CVPR.2015.7298731

RBPNET: An Asymptotic Residual Back-Projection Network for Super Resolution of Very Low Resolution Face Image

Xuebo Wang[1], Yao Lu[1(✉)], Xiaozhen Chen[1], Weiqi Li[1], and Zijian Wang[1,2]

[1] Beijing Laboratory of Intelligent Information Technology,
Beijing Institute of Technology, Beijing, China
vis_yl@bit.edu.cn
[2] China Central Television, Beijing, China

Abstract. The super resolution of a very low resolution face image is a challenge task in computer vision, because it is difficult to learn a nonlinear mapping of input-to-target space by deep neural network in one step upsampling. In this paper, we propose an asymptotic Residual Back-Projection Network (RBPNet) to gradually learn residual between the reconstructed face image and the ground truth by self-supervision mechanism. We map the reconstructed high-resolution feature map back to the original low-resolution feature space, use the original low-resolution feature map as a reference to self-supervising the learning of the various layers. The real high-resolution feature maps are approached gradually by iterative residual learning. Meanwhile, we explicitly reconstruct the edge map of face image and embed it into the reconstruction of high-resolution face image to reduce distortion of super-resolution results. Extensive experiments demonstrate the effectiveness and advantages of our proposed RBPNet qualitatively and quantitatively.

Keywords: Super resolution · Very low resolution face image · Residual learning · Back projection · Self-supervision

1 Introduction

In order to meet the demand of face detection and recognition, face image super-resolution (face SR) has been paid much more attention in recent years. It aims to reconstruct a high-resolution face image from a low resolution face image and improve the visual effect and the accuracy of face detection and recognition.

Recently, learning-based face SR approaches [1,13–15,17] have shown better performance than traditional methods. However most current face SR methods can get pleasing results only when upscale factors is not large ($2\times$, $3\times$, $4\times$) and input low resolution image has middle-level resolution (64×64, 32×32) as input. When the resolution of an input face image is lower (16×16), the results of

© Springer Nature Switzerland AG 2019
T. Gedeon et al. (Eds.): ICONIP 2019, LNCS 11954, pp. 175–186, 2019.
https://doi.org/10.1007/978-3-030-36711-4_16

predicting high-resolution face images by these methods of one-step upsampling are unsatisfactory. Lai [9] proposes deep laplacian pyramid networks for fast and accurate super-resolution (LapSRN), which is used to reconstruct generic images, to progressively reconstruct the sub-band residuals of high-resolution images using more supervision information at each level in pyramid. However, LapSRN needs more ground truth as image labels and manipulates the prediction of the neural network, which limits the predictive power of neural networks.

We propose a novel neural network RBPNet: an asymptotic Residual Back-Projection Network to super-resolve very low resolution face image by gradually residual learning using self-supervision information. In order to avoid to introduce more supervised labels in the neural network, our intuition is using the original low-resolution face image as a reference. Inspired by the early SR algorithm of iterative back-projection [7], we propose to project the reconstructed high-resolution feature map back to the original low-resolution feature space to supervise reconstructed HR face images (self-supervision mechanism) and learn to map the residuals of low-resolution feature space to high-resolution feature space. It is not enough to approximate the real high-resolution face image with only one-step residual learning, so we iteratively learn the residuals between the generated image and ground truth by multiple steps. Our network successfully super-resolve a very low resolution face image of 16×16 pixels to its $8\times$ larger version.

Meanwhile, we take the global face structure into account instead of considering only local information to keep the reconstructed face image structure undistorted. Zhu et al. [17] propose deep Cascaded Bi-Network (CBN) to localize facial components in LR face images and then upsample them progressively. However, localizing these facial components with high accuracy is generally a difficult task in very low resolution face images. Instead of localizing facial components, we use face edge map as global face structure information. Edge prior has been used in image super-resolution to make the reconstructed high-resolution image sharper [2,12]. In contrast to previous methods, the edge map in our method not only can make the image sharper but also can be served as the global information to make the resultant image not distorted. We keep the reconstructed face image undistorted by explicitly predicting the edge map of the face image and embedding it into the reconstruction process of the face image.

Contributions of our work can be summarized as:

(1) We present a novel end-to-end framework RBPNet to super-resolve very low resolution face image. The network gradually learns high-resolution residual images by self-supervision mechanism, and finally approximate real high-resolution images.

(2) The proposed network explicitly learns the edge map of high-resolution face image and embed it into the reconstruction of high-resolution face image to maintain the global structure of face image. We demonstrate the validity of the method qualitatively and quantitatively.

2   Related Work

2.1   Single Image Super-Resolution (SISR)

With the improvement of computing performance, many neural network based super-resolution methods have emerged and demonstrated better performance than traditional methods. Image Super-Resolution using deep Convolutional Networks (SRCNN) [3] is the pioneering work of deep learning for super-resolution reconstruction. It first upsamples the low resolution image to the desired size by bicubic interpolation, and then learns the mapping of low-resolution and high resolution image patches through only three convolution layers. Real-time single image and video super-resolution using an Efficient Sub-Pixel Convolutional neural Network (ESPCN) [11] proposes a sub-pixel convolution layer to improve the computational efficiency of the network. Li et al. [10] present a two-channel convolutional neural network (SDSR) to restore the general outline of the image and detailed texture information simultaneously. Image super-resolution via a Densely Connected Recursive Network (DCRN) [4] is proposed to reconstruct high-quality images with fewer parameters and less computation time. LapSRN [9] uses a cascading network to learn high-frequency residual details progressively, enabling 8× super resolution.

2.2   Back-Projection

Back-projection [7] is well known as the efficient iterative procedure to minimize the reconstruction error. Recent works [5,16] have proven the effectiveness of back projection on super-resolution. Zhao et al. [16] propose a method to refine high-frequency texture details with an iterative projection process. Deep Back-Projection Networks for super-resolution (DBPN) [5] constructs mutually-connected up- and down-sampling to imitate the process of super resolution and image degradation to learn more about degradation patterns.

Different from the above methods, we propose RBPNet to project the reconstructed high-resolution feature map back to the original low-resolution feature space to supervise reconstructed HR face images (self-supervision mechanism) and learn to map the residuals of low-resolution feature space to high-resolution feature space to complement the residual information onto the high-resolution feature map, which is a process from coarse to fine.

3   Proposed Method

Our asymptotic residual network with edge map embedded is composed of two branches: an upsampling branch that upsamples original LR face images and their LR edge maps simultaneously and a edge map embedded branch that explicitly embeds edge map in the reconstruction process. The framework of the proposed network is shown in Fig. 1.

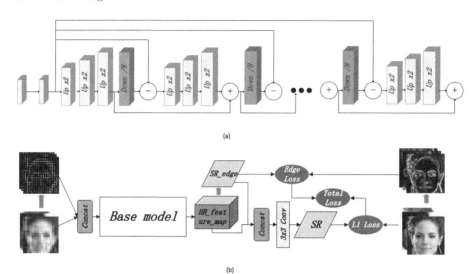

Fig. 1. The architecture of our network. (a) Base model: asymptotic residual back-projection network (b) The network of embedding edge maps explicitly into the reconstruction of face images.

3.1   Asymptotic Residual Back-Projection Network

Let I_{LR} (the concatenation of LR face images and LR edge maps) and I_{SR} denote the input and output images respectively. In order to improve the expressive ability of residual learning, we map it to the high-dimensional feature space. As shown in Fig. 1(a), we extract shallow feature F_0^L from I_{LR}, so that:

$$F_0^L = f_{shallow}(I_{LR}) \tag{1}$$

Next, we upsample F_0^L to the desired size (128×128) using deconvolution (More detailed deconvolution operations can be found in the experimental section). In order to get the difference between real HR feature map F_1^H and reconstructed HR feature map F_0^H, we use a simple downsampling convolution to project reconstructed HR feature map F_0^H back to the LR feature map F_1^L:

$$F_0^H = f_{up}(F_0^L; \alpha_0) \tag{2}$$

$$F_1^L = f_{down}(F_0^H; \theta_0) \tag{3}$$

where α_0 and θ_0 denotes (de)convolution parameters in 0_{th} step. We will get the difference (also know as residual) of original F_0^L and F_1^L. Then we learn residual mapping to map the residual in LR feature space to HR feature space and we will get the difference e_1 between F_1^H and F_0^H. The final output is the summation of F_0^H and the difference e_1:

$$e_1 = f_{up}((F_1^L - F_0^L); \gamma_0) \tag{4}$$

$$F_1^H = F_0^H + e_1 \qquad (5)$$

where γ_0 denotes deconvolution parameters in 0_{th} step. We only show one-step residual learning.

Asymptotic residual back-projection aims to learn the residual between the real high resolution feature map and reconstructed high resolution feature map, described as $F_i^H - F_{i-1}^H$. In the first step, the real residual is $F_1^H - F_0^H$. F_1^H is the real high resolution feature map which is the result we desire, but it can't be obtained directly. On the contrary, the real low resolution feature map can be obtained. So we project the learned high resolution feature map F_0^H back to low resolution space, and the residual of low resolution feature map is $F_1^L - F_0^L$. In the process of back-projection, it is inevitable to introduce error. So we need multi-step residual learning to reduce errors and make the reconstructed HR feature map approximate to the real HR feature map. Multi-step residual learning is to repeat the operations of Eqs. 2, 3, 4, 5. Each residual reference value is always the original LR feature map F_0^H, as shown in Fig. 3(b). The final residual of our predicted $\hat{F}_n^H$ can be described as follow:

$$\hat{F}_n^H = F_{n-1}^H + f_{up}((F_n^L - F_0^L); \gamma_i) \qquad (6)$$

where n denotes the number of steps of residual learning.

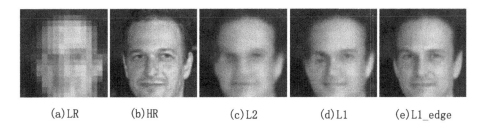

| (a) LR | (b) HR | (c) L2 | (d) L1 | (e) L1_edge |

Fig. 2. Comparisons of different losses for the super-resolution by our RBPNet. (a) original LR inputs. (b) Original HR images. (c) $L = L_p = L_1$ (d) $L = L_p = L_2$. (e) $L = L_p + L_e = L_1 + L_e$.

3.2   Edge Map Embedding Network

In order to ensure structure consistency between LR face images and HR face images, we use edge map as prior. In contrast to the other priors such as textures that are usually difficult to recover after image degradation, edges are much easier to detect in LR images. As shown in Fig. 2(c), (d) and (e), embedding edge map into the reconstruction of high-resolution face images effectively reduces distortion of super resolution results. To extract edges, we first apply an off-the-shelf edge detector (Sobel in this paper) on LR face images and HR face images respectively. As shown in Fig. 1(b), we concatenate extracted LR edge maps with LR face images.

We reconstruct HR images and edge maps simultaneously. Reconstructed high resolution feature maps include two parts. One is for HR image recovery and the other one is for edge prediction in the HR image. We extract HR edge map from HR feature maps for comparing with ground truth of original HR edge map extracted from original HR images.

$$F_{edge} = f_{edge}(F_{output}; \mu) \tag{7}$$

where μ denotes the parameter of SR edge extracted layer. Finally, we reconstruct high-resolution images with SR edge map embedding:

$$I_{SR} = f_{reconstruction}([F_{edge}, F_{output}], z) \tag{8}$$

where z denotes the parameter of reconstruction layer.

3.3   Loss Function

In this section, we describe the loss function used in our network. To illustrate simplicity, let x, y and $\hat{y}$ denote LR, restored HR images and the ground truth. The loss function consists of two parts: Pixel-wise Loss and Edge-wise loss, as shown in Eq. 9, we apply pixel-wise l_1 loss to enforce the similarity of restored HR images and the ground truth and apply edge-wise l_2 loss to enforce the similarity of restored edge map and the real one extracted from ground truth.

$$\mathcal{L} = \alpha\mathcal{L}_p + \beta\mathcal{L}_e = \frac{1}{N} \sum_{i=1}^{N} (\alpha|G_w(x_i) - y_i| + \beta\|H(G_w(x_i)) - y_i\|_2^2) \tag{9}$$

Where $G_w(x_i)$ represent the restored face images, x_i and y_i denote the LR input face image and its HR ground-truth counterpart respectively. H is Sobel operator in our experiment. N is the number of training samples in each batch. Where α, β are the trade-off weights. We set α and β to 1 empirically. Specifically, we use Adam optimization algorithm [8] to update the parameters. The initial learning rate is set to 10^{-4} and decreased by a factor of 10 every 3×10^4 iterations.

4   Experiment Result

4.1   Implementation Details

We set the convolution kernel size to 3×3, padding to 1 and stride to 1 in the feature extraction layers (followed by a convolution layer with a kernel size of 1×1), high-resolution edge map extraction layer and reconstruction layer. We set all the convolution kernel size to 12×12, padding to 2 and stride to 8 in downsampling layer to downsample feature maps by a factor of eight. We use 6×6 convolution kernel size with 2 striding and 2 padding in pyramid upsampling layer. More detailed parameter settings are shown in Table 1. All convolution layers are followed by PReLu activation function [6] (no activation function in the reconstruction layer). We set the number of channels for all intermediate convolution layers to 64. We use the method described in [6] to initialize the weight of the convolution filters. The weights of the transposed convolution filters are initialized from bilinear interpolation kernel. We use batch size of 8 with pixels of 16×16 for LR image, while HR image size is 128×128 for training. All experiments were conducted using Pytorch on NVIDIA TITAN X GPUs. The network converges after 10^5 iterations.

4.2 Datasets for Training and Testing

Our experiments are performed on CelebA datasets without augmentation, which is a large-scale face attributes dataset with about 0.2 million 128×128 face images. We randomly sampling 5000 images as verification set images, 1000 images as test set images, and other images as training set images. To produce LR images of 16×16 pixels, we use bicubic to downsample the HR image by a factor of eight.

We compare the proposed RBPNet with four state-of-the-art face super-resolution algorithms: DBPN [5], LapSRN [9], CBN [17], URDGN [14]. We evaluate the reconstructed SR images with two commonly used image quality metrics: PSNR and SSIM. All of the compared method use the same test dataset for testing. The test dataset is randomly sampling from the CelebA. DBPN [5] and LapSRN [9] were trained for super-resolving generic images, so we retrain them on celebA training set to suit better for face images.

Table 1. Network configuration

	DBPN	RBPNet-B	RBPNet-L	RBPNet-F
Input (16 × 16 pixels)				[Input, edge map]
Extract features	Conv(3-1-1,256) Conv(1-1-0,64)	Conv(3-1-1,256) Conv(1-1-0,64)	Conv(3-1-1,256) Conv(1-1-0,64)	Conv(3-1-1,256) Conv(1-1-0,64)
Up(×7)	Deconv(12-8-2,64) Conv(12-8-2,64) Deconv(12-8-2,64)	**Deconv(12-8-2,64)**	**Deconv(6-2-2,64) Deconv(6-2-2,64) Deconv(6-2-2,64)**	Deconv(6-2-2,64) Deconv(6-2-2,64) Deconv(6-2-2,64)
Down(×6)	Conv(12-8-2,64) Deconv(12-8-2,64) Conv(12-8-2,64)	**Conv(12-8-2,64)**	Conv(12-8-2,64)	Conv(12-8-2,64)
Extract edge	✗	✗	✗	**Conv(3-1-1,1)**
Reconstruction	Conv(3-1-1,3)	Conv(3-1-1,3)	Conv(3-1-1,3)	Conv(3-1-1,3)
Output (128 × 128 pixels)				[Output, edge map]

4.3 Model Analysis

Comparison with DBPN: In order to clearly explain the difference between our proposed model and DBPN, and demonstrate the validity of our model, we construct RBPNet-B as our base model. For a fair comparison, we removed (a)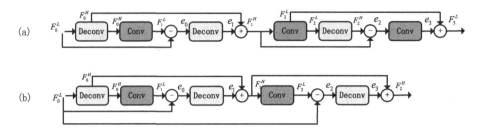

(b)

Fig. 3. Difference between DBPN and our RBPNet. (a) The up- and down-projection unit in DBPN [5] (b) The residual back-projection unit in our RBPNet

the dense connection in DBPN. The specific network configuration is shown in Table 1. Here, let $(de)conv(k - s - p, c)$ be a (de) convolution layer, where k, s, p denotes (de)convolution kernel size, (de)convolution stride and padding size respectively, c denotes the number of (de)convolution kernels. Our RBPNet-B is composed of four parts like DBPN: extract features, upsampling, downsampling, reconstruction. Note that the up- and down- sampling layers are alternated. In order to enlarge the original image, the number of upsampling layers are one more than the number of downsampling layers. Our RBPNet-B is the same as the DBPN, using 7 upsampling layers and 6 downsampling layers.

In order to make a fair comparison with DBPN, our network configuration is basically the same as DBPN. The difference is that we only use one (de)convolution layer in up- and down- sampling layers.

The main difference between RBPNet-B and DBPN is the **data flow**. As shown in Fig. 3, we use the original low-resolution feature map as the supervised information, continuously supervise the high-resolution feature map obtained by upsampling and complement the residual information onto the high-resolution feature map, which is a process from coarse to fine. However, DBPN constructs mutually-connected up- and down-sampling to imitate the process of super resolution and image degradation to learn more about degradation patterns, as the author of DBPN mentioned in the abstract.

As shown in Table 3, our RBPNet-B has about 20% fewer parameters and higher PSNR than DBPN. Through the improvement of the data flow, our RBPNet-B gains 0.15dB higher than DBPN on PSNR using fewer parameters. This evidence show that our network is more effective than DBPN to super-resolve a very low resolution face image of 16×16 pixels to its $8\times$ larger version in a coarse-to-fine manner. As shown in Fig. 4, we visualize activation maps in upsampling layers. All activation maps are sampled from the 52nd channel of the upsampling layers, whose contrast is more strongly suitable for presentation. Upsampling activation maps at different stages show that high-resolution feature maps are generated from coarse to fine, which is in line with the original intention of design.

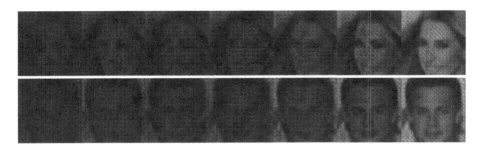

Fig. 4. Sample of activation maps from up-projection units in RBPNet-B where n = 7. Each feature has been enhanced using the same grayscale colormap for visibility.

Pyramid Upsampling: In order to further reduce the difficulty of upsampling on the network, we improve the one-step upsampling in the upsampling layers to multi-step pyramid upsampling. Here, rather than using 12×12 deconvolution kernel, we use three 6×6 deconvolution kernel to magnify low-resolution face images by 8 times through three steps. The specific network parameters are shown in the Table 1, which we call as RBPNet-L. We incorporate three non-linear rectification layers instead of a single one, which makes the decision function more discriminative. In addition, we have further reduced the parameters of the network: assuming that both the input and the output of a three-layer 6×6 deconvolution stack has C channels ($C = 64$ in our network), the stack is parameterized by $3 \cdot 6^2 \cdot C^2 = 108C^2$ weights; at the same time, a single 12×12 deconvolution layer would require $12 \cdot C^2 = 144C^2$ parameters. As shown in Table 3, pyramid upsampling achieves better results with fewer parameters than using one-step upsampling.

Table 2. Objective comparison

Methods	Bicubic	LapSRN [9]	DBPN [5]	URDGN [14]	CBN [17]	Our
PSNR	22.2025	23.9884	24.0100	23.6326	23.8004	**24.2391**
SSIM	0.5653	0.6810	0.6812	0.6710	0.6723	**0.6921**

Edge Map Embedding: We refer the network embedding the edge map as RBPNet-F. As shown in Table 1, RBPNet-F has four input channels, including three channels of input image and one low-resolution edge map. Before reconstructing the high-resolution image, we extract the edge map from the high-resolution feature maps, use the ground truth of edge map as the supervised information, and finally embed the high-resolution edge map into the reconstruction of the high-resolution image. In Fig.2, it is shown that embedding the edge map explicitly into the reconstruction of the high-resolution image can reduce the distortion.

Table 3. Quantitative analysis in ablation study.

	PSNR	SSIM	Parameters
DBPN	24.0100	0.6812	2.3×10^7
RBPNet-B	24.1621	0.6897	1.8×10^7
RBPNet-L	24.2305	0.6901	1.2×10^7
RBPNet-All	24.2421	0.6935	1.3×10^7

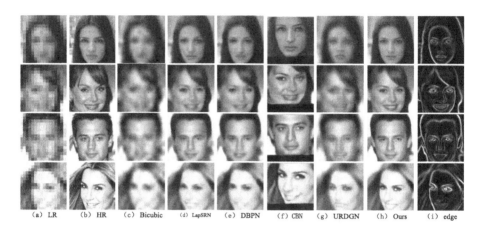

(a) LR   (b) HR   (c) Bicubic   (d) LapSRN   (e) DBPN   (f) CBN   (g) URDGN   (h) Ours   (i) edge

Fig. 5. Visual comparison for 8× face SR on celebA test sets.

4.4   Comparison with the State-of-the-arts

Table 2 shows quantitative comparisons for 8× face super-resolution, where the best algorithm has been highlighted on Table 2. From Table 2, we can find that our RBPNet(RBPNet-All) achieves better performance than the existing methods on the unified evaluation index including PSNR and SSIM.

In Fig. 5, we show visual comparisons for 8× face super-resolution on celebA test set. The reconstructed face images by CBN [17] (see Fig. 5(f)) look incompatible with other results, because the author [17] applied the affine transformation on the face images before super-resolving. As shown in Fig. 5, by progressively self-supervised residual learning, our network generates the face images that are closer to the real face images than LapSRN [9] and DBPN [5]. The proposed network explicitly learns the edge map of high-resolution face images and embed it into the reconstruction of high-resolution face images to maintain the global structure of face images. So the face images generated by our RBPNet further reduce distortion than CBN [17] and URDGN [14]. As shown in Fig. 5(i), we accurately restored the global structure of the face images.

5   Conclusion

We propose an asymptotic Residual Back-Projection Network(RBPNet) for super resolution of very low resolution face image. Unlike previous methods predicting high-resolution images by one-step learning, which tends to generate over-smoothed images, we propose to project the reconstructed high-resolution feature map back to the original low-resolution feature space to supervise reconstructed HR face images (self-supervision mechanism) and learn to map the residuals in low-resolution feature space to high-resolution feature space. We gradually approach the real high-resolution feature maps by multi-step residual learning. Extensive experiments demonstrate that our RBPNet achieves better performance than the state-of-the-art quantitatively and qualitatively.

References

1. Dahl, R., Norouzi, M., Shlens, J.: Pixel recursive super resolution. In: IEEE International Conference on Computer Vision, ICCV 2017, Venice, Italy, 22–29 October 2017, pp. 5449–5458 (2017)
2. Dai, S., Han, M., Xu, W., Wu, Y., Gong, Y.: Soft edge smoothness prior for alpha channel super resolution. In: 2007 IEEE Computer Society Conference on Computer Vision and Pattern Recognition (CVPR 2007), Minneapolis, Minnesota, USA, 18–23 June 2007 (2007)
3. Dong, C., Loy, C.C., He, K., Tang, X.: Image super-resolution using deep convolutional networks. IEEE Trans. Pattern Anal. Mach. Intell. **38**, 295–307 (2016)
4. Feng, Z.-X., Lai, J., Xie, X., Zhu, J.-Y.: Image super-resolution via a densely connected recursive network. Neurocomputing **316**, 270–276 (2018)
5. Haris, M., Shakhnarovich, G., Ukita, N.: Deep back-projection networks for super-resolution. In: 2018 IEEE Conference on Computer Vision and Pattern Recognition, CVPR 2018, Salt Lake City, UT, USA, 18–22 June 2018, pp. 1664–1673 (2018)
6. He, K., Zhang, X., Ren, S., Sun, J.: Delving deep into rectifiers: surpassing human-level performance on imagenet classification. In: 2015 IEEE International Conference on Computer Vision, ICCV 2015, Santiago, Chile, 7–13 December 2015, pp. 1026–1034 (2015)
7. Irani, M., Peleg, S.: Improving resolution by image registration. CVGIP: Graph. Model. Image Process. **53**(3), 231–239 (1991)
8. Kingma, D.P., Ba, J.: Adam: a method for stochastic optimization. CoRR, abs/1412.6980 (2014)
9. Lai, W.-S., Huang, J.-B., Ahuja, N., Yang, M.-H.: Deep Laplacian pyramid networks for fast and accurate super-resolution. In: 2017 IEEE Conference on Computer Vision and Pattern Recognition, CVPR 2017, Honolulu, HI, USA, 21–26 July 2017, pp. 5835–5843 (2017)
10. Li, S., Fan, R., Lei, G., Yue, G., Hou, C.: A two-channel convolutional neural network for image super-resolution. Neurocomputing **275**, 267–277 (2018)
11. Shi, W., et al.: Real-time single image and video super-resolution using an efficient sub-pixel convolutional neural network. In: 2016 IEEE Conference on Computer Vision and Pattern Recognition (CVPR), pp. 1874–1883. IEEE (2016)

12. Tai, Y.-W., Liu, S., Brown, M.S., Lin, S.: Super resolution using edge prior and single image detail synthesis. In: The Twenty-Third IEEE Conference on Computer Vision and Pattern Recognition, CVPR 2010, San Francisco, CA, USA, 13–18 June 2010, pp. 2400–2407 (2010)
13. Yang, C.-Y., Liu, S., Yang, M.-H.: Structured face hallucination. In: 2013 IEEE Conference on Computer Vision and Pattern Recognition, Portland, OR, USA, 23–28 June 2013, pp. 1099–1106 (2013)
14. Yu, X., Porikli, F.: Ultra-resolving face images by discriminative generative networks. In: Leibe, B., Matas, J., Sebe, N., Welling, M. (eds.) ECCV 2016. LNCS, vol. 9909, pp. 318–333. Springer, Cham (2016). https://doi.org/10.1007/978-3-319-46454-1_20
15. Xin, Y., Porikli, F.: Imagining the unimaginable faces by deconvolutional networks. IEEE Trans. Image Process. **27**(6), 2747–2761 (2018)
16. Zhao, Y., Wang, R., Jia, W., Wang, W., Gao, W.: Iterative projection reconstruction for fast and efficient image upsampling. Neurocomputing **226**, 200–211 (2017)
17. Zhu, S., Liu, S., Loy, C.C., Tang, X.: Deep cascaded Bi-network for face hallucination. In: Leibe, B., Matas, J., Sebe, N., Welling, M. (eds.) ECCV 2016. LNCS, vol. 9909, pp. 614–630. Springer, Cham (2016). https://doi.org/10.1007/978-3-319-46454-1_37

Accurate Single Image Super-Resolution Using Deep Aggregation Network

Xiaozhen Chen[1], Yao Lu[1(✉)], Xuebo Wang[1], Weiqi Li[1], and Zijian Wang[1,2]

[1] Beijing Laboratory of Intelligent Information Technology,
Beijing Institute of Technology, Beijing, China
vis_yl@bit.edu.cn
[2] China Central Television, Beijing, China

Abstract. Recent studies have shown that effectively combining rich representations of convolution neural network can significantly boost the performance of single image super resolution. Although dense skip connections can aggressively reduce depth and parameter count by feature reuse, it is a memory-intensive fusion operation. In this paper, we proposed a tree-structured deep aggregation block that spans the spectrum of layers to achieve more accuracy with less parameters and memory in super-resolution. Most of methods fuse the all features of blocks by a simple one-step aggregation. But it don't robust enough for train data with discrepancy. So we propose a recursive aggregation structure to get rich semantic information and perform better on propagation features and gradient. We performed our method on three benchmark datasets and get a comparable result in PSNR (Peak Signal-to-Noise Ratio) and SSIM (Structural SIMilarity) compared with state-of-the-art methods.

Keywords: Super-resolution · Dense skip connection · Deep aggregation · Residual unit · Recursive aggregation

1 Introduction

Single image Super-Resolution (SISR) aims to reconstruct high resolution images from low resolution images, which is used in various computer vision tasks, such as medical imaging, satellite imaging, security and surveillance [18]. Many super-resolution methods [6,7,13,15] based convolution neural network have been proposed and achieved promising results with deeper and wider network.

Kim et al. increased the network depth in VDSR [6] and DRCN [7] using gradient clipping, skip connection, or recursive-supervision to ease the difficulty of training in deep convolutional neural network. Tai et al. [13] adopted residual learning and recursive learning to deeper the network in DRRN [13]. However, compared with SRDensenet [15], these methods have relatively low results in PSNR and SSIM because the depth of their network are relatively shallow relative to SRDensenet. SRDenseNet [15] uses dense skip connection to deepen its network to improve the performance of super-resolution. But it is obviously not

T. Gedeon et al. (Eds.): ICONIP 2019, LNCS 11954, pp. 187–198, 2019.
https://doi.org/10.1007/978-3-030-36711-4_17

an efficient way to fuse all layer features by dense concatenation, which also is a memory-intensive fusion operation.

In order to make use of the features arranged from low-level to high-level in neural network more effectively, we propose a novel framework named Deep Aggregation Super-Resolution Network (DASRNet). Firstly, we use a residual unit (RU) to extract features from different layers. And then, we use a deep aggregation block (DAB), which hierarchically connect in a tree structure, to aggregation these features effectively which also can alleviate gradients vanishing with less parameters and more efficient memory. In order to rich the fusion features, we use four deep aggregation blocks of different depth. Finally, we use a recursive aggregation (RA) operation instead of a simple one-step aggregation to merge the features from the blocks. Because it fuses semantic information for reconstructing high-resolution images better.

In summary, our main contributions are three-folds:

(1) We propose a new end-to-end framework *Deep Aggregation Super-Resolution Network (DASRNet)* for reconstructing high-resolution image from low-resolution image. The network not only makes full use of the features from the low-level to high-level, but also reduce redundant information and computational consumption, and get a comparable result compared with state-of-the-art methods.
(2) We propose a unified deep aggregation block (DAB) to extends skip connections in a tree structure that cross the stages and deeply fusion than dense concatenation. And it achieve more accuracy with less parameters and memory.
(3) We propose a method to aggregate the Deep Aggregation Block (DAB) features recursively, which reduces the pressure for final feature fusion comparing with one-step aggregation through just one aggregation node.

2   Related Works

2.1   Single Image Super-Resolution Using Convolutional Neural Network

Recently, the methods of deep convolutional neural network have achieved dramatic performance against traditional methods in reconstructing high-resolution image from low-resolution image. SRCNN [3] is first method using convolutional neural network to solve the super-resolution problem, and only uses 3-layers convolution, but achieves a better performance compared with the best method at that time. VDSR [6] introduces global residual learning in deep convolutional neural network, alleviate the problem of gradient vanishing and improve the effect of super resolution compared with SRCNN [3]. DRCN [7] firstly proposed recursive learning (up to 16 recursions), and no additional parameters are added in additional convolutions. Inspired by DRCN [7] and ResNet [4], DRRN [13] deepen the network using both local and global residual learnings to achieve better results. In addition, it is difficult to obtain a larger upsampling factor

(8 times or more) using one-step upsampling in reconstructing a high-resolution image. Lai et al. [9] propose deep laplacian pyramid network to progressively reconstruct the sub-band residuals of high-resolution images meanwhile generating multi-scale predictions in one feed-forward pass through the progressive reconstruction. To further deepen the network of super resolution, Tong et al. [15] proposed SRDenseNet to fuse all of the feature maps in each dense block to alleviate the vanishing-gradient problem of very deep networks.

2.2   Recursive Aggregation

Aggregation is the combination of different layers by skip connection using 1×1 conv to implement throughout a network. Network-in-network [11] demonstrated channel mixing as a technique to fuse features, control dimensionality, and go deeper. Recursive aggregation use a deep representation backbone architecture to merge features which arrange from the lowest and the deepest. The backbone architecture is shown in Fig. 1(b). Although, SRDenseNet propose one-step aggregation also merge the different depth features, but it don't performs well on propagation features and gradient.

The recursive aggregation function using a series of layers $x_1,...,x_n$ is formulated as Eq. 1. Where A is the aggregation node.

$$A(x_1, ..., x_n) = \begin{cases} x_1 & \text{if } n = 1 \\ A(A(x_1, ..., x_{n-1}), x_n) & \text{if } n = others \end{cases} \tag{1}$$

2.3   Deep Aggregation

Aggregation architectures are most closely related to leading approaches for fusing hierarchical features which was proposed at the first time in DLA [16]. In their paper, they use the method to fuse semantic, or aggregate across channels and depths, and improves inference of what. Deep aggregation is a structure of compositional, nonlinear, and the earliest aggregated layer passed through multiple aggregations. Deep aggregation merges convolution blocks in a tree to preserve and combine feature channels. Rather than only routing intermediate aggregations further up the tree, we instead feed the output of an aggregation node back into the backbone as the input to the next sub-tree. This propagates the aggregation of all previous blocks instead of the preceding block alone to better preserve features. Avoiding to the re-learning of reductant features, deep aggregation merge the aggregation nodes of the same depth, as show in Fig. 1. The hierarchical deep aggregation function T_n, with depth n, is formulated as:

$$T_n(x) = N(R_{n-1}^n(x), R_{n-2}^n(x), ..., R_1^n, L_1^n(x), L_2^n(x)) \tag{2}$$

Where N is the aggregation node. Where B represents a convolution block. R and L are defined as:

$$L_2^n = B(L_1^n(x)), L_1^n = B(R_1^n(x)) \tag{3}$$

$$R_m^n(x) = \begin{cases} T_m(x) & \text{if } m = n - 1 \\ T_m(R_{m+1}^n(x)) & \text{if } others \end{cases} \quad (4)$$

Although, Dense skip connections share the same insight on the features reuse and reducing the channels from the precede layer passed to the next layers. Densely connected networks (DenseNet) [5] are the dominant family of architectures for semantic fusion, designed to better propagate features and losses through skip connections that concatenate all the layers in stages. But it have been incorporated to combine layers, these connections have been shallow themself.

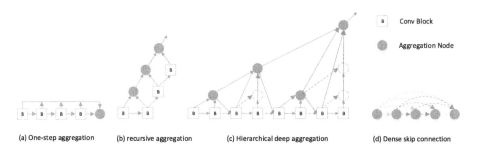

(a) One-step aggregation   (b) recursive aggregation   (c) Hierarchical deep aggregation   (d) Dense skip connection

Fig. 1. (a) shows the architecture of one-step aggregation. (b) is the iterator deep aggregation. (c) is the Hierarchical deep aggregation. The architecture is simplified from a tree, it delete a close connection resulting redundant parameters. The yellow dotted lines indicate truncated redundant connections. To maintain the integrity of the connection, some connections are added, indicated by the green arrows. (d) is a dense skip connection. (Color figure online)

3   Method

3.1   Proposed Network

For reconstructing HR images from LR images, we use an end-to-end framework Deep Aggregation Super-Resolution Networks (DASRNet) inspired by Yu et al. [16]. In their work, they aggregate rich features that span levels from low to high, scales from small to large, and resolutions from fine to coarse in visual recognition required rich representations. But in our work, we only aggregate hierarchical features from different levels to reduce the redundant information and memory consumption. As show in Fig. 1(c), the basic frame of deep aggregation block is consist of two residual units extracted different depth features and one aggregation node. In order to improve the efficiency of information passing at each layer, we use the structure of optimized tree to make skip connections efficiently instead of dense skip connections. In dense skip connections, they accept a lot of redundant information at each subsequent layer of the receiving information, and it will increase their computational and memory consumption.

After extracting the aggregation features of different depth with DAB, we progressively fuse them by recursive aggregation (RA) to exploit global residual reconstructed high-resolution images. Finally, we reconstruct the HR images by upsampling them.

Shallow feature extraction can be expressed as follows:

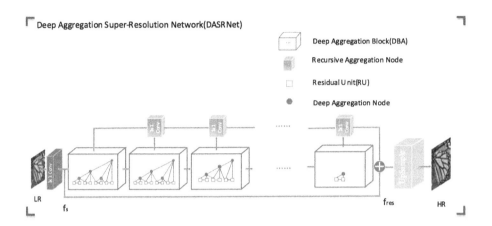

Fig. 2. Neural network structure of our method. The whole network is composed of feature extraction network, which realized by global residual learning, and upsampling layers. The feature extraction network is composed of 8 DAB, each of which deeply aggregated from a different number of RU aggregations to extracts different fine-grained features of the network and then merges them.

$$f_s = F_s(I^{LR}) \tag{5}$$

Where $F_s(.)$ is the operation of shallow feature extraction. We use $F_{ru}(.)$ to denote extracting features by RU, d denotes the dth extraction feature, the smallest unit RU of the deep aggregation layer can be expressed as:

$$f_{ru}^d = F_{ru}(f_{ru}^{d-1}) \tag{6}$$

3.2   Incorporating by Aggregation Node

Aggregation Node is the basic model to incorporate the features extracted from two adjacent residual units. On the one hand, there is lots of redundant information between adjacent layers, in which may have a lot of similar information can be removed when merging. On the other hand, in order to reduce the computational complexity of the later layer, we need to fuse the information of the current layer and transfer it back. In Fig. 1(c), the aggregation node is mainly represented as the merging, and the number is not fixed in different connection points. For example, two-node aggregation can be expressed in terms of the formula as Eq. 7. Where F_a denotes the operation of the aggregation node, and i represents the ith aggregation node.

$$f_a^i = F_a(f_{ru}^{2i-1}, f_{ru}^{2i})$$

(7)

3.3   Hierarchial Deep Aggregation

In order to preserve and fuse channel features, deep aggregation combine the block and stage of features extract from residual units. The shallow layer and deep layer together can learn more rich combination, thus across more features hierarchical structure. Instead of only routing intermediate aggregations further up the tree, we instead feed the output of an aggregation node back into the backbone as the input to the next sub-tree. This will spread all previous block polymerization, not only spread in front of the block, to better retention properties. In order to improve the efficiency, we merge the same depth of aggregation node. The aggregation features of each layer are obtained by local residual learning, as shown in Fig. 1(c).

The recursive deep aggregation function f_a^n, with depth n, is formulated as Eq. 8. And the relationship between f_{ru1}^n and f_{ru2}^n is defined as Eq. 9. When $n = 1$, the formula denotes our base model in Fig. 2(c). In our network, the max value of $n = 4$.

$$f_a^n = F_a(f_a^{n-1}, f_a^{n-2}, ..., f_{ru1}^n, f_{ru2}^n)f_{ru2}^n = F_{ru}(f_{ru1}^n)$$

(8)

$$f_{ru2}^n = F_{ru}(f_{ru1}^n)$$

(9)

3.4   Fusion of DAB Feature

We use four groups of deep aggregation block (DAB) at different depths to make full use of the aggregation features, the aggregation depths of these four DAB are gradually decreasing. And the maximum depth of recursion is four, there are two depths of each aggregation in our network. After extracting local aggregation features with a sets of different deep of aggregation block, we further propose to fuse aggregation features by a recursively method in a global way. So then the global residuals f_{res} learned through the 8 deep aggregation blocks can be expressed as:

$$f_{res} = F_A(F_A(f_{a1}^4, ..., f_{a1}^1), f_{a2}^1)$$

(10)

In the above formula, $F_A(.)$ denotes the operation of fusing the different block features. So the high-resolution image which reconstructed from the aggregation network can be expressed as Eq. 11. I^{SR} and $F_{up}(.)$ denote the reconstructed high-resolution image and the operation of upsampling respectively.

$$I^{SR} = F_{up}(f_s^{-1} + f_{res})$$

(11)

4 Experiments

4.1 Datasets and Metrics

We train our end-to-end neural network with DIV2K dataset [14] which is a publicly available benchmark dataset for super-resolution. The DIV2K dataset consists of 800 training images with the size of 3K approximately, 100 validation images, and 100 test images. During testing, the dataset Set5 [1] and Set14 [17] are often used for SR benchmark. The BSD100 [12] from Berkeley segmentation dataset 100 consisting of 100 natural images were used for testing. Our experiments is performed using three scale factor of $2\times$, $3\times$, $4\times$ between LR and the HR images. We use the unified image quality evaluation standard: peak signal-to-noise ratio (PSNR) [2] and the structural similarity (SSIM) [19] to test the resultant images. Since super-resolution was performed in luminance channel in YCbCr colour space, the PSNR and SSIM is calculated on Y-channel of images.

4.2 Implementation Details

For parameters, we extract 128 feature maps from the original high-resolution image as formulated in Eq. 5. On the recursive aggregation layer, the output and input feature maps are 128. In order to ensure that each RAL has the same input, rather than treating the first RAL individually, we perform dimensional reduction operations on the extracted shallow features as formulated in Eq. 5. In addition, we find that the extracted shallow features as many as possible is conducive to the reconstruction of low-resolution images. In our research, it is reflected in the fact that if the shallow features extracted are 128, the PSNR of the reconstructed high-resolution image is 0.8 dB less than that of 256. Finally, our upsampling network is composed of deconvolution network. In particular, when the magnification factor is 4, we use two deconvolution with the parameters of $kernel size = 4$, $stride = 2$, $padding = 1$, and a 1×1 conv between the two deconvolution.

For training, we randomly crop sub-image with size of 164×164 from HR image space, downsample all the sub-images by bicubic interpolation with the same as SRCNN as our inputs. We augment the training data with random horizontal flips and 90 rotations. Each image has been transformed into YCbCr space and only the Y-channel was used for training. We train our model with ADAM optimizer [8] by setting $\beta = (0.9, 0.999)$, and $e = 10^{-8}$, weight decay $= 10^{-4}$. We set minibatch size as 16. The learning rate was initially set to 10^{-4} and decreased by a factor of 10 after 3×10^5 iterations. We implemented the proposed networks with Pytorch framework and trained them using NVIDIA Titan x GPUs. It takes 4 days to train our model.

Table 1. The $4\times$ PSNR of the network structure of different aggregation depth on Set5 and Set14. L and R denote the number of the DAB and the deepth of the aggregation respectively. "*in*" represents that the method of sorting by aggregation depth, and the meaning of "*de*" is the opposite of "*in*". "64" is used to mark the DAB feature maps of input and output and marked as feat. "*single*" shows that one DAB at each aggregation depth in the overall network structure.

Name	DASR_8L_1R	DASR_4L_2R	DASR_in_single	DASR_64	DASR_de_single	DASR
Set5	31.78	31.84	32.03	32.14	32.23	32.31
Set14	28.18	28.26	28.40	28.53	28.63	28.70

4.3   Ablation Investigation

We perform experiment on the design of network structures with different depth aggregation block and get the results in the Table 1 which arranged from left to right as the PSNR values increase. Compared the value of DASR_8L_1R with DASR_4L_2R, we found that the deep of aggregation need moderation. For deep convolutional network, if there is no skip connection from the deep layer to the shallow layer, the gradient will gradually decrease in the backward and forward return transmission, leading to the problem of gradient vanishing in the process of gradient return transmission. On other hands, if the aggregation depth is increased, the network parameters and the computational cost will be increased, so that the network cannot be extended. Besides, In order to extract features from different recursion depths, we used four different aggregation depths in the network structure. From the PSNR value of DASR_in_single and DASR_de_single, we conclude that deep aggregation is necessary for shallow features. In our network, the feat is 128, but we experiment on $feat = 64$, and get the weak result. Finally, for increasing the deep of our network, each layer with a different depth of aggregation is followed by an identical layer. This increases the PSNR value a little, but doubles the amount of computation and memory consumption. Considering both the performance and number of parameters, we choose DASR (de $= 1$, feat $= 128$, single $= 0$, L $= 8$) as our best model.

4.4   Comparison

We now provide quantitative and qualitative comparisons. For fair comparison, we also construct a DASR_8L_8C(L $= 8$, C $=$ conv) structure, which has the same depth as SRDenseNet, but fewer parameters. In Table 2, the difference between DASR_8L_8C and SRDenseNet in the commonly used evaluation PSNR and SSIM is about 0.3% points. Besides, the parameter number of the SRDenseNet structure is about 77 millions which is twice as much as DASR_8L_8C skipped connections selectively instead of dense connections. DASR_de_single not only

Table 2. Benchmark results with bicubic degradation model. Average PSNR/SSIM values for scaling factor 2, 3, and 4. The best result is red. The bold is our result.

Dataset	Set5			Set14			BSD100		
Scale	X2	X3	X4	X2	X3	X4	X2	X3	X4
Bicubic	33.66/0.9299	30.39/0.8682	28.42/0.8104	30.24/0.8688	27.55/0.7742	26.00/0.7027	29.56/0.8431	27.21/0.7385	25.96/0.6675
SRCNN	36.66/0.9542	32.75/0.9090	30.48/0.8628	32.45/0.9067	29.30/0.8215	27.50/0.7513	31.36/0.8879	28.41/0.7863	26.90/0.7107
LapSRN	37.52/0.9591	33.82/0.9227	31.54/0.8855	33.08/0.9133	29.79/0.8320	28.19/0.7720	31.80/0.8950	28.82/0.7973	27.32/0.7280
VDSR	37.53/0.9587	33.60/0.9213	31.35/0.8838	33.03/0.9124	29.77/0.8314	28.01/0.7674	31.90/0/8960	28.82/0.7976	27.29/0.7251
DRCN	37.63/0.9588	33.82/0.9226	31.53/0.8854	33.04/0.9118	29.76/0.8311	28.02/0.7670	31.85/0.8942	28.80/0.7963	27.23/0.7233
DRRN	37.74/0.9591	34.03/0.9244	31.68/0.8888	33.23/0.9136	29.96/0.8349	28.21/0.7721	32.05/0.9730	28.95/0.8004	27.38/0.7284
SRDenseNet	-/-	-/-	32.02/0.8934	-/-	-/-	28.50/0.7782	-/-	-/-	27.53/0.7738
DASR_8L_8C	37.91/0.9604	32.21/0.9300	31.85/0.8894	33.39/0.9143	30.11/0.8365	28.38/0.7833	32.21/0.9802	29.10/0.8120	27.43/0.7653
DASR_de_single	38.00/0.9578	34.46/0.9230	32.23/0.8956	33.89/0.9202	30.35/0.8433	28.71/0.7820	32.12/0.8990	29.02/0.8057	27.72/0.7794
DASR	**38.13/0.9600**	**34.59/0.9250**	**32.36/0.8970**	**33.89/0.9211**	**30.50/0.8459**	**28.72/0.7832**	**32.30/0.9000**	**29.25/0.8079**	**27.73/0.7404**
EDSR [10]	38.20/0.9606	34.76/0.9290	32.62/0.8984	34.02/0.9204	30.66/0.8481	28.94/0.7901	32.37/0.9018	29.32/0.8104	27.79/0.7437

has fewer layers than SRDenseNet, but also has an increase of 0.21 dB and 0.0022 over 4× on PSNR and SSIM. DRRN is the first deep recursive network proposed, and explores the depth of recursion (expressed as U in their pater) and the number of recursion units (expressed as B in their paper). They finally found the DRRN_B1U9 [13] is best model for solving the problem of super-resolution. At the same time, when they increase the recursion depth to 25(DRRN_B1U25), the result of DRRN_B1U25 on PSNR and SSIM is almost the same as DRRN_B1U9 [13]. Therefore, as the aggregation depth increases, the performance of the model will gradually reach the bottleneck layer. In our network model, the recursion depth is no more than 4 layers, but it perform better than DRRN in PSNR and SSIM. This indicates that the aggregation network improves the performance of deep aggregation network to some extent. The Table 3 shows that the number of layers in the network structure of various super-resolution solutions and their performance on upsampling 4× on the benchmark of Set5. In Fig. 3, we show visual comparisons for 4× image super-resolution on BSD100 test set. The reconstructed images by SRCNN [3] look incompatible with other results. As shown in Fig. 3, by the method of aggregation, our network generates the images that are closer to the real images than the results from other networks which are similar to our network. Although, our method can't reach the best of EDSR, but it proved feasible and effective on the task of single image super-resolution. Above all, our final model DASRNets is comparable in PSNR evaluation.

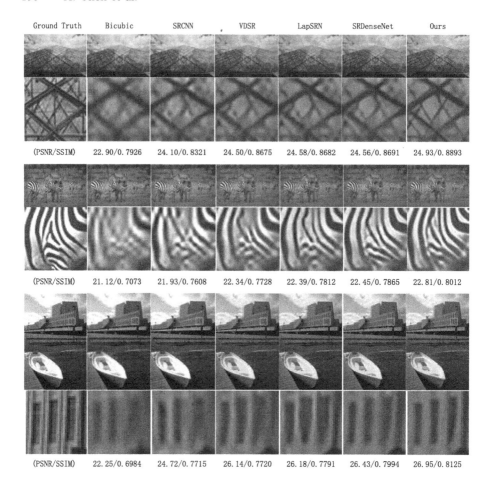

Fig. 3. Super-resolution results for "img045" (top figure), "img052" (middle figure) and "img092" (bottom figure) from BSD100 with an upscaling factor of 4. PSNR and SSIM values are shown on the bottom of each sub-figure.

Table 3. The number of layers, the number of parameters and the PSNR values by upsampling $4\times$ on the Set5 dataset.

Name	SRCNN	DRCN	VDSR	DRRN	SRDenseNet	DASR_8L_8C	DASR_de_single	DASR
Layer	3	16	20	22	66	42	66	82
Parameters	57K	1.77M	665K	297K	7.38M	5.10M	5.85M	**6.12M**
Set5_x4	30.48	31.53	31.35	31.68	32.02	31.85	32.23	**32.31**

5   Conclusion

In this paper, we propose DASRNet for single image super-resolution, where deep aggregation block (DAB)serves as the basic build module. In our network, We use the layers with different depths to aggregate features extracted from the smallest unit (RU), and progressively fuse them to learn the residual features between the HR and LR feature space. By fully using local and global features, our DASRNet leads to a aggregation feature fusion and deep supervision. Extensive benchmark experiments and analysis show that DASRNet is a deep, concise, and comparable model for SISR.

References

1. Bevilacqua, M., Roumy, A., Guillemot, C., Alberi-Morel, M.-L.: Low-complexity single-image super-resolution based on nonnegative neighbor embedding. In: British Machine Vision Conference, BMVC 2012, Surrey, UK, 3–7 September 2012, pp. 1–10 (2012)
2. Burnett, I.S. (ed.): Fourth International Workshop on Quality of Multimedia Experience, QoMEX 2012, Melbourne, Australia, 5–7 July 2012. IEEE (2012)
3. Dong, C., Loy, C.C., He, K., Tang, X.: Learning a deep convolutional network for image super-resolution. In: Fleet, D., Pajdla, T., Schiele, B., Tuytelaars, T. (eds.) ECCV 2014. LNCS, vol. 8692, pp. 184–199. Springer, Cham (2014). https://doi.org/10.1007/978-3-319-10593-2_13
4. He, K., Zhang, X., Ren, S., Sun, J.: Deep residual learning for image recognition. CoRR, abs/1512.03385 (2015)
5. Huang, G., Liu, Z., Van Der Maaten, L., Weinberger, K.Q.: Densely connected convolutional networks. In: Computer Vision and Pattern Recognition, pp. 2261–2269 (2017)
6. Kim, J., Kwon Lee, J., Mu Lee, K.: Accurate image super-resolution using very deep convolutional networks. In: 2016 IEEE Conference on Computer Vision and Pattern Recognition, CVPR 2016, Las Vegas, NV, USA, 27–30 June 2016, pp. 1646–1654 (2016)
7. Kim, J., Kwon Lee, J., Mu Lee, K.: Deeply-recursive convolutional network for image super-resolution. In: 2016 IEEE Conference on Computer Vision and Pattern Recognition, CVPR 2016, Las Vegas, NV, USA, 27–30 June 2016, pp. 1637–1645 (2016)
8. Kingma, D.P., Ba, J.: Adam: a method for stochastic optimization. In: 3rd International Conference on Learning Representations, ICLR 2015, San Diego, CA, USA, 7–9 May 2015, Conference Track Proceedings (2015)
9. Lai, W.-S., Huang, J.-B., Ahuja, N., Yang, M.-H.: Deep Laplacian pyramid networks for fast and accurate super-resolution. CoRR, abs/1704.03915 (2017)
10. Lim, B., Son, S., Kim, H., Nah, S., Mu Lee, K.: Enhanced deep residual networks for single image super-resolution. In: 2017 IEEE Conference on Computer Vision and Pattern Recognition Workshops, CVPR Workshops 2017, Honolulu, HI, USA, 21–26 July 2017, pp. 1132–1140 (2017)
11. Lin, M., Chen, Q., Yan, S.: Network in network. In: International Conference on Learning Representations (2014)
12. Martin, D.R., Fowlkes, C.C., Tal, D., Malik, J.: A database of human segmented natural images and its application to evaluating segmentation algorithms and measuring ecological statistics. In: ICCV, pp. 416–425 (2001)
13. Tai, Y., Yang, J., Liu, X.: Image super-resolution via deep recursive residual network. In: 2017 IEEE Conference on Computer Vision and Pattern Recognition, CVPR 2017, Honolulu, HI, USA, 21–26 July 2017, pp. 2790–2798 (2017)

14. Timofte, R., Agustsson, E., Van Gool, L., Yang, M.-H., et al.: NTIRE 2017 challenge on single image super-resolution: methods and results. In: 2017 IEEE Conference on Computer Vision and Pattern Recognition Workshops, CVPR Workshops 2017, Honolulu, HI, USA, 21–26 July 2017, pp. 1110–1121 (2017)

15. Tong, T., Li, G., Liu, X., Gao, Q.: Image super-resolution using dense skip connections, pp. 4809–4817 (2017)

16. Yu, F., Wang, D., Darrell, T.: Deep layer aggregation. CoRR, abs/1707.06484 (2017)

17. Zeyde, R., Elad, M., Protter, M.: On single image scale-up using sparse-representations. In: Boissonnat, J.-D., Chenin, P., Cohen, A., Gout, C., Lyche, T., Mazure, M.-L., Schumaker, L. (eds.) Curves and Surfaces 2010. LNCS, vol. 6920, pp. 711–730. Springer, Heidelberg (2012). https://doi.org/10.1007/978-3-642-27413-8_47

18. Zhang, L., Zhang, H., Shen, H., Li, P.: A super-resolution reconstruction algorithm for surveillance images. Sig. Process. **90**(3), 848–859 (2010)

19. Zhao, H., Gallo, O., Frosio, I., Kautz, J.: Loss functions for neural networks for image processing. CoRR, abs/1511.08861 (2015)

Reinforcing LiDAR-Based 3D Object Detection with RGB and 3D Information

Wenjian Liu and Yue Zhou[✉]

School of Electronic Information and Electrical Engineering,
Shanghai Jiao Tong University, Shanghai 200240, China
{liuwenjian,zhouyue}@sjtu.edu.cn

Abstract. LiDAR-based 3D object detection is efficient for autonomous driving because high accuracy LiDAR information is extremely useful for 3D proposals generation and 3D boxes regression. However, some background and foreground objects may have similar appearances in point clouds. Therefore the accuracy of LiDAR-based 3D object detection is hard to be improved. In this paper, we propose a three-stage 3D object detection method called RGB3D to reinforce LiDAR-based 3D object detection by using an RGB-D classifier with a 3D classifier in parallel. We also apply proper training method to improve the performance of the added classifiers. The 3D classifier is trained by using higher IoU threshold with refined 3D information, and the RGB-D classifier is trained with resized 2D RoIs projected from refined 3D boxes. Extensive experiments are conducted on the KITTI object detection benchmark. The results show that the proposed method is effective.

Keywords: 3D object detection · Autonomous driving · Convolutional neural networks · Computer vision

1 Introduction

Autonomous driving is highly dependent on reliable and robust environment perception, and object detection is one of the fundamental requirements for autonomous driving to obtain environment information. While deep learning has achieved remarkable progress on 2D object detection task to obtain categories, pixel locations and pixel sizes of objects in an image, the detected 2D bounding boxes without 3D environment information are not reliable for autonomous driving. In contrast, 3D object detection is a task used to determine the categories, locations, sizes and orientations of targets in a 3D scene from images and point clouds, etc. 3D object detection helps to obtain more geometry information of interested objects than 2D object detection. Therefore 3D object detection becomes a crucial requirement for autonomous driving. Nevertheless, the performance of 3D object detection is still need to be improved for application. Benefit from the high accuracy of LiDAR 3D point clouds, recent state-of-the-art 3D object detection systems show that algorithms using raw point cloud information

© Springer Nature Switzerland AG 2019
T. Gedeon et al. (Eds.): ICONIP 2019, LNCS 11954, pp. 199–209, 2019.
https://doi.org/10.1007/978-3-030-36711-4_18

or LiDAR information [7,17,22,23] outperform algorithms using only monocular or stereo information [8,14,20] with remarkable margins in KITTI 3D object detection benchmark [3]. Despite of the differences with feature extraction methods among point clouds, images and other information, the most pipelines of recent state-of-the-art methods such as [2,6,17] consist of region proposal stage and refine stage. These methods generate 3D proposals in the first stage and refines the proposals in the second stage. The classifier in the second stage predict the classes of objects from 3D proposals generated by the network in the first stage without the information of the regressed 3D boxes after the second stage. Therefore an added classifier as the third stage to classify the refined 3D bounding boxes from the second stage can improve the performance of 3D objective detection. Another problem about LiDAR-based 3D object detection is that there are a number of background objects are predicted as foreground objects with high confidence by the second stage because point clouds of background and foreground objects may have similar appearance or space distribution. It is hard for the LiDAR-based network to be trained for their separation. Therefore image classifier is qualified to solve the problem because of their obvious differences in RGB images, as shown in Fig. 1.

In this paper, we propose a three stage 3D object detection method called RGB3D to reinforce the performance of two-stage LiDAR-based 3D object detection by extending the second stage with an RGB-D image classifier and an accurate 3D classifier. We use the three-stage framework to make the detection results classified with high quality. Our contributions are summarized as below:

1. We propose a low coupling framework to combine 2D image and 3D point cloud information.
2. We combine the confidence predictor in two-stage LiDAR-based 3D detector with an accurate classify stage.
3. We apply efficient training methods for the proposed networks.

2   Related Work

In this part, we will briefly review previous works on 3D object detection. We organize our reviews into three categories according to the form of input data.

2.1   3D Object Detection from Raw Point Clouds

Recent 3D object detection from raw point clouds focuses on extracting point-wise features or associate point-wise features to some voxel-level features to generate 3D proposals. A large number of them are based on LiDAR data. VoxelNet [23] groups point-wise features into voxels, then uses 3D convolution to process voxel-wise features. SECOND [22] applies sparse convolution to increase the speed of processing voxel-wise features. PointPillars [7] provides a method for encoding features on pillars of the point cloud to predict 3D boxes. In two stage method, a refine stage is implied to obtain accurate 3D boxes. [17] generates 3D

Fig. 1. LiDAR-based 3D detection results with high confidence scores (before Non-Maximum Suppression) are projected to this front-view image. In this figure, if our RGB-D classification results of these projected bounding boxes are with high confidence scores as well, the color of the boxes is green, else the color of the corresponding boxes changes to red. In this figure, our RGB-D classifier helps LiDAR-based 3D object detector to distinguish the misclassified background. (Color figure online)

proposals from segmented foreground point clouds, then extracts semantic and local spatial features from sampled point cloud for refining the 3D proposals. These methods have achieved high performance and can be easily modified or associated with other methods.

2.2   3D Object Detection from Images

To estimate positions and orientations in 3D coordinate system from monocular images or stereo images without depth information is a tough challenge. [8] proposes a method to study constraints from semantic and geometry information in stereo images, and the method achieves remarkable performance. [14] combines a novel instance depth estimation method among 2D detection, 3D localization and local corner regression as four sub-networks to estimate 3D boxes from monocular images. [20] introduces a novel pipeline to generate 3D point clouds from monocular or stereo images and then applies LiDAR-based 3D detection methods to regress 3D boxes, which closes the gap in 3D detection between image-based methods and LiDAR-based methods.

2.3   3D Object Detection from Point Clouds with Images

Benefit from reliable precision on mature 2D object detection method [1,4,9, 15,16] and the progress of point set deep learning [5,12,13], recent 3D detection methods from point clouds with 2D detectors have achieved remarkable progress. F-PointNet [11] first limits down the local process region of point clouds from bounding boxes detected by 2D detector and then uses methods in PointNet [12] to process points in accurate local coordinates. RoarNet [18] improves the 2D detector and applies geometric constrain and monocular pose estimation to regress 3D boxes. In this work, a two-stage refine network is implemented and the refine network sharply improves mAP performance. Frustum ConvNet [21] proposes a novel method aggregates point-wise features as frustum-level features then uses FCN [10] to estimate 3D boxes of objects. These methods associate 2D detection methods with point-wise features for 3D object detection and achieved extremely high mAP on KITTI [3] 3D object detection benchmark.

3 Our Proposed Approach

In this section, we present the architecture of our proposed method, then we describe the relevant details. We assume that a front view RGB image captured by a camera is available accompanying the LiDAR 3D point cloud, and the corresponding parameters of the camera and the LiDAR are known.

3.1 Network Architecture

Our framework RGB3D is a three-stage 3D object detection method shown in Fig. 2. We follow the architecture described in [17] to generate proposals in the first stage and refine the proposals in the second stage. In our third stage, we use the regressed 3D boxes to train a 3D classifier and an RGB-D classifier. The 3D classifier is the same as the second stage described in [17] but the regression head is removed. The 3D classifier is trained with regressed proposals from the second stage at higher IoU threshold. The regressed 3D bounding boxes in the second stage are projected to front view image to generate 2D RoIs. The RGB-D classifier is trained by using these 2D RoIs with the depths of their corresponding 3D boxes, and the RGB-D classifier is used to help the 3D classifier to exclude misclassification such as background, which is hard to be classified with point cloud information. In the inference stage, the output of each classifier will be added before normalization. The final normalized classification scores of 3D boxes can be formulated as below:

$$
\begin{aligned}
score(x, I) &= sigmoid(pred(x) + cls(x, I)) \\
cls(x, I) &= cls_{3D}(reg(x)) + cls_{RGB-D}(proj(reg(x), I), depth(reg(x)))
\end{aligned}
\tag{1}
$$

where $score$ outputs the final normalized classification scores of the 3D Boxes, x indicates 3D RoIs generated by the first stage, I indicates the corresponding front view image, $pred$ is the classifier in the second stage, cls is the classifier in the third stage, reg is the regressor in the second stage, cls_{3D} is the 3D classifier in the third stage, cls_{RGB-D} is the RGB-D classifier in the third stage, $proj$ calculates projected 2D boxes and generates resized 2D RoIs, $depth$ calculates the depths of refined 3D boxes.

3.2 Point Cloud Reclassification Network

The point cloud based classifier can outperform 2D classifier for occluded objects and dark lighting objects, and the performance of the second-stage classifier

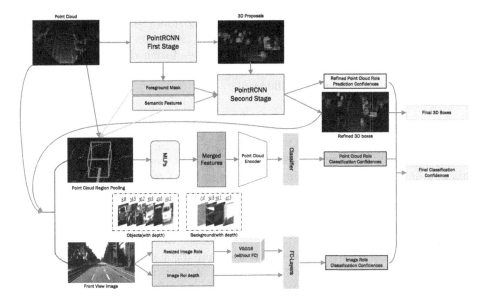

Fig. 2. The 3-stage RGB3D architecture for 3D object detection.

can be improved by using a resampling mechanism described in [1]. Existing two-stage 3D object detection methods generate proposals firstly and further regress the proposals, at the same time their classification heads predict the classes from extracted features of proposals. However the classification heads cannot meet the regressed boxes. Therefore we extend the two-stage LiDAR based 3D object detector PointRCNN [17] with the more accurate classifier by using resampling mechanism. After proposals of point clouds are obtained from the first stage, the proposals are labeled according to their IoU with ground truth bounding boxes. The second stage of PointRCNN [17] is trained from 0.6 IoU point clouds. The distribution of regressed 3D boxes is more close to ground truth, which means that there are enough acceptable positive samples to train a more accurate classifier and the regression head in the third stage need to be removed. Experiments in Table 4 show that the model of 3D classifier trained with 0.7 IoU in the third stage can improve the performance of the whole framework than the model trained with 0.6 IoU in the second stage.

3.3   RGB-D Classifier

Point cloud based methods can regress the 3D box accurately but may classify regressed false 3D boxes as positive or ignore true 3D boxes because of the limited information of point clouds, while the object is easy to classify in images. Inspired by [11] and [1], we propose an RGB-D classifier to solve the stated problems. The RGB-D classifier is aimed at utilizing 2D image information of the objects to find out the hard to be classified proposals in point clouds, which are obviously in a front view image with depth information of 3D boxes. The depth information is used because the resized 2D RoIs are different according to their depth in an image. The RGB-D classifier uses a changed VGG16-D [19] with batch normalization to classify the confidence of refined 3D proposals. The RGB-D classifier uses 2D RoIs with the depths of their corresponding 3D boxes to evaluate their classification confidences.

4   Experiment

In this paper, all experiments use the KITTI [3] object detection benchmark dataset which contains 7481 training samples and 7518 testing samples to detect cars, pedestrians and cyclists. We follow the train/val split mentioned in [2] to divide the training samples into *train* split (3712 samples) and *val* split (3769 samples). The proposed network is trained with the *train* split and evaluated with the *val* split. In this section, we first introduce the implementation details of the proposed network. Then we perform a comparison with other 3D detection methods in KITTI [3] benchmark *val* split and *test* set by comparing validation results with labels of *val* split and submitting test results to official test server, and test result of RGB3D will be published on the server. Finally, we analyze the effectiveness of each module by conducting extensive ablation studies. All the experiments are focused on car class.

4.1   Implementation Details

The 3D classifier in the third stage is trained from a pretrained second stage model. The training data consists of proposals generated by the first stage and refined from the regressor in the second stage. The labels of these proposals depend on their IoU with ground truth 3D bounding boxes. The foreground IoU threshold for positive label is set to 0.7, while the second stage is trained with foreground IoU threshold as 0.6. To train the 3D classifier, only parameters of the 3D classification head in the third stage are updated during training, and other parameters will not change. We follow the training parameters described in [17], but learning rate is set to 0.0002, batch size is 2, and we use binary cross-entropy loss to train the network for 35 epochs. We finally select the model saved at the 19th epoch to evaluate the performance of the proposed method.

The RGB-D classifier uses a changed VGG16-D [19] with batch normalization to classify the confidence of refined 3D proposals. To train the classifier, the fixed quantity proposals generated by the first stage in each point cloud of a scene are projected to the 2D image of the scene as 2D rectangle RoIs, these 2D RoIs are labeled according to their 3D IoU with ground truth 3D boxes. The 3D boxes that does not intersect with ground truth 3D boxes are regarded as background boxes, their 2D RoIs are labeled as zero. For those 3D boxes intersected with ground truth boxes, the foreground threshold is set to 0.45 and foreground 3D boxes are labeled as 1. Ground truth 3D boxes with label 1 are added to them by randomly replacing the same number proposals. 3D boxes that intersects with 3D ground truth but have low IoU are changed to background 3D boxes with label 0 before projection. 2D RoIs are resized as $112*112*3$ images. If there is no background in a scene, or the projected 2D RoI cannot be resized, their resized RoIs will be random generated $112*112*3$ images with label 0. All the resized RoIs in an image are regarded as a batch to train the classifier, the batch size is number of proposals in a scene, which is set to 64. Batch size of scenes (point cloud with a front view image) is set to 1. The extracted features of resized RoIs will concate with the depth of their 3D boxes. The input size of fully connected layers (FC-layers) is changed to match the features. We use a pretrained VGG16 model without parameters of FC-layers. The start learning rate is set to 0.0002. The network is trained by Adam optimizer and binary cross-entropy loss for 40 epochs, and we select the model saved at the 21th epoch. Figure 3 shows the corresponding data in training images preparation pipeline.

3D Proposals

2D ROIs

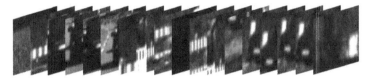

Resized 2D ROIs

Fig. 3. Training data generation for the RGB-D classifier, 2D boxes in red are background, 2D boxes in green are foreground, resized RoIs determined by pink 2D boxes will be changed. (Color figure online)

4.2 3D Object Detection on KITTI

In this part, we conduct experiments on KITTI [3] object detection *val* split and test set as mentioned above. 3D object detection, 2D object detection and BEV detection are evaluated by average precision (AP), orientation estimation is evaluated by average orientation similarity (AOS) [3].

Evaluation Using the KITTI Validation Split. We compare the proposed method with the baseline 3D object detection method [17] on KITTI [3] *val* split, results of AP are demonstrated in Table 1, higher is better. The results show that the proposed method is effective as expected.

Table 1. 3D and 2D object detection results on KITTI *val* split.

Method	3D object detection			2D object detection		
	Easy	Moderate	Hard	Easy	Moderate	Hard
PointRCNN (baseline) [17]	89.1975	78.8519	77.9147	96.9105	89.5363	88.7479
Ours	89.7637	79.5088	78.5762	98.5520	90.0777	89.5431

Evaluation Using the KITTI Test Set. We submit the prediction result of test set by the proposed method to KITTI [3] official test server and compare the test result with other 3D object detection methods. Results are demonstrated in Tables 2 and 3. Results of 3D and 2D object detection are demonstrated in Table 2. Results of orientation estimation [3] and bird's eye view (BEV) detection are demonstrated in Table 3. 3D object detection, 2D object detection and BEV detection are evaluated by average precision (AP), orientation estimation is evaluated by average orientation similarity (AOS) [3]. For each metric, higher result is better, and the best result is in red, the second best result is in blue. By only using the 3D classifier (no images), the 3D object detection performance especially for moderate and hard objects are competitive. After adding RGB-D classifier, 3D object detection AP for easy objects with slight occlusion and clustering are improved, and the final results for other metrics are improved obviously. Results of orientation estimation and bird's eye view detection show that our method has accurate 3D position and orientation values. The results show that our proposed method RGB3D improves the 3D detection precision effectively and has competitive performance compared with other methods. More details can be found on the KITTI 3D Object Detection Benchmark Leader Board [3]: http://www.cvlibs.net/datasets/kitti/eval_object.php? obj_benchmark=3d.

Table 2. 3D and 2D object detection results on KITTI *test* set.

Method	Modality	3D object detection			2D object detection		
		Easy	Moderate	Hard	Easy	Moderate	Hard
F-PointNet [11]	LiDAR+RGB	81.20	70.39	62.19	90.78	90.00	80.80
F-ConvNet [21]	LiDAR+RGB	85.88	76.51	68.08	90.44	89.79	80.66
AVOD-FPN [6]	LiDAR+RGB	81.94	71.88	66.38	89.99	87.44	80.05
PointPillars [7]	LiDAR	79.05	74.99	68.30	90.33	89.22	87.04
SECOND [22]	LiDAR	83.13	73.66	66.20	90.40	88.40	80.21
PointRCNN [17]	LiDAR	85.94	75.76	68.32	90.74	89.32	85.73
Ours (no images)	LiDAR	85.58	76.00	68.52	90.72	89.59	88.09
Ours	LiDAR+RGB	85.72	75.92	68.29	90.75	89.71	88.21

Table 3. Orientation estimation and BEV detection results on KITTI *test* set.

Method	Modality	Orientation estimation			Bird's eye view detection		
		Easy	Moderate	Hard	Easy	Moderate	Hard
F-PointNet [11]	LiDAR+RGB	–	–	–	88.70	84.00	75.33
F-ConvNet [21]	LiDAR+RGB	90.41	89.60	80.39	89.69	83.08	74.56
AVOD-FPN [6]	LiDAR+RGB	89.95	87.13	79.74	88.53	83.79	77.90
PointPillars [7]	LiDAR	90.19	88.76	86.38	88.35	86.10	79.83
SECOND [22]	LiDAR	87.84	81.31	71.95	88.07	79.37	77.95
PointRCNN [17]	LiDAR	90.73	89.22	85.53	89.47	85.68	79.10
Ours (no images)	LiDAR	90.71	89.49	87.88	89.68	86.80	79.37
Ours	LiDAR+RGB	90.74	89.60	87.98	89.71	86.98	79.35

4.3   Ablation Studies

To explore the effect of our proposed 3D object detection methods, we do ablation studies on KITTI [3] *val* split.

Average Precision on KITTI Validation Split. The results of average precision are demonstrated in Table 4. L denotes LiDAR-based 3D object Detector, I denotes added image (with depth) classifier. P denotes added point cloud classifier using our training methods. P' denotes added point cloud classifier simply copy stage 2 parameters without training. The results show that the adoption of the point cloud classifier and the RGB-D classifier in the third stage could improve the 3D detection precision obviously.

Table 4. 3D and 2D object detection results on KITTI *val* split.

Method	3D object detection			2D object detection		
	Easy	Moderate	Hard	Easy	Moderate	Hard
L	89.1975	78.8519	77.9147	96.9105	89.5363	88.7479
L+P	89.6146	79.2477	78.3812	98.2835	89.7282	89.2224
L+P'	89.4974	79.0964	78.1960	98.2649	89.7614	89.0974
L+I	89.6127	79.3134	78.2544	98.5196	90.0693	89.4110
L+P+I	89.7637	79.5088	78.5762	98.5520	90.0777	89.5431

Time Performance. To analyze the consumption of added classifiers, we conduct experiments to compare the GPU consumption and inference speed of proposed parts. All the results are tested by using PyTorch on an Intel E5-2620 v4 CPU with an NVIDIA TITAN Xp, and inference batch size is set to 1. We calculate the GPU memory consumption and inference speed. The metric of inference speed is Hz, which means the number of scenes (A scene includes an

Table 5. Time performance on KITTI *val* split

Method	GPU memory usage	Speed	AP (Moderate)
L	1997 MB	6.48 Hz	78.8519
L+P	2005 MB	4.15 Hz	79.2477
L+I	4597 MB	3.25 Hz	79.3134
L+P+I	4612 MB	2.55 Hz	79.5088

Fig. 4. Final results of our proposed model on the KITTI *test* set. The upper part of each sample is the front view image with projected 3D bounding boxes and the lower part of each sample is point cloud with 3D bounding boxes.

image and the corresponding point cloud) are calculated in a second. The results are demonstrated in Table 5. The names of methods have the same meaning as that in Table 4. Results show that the consumption is increased by adding new stage for better precision and the result is acceptable.

5   Conclusion

In this paper, we propose a low coupling three-stage 3D object detection framework. The proposed framework can be easily changed to combine two-stage LiDAR-based 3D detection methods and image classification methods to receive better performance. We also propose the method to train the third stage to receive improved performance with pretrained models. Figure 4 shows some results of our proposed model on the KITTI [3] test set. Results show the performance of our proposed method is effective.

Acknowledgment. This work is supported by Shanghai Automotive Industry Sci-Tech Development Foundation (No. 1823).

References

1. Cai, Z., Vasconcelos, N.: Cascade R-CNN: delving into high quality object detection. In: CVPR (2018)
2. Chen, X., Ma, H., Wan, J., Li, B., Xia, T.: Multi-view 3D object detection network for autonomous driving. In: IEEE Conference on Computer Vision & Pattern Recognition (2017)

3. Geiger, A., Lenz, P., Urtasun, R.: Are we ready for autonomous driving? The KITTI vision benchmark suite. In: Conference on Computer Vision and Pattern Recognition (CVPR) (2012)
4. He, K., Gkioxari, G., Dollar, P., Girshick, R.: Mask R-CNN. IEEE Trans. Pattern Anal. Mach. Intell. (2017)
5. Jiang, M., Wu, Y., Zhao, T., Zhao, Z., Lu, C.: PointSIFT: a sift-like network module for 3D point cloud semantic segmentation (2018)
6. Ku, J., Mozifian, M., Lee, J., Harakeh, A., Waslander, S.: Joint 3D proposal generation and object detection from view aggregation. In: IROS (2018)
7. Lang, A.H., Vora, S., Caesar, H., Zhou, L., Yang, J., Beijbom, O.: PointPillars: fast encoders for object detection from point clouds. In: CVPR (2019)
8. Li, P., Chen, X., Shen, S.: Stereo R-CNN based 3D object detection for autonomous driving. In: CVPR (2019)
9. Liu, W., et al.: SSD: single shot multibox detector. In: Leibe, B., Matas, J., Sebe, N., Welling, M. (eds.) ECCV 2016. LNCS, vol. 9905, pp. 21–37. Springer, Cham (2016). https://doi.org/10.1007/978-3-319-46448-0_2
10. Long, J., Shelhamer, E., Darrell, T.: Fully convolutional networks for semantic segmentation. Arxiv 79, November 2014
11. Qi, C.R., Liu, W., Wu, C., Su, H., Guibas, L.J.: Frustum pointNets for 3D object detection from RGB-D data. arXiv preprint arXiv:1711.08488 (2017)
12. Qi, C.R., Su, H., Mo, K., Guibas, L.J.: PointNet: deep learning on point sets for 3D classification and segmentation. arXiv preprint arXiv:1612.00593 (2016)
13. Qi, C.R., Yi, L., Su, H., Guibas, L.J.: PointNet++: deep hierarchical feature learning on point sets in a metric space. arXiv preprint arXiv:1706.02413 (2017)
14. Qin, Z., Wang, J., Lu, Y.: MonoGRNet: a geometric reasoning network for 3D object localization. In: The Thirty-Third AAAI Conference on Artificial Intelligence (AAAI-19) (2019)
15. Redmon, J., Divvala, S., Girshick, R., Farhadi, A.: You only look once: unified, real-time object detection. In: Computer Vision & Pattern Recognition (2016)
16. Ren, S., He, K., Girshick, R., Sun, J.: Faster R-CNN: towards real-time object detection with region proposal networks. IEEE Trans. Pattern Anal. Mach. Intell. 39(6), 1137–1149 (2017)
17. Shi, S., Wang, X., Li, H.: PointRCNN: 3D object proposal generation and detection from point cloud. In: The IEEE Conference on Computer Vision and Pattern Recognition (CVPR), June 2019
18. Shin, K., Kwon, Y.P., Tomizuka, M.: RoarNet: a robust 3D object detection based on region approximation refinement (2018)
19. Simonyan, K., Zisserman, A.: Very deep convolutional networks for large-scale image recognition. Comput. Sci. (2014)
20. Wang, Y., Chao, W.L., Garg, D., Hariharan, B., Campbell, M., Weinberger, K.: Pseudo-LiDAR from visual depth estimation: bridging the gap in 3D object detection for autonomous driving. In: CVPR (2019)
21. Wang, Z., Jia, K.: Frustum convNet: sliding frustums to aggregate local point-wise features for amodal 3D object detection (2019)
22. Yan, Y., Mao, Y., Li, B.: Second: sparsely embedded convolutional detection. Sensors 18, 3337 (2018). https://doi.org/10.3390/s18103337
23. Yin, Z., Tuzel, O.: VoxelNet: end-to-end learning for point cloud based 3D object detection (2017)

Cross-View Image Retrieval - Ground to Aerial Image Retrieval Through Deep Learning

Numan Khurshid$^{(\boxtimes)}$ (ID), Talha Hanif(ID), Mohbat Tharani(ID), and Murtaza Taj(ID)

Computer Vision and Graphics Lab, School of Science and Engineering,
Lahore University of Management Sciences, Lahore, Pakistan
{15060051,16060073,murtaza.taj}@lums.edu.pk, 1181864@lhr.nu.edu.pk

Abstract. Cross-modal retrieval aims to measure the content similarity between different types of data. The idea has been previously applied to visual, text, and speech data. In this paper, we present a novel cross-modal retrieval method specifically for multi-view images, called Cross-view Image Retrieval *CVIR*. Our approach aims to find a feature space as well as an embedding space in which samples from street-view images are compared directly to satellite-view images (and vice-versa). For this comparison, a novel deep metric learning based solution *"DeepCVIR"* has been proposed. Previous cross-view image datasets are deficient in that they (1) lack class information; (2) were originally collected for cross-view image geolocalization task with coupled images; (3) do not include any images from off-street locations. To train, compare, and evaluate the performance of cross-view image retrieval, we present a new 6 class cross-view image dataset termed as *CrossViewRet* which comprises of images including freeway, mountain, palace, river, ship, and stadium with 700 high-resolution dual-view images for each class. Results show that the proposed DeepCVIR outperforms conventional matching approaches on CVIR task for the given dataset and would also serve as the baseline for future research.

Keywords: Cross-modal retrieval · Cross-view image retrieval · Cross-view image matching · Deep metric learning

1 Introduction

Cross-view image matching (CVIM) attracted considerable attention of the researchers due to its growing applications in the fields of image geolocalization, GIS mapping, autonomous driving, augmented reality navigation, and robot rescue [1,5]. Another key factor is the rapid increase in high resolution satellite and street-view imagery provided by platforms such as Google and Flickr. One of the most challenging task to address CVIM is to devise an effective method to fill-in the heterogeneity gap of the two types of images [14,18].

© Springer Nature Switzerland AG 2019
T. Gedeon et al. (Eds.): ICONIP 2019, LNCS 11954, pp. 210–221, 2019.
https://doi.org/10.1007/978-3-030-36711-4_19

| Freeway | Mountain | Palace | River | Ship | Stadium |

Fig. 1. Some of the sample images from the developed *CrossViewRet* dataset, presenting 6 distinct classes. Apart from view-point variations these images also exhibit seasonal changes, varying illumination, and different spatial resolution.

We introduce cross-view image retrieval (CVIR) which is a special type of cross-modal retrieval, which aims to enable flexible search and collect method across dual-view images. For query image taken from one view-point (say ground-view) it searches for all the similar images taken from the other view-point (say aerial-view) in the database. The idea has evolved from the notion of cross-view image matching with one key difference. In standard cross-view image matching a ground-view image is matched to its respective aerial-view image while relying only on the content of the images. We in contrast introduce CVIR in which the system for the given query image searches for all the similar images in a database considering contextual class information embedded in visual descriptors of the images.

Common practice for conventional retrieval system is representation learning. It tries to transform images to a feature space where distance between them could be measured directly [3]. However, in our case these representative features must be transmuted to another common embedding space to bridge the heterogeneity gap and compute similarity between them.

In this paper, we present a novel cross-view image retrieval method, termed as Deep Metric Learning based cross-view image retrieval (DeepCVIR). This method aims to retain the discrimination among visual features from different semantic groups and reduces the dual-view image disparities as well. Intended to achieve this objective, class information is retained in the learned feature space and pairwise label information are retained in the embedding space for all the images. This is done by minimizing the discrimination loss of the images in both the feature space as well as embedding space to ensure the learned embeddings to be both discriminative in class information and view invariant in nature. Figure 2 illustrates our proposed framework in detail.

The remainder of this paper is organized as follows: Sect. 2 reviews the related work in cross-view image matching and cross-modal learning. Section 3 presents the proposed model including problem formulation, DeepCVIR and implementation details. Section 4 explains the experimental setup including dataset while Sect. 5 provides the results and analysis. Section 6 concludes the paper.

2 Related Work

Recent applications of cross-modal retrieval especially for text, speech, and images in big-data opened new avenues which require improved solution for the recent problems. Existing technique applies cross-modal retrieval techniques to multi-modal data but do not address variety of data in any single modality such as multi-view image retrieval [15].

Cross-view image matching could be taken as one of the potential problems for which Vo *et al.* cross-matched and geo-localized street-view images of the 11 cities of United States to their respective satellite-view images [13]. In which experimentation using various versions of Siamese and Triplet networks for feature extraction with distance-based logistic loss have been carried out. While validating the approach on another similar dataset *CV-USA* Hu *et al.* combined local features and global descriptors [5]. One of the major short comings of both these datasets is that the street-view images are obtained from Google satellite image repository which totally ignores the off-street images. Another way to cross-match images is to detecting and matching the content of the images e.g. matching buildings in the street-view query image to the building in the aerial images [12]. This particular approach intuitively failed to perform in the area lacking any tall structures or buildings with prominent features. Researchers have even tried to predict the ground-level scene layout from their respective aerial images, however, the same approach could not be extended for accurate image matching and retrieval purpose [17].

Image retrieval on the other hand has already been progressively used for multi-modal matching in the field of information retrieval [14]. The approach has been validated for applications to match sentences to images, ranking images, and free-hand sketch based image retrieval [6–8,15,18]. Moreover, metric learning networks have been previously introduced for template matching tasks [16]. We introduce cross-view image retrieval, employing the combination of metric learning and image retrieval technique for class-based cross-view image matching.

3 Proposed Method

One of the core ideas of this paper is to identify an efficient framework for CVIR using the contextual information of the scene in image. The detailed approach is presented in four different subsections: (a) Problem Formulation, (b) Deep Feature Extraction, (c) Feature Matching, (d) DeepCVIR. Figure 2 visually explains the overall architecture of the proposed approach.

3.1 Problem Formulation

We focus on the formulation of CVIR problem for CrossViewRet dataset $\mathcal{D}$ without losing generality of the topic. Dataset $\mathcal{D}$ contains two subsets: ground-view images $\mathcal{D}_g$ and aerial-view images $\mathcal{D}_a$. In ground-to-aerial retrieval for the

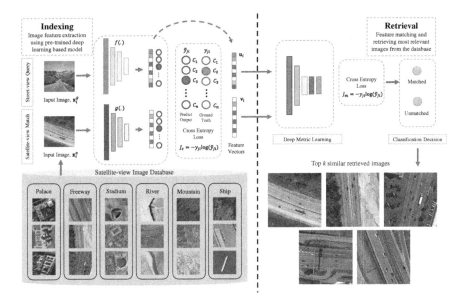

Fig. 2. Overall process of Cross-view Image Retrieval involving: (a) Indexing step which identifies the features of the query image and image to be matched (from database), (b) Retrieval step matches image features and visualize the top k relevant images based upon the retrieval score.

given query image $x^g \in \mathcal{D}_g$ we aim to retrieve the set of all the relevant images $\mathcal{D}_{rel}$, where $\mathcal{D}_{rel} \subset \mathcal{D}_a$. Similarly, this problem could also be formulated for aerial-to-ground search and retrieval by replacing query image with x_a and search data as $\mathcal{D}_g$. For this purpose, we assume a collection of n instances of ground-view and aerial-view image pairs, denoted as $\Psi = \{(x_i{}^a, x_i{}^g)\}_{i=1}^n$, where x_i^g is the input ground-view image sample and x_i^a is the input aerial-view image sample for the ith instance. Each pair of instances $(x_i{}^a, x_i{}^g)$ has been assigned a semantic label y_{ji}. If ith instance belongs to jth class, $y_{ji} = 0$, otherwise $y_{ji} = 1$.

3.2   Deep Supervised Feature Learning

Representation learning also termed as *"Indexing"* in CVIR refers to learn two functions for dual-view images containing same class information: $u_i = f(x_i^g; \phi_g) \in \mathcal{R}^d$ for the ground-view image and $v_i = f(x_i^a; \phi_a) \in \mathcal{R}^d$ for aerial-view image, where d is the dimensionality of features in their respective feature spaces. ϕ_g and ϕ_a in the above two functions are the trainable weights of the street-view and satellite-view feature learning networks. Feature extraction step for the cross-view image pair is influenced by benchmark deep supervised convolutional neural networks including VGG, ResNet-50, and Tiny-Inception-ResNet-v2 pretrained networks [10]. These networks are selected due to their exceptional performance in object recognition and classification task. Unlike traditional Siamese network, here two separate feature learning networks (without weight sharing policy) are employed for extracting features of street and satellite view images. Features acquired through this technique implicitly retain the class information of the images irrespective of their visual viewpoint. Although, these representations might not be projected in the combined feature space for both views still they share same dimensional footprint and could be compared in an embedding space through matching. Figure 2 (left side) shows the overall indexing procedure in detail.

3.3   Feature Matching and Retrieval

Features of the cross-view image pair are matched either through distance computation, metric learning, or deep networks with specialized loss functions. Traditionally, matching techniques employ distance computation method of the paired data $(\mathbf{u}_i, \mathbf{v}_j)$. For instance, Euclidean distance for feature embeddings of this paired data could be computed as

$$D(\Psi) = \|\mathbf{u}_i - \mathbf{v}_j\|_2 \tag{1}$$

where $\|.\|_2$ denotes L2-norm operation. In distance metric learning especially contrastive embedding, a loss function implemented on top of point-wise distance operation, is minimized to learn the association of similar and dissimilar data pairs. It is mathematically computed as

$$J_{con} = \sum_{i,j} \ell_{ij} D(\Psi)^2 + (1 - \ell_{ij}) h(\alpha - D(\Psi)^2) \tag{2}$$

where $\ell_{ij} \in 0, 1$ indicates the labels of the paired data, 0 representing similar pair and 1 otherwise. $h(.) = max(0, h)$ is hinge loss function and $D(\Psi)$ is taken from (1). α is used to penalize the dissimilar pair distances for being smaller than this predefined margin using hinge loss in the second part of (2). Similarly, Mahalanobis distance between the cross-view image pair features is computed as

$$J_{ma} = ((\mathbf{u}_i - \mathbf{v}_j)' \mathbf{C}^{-1} (\mathbf{u} - \mathbf{v}))^{\frac{1}{2}} \tag{3}$$

where x_i and z_j are two points from the same distribution which has covariance matrix $\mathbf{C}$. The Mahalanobis distance is the same as the Euclidean distance if the covariance matrix becomes the identity matrix. variation in each component of the point.

For each of the these matching measure if the retrieval score comes out to be less than the given threshold (say 0.5), the feature pair is categorized as similar and dissimilar otherwise. For image retrieval top k images are visualized as relevant to the query image as shown in Fig. 2.

3.4   DeepCVIR: A DML Based Framework for Feature Matching

The idea of transforming images from feature space to embedding space could be applied by incorporating a deep learning model technically called as deep metric learning network (DML) [11,16]. We in this research propose a residual deep metric learning architecture optimized with the well known binary cross-entropy loss.

Reshaping 1D Features in DeepCVIR. To exploit the contextual information of the objects in image features we reshape 1D features (1024×1) from indexing step to 2D features (32×32) in retrieval step. 2D convolution layers are then employed to extract significant information from concatenated 2D features of the matching images.

Residual Blocks in DeepCVIR. This DML network inspired from residual learning comprises the combination of two standard residual units presented in [4]. The first residual unit consists of two convolution layers with an identity path while the second one comprise a 1×1 convolutional shortcut with two convolution layers. We tested three variations of DML for DeepCVIR. S-DeepCVIR consists of only one residual block (two residual units). For D-DeepCVIR and T-DeepCVIR, two and three stacked residual blocks are additionally used in this network, respectively. The rest of the network structure remains the same for all the three variations. Each DeepCVIR network has been terminated by the combination of three pairs of fully connected and activation layers for instigation of non-linear learning.

4   Experimental Setup

Cross-view image retrieval could be inherently divided into two sub-tasks namely Street-to-satellite retrieval and Satellite-to-street retrieval. If for the given street-view query image, satellite-view relevant images are retrieved it is referred to as Str2Sat while the vice-versa case is referred to as Sat2Str in the rest of the paper. We also investigate the effects of employing different activation functions in DML networks.

4.1   Dataset

In this research a new dataset *CrossViewRet* has been developed to evaluate and compare the performance of DeepCVIR framework. Previous cross-view image datasets are deficient in that they (1) lack class information about the content of the image; (2) were originally collected for cross-view image geolocalization task with coupled images; (3) were specifically acquired for the purpose of autonomous vehicles therefore they do not include any images having off-street locations. CrossViewRet comprise of images containing 6 classes including freeway, mountain, palace, river, ship, and stadium with 700 high resolution dual-view images for each class. The satellite-view images are collected from the benchmark NWPU-RESISCS-45 dataset, while respective street-view images of

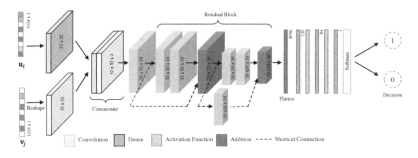

Fig. 3. The proposed Deep Metric Learning network (S-DeepCVIR) employed for DeepCVIR technique consists of only one residual block (two residual units). For D-DeepCVIR and T-DeepCVIR, two and three stacked residual blocks are additionally used in this network, respectively. The rest of the network structure remains the same for all the three variations.

each class are downloaded from Flickr image dataset[1] using Flickr API [2]. The downloaded street-view images are then cross checked by human annotators and images with obvious visual descriptions of the classes are selected for each class. The spatial resolution of satellite-view images is 256×256 and the street-view images are of variable sizes; however, they have been resized before employing for experimentation. The dataset has been made public for future use[2] (Fig. 1).

CrossViewRet is a very complex dataset. Unlike existing cross-view dataset [5,13] which contain ground and aerial images of the same location. We, on the other hand, do not constraint the images to be of same geo-location. Rather, we focus on visual contents in the scene regardless of any transformation in the images, weather conditions, and variation in day and night time in the scene. As shown in Fig. 1, the ground view in sample image of mountain class contains snow whereas its target aerial view image does not. Similarly, the ground view images of palace and stadium class are taken during night and aerial view contains day time drone images. However, the aerial view in river example is satellite image which is totally different than top view drone images.

4.2 Implementation Details

We use two independent networks for feature learning and embedding learning. In case of feature learning VGGNet, ResNet, and Inception-ResNet-v2 with pre-trained ImageNet weights are fine-tuned. Two independent sub-networks have been employed for learning the discriminating class-wise features of both the views. The architecture of the proposed DML network has been explained in Sect. 3.4. The standard 80/20 train-validation splitting criteria was used for CVIR dataset to fine-tune and train all the feature networks and variants of DML networks respectively. Query images used for evaluation were randomly taken from the validation split of the data.

---

[1] www.flickr.com.
[2] https://cvlab.lums.edu.pk/category/projects/imageretrieval.

Deep learning networks have been trained on a Nvidia RTX 2080Ti GPU in Keras. For training feature networks, we employ Stochastic Gradient Descent (SGD) with initial learning rate 0.00001 and a learning rate decay with patience 5. For DML network, ADAM with initial learning rate of 0.001 has been used. Early stopping criteria of 15 epochs has been used to halt training for all the networks.

4.3 Evaluation Metric

We evaluated the performance of cross-view image retrieval with not only the standard measures of Precision, Recall, and F1-Score but also evaluated Average Normalized Modified Retrieval Rank (ANMRR), Mean Average Precision (mAP), and P@K (read as Precision at K) [9]. P@K is the percentage of queries which the ground truth image class are in one of the first K retrieved results. Here we only employ P@5 measure for our analysis.

Table 1. Performance comparison of features computed with state-of-the art-architectures (IncepRes-v2=Tiny-Inception-ResNet-v2).

Feature network	Similarity measure	ANMRR↓	mAP↑	p@5↑	Precision	Recall	F1-score
ResNet-50	Euclidean	0.42	0.17	0.16	0.50	0.50	0.50
IncepRes-v2		0.42	0.17	0.16	0.50	0.50	0.50
VGG-16		0.41	0.18	0.15	0.48	0.48	0.48
ResNet-50	Contrastive	0.05	0.90	0.88	0.50	0.50	0.50
IncepRes-v2		0.40	0.20	0.16	0.50	0.50	0.50
VGG-16		0.29	0.41	0.40	0.50	0.50	0.50
ResNet-50	Mahalanobis	0.42	0.17	0.16	0.50	0.50	0.50
IncepRes-v2		0.42	0.16	0.15	0.50	0.50	0.50
VGG-16		0.42	0.17	0.19	0.50	0.50	0.50
ResNet-50	DeepCVIR-DML	0.03	0.93	0.94	0.94	0.94	0.94
IncepRes-v2		0.29	0.22	0.23	0.52	0.52	0.52
VGG-16		**0.02**	**0.96**	**0.97**	**0.96**	**0.96**	**0.96**

5 Results

Validation of the proposed DeepCVIR approach for this type of challenging dataset demands extensive assessment. We therefore provide a comparative analysis of the approach using various state-of-the-art techniques as well as variants of the proposed method.

5.1 Deep Features and Their Matching Techniques

Various deep features have been previously used for the task of same-view image retrieval; however, view-invariant features of multi-modal images plays a pivotal

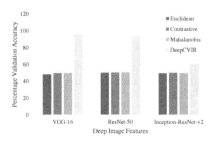
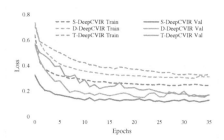

a) Features vs. Similarity Metric   b) Convergence rate of DeepCVIR

Fig. 4. Additional results: (a) showing the performance of similarity measuring techniques with various deep supervised features and, (b) showing the convergence rate of {S,T, and D}-DeepCVIR networks during training and validation.

role in CVIR. Table 1 shows that although Inception-ResNet-v2 may outperform the VGGNet and ResNet on ImageNet challenge yet it failed to extract the most optimal features for cross-view image matching. In addition, the performance of various distance computation methods illustrates that the problem is more complex and could not be solved by linear distances i.e. Euclidean or Contrastive loss embedding. Figure 4(a) also confirms the improvement of learning behavior in term of percentage validation accuracy.

5.2   Feature Matching Through DeepCVIR

The proposed DeepCVIR architecture involves the contribution of DML network which assists the learning process by efficient learning of the embedding space to discriminate similar and dissimilar pairs. However, to evaluate the learning routine of the DML network we tried variants of DML with the single, double and triple combination of the proposed residual blocks termed as S-DeepCVIR, D-DeepCVIR, and T-DeepCVIR, respectively.

Table 2. Comparison of different variations of proposed architecture.

DML type	Feature type	Activation function	ANMRR ↓	mAP↑	p@5↑	Precision	Recall	F1-score
S-DeepCVIR	ResNet-50	eLU	0.04	0.93	0.94	0.50	0.50	0.50
S-DeepCVIR		Leaky ReLU	0.03	0.93	0.94	0.94	0.94	0.94
S-DeepCVIR		ReLU	0.03	0.93	0.95	0.93	0.93	0.93
D-DeepCVIR	ResNet-50	ReLU	0.04	0.92	0.94	0.92	0.92	0.92
T-DeepCVIR		ReLU	0.05	0.89	0.92	0.90	0.90	0.90
S-DeepCVIR	VGG-16	Leaky ReLU	**0.02**	**0.96**	**0.97**	**0.96**	**0.96**	**0.96**
D-DeepCVIR		Leaky ReLU	0.02	0.95	0.97	0.95	0.95	0.95
T-DeepCVIR		Leaky ReLU	0.02	0.96	0.98	0.95	0.95	0.95

Impact of the Number of Residual Blocks in DeepCVIR. In general increasing the number of residual blocks in a network supports the overall performance; however, in our case S-DeepCVIR with least number of residual blocks outperforms the rest of the DeepCVIR networks. This was beyond our anticipation, but one cannot neglect the simplicity of this task as compare to other recognition tasks. It could be concluded that the number of learnable parameters of S-DeepCVIR are enough to separate similar and dissimilar features. ANMRR and mAP values in Table 2 illustrates that although all the variants of DeepCVIR performed better than other matching techniques still S-DeepCVIR performed extraordinarily for the given task of Str2Sat as well as Sat2Str. Their convergence curves illustrated in Fig. 4(b) due to their less number of learnable parameters, represents significantly earlier and much lower loss with respect to the number of epochs as compare to rest of the combinations.

5.3 Str2Sat vs. Sat2Str Evaluation

Our proposed S-DeepCVIR framework performs equally well on both Str2Sat and Sat2Str tasks. Results in Table 3 shows that although the average ANMRR values remain comparative for all the variants of DeepCVIR architecture still S-DeepCVIR with VGG features achieves minimum average ANMRR of 0.025 and maximum mAP score.

5.4 t-SNE Visualization of the Learned Embeddings

t-SNE plot is a very effective tool to visualize the data in two dimensional plane for better analysis. We adapted this approach to witness and validate the contribution of DML in transforming features to embedding space. Figure 5(a, f) shows that image features are distributed among the whole region of the plot and hence it is very difficult to measure the correspondence among same and different feature just by using a linear distance. DML separates them into distinguishable clusters.

Although no class information was explicitly provided to the network during training still it successfully clustered the similar pairs into six different classes. It is also observed from the figures that use of different activation functions and multiple residual blocks does not contribute to improvement of the overall result.

Table 3. Performance comparison of VGG-16 features with {S,T, and D}-DeepCVIR networks for Street-to-satellite (Str2Sat) and Satellite-to-street (Sat2Str) retrieval task.

Features	DeepCVIR	Str2Sat			Sat2Str			Average ANMRR
		ANMRR↓	mAP↑	p@5↑	ANMRR↓	mAP↑	p@5↑	
VGG-16	S-DeepCVIR	**0.02**	**0.96**	**0.97**	**0.03**	**0.92**	**0.92**	0.025
VGG-16	D-DeepCVIR	0.02	0.95	0.97	0.03	0.91	0.91	0.025
VGG-16	T-DeepCVIR	0.02	0.96	0.98	0.03	0.91	0.91	0.025

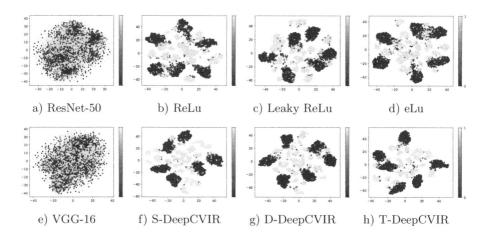

| a) ResNet-50 | b) ReLu | c) Leaky ReLu | d) eLu |

| e) VGG-16 | f) S-DeepCVIR | g) D-DeepCVIR | h) T-DeepCVIR |

Fig. 5. t-SNE plots showing learning behavior of DML for: ResNet-50 features trained with S-DeepCVIR employing various activation functions (in top row), and VGG-16 features using different number of residual blocks in DML network (in bottom row).

6 Conclusion

We propose a cross-view image retrieval system for which we developed a cross-view dataset named CrossViewRet. The dataset consists of street-view and satellite-view images for 6 distinct classes having 700 images per class. The proposed DeepCVIR system consists of two parts: (a) a fine-tuned deep feature network, and (b) a deep metric learning network trained on image pairs from CrossViewRet dataset. Given features for two images, the proposed residual DML network decides if the two images belong to the same class. In addition an ablative study and a detailed empirical analysis on different activation functions and number of residual blocks in DML network have also been performed. This shows that our proposed DeepCVIR network performed significantly well for the problem of cross-view retrieval.

References

1. Arth, C., Schmalstieg, D.: Challenges of large-scale augmented reality on smartphones, pp. 1–4. Graz University of Technology, Graz (2011)
2. Cheng, G., Han, J., Lu, X.: Remote sensing image scene classification: benchmark and state of the art. Proc. IEEE **105**(10), 1865–1883 (2017)
3. Göksu, Ö., Aptoula, E.: Content based image retrieval of remote sensing images based on deep features. In: 26th Signal Processing and Communications Applications Conference (SIU), pp. 1–4 (2018)
4. He, K., Zhang, X., Ren, S., Sun, J.: Identity mappings in deep residual networks. In: Leibe, B., Matas, J., Sebe, N., Welling, M. (eds.) ECCV 2016. LNCS, vol. 9908, pp. 630–645. Springer, Cham (2016). https://doi.org/10.1007/978-3-319-46493-0_38

5. Hu, S., Feng, M., Nguyen, R.M., Hee Lee, G.: CVM-Net: cross-view matching network for image-based ground-to-aerial geo-localization. In: Proceedings of the IEEE Conference on Computer Vision and Pattern Recognition, pp. 7258–7267 (2018)
6. Lin, Z., Ding, G., Hu, M., Wang, J.: Semantics-preserving hashing for cross-view retrieval. In: Proceedings of the IEEE Conference on Computer Vision and Pattern Recognition, pp. 3864–3872 (2015)
7. Liu, L., Shen, F., Shen, Y., Liu, X., Shao, L.: Deep sketch hashing: fast free-hand sketch-based image retrieval. In: Proceedings of the IEEE Conference on Computer Vision and Pattern Recognition, pp. 2862–2871 (2017)
8. Ma, L., Lu, Z., Shang, L., Li, H.: Multimodal convolutional neural networks for matching image and sentence. In: Proceedings of the IEEE Conference on Computer Vision and Pattern Recognition, pp. 2623–2631 (2015)
9. Napoletano, P.: Visual descriptors for content-based retrieval of remote-sensing images. Int. J. Remote Sens. 39(5), 1–34 (2018)
10. Nazir, U., Khurshid, N., Bhimra, M.A., Taj, M.: Tiny-Inception-ResNet-v2: using deep learning for eliminating bonded labors of brick kilns in South Asia. In: Proceedings of the IEEE Conference on Computer Vision and Pattern Recognition Workshops, pp. 39–43 (2019)
11. Tharani, M., Khurshid, N., Taj, M.: Unsupervised deep features for remote sensing image matching via discriminator network. arXiv preprint arXiv:1810.06470 (2018)
12. Tian, Y., Chen, C., Shah, M.: Cross-view image matching for geo-localization in urban environments. In: Proceedings of the IEEE Conference on Computer Vision and Pattern Recognition, pp. 3608–3616 (2017)
13. Vo, N.N., Hays, J.: Localizing and orienting street views using overhead imagery. In: Leibe, B., Matas, J., Sebe, N., Welling, M. (eds.) ECCV 2016. LNCS, vol. 9905, pp. 494–509. Springer, Cham (2016). https://doi.org/10.1007/978-3-319-46448-0_30
14. Wang, K., Yin, Q., Wang, W., Wu, S., Wang, L.: A comprehensive survey on cross-modal retrieval. arXiv preprint arXiv:1607.06215 (2016)
15. Wei, Y., et al.: Cross-modal retrieval with CNN visual features: a new baseline. IEEE Trans. Cybern. 47(2), 449–460 (2017)
16. Han, X., Leung, T., Jia, Y., Sukthankar, R., Berg, A.C.: MatchNet: unifying feature and metric learning for patch-based matching. In: Proceedings of IEEE Conference on Computer Vision and Pattern Recognition, pp. 3279–3286 (2015)
17. Zhai, M., Bessinger, Z., Workman, S., Jacobs, N.: Predicting ground-level scene layout from aerial imagery. In: Proceedings of the IEEE Conference on Computer Vision and Pattern Recognition, pp. 867–875 (2017)
18. Zhen, L., Hu, P., Wang, X., Peng, D.: Deep supervised cross-modal retrieval. In: Proceedings of the IEEE Conference on Computer Vision and Pattern Recognition, pp. 10394–10403 (2019)

Direct Image to Point Cloud Descriptors Matching for 6-DOF Camera Localization in Dense 3D Point Clouds

Uzair Nadeem[1]([✉])[iD], Mohammad A. A. K. Jalwana[1][iD],
Mohammed Bennamoun[1][iD], Roberto Togneri[1][iD], and Ferdous Sohel[2][iD]

[1] The University of Western Australia, Perth, Australia
{uzair.nadeem,mohammad.jalwana}@research.uwa.edu.au,
{mohammed.bennamoun,roberto.togneri}@uwa.edu.au
[2] Murdoch University, Perth, Australia
f.sohel@murdoch.edu.au

Abstract. We propose a novel concept to directly match feature descriptors extracted from RGB images, with feature descriptors extracted from 3D point clouds. We use this concept to localize the position and orientation (pose) of the camera of a query image in dense point clouds. We generate a dataset of matching 2D and 3D descriptors, and use it to train a proposed Descriptor-Matcher algorithm. To localize a query image in a point cloud, we extract 2D key-points and descriptors from the query image. Then the Descriptor-Matcher is used to find the corresponding pairs 2D and 3D key-points by matching the 2D descriptors with the pre-extracted 3D descriptors of the point cloud. This information is used in a robust pose estimation algorithm to localize the query image in the 3D point cloud. Experiments demonstrate that directly matching 2D and 3D descriptors is not only a viable idea but can also be used for camera pose localization in dense 3D point clouds with high accuracy.

Keywords: 3D to 2D matching · Multi-domain descriptor matching · 6-DOF pose estimation · Image localization

1 Introduction

With the recent advances in the computational power of modern machines, there has been a steep increase in the popularity of 3D vision and its applications. A lot of research is being carried out using RGB-D images, point clouds and 3D meshes. This is also supported by new hardware and software products that use 3D data for various applications. For example, Microsoft Windows 10 has now a dedicated library for point clouds and meshes named "3D Objects", as well as 3D Paint and 3D Builder software. The quality and capabilities of 3D sensors have also improved a lot, and at the same time, costs have come down. Many of the latest smart-phones have a dedicated 3D sensor along with one or more RGB cameras.

© Springer Nature Switzerland AG 2019
T. Gedeon et al. (Eds.): ICONIP 2019, LNCS 11954, pp. 222–234, 2019.
https://doi.org/10.1007/978-3-030-36711-4_20

(a)   (b)   (c)

Fig. 1. (a) A section of the 3D point cloud from Shop Facade dataset [1]. (b) An RGB query image to be localized in 3D point cloud (c) Visualization of the area of the 3D point cloud, identified by our technique as the location of the query image.

Despite the progress in the fields of 3D and 2D vision, there is still a need to develop better techniques for the fusion of 2D and 3D information. Both 2D and 3D data can complement each other in many ways for improved performance and efficiency. Techniques that can combine 2D and 3D data have many potential applications, e.g., recognizing an object in an image using its 3D model, locating objects or regions of interest from RGB images in 3D maps, face recognition and verification, as well as 2D image localization in a 3D point cloud. Moreover, most of the vision data that is currently available is in the form of 2D images (or videos). A technique that can bridge the gap between the 2D and 3D data will highly be beneficial to improve 3D vision systems using 2D data. In this paper we propose a technique to match feature descriptors extracted from 2D images and 3D point clouds and demonstrate their application for the task of 6-DOF camera pose (position and orientation) estimation of 2D images in a 3D point cloud.

Camera pose estimation is a popular research topic now-a-days because of its numerous applications e.g., for place recognition, augmented reality, robotic navigation, robot pose estimation, grasping, and in Simultaneous Localization and Mapping (SLAM) problem. Current techniques for camera localization comprise of two major categories: (ii) Regression Networks-based methods and (i) Handcrafted features-based methods. The regression networks-based methods usually require a lot of data for training and have high requirements for computational resources, such as powerful GPUs. Most of the feature-based techniques use local or global features that are extracted from 2D images. For 3D models they use sparse 3D point clouds generated from the Structure from Motion (SfM) pipeline [2]. Once the 3D model is generated from SfM, the approach provides a one-to-one correspondence between the pixels of the images and the 3D points in the SfM model. This correspondence has been used to create systems that can localize images in the sparse point cloud, generated by SfM. However, with the advances in 3D scanning technology, it is possible to directly generate 3D point clouds of large areas without using the SfM pipeline e.g., Microsoft Kinect, LIDAR, Faro 3D scanner or Matterport scanners can be used to directly generate the point cloud of a scene. This is a much more practical approach to

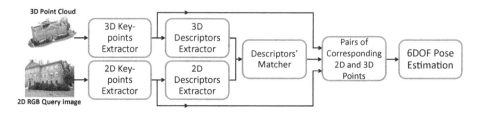

Fig. 2. A block diagram of the test pipeline of the proposed technique. We extract 3D key-points and descriptors from the dense 3D Point Cloud. 2D key-points and descriptors are extracted from the 2D RGB Query Image. Then our proposed 'Descriptor-Matcher' algorithm directly matches the 2D descriptors with the 3D descriptors to generate correspondence between points in 2D image and 3D point cloud. This is then used with a robust pose estimation algorithm to estimate the 6-DOF pose of the query image in the 3D point cloud.

generate 3D models, compared to SfM as the generated point clouds are denser and the quality of the models generated by 3D scanners is much better than the ones obtained by SfM. Although it may be possible to generate sparse point clouds from the dense ones by randomly downsampling them, it is not possible to generate one-to-one correspondences between the 3D vertices and the pixels of the 2D images. In such a scenario, many of the current image localization techniques cannot be used since they heavily rely on the information that is generated by the SfM.

In this paper we propose a novel camera localization technique. Our technique can localize images directly in dense point clouds, that are acquired by 3D scanners, by directly matching the 2D descriptors extracted from images with the 3D descriptors that are extracted from the point clouds. Figure 1 shows the dense point cloud of the Shop Facade dataset [1] along with a query image localized by our technique in the point cloud. Specifically, we train a 2D-3D Descriptor matching classifier, that we call 'Descriptor-Matcher', using a training set of corresponding 2D and 3D descriptors. To localize an image, we extract key-points and descriptors from the query image using 2D key-points and descriptors techniques such as Scale Invariant Features Transform (SIFT) key-points and SIFT descriptors [3]. Similarly, we extract 3D key-points and descriptors from the point cloud e.g., 3D-SIFT key-points [3,4] or 3D-Harris key-points [4,5] and Rotation Invariant Features Transform (RIFT) descriptors [6]. Then we use the trained Descriptor-Matcher to find matching pairs of 2D and 3D descriptors. We use this information to identify the points from the image that match with points in the 3D point cloud. The matching pairs of 2D and 3D points are used in a robust pose estimation algorithm to estimate the orientation and the location of camera in the 3D point cloud (see Sect. 3.3). Figure 2 shows the steps of the proposed technique to estimate the camera pose.

To the best of our knowledge, our contribution is the first: **(i)** to directly match 2D descriptors from RGB images with 3D descriptors that are extracted from dense point clouds, and **(ii)** to localize 6-DOF Camera pose in dense 3D point clouds by directly matching 2D and 3D descriptors.

The rest of this paper is organized as follows. Section 2 discusses the different types of techniques that have the goal to localize or geo-register an image. The proposed technique is presented in Sect. 3. Section 4 reports the experimental setup and a detailed evaluation of our results along with a comparison with other approaches. The paper is concluded in Sect. 5.

2 Related Work

Localizing the position of an image and estimating its pose is an active area of research. Two major approaches are used for this purpose: **(i)** handcrafted features-based methods, and **(ii)** network-based pose regression.

(i) Handcrafted features-based methods mainly emphasize on locating an image in an area i.e., many of the image localization datasets do not provide the ground truth camera pose, therefore, the localization techniques only use the number of inliers found with RANSAC [7] as a registration metric. For example, if the RANSAC finds 12 inliers for the query image, the image is considered registered. This is a very crude metric and does not actually show the performance of these techniques. These works are further of two types, **(i.a)** image retrieval based methods, and **(i.b)** SfM-based methods.

(i.a) Image retrieval based methods treat the problem as a pure image based problem where for a given query image, retrieval techniques are used to find a set of similar images from a database of geo-tagged images. This set of images is then used to triangulate the pose of the camera [8,9]. As evident by the approach, they cannot be used to localize images in a 3D model. Also since the estimated pose is based on the poses of the retrieved similar images, which are not necessarily close, so this approximation is inaccurate compared to the techniques that use the SfM model for localization [10].

(i.b) SfM-based methods use structure from motion based 3D models for localization. These methods are more accurate than the image retrieval based methods. In SfM each point is triangulated from multiple images' key-points and is then associated with those corresponding feature descriptors [2]. The commonly used image features include SIFT, SURF, ORB etc. Irschara et al. [11] created the SfM model from the training images and then used image retrieval techniques to find training images similar to the query image. The retrieved images were used with the SfM model to improve the localization accuracy. Li et al. [12] further enhanced the performance by directly comparing the query image and 3D point features, instead of using retrieval methods. Sattler et al. [13] used a visual vocabulary of 16M words for localization in larger point clouds. Sattler et al. [10] extended their work by using a prioritized matching system to improve the image localization results.

These works require that the point cloud be generated from the SfM based techniques, due to the fact that 3D points are assigned features based on the known poses of images that constructed them. Each point in the 3D model generated from SfM is created from key-points that are extracted from a number of 2D images. Some works consider a function of the 2D descriptors corresponding to those key-points as the 3D descriptors (e.g., average of 2D descriptors). However, such approximation and assignment of 3D descriptors is only possible if the 3D model is generated from the SfM using a large number of images. Moreover, since 3D descriptors are a function of the 2D image descriptors, the matching between image descriptors and SfM model's descriptors is not a 2D to 3D matching problem in the true sense, but rather a 2D to 2D descriptor matching problem. The recent arrival of cheap 3D sensors allow to directly capture large scale point clouds, avoiding the time consuming generation of 3D models from hundred or thousands of images. The above mentioned techniques cannot localize images in the point clouds captured by 3D scanners.

(ii) **Network-based pose regression methods** use neural networks for pose estimation. PoseNet, developed by Kendall et al. [1], is a CNN based neural network which learns to regress input image to the pose. However, it has a low accuracy. Kendall et al. [14] and Walch et al. [15] enhanced Posenet by improving the loss function and architecture of the network, respectively. Instead of directly regressing the pose, Brachmann et al. [16] introduced the differentiable RANSAC for using it as a trainable component in their deep network pipeline based on the work of [17].

In contrast to SfM-based techniques, our technique is the first approach which extracts 3D key-points and descriptors from the point cloud and matches them with the features extracted from the 2D images. This allows our technique to find the pose of the query image in the 3D model that can be obtained from any scanner. Moreover, as the proposed technique can work with high density point clouds, the 3D features have better quality which helps our technique in localization.

3   Technique

The proposed technique provides a novel way to estimate poses of query images in a 3D point cloud. Our technique can work with point clouds that are acquired from any scanner. Moreover, our technique can work in both indoor and outdoor scenarios. As the popular datasets for pose estimation or image localization do not provide dense 3D point clouds and poses to train and query images using the dense model, we used the COLMAP's Multi View Stereo (MVS) [18] pipeline to generate dense 3D point clouds from images in publicly available datasets.

To train the Descriptor-Matcher, we need a dataset of pairs of 2D and 3D descriptors which correspond to the same point in the 2D image and the 3D point cloud, respectively. Once the Descriptor-Matcher is trained, our technique does not require any type of intermediate information (e.g., from SfM) to localize the query image and estimate its pose.

3.1   Dataset Creation

To train the Descriptor-Matcher to match the 2D descriptors with the 3D descriptors, we need a dataset of corresponding 2D and 3D descriptors. Any manual creation of such a dataset on a large scale will be tedious and imprac-tical. We devised a way to automatically mine matching 2D and 3D descriptors from a given set of training images, and a dense 3D point cloud that may have been generated from any scanner. Given a dataset with N number of training images and M number of query images, we use the COLMAP's MVS [18] to generate the dense 3D point clouds. COLMAP generates a sparse 3D model [2] (called sparse point cloud) in an intermediate step to the construction of the dense point cloud. This provides the poses of the training and the query images, with respect to the sparse 3D point cloud. For the quantitative evaluation of the proposed technique, we need the poses of the query images with respect to the point cloud obtained from 3D scanner (called the Dense 3D point cloud). The sparse point cloud can be registered with point clouds obtained from any 3D scanner, to get the poses of the training and the query images with respect to the dense 3D point cloud. For our experiments we used the point clouds generated from MVS as the dense point cloud.

For the dataset creation, we first extract the 3D key-points and descriptors from the dense point cloud [4]. Similar to [10,12,19], we remove all the points in the point cloud that were generated using only the query images to ensure that no information from the query set is used for the generation of the training dataset. After applying the 3D key-point detector and descriptors on the dense point cloud we get a set of 3D key-points:

$$keys_{3D} = \bigcup_{i=1}^{N_{k3}} (x_i, y_i, z_i) \tag{1}$$

and their corresponding 3D descriptors:

$$desc_{3D} = \bigcup_{i=1}^{N_{k3}} (d_i^1, d_i^2, d_i^3, ...d_i^m) \tag{2}$$

where N_{k3} is the number of detected key-points and m is the length of the used 3D descriptor. Let PC_s be the sparse point cloud obtained after removing the points that were created using the query images:

$$PC_s = \bigcup_{j=1}^{N_p} (x_j, y_j, z_j) \tag{3}$$

where N_p is the number of points that are left in the point cloud. We find the Euclidean distances between the elements of $keys_{3D}$ and PC_s and keep only those points whose difference is less than a threshold α. Let ζ be the set of the pair of indices, corresponding to the points of N_{k3} and PC_s, that are equal within an error threshold α:

$$\zeta = \bigcup (i, j) \quad \forall ||(x_i - x_j), (y_i - y_j), (z_i - z_j))|| < \alpha$$
$$where \quad i = 1, 2, 3, ..., N_{k3}, \quad j = 1, 2, 3, ..., N_p. \tag{4}$$

It is to be noted that the resulting ζ usually contains less than 10% of the key-points that are detected from the dense point cloud. The fact that our technique produces good results on the query images (see Sect. 4), despite never being trained on more than 90% of the training 3D key-points, shows the high generalization capability of the proposed technique. Since the sparse point cloud, created by COLMAP [2], contains the correspondence information between the pixels from the training images that were used to create 3D points in the sparse point cloud, we use this information along with ζ to find the 2D key-points corresponding to the key-points obtained from the dense point cloud which are included in the set ζ. This creates a correspondence between the 3D key-points from the dense point cloud and the 2D key-points from the training images. Note that this is a one-to-many correspondence, since one 3D point in a point cloud may appear in many 2D images. We convert this set of key-points correspondences from one-to-many to one-to-one by duplicating each 3D key-point as many times as their are corresponding 2D key-points for that point. This gives us a one-to-one set of matching 2D and 3D key-points. We retrieve the corresponding descriptors for 3D key-points from $desc_{3D}$ and apply 2D descriptor extraction on the 2D key-points to obtain a dataset of corresponding 2D and 3D descriptors.

3.2   Training

We use the generated dataset to train the Descriptor-Matcher. We pose the problem of matching 2D and 3D descriptors as a binary classification problem. Empirically, we found that the Random Forest classifier [20] is the most suited for this problem, due to its robustness, speed, resistance to over-fitting and good generalization ability. We concatenated the corresponding 3D and 2D descriptors from the training dataset and used them as positive samples. To generate negative samples, we generate one-to-one matches between the 3D and the 2D descriptors from the training set, such that the distance between their corresponding key-points is greater than a threshold β. Due to the large number of negative samples, we randomly select a small subset of them. We used the positive and the negative samples to train our Descriptor-Matcher.

3.3   Testing

To localize a given query image at test time, we extract 2D key-points and descriptors from the query image. Similarly, we extract 3D key-points and descriptors from the point cloud in which the query image is to be localized. We then use the Descriptor-Matcher to find the matching 2D and 3D descriptors. We retrieve the corresponding 2D and 3D key-points of the matching 2D and 3D descriptors based on the output of the Descriptor-Matcher and use them as the matching pairs of points in the 2D image and the 3D point cloud. Just like any other classifier, there is the possibility of false positives in the resulting matches. We therefore use a robust pose estimation algorithm to estimate the location and orientation of the 2D image. Our pose estimation algorithm is a combination of P3P [21] and MLESAC [22] algorithms. MLESAC is a generalized and improved version of RANSAC [7] that not only tries to maximize the number of inliers but also maximizes the likelihood [22]. This provides us with the position and viewing direction of the camera used to capture the query image in the 3D point cloud. We can use this position and orientation to map the image on the 3D point cloud. Figure 2 shows the testing pipeline of the proposed technique.

4   Experiments and Analysis

To evaluate the performance of our technique, we carried out experiments on publicly available popular datasets. We used the Heads, Fire and Pumpkin datasets from the RGB-D 7-Scenes Database [17] to evaluate our technique for indoor scenarios. For outdoor scenarios, we used the South Building [23], Notre Dame [24], Shop Facade [1] and Old Hospital [1] datasets.

The quality of the point clouds generated from MVS turned out to be poor as they contained a large amount of noise. To reduce the noise, we used the Statistical Outlier Removal Filter (SOR) [4]. SOR computes the mean distance between points in a local neighbourhood, and removes those points that are far apart based on a statistical threshold.

We extracted SIFT key-points and descriptors [3] from the 2D images and 3D SIFT key-points [4] and RIFT descriptors [6] from the dense 3D point cloud. 3D SIFT key-point extraction is an extension of the 2D SIFT key-point extraction algorithm [3] for point clouds. We used $\alpha = 0.01$ and $\beta = 0.1$ in all our experiments. We used Gini's Diversity Index as a measure of node impurity for the splitting of nodes in the trees of Random Forest. In order to optimize other parameters of Random Forest in the Descriptor-Matcher, we held out 15% of the training dataset (see Sect. 3.1) for the validation set and trained the Random Forest on the remaining 85% of the data. The validation set was used to optimize the parameters of the Random Forest. These optimal parameters were then used to train the Random Forest using the complete training dataset.

4.1   Evaluation Metric

We calculated the errors in position and rotation of the query images with respect to the ground truth. For errors in position we used the distance between the ground truth and the predicted positions of the camera in the point cloud for the evaluation metric. For rotational error, we calculated the smallest angle between the viewing direction of the ground truth orientation and the predicted orientation of the query image's camera. If R_g is the ground truth rotation matrix and R_p is the predicted rotation matrix then the rotational error ϕ in degrees is calculated as follows:

$$\phi = \frac{\pi}{180} * cos^{-1}\left(\frac{trace(R_g \times transpose(R_p)) - 1}{2}\right) \tag{5}$$

Table 1. Median and percentile localization errors for the outdoor datasets: South Building [23], Notre Dame [24], Shop Facade [1] and Old Hospital [1]. P stands for percentile, e.g., P 25% means the maximum error for 25% of the data when errors are sorted in the ascending order.

Dataset ↓	Errors ↓\Metrics →	Median	P 25%	P 50%	P 75%	P 90%
South Building	Position Error (m)	0.12 m	0.086 m	0.12 m	0.15 m	0.21 m
	Angle Error (degrees)	0.61°	0.36°	0.61°	0.93°	1.26 °
Notre Dame	Position Error (m)	4.04 m	2.15 m	4.04 m	15.66 m	33.59 m
	Angle Error (degrees)	4.10°	2.18°	4.10°	14.63°	27.60°
Shop Facade	Position Error (m)	0.23 m	0.09 m	0.23 m	1.73 m	11.07 m
	Angle Error (degrees)	1.60°	0.67°	1.60°	15.08°	86.72°
Old Hospital	Position Error (m)	0.53 m	0.17 m	0.53 m	5.72 m	23.84 m
	Angle Error (degrees)	1.12°	0.56°	1.12°	32.91°	97.38°

4.2   Outdoor Datasets

South Building. The South Building dataset [23] consists of images of the "South Building" at the university of North Carolina, Chapel Hill. The dataset contains images from all the sides of the building. We randomly selected 10% of the images for the query set and the remaining images were used for the training set. The images in this dataset were acquired from different viewpoints, orientations, and occlusions were present due to the trees. South Building also has repetitive patterns. Moreover, due to the symmetric nature of the building, it is difficult to differentiate images from different sides of the building. Table 1 shows the results of the proposed technique on the test set. The proposed technique was able to register all the images of the query set. We report the median as well as the percentile errors for the intervals of 25%, 50%, 75% and 90% data, for both position (in meters) and angle (in degrees).

Table 2. Median and percentile localization errors for the indoor datasets: Heads, Fire and Pumpkin from the Seven Scenes RGBD database [17]. P stands for percentile, e.g., P 25% means the maximum error for 25% of the data when errors are sorted in the ascending order.

Dataset ↓	Errors ↓\Metrics →	Median	P 25%	P 50%	P 75%	P 90%
Heads	Position Error (m)	0.01 m	0.008 m	0.01 m	0.09 m	0.67 m
	Angle Error (degrees)	1.82°	0.84°	1.82°	7.43°	100.48°
Fire	Position Error (m)	0.02 m	0.006 m	0.02 m	0.45 m	1.06 m
	Angle Error (degrees)	1.56°	0.86°	1.56°	50.44°	147.05°
Pumpkin	Position Error (m)	0.01 m	0.007m	0.01 m	0.02 m	1.93 m
	Angle Error (degrees)	0.66°	0.40°	0.66°	1.30°	131.23°

Table 3. Median errors for position and orientation estimation of our technique compared to other approaches on indoor and outdoor datasets. Pos stands for median positional error in meters and Ang stands for rotational error in degrees.

Methods→	PoseNet [1] ICCV'15		Geom. Loss Net [14] CVPR'17		VLocNet [25] ICRA'18		DSAC [16] CVPR'17		Active Search [10] TPAMI'17		Ours	
Methods' Type→	Network-based		Network-based		Network-based		Network + RANSAC		SfM-based		2D to 3D Descriptors Matching	
Datsets↓	Pos (m)	Ang	Pos (m)	Ang	Pos (m)	Ang	Pos (m)	Ang	Pos (m)	Ang	Pos (m)	Ang
Shop Facade	1.46	4.04°	1.05	4°	0.59	3.53°	0.09	0.4°	0.12	0.4°	0.23	1.6°
Old Hospital	2.31	2.69°	2.17	2.9°	1.07	2.41°	0.33	0.6°	0.44	1°	0.53	1.12°
Heads	0.29	6°	0.17	13°	0.05	6.64°	0.03	2.7°	0.02	1.5°	0.01	1.82°
Fire	0.47	7.33°	0.27	11.3°	0.04	5.34°	0.04	1.5°	0.03	1.5°	0.02	1.56°
Pumpkin	0.47	4.21°	0.26	4.8°	0.04	2.28°	0.05	2°	0.08	3.1°	0.01	0.66°

Notre Dame. The Notre Dame dataset [24] contains random pictures of the Notre Dame Cathedral and its surrounding areas in Paris, France. There is very high variation in the images in terms of scale, illumination and orientation. The dataset contains 716 images. The scale of the pictures varies from close ups of the graffiti on the cathedral to ones taken from hundreds of meters away from the building. The pictures are both in landscape and portrait orientation. We did not correct the orientation of the pictures and used them as they were, for training and testing purposes. Moreover, this dataset contains picture that were taken at different times of the day including day, night and dusk. The pictures taken at night look strikingly different from the ones taken at day time. We randomly selected 10% of the images as the held out query set and used the remaining pictures for training. Our technique successfully registered 57 query images out of 72. Among the pictures that were not registered, 4 were not part of the 3D Model so these were successful rejections by our technique. Table 1 shows the localization results on the Notre Dame dataset for the registered images.

Shop Facade. The Shop Facade dataset, from the Cambridge Landmarks database [1], consists of 334 images from the intersection of two streets in Cambridge, with a focus on the shops at the intersection. We used the standard train-query split defined by the authors of the dataset. The query set contains 103 images [1]. Our technique successfully localized all the images in the query set. Table 1 shows the median errors in position and rotation along with the percentile errors on the Shop Facade dataset.

Old Hospital. The Old Hospital dataset is part of the Cambridge Landmarks database [1]. This dataset contains 1077 images. The dataset suffers from the challenges of high symmetry and repetitive patterns in the buildings. We used the data split defined by the authors of the dataset [1] to generate the training and the query sets. The query set contains 182 images. We were able to register all the images of the query set in the 3D model. Table 1 shows the percentile errors in the location and the orientation of the localized images for the intervals of 25%, 50%, 75%, and 90% data.

4.3 Indoor Datasets

To test the performance of the proposed technique in indoor conditions we used the Heads, Pumpkin and Fire datasets. For indoor datasets, the quality of the generated point clouds from MVS was much worse than what would have been achieved, had a Kinect or some other 3D scanner been used. We only applied SOR filter to the generated point cloud and used it for our experiments. The results of our technique on the indoor datasets demonstrate its robustness against noise in point clouds.

Heads. The Heads dataset [17] for indoor localization is part of the seven scenes RGBD database. As the name indicates, it contains multiple models of heads, along with monitors, and other items in a room. The dataset consists of 2000 images. We used the standard train-query split as defined by the authors of the dataset. Table 2 shows the median and percentile errors of our technique.

Fire. Fire dataset [17] is composed of 4000 images. It is part of the seven scenes RGBD database. The scene consists of an area with fire equipment, chair and some other stuff. For the train and query sets, we used the standard split defined by the authors of the dataset [17]. We were able to localize all the images in the query set using our technique. Table 2 shows the different types of errors of our technique on the Fire dataset.

Pumpkin. Pumpkin dataset is one of the datasets in the seven scenes RGBD database [17]. It contains 6000 images in total of a kitchen and surrounding area. We used the standard distribution of images for the training and the query sets as defined by the authors of the dataset. The percentile and the median positional and rotational errors are shown in Table 2. The proposed technique successfully registered all the images in the query set.

4.4 Comparison with Other Approaches

Although the main purpose of our technique is to localize images in dense point clouds, we also compared the performance of our technique with popular and state-of-the-art SfM and Network based approaches that used the same datasets. We report the median location and orientation errors, on five of the common datasets between the different works, as only median errors were reported by other methods. Despite the large differences between the approaches, we achieved competitive accuracies for the outdoor datasets. For the indoor datasets, we achieved the best accuracies for position estimation. Table 3 shows the median errors of our technique as compared to other SfM-based and Network-based pose estimation methods.

5   Conclusion and Future Work

This paper has introduced a novel concept to directly compare 3D and 2D descriptors extracted using 3D and 2D feature techniques, respectively. We have demonstrated the performance of this technique for the application of 6-DOF pose localization of a query image in a dense 3D point cloud. This approach makes the localization pipeline much simpler compared to SfM or neural network based approaches. Unlike SfM-based approaches, the proposed technique can localize images in point clouds that have been directly generated from any 3D scanner. Our technique can work in both indoor and outdoor environments. Experiments show that the proposed technique achieves competitive or superior pose estimation accuracy, compared to other approaches. In the future, we will further refine our technique, followed by more detailed experimentation on other datasets and demonstrate its use for other tasks that can benefit from complementing 2D with 3D data.

Acknowledgments. This work was supported by the SIRF scholarship from the University of Western Australia (UWA) and by the Australian Research Council under Grant DP150100294.

References

1. Kendall, A., Grimes, M., Cipolla, R.: PoseNet: a convolutional network for real-time 6-DOF camera relocalization. In: International Conference on Computer Vision, pp. 2938–2946. IEEE (2015)
2. Schönberger, J.L., Frahm, J.-M.: Structure-from-motion revisited. In: Conference on Computer Vision and Pattern Recognition. IEEE (2016)
3. Lowe, D.G.: Distinctive image features from scale-invariant keypoints. Int. J. Comput. Vision **60**(2), 91–110 (2004)
4. Rusu, R.B., Cousins, S.: Point cloud library (PCL). In: International Conference on Robotics and Automation, pp. 1–4. IEEE (2011)
5. Harris, C.G., Stephens, M., et al.: A combined corner and edge detector. In: Alvey Vision Conference, vol. 15, pp. 10–5244. Citeseer (1988)
6. Lazebnik, S., Schmid, C., Ponce, J.: A sparse texture representation using local affine regions. IEEE Trans. Pattern Anal. Mach. Intell. **27**(8), 1265–1278 (2005)
7. Fischler, M.A., Bolles, R.C.: Random sample consensus: a paradigm for model fitting with applications to image analysis and automated cartography. Commun. ACM **24**(6), 381–395 (1981)
8. Chen, D.M., et al.: City-scale landmark identification on mobile devices. In: Conference on Computer Vision and Pattern Recognition, pp. 737–744. IEEE (2011)
9. Zamir, A.R., Shah, M.: Accurate image localization based on google maps street view. In: Daniilidis, K., Maragos, P., Paragios, N. (eds.) ECCV 2010. LNCS, vol. 6314, pp. 255–268. Springer, Heidelberg (2010). https://doi.org/10.1007/978-3-642-15561-1_19

10. Sattler, T., Leibe, B., Kobbelt, L.: Efficient & effective prioritized matching for large-scale image-based localization. IEEE Trans. Pattern Anal. Mach. Intell. **39**(9), 1744–1756 (2017)
11. Irschara, A., Zach, C., Frahm, J.-M., Bischof, H.: From structure-from-motion point clouds to fast location recognition. In: Conference on Computer Vision and Pattern Recognition, pp. 2599–2606. IEEE (2009)
12. Li, Y., Snavely, N., Huttenlocher, D.P.: Location recognition using prioritized feature matching. In: Daniilidis, K., Maragos, P., Paragios, N. (eds.) ECCV 2010. LNCS, vol. 6312, pp. 791–804. Springer, Heidelberg (2010). https://doi.org/10. 1007/978-3-642-15552-9_57
13. Sattler, T., Havlena, M., Radenovic, F., Schindler, K., Pollefeys, M.: Hyperpoints and fine vocabularies for large-scale location recognition. In: International Conference on Computer Vision, pp. 2102–2110. IEEE (2015)
14. Kendall, A., Cipolla, R.: Geometric loss functions for camera pose regression with deep learning. In: Conference on Computer Vision and Pattern Recognition, pp. 5974–5983. IEEE (2017)
15. Walch, F., Hazirbas, C., Leal-Taixe, L., Sattler, T., Hilsenbeck, S., Cremers, D.: Image-based localization using LSTMs for structured feature correlation. In: International Conference on Computer Vision, pp. 627–637. IEEE (2017)
16. Brachmann, E., et al.: DSAC-differentiable RANSAC for camera localization. In: Conference on Computer Vision and Pattern Recognition, pp. 6684–6692. IEEE (2017)
17. Shotton, J., Glocker, B., Zach, C., Izadi, S., Criminisi, A., Fitzgibbon, A.: Scene coordinate regression forests for camera relocalization in RGB-D images. In: Conference on Computer Vision and Pattern Recognition, pp. 2930–2937. IEEE (2013)
18. Schönberger, J.L., Zheng, E., Frahm, J.-M., Pollefeys, M.: Pixelwise view selection for unstructured multi-view stereo. In: Leibe, B., Matas, J., Sebe, N., Welling, M. (eds.) ECCV 2016. LNCS, vol. 9907, pp. 501–518. Springer, Cham (2016). https:// doi.org/10.1007/978-3-319-46487-9_31
19. Sattler, T., et al.: Benchmarking 6DOF outdoor visual localization in changing conditions. In: Conference on Computer Vision and Pattern Recognition, pp. 8601–8610. IEEE (2018)
20. Breiman, L.: Random forests. Mach. Learn. **45**(1), 5–32 (2001)
21. Gao, X.-S., Hou, X.-R., Tang, J., Cheng, H.-F.: Complete solution classification for the perspective-three-point problem. IEEE Trans. Pattern Anal. Mach. Intell. **25**(8), 930–943 (2003)
22. Torr, P.H., Zisserman, A.: MLESAC: a new robust estimator with application to estimating image geometry. Comput. Vis. Image Underst. **78**(1), 138–156 (2000)
23. Hane, C., Zach, C., Cohen, A., Angst, R., Pollefeys, M.: Joint 3D scene reconstruction and class segmentation. In: Conference on Computer Vision and Pattern Recognition, pp. 97–104. IEEE (2013)
24. Snavely, N., Seitz, S.M., Szeliski, R.: Modeling the world from internet photo collections. Int. J. Comput. Vision **80**(2), 189–210 (2008)
25. Valada, A., Radwan, N., Burgard, W.: Deep auxiliary learning for visual localization and odometry. In: International Conference on Robotics and Automation, pp. 6939–6946. IEEE (2018)

Learning from Incomplete Data

Improving Object Detection with Consistent Negative Sample Mining

Xiaolian Wang[1,2], Xiyuan Hu[1,2], Chen Chen[1,2(✉)], Zhenfeng Fan[1,2],
and Silong Peng[1,2,3]

[1] Institute of Automation, Chinese Academy of Sciences, Beijing, China
{wangxiaolian2016,xiyuan.hu,chen.chen,
fanzhenfeng2016,silong.peng}@ia.ac.cn
[2] University of Chinese Academy of Sciences, Beijing, China
[3] Beijing ViSystem Corporation Limited, Beijing, China

Abstract. In object detection, training samples are divided into negatives and positives simply according to their initial positions on images. Samples which have low overlap with ground-truths are assigned to negatives, and positives otherwise. Once allocated, the negative and positive set are fixed in training. A usually overlooked issue is that certain negatives do not stick to their original states as training proceeds. They gradually regress towards foreground objects rather than away from them, which contradicts the nature of negatives. Training with such inconsistent negatives may confuse detectors in distinguishing between foreground and background, and thus makes training less effective. In this paper, we propose a *consistent negative sample mining* method to filter out biased negatives in training. Specifically, the neural network takes the regression performance into account, and dynamically activates consistent negatives which have both low input IoUs and low output IoUs for training. In the experiments, we evaluate our method on PASCAL VOC and KITTI datasets, and the improvements on both datasets demonstrate the effectiveness of our method.

Keywords: Object detection · Sample mining · Consistent negatives

1 Introduction

Deep learning [1] has become a powerful technology and brought great success to many fields such as object detection, video captioning, speech recognition, machine translation and so on. The learning of Deep Neural Networks (DNNs) heavily relies on data, thus a proper set of training samples is very important. Unlike image classification, positives/negatives are sampled from different positions of images in object detection. Specifically, most modern detectors [3–9, 11, 12, 20] first create a large pool of prior boxes with various sizes (also named *default boxes* in [4], *grid cells* in [7] and *anchors* in [3]) densely tiled on images before training, which serve as reference for predicting objects [3].

© Springer Nature Switzerland AG 2019
T. Gedeon et al. (Eds.): ICONIP 2019, LNCS 11954, pp. 237–247, 2019.
https://doi.org/10.1007/978-3-030-36711-4_21

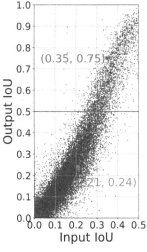

(b) Negative prior boxes

(a) IoU distribution of negatives	(c) Regressed boxes

Fig. 1. (a) IoU distribution of negatives before and after regression when $\mu_n = 0.5$. Negatives above the red line are considered to be inconsistent. The orange and red dots correspond to the orange and red boxes in right figures, respectively. (b) Visualization of the two negative prior boxes. (c) Visualization of regressed boxes predicted by the two negatives. The green boxes are ground-truths. (Color figure onine)

Then the Intersection over Union (IoU) between each prior box and its nearest ground-truth object is computed. A box is positive if it is the best match of any ground-truth or the IoU is higher than a positive threshold μ_p, otherwise assigned to a negative if the IoU is lower than a negative threshold μ_n ($\mu_n \leq \mu_p$). The other unassigned prior boxes are neutrals, and do not contribute to the training process.

It is generally believed that in training the negativity and positivity of samples are consistent with initialization, thus the negative and positive set are fixed to iteratively optimize models towards targets. However, the premise of applying fixed sample sets fails, as we observe inconsistency in negatives. Certain negative boxes are attracted to objects rather than stay in the background as the data-driven optimization proceeds. We depict the distribution of negatives' IoUs before and after regression when $\mu_n = 0.5$ in Fig. 1(a) for better illustration. The x-axis is *input IoU*, which is referred to as the initial overlap between prior boxes and their nearest objects. The y-axis is *output IoU*, denoting the IoU between the regressed box and its nearest ground-truth instance. After regression, only negatives below the red line adhere to the initial allocation principle to have IoUs smaller than μ_n. We further visualize behaviors of two negatives (the orange and red dot in Fig. 1(a)) in right figures, where initial positions of negatives are shown in Fig. 1(b), and the regressed boxes are shown in Fig. 1(c). The orange box consistently keeps a low overlap with its nearest object, while the red one regresses to a tight box around the car.

Negatives serve to guide detectors in learning discriminative background features, but training with inconsistent negatives may result in optimization ambiguity. In this study, a *consistent negative sample mining* method is proposed to address the inconsistency issue. Instead of throwing all stiffly pre-assigned negatives into training, we dynamically activate them based on their regression performance to mine consistent negatives throughout training, thus the biased negative set can be adaptively adjusted. In the experiments, we evaluate our method on PASCAL VOC [28] and KITTI [27], and achieve notable improvement on both datasets.

2 Related Work

In previous literature, the allocation of negatives/positives is an empirical and one-time operation based on samples' initial positions on images, and the choice of (μ_n, μ_p) varies among detectors. The single-threshold $\mu_p = \mu_n = 0.5$ [2,4,5,12–20] may be the most popular setting. Other detectors embed neutrals between negatives and positives to soften the division. They adopt dual-thresholds such as (0.4, 0.5) [9,11], (0.3, 0.45) [21], (0.3, 0.5) [22] and (0.3, 0.7) [3,23–26]. For cascade-like detectors [6,29], multiple thresholds are applied for different stages. In [6], authors adopt three single-thresholds $\{0.5, 0.6, 0.7\}$ in three stages, respectively. In [29], thresholds are set to $\{(0.3, 0.5), (0.4, 0.6), (0.5, 0.7)\}$ in three steps.

These detectors focus on the IoU distance between the positive and negative set, and an effective initialization for positives. However, they overlook the inconsistency of biased negatives in training and cannot handle this problem with static sample allocation. Our consistent negative sample mining method is a dynamic operation and can address the inconsistency issue without introducing new parameters.

3 Consistent Negative Sample Mining

This section describes our consistent negative sample mining method for training detectors. We first introduce consistent negatives in Sect. 3.1, then propose a dynamic loss which differs from the standard function in Sect. 3.2. Practical operations are further specified in Sect. 3.3. We finally discuss the differences between our method and previous sample mining in Sect. 3.4.

3.1 Consistent Negative Samples

Let $\mathcal{S}$ be the set of prior boxes sampled from images before training, and $\mathcal{G}$ be the ground-truth box set. We then refer to $I(s; k)$ as the input IoU of sample $s \in \mathcal{S}$, and $O(s; k)$ as its output IoU in the k-th training step:

$$I(s; k) = \max_{g \in \mathcal{G}} \text{IoU}(s, g)$$
$$O(s; k) = \max_{g \in \mathcal{G}} \text{IoU}(R(s; k), g) \tag{1}$$

where $R(s; k)$ denotes the regressed box of sample s in the k-th iteration. The initial negative set $\mathcal{N}_0$ is determined by the negative threshold μ_n:

$$\mathcal{N}_0 = \{s \in \mathcal{S} | I(s; 0) < \mu_n\}. \tag{2}$$

Now our purpose is to mine the consistent negative set $\mathcal{N}_k \subseteq \mathcal{N}_0$ throughout training.

The sample s is considered to be a consistent negative in the k-th training step only if it satisfies the following conditions:

$$I(s; k) < \mu_n \quad \text{and} \quad O(s; k) < \mu_n. \tag{3}$$

Note that

$$I(s; k) = I(s; 0), \quad \forall k \in \{1, 2, \ldots, K\} \tag{4}$$

where K is the number of training steps, thus our consistent negative set $\mathcal{N}_k$ is defined as

$$\mathcal{N}_k = \{s \in \mathcal{S} | I(s; k) < \mu_n, O(s; k) < \mu_n\} = \{s \in \mathcal{N}_0 | O(s; k) < \mu_n\}. \tag{5}$$

These dynamically selected negatives have low input IoUs as well as low output IoUs, ensuring the negative set composed of samples consistently performing as background.

3.2 Loss Function

Object detectors are usually optimized by a joint objective function [2–4] composed of the loss for classification (cls) and localization (loc):

$$L(c_s, r_s) = \sum_{s \in \mathcal{P}} (L_{\text{cls}}(c_s) + \alpha L_{\text{loc}}(r_s)) + \sum_{s \in \mathcal{N}_0} L_{\text{cls}}(c_s), \tag{6}$$

where $\mathcal{P}$ is the positive set, α is a weight term commonly set to 1, c_s is estimated classification confidence and r_s is regressed location offsets of sample s. Negatives have no ground-truth positions, thus no regression optimization is imposed on negatives.

The second negative loss term is static and not aware of the existence of inconsistent negatives among the initial allocation. We thus propose a dynamic classification loss term $L_{\text{Neg}}^{\text{CN}}$ for consistent negatives as follow:

$$L_{\text{Neg}}^{\text{CN}}(c_s; k) = \sum_{s \in \mathcal{N}_k} L_{\text{cls}}(c_s; k). \tag{7}$$

The overall objective function is

$$L(c_s, r_s; k) = \sum_{s \in \mathcal{P}} (L_{\text{cls}}(c_s) + \alpha L_{\text{loc}}(r_s)) + \sum_{s \in \mathcal{N}_k} L_{\text{cls}}(c_s; k). \tag{8}$$

Different from the original negative loss term which simply supervises negative classification scores, the newly introduced $L_{\text{Neg}}^{\text{CN}}(c_s; k)$ inherently takes the regression behavior of negatives into consideration, as the classification loss can only sum over samples from the consistent negative set $\mathcal{N}_k$ which is dynamically constructed according to the regressed positions of negatives.

Algorithm 1. Training Detectors with Consistent Negative Sample Mining

Input: $\mathcal{S}, \mathcal{G}, \mathcal{P}, \mathcal{N}_0, R(\cdot), \mu_n, K$

    $\mathcal{S}$ is the set of all prior boxes
    $\mathcal{G}$ is the set of ground-truth boxes
    $\mathcal{P}$ is the set of positives
    $\mathcal{N}_0$ is the set of initial negatives
    $R(\cdot)$ is the function mapping prior boxes to regressed boxes
    μ_n is the negative allocation threshold
    K is the number of training steps

1: **for** $k \leftarrow 1, 2, \ldots, K$ **do**
2:     $\mathcal{N}_k \leftarrow \varnothing$
3:     **for** $s \in \mathcal{N}_0$ **do**
4:         **if** $\max\limits_{g \in \mathcal{G}} \text{IoU}(R(s;k), g) < \mu_n$ **then**
5:             $\mathcal{N}_k \leftarrow \mathcal{N}_k \cup \{s\}$
6:         **end if**
7:     **end for**
8:     Train the detector with the positive set $\mathcal{P}$ and current negative set $\mathcal{N}_k$
9: **end for**

3.3 Training Process

We summarize the implementation of our method in Algorithm 1. As a dynamic refinement of the negative set, we embed this module after the sample allocation process to provide detectors with beneficial negatives related to the training status. The negative set is adjusted in each training step, and those inconsistent negatives $s \in \mathcal{N}_0 \backslash \mathcal{N}_k$ are adaptively excluded from training to reduce optimization ambiguity between foreground and background.

The proposed module can also be inserted into the calculation of classification loss to serve as a reweighting of negatives. Only the weights of consistent negatives are activated to 1 while others are 0 in the negative loss term.

Furthermore, since no modification of the neural network architecture is required, our approach can be conveniently applied in various detectors.

3.4 Discussion

Our method is a kind of sample mining but has totally different intentions from previous approaches such as *Online Hard Example Mining* (OHEM) [10] and *Focal Loss* (FL) [11]. These methods are proposed base on a consensus that training with vast number of easy samples may hinder the improvement of detection performance. Thus they discard or lower the weights of samples with small classification losses, and focus on training with the hard ones.

We ascribe one of reasons for ineffective training to the inconsistency of negatives and hold the view that training with consistent negatives is also important as hard samples. These two approaches promote the optimization process from two different perspectives: one discounts the effect of well-classified samples while the other one mitigates the impact of biased negatives which regress to foreground. Consistent negatives are not necessarily hard samples which have large classification losses and vice versa. Thus the methods of mining consistent negatives and mining hard samples complement each other, and can be combined together to further benefit object detection as experimentally demonstrated in Sect. 4.3.

4 Experiments

4.1 Experimental Configuration

Datasets. We evaluate the proposed method on two datasets, PASCAL VOC [28] and KITTI [27]. PASCAL VOC is a generic object detection dataset composed of 20 categories. We use the VOC 2007 and VOC 2012 *trainval* sets for training, and test on the VOC 2007 *test* set. The KITTI dataset is a large benchmark for autonomous driving and we evaluate our method mainly on the *car* subset. Following previous object detection works, results evaluated by mean Average Precision (mAP) and Average Precision (AP) at the matching IoU of 0.5 are reported for PASCAL VOC and KITTI, respectively.

Implementation Details. All experiments are conducted on Keras [33] platform. In our implementation, the mining of consistent negatives proceeds in sequence as shown in Algorithm 1, thus the time of training increases with the number of initial negatives. We provide a quicker version: only check samples with input IoUs between 0.1 and μ_n. This operation is based on the observation that prior boxes with input IoUs lower than 0.1 are mostly background-like in training, thus they can be permanently activated as negatives. Moreover, parallel implementation can be developed to further accelerate the process, since the behavior examination of negatives is independent of each other.

4.2 Comparison with State-of-the-Arts on PASCAL VOC

We first evaluate our method on PASCAL VOC dataset. We apply consistent negatives in two baseline frameworks, the classical object detector SSD [4] as well as the recent RefineDet [20], respectively. For fair comparison, we reproduce the results of the two baseline detectors in Keras[1], which are denoted by the symbol * in Table 1. Following the works listed in Table 1, SSD and RefineDet are pre-trained on MS COCO [30] dataset. We fine-tune the resulting models using SGD with initial learning rate 10^{-4}, 0.9 momentum and 0.0005 weight decay. For SSD, we set the batch size to 32 and train the model with 10^{-4} learning rate for the first 40 epochs (approximately $21k$ iterations), then 10^{-5} and 10^{-6} for another two 10 epochs. For RefineDet, we set the batch size to 24 and train the model with 10^{-4} learning rate for the first 48 epochs (approximately $33k$ iterations), then 10^{-5} and 10^{-6} for another two 12 epochs. Our detection results along with other recent top-performing detectors are reported in Table 1.

---

[1] Our codes are based on https://github.com/pierluigiferrari/ssd_keras.

Table 1. Detection results on PASCAL VOC 2007 *test* set. The symbol * represents results of our reproduction, and *CNSM* is short for *Consistent Negative Sample Mining*.

Method	Backbone	Input size	mAP
Faster R-CNN [3]	VGG-16	~1000 × 600	78.8
Faster R-CNN+++ [34]	ResNet-101	~1000 × 600	85.6
R-FCN ms train [5]	ResNet-101	-	83.6
R-FCN++ ms train [35]	ResNet-101	-	84.9
SSD300 [4]	VGG-16	300 × 300	79.6
SSD512 [4]	VGG-16	512 × 512	81.6
RON320 [22]	VGG-16	320 × 320	78.7
RON384 [22]	VGG-16	384 × 384	80.2
RON320++ [22]	VGG-16	-	80.3
RON384++ [22]	VGG-16	-	81.3
DSOD300 [31]	DS/64-192-48-1	300 × 300	81.7
DES300 [32]	VGG-16	300 × 300	82.7
DES512 [32]	VGG-16	512 × 512	84.3
RefineDet320 [20]	VGG-16	320 × 320	84.0
RefineDet512 [20]	VGG-16	512 × 512	85.2
SSD300*	VGG-16	300 × 300	80.2
SSD300*+CNSM	VGG-16	300 × 300	80.9
RefineDet320*	VGG-16	320 × 320	84.2
RefineDet320*+CNSM	VGG-16	320 × 320	**86.2**

As shown in Table 1, we obtain +0.7 mAP gain on SSD300 compared with our reproduction 80.2. Note that RON384 [22] also achieves a similar gain (+0.6 mAP) above the original SSD result 79.6. However, RON384 applies a complex architecture designed on SSD with objectness prior, and enlarges the input resolutions to get better performance. Thus being a basic sample mining process, our method makes quite meaningful improvement in detection. As for RefineDet320, the detector applying consistent negatives obtains significant performance of 86.2 mAP, which is +2.0 mAP better than the reproduced baseline 84.2. RefineDet contains an anchor refinement module which first distinguishes between objects and background, and then filters out well-classified negatives to solve the class imbalance issue to some extent. Our method is embedded after this module to first refine the negative set, and then boost the performance together with easy-negatives filtering.

4.3 Extension Experiments on KITTI

We further evaluate the performance of our method on the *car* subset of KITTI dataset. All experiments in this section are conducted on SSD300, and we refer to

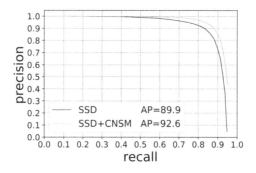

Fig. 2. Precision-Recall curves on the *car* subset of KITTI *val* set.

CNSM which appears in Table 2 and Fig. 2 as the short for *Consistent Negative Sample Mining.*

Table 2. Performance of sample mining methods on the *car* subset of KITTI *val* set.

Method	AP	AP_{small}	AP_{medium}	AP_{large}	Training time (ms/image)
Initial	89.2	83.8	93.1	96.4	95.28
Initial+CNSM	**91.2**	**86.8**	**95.0**	**97.3**	97.36
Gain	+2.0	**+3.0**	+1.9	+0.9	-
OHEM	91.3	87.8	94.5	96.4	95.69
OHEM+CNSM	**92.6**	**89.4**	**95.3**	**97.1**	98.75
Gain	+1.3	**+1.6**	+0.8	+0.7	-
FL	90.5	85.9	93.6	97.1	101.94
FL+CNSM	**92.5**	**89.2**	**95.0**	**97.1**	108.89
Gain	+2.0	**+3.3**	+1.4	+0.0	-

Performance of Two-Class Object Detection. The precision-recall curves of *car* subset are shown in Fig. 2. At the same recall rate, SSD applying consistent negatives achieves higher precision than the vanilla SSD, resulting in +2.7 AP gain in total. This increment is greater than the average gain of multi-class detection results observed on PASCAL VOC for SSD (+0.7). The reason might be that our approach is a class-agnostic sample mining method and focuses on keeping the distinction between all foreground objects and background, thus the pertinence of detecting a specific category is weakened when coping with multiple classes. As for two-class (including background) object detection, mining representative negatives is equivalent to directly discriminating between the target class and non-objects, thus the performance of detectors can be significantly improved. Similar results are further observed on the *pedestrian* and *cyclist* subset, where vanilla SSD achieves 56.0% and 78.7% AP while applying CNSM boosts performance to 68.8% and 82.1%, respectively.

Relation with Hard Sample Mining Methods. We explore the relation between our consistent negative sample mining and hard sample mining methods such as OHEM and FL on negatives. We embed our approach into three baseline implementations: training initialized negatives without sample mining (denoted by *Initial*), training with OHEM and FL. For FL, we follow the original paper [11] to adopt sigmoid loss in classification, and we apply the typical softmax loss to the other two settings. As shown in Table 2, *Initial+CNSM* gets comparable results (91.2 AP) with *OHEM*[2] (91.3 AP), verifying the argument in Sect. 3.4 that training with consistent negatives is important and effective for detectors as mining hard negatives. Furthermore, detectors applying CNSM are about +2.0, +1.3 and +2.0 AP higher than their corresponding baselines, respectively. This implies that our method is complementary to hard sample mining methods, and detectors can further benefit from combining the two applications together.

We also report the detection performance on different sizes of objects in Table 2 and observe the highest AP increment is on *small* in all the three implementations. Training with consistent negatives focuses detectors on learning discriminative foreground and background features, thus more small objects can be correctly detected in our method. The average time of training an image is also summarized. The proposed method improves the detection performance only at a marginal cost of computational time, i.e. an average of 4.03 ms per image across the three settings.

5 Conclusion

We propose a consistent negative sample mining method for the training of detectors. The main idea is to mitigate the impact of biased negative set which inappropriately sticks to the initialization. Specifically, we pick out samples consistently regressed as background from initialized negatives to build a dynamic negative set for each training step. Our approach can be conveniently combined with hard sample mining to further improve detection performance. Experimental results on PASCAL VOC and KITTI dataset demonstrate the effectiveness of our method. We hope this work can be one of the small steps focusing on the basic issues for the advance of object detection.

Acknowledgments. All correspondences should be forwarded to Chen Chen, the corresponding author, via chen.chen@ia.ac.cn. This work was supported by the National Science Foundation of China under Grant NSFC 61906194.

---

[2] Softmax loss is used in both *Initial* and *OHEM*, thus *Initial+CNSM* can be compared with *OHEM* to evaluate the effectiveness of CNSM.

References

1. LeCun, Y., Bengio, Y., Hinton, G.: Deep learning. Nature **521**(7553), 436 (2015)
2. Girshick, R.: Fast R-CNN. In: Proceedings of the IEEE Conference on Computer Vision and Pattern Recognition, pp. 1440–1448 (2015)
3. Ren, S., He, K., Girshick, R., Sun, J.: Faster R-CNN: towards real-time object detection with region proposal networks. In: International Conference on Neural Information Processing Systems, vol. 39, pp. 91–99. MIT Press, Cambridge (2015)
4. Liu, W., et al.: SSD: single shot multibox detector. In: Leibe, B., Matas, J., Sebe, N., Welling, M. (eds.) ECCV 2016. LNCS, vol. 9905, pp. 21–37. Springer, Cham (2016). https://doi.org/10.1007/978-3-319-46448-0_2
5. Li, Y., He, K., Sun, J., Dai, J.: R-FCN: object detection via region-based fully convolutional networks. In: Advances in Neural Information Processing Systems, pp. 379–387 (2016)
6. Cai, Z., Vasconcelos, N.: Cascade R-CNN: delving into high quality object detection. In: Proceedings of the IEEE Conference on Computer Vision and Pattern Recognition, pp. 6154–6162 (2018)
7. Redmon, J., Divvala, S., Girshick, R., Farhadi, A.: You only look once: unified, real-time object detection. In: Proceedings of the IEEE conference on Computer Vision and Pattern Recognition, pp. 779–788 (2016)
8. Redmon, J., Farhadi, A.: YOLO9000: better, faster, stronger. In: Proceedings of the IEEE Conference on Computer Vision and Pattern Recognition, pp. 7263–7271 (2017)
9. Yang, T., Zhang, X., Zhang, W., Sun, J.: MetaAnchor: learning to detect objects with customized anchors. In: International Conference on Neural Information Processing Systems (2018)
10. Shrivastava, A., Gupta, A., Girshick, R.: Training region-based object detectors with online hard example mining. In: Proceedings of the IEEE Conference on Computer Vision and Pattern Recognition (2016)
11. Lin, T.-Y., Goyal, P., Girshick, R., He, K., Dollar, P.: Focal loss for dense object detection. In: Proceedings of the IEEE International Conference on Computer Vision, pp. 2980–2988 (2017)
12. He, K., Gkioxari, G., Dollar, P., Girshick, R.: Mask R-CNN. In: Proceedings of the IEEE International Conference on Computer Vision, pp. 2961–2969 (2017)
13. Li, Y., Chen, Y., Wang, N., Zhang, Z.: Scale-aware trident networks for object detection (2019). arXiv preprint arXiv:1901.01892
14. Wang, X., Xiao, T., Jiang, Y., Shao, S., Sun, J., Shen, C.: Repulsion loss: detecting pedestrians in a crowd. In: Proceedings of the IEEE Conference on Computer Vision and Pattern Recognition (2018)
15. Brazil, G., Yin, X., Liu, X.: Illuminating pedestrians via simultaneous detection and segmentation. In: Proceedings of the IEEE International Conference on Computer Vision, pp. 4960–4969 (2017)
16. Wang, X., Jung, C., Hero, A.O.: Part-level fully convolutional networks for pedestrian detection. In: International Conference on Acoustics, Speech and Signal Processing, pp. 2267–2271 (2017)
17. Fu, C.-Y., Liu, W., Ranga, A., Tyagi, A., Berg, A.C.: DSSD: deconvolutional single shot detector (2017). arXiv preprint arXiv:1701.06659
18. Zhou, P., Ni, B., Geng, C., Hu, J., Xu, Y.: Scale-transferrable object detection. In: Proceedings of the IEEE Conference on Computer Vision and Pattern Recognition (2018)

19. Du, X., El-Khamy, M., Lee, J., Davis, L.: Fused DNN: a deep neural network fusion approach to fast and robust pedestrian detection. In: Applications of Computer Vision, pp. 953–961 (2017)
20. Zhang, S., Wen, L., Bian, X., Lei, Z., Li, S.Z.: Single-shot refinement neural network for object detection. In: Proceedings of the IEEE Conference on Computer Vision and Pattern Recognition, pp. 4203–4212 (2018)
21. Kong, T., Yao, A., Chen, Y., Sun, F.: HyperNet: towards accurate region proposal generation and joint object detection. In: Proceedings of the IEEE Conference on Computer Vision and Pattern Recognition, pp. 845–853 (2016)
22. Kong, T., Sun, F., Yao, A., Liu, H., Lu, M., Chen, Y.: RON: reverse connection with objectness prior networks for Object Detection. In: Proceedings of the IEEE Conference on Computer Vision and Pattern Recognition (2017)
23. He, K., Zhang, X., Ren, S., Sun, J.: Spatial pyramid pooling in deep convolutional networks for visual recognition. In: Proceedings of the European Conference on Computer Vision, pp. 346–361 (2014)
24. Lin, T., Dollr, P., Girshick, R., He, K., Hariharan, B., Belongie, S.: Feature pyramid networks for object detection. In: Proceedings of the IEEE Conference on Computer Vision and Pattern Recognition (2017)
25. Li, Z., Peng, C., Yu, G., Zhang, X., Deng, Y., Sun, J.: Light-head R-CNN: in defense of two-stage object detector (2017). arXiv preprint arXiv:1711.07264
26. Rao, Y., Lin, D., Lu, J., Zhou, J.: Learning globally optimized object detector via policy gradient. In: Proceedings of the IEEE Conference on Computer Vision and Pattern Recognition (2018)
27. Geiger, A., Lenz, P., Urtasun, R.: Are we ready for autonomous driving? The KITTI vision benchmark suite. In: Proceedings of the IEEE Conference on Computer Vision and Pattern Recognition (2012)
28. Everingham, M., Van Gool, L., Williams, C.K., Winn, J., Zisserman, A.: The pascal visual object classes (VOC) challenge. J. Int. J. Comput. Vis. **88**(2), 303–338 (2010)
29. Liu, W., Liao, S., Hu, W., Liang, X., Chen, X.: Learning efficient single-stage pedestrian detectors by asymptotic localization fitting. In: Proceedings of the European Conference on Computer Vision (2018)
30. Lin, T., et al.: Microsoft COCO: common objects in context. In: Proceedings of the European Conference on Computer Vision, pp. 740–755 (2014)
31. Shen, Z., Liu, Z., Li, J., Jiang, Y., Chen, Y., Xue, X.: DSOD: learning deeply supervised object detectors from scratch. In: Proceedings of the IEEE International Conference on Computer Vision (2017)
32. Zhang, Z., Qiao, S., Xie, C., Shen, W., Wang, B., Yuille, A.L.: Single-shot object detection with enriched semantics. In: Proceedings of the IEEE Conference on Computer Vision and Pattern Recognition (2018)
33. Chollet, F.: Keras (2015). https://github.com/fchollet/keras
34. He, K., Zhang, X., Ren, S., Sun, J.: Deep residual learning for image recognition. In: Proceedings of the IEEE Conference on Computer Vision and Pattern Recognition (2016)
35. Li, Z., Chen, Y., Yu, G., Deng, Y.: R-FCN++: towards accurate region-based fully convolutional networks for object detection. In: AAAI Conference on Artificial Intelligence (2018)

A Model Selection Criterion for LASSO Estimate with Scaling

Katsuyuki Hagiwara[✉]

Faculty of Education, Mie University, 1577 Kurima-Machiya-cho,
Tsu 514-8507, Japan
hagi@edu.mie-u.ac.jp

Abstract. There have been several studies to relax a bias problem in
LASSO (Least Absolute Shrinkage and Selection Operator). In this article, we considered to solve a bias problem of LASSO estimator by scaling
and derived a model selection criterion under the scaling method. The
proposed scaling value is valid to compensate the excessive shrinkage
of LASSO estimator and is easy to compute by using LASSO estimator. Moreover, we derived SURE (Stein's Unbiased Risk Estimate) as a
model selection criterion. This analytic solution is also a benefit of the
proposed scaling value. Furthermore, we verified the risk estimate and
confirmed its effectiveness through a simple numerical example.

Keywords: Sparse modeling · LASSO · SURE · Scaling

1 Introduction

A sparse modeling is a major topic in machine learning and statistics. Especially, LASSO (Least Absolute Shrinkage and Selection Operator) is a popular
method that has been extensively studied [4–6,8,10,12,13,17,18]. LASSO is an
ℓ_1 penalized least squares method and has a nature of soft-thresholding that
implements thresholding and shrinkage of coefficients; e.g. [3]. These two properties are simultaneously controlled by a single regularization parameter. This
causes an excessive shrinkage, thus, a large bias that is directly related to a
consistency of model selection by LASSO. This fact has been pointed out by
[6,9,10]. Several methods have been proposed for solving this problem such as
adaptive LASSO [17], relaxed LASSO [10], SCAD [6] and MCP [16]. From a theoretical point of view, adaptive LASSO, SCAD and MCP have been shown to
have nice asymptotic properties under an appropriate choice of the regularization
parameter; i.e. oracle property. Despite of these excellent theoretical analyses,
the choice of the regularization parameter relies on the cross validation in their
applications and theoretical studies for model selection seem to be restrictive for
these methods. Contrastly, for LASSO and its variants, [4,13,18] have derived
SURE (Stein's Unbiased Risk Estimate) which is an analytic C_p-type model
selection criterion for choosing the regularization parameter.

© Springer Nature Switzerland AG 2019
T. Gedeon et al. (Eds.): ICONIP 2019, LNCS 11954, pp. 248–259, 2019.
https://doi.org/10.1007/978-3-030-36711-4_22

In this article, we consider a method for improving a bias problem of LASSO and, simultaneously give SURE under the method. The new method is to introduce a scaling for LASSO estimator; i.e. scalar times of LASSO estimator [7]. We here employ an appropriate empirical scaling value which actually improves the excessive shrinkage, thus a bias in LASSO. The empirical scaling value has a simple form that is calculated by using LASSO estimator; i.e. LASSO estimator is plugged into the scaling value and, thus, our method is the two stage estimation. Therefore, in our method, we just need LASSO estimator that can be obtained by a fast and stable method such as LARS (Least Angle Regression) [5] under LASSO modification or coordinate descent [14]. This is a benefit of our method in comparing with the other methods including non-convex methods. In addition, a simplicity of our scaling method enables us to derive SURE.

Our scaling method is closely related to adaptive LASSO and relaxed LASSO. Adaptive LASSO controls biases by coefficient-wise weights in ℓ_1 regularizer, in which the least squares estimators are plugged into the weights. As an improvement of adaptive LASSO, multi-step adaptive LASSO has been proposed in [1]; see also [15]. Multi-step adaptive LASSO employ adaptive LASSO at each cycle, in which LASSO estimators are employed as initial estimators in weights. Multi-step adaptive LASSO is similar to our scaling method since it also employs LASSO estimator in the weights. On the other hand, in relaxed LASSO, shrinkage and thresholding parameters are introduced differently. Relaxed LASSO can be viewed as controlling an amount of shrinkage independently of a threshold level. In this point of view, in our scaling method, thresholding is achieved by LASSO and an amount of shrinkage is controlled by a scaling value. Unfortunately, unlike our scaling method, analytic studies of model selection have not been discussed for these methods.

In Sect. 2, we give a regression framework including LASSO and a definition of risk with its Stein's formula. In Sect. 3, we introduce a scaling of LASSO estimator. Especially, we give a reasonable empirical scaling value and derive SURE under the given scaling value. In Sect. 4, we verify our results in Sect. 3 through a simple numerical example. Section 5 is devoted for conclusions and future works.

2   LASSO with Scaling

2.1   Regression Problem and LASSO

Let $\boldsymbol{x} = (x_1, \ldots, x_m)$ and y be explanatory variables and a response variable, for which we have n samples : $\{(x_{i,1}, \ldots, x_{i,m}, y_i) : i = 1, \ldots, n\}$. We define $\boldsymbol{x}_j = (x_{1,j}, \ldots, x_{n,j})' \in \mathbb{R}^n$ for $j = 1, \ldots, m$, where $'$ stands for the transpose operator. We define $\mathbf{X} = (\boldsymbol{x}_1, \ldots, \boldsymbol{x}_m)$ and $\boldsymbol{y} = (y_1, \ldots, y_n)'$. In this article, we assume that $m \leq n$ holds and $\boldsymbol{x}_1, \ldots, \boldsymbol{x}_m$ are linearly independent. Therefore, $\mathbf{X}'\mathbf{X}$ is not singular here. Let $\varepsilon_1, \ldots, \varepsilon_n$ be i.i.d. samples from $N(0, \sigma^2)$; i.e. normal distribution with mean 0 and variance σ^2. Thus, by defining $\boldsymbol{\varepsilon} = (\varepsilon_1, \ldots, \varepsilon_n)'$, $\boldsymbol{\varepsilon} \sim N(\mathbf{0}_n, \sigma^2 \mathbf{I}_n)$, where $\mathbf{0}_n$ is an n-dimensional zero vector and $\mathbf{I}_n$ is an $n \times n$ identity matrix. We assume $\boldsymbol{y} = \boldsymbol{\mu} + \boldsymbol{\varepsilon}$, where $\boldsymbol{\mu} = (\mu_1, \ldots, \mu_n)'$.

We therefore have $\boldsymbol{\mu} = \mathbb{E}\boldsymbol{y}$, where $\mathbb{E}$ is the expectation with respect to the joint probability distribution of $\boldsymbol{y}$. We consider a regression problem by $\mathbf{X}\boldsymbol{b}$, where $\boldsymbol{b} = (b_1, \ldots, b_m)$ is a coefficient vector. Let $\widehat{\boldsymbol{b}} = (\widehat{b}_1, \ldots, \widehat{b}_m)$ be an estimator of $\boldsymbol{b}$. LASSO is a method for obtaining coefficient estimators that minimize ℓ_1 regularized cost function defined by

$$C_\lambda(\boldsymbol{b}) = \|\boldsymbol{y} - \mathbf{X}\boldsymbol{b}\|^2 + \lambda\|\boldsymbol{b}\|_1, \tag{1}$$

where $\|\cdot\|$ is the Euclidean norm and $\|\cdot\|_1$ is the ℓ_1 norm. $\lambda \geq 0$ is a regularization parameter. The second term of the right hand side of (1) is called ℓ_1 regularizer. Let $\widehat{\boldsymbol{b}}_\lambda = (\widehat{b}_{1,\lambda}, \ldots, \widehat{b}_{m,\lambda})$ be a LASSO solution. Since LASSO is known to yield a sparse representation under an appropriate choice of λ, some of elements in $\widehat{\boldsymbol{b}}_\lambda$ are exactly zeros. We denote a LASSO output vector by $\widehat{\boldsymbol{\mu}}_\lambda = (\widehat{\mu}_{\lambda,1}, \ldots, \widehat{\mu}_{\lambda,n})'$ that is given by $\widehat{\boldsymbol{\mu}}_\lambda = \mathbf{X}\widehat{\boldsymbol{b}}_\lambda$. We define $\widehat{B}_\lambda = \{i : \widehat{b}_{i,\lambda} \neq 0\}$ and $\widehat{k}_\lambda = |\widehat{B}_\lambda|$. $\widehat{B}_\lambda$ is called an active set or support.

Let $\mathbf{X}_{\widehat{B}_\lambda}$ be an $n \times \widehat{k}_\lambda$ matrix whose column vectors are $\{\boldsymbol{x}_j : j \in \widehat{B}_\lambda\}$. We write $\widehat{\mathbf{X}}_\lambda = \mathbf{X}_{\widehat{B}_\lambda}$ for simplicity. Also we define $\widehat{\boldsymbol{\beta}}_\lambda$ as a $\widehat{k}_\lambda$-dimensional vector whose elements are $\{\widehat{b}_k : k \in \widehat{B}_\lambda\}$. We write $\widehat{\boldsymbol{\beta}}_\lambda = (\widehat{\beta}_{1,\lambda}, \ldots, \widehat{\beta}_{\widehat{k},\lambda})'$; i.e. $\widehat{\beta}_{k,\lambda}$ is a member of $\{\widehat{b}_k : k \in \widehat{B}_\lambda\}$ under an appropriate enumeration. Under this definition, we have $\widehat{\boldsymbol{\mu}}_\lambda = \widehat{\mathbf{X}}_\lambda\widehat{\boldsymbol{\beta}}_\lambda$ since $\widehat{b}_{k,\lambda} = 0$ for $k \notin \widehat{B}_\lambda$. Let $\widehat{\mathbf{S}}_\lambda = (\widehat{S}_{1,\lambda}, \ldots, \widehat{S}_{\widehat{k},\lambda})'$ be a sign vector of $\widehat{\boldsymbol{\beta}}_\lambda$; i.e.

$$\widehat{S}_{j,\lambda} = \begin{cases} 1 & \widehat{\beta}_{j,\lambda} > 0 \\ 0 & \widehat{\beta}_{j,\lambda} = 0 \\ -1 & \widehat{\beta}_{j,\lambda} < 0 \end{cases}. \tag{2}$$

2.2   Some Facts on LASSO Estimate

It is well known that

$$\widehat{\boldsymbol{\beta}}_\lambda = (\widehat{\mathbf{X}}_\lambda'\widehat{\mathbf{X}}_\lambda)^{-1}\left(\widehat{\mathbf{X}}_\lambda'\boldsymbol{y} - \lambda\widehat{\mathbf{S}}_\lambda\right). \tag{3}$$

holds if $\mathbf{X}'\mathbf{X}$ is not singular [4,18]. Then, we have

$$\widehat{\boldsymbol{\mu}}_\lambda = \widehat{\mathbf{H}}_\lambda\boldsymbol{y} - \lambda\widehat{\boldsymbol{q}}_\lambda, \tag{4}$$

where $\widehat{\mathbf{H}}_\lambda = \widehat{\mathbf{X}}_\lambda(\widehat{\mathbf{X}}_\lambda'\widehat{\mathbf{X}}_\lambda)^{-1}\widehat{\mathbf{X}}_\lambda'$ and $\widehat{\boldsymbol{q}}_\lambda = \widehat{\mathbf{X}}_\lambda(\widehat{\mathbf{X}}_\lambda'\widehat{\mathbf{X}}_\lambda)^{-1}\widehat{\mathbf{S}}_\lambda$. It is easy to check that $\widehat{\mathbf{H}}_\lambda$ is an idempotent matrix.

We define $\widetilde{\boldsymbol{\beta}}_\lambda = (\widehat{\mathbf{X}}_\lambda'\widehat{\mathbf{X}}_\lambda)^{-1}\widehat{\mathbf{X}}_\lambda'\boldsymbol{y}$. This is the least squared estimator under $\widehat{\mathbf{X}}_\lambda$, thus in a post estimation. Note that this is not a linear estimator of $\boldsymbol{y}$ since $\widehat{\mathbf{X}}_\lambda$ is already chosen according to $\boldsymbol{y}$. We also define $\widetilde{\boldsymbol{\mu}}_\lambda = \widehat{\mathbf{X}}_\lambda\widetilde{\boldsymbol{\beta}}_\lambda$. Obviously, this can be written as $\widetilde{\boldsymbol{\mu}}_\lambda = \widehat{\mathbf{H}}_\lambda\boldsymbol{y}$. Therefore, (4) can be written as

$$\widehat{\boldsymbol{\mu}}_\lambda = \widetilde{\boldsymbol{\mu}}_\lambda - \lambda\widehat{\boldsymbol{q}}_\lambda. \tag{5}$$

We summarize some facts that are derived by (4) and are used in this article.

Lemma 1. *The following equations hold.*

$$\widehat{\boldsymbol{\mu}}_\lambda'\widehat{\boldsymbol{q}}_\lambda = \|\widehat{\boldsymbol{\beta}}_\lambda\|_1 \tag{6}$$

$$\|\widehat{\boldsymbol{\mu}}_\lambda\|^2 = \widehat{\boldsymbol{\mu}}_\lambda'\boldsymbol{y} - \lambda\widehat{\boldsymbol{q}}_\lambda'\boldsymbol{y} + \lambda^2\|\widehat{\boldsymbol{q}}_\lambda\|^2 \tag{7}$$

$$\|\widehat{\boldsymbol{\mu}}_\lambda\|^2 = \widehat{\boldsymbol{\mu}}_\lambda'\boldsymbol{y} - \lambda\|\widehat{\boldsymbol{\beta}}_\lambda\|_1 \tag{8}$$

$$\mathbf{H}_\lambda\widehat{\boldsymbol{\mu}}_\lambda = \widehat{\boldsymbol{\mu}}_\lambda. \tag{9}$$

Proof. In this proof, we drop λ from symbols for simplifying the description of terms. By (4), we have

$$\widehat{\boldsymbol{\mu}}'\widehat{\boldsymbol{q}} = \widehat{\boldsymbol{q}}'\widehat{\boldsymbol{\mu}} = \widehat{\mathbf{S}}'(\widehat{\mathbf{X}}'\widehat{\mathbf{X}})^{-1}\widehat{\mathbf{X}}'\widehat{\mathbf{X}}(\widehat{\mathbf{X}}'\widehat{\mathbf{X}})^{-1}(\widehat{\mathbf{X}}'\boldsymbol{y} - \lambda\widehat{\mathbf{S}}) = \widehat{\mathbf{S}}'\widehat{\boldsymbol{\beta}}. \tag{10}$$

We then obtain (6) by the definition of $\widehat{\mathbf{S}}$.

We define $\widehat{\mathbf{P}} = \mathbf{I}_n - \widehat{\mathbf{H}}$. By the definition of $\widehat{\mathbf{H}}$ and $\widehat{\mathbf{P}}$, we have

$$\widehat{\boldsymbol{q}}'\widehat{\mathbf{H}}\boldsymbol{y} = \widehat{\boldsymbol{q}}'\boldsymbol{y} \tag{11}$$

and, thus,

$$\widehat{\boldsymbol{q}}'\widehat{\mathbf{P}}\boldsymbol{y} = \widehat{\boldsymbol{q}}'\boldsymbol{y} - \widehat{\boldsymbol{q}}'\widehat{\mathbf{H}}\boldsymbol{y} = 0. \tag{12}$$

Since $\widehat{\mathbf{H}}$ is an idempotent matrix, we have $\widehat{\mathbf{H}}\widehat{\mathbf{P}} = O_n$, where O_n is an $n \times n$ zero matrix. Thus, by (3), (7) is obtained as

$$\widehat{\boldsymbol{\mu}}'\boldsymbol{y} - \|\widehat{\boldsymbol{\mu}}\|^2 = \widehat{\boldsymbol{\mu}}'(\boldsymbol{y} - \widehat{\boldsymbol{\mu}}) = (\widehat{\mathbf{H}}\boldsymbol{y} - \lambda\widehat{\boldsymbol{q}})'(\widehat{\mathbf{P}}\boldsymbol{y} + \lambda\widehat{\boldsymbol{q}}) = \lambda\widehat{\boldsymbol{q}}'\boldsymbol{y} - \lambda^2\|\widehat{\boldsymbol{q}}\|^2. \tag{13}$$

Moreover, by (11), (4) and (6), we have

$$\lambda\widehat{\boldsymbol{q}}'\boldsymbol{y} - \lambda^2\|\widehat{\boldsymbol{q}}\|^2 = \lambda\widehat{\boldsymbol{q}}'\widehat{\mathbf{H}}\boldsymbol{y} - \lambda^2\|\widehat{\boldsymbol{q}}\|^2 = \lambda\widehat{\boldsymbol{q}}'(\widehat{\mathbf{H}}\boldsymbol{y} - \lambda\widehat{\boldsymbol{q}}) = \lambda\widehat{\boldsymbol{q}}'\widehat{\boldsymbol{\mu}} = \lambda\|\widehat{\boldsymbol{\beta}}\|_1. \tag{14}$$

Finally, by the definition of $\widehat{\mathbf{H}}$ and $\widehat{\boldsymbol{\mu}}$, we obtain

$$\widehat{\mathbf{H}}\widehat{\boldsymbol{\mu}} = \widehat{\mathbf{X}}(\widehat{\mathbf{X}}'\widehat{\mathbf{X}})^{-1}\widehat{\mathbf{X}}'\widehat{\mathbf{X}}(\widehat{\mathbf{X}}'\widehat{\mathbf{X}})^{-1}(\widehat{\mathbf{X}}'\boldsymbol{y} - \lambda\widehat{\mathbf{S}}) = \widehat{\boldsymbol{\mu}}. \tag{15}$$

2.3 Definition of Risk and Its Stein's Formula

Let $\widehat{\boldsymbol{\mu}} = (\widehat{\mu}_1, \ldots, \widehat{\mu}_n)' \in \mathbb{R}^n$ be a regression estimate of $\boldsymbol{\mu} = \mathbb{E}[\boldsymbol{y}]$. A prediction performance of $\widehat{\boldsymbol{\mu}}$ is measured by a risk that is defined by

$$R_n = \frac{1}{n}\mathbb{E}\left[\|\widehat{\boldsymbol{\mu}} - \boldsymbol{\mu}\|^2\right], \tag{16}$$

where $\mathbb{E}$ is the expectation with respect to the joint probability distribution of $\boldsymbol{y}$. It is easily verified that

$$R_n = \frac{1}{n}\mathbb{E}\left[\|\widehat{\boldsymbol{\mu}} - \boldsymbol{y}\|^2\right] - \sigma^2 + \mathrm{DF}_n, \tag{17}$$

where

$$\mathrm{DF}_n = \frac{2}{n}\mathbb{E}\left[(\widehat{\boldsymbol{\mu}} - \mathbb{E}[\widehat{\boldsymbol{\mu}}])'(\boldsymbol{y} - \boldsymbol{\mu})\right] \tag{18}$$

that is a covariance between $\widehat{\boldsymbol{\mu}}$ and $\boldsymbol{y}$. DF_n is often called the degree of freedom. Let $\partial\widehat{\boldsymbol{\mu}}/\partial\boldsymbol{y}$ be an $n \times n$ matrix whose (i,j) entry is $\partial\widehat{\mu}_i/\partial y_j$. We define

$$\nabla \cdot \widehat{\boldsymbol{\mu}} = \mathrm{trace}\frac{\partial\widehat{\boldsymbol{\mu}}}{\partial\boldsymbol{y}} = \sum_{i=1}^{n} \frac{\partial\widehat{\mu}_i}{\partial y_i} \tag{19}$$

in which trace denotes the trace of a matrix. In [11], it has been shown that

$$\mathrm{DF}_n = \frac{2\sigma^2}{n}\mathbb{E}\left[\nabla \cdot \widehat{\boldsymbol{\mu}}\right] \tag{20}$$

holds if $\widehat{\mu}_i = \widehat{\mu}_i(\boldsymbol{y}) : \mathbb{R}^n \mapsto \mathbb{R}$, $i = 1,\ldots,n$ are almost differentiable in the term of [11] and the expectation in the right hand side exists. $\nabla \cdot \widehat{\boldsymbol{\mu}}$ is called a divergence of $\widehat{\boldsymbol{\mu}}$. By this result,

$$\widehat{R}_n(\sigma^2) = \frac{1}{n}\|\widehat{\boldsymbol{\mu}} - \boldsymbol{y}\|^2 - \sigma^2 + \frac{2\sigma^2}{n}\nabla \cdot \widehat{\boldsymbol{\mu}} \tag{21}$$

is an unbiased estimator of a risk R_n. $\widehat{R}_n(\sigma^2)$ is called SURE (Stein's Unbiased Risk Estimate). We can then construct a C_p-type model selection criterion by replacing σ^2 with an appropriate estimate $\widehat{\sigma}^2$; e.g. [18].

In [4,13,18], it has been shown for LASSO that a divergence of estimate is given by the number of non-zero coefficients and, thus, SURE is given by

$$\widehat{R}(\lambda,\sigma^2) = \frac{1}{n}\|\widehat{\boldsymbol{\mu}}_\lambda - \boldsymbol{y}\|^2 - \sigma^2 + \frac{2\sigma^2}{n}\widehat{k}_\lambda \tag{22}$$

3   LASSO with Scaling

3.1   LASSO with Scaling

We now consider to assign a positive single scaling parameter to the LASSO estimator [7]. More precisely, the scaling parameter is denoted by $\alpha > 0$ and the modified LASSO estimator with scaling is given by $\alpha\widehat{\boldsymbol{\beta}}_\lambda$, where $\widehat{\boldsymbol{\beta}}_\lambda$ is a vector of non-zero elements of LASSO estimator. The output vector with a single scaling parameter is given by $\widehat{\boldsymbol{\mu}}_{\lambda,\alpha} = \alpha\widehat{\boldsymbol{\mu}}_\lambda$. Thus, $\widehat{\boldsymbol{\mu}}_{\lambda,1}$ is a LASSO output vector. We write $\widehat{\boldsymbol{\mu}}_{\lambda,\alpha} = (\widehat{\mu}_{\lambda,\alpha,1},\ldots,\widehat{\mu}_{\lambda,\alpha,n})'$, where $\widehat{\mu}_{\lambda,\alpha,k} = \alpha\widehat{\mu}_{\lambda,k}$. By (20) and (22), it is easy to obtain

$$\frac{1}{n}\mathbb{E}\left[\|\widehat{\boldsymbol{\mu}}_{\lambda,\alpha} - \boldsymbol{\mu}\|^2\right] = \frac{1}{n}\mathbb{E}\left[\|\widehat{\boldsymbol{\mu}}_{\lambda,\alpha} - \boldsymbol{y}\|^2\right] - \sigma^2 + \frac{2\sigma^2\alpha}{n}\mathbb{E}\left[\widehat{k}_\lambda\right]. \tag{23}$$

Therefore, as in [7], the optimal α that minimizes the risk is given by

$$\alpha_{\mathrm{opt}} = \frac{\left(\mathbb{E}\widehat{\boldsymbol{\mu}}_\lambda'\boldsymbol{y} - \sigma^2\mathbb{E}\widehat{k}_\lambda\right)}{\mathbb{E}\|\widehat{\boldsymbol{\mu}}_\lambda\|^2}. \tag{24}$$

The direct estimate of α_{opt} may be unstable and we consider

$$\widehat{\alpha} = \frac{\widehat{\boldsymbol{\mu}}'_\lambda \boldsymbol{y} + \delta}{\|\widehat{\boldsymbol{\mu}}_\lambda\|^2 + \delta} \tag{25}$$

as a stable empirical scaling value, where δ is a fixed positive constant. Note that δ is not a tuning parameter (hyper-parameter) and is a constant for stabilizing $\widehat{\alpha}$. Therefore, it is set to be a small value, say, 10^{-6} in applications. By (8), we can write

$$\widehat{\alpha} = 1 + \frac{\lambda \|\widehat{\boldsymbol{\beta}}_\lambda\|_1}{\|\widehat{\boldsymbol{\mu}}_\lambda\|^2 + \delta}. \tag{26}$$

Therefore, $\widehat{\alpha} \geq 1$ holds; i.e. it really behaves as an expansion parameter. Moreover, $\widehat{\alpha} \simeq 1$ for a small λ. This is a nice property since the bias problem in LASSO is serious when λ is large and is not essential when it is small. We have two facts relating to $\widehat{\alpha}$. The first one shows an effect of the introduction of $\widehat{\alpha}$.

Lemma 2.
$$\|\boldsymbol{y} - \widetilde{\boldsymbol{\mu}}_\lambda\|^2 \leq \|\boldsymbol{y} - \widehat{\boldsymbol{\mu}}_{\lambda,\widehat{\alpha}}\|^2 \leq \|\boldsymbol{y} - \widehat{\boldsymbol{\mu}}_{\lambda,1}\|^2 \tag{27}$$

holds.

Proof. The first inequality is obvious because $\widetilde{\boldsymbol{\mu}}_\lambda$ is the least squares solution under $\widehat{\mathbf{X}}_\lambda$; i.e. it is a projection of $\boldsymbol{y}$ onto a linear subspace determined by column vectors of $\widehat{\mathbf{X}}_\lambda$. For simplicity, we define $m_2 = \|\widehat{\boldsymbol{\mu}}_{\lambda,1}\|^2$ and $p_1 = \lambda\|\widehat{\boldsymbol{\beta}}_\lambda\|_1$. We then obtain

$$\begin{aligned}
\|\boldsymbol{y} - \widehat{\boldsymbol{\mu}}_{\lambda,\widehat{\alpha}}\|^2 &= \|\boldsymbol{y} - \widehat{\alpha}\widehat{\boldsymbol{\mu}}_{\lambda,1}\|^2 \\
&= \|\boldsymbol{y} - \widehat{\boldsymbol{\mu}}_{\lambda,1} + \widehat{\boldsymbol{\mu}}_{\lambda,1} - \widehat{\alpha}\widehat{\boldsymbol{\mu}}_{\lambda,1}\|^2 \\
&= \|\boldsymbol{y} - \widehat{\boldsymbol{\mu}}_{\lambda,1}\|^2 + (1 - \widehat{\alpha})^2 m_2 + 2(1 - \widehat{\alpha})p_1 \\
&= \|\boldsymbol{y} - \widehat{\boldsymbol{\mu}}_{\lambda,1}\|^2 + (1 - \widehat{\alpha})^2 m_2 - 2(1 - \widehat{\alpha})^2 (m_2 + \delta) \\
&= \|\boldsymbol{y} - \widehat{\boldsymbol{\mu}}_{\lambda,1}\|^2 - (1 - \widehat{\alpha})^2 (m_2 + 2\delta),
\end{aligned} \tag{28}$$

where we used (8) in the third line and (26) in the fourth line.

Therefore, the introduction of $\widehat{\alpha}$ surely reduces the residual sum compared to a LASSO estimate. This implies that $\widehat{\alpha}$ moves the LASSO estimator toward the least squares estimator at each λ. In a particular case, we have the following fact for the second term of the last equality in (28).

Lemma 3. *For simplicity, we consider a specific case where $\delta = 0$. We assume that $\|\widehat{\boldsymbol{\beta}}_\lambda\|_1 \neq 0$ holds. Let $\rho_{\min}$ and $\rho_{\max}$ be the minimum and maximum eigenvalues of $\mathbf{X}'\mathbf{X}/n$ and assume $\rho_{\min} > 0$. Then, we have*

$$\frac{\lambda^2}{n\rho_{\max}} \leq \|\boldsymbol{y} - \widehat{\boldsymbol{\mu}}_{\lambda,1}\|^2 - \|\boldsymbol{y} - \widehat{\boldsymbol{\mu}}_{\lambda,\widehat{\alpha}}\|^2 \leq \frac{\lambda^2 m}{n\rho_{\min}}. \tag{29}$$

Proof. Since

$$(1 - \widehat{\alpha})^2(m_2 + 2\delta) = \lambda^2\|\widehat{\boldsymbol{\beta}}_\lambda\|_1^2 \frac{\|\widehat{\boldsymbol{\mu}}_{\lambda,1}\|^2 + 2\delta}{(\|\widehat{\boldsymbol{\mu}}_{\lambda,1}\|^2 + \delta)^2} = \frac{\lambda^2\|\widehat{\boldsymbol{\beta}}_\lambda\|_1^2}{\|\widehat{\boldsymbol{\mu}}_{\lambda,1}\|^2} \tag{30}$$

holds in case of $\delta = 0$, we have

$$\frac{\lambda^2\|\widehat{\boldsymbol{\beta}}_\lambda\|_1^2}{n\rho_{\max}\|\widehat{\boldsymbol{\beta}}_\lambda\|^2} \leq (1 - \widehat{\alpha})^2(m_2 + 2\delta) \leq \frac{\lambda^2\|\widehat{\boldsymbol{\beta}}_\lambda\|_1^2}{n\rho_{\min}\|\widehat{\boldsymbol{\beta}}_\lambda\|^2}. \tag{31}$$

By the equivalence of the norms and (28), we have (29) since $\widehat{k}_\lambda \leq m$.

Therefore, the difference between the residuals of LASSO without and with scaling is large when λ is large; i.e. in a sparse situation. This fact implies that the effect of $\widehat{\alpha}$ may be large in a sparse situation.

3.2   Model Selection Criterion Under Empirical Scaling

Now, we consider to derive a C_p-type model selection criterion for $\widehat{\boldsymbol{\mu}}_{\lambda,\widehat{\alpha}}$. For this purpose, we derive an unbiased estimate of a risk for $\widehat{\boldsymbol{\mu}}_{\lambda,\widehat{\alpha}}$. To do this, we need to calculate the degree of freedom of $\widehat{\boldsymbol{\mu}}_{\lambda,\widehat{\alpha}}$.

Theorem 1.

$$\mathrm{DF}_n^{\mathrm{sca}}(\lambda) = \frac{2}{n}\mathbb{E}\left[(\widehat{\boldsymbol{\mu}}_{\lambda,\widehat{\alpha}} - \mathbb{E}[\widehat{\boldsymbol{\mu}}_{\lambda,\widehat{\alpha}}])'(\boldsymbol{y} - \boldsymbol{\mu})\right] = \frac{2\sigma^2}{n}\mathbb{E}\left[\widehat{d}_1 + \widehat{d}_2\right], \tag{32}$$

holds, where

$$\widehat{d}_1 = (1 - \widehat{\alpha})\frac{\|\widehat{\boldsymbol{\mu}}_\lambda\|^2 - \delta}{\|\widehat{\boldsymbol{\mu}}_\lambda\|^2 + \delta} \tag{33}$$

$$\widehat{d}_2 = \widehat{\alpha}\widehat{k}_\lambda. \tag{34}$$

Proof. We drop λ from expressions for simplicity since we fix λ below. We thus write $\widehat{\boldsymbol{\beta}} = \widehat{\boldsymbol{\beta}}_\lambda$, $\widehat{\mathbf{S}} = \widehat{\mathbf{S}}_\lambda$, $\widehat{\boldsymbol{\mu}}_\alpha = \widehat{\boldsymbol{\mu}}_{\lambda,\alpha}$, $\widehat{B} = \widehat{B}_\lambda$ and $\widehat{k} = \widehat{k}_\lambda$.

We can write $\widehat{\boldsymbol{\mu}}_\alpha = \alpha\mathbf{X}_{\widehat{B}}\widehat{\boldsymbol{\beta}}$. Especially, $\widehat{\boldsymbol{\mu}}_1$ is a LASSO output. For simplicity, we write $\widehat{\boldsymbol{\mu}} = \widehat{\boldsymbol{\mu}}_1$ below. We denote the kth member of $\widehat{\boldsymbol{\mu}}_\alpha$ by $\widehat{\mu}_{\alpha,k}$. In [4], it has been shown that, for any fixed λ, $\widehat{\mu}_{1,k} : \mathbb{R}^n \mapsto \mathbb{R}$, $k = 1,\ldots,n$ are almost differentiable. By (25), $\widehat{\alpha}\widehat{\mu}_{1,k} : \mathbb{R}^n \mapsto \mathbb{R}$ is calculated by arithmetic operations of the components of $\boldsymbol{y}$ and $\widehat{\boldsymbol{\mu}}$. Therefore, $\widehat{\alpha}\widehat{\mu}_{1,k}$ is almost differentiable since it essentially requires a coordinatewise absolutely continuity. As a result, Stein's lemma can be applied to $\widehat{\mu}_{\widehat{\alpha},k}$ and, by (20), we have

$$\mathrm{DF}_n^{\mathrm{sca}}(\lambda) = \frac{2\sigma^2}{n}\mathbb{E}\left[\nabla \cdot \widehat{\boldsymbol{\mu}}_{\widehat{\alpha}}\right], \tag{35}$$

where

$$\nabla \cdot \widehat{\boldsymbol{\mu}}_{\widehat{\alpha}} = \mathrm{trace}\frac{\partial\widehat{\boldsymbol{\mu}}_{\widehat{\alpha}}}{\partial\boldsymbol{y}} = \sum_{i=1}^n \frac{\partial\mu_{\widehat{\alpha},i}}{\partial y_i}. \tag{36}$$

Since

$$\sum_{i=1}^{n} \frac{\partial}{\partial y_i} \widehat{\mu}_{\widehat{\alpha},i} = \sum_{i=1}^{n} \widehat{\mu}_{1,i} \left(\frac{\partial}{\partial y_i} \widehat{\alpha} \right) + \widehat{\alpha} \sum_{i=1}^{n} \left(\frac{\partial}{\partial y_i} \widehat{\mu}_{1,i} \right), \tag{37}$$

holds, we have

$$\nabla \cdot \widehat{\boldsymbol{\mu}}_{\widehat{\alpha}} = \widehat{\boldsymbol{\mu}}' \left(\frac{\partial \widehat{\alpha}}{\partial \boldsymbol{y}} \right) + \widehat{\alpha} \nabla \cdot \widehat{\boldsymbol{\mu}}, \tag{38}$$

where $\partial \widehat{\alpha} / \partial \boldsymbol{y}$ is an n-dimensional vector whose ith entry is $\partial \widehat{\alpha} / \partial y_i$.

For the second term of (38), it has been shown in [4] that

$$\frac{\partial \widehat{\boldsymbol{\mu}}}{\partial \boldsymbol{y}} = \widehat{\mathbf{H}} \tag{39}$$

holds and, thus,

$$\nabla \cdot \widehat{\boldsymbol{\mu}} = \text{trace} \widehat{\mathbf{H}} = \widehat{k} \tag{40}$$

holds almost everywhere. Therefore, the second term of (38) is equal to $\widehat{d}_2$.

We evaluate the first term below. To do this, we note that, as shown in [4,13], the active set and the sign vector of $\widehat{\boldsymbol{\beta}}_\lambda$ are locally constants almost everywhere. Thus, $\widehat{\boldsymbol{q}}$ is locally constant almost everywhere. This fact is also used to show (39). Since

$$\frac{\partial}{\partial y_k} \|\widehat{\boldsymbol{\mu}}\|^2 = \frac{\partial}{\partial y_k} \sum_{j=1}^{n} \widehat{\mu}_j^2 = 2 \sum_{j=1}^{n} \widehat{\mu}_j \frac{\partial \widehat{\mu}_j}{\partial y_k}, \tag{41}$$

we have

$$\frac{\partial \|\widehat{\boldsymbol{\mu}}\|^2}{\partial \boldsymbol{y}} = 2 \left(\frac{\partial \widehat{\boldsymbol{\mu}}}{\partial \boldsymbol{y}} \right) \widehat{\boldsymbol{\mu}} = 2 \widehat{\mathbf{H}} \widehat{\boldsymbol{\mu}} = 2 \widehat{\boldsymbol{\mu}} \tag{42}$$

by (39) and (9). On the other hand, we have

$$\frac{\partial \widehat{\boldsymbol{\mu}}' \boldsymbol{y}}{\partial \boldsymbol{y}} = \frac{\partial}{\partial \boldsymbol{y}} \left\{ \|\widehat{\boldsymbol{\mu}}\|^2 + \lambda \widehat{\boldsymbol{q}}' \boldsymbol{y} - \lambda^2 \|\widehat{\boldsymbol{q}}\|^2 \right\} = 2 \widehat{\boldsymbol{\mu}} + \lambda \widehat{\boldsymbol{q}} \tag{43}$$

by (42), (7) and local constancy of $\widehat{\boldsymbol{q}}$.

By (42), (43) and (7), we have

$$\begin{aligned}
\frac{\partial \widehat{\alpha}}{\partial \boldsymbol{y}} &= \frac{(\|\widehat{\boldsymbol{\mu}}\|^2 + \delta) \frac{\partial}{\partial \boldsymbol{y}} \widehat{\boldsymbol{\mu}}' \boldsymbol{y} - (\widehat{\boldsymbol{\mu}}' \boldsymbol{y} + \delta) \frac{\partial}{\partial \boldsymbol{y}} \|\widehat{\boldsymbol{\mu}}\|^2}{(\|\widehat{\boldsymbol{\mu}}\|^2 + \delta)^2} \\
&= \frac{(\|\widehat{\boldsymbol{\mu}}\|^2 + \delta)(2\widehat{\boldsymbol{\mu}} + \lambda \widehat{\boldsymbol{q}}) - 2(\widehat{\boldsymbol{\mu}}' \boldsymbol{y} + \delta) \widehat{\boldsymbol{\mu}}}{(\|\widehat{\boldsymbol{\mu}}\|^2 + \delta)^2} \\
&= \frac{(\|\widehat{\boldsymbol{\mu}}\|^2 + \delta)(2\widehat{\boldsymbol{\mu}} + \lambda \widehat{\boldsymbol{q}}) - 2\widehat{\alpha} (\|\widehat{\boldsymbol{\mu}}\|^2 + \delta) \widehat{\boldsymbol{\mu}}}{(\|\widehat{\boldsymbol{\mu}}\|^2 + \delta)^2} \\
&= \frac{1}{\|\widehat{\boldsymbol{\mu}}\|^2 + \delta} \left\{ 2\widehat{\boldsymbol{\mu}} + \lambda \widehat{\boldsymbol{q}} - 2\widehat{\alpha} \widehat{\boldsymbol{\mu}} \right\},
\end{aligned} \tag{44}$$

where the third line comes from (25). Therefore, we obtain

$$
\begin{aligned}
\widehat{\boldsymbol{\mu}}' \left(\frac{\partial \widehat{\alpha}}{\partial \boldsymbol{y}} \right) &= \frac{1}{\|\widehat{\boldsymbol{\mu}}\|^2 + \delta} \left\{ 2\|\widehat{\boldsymbol{\mu}}\|^2 + \lambda \widehat{\boldsymbol{\mu}}' \widehat{\boldsymbol{q}} - 2\widehat{\alpha}\|\widehat{\boldsymbol{\mu}}\|^2 \right\} \\
&= \frac{1}{\|\widehat{\boldsymbol{\mu}}\|^2 + \delta} \left\{ 2\|\widehat{\boldsymbol{\mu}}\|^2 + \lambda \|\widehat{\boldsymbol{\beta}}\|_1 - 2\widehat{\alpha}\|\widehat{\boldsymbol{\mu}}\|^2 \right\} \\
&= \frac{2}{\|\widehat{\boldsymbol{\mu}}\|^2 + \delta}(1 - \widehat{\alpha})\|\widehat{\boldsymbol{\mu}}\|^2 + \frac{\lambda \|\widehat{\boldsymbol{\beta}}\|_1}{\|\widehat{\boldsymbol{\mu}}\|^2 + \delta} \\
&= \frac{2}{\|\widehat{\boldsymbol{\mu}}\|^2 + \delta}(1 - \widehat{\alpha})\|\widehat{\boldsymbol{\mu}}\|^2 - (1 - \widehat{\alpha}) \\
&= \widehat{d}_1, \qquad\qquad\qquad\qquad\qquad\qquad\qquad\qquad (45)
\end{aligned}
$$

where we used (6), (8) and (25).

By this theorem, the risk for $\widehat{\boldsymbol{\mu}}_{\lambda,\widehat{\alpha}}$ is given by

$$
R_n^{\mathrm{sca}}(\lambda) = \frac{1}{n}\mathbb{E}\left[\|\boldsymbol{\mu} - \widehat{\boldsymbol{\mu}}_{\lambda,\widehat{\alpha}}\|^2\right] = \frac{1}{n}\mathbb{E}\left[\|\boldsymbol{y} - \widehat{\boldsymbol{\mu}}_{\lambda,\widehat{\alpha}}\|^2\right] - \sigma^2 + \mathrm{DF}_n^{\mathrm{sca}}(\lambda). \qquad (46)
$$

Therefore, SURE for LASSO with scaling is given by

$$
\widehat{R}_n^{\mathrm{sca}}(\lambda, \sigma^2) = \frac{1}{n}\|\boldsymbol{y} - \widehat{\boldsymbol{\mu}}_{\lambda,\widehat{\alpha}}\|^2 - \sigma^2 + \frac{2\sigma^2}{n}\left(\widehat{d}_1 + \widehat{d}_2\right), \qquad (47)
$$

where $\widehat{d}_1$ and $\widehat{d}_2$ are defined by (33) and (34) respectively.

3.3   Estimate of Noise Variance

To compute a C_p-type model selection criterion based on SURE, we need an appropriate estimate of σ^2. For estimating the noise variance in a regression problem, [2] has recommended to apply

$$
\widehat{\sigma}_{\mathrm{CE}}^2 = \frac{\boldsymbol{y}'(\mathbf{I}_n - \mathbf{H}_\gamma)^2 \boldsymbol{y}}{\mathrm{trace}[(\mathbf{I}_n - \mathbf{H}_\gamma)^2]}, \qquad (48)
$$

where $\mathbf{H}_\gamma = \mathbf{X}(\mathbf{X}'\mathbf{X} + \gamma \mathbf{I}_n)^{-1}\mathbf{X}'$ with $\gamma > 0$. $\mathbf{H}_\gamma$ can be viewed as the hat matrix in a ridge regression with a ridge parameter $\gamma > 0$ or, equivalently, an ℓ_2 regularization with a regularization parameter γ. Since the purpose to introduce γ here is to stabilize an estimate of the noise variance. Therefore, we just set γ to a small value, say, 10^{-6} in applications. Especially, this is effective when m is large; i.e. when a colinearity problem arises under a full model.

4   Numerical Example

In this section, through a simple numerical example, we verify our result on SURE for LASSO with scaling and compare our method with the naive LASSO.

We refer to LASSO with scaling $\widehat{\alpha}$ as LASSO-S. We here refer to $\widehat{R}_n(\lambda, \widehat{\sigma}_{\mathrm{CE}}^2)$ in (22) and $\widehat{R}_n^{\mathrm{sca}}(\lambda, \widehat{\sigma}_{\mathrm{CE}}^2)$ in (47) as SUREs of LASSO and LASSO-S respectively; i.e. the noise variance is replaced with $\widehat{\sigma}_{\mathrm{CE}}^2$ defined in (48). These are fully empirical and, thus, can be applied as model selection criteria.

For $u \in \mathbb{R}$, we define $g_\tau(u, \xi) = \exp\left\{-(u-\xi)^2/(2\tau)\right\}$, where $\xi \in \mathbb{R}$ and $\tau > 0$. Let u_i, $i = 1, \ldots, n$ be equidistant points in $[-5, 5]$. Let $\{\xi_1, \ldots, \xi_m\}$ be a subset of $\{u_1, \ldots, u_n\}$, where $m \leq n$. We take $\xi_j = u_{(n/m)j}$, $j = 1, \ldots, m$ by assuming n/m is an integer. We define $n \times m$ matrix $\mathbf{X}_1$ whose (i,j) entry is $g_\tau(u_i, \xi_j)$. Let $\mathbf{X}_2$ be a normalized version of $\mathbf{X}_1$. By taking account of the intercept, we construct a design matrix by $\mathbf{X} = (\mathbf{1}_n, \mathbf{X}_2)$. Therefore, we consider a curve fitting problem using a linear combination of m Gaussian basis functions whose centers are input data points that are appropriately chosen. We generate y_i by $y_i = \sum_{k=1}^m \beta_k^* g_\tau(u_i, \xi_k) + \varepsilon_i$, where $\varepsilon_i \sim N(0, \sigma^2)$. We define $K^* = \{k | \beta_k^* \neq 0\}$ and consider the case where $|K^*| \ll m$. This corresponds to the case that there exists an exact sparse representation; i.e. there is a small true representation.

We set $n = 100$, $m = 50$, $\sigma^2 = 1$, $K^* = \{5, 18, 31, 45\}$ and $(\beta_5^*, \beta_{18}^*, \beta_{31}^*, \beta_{45}^*) = (1, -2, 2, -1)$; i.e. ξ_j's of non-zero coefficients are almost equally positioned. We also set $\delta = 1/n$ for LASSO-S and $\gamma = 10^{-6}$ in calculating $\widehat{\sigma}_{\mathrm{CE}}^2$. We here consider two cases of $\tau = 0.1$ and $\tau = 0.4$. In both cases, some Gaussian functions that are close to each other are relatively correlated. However, 4 Gaussian functions with non-zero coefficients (components of a target function) are nearly orthogonal in the former case while those are still correlated in the latter case. This condition of correlation among components in a target function affects the consistency of model selection of LASSO, adaptive LASSO and MCP.

We here employ LARS-LASSO for calculating LASSO path and use "lars" package in R [5]. Since the regularization parameter corresponds to the number of un-removed coefficients, we here observe the relationship between the number of un-removed coefficients and risk. Since we know the true representation, we can calculate the actual risk by the mean squared error between the true output and estimated output. We repeat this procedure for 1000 times and calculate averages of actual risks and SUREs.

The averages of actual risks and SUREs of LASSO and LASSO-S are depicted in Fig. 1. The horizontal axis is an average of the number of non-zero coefficients (members in active set) at the each step in LARS-LASSO, in which the average is taken for 1000 trials. In Fig. 1, we depict the results at some specific steps (not the results at all steps) for the clarity of graphs. We have some remarks on these results. Firstly, SURE is well consistent with the actual risk for both of LASSO and LASSO-S. Especially, the consistency for LASSO-S verifies Theorem 1. Note that these are the results when we employ $\widehat{\sigma}^2$. Secondly, when the number of non-zero coefficients is small (λ is large), LASSO-S shows a lower risk compared to LASSO. This is notable in $\tau = 0.1$; i.e. components of a target function are nearly orthogonal. Lastly, the number of non-zero coefficients at which an averaged risk is minimized is smaller for LASSO-S than LASSO. As a result, we can expect that the proposed scaling method can solve a bias problem of LASSO

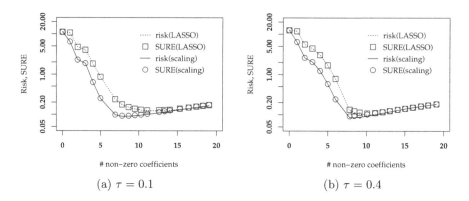

(a) $\tau = 0.1$ (b) $\tau = 0.4$

Fig. 1. Averages of actual risks and SUREs for LASSO and LASSO-S.

and $\widehat{R}_n^{\mathrm{sca}}(\lambda, \widehat{\sigma}_{\mathrm{CE}}^2)$ can be a good selector of λ under the proposed scaling method; i.e. it can choose a sparse model with low risk compared to the naive LASSO.

5 Conclusions and Future Works

LASSO is known to suffer from a bias problem that is caused by excessive shrinkage. In this article, we considered to improve it by a simple scaling method. We gave an appropriate empirical scaling value that expands the LASSO estimator and actually moves the LASSO estimator close to the least squares estimator in the post estimation. This is shown to be especially effective when the regularization parameter is large; i.e. a sparse representation. Since it can be calculated based of the LASSO estimator, we just run a fast and stable LASSO optimization procedure such as LARS-LASSO or coordinate descent. We also derived SURE under the modified LASSO with scaling. This analytic solution for model selection is also a benefit of the proposed scaling method. As a result, we gave a fully empirical sparse modeling procedure by a scaling method. In a simple numerical example, we verified that the proposed scaling method actually improves the bias problem of LASSO and the obtained SURE can be a good model selection criterion. As future works, we need performance comparisons with the other methods such as MCP and more application results of our scaling method. As an extension, instead of assigning a single scaling value for all coefficients, we consider to assign coefficient-wise scaling values to improve the prediction performance. Furthermore, we need to consider a scaling method when the input dimension is larger than the number of data.

Acknowledgements. This work was supported in part by Japan Society for the Promotion of Science (JSPS) KAKENHI Grant Number 18K11433.

References

1. Bühlmann, P., Meier, L.: Discussion: one-step sparse estimates in nonconcave penalized likelihood models. Ann. Stat. **36**, 1534–1541 (2008)
2. Carter, C.K., Eagleson, G.K.: A comparison of variance estimators in nonparametric regression. J. R. Stat. Soc. B **54**, 773–780 (1992)
3. Donoho, D.L., Johnstone, I.M.: Ideal spatial adaptation via wavelet shrinkage. Biometrika **81**, 425–455 (1994)
4. Dossal, C., Kachour, M., Fadili, J., Peyré, G., Chesneau, C.: The degrees of freedom of the LASSO for general design matrix. Statistica Sinica **23**, 809–828 (2013)
5. Efron, B., Hastie, T., Johnstone, I., Tibshirani, R.: Least angle regression. Ann. Stat. **32**, 407–499 (2004)
6. Fan, J., Li, R.: Variable selection via nonconcave penalized likelihood and its oracle properties. J. Am. Statist. Assoc. **96**, 1348–1360 (2001)
7. Hagiwara, K.: A problem in model selection of LASSO and introduction of scaling. In: Hirose, A., Ozawa, S., Doya, K., Ikeda, K., Lee, M., Liu, D. (eds.) ICONIP 2016. LNCS, vol. 9948, pp. 20–27. Springer, Cham (2016). https://doi.org/10.1007/978-3-319-46672-9_3
8. Knight, K., Fu, W.: Asymptotics for LASSO-type estimators. Ann. Stat. **28**, 1356–1378 (2000)
9. Leng, C.L., Lin, Y., Wahba, G.: A note on the LASSO and related procedures in model selection. Statistica Sinica **16**, 1273–1284 (2006)
10. Meinshausen, N.: Relaxed LASSO. Comput. Stat. Data Anal. **52**, 374–393 (2007)
11. Stein, C.: Estimation of the mean of a multivariate normal distribution. Ann. Stat. **9**, 1135–1151 (1981)
12. Tibshirani, R.: Regression shrinkage and selection via the LASSO. J. R. Stat. Soc. Ser. B. **58**, 267–288 (1996)
13. Tibshirani, R., Taylor, J.: Degrees of freedom in LASSO problems. Ann. Stat. **40**, 1198–1232 (2012)
14. Wu, T.T., Lange, K.: Coordinate descent algorithms for LASSO penalized regression. Ann. Appl. Stat. **2**, 224–244 (2008)
15. Xiao, N., Xu, Q.S.: Multi-step adaptive elastic-net: reducing false positives in high-dimensional variable selection. J. Stat. Comput. Simul. **85**, 3755–3765 (2015)
16. Zhang, C.H.: Nearly unbiased variable selection under minimax concave penalty. Ann. Stat. **38**, 894–942 (2010)
17. Zou, H.: The adaptive LASSO and its oracle properties. J. Am. Stat. Assoc. **101**, 1418–1492 (2006)
18. Zou, H., Hastie, T., Tibshirani, R.: On the degree of freedom of the LASSO. Ann. Stat. **35**, 2173–2192 (2007)

Geometric Mean Metric Learning for Label Distribution Learning

Yansheng Zhai[1] and Jianhua Dai[2(✉)]

[1] College of Intelligence and Computing, Tianjin University, TianJin 300350, China
`yszhai@tju.edu.cn`
[2] Hunan Provincial Key Laboratory of Intelligent Computing and Language Information Processing, College of Information Science and Engineering, Hunan Normal University, ChangSha 410081, China
`jhdai@hunnu.edu.cn`

Abstract. Label distribution learning is an extend multi-label learning paradigm, especially it can preserve the significance of the labels and the related information among the labels. Many studies have shown that label distribution learning has important applications in label ambiguity. However, some classification information in the labels is not effectively utilized. In this paper, we use the classification information in the labels, and combine with the geometric mean metric learning to learn a new metric in the feature space. Under the new metric, the similar samples of the label space are as close as possible, and dissimilar samples are as far as possible. Finally, the GMML-kLDL model is proposed by combining the classification information in the labels and the neighbor information in the features. The experimental results show that the model is effective in label distribution learning and can effectively improve the prediction performance.

Keywords: Label distribution learning · Geometric mean metric learning · k-neighborhood learning

1 Introduction

The processing of label ambiguity is very hot in the field of machine learning. At present, single-label learning and multi-label learning [13] have a wide range of applications in label ambiguity research. Single-label learning, each sample corresponds to a label, which is a simple classification problem. Multi-label learning, each sample corresponding to a set of labels, indicating whether the sample has the labels. If the sample has a label, it is marked as 1, and if it does not have the label, it is marked as 0 or -1. It solves the problem of a sample with multiple labels. In order to preserve the original label information, label distribution learning [2] uses the label distribution instead of the original discrete label set to indicate the significance of each label. Label distribution learning is a new supervised learning paradigm described by label distribution or histogram.

© Springer Nature Switzerland AG 2019
T. Gedeon et al. (Eds.): ICONIP 2019, LNCS 11954, pp. 260–272, 2019.
https://doi.org/10.1007/978-3-030-36711-4_23

After label distribution learning was proposed, many researchers applied label distribution learning to deal with the problem of label ambiguity and achieved good results, such as age facial estimation problem [5], emotion recognition problem [16], head gesture recognition problem [4], movies scoring problem [10] and text mining problem [15]. Although label distribution learning has achieved good results in many fields, most label distribution learning algorithms can not effectively use the correlation and classification information of labels to improve the prediction performance. Some methods such as [14] and [6] use the local correlation of the labels, effectively improve the prediction performance of label distribution learning. In this work, we use label classification information to learn a new metric in the feature space. Under the new metric, the samples with similar labels have smaller distances in the feature space, and the samples with different labels have further distances. Then, the GMML-kLDL model is proposed according to the k-nearest neighbor classification. The model uses the geometric mean metric learning [12] to learn a new metric with the label classification information, then calculates the neighbor information of the samples through the new metric to predict the unlabeled label distribution learning data.

The main contributions of this paper are as follows:

1. We use the classification information in the label space and geometric mean metric learning to learn a new metric. Under this metric, it will be easier to use the neighbor samples information.
2. We propose a classification method in the label distribution, which uses the label manifold to assign weights to the neighbor samples to determine the probability that the neighbor samples belong to the same class.
3. We propose the GMML-kLDL model based on the k-nearest neighbor learning and label classification information, which effectively improves the predictive performance of label distribution learning. This is the first time to add geometric mean metric learning to label distribution learning.

In the next work, I will introduce the related work first, then propose the model, the solution to the problem and the experimental analysis. Finally, we summarize the full text.

2   Related Work

2.1   Label Distribution Learning

At present, label distribution learning models mainly have the following three design strategies [1]. The first is the problem conversion category. The method converts the label distribution learning problem into single-label learning problem or multi-label learning problem, then calculates the label distribution through existing single-label learning algorithms or multi-label learning algorithms. The main representative algorithms are PT-SVM and PT-bayes. The second is the algorithm adjustment category, which adapts the existing single-label learning algorithms or multi-label algorithms to the current label distribution learning problem. The main representative algorithm is AA-BP. In addition, there are some special algorithm strategies that are directly applicable to label distribution learning. A representative algorithm is BFGS-LLD [1].

2.2 Geometric Mean Metric Learning

Geometric Mean Metric Learning(GMML) [12] is an algorithm proposed by Pour et al. The main innovation of this method is to add items of dissimilar points to the objective function. It is similar to the original metric learning method MMC [11], the distance among similar points is measured by matrix $\boldsymbol{A}$ to make the distance of similar points as close as possible. But unlike the previous algorithms, they proposed using $\boldsymbol{A}^{-1}$ to measure the distance among dissimilar points. In this way, an objective function can be used to make the distance among similar points as small as possible, and the distance among dissimilar samples is as large as possible. The new objective function is:

$$\min_{\boldsymbol{A} \succ 0} \sum_{(x,y) \in S} d_{\boldsymbol{A}}(x,y) + \sum_{(x,y) \in D} d_{\boldsymbol{A}^{-1}}(x,y) \tag{1}$$

where S is a set of similar point pairs and D is a set of dissimilar point pairs. $\sum_{(x,y) \in S} d_{\boldsymbol{A}}(x,y)$ can ensure that the distance among the similar points is as small as possible by Mahalanobis distance. In addition, according to the theorem: suppose $\boldsymbol{A}$ and $\boldsymbol{B}$ are positive definite matrices, if $\boldsymbol{A} \succ \boldsymbol{B}$, then $\boldsymbol{B}^{-1} \succ \boldsymbol{A}^{-1}$. So it can maximize $d_{\boldsymbol{A}}(x,y)$ by minimizing $d_{\boldsymbol{A}^{-1}}(x,y)$. Therefore, $\sum_{(x,y) \in D} d_{\boldsymbol{A}^{-1}}(x,y)$ can guarantee that the distance among dissimilar points are as far as possible under the metric of Mahalanobis distance.

3   The Proposed Approach

3.1   Notations

Symbol definition rule: bold uppercase letters and their combination represent matrices or sets. Bold lowercase letters and their combinations represent column vectors. Non-bold letters indicate scalar.

3.2   Formulation

Let the training set be $\boldsymbol{S} = \{(\boldsymbol{x}_1, \boldsymbol{d}_1), (\boldsymbol{x}_2, \boldsymbol{d}_2), ..., (\boldsymbol{x}_n, \boldsymbol{d}_n)\}$. We denote $\boldsymbol{X} = [\boldsymbol{x}_1, ..., \boldsymbol{x}_n]^T \in \mathbb{R}^{n \times d}$ and $\boldsymbol{D} = [\boldsymbol{d}_1, ..., \boldsymbol{d}_n]^T$, where $\boldsymbol{x}_i$ is an instance, $\boldsymbol{d}_i = [d_i^1, ..., d_i^L]^T$ is the label distribution of the instance $\boldsymbol{x}_i$, and d_i^j represents the description degree of $\boldsymbol{x}_i$, which satisfies $\sum_{j=1}^{L} d_i^j = 1$. The goal of LDL is to learn a mapping function $f : \boldsymbol{X} \to \boldsymbol{D}$ to predict the labels.

We define $\boldsymbol{adv}_i = [adv_i^1, adv_i^2, ..., adv_i^L]^T$ denotes the advantage labels of sample $\boldsymbol{x}_i$. $d_m = \frac{1}{L}$ is the average of the sample labels. if $d_i^j \geq d_m$ then $adv_i^j = 1$, otherwise $adv_i^j = 0$. The advantage labels indicate the labels that are dominant in the label distribution. For each training instance $\boldsymbol{x}_i (i = 1, 2, ..., n)$, $\boldsymbol{X}_S(\boldsymbol{x}_i) =$

$\{x_j|j = 1, 2, ..., n, j \neq i, adv_i = adv_j\}$, which represents a set of samples with the same advantage labels as x_i. $X_D(x_i) = \{x_j|j = 1, 2, ..., n, j \neq i, adv_i \cap adv_j = \phi\}$ represents a sample set with completely different advantage labels from x_i. $N_k^S(x_i)$ represents a set of k neighbor samples with the same advantage labels as x_i. $N_D(x_i) = \{x_j \mid \parallel x_j - x_i \parallel < \max_{x_a \in N_k^S(x_i)} \parallel x_a - x_i \parallel\}, x_j \in X_D$ represents a set of samples whose Euclidean distance are less than k nearest neighbors in the set of samples with different advantage labels with x_i.

The main purpose of this paper is to learn a new metric on the label distribution data. Under this metric, samples belonging to the same class should have a smaller distance in the feature space, and samples belonging to different classes should have a larger distance in the feature space. In order to solve this problem, it is necessary to provide sample pairs belonging to the same class and sample pairs belonging to different classes. Based on the manifold representation of the labels, we consider the k-nearest neighbor samples with the same advantage labels as x_i to be the same class as x_i. At the same time, if $x_j \in N_D(x_i)$, then it is considered to be different from the class of x_i. The relevant definitions are as follows:

$$\begin{cases} S^+ = \{(x_i, x_j) \mid x_j \in N_k^S(x_i)\}(i = 1, ..., n) \\ D^+ = \{(x_i, x_j) \mid x_j \in N_D(x_i)\}(i = 1, ..., n) \end{cases} \quad (2)$$

In addition, according to the relative probability that the k-nearest neighbor samples of x_i belong to the same class, we set weights for each sample pair $(x_i, x_j), x_j \in N_k^S$. Therefore, the objective function is defined as:

$$\min_{M \succ 0} \sum_{i=1}^{n} \sum_{x_j \in N_k^S} w_{i,j} d_M(x_i, x_j) + \sum_{(x_i, x_j) \in D^+} d_{M^{-1}}(x_i, x_j) \quad (3)$$

The first term of the formula ensures that similar samples are as close as possible in the measure of Mahalanobis distance, and the second term guarantees that the distances between dissimilar samples are as far as possible. $w_i = [w_{i,1}, w_{i,2}, ..., w_{i,j}]^T (x_j \in N_k^S(x_i), j = 1, 2, ..., k)$ represents a weight vector, indicating the relative probability that the neighbor samples $N_k^S(x_i)$ of x_i belong to the same class as x_i. In order to maintain the locality of the label, we use the neighbor information of the label to represent the label, which is used to calculate the relative probability that the labels belongs to the same class. For convenience of computation, we assume that each label distribution can be optimally represented linearly by its neighbor label distributions [8,17]. Then the calculation of the weight vector w_i can be obtained by minimizing the following formula:

$$\min_{w_i} \parallel d_i - \sum_{j=1}^{k} w_{i,j} d_j \parallel^2 \quad (4)$$

$$s.t \ \mathbf{1}^T w_i = 1, w_{i,j} > 0$$

where $\boldsymbol{w}_i = [w_{i,1}, w_{i,2}, ..., w_{i,k}]^T$, $\boldsymbol{1}^T$ is an all 1 vector. The minimization of the above formula can be solved by the least square method.

$$\min_{\boldsymbol{w}_i} \boldsymbol{w}_i^T \boldsymbol{G}_i \boldsymbol{w}_i$$
$$s.t \ \ \boldsymbol{1}^T \boldsymbol{w}_i = 1 \tag{5}$$

where $\boldsymbol{G}_i$ is the local *Gram* matrix of the label, $\boldsymbol{G}_i^{jk} = (\boldsymbol{d}_i - \boldsymbol{d}_j)^T (\boldsymbol{d}_i - \boldsymbol{d}_k)$, $\boldsymbol{x}_j \in N_k^S$. The solution of formula Eq. 5 can solve the problem using quadratic programming.

4   Solution

In order to solve the objective function, we use the trace to rewrite the formula to get the following formula:

$$\min_{\boldsymbol{M} \succ 0} \sum_{i=1}^{n} \sum_{\boldsymbol{x}_j \in N_k^S} w_{i,j} \boldsymbol{d}_M(\boldsymbol{x}_i - \boldsymbol{x}_j) + \sum_{i=1}^{n} \sum_{\boldsymbol{x}_j \in N_D} \boldsymbol{d}_{M^{-1}}(\boldsymbol{x}_i - \boldsymbol{x}_j)$$

$$= \min_{\boldsymbol{M} \succ 0} \sum_{i=1}^{n} \sum_{\boldsymbol{x}_j \in N_k^S} w_{i,j} (\boldsymbol{x}_i - \boldsymbol{x}_j)^T \boldsymbol{M}(\boldsymbol{x}_i - \boldsymbol{x}_j) + \sum_{i=1}^{n} \sum_{\boldsymbol{x}_j \in N_D} (\boldsymbol{x}_i - \boldsymbol{x}_j)^T \boldsymbol{M}^{-1}(\boldsymbol{x}_i - \boldsymbol{x}_j)$$

$$= \min_{\boldsymbol{M} \succ 0} \sum_{i=1}^{n} \sum_{\boldsymbol{x}_j \in N_k^S} w_{i,j} tr(\boldsymbol{M}(\boldsymbol{x}_i - \boldsymbol{x}_j)(\boldsymbol{x}_i - \boldsymbol{x}_j)^T)$$

$$+ \sum_{i=1}^{n} \sum_{\boldsymbol{x}_j \in N_D} tr(\boldsymbol{M}^{-1}(\boldsymbol{x}_i - \boldsymbol{x}_j)(\boldsymbol{x}_i - \boldsymbol{x}_j)^T)$$

$$= \min_{\boldsymbol{M} \succ 0} tr(\boldsymbol{M}\boldsymbol{S}) + tr(\boldsymbol{M}^{-1}\boldsymbol{D}) \tag{6}$$

Add a regular item [7] to the objective function:

$$\min_{\boldsymbol{M} \succ 0} tr(\boldsymbol{M}\boldsymbol{S}) + tr(\boldsymbol{M}^{-1}\boldsymbol{D}) + \lambda D_{sld}(\boldsymbol{M}, \boldsymbol{M}_0) = \min_{\boldsymbol{M} \succ 0} f(\boldsymbol{M}) \tag{7}$$

Here, $\boldsymbol{M}_0$ is a priori matrix, and $\boldsymbol{D}_{sld}$ is a symmetric *DetLog* divergence.

$$D_{sld}(\boldsymbol{M}, \boldsymbol{M}_0) = tr(\boldsymbol{M}\boldsymbol{M}_0^{-1}) + tr(\boldsymbol{M}^{-1}\boldsymbol{M}_0) - 2d \tag{8}$$

where matrices $\boldsymbol{S}$ and $\boldsymbol{D}$ denote

$$\begin{cases} \boldsymbol{S} = \sum_{i=1}^{n} \sum_{\boldsymbol{x}_j \in N_k^S} w_{i,j} (\boldsymbol{x}_i - \boldsymbol{x}_j)(\boldsymbol{x}_i - \boldsymbol{x}_j)^T \\ \boldsymbol{D} = \sum_{i=1}^{n} \sum_{\boldsymbol{x}_j \in N_D} (\boldsymbol{x}_i - \boldsymbol{x}_j)(\boldsymbol{x}_i - \boldsymbol{x}_j)^T \end{cases} \tag{9}$$

It is assumed by most problems in reality that the matrix $\boldsymbol{S}$ and the matrix $\boldsymbol{D}$ are positive definite matrices, and the function $f(\boldsymbol{M})$ is both strictly convex and strictly geodesically convex. Therefore, when $\nabla f(\boldsymbol{M})$ has a solution, the solution is globally optimal.

By deriving $f(M)$ for M, we can get

$$\nabla f(M) = S - M^{-1}DM^{-1} + \lambda(M_0^{-1} - M^{-1}M_0M^{-1}) \qquad (10)$$

Let $\nabla f(M) = 0$, we get

$$M(S + \lambda M_0)M = (D + \lambda M_0), \qquad (11)$$

which is a *Riccati* equation. Since the matrix $S + \lambda M_0$ and the matrix $D + \lambda M_0$ are positive define matrices. Then it has unique positive solution, that is

$$M = (S + \lambda M_0)^{-1} \#_{\frac{1}{2}} (D + \lambda M_0) = S_\lambda^{\frac{1}{2}}(S_\lambda^{\frac{1}{2}} D_\lambda S_\lambda^{\frac{1}{2}})^{\frac{1}{2}} S_\lambda^{\frac{1}{2}} \qquad (12)$$

where $S_\lambda = S + \lambda M_0$, $D_\lambda = D + \lambda M_0$.

5 Weighting

It is meaningless to scale the solution of M by a constant to keep the balance of S and D, so we assign similar matrix and dissimilar matrix weights in the perspective of geodesy. We use the method of paper [12] to assign weights, which is equivalent to the following optimization problem.

$$\min \ h(M) = (1-t)\delta_R^2(M, S^{-1}) + t\delta_R^2(M, D) \qquad (13)$$

where δ_R is the Riemannian distance on the symmetric positive definite matrix.

$$\delta_R(X, Y) = \| \log(Y^{-\frac{1}{2}}XY^{-\frac{1}{2}}) \|_F \quad for \quad X, Y \succ 0 \qquad (14)$$

The solution to this optimization problem is $M = S^{-1} \#_t D$, so the regularized solution is

$$M = (S + \lambda M_0^{-1})^{-1} \#_t (D + \lambda M_0), t \in [0, 1] \qquad (15)$$

For $t \in [0, 1]$, $S^{-1} \#_t D$ is the geometric mean of S^{-1} to D. Equation 12 is the solution for $t = \frac{1}{2}$

6 Prediction Model

In order to make full use of the learned metric matrix M and the advantage label class information contained in the label distribution, we divide the training set into h classes according to the advantage labels, and the number of samples in each class is m_i. m_i means that the ith class has a total of m_i samples. The label distribution center of each advantage class set is the average of the label distribution of all samples in the class, ie $c_j = \frac{1}{m_j} \sum_{i=1}^{m_j} d_i$. d_i belongs to the same class. c_j denotes the label distribution center of the advantage label distribution class j, $C = [c_1, c_2, ..., c_h]$. The feature center is the average value of each sample feature vector, that is $a_j = \frac{1}{m_j} \sum_{i=1}^{m_j} x_i$. a_j represents the feature center of class j.

We know that when predicting a new sample, the label distribution of the sample is not only affected by its k-nearest neighbor label distribution, but also by the class it belongs to. If in a k-nearest neighbor of a sample, most of the neighbors belong to the same advantage class, then the sample is likely to have the characteristics of the advantage class. So we have defined the following calculations. Suppose the test sample is x_t

(1) The matrix M is used to calculate the label distribution and corresponding distance of the k-nearest neighbor samples of x_t

$$dist_{t,i} = (x_t - x_i)^T M (x_t - x_i), i = 1, 2, ..., m \tag{16}$$

(2) The matrix M is used to calculate the distance of the sample x_t to the center of each advantage class.

$$Cdist_{t,i} = (x_t - a_i)^T M (x_t - a_i), i = 1, 2, ..., h \tag{17}$$

(3) We sort the distance from small to large, select the distance of the first k samples, and count the number of samples belonging to each advantage class in the k samples as $u_{t,i}$. $u_{t,i}$ indicates that in the k-nearest neighbor of x_t, the number of samples belonging to the i-th class is $u_{t,i}$, $u_{t,i} \in [0, k]$. The label distribution of k samples is $D_k = [d_1, d_2, ..., d_k]$. $Rank_k(.)$ means sorting the values, and taking the first k values to form a vector. The closer the k-nearest neighbor is, the greater the impact on the label distribution, so we take the reciprocal distance. The more samples of the same class in the k-nearest neighbor, the more influence the class has on the results of the label distribution, so we weight it.

$$rdis = [rdis_1, rdis_2, ..., rdis_k] = Rank_k([dist_{t,1}, dist_{t,2}, ..., dist_{t,m}])$$
$$Cdist = \frac{1}{k}[\frac{u_{t,1}}{Cdist_{t,1} + \delta}, \frac{u_{t,2}}{Cdist_{t,2} + \delta}, ..., \frac{u_{t,h}}{Cdist_{t,h} + \delta}]^T \tag{18}$$
$$dis = [\frac{1}{rdis_1 + \delta}, \frac{1}{rdis_2 + \delta}, ..., \frac{1}{rdis_k + \delta}]^T$$

δ prevents the denominator from being 0. Generally take 0.01.

dis and $Cdis$ are spliced into a vector $z = [z_1, z_2, ..., z_{k+h}]^T = [dis; Cdist_t]$. The distance matrix is processed by the $softmax$ function to obtain the weight metrix $w = [w_1, w_2, ..., w_{k+h}]^T$

$$w_i = \frac{\exp(z_i)}{\sum_{j=1}^{k+h} \exp(z_j)} \quad (i = 1, ..., k + h) \tag{19}$$

The label set is $U = [D_k, C]$, and the dimension is $n \times (k + h)$. The predicted label distribution is

$$p = Uw \tag{20}$$

Algorithm 1. GMML-kLDL

Data: training set $\{X, D\}$, λ, M_0, t, K, k
Result: the label distribution p_t
1 Train;
2 initialize λ , M_0, t, K, k;
3 **for** $i = 1; i \le n; i + +$ **do**
4   calculate $X^S(x_i)$, $X_D(x_i)$, $N_K^S(x_i)$, $N_D(x_i)$;
5   calculate w_i by Eq.5;
6 **end**
7 calculate S and D;
8 $S = \sum_{i=1}^n \sum_{x_j \in N_K^S} w_{i,j}(x_i - x_j)(x_i - x_j)^T$;
9 $D = \sum_{i=1}^n \sum_{x_j \in N_D}(x_i - x_j)(x_i - x_j)^T$;
10 calculate $M = (S + \lambda M_0^{-1})^{-1} \#_t (D + \lambda M_0)$;
11 Test;
12 calculate U, w by Eq.16, Eq.17, Eq.18 and Eq.19;
13 return $p = Uw$;

Proof: p conforms to the definition of the label distribution, ie if $p = [p_1, p_2, ..., p_n]^T$, and $0 \le p_i$, $\sum_{i=1}^n p_i = 1$

We all know $U = [d_1, d_2, ..., d_{k+h}]$, $d_i = [d_i^1, d_i^2, ..., d_i^n]^T$ and $\sum_{j=1}^n d_i^j = 1, 0 \le d_i^j$. It can get $\sum_{i=1}^{k+h} w_i = 1, 0 \le w_i$ from the definition of w

$$p = Uw = \sum_{i=1}^{k+h} d_i w_i = [\sum_{j=1}^{k+h} d_j^1 w_j, \sum_{j=1}^{k+h} d_j^2 w_j, ..., \sum_{j=1}^{k+h} d_j^n w_j]^T \quad (21)$$

we can get $p_n = \sum_{j=1}^{k+h} d_j^n w_j \ge 0, \sum_{i=1}^n p_i = \sum_{i=1}^n n \sum_{j=1}^{k+h} d_j^i w_j = \sum_{j=1}^{k+h} w_j \sum_{i=1}^n d_j^i = 1$

7   Experiment

In this section, we will compare the model with existing advanced models to evaluate the effectiveness of the model.

7.1   Datasets

These 11 datasets cover areas such as biometric classification and sentiment analysis. Due to page restrictions, we only provide brief statistics for the datasets in Table 1.

Table 1. Specific information of the datasets

Dataset	cold	spo	spo5	dtt	heat	spoem	diau	elu	cdc	alpha	SJAFFE
Sample	2465	2465	2465	2465	2465	2465	2465	2465	2465	2465	213
Feature	24	24	24	24	24	24	24	24	24	24	243
Labels	4	6	3	4	6	2	7	14	15	18	6

7.2   Experimental Evaluation Method

A total of six evaluation methods were selected as the evaluation indicators of the algorithm performance. The first one is the distance evaluation indicators (*Chebyshev, Clark, Canberra, KL divercence*), the smaller the value, the better. The second is the similarity evaluation indicators (*Cosine, Intersection*), the larger the value, the better (Table 2).

Table 2. Evaluation measures for LDL algorithms

Name	Formula
Chebyshev $\downarrow$	$Chebyshev(P,Q) = max_i|P_i - Q_i|$
Clark $\downarrow$	$Clark(P,Q) = \sqrt{\sum_{i=1}^{c} \frac{(P_i-Q_i)^2}{(P_i+Q_i)}}$
Canberra $\downarrow$	$Canbera(P,Q) = \sum_{i=1}^{c} \frac{|P_i-Q_i|}{P_i+Q_i}$
Kullback − Leibler $\downarrow$	$KL(P,Q) = \sum_{j=1}^{c} P_j \ln \frac{P_j}{Q_j}$
Cosine $\uparrow$	$Cosine(P,Q) = \frac{\sum_{i=1}^{c} P_i Q_i}{\sqrt{\sum_{i=1}^{c} P_i^2}\sqrt{\sum_{i=1}^{c} Q_i^2}}$
Intersection $\uparrow$	$Intersection(P,Q) = \sum_{j=1}^{c} \min(P_j - Q_j)$

7.3   Comparison Algorithm

According to the previous sections, we compare the proposed algorithm GMML-kLDL with the most advanced label distribution learning algorithms. In the problem conversion algorithm, PT-SVM is selected, AA-BP is selected in the algorithm transformation, and the special design algorithm BFGS-LLD is used.

7.4   Parameter Settings

According to the paper [9], we set AA-BP [9], PT-SVM [3], BFGS-LLD [1] as the best settings. For the GMML-kLDL algorithm, we set $k = 30$ (in k-nearest neighbor classifier), K from 1 to 20, the step size is 1. t is from 0.1 to 1, the step is 0.1, M_0 is the identity matrix, $\lambda = 0.1$

Table 3. The performance measure: *intersection* ↑

Dataset	AA-BP	PT-SVM	BFGS-LLD	GMML-kLDL	K	t
Yeastcold	0.9338 ± 0.0025	0.9340 ± 0.0064	0.9407 ± 0.0023	**0.9413 ± 0.0027**	10	0.4
Yeastspo	0.9046 ± 0.0044	0.9089 ± 0.0188	0.9154 ± 0.0055	**0.9158 ± 0.0051**	10	0.4
Yeastspo5	0.9043 ± 0.0065	0.9047 ± 0.0048	0.9086 ± 0.0054	**0.9102 ± 0.0051**	10	0.1
Yeastdtt	0.9478 ± 0.0020	0.9554 ± 0.0018	0.9583 ± 0.0013	**0.9587 ± 0.0011**	10	0.3
Yeastheat	0.9228 ± 0.0053	0.9371 ± 0.0019	0.9401 ± 0.0012	**0.9412 ± 0.0011**	10	0.4
yeastspoem	0.9066 ± 0.0047	0.9083 ± 0.0057	0.9131 ± 0.0052	**0.9138 ± 0.0039**	10	0.5
Yeastdiau	0.9206 ± 0.0066	0.9283 ± 0.0042	0.9403 ± 0.0028	**0.9587 ± 0.0011**	10	0.3
Yeastelu	0.8875 ± 0.0053	0.9561 ± 0.0013	**0.9588 ± 0.0012**	0.9587 ± 0.0012	10	0.7
Yeastcdc	0.8792 ± 0.0066	0.9553 ± 0.0022	**0.9573 ± 0.0027**	0.9571 ± 0.0027	10	0.2
Yeastalpha	0.8627 ± 0.0068	0.9598 ± 0.0023	**0.9622 ± 0.0025**	0.9620 ± 0.0025	10	0.3
SJAFFE	0.8297 ± 0.0231	0.8435 ± 0.0163	0.8409 ± 0.0149	**0.8594 ± 0.0182**	15	0.3
Average	0.9000 ± 0.0067	0.9265 ± 0.0060	0.9305 ± 0.0040	**0.9343 ± 0.0041**	–	–

7.5 Experimental Result

Tables 4 and 3 show the experimental results of several algorithms on different evaluation indicators on multiple datasets. Here, we choose two evaluation indicators *Chebyshev* (the smaller the better), and the *Intersection* (the bigger the better). Other evaluation indicators are shown in Fig. 1. We used the ten-fold cross-validation method to evaluate the predicted performance, so the experimental results were given in the form of (average ± standard deviation) and the best-ranked results were bolded.

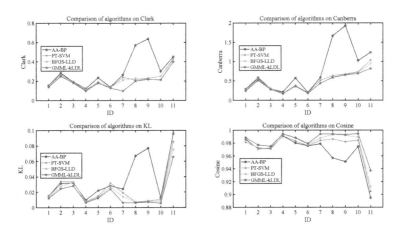

Fig. 1. Algorithm performance comparison

Table 4. The performance measure: *chebyshev* ↓

Dataset	AA-BP	PT-SVM	BFGS-LLD	GMML-kLDL	K	t
Yeastcold	0.0572 ± 0.0020	0.0574 ± 0.0056	0.0512 ± 0.0018	**0.0506 ± 0.0020**	10	0.4
Yeastspo	0.0651 ± 0.0031	0.0629 ± 0.0164	0.0584 ± 0.0038	**0.0571 ± 0.0036**	10	0.4
Yeastspo5	0.0957 ± 0.0065	0.0953 ± 0.0048	0.0914 ± 0.0054	**0.0898 ± 0.0051**	10	0.1
Yeastdtt	0.0450 ± 0.0018	0.0388 ± 0.0020	0.0361 ± 0.0013	**0.0358 ± 0.0013**	10	0.3
Yeastheat	0.0535 ± 0.0032	0.0443 ± 0.0015	0.0423 ± 0.0009	**0.0415 ± 0.0011**	10	0.4
Yeastspoem	0.0934 ± 0.0047	0.0917 ± 0.0057	0.0869 ± 0.0052	**0.0862 ± 0.0039**	10	0.5
Yeastdiau	0.0486 ± 0.0041	0.0446 ± 0.0031	0.0370 ± 0.0015	**0.0358 ± 0.0013**	10	0.3
Yeastelu	0.0404 ± 0.0019	0.0170 ± 0.0006	0.0163 ± 0.0006	0.0163 ± 0.0009	10	0.7
Yeastcdc	0.0409 ± 0.0020	0.0171 ± 0.0010	0.0163 ± 0.0006	0.0163 ± 0.0010	10	0.2
Yeastalpha	0.0398 ± 0.0018	0.0140 ± 0.0009	0.0135 ± 0.0009	0.0135 ± 0.0008	10	0.3
SJAFFE	0.1261 ± 0.0207	0.1204 ± 0.0159	0.1183 ± 0.0135	**0.1125 ± 0.0157**	15	0.3
Average	0.0642 ± 0.0047	0.0549 ± 0.0052	0.0516 ± 0.0032	**0.0506 ± 0.0033**	–	–

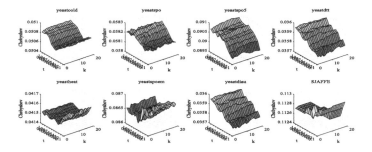

Fig. 2. Parameter analysis

7.6   Experiment Analysis

1. From Tables 4, 3 and Fig. 1, we can see that the GMML-kLDL model still achieves good predictive performance compared to the most advanced learning algorithms. The GMML-kLDL model has obvious advantages in several datasets with a small number of labels. The advantage is not obvious in the datasets with a large number of labels, but the predictive performance can also be in the forefront. Analyzing the experimental datasets with insignificant advantages, the value of the label distribution is relatively average. Therefore, the difference among the samples is fuzzy, and the accuracy of dividing the similar matrices and the dissimilar matrices is not high, so the performance improvement is not obvious.

2. Figure 2 is the parameter analysis diagram of the parameter k and the parameter t. Due to space limitations, only the analysis diagrams of 8 datasets are shown here. From Fig. 2, we can see that when t takes the appropriate value, it can effectively improve the performance of the model.

8 Conclusion

In this paper, we use the geometric mean metric learning, combined with the label classification information to propose the GMML-kLDL model. The model uses the label classification information to adjust the feature space of the samples, and learns a new metric matrix M. Finally, the label distribution is predicted by combining the label classification information, and obtains good experimental results. In the future work, we will continue to study the relationship among features and improve the performance of label distribution learning.

Acknowledgment. This work was partially supported by the National Natural Science Foundation of China (Nos. 61976089, 61473259, 61070074, 60703038) and the Hunan Provincial Science & Technology Program Project (Nos. 2018RS3065, 2018TP1018).

References

1. Geng, X.: Label distribution learning. IEEE Trans. Knowl. Data Eng. **28**(7), 1734–1748 (2014)
2. Geng, X., Ji, R.: Label distribution learning. In: IEEE International Conference on Data Mining Workshops, pp. 377–383 (2014)
3. Geng, X., Wang, Q., Xia, Y.: Facial age estimation by adaptive label distribution learning. In: International Conference on Pattern Recognition, pp. 4465–4470 (2014)
4. Geng, X., Xia, Y.: Head pose estimation based on multivariate label distribution. In: Computer Vision and Pattern Recognition, pp. 1837–1842 (2014)
5. Geng, X., Yin, C., Zhou, Z.: Facial age estimation by learning from label distributions. IEEE Trans. Pattern Anal. Mach. Intell. **35**(10), 2401–2412 (2013)
6. Jia, X., Li, W., Liu, J., Zhang, Y.: Label distribution learning by exploiting label correlations. In: Proceedings of the Thirty-Second AAAI Conference on Artificial Intelligence, New Orleans, Louisiana, USA, 2–7 February 2018 (2018)
7. Schölkopf, B., Platt, J., Hofmann, T.: Large margin component analysis. In: International Conference on Neural Information Processing Systems, pp. 1385–1392 (2006)
8. Wikipedia contributors: Semi-supervised learning – Wikipedia, the free encyclopedia (2018)
9. Geng, X., Smith-Miles, K., Zhou, Z.-H.: Facial age estimation by learning from label distributions. In: Proceedings of the 24th AAAI Conference on Artificial Intelligence, pp. 451–456 (2010)
10. Xin, G., Peng, H.: Pre-release prediction of crowd opinion on movies by label distribution learning. In: International Conference on Artificial Intelligence, pp. 3511–3517 (2015)
11. Xing, E.P.: Distance metric learning, with application to clustering with side-information. In: International Conference on Neural Information Processing Systems, pp. 521–528 (2002)
12. Zadeh, P., Hosseini, R., Sra, S.: Geometric mean metric learning. In: Proceedings of the 33nd International Conference on Machine Learning, ICML 2016, New York City, NY, USA, 19–24 June 2016, pp. 2464–2471 (2016)

13. Zhang, M., Zhou, Z.: ML-KNN: a lazy learning approach to multi-label learning. Pattern Recogn. **40**(7), 2038–2048 (2007)
14. Zheng, X., Jia, X., Li, W.: Label distribution learning by exploiting sample correlations locally. In: Proceedings of the Thirty-Second AAAI Conference on Artificial Intelligence, New Orleans, Louisiana, USA, 2–7 February 2018 (2018)
15. Zhou, D., Zhang, X., Zhou, Y., Zhao, Q., Geng, X.: Emotion distribution learning from texts. In: Conference on Empirical Methods in Natural Language Processing, pp. 638–647 (2016)
16. Zhou, Y., Xue, H., Geng, X.: Emotion distribution recognition from facial expressions. In: Proceedings of the 23rd ACM International Conference on Multimedia, pp. 1247–1250. ACM (2015)
17. Zhou, Y., Gu, H.: Geometric mean metric learning for partial label data. Neurocomputing **275**, 394–402 (2018)

Explicit Center Selection and Training for Fault Tolerant RBF Networks

Hiu Tung Wong[1], Zhenni Wang[1], Chi-Sing Leung[1(✉)], and John Sum[2]

[1] City University of Hong Kong, Kowloon Tong, Hong Kong
eeleungc@cityu.edu.hk
[2] Institute of Technology Management, National Chung Hsing University,
Taichung City, Taiwan

Abstract. Although some noise tolerant center selection training algorithms for RBF networks have been developed, they usually have some disadvantages. For example, some of them cannot select the RBF centers and train the network simultaneously. Others do not allow us to explicitly define the number of RBF nodes in the resultant network, and we need to go through a time consuming procedure to tune the regularization parameter such that the number of RBF nodes used satisfies our pre-specified value. Therefore, it is important to develop some noise resistant algorithms that allow us to specify the number of RBF nodes in the resultant network. In addition, they should be able to train the network and to select RBF nodes simultaneously. This paper formulates the RBF training problem as a generalized M-sparse problem. We first define a noise tolerant objective function for RBF networks. Afterwards, we formulate the training problem as a generalized M-sparse problem, in which the objective function is the proposed noise tolerant training objective function and the constraint is an ℓ_0-norm of the weight vector. An iterative algorithm is then developed to solve this generalized M-sparse problem. From simulation experiments, the proposed algorithm is superior to the state-of-art noise tolerant algorithms. In addition, the proposed algorithm allows us to explicitly define the number of RBF nodes in the resultant network. We prove that the algorithm converges and that the fixed points of the proposed algorithms are the local minimum of this generalized M-sparse problem.

Keywords: RBF network · Center selection · Fault tolerance

1 Introduction

The radial basis function (RBF) network model is widely used in many tasks, including nonlinear regression, classification and system control, due to its simple network structure. The training process of an RBF network involves two steps. The first step is to select the RBF centers from the training samples. The second one is to estimate the output weights between the RBF hidden layer and the output layer. Many approaches have been proposed to select RBF centers. One

© Springer Nature Switzerland AG 2019
T. Gedeon et al. (Eds.): ICONIP 2019, LNCS 11954, pp. 273–285, 2019.
https://doi.org/10.1007/978-3-030-36711-4_24

commonly used approach is the clustering approach [1]. The orthogonal least squares (OLS) algorithm [2] is another widely used approach for center selection. Using the OLS algorithm, the centers are selected by evaluating an error reduction ratio in a forward selection manner. The center selection can also be implemented using support vector regression (SVR) approach [3].

When implementing an RBF network, imperfection can affect the performance of the network. For example, round-off errors may happen in the trained weights. The behavior of round-off errors can be described as multiplicative weight noise [4,5]. Also, in the analog implementation, the precision error of an analog component is proportional to its nominal value. Hence it is important to embed the capability to resist multiplicative noise in the training process. However, those aforementioned center selection approaches do not consider the existence of multiplicative weight noise. Therefore, the performance of those approaches cannot be guaranteed, when the resultant network is affected by multiplicative noise. Based on regularization and OLS center selection, a fault tolerant approach was proposed in [5]. This approach has a good performance in fault tolerance. However, this approach cannot perform the center selection and network training simultaneously. In [6], an ADMM based algorithm with an ℓ_1-norm regularizer was proposed. Its performance is much better many existing algorithms, including OLS, fault tolerant OLS and SVR. However, in this ADMM ℓ_1-norm based approach, we cannot explicitly specify the number of RBF nodes in the resultant network. The number of RBF nodes in the resultant network depends on the regularization parameter of the ℓ_1-norm regularizer. Also, there is no analytic expression to describe the relationship between the ℓ_1-norm regularization parameter and the number of RBF nodes in the resultant network.

In this paper, a noise resistant algorithm is proposed to train an RBF network and select the RBF center simultaneously. In addition, in the algorithm, we can specify the number of RBF nodes in the resultant network. A noise resistant training objective is constructed based on the multiplicative weight noise model. Afterward, a constrained optimization problem is defined, in which the training objective is the noise resistant objective and the constraint is the number of RBF nodes in the resultant network, i.e., the ℓ_0-norm of the output weight vector. Our training problem can be considered as a generalized M-sparse problem. We then derive an iterative algorithm to solve the constrained optimization problem based on the iterative hard threshold (IHT) concept [7]. The convergent property of the proposed algorithm is then presented. The Simulation results show that the noise tolerant performance of the proposed algorithm is better than that of the state-of-art noise tolerant algorithms.

The rest of this paper is organized as follows. The background of the RBF network and the IHT concept are given in Sect. 2. The proposed fault algorithm is developed and analyzed in Sect. 3. Simulation results are provided in Sect. 4. A concluded remarked is given in Sect. 5.

2   Background

2.1   Standard RBF Network

We consider that the RBF network model is designed for nonlinear regression. The training data set is denoted as $\mathcal{T} = \{(\boldsymbol{x}_1, y_1), \cdots, (\boldsymbol{x}_N, y_N)\}$, where $\boldsymbol{x}_i \in \mathbb{R}^K$ is the i-th training input vector and y_i is the i-th training output.

Given an input vector $\boldsymbol{x}$, the output of the RBF network is given by

$$\varphi(\boldsymbol{x}) = \sum_{j=1}^{M} a_j \rho_j(\boldsymbol{x}), \tag{1}$$

where M is the number of RBF nodes in the hidden layer, a_j is the weight between j-th hidden layer node and the output layer, $\rho_j(\boldsymbol{x}) = \exp(-\xi \|\boldsymbol{x} - \boldsymbol{c}_j\|^2)$ is the output of the j-th RBF node, ξ is a parameter that controls the RBF width, $\boldsymbol{c}_j$ is the RBF center vector of the j-th RBF, and the centers $\boldsymbol{c}_j$'s are usually selected from the training input vectors $\{\boldsymbol{x}_1, \cdots, \boldsymbol{x}_N\}$. The training set mean square error (MSE) is given by

$$\varepsilon = \frac{1}{N} \sum_{i=1}^{N} (y_i - \varphi(\boldsymbol{x}_i))^2 = \frac{1}{N} \sum_{i=1}^{N} (y_i - \sum_{j=1}^{M} a_j \rho_j(\boldsymbol{x}))^2 = \frac{1}{N} \|\boldsymbol{y} - \boldsymbol{Pa}\|_2^2, \tag{2}$$

where $\boldsymbol{y} = [y_1, ..., y_N]^T$, $\boldsymbol{P}$ is and $N \times M$ matrix and $P_{(i,j)} = \rho_j(\mathbf{x}_i) = \exp(-\xi \|\boldsymbol{x}_i - \boldsymbol{c}_j\|^2)$, and $\boldsymbol{a} = [a_1, \cdots, a_M]^T$.

If we use all training input vectors as RBF centers, then $\boldsymbol{c}_j = \boldsymbol{x}_j$, and $j = 1, \cdots, N$. The network output is given by $\varphi(\boldsymbol{x}) = \sum_{j=1}^{N} \alpha_j \rho_j(\boldsymbol{x})$, where $\rho_j(\boldsymbol{x}) = \exp(-\xi \|\boldsymbol{x} - \boldsymbol{x}_j\|^2)$. Equation (2) is still given by

$$\varepsilon = \frac{1}{N} \sum_{i=1}^{N} (y_i - \varphi(\boldsymbol{x}_i))^2 = \frac{1}{N} \|\boldsymbol{y} - \boldsymbol{Pa}\|_2^2,$$

where $\boldsymbol{P}$ becomes an $N \times N$ matrix with $P_{ij} = \rho_j(\mathbf{x}_i) = \exp(-\xi \|\boldsymbol{x}_i - \boldsymbol{x}_j\|^2)$. It should be noticed that in Sect. 3 we will present an algorithm to select M centers from $\{\boldsymbol{x}_1, \cdots, \boldsymbol{x}_N\}$.

2.2   Iterative Hard Threshold Algorithm

The IHT concept [7] can solve the M-sparse problem, given by

$$\min_{\boldsymbol{\alpha}} \|\boldsymbol{y} - \boldsymbol{\Phi\alpha}\|_2^2, \quad \text{s.t. } \|\boldsymbol{\alpha}\|_0 \leq M, \tag{3}$$

where $\boldsymbol{y} \in \mathbb{N}$ is the target output, $\boldsymbol{\Phi}$ is an $N \times N_1$ ($N \leq N_1$) matrix, and $\leq N_1 \leq M$. In the M-sparse problem, we would like minimize the squared error with a weighted sum of M columns of $\boldsymbol{\Phi}$. A surrogate function is first introduced, given by

$$L_M^S(\boldsymbol{\alpha}, \boldsymbol{z}) = \|\boldsymbol{y} - \boldsymbol{\Phi\alpha}\|_2^2 - \|\boldsymbol{\Phi\alpha} - \boldsymbol{\Phi z}\|_2^2 + \|\boldsymbol{\alpha} - \boldsymbol{z}\|_2^2. \tag{4}$$

Note that $L_M^S(\boldsymbol{\alpha}, \boldsymbol{\alpha}) = \|\boldsymbol{y} - \boldsymbol{\Phi}\boldsymbol{\alpha}\|_2^2$. Given a fixed $\boldsymbol{z}$, minimizing the objective stated in (4) is achieved at

$$\hat{\alpha}_i = z_i + \boldsymbol{\phi}_i^{\mathrm{T}}\mathbf{y} - \boldsymbol{\phi}_i^{\mathrm{T}}\boldsymbol{\Phi}\boldsymbol{z}, \tag{5}$$

where $\boldsymbol{\phi}_i$ is the i-th column of $\boldsymbol{\Phi}$. Considering the constrain that limiting $\|\boldsymbol{\alpha}\|_0 \leq M$, the minimum of the objective (4) can be obtained as

$$\hat{\boldsymbol{\alpha}} = H_M(\boldsymbol{z} + \boldsymbol{\Phi}^{\mathrm{T}}(\boldsymbol{y} - \boldsymbol{\Phi}\boldsymbol{z}), \tag{6}$$

where H_M is an element wise hard thresholding operator H_M. Given a vector $\boldsymbol{v} \in \mathbb{R}^{N_1}$,

$$H_M(v_i) = \begin{cases} 0, & \text{if } |v_i| < q \\ v_i, & \text{if } |v_i| \geq q, \end{cases} \tag{7}$$

where q is the M-th largest element of $\{|v_1|, \cdots, |v_{N_1}|\}$. If the number of nonzero elements in $\boldsymbol{v}$ is less than M, then q is the smallest nonzero element of $\{|v_1|, \cdots, |v_{N_1}|\}$.

In the IHT for the M-sparse problem, it sets $\boldsymbol{z}$ as $\boldsymbol{\alpha}^n$ and $\hat{\boldsymbol{\alpha}}$ as $\boldsymbol{\alpha}^{n+1}$. The iteration is then given by

$$\boldsymbol{\alpha}^{n+1} = H_M(\boldsymbol{\alpha}^n + \boldsymbol{\Phi}^{\mathrm{T}}(\boldsymbol{y} - \boldsymbol{\Phi}\boldsymbol{\alpha}^n)). \tag{8}$$

From [7], during the iterative process, the original cost function $\|\boldsymbol{y} - \boldsymbol{\Phi}\boldsymbol{\alpha}\|_2^2$ does not increase. The condition of the convergence is that $\|\boldsymbol{\Phi}\|_2 < 1$. Also, a fixed point of the IHT algorithm is a local minimum of the M-sparse problem. It should be noticed that the M-sparse problem is NP hard. It is not possible to discuss the convergence of global minimum.

3   Proposed Algorithm

3.1   RBF Network with Weight Noise

Consider that all training input vectors are used as centers, i.e., $\varphi(\boldsymbol{x}) = \sum_{j=1}^{N} \alpha_j \rho_j(\boldsymbol{x})$. For multiplicative weight noise, a noisy weight is modeled as

$$\tilde{a}_j = a_j + \kappa_j a_j, j = 1, \cdots, N, \tag{9}$$

where κ_j is a zero mean random variable that models the effect of multiplicative weight noise. In addition, κ_j's are independent with the same distribution, and their variance is equal to σ_κ^2. The intensity of the overall effect $\kappa_j a_j$ depends on σ_κ^2 and the magnitude of a_j. The statistics of κ_j's are given by

$$E(\kappa_j) = 0, \quad E(\kappa_j^2) = \sigma_\kappa^2, \text{ and } E(\kappa_j \kappa_{j'}) = 0 \; \forall j \neq j', \tag{10}$$

where $E(\cdot)$ is the expectation operator. The training set MSE of a noisy RBF network is modeled as

$$
\begin{aligned}
\tilde{\varepsilon} &= \frac{1}{N}\|\boldsymbol{y} - \boldsymbol{P}\tilde{\boldsymbol{a}}\|_2^2 \\
&= \frac{1}{N}\sum_{i=1}^{N}\bigg(y_i^2 - 2y_i\sum_{j=1}^{N}(a_j + \kappa_j a_j)\rho_j(\boldsymbol{x}_i) \\
&\quad + \sum_{j=1}^{N}\sum_{j'=j}^{N} a_j a_{j'}(1 + \kappa_j\kappa_{j'})\rho_j(\boldsymbol{x}_i)\rho_{j'}(\boldsymbol{x}_i) \\
&\quad + \sum_{j=1}^{N}\sum_{j'=1}^{N}(\kappa_j + \kappa_{j'})a_j a_{j'}\rho_j(\boldsymbol{x}_i)\rho_{j'}(\boldsymbol{x}_i)\bigg).
\end{aligned}
\tag{11}
$$

Combining (10) and (11), the expected training MSE is given by

$$
F(\boldsymbol{a}) = \frac{1}{N}\|\boldsymbol{y} - \boldsymbol{P}\boldsymbol{a}\|_2^2 + \boldsymbol{a}^{\mathrm{T}}\boldsymbol{\Theta}\boldsymbol{a},
\tag{12}
$$

where $\boldsymbol{\Theta} = \mathrm{diag}((\sigma_\kappa^2/N)\boldsymbol{P}^{\mathrm{T}}\boldsymbol{P})$ is a diagonal matrix whose elements are equal to the diagonal elements of $(\sigma_\kappa^2/N)\boldsymbol{P}^{\mathrm{T}}\boldsymbol{P}$. Instead of using the training objective (2), when the network is affected by multiplicative weight noise, it is more reasonable to train the network using the expected MSE $F(\boldsymbol{a})$, stated as in (12), as the objective function.

3.2   Algorithm Development

Let us restrict the number of RBF nodes to be M in the resultant network. Then the noise resistant training problem is a constrained optimization problem, given by

$$
\min_{\boldsymbol{\alpha}} \frac{1}{N}\|\boldsymbol{y} - \boldsymbol{P}\boldsymbol{a}\|_2^2 + \boldsymbol{a}^{\mathrm{T}}\boldsymbol{\Theta}\boldsymbol{a}, \quad \text{s.t. } \|\boldsymbol{\alpha}\|_0 \le M.
\tag{13}
$$

The problem stated in (13) is identical to minimize the following objective function:

$$
\tilde{F}(\boldsymbol{a}) = \frac{1}{N}\|\boldsymbol{y} - \boldsymbol{P}\boldsymbol{a}\|_2^2 + \boldsymbol{a}^{\mathrm{T}}\boldsymbol{\Theta}\boldsymbol{a} + \mathrm{i}(\boldsymbol{a}) = F(\boldsymbol{a}) + \mathrm{i}(\boldsymbol{a}),
\tag{14}
$$

where

$$
\mathrm{i}(\boldsymbol{a}) =
\begin{cases}
0, & \text{if } \|\mathbf{a}\|_0 \le M \\
\infty, & \text{if } \|\mathbf{a}\|_0 > M
\end{cases}
\tag{15}
$$

is an indicator function.

Borrowing the concept from IHT, we construct two surrogate objective functions for (12) and (14), given by

$$
\begin{aligned}
F_M(\boldsymbol{a}, \boldsymbol{z}) = {} & \frac{1}{N}\|\boldsymbol{y} - \boldsymbol{Pa}\|_2^2 + \boldsymbol{a}^{\mathrm{T}}\boldsymbol{\Theta}\boldsymbol{a} - \frac{1}{N}\|\boldsymbol{Pa} - \boldsymbol{Pz}\|_2^2 \\
& - (\boldsymbol{a} - \boldsymbol{z})^{\mathrm{T}}\boldsymbol{\Theta}(\boldsymbol{a} - \boldsymbol{z}) + \frac{1}{2\beta}\|\boldsymbol{a} - \boldsymbol{z}\|_2^2,
\end{aligned}
\tag{16}
$$

$$
\begin{aligned}
\tilde{F}_M(\boldsymbol{a}, \boldsymbol{z}) = {} & \frac{1}{N}\|\boldsymbol{y} - \boldsymbol{Pa}\|_2^2 + \boldsymbol{a}^{\mathrm{T}}\boldsymbol{\Theta}\boldsymbol{a} - \frac{1}{N}\|\boldsymbol{Pa} - \boldsymbol{Pz}\|_2^2 \\
& - (\boldsymbol{a} - \boldsymbol{z})^{\mathrm{T}}\boldsymbol{\Theta}(\boldsymbol{a} - \boldsymbol{z}) + \frac{1}{2\beta}\|\boldsymbol{a} - \boldsymbol{z}\|_2^2 + \mathrm{i}(\boldsymbol{a}),
\end{aligned}
\tag{17}
$$

where $\beta > 0$. We will discuss the rule of selecting β in the rest of the paper. Note that $F(\boldsymbol{a}) = F_M(\boldsymbol{a}, \boldsymbol{a})$ and $\tilde{F}(\boldsymbol{a}) = \tilde{F}_M(\boldsymbol{a}, \boldsymbol{a})$.

To solve the optimization problem, let us consider the minimization of $F_M(\boldsymbol{a}, \boldsymbol{z})$ with respect to $\boldsymbol{a}$. From basic algebra,

$$
F_M(\boldsymbol{a}, \boldsymbol{z}) \propto \frac{1}{2\beta}\|\boldsymbol{a}\|^2 - \frac{2}{2\beta}\boldsymbol{a}^T\left(2\beta(\frac{1}{N}\boldsymbol{P}^{\mathrm{T}}\boldsymbol{y} - (\frac{1}{N}\boldsymbol{P}^{\mathrm{T}}\boldsymbol{P} + \boldsymbol{\Theta})\boldsymbol{z}) + \boldsymbol{z}\right)
\tag{18}
$$

$$
= \frac{1}{2\beta}\sum_{j=1}^{N} a_j^2 - \frac{2}{2\beta}\sum_{j=1}^{N} a_j \left[2\beta(\frac{1}{N}\boldsymbol{P}^{\mathrm{T}}\boldsymbol{y} - (\frac{1}{N}\boldsymbol{P}^{\mathrm{T}}\boldsymbol{P} + \boldsymbol{\Theta})\boldsymbol{z}) + \boldsymbol{z}\right]_j,
\tag{19}
$$

where $[\cdot]_j$ denotes the j-th element of a vector. Clearly, the minimum of $F_M(\boldsymbol{a}, \boldsymbol{z})$ is attained at

$$
\hat{a}_j = z_j - 2\beta\left[(\frac{1}{N}\boldsymbol{P}^{\mathrm{T}}\boldsymbol{P} + \boldsymbol{\Theta})\boldsymbol{z} - \frac{1}{N}\boldsymbol{P}^{\mathrm{T}}\boldsymbol{y})\right]_j.
\tag{20}
$$

At this minimum, we have

$$
F_M(\boldsymbol{a}, \boldsymbol{z}) \propto -\frac{1}{2\beta}\sum_{j=1}^{N} \hat{a}_j^2.
\tag{21}
$$

Hence the minimum of $\tilde{F}_M(\boldsymbol{a}, \boldsymbol{z})$ is attained by selecting the largest M values of $|\hat{a}_j|$'s, given by

$$
\hat{\boldsymbol{a}} = H_M\left(\boldsymbol{z} - 2\beta((\frac{1}{N}\boldsymbol{P}^{\mathrm{T}}\boldsymbol{P} + \boldsymbol{\Theta})\boldsymbol{z} - \frac{1}{N}\boldsymbol{P}^{\mathrm{T}}\boldsymbol{y})\right),
\tag{22}
$$

where $H_M(\cdot)$ is the hard threshold operation stated in (7).

By setting $\boldsymbol{a}^n = \boldsymbol{z}$, the iterative algorithm for minimizing the noise resistant objective is given by

$$
\boldsymbol{a}^{n+1} = H_M\left(\boldsymbol{a}^n - 2\beta((\frac{1}{N}\boldsymbol{P}^{\mathrm{T}}\boldsymbol{P} + \boldsymbol{\Theta})\boldsymbol{a}^n - \frac{1}{N}\boldsymbol{P}^{\mathrm{T}}\boldsymbol{y})\right).
\tag{23}
$$

We call the algorithm stated in (23) as the **noise resistant IHT**.

3.3 Convergence

Although the proposed noise resistant IHT is based on the IHT concept, our objective function is different from the standard squared error used in the IHT concept. Also, our surrogate objective functions, stated in (16) and (17), are different from the surrogate objective functions used in the standard IHT. Hence we need to investigate the convergence of the proposed noise resistant IHT. Since ℓ_0-norm problems are NP-hard, it is impossible to prove that the proposed noise resistant IHT algorithm globally converges to the global minimum. In this paper, we prove that $\{a^n\}$ converges, and that fixed points of the proposed noise resistant IHT are local minimums of the constrained optimization problem stated in (3). Note that solving the problem stated in (3) is identical to minimize the objective function stated in (14).

First at all, we prove that the algorithm has the following important theorem.

Theorem 1: *If $\beta \leq \frac{1}{2\lambda_{max}}$, the proposed noise resistant IHT algorithm will not increase the noise resistant objective value stated in (14), where λ_{max} is the maximum eigenvalue of $(\frac{1}{N}\boldsymbol{P}^T\boldsymbol{P} + \boldsymbol{\Theta})$.*

Proof: Since $\boldsymbol{\Theta} = \frac{1}{N}\text{diag}(\boldsymbol{P}^T\boldsymbol{P})$, $\frac{1}{N}\boldsymbol{P}^T\boldsymbol{P}^T + \boldsymbol{\Theta}$ is positive definite with a positive maximum eigenvalue λ_{max}. It is not difficult to see that

$$-\frac{1}{N}\|\boldsymbol{Pa} - \boldsymbol{Pz}\|_2^2 - (\boldsymbol{a} - \boldsymbol{z})^T\boldsymbol{\Theta}(\boldsymbol{a} - \boldsymbol{z}) + \frac{1}{2\beta}\|\boldsymbol{a} - \boldsymbol{z}\|_2^2$$
$$= (\boldsymbol{a} - \boldsymbol{z})^T(\frac{1}{2\beta}\boldsymbol{I} - \frac{1}{N}\boldsymbol{P}^T\boldsymbol{P} - \boldsymbol{\Theta})(\boldsymbol{a} - \boldsymbol{z}), \tag{24}$$

where $\boldsymbol{I}$ is an identity matrix. As "$\frac{1}{N}\boldsymbol{P}^T\boldsymbol{P}^T + \boldsymbol{\Theta}$" is positive definite, if $\beta \leq \frac{1}{2\lambda_{max}}$, then

$$(\boldsymbol{a} - \boldsymbol{z})^T(\frac{1}{2\beta}\boldsymbol{I} - \frac{1}{N}\boldsymbol{P}^T\boldsymbol{P} - \boldsymbol{\Theta})(\boldsymbol{a} - \boldsymbol{z}) > 0, \tag{25}$$

for any nonzero $(\boldsymbol{a} - \boldsymbol{z})$. Hence if $\beta \leq \frac{1}{2\lambda_{max}}$, then

$$\tilde{F}(\boldsymbol{a}^{n+1}) < \tilde{F}(\boldsymbol{a}^{n+1}) + (\boldsymbol{a}^{n+1} - \boldsymbol{a}^n)^T(\frac{1}{2\beta}\boldsymbol{I} - \frac{1}{N}\boldsymbol{P}^T\boldsymbol{P} - \boldsymbol{\Theta})(\boldsymbol{a}^{n+1} - \boldsymbol{a}^n)$$
$$= \tilde{F}_M(\boldsymbol{a}^{n+1}, \boldsymbol{a}^n). \tag{26}$$

Since $\boldsymbol{a}^{n+1}$ is a minimization of $\tilde{F}_M(\boldsymbol{a}, \boldsymbol{a}^n)$, we have

$$\tilde{F}_M(\boldsymbol{a}^{n+1}, \boldsymbol{a}^n) \leq \tilde{F}_M(\boldsymbol{a}^n, \boldsymbol{a}^n) = \tilde{F}(\boldsymbol{a}^n). \tag{27}$$

Hence, from (26) and (27), we have $\tilde{F}(\boldsymbol{a}^{n+1}) < \tilde{F}(\boldsymbol{a}^n)$. The proof is completed. ∎

Since $\tilde{F}(\boldsymbol{a})$ is lower bounded, we can say that the sequence $\{a^n\}$ converges some fixed points. We show some additional important properties of the fixed points. The noise resistant IHT stated in (22) can be expressed as

$$a_j^{n+1} = H_M\left(a_j^n - 2\beta(\frac{1}{N}\boldsymbol{p}_j^T\boldsymbol{Pa}^n - \frac{1}{N}\boldsymbol{p}_j^T\boldsymbol{y} + \Theta_{jj}a_j^n)\right), \tag{28}$$

where p_j is the j-th column of P, and Θ_{jj} is the j-th diagonal element of Θ. Note that Θ is a diagonal matrix. Let a^* is a fixed point. Clearly, $a^* = H_M(a^*)$, $\|a^*\|_0 \leq M$, and

$$a_j^* = H_M\left(a_j^* - 2\beta\left(\frac{1}{N}p_j^{\mathrm{T}}(Pa^* - y) + \Theta_{jj}a_j^*\right)\right). \tag{29}$$

We define two index sets $\mathcal{S}_1 = \{j : a_j^* \neq 0\}$ and $\mathcal{S}_0 = \{j : a_j^* = 0\}$. If j belongs to $\mathcal{S}_1$, then (29) holds, if and only if $\left|\frac{1}{N}p_j^{\mathrm{T}}(Pa^* - y) + \Theta_{jj}a_j^*\right| = 0$. If j belongs to $\mathcal{S}_0$, then (29) holds, if and only if $\left|\frac{1}{N}p_j^{\mathrm{T}}(Pa^* - y) + \Theta_{jj}a_j^*\right| \leq l^*/2\beta$, where l^* is the smallest element in $\{|a_j^*| : j \in \mathcal{S}_1\}$, i.e., it is the smallest nonzero absolute value in $\{a_1^*, \cdots, a_N^*\}$. Hence we have an important property of a fixed point given by Property 1.

Property 1: *A necessary and sufficient condition for a point a^* to be a fixed point of the proposed noise resistant IHT is given by*

$$\left|\frac{1}{N}p_j^{\mathrm{T}}(Pa^* - y) + \Theta_{jj}a_j^*\right| \begin{cases} = 0, & \text{if } i \in \mathcal{S}_1 \\ \leq l^*/2\beta, & \text{if } i \in \mathcal{S}_0. \end{cases} \tag{30}$$

Based on Property 1, we obtain two additional properties for fixed points. The first one considers that $\|a^*\|_0 < M$. The second one considers that $\|a^*\|_0 = M$.

Consider that $\|a^*\|_0 < M$. That means there are less than M elements of "$a_j^* - 2\beta(\frac{1}{N}p_j^{\mathrm{T}}(Pa^* - y) + \Theta_{jj}a_j^*)$" with nonzero values. That implies that, for all $j \in \mathcal{S}_0$,

$$a_j^* - 2\beta\left(\frac{1}{N}p_j^{\mathrm{T}}(Pa^* - y) + \Theta_{jj}a_j^*\right) = 0. \tag{31}$$

Hence

$$\frac{1}{N}p_j^{\mathrm{T}}(Pa^* - y) + \Theta_{jj}a_j^* = 0, \ \forall j \in \mathcal{S}_0. \tag{32}$$

Also, for all $j \in \mathcal{S}_1$, from Property 1, we also have

$$\frac{1}{N}p_j^{\mathrm{T}}(Pa^* - y) + \Theta_{jj}a_j^*) = 0, \ \forall j \in \mathcal{S}_1. \tag{33}$$

To sum up, for $\|a^*\|_0 < M$, since Θ is a full rank matrix, we have

$$a^* = \left(\frac{1}{N}P^{\mathrm{T}}P + \Theta\right)^{-1}P^{\mathrm{T}}y. \tag{34}$$

Hence we have the second property, given by Property 2.

Property 2: *Given a fixed point a^* with $\|a^*\|_0 < M$, it is the minimum solution of the noise resistant objective function, given by $\frac{1}{N}\|y - Pa\|_2^2 + a^{\mathrm{T}}\Theta a$ and satisfies the ℓ_0-norm constraint.*

Consider that $\|a^*\|_0 = M$. Let $P_{\mathcal{S}_1}$ be the collection of the columns p_j's with $j \in \mathcal{S}_1$, let $a_{\mathcal{S}_1}$ be the collection of the elements a_j's with $j \in \mathcal{S}_1$, and $\Theta_{\mathcal{S}_1}$

Table 1. Properties of four datasets

Data set	Number of feature	Training set size	Testing set size
ASN	5	1052	451
Auto-mpg	8	274	118
Concrete	8	721	309
Energy efficiency	8	538	230

be the a diagonal matrix whose elements are taken from $\boldsymbol{\Theta}$ with $j \in \mathcal{S}_1$. From Property 1, we have

$$a^*_{\mathcal{S}_1} = (\frac{1}{N}\boldsymbol{P}^{\mathrm{T}}_{\mathcal{S}_1}\boldsymbol{P}_{\mathcal{S}_1} + \boldsymbol{\Theta}_{\mathcal{S}_1})^{-1}\boldsymbol{P}^{T}_{\mathcal{S}_1}\boldsymbol{y}. \tag{35}$$

Clearly, $a^*_{\mathcal{S}_1}$ is the minimum solution of $\frac{1}{N}\|\boldsymbol{y} - \boldsymbol{P}_{\mathcal{S}_1}\boldsymbol{a}_{\mathcal{S}_1}\|^2_2 + \boldsymbol{a}^{T}_{\mathcal{S}_1}\boldsymbol{\Theta}_{\mathcal{S}_1}\boldsymbol{a}_{\mathcal{S}_1}$. Hence, we obtain another property of fixed points, given by Property 3.

Property 3: *Given a fixed point* $\boldsymbol{a}^*$ *with* $\|\boldsymbol{a}^*\|_0 = M$ *and its support equal to* $\mathcal{S}_1$, *for all* $\boldsymbol{a}$ *with the support* $\mathcal{S}_1$, $\tilde{F}(\boldsymbol{a}^*) \leq \tilde{F}(\boldsymbol{a}^*)$.

From Property 2 and Property 3, we can obtain an important theorem about local minimum, given by Theorem 2.

Theorem 2: *A fixed point of the proposed noise resistant IHT algorithm is the local minimum of the original objective function.*

Proof: Note that a fixed point must satisfy the constraint, i.e., $\|\boldsymbol{a}^*\|_0 \leq M$. We need to show that there exists a $\epsilon > 0$, for any perturbation $\boldsymbol{\Delta}$ with $\|\boldsymbol{\Delta}\|_2 < \epsilon$, $\tilde{F}(\boldsymbol{a}^*) \leq \tilde{F}(\boldsymbol{a}^* + \boldsymbol{\Delta})$. The proof considers three cases: $\|\boldsymbol{a}^*\|_0 < M$, $\|\boldsymbol{a}^*\|_0 = M$ with the support of $\boldsymbol{\Delta}$ equal to the support of $\boldsymbol{a}^*$, and $\|\boldsymbol{a}^*\|_0 = M$ with the support of $\boldsymbol{\Delta}$ not equal to the support of $\boldsymbol{a}^*$.

For the first case, $\|\boldsymbol{a}^*\|_0 < M$, from Property 2, $\boldsymbol{a}^*$ is the minimum solution.

For the second case, $\|\boldsymbol{a}^*\|_0 = M$ with the support of $\boldsymbol{\Delta}$ equal to the support of $\boldsymbol{a}^*$, from Property 3, we have $\tilde{F}(\boldsymbol{a}^*) \leq \tilde{F}(\boldsymbol{a}^* + \boldsymbol{\Delta})$.

For the third case, $\|\boldsymbol{a}^*\|_0 = M$ with the support of $\boldsymbol{\Delta}$ not equal to the support of $\boldsymbol{a}^*$. Let Δ_j be a nonzero element not in the support of $\boldsymbol{a}^*$. To maintain the constraint, there should be an element $a^*_{j'}$ of $\boldsymbol{a}^*$ in the support of $\boldsymbol{a}^*$ such that $a^*_{j'} + \Delta_{j'} = 0$. Clearly, we can multiply $\boldsymbol{\Delta}$ with a positive $c_o < 1$, and thus $a^*_{j'} + c_o\Delta_{j'} \neq 0$. Hence, the constraint is not held. That means, the neighborhoods $\boldsymbol{a}^* + c_o\boldsymbol{\Delta}$ of $\boldsymbol{a}^*$ (with their supports not equal to the support of $\boldsymbol{a}^*$) do not satisfy the constraint. Thus, we have $\tilde{F}(\boldsymbol{a}^*) \leq \tilde{F}(\boldsymbol{a}^* + c_o\boldsymbol{\Delta})$. Note that if the constraint is not satisfied, the term $\mathrm{i}(\boldsymbol{a}^* + c_o\boldsymbol{\Delta})$ in $\tilde{F}(\boldsymbol{a}^* + c_o\boldsymbol{\Delta})$ is equal to ∞. The proof is completed. ∎

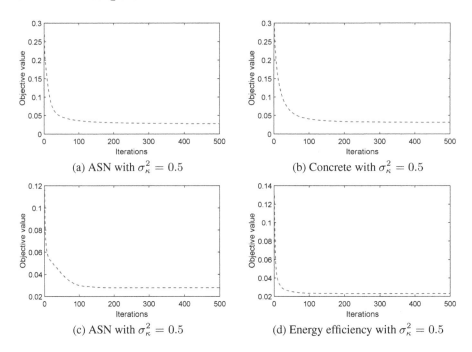

Fig. 1. The convergence of objective value for various datasets. (a) ASN. (b) Concrete.

4   Simulations

This section evaluates the performance of the proposed noise resistant IHT with some real life datasets. The datasets are Airfoil Self-Noise (ASN), Auto-MPG, Concrete and Energy efficiency. They are download from UCI machine learning repository [8]. The properties of the four datasets are shown in Table 1. In each dataset, we randomly select 70% of the data as the training data, and the rest are used for testing. The input data and target outputs are normalized to the range of $[0, 1]$. For each dataset, we try several values of RBF width parameter ξ and select $\xi = 0.1$ as the overall performance are satisfactory. Three noise levels, $\sigma_\kappa^2 = \{0.1, 0.3, 0.5\}$, are considered.

4.1   Experiment 1: Convergence

In this experiment, we discuss the convergence of the proposed algorithm. We use two datasets, ASN and Concrete, to illustrate the convergence of the proposed noise resistant IHT. The fault level is $\sigma_\kappa^2 = 0.5$. As shown in Fig. 1, value of the training objective decrease. We can see that the proposed algorithm converges around 100 to 200 iterations. For the other two datasets, the values of the training objective have similar convergence behavior.

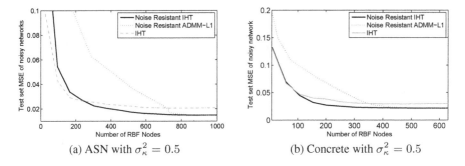

(a) ASN with $\sigma_\kappa^2 = 0.5$ (b) Concrete with $\sigma_\kappa^2 = 0.5$

Fig. 2. Test set MSE versus number of nodes. (a) ASN dataset. (b) Concrete dataset.

4.2 Experiment 2: Comparison with Others Algorithms

This subsection studies the performance of the proposed noise resistant IHT algorithm. Two comparison algorithms are considered.

The first one is the IHT algorithm. It gives us a baseline on the noise resistant ability, when the noise resistant regularization term $a^T \Theta a$ is not considered in the objective function. In the IHT algorithm, we can easily control the number of nodes in the resultant networks because we can set the M value in the constraint.

The second algorithm is the noise resistant ADMM-ℓ_1 [6]. This algorithm is much better other RBF center selection algorithms, including the noise resistant OLS [9], the orthogonal forward regression (OFR) algorithm [10], and the Homotopy (HOM) algorithm [11]. In the noise resistant ADMM-ℓ_1 algorithm, we can control the number of nodes in the resultant network by tuning the regularization parameter of the ℓ_1 term. However, there is not analytical way to determine regularization parameter.

Table 2. Average testing MSE of Noise Resistant IHT, IHT and Noise Resistant ADMM-L1 over 50 trials under different node noise.

Data set	Number of Node	Noise level	Noise Resistant IHT		IHT		Noise Resistant ADMM-L1	
			Average MSE	SD	Average MSE	SD	Average MSE	SD
ASN	400	$\sigma_\kappa^2 = 0.1$	0.0127	0.0008	0.0128	0.0008	0.0243	0.0022
		$\sigma_\kappa^2 = 0.3$	0.0167	0.0012	0.0180	0.0008	0.0381	0.0026
		$\sigma_\kappa^2 = 0.5$	0.0200	0.0015	0.0232	0.0009	0.0465	0.0025
Auto-mpg	150	$\sigma_\kappa^2 = 0.1$	0.0122	0.0018	0.0148	0.0017	0.0182	0.0027
		$\sigma_\kappa^2 = 0.3$	0.0157	0.0017	0.0256	0.0023	0.0270	0.0035
		$\sigma_\kappa^2 = 0.5$	0.0201	0.0023	0.0364	0.0035	0.0332	0.0046
Concrete	300	$\sigma_\kappa^2 = 0.1$	0.0160	0.0018	0.0164	0.0018	0.0178	0.0020
		$\sigma_\kappa^2 = 0.3$	0.0211	0.0021	0.0239	0.0020	0.0297	0.0030
		$\sigma_\kappa^2 = 0.5$	0.0255	0.0025	0.0314	0.0023	0.0417	0.0048
Energy efficiency	300	$\sigma_\kappa^2 = 0.1$	0.0168	0.0031	0.0176	0.0030	0.0270	0.0036
		$\sigma_\kappa^2 = 0.3$	0.0216	0.0037	0.0314	0.0038	0.0463	0.0063
		$\sigma_\kappa^2 = 0.5$	0.0257	0.0039	0.0452	0.0047	0.0544	0.0073

Figure 2 shows the performance of the three algorithms versus the number of RBF nodes used. From the figure, when all the RBF nodes are used, the performance of the IHT is worse than that the noise resistant IHT and the noise resistant ADMM-ℓ_1.

It is because there is no noise resistant term in the objective function of the IHT. For the noise resistant IHT and the noise resistant ADMM-ℓ_1, when all the RBF nodes are used (the node selection process is not active), it is not surprising that they have similar performance.

Now we discuss the situation that we do not use all the nodes. From the figure, for the ASN dataset, when around 400 to 700 RBF nodes are used, the performance of the noise resistant IHT is the best. For the Concrete dataset, when around 150 to 350 RBF nodes are used only, the test set MSE of the noise resistant IHT is the best.

For the ASN dataset, the test set MSE values of the three algorithms decrease, as the number of nodes increases. The MSE value of the IHT does not decrease significantly when the number of nodes is around 200, but the MSE value is a bit high around 0.02652. The MSE value of the noise resistant IHT does not decrease significantly when the number of nodes is around 400, and the MSE value is around 0.02000. For the noise resistant ADMM-ℓ_1, when around 400 nodes are used. Its MSE is very high around 0.0600.

To sum up, with the same number of nodes (not all the nodes are used), the test set MSE values of the proposed noise resistant IHT is lower than those of the noise resistant ADMM-ℓ_1 and the IHT. Hence we can conclude that the proposed noise resistant IHT have a better node selection ability under noisy condition.

To further investigate the performance differences among the three algorithms. We consider three noise levels $\sigma_\kappa^2 = \{0.1, 0.3, 0.5\}$. The simulations are repeated for 10 times of random partitioning of test set and training set. Table 2 summarized the test set MSE results. In the simulations, the number of nodes used is limited to around half of the number of training samples. From the table, the proposed noise resistant IHT outperforms the two comparison algorithms. For example, for the ASN data set with $\sigma_\kappa^2 = 0.5$, Using the IHT and the noise resistant ADMM-ℓ_1, the average MSEs are equal to 0.0232 and 0.0465, respectively. With the proposed noise resistant IHT, we further reduce the MSE to 0.0200.

5   Conclusion

In this paper, we propose a noise resistant training objective for training RBF networks. We then formulate the training problem as a generalized M-sparse problem, in which the objective function is the proposed noise resistant training objective and the constraint is an ℓ_0-norm of the weight vector. The ℓ_0-norm limits the number of RBF nodes to the pre-defined value. Based on the hard thresholding concept, we develop an iterative algorithm to solve the generalized M-sparse problem. In theoretical side, we prove that the proposed noise resistant

IHT converges. Also, any fixed points of the proposed algorithm are the local minimum of the generalized M-sparse problem. From the simulation result, when not all the training input vectors are used as RBF nodes, the performances of the proposed noise resistant IHT are much better than those of comparison algorithms.

Acknowledgments. The work was supported by a research grant from City University of Hong Kong (9610431).

References

1. Chen, S.: Nonlinear time series modelling and prediction using Gaussian RBF networks with enhanced clustering and RLS learning. Electron. Lett. **31**(2), 117–118 (1995)
2. Gomm, J.B., Yu, D.L.: Selecting radial basis function network centers with recursive orthogonal least squares training. IEEE Trans. Neural Netw. **11**(2), 306–314 (2000)
3. Drucker, H., Burges, C.J., Kaufman, L., Smola, A.J., Vapnik, V.: Support vector regression machines. In: Advances in Neural Information Processing Systems, pp. 155–161 (1997)
4. Han, Z., Feng, R.B., Wan, W.Y., Leung, C.S.: Online training and its convergence for faulty networks with multiplicative weight noise. Neurocomputing **155**, 53–61 (2015)
5. Leung, C.S., Wan, W.Y., Feng, R.: A regularizer approach for RBF networks under the concurrent weight failure situation. IEEE Trans. Neural Netw. Learn. Syst. **28**(6), 1360–1372 (2017)
6. Wang, H., Feng, R., Han, Z.F., Leung, C.S.: ADMM-based algorithm for training fault tolerant RBF networks and selecting centers. IEEE Trans. Neural Netw. Learn. Syst. **29**(8), 3870–3878 (2018)
7. Blumensath, T., Davies, M.E.: Iterative thresholding for sparse approximations. J. Fourier Anal. Appl. **14**(5–6), 629–654 (2008)
8. Lichman, M.: UCI machine learning repository (2013). http://archive.ics.uci.edu/ml
9. Leung, C.S., Wan, W.Y., Feng, R.: A regularizer approach for RBF networks under the concurrent weight failure situation. IEEE Trans. Neural Netw. Learn. Syst. **28**(6), 1360–1372 (2017)
10. Hong, X., Chen, S., Gao, J., Harris, C.J.: Nonlinear identification using orthogonal forward regression with nested optimal regularization. IEEE Trans. Cybern. **45**(12), 2925–2936 (2015)
11. Malioutov, D.M., Cetin, M., Willsky, A.S.: Homotopy continuation for sparse signal representation. In: 2005 Proceedings of IEEE International Conference on Acoustics, Speech, and Signal Processing (ICASSP 2005), vol. 5, pp. v/733–v/736 (2005)

Learning with Incomplete Labels for Multi-label Image Annotation Using CNN and Restricted Boltzmann Machines

Jonathan Mojoo$^{(\boxtimes)}$, Yu Zhao, Muthusubash Kavitha, Junichi Miyao, and Takio Kurita

Department of Information Engineering,
Hiroshima University, Higashi-hiroshima, Hiroshima 739-8521, Japan
jonathanmojoo@yahoo.com

Abstract. Multi-label image annotation based on convolutional neural networks (CNN) has seen significant improvements in recent years. One problem, however, is that it is difficult to prepare complete labels for the training images and usually training data has missing or incomplete labels. Restricted Boltzmann Machines (RBM) can explore the co-occurrence distribution of the labels and estimate the missing labels efficiently. Hence we intend to propose a novel learning model for multi-label image annotation with missing labels based on CNNs, which aims to regenerate the missing labels for an image by learning the generative model of labels using an RBM. Firstly, label sets are reconstructed by the pre-trained RBM model which is trained on data with some missing labels. Then the reconstructed label sets are used as a teacher signal to train the CNN. The effectiveness of the proposed approach is confirmed by comparing the performance with baseline CNNs using various performance evaluation metrics on two different data sets. Experimental results prove that our RBM-CNN formulation exceeds the performance of the baseline CNN.

Keywords: Multi-label image annotation · Restricted Boltzmann Machines · Convolutional neural network

1 Introduction

With the recent exponential growth of the web, handling and retrieving large quantities of images and videos requires efficient automatic image annotation or tagging. Image annotation involves specifying the most relevant labels for any given image, that demonstrate its visual content. During the past decade, automated annotation with multi-label learning has been widely researched [14, 18]. Most of the conventional frameworks assume that all instances in the training set have complete labels. However, this is not the case with a lot of real-life image

This work was partly supported by JSPS KAKENHI Grant Number 16K00239.

T. Gedeon et al. (Eds.): ICONIP 2019, LNCS 11954, pp. 286–298, 2019.
https://doi.org/10.1007/978-3-030-36711-4_25

sets, which may be only partially annotated due to intrinsic uncertainty among the training instances and the human factor. As a result, training with these incomplete labels may not accurately predict the relationship between input instances and their true label vectors. Thus building an efficient generative model for missing labels is important and also considered as one of the most challenging tasks in image annotation. Several approaches in recent research have proved that significant improvements can be achieved by CNN utilizing missing labels restricted with label similarity information [20,21]. However, these methods use complex label relationships in the CNN training process. Alternatively, some researchers have proposed incorporating additional co-occurrence distribution of label information in CNN to compensate for missing or incorrect labels and improve the prediction performance [12,23]. Some approaches attempt to model co-occurrence dependency information based on graphical representation [19] and pairwise probabilities [2] but these usually need to include large numbers of parameters, which does not scale well for large label sets.

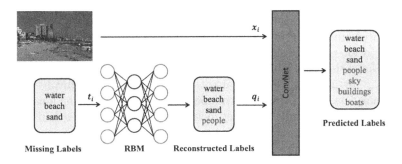

Fig. 1. The architecture of the proposed CNN+RBM model for multi-label annotation. Before input into the CNN, the missing labels are firstly reconstructed by the pretrained Restricted Boltzmann Machines.

In this study, we propose a novel idea for multi-label learning with incomplete labels by combining a Restricted Boltzmann Machine (RBM) with a CNN. RBMs are primarily used to learn generative models [15], although they can be adapted to learn supervised discriminative models [9]. We use the RBM to generate additional labels (assumed to be missing) for images used to train a CNN for multi-label image annotation. Our reasoning is that by supplementing each training example with labels based on co-occurrence relationships learned from the entire set, we can improve the model's capability to generalize to unseen data. Our work is similar in essence to the approach presented in [16], where RBMs are used for collaborative filtering for movie recommendation. In our case, each hidden unit learns to model dependency between different labels. The learned weights between visible and hidden layers hold co-occurrence information. The illustration of our proposed method is shown in Fig. 1. The proposed approach requires relatively less hyper-parameter tuning to build co-occurrence relationships between the input label vectors. In this study, we demonstrate that an RBM and CNN combination can more accurately predict the relationship of input instances with different label missing-rates using various performance evaluation metrics. We compare the proposed method with the baseline multi-label CNN approach on two real world data sets.

2   Related Works

In this section, we review several multi-label image annotation algorithms. Then we look at a few proposed solutions for the problem of missing labels and label co-dependence in training data.

2.1   Multi-label Image Annotation

Typical classification problems consist of samples which belong to only one of several defined categories. Some researchers even opt to exclude samples with multiple labels or select one label that best matches the image. However, most real-world images necessarily belong to multiple categories. Most approaches to multi-label annotation begin by transforming the problem from one of multi-label annotation to one of single-label classification [1,17]. Binary relevance (BR) [22] is perhaps the most popular transformation of this kind and is considered the baseline for multi-label image annotation. This approach involves learning several binary classifiers, one for each label in the label space. The idea of binary relevance has been extended to deep neural networks, where each node in the output layer predicts a score for a single label [3,7,13].

2.2   Missing Labels and Label Co-occurrence Dependency

While binary relevance is preferred among the various problem transformation techniques, it has been argued that it may lack the ability to model label co-occurrence, which is crucial to multi-label image annotation. Various techniques have been proposed to incorporate label co-occurrence information in training algorithms. Utilizing label inter-dependency information found in ground truth data can also solve the problem of inaccurate or missing labels. J. Wang et al. [19] proposed a framework that combines a CNN and an RNN, where the CNN acts as a feature extractor, and the RNN models image-label relationships and label dependency. Label dependency is incorporated by representing a multi-label annotation as an ordered path of label predictions. Another approach is presented in [3], which consists of a deep neural network-based Canonical-Correlated Autoencoder that can exploit label inter-dependency during both label embedding and prediction processes. The authors also claim that it can easily be extended to the case of missing labels. The approach presented in [11] also uses an RBM, with the main difference being that while they use a 'conditional RBM' network to both predict labels and fine tune those predicted labels, we train our RBM to reconstruct the training labels that are used to train a separate multi-label prediction CNN.

Fig. 2. Restricted Boltzmann Machine

3   Proposed Method

3.1   Train Restricted Boltzmann Machine with Missing Labels

We use training samples with missing labels to train the RBM model. A Restricted Boltzmann machine (RBM) is a 2-layer neural network which contains visible units $v \in \{0,1\}^N$ and hidden units $h \in \{0,1\}^H$ where N and H are the numbers of visible and hidden units, respectively (Fig. 2). It is an energy-based model and can be used to encode the dependencies between the visible units. In the learning process, we minimize the energy function of a certain state (v, h), defined as

$$E(v, h) = -b^T v - c^T h - v^T W h \qquad (1)$$

$$= -\sum_{i=1} b_i v_i - \sum_{j=1} c_j h_j - \sum_{i,j} v_i h_j w_{ij} \qquad (2)$$

with the parameter $\theta = \{W, b, c\}$. W denotes the weights between the 2 layers, and b and c represent visible and hidden unit biases, respectively. If there are no connections between hidden units, then the probability distribution of v is given as

$$p(v) = \frac{1}{Z} \sum_h p(v, h) = \frac{1}{Z} \sum_h e^{-E(v,h)} \qquad (3)$$

where Z is the normalization factor by the summation of over all possible pairs of visible and hidden vectors.

$$Z = \sum_{v,h} e^{-E(v,h)} \qquad (4)$$

Because both visible and hidden units can only have state of 0 or 1, then the conditional probability of a visible and hidden unit value being set to 1 is defined as

$$p(h_i = 1 | v) = \sigma(\sum_{j=1}^{M} w_{ij} v_j + c_i) \qquad (5)$$

$$p(v_j = 1 | h) = \sigma(\sum_{i=1}^{N} w_{ij} h_i + b_j) \qquad (6)$$

where σ denotes the logistic sigmoid function. The log-likelihood for a single training example v is given as

$$\ln \mathcal{L}(\boldsymbol{\theta}|\boldsymbol{v}) = \ln p(\boldsymbol{v}|\boldsymbol{\theta}) = \ln \frac{1}{Z} \sum_h e^{-E(\boldsymbol{v},\boldsymbol{h})} \tag{7}$$

According to [6] the process of calculating the gradient function $\boldsymbol{\theta}$ is

$$\frac{\partial \ln \mathcal{L}(\boldsymbol{\theta}|\boldsymbol{v})}{\partial w_{ij}} = p(h_i = 1|\boldsymbol{v})v_j - \sum_v p(\boldsymbol{v})p(h_i = 1|\boldsymbol{v})v_j \tag{8}$$

$$\frac{\partial \ln \mathcal{L}(\boldsymbol{\theta}|\boldsymbol{v})}{\partial b_j} = v_j - \sum_v p(\boldsymbol{v})v_j \tag{9}$$

$$\frac{\partial \ln \mathcal{L}(\boldsymbol{\theta}|\boldsymbol{v})}{\partial c_i} = p(h_i = 1|\boldsymbol{v}) - \sum_v p(\boldsymbol{v})p(h_i = 1|\boldsymbol{v}) \tag{10}$$

Computing the second term of Eqs. 8, 9 and 10, one can approximate the expectation by samples obtained by Gibbs sampling. In the learning process, Gibbs chain runs for only k steps [8], which is called k-step contrastive divergence learning (CD-k).

3.2   Reconstruction of Labels by Pre-trained RBM Model

Let $D = \{(\boldsymbol{x}_i, \boldsymbol{t}_i)\}_{i=1}^M = \{X, T\}$ denote a set of training samples. Here $\boldsymbol{x}_i$ is the i-th sample used as input to the neural network and $\boldsymbol{t}_i = \left[t_i^{(1)} \cdots t_i^{(N)}\right]^T$ are the training labels (supposedly containing missing labels) which denotes the binary vector representation of the i-th sample. $t_i^{(j)} = 1$ when the j-th label is annotated to the i-th image, otherwise $t_i^{(j)} = 0$. M and N are the numbers of samples and labels respectively. According to the RBM, the number of hidden units H is less than the number of visible units N ($H < N$).

   Suppose $\mathcal{R}(\boldsymbol{x})$ is the reconstruction function of the pre-trained RBM model for training label set T. The reconstructed label set $\boldsymbol{q}$ of the original label set $\boldsymbol{t}$ can be obtained using the equation $\boldsymbol{q} = \mathcal{R}(\boldsymbol{t}) = \left[q^{(1)} \cdots q^{(N)}\right]^T$. The label reconstruction algorithm used in this study is presented in Algorithm 1.

3.3   Training the CNN Using RBM Reconstructed Labels

Let $D_{new} = \{(\boldsymbol{x}_i, \boldsymbol{q}_i)\}_{i=1}^M = \{X, Q\}$ denote the newly reconstructed training samples. We use T to train the CNN. AlexNet [10] is used as the CNN architecture, which has 5 convolution layers and 2 fully connected layers. Because both the true and predicted values are given by the state $\{0, 1\}$, we use sigmoid cross

Algorithm 1. Label reconstruction algorithm $\mathcal{R}$

1: Given missing label set $t = \left[t^{(1)} \cdots t^{(N)}\right]^T$
   ▷ Prop up
2: **for** $i = 0, \ldots, H$ **do**
3:     $h_i \leftarrow \sigma(\sum_{j=1}^{N} w_{ij} t^{(j)} + c_i)$
   ▷ Prop down
4: **for** $j = 0, \ldots, N$ **do**
5:     $v_j \leftarrow \sigma(\sum_{i=1}^{H} w_{ij} h_i + b_j)$
   ▷ Get binomial samples of the visible units based on their activation v
6: **for** $j = 0, \ldots, N$ **do**
7:     $q^{(j)} \leftarrow binomial(v_j)$
   ▷ Keep all the elements in t which are equal to 1
8: **for** $j = 0, \ldots, N$ **do**
9:     **if** $t^{(j)} = 1$ **then**
10:        $q^{(j)} \leftarrow t^{(j)}$

entropy to evaluate dissimilarity between them. The loss function used to train the CNN is

$$H(y, \hat{y}) = -y \log \hat{y} - (1 - y) \log (1 - \hat{y}) \tag{11}$$

where y and $\hat{y}$ denotes true and predicted values, respectively. The original objective function of the CNN is

$$J = \sum_{i=1}^{M} \sum_{j=1}^{N} H({t_j}^{(i)}, {\hat{y}_j}^{(i)}) \tag{12}$$

We used the newly reconstructed N_{new} as a teacher signal and thus the objective function becomes

$$J' = \sum_{i=1}^{M} \sum_{j=1}^{N} H({q_j}^{(i)}, {\hat{y}_j}^{(i)}) \tag{13}$$

Let $\mathcal{S}(x)$ be the function learned by the CNN for the input image x. Then the estimated labels $\hat{y}$ can be obtained by feeding image x from the test data set to the trained CNN model as

$$\hat{y} = \mathcal{S}(x). \tag{14}$$

The value of the each element in the estimated vector $\hat{y}$ can be considered as the probability of the corresponding label.

4   Experiments

4.1   Datasets and Settings

We use Corel5K [5] and NUS-WIDE-LITE [4] data sets to evaluate our proposed method. The Corel5K data set contains 4500 training and 499 testing samples with 260 labels. The average number of labels assigned to each sample is 3.4. The NUS-WIDE-LITE data set contains 27807 training and 27808 testing samples with 81 labels. The average number of labels assigned to each sample is 1.6. We randomly remove 30 % of the labels from each sample to simulate missing labels and they are used to train the RBM and baseline CNN model. In the RBM structure, the number of visible units is set to the number of labels in the data set. The images are normalized and re-scaled to the same size before inputting them into the CNN. The number of training epochs is 500. The CNN is trained with the reconstructed teacher signal based on the objective given by Eq. 13.

4.2   PCA of Hidden Units in the Trained RBM

To explain the distribution of co-occurrence information, we used two-dimensional principal component analysis (PCA) on the hidden units of the trained RBM. As shown in Fig. 3, we input all one-hot label vectors of the data set into the trained RBM and plotted the PCA results of its hidden units. Figure 4 shows all the 81 labels in NUS-WIDE-LITE data set, we can observe that the distance between the labels with similar co-occurrence relations are closer than the labels with disparate co-occurrence relations.

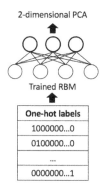

Fig. 3. PCA of hidden units with one-hot labels

4.3   Pre-processing of RBM Training Data

There are some labels that do not appear in any training samples before reconstruction by the RBM, which means they have no co-occurrence relation with other labels in all the training samples. At the same time, there are some samples which only have one label, that is, the label in that sample is independent. Therefore, we removed labels that do not appear in any samples (indicated by the column 'Pre-process 1' in Table 1) and samples that have a single label (indicated by 'Pre-process 2'). We also tried a combination of the two pre-processing steps (indicated by the column 'Combined').

To evaluate the label reconstruction capability of the RBM, we select 100 images from the dataset and manually assign additional appropriate labels to these images. These manually completed labels are used as the ground-truth labels. Figure 5 shows a sample image, with the labels given in the dataset and the manually assigned labels.

Table 1. Micro-F1 Score Labels (%) with 100 ground-truth test samples (RBM training epoch = 2000).

Label missing-rate	Before Pre-process	Pre-process 1	Pre-process 2	Combined
0% Missing	75.42	–	**76.40**	–
10% Missing	76.10	–	**76.50**	–
30% Missing	75.79	**77.61**	75.36	77.14
50% Missing	73.78	73.59	73.83	**74.30**

Table 1 shows the result of training data reconstruction by RBM. We compare the labels reconstructed by a trained RBM with the ground-truth labels we manually assigned using the micro-f1 score, at different label missing-rates (0%, 10%, 30% and 50%). The second column represents the results without label-data pre-processing, and columns 3 to 5 are the results with label-data pre-processing, as described at the beginning of this section. The best result for each

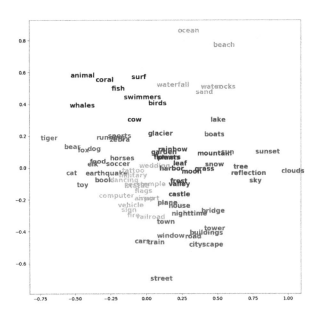

Fig. 4. PCA of hidden units(50) with 81 labels of NUS-WIDE-LITE data set. The labels with similar co-occurrence have short distance.

label missing-rate is marked with bold font. From this table, we observe that the RBM is able to reliably recover missing labels, up to 30% label missing-rate. We also observe that the RBM learns better with data that has been pre-processed by removing labels with no instances, removing examples with single labels, or both.

4.4   Reconstructed and Predicted Labels of the Training Data

Figure 6 presents some example images from the Corel5K training data set and their original labels, indicated as 'Incomplete'. The labels reconstructed by the RBM and the labels predicted by the CNN are indicated as 'Reconstructed' and 'Predicted' respectively under each image. The correct additional labels are highlighted in red whereas the incorrect labels are highlighted in blue. We observe that the trained RBM model manages to adds some reasonable labels based on the original label in most cases. We also note that while the RBM introduces some false negatives, the number of relevant labels it adds to the training samples is larger, leading to an overall improvement of both train and test data prediction.

4.5   Prediction Results on the Test Data

On the test data sets, we compare the prediction performance of our proposed CNN + RBM model with the baseline CNN model which is trained by the objective function in Eq. 12. We measured the performance using three evaluation metrics: precision (P), recall (R) and F1 score. In addition, to select the most suitable labels we use 2 kinds of label selection thresholds: labels whose predicted probability are over 0.1 and the top 3 ranked labels. Tables 2 and 3 show the performance of the proposed approach with various numbers of RBM hidden units over the baseline CNN using Corel5K and NUS-WIDE-LITE data set, respectively. We note that the results obtained by our proposed method outperform the baseline CNN on both datasets. Our approach performs notably better when using the Top-3 thresholding technique, which we interpret to mean

Fig. 5. Example of manually completed image labels. Dataset-provided labels: water, beach, people. Manually supplied labels: sea, water, beach, coast, people, sky, clouds, tree, horizon

Incomplete: sun,clouds,boats   **Incomplete**: cars,tracks,turn
Reconstructed: sun,clouds,boats,   **Reconstructed**: cars,tracks,turn,
        ships,balcony   prototype
Predicted: sun,clouds,boats,sky,   **Predicted**: cars,tracks,turn,wall,
        water,land,sunset,tree   prototype,formula,grass

Fig. 6. Training data annotation sample results on Corel5K data set. (Color figure online)

Original:statue,museum,art   **Original**:stone,temple,sculpture,pillar
Predicted:statue,stone,buildings,   **Predicted**:stone,temple,sculpture,pillar,
        sculpture,window   buildings,castle,statue,window

Fig. 7. Test data annotation sample results on Corel5K data set. Original labels and predicted labels by CNN+RBM model. Additional inappropriate labels are highlighted in blue. (Color figure online)

our approach has a higher accuracy in the top labels assigned to images. We also note that optimal performance is achieved when the number of hidden units is set to 50. We deduce that setting this parameter too high causes the RBM to over-fit, thereby encoding label dependencies that do not generally hold for unseen data. Figure 7 shows some example images from the Corel5K test set. The additional labels predicted by our proposed (CNN+RBM) model are shown in red font.

Furthermore, to confirm the learning ability with incomplete labels, we remove some labels and observe the performance at different label removal rates (10%, 30%, 50%, 70%) and compare the results in terms of precision, recall and F1-score against the baseline CNN. The results are shown in Fig. 8. Performance for both methods understandably deteriorates at very high label missing-rates but we note that our proposed method performs better than the baseline CNN across different rates of missing labels.

Table 2. Multi-label annotation results on Corel5K (260 labels) with different number of hidden units. Better results are marked with bold font. P, R, Micro-F1 represent precision, recall and F1 score respectively.

Algorithms	Probability ≥ 0.1(%)			Top-3(%)		
	P	R	F1	P	R	F1
Baseline CNN	**14.52**	22.80	16.96	15.98	18.39	16.94
CNN+RBM(hidden = 50)	14.10	**24.84**	**17.37**	**17.38**	**20.08**	**18.43**
CNN+RBM(hidden = 100)	14.13	23.97	17.12	16.48	19.07	17.52
CNN+RBM(hidden = 200)	14.15	24.13	17.14	16.73	19.34	17.75

Table 3. Multi-label annotation results on NUS-WIDE-LITE (81 labels) with different numbers of hidden units. The best results are marked with bold font. P, R, and F1 represent precision, recall and Micro-F1 score respectively.

Algorithms	Probability ≥ 0.1(%)			Top-3(%)		
	P	R	F1	P	R	F1
Baseline CNN	6.93	8.15	6.37	6.85	9.70	7.40
CNN+RBM(hidden = 30)	8.02	12.59	8.49	8.56	12.17	9.34
CNN+RBM(hidden = 50)	**8.46**	**14.40**	**9.24**	**8.64**	**12.20**	**9.37**

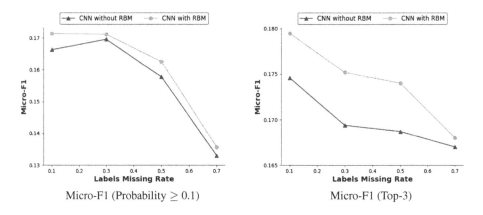

Micro-F1 (Probability ≥ 0.1)   Micro-F1 (Top-3)

Fig. 8. Comparisons of our predicted results in terms of precision, recall and Micro-F1 score with the baseline CNN on Corel5K data set using different label missing-rates. Each column presents the results based on the three label selection criteria.

5   Conclusion

We proposed a multi-label learning framework consisting of a CNN combined with a Restricted Boltzmann Machine as a label reconstruction algorithm for multi-label annotation with incomplete labels. The CNN trained with labels reconstructed by an RBM achieved satisfactorily better performance in recovering missing labels compared to the one trained with original ground truth labels. The potential ability of the RBM in estimating missing labels by learning co-occurrence relations is demonstrated in our experiments using different label selection criteria and label missing-rates. The F1-score value of the CNN+RBM model shows that it outperforms the baseline CNN, thus confirming the effectiveness of the proposed approach in learning with incomplete labels for the image annotation task. For future work, we would like to evaluate our method on more data sets and compare performance with our previously proposed methods which adopted Hayashi's quantification [12] and Word2Vec [23] methods for missing labels estimation.

Acknowledgments. This work was partly supported by JSPS KAKENHI Grant Number 16K00239.

References

1. Boutell, M.R., Luo, J., Shen, X., Brown, C.M.: Learning multi-label scene classification. Pattern Recogn. **37**(9), 1757–1771 (2004)
2. Chen, X., Mu, Y., Yan, S., Chua, T.S.: Efficient large-scale image annotation by probabilistic collaborative multi-label propagation. In: Proceedings of the 18th ACM International Conference on Multimedia, pp. 35–44 (2010)
3. Yeh, C.K., Wu, W.C., Ko, W.-J., Wang, Y.C.F.: Learning deep latent space for multi-label classification. In: AAAI, pp. 2838–2844 (2017)
4. Chua, T.S., Tang, J., Hong, R., Li, H., Luo, Z., Zheng, Y.T.: NUS-WIDE: a real-world web image database from National University of Singapore. In: Proceedings of ACM Conference on Image and Video Retrieval, CIVR 2009, 8–10 July 2009
5. Duygulu, P., Barnard, K., de Freitas, J.F.G., Forsyth, D.A.: Object recognition as machine translation: learning a lexicon for a fixed image vocabulary. In: Heyden, A., Sparr, G., Nielsen, M., Johansen, P. (eds.) ECCV 2002. LNCS, vol. 2353, pp. 97–112. Springer, Heidelberg (2002). https://doi.org/10.1007/3-540-47979-1_7
6. Fischer, A., Igel, C.: An introduction to restricted Boltzmann machines. In: Alvarez, L., Mejail, M., Gomez, L., Jacobo, J. (eds.) CIARP 2012. LNCS, vol. 7441, pp. 14–36. Springer, Heidelberg (2012). https://doi.org/10.1007/978-3-642-33275-3_2
7. Gong, Y., Jia, Y., Leung, T., Toshev, A., Ioffe, S.: Deep convolutional ranking for multilabel image annotation. arXiv preprint arXiv:1312.4894 (2013)
8. Hinton, G.: Training products of experts by minimizing contrastive divergence. Neural Comput. **14**(8), 1771–1800 (2002)
9. Hugo, L., Michael, M., Razvan, P., Yoshua, B.: Learning algorithms for the classification restricted Boltzmann machine. J. Mach. Learn. Res. **13**(1), 643–669 (2012)
10. Krizhevsky, A., Sutskever, I., Hinton, G.E.: ImageNet classification with deep convolutional neural networks. In: Pereira, F., Burges, C.J.C., Bottou, L., Weinberger, K.Q. (eds.) Advances in Neural Information Processing Systems 25, pp. 1097–1105 (2012)
11. Li, X., Zhao, F., Guo, Y.: Conditional restricted Boltzmann machines for multi-label learning with incomplete labels. In: AISTATS, pp. 635–643 (2015)

12. Mojoo, J., Kurosawa, K., Kurita, T.: Deep CNN with graph Laplacian regularization for multi-label image annotation. In: ICIAR, pp. 19–26 (2017)
13. Nam, J., Kim, J., Loza Mencía, E., Gurevych, I., Fürnkranz, J.: Large-scale multi-label text classification — revisiting neural networks. In: Calders, T., Esposito, F., Hüllermeier, E., Meo, R. (eds.) ECML PKDD 2014. LNCS (LNAI), vol. 8725, pp. 437–452. Springer, Heidelberg (2014). https://doi.org/10.1007/978-3-662-44851-9_28
14. Qi, G.J., Hua, X.S., Rui, Y., Tang, J., Mei, T., Zhang, H.J.: Correlative multi-label video annotation. In: Proceedings of the 15th International Conference on Multimedia, pp. 17–26 (2007)
15. Salakhutdinov, R., Hinton, G.: Deep Boltzmann machines. In: van Dyk, D., Welling, M. (eds.) Proceedings of the Twelth International Conference on Artificial Intelligence and Statistics. Proceedings of Machine Learning Research, vol. 5, pp. 448–455. PMLR, Hilton Clearwater Beach Resort, Clearwater Beach, 16–18 April 2009. http://proceedings.mlr.press/v5/salakhutdinov09a.html
16. Salakhutdinov, R., Mnih, A., Hinton, G.: Restricted Boltzmann machines for collaborative filtering. In: Proceedings of the 24th International Conference on Machine Learning, ICML 2007, pp. 791–798. ACM (2007)
17. Tsoumakas, G., Katakis, I., Vlahavas, I.: Mining multi-label data. In: Maimon, O., Rokach, L. (eds.) Datamining and Knowledge Discovery Handbook, pp. 667–685. Springer, Boston (2009). https://doi.org/10.1007/978-0-387-09823-4_34
18. Wang, C., Yan, S., Zhang, L., Zhang, H.J.: Multi-label sparse coding for automatic image annotation. In: The IEEE Conference on Computer Vision and Pattern Recognition (CVPR), pp. 1643–1650 (2009)
19. Wang, J., Yang, Y., Mao, J., Huang, Z., Huang, C., Xu, W.: CNN-RNN: a unified framework for multi-label image classification. In: The IEEE Conference on Computer Vision and Pattern Recognition (CVPR), pp. 2285–2294 (2016)
20. Wu, B., Liu, Z., Wang, S., Hu, B.G., Ji, Q.: Multi-label learning with missing labels. In: The 22nd International Conference on Pattern Recognition (ICPR), pp. 2279–2289 (2014)
21. Wu, B., Lyu, S., Ghanem, B.: ML-MG: multi-label learning with missing labels using a mixed graph. In: The IEEE International Conference on Computer Vision (ICCV), pp. 4157–4165 (2015)
22. Zhang, M.L., Li, Y.K., Liu, X.Y., Geng, X.: Binary relevance for multi-label learning: an overview. Front. Comput. Sci. 12, 1–12 (2018)
23. Zhao, Y., Miyao, J., Kurita, T.: Multi-label image annotation via CNN with graph Laplacian regularization based on Word2Vec. In: IW-FCV (2018)

Learning-Based Confidence Estimation
for Multi-modal Classifier Fusion

Uzair Nadeem[1(✉)] , Mohammed Bennamoun[1] , Ferdous Sohel[2] ,
and Roberto Togneri[1]

[1] The University of Western Australia, Perth, Australia
uzair.nadeem@research.uwa.edu.au
{mohammed.bennamoun,roberto.togneri}@uwa.edu.au
[2] Murdoch University, Perth, Australia
f.sohel@murdoch.edu.au

Abstract. We propose a novel confidence estimation method for predictions from a multi-class classifier. Unlike existing methods, we learn a confidence-estimator on the basis of a held-out set from the training data. The predicted confidence values by the proposed system are used to improve the accuracy of multi-modal emotion and sentiment classification. The scores of different classes from the individual modalities are superposed on the basis of confidence values. Experimental results demonstrate that the accuracy of the proposed confidence based fusion method is significantly superior to that of the classifier trained on any modality separately, and achieves superior performance compared to other fusion methods.

Keywords: Confidence estimation · Multi-modal fusion · Emotion classification · Sentiment analysis

1 Introduction

For the real life deployment of any machine learning classifier, it is not only important that the classifier should have a high accuracy, but it should also be able to predict correct classes with high confidence. Methods to determine the confidence of classification can improve the reliability of the classification systems. For binary classification, the maximum of the probability of the sample to belong to the positive or the negative class is usually taken as the confidence of classification. For multi-class classification the probability of the predicted class is generally considered as the classification confidence. While this concept may give an idea of the confidence, it is not sufficient for any useful purpose, as it ignores the relationships between the scores of the remaining classes.

To overcome this shortcoming, many methods have been proposed in the literature to evaluate the confidence of classification, ranging from simple heuristic formulae to complex and elaborate mechanisms [1,2]. We propose a novel learning based method to determine the confidence of the results predicted by a

© Springer Nature Switzerland AG 2019
T. Gedeon et al. (Eds.): ICONIP 2019, LNCS 11954, pp. 299–312, 2019.
https://doi.org/10.1007/978-3-030-36711-4_26

classifier. The proposed method can be used with any type of classifier We use the confidence values from our approach to improve the classification accuracy for the tasks with more than one source of data.

The progress of modern computing has allowed the use of data from multiple sources to make an improved decision for any task. Data from one source can complement the shortcomings of the data from another source. This usually results in an improvement in the decision making process. The use of multi-source data, also known as multi-modal data, has improved the classification accuracy in many practical tasks, e.g., biometrics [3–5], emotion analysis [6,7] and sentiment analysis [7–10].

A major challenge to use multi-modal data is to find the best approach to combine the data from different modalities [11]. A multi-modal system has usually two major components: an individual classifier for each modality and a mechanism to combine the results of all modalities for an improved overall accuracy. This paper proposes a novel method for the combination of multiple modalities, which can be used as an add-on to any combination of classifiers, and produces competitive or superior overall accuracies, compared to other methods of fusion.

The information from different modalities can be combined at an early, late or intermediate stage (see Sect. 2). In practical scenarios, the data from some modality may get corrupted or become unreliable. A decision using early or intermediate stage fusion, will not be able to produce reliable results in such a scenario, as it strictly requires the data from all the modalities [11]. We propose a novel late fusion method for the combination of information from different sources based on the confidence values predicted by our method. We first train the independent classifiers for each modality. The trained classifiers are used to estimate the classification scores on the samples in a development set, which was initially held out from the training set. The scores on the development set are then used to train a class balanced confidence-estimator for each modality. The confidence-estimator predicts the confidence value for the classifications by the original classifiers. At the test time, we combine the results from the classifiers of different modalities, weighted by the confidence values from the confidence-estimators, to improve the combined classification accuracy (see Sect. 3). Figures 1 and 2 show the training and testing pipelines, respectively, of the proposed multi-modal classification system.

The proposed method is unique in the way that the value of confidence is independent of the main classifier. In this way the combination of different modalities using the predicted confidences does not lead to over-fitting, which is a major challenge for early and intermediate stage fusion methods. Moreover if the data of any modality is corrupted, it can simply be excluded from the decision making process and we can still get reliable results, as shown by bi-modal results in Sects. 4.2 and 4.3. There are many different methods to determine the quality of data for each modality [12]. However, it is out of the scope of this paper. The main contributions of this paper are: (i) a novel learning based method to determine the confidence of classification from any multi-class classifier, and (ii) a novel method for confidence based fusion of classifiers, which are trained on the data of different modalities, to improve the final classification accuracy. The proposed method can also be used as an add-on to already trained classifiers, and is able to produce reliable results even if the data from any modality is missing.

2 Related Work

The methods for fusing information from different sources or modalities can be divided into three major types: early fusion, late fusion and intermediate fusion. In **early fusion** the data from different sources is assembled together before training any machine learning algorithm. One simple yet effective approach is to concatenate the features of different modalities and then learn on the concatenated features as used in [13,14].

Late fusion methods train the algorithms on individual modalities and then use different techniques to combine the separate decisions, depending on whether the task at hand is classification or regression. One of the common methods of decision fusion is to use majority voting for classification, or to use mean of predictions for regression [4,15]. Another approach is to use a weighted combination of the individual decisions. Some works use heuristic formulae [2] or metrics for the quality of data [12] and use them to weigh the individual modalities and then combine them for a final decision.

Intermediate fusion techniques perform some initial processing or learning on the features of individual modalities and then use the features from the initial classifiers in a second stage classifier for a final decision. Most techniques in this category are deep learning based. The features from the penultimate layers of the networks, trained for individual modalities, are used to train a final network [16]. The features may be combined in several different ways, e.g., concatenation or cross-product [17].

Early fusion techniques work on the combination of data from different modalities and can identify the relationships between the features of the different modalities. However, they fail to fully use the patterns in the features of each individual modality. Thus, intermediate fusion methods claim that they can take advantage of both intra and inter-modalities' patterns. One of the prominent intermediate fusion methods for emotion and sentiment classification is contextual-LSTM [8,9] by Poria et al. They first extract uni-modal features from the utterances (an uninterrupted sentence or dialogue by an individual) without considering the context of the utterances. Then they use an attention based network to fuse the extracted features of all the different modalities. This is followed by an attention based contextual LSTM network to get the final classification of emotions or sentiments. We used this work as a baseline to compare the results of our proposed confidence based fusion method, as it is one of the state-of-the art approaches for the fusion of modalities and its results and codes

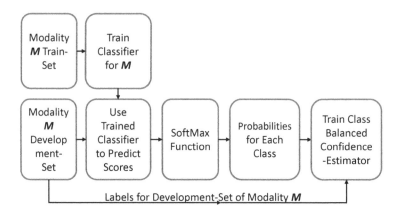

Fig. 1. A block diagram of the confidence estimation and the training pipeline of a modality in the proposed method. The same procedure is followed for each modality in a multi-modal system.

are publicly available[1]. Moreover, unlike many multi-modal fusion works [16,17], its results are available for multiple multi-class datasets.

Late fusion methods are simpler, compared to the intermediate fusion methods [11]. Moreover, one of the serious drawbacks of early and intermediate fusion methods is that, they require data from all the modalities, as they train classifiers on the fusion of features of different modalities [11]. Therefore, in such practical scenarios, when there are high chances of data corruption or data quality is of concern, they fail to produce good results [18]. Late fusion methods have the advantage that they can easily exclude any individual modality from the decision making process, if the data of that modality is corrupted, unreliable or not of good quality. In contrast to heuristic approaches that are used by other late fusion methods [2], the proposed method uses learning-based confidence estimation for the fusion of the decisions from the individual modalities. This helps our technique to take improved decisions for any nature of data and type of classifiers. For the case of corrupted data of any modality, we can set the confidence value to zero for that specific modality (see Sect. 3). As early and intermediate fusion methods work on the combination of features of different modalities, they usually have much higher features to samples ratio, compared to late fusion methods. This usually results in over-fitting of classifiers. Although it may be possible to avoid over-fitting by optimizing parameters on a validation-set, it often leads to sub-optimal results in the absence of a large amount of data. As the proposed technique estimates confidence values are independently of the classifier or the train-set, it is inherently robust to over-fitting resulting from fusion, and thus any number of modalities can be combined.

---

[1] https://github.com/soujanyaporia/multimodal-sentiment-analysis.

3   Learned Confidence Estimation for Multi-modal Fusion

We propose a novel method to estimate the confidence of a multi-class classification task. Our technique can work as a simple add-on step to any existing classifier. The confidence values can be used to increase the accuracy of the overall system in a multi-modal scenario.

3.1   Training

Suppose, we have N number of training samples, each with data from M number of modalities for a classification task with C number of classes. According to standard machine learning practice, the N training samples are randomly divided into a train-set, $T = [x^1, x^2, x^3, ..., x^K]$, and a development-set, $D = [x^1, x^2, x^3, ..., x^P]$, where x^i is a sample in the training set and K and P are the number of samples kept in the train-set and the development-set, respectively, such that $K + P = N$. Then, we train independent classifiers for each modality, $1, 2, 3, ..., M$ using the train-set T. Since our proposed technique is mainly concerned with the confidence estimation and the fusion of the modalities, the nature or the type of the classifiers is not important for our method. We use deep learning based classifiers in our experiments (Sect. 4). Let $\zeta_m()$ be the trained classifier for the modality m, where $m = 1, 2, 3, ..., M$. We use the trained classifiers $\zeta_m()$ to estimate the scores for each class for the samples in the development-set D.

$$\varphi_m^i = [s_m^{i,1}, s_m^{i,2}, s_m^{i,3}, ..., s_m^{i,C}] = \zeta_m(x_m^i),$$
$$where \quad i = 1, 2, 3, ..., P \quad and \quad m = 1, 2, 3, ..., M. \tag{1}$$

where $s_m^{i,c}$ is the score obtained for the class c by applying the classifier $\zeta_m()$ on the ith sample x_m^i and φ_m^i is a row vector containing the scores of all the classes for the sample x^i and the modality m.

We then create a dataset to train a modality specific confidence-estimator for the predictions from the classifier $\zeta_m()$. For this purpose, we first use the SoftMax function to convert the scores obtained with the development-set D into probabilities, i.e., the scores should be in the range $[0–1]$ and the sum of scores should be equal to 1 for each sample x_m^i.

$$\vartheta_m^i = \frac{exp(\varphi_m^i)}{\sum_1^C (exp(\varphi_m^i))} = \frac{[exp(s_m^{i,1}), ..., exp(s_m^{i,C})]}{\sum_1^C (exp(\varphi_m^i))},$$
$$\forall \quad i = 1, 2, 3, ..., P \quad and \quad m = 1, 2, 3, ..., M. \tag{2}$$

Next, for each modality, we concatenate the probability vectors ϑ_m^i horizontally to create a matrix of dimensions $P \times C$. Each row of the matrix is treated as a sample for the training of the confidence-estimator. We pose the training of the confidence-estimator as a binary classification problem. All the probability vectors ϑ_m^i which have the highest value for the correct class are given a positive label (1), and the remaining vectors are given a negative label (0). This dataset is then used to train an ensemble of boosted trees for each modality [19,20]. We use boosted trees because, empirically, we found that they give a reliable performance along with efficiency and robustness. However, one of the major challenges in the generated dataset is class imbalance. An easy classification task will have a bias towards the positive samples, while a difficult classification task will be biased towards the negative samples. To overcome this difficulty we grow trees in such a way that they always contain the same number of positive and negative samples i.e., we randomly under-sample the majority class such that it becomes equal to the minority class for each tree in the ensemble [21]. We use Gini's Diversity Index as a measure of node impurity for the splitting of nodes in a tree, defined as:

$$1 - \sum_c \alpha^2(c) \tag{3}$$

where the sum is over the classes c at a node, and $\alpha(c)$ is the observed fraction of classes with class c which reach the node. E.g., a node that contains samples from more than one class will have a positive value for the Gini index and the value of the Gini index will be zero for a node with samples of only one class. We use AdaBoost algorithm [19,20] for the boosting of trees. A block diagram of the training pipeline of the proposed technique is shown in Fig. 1.

3.2   Testing

To determine the unknown class χ^q of a multi-modal query sample q at test time, we first use the modality specific classifiers to predict the scores for each class:

$$\varphi_m^q = [s_m^{q,1}, s_m^{q,2}, s_m^{q,3}, ..., s_m^{q,C}] = \zeta_m(q_m), \quad where \quad m = 1,2,3,...,M. \tag{4}$$

Next, similar to the steps taken during training, we convert the scores in the vector φ_m^q to probabilities using the SoftMax function:

$$\vartheta_m^q = \frac{exp(\varphi_m^q)}{\sum_1^C (exp(\varphi_m^q))} = \frac{[exp(s_m^{q,1}), ..., exp(s_m^{q,C})]}{\sum_1^C (exp(\varphi_m^q))}, \tag{5}$$
$$where \quad m = 1,2,3,...,M.$$

Then, we use the trained class balanced confidence-estimators to determine the level of confidence γ_m^q for the scores predicted by the original classifier $\zeta_m()$. For this purpose, instead of taking the confidence output as a binary decision, we consider it as a continuous variable in the range $[0{-}1]$. We propose to define the confidence value γ_m^q for a modality m and a query sample q as:

$$\gamma_m^q = \frac{\sum_1^T \rho_m^+}{\sum_1^T \rho_m^+ + \sum_1^T \rho_m^-}, \quad where \quad m = 1,2,3,...,M. \tag{6}$$

where ρ_m^+ is the probability for correct classification and ρ_m^- is the probability for wrong classification, as predicted by the individual trees of the ensemble and the summation is over all the trees of the ensemble. Next, we superpose the probability vectors ϑ_m^q for all the modalities $1, 2, 3, ..., M$, scaled by their respective confidence scores γ_m^q:

$$\omega^q = \sum_{m=1}^{M} \gamma_m^q \times \vartheta_m^q \tag{7}$$

Finally, the class with the maximum value of the superposed scores w^q is declared as the predicted class of the query sample.

$$\chi^q = argmax(\omega^q) \tag{8}$$

where χ^q is the required predicted class of the query sample q. Figure 2 shows a block diagram of the testing pipeline of the proposed multi-modal classification system.

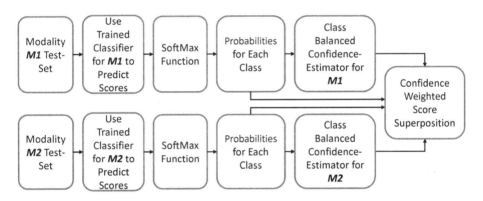

Fig. 2. A block diagram of the testing pipeline of the proposed multi-modal classification method. The method can be extended to any number of modalities (See Sect. 3)

4   Experiments and Analysis

To demonstrate the performance of our technique for the estimation of the confidence of any multi-class classification and its effectiveness for accuracy improvement in multi-modal scenarios, we carried out detailed experiments on a number of publicly available datasets, with more than two classes, for sentiment and emotion analysis. We compared our multi-modal results with other methods and fusion techniques which use the same classifiers as the basic units. For emotion classification we used IEMOCAP [6] and MELD [7] datasets, while for sentiment analysis we used MOSEI [10] and MELD [7] datasets.

   We set the leaning rate for AdaBoost algorithm [19, 20] to 0.1 in all our experiments. To optimize the number and size of trees in the confidence-estimators, we used five-fold cross validation to grid-search the number of trees in the set [5, 10, 20, 30, 60, 90, 120, 150, 300, 600, 900, 1200] and the maximum number of splits in the range 1–30. However, from our experiments on all the datasets, we concluded that we can set the number of trees to 30 and the maximum number of node splits in a tree to 20, with only a slight loss in accuracy.

We used Multi-class classification accuracy (Acc), weighted F1-scores (F1) and Multimodal-Improvement (M-Imp) for the comparison of techniques. Multi-class classification accuracy (Acc) is defined as the number of utterances that are correctly predicted in the test set divided by the total number of utterances in the test set. We also calculated the weighted F1-scores (F1) for all techniques, where F1-score is defined as the harmonic mean of precision and recall. Moreover, as the main purpose of the proposed method is the fusion of modalities for the improvement in accuracies, we also report the Multimodal-Improvement (M-Imp). It is defined as the difference in the percentage accuracy of the modality with the highest accuracy from that achieved by the fusion of modalities for any given technique. For example, if a method takes a decision on the combination of audio and visual modalities, then the accuracy of that system minus the maximum accuracy that can be achieved with either the audio data or the visual data, using the same system, is called Multimodal-Improvement.

We compared our technique with Contextual-LSTM [8,9] (Intermediate fusion) and Feature Concatenation based early fusion (Feat-Cat). For both these methods we used the codes provided by the authors[2]. For comparison with late fusion methods, we substituted the fusion method in our technique with Majority Voting and Mean Scores. In Majority Voting, the class predicted by the majority of modalities is taken as the final predicted class. For Mean Scores, we take the class-wise average of the probability vectors ϑ_m^q for all the modalities and the class with the highest value is declared as the unknown class χ^q. To show the advantage of our predicted confidence value, compared to the scores predicted by a classifier, we also report the results for Weighted Mean Scores. For Weighted Mean Scores, we used the highest probability from the uni-modal classifier to weigh the probabilities from that classifier, and then took class-wise mean over all the probabilities. The class with the highest resulting score was declared as the unknown class χ^q.

4.1 MELD Dataset

The Multi-modal Emotion Lines Dataset (MELD) [7] is one of the largest publicly available datasets for emotion and sentiment analysis. One of the main purposes of the MELD dataset is to explore the role of context in conversation for emotion and sentiment analysis. MELD contains data from the three modalities: text, audio and video. It contains approximately 13000 utterances from 1433 dialogues of a famous TV show. For emotion classification it has seven classes,

---

[2] https://github.com/soujanyaporia/multimodal-sentiment-analysis.
https://github.com/SenticNet/MELD.

Anger, Disgust, Fear, Joy, Neutral, Sadness and Surprise, while for sentiment analysis it has three classes: Positive, Negative and Neutral.

We used this dataset for both emotion and sentiment classification, and used the standard training, development and test splits as defined by the authors of the dataset [7]. As only the results for the fusion of two modalities, audio and text, have been reported in [7], we also carried out our experiments for the same two modalities. For a fair comparison of the fusion capability of the proposed technique compared to other methods, we used the features provided by the authors of [7]. Specifically, we used the GloVe vectors representation [22] for the textual features. For the audio features, the OpenSmile toolkit [23] was used to extract features. The L2-based feature selection was then applied with sparse estimators to reduce the dimensionality of the audio features.

For the audio classifier we used two stacked bi-directional LSTMs [24], each with 300 neurons and a drop-out rate of 40%. This was followed by a fully connected layer with seven neurons for emotion classification and three neurons for sentiment classification and a SoftMax layer. For text based classification a CNN-LSTM model was used. The model comprised of three parallel convolutional layers with different filter sizes. This was followed with MaxPooling for each layer. The feature-maps from each layer were then concatenated. Then, a fully connected layer was used with 100 neurons before passing the features to two stacked bi-directional LSTMs, each with 300 neurons and a drop-out rate of 30%. Finally, a fully connected layer and a SoftMax layer were used for classification. We set the batch size to 10 and used the Adam [25] optimizer to train the network on the train-set. We monitored the accuracy on the development-set and stopped the training when the accuracy ceased to improve. Table 1 shows the results of our method, compared to other methods. The proposed fusion method achieved a superior performance on all the three metrics, compared to the other methods. It should be noted that for emotion classification, only the proposed fusion technique was able to improve the accuracy, compared to the individual modalities (M-Imp). This may be due to a large difference of 11.5% between the uni-modal accuracies achieved by the textual and audio modalities. This combined with a large number of classes made it harder to achieve any improvement

Table 1. Multi-class classification accuracy (Acc), weighted F1-scores (F1) and Multimodal-Improvement (M-Imp) of our technique compared to other methods on MELD dataset. Modalities: A = Audio, T = Text.

Dataset →	MELD-Sentiments 3 classes			MELD-Emotions 7 classes		
Method↓/Metric→	Acc (%)	F1	M-Imp (%)	Acc (%)	F1	M-Imp (%)
Majority Voting (A+T)	60.46	0.5695	−5.86	53.10	0.4267	−7.40
Mean Scores (A+T)	66.36	0.6585	+0.04	60.31	0.5674	−0.19
Weighted Mean Scores (A+T)	66.28	0.6578	−0.04	60.08	0.5661	−0.42
Feature-Cat (A+T)	64.47	0.6392	−1.85	59.23	0.5871	−1.27
Contextual-LSTM [8,9] (A+T)	66.74	0.6668	+0.42	60.34	0.5931	−0.16
Ours (A+T)	**67.31**	**0.6720**	**+0.99**	**61.15**	**0.5947**	**+0.65**

Table 2. Multi-class classification accuracy (Acc), weighted F1-scores (F1) and Multimodal-Improvement (M-Imp) of our technique compared to other methods on MOSEI dataset. Modalities: A = Audio, T = Text, V = Visual.

Dataset →	MOSEI-Sentiments 3 classes		
Method ↓/Metric→	Acc (%)	F1	M-Imp (%)
Majority Voting (A+T+V)	59.40	0.5273	+0.19
Mean Scores (A+T+V)	59.34	0.5250	+0.13
Weighted Mean Scores (A+T+V)	59.17	0.5206	−0.04
Feature-Cat (A+T+V)	58.77	0.5698	+1.15
Contextual-LSTM [8,9] (A+T+V)	59.44	0.5845	+1.82
Ours (A+T)	60.03	0.5320	+0.82
Ours (A+V)	58.74	0.5143	+1.82
Ours (T+V)	60.61	0.5495	+1.40
Ours (A+T+V)	**62.47**	**0.5853**	**+3.26**

in accuracy over the individual modalities. Reduction in multi-modal accuracy, compared to the accuracies of individual modalities, for various techniques and emotions was also observed by the authors of MELD dataset [7].

4.2   MOSEI

The CMU Multi-modal Opinion Sentiment and Emotion Intensity (MOSEI) [10] is the largest dataset for sentiment. It contains 23,453 annotated video segments of more than 65 h (combined) for 1,000 different speakers and provides annotated data for the visual, text and audio modalities.

Similar to [9], we used the dataset for a three class (positive, negative and neutral) sentiment classification task. We randomly divided the data into train, development and test sets such that they approximately contain 70%, 10% and 20% of the data, and there is no overlap of speakers between any two sets. We used the features provided by the authors of [8,9][3]. The OpenSmile [23] toolkit was used to extract audio features. For visual features, a 3D-CNN was used. For textual features, utterances were first converted to matrices by concatenating the Google Word2Vec features [26] of each word in the utterance. Then a CNN was used to extract features from the matrices for each utterance. Each video was padded or trimmed to a length of 98 utterances.

For each modality, a bi-directional Gated Recurrent Unit (GRU) [27] of size 100 was followed by two fully connected layers of sizes 100 and three, respectively. Finally, a SoftMax layer was used for classification with Adam [25] optimizer. We used a batch size of 20. We trained the network on train-set and monitored the performance on the development-set. We stopped the training when the accuracy ceased to improve on the development-set. Table 2 shows the results of

---

[3] https://github.com/soujanyaporia/multimodal-sentiment-analysis.

Table 3. Multi-class classification accuracy (Acc), weighted F1-scores (F1) and Multimodal-Improvement (M-Imp) of our technique compared to other methods on IEMOCAP dataset. Modalities: A = Audio, T = Text, V = Visual.

Dataset →	IEMOCAP-Emotions 6 classes			IEMOCAP-Emotions 4 classes		
Method ↓/Metric→	Acc (%)	F1	M-Imp (%)	Acc (%)	F1	M-Imp (%)
Majority Voting (A+T+V)	61.34	0.6143	−2.44	74.03	0.7423	−2.27
Mean Scores (A+T+V)	67.68	0.6805	+3.90	80.19	0.8023	+3.89
Weighted Mean Scores (A+T+V)	66.95	0.6752	+3.17	79.55	0.7972	+3.25
Feature-Cat (A+T+V)	63.46	0.6321	+2.68	76.40	0.7659	+0.37
Contextual-LSTM [8,9] (A+T+V)	63.96	0.6386	+3.18	77.15	0.7764	+1.12
Ours (A+T)	66.63	0.6771	+2.85	80.52	0.8066	+4.22
Ours (A+V)	54.04	0.5637	+1.36	68.83	0.6989	+3.57
Ours (T+V)	67.21	0.6701	+3.43	76.62	0.7644	+0.32
Ours (A+T+V)	**68.73**	**0.6959**	**+4.95**	**84.42**	**0.8434**	**+8.12**

sentiment classification of the proposed technique, compared to the individual modalities and [9]. We also report the results of the possible bi-modal fusion of the different modalities for our technique, which shows the performance of our technique for the case when the data of any modality is missing. The proposed technique achieved the highest performance on all the metrics.

4.3 IEMOCAP

The Interactive Emotional Dyadic Motion Capture (IEMOCAP) dataset is the most popular dataset for multi-modal emotion analysis. This dataset consists of dyadic conversation between pairs of speakers from a pool of ten speakers and comprises approximately twelve hours of data. It contains the data for audio, visual and text modalities as well as the motion capture data.

Different works have used very different protocols for experiments on this dataset, including a different number and combinations of classes, and different ratios of train-test splits. We conducted our experiments using two of the popular protocols. Specifically, we used the dataset for 6-class and 4-class emotion classification. For 4-Class classification, we used the data with the labels: anger, happiness, neutral and sadness. For 6-class classification, in addition to the previously mentioned four classes, we also used the data for excitement and frustration classes. We randomly selected approximately 20% of the data for the test-set, 70% of the data for the train-set, and 10% of the data for the development-set, with no overlap of speakers between the training and the test sets.

We used the same features for IEMOCAP dataset as used by the authors of [8,9][4]. For textual features, Google Word2Vec [26] was used to convert each word in an utterance to a feature vector and then the words' vectors were concatenated to form a matrix. A CNN was used on these matrices and the resulting features were used for the textual modality. Audio features were extracted with the help

---

[4] https://github.com/soujanyaporia/multimodal-sentiment-analysis.

of the OpenSmile [23] toolkit while a 3D-CNN was used for visual features. Each video was padded or trimmed to a length of 110 utterances.

For uni-modal classification on all the modalities, we used a bi-directional Gated Recurrent Unit (GRU) [27] with size 100, followed by two fully connected layers of sizes 100 and the number of outputs (four or six), respectively. At the output, we used a SoftMax layer for classification and the Adam [25] optimizer. We trained the network with a batch size of 20 on the train-set for as long as the accuracy kept improving on the development-set. Table 3 shows the results of the proposed technique as compared to other methods. Our technique, using all the three modalities, achieved the highest performance for both 4-class and 6-class classification.

5   Conclusion

We have proposed a novel learning-based confidence-estimation method for multi-class classification. A confidence-estimator ensemble was trained to predict the confidence values from the scores of a classifier. The predicted confidence values can effectively be used to increase the accuracy in a multi-modal scenario. Extensive experiments demonstrated that the proposed method not only achieved superior accuracy for multi-modal classification, compared to other methods, but also achieved higher improvement over the accuracy of the individual modalities.

Acknowledgments. We greatly acknowledge NVIDIA for providing a Tesla K40c GPU for the experiments involved in this research. This work was supported by the SIRF scholarship from the University of Western Australia (UWA) and by Australian Research Council under Grant DP150100294.

References

1. Devarakota, P.R., Mirbach, B., Ottersten, B.: Confidence estimation in classification decision: a method for detecting unseen patterns. In: Advances in Pattern Recognition, pp. 290–294. World Scientific (2007)
2. Alam, M.R., Bennamoun, M., Togneri, R., Sohel, F.: A confidence-based late fusion framework for audio-visual biometric identification. Pattern Recogn. Lett. **52**, 65–71 (2015)
3. El-Sayed, A.: Multi-biometric systems: a state of the art survey and research directions. Int. J. Adv. Comput. Sci. Appl. **6**, 128–138 (2015)
4. Nadeem, U., Shah, S.A.A., Bennamoun, M., Togneri, R., Sohel, F.: Real time surveillance for low resolution and limited-data scenarios: an image set classification approach. arXiv preprint arXiv:1803.09470 (2018)
5. Nadeem, U., Shah, S.A.A., Bennamoun, M., Sohel, F., Togneri, R.: Efficient image set classification using linear regression based image reconstruction. In: Proceedings of the IEEE Conference on Computer Vision and Pattern Recognition Workshops, pp. 99–108 (2017)
6. Busso, C., et al.: IEMOCAP: interactive emotional dyadic motion capture database. Lang. Resour. Eval. **42**(4), 335 (2008)

7. Poria, S., Hazarika, D., Majumder, N., Naik, G., Cambria, E., Mihalcea, R.: MELD: a multimodal multi-party dataset for emotion recognition in conversations. In: Proceedings of the 57th Annual Meeting of the Association for Computational Linguistics (2019)
8. Poria, S., Cambria, E., Hazarika, D., Majumder, N., Zadeh, A., Morency, L.-P.: Context-dependent sentiment analysis in user-generated videos. In: Proceedings of the 55th Annual Meeting of the Association for Computational Linguistics (Volume 1), pp. 873–883 (2017)
9. Poria, S., Cambria, E., Hazarika, D., Majumder, N., Zadeh, A., Morency, L.-P.: Multi-level multiple attentions for contextual multimodal sentiment analysis. In: IEEE International Conference on Data Mining, pp. 1033–1038 (2017)
10. Zadeh, A.B., Liang, P.P., Poria, S., Cambria, E., Morency, L.-P.: Multimodal language analysis in the wild: CMU-MOSEI dataset and interpretable dynamic fusion graph. In: Proceedings of the 56th Annual Meeting of the Association for Computational Linguistics (Volume 1: Long Papers), pp. 2236–2246 (2018)
11. Baltrušaitis, T., Ahuja, C., Morency, L.-P.: Multimodal machine learning: a survey and taxonomy. IEEE Trans. Pattern Anal. Mach. Intell. **41**(2), 423–443 (2018)
12. Poh, N., Kittler, J.: A unified framework for biometric expert fusion incorporating quality measures. IEEE Trans. Pattern Anal. Mach. Intell. **34**(1), 3–18 (2011)
13. Poria, S., Chaturvedi, I., Cambria, E., Hussain, A.: Convolutional MKL based multimodal emotion recognition and sentiment analysis. In: IEEE 16th International Conference on Data Mining, pp. 439–448. IEEE (2016)
14. Wang, H., Meghawat, A., Morency, L.-P., Xing, E.P.: Select-additive learning: improving generalization in multimodal sentiment analysis. In: IEEE International Conference on Multimedia and Expo, pp. 949–954. IEEE (2017)
15. Wörtwein, T., Scherer, S.: What really matters–an information gain analysis of questions and reactions in automated PTSD screenings. In: Seventh International Conference on Affective Computing and Intelligent Interaction, pp. 15–20. IEEE (2017)
16. Nojavanasghari, B., Gopinath, D., Koushik, J., Baltrušaitis, T., Morency, L.-P.: Deep multimodal fusion for persuasiveness prediction. In: Proceedings of the 18th ACM International Conference on Multimodal Interaction, pp. 284–288. ACM (2016)
17. Zadeh, A., Chen, M., Poria, S., Cambria, E., Morency, L.-P.: Tensor fusion network for multimodal sentiment analysis. In: Proceedings of the Conference on Empirical Methods in Natural Language Processing, pp. 1103–1114 (2017)
18. Wagner, J., Andre, E., Lingenfelser, F., Kim, J.: Exploring fusion methods for multimodal emotion recognition with missing data. IEEE Trans. Affect. Comput. **2**(4), 206–218 (2011)
19. Schapire, R.E., Freund, Y., Bartlett, P., Lee, W.S., et al.: Boosting the margin: a new explanation for the effectiveness of voting methods. Ann. Stat. **26**(5), 1651–1686 (1998)
20. Friedman, J.H.: Greedy function approximation: a gradient boosting machine. Ann. Stat. **29**, 1189–1232 (2001)
21. Seiffert, C., Khoshgoftaar, T.M., Van Hulse, J., Napolitano, A.: RUSBoost: a hybrid approach to alleviating class imbalance. IEEE Trans. Syst. Man Cybern.-Part A: Syst. Hum. **40**(1), 185–197 (2009)
22. Pennington, J., Socher, R., Manning, C.: Glove: global vectors for word representation. In: Proceedings of the Conference on Empirical Methods in Natural Language Processing, pp. 1532–1543 (2014)

23. Eyben, F., Wöllmer, M., Schuller, B.: OpenSMILE : the Munich versatile and fast open-source audio feature extractor. In: Proceedings of the 18th ACM International Conference on Multimedia, pp. 1459–1462. ACM (2010)
24. White, L., Togneri, R., Liu, W., Bennamoun, M.: Neural Representations of Natural Language, vol. 783. Springer, Singapore (2018). https://doi.org/10.1007/978-981-13-0062-2
25. Kingma, D.P., Ba, J.: Adam: a method for stochastic optimization. arXiv preprint arXiv:1412.6980 (2014)
26. Mikolov, T., Chen, K., Corrado, G., Dean, J.: Efficient estimation of word representations in vector space. arXiv preprint arXiv:1301.3781 (2013)
27. Cho, K., et al.: Learning phrase representations using RNN encoder-decoder for statistical machine translation. arXiv preprint arXiv:1406.1078 (2014)

Model Compression and Optimisation

Siamese Network for Classification with Optimization of AUC

Hideki Oki$^{(\boxtimes)}$, Junichi Miyao$^{(\boxtimes)}$, and Takio Kurita$^{(\boxtimes)}$

Department of Information Engineering, Hiroshima University,
1-4-1 Kagamiyama, Higashi-Hiroshima 739-8527, Japan
{m181021,miyao,tkurita}@hiroshima-u.ac.jp

Abstract. It is known that RankSVM can optimize area under the ROC curve (AUC) for binary classification by maximizing the margin between the positive class and the negative class. Since the objective function of Siamese Network for rank learning is the same as RankSVM, Siamese Network can also optimize AUC for binary classification. This paper proposes a method for binary classification by combining Siamese Network for rank learning with logistic regression. The effectiveness is investigated by comparing the AUC scores of the proposed method with the standard Convolutional Neural Network. Then the proposed method is extended to multi-class classification problem by using Siamese Network and multi-nominal logistic regression. We extend the proposed binary classifier to multi-class classification by using one-vs-others approach.

Keywords: Siamese Network · Rank learning · AUC score · Logistic regression · Multinomial logistic regression

1 Introduction

The original form of Support Vector Machine (SVM) was first invented by Vapnik et al. [1] in 1963. Also, the current standard from of soft-margin SVM was proposed by Cortes et al. [2] in 1995. It is known that the standard SVM is formulated as convex optimization problem and has unique global optima. Also, we can easily extend the linear SVM to the nonlinear SVM by introducing kernel learning. The SVM is defined to solve the binary classification problem but the idea of SVM can be extended to other tasks. For example, RankSVM was proposed by Herbrich et al. [3] for learning to rank. RankSVM maximizes the margin between samples that are highly relevant to the query and those that are less relevant to the query whereas the standard SVM maximizes the margin between classification boundaries and training samples. RankSVM is the pairwise learning model and is currently used most frequently as a baseline in the field of rank learning such as information retrieval. O. Chapelle et al. [4] show that RankSVM can optimize AUC score for binary classification. This is realized by optimizing the parameters of RankSVM as maximizing the margin between positive class and negative class. However, it is difficult to estimate the class from

© Springer Nature Switzerland AG 2019
T. Gedeon et al. (Eds.): ICONIP 2019, LNCS 11954, pp. 315–327, 2019.
https://doi.org/10.1007/978-3-030-36711-4_27

the output value only by maximizing the margin of the positive class and the negative class. Therefore, O. Chapelle et al. manually adjust the output value at the learning stage so that the output value for the positive class is larger than the output value for the negative class.

Meanwhile, a deep neural network model such as deep Convolutional Neural Network (CNN) has been widely used in the field of pattern recognition since deep CNN proposed by Krizhevsky et al. [5] won the ILSVRC 2012 with higher recognition accuracy than the conventional methods. To enable pairwise learning by deep neural networks, models such as Siamese Neural Network [6–8] have been developed and used for rank learning. This model contributes to solving the problems of information retrieval or person identification. Siamese Neural Network maximizes the distance between the sample that is highly relevant to the query and the sample that is less relevant to the query. Also, Siamese Neural Network minimizes the distance between samples that are highly relevant to the query or between those that are less relevant to the query. This objective function of Siamese Network is the same function as RankSVM. This means that Siamese Network can also optimize AUC for binary classification.

To the best of our knowledge, we can not find the research in which Siamese Network is used for optimizing AUC for the classification tasks. In this paper we experimentally confirm whether AUC can be optimized by Siamese Network for rank learning.

In experiment, we train the standard CNN model with a sigmoid cross-entropy loss for the binary classification task for image. Then we train the model which was trained by using Siamese Network for rank learning. We then compare the AUC scores from both models for verification.

In RankSVM, the output value was adjusted manually so that the class can be estimated from the output value. Instead of manually adjusting the output value of Siamese Network, we decided to divide the learning into two stages. The first stage, maximizes margin of positive class and negative class by optimizing loss of Siamese Network. In the second stage, we make it possible to estimate the class from the output by learning logistic regression model using the feature vector obtained from this Siamese Network to express posterior probability. By doing this, we think that the value for estimating the class more natural can be obtained from Siamese Network.

Then, the model using Siamese Network for binary classification is extended to multi-class classification for images by using Siamese Network and multinomial logistic regression. We extend by using one-vs-others approach. The AUC of the proposed model is also compared with the standard deep CNN model for multi-class classification.

The paper is organized as follows. In Sect. 2, related works such as Deep CNN, Siamese Networks, and Rank SVM are explained. Then the proposed methods both for binary classification and multi class classification are described in Sect. 3. Experimental results are shown in Sect. 4. Section 5 is for conclusion and future works.

2   Related Works

2.1   Deep Convolutional Neural Network

The deep CNN has been proven to be effective and has been applied many applications such as for image classification [5,9], object detection [10], image segmentation [11] and so on.

The computation within the convolution layers is regarded as a filtering process of the input image as

$$f_{p,q}^{(c)} = h\left(\sum_{r=0}^{convy-1} \sum_{s=0}^{convx-1} w_{r,s}^{(c)} f_{p+r,q+s}^{(c-1)} + b^{(c)} \right) , \tag{1}$$

where $w_{r,s}^{(c)}$ is the weight of the neuron indexed as (r, s) in the c-th convolution layer and $b^{(c)}$ is the bias of the c-th convolution layer. The size of the convolution filter is given as $convx \times convy$. The activation function of each neuron is denoted as h. Usually, pooling layers are added after the convolution layers. The pooling layer performs downsampling for reducing computational costs and enhancing against micro position changes. Fully-connected layers like multi layer perceptron is connected to the convolution layers which is used to construct the classifier.

2.2   Siamese Neural Network

The Siamese Neural Network [6–8] consists of two identical networks joined at their outputs as shown in Fig. 1. The two networks extract feature vectors from two different samples. Usually, the weights of the two networks are shared, the objective function of the optimization for training the parameters of the networks is defined by using these extracted feature vectors. The parameters of the Siamese Network are trained to distinguish between similar and dissimilar pairs of the training samples. This network architecture is usually used for metric learning, and a contrastive loss over the metric defined on the trained representation is used as the objective function for the optimization. The objective function is defined as

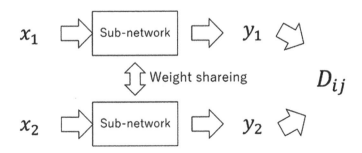

Fig. 1. Siamese Network

$$E = \frac{1}{2N} \sum_i^N \sum_j^N l_{ij}(D_{ij})^2 + (1 - l_{ij})max(m - D_{ij},\ 0)^2 \qquad (2)$$

$$D_{ij} = ||\boldsymbol{y}_i - \boldsymbol{y}_j||_2^2 \qquad (3)$$

where m is a parameter indicating the distance between clusters and D_{ij} represents the distance between the pair of the outputs $\boldsymbol{y}_i$ and $\boldsymbol{y}_j$ of each network for the sample pair $\boldsymbol{x}_i$ and $\boldsymbol{x}_j$. N is the number of sample pairs. A label l is assigned for each sample pair such that label is $l_{ij} = 1$ when the pair i and j is similar and label is $l_{ij} = 0$ when the pair i and j is dissimilar. After the training of Siamese Network, the outputs for dissimilar pair will be dissimilar while the outputs for similar pair become similar.

2.3   Rank SVM

The RankSVM is a ranking model minimizing margin-based pairwise loss [3]. RankSVM was trained to minimize the loss function defined by

$$\frac{1}{2}||\boldsymbol{w}||^2 + \lambda \sum_{i \in P, j \in N} max(0, 1 - \boldsymbol{w}^T(\boldsymbol{x}_i - \boldsymbol{x}_j))^2 \qquad (4)$$

where P is a set of positive training samples, and N is a set of negative training samples. λ is a parameter of $\lambda > 0$, $\boldsymbol{w}$ is a weight. And $(\boldsymbol{x}_i, \boldsymbol{x}_j)$ is a pair of training samples given a positive label and a negative label. As can be seen from equation (4), among the pairs of the positive vector and the negative vector, the loss becomes large when the pair is incorrectly ranked.

Chapelle et al. [4] proposed a fast optimization method for RankSVM based on the primal Newton method. Also, O. Chapelle et al. showed that RankSVM can be used for binary classification and can improve area under the ROC curve (AUC) defined as

$$AUC = \frac{|\{(i,j)|t_i = 1, t_j = 0, f(\boldsymbol{x}_i) > f(\boldsymbol{x}_j)\}|}{|\{i|t_i = 1\}| \times |\{j|t_j = 0\}|} \qquad (5)$$

where $t_i \in \{1, 0\}$ is a label assigned to i-th training sample and $|S|$ denotes the number samples in the set S. $f(\boldsymbol{x}_i)$, $f(\boldsymbol{x}_j)$ are outputs of RankSVM for samples $\boldsymbol{x}_i$, $\boldsymbol{x}_j$. The denominator is the product of the number of positive samples and the number of negative samples and the numerator is the number of pairs that positive and negative samples could be classified correctly. In order to optimize the loss defined by the equation (4), the ranking of $\boldsymbol{x}_i$ and $\boldsymbol{x}_j$ must be correct. That means that the AUC score should be high. This has been introduced as a special case of RankSVM.

3   Proposed Methods

Chappell et al. [4] show that RankSVM can be used to construct a binary classifier for optimizing the AUC. Binary classification is realized by using RankSVM and by maximizing the margin of positive sample and negative sample. Since the Siamese Network for rank learning uses the same loss function with RankSVM, the Siamese Network also can be used to construct a binary classifier for optimizing the AUC. In this paper, we propose to use the Siamese Network for rank learning for constructing a binary classifier. Then the proposed method is extended to multi-class classification problem.

3.1   Binary Classification

In order to perform binary classification, consider the Siamese Network which classify the positive class and the negative class as shown in Fig. 2. The output of each network y is assumed to be scalar, namely the dimension of the output is 1. Similar with the standard Siamese Network, the weights of the two networks are shared. ReLU is used as an activation function for each convolution layer and hidden layer (Eq. (6)).

$$h(x) = max(0, x) \tag{6}$$

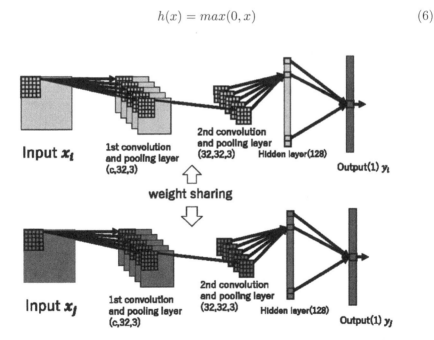

Fig. 2. Siamese Network for binary classification

The objective function of the Siamese Network for binary classification is defined as

$$E = \frac{1}{2N} \sum_i^N \sum_j^N l_{ij}(D_{ij})^2 + (1 - l_{ij})max(m - D_{ij},\, 0)^2 \tag{7}$$

$$D_{ij} = ||y_i - y_j||_2^2 \tag{8}$$

where m is a parameter indicating the distance between clusters and D_{ij} is the distance between the pair of the outputs y_i and y_j of each network for the sample pair x_i and x_j. For the binary classification, the label is defined as $l_{ij} = 1$ whenever the pair of inputs x_i and x_j belongs to the same class, and the label is defined as $l_{ij} = 0$ whenever the pair of inputs belongs to the different class.

The objective function of the Siamese Network depends on the distances between pair of samples and the order of the output of positive class y_+ and the output of negative class y_- is not specified. On the other hand, AUC assumes the order $y_+ > y_-$. This means that there is a possibility to be inconsistent in the order of the outputs. To make consistent and to estimate the posterior probability $P(l = 1|x)$, we apply the logistic regression to the output of the trained network y. The logistic regression model is given by

$$P(l = 1|x) \approx \hat{y} = \sigma(wy + b) \tag{9}$$

where w and b is the parameters of the model and $\sigma(\cdot)$ is the sigmoid function. Usually the log-likelihood of the logistic regression for N training samples is defined by

$$\hat{E} = \sum_{i=1}^N \{t_i log(\hat{y}_i) + (1 - t_i)log(1 - \hat{y}_i)\}\,. \tag{10}$$

The optimum parameters w and b are obtained by maximizing this log-likelihood.

In the proposed method, Siamese Network is regarded as a feature extractor and the obtained features are classified by logistic regression model. As can be seen from Eq. (10), it is obvious that the output value becomes larger for the positive class.

3.2   Multi-class Classification

We extend the proposed binary classifier to multi-class classification by using one-vs-others approach. Figure 3 shows the proposed Siamese Network for multi-class classification. Similar with the Siamese Network for binary classification, the K features $y^{(1)}, y^{(2)}, \ldots, y^{(K)}$ for K classes classification are extracted by deep CNN.

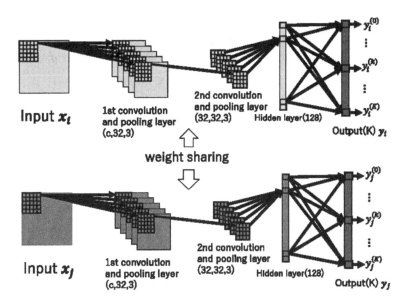

Fig. 3. Siamese Network for multi-class classification

Each unit in the output layer of Siamese Network extracts a feature to classify the corresponding class and the other classes. The contrastive loss of this network is defined as

$$L_k = \frac{1}{2N} \sum_i^N \sum_j^N l_{ij}^{(k)} (D_{ij}^{(k)})^2 + (1 - l_{ij}^{(k)}) max(m - D_{ij}^{(k)}, 0)^2 \qquad (11)$$

$$D_{ij}^{(k)} = |y_i^{(k)} - y_j^{(k)}|^2 \qquad (12)$$

where $l_{ij}^{(k)}$ is a label in the binary classification when the k-th class is regarded as a positive class and the other classes are regarded as a negative class. The distance $D_{ij}^{(k)}$ is defined as the distance between the pair of outputs $y_i^{(k)}$ and $y_j^{(k)}$ of the k-th unit.

The average of K contrastive losses L_k

$$E = \frac{1}{K} \sum_k^K L_k \qquad (13)$$

is used to obtain the weights of the Siamese Network.

To estimate the posterior probability of each class from the features calculated by the Siamese Network, we use the multi-nominal logistic regression. The model of the multi-nominal logistic regression for the input vector $\boldsymbol{y}_n$ is given as

$$\hat{\boldsymbol{y}}_n = S(W\boldsymbol{y}_n + \boldsymbol{b}) \tag{14}$$

where W and $\boldsymbol{b}$ are the coefficient matrix and the bias vector respectively. Also, $S(\cdot)$ is a softmax function. Similar with the binary logistic regression, the log-likelihood for the training samples is defined as

$$\hat{E} = \sum_n^N \boldsymbol{t}_n^T log(\hat{\boldsymbol{y}}_n) \tag{15}$$

where $log(\hat{\boldsymbol{y}}_n)$ is the logarithm of each element of $\hat{\boldsymbol{y}}_n$. This is used to obtain the optimum parameters W and $\boldsymbol{b}$ of the model. It is known that this log-likelihood is the same as the cross entropy loss except the sign.

4   Experiments

In the experiment, we used Fashion-MNIST dataset and CIFAR-10 dataset. Fashion-MNIST is a dataset in which grayscale images of 10 kinds of clothing items such as "trouser" and "dress" are included. The image size is 28×28, it has 6,000 train images per class and 1,000 test images per class. CIFAR-10 is a dataset in which color images of 10 kinds of objects such as "automobile" and "dog" are included. The image size is 32×32, it has 5,000 train images per class and 1,000 test images per class.

At first, the effectiveness of the proposed approach for binary classification is investigated by comparing the proposed method with the standard CNN. Then the effectiveness for multi-class classification is investigated.

4.1   Binary Classification

At first we consider binary classification problems in which a specific target class and the other classes are classified. Since there are ten classes in the datasets (Fashion-MNIST and CIFAR-10), we trained ten different networks for binary classification. The Siamese Networks for binary classification shown in Fig. 2 are trained. The experiment was performed changing the parameter m in the loss of the Siamese Network in the range of 1 to 10. It was found that the larger the m, the higher the score, but above 5 the learning becomes unstable. Therefore, m was set to 5. The learning rate of SGD with momentum is initially set at 0.001 and divided by 10 every 100 epochs. The momentum parameter is set to 0.9. Then the parameters of the logistic regression model are determined to estimate the posterior probability of the target class.

For the comparison, the standard CNN with the same network structure with the Siamese Network is also trained as the baseline model. The sigmoid function is used as the activation function of the output layer of the standard CNN and the binary cross entropy is used as the loss function. AUC scores for the proposed model and the standard CNN are calculated. For each model, the parameters of the networks are trained five times with different initial values and the average of the AUC scores are calculated for each target class.

The average AUC scores for Fashion-MNIST dataset are shown in Table 1. Table 2 shows the average AUC scores for CIFAR-10 dataset. It is noticed that the average AUC scores of the proposed method are better than the standard CNN for many cases. Especially for CIFAR-10 dataset almost all the average AUC scores of the proposed method are better than the standard CNN.

For reference, Fig. 4 shows the ROC curve for binary classification between "deer" and the other classes for CIFAR-10 dataset.

Table 1. AUC of binary classification (Fasion-MNIST)

Target class	Baseline	Siamese	Target class	Baseline	Siamese
Class "t-shirt"	**0.9889**	0.9850	Class "sandal"	0.9996	**0.9998**
Class "trouser"	0.9992	**0.9999**	Class "shirt"	**0.9723**	0.9720
Class "pullover"	**0.9891**	0.9854	Class "sneaker"	0.9989	**0.9990**
Class "dress"	**0.9955**	0.9928	Class "bag"	0.9985	**0.9996**
Class "coat"	0.9891	**0.9909**	Class "ankle boot"	0.9988	**0.9989**

Table 2. AUC of binary classification (CIFAR-10)

Class	Baseline	Siamese	Class	Baseline	Siamese
Class "airplane"	0.9554	**0.9599**	Class "dog"	0.9292	**0.9323**
Class "automobile"	0.9783	**0.9827**	Class "frog"	0.9710	**0.9719**
Class "bird"	0.9066	**0.9076**	Class "horse"	0.9630	**0.9653**
Class "cat"	**0.8879**	0.8581	Class "ship"	0.9771	**0.9789**
Class "deer"	0.9303	**0.9402**	Class "truck"	0.9735	**0.9785**

4.2 Multi-class Classification

Here we investigate the effectiveness of the proposed method for multi-class classification. The proposed model is trained by using Fashion-MNIST dataset and CIFAR-10 dataset. The learning rate of SGD with momentum is initially set to 0.01 and divided by 10 at every 100 epochs. The momentum parameter is set to 0.9. The parameter m in the loss function of Siamese Network is set to 10. As

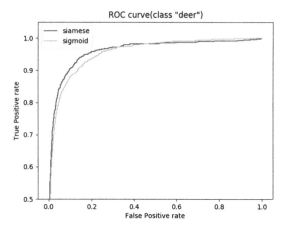

Fig. 4. ROC curve for binary classification between "deer" and the other objects in CIFAR-10 dataset.

the baseline model, the standard CNN with softmax function as the activation function of the output layer is also trained to minimize the cross entropy loss. Similar with the binary classification, the average AUC scores are measured for the proposed method and the standard CNN. The recognition accuracies for each model are also calculated. In the case of multi-class classification, we regard that each unit of the output layer solves the binary classification problem classifying the target class and the other classes and the average of the AUC scores of each output unit is calculated as the AUC score for each model. For each model, the parameters of the networks are trained five times with different initial values and the average of the AUC scores are calculated.

The results are shown in Table 3. It is noticed that both of the average AUC score and the recognition accuracy of the proposed method is better than the standard CNN for multi-class classification. Particularly in classification of CIFAR10, the recognition accuracy is about 3% better than the standard CNN.

ROC curves for CIFAR-10 dataset are shown in the Fig. 5. It is noticed that the proposed method gives better results than the standard CNN.

Table 3. AUC and accuracy for multi-class classification

AUC	Baseline	Siamese	Accuracy	Baseline	Siamese
fasionMNIST	0.9932	**0.9941**	fasionMNIST	0.9040	**0.9163**
CIFAR10	0.9601	**0.9635**	CIFAR10	0.7219	**0.7538**

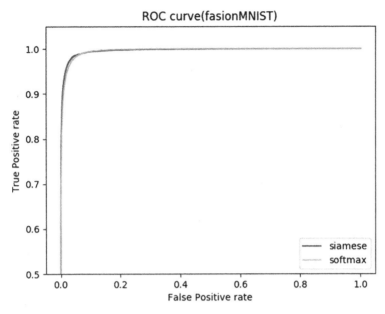

(a) ROC curve for Fashion-MNIST dataset

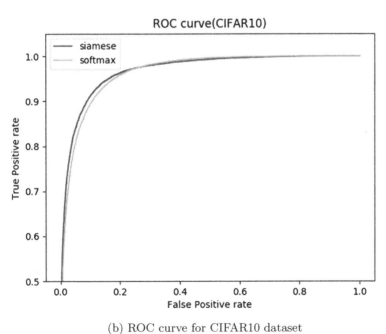

(b) ROC curve for CIFAR10 dataset

Fig. 5. ROC curve for multi-class classification

5   Conclusion and Future Works

This paper investigates the effectiveness of the Siamese Network for rank learning for binary classification and multi-class classification. It was found that the proposed approach can achieve better AUC scores than the standard CNN. In addition, it is confirmed that the logistic regression model that estimates the posterior probability from the output of Siamese Network also works effectively to optimize AUC.

In this paper, we performed two stages of learning to estimate posterior probability. As future work, we would like to develop a one stage model that simultaneously performs margin maximization and estimation of the posterior probability.

The Triplet Network is proposed by Hoffer et al. [12] to use triples of the samples as an extension of the Siamese Network which uses the pairwise samples in the training. They claim that we can extract feature vectors from triplicate samples and extract embedded representations for classification by clustering their feature vectors. Similar with the proposed Siamese Network based methods, the posterior probability is estimated by logistic regression from the representation obtained by the Triplet Network. However, the results are inferior to the standard CNN based methods for many datasets. We have to find a way to extend the proposed binary classification based method with Siamese Network to the Triplet Network based method.

Acknowledgments. This work was partly supported by JSPS KAKENHI Grant Number 16K00239.

References

1. Vapnik, V., Lerner, A.: A pattern recognition using generalized portrait method. Autom. Remote Control **24**(6), 774–780 (1963)
2. Cortes, C., Vapnik, V.: Support vector networks. Mach. Learn. **20**, 273–297 (1995)
3. Herbrich, R., Graepel, T., Obermayer, K.: Large margin rank boundaries for ordinal regression. In: Smola, B., Schoelkopf, S. (eds.) Advances in Large Margin Classifiers. MIT Press, Cambridge (2000)
4. Chapelle, O., Keerthi, S.S.: Efficient algorithms for ranking with SVMs. Inf. Retr. **13**, 201–215 (2010)
5. Krizhevsky, A., Sutskever, I., Hinton, G.E.: ImageNet classification with deep convolutional neural networks. In: Proceedings of Conference Neural Information Processing Systems, pp. 1097–1105 (2012)
6. Bromley, J., Guyon, I., LeCun, Y., Säckinger, E., Shah, R.: Signature verification using a Siamese time delay neural network. In: Advances in Neural Information Processing Systems, NIPS 1993, vol. 6 (1993)
7. Chopra, S., Hadsell, R. LeCun, Y.: Learning a similarity metric discriminatively, with application to face verification. In: Proceedings of the IEEE Computer Society Conference on Computer Vision and Pattern Recognition, CVPR 2005, vol. 1, pp. 539–546 (2005)

8. Hadsell, R., Chopra, S., LeCun, Y.: Dimensionality reduction by learning an invariant mapping. In: Proceedings of 2006 IEEE Computer Society Conference on Computer Vision and Pattern Recognition CVPR 2006, vol. 2, pp. 1735–1742 (2006)
9. He, K., Zhang, X., Ren, S., Sun, J.: Deep residual learning for image recognition. In: Proceedings of CVPR 2016 (2016)
10. He, K., Gkioxari, G., Dollár, P., Girshick, R.: Mask R-CNN. In: Proceedings of ICCV 2017 (2017)
11. Ronneberger, O., Fischer, P., Brox, T.: U-Net: convolutional networks for biomedical image segmentation. In: Navab, N., Hornegger, J., Wells, W.M., Frangi, A.F. (eds.) MICCAI 2015. LNCS, vol. 9351, pp. 234–241. Springer, Cham (2015). https://doi.org/10.1007/978-3-319-24574-4_28
12. Hoffer, E., Ailon, N.: Deep metric learning using triplet network. In: Feragen, A., Pelillo, M., Loog, M. (eds.) SIMBAD 2015. LNCS, vol. 9370, pp. 84–92. Springer, Cham (2015). https://doi.org/10.1007/978-3-319-24261-3_7

Attention-Based Audio-Visual Fusion for Video Summarization

Yinghong Fang, Junpeng Zhang, and Cewu Lu$^{(\boxtimes)}$

Department of Computer Science and Engineering,
Shanghai Jiao Tong University, Shanghai, China
{yhfang,jpzhang1995,lucewu}@sjtu.edu.cn

Abstract. Video summarization compresses videos while preserving the most meaningful content for users. Many image-based works focus on how to effectively utilize video visual cues to choose keyframes. However, apart from visual content, videos also contain useful audio information. In this paper, we propose a novel attention-based audio-visual fusion framework which integrates the audio information with visual information. Our framework is composed of two key components: asymmetrical self-attention mechanism, and odd-even attention. The asymmetrical self-attention mechanism addresses the problem that visual information is more strongly related to video summarization than audio information. The odd-even attention focuses on alleviating the memory requirements. Besides, we create ViAu-SumMe, an audio-visual dataset, which is based on SumMe dataset. Experimental results on the dataset show that our proposed method outperforms the state-of-the-art methods.

Keywords: Video summarization · Audio-visual fusion · Self-attention

1 Introduction

With the development of the internet and mobile devices, a large number of online videos have been produced. For example, on YouTube, nearly 300 h of videos are uploaded per minute [1]. It is infeasible to watch these videos which are created in one minute, not to mention all the videos uploaded in a day. Therefore, it becomes increasingly important to develop techniques which can quickly browse enormous video data. Video summarization has become one of the most promising solutions.

Video summarization aims to select the most representative frames. In this way, it retains valuable information while compressing video data. Most state-of-the-art methods [2,17,18] utilize only image features to select frames. However, in addition to images, videos also contain rich audio information, which is beneficial to this task. For example, fans will cheer and applaud when their team scores in a rugby match. If an algorithm can integrate both audio and visual cues, the summarization result may be more accurate. However, as discussed in [6,8, 14], how to effectively combine these two features is still a problem. The visual

© Springer Nature Switzerland AG 2019
T. Gedeon et al. (Eds.): ICONIP 2019, LNCS 11954, pp. 328–340, 2019.
https://doi.org/10.1007/978-3-030-36711-4_28

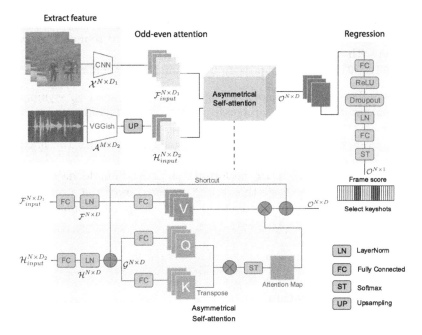

Fig. 1. Illustration of our method. The first row is the whole pipeline and the second row describes the details of the green block which represents asymmetrical self-attention. The inputs for asymmetrical self-attention are: (1) image features $\mathcal{F}_{input}$, (2) audio features $\mathcal{H}_{input}$. A regression network is attached to the end of the asymmetrical self-attention block. The frame score from regression network is used to select keyshots. (Color figure online)

modality is dominant for the task of video summarization, and acoustic modality only captures important moments. Therefore, simply fusing these two type of data does not improve much, and may even reduce accuracy.

Motivated by this, in this paper, we propose a novel audio-visual multimodal learning framework for video summarization based on our designed asymmetrical self-attention mechanism. Generally, the interaction between audio and visual modalities is based on two-way interaction. However, in our learning framework, we use one-way interaction; that is, only the visual modality is affected by the audio modality. In order to address this problem, we design a multimodal learning framework which is consist of three key components: the query module, the key module, and the value module. Since visual data is more relevant to importance scores, we only use images as input to the value module. For the query module and key module, both image and audio are fed into each of them. In this way, the importance scores of frames with similar sound semantics will be enhanced by each other.

Besides, self-attention requires a large memory space when the video sequence is particularly long. Because unlike RNN, it computes the entire sequence at a time. To ease this problem, we propose odd-even attention, which applies local attention and propagates knowledge in different rounds. In even round, local data exchanges information with its right neighbor, and in odd round, it exchanges information with its left neighbor (or vice versa).

The contributions of this paper can be summarized as follows:

1. A novel audio-visual multimodal learning framework based on asymmetrical self-attention mechanism is proposed to effectively integrates the audio and visual data.
2. An odd-even self-attention schema is designed to minimize the maximum memory requirement.
3. Quantitative experiments are performed on ViAu-SumMe dataset, which show that audio can facilitate this task. Also, the comparison results between symmetrical methods and our method verify the point that asymmetrical attention is efficient for this task.

2   Related Work

2.1   Video Summarization

Conventional video summarization method considered physical characteristics of an image. For example, a dynamic sampling rate based on motion intensity was proposed in [10], where a higher local temporal rate is given to high visual activity. In addition to motion intensity, singular value decomposition can also be used to summary videos [3]. But these methods failed to capture the semantic properties of videos.

Recently, deep learning has become a promising technique in video summarization. Deep learning based methods for video summarization can be divided into two categories, unsupervised learning and supervised learning. As for unsupervised learning for video summarization, Zhou et al. [18] designed a diversity-representative reward to generate summaries in a framework based on reinforcement learning. In [16], cycle-consistence was also used to evaluate the quality of the generated summary, where there were two dual generators, one to generate a summary video from the original video and another to generate original video from the summary video. As for the supervised learning for video summarization, Zhang et al. [17] proposed dppLSTM, which used LSTM to obtain temporal dependency and DPP to ensure significant diversity. To make the summary more semantic, Wei et al. [15] added text supervision to choose more semantically relevant video segments. The task of video summarization was regarded as a generalization problem of semantic segmentation as well [13]. The above representative works mainly leverages RNN, which is computationally demanding in comparison with fully connected networks. In order to alleviate this problem, Jiri et al. [2] applied self-attention mechanism which only requires one forward pass and supports computing in parallel. Audio also involves much semantic information, but it was not utilized in previously mentioned cases.

2.2   Audio-Visual Fusion

Videos contain audio information which is beneficial to video summarization task. Some of the earliest audio-visual fusion methods simply concatenate or sum up features. Petridis *et al.* [11] concatenated the visual feature and audio feature which were extracted from BiLSTM. In [19], Zhou *et al.* introduced a weighted sum of multiple modalities. Later, co-attention was put forward to fuse two different features [9]. These two features were first aligned via their similarity matrix and then added them.

All of these are two-way interactions, that is, not only visual feature is affected by acoustic representation, but acoustic representation also learns from visual feature. The final feature is the concatenation of visual feature and acoustic feature. However, for video summarization, visual modality is more dominant and sufficient. Therefore, in our work, we use the visual feature that affected by audio feature as the final feature. It is a one-way interaction. For one-way interaction, in the field of automatic speech recognition, Sterpu *et al.* [14] appended the outputs of video encoder into audio encoder so that only the acoustic modality is affected by the visual feature. Our method is also a one-way interaction, that is, only the visual data is affected by acoustic data. We integrate this insight into attention mechanism and apply it to video summarization area.

3   Our Method

In this section, we first introduce the whole pipeline of our work in Sect. 3.1. Besides, Sect. 3.2 describes asymmetrical self-attention, which is a one-way audio-visual multimodal fusion mechanism, and Sect. 3.3 explains odd-even attention to save memory space.

3.1   Overview

The task of video summarization is to select some representative frames for a given video. Usually, there are three steps. First, the importance score s_i of each frame is predicted. Second, the input video is divided into several shots using the kernel time segmentation algorithm [12]. Finally, following [2,17,18], we use the frame importance score to select some shots. In this paper, we mainly focus on the first step. As illustrated in Fig. 1, visual features $\mathcal{X}^{N \times D_1}$ and audio features $\mathcal{A}^{M \times D_2}$ are extracted by the CNN network and the VGGish network, respectively. In order to make the two features have the same length, audio features $\mathcal{A}^{M \times D_2}$ are linearly interpolated into $\mathcal{H}_{input}^{N \times D_2}$, and $\mathcal{F}_{input}^{N \times D_1}$ is the same as $\mathcal{X}^{N \times D_1}$. Then, both the visual features $\mathcal{F}_{input}^{N \times D_1}$ and audio features $\mathcal{H}_{input}^{N \times D_2}$ are fed into the block of asymmetrical self-attention. The output features $\mathcal{O}^{N \times D}$ go through a regression network to generate a score for each input frame, where the regression network is designed based on [2].

3.2   Asymmetrical Self-attention Based Audio-Visual Fusion

Usually when audio and visual are fused, they are considered to have same weight. However, for the video summary problem, the visual features are more dominant, while the audio features cannot be ignored. Therefore, we propose an asymmetrical self-attention based audio-visual fusion mechanism, which relies more on visual data when fusing audio and visual information.

The asymmetrical self-attention is composed of three modules, namely the query module Q, the key module $\mathcal{K}$, and the value module $\mathcal{V}$. As shown in Fig. 2, the query module and the key module contain both the visual features and audio features while the key module only has the audio features. We first build the inputs to these three modules and then describe the operations between the three modules.

For the query module and the key module, the input is $\mathcal{G}^{N \times D}$, which is the fusion of visual features $\mathcal{F}_{input}^{N \times D_1}$ and audio features $\mathcal{H}_{input}^{N \times D_2}$. In order to fuse these two features, we add them together after having same number of channels, that is,

$$\mathcal{G} = LayerNorm(\mathcal{F}) + LayerNorm(\mathcal{H}),$$
$$\mathcal{F} = \mathcal{F}_{input}\mathcal{W}_1, \quad \mathcal{H} = \mathcal{H}_{input}\mathcal{W}_2, \tag{1}$$

where $\mathcal{W}_1^{D_1 \times D}$ and $\mathcal{W}_2^{D_2 \times D}$ are transformation matrices and D is the dimension of final feature. For key module, the input is only the transformed visual feature $\mathcal{F}$.

Secondly, we describe the operations between these three modules. Asymmetrical attention is illustrated as,

$$Asy\_Attention(Q(\mathcal{G}), \mathcal{K}(\mathcal{G}), \mathcal{V}(\mathcal{F})) = softmax\left(\frac{Q(\mathcal{G})\mathcal{K}(\mathcal{G})^T}{\sqrt{d_k}}\right)\mathcal{V}(\mathcal{F}), \tag{2}$$

$$Q(\mathcal{G}) = \mathcal{G}\mathcal{W}_q, \mathcal{K}(\mathcal{G}) = \mathcal{G}\mathcal{W}_k, \mathcal{V}(\mathcal{G}) = \mathcal{F}\mathcal{W}_v, \tag{3}$$

where $\mathcal{W}_q, \mathcal{W}_k, \mathcal{W}_v$ are the weight matrices, d_k is the number of channels for $Q(\mathcal{G})$.

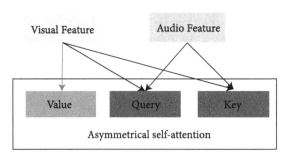

Fig. 2. Asymmetrical self-attention schema. Both visual features and audio features are fed into the query module and the key module. But only visual features are entered into the value module.

For traditional attention, it can be expressed as

$$Attention(Q(\mathcal{U}), \mathcal{K}(\mathcal{U}), \mathcal{V}(\mathcal{U})) = softmax\left(\frac{Q(\mathcal{U})\mathcal{K}(\mathcal{U})^T}{\sqrt{d_k}}\right)\mathcal{V}(\mathcal{U}), \quad (4)$$

where $\mathcal{U} = \mathcal{F}; \mathcal{H}$, which is the concatenation of $\mathcal{F}$ and $\mathcal{H}$.

It is symmetrical, because the image features and audio representation interact with each other equally. More generally, let M donates model, F is input image feature, H is input audio feature. If it is symmetrical, then $M(F, H) = M(H, F)$. If it is asymmetrical, that is, $M(F, H) \neq M(H, F)$.

3.3 Odd-Even Attention

As we can see, the memory cost of the self-attention mechanism is about $N * D$ compared to the RNN-based approach that only processes one frame at a time. For long video, it demands large GPU space. A common way to alleviate this problem is to divide the entire video into several segments and process them separately. However, in this way, only local features are shared between frames in the same part. In order to reduce the memory cost, we propose odd-even attention. As shown in Fig. 3, we first split the video into K *segments* that do not overlap with each other. The algorithm then consists of two rounds of each epoch, one odd round and one even round. In the odd round, each odd indexed segment is concatenated with its left neighbor and applies asymmetrical self-attention, and each even numbered segment is concatenated with its right neighbor and applies asymmetrical self-attention. In even round, conversely, each odd numbered frame exchanges information with its right neighbor. The memory cost of this algorithm is $2 * (N/K) * D$. Furthermore, it is worth noting that each paired segments can independently perform asymmetrical self-attention in parallel.

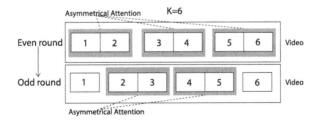

Fig. 3. Odd-even attention with $K = 6$ segments. The input video is splitted into K segments. The first row represents an even round and the second one is an odd round. In each round, two adjacent segments are grouped into one super segment and then an asymmetrical self-attention is performed for each super segment. The difference is that in even rounds the odd indexed segment is grouped with its right neighbor, and in odd rounds it is grouped with its left neighbor.

4   Experimental Results

4.1   Dataset

SumMe [4] is a widely used video summarization dataset containing 25 videos, each of which is annotated with keyshots by 15–20 users. But some of the videos in this dataset lack audio channels, and we created a ViAu-SumMe dataset where each video had an audio channel. Our ViAu-SumMe dataset is based on SumMe, where we only select videos with audio. The five deleted videos are *Scuba, Car railcrossing, Eiffel Tower, Excavators river crossing*, and *Saving dolphines*. It contains 20 videos for training and testing. We use standard 5-fold cross-validation, which randomly select 80% of the videos for training and the remaining 20% videos for testing.

4.2   Implementation Details

We first describe feature extraction, and then explain the training details.

Visual Feature Extraction. In order to remove redundancy in adjacent frames, frames are sampled under uniform sampling. We compute for each frame a 1024-D feature $f_i \in \mathbb{R}^{1024}$ ($i \in \{1, ..., N\}$) using pretrained GoogleNet. The entire feature for a video is donated by $\mathcal{F}_{input} = \{f_1, ..., f_N\}$, where f_i is the i-th frame feature, and N is the total number of frames.

Audio Feature Extraction. In order to have a good representation of the sound, features are extracted using audioset [5] model. The number of audio features is not equal to the length of the total frames, donated by $\mathcal{H}_{input} = \{h_1, ..., h_M\}$ with $h_i \in \mathbb{R}^{128}$, where M is the size of the extracted audio features, and M is not equal to N. Hence, these features are linearly interpolated so that their length is the same as the number of frames. Audio feature h_i is interpolated as follows,

$$h_i^* = (1 - r) * h_l + r * h_{l+1},$$
$$p = \frac{i * M}{N}, l = \lfloor p \rfloor, r = p - \lfloor p \rfloor, \tag{5}$$

where $i \in \{1, ..., N\}$, M be the total number of audio features, and h_i^* are the interpolated audio features for frame i. For convenience, the symbol h_i in the following paragraph represents the interpolated feature h_i^*.

Feature Transformation. The visual feature $f_i \in \mathbb{R}^{1024}$ and audio feature $h_i \in \mathbb{R}^{128}$ are different in both dimension and semantics. For dimensional differences, two features are linearly transformed so that the projected features have the same inner dimension D. Visual feature f_i and audio feature h_i are linearly projected as follows, as briefly described in Eq. 1,

$$f_{i,j} = u_{i,j,1} f_{i,1} + ... + u_{i,j,1024} f_{i,1024},$$
$$h_{i,j} = w_{i,j,1} h_{i,1} + ... + w_{i,j,128} h_{i,128}, \tag{6}$$

where $i \in \{1, ..., N\}$, $j \in \{1, ..., D\}$, $u_{i,j,k}$ is the weight matrix for the visual feature, $w_{i,j,k}$ is the weight matrix for the audio feature, and D is the final feature dimension.

For semantic differences, they are normalized by layer norm before entering asymmetrical self-attention. Visual feature f_i and audio feature h_i are normalized as follows,

$$f_i = \frac{f_i - E(f_i)}{\sqrt{Var(f_i)}}, \quad h_i = \frac{h_i - E(h_i)}{\sqrt{Var(h_i)}}, \tag{7}$$

where $E(f_i)$ and $Var(f_i)$ are the mean and variance for f_i, respectively, and $E(h_i)$ and $Var(h_i)$ are the mean and variance for h_i, respectively.

Training Details. For training details, we follow the training setting in [2]. Mini-batch size is set to 64, and Adam [7] optimizer is used. The learning rate is set to 5e-4 and the network is trained for 300 epochs. Our framework is implemented in Pytorch.

4.3 Evaluation

We follow the evaluation protocol as in [2,9,17,18] by using F-score as the evaluation criterion for final results. The predicted summaries are compared to labeled summaries by many users, and the highest F-score is taken as the final score in all F-scores. This is because different users have different preferences, and summaries are considered to be the correct output as long as it matches one user's preference. F-score is calculated as follows,

$$precision = \frac{|PS \cap TS|}{|PS|}, recall = \frac{|PS \cap TS|}{|TS|},$$
$$F = \frac{2 * precision * recall}{precision + recall}, \tag{8}$$

where PS are the green segments in predicted summaries, TS is the segment in target summaries. $PS \cap TS$ are the yellow segments in the third row in Fig. 4.

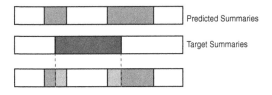

Fig. 4. F-score. The parts marked in green in the first line are predicted summaries, the part marked in red in the second line are target summaries, and the yellow parts in the third row are the intersection of predicted summaries and target summaries. (Color figure online)

4.4 Comparison with State-of-the-Art Methods

The quantitative results on ViAu-SumMe dataset are given in Table 1. We divide the experiment into two parts, no-audio and audio. Specifically, DR-DSN [18], DppLSTM [17], Attention [2] are no-audio methods. CoAttention [9], Concatenation, and our asymmetrical self-attention are three methods using audio. In these audio-based methods, CoAttention [9] and Concatenation use asymmetric mechanism, and our asymmetrical self-attention method applies symmetric mechanism. More qualitative results are shown in Fig. 6. It can be seen that there are some similarities between the selected segments.

Adding Audio Information. DR-DSN [18], DppLSTM [17], and Attention [2] are three state-of-the-art methods which do not leverage audio information. Compared to these methods, CoAttention [9] and our asymmetrical attention method use audio information and show higher F-score. The F-scores of CoAttention and our method increase from 52.35 to 55.85 and from 52.35 to 60.00, respectively. It proves that audio contributes to video summarization.

Using Asymmetrical Attention. We also compare our method with CoAttention [9], which is a symmetrical mechanism. It shows that our asymmetrical attention method achieves 3.15 higher. For the concatenation method of another symmetric mechanism based method listed in the table, we first concatenate the audio features and visual features, then we apply self-attention. Compared to this method, our method also has a 2.6% improvement. The reason is that the visual features are the primary factors in predicting the importance score of the frame.

Table 1. Comparison of our asymmetrical attention method with the start-of-the-art methods on ViAu-SumMe dataset.

	Methods	Asymmetircal	F-score
No-audio	DR-DSN [18]	/	47.54
	DppLSTM [17]	/	48.14
	Attention [2]	/	52.35
Audio	CoAttention [9]	No	55.85
	Concatenation	No	58.49
	Our method	Yes	**60.00**

4.5 Ablation Study

Odd-Even Attention. As shown in Table 2, we compare F-score and memory costs after using attention mechanism with different number of segments and different normalization ways. Odd-even attention reduces the F-score when applying batch normalization. But, odd-even attention not only reduces memory requirements but also improves F-score when using layer normalization. This is because layer normalization has the same effect under different partitioning schemes.

Table 2. F-score using odd-even attention under different number of segments and normalization methods. K is the number of segments.

Normalization	K	S_1	S_2	S_3	S_4	S_5	Avg F-Score	Memory
Batch norm	1	53.46	62.20	69.10	46.28	63.51	58.91	N*D
	4	49.71	61.26	63.30	51.41	57.14	56.56	N*D/2
	10	51.00	64.22	59.52	50.21	60.18	57.03	N*D/5
	20	47.71	62.53	57.13	45.17	54.18	53.35	N*D/10
Layer norm	1	53.91	62.16	53.85	59.49	59.06	57.69	N*D
	4	58.98	60.56	59.31	56.21	62.79	59.57	N*D/2
	10	54.50	66.62	59.73	57.44	61.70	**60.00**	N*D/5
	20	51.94	63.66	62.94	58.95	58.11	59.12	N*D/10

Normalization First or Fusion First. There are two types of information, audio and visual. We need to normalize them and add them. There are two possibilities for the order of these two operations. The first one is to sum and then normalize these two pieces of information, and the second one is to normalize and then sum them. As shown in Fig. 5, normalization first gets a higher average score.

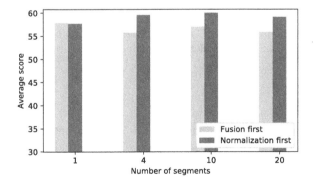

Fig. 5. F-score using fusion first or normalization first under different number of segments.

Different Number of Inner Features. We can see from Table 3, when the number of channels is 512, it gets the best score. The accuracy curve with the number of internal channels is an inverted U-shaped curve.

Table 3. F-score with different number of kernels

# of kernels	S_1	S_2	S_3	S_4	S_5	Avg
64	44.60	60.02	49.48	53.28	58.91	53.26
128	49.56	57.13	55.91	53.02	52.63	53.65
256	57.76	56.54	55.03	53.20	57.56	56.02
512	53.91	62.16	53.85	59.48	59.05	**57.69**
1024	52.83	57.25	50.73	56.30	59.82	55.38

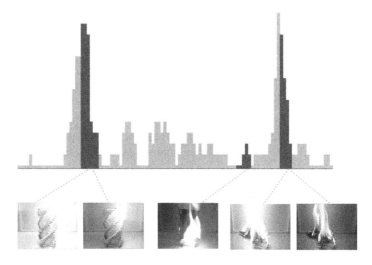

Fig. 6. Ground truth frame scores (red), selected frames (blue), and corresponding frames for *Fire Doimino* video. (Color figure online)

5   Conclusion

In this paper, we proposed asymmetrical self-attention and odd-even attention mechanism. Asymmetrical self-attention dealed with audio-visual fusion and odd-even attention reduced the memory cost. The experimental results showed that compared with the non-audio method, audio-visual fusion led to an improvement of 3.5 (F-score), and our asymmetrical self-attention based method is better than symmetrical fusion with 1.51 (F-score) improvement. Besides, our odd-even attention mechanism reduced memory requirements to one-fifth of the original memory requirements.

References

1. 37 Mind blowing youtube facts, figures and statistics – 2019 (2019). https://merchdope.com/youtube-stats/
2. Fajtl, J., Sokeh, H.S., Argyriou, V., Monekosso, D., Remagnino, P.: Summarizing videos with attention (2018)
3. Gong, Y., Liu, X.: Video summarization using singular value decomposition. In: Proceedings IEEE Conference on Computer Vision and Pattern Recognition. CVPR 2000 (Cat. No. PR00662), vol. 2, pp. 174–180. IEEE (2000)
4. Gygli, M., Grabner, H., Riemenschneider, H., Van Gool, L.: Creating summaries from user videos. In: Fleet, D., Pajdla, T., Schiele, B., Tuytelaars, T. (eds.) ECCV 2014. LNCS, vol. 8695, pp. 505–520. Springer, Cham (2014). https://doi.org/10.1007/978-3-319-10584-0_33
5. Hershey, S., et al.: CNN architectures for large-scale audio classification. In: 2017 IEEE International Conference on Acoustics, Speech and Signal Processing (ICASSP), pp. 131–135. IEEE (2017)
6. Katsaggelos, A.K., Bahaadini, S., Molina, R.: Audiovisual fusion: challenges and new approaches. Proc. IEEE 103(9), 1635–1653 (2015)
7. Kingma, D.P., Ba, J.: Adam: a method for stochastic optimization. arXiv preprint arXiv:1412.6980 (2014)
8. Lahat, D., Adali, T., Jutten, C.: Multimodal data fusion: an overview of methods, challenges, and prospects. Proc. IEEE 103(9), 1449–1477 (2015)
9. Lu, J., Yang, J., Batra, D., Parikh, D.: Hierarchical question-image co-attention for visual question answering. In: Advances In Neural Information Processing Systems, pp. 289–297 (2016)
10. Nam, J., Tewfik, A.H.: Video abstract of video. In: 1999 IEEE Third Workshop on Multimedia Signal Processing (Cat. No. 99TH8451), pp. 117–122. IEEE (1999)
11. Petridis, S., Wang, Y., Li, Z., Pantic, M.: End-to-end audiovisual fusion with LSTMs. arXiv preprint arXiv:1709.04343 (2017)
12. Potapov, D., Douze, M., Harchaoui, Z., Schmid, C.: Category-specific video summarization. In: Fleet, D., Pajdla, T., Schiele, B., Tuytelaars, T. (eds.) ECCV 2014. LNCS, vol. 8694, pp. 540–555. Springer, Cham (2014). https://doi.org/10.1007/978-3-319-10599-4_35
13. Rochan, M., Ye, L., Wang, Y.: Video summarization using fully convolutional sequence networks. In: Ferrari, V., Hebert, M., Sminchisescu, C., Weiss, Y. (eds.) ECCV 2018. LNCS, vol. 11216, pp. 358–374. Springer, Cham (2018). https://doi.org/10.1007/978-3-030-01258-8_22
14. Sterpu, G., Saam, C., Harte, N.: Attention-based audio-visual fusion for robust automatic speech recognition. In: Proceedings of the 2018 on International Conference on Multimodal Interaction, pp. 111–115. ACM (2018)
15. Wei, H., Ni, B., Yan, Y., Yu, H., Yang, X., Yao, C.: Video summarization via semantic attended networks. In: Thirty-Second AAAI Conference on Artificial Intelligence (2018)
16. Yuan, L., Tay, F.E., Li, P., Zhou, L., Feng, J.: Cycle-SUM: cycle-consistent adversarial LSTM networks for unsupervised video summarization. arXiv preprint arXiv:1904.08265 (2019)
17. Zhang, K., Chao, W.-L., Sha, F., Grauman, K.: Video summarization with long short-term memory. In: Leibe, B., Matas, J., Sebe, N., Welling, M. (eds.) ECCV 2016. LNCS, vol. 9911, pp. 766–782. Springer, Cham (2016). https://doi.org/10.1007/978-3-319-46478-7_47

18. Zhou, K., Qiao, Y., Xiang, T.: Deep reinforcement learning for unsupervised video summarization with diversity-representativeness reward. In: Thirty-Second AAAI Conference on Artificial Intelligence (2018)
19. Zhou, P., Yang, W., Chen, W., Wang, Y., Jia, J.: Modality attention for end-to-end audio-visual speech recognition. arXiv preprint arXiv:1811.05250 (2018)

RLDR-Pruning: Restricted Linear Dimensionality Reduction Approach for Model Compression

Xiaoru Liu, Jing Wu, and Chengnian Long[✉]

Department of Automation, School of Electronic Information and Electrical
Engineering, Shanghai Jiao Tong University and Key Laboratory of System Control
and Information Processing, Ministry of China, Shanghai, China
{lxr_orz,jingwu,longcn}@sjtu.edu.cn

Abstract. This paper studies pruning a trained deep neural network
for resource-constrained devices. In general, pruning a trained CNN is
an iterative process: start with a trained CNN; choose and prune *the
least important* parameter; fine-tune to get another trained CNN. It
is reasonable to define *the least important* parameter as the parameter
that leads to the minimum accuracy drop after pruning and fine-tuning.
However, directly searching such parameter is computationally infeasible because of fine-tuning. Therefore, current methods ignore fine-tuning
when choosing parameter to prune. We take fine-tuning into consideration and propose our RLDR-pruning method. To make the searching
feasible in our method, we first model the fine-tuning process and propose an one-step process called *mini-tuning*. Then, our RLDR-pruning
replaces fine-tuning with *mini-tuning* when searching *the least important* parameter. Via experiments on classification tasks, we demonstrate
that RLDR-pruning achieves significantly higher inference accuracy than
existing techniques based on similar parameter optimization capabilities.

Keywords: RLDR-pruning · Model the fine-tuning · *Mini-tuning*

1 Introduction

Convolutional Neuron Networks (CNN) have achieved great success in Computer Vision (CV) tasks and became widely used in image classification [1,2,4,5],
object detection, semantic segmentation [11,12], depth prediction [13] and lots
of other CV tasks [9]. Although CNN achieves higher accuracy in these tasks, it
demands much more computational resources than tradition methods.

Therefore, resource efficient inference becomes crucial for the application of
neuron networks. Pruning is one of the ways to improve inference efficiency first
studied by [14] and [15]. They select parameters to prune according to a second-
order Taylor expansion to improve generalization during the training. Sharing
the similar idea, [18] and [17] remove or set some parameters to zero during
training, aiming at increasing model sparsity and inference resource efficiency.

© Springer Nature Switzerland AG 2019
T. Gedeon et al. (Eds.): ICONIP 2019, LNCS 11954, pp. 341–352, 2019.
https://doi.org/10.1007/978-3-030-36711-4_29

Other works prune a CNN after fully training. [6] directly prune the weights under a pre-set threshold. [16] use the first-degree Taylor polynomial to choose the parameters to prune. These works have the similar iterative pruning process: (1) Start with a trained CNN. (2) Prune *the least important* parameter. (3) Fine-tune to get another trained CNN. Criterion for choosing *the least important* parameter to prune determines the performance of a pruning method.

In most of the previous works, they define *the least important* parameter as the parameter that leads to the minimum accuracy drop after pruned. We innovatively take fine-tuning into consideration and define *the least important* parameter as the parameter that leads to the minimum accuracy drop after pruning and fine-tuning. However, directly searching is computationally infeasible. To compute the accuracy drop for one parameter, we need to prune this parameter then fine-tune the rest of network to get another trained CNN. Then the accuracy drop is the accuracy gap between the old CNN and the new one. For a ResNet-50 [1] with 20 million parameters, we need to fine-tune the network 20 million times to prune one parameter. Therefore, we first build a model for fine-tuning process to estimate the result of fine-tuning in a little amount of computation. We call it *mini-tuning* which modifies the remaining parameters after pruning to improve accuracy. When computing the accuracy drop for each parameter, we replace fine-tuning process with our *mini-tuning*. We show that find out *the least important* parameter becomes solving a Restricted Linear Dimensional Reduction problem by aforesaid replacement. Thus, our pruning method is called RLDR-pruning. Our approach has the following contributions:

A Better Definition of *the Least Important* Parameter. We are the first to take fine-tuning into consideration when choosing *the least important* parameter. As shown in Fig. 1, pruning can be deemed as a structure searching problem. Under our definition, our pruning method aims at greedily searching the structure which achieves the highest accuracy during each pruning step. Therefore, our definition of *the least important* parameter is better than all the previous works.

Modelling the Fine-Tuning Process. We are the first to model the fine-tuning process. To make greedy search computationally feasible, we model the fine-tuning process then propose the *mini-tuning* so as to approximate the accuracy after fine-tuning using a little amount of computation. Experiments show that our *mini-tuning* can improve accuracy after pruning.

RLDR-Pruning Method. Our proposed RLDR-pruning method similarly starts with a trained CNN. By replacing fine-tuning with *mini-tuning*, our method then greedily search the parameter that leads to the minimum accuracy drop after pruning and our *mini-tuning* as shown in Fig. 1. After we prune *the least important* parameter we found, we still fine-tune the network since *mini-tuning* is an approximation of fine-tuning process.

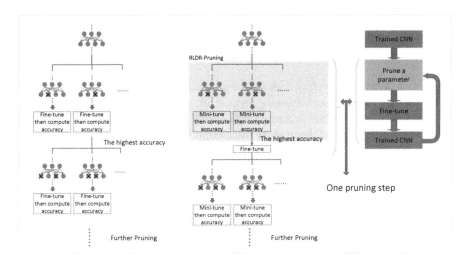

Fig. 1. Left: Treating pruning as a smaller structure searching problem. A greedy search chooses the structure that achieves the highest accuracy during each pruning step. However, it is computationally infeasible. **Middle**: Our RLDR-pruning is also a searching process as shown in blue mask. We replace fine-tuning with *mini-tuning* then greedy search the structure that achieves the highest accuracy. We then fine-tune the structure chosen by our method. **Right**: A general iterative pruning process. Different methods have different criteria to choose the least important parameter.

2 Background Knowledge and Related Work

2.1 Convolution Neuron Networks

As shown in Fig. 2, there are several components in a typical CNN block: convolution layer, fully connected layer, batch normalization layer, and active function. Convolution layers can be deemed as fully connected layer sliding over the feature maps. Therefore, these two layers can be formulated as

$$Y = WX, \tag{1}$$

where X is a n-dimensional column vector, Y is a m-dimensional column vector and W is a $m \times n$ matrix which is called weights. Specifically for a convolution layer, X is a vectorized patch of the input feature map, and each row of W is a vectorized convolution kernel. Then the length vector Y is the amount of output channels.

Usually, batch normalization layer follows behind to adjust the means and variances of Y, formulated as

$$Z = \beta \frac{Y - E(Y)}{\sqrt{D(Y)}} + \gamma = Scale(Shift(\bar{Y})). \tag{2}$$

Here we simplify the batch normalization formulation given by [7]. $\bar{Y}$ is the centralized Y satisfying $\bar{Y} = Y - E(Y)$. $Shift()$ adds a constant number and

$Scale()$ multiplies a constant number. After that, Z gets through Rectified Linear Units (ReLU) [2] function formulated as $T = relu(Z) = maximum(Z, 0)$, where T is the output activations of this block and the input activations of the next block.

Statistics of middle layers are useful for analyzing a network. For a layer which inputs a feature map tensor with size $[n, w, h, d]$, representing batch size, weight, height and depth, there are n samples of input random variables. However, if this is a convolution layer deemed as fully connected layer sliding on the input feature map and processing m patches in all, then there are $n \times m$ samples. Then statistics are computed based on these samples.

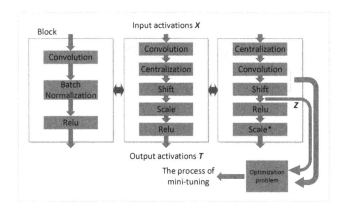

Fig. 2. Different arrangement of layers in a block. After pruning one activation from X, *mini-tuning* should minimize Z by modifying parameters in *Convolution* and *Shift*.

2.2   Network Pruning

When using a trained CNN, most of the computation and parameters exist in the convolution layers, which is matrix multiplications shown as Eq. (1). Deleting one element in a matrix can only increase its sparsity. Therefore, we focus on criteria that directly prune convolution kernels. Pruning a convolution kernel is equivalent to pruning the activations from corresponding channel and there are several criteria to identify *the least important* activations.

Taylor Criterion. Taylor Criterion [16] defines *the least important* activation as the activation that leads to the minimum loss function's variation after pruned. To approximate this variation, they write loss function C as a function of activations x_i then expand C at zero point. They take the first-degree of Taylor expansion to approximate the relationship between variation of x_i and variation of C.

$$|\frac{1}{M} \sum_{i \in K_j} \frac{\partial C}{\partial x_i} x_i|, \tag{3}$$

where $\{x_i | i \in K_j\}$ is all the activation outputted by the jth convolution kernel and M is the number of them. The above formula gives each activation a *score*. When pruning, they delete the activation with the lowest *score*.

Statistics of Activation. Mean activation is an intuitive but reasonable criterion. When an activation's value is always small, it means this convolution kernels fail to detect any useful information for the task at hand. Therefore, the convolution kernels that always output small activations can be removed. Along with the notation above, it evaluates the importance of a convolution kernel as:

$$\frac{1}{M} \sum_{i \in K_j} x_i. \tag{4}$$

Similarly, they delete the activation with the lowest *score*.

3   Method

Similar with previous works, our RLDR-pruning is a iterative process: (1) Start with a fully trained CNN. (2) Prune activations according to statistics. (3) Fine-tune the rest of the network. (4) Decide whether jump to step 2 or stop pruning.

In step (2), we aim at pruning one channel from the current network. Brutally searching the structure which achieves the highest accuracy after fine-tuning needs thousands of GPUs to simultaneously fine-tune different structures then compute the accuracy to choose the highest one. To make this process more computational feasible, we start with modelling the fine-tuning process.

We model fine-tuning as a process which modifies the rest of the pruned network to improve the accuracy. Now we want to find a way to modify the rest of the network after pruning to improve accuracy as much as we can. Because the pruned network is smaller than the original one, and the original one is already fully trained. Therefore, no matter how we fine-tune, the accuracy that the pruned network can achieve is no higher than the accuracy of the original one. To achieve the original accuracy, the output of the pruned network, which called logits, should equal to the output of the original one for any input image. Along with this, we assume that fine-tuning process narrows the difference between the logits of the original network and the pruned one. To mathematically define this difference, we treat the input of a network as random variables. Therefore, the logits also become random variables. Since the distribution of the input random variables stay unchanged before and after pruning, we define them as random vector X^1. We denote the CNN before and after pruning as $f()$ and $\tilde{f}()$. We have $logits = f(X^1)$ and $\widetilde{logits} = \tilde{f}(X^1)$. Then, we define the difference δ_{logits} of logits before and after pruning as

$$\delta_{logits} = E(|logits - \widetilde{logits}|_2^2). \tag{5}$$

Now we show how pruning changes δ_{logits}. When pruning one input activation of the kth block, the output activation of this block is changed, which is the input activation of the next block and leads to a series of variation in the blocks below. If it is possible to preserve the output activations of the kth block after pruning, there will be no variation on logits. Therefore, after pruning one input activation of the kth block, our fine-tuning model modifies the parameters in the kth block to preserve the distribution of this block's output activations. Denoting the kth block's output activation as T^k and $\tilde{T}^k$ before and after pruning. Our fine-tuning model should narrow the difference of the kth block's output activation δ_{T^k} by modifying this block's parameters:

$$\delta_{T^k} = E(|T^k - \tilde{T}^k|_2^2). \tag{6}$$

Under most of the situations, δ_{T^k} will not be zero no matter how we modify this block's parameters because that information from the pruned input activation is completely lost. However, if the pruned activation is not important, δ_{T^k} will be small enough to be treated as zero. Then, no more modification is needed in all the blocks below.

Therefore, after pruning one input activation of the kth block, we model the fine-tuning process as a modification on the kth block's parameters to minimize δ_{T^k}. In this way, only one non-linear function is involved, making this problem easier to solve. We call the process that models fine-tuning the *mini-tuning*.

3.1   Mini-tuning

In this section, we demonstrate the deduction of our one-step *mini-tuning*. Following the aforesaid assumption and approximation, we can deem a trained CNN as a series of cascading linear transform bounded by non-linear active functions. After pruning, we only modify the parameters in this block using *mini-tuning* to minimize the variations of this block's output activations T. However, a cascading information process system have another requirement: the variances and means of each block's input should be preserved. Therefore, we rearrange the computational steps in a block as shown in the right of Fig. 2. Here $Scale^*$ multiplies the input random variables with constants, which change once after pruning once, to preserve the variances of output random variables. It's easy to prove that

$$E(|Z - \tilde{Z}|_2^2) \geq E(|relu(Z) - relu(\tilde{Z})|_2^2). \tag{7}$$

Therefore, instead of preserving T, we skip $Scale^*$ and $Relu$ and preserve Z. We show in the next paragraph that means of output activations will be preserved by minimizing the variation of Z.

We first consider 1×1 convolution and assume that we have pruned one activation from the input activation X. As shown in Fig. 3, pruning one activation from convolution is equivalent to pruning one channel from the feature map. And pruning one activation is equivalent to set corresponding column of W to zero. Following Eq. (1) and denoting centralized X as $\bar{X}$, when the pth activation is pruned, we formulate an optimization problem whose solution is

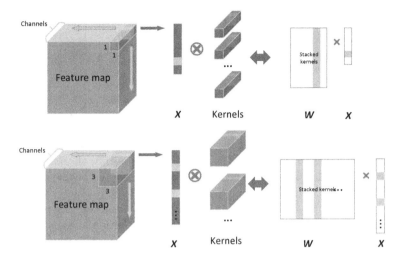

Fig. 3. Green parts mean the parameters pruned or assigned to zeros. **Top:** For 1×1 convolution, pruning one activation is equivalent to pruning one channel from feature map. By converting convolution into matrix multiplication, pruning one activation in X is equivalent to set green parameters in W to zero. **Bottom:** Similar story for 3×3 convolution. (Color figure online)

our *mini-tuning*:

$$
\begin{aligned}
\min_{\tilde{W},\tilde{\beta}} \quad & E(|Z - \tilde{Z}|_2^2) \\
s.t. \quad & \tilde{W}_{\cdot p} = \mathbf{0}, \\
where \quad & Z = W\bar{X} + \beta, \\
& \tilde{Z} = \tilde{W}\bar{X} + \tilde{\beta}.
\end{aligned} \tag{8}
$$

Here all the notations with hat $\tilde{\ }$ mean the value of the same variable after pruning. $\tilde{W}_{\cdot p}$ is the pth column of $\tilde{W}$ and β comes from the *Shift* layer. We can compute the solution by differentiating Eq. (8) and get

$$
\begin{cases}
\tilde{\beta} = E((W - \tilde{W})\bar{X} + \beta) \\
\tilde{W}_{ij} = 0, & j = p \\
\tilde{W}_{ij} = W_{ij} + \sum_{k \neq j} \dfrac{COV(\bar{X}_i, \bar{X}_k)}{D(\bar{X}_i)}(W_{ik} - \tilde{W}_{ik}), & j \neq p
\end{cases} \tag{9}
$$

It still too complicated to get $\tilde{W}$. Therefore, we consider the situation where only X_p and X_q satisfying $COV(X_p, X_q) \neq 0$. In real situation, we approximately find $X_q = \underset{X_i}{argmax}\, \rho_{X_p X_i} = \underset{X_i}{argmax}\, \dfrac{COV(X_p, X_i)}{\sqrt{D(X_p)}\sqrt{D(X_i)}}$ and ignore other correlations. Then solution becomes

$$\begin{cases} \tilde{\beta} = E((W - \tilde{W})\bar{X} + \beta) \\ \tilde{W}_{ip} = 0 \\ \tilde{W}_{iq} = W_{iq} + \dfrac{COV(\bar{X}_q, \bar{X}_p)}{D(\bar{X}_q)} W_{ip} \\ \tilde{W}_{ij} = W_{ij}, \qquad\qquad j \neq p, q. \end{cases} \tag{10}$$

Eq. (10) gives the one-step computational process of *mini-tuning*. After pruning, we find another activation that is highly related with the pruned one and modify its connecting weights in convolution layer. Then we modify the parameters in batch normalization layer to keep the means and variances of output activations unchanged.

For the situation of 3×3 convolution, pruning a channel is equivalent to pruning nine input activations from the aspect of convolution as shown in Fig. 3. In analogy to the *mini-tuning* for 1×1 convolution, we do the same operation to each of the nine activations for 3×3 convolution.

3.2   RLDR-criterion

In this section, we explain our *RLDR-pruning* method to choose the activation to prune. We first give the formulation whose solution is our method. It is a linear dimensional reduction problem because we try to use less input activations to compute the output activations. Also, we are restricted to not use linear transformation to solve this problem because putting linear transformation in a network will increase the amount of computation.

$$\begin{aligned} &\underset{\tilde{W}, \tilde{\beta}}{min} && E(|Z - \tilde{Z}|_2^2) \\ &s.t. && ZeroColumn(\tilde{W}) = 1, \\ &where && Z = W\bar{X} + \beta, \\ & && \tilde{Z} = \tilde{W}\bar{X} + \tilde{\beta}. \end{aligned} \tag{11}$$

The only difference between Eqs. (11) and (8) is the constrain to $\tilde{W}$. Here, $ZeroColumn(\tilde{W})$ means the number of zero column in $\tilde{W}$ for 1×1 convolution. As for 3×3 convolution, it means the number of corresponding sets of zero columns. In Eq. (8), we already know which activation to prune then minimize the variation $E(|Z - \tilde{Z}|_2^2)$. Here, we also need to decide which activation to prune. In this way, it becomes an integer programming problem.

As shown in the blue mask in Fig. 1, we directly search the solution of Eq. (11): For each input activation in the network, we compute the $E(|Z - \tilde{Z}|_2^2)$ as a *score* after pruning and *mini-tuning*. Then we choose the activation with the lowest *score* as the *least important* activation.

We denote the *score* of input activation X_p as $\delta_Z(X_p)$. Then we have

$$\delta_Z(X_p) = \sum_i W_{ip}^2 D\left(X_p - \frac{COV(X_q, X_p)}{D(X_q)} X_q\right). \tag{12}$$

Eq. (12) computes the variation of Z as a *score* in the same block where X_p is after pruning and *mini-tuning*. Inside a block, we can evaluate the importance of each activation by the *score*. However, activations form different blocks cannot be compared by this *score*. Therefore, we normalize the *score* so that we can compare activations from different blocks. X_k^l denotes for the kth input activation in l^{th} layer:

$$\Theta_{X_k^l} = \frac{\delta_Z(X_k^l)}{\sqrt{\sum_i (\delta_Z(X_i^l))^2}} \tag{13}$$

Eq. (13) gives a *score* that we use to choose the *least important* activation from the whole network in our *RLDR-pruning* method.

4   Experiment

We implement our pruning method in Tensorflow. We take a full pre-activation ResNet-50 [20] trained on ImageNet and fine-tune it on Birds-200 [8]. After achieving accuracy of 73%, we prune parameters while preserving the accuracy on Birds-200. We carried out the experiments on one NVIDIA GTX1080 GPU. Our batch size is 24 and input images are randomly cropped from Birds-200 with size of 224×224. When computing statistics and fine-tuning, we use training set. We use test set only to computing accuracy.

Statistics of Activations. Directly collect large samples then compute statistics requires huge computational resource. Therefore, in order to compute statistic R, we input a batch of images each time and batch-wisely compute an approximation R_i. After N iterations, we compute the mean value $\overline{R} = \frac{1}{N} \sum_i R_i$. Then, the average value $\overline{R}$ approximates an unbiased approximation of the statistic R. In all the experiments, we run 1000 iterations to compute the statistics. Then we prune the network and *mini-tune* according to the statistics.

Fine-tuning. In all experiments that need fine-tuning, we set learning rate to 0.001 and use momentum optimizer provided in Tensorflow. We run 1000 iterations to complete fine-tuning. During fine-tuning, we update the moving means and variances in batch normalization layers to preserve the means and variances of the output activations.

Pruning Objective. We evaluate inference efficiency of a pruned network by the amount of parameters and floating-point operations (FLOPs). Therefore, our pruning objective is to preserve accuracy with less parameters and FLOPs.

4.1   Mini-tuning

In our first experiment, the pruning process is shown in the right side of Fig. 1. We use Taylor criterion to choose parameters for pruning. We separately test the situation where we use fine-tuning as shown in the right side of Fig. 1, where we

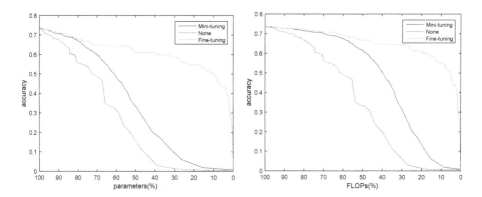

Fig. 4. To test *mini-tuning*, we use Taylor criterion and iterative pruning process shown in the right of Fig. 1. **Fine-tuning**: The original pruning process. **Mini-tuning**: Replacing fine-tuning with *mini-tuning*. **None**: Removing fine-tuning. It shows that the proposed *mini-tuning*, to some extend, functions as fine-tuning.

replace fine-tuning with *mini-tuning* and where we directly remove fine-tuning. If our *mini-tuning* is a good model of fine-tuning, it will have two functions: (1) Improving accuracy after pruning in each pruning step. (2) Helping criterion to choose a less important parameter in the next iteration. And they will improve the pruning result.

Figure 4 shows that using *mini-tuning* achieves better pruning curve than doing nothing does. However, using fine-tuning achieves the best pruning curve. During the first several pruning iterations, curves of *mini-tuning* is close to curves of fine-tuning. It means *mini-tuning* functions well as a replacement for fine-tuning. However, the gap between *mini-tuning* and fine-tuning accumulates as pruning goes on, leading to drastic accuracy drop. Therefore, *mini-tuning* is a good replacement for fine-tuning when selecting the parameter to prune. We still fine-tune the pruned network after each pruning as shown in the middle of Fig. 1.

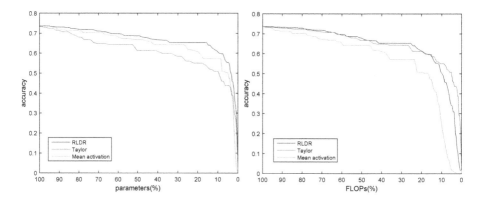

Fig. 5. Using different criteria to prune then fine-tuning.

4.2 RLDR-Pruning

Then we compare RLDR-criterion with Taylor criterion and mean activation criterion. We fine-tune the whole network after pruning. As showed in Fig. 5, our criterion achieves highest parameter efficiency all along. And mean activation criterion achieves higher parameter efficiency than Taylor criterion dose in most situations. For FLOPs efficiency, our criteria achieve slightly better result than Taylor criterion until reaching 10% FLOPs where accuracy of our criterion drops faster than accuracy of Taylor criterion. But our criterion still better than mean activation all along.

Table 1 shows the least parameters and FLOPs each method requires to achieve the same accuracy. Overall, our criterion achieves higher compress rate than the other two in most situations.

Table 1. The amount of parameters and FLOPs needed by each method to achieve required accuracy on Birds-200. Comparing with the other two, network pruned with RLDR-criterion needs less parameters and FLOPs to achieve the same accuracy in most situations.

Criterion	Accuracy = 0.7		Accuracy = 0.65		Accuracy = 0.6	
	Parameters	FLOPs	Parameters	FLOPs	Parameters	FLOPs
Mean activation	15.89 M	5.35 G	9 M	3.78 G	4.15 M	2.4 G
Taylor	17.7 M	**3.97 G**	15 M	2.76 G	10.4 M	1.53 G
RLDR	**13.3 M**	3.99 G	**6 M**	**2.29 G**	**1.96 M**	**1.11 G**

5 Conclusion

In this paper, we model the fine-tuning process to greedy search the optimum smaller structure. Our deducted RLDR-pruning method jointly consider activation's variance after decorrelation and its corresponding weights, which can be deemed as a combination of minimum weight criterion and decorrelated activation variance criterion. Experiments show that our method outperforms the state-of-art pruning methods. Therefore, RLDR-pruning method can compress a trained network until satisfying the resource constraints while achieving higher accuracy than current methods for resource-constrained devices.

Acknowledgement. This work was supported in part by the National Nature Science Foundation of China under Grants 61673275, 61873166.

References

1. He, K., Zhang, X., Ren, S., Sun, J.: Identification of common molecular subsequences. J. Mol. Biol. **147**, 195–197 (1981)

2. Krizhevsky, A., Sutskever, I., Hinton, G.E.: ImageNet classification with deep convolutional neural networks. In: Advances in Neural Information Processing Systems, pp. 1097–1105 (2012)

3. Zeiler, M.D., Fergus, R.: Visualizing and understanding convolutional networks. In: Fleet, D., Pajdla, T., Schiele, B., Tuytelaars, T. (eds.) ECCV 2014. LNCS, vol. 8689, pp. 818–833. Springer, Cham (2014). https://doi.org/10.1007/978-3-319-10590-1_53

4. Szegedy, C., et al.: Going deeper with convolutions. arXiv preprint arXiv:1409.4842 (2014)

5. Sandler, M., Howard, A., Zhu, M., Zhmoginov, A., Chen, L.C.: MobileNetv 2: inverted residuals and linear bottlenecks. In: Proceedings of the IEEE Conference on Computer Vision and Pattern Recognition, pp. 4510–4520 (2018)

6. Han, S., Pool, J., Tran, J., Dally, W.: Learning both weights and connections for efficient neural network. In: Advances in Neural Information Processing Systems, pp. 1135–1143 (2015)

7. Ioffe, S., Szegedy, C.: Batch normalization: accelerating deep network training by reducing internal covariate shift. arXiv preprint arXiv:1502.03167 (2015)

8. Wah, C., Branson, S., Welinder, P., Perona, P., Belongie, S.: The Caltech-UCSD Birds-200-2011 dataset (2011)

9. Zamir, A.R., Sax, A., Shen, W., Guibas, L.J., Malik, J., Savarese, S.: Taskonomy: disentangling task transfer learning. In: Proceedings of the IEEE Conference on Computer Vision and Pattern Recognition, pp. 3712–3722 (2018)

10. Russakovsky, O., et al.: ImageNet large scale visual recognition challenge. Int. J. Comput. Vis. **115**(3), 211–252 (2015)

11. Redmon, J., Farhadi, A.: Yolov3: an incremental improvement. arXiv preprint arXiv:1804.02767 (2018)

12. Chen, L.C., Papandreou, G., Schroff, F., Adam, H.: Rethinking Atrous Convolution for Semantic Image Segmentation. arXiv preprint arXiv:1706.05587 (2017)

13. Laina, I., Rupprecht, C., Belagiannis, V., Tombari, F., Navab, N.: Deeper depth prediction with fully convolutional residual networks. In: 2016 Fourth International Conference on 3D Vision (3DV), pp. 239–248. IEEE, October 2016

14. LeCun, Y., Denker, J.S., Solla, S.A.: Optimal brain damage. In: Advances in Neural Information Processing Systems, pp. 598–605 (1990)

15. Hassibi, B., Stork, D.G.: Second order derivatives for network pruning: optimal brain surgeon. In: Advances in Neural Information Processing Systems, pp. 164–171 (1993)

16. Molchanov, P., Tyree, S., Karras, T., Aila, T., Kautz, J.: Pruning convolutional neural networks for resource efficient transfer learning. arXiv preprint arXiv:1611.06440, 3 (2016)

17. Luo, J.H., Wu, J., Lin, W.: ThiNet: a filter level pruning method for deep neural network compression. In: Proceedings of the IEEE International Conference on Computer Vision, pp. 5058–5066 (2017)

18. Zhu, M., Gupta, S.: To prune, or not to prune: exploring the efficacy of pruning for model compression. arXiv preprint arXiv:1710.01878 (2017)

19. LeCun, Y., Bottou, L., Bengio, Y., Haffner, P.: Gradient-based learning applied to document recognition. Proc. IEEE **86**(11), 2278–2324 (1998)

20. He, K., Zhang, X., Ren, S., Sun, J.: Identity mappings in deep residual networks. In: Leibe, B., Matas, J., Sebe, N., Welling, M. (eds.) ECCV 2016. LNCS, vol. 9908, pp. 630–645. Springer, Cham (2016). https://doi.org/10.1007/978-3-319-46493-0_38

Adaptive Neuro-Surrogate-Based Optimisation Method for Wave Energy Converters Placement Optimisation

Mehdi Neshat[1], Ehsan Abbasnejad[2], Qinfeng Shi[2], Bradley Alexander[1(✉)], and Markus Wagner[1]

[1] Optimisation and Logistics Group, School of Computer Science, University of Adelaide, Adelaide, Australia
bradley.alexander@adelaide.edu.au
[2] The Australian Institute for Machine Learning, University of Adelaide, Adelaide, Australia

Abstract. Installed renewable energy capacity has expanded massively in recent years. Wave energy, with its high capacity factors, has great potential to complement established sources of solar and wind energy. This study explores the problem of optimising the layout of advanced, three-tether wave energy converters in a size-constrained farm in a numerically modelled ocean environment. Simulating and computing the complicated hydrodynamic interactions in wave farms can be computationally costly, which limits optimisation methods to using just a few thousand evaluations. For dealing with this expensive optimisation problem, an adaptive neuro-surrogate optimisation (ANSO) method is proposed that consists of a surrogate Recurrent Neural Network (RNN) model trained with a very limited number of observations. This model is coupled with a fast meta-heuristic optimiser for adjusting the model's hyper-parameters. The trained model is applied using a greedy local search with a backtracking optimisation strategy. For evaluating the performance of the proposed approach, some of the more popular and successful Evolutionary Algorithms (EAs) are compared in four real wave scenarios (Sydney, Perth, Adelaide and Tasmania). Experimental results show that the adaptive neuro model is competitive with other optimisation methods in terms of total harnessed power output and faster in terms of total computational costs.

Keywords: Evolutionary Algorithms · Local search · Surrogate-based optimisation · Sequential deep learning · Gray Wolf Optimiser · Wave Energy Converters · Renewable energy

1 Introduction

As the global demand for energy continues to grow, the advancement and deployment of new green energy sources are of paramount significance. Due to

© Springer Nature Switzerland AG 2019
T. Gedeon et al. (Eds.): ICONIP 2019, LNCS 11954, pp. 353–366, 2019.
https://doi.org/10.1007/978-3-030-36711-4_30

high capacity factors and energy densities compared to other renewable energy sources, ocean wave energy has attracted research and industry interest for a number of years [6]. Wave Energy Converters (WECs) are typically laid out in arrays and, to maximise power absorption, it is crucial to arrange them carefully with respect to each other [5]. The number of hydrodynamic interactions increases quadratically with the number of WEC's in the array. Modelling these interactions for a single moderately-sized farm layout can take several minutes. Moreover, the optimisation problem for farm-layouts is multi-modal and usually requires many evaluations to explore the search space adequately. There is scope to improve the speed of this search process through the use of a learned surrogate model. The key challenge is to train such a model fast enough to allow an overall reduction in optimisation time. This paper proposes a new hybrid adaptive neuro-surrogate model (ANSO) for maximizing the total absorbed power of WECs layouts in detailed models of four real wave regimes from the southern coast of Australia (Sydney, Adelaide, Perth and Tasmania). Our approach utilizes a neural network that acts as a surrogate for estimating the best position for placement of the converters. The key contributions of this paper are:

1. Designing a neuro-surrogate model for predicting total wave farm energy by training of recurrent neural network (RNNs) using data accumulated from evaluations of farm layouts.
2. The use of the Grey Wolf Optimiser [14] to tune hyper-parameters for each surrogate.
3. A new symmetric local search heuristic with greedy WEC position selection combined with a backtracking optimisation (BO) step to improve the layouts further for fine adjustments.

We demonstrate that the adaptive framework described outperforms previously published results in terms of both optimisation speed (even when surrogate model training time is included) and total absorbed power output for 16-WEC layouts.

Related Work. In this application domain, neural networks have been, primarily, utilized for predicting the wave features (height, period and direction) [2]. In early work, Alexandre et al. [1] applied a hybrid Genetic Algorithm (GA) and an extreme learning machine (ELM) (GA-ELM) for reconstructing missing parameters from readings from nearby sensor buoys. The same study [3] investigated a combination of the grouping GA and ELM (GGA-ELM) for feature extraction and wave parameter estimation. A later approach [4], combined the GGA-ELM with Bayesian Optimisation for predicting the ocean wave features. This combination improved the model significantly at the cost of increased computation time. Sarkar et al. [18] combined machine learning and optimisation of arrays of, relatively simple, oscillating surge WECs. They were able to use this technique to effectively optimise arrays of up to 40 WEC's – subject to fixed spacing constraints. Recently, James et al. [11] used two different supervised ML methods (MLP and SVM) to estimate WEC layout performance and characterise the wave environment [11]. However, the models produced required a large training data-set and manual tuning of hyper-parameters.

In work optimising WEC control parameters, Li et al. [12] trained a feed-forward neural network (FFNN) to learn key temporal relationships between wave forces. While the model required many samples to train it exhibited high accuracy and was used effectively in parameter optimisation for the WEC controller. Recently, Lu et al. [13] proposed a hybrid WECs power take-off controller which consists of a recurrent wavelet-based Elman neural network (RWENN) with an online back-propagation training method and a modified gravitational search algorithm (MGSA) for tuning the learning rate and improving learning capability. The method was used to control the rotor acceleration of the combined offshore wind and wave power converter arrangements. Finally, recent work by Neshat et al. [17] evaluated a wide variety of EAs and hybrid methods by utilizing an irregular wave model with seven wave directions and found that a mixture of a local search combined with the Nelder-Mead simplex method achieved the best array configurations in terms of the total power output.

2   Wave Energy Converter Model

We use a hydrodynamic Wave-Energy Converter (WEC) model for fully submerged three-tether buoys. Each tether is attached to a converter installed on the seafloor [19]. The relevant fixed model parameters in this research are: Buoy number $= 16$, Buoy radius $= 5$ m, Submergence depth $= 3$ m, Water depth $= 30$ m, Buoy mass $= 376$ t, Buoy volume $= 523.60$ m^2 and Tether angle $= 55°$.

System Dynamics and Parameters. The total energy produced by each buoy in an array is modelled as the sum of three forces [20]:

1. The power of wave excitation ($F_{exc,p}(t)$) includes the forces of the diffracted and incident ocean waves when all generator's locations are fixed.
2. The force of radiation ($F_{rad,p}(t)$) is the derived power of an oscillating buoy independent of incident waves.
3. Power take-off force ($F_{pto,p}(t)$) is the force exerted on the generators by their tethers.

Interactions between buoys are captured by the $F_{exc,p}(t)$ term. These interactions can be destructive or constructive, depending on buoys' relative angles, distances and surrounding sea conditions. Equation 1 shows the power accumulating to buoy number p in a buoy array:

$$M_p \ddot{X}_p(t) = F_{exc,p}(t) + F_{rad,p}(t) + F_{pto,p}(t) \tag{1}$$

where M_p is the displacement of the p_{th} buoy, $\ddot{X}_p(t)$ is a vector of body acceleration in terms of surge, heave and sway. The last term, modelling the power take-off system, is simulated as a linear spring and damper. Two control factors are involved for each mooring line: the damping B_{pto} and stiffness K_{pto} coefficients. Therefore the Eq. (1) can be written:

$$\left((M_\Sigma + A_\sigma(\omega))j\omega + B_\sigma(\omega) - \frac{K_{pto,\Sigma}}{\omega}j + B_{pto,\Sigma}\right)\ddot{X}_\Sigma = \hat{F}_{exc,\Sigma} \tag{2}$$

where $A_\Sigma(\omega))$ and $B_\Sigma(\omega)$ are hydrodynamic parameters which are derived from the semi-analytical model based on [22]. Hence, the total power output of a buoy array is:

$$P_\Sigma = \frac{1}{4}(\hat{F}^*{}_{exc,\Sigma}\ddot{X}_\Sigma + \ddot{X}^*{}_\Sigma \hat{F}_{exc,\Sigma}) - \frac{1}{2}\ddot{X}^*{}_\Sigma B \ddot{X}^*{}_\Sigma \quad (3)$$

The calculations in Eq. 3, are very computationally demanding and increase quadratically with the number of buoys. It is also true that, with constructive interference the total power output can scale super–linearly with the number of buoys.

3   Optimisation Setup

The optimisation problem studied in this work can be expressed as: $P_\Sigma^* = argmax_{\mathbf{x},\mathbf{y}} P_\Sigma(\mathbf{x},\mathbf{y})$, where $P_\Sigma(\mathbf{x},\mathbf{y})$ is the average whole-farm power given by placing buoys in a field at x-positions: $\mathbf{x} = [x_1,\ldots,x_N]$ and corresponding y positions: $\mathbf{y} = [y_1,\ldots,y_N]$. The the number of buoys in this work is $N = 16$.

Constraints. There is a square-shaped boundary constraint for placing all buoy positions (x_i, y_i): $l \times w$ where $l = w = \sqrt{N * 20000}\,m$. This gives $20\,000\,\mathrm{m}^2$ of the farm-area per-buoy. To maintain a safety distance, buoys must also be at least $50\,\mathrm{m}$ away from each other. For any layout $\mathbf{x}, \mathbf{y}$ the sum-total of the inter-buoy distance violations, measured in metres, is:

$$Sum_{dist} = \sum_{i=1}^{N-1} \sum_{j=i+1}^{N} (dist((x_i, y_i), (x_j, y_j)) - 50)$$

if $dist((x_i, y_i), (x_j, y_j)) < 50$, where $dist((x_i, y_i), (x_j, y_j))$ is the L2 (Euclidean) distance between buoys i and j. The penalty applied to the farm power output (in Watts) is $(Sum_{dist} + 1)^{20}$. This steep penalty smoothly handles constraint violations during search. Buoy placements which are outside of the farm area are handled by reiterating the positioning process.

Computational Resources. In this work, depending on the optimisation method, the average evaluation time for a candidate layout can vary greatly. To ensure a fair comparison of methods the maximum budget for all optimisation methods is three days of elapsed time on a dedicated high-performance shared-memory parallel platform. The compute nodes have 2.4 GHz Intel 6148 processors and 128 GB of RAM. The meta-heuristic frameworks as well as the hydrodynamic simulator for $P_\Sigma(\mathbf{x},\mathbf{y})$ are run in MATLAB R2018. This configuration allows up to 12 worker threads to be run in parallel. We optimise search methods to use as many of these threads as each search method allows.

4   Methodology

In this study, the optimisation approaches employ one of two strategies. The first is, optimising all decision variables (buoy placements) at the same time. We compare five population-based EAs that use this strategy. Second, based on [17], we place buoys sequentially.

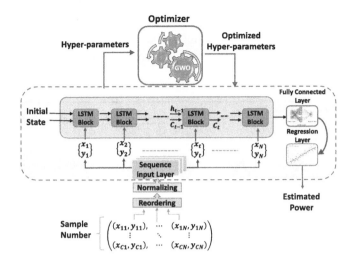

Fig. 1. The Neuro-Surrogate model architecture

4.1 Evolutionary Algorithms (EAs)

Five popular off-the-shelf EAs are compared in the first strategy to optimise all problem dimensions. These EAs include: (1) Differential Evolution (DE) [21], with a configuration of $\lambda = 30$ (population size), $F = 0.5$ and $P_{cr} = 0.5$; (2) covariance matrix adaptation evolutionary-strategy (CMA-ES) [9] with the default settings and $\lambda =$DE configurations; (3) a $(\mu + \lambda)$EA that mutates buoys' position with a probability of $1/N$ using a normal distribution ($\sigma = 0.1 \times (U_b - L_b)$) when $\mu = 50$ and $\lambda = 25$; and (4) Particle Swarm optimisation (PSO) [8], with $\lambda=$ DE configurations , $c_1 = 1.5, c_2 = 2, \omega = 1$ (linearly decreased).

4.2 Sequential Placement Algorithms

Previous research [15–17] found that employing a neighbourhood search around the previously placed-buoys could help tune placements to exploit constructive interactions between buoys. The following two methods employ such local search.

Local Search + Nelder-Mead (LS-NM). LS-NM [17] is one of the most effective WEC placement methods. LS-NM places each buoy by sampling at a normally-distributed random deviation ($\sigma = 70$ m) from the previous buoy location. The best-sampled location is then optimised using N_s iterations of the Nelder-Mead search method. This process is repeated until all buoys are placed.

Adaptive Neuro-Surrogate Optimisation Method (ANSO). Here, we devise a novel approach with the intuition that (a) sequential placement of the converters provide a simple, yet effective baseline and (b) we can *learn* a surrogate to mimic the potential power output for an array of buoys during this placement process. ANSO follows a three step solution shown in Algorithm 1.

Algorithm 1. *ANSO*

1: **procedure** ADAPTIVE NEURO-SURROGATE OPTIMISATION (ANSO)
2: **Initialization**
3: $size = \sqrt{N} * 20000$ ▷ Farm size
4: $Res = 3$ ▷ angle resolution
5: $angle = \{0, Res, 2 \times Res, \dots, 360 - Res\}$ ▷ symmetric samples angle
6: $iters = Size([angle])$ ▷ Number of symmetric samples
7: $EvalSet = \{2^{nd}, 3^{rd}, 5^{th}, \dots, 15^{th}\}$ ▷ Set of evaluated buoys
8: $EstimSet = \{4^{th}, 6^{th}, 8^{th}, \dots, 16^{th}\}$ ▷ Set of estimated buoys
9: $S = \{\langle x_1, y_1 \rangle, \dots, \langle x_N, y_N \rangle\} = \perp$ ▷ Positions
10: $S_{(1)} = \{\langle size, 0 \rangle\}$ ▷ first buoy position
11: $energy = Eval([S_{(1)}])$
12: $bestPosition = S_{(1)};$
13:     **for** i in $[2, .., N]$ **do**
14:         $bestEnergy = 0;$
15:         **if** $i \in Evalset$ **then**   ▷ layouts should be evaluated by Simulator
16:             **for** j in $[1, .., iters]$ **do**
17:                 $(Sample_j, energy_j) = SymmetricSampleEval(angle_j, S_{(i-1)})$
18:                 **if** $Sample_j$ *is feasible* & $energy_j > bestEnergy$ **then**
19:                     $tPos = Sample_j$ ▷ Temporary buoy position
20:                     $bestEnergy = energy_j$
21:                     $bestAngle = j$
22:                 **end if**
23:             **end for**
24:             **if** *No feasible solution is found* **then**
25:                 $(Sample_1, energy_1) = rand(S_{(i-1)})$
26:             **end if**
27:             $(Es_1, Es_2) = SymmetricSampleEval(bestAngle \pm Res/2, S_{(i-1)})$
28:             $(S_{(i)}, energy) = FindbestS(tPos, Es_1, Es_2)$
29:             $DataSet_i = UpdateData(Sample, energy)$
30:         **else**   ▷ layouts should be estimated by the LSTM
31:             $(HyperParameters_i) = Optimise\text{-}Hyper(DataSet_i)$ ▷ Optimising by GWO
32:             $(Deep_i) = reTrain(Deep_i, DataSet_i, HyperParameters_i)$
33:             **for** j in $[1, .., iters]$ **do**
34:                 $(Sample_j, energy_j) = SymmetricSampleEstim(angle_j, S_{(i-1)}, Deep_i)$
35:                 **if** $Sample_j$ *is feasible* & $energy_j > bestEnergy$ **then**
36:                     $tPos = Sample_j$ ▷ Temporary buoy position
37:                     $bestEnergy = energy_j$
38:                     $bestAngle = j$
39:                 **end if**
40:             **end for**
41:         **end if**
42:     **end for**
43:     $(bestPosition', bestEnergy') = BackTrackingOp(bestPosition)$
44:     **return** $bestPosition', bestEnergy'$ ▷ Final Layout
45: **end procedure**

Symmetric Local Search (SLS): Inspired by LS-NM [16,17], in the first step we sequentially place buoys by conducting a symmetric local search (SLS) for each placement. SLS starts by placing the first buoy in the bottom corner of the field and then, for each subsequent buoy position, uniformly makes N_{iters} feasible local samples in sectors commencing at angles: $\{angles = [0°, Res°, 2 \times Res°, ..., 360 - Res°]\}$ and bounded by a radial distance between $50 + R_1 m$ and $50 + R_2 m$. From these the best sample is chosen Next, two extra neighbourhood samples are made near the best sample $(\pm Res/2)$ to further refine the placements. From these three, the sample with the highest absorbed power is then selected.

Learning the Neuro-Surrogate Model: As previously noted, the hydrodynamic simulator is computationally expensive to run. To speed up optimisation, we train a fast and accurate neuro-surrogate to estimate the power of layouts based on the position of the next buoy: (x_i, y_i). The key challenges to overcome in designing a neuro-surrogate are: (1) *function complexity*: a highly nonlinear and complex relationship between buoys' positions and absorbed farm power, (2) *changing dataset*: as more evaluations of the placements are performed, new data for training is collected that has to be incorporated, and, (3)*efficiency*: training time plus the hyper-parameter tuning has to be included in our computational budget.

For handling these challenges, we use a combination of recurrent networks with long-term-short-term-memory (LSTM) cells [10] (sequential learning strategy), and, an optimiser (GWO) [14] for tuning the network hyper-parameters for estimating the power of the layouts. The overall framework is shown in Fig. 1. The proposed LSTM network is designed for sequence-to-one regression in which the input layer takes 2D buoy positions (x_i, y_i) and the output of the regression layer is the estimated layout power. The LSTM training process is done using the back-propagation algorithm, in which the gradient of the cost function (in this case the mean squared error between the true ground-truth and the estimated output of the LSTM) at different layers is computed to update the weights.

For tuning the hyper-parameters of the LSTM we use the ranges: Mini-Batch size (5–100), learning rate (10^{-4}–10^{-1}), the maximum number of training epochs (50–600), LSTM layer number (one or two) and hidden node number (10–150). At each step of the position optimisation, a fast and effective meta-heuristic algorithm (GWO) [14] is used. This is because the collected data-set is dynamic in terms of input length (increases over time) and the arrangement of buoys. This hybrid idea embeds an adaptive learning process that converges in just a few evaluations (Fig. 5)), is accurate and easily scaled.

Backtracking Optimisation: The third component of ANSO is applying a backtracking optimisation strategy (BO). This is because the initial placements described above are based on greedy selection, the previous buoys' positions are revisited during this phase. Consequently, introducing backtracking can help maximise the power of the layouts. For this part, a 1+1EA [7] is employed. In each iteration, a buoy's position (x_i, y_i) with a normally distributed perturbation with standard deviation σ which is decreased linearly using an adaptive probability rate P_m. Each mutated position is evaluated by the simulator. Equation 4 shows how BO's control parameters are calculated.

$$\sigma_{iter} = \sigma_{Max} \times 0.08 \times iter/iter_{Max} \ \forall \ iter \in \{1, ..., iter_{Max}\}$$
$$P_{m_i} = (1/N) \times (1/(Power_{Buoy_i}/Max_{Power})) + \omega_i \ \forall \ i \in \{1, ..., N\} \quad (4)$$

where σ_{Max} is the initial mutation step size at $10\,\mathrm{m}$ and P_{m_i} shows the mutation probability of each buoy in the layout. Through these equations, the highest mutation probability rate is allocated to that buoy with the lowest power, based on the a-priori assumption that these buoys have most scope for improvement. In addition, the ω_i coefficient ranges from 0.1 (for the lowest power buoy) to 0 (highest power buoy). The allocated run time for the BO method is one hour. Algorithm 1 describes ANSO in detail.

5   Experiments

The adaptive tuning of hyper-parameters in ANSO allows it to match the needs of each layout problem. Moreover, no pre-processing time is required for collecting the relevant training data-set, ANSO is able to collect the required training data in real-time during the sampling and optimisation of previous buoy positions.

Table 1. Performance comparison of various heuristics for the 16-buoy case, based on maximum, median and mean power output layout of the best solution per experiment.

	DE	CMA-ES	PSO	$(\mu+\lambda)$ EA	LS-NM	ANSO-S_1	ANSO-S_2	ANSO-S_3	ANSO-S_4	ANSO-S_1-B	ANSO-S_2-B	ANSO-S_3-B	ANSO-S_4-B
Perth wave scenario (16-buoy)													
Max	1474381	1490404	1463608	1506746	1501145	1544546	1533055	1554926	1555446	1552108	1549299	1554833	**1559535**
Min	1455256	1412438	1433776	1486397	1435714	1513894	1489365	1531290	1543637	1535508	1502373	1543384	1549517
Mean	1462331	1476503	1450589	1494311	1479345	1534032	1514147	1543361	1550171	1544832	1525112	1549276	**1556073**
Median	1462697	1482974	1448835	1493109	1490195	1535162	1516162	1544076	1551105	1544733	1523082	1549701	**1556091**
STD	4742.1	23004.6	8897.7	6227.9	23196.4	7991.1	12092.2	7441.2	3333.5	5531.3	12663.7	4006.2	2783.2
Adelaide wave scenario (16-buoy)													
Max	1494124	1501992	1475991	1517424	1523773	1563935	1563249	1583623	1585626	1576713	1571181	**1589830**	1588297
Min	1468335	1478052	1452804	1488276	1496878	1558613	1520681	1565725	1571131	1566240	1527665	1567491	1576009
Mean	1479247	1488783	1461579	1502708	1513070	1561624	1541404	1573125	1575439	1572454	1552201	**1581643**	1578365
Median	1479707	1487430	1460687	1501805	1515266	1562548	1541101	1576658	1575092	1573763	1552663	**1582515**	1577353
STD	7704.9	8167.9	6670.9	8443.2	7434.7	2154.3	12366.9	7572.5	3676.1	3639.8	12373.1	6481.1	3428.9
Sydney wave scenario (16-buoy)													
Max	1520654	1529809	1525938	1528934	1524164	1523552	1523353	1523549	1524974	1531566	**1532200**	1528619	1531155
Min	1515231	1520031	1508729	1516014	1487836	1509677	1493596	1500115	1514248	1517559	1506128	1513182	1520086
Mean	1518047	1524054	1519251	1522625	1507594	1517627	1514384	1514300	1520597	1524357	1523382	1521277	**1526443**
Median	1518014	1523440	1520319	1522234	1507898	1518667	1516523	1518055	1521351	1524767	1524356	1522289	**1527839**
STD	1880.1	2767.8	5818.1	3887.1	10929.2	4871.7	8811.3	8642.02	4021.8	4161.7	6710.5	6393.02	3481.1
Tasmania wave scenario (16-buoy)													
Max	3985498	4063049	3933518	4047620	4082043	4144344	4085915	4121312	4135256	**4162505**	4104237	4143536	4160738
Min	3935990	3935833	3893456	3992362	3904892	4025709	4021772	4071497	4113146	4053715	4043849	4103441	4128702
Mean	3956691	4000087	3914316	4019472	4008228	4072874	4042537	4093453	4122447	4095608	4071852	4123334	**4145569**
Median	3951489	3994739	3914764	4019623	4020515	4066904	4033063	4091620	4121959	4079286	4074154	4124520	**4144359**
STD	17243.1	37701.2	13758.4	18377.5	54771.9	33897.8	19819.9	17367.4	6422.9	34789.9	16516.9	12411.4	10085.3

In this work, we test four strategies for buoy placement under ANSO these vary in the membership of the *EvalSet* – the set of buoys evaluated by the full simulator and the sample set used to train the neuro-surrogate model. The

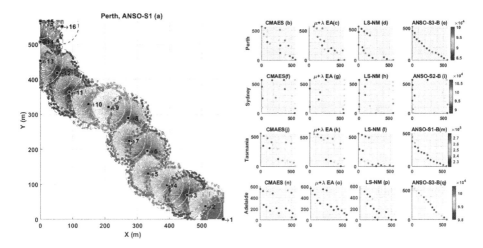

Fig. 2. The best-obtained 16-buoy layouts: figure (a) presents how the proposed hybrid method can optimise buoys position and estimate the power of some buoys $(4^{th}, 6^{th}, ..., 16^{th})$ sequentially. Two rings around each buoy show the exploration space($Res = 3°$, $\Delta R = 20$ m). Other figures show the best layouts arrangement of the four real wave scenarios based on Table 1.

Table 2. The average ranking of the proposed methods for ρ by Friedman test.

Rank	Adelaide		Perth		Sydney		Tasmania	
1	**ANSO-S_3-B**	**(1.75)**	**ANSO-S_4-B**	**(1.08)**	**ANSO-S_4-B**	**(3.00)**	**ANSO-S_4-B**	**(1.25)**
2	ANSO-S_4-B	(2.08)	ANSO-S_4	(3.08)	ANSO-S_1-B	(4.17)	ANSO-S_3-B	(2.75)
3	ANSO-S_3	(3.67)	ANSO-S_3-B	(3.17)	CMA-ES	(4.33)	ANSO-S_4	(3.00)
4	ANSO-S_4	(3.67)	ANSO-S_1-B	(4.00)	ANSO-S_2-B	(4.50)	ANSO-S_1-B	(4.67)
5	ANSO-S_1-B	(4.00)	ANSO-S_3	(4.42)	ANSO-S_3-B	(5.08)	ANSO-S_3	(5.00)
6	ANSO-S_1	(6.08)	ANSO-S_1	(6.00)	$(\mu + \lambda)$EA	(6.00)	ANSO-S_2-B	(6.00)
7	ANSO-S_2-B	(6.75)	ANSO-S_2-B	(6.50)	ANSO-S_4	(7.08)	ANSO-S_1	(6.33)
8	ANSO-S_2	(8.08)	ANSO-S_2	(8.00)	PSO	(7.92)	ANSO-S_2	(8.33)
9	LS-NM	(9.17)	$(\mu + \lambda)$EA	(9.25)	ANSO-S_1	(8.42)	LS-NM	(9.25)
10	$(\mu + \lambda)$EA	(9.92)	LS-NM	(10.50)	DE	(9.58)	$(\mu + \lambda)$EA	(9.42)
11	CMAES	(11.00)	CMA-ES	(10.67)	ANSO-S_3	(9.67)	CMA-ES	(10.25)
12	DE	(11.83)	DE	(11.83)	ANSO-S_2	(10.00)	DE	(11.75)
13	PSO	(13.00)	PSO	(12.50)	LS-NM	(11.25)	PSO	(13.00)

strategies tested are: (1) With $EvalSet = \{2^{nd}, 3^{rd}, 5^{th}, ..., 15^{th}\}$ so the neuro-surrogate is used to place buoys: $4, 6, 8, ..., 16$. The neuro-surrogate is trained prior to each placement using sampled positions used for the previous buoy placement. (2) Use $EvalSet = \{2^{nd}, 3^{rd}, 6^{th}, 9^{th}, ..., 15^{th}\}$ so the neuro-surrogate is used to place buoys: $4, 5, 7, 8, 10, 11, 13, 14, 16$. As with strategy 1 above, the previous sampled positions evaluated by the simulator are used to train the

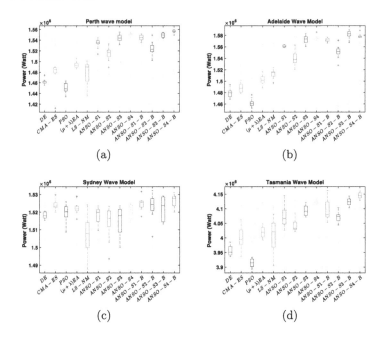

Fig. 3. Comparison of the algorithms' effectiveness for 16-buoy layouts in four real wave scenarios (Perth (a), Adelaide (b), Sydney (c), Tasmania (d)). The optimisation results show the best solutions of 10 independent runs.

neuro-surrogate model. (3) The same setup as the first strategy but the LSTM is trained by *all* previous simulator samples. (4) All evaluations are done by the simulator.

From these experiments, Table 1 shows the statistical results of the maximal power output of the 13 compared heuristics for 10 independent runs each for four real wave scenarios. As shown in Table 1, ANSO-S_4-B is best, on average, in Sydney, Perth and Tasmania. ANSO-S_3-B shows the best performance in Adelaide. However, all methodologies using the neuro-surrogate are competitive in terms of performance. The results of applying the Friedman test are shown in Table 2. Algorithms are ranked according to their best configuration for each run. Again, ANSO-S_3-B obtained first ranking in the Adelaide wave model and non-neuro-surrogate ANSO-S_4-B algorithm ranks highest in other scenarios. The best 16-buoy layouts of the 4 compared algorithms (CMAES, $(\mu + \lambda)$EA, LS-NM and the best-performing versions of ANSO) are shown in Fig. 2. The sampling used by the optimisation process of ANSO-S_1 is shown in Fig. 2(a). It shows how ANSO-S_1 explores each buoy's neighbourhood and modifies positions during backtracking.

Figure 3 shows box-and-whiskers plots for the best solutions' power output per-run for all approaches and all wave scenarios. It can be seen that the best mean performance is given by ANSO-S_4-B in three of four wave scenarios. In the Adelaide case study, ANSO-S_3-B performs best. Another interesting observation

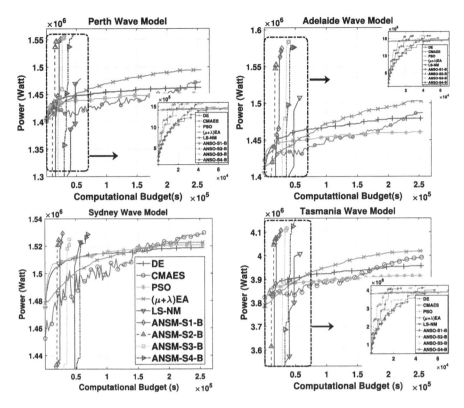

Fig. 4. Evolution and convergence rate of the average power output of the nine algorithms for four real wave models. A zoomed version of the plots is provided to give a better view of convergence speed.

is that, among population-based EAs, $(\mu + \lambda)$EA excels. However, both ANSO and LS-NM outperform all population-based methods.

Figure 4 shows the convergence diagrams of the average power output of the nine compared algorithms. In all wave scenarios, ANSO-S_2-B has the ability to converge very fast because it estimates two sequentially placed buoy's layout's power after each training process instead of evaluating one of these using the expensive simulator. Thus ANSO-S_2-B is, respectively, 3, 4.5 and 14.6 times faster, on average, than ANSO-S_4-B, LS-NM and $(\mu + \lambda)EA$. Note again, that these timings include training and configuration times.

For the neuro-surrogate model to produce accurate and reliable power estimation, we need to obtain good settings for hyper-parameters. Finding the best configuration for these parameters in such a continuous, multi-modal and complex search space is not a trivial challenge. Figure 5 shows the GWO performance for tuning the LSTM hyper-parameters for ANSO-S_1. The Pearson correlation coefficient test values (R-value) for all trained LSTMs estimates is $\bar{R} >= 0.7$. The most challenging training process is related to the power estimation of the

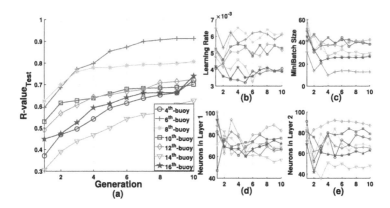

Fig. 5. Evolutionary (GWO) hyper-parameters optimisation: (a) test-set accuracy of the mean best configuration by cross-validation per generation. (b) and (c) learning rate and minibatch size for estimating the power of the seven buoys. Both (d) and (e) optimised neurons number in the first and second LSTM layers.

14th buoy because ANSO is faced with the boundary constraint of the search space, so the arrangement of the layouts change. Our code and auxiliary material are publicly available: https://cs.adelaide.edu.au/~optlog/research/energy.php.

6   Conclusions

Optimising the arrangement of a large WEC farm is computationally intensive, taking days in some cases. Faster and smarter optimisation methods are needed. We have shown that a neuro-surrogate optimisation approach, with online training and hyper-parameter optimisation, is able to outperform previous methods in terms of layout performance -3.2% to 3.6% better, respectively than $(\mu + \lambda)EA$ and LS-NM. Moreover, even including the time for training and tuning the LSTM network the neuro-surrogate model finishes optimisation faster than previous methods. Thus better results are obtained in less time – up to 14 times faster than the $(\mu + \lambda)EA$. The approach is also highly adaptable with the model's and its hyper-parameters being tuned online for each environment. Future work will include a more detailed analysis of the training setup of the neuro-surrogate to further focus training to the sectors most relevant to buoy placement and to further adapt training for placement of buoys once the farm boundary has been reached.

References

1. Alexandre, E., Cuadra, L., Nieto-Borge, J., Candil-Garcia, G., Del Pino, M., Salcedo-Sanz, S.: A hybrid genetic algorithm–extreme learning machine approach for accurate significant wave height reconstruction. Ocean Model. **92**, 115–123 (2015)

2. Bhattacharya, B., Shrestha, D., Solomatine, D.: Neural networks in reconstructing missing wave data in sedimentation modelling. In: Proceedings of the XXXth IAHR Congress, vol. 500, pp. 770–778, Thessaloniki (2003)
3. Cornejo-Bueno, L., Aybar-Ruíz, A., Jiménez-Fernández, S., Alexandre, E., Nieto-Borge, J.C., Salcedo-Sanz, S.: A grouping genetic algorithm–extreme learning machine approach for optimal wave energy prediction. In: 2016 IEEE Congress on Evolutionary Computation (CEC), pp. 3817–3823. IEEE (2016)
4. Cornejo-Bueno, L., Garrido-Merchán, E.C., Hernández-Lobato, D., Salcedo-Sanz, S.: Bayesian optimization of a hybrid system for robust ocean wave features prediction. Neurocomputing **275**, 818–828 (2018)
5. De Andrés, A., Guanche, R., Meneses, L., Vidal, C., Losada, I.: Factors that influence array layout on wave energy farms. Ocean Eng. **82**, 32–41 (2014)
6. Drew, B., Plummer, A.R., Sahinkaya, M.N.: A review of wave energy converter technology. Proc. Inst. Mech. Eng. Part A: J. Power Energy **223**(8), 887–902 (2009)
7. Droste, S., Jansen, T., Wegener, I.: On the analysis of the $(1+1)$ evolutionary algorithm. Theor. Comput. Sci. **276**(1–2), 51–81 (2002)
8. Eberhart, R., Kennedy, J.: A new optimizer using particle swarm theory. In: Proceedings of the Sixth International Symposium on Micro Machine and Human Science, MHS 1995, pp. 39–43. IEEE (1995)
9. Hansen, N.: The CMA evolution strategy: a comparing review. In: Lozano, J.A., Larrañaga, P., Inza, I., Bengoetxea, E. (eds.) Towards a New Evolutionary Computation Studies in Fuzziness and Soft Computing, vol. 192, pp. 75–102. Springer, Heidelberg (2006). https://doi.org/10.1007/3-540-32494-1_4
10. Hochreiter, S., Schmidhuber, J.: Long short-term memory. Neural Comput. **9**(8), 1735–1780 (1997)
11. James, S.C., Zhang, Y., O'Donncha, F.: A machine learning framework to forecast wave conditions. Coast. Eng. **137**, 1–10 (2018)
12. Li, L., Yuan, Z., Gao, Y.: Maximization of energy absorption for a wave energy converter using the deep machine learning. Energy **165**, 340–349 (2018)
13. Lu, K.H., Hong, C.M., Xu, Q.: Recurrent wavelet-based elman neural network with modified gravitational search algorithm control for integrated offshore wind and wave power generation systems. Energy **170**, 40–52 (2019)
14. Mirjalili, S., Mirjalili, S.M., Lewis, A.: Grey wolf optimizer. Adv. Eng. Softw. **69**, 46–61 (2014)
15. Neshat, M., Alexander, B., Sergiienko, N., Wagner, M.: A new insight into the position optimization of wave energy converters by a hybrid local search. arXiv preprint arXiv:1904.09599 (2019)
16. Neshat, M., Alexander, B., Sergiienko, N.Y., Wagner, M.: A hybrid evolutionary algorithm framework for optimising power take off and placements of wave energy converters. In: Proceedings of the Genetic and Evolutionary Computation Conference, GECCO 2019, pp. 1293–1301. ACM, New York (2019)
17. Neshat, M., Alexander, B., Wagner, M., Xia, Y.: A detailed comparison of metaheuristic methods for optimising wave energy converter placements. In: Proceedings of the Genetic and Evolutionary Computation Conference, GECCO 2018, pp. 1318–1325. ACM, New York (2018)
18. Sarkar, D., Contal, E., Vayatis, N., Dias, F.: Prediction and optimization of wave energy converter arrays using a machine learning approach. Renew. Energy **97**, 504–517 (2016)
19. Scruggs, J., Lattanzio, S., Taflanidis, A., Cassidy, I.: Optimal causal control of a wave energy converter in a random sea. Appl. Ocean Res. **42**, 1–15 (2013)

20. Sergiienko, N.Y.: Three-tether wave energy converter: hydrodynamic modelling, performance assessment and control. Ph.D. thesis (2018)
21. Storn, R., Price, K.: Differential evolution-a simple and efficient heuristic for global optimization over continuous spaces. J. Global Optim. **11**(4), 341–359 (1997)
22. Wu, G.: Radiation and diffraction by a submerged sphere advancing in water waves of finite depth. Proc. R. Soc. Lond. A **448**(1932), 29–54 (1995)

Lightweight Modal Regression for Stand Alone Embedded Systems

Taiki Watanabe and Koichiro Yamauchi[✉]

Chubu University, Matsumoto-cho 1200, Kasugai, Aichi, Japan
tp18015-8999@sti.chubu.ac.jp, k_yamauchi@isc.chubu.ac.jp
http://sakura.cs.chubu.ac.jp/

Abstract. Although the CPU power of recent embedded systems has increased, their storage space is still limited. To overcome this limitation, most embedded devices are connected to a cloud server so they can outsource heavy calculations. However, some applications must handle private data, meaning internet connections are undesirable based on security concerns. Therefore, small devices that handle private data should be able to work without internet connections. This paper presents a limited modal regression model that restricts the number of internal units to a certain fixed number. Modal regression can be used for multivalued function approximation with limited sensory inputs. In this study, a kernel density estimator (KDE) with a fixed number of kernels called "limited KDE" was constructed. We will demonstrate how to implement the limited KDE and how to construct a lightweight algorithm for modal regression using a system-on-chip field-programmable gate array device.

Keywords: Multivalued function · Regression · Modal regression · Kernel Density Estimator (KDE) · Incremental learning

1 Introduction

Recent developments in embedded systems have enabled the completion of costly computations on edge devices. However, the storage capacity and computational power of such devices are still less than those of enterprise servers. Therefore, most heavy computations are outsourced to a cloud server. This means that such edge devices must be connected to the internet. If data privacy is not a major concern, this is convenient method for performing high-cost computations. However, based on security concerns, some applications should not use active internet connections.

In this study, we constructed a standalone system to overcome security issues. In such a system, all heavy calculations must be completed on an edge device. To this end, Yamamoto and Yamauchi (2019) proposed "swap kernel regression," which is a kernel method for regression that collaborates with secondary storage.

A part of this research was supported by a Special grant of Chubu University.

© Springer Nature Switzerland AG 2019
T. Gedeon et al. (Eds.): ICONIP 2019, LNCS 11954, pp. 367–379, 2019.
https://doi.org/10.1007/978-3-030-36711-4_31

Therefore, swap kernel regression moves kernels whose output values are small enough to ignore into secondary storage while moving essential kernels from secondary storage into main memory. This system requires a method for identifying essential kernels in secondary storage before calculating their outputs. In other words, this system has difficulty in detecting target kernels accurately prior to replacement. Therefore, it is difficult to implement this system using the page replacement algorithm used in most operating systems.

The goal of our study was to construct a multivalued function approximator for a small devices using a technique similar to swap-kernel regression. The proposed method can be easily applied to system-on-chip (SoC) field-programmable gate array (FPGA) devices. Multivalued functions are typically implemented for information processing in partially observable environments. Good examples of such partially observable environments can be found in the reinforcement learning field (e.g. Kaelbling et al. (1998)Kaelbling, Littman, and Cassandra). Recently, one researcher demonstrated that maximum power point tracking for photovoltaic devices also includes this type of problem Yamauchi (2018). In such situations, a problem solver typically generates several solution candidates for a current sensory input. Because limited sensory inputs only represent a portion of the current situation, such systems must detect hidden states based on limited sensory inputs.

Multivalued function approximation can be realized using modal regression Einbeck and Tutz (2006), Yao et al. (2012) and Sasaki et al. (2016). Modal regression is an application of the kernel density estimator (KDE) that can be used to manage learning algorithms Yamauchi and Bhargav (2018). The KDE is also suitable for realizing incremental learning, meaning it is suitable for practical applications. However, the KDE simply increases the number of kernels with an increasing number of learning samples. This increase in the number of kernels wastes the computational power of a system. In Yamauchi (2018), we proposed a method that facilitates learning using a fixed number of kernels. In this study, we improved on the method above by introducing a lightweight modal regression algorithm that restricts the number of kernels to be calculated.

The remainder of this paper is organized as follows. Section 2 describes related works. Section 3 reviews the KDE and modal regression. Section 4 shows the modal regression on a fixed budget. Section 5 presents an example of hardware implementation. Section 6 discusses the proposed lightweight model for embedded systems. Section 7 presents experimental results and Sect. 8 concludes the paper.

2   Related Works

David et al. proposed a novel method called support vector data description (SVDD) TAX and DUIN (2004). SVDD represents a data distribution using a small number of kernels. Although SVDD seems to be suitable for implementing a compact data model for embedded systems, it does not support incremental learning, unlike our proposed method.

Cao et al. proposed a method called "SOMKE." Cao et al. (2012), which aims to reduce the computational complexity of the KDE, similar to our method. The SOMKE method generates a small number of kernel centroids using a self-organizing feature map (SOM). The resulting network reduces computational complexity by reducing the total number of kernels. In contrast, our system mainly focuses on the kernels that must be calculated for regression of a current input.

Although the method proposed in this paper is based on swap-kernel regression Yamamoto and Yamauchi (2019), our model does not include secondary storage. Instead, the main and secondary storage modules in the swap-kernel regression model correspond to an FPGA-based accelerator and CPU core with corresponding main memory, respectively (see Fig. 1).

3   Modal Regression

Modal regression Einbeck and Tutz (2006) approximates a multivalued function by searching for local peaks in a given sample distribution. Modal regression combined the KDE with the partial mean shift (PMS) method.

3.1   KDE

The KDE is a variation of a Parzen window Parzen (1962). Let χ be a set of given samples and $\chi = \{(\boldsymbol{x}, y) \mid \boldsymbol{x} \in \mathbb{R}\}$. The estimator approximates the given sample distribution function using a number of kernels called a support set, which is denoted as S_t. The kernels used are Gaussian kernels and

$$p(\boldsymbol{X}) \propto \hat{p}(\boldsymbol{X}) \equiv \sum_{i \in S_t} K \left(\frac{\|\boldsymbol{x} - \boldsymbol{X}_i\|}{h_x} \right), \tag{1}$$

where $K \left(\frac{\|\boldsymbol{x} - \boldsymbol{X}_i\|}{h_x} \right) \equiv \exp \left(-\frac{\|\boldsymbol{x} - \boldsymbol{X}_i\|^2}{h_x^2} \right)$. As mentioned in Sasaki et al. (2016), the KDE used for modal regression should approximate the peak points of a distribution, rather than the distribution itself.

3.2   PMS

Modal regression searches for the local peaks in a distribution model represented by the KDE. The PMS method facilitates rapid convergence to the nearest peak from an initial point. We denote the initial point as $\boldsymbol{x}_0$, which represents the starting point for the search for peak points. Modal regression iteratively modifies the current value of y as follows:

$$y_{new} \leftarrow \frac{\sum_{i \in S_t} y_{old} K \left(\frac{|y_{old} - y_i|}{h_y} \right) K \left(\frac{\|\boldsymbol{X} - \boldsymbol{X}_i\|}{h_x} \right)}{\sum_{j \in S_t} K \left(\frac{|y_{old} - y_j|}{h_y} \right) K \left(\frac{\|\boldsymbol{X} - \boldsymbol{X}_j\|}{h_x} \right)}, \tag{2}$$

where $\boldsymbol{X}$ denotes $\boldsymbol{X} = [x_1, \cdots x_N, y]^T$. It should be noted that $\boldsymbol{X}$ includes y.

4   Modal Regression on a Fixed Budget

The original modal regression model records all given samples $\chi =$ $\{(\boldsymbol{x}, y) \mid \boldsymbol{x} \in \mathbb{R}\}$ by allocating the same number of kernels, each of which has a centroid of $\boldsymbol{u}_i = [\boldsymbol{x}_i \; y_i]^T$. However, if the storage space is limited to a certain capacity, the number of kernels are also restricted. To overcome this issue, we developed a minimum modal regression model in our previous work Yamauchi and Bhargav (2018). Minimum modal regression learns a set of given samples incrementally, but does not allocate a new kernel if an input is similar an existing kernel centroid. Instead, it projects the current sample onto the space spanned by existing kernels. However, this method does not restrict the number of kernels to a fixed budget. In another study, we improved on this method to realize incremental learning for a kernel density estimator with fixed storage space Yamauchi (2018). Additionally, the PMS method was modified to reduce the set of kernels calculated for a current input. Instead of calculating new kernels, existing kernels are divided into several groups using the fuzzy c-means method.

4.1   KDE on a Fixed Budget

In our previous work, we proposed a modal regression method with a minimum number of kernels Yamauchi and Bhargav (2018). Although this method reduces kernel usage to a minimum number, the number is not bounded. We also extended this method to create a definite bound on kernel size Yamauchi (2018). In this study, we will extend the method proposed in Yamauchi (2018). In the following explanations, we denote the Gaussian kernel $K \left(\frac{\|\boldsymbol{X} - \boldsymbol{X}_t\|}{h_x} \right)$ as the dot product of two vectors $k(\boldsymbol{x}_t, \cdot)$ and $k(\boldsymbol{x}, \cdot)$ in the Hilbert space[1] to represent the learning algorithm using simple algebraic equations. Therefore, $K \left(\frac{\|\boldsymbol{X} - \boldsymbol{X}_t\|}{h_x} \right) = \langle k(\boldsymbol{x}_t, \cdot), k(\boldsymbol{x}, \cdot) \rangle$, where $\langle \cdot, \cdot \rangle$ denotes the dot product.

The proposed method utilizes three strategies to perform KDE learning. The following paragraphs outline these three strategies.

Allocation of New Kernels. Typically, the KDE allocates a new kernel when a new sample $\boldsymbol{X}_t = [\boldsymbol{x}_t \; y_t]^T$ is introduced, as shown below. Let $\hat{P}_t$ be the predicted distribution from the KDE at the t-th round.

$$\hat{P}_t = \hat{P}_{t-1} + K(\boldsymbol{X}_t, \cdot), \quad S_t = S_{t-1} \cup \{t\}, \tag{3}$$

where S_t denotes the set of support set at the t-th round. However, if current sample $\boldsymbol{X}_t = [\boldsymbol{x}_t \; y_t]^T$ is similar to one of the existing kernel centroids, the KDE should not waste a new kernel to represent the new sample under a fixed budget conditions, but it should modify the current distribution to reflect $\boldsymbol{X}_t = [\boldsymbol{x}_t \; y_t]^T$. To modify current the distribution without allocating new kernels, the proposed method introduces the extension coefficient for each kernel W_i. Specifically, W_i

---

[1] Note that Gaussian kernel satisfies the condition for the reproduction kernel.

represents frequency of appearing similar inputs around the i-th kernel centroid. Therefore,

$$\hat{P}_{t-1} \equiv \sum_{i \in S_{t-1}} W_i K(\boldsymbol{X}_i, \cdot) \tag{4}$$

Therefore, Eq. (3) is rewrote as

$$\hat{P}_t = \hat{P}_{t-1} + W_t K(\boldsymbol{X}_t, \cdot), \quad S_t = S_{t-1} \cup \{t\}. \tag{5}$$

Note that the initial value of W_t is 1.

Adjustment of Kernel Centroids. The nearest kernel centroid relative to the current sample is moved toward the current sample. However, if the nearest kernel centroid is too far from the current sample, it should not be moved. To estimate the suitability of using this option, the output value of the nearest kernel for the current sample is evaluated. If $K\left(\frac{\|\boldsymbol{X}_t - \boldsymbol{X}_{n^*}\|}{h_x}\right) > \epsilon$, where $n^* = \arg\min_j \|\boldsymbol{X}_t - \boldsymbol{X}_j\|^2$,

$$\boldsymbol{X}_{n^*} = \boldsymbol{X}_{n^*} + \frac{1}{W_{n^*}}(\boldsymbol{X}_t - \boldsymbol{X}_{n^*}) \tag{6}$$

Next, the extension parameter for the nearest kernel W_{n^*} is updated as

$$W_{n^*} = W_{n^*} + 1 \tag{7}$$

Therefore, if the current instance is similar to the j-th kernel centroid, W_j increases.

Pruning the Least-Recently-Activated Kernel with Replacement. If there are no kernels to be replaced with a new kernel, the proposed method identifies a kernel to be pruned using the "least recently and frequently used" (LRFU) evaluation function Lee et al. (2001). The LRFU was originally proposed for the page replacement algorithm by operating systems. To detect the least-recently-activated kernel, each kernel has an additional parameter value n_i which represents the maximum number of activated inputs. Therefore, the n_{n^*} for the nearest kernel n^* is incremented as

$$n_{n^*} = n_{n^*} + 1, \tag{8}$$

while the n_i values for all kernels are reduced as follows

$$n_i = (1 - \gamma)n_i, \tag{9}$$

where $0 < \gamma \ll 1$.

Therefore, the kernel whose n_i is the smallest is replaced by the new kernel. The pruning process is represented as follows.

$$\hat{P}_t = \hat{P}_{t-1-p^*} + W_t K(\boldsymbol{X}_t, \cdot), \quad p^* = \arg\min_i n_i. \tag{10}$$

where $W_t = 1$. Note that the n_t value for the newly allocated kernel is set to t as an initial value. Algorithm 1 summarizes the process described above.

Algorithm 1. Kernel density estimator on a budget

Require:
  {Previous KDE}, $\hat{\boldsymbol{P}}_{t-1}$
  {current input}, $\boldsymbol{x}_t$
  {Previous Support Set}, S_{t-1}
  {Redundancy threshold}, ε
  if $|S_{t-1}| < B$ **then**
    $W_t = 1$
    $\hat{\boldsymbol{P}}_t = \hat{\boldsymbol{P}}_{t-1} + W_t K(\boldsymbol{x}_t, \cdot)$
    $C_t = C_{init}$ {initialization of LRFU parameter}
    $S_t = S_{t-1} \cup \{t\}$
  else
    $n^* = \arg\min_j \|\boldsymbol{x}_t - \boldsymbol{x}_j\|^2$
    if $K\left(\frac{\|\boldsymbol{X}_t - \boldsymbol{X}_{n^*}\|}{h_x}\right) > \epsilon$ **then**
      $\boldsymbol{X}_{n^*} = \boldsymbol{X}_{n^*} + \frac{1}{W_{n^*}}(\boldsymbol{X}_t - \boldsymbol{X}_{n^*})$ {Update centroid.}
      $W_{n^*} = W_{n^*} + 1$
    else
      $u^* = \arg\min_k C_k$ {Find the LRFU kernel.}
      $W_{i^*} += W_{u^*}$ where $i^* = \arg\min_{i \neq u^*} \|\boldsymbol{x}_i - \boldsymbol{x}_{u^*}\|^2$
      $\boldsymbol{X}_{u^*} = \boldsymbol{X}_t$
    end if
  end if
  for all $i \in S_{t-1}$ **do**
    $C_i = (1 - \gamma)C_i$ {Update LRFU parameter}
  end for
  RETURN $\hat{\boldsymbol{P}}_t$

4.2 Weighted PMS

The KDE with a fixed budget described in the previous section maintains the limited size of the support set by applying pruning with replacement. In this process, the expansion parameter of each kernel W_i has a certain value that represents the target distribution. Therefore, $W_i > 1$ indecates that the i-th kernel shares the duty of more than one kernel. In our previous work Yamauchi and Bhargav (2018), we have improved the PMS method to adjust the solution according to the expansion parameters, as follows.

$$y_{new} \leftarrow \frac{\sum_{i \in A_t} y_{old} W_i K\left(\frac{|y_{old}-y_i|}{h_y}\right) K\left(\frac{\|\boldsymbol{X}-\boldsymbol{X}_i\|}{h_x}\right)}{\sum_{j \in A_t} W_j K\left(\frac{|y_{old}-y_j|}{h_y}\right) K\left(\frac{\|\boldsymbol{X}-\boldsymbol{X}_j\|}{h_x}\right)} \tag{11}$$

where A_t denotes the set of kernels to be calculated and $A_t \subseteq S_t$. A_t is adjusted to reduce the computational complexity, which will be discussed further in Subsect. 6.2.

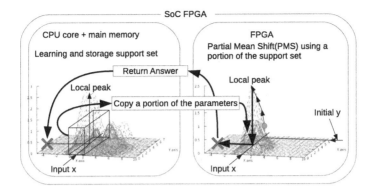

Fig. 1. Schematic of the proposed system on SoC FPGA.

5   Hardware Implementation

The main goal of this study was the implementation of modal regression on a budget on small-scale hardware, such as an FPGA. We utilized the XILINX PYNQ-Z1 SoC FPGA, which is a hybrid of the ARM-core and FPGA. In the proposed method, the ARM-core performs learning and the FPGA executes weighted PMS. The parameters generated during learning are sent to the FPGA and the results calculated by the FPGA are sent back to the ARM-core. The schematic of the proposed system is shown in Fig. 1.

In this study, we developed the circuit for the FPGA using the Xilinx Vivard High-Level Synthesis software. The developed circuit facilitates rapid calculations for Gaussian kernel functions and the weighted PMS method using pipeline processing.

As shown in Fig. 1, the proposed system uploads a portion of the parameters for modal regression to the FPGA prior to calculation. This helps to save hardware resources and reduce computational complexity. The following section presents the proposed lightweight model.

6   Lightweight Model

The proposed method selects a portion of the kernels to be calculated for a current input and sends the associated parameters to the FPGA. To accomplish this task, we introduce some additional cluster kernels. Each kernel in the proposed method has attribute values that represent how close each kernel is to the cluster kernels. Therefore, if the current input is closest to one of the cluster kernels, only the existing kernels whose attribute values for the closest cluster kernel are greater than a predefined threshold are sent to the FPGA and calculated. There are many clustering algorithms that can be used for selection operations. For example, k-means method MacQueen (1967) accomplish the clustering of existing kernel centroids and produces crisp clustering results. However, crisp clustering sometimes leads to inaccurate PMS results. To avoid this issue, fuzzy c-means clustering Dunn (1973) was employed to generate cluster centroids and perform clustering on existing kernels.

In this case, each existing kernel has values indicating its degree of belonging to all clusters. The system chooses the kernels whose degrees of belonging to the closest cluster are greater than a predefined threshold for calculation.

6.1 Clustering Existing Kernels

Fuzzy c-means method requires a fixed number of cluster centers. Fuzzy c-means clustering requires a fixed number of cluster centroids and is outlined below.

Step1 Initialize cluster centroids by initializing x_i as a random vector.
Step2 Detect the cluster centroid x_k as

$$X_k = \frac{\sum_j^N (u_{kj})^m X_j}{\sum_j^N (u_{kj})^m}, \tag{12}$$

where x_i denotes the i-th cluster centroid, u_{ij} denotes the degree of belonging of the i-th centroid to the j-th cluster, and m denotes the weighting exponent, which was set to 1.3 in our experiments.
Step3 Update the degree of belonging for each cluster to minimize quantization error as follows:

$$u_{ik} = \left[\sum_j^c \left(\frac{\|X_i - X_k\|}{\|X_i - X_j\|} \right)^{\frac{2}{m-1}} \right]^{-1}, \quad X_i \neq X_k, \tag{13}$$

where $k = 1, 2, \cdots$.
Step4 If the magnitude of parameter change is smaller than that in the previous iteration, the system stops the modification of parameters. Otherwise, the system returns to Step2.

6.2 Lightweight PMS

To reduce computational complexity, the proposed system uses c-means clustering to reduce the number of kernels to be calculated for the current input. Initially, the proposed method detects the cluster kernels that are closest to the current input. We denote the current input as x_t, and the suffix of the closest cluster kernel is

$$j^* = \arg\min_i \|x_t - x_i\|^2 \tag{14}$$

Note that the vectors x_t and x_i do not include the dimensions for y^2. The system predicts appropriate y values such that $X = [x, y]^T$ are the local peaks of $\hat{p}(X)$. Next, the set of kernels to be calculated is defined as

$$A_t = \{i | u_{j^* i} > \epsilon\}. \tag{15}$$

---

[2] Remember that X in Eq. (2) includes the output dimension and $X = [x, y]^T$.

The set A_t is used to restrict the number of kernels for weighted PMS (see Eq. (11)).

7 Experiments

In this study, we tested whether or not limited modal regression works on a synthetic noisy dataset and a real traffic flow dataset.

The synthetic dataset consisted of 10000 samples from a noisy sigmoidal function, whose outputs are sigmoidal function outputs with noise generated from a normal distribution $\mathcal{N}(0,1)$.

The performance of the proposed method was evaluated based on accuracy and processing time. The accuracy of the proposed method was evaluated using the synthetic dataset. Specifically, the differences between resultant regression outputs and the outputs from the source functions were evaluated.

The calculation speed of the lightweight version of the proposed method was compared to that of the proposed method without the lightweight optimization, which was described in Sect. 6.

7.1 Evaluation of Accuracy and Processing Time for Single-Valued Regression

Accuracy evaluation was conducted using the synthetic dataset of noisy sig-moidal function outputs. A dataset with 10000 samples in the form of (x_t, y_t) was obtained as follows:

$$y_t = Y_t[x_t] + n, \quad n \sim \mathcal{N}(0,1), \tag{16}$$

where Y_t is

$$Y_t[x_t] = \frac{10}{1 + \exp(-x_t)}. \tag{17}$$

The 10000 samples were fed into the proposed methods and other existing methods sequentially. The regression outputs from the proposed methods were then compared to (x_t, Y_t). We denote the regression output from the modal regressor as $\hat{y}(x_t)$. The mean squared error for all samples was calculated as follows:

$$E = \frac{1}{N} \sum_t^N (Y_t[x_t] - \hat{y}(x_t))^2. \tag{18}$$

The hyperparameters for the proposed method were $h_x = 0.5$ and $h_y = 0.5$, and the number of kernels was set to 100. The number of cluster kernels was varied from one to six. It should be noted that the proposed method with only one cluster kernel is equivalent to the method without the lightweight optimization.

Figure 2 presents the resultant regression outputs from the proposed method.

One can see that the regression outputs (red curve) have the shape of a sigmoid-like function. We evaluated the mean squared error using Eq. (18), as

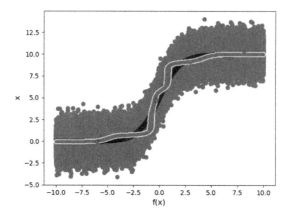

Fig. 2. Example regression outputs for the noisy sigmoid function dataset (blue points and red curve represent the learning samples and regression outputs, respectively). (Color figure online)

well as the processing time, while changing the number of cluster kernels. The results are listed in Table 1. One can see that as the number of cluster kernels increases, the mean squared error also increases. This is because as the number of cluster kernels increases, the number of kernels calculated for each sample decreases.

Table 1. Mean squared errors and processing times for different numbers of cluster kernels.

# of cluster kernles	1	3	4	5	6
Processing time	345.48 [sec]	235.38 [sec]	225.83 [sec]	215.07 [sec]	200.641 [sec]
Mean square errors	0.1878	0.1886	0.1894	0.1897	0.2198

The proposed lightweight method completed the regression process 33% faster than the method without the lightweight optimization. Additionally, the memory usage of the proposed lightweight method is approximately 30% lower than that of the normal modal regressor.

Evaluation Using the Traffic Flow Dataset. The traffic flow dataset contains data regarding carriageway flow versus speed flow on a highway in England MIDIAS Site 1030(LM205). This dataset is available at http://tris. highwaysengland.co.uk/detail/trafficflowdata. The data expresses the relationships between car speed and traffic volume during the month of January, 2006. Data were collected every 15 min and the dataset contains data from four 24 h periods. The data distribution of the first period is similar to those of the other periods. Therefore, we only considered the first 24 h period (8580 instances) of data. Additionally, the velocity and volume data were normalized via division by 140 and 1400, respectively.

We compared the regression results of the proposed lightweight version to those of normal modal regression on a budget. For the proposed method, the number of kernels was set to 200. The comparison results are presented in Fig. 3.

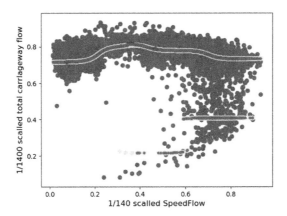

Fig. 3. Responses of the lightweight version of modal regression on a budget and those of the proposed method without the lightweight optimization. Red and yellow curves are the responses of the lightweight method and the method without the lightweight optimization, respectively. The green points represent the cluster centroid positions for the lightweight version of the proposed method. (Color figure online)

One can see that almost all of the responses of the proposed lightweight method are duplicates of those of normal modal regression on a budget.

The calculation speeds of the proposed lightweight model, normal modal regression on a budget, and modal regression on a budget implemented on an SoC FPGA were analyzed. Figure 3 reveals that the results of the lightweight version of the proposed method are nearly the same as those of the proposed method without the lightweight optimization. We also examined the processing times of these two methods, as shown in Table 2.

Table 2. Comparison of processing times

Proposed method	53.54 [sec]
Lightweighted proposed method	37.66 [sec]

From Table 2, one can see that the processing time of the lightweight version of the proposed method is approximately 30% less than that of the method without the lightweight optimization.

Finally, we analyzed the speed of the weighted PMS method accelerated by an FPGA. We compared the ARM-core based calculation speed to the FPGA calculation speed for the PMS method using the traffic flow dataset. The results are listed in Table 3. One can see that the calculation speed of the proposed method is approximately 41% faster than that of ARM-core based normal PMS.

Table 3. Comparison of calculation speeds for the PMS method

Existing method on the ARM-core	1559.877 [sec]
Proposed method on the ARM-core	1050.899 [sec]
Proposed method with accelered by FPGA	957.997 [sec]

8   Conclusion

This paper proposed a lightweight modal regression method for embedded systems. To make facilitate modal regression on embedded devices, the proposed method reduces not only the number of kernels used, but also the computational complexity of PMS by selecting optimal kernels for PMS. To this end, the proposed method divides kernels into several groups and chooses one group to calculate an output for the current input.

We conducted computer simulations of the proposed method to evaluate the accuracy and speed of regression. The proposed method performs more than 38% faster than a system that does not reduce in the number of kernels used for calculating the PMS while maintaining similar accuracy.

By using modal regression, we can handle problem domains in which a portion of the sensory inputs are not available. Under such conditions, multiple solution candidates should be generated by a regressor. The proposed method can quickly generate several candidate solutions and is useful for many practical applications such as those proposed in Yamauchi (2018).

Furthermore, we implemented one part of the proposed method on an SoC FPGA. Preliminary experimental results suggest that a hardware implementation of modal regression can increase its processing speed. In the near future, we will attempt to implement the entire algorithm on an SoC FPGA.

Although the proposed method is based on swap-kernel regression Yamamoto and Yamauchi (2019), it does not use any secondary storage. The secondary storage used by swap-kernel regression corresponds to the ARM-core and its main memory in our model. However, it is easy to extend our current model to utilize secondary storage.

References

Cao, Y., He, H., Man, H.: SOMKE: kernel density estimation over data streams by sequences of self-organizing maps. IEEE Trans. Neural Netw. Learn. Syst. **23**(8), 1254–1268 (2012). https://doi.org/10.1109/TNNLS.2012.2201167

Dunn, J.C.: A fuzzy relative of the isodata process and its use in detecting compact well-separated clusters. J. Cybern. **3**(3), 32–57 (1973). https://doi.org/10.1080/01969727308546046

Einbeck, J., Tutz, G.: Modelling beyond regression functions: an application of multimodal regression to speed flow data. Appl. Stat. **55**(4), 461–475 (2006). https://doi.org/10.1111/j.1467-9876.2006.00547.x

Kaelbling, L.P., Littman, M.L., Cassandra, A.R.: Planning and acting in partially observable stochastic domains. Artif. Intell. **101**, 99–134 (1998). https://doi.org/10.1016/S0004-3702(98)00023-X

Lee, D., Noh, S., Min, S., Choi, J., Kim, J., Cho, Y., Sang, K.C.: LRFU: a spectrum of policies that subsumes the least recently used and least frequently used policies. IEEE Trans. Comput. **50**(12), 1352–1361 (2001)

MacQueen, J.: Some methods for classification and analysis of multivariate observations. In: Cam, L.M.L., Neyman, J. (eds.) Proceedings of the Fifth Berkeley Symposium on Mathematical Statistics and Probability, vol. 1, pp. 281–297. University of California Press, Berkeley (1967)

Parzen, E.: On estimation of a probability density function and mode. Ann. Math. Stat. **33**(3), 1065–1076 (1962). https://doi.org/10.1214/aoms/1177704472

Sasaki, H., Ono, Y., Sugiyama, M.: Modal regression via direct log-density derivative estimation. In: Hirose, A., Ozawa, S., Doya, K., Ikeda, K., Lee, M., Liu, D. (eds.) ICONIP 2016. LNCS, vol. 9948, pp. 108–116. Springer, Cham (2016). https://doi.org/10.1007/978-3-319-46672-9_13

Tax, D.M., Duin, R.P.: Support vector data description. Mach. Learn. **54**(1), 45–66 (2004). https://doi.org/10.1023/B:MACH.0000008084.60811.49

Yamamoto, M, Yamauchi, K.: Swap kernel regression. In: Tetko, I.V., Kůrková, V., Karpov, P., Theis, F. (eds.) ICANN 2019. LNCS, vol. 11728, pp. 579–592. Springer, Cham (2019). https://doi.org/10.1007/978-3-030-30484-3_47

Yamauchi, K.: A Quick Maximum Power Point Tracking Method Using an Embedded Learning Algorithm for Photovoltaics on Roads, pp. 85–106. InTechOpen (2018). https://doi.org/10.5772/intechopen.79711

Yamauchi, K., Bhargav, V.N.: Minimum modal regression. In: Marsico, M.D., di Baja, G.S., Fred, A. (eds.) ICPRAM2018 7th International Conference on Pattern Recognition Applications and Methods, pp. 448–455 (2018)

Yao, W., Lindsay, B.G., Li, R.: Local modal regression. Stat. J. Nonparametr. **24**(3), 647–663 (2012). https://doi.org/10.1080/10485252.2012.678848

Sparse Modeling of Nonlinear Dynamics in Heterogeneous Reactions

Masaki Ito[1], Tatsu Kuwatani[2], Ryosuke Oyanagi[2], and Toshiaki Omori[1(✉)]

[1] Department of Electrical and Electronic Engineering,
Graduate School of Engineering, Kobe University,
1-1 Rokkodai-cho, Nada-ku, Kobe 657-8501, Japan
omori@eedept.kobe-u.ac.jp
[2] Research Institute for Marine Geodynamics,
Japan Agency for Marine-Earth Science and Technology,
2-15 Natsushima-cho, Yokosuka 237-0061, Japan

Abstract. Surface heterogeneous reactions are chemical reactions with conjugation of multiple phases, and they have the intrinsic nonlinearity of their dynamics caused by the effect of surface-area between different phases. We propose a sparse modeling approach for extracting nonlinear dynamics of surface heterogeneous reactions from noisy observable data. We employ sparse modeling algorithm and sequential Monte Carlo algorithm to partial observation problem, in order to simultaneously extract substantial reaction terms and surface models from a number of candidates. Using our proposed method, we show that the rate constants of dissolution and precipitation reactions, which are typical examples of surface heterogeneous reactions, necessary surface models and reaction terms underlying observable data were successfully estimated only from the observable temporal changes in the concentration of the dissolved intermediate product.

Keywords: Sparse modeling · Heterogeneous reactions · Nonlinear dynamics · Probabilistic time series analysis

1 Introduction

It is essential to extract underlying dynamics from observed time series data in natural sciences. In general, the dynamics is nonlinear and there are a lot of candidate nonlinear terms. Furthermore, observed time series data is generally noisy. Therefore, it is important to develop a data driven method that can extract only substantial elements from a lot of candidates by using noisy observed time series data.

In recent years, sparse modeling is attracting as a means of extracting important factors from high-dimensional natural science data. Sparse modeling has been widely applied to various fields in the natural sciences such as physics [1], brain science [2] and earth sciences [3]. In particular, it is necessary to establish

© Springer Nature Switzerland AG 2019
T. Gedeon et al. (Eds.): ICONIP 2019, LNCS 11954, pp. 380–391, 2019.
https://doi.org/10.1007/978-3-030-36711-4_32

a method for estimation of the dynamics from time series data by using such sparse modeling.

Among the nonlinear dynamics in natural sciences, we focused on heterogeneous reactions. These reactions are chemical reactions with conjugation of multiple phases [4] and observed time series data is noisy and the dynamics is nonlinear [5,6]. It is necessary to extract important reactions from many candidates since there are many types of heterogeneous reactions which are linear or nonlinear in surface area reactions and reaction terms [7]. These candidates depend on rate constants. In order to correctly estimate heterogeneous reaction dynamics inside the earth, we introduce sparse modeling for nonlinear dynamics in heterogeneous reactions.

In this study, we propose an effective method to simultaneously estimate rate constants and concentrations from nonlinear dynamics of heterogeneous reaction by using sparse modeling and sequential Monte Carlo method. First, we formulate state space model of nonlinear dynamics for heterogeneous reactions including multiple candidates. Next, we use sequential Monte Carlo method to understand the model. We introduce sparse modeling in order to estimate true rate constants from many candidates. Using the proposed method, we experiment with simulation data and show that nonlinear dynamics for heterogeneous reactions can be estimated from noisy data.

2   Estimation Algorithm

2.1   Heterogeneous Reactions

Heterogeneous reactions are chemical reactions with conjugation of multiple phases. In the earth's crust, solid and liquid phases interact, dissolve and precipitate. For example, serpentinization in oceanic lithosphere (hydrolysis reaction with peridotite-water interaction) is a storage process of water brought into the earth's deep region. It significantly changes the physical properties of the oceanic lithosphere and also affects the occurrence of earthquakes in subduction zone [6]. It is important to understand heterogeneous reactions in order to figure out the dynamics of rock formation near surface of the earth.

We show in Fig. 1 surface heterogeneous reactions in the laboratory. In the reactions, solid reactant $N^{(\mathrm{r})}$ dissolves into liquid intermediate product C and liquid intermediate product C precipitates into solid product $N^{(\mathrm{p})}$.

We assume that simple heterogeneous surface reactions obey following differential equations [4,8].

$$\frac{dN^{(\mathrm{r})}}{dt} = k^{(\mathrm{r})} S^{(\mathrm{r})} \left(N^{(\mathrm{r})} \right) \left(C - C_{eq}^{(\mathrm{r})} \right) \tag{1}$$

$$\frac{dN^{(\mathrm{p})}}{dt} = k^{(\mathrm{p})} S^{(\mathrm{p})} \left(N^{(\mathrm{p})} \right) \left(C - C_{eq}^{(\mathrm{p})} \right) \tag{2}$$

$$\frac{dN^{(\mathrm{r})}}{dt} + \frac{dC}{dt} + \frac{dN^{(\mathrm{p})}}{dt} = 0 \tag{3}$$

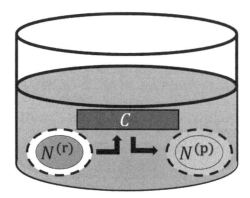

Fig. 1. An example of surface heterogeneous reactions consisting of reactant $N^{(r)}$, intermediate product C and product $N^{(p)}$. Solid reactant dissolves into liquid intermediate product and it precipitates into solid product. These reactions depend on rate constants $k^{(r)}$ and $k^{(p)}$ and surface area reactions $S^{(r)}(N^{(r)})$ and $S^{(p)}(N^{(p)})$.

where $C_{eq}^{(r)}$ and $C_{eq}^{(p)}$ are solubility coefficients and constants. $k^{(r)}$ and $k^{(p)}$ are rate constants and $S^{(r)}(N^{(r)})$ and $S^{(p)}(N^{(p)})$ indicates surface area reactions. The parameters with (r) and (p) respectively relate to reactant and product. Rate constants $k^{(r)}$ and $k^{(p)}$, and surface area reactions $S(N)$ are very important for heterogeneous reactions.

$k^{(r)}$ and $k^{(p)}$ are rate constants. These constants indicate how fast the reactants $N^{(r)}$ dissolve and products $N^{(p)}$ precipitates and do not depend on the concentration, but on the temperature. These two rate constants are important values to determine what kind of mineral dissolves into liquid intermediate product and precipitates into solid product.

$S^{(r)}(N^{(r)})$ and $S^{(p)}(N^{(p)})$ indicates surface area reactions between two different solid and liquid phases and there are many types of surface area reaction. They have a strong influence on heterogeneous surface reaction. The formula of surface area reaction $S(N)$ is expressed as follows.

$$S(N) \propto N^{\alpha} \tag{4}$$

where α is the order of surface area reaction. $S(N)$ depends on the number N of moles of solid phase and it is proportional to α-th power of N.

We show typical time course of heterogeneous reaction when α is unity in Fig. 2. When the time is zero, solid reactant $N^{(r)}$ only exsists and dissolves into liquid intermediate product C as time passes. When intermediate product C dissolves sufficiently, it precipitates into solid product $N^{(p)}$. With more time, solid reactant $N^{(r)}$ almost disappears and intermediate product C and solid product $N^{(p)}$ become constant. The heterogeneous reactions depend on surface area.

However, inside the actual earth, we can assume more complicated heterogeneous reactions than them. For example, there are many types of surface area

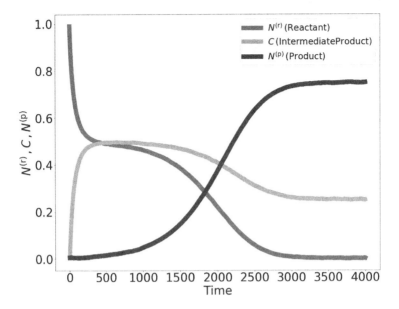

Fig. 2. A typical behavior of heterogeneous reactions. At $t = 0$, solid reactant $N^{(\mathrm{r})}$ only exists and dissolves into liquid intermediate product C as time passes. When intermediate product C dissolves sufficiently, it precipitates into solid product $N^{(\mathrm{p})}$. With more time, solid reactant $N^{(\mathrm{r})}$ almost disappears and intermediate product C and solid product $N^{(\mathrm{p})}$ become constant. The heterogeneous reactions depend on surface area.

reactions and a multiplier of intermediate product C [7]. Therefore, we must develop a method which estimates more complicated heterogeneous reactions such as a lot of nonlinear reactions and surface area reactions.

2.2 Differential Equations of More Complicated Surface Heterogeneous Reactions

In order to estimate more complicated heterogeneous reactions which have many candidates of nonlinear reactions and surface area reactions, we improve simple heterogeneous surface reactions which obeys Eqs. (1)–(3). We consider multiple surface area reactions and a multiplier of intermediate product C. Furthermore, we assume a multiplier of the difference between intermediate product and solubility coefficient, $(C^m - C_{eq})$. Therefore, we assume heterogeneous reactions that simultaneously consider linear and nonlinear dynamics in C^m $(m = 1, 2, \cdots, M)$ and $(C^m - C_{eq})^n$ $(n = 1, 2, \cdots, N)$. The complicated heterogeneous reactions are expressed by the following differential equations.

$$\frac{dN^{(\mathrm{r})}}{dt} = \sum_{l=1}^{L}\sum_{m=1}^{M}\sum_{n=1}^{N} k_{l,m,n}^{(\mathrm{r})} S_l^{(\mathrm{r})} \left(N^{(\mathrm{r})}\right)\left(C^m - C_{eq}^{(\mathrm{r})}\right)^n \tag{5}$$

$$\frac{dN^{(\mathrm{p})}}{dt} = \sum_{l=1}^{L}\sum_{m=1}^{M}\sum_{n=1}^{N} k_{l,m,n}^{(\mathrm{p})} S_l^{(\mathrm{p})} \left(N^{(\mathrm{p})}\right)\left(C^m - C_{eq}^{(\mathrm{p})}\right)^n \tag{6}$$

$$\frac{dN^{(\mathrm{r})}}{dt} + \frac{dC}{dt} + \frac{dN^{(\mathrm{p})}}{dt} = 0 \tag{7}$$

where l denotes the type of surface area model. m is a multiplier of intermediate product C. n is a multiplier of reaction terms $(C^m - C_{eq})$.

As for surface area reactions, Fig. 3 shows typical their models and formulas for them are expressed as follows.

$$S_1\left(N\right) \propto N^{\frac{2}{3}} \tag{8}$$

$$S_2\left(N\right) \propto N^1 \tag{9}$$

In the Fig. 3, the top figure indicates Eq. (8). This surface area reaction keeps the geometrical shape before and after heterogeneous reactions. If the reactant is a sphere of radius $r(t)$, the volume of sphere $N(t) \propto \frac{4}{3}\pi r^3(t)$ is established. In the Fig. 3, the bottom figure indicates Eq. (9). This surface area reaction changes in proportion to the number of moles of the reactant and it is called the bulk reaction.

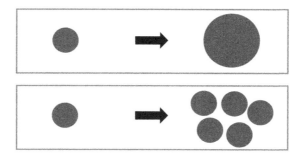

Fig. 3. Two surface area reaction models of heterogeneous reactions between solid and liquid phases. The top figure indicates a surface area reaction which keeps the geometrical shape before and after heterogeneous reactions. The bottom figure indicates a surface area reaction which changes in proportion to the number of moles of the reactant before and after heterogeneous reactions.

By considering many types of surface area reactions, a multiplier of intermediate product C and a multiplier of reaction terms $(C^m - C_{eq})$, our research includes more complex nonlinear terms than simple heterogeneous surface reactions and it is possible to handle many heterogeneous reactions. Such three factors enable us to determine nonlinear dynamics in heterogeneous reactions by estimation of rate constants $\boldsymbol{k} = \left\{ k^{(\mathrm{r})}_{l,m,n}, k^{(\mathrm{p})}_{l,m,n} \right\}$. Therefore, we must estimate them accurately.

2.3 State-Space Model for Surface Heterogeneous Reactions

Before estimating the rate constants $\boldsymbol{k} = \left\{ k^{(\mathrm{r})}_{l,m,n}, k^{(\mathrm{p})}_{l,m,n} \right\}$, it is necessary to determine solid reactant $N^{(\mathrm{r})}(t)$, liquid intermediate product $C(t)$ and solid product $N^{(\mathrm{p})}(t)$. In order to estimate them, we propose nonlinear state-space model for surface heterogeneous reactions and Fig. 4 shows graphical model of it according to Eqs. (5)–(7).

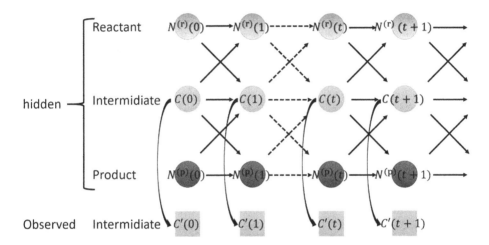

Fig. 4. Graphical model of surface heterogeneous reactions. According to Eqs. (5)–(7), solid reactant $N^{(\mathrm{r})}(t)$ and liquid intermediate product $C(t)$ affect solid product $N^{(\mathrm{p})}(t)$. Only the noisy liquid intermediate product can be observed as $C'(t)$. We estimate hidden variables $N^{(\mathrm{r})}(t)$, $C(t)$ and $N^{(\mathrm{p})}(t)$ based on observed variable $C'(t)$.

State-space model is composed of observation model and system model. Observation model represents relationship between hidden variables and observation variables. In our research, solid reactant $N^{(\mathrm{r})}$, liquid intermediate product C and solid product $N^{(\mathrm{p})}$ are hidden variables and noisy liquid intermediate product C' is an observation variable. Our observation model is expressed as follows.

$$C'(t) = C(t) + \xi(t) \tag{10}$$

where $\xi(t)$ indicates an observation noise and obeys the normal distribution. System model denotes relationship between hidden variables and other hidden variables. System model obeys Eqs. (5)–(7).

State-space model estimates hidden variables x_t $(t = 1, \cdots, T)$ based on an observed variable y_t $(t = 1, \cdots, T)$. In our research, $x_t = [N^{(\mathrm{r})}(t), C(t), N^{(\mathrm{p})}(t)]$ and $y_t = [C'(t)]$ are established. We consider the case of estimating the hidden variables x_t when we obtain the observed variable $y_{1:T} = [y_1, \cdots, y_T]$. The prediction distribution from time $t - 1$ to t is expressed as follows [9,10].

$$p(x_t|y_{1:t-1}) = \int p(x_t|x_{t-1}) p(x_{t-1}|y_{1:t-1}) dx_{t-1} \tag{11}$$

where $p(x_t|x_{t-1})$ is system model. $p(x_{t-1}|y_{1:t-1})$ is filter distribution at the time $t - 1$ and it is expressed as follows at the time t.

$$p(x_t|y_{1:t}) = \frac{p(y_t|x_t) p(x_t|y_{1:t-1})}{p(y_t|y_{1:t-1})} \tag{12}$$

where $p(y_t|y_{1:t-1}) = \int p(y_t|x_t)p(x_t|y_{1:t-1})dx_t$ is established. $p(x_t|y_{1:t-1})$ is the observation model and $p(x_t|y_{1:t-1})$ is a prediction distribution.

In order to obtain this state-space model, we use particle filter. It is a estimation algorithm of nonlinear and non-Gaussian state-space model and a kind of sequential Monte Carlo method. The feature of the particle filter is to estimate a conditional distribution by using the hidden variables x_t created by from hundreds to millions of particles and calculating likelihoods w_t with the observed variable y_t at that time. We suppose that the number of particles is N and $X_{t|t} = [x_{t|t}^{(i)}]_{i=1}^{N}$ is set of the hidden variables at the time t. For each time $t = 1, \cdots, T$, the particle filter estimates $X_{t|t}$ in the following way.

1. We make an N-dimensional random number $X_{0|0} = [x_{0|0}^{(i)}]_{i=1}^{N}$.
2. For each time $t = 1, \cdots, T$, we perform steps (a), (b) and (c).
   (a) For each particles i $(i = 1, \cdots, N)$, we perform steps (i) and (ii).
       i. According to Eq. (11), we estimate the prediction distribution of $N_{t-1|t-1}^{(\mathrm{r})}$, $C_{t-1|t-1}$, $N_{t-1|t-1}^{(\mathrm{p})}$ and obtain $N_{t|t-1}^{(\mathrm{r})}$, $C_{t|t-1}$, $N_{t|t-1}^{(\mathrm{p})}$
       ii. We assume that the conditional distribution follows Gaussian distribution and use Eq. (13) to calculate the likelihood $w_t^{(i)}$ based on the concentration of observed intermediate products C'_t at time t.

$$w_t^{(i)} = p\left(y_t|x_{t:t-1}^{(i)}\right) = \frac{1}{\sqrt{2\pi\sigma^2}} \exp\left(-\frac{\left(C'_t - C_{t:t-1}^{(i)}\right)^2}{2\sigma^2}\right) \tag{13}$$

   where σ is standard deviation of observation noise.
   (b) We solve $W_t = \sum_{i=1}^{N} w_t^{(i)}$.
   (c) We resample $x_{t|t-1}^{(i)}$ from $X_{t|t-1} = \{x_{t|t-1}^{(1)}, \cdots, x_{t|t-1}^{(N)}\}$ according to the probability of $\tilde{w}_t^{(i)} = w_t^{(i)}/W_t$ and generate $X_{t|t} = \{x_{t|t}^{(1)}, \cdots, x_{t|t}^{(N)}\}$.

By this method, it is possible to estimate the hidden variables of solid reactant $N^{(\mathrm{r})}$, liquid intermediate product C and solid product $N^{(\mathrm{p})}$ from the noisy observed liquid intermediate product C'.

2.4   Sparse Modeling Algorithm for Rate Constants

Rate constants k play a very important role in determining not only reaction rates, but also surface area reactions, linear or nonlinear of reaction term ($C^m - C_{eq}$) and intermediate product C in Eqs. (5) and (6). We use sparse modeling to estimate rate constants k. On the case that the information is much, but the meaningful information is only a part, sparse modeling extract only some important information. According to Eqs. (5)–(7), the following formula can be derived [2].

$$-\frac{C(t+\Delta t) - C(t)}{\Delta t} = \sum_{l=1}^{L}\sum_{m=1}^{M}\sum_{n=1}^{N} k_{l,m,n}^{(r)} S_l^{(r)} \left(N^{(r)}(t)\right) \left(C^m(t) - C_{eq}^{(r)}\right)^n$$

$$+ \sum_{l=1}^{L}\sum_{m=1}^{M}\sum_{n=1}^{N} k_{l,m,n}^{(p)} S_l^{(p)} \left(N^{(p)}(t)\right) \left(C^m(t) - C_{eq}^{(p)}\right)^n \quad (14)$$

where we discretize time in the differential equation according to Eqs. (5)–(7) and obtain time step interval Δt. we can understand the left-handside of Eq. (14) is expressed by a linear sum of product of rate constants $k_{l,m,n}$ and the reaction term $S_l(N(t))(C^m(t) - C_{eq})^n$. In Eq. (5), we use Lasso which is a kind of sparse modeling method and Lasso is expressed as follows [11].

$$k' = \arg\min_{k} \left\{||C' - k^{\mathrm{T}} A||_2^2 + \lambda ||k||_1\right\} \quad (15)$$

where C' is the observable noisy data of liquid intermediate product. A is a matrix, called a design matrix, λ is a regularization coefficient that controls a relative importance of a data-dependent error $||C' - k^{\mathrm{T}} A||_2^2$ and a regularization term $||k||_1$. In order to obtain an appropriate value of λ, we use S-fold cross-validation error [11].

Figure 5 shows a conceptual diagram of the estimation method of surface area reaction by using Lasso in heterogeneous reaction. We assume the rate constants k and Lasso extracts only the necessary heterogeneous reactions by estimating each value of the rate constant with zero or non zero.

3   Expeiment

Our proposed method is a combination of sequential Monte Carlo and sparse modeling. We estimate hidden variables of solid reactant $N^{(r)}$, liquid intermediate product C and solid product $N^{(p)}$ from a noisy observed liquid intermediate product C' by using sequential Monte Carlo method. We use sparse modeling to estimate the rate constants $k = \left\{k_{l,m,n}^{(r)}, k_{l,m,n}^{(p)}\right\}$. By alternately performing these two calculations a sufficient times, we can simultaneously estimate $N^{(r)}, C, N^{(p)}$ and $k = \left\{k_{l,m,n}^{(r)}, k_{l,m,n}^{(p)}\right\}$. Note that the regularization coefficient λ is optimized in terms of cross-validation error. Figure 6 shows a conceptual diagram of our proposed method.

Many types of
heterogeneous reactions

Estimating each value of the rate
constants k with zero or non zero

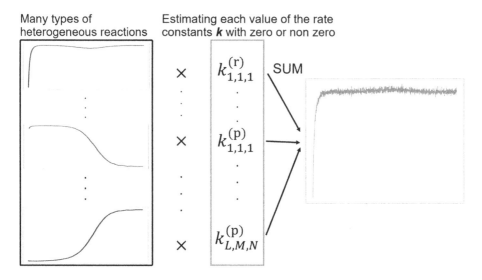

Fig. 5. The concept of sparse modeling for nonlinear dynamics in heterogeneous reactions. The proposed method with sparse modeling extracts only the necessary rate constants $k_{l,m,n}^{(r)}$ and $k_{l,m,n}^{(p)}$ from many candidates of them and estimates each value of the rate constant with zero or nonzero value.

We validate the proposed method using simulation data. In Eqs. (5) and (6), we set $L = 2, M = 2, N = 2$. L denotes the type of surface area model, M is a multiplier of intermediate product C and N is a multiplier of the reaction term ($C^n - C_{eq}$). Therefore, the number of rate constants k is 16. In the simulation data, only rate constants $k_{2,1,1}^{(r)}$ and $k_{2,1,1}^{(p)}$ have nonzero value and the other 14 rate constants have zero values.

Figure 7(a) shows the observed noisy data of liquid intermediate product C' and Fig. 7(b) shows the result of estimating hidden variables of solid reactant $N^{(r)}$, liquid intermediate product C and solid product $N^{(p)}$ from observed liquid intermediate product C'. The dotted lines represent true values and solid lines represent estimated values. As shown in Fig. 7(b), we find that estimated values, $N^{(r)}$, C and $N^{(p)}$ are similar to true values. Therefore, by the only noisy observed liquid intermediate product C', we can estimate hidden variables $N^{(r)}$, C and $N^{(p)}$.

Also, Fig. 8 shows the result of estimating the 16 rate constants k. As shown in Fig. 8, the proposed method with sparse modeling correctly extracts only necessary rate constants $k_{2,1,1}^{(r)}$ and $k_{2,1,1}^{(p)}$ from many candidates of them and estimates each value of the rate constant with zero or nonzero value. Furthermore, the proposed method can estimate not only whether rate constants k is a non-zero value or a zero value, but also variables of $k_{2,1,1}^{(r)}$ and $k_{2,1,1}^{(p)}$ successfully.

As mentioned in Sect. 2.2, there are two types of surface area reactions. A surface area reaction which expands or contracts while maintaining the geometrical shape is estimated by $k_{1,m,n}^{(r)}$, $k_{1,m,n}^{(p)}$. Also, a surface area reaction which

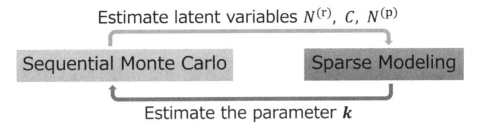

Fig. 6. A conceptual diagram of our proposed method. Sequential Monte Carlo estimate the hidden variables of solid reactant $N^{(\mathrm{r})}$, liquid intermediate product C and solid product $N^{(\mathrm{p})}$ and sparse modeling estimate the rate constants $k = \left\{ k^{(\mathrm{r})}_{l,m,n}, k^{(\mathrm{p})}_{l,m,n} \right\}$.

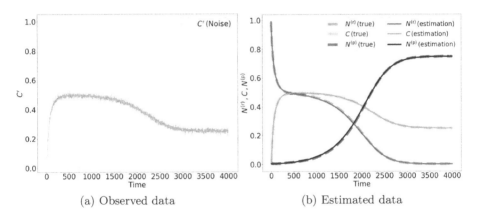

(a) Observed data   (b) Estimated data

Fig. 7. (a) shows noisy observed liquid intermediate product C'. (b) shows estimated hidden variables of solid reactant $N^{(\mathrm{r})}$, liquid intermediate product C and solid product $N^{(\mathrm{p})}$ from noisy observed liquid intermediate product C'. The dotted lines represent true values and solid lines represent estimated values. We can understand that estimated values, $N^{(\mathrm{r})}$, C and $N^{(\mathrm{p})}$ are similar to true values. Therefore, by only observed liquid intermediate product C', we can estimate hidden variables $N^{(\mathrm{r})}$, C and $N^{(\mathrm{p})}$.

changes in proportion to the number of moles of reactant is estimated by $k^{(\mathrm{r})}_{2,m,n}$, $k^{(\mathrm{p})}_{2,m,n}$. In our research, $k^{(\mathrm{r})}_{2,1,1}$ and $k^{(\mathrm{p})}_{2,1,1}$ have nonzero value and the others have almost zero value. Therefore, it indicates that our proposed method can distinguish the difference between these two surface area reactions and extract the heterogeneous reaction of $n = 1$ and $m = 1$ from candidate linear and nonlinear terms $(C^m - C_{eq})^n$.

4   Conclusion

We have proposed a sparse modeling approach for extracting nonlinear dynamics of surface heterogeneous reactions from noisy observable data. The features of

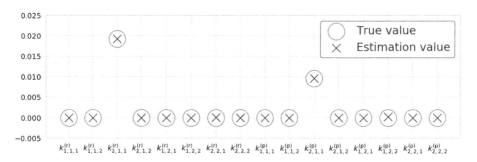

Fig. 8. Estimated rate constants $\boldsymbol{k} = \left\{ k_{l,m,n}^{(\mathrm{r})}, k_{l,m,n}^{(\mathrm{p})} \right\}$. In $k_{l,m,n}$, l denotes a type of surface area model, m is a multiplier of intermediate product C and n is a multiplier of a difference between intermediate product and solubility coefficient, $(C^m - C_{eq})$. Circles show the true values, whereas crosses show the estimated values. Circles and crosses overlap in almost all parameters.

our proposed method categorizes three aspects, l $(l = 1, 2, \cdots, L)$ types of surface area reactions, a multiplier of intermediate product C^m $(m = 1, 2, \cdots, M)$ and a multiplier of reaction term $(C^m - C_{eq})^n$ $(n = 1, 2, \cdots M)$. Therefore, we consider many candidates of heterogeneous reactions. We focused on the nonlinear dynamics that the reactions depend on surface area reaction of liquid phase and solid phase and formulated state space model in order to estimate the concentrations of heterogeneous reactions. By introducing sequential Monte Carlo algorithm, we estimated the hidden variables of solid reactant, liquid intermediate product and solid product from the observable noisy data of liquid intermediate product. Also, we used sparse modeling to estimate rate constants and determine a surface area reaction.

In order to confirm the effectiveness of our proposed method, we validated it using simulation data. We showed that our proposed method can successfully estimate hidden variables of solid reactant $N^{(\mathrm{r})}$, liquid intermediate product C, solid product $N^{(\mathrm{p})}$ and rate constants $\boldsymbol{k} = \left\{ k_{l,m,n}^{(\mathrm{r})}, k_{l,m,n}^{(\mathrm{p})} \right\}$ from an only noisy observed liquid intermediate product.

Acknowledgments. This work is partially supported by Grants-in-Aid for Scientific Research for Innovative Areas "Initiative for High-Dimensional Data driven Science through Deepening of Sparse Modeling" [JSPS KAKENHI Grant No. JP25120010] and for Scientific Research [JSPS KAKENHI Grant No. JP16K00330], and a Fund for the Promotion of Joint International Research (Fostering Joint International Research) [JSPS KAKENHI Grant No. JP15KK0010] from the Ministry of Education, Culture, Sports, Science and Technology of Japan, and Core Research for Evolutional Science and Technology (CREST) [Grant No. JPMJCR1914], Japan Science and Technology Agency, Japan.

References

1. Yang, J., Wright, J., Huang, T.S., Ma, Y.: Image super-resolution via sparse representation. IEEE Trans. Image Process. **19**(11), 2861–2873 (2010)
2. Otsuka, S., Omori, T.: Estimation of neuronal dynamics based on sparse modeling. Neural Netw. **109**, 137–146 (2019)
3. Honma, M., et al.: Imaging black holes with sparse modeling. J. Phys.: Conf. Ser. **699**, 012006 (2016)
4. Omori, T., Kuwatani, T., Okamoto, A., Hukushima, K.: Bayesian inversion analysis of nonlinear dynamics in surface heterogeneous reactions. Phys. Rev. E **94**(3), 033305 (2016)
5. Zhu, C., Lu, P., Zheng, Z., Ganor, J.: Coupled alkali feldspar dissolution and secondary mineral precipitation in batch systems: 4. numerical modeling of kinetic reaction paths. Geochimica et Cosmochimica Acta **74**(14), 3963–3983 (2010)
6. Okamoto, A., Ogasawara, Y., Ogawa, Y., Tsuchiya, N.: Progress of hydration reactions in olivine-H_2O and orthopyroxenite-H_2O systems at $250°C$ and vapor-saturated pressure. Chem. Geol. **289**(3–4), 245–255 (2011)
7. Lasaga, A.C.: Kinetic Theory in the Earth Sciences. Princeton University Press, Princeton (2014)
8. Atkins, P., Paula, J.: Physical Chemistry, 7th edn. Oxford University Press, Oxford (2002)
9. Kitagawa, G.: Non-gaussian state—space modeling of nonstationary time series. J. Am. Stat. Assoc. **82**(400), 1032–1041 (1987)
10. West, M., Harrison, J.: Bayesian Forecasting and Dynamic Models. Springer, Heidelberg (2006)
11. Bishop, C.M.: Pattern Recognition and Machine Learning. Springer, Heidelberg (2006)

Neural Learning Models

Sparse Least Squares Low Rank
Kernel Machines

Di Xu[1]([✉]), Manjing Fang[1], Xia Hong[2], and Junbin Gao[1]

[1] Discipline of Business Analytics, The University of Sydney Business School,
The University of Sydney, Sydney, NSW 2006, Australia
{dixu3140,mfan9400}@uni.sydney.edu.au, junbin.gao@sydney.edu.au
[2] Department of Computer Science, University of Reading, Reading RG6 6AH, UK
x.hong@reading.ac.uk

Abstract. A general framework of low rank least squares support vector machine (LR-LSSVM) is introduced in this paper. The special structure of controlled model size of the low rank kernel machine brings in remarkable sparsity and hence gigantic breakthrough in computational efficiency. In the meantime, a two-step optimization algorithm with three regimes for gradient descent is proposed. For demonstration purpose, experiments are carried out using a novel robust radial basis function (RRBF), the performances of which mostly dominate.

Keywords: Least squares support vector machine · Low Rank
Kernels · Robust RBF function · End-to-end modeling

1 Introduction

With the proliferation of big data, one wishes to build sparse models with more efficient algorithms in the settings of practical nonlinear modeling. Kernel machines (KMs) have attracted great attention since support vector machines (SVM) was introduced [8]. In fact, KMs have extended SVM by implementing the linearity in high dimensional feature space under the feature mapping implicitly determined by Mercer kernel function. As one of the most well-known members of the KM family, SVM has good generalization and insensitivity to overfitting [7].

The Performance of SVM greatly depends on kernel types, among which Gaussian RBF kernel normally champions others. Nonetheless, Gaussian RBF has non-negligible deficiencies in nonlinear boundary separation and therefore further optimization of its structure is intensively needed. Amari and Wu [1] modified kernels using a so-called information-geometric and data-dependent method to boost the performance of kernelized SVM. Yu *et al.* [12] enhanced kernels by taking advantages of regularization.

One of the main advantages of standard SVM is its model sparsity determined by the so-called support vectors. However, sparsity is not pre-determined and a computationally demanding quadratic programming problem has to be

© Springer Nature Switzerland AG 2019
T. Gedeon et al. (Eds.): ICONIP 2019, LNCS 11954, pp. 395–406, 2019.
https://doi.org/10.1007/978-3-030-36711-4_33

optimized in order to obtain support vectors [5]. Thus, a massive progress in proposing computationally efficient SVM algorithms has been explored. One of the examples is the introduction of least squares SVM (LSSVM) [9]. Instead of the margin constraints in the standard SVM, equality constraints are introduced in LSSVM. The resulting quadratic programming problem can be solved by a set of linear equations [9]. Nevertheless, equality constraints of LSSVM lead to an evaluation of all possible pairs of data in kernel functions. Therefore, LSSVM loses the sparsness in the standard SVM and is infeasible for large scale data learning. To make LSSVM sparse, researchers considered extending LSSVM to the Ramp loss function and produce sparse models with extra computational complexity, see [6]. This strategy has been extended to more general insensitive loss functions in [11]. Recently, Zhu et al. [13] proposed a way to select effective patterns from training datasets for fast support vector regression learning. However, there is not yet extension in classification. Chen [2] proposed a method for building a sparse kernel model by extending the so-called orthogonal least squares (OLS) algorithm [3] and kernel techniques. Based on the so-called significant vectors, Gao et al. [4] proposed a more straightforward way to learn the significant regressors from training data for the kernel regression modelling.

Almost all the aforementioned modelling methods extract patterns from the entire training dataset. Recently, Hong *et al.* [5] proposed a new LR-LSSVM based on simplex basis functions (LR-LSSVM-SBF), successfully building a sparse and fast modeling algorithm. The model size is no longer determined by the given training data while the key patterns will be learnt straightaway. We further explore this idea and extend it to fit a kind of robust radial basis functions. The main contributions of this paper are summarized as follows,

1. Given that the aforementioned models learn the data patterns under regression settings, this paper focuses on classification settings with a controlled or pre-defined model size;
2. The kernel function proposed in this paper takes the form of composition of basis function components which are adaptive to the training data. This composition form opens the door for a fast closed form solution, avoiding the issue of kernel matrix inversion in the case of large scale datasets;
3. A new criterion is proposed for the final model selection in terms of pattern parameters of location and scale of basis functions; and
4. A two-step optimization algorithm is proposed to simplify the learning procedure.

The rest of this paper is organized as follows. In Sect. 2, we present a brief background on several related models. Section 3 proposes our robust RBF kernel function and its classification model. Section 4 describes the artificial and real-world datasets and conducts several experiments to demonstrate the performance of the model and algorithm. And Sect. 5 concludes the paper.

2 Background and Notation

In this section, we start introducing necessary notation for the purpose of presenting our model and algorithm. We mainly consider binary classification problems. For the multi-class classification problems, as usual, the commonly used heuristic approach of "one-vs-all" or "one-vs-one" can be adopted.

Given a training dataset $\mathcal{D} = (\boldsymbol{X}, \boldsymbol{t}) = \{(\boldsymbol{x}_n, t_n)\}_{n=1}^N$ where N is the number of data, $\boldsymbol{x}_n \in \mathbb{R}^D$ is the feature vector and $t_n \in \{-1, 1\}$ is the label for the n-th data, respectively.

KM methods have been used as a universal approximator in data modeling. The core idea of the KMs is to implement a linear model in a high dimensional feature space by using a feature mapping ϕ defined as [8]

$$\boldsymbol{x} \in \mathbb{R}^D \rightarrow \phi(\boldsymbol{x}) \in \mathcal{F},$$

which induces a *Mercer* kernel function in the input space

$$k(\boldsymbol{x}_i, \boldsymbol{x}_j) = \langle \phi(\boldsymbol{x}_i), \phi(\boldsymbol{x}_j) \rangle,$$

where $\langle \cdot, \cdot \rangle$ is the inner product on the feature space $\mathcal{F}$.

In general, an affine linear model of KMs is defined as

$$y(\boldsymbol{x}) = \langle \phi(\boldsymbol{x}), \boldsymbol{w} \rangle + b, \tag{1}$$

where $b \in \mathbb{R}$ is the bias parameter and $\boldsymbol{w} \in \mathcal{F}$ is the parameter vector of high dimensionality, most likely in infinite dimension. It is infeasible to solve for the parameter vector $\boldsymbol{w}$ directly. Instead, the so-called kernel trick transforms the infinite dimension problem to a finite dimension problem by relating the parameters $\boldsymbol{w}$ to the data as

$$\boldsymbol{w} = \sum_{n=1}^N a_n t_n \phi(\boldsymbol{x}_n). \tag{2}$$

A learning algorithm will focus on solving for N parameters $\boldsymbol{a} = (a_1, a_2, ..., a_N)^T \in \mathbb{R}^N$ under an appropriate learning criterion.

For the sake of convenience, define

$$\boldsymbol{k}(\boldsymbol{x}, \boldsymbol{X}) = \left[k(\boldsymbol{x}, \boldsymbol{x}_1)\ k(\boldsymbol{x}, \boldsymbol{x}_2) \cdots k(\boldsymbol{x}, \boldsymbol{x}_N) \right]^T \in \mathbb{R}^N.$$

Then, under (2), model (1) can be expressed in terms of new parameters $\boldsymbol{a}$ as[1]

$$y(\boldsymbol{x}) = \boldsymbol{k}(\boldsymbol{x}, \boldsymbol{X})^T (\boldsymbol{a} \circ \boldsymbol{t}) + b. \tag{3}$$

where $\circ$ means the component-wise product of two vectors.

---

[1] If we are considering a regression problem, there is no need to add t_n in the model (3).

All the KMs algorithms are involved with the so-called kernel matrix, as defined below

$$K = \begin{bmatrix} k(\boldsymbol{x}_1, \boldsymbol{x}_1) & \cdots & k(\boldsymbol{x}_1, \boldsymbol{x}_N) \\ \vdots & \ddots & \vdots \\ k(\boldsymbol{x}_N, \boldsymbol{x}_1) & \cdots & k(\boldsymbol{x}_N, \boldsymbol{x}_N) \end{bmatrix} \in \mathbb{R}^{N \times N}$$

and

$$\boldsymbol{\Omega} = \begin{bmatrix} t_1 t_1 k(\boldsymbol{x}_1, \boldsymbol{x}_1) & \cdots & t_1 t_N k(\boldsymbol{x}_1, \boldsymbol{x}_N) \\ \vdots & \ddots & \vdots \\ t_N t_1 k(\boldsymbol{x}_N, \boldsymbol{x}_1) & \cdots & t_N t_N k(\boldsymbol{x}_N, \boldsymbol{x}_N) \end{bmatrix} \in \mathbb{R}^{N \times N}.$$

Both K and $\boldsymbol{\Omega}$ are symmetric matrices of size $N \times N$.

In the following subsections, LSSVM and sparse least square support vector machine using simplex basis function (LSSVM-SBF) [5] are outlined.

2.1 LSSVM

To reduce the computational complexity of the standard SVM, the least square support vector machine introduces the equality constraints.

The standard LSSVM is formulated in the following programming problem

$$\min_{w,b,\eta} \frac{1}{2} \|\boldsymbol{w}\|_{\mathcal{F}}^2 + \frac{\gamma}{2} \sum_{n=1}^{N} \eta_n^2, \quad \text{s.t. } t_n(\langle \boldsymbol{w}, \boldsymbol{\phi}(\boldsymbol{x}_n) \rangle + b) = 1 - \eta_n, \ n = 1, ..., N, \quad (4)$$

where $\gamma > 0$ is a penalty parameter.

With the given equality constraints, the Lagrangian multiplier method produces a kernel model (3) such that the parameters $\boldsymbol{a}$ and b are given by the following set of closed form linear equations

$$\begin{bmatrix} b \\ \boldsymbol{a} \end{bmatrix} = \begin{bmatrix} 0 & \boldsymbol{t}^T \\ \boldsymbol{t} & \boldsymbol{\Omega} + \boldsymbol{I}/\gamma \end{bmatrix}^{-1} \begin{bmatrix} 0 \\ 1 \end{bmatrix} \tag{5}$$

where $\boldsymbol{I}$ is the identity matrix of size $N \times N$. However, the computational hurdle lies in the massive matrix inverse in (5) which has complexity of order $O(N^3)$.

2.2 LSSVM-SBF

Despite of a closed form solution obtained by LSSVM, the model is still limited in computational burden and non-sparsity. Alternatively, the novel LSSVM-SBF [5] overcomes these two issues by introducing the so-called low rank Simplex Basis Function (SBF) kernel, which is defined as follows,

$$\phi_j(\boldsymbol{x}; \boldsymbol{\mu}_j, \boldsymbol{c}_j) = \max \left\{ 0, 1 - \sum_{i=1}^{D} \mu_{i,j} |x_i - c_{i,j}| \right\}, \tag{6}$$

where $c_j = [c_{1,j}, \cdots, c_{D,j}]^T \in \mathbb{R}^D$ and $\mu_j = [\mu_{1,j}, \cdots, \mu_{D,j}]^T \in \mathbb{R}_+^D$ are the center and shape vectors. The proposed new kernel in [5] is defined as

$$k(x', x'') = \sum_{j=1}^{M} \phi_j(x'; \mu_j, c_j)^T \phi_j(x''; \mu_j, c_j) \tag{7}$$

in which the SBF kernels use only $M \ll N$ basis functions, where M is a pre-defined model size.

With the low rank kernel structure defined as (7), the closed form solution (5) for a and b can be rewritten as, see [5],

$$\begin{bmatrix} b \\ a \end{bmatrix} = q - P\tilde{\Phi}(I + \tilde{\Phi}^T P\tilde{\Phi})^{-1}\tilde{\Phi}^T q, \tag{8}$$

where

$$P = \frac{1}{N}\begin{bmatrix} -1/\gamma & t^T \\ t & \gamma(NI - tt^T) \end{bmatrix}, \quad q = \frac{1}{N}\begin{bmatrix} t^T 1 \\ \gamma(NI - tt^T) \end{bmatrix}, \quad \tilde{\Phi} = \begin{bmatrix} 0 & \cdots & 0 \\ t \circ \phi_1 & \cdots & t \circ \phi_M \end{bmatrix}$$

with $\phi_j = [\phi_j(x_1; \mu_j, c_j), \phi_j(x_2; \mu_j, c_j), ..., \phi_j(x_N; \mu_j, c_j)]^T$, i.e., the vector of basis function values at the training inputs.

The new solution (8) only involves the matrix inverse of size $M \times M$, which is superior to (5) where the inverse is of size $N \times N$.

3   The Proposed Model and Its Algorithm

From Subsect. 2.2, we have found that the special choice of low rank SBF kernel as defined in (6) and (7) brings model efficiency. To extend the idea of using low rank kernel, in this section, we propose a general framework for fast algorithm and validate it with several examples.

We would like to emphasize that our idea of using low rank kernel is inspired by the original low rank kernel approximation such as Nyström approximation [10]. However the standard low rank kernel methods aim to approximate a given kernel function, while our approach involves learning (basis) functions and constructs the kernel with composite structure in order to assist fast algorithms.

3.1   The Low Rank Kernels and Models

Consider M learnable "basis" functions

$$\phi_j(x; \lambda_j) : j = 1, 2, ..., M. \tag{9}$$

with adaptable parameters λ_j ($j = 1, 2, ..., M$). In the case of SBF in (6), we have in total $2D$ parameters

$$\lambda_j = \{\mu_j, c_j\}.$$

As another example, we will consider the so-called robust RBF

$$\phi_j(\boldsymbol{x}; \boldsymbol{\mu}_j, \boldsymbol{c}_j) = \exp\left\{ -\sum_{i=1}^{D} \mu_{i,j}|x_i - c_{i,j}| \right\}. \tag{10}$$

Similar to the SBF, while $c_{i,j}$ determines the location of $\phi_j(\boldsymbol{x}; \boldsymbol{\mu}_j, \boldsymbol{c}_j)$ in the ith dimensional direction, $\mu_{i,j}$ restricts the sharpness of $\phi_j(\boldsymbol{x}; \boldsymbol{\mu}_j, \boldsymbol{c}_j)$ in the ith dimension. In fact, the SBF (6) can be regarded as the first order approximation of the robust RBF in terms of $\exp\{-t\} = 1 - t + \frac{1}{2!}t^2 + \cdots$. We expect the robust RBF will have better modeling capability.

More generally, each learnable basis function $\phi_j(\boldsymbol{x}; \boldsymbol{\lambda}_j)$ can be a deep neural network. We will leave this for further study.

Given a set of learnable basis functions (9), define a finite dimensional feature mapping

$$\boldsymbol{\phi}_r : \boldsymbol{x} \in \mathbb{R}^D \to \boldsymbol{\phi}_r(\boldsymbol{x}) = \begin{bmatrix} \phi_1(\boldsymbol{x}; \boldsymbol{\lambda}_1) \\ \vdots \\ \phi_M(\boldsymbol{x}; \boldsymbol{\lambda}_M) \end{bmatrix} \in \mathcal{F}.$$

This feature mapping naturally induces the following learnable low rank kernel

$$k(\boldsymbol{x}', \boldsymbol{x}'') = \sum_{j=1}^{M} \phi_j(\boldsymbol{x}'; \boldsymbol{\lambda}_j)^T \phi_j(\boldsymbol{x}''; \boldsymbol{\lambda}_j). \tag{11}$$

Consider the "linear" model $y(\boldsymbol{x}) = \langle \boldsymbol{w}, \boldsymbol{\phi}_r(\boldsymbol{x}) \rangle + b$ and define the following low rank LSSVM (LR-LSSVM)

$$\min_{w,b,\eta} \frac{1}{2}\|\boldsymbol{w}\|_{\mathcal{F}}^2 + \frac{\gamma}{2}\sum_{n=1}^{N}\eta_n^2, \quad \text{s.t. } t_n(\langle \boldsymbol{w}, \boldsymbol{\phi}_r(\boldsymbol{x_n}) \rangle + b) = 1 - \eta_n, \ n = 1, ..., N.$$
$$\tag{12}$$

The LR-LSSVM problem takes the same form as the standard LSSVM (4), however our low rank kernel carries composition structure and is learnable with adaptable parameters. In the following subsections, we propose a two-steps alternative algorithm procedure to solve the LR-LSSVM.

3.2   Solving LR-LSSVM with Fixed Feature Mappings

When all the feature mappings $\phi_j(j = 1, 2, ..., M)$ are fixed, problem (12) gives back to the standard LSSVM. Denote $\boldsymbol{\eta} = [\eta_1, \eta_2, ..., \eta_N]^T$ and consider the Lagrangian function

$$L(\boldsymbol{w}, b, \boldsymbol{\eta}; \boldsymbol{a}) = \frac{\gamma}{2}\|\boldsymbol{\eta}\|^2 + \frac{1}{2}\|\boldsymbol{w}\|^2 - \sum_{n=1}^{N} a_n\{t_n(\langle \boldsymbol{w}, \boldsymbol{\phi}_r(\boldsymbol{x_n}) \rangle + b) - 1 + \eta_n\},$$

where $\boldsymbol{a} = [a_1, a_2, ..., a_N]^T$ are Lagrange multipliers for all the equality constraints. We now optimize out $\boldsymbol{w}$, b and $\boldsymbol{\eta}$ to give

$$\frac{\partial L}{\partial \boldsymbol{w}} = \mathbf{0} \to \boldsymbol{w} = \boldsymbol{\Phi}^T(\boldsymbol{a} \circ \boldsymbol{t}), \quad \frac{\partial L}{\partial b} = 0 \to \boldsymbol{t}^T \circ \boldsymbol{a} = 0, \quad \frac{\partial L}{\partial \boldsymbol{\eta}} = \mathbf{0} \to \boldsymbol{a} = \gamma\boldsymbol{\eta} \tag{13}$$

where

$$\boldsymbol{\Phi} = \begin{bmatrix} \phi_1(\boldsymbol{x}_1;\lambda_1) & \cdots & \phi_M(\boldsymbol{x}_1;\lambda_M) \\ \vdots & \cdots & \vdots \\ \phi_1(\boldsymbol{x}_N;\lambda_1) & \cdots & \phi_M(\boldsymbol{x}_N;\lambda_M) \end{bmatrix} \in \mathbb{R}^{N\times M}. \tag{14}$$

Furthermore, setting the partial derivative with respect to each Lagrange multiplier and after a long algebraic manipulation, the solution for the dual problem is given by

$$\begin{bmatrix} b \\ a \end{bmatrix} = \left\{ \begin{bmatrix} 0 & t^T \\ t & I/\gamma \end{bmatrix} + \widetilde{\boldsymbol{\Phi}}\widetilde{\boldsymbol{\Phi}}^T \right\}^{-1} \begin{bmatrix} 0 \\ 1 \end{bmatrix}. \tag{15}$$

where $\widetilde{\boldsymbol{\Phi}}$ the $(N+1) \times M$ is the matrix with one row of all zeros on the top of matrix $\mathrm{diag}(t)\boldsymbol{\Phi}$.

Applying the matrix inversion formula to (15) results in the exactly same solution as (8). Once a and b are worked out, the final model can be written as

$$y(\boldsymbol{x}) = \sum_{j=1}^{M} \theta_j \phi_j(\boldsymbol{x};\lambda_j) + b, \tag{16}$$

where

$$\theta_j = \sum_{n=1}^{N} a_n t_n \phi_j(\boldsymbol{x}_n;\lambda_j).$$

Thus the final model is expressed in terms of sparse form of size M.

3.3   Training Learnable Low Rank Kernels

Given a, b which are solved by the closed-form solution in the first step, we estimate the kernel parameters λ_j $(j = 1,\ldots,M)$ using a gradient descent algorithm. The algorithm seeks to maximize the magnitude of model outputs, which leads to overall further distance from the model outputs to the existing decision boundary. Taking the robust RBF functions (10) as an example, this objective function can be expressed as

$$J^{(j)}(\boldsymbol{c}_j, \boldsymbol{\mu}_j) = \sum_{n=1}^{N} |y(\boldsymbol{x}_n)|. \tag{17}$$

Another objective function is

$$J^{(j)}(\boldsymbol{c}_j, \boldsymbol{\mu}_j) = \sum_{n=1}^{N} t_n y(\boldsymbol{x}_n), \tag{18}$$

which gives similar results as (17).

Denote $\text{sign}(\boldsymbol{y}) = [\text{sign}(y(\boldsymbol{x}_1)), \dots, \text{sign}(y(\boldsymbol{x}_N))]^T$. Given the objective function above, we have

$$
\begin{cases}
\dfrac{\partial J^{(j)}}{\partial \mu_{i,j}} = [\text{sign}(\boldsymbol{y})]^T \dfrac{\partial \boldsymbol{K}}{\partial \mu_{i,j}}(\boldsymbol{a} \circ \boldsymbol{t}) & i = 1, \dots, D \\[3mm]
\dfrac{\partial J^{(j)}}{\partial c_{i,j}} = [\text{sign}(\boldsymbol{y})]^T \dfrac{\partial \boldsymbol{K}}{\partial c_{i,j}}(\boldsymbol{a} \circ \boldsymbol{t}) & i = 1, \dots, D
\end{cases}
\tag{19}
$$

in which

$$
\frac{\partial \boldsymbol{K}}{\partial \mu_{i,j}} = \left(\frac{\partial \phi_j}{\partial \mu_{i,j}}\right)\phi_j^T + \phi_j\left(\frac{\partial \phi_j}{\partial \mu_{i,j}}\right)^T; \quad \frac{\partial \boldsymbol{K}}{\partial c_{i,j}} = \left(\frac{\partial \phi_j}{\partial c_{i,j}}\right)\phi_j^T + \phi_j\left(\frac{\partial \phi_j}{\partial c_{i,j}}\right)^T
\tag{20}
$$

where

$$
\frac{\partial \phi_j}{\partial \mu_{i,j}} = \left[\frac{\partial \phi_j(\boldsymbol{x}_1)}{\partial \mu_{i,j}}, \dots, \frac{\partial \phi_j(\boldsymbol{x}_N)}{\partial \mu_{i,j}}\right]^T; \quad \frac{\partial \phi_j}{\partial c_{i,j}} = \left[\frac{\partial \phi_j(\boldsymbol{x}_1)}{\partial c_{i,j}}, \dots, \frac{\partial \phi_j(\boldsymbol{x}_N)}{\partial c_{i,j}}\right]^T
\tag{21}
$$

which are calculated by, for $i = 1, \dots, D$,

$$
\frac{\partial \phi_j(\boldsymbol{x}_n)}{\partial \mu_{i,j}} = -|x_{i,n} - c_{i,j}|\phi_j(\boldsymbol{x}_n; \boldsymbol{\mu}_j, \boldsymbol{c}_j),
\tag{22}
$$

$$
\frac{\partial \phi_j(\boldsymbol{x}_n)}{\partial c_{i,j}} = \mu_{i,j}\text{sign}(x_{i,n} - c_{i,j})\phi_j(\boldsymbol{x}_n; \boldsymbol{\mu}_j, \boldsymbol{c}_j).
\tag{23}
$$

where $\phi_j(\boldsymbol{x}; \boldsymbol{\mu}_j, \boldsymbol{c}_j)$ is defined in (10).

Meanwhile, we should also consider the positivity constraints for the shape parameters vector $\boldsymbol{\mu}_j$ and thus, we have the following constrained normalized gradient descent algorithm, which is, for $i = 1, \dots, D$,

$$
\begin{cases}
c_{i,j} = c_{i,j} + \eta \cdot \dfrac{\partial J^{(i)}}{\partial c_{i,j}} \Big/ \left\|\dfrac{\partial J^{(i)}}{\partial \boldsymbol{c}_j}\right\| \\[4mm]
\tilde{\mu}_{i,j} = \mu_{i,j} + \eta \cdot \dfrac{\partial J^{(i)}}{\partial \mu_{i,j}} \Big/ \left\|\dfrac{\partial J^{(i)}}{\partial \boldsymbol{\mu}_j}\right\| \\[4mm]
\mu_{i,j} = \max(0, \tilde{\mu}_{i,j})
\end{cases}
\tag{24}
$$

where $\eta > 0$ is a preset learning rate. By applying (19) to (24) to all M Robust RBF units while keeping $b, \boldsymbol{a}$ to their current values and other RBF units constant, we manage to update all RBF kernels.

3.4   Initialization of Robust Radial Basis Functions

As is shown in (16), the model requires a preset kernel model size M and a set of initial kernel parameters $\boldsymbol{\lambda}_j$, $j = 1, \dots, M$. In the case of robust RBFs, both $\boldsymbol{c}_j$ and $\boldsymbol{\mu}_j$ need to be initialized. The initialization of the center vector $\boldsymbol{c}_j$ can be obtained using a clustering algorithm. We propose a k-medoids algorithm here to solve for the Robust RBF centers since it is more robust to unbalanced distribution of data. It seeks to divide the data points into M subsets and iteratively adjust the centers c_j of each subset S_j until reaching convergence while minimizing the clustering objective objection given by

$$J = \sum_{j=1}^{M} \sum_{x_n \in S_j} \|x_n - c_j\| \tag{25}$$

where the centers c_j of each subset are the members of that subset. As for the initial values of the shaping parameters μ_j, we preset $\mu_{i,j}$ as a predetermined constant for all basis functions, e.g., $1\,\mathrm{s}$.

3.5   The Overall Algorithm and Its Complexity

Algorithm 1^2 summarizes the overall procedure of LR-LSSVM using the example of robust RBF kernel. The algorithm starts with the k-medoids clustering algorithm for initialization of the robust RBF centres in Sect. 3.2, then the fast LSSVM solution is achieved and the gradient descent algorithm in Sect. 3.3 or 3.6 are alternatively applied for a predefined number of iterations. A simple complexity analysis indicates that the overall computational complexity is $O(M^2 N)$ which is dominated by the gradient descent algorithm for training learnable basis functions, scaled by the iteration number. Many examples in Sect. 4 have shown that a minor size M gives competitive model prediction performance. In this sense, the newly proposed algorithm has a complexity of $O(N)$. The lower complexity benefits from the special structure of low rank kernel functions. It should be pointed out again that the proposed framework contains the SBF model in [5] as a special case, that the framework can be applied for more generic extension, for example using deep neural networks for learning kernel functions.

Algorithm 1. The Proposed LR-LSSVM Algorithm with robust RBF kernel

---

Input: Dataset $\mathcal{D}$. Model size M. Regularization parameter γ. Initial shape parameter μ_j. Iteration number T.
Output: The obtained model parameters a, b, $\lambda_j = (c_j, \mu_j)$ for $j = 1, 2, ..., M$.
  1: Apply the k-medoids clustering algorithm to initialize c_j ($j = 1, 2, ..., M$). Set all $\mu_{i,j}$ to a constant μ.
  2: **for** $t = 1, 2, ..., T$ **do**
  3:    Form $\boldsymbol{\Phi}$ from the dataset $\mathcal{D}$ and the current kernel parameters $\lambda_j = (c_j, \mu_j)$ for $j = 1, 2, ..., M$;
  4:    Construct $\widetilde{\boldsymbol{\Phi}}$ by adding one row of $\mathbf{0}$ on the top of matrix $\mathrm{diag}(t)\boldsymbol{\Phi}$;
  5:    Update b and a according to the closed form solution (8);
  6:    **for** $j = 1, 2, ..., M$ **do**
  7:       Apply (19) to (24) to adjust $\lambda_j = (c_j, \mu_j)$
  8:    **end for**
  9: **end for**

---

^{2} The algorithm can be easily adopted to any learnable kernels.

3.6   The Differentiable Objective Functions

The objective defined in (17) is non-differentiable. For the purpose of maximizing the magnitude of model outputs, we propose the following squared objective which is differentiable, for $j = 1, 2, ..., M$,

$$F^{(j)}(c_j, \mu_j) = \sum_{n=1}^{N} y(x_n)^2. \tag{26}$$

It is not hard to prove that

$$\frac{\partial F^{(j)}}{\partial \nu} = (a \circ t)^T \left(K \frac{\partial K}{\partial \nu} + \frac{\partial K}{\partial \nu} K \right) (a \circ t) + 2b(a \circ t)^T \frac{\partial K}{\partial \nu} \mathbf{1} \tag{27}$$

where $\frac{\partial K}{\partial \nu}$ is the matrix given by (19) and (20), and ν means either $\mu_{i,j}$ or $c_{i,j}$.

Table 1. The misclassification rate (%) on different datasets.

Models	Synthetic		Titanic		Diabetes		German Credit	
	Mis rate	Size	Mis rate	Size	Mis rate	Size	Mis rate	Size
Adaboost with RBF	N/A	N/A	22.6 ± 1.2	4	26.5 ± 1.9	15	27.5 ± 2.5	8
QPReg-AdaBoost	N/A	N/A	22.7 ± 1.1	4	25.4 ± 2.2	15	25.3 ± 2.1	8
SVM with RBF kernel	N/A	N/A	22.4 ± 1.0	N/A	23.5 ± 1.7	N/A	23.6 ± 2.1	N/A
LSSVM-Gaussian ($\sigma = 1$)	9.2	250	N/A	N/A	N/A	N/A	N/A	N/A
LSSVM-SBF	8.3	4	22.5 ± 0.8	2	23.5 ± 1.7	5	24.9 ± 1.9	3
M1	8.0	3	22.3 ± 0.8	2	23.8 ± 1.7	5	25.6 ± 2.3	2
M2	8.3	3	22.6 ± 1.5	3	23.5 ± 2.0	4	24.7 ± 1.9	2
M3	8.0	3	22.4 ± 0.8	2	24.7 ± 2.0	5	25.6 ± 2.4	2

4   Experimental Studies

In this section, validations are conducted on synthetic, Titanic, Diabetes, and German Credit datasets. The descriptions of data and model parameters are in Table 2, where M1, M2 and M3 are the proposed models by using absolute (17), squared (26) and target (18) objectives, respectively. D is the input dimension of dataset. No. Train and No. Test are the number of realizations in each group, while 100 means that the group is divided into 100 subsets. μ, γ, η, and T are steepness, penalization, learning rate and times of iteration. Outcomes of the proposed and benchmark models are shown in Table 1 with $\sigma = 1.0$ being the optimal value for LSSVM-Gaussian among 0.5–3, step 0.5 and the first five benchmarks in the table citing from [5].

Overall, LR-LSSVM mostly stands out in synthetic, Titanic and Diabetes, while remains comparable in German Credit. Within LR-LSSVM, RRBF using square objective is fairly unstable with good performance in Diabetes whereas

Table 2. The parameter setting of different datasets.

Parameters	Synthetic			Titanic			Diabetes			German Credit		
	M1	M2	M3	M1	M2	M3	M1	M2	M3	M1	M2	M3
D		2			3			8			20	
No. train		250			100×150			100×468			100×700	
No. test		1000			100×2051			100×300			100×300	
μ		0.2		0.03	0.001	0.001	0.01	0.001	0.0001		0.005	
γ		100		50000	500000	50000		50000			200000	
η	0.0008	0.0005	0.0008	0.0005	0.0001	0.0001		0.001			0.003	
T	150	20	150		100			100			100	

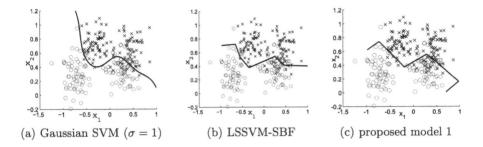

(a) Gaussian SVM ($\sigma = 1$)   (b) LSSVM-SBF   (c) proposed model 1

Fig. 1. The decision boundaries for synthetic dataset

less ideal in the rest. Thus, inference that square-objectived LR-LSSVM-RRBF suits more for high-dimensional cases would be made, still more validations needed for solid conclusion. The size column of Table 1 represents model sparsity. Superb sparseness of LR-LSSVM can be easily observed within this column and thus lead to notable progress of computational speed. Figure 1 depicts the decision boundaries of some typical models in Synthetic dataset, in which the decision boundary of Gaussian LSSVM is smooth and round whereas that of LR-LSSVM local-linearly wiggles. Plus, though both of locally linear traits, the lineshape of decision boundary of LR-LSSVM-RRBF significantly deviates from that of LR-LSSVM-SBF.

5   Conclusions

In this paper, we present a general framework of fast LR-LSSVM and take a RRBF kernel as demonstration. After kernel parameter initialization with k-medriods clustering, training alternates between closed form solution of a, b and gradient descent of c, μ. Three objective functions are suggested for gradient descent, where solely the second one is differentiable. In the end, experiments are conducted on synthetic and real-world cases.

References

1. Amari, S., Wu, S.: Improving support vector machine classifiers by modifying kernel functions. Neural Netw. **12**(6), 783–789 (1999). https://doi.org/10.1016/s0893-6080(99)00032-5
2. Chen, S.: Local regularization assisted orthogonal least squares regression. NeuroComputing **69**, 559–585 (2006)
3. Chen, S., Cowan, C., Grant, P.: Orthogonal least squares learning algorithm for radial basis function networks. IEEE Trans. Neural Netw. **2**(2), 302–309 (1991)
4. Gao, J., Shi, D., Liu, X.: Critical vector learning to construct sparse kernel regression modelling. Neural Netw. **20**(7), 791–798 (2007)
5. Hong, X., Wei, H., Gao, J.: Sparse least squares support vector machine using simplex basis function. IEEE Trans. Cybern. XX, Submission No. CYB-E-2018-06-1246 (2018)
6. Liu, D., Shi, Y., Tian, Y., Huang, X.: Ramp loss least squares support vector machine. J. Comput. Sci. **14**, 61–68 (2016)
7. Lotte, F., Congedo, M., Lécuyer, A., Lamarche, F., Arnaldi, B.: A review of classification algorithms for EEG-based brain-computer interfaces. J. Neural Eng. **4**(2), R1–13 (2007). https://doi.org/10.1088/1741-2560/4/2/r01
8. Schölkopf, B., Smola, A.J.: Learning with Kernels. MIT Press, Cambridge (2002)
9. Suykens, J., Vandewalle, J.: Least squares support vector machine classifiers. Neural Process. Lett. **9**, 293–300 (1999)
10. Williams, C., Seeger, M.: Using the Nyström method to speed up kernel machines. In: Proceedings of NIPS, pp. 682–688 (2001)
11. Ye, Y., Gao, J., Shao, Y., Li, C., Jin, Y.: Robust support vector regression with general quadratic non-convex ϵ-insensitive loss. ACM Trans. Knowl. Discov. Data XX, submitted (2019)
12. Yu, K., Xu, W., Gong, Y.: Deep learning with kernel regularization for visual recognition. In: NIPS, vol. 21, pp. 1889–1896 (2009)
13. Zhu, F., Gao, J., Xu, C., Yang, J., Tao, D.: On selecting effective patterns for fast support vector regression training. IEEE Trans. Neural Netw. Learn. Syst. **29**(8), 3610–3622 (2018)

Proposal of Online Regularization for Dynamical Structure Optimization in Complex-Valued Neural Networks

Tianben Ding[1,2] and Akira Hirose[1(✉)]

[1] Department of Electrical Engineering and Information Systems,
The University of Tokyo, Tokyo 153-8656, Japan
`ahirose@ee.t.u-tokyo.ac.jp`
[2] Department of Electrical and Systems Engineering,
Washington University in St. Louis, St. Louis, MO 63130, USA

Abstract. We propose online-learning complex-valued neural networks (CVNN) to predict future channel states in fast fading multipath mobile communications. A communication channel is represented by complex amplitude. Then, CVNNs are intrinsically suitable for fading channel prediction by utilizing its high generalization ability in the complex-amplitude domain. In this paper, we introduce regularization dynamics to make the CVNN structure dynamically changing in accordance with the changes in the multipath situations. We demonstrate the online adaptability when the scattering environment changes.

Keywords: Adaptive communications · Channel prediction · Complex-valued neural network (CVNN) · Fading

1 Introduction

Channel prediction is expected to play an important role in the near future mobile communications [5,7,11,15,31]. There exist several works on the channel prediction in mobile communications based on, for example, linear [4,27] and autoregressive (AR) model extrapolation [2,12,16,32]. They have low computational complexity suitable for real-time operation in mobile communications. However, simple linear or AR-based methods provide limited performance in rapid channel changes environment [8].

Neural-network-based channel prediction methods have also been studied very actively due to the recent successful development of artificial neural networks in various engineering fields. The generalization ability of neural networks provides flexible representation of complicated channel-state changes and high prediction capability. Researchers proposed an echo-state-network (ESN) based

A. Hirose—A part of this work was supported by JSPS KAKANHI under Grant 15H02756 and Grant 18H04105, and a part by Tohoku University RIEC Cooperative Research Project.

© Springer Nature Switzerland AG 2019
T. Gedeon et al. (Eds.): ICONIP 2019, LNCS 11954, pp. 407–418, 2019.
https://doi.org/10.1007/978-3-030-36711-4_34

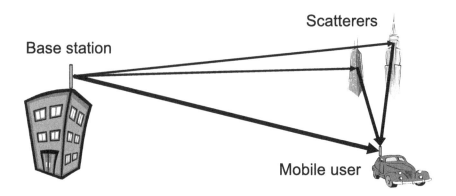

Fig. 1. Multipath situation in mobile communications.

prediction method [37], an extreme-learning-machine (ELM) based one [33], as well as real-valued recurrent-neural-network (RNN) based ones [26,28]. The authors also proposed a method [8] based on a multiple-layer complex-valued neural network (ML-CVNN) by focusing rotary motion nature of the channel state in the complex plane. This method gave us superb channel prediction performance in many practical communication scenarios.

In neural-network-based applications in general, the network size is critical to the application performance because it affects the generalization characteristics and calculation cost [19,29]. For example, a too small network is not enough to represent the complexity of targets, showing low convergence properties. On the other hand, a too large network requires expensive calculation costs, and most importantly, it causes overfitting.

However, in our previous prediction method, we empirically set and fixed the structure of the CVNN (the number of input terminals and neurons in the hidden layer) based on its prediction accuracy in a series of simulations with several communication situations. Although the structure shows a high prediction performance on some simulated and experimentally observed fading channels [8], this manual pre-tuning of the network parameters is time consuming and not efficient. Mobile communications in the real world is forced to work in diverse communication environments. As a result, an *a priori* tuned structure is no longer optimal for other practical communication environment, but the most suitable neural-network structure is dynamically changing accordingly.

In this paper, we propose a new ML-CVNN-based channel prediction scheme by introducing regularization in the complex domain. We work with a large-size network platform and then let it automatically find, or self-adjust to, a suitable structure within the platform that uses only a limited portion of the network in order to achieve a good generalization. The self-adjustment is performed by imposing a sparse constraint [13] to the connection weight updates. The sparse constraint suppresses the redundant connection weights to be zeros, and equivalently constructs a smaller scaled network using only the remaining non-zero connections [9].

In order to follow the time fluctuation in the channel state to make the network structure optimized, we develop an online training-and-prediction framework with a dynamically changing structure. We update the network by using a set of the most recent channel immediately before the prediction with a small learning iteration number. Then we keep the updated network structure temporarily for the next training-and-predicting time frame. In this way, we change the non-zero connection distribution from time-to-time in the structure so that it keeps the most suitable size of the network for the situations of prediction.

In each training phase, we use a backpropagation of teacher signal (BPTS) [20], rather than the standard error-backpropagation. The BPTS-based update method is simpler with a lower computational cost, which is preferred for mobile communications. We demonstrate that the new channel prediction method with the online adaptive CVNN structure presents highly accurate predictions under fluctuating communication environment.

2   Online Regularization in CVNN

2.1   Channel Model

Channel states of communications are distorted mainly by multipath interference caused by scattering in the communication environment. In addition, movement of mobile users and/or scatterers causes rapid and irregular channel changes in time. Figure 1 illustrates such a multipath situation. Generally, a signal received at a communication end $y(t)$ at time t is modeled with time-varying channel $c(t)$ as

$$y(t) = c(t)s(t) + n(t) \tag{1}$$

where $s(t)$ and $n(t)$ are transmitted signal and additive white Gaussian noise (AWGN), respectively. According to the Jakes model [23], fading channel $c(t)$ as a function of time t is modeled as a summation of individual M complex signal paths $c_m(t)$ at a receiver and expressed as

$$c(t) = \sum_{m=1}^{M} c_m(t) = \sum_{m=1}^{M} a_m e^{j(2\pi f_m t + \phi_m)} \tag{2}$$

where a_m, f_m, and ϕ_m are amplitude, Doppler frequency, and phase shift of each single path m, and M is the total path number. The Doppler frequency due to movement of a mobile user is given by

$$f_m = \frac{f_c}{c} v_m \cos \psi_m \tag{3}$$

where v and c are speed of the mobile user and the speed of light, respectively, f_c is the carrier frequency of the communication, and ψ is the incident radio wave angle with respect to the motion of the mobile user.

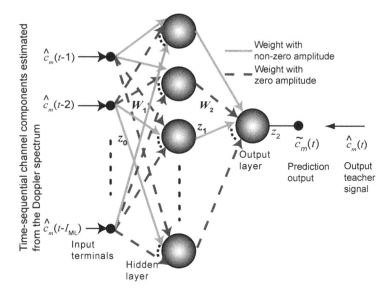

Fig. 2. Construction of the complex-valued neural network, in which the solid arrows show non-zero-amplitude connections while dashed arrows represent zero-amplitude ones.

Observed channel $c(t)$ in an actual communication can be decomposed into multiple path components $c_m(t)$ in the frequency domain based on this model. Different path components with different incident angles ψ appear as separate peaks in a Doppler frequency spectrum. Hence, the parameters of each path component can be estimated by finding peak amplitudes and Doppler frequencies for a_m and f_m in the Doppler spectrum and the corresponding phase shifts for ϕ_m in the phase spectrum. Chirp z-transform (CZT) with a Hann window provides low calculation cost and a smooth frequency-domain interpolation useful for an accurate estimation of the parameters in the region close to zero frequency [34]. By sliding the Hann window in the past and by repeating the parameter estimation process, we can obtain separated path components at different time points. We focus on the fact that the separated channel states $c_m(t)$ have rotary locus in the complex plane and, then, predict its change in time for obtaining the future channel by using CVNNs.

2.2   Proposal of Online-Regularizing CVNN

The changes in the separated channel components $c_m(t)$ can be predicted by ML-CVNNs [8]. CVNN is a framework suitable for treating signal rotation and scaling adaptively in the complex plane by use of its high generalization ability [19,21]. It has been receiving more attentions in various applications that intrinsically require dealing with complex values [1,17,25,36].

With a basic ML-CVNN consisting of a layer of I_{ML} input terminals, a hidden-neuron layer with K_{ML} neurons and an output neuron, we can predict the complex-valued $c_m(t)$ from a set of past channel components, $c_m(t-1)$, ..., $c_m(t - I_{\mathrm{ML}})$ for paths $m = 1, ..., M$.

The input terminals distribute input signals, $c_m(t-1)$, ..., $c_m(t - I_{\mathrm{ML}})$, to the hidden-layer neurons as their inputs z_0. In the same way, the outputs of the hidden-layer neurons z_1 are passed to the output-layer neuron as its input. The neurons in the hidden layer are fully connected with the input terminals and the output-layer neuron. The output of the output-layer neuron z_2 is the prediction result $\tilde{c}_m(t)$. The connection weight w_{lki} to ith input at kth neuron in layer l is expressed by its amplitude $|w_{lki}|$ and phase θ_{lki}. The internal state u_{lk} of kth neuron in lth layer is obtained as the summation of its inputs $z_{(l-1)}$ weighted by $\boldsymbol{w}_{lk} = [w_{lki}]$, i.e.,

$$u_{lk} \equiv \sum_i w_{lki} z_{(l-1)i} = \sum_i |w_{lki}||z_{(l-1)i}|e^{j(\theta_{lki} + \theta_{(l-1)i})} \tag{4}$$

where $z_{(l-1)i} = |z_{(l-1)i}|e^{j\theta_{(l-1)i}}$. The output z_{lk} is given by adopting an amplitude-phase-type activation function f_{ap} to u_{lk} as

$$z_{lk} = f_{\mathrm{ap}}(u_{lk}) = \tanh(|u_{lk}|)e^{(j\arg(u_{lk}))} \tag{5}$$

In our previous work, the connection weights $\boldsymbol{W}_l = [\boldsymbol{w}_{lk}] = [w_{lki}]$ in the ML-CVNN are updated as follows. The ML-CVNN regards the past known channel component $\hat{c}_m(t)$ as an output teacher signal, while the preceding channel components associated with the same path $\hat{c}_m(t-1), ..., \hat{c}_m(t - I_{\mathrm{ML}})$ as the input teacher signals. The weights are updated based on the steepest descent method so that they minimize the difference

$$E_l \equiv \frac{1}{2}|z_l - \hat{z}_l|^2 \tag{6}$$

where z_l and $\hat{z}_l$ denote temporary output signals and the teacher signals, respectively, in layer l. The teacher signals in the hidden layer $\hat{z}_1$ are the signals obtained through the backpropagation of the teacher signal (BPTS) of the output layer $\hat{z}_2$ [18–20]. The weight updates are performed at each estimated channel components by sliding the teacher signal and the input set in the time domain. We stop the update at a certain small number of iteration R_{ML} in the update process for $\hat{c}_m(t)$ and keep the updated weights as the initial values in the following weight update for $\hat{c}_m(t+1)$. With this procedure, we reduce the learning cost to follow the weak regularity of the separated channel components $c_m(t)$ and to achieve a channel prediction with high accuracy.

There are a number of preceding studies to get optimized structures of neural networks in general [3,14,22,24,29,30,35]. In this paper, we propose a new channel prediction method based on a dynamic network that prunes and grows connections depending on the fluctuating communication situations by introducing regularization in the complex domain.

Figure 2 shows the construction of the CVNN. Here, we introduce the sparse constraint as a penalty function using L_1-norm [6,10,13]. That is, the objective function we use to update the weights in layer l is expressed as

$$\arg\min_{\boldsymbol{W}_l} E'_l = \arg\min_{\boldsymbol{W}_l}(\frac{1}{2}|\boldsymbol{z}_l - \hat{\boldsymbol{z}}_l|^2 + \alpha\|\boldsymbol{W}_l\|_1) \tag{7}$$

where α is a coefficient to express degrees of the penalty. Minimizing this term means restricting non-zero weight number to get its minimal number in the network. We use the steepest descent method in the complex domain to update the weights here [19]. Thus, the weight amplitude $|w_{lki}|$ and the phase θ_{lki} are renewed as

$$
\begin{aligned}
|w_{lki}|(r+1) =& |w_{lki}|(r) - \kappa_1 \frac{\partial E'_l}{\partial(|w_{lki}|)}\\
=& |w_{lki}|(r) - \kappa_1\Big\{(1 - |z_{lk}|^2)\\
& \times (|z_{lk}| - |\hat{z}_{lk}|\cos(\theta_{lk} - \hat{\theta}_{lk}))|z_{(l-1)i}|\cos\theta_{lki}^{\mathrm{rot}}\\
& - |z_{lk}||\hat{z}_{lk}|\sin(\theta_{lk} - \hat{\theta}_{lk})\frac{|z_{(l-1)i}|}{|u_{lk}|}\sin\theta_{lki}^{\mathrm{rot}}\\
& + \alpha\Big\}
\end{aligned}
\tag{8}
$$

$$
\begin{aligned}
\theta_{lki}(r+1) =& \theta_{lki}(r) - \kappa_2 \frac{1}{|w_{lki}|}\frac{\partial E'_l}{\partial\theta_{lki}}\\
=& \theta_{lki}(r) - \kappa_2\Big\{(1 - |z_{lk}|^2)\\
& \times (|z_{lk}| - |\hat{z}_{lk}|\cos(\theta_{lk} - \hat{\theta}_{lk}))|z_{(l-1)i}|\sin\theta_{lki}^{\mathrm{rot}}\\
& + |z_{lk}||\hat{z}_{lk}|\sin(\theta_{lk} - \hat{\theta}_{lk})\frac{|z_{(l-1)i}|}{|u_{lk}|}\cos\theta_{lki}^{\mathrm{rot}}\Big\}
\end{aligned}
\tag{9}
$$

where $\theta_{lki}^{\mathrm{rot}} \equiv \theta_{lk} - \theta_{(l-1)i} - \theta_{lki}$, r is the index of learning iteration, and κ_1 and κ_2 are learning constants.

This update rule has an additional term $+\alpha$ in the amplitude $|w_{lki}|$ update in comparison to the previous ML-CVNN-based method because of the penalty term. The phase update rule does not change in this regularization. This is the complex-domain regularization.

For simplicity and lower computational consumption, the BPTS is kept to use in this work for getting the teacher signal $\hat{\boldsymbol{z}}_1$ in the hidden layer from the teacher signal in the output layer $\hat{\boldsymbol{z}}_2$ as [18]

$$\hat{\boldsymbol{z}}_1 = (f_{\mathrm{ap}}(\hat{z}_2^*\boldsymbol{W}_2))^* \tag{10}$$

where $(\cdot)^*$ represents the complex conjugate or hermite conjugate.

To predict the channel, we update the connection weights by time-sliding the input and output teacher signals by using the channel components $\hat{c}_m(t)$ estimated sequentially from the Doppler spectrum as we did in the previous work [8]. That is, a set of weights, updated by using the complex-valued estimation

Table 1. Communication parameters

Parameter	Value
QPSK symbol number	1612
Number of OFDM subcarriers	64
Number of OFDM guard bands	6 left, 6 right
Number of OFDM symbols	31
Length of OFDM cyclic prefix	16
TDD frame length	4.96 ms
TDD symbol number in a frame	2480 symbols
Sampling rate	500 kHz

Table 2. Channel prediction parameters

Parameter	Value
CZT size	8 TDD frames
ML-CVNN input terminals I_{ML}	30
ML-CVNN hidden-neuron number K_{ML}	30
ML-CVNN weight update iterations R_{ML}	10

$\hat{c}_m(t)$ as the output teacher signal (for prediction $\tilde{c}_m(t)$ in Fig. 2) and $\hat{c}_m(t - 1), ..., \hat{c}_m(t - I_{\mathrm{ML}})$ as the input teacher signals, are kept in the network and used as the initial weights in the following update by regarding $\hat{c}_m(t + 1)$ as the new output teacher signal (for prediction $\tilde{c}_m(t + 1)$) and $\hat{c}_m(t), ..., \hat{c}_m(t - I_{\mathrm{ML}} + 1)$ as the new input teacher signals. The weight update is performed until the latest channel component is used for prediction of the future channel. The combination of the penalty term and the prediction scheme in the time domain is expected to keep the structure with a suitable size for the channel prediction depending on the fluctuating communication environment.

3   Numerical Experiments

We evaluate the performance of the channel prediction based on the ML-CVNN with the penalty in simulations and experiments. We assume orthogonal frequency-division multiplexing (OFDM) with quadrature phase shift keying (QPSK) modulation, and time division duplex (TDD) as the communication scheme in this paper. Table 1 lists the system parameters.

In this section, we characterize the influence of the degree of penalty α on the neural network size and prediction accuracy for simulated fading channels. The geometrical setup is shown in Fig. 3. We consider communications between a base station (BS) and a mobile user (MU) moving away from the BS at 12 m/s with a certain moving angle. There are two scatterers making 2 paths in addition to the line-of-sight path. The carrier frequency is 2 GHz here.

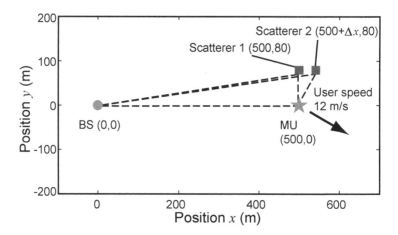

Fig. 3. Geometrical setup used in the simulation. There are two scatters separate by Δx m, a base station (BS), and a mobile user (MU) in an open communication space. The line of sight between the BS and the MU is considered. The MU moves in the direction of the arrow ($-30°$ from the x axis) with a velocity of $12\,\text{m/s}$.

We predict channel changes in a TDD frame based on its preceding channel states. The past path characteristics are estimated by using CZT with the Hann window. A window with 8-TDD-frame length is applied to the past channel states for estimating the path parameters, $a_m(t)$, $f_m(t)$, $\phi_m(t)$, based on peaks in Doppler spectra and corresponding phase spectra. Then, the past path characteristics $c_m(t)$ are composed by using the parameters, and assigned as the estimated characteristics at the center of the window. We shift the window center at a TDD-frame interval for estimating multipath characteristics at every TDD frame. The details of the time frames are explained in our previous work [8].

To evaluate the performance in various channel changes, we change the scatterer distance Δx shown in Fig. 3 from $\Delta x = 0.5$ to $20\,\text{m}$ with $0.5\,\text{m}$ step, and performed 100 independent predictions at each scatterer distance along with the movement of MU. We start with the neural network with the parameters listed in Table 2. The penalty prunes and grows the network connections, 30×30 in the hidden layer and 30×1 in the output layer, online as the communication situation changes.

Figure 4(a) shows the mean of the network size at each scatterer distance condition. A connection weight is counted as non-zero if its amplitude satisfies

$$|w_{lki}| \geq \max(|\boldsymbol{W}_l|)/100 \tag{11}$$

Otherwise, the weight was considered as a zero weight. If a weight in the output layer ($l = 2$) is counted as a zero weight, all the weights in the hidden layer connecting themselves to the corresponding neurons are also considered as zero weights in order to fairly compare the penalty effect on the entire net-

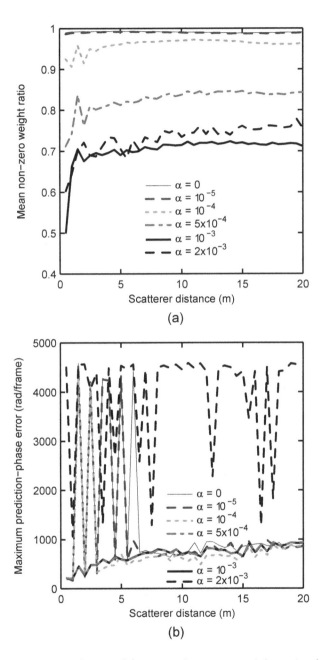

Fig. 4. Simulation results showing (a) averaged non-zero weight ratios (network size) and (b) maximum predicted phase errors against scatterer distance Δx in Fig. 3 for various penalty coefficient α.

work. The network sizes of the ML-CVNN with various penalty coefficients ($\alpha = 0, 10^{-5}, 10^{-4}, 5 \times 10^{-4}, 10^{-3}, 2 \times 10^{-2}$) have been evaluated, and the mean connection numbers for 100 trials in each condition have been normalized by the maximum possible connections to show the non-zero connection ratio. Corresponding prediction accuracy is calculated by accumulating predicted phase errors within the prediction frame. Figure 4(b) presents the maximum estimated phase errors in each communication condition, showing stability of the prediction.

We find in Fig. 4(a) that the non-zero weight number consisting effective network decreases as the penalty coefficient α increases as we expect, whereas a network without the penalty ($\alpha = 0$) keeps almost all of the connections active for all communication conditions. In Fig. 4(b), the smaller networks achieved by the penalty show better prediction stability compared to the conventional CVNN-based method ($\alpha = 0$). The results also presents that the proposed prediction method reaches its best performance with a penalty coefficient around $\alpha = 5 \times 10^{-4} \sim 10^{-3}$, and that α larger than this value introduces instability to the channel prediction again. These results show that the proposed prediction method with an appropriate α can prune redundant connections in its network automatically to achieve higher prediction accuracy even in prediction conditions difficult for the conventional method.

4   Conclusion

We proposed the online adaptive channel prediction method based on ML-CVNNs with self-optimizing dynamic structures. The penalty function based on L_1-norm of the CVNN weights realizes the adaptive CVNN structure without large increase of calculation costs for the weight updates to achieve highly accurate and robust channel prediction of rapidly changing fading.

References

1. Arima, Y., Hirose, A.: Performance dependence on system parameters in millimeter-wave active imaging based on complex-valued neural networks to classify complex texture. IEEE Access **5**, 22927–22939 (2017). http://ieeexplore.ieee.org/document/8036195/
2. Arredondo, A., Dandekar, K., Xu, G.: Vector channel modeling and prediction for the improvement of downlink received power. IEEE Trans. Commun. **50**(7), 1121–1129 (2002). http://ieeexplore.ieee.org/document/1021044/
3. Barakat, M., Druaux, F., Lefebvre, D., Khalil, M., Mustapha, O.: Self adaptive growing neural network classifier for faults detection and diagnosis. Neurocomputing **74**(18), 3865–3876 (2011). https://doi.org/10.1016/j.neucom.2011.08.001. http://linkinghub.elsevier.com/retrieve/pii/S0925231211004425
4. Bui, H.P., Ogawa, Y., Nishimura, T., Ohgane, T.: Performance evaluation of a multi-user MIMO system with prediction of time-varying indoor channels. IEEE Trans. Antennas Propag. **61**(1), 371–379 (2013). http://ieeexplore.ieee.org/document/6280628/

5. Bui, N., Cesana, M., Hosseini, S.A., Liao, Q., Malanchini, I., Widmer, J.: A survey of anticipatory mobile networking: context-based classification, prediction methodologies, and optimization techniques. IEEE Commun. Surv. Tutorials **19**(3), 1790–1821 (2017). http://ieeexplore.ieee.org/document/7904647/

6. Candès, E.J., Romberg, J.K., Tao, T.: Stable signal recovery from incomplete and inaccurate measurements. Commun. Pure Appl. Math. **59**(8), 1207–1223 (2006). https://doi.org/10.1002/cpa.20124

7. Cho, Y.S., Kim, J., Yang, W.Y., Kang, C.G.: MIMO-OFDM Wireless Communications with MATLAB®. Wiley, Chichester (2010). https://doi.org/10.1002/9780470825631

8. Ding, T., Hirose, A.: Fading channel prediction based on combination of complex-valued neural networks and chirp Z-transform. IEEE Trans. Neural Netw. Learn. Syst. **25**(9), 1686–1695 (2014). https://doi.org/10.1007/978-3-319-12637-1_22. http://ieeexplore.ieee.org/document/6755477/

9. Ding, T., Hirose, A.: Fading channel prediction based on self-optimizing neural networks. In: Loo, C.K., Yap, K.S., Wong, K.W., Teoh, A., Huang, K. (eds.) ICONIP 2014. LNCS, vol. 8834, pp. 175–182. Springer, Cham (2014). https://doi.org/10.1007/978-3-319-12637-1_22

10. Donoho, D.L., Tanner, J.: Counting faces of randomly projected polytopes when the projection radically lowers dimension. J. Am. Math. Soc. **22**(1), 1–53 (2008). http://www.ams.org/journal-getitem?pii=S0894-0347-08-00600-0

11. Duel-Hallen, A.: Fading channel prediction for mobile radio adaptive transmission systems. Proc. IEEE **95**(12), 2299–2313 (2007). http://ieeexplore.ieee.org/document/4389753/

12. Duel-Hallen, A., Hallen, H., Yang, T.-S.: Long range prediction and reduced feedback for mobile radio adaptive OFDM systems. IEEE Trans. Wirel. Commun. **5**(10), 2723–2733 (2006). http://ieeexplore.ieee.org/document/1705934/

13. Elad, M.: Sparse and Redundant Representations: From Theory to Applications in Signal and Image Processing. Springer, Berlin (2010)

14. Elman, J.L.: Learning and development in neural networks: the importance of starting small. Cognition **48**(1), 71–99 (1993). http://linkinghub.elsevier.com/retrieve/pii/0010027793900584

15. Eraslan, E., Daneshrad, B., Lou, C.Y.: Performance indicator for MIMO MMSE receivers in the presence of channel estimation error. IEEE Wirel. Commun. Lett. **2**(2), 211–214 (2013). http://ieeexplore.ieee.org/document/6425374/

16. Eyceoz, T., Duel-Hallen, A., Hallen, H.: Deterministic channel modeling and long range prediction of fast fading mobile radio channels. IEEE Commun. Lett. **2**(9), 254–256 (1998). http://ieeexplore.ieee.org/document/718494/

17. Hara, T., Hirose, A.: Plastic mine detecting system using complex-valued self-organizing map that deals with multiple-frequency interferometric images. Neural Netw. **17**(8–9), 1201–1210 (2004)

18. Hirose, A.: Applications of complex-valued neural networks to coherent optical computing using phase-sensitive detection scheme. Inf. Sci.-Appl. **2**, 103–117 (1994)

19. Hirose, A.: Complex-Valued Neural Networks, vol. 400, 2nd edn. Springer, New York (2012)

20. Hirose, A., Eckmiller, R.: Coherent optical neural networks that have optical-frequency-controlled behavior and generalization ability in the frequency domain. Appl. Optics **35**(5), 836 (1996). https://doi.org/10.1002/rnc.592. https://www.osapublishing.org/abstract.cfm?URI=ao-35-5-836

21. Hirose, A., Yoshida, S.: Generalization characteristics of complex-valued feedforward neural networks in relation to signal coherence. IEEE Trans. Neural Netw. Learn. Syst. **23**, 541–551 (2012)
22. Ishikawa, M.: Structural learning with forgetting. Neural Netw. **9**(3), 509–521 (1996). http://linkinghub.elsevier.com/retrieve/pii/0893608096836963
23. Jakes, W.: Microwave Mobile Communications, 2nd edn. Wiley, New York (1994). http://ieeexplore.ieee.org/xpl/bkabstractplus.jsp?bkn=5263365%5Cnieeexplore.ieee.org/search/srchabstract.jsp?arnumber=5263390
24. Karnin, E.: A simple procedure for pruning back-propagation trained neural networks. IEEE Trans. Neural Netw. **1**(2), 239–242 (1990). http://ieeexplore.ieee.org/document/80236/
25. Kawata, S., Hirose, A.: Frequency-multiplexed logic circuit based on a coherent optical neural network. Appl. Opt. **44**(19), 4053–4059 (2005)
26. Liu, W., Yang, L.L., Lajos, H.: Recurrent neural network based narrowband channel prediction. In: 2006 IEEE 63rd Vehicular Technology Conference, vol. 5, pp. 2173–2177. IEEE (2006). http://ieeexplore.ieee.org/document/1683241/
27. Maehara, F., Sasamori, F., Tkahata, F.: Linear predictive maximal ratio combining transmitter diversity for OFDM-TDMA/TDD systems. IEICE Trans. Commun. **E86–B**(1), 221–229 (2003)
28. Potter, C., Venayagamoorthy, G.K., Kosbar, K.: RNN based MIMO channel prediction. Signal Process. **90**(2), 440–450 (2010). http://linkinghub.elsevier.com/retrieve/pii/S0165168409003120
29. Ramachandram, D., Taylor, G.W.: Deep multimodal learning: a survey on recent advances and trends. IEEE Signal Process. Mag. **34**(6), 96–108 (2017). http://ieeexplore.ieee.org/document/8103116/
30. Reed, R.: Pruning algorithms-a survey. IEEE Trans. Neural Netw. **4**(5), 740–747 (1993). http://ieeexplore.ieee.org/document/248452/
31. Ren, X., Wu, J., Johansson, K.H., Shi, G., Shi, L.: Infinite horizon optimal transmission power control for remote state estimation over fading channels. IEEE Trans. Autom. Control **63**(1), 85–100 (2018). http://ieeexplore.ieee.org/document/7935515/
32. Sharma, P., Chandra, K.: Prediction of state transitions in rayleigh fading channels. IEEE Trans. Veh. Technol. **56**(2), 416–425 (2007). http://ieeexplore.ieee.org/document/4138045/
33. Sui, Y., Yu, W., Luo, Q.: Jointly optimized extreme learning machine for short-term prediction of fading channel. IEEE Access **6**, 49029–49039 (2018). https://ieeexplore.ieee.org/document/8457080/
34. Tan, S., Hirose, A.: Low-calculation-cost fading channel prediction using chirp Z-transform. Electron. Lett. **45**(8), 418 (2009). http://digital-library.theiet.org/content/journals/10.1049/el.2009.3472
35. Lu, T.-C., Yu, G.-R., Juang, J.-C.: Quantum-based algorithm for optimizing artificial neural networks. IEEE Trans. Neural Netw. Learn. Syst. **24**(8), 1266–1278 (2013). http://ieeexplore.ieee.org/document/6507335/
36. Valle, M.E.: Complex-valued recurrent correlation neural networks. IEEE Trans. Neural Netw. Learn. Syst. **25**(9), 1600–1612 (2014). http://ieeexplore.ieee.org/lpdocs/epic03/wrapper.htm?arnumber=6866912
37. Zhao, Y., Gao, H., Beaulieu, N.C., Chen, Z., Ji, H.: Echo state network for fast channel prediction in ricean fading scenarios. IEEE Commun. Lett. **21**(3), 672–675 (2017). http://ieeexplore.ieee.org/document/7755792/

Set Aggregation Network as a Trainable Pooling Layer

Łukasz Maziarka[1,2], Marek Śmieja[1(✉)], Aleksandra Nowak[1], Jacek Tabor[1], Łukasz Struski[1], and Przemysław Spurek[1]

[1] Faculty of Mathematics and Computer Science, Jagiellonian University, Łojasiewicza 6, 30-348 Kraków, Poland
marek.smieja@ii.uj.edu.pl
[2] Ardigen, Podole 76, 30-394 Kraków, Poland

Abstract. Global pooling, such as max- or sum-pooling, is one of the key ingredients in deep neural networks used for processing images, texts, graphs and other types of structured data. Based on the recent DeepSets architecture proposed by Zaheer et al. (NIPS 2017), we introduce a Set Aggregation Network (SAN) as an alternative global pooling layer. In contrast to typical pooling operators, SAN allows to embed a given set of features to a vector representation of arbitrary size. We show that by adjusting the size of embedding, SAN is capable of preserving the whole information from the input. In experiments, we demonstrate that replacing global pooling layer by SAN leads to the improvement of classification accuracy. Moreover, it is less prone to overfitting and can be used as a regularizer.

Keywords: Global pooling · Structured data · Representation learning · Convolutional neural networks · Set processing · Image processing

1 Introduction

Deep neural networks are one of the most powerful machine learning tools for processing structured data such as images, texts or graphs [9,18]. While convolutional or recurrent neural networks allow to extract a set of meaningful features, it is not straightforward how to vectorize their output and pass it to the fully connected layers.

One typical approach to this problem relies on flattening the given tensor. However, the flattened vector may contain a lot of redundant information, which in turn may lead to overfitting. Moreover, flattening cannot be followed by a dense layer (e.g. in classification models), when the input has varied size [2, 11]. This situation often appears in graphs and texts classification, but is also common in learning from images of different resolutions [1,4,7].

In order to produce a fixed-length vector, a maximum or sum function may be applied to the learned data representations. This operation is commonly known

© Springer Nature Switzerland AG 2019
T. Gedeon et al. (Eds.): ICONIP 2019, LNCS 11954, pp. 419–431, 2019.
https://doi.org/10.1007/978-3-030-36711-4_35

as the global pooling. In image recognition the data is frequently aggregated by computing the average value over the channels of the feature map tensor obtained by the backbone network. Such vector is then passed to the predictor head. This is the case in numerous large scale networks such as ResNet [6], DenseNet [8] or, more recent, Amoeba-Net [17]. In Graph Neural Networks the representation of a given node is usually computed by recursively mean-pooling the representations of its neighbours [12,22]. Despite its wide applicability, the global pooling layer is not able to fully exploit the information from the input data, because it does not contain trainable parameters. Moreover, the global pooling cannot adjust the dimensionality of the representation, because the size of its result is solely determined by the number of input channels.

An additional requirement often imposed on the aggregation function is the invariance to the permutation of the input. This constraint arises as a consequence of set processing, and is present, for instance, in 3D point cloud recognition [15] and graph analysis [22]. The issue of efficiently learning a representation of permutation invariant inputs was recently studied by Zaheer et al. [23], who proposed a unified methodology for the processing of sets by neural networks. Their model, called DeepSets, is based on the idea of summing the representations of the sets elements. This concept was also further developed by [14] who define the pooling function as the average of permutation-sensitive maps of all reorderings of the sequence of the set members. Those permutation-sensitive functions may be modeled by recurrent networks and allow for learning representations that utilize high order dependencies between the set points already at the aggregation time. Neural networks capable of processing sets where also analyzed by [19], who prove that the studied permutation invariant/equivariant deep models are universal approximators of permutation invariant/equivariant functions.

In this paper, we propose Set Aggregation Network (SAN), an alternative to the global pooling operation, which guarantees no information loss. For this purpose, we adapt the DeepSets architecture to embed a set of features retrieved from structured data into a vector of fixed length. Contrary to pooling operation, the parameters of SAN are trainable and we can adjust the size of its representation. In addition to Zaheer et al. [23], we prove that for a sufficiently large latent space, SAN learns a unique representation of every input set, which justifies this approach from a theoretical perspective (Theorem 1).

Our experimental results confirm that replacing global pooling by SAN leads to the improvement of classification accuracy of convolutional neural networks used in classification (Sect. 4). Moreover, SAN is less prone to overfitting, which allows to use it as a regularizer. The experiments were carried out on a small network architecture as well as on the large-scale ResNet model.

2   Set Aggregation Network

Suppose that we want to process structured data $X = (x_i)_i \subset \mathbb{R}^D$ by the use of a neural network. Some practical examples of X may include a sequence of word

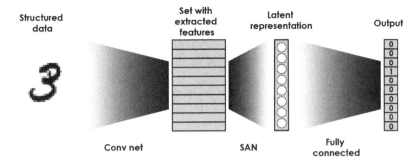

Fig. 1. SAN is an intermediate network which is responsible for learning a vector representation using a set of features extracted from of structured data.

embeddings, image represented as a set of pixels or a graph structure. In this paper, we study one of the typical architectures used for processing such data. It consists of two networks combined with an intermediate pooling layer:

$$X = (x_i)_i \xrightarrow{\Psi} (\Psi x_i)_i \xrightarrow{\text{Pool}} \text{Pool}\{\Psi(x_i) : i\} \xrightarrow{\Phi} \mathbb{R}^N. \tag{1}$$

The first network $\Psi : \mathbb{R}^{aD} \to \mathbb{R}^K$, where $a \in \mathbb{N}$, is responsible for extracting meaningful features of structured data. In the case of images it can be a convolutional network, while for a sequential data, such as texts, it may be a recurrent neural network. This network transforms elements of X sequentially and produces a set (or sequence) of K-dimensional vectors. Depending on the size of X (length of a sentence or image resolution), the number of vectors returned by Ψ may vary. To make the response of Ψ equally-sized, a global pooling is applied, which returns a single K-dimensional vector. A pooling layer, commonly implemented as a sum or maximum operation over the set of K-dimensional vectors, gives a vector representation of structured object. Finally, a network $\Phi : \mathbb{R}^K \to \mathbb{R}^N$ maps the resulting representation to the final output.

The basic problem with the above pipeline lies in the pooling layer. Global pooling "squashes" a set of K-dimensional vectors into a single output with K attributes. A single K-dimensional output vector may be insufficient to preserve the whole information contained in the input set (especially for large sets and small K), which makes a pooling operation the main bottleneck of the above architecture. In this paper, we would like to address this problem. We focus on defining more suitable aggregation network, which will be able to learn a sufficiently rich latent representation of structured data.

To replace a pooling layer, we extend DeepSets architecture introduced in [23] to the case of structured data. In consequence, we define an aggregation network, which embeds a set of extracted features to a fixed-length representation. First, we recall a basic idea behind pioneering work of Zaheer et al. and explain its use as an alternative to the classical pooling layer. In the next section, we prove that this framework is able to preserve the whole information contained in the set structure.

Let $f : \mathbb{R}^D \supset X \to y \in Y$ be a function, which maps sets $X = (x_i)_i$ to some target values $y \in Y$. Since f deals with sets, then the response of f should be invariant to the ordering of set elements. Zaheer et al. [23] showed that to realize this requirement f has to be decomposed in the form:

$$f(X) = \rho(\sum_i \tau(x_i)), \tag{2}$$

for suitable transformations ρ, τ. In the case of neural networks, f can be implemented by constructing two networks τ and ρ. The first network processes elements of a given set X sequentially. Next, the response of τ is summarized over the whole elements of X and a single vector is returned. Finally, a network ρ maps the resulting representation to the final output.

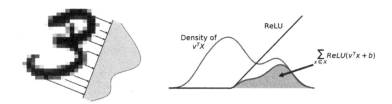

Fig. 2. The idea of our approach is to aggregate information from projections of a set onto several one-dimensional subspaces (left). Next non-linear activation function is applied to every set element and the results are aggregated (right).

One can directly adapt the above architecture to the pipeline considered in this paper. Namely, instead of taking the maximum or sum pooling over the set of extracted features, we define a separate neural network τ to compute the summarized activation for all set elements (the role of ρ is played by a network Φ in our framework). We refer to this network as set aggregation network (SAN), see Fig. 1. If τ contains M output neurons, then we get M-dimensional vector representation of the structured data. In contrast to pooling operation, which always returns K-dimensional vector (K is a dimension of input feature vectors), the size of representation produced by SAN may be adjusted to a given problem. Moreover, their parameters are trainable and thus we allow for learning the most convenient representation of structured data. Although SAN is designed to process permutation invariant structures (sets), one may add special attributes to indicate the ordering of extracted features. One way is to use the normalization of the elements index or its trigonometric transformation [20, Sect. 3.5].

The following remark shows that max-pooling is a special case of SAN.

Remark 1. Observe that max-pooling is a special case of SAN. Clearly, for non-negative scalar data $X = (X_i) \subset \mathbb{R}$ and function $\tau_p(x) = x^p$, we have:

$$\tau^{-1}(\sum_i \tau(x_i)) \to \max_i(x_i), \text{ as } p \to \infty. \tag{3}$$

To obtain a maximum, we use τ as the activity function in aggregative neuron, which is followed by a layer with its inverse. By extending this scheme, we can get a maximum value for every coordinate. Additionally, to deal with negative numbers, we first take the exponent followed by logarithm after the aggregation.

3   Theoretical Analysis

Although Zaheer et al. theoretically derived the form of f as the only permutation invariant transformation operating on sets, there is no guarantees that this network is capable of learning a unique representation for every set. In this section we address this question and show that if τ is a universal approximator, then $\sum_{x \in X} \tau(x)$ gives a unique embedding of every set X in a vector space.

Before a formal proof, we first give an illustrative argument for this fact. A typical approach used in computer tomography applies Radon transform [5,16] to reconstruct a function (in practice the 2D or 3D image) from the knowledge of its integration over all one-dimensional lines. A similar statement is given by the Cramer-Wold Theorem [3], which says that for every two distinct measures one can find their one-dimensional projection which discriminates them. This implies that without loss of information we can process the set $X \subset \mathbb{R}^K$ through its all one-dimensional projections $v^T X \subset \mathbb{R}$, where $v \in \mathbb{R}^K$.

In consequence, we reduce the question of representing a multidimensional set to the characterization of one-dimensional sets. Next, one can easily see that the one-dimensional set $S \subset \mathbb{R}$ can be retrieved from the knowledge of aggregated ReLU on its translations: $b \to \sum_i \mathrm{ReLU}(s_i + b)$, see Fig. 2. Summarizing the above reasoning, we obtain that the full knowledge of a set $X \subset \mathbb{R}^K$ is given by the scalar function

$$\mathbb{R}^K \times \mathbb{R} \ni (v, b) \to \sum_i \mathrm{ReLU}(v^T x_i + b). \tag{4}$$

Now, given M vectors $v_i \in \mathbb{R}^K$ and biases $b_i \in \mathbb{R}$, we obtain the fixed-size representation of the set $X \subset \mathbb{R}^K$ as a point in $\mathbb{R}^M$ given by

$$[\sum_i \mathrm{ReLU}(v_1^T x_i + b_1), \ldots, \sum_i \mathrm{ReLU}(v_M^T x_i + b_M)] \in \mathbb{R}^M. \tag{5}$$

The above transformation directly coincides with a single layer SAN parametrized by ReLU function. Thus for a sufficiently large number of neurons, SAN allows to uniquely identify every input set.

Now, we show formally that the above reasoning can be extended to a wide range of activity functions. For this purpose, we will use the UAP (universal approximation property). We say that a family of neurons $\mathcal{N}$ has UAP if for every compact set $K \subset \mathbb{R}^D$ and a continuous function $f : K \to \mathbb{R}$ the function f can be arbitrarily close approximated with respect to supremum norm by $\mathrm{span}(\mathcal{N})$ (linear combinations of elements of $\mathcal{N}$). We show that if a given family of neurons satisfies UAP, then the corresponding SAN allows to distinguish any two sets:

Theorem 1. *Let X, Y be two sets in $\mathbb{R}^D$. Let $\mathcal{N}$ be a family of functions having UAP.*
If

$$\tau(X) = \tau(Y) \text{ , for every } \tau \in \mathcal{N}, \tag{6}$$

then $X = Y$.

Proof. Let μ and ν be two measures representing sets X and Y, respectively, i.e. $\mu = \mathbf{1}_X$ and $\nu = \mathbf{1}_Y$. We show that if $\tau(X) = \tau(Y)$ then μ and ν are equal.

Let $R > 1$ be such that $X \cup Y \subset B(0, R-1)$, where $B(a, r)$ denotes the closed ball centered at a and with radius r. To prove that measures μ, ν are equal it is sufficient to prove that they coincide on each ball $B(a, r)$ with arbitrary $a \in B(0, R-1)$ and radius $r < 1$.

Let ϕ_n be defined by

$$\phi_n(x) = 1 - n \cdot d(x, B(a, r)) \text{ for } x \in \mathbb{R}^D, \tag{7}$$

where $d(x, U)$ denotes the distance of point x from the set U. Observe that ϕ_n is a continuous function which is one on $B(a, r)$ an and zero on $\mathbb{R}^D \setminus B(a, r+1/n)$, and therefore ϕ_n is a uniformly bounded sequence of functions which converges pointwise to the characteristic funtion $\mathbf{1}_{B(a,r)}$ of the set $B(a, r)$.

By the UAP property we choose $\psi_n \in \text{span}(\mathcal{N})$ such that

$$\sup_{x \in B(0,R)} |\phi_n(x) - \psi_n(x)| \leq 1/n. \tag{8}$$

Thus ψ_n restricted to $B(0, R)$ is also a uniformly bounded sequence of functions which converges pointwise to $\mathbf{1}_{B(a,r)}$. Since $\psi_n \in \mathcal{N}$, by (6) we get

$$\sum_{x \in X} \mu(x)\psi_n(x) = \sum_{y \in Y} \nu(y)\psi_n(y). \tag{9}$$

Now by the Lebesgue dominated convergence theorem we trivially get

$$\begin{aligned}
\sum_{x \in X} \mu(x)\psi_n(x) &= \int_{B(0,R)} \psi_n(x) d\mu(x) \rightarrow \mu(B(a, r)), \\
\sum_{y \in Y} \nu(y)\psi_n(y) &= \int_{B(0,R)} \psi_n(x) d\nu(x) \rightarrow \nu(B(a, r)),
\end{aligned} \tag{10}$$

which completes proof.

4   Experiments

We apply SAN to typical architectures used for processing images. Our primary goal is to compare SAN with global pooling in various settings. First, we focus on classifying images of the same sizes using a small convolutional neural network. Next, we extend this experiment to the case of images with varied resolutions. Finally, we consider a large scale ResNet architecture and show that replacing a global pooling layer by SAN leads to the improvement of classification performance. Our implementation is available at github[1].

---

[1] https://github.com/gmum/set-aggregation.

Table 1. Architecture summary of a small neural network (N is the size of the input to the layer, and D is the number of output neurons from the SAN layer).

Flatten			Max/Avg-pooling			SAN		
Type	Kernel	Outputs	Type	Kernel	Outputs	Type	Kernel	Outputs
Conv 2d	3 × 3	32	Conv 2d	3 × 3	32	Conv 2d	3 × 3	32
Max pooling	2 × 2		Max pooling	2 × 2		Max pooling	2 × 2	
Conv 2d	3 × 3	64	Conv 2d	3 × 3	64	Conv 2d	3 × 3	64
Max pooling	2 × 2		Max pooling	2 × 2		Max pooling	2 × 2	
Conv 2d	3 × 3	64	Conv 2d	3 × 3	64	Conv 2d	3 × 3	64
Flatten			Max/Avg pooling	N × N		SAN		D
Dense		128	Dense		D	Dense		10
Dense		10	Dense		10			

4.1 Small Classification Network

We considered a classification task on CIFAR-10 [13], which consists of 60 000 color images of the size 32×32 and the Fashion-MNIST, composed of 70 000 gray-scale pictures of size 28×28 [21]. We used small neural networks with 3 convolutional layers with ReLU activity function and a max-pooling between them, see Table 1 for details.

To aggregate resulted tensor we considered the following variants:

– **flatten:** We flattened a tensor to preserve the whole information from the previous network.
– **conv-1x1:** We applied 1×1 convolutions with one channel and flattened the output. This reduces the number of parameters in subsequent dense layer compared to the classical flatten approach.
– **max-pooling:** We applied max pooling along spatial dimensions (width and height of a tensor) to reduce the dimensionality. In consequence, we obtained a vector of the size equal the depth of the tensor.
– **avg-pooling:** We considered a similar procedure as above, but instead of max pooling we used average pooling.
– **SAN:** We used a single layer SAN as an alternative aggregation. The resulting tensor was treated as a set of vectors with sizes equal to the depth of the tensor. Moreover, the (normalized) indices were added to every vector to preserve the information about local structure.

SAN allows to select the number of output neurons. For the experiment, we considered the following numbers of output neurons: $\{128, 256, 512, 1024, 2048, 4096\}$. To use the same number of parameters for global pooling and conv1x1 approaches we followed them by a dense network with identical number of neurons to SAN. In the case of flatten, we obtained a comparable number of parameters to the other networks trained on the size 4 096. In each case we used additional two dense layers, except for the SAN model, where only one dense layer was used. All models were trained using adam optimizer with a learning rate 10^{-3} and batch size 256. We used 5 000

Table 2. Classification accuracy on a small network (images with the same resolutions) for different number of parameters used in aggregation layer.

Size	Fashion MNIST					CIFAR 10				
	Flatten	Avg-pool	Max-pool	conv-1x1	SAN	Flatten	Avg-pool	Max-pool	conv-1x1	SAN
128	–	0.852	0.901	**0.916**	0.912	–	0.624	0.690	0.731	**0.738**
256	–	0.877	0.908	**0.916**	0.911	–	0.649	0.697	0.738	**0.739**
512	–	0.879	0.906	**0.918**	0.910	–	0.671	0.701	0.722	**0.730**
1024	–	0.888	0.914	0.912	**0.915**	–	0.659	0.683	0.722	**0.756**
2048	–	0.889	0.912	0.914	**0.919**	–	0.697	0.686	0.707	**0.733**
4096	**0.919**	0.912	0.900	0.914	0.912	0.720	0.738	0.708	0.709	**0.762**

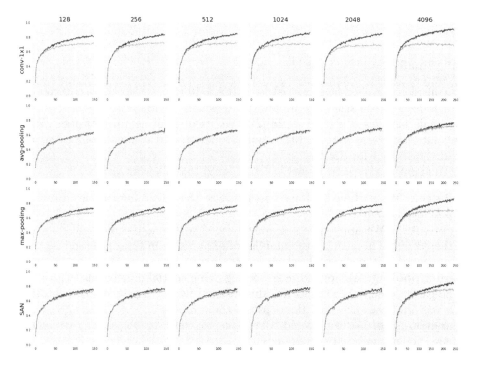

Fig. 3. Train (blue) and test accuracy (red) on CIFAR-10 (images with the same resolutions) for different number of parameters used in aggregation layer. (Color figure online)

images for the validation set, 5 000 images for the test set for both CIFAR-10 and Fashion-MNIST. We trained every model on the remaining images.

It is evident from Table 2 that SAN outperformed all reported operations on CIFAR-10. In addition, it gave higher accuracy than flatten when both approaches have a comparable number of parameters (last row). We verified that lower results of flatten were caused by its slight overfitting to the training data. Adding dropout to flatten makes both approaches comparable. In the case of significantly simpler Fashion-MNIST dataset, the differences between all

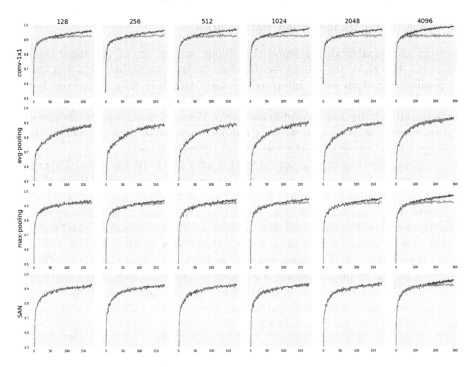

Fig. 4. Train (blue) and test accuracy (red) on Fashion-MNIST (images with the same resolutions) for different number of parameters used in aggregation layer. (Color figure online)

methods are smaller. SAN achieved an identical accuracy to flatten for the size 2048. Note however, that the flatten approach uses twice as much parameters as SAN. This demonstrates that by the use of SAN the network can be simplified without any loss in accuracy.

To get more insight to the results, we present learning curves for CIFAR-10 and Fashion-MNIST in Figs. 3 and 4, respectively. It is evident that max-pooling and conv-1x1 highly overfitted to training data, especially on the more demanding CIFAR-10 dataset. Although avg-pooling presented comparable accuracy on train and test sets, its overall performance was quite low, and matched that of the other methods only for high number of the parameters. In contrast, SAN provided high accuracy and did not suffer from high overfitting to training data. In addition, for the Fashion-MNIST experiment, SAN converged to high performance (over 90%) much faster than the corresponding avg-pooling approach.

This experiment partially confirms our theoretical result that for a sufficient number of neurons, SAN is able to preserve the whole information contained in the input. On the other hand, it shows that SAN can work as a regularizer, which prevents the model from overfitting.

4.2 Classifying Images with Varied Sizes

Most classification models assume that input images are of the same size. If this is not the case, we are forced to scale images at preprocessing stage or use pooling operation as an intermediate layer to apply fully connected layers afterwards. In this experiment, we compared SAN with max-pooling and avg-pooling in classifying images of different sizes. We used analogical architecture as in previous section. Note that we were unable to use flatten or conv-1x1, because the output from convolutional network had different sizes.

We again considered Fashion-MNIST and CIFAR-10 datasets. To create examples with different sizes we used bicubic interpolation on randomly selected images[2]. We examined two cases. In the first one, the network was trained only on images with original resolution, but tested on images with different resolutions. In the second case, scaled images were used both in training and testing.

The results presented in Table 3 show that **SAN** produced more accurate results than both global pooling approaches for almost every image resolution. Observe that the results are worse when only images with 32×32 size were used in train set. It can be explained by the fact that convolutional filters were not trained to recognize relevant features from images with different scales. In this case, the differences are even higher.

Table 3. Classification accuracy for images with varied resolutions.

Dataset	Image size	Trained on all resolutions			Trained only on original resolution		
		Max-pool	Avg-pool	SAN	Max-pool	Avg-pool	SAN
Fashion MNIST	14×14	0.8788	0.8753	**0.8810**	0.2519	0.270	**0.2884**
	22×22	0.8969	0.9002	**0.9064**	0.7380	0.801	**0.8247**
	28×28	0.9023	0.9078	**0.9111**	0.9062	0.904	**0.9150**
	42×42	0.9020	**0.9041**	0.9033	0.5548	0.6511	**0.6893**
	56×56	0.8913	0.8960	**0.8966**	0.3274	0.3809	**0.4515**
CIFAR-10	16×16	0.5593	0.5820	**0.6305**	0.3251	0.2714	**0.3808**
	24×24	0.6450	0.6935	**0.7317**	0.6409	0.6130	**0.6956**
	32×32	0.6729	0.7018	**0.7565**	0.7131	**0.7637**	0.7534
	40×40	0.6739	0.6914	**0.7430**	0.6512	0.6780	**0.7234**
	48×48	0.6770	0.6625	**0.7626**	0.5325	0.5366	**0.6264**

4.3 Large Scale ResNet Experiment

In previous experiments we deliberately use a rather simple network in order the examine the effect of only alternating the aggregation method. This allows for the assessment of the methods performance in isolation from any additional layers which could further improve models regularization effect and which are

---

[2] For CIFAR-10, original images of size 32×32 were scaled to $16 \times 16, 24 \times 24, 32 \times 32, 40 \times 40, 48 \times 48$. For Fashion-MNIST, images of size 28×28 were scaled to $14 \times 14, 22 \times 22, 42 \times 42, 56 \times 56$.

necessary to efficiently train a vast network (such as, for instance, batch norm [10]). In this experiment, we tested the impact of using SAN in a large-scale network.

Table 4. Test accuracy on CIFAR-10 using the ResNets architecture. The first column corresponds to the original ResNet model. The ResNet-avg/max/conv-1x1 models come with an additional penultimate dense layer of size 4096, in order to match the number of parameters in SAN .

	Original	ResNet-avg	ResNet-max	ResNet-conv1x1	ResNet-SAN
Error	0.0735	0.0724	0.0782	0.0780	**0.0697**

For this purpose we chose the ResNet-56 model [6], which consists of 56 layers. The original ResNet uses the global average pooling approach followed by a dense layer, which projects the data into the output dimension. Our modification relies on replacing global pooling by SAN. As introduction of the SAN with 4096 vectors comes at a cost of increased number of parameters, we added an additional, penultimate dense layer with hidden dimension 4096 to the ResNet for the average- and the max-pooling, and the conv-1x1, in order to allow for fair comparison.

The results for CIFAR-10 dataset are reported in Table 4. It is evident that the introduction of SAN to the original ResNet architecture led to the improvement of classification accuracy. Moreover, SAN outperformed other aggregation approaches.

5   Conclusion

In this paper, we proposed a novel aggregation network, SAN, for processing structured data. Our architecture is based on recent methodology used for learning from permutation invariant structures (sets) [23]. In addition, to Zaheer's work, we showed that for a sufficiently large number of neurons, SAN allows to preserve the whole information contained in the input. This theoretical result was experimentally confirmed applying convolutional network to image data. Conducted experiments demonstrated that the replacing of global pooling by SAN in typical neural networks used for processing images leads to higher performance of the model.

Acknowledgements. This work was partially supported by the National Science Centre (Poland) grants numbers: 2018/31/B/ST6/00993, 2017/25/B/ST6/01271 and 2015/19/D/ST6/01472.

References

1. Brin, S., Page, L.: The anatomy of a large-scale hypertextual web search engine. Comput. Netw. ISDN Syst. **30**(1–7), 107–117 (1998)
2. Ciresan, D.C., Meier, U., Masci, J., Maria Gambardella, L., Schmidhuber, J.: Flexible, high performance convolutional neural networks for image classification. In: IJCAI Proceedings-International Joint Conference on Artificial Intelligence, Barcelona, Spain, vol. 22, p. 1237 (2011)
3. Cramér, H., Wold, H.: Some theorems on distribution functions. J. London Math. Soc. **1**(4), 290–294 (1936)
4. Frasconi, P., Gori, M., Sperduti, A.: A general framework for adaptive processing of data structures. IEEE Trans. Neural Netw. **9**(5), 768–786 (1998)
5. van Ginkel, M., Hendriks, C.L., van Vliet, L.J.: A short introduction to the radon and hough transforms and how they relate to each other. Delft University of Technology (2004)
6. He, K., Zhang, X., Ren, S., Sun, J.: Deep residual learning for image recognition. In: 2016 IEEE Conference on Computer Vision and Pattern Recognition (CVPR), pp. 770–778, June 2016. https://doi.org/10.1109/CVPR.2016.90
7. He, K., Zhang, X., Ren, S., Sun, J.: Spatial pyramid pooling in deep convolutional networks for visual recognition. IEEE Trans. Pattern Anal. Mach. Intell. **37**(9), 1904–1916 (2015)
8. Huang, G., Liu, Z., Weinberger, K.Q.: Densely connected convolutional networks. In: 2017 IEEE Conference on Computer Vision and Pattern Recognition (CVPR), pp. 2261–2269 (2017)
9. Iizuka, S., Simo-Serra, E., Ishikawa, H.: Globally and locally consistent image completion. ACM Trans. Graph. (TOG) **36**(4), 107 (2017)
10. Ioffe, S., Szegedy, C.: Batch normalization: accelerating deep network training by reducing internal covariate shift. In: Proceedings of the 32nd International Conference on International Conference on Machine Learning, ICML 2015, vol. 37. pp. 448–456. JMLR.org (2015)
11. Karpathy, A., Fei-Fei, L.: Deep visual-semantic alignments for generating image descriptions. In: Proceedings of the IEEE Conference on Computer Vision and Pattern Recognition, pp. 3128–3137 (2015)
12. Kipf, T.N., Welling, M.: Semi-supervised classification with graph convolutional networks. arXiv preprint arXiv:1609.02907 (2016)
13. Krizhevsky, A., Hinton, G.: Learning multiple layers of features from tiny images. Technical report, Citeseer (2009)
14. Murphy, R.L., Srinivasan, B., Rao, V., Ribeiro, B.: Janossy pooling: learning deep permutation-invariant functions for variable-size inputs. In: International Conference on Learning Representations (2019). https://openreview.net/forum?id=BJluy2RcFm
15. Qi, C.R., Su, H., Mo, K., Guibas, L.J.: PointNet: deep learning on point sets for 3D classification and segmentation. In: 2017 IEEE Conference on Computer Vision and Pattern Recognition (CVPR), pp. 77–85 (2017)
16. Radon, J.: On the determination of functions from their integral values along certain manifolds. IEEE Trans. Med. Imaging **5**(4), 170–176 (1986)
17. Real, E., Aggarwal, A., Huang, Y., Le, Q.V.: Regularized evolution for image classifier architecture search. arXiv preprint arXiv:1802.01548 (2018)

18. Ronneberger, O., Fischer, P., Brox, T.: U-net: convolutional networks for biomedical image segmentation. In: Navab, N., Hornegger, J., Wells, W.M., Frangi, A.F. (eds.) MICCAI 2015. LNCS, vol. 9351, pp. 234–241. Springer, Cham (2015). https://doi.org/10.1007/978-3-319-24574-4_28
19. Sannai, A., Takai, Y., Cordonnier, M.: Universal approximations of permutation invariant/equivariant functions by deep neural networks. arXiv preprint arXiv:1903.01939 (2019)
20. Vaswani, A., et al.: Attention is all you need. In: Advances in Neural Information Processing Systems, pp. 5998–6008 (2017)
21. Xiao, H., Rasul, K., Vollgraf, R.: Fashion-MNIST: a novel image dataset for benchmarking machine learning algorithms. arXiv preprint arXiv:1708.07747 (2017)
22. Xu, K., Hu, W., Leskovec, J., Jegelka, S.: How powerful are graph neural networks? In: International Conference on Learning Representations (2019). https://openreview.net/forum?id=ryGs6iA5Km
23. Zaheer, M., Kottur, S., Ravanbakhsh, S., Poczos, B., Salakhutdinov, R.R., Smola, A.J.: Deep sets. In: Advances in Neural Information Processing Systems, pp. 3391–3401 (2017)

Exploring Latent Structure Similarity for Bayesian Nonparameteric Model with Mixture of NHPP Sequence

Yongzhe Chang[1,2(✉)], Zhidong Li[1,3], Ling Luo[4], Simon Luo[1], Arcot Sowmya[2], Yang Wang[1,3], and Fang Chen[1,3]

[1] Data 61 CSIRO, Sydney, Australia
{yongzhe.chang,zhidong.li,simon.luo,yang.wang,fang.chen}@data61.csiro.au
[2] University of New South Wales, Kensington, Australia
{yongzhe.chang,arcot.sowmya}@unsw.edu.au
[3] University of Technology Sydney, Ultimo, Australia
{zhidong.li,yang.wang,fang.chen}@uts.edu.au
[4] The University of Melbourne, Melbourne, Australia
ling.luo@unimelb.edu.au

Abstract. Temporal point process data has been widely observed in many applications including finance, health, and infrastructures, so that it has become an important topic in data analytics domain. Generally, a point process only records occurrence of a type of event as 1 or 0. To interpret the temporal point process, it is important to estimate the intensity of the occurrence of events, which is challenging especially when the intensity is dynamic over time, for example non-homogeneous Poisson process (NHPP) which is exactly what we will analyse in this paper. We performed a joint task to determine which two NHPP sequences are in the same group and to estimate the intensity resides in that group. Distance dependent Chinese Restaurant Process (ddCRP) provides a prior to cluster data points within a Bayesian nonparametric framework, alleviating the required knowledge to set the number of clusters which is sensitive in clustering problems. However, the distance in previous studies of ddCRP is designed for data points, in this paper such distance is measured by dynamic time warping (DTW) due to its wide application in ordinary time series (e.g. observed values are in $\mathcal{R}$). The empirical study using synthetic and real-world datasets shows promising outcome compared with the alternative techniques.

Keywords: NHPP · ddCRP · DTW

1 Introduction

A temporal point process is basically a random list process whose observations are times of events. A simple temporal point process can be typically modeled by its intensity λ which related to time t, familiarity with Poisson process [18] and

© Springer Nature Switzerland AG 2019
T. Gedeon et al. (Eds.): ICONIP 2019, LNCS 11954, pp. 432–444, 2019.
https://doi.org/10.1007/978-3-030-36711-4_36

Hawkes process [9]. In the real world, many phenomena can be represented as temporal point process, for example the happening of earthquakes, customers' shopping records and patients' hospitalization records etc. For these examples, one common issue is that we do not know how many time of events may occur and at what time. However, latent pattern may behind superficial phenomenon, for instance an earthquake can cause aftershocks. An essential target is to estimate intensity function of temporal point process in order to predict the future events.

A non-homogeneous Poisson process (NHPP) is a counting process with its average rate of arrivals varying with time. In general, intensity function of NHPP can be any arbitrary function over temporal variables, due to this fact, it is difficult to recover the true underlying intensity function form in many cases. Therefore it is challenging in estimating intensity function for temporal point process directly. Moreover, estimation for intensity function may suffer from the model selection problem and the insufficient power of intensity functions to represent complex real-world problems.

For a given NHPP, we can first estimate intensity function then cluster them according to each intensity function, assign those NHPP with same or similar intensity functions, for example [14] discussed Bayesian nonparametric methods in clustering and in [19], Chinese restaurant process (CRP) Dirichlet mixture model and Hierarchical Dirichlet mixture model were used in achieving the goal. When using Bayesian nonparametric methods in clustering, the framework of Bayesian nonparametric prior and a mixture component is usually being used, such as in [7] they combined a nonparamatric prior with Dirichlet allocation in learning topic hierarchies from data.

However, Bayesian nonparametric clustering methods are complicated and slow, especially for clustering NHPP. First, in order to be more efficient, the likelihood is preferable to be conjugate to the prior, otherwise Monte Carlo Markov chain (MCMC) should be utilzied for inference, which is tractable but less efficient. Second, each object being clustered itself is a Bayesian nonparametric process, e.g. the intensity is formulated as a transformed Gaussian process (GP) which guarantees the intensity being positive. However, as a well known result, the complexity of GP inference is cubic so the inference algorithm becomes extremely inefficient. Thirdly, in Bayesian nonparametric clustering, the highly similar components can still be assigned to different clusters due to sampling randomness, which leads to a undesirable result.

Considering the problems above, in this paper, we proposed a Bayesian nonparametric model which is a DTW based ddCRP model and we shortly named it DTW-ddCRP model, to discover latent pattern of intensity function and cluster NHPP, which is much faster and easier for inference than CRP based clustering model mentioned above. In our model, we used DTW distance measurement for similarity learning and reflecting structure information within processes, then we proposed ddCRP-based model to study the partition of failure event processes. DTW distance measurement is an accurate measure in looking for the nearest neighbor and ddCRP gives partition result without knowing the number of partitions at first. However, DTW can only find out the nearest one, ddCRP has the ability of deciding whether the two customer should be put into one cluster because of the setting of scalar α and decay function parameter. We combined ddCRP with DTW distance measure, and used Gibbs sampler in the inference part of our model. It makes contribution via tackling the challenges in the temporal point process pattern learning: clustering temporal point processes without knowing latent pattern, which is especially latent dynamic intensity here; estimating latent dynamic intensity of water mains failure bursts by inferring the probability of which cluster one failure event process would in; then according to the ddCRP inference, the label of each table (cluster) can be obtained, which is an approximation of water mains failure intensity.

2   Related Work

In this section, we give a brief introduction about related work. Section 2.1 introduces sequence similarity learning method especially what we use in our model, the DTW distance measurement. In Sect. 2.2 we will describe Bayesian nonparametric methods in clustering and parameter estimation work, distance dependent Chinese restaurant process.

2.1   Clustering for Time-Series and DTW Distance

Clustering for time-series has been shown effective in providing useful information in various domain and attracted increasing interest as a part of the effort in the temporal data mining research [12]. In [8], Han and Kamber classified clustering methods into five main categories: hierarchical methods, density-based methods, partitioning methods, grid-based methods, and model-based methods.

In clustering model for time-series, the distance measurement approach is an important part. The most popular distance measurements for time-series data include Euclidean distance, Hausdorff distance, HMM-based distance and DTW distance, etc [2]. Each of these distance measurements has its advantages and disadvantages, for example the Euclidean distance in simple but can only be used when different sequences have same length; the DTW distance is computational expensive but can treat with different length of sequences. In our model, we chose DTW distance measurement mainly because its good performance on measuring sequences with different length.

DTW algorithm is a distance learning measurement by obtaining the optimal alignment between two time series, especially when the two sequences vary in speed, and has been widely used in time series clustering not only in academic domain, but also in many industrial projects [13] in the past decades. These applications include image processing, data mining, computer graphics and so on. It is one of the best measurement in searching for the nearest neighbor [6], defined for time series by measuring the distance between temporal sequences that vary in frequency and length. As all known, the expensive calculation problem is always the key problem for distance measurements, researchers have done plenty of contribution to speed it up and have a better performance, for example [16] and [15].

2.2   Joint Model for Clustering and Parameter Estimation

The Chinese restaurant process (CRP) [4] is a probability distribution over partitions. It is a popular representation of Dirichlet process (DP) and emphasis the clustering nature of DP. CRP assumes a prior distribution over the clusters of customers and is widely used in Bayesian nonparametric mixture models. It gives the probability of which table a coming customer may sit at by assuming that there are infinite tables in the Chinese restaurant. The CRP model is exchangeable because the change of the coming order of customers does not change the distribution of partition and each customer's probability assigned to any particular table only depends on how many customers already sit at that table. A concentration parameter α determines the probability that the customer sits at a new table or not. So it is obvious that a table with more customers has higher probability on attracting a new coming customer. The CRP is a widely used clustering method especially on mixture models and open-ended problems.

However, in CRP model, there is no relation among customers, which may assign those customers that have similar pattern into different tables. Then ddCRP [3] was introduced to solve this problem that can model random partitions on non-exchangeable data. Unlike CRP, in ddCRP one customer does not choose which table to sit at directly, but choose the customer who has the nearest distance between him to sit with, which can be comprehended as the ddCRP modifies the CRP by determining the table assignment via customer relations. It is a widely used method that provide a Bayesian nonparametric prior for clustering models and mixture models. Different from k-means and other clustering methods, with ddCRP prior we can learn the number of clusters automatically from data without knowing it beforehand. Also in the preliminary work section we will expound this distribution elaborately.

3   Model and Inference

3.1   Preliminary Work

To solve NHPP clustering problem, a DP and Gaussian process (GP) mixture model can be used. Assume we have n observations that are NHPP $X = (\mathbf{x}_1, \mathbf{x}_2, ..., \mathbf{x}_n)$, here we don't know intensity function for each process, assume intensity functions are $\Lambda = (\lambda_{t1}, \lambda_{t2}, ..., \lambda_{tK})$, then equation below can achieve estimation of each intensity and clustering these NHPP:

$$P(\Lambda, Z|X) \propto P(X|\Lambda, Z)P(Z|\alpha)P(\Lambda) \tag{1}$$

In Eq. (1), Z is vector of sitting configuration, where each element is the table $z_i = k$ for $\mathbf{x}_i$; $P(X|\Lambda, Z)$ is likelihood; $P(Z|\alpha)$ is a DP prior to figure out Z, which means DP prior determines the number of clusters; $P(\Lambda) = GP(\lambda_1)GP(\lambda_2)...GP(\lambda_n)$ that samples intensity for each NHPP. By doing this, we can not only get intensity function for each process, but also handle the clustering problem. However, the question is, for NHPP its intensity λ is a function on time which is a smooth function, not discrete vector that means sampling intensity for each NHPP may be a infinity work. So it is extremely hard to do inference, even it can be done theoretically, this would be incredibly slow.

Since the GP-DP mixture model is very complicated in the inference part and to my knowledge, no one had used this kind of model before, we can use DP mixture of Beta distribution plus CRP to approximate the GP-DP model. In [11], the author used DP mixture of Beta distribution model to estimate intensity, which can be used in estimating the intensity function of NHPP. With the estimated intensity result, a CRP model can be used for final clustering. However, when the dataset is large, this method became very slow. Considering calculation efficiency, we need to propose another model that can solve this NHPP clustering problem more efficiently, which is exactly our DTW-ddCRP model.

In DTW distance measurement, suppose we have two time series $\mathbf{x} = \{x_i\}_{i=1}^{m}$ and $\mathbf{y} = \{y_j\}_{j=1}^{n}$. To find the alignment of two sequences using DTW, we should first construct an $n * m$ matrix where the (i, j) element of this matrix is the distance $d(x_i, y_j)$ between point x_i and y_j, and this distance can be Manhattan distance or Euclidean distance or other kind of distance.Then we define a cumulative distance $D(i, j)$ as bellow:

$$D(i, j) = d(x_i, y_j) + min\{D(i - 1, j - 1), D(i - 1, j), D(i, j - 1)\}. \quad (2)$$

DTW algorithm begins at element $d(x_1, y_1)$ and ends at element $d(x_m, y_n)$ so the final $D(m, n)$ is the DTW distance between time series $\mathbf{x}, \mathbf{y}$. The time complexity of DTW algorithm is $O(mn)$.

The ddCRP model determines table assignment via customer's link, which leads to a result that each customer is more likely to be clustered with other customers that are near it in an external sense. These customer assignments are generated according to the distribution below:

$$p(c_i = j | M_D, \alpha) \propto \begin{cases} f(d_{ij}) & if \ i \neq j \\ 3.\alpha & if \ i = j \end{cases} \quad (3)$$

Here we set up c_i that denotes the ith sequence's assignment, which is the index of sequence i with which sequence being put into the same cluster. Let d_{ij} denote the DTW distance between sequence i and sequence j. Let M_D denote the distance matrix of all the time series sequences, and f is the decay function. The decay function mediates how the distance of two data points affects the probability that they connect to each other, for example their probability of belonging to the same cluster. According to [3], there are three kind of decay functions, the window decay $f(d) = 1[d < a]$ which only considers customers at most distance a from the current customer; the exponential decay $f(d) = e^{-d/a}$ which decays the probability of exponentially link to an earlier customer with the current customer; and the logistic decay $f(d) = exp(-d + a)/(1 + exp(-d + a))$ which is a smooth version of the window decay. In general, ddCRP shows the probability of sequence i and j being in the same cluster, which conditioned on the distance measurement.

From Eq. (3) we note that the probability of which table would one customer sit at has relation with the distance, decay function and scalar α, which means that, if one customer have a connection with another one according to the customer links, they may have high probability sitting together at one table. However, Eq. (3) is only a prior, likelihood and setting of hyperparameters also contribute much to final assignments.

3.2 Model

In this section, we will give a formal and detailed description of the proposed DTW-ddCRP model on NHPP.

In the DTW-ddCRP model, our target is to estimate intensity $\lambda_i(t)$ for each NHPP i via time t by clustering different processes, so both intensity and clustering are latent. Each NHPP is described by $\mathbf{x}_i = \{x_{t_i}\}$ where each x_{t_i} is the event time for tth event in $\mathbf{x}_i$, where $t_i = 1...n_i$. DTW algorithm is used in the first stage to obtain distances d_{ij} for any pair of pipes i and j. This distance is later input into decay function f in ddCRP and the purpose is to estimate $\lambda_i(t)$. However, if we assume that the structure information has been compared in DTW, we can use the statistic information as simpler distributions instead of the stochastic process assumption. Here we assume that each component k follows a Poisson distribution with latent parameter $\theta = (\theta_1, \theta_2, ..., \theta_k)$, and corresponding prior is a gamma distribution with hyper-parameters α^*, β. Given two point process $\mathbf{x}_i$ and $\mathbf{x}_j$ $0 \le i, j \ge N$, we assume that $c_{ij} = 1$ indicates there is a link between them and $c_{ij} = 0$ indicates the opposite. Our target is to estimate $E(C)$ where $C \in {0, 1}^{N \times N}$, and each element is $c_{i,j}$. To obtain $E(C)$, the posterior distribution $P(C|X, f, \Theta)$ will be estimted via our model. Here $X = (\mathbf{x}_1, \mathbf{x}_2, ..., \mathbf{x}_n)$ is the dataset of all point processes, f is the decay function, and Θ includes all hyper-parameters. The connection matrix C represents which processes are linked together. Here both $\mathbf{c}$ and θ are latent. Here is the generative process:

1. For all $\mathbf{x}_i$, calculate $\mathbf{M}_D = d(\mathbf{x}_i, \mathbf{x}_j)$ as DTW distance matrix for each pair of processes in dataset X;
2. For each i, a connect $c_{ij} = 1/0$ can be generated using the probability represented in (3). For all the pipes can be linked to the same pipe, we denote the set of them to be a cluster. Then we use k to index all the clusters, and $z(x_i) = k$ to represent the transfer from clusters to the index.
3. For each cluster k, draw a cluster parameter $\theta_k \sim Gamma(\alpha^*, \beta)$. Note that θ_k does not change with t so it is much simplified version to $\lambda_i(t)$. θ_k is inferred as the model variable.
4. For each water main failure burst process, generate the number of failures by $n_i \sim Poisson(\theta_k)$.

Here we can write the posterior as: $P(C|X, \mathbf{M}_D) = \int_\lambda P(C, \lambda|X, \mathbf{M}_D) P(\lambda|\alpha^*, \beta)d\lambda$. The $P(C, \lambda|X, \mathbf{M}_D) \sim P(X|C, \lambda)P(C|d(\mathbf{x}_i, \cdot))$. Here $P(X|C, \lambda)$ is the likelihood, we use Poisson distribution. $P(C|d(\mathbf{x}_i, \cdot))$ is the ddCRP prior distribution in Eq. (3). Our model can save effort as we avoided the estimation of the likelihood using Poisson process and Gaussian process as prior. We will see the details in the inference part.

3.3   Model Inference

In this section, we will give the detailed inference method for inferring model parameters from water main failure burst process.

The inference itself analytically complicate for ddCRP-based models due to the combinatorial nature in partitions and intractable structure of the model. So, for our model we used approximated inference, the Gibbs sampler [10] particularly, due to the fact that the hyperparameters on our model are conjugate priors of our model parameters.

The key part of the inference is the inference of index for each cluster and the assignment of each customer, which in our model is the assignment of non-homogeneous Poisson processes.

As introduced in Sect. 3.2, the prior is $p(c_i|D, f, \alpha)$, the likelihood of the observation is $p(x_i|z(c_{-i} \cup c_i), G_0)$, $z(c_{-i} \cup c_i)$ is the current partition, G_0 is denote the base measure. So the posterior is then:

$$p(c_i|c_{-i}, X, \Theta) \propto p(c_i|M_D, \alpha)p(X|z(c_{-i} \cup c_i), \Theta, G_0) \qquad (4)$$

where Θ is the hyperparameters of our model and $\Theta = M_D, f, G_0$. As our cluster parameter θ is draw by Gamma distribution and our observations are Possion processes, so posterior became into:

$$p(c_i|c_{-i}, X, M_D, \alpha^*, \beta) \propto p(c_i|M_D, \alpha)p(X|z(c_{-i} \cup c_i), \alpha^*, \beta) \qquad (5)$$

Then we can decompose the likelihood term as below:

$$p(X|z(c_{-i} \cup c_i), \Theta, \alpha^*, \beta, \lambda) = \prod_{k=1}^{|z(C)|} p(X_{z(c_{1:n})=k}|\Theta, \alpha^*, \beta, \lambda) \qquad (6)$$

In Eq. 6, we define $|z(C)|$ as the number of unique clusters and $X_{z(c_{1:n})=k}$ as the set of $\mathbf{x}_i$ that are generated from cluster k. For each particular cluster, we then marginalized out the mixture component λ because the dataset of observations from each cluster are drawn independently from the same intensity, which itself is drawn from Gamma distribution, so the marginal probability is:

$$p(X|z(c_{-i} \cup c_i), \Theta, \alpha^*, \beta) = \int \prod_{k=1}^{|z(C)|} p(X_{z(c_{1:n})=k}|\Theta, \alpha^*, \beta, \lambda)d\lambda \qquad (7)$$

Then comes to the sampling part, where we use Gibbs sampling [6] that is a simple form of MCMC inference [17]. The first stage is to remove or reassign the customer link c_i, where we either leave the old cluster structure inact or split the cluster that was assigned to the coming ith customer. Then the second stage is to consider the prior probability of such new customer and corresponding changes it takes to the likelihood term. Suppose we have l and m that represent the indices that joined with index k, then resampling customer assignments from

$$p(c_i|c_{-i}, X, \Theta) \propto \begin{cases} p(c_i|M_D, \alpha)\Phi(\boldsymbol{X}, z, \alpha^*, \beta) & if \ c_i \ joins \ l \ and \ m, \\ p(c_i|M_D, \alpha) & otherwise, \end{cases} \tag{8}$$

where Φ is defined as:

$$\Phi(X, z, \alpha^*, \beta) = \frac{p(X_{z(C)=k}|\alpha^*, \beta)}{p(X_{z(C)=l}|\alpha^*, \beta)p(X_{z(C)=m}|\alpha^*, \beta)} \tag{9}$$

4 Empirical Study

In this section, we conduct the comparison experiments on different datasets on both synthetic data and real-world data.

4.1 Synthetic Data

In this section we are going to test model performance on synthetic data which include three steps: the first step is data generation; the second step is to cluster generated data using our DTW-ddCRP model and hyper-parameter discussion; the third step is comparing model performance with other three baseline measures and hyperparameter discussion.

Generating NHPP. The first step is to generate NHPP as our synthetic data. We generate NHPP on temporal domain T, where $T \in R^{\mathcal{D}}$, and $\lambda(t)$ denotes the intensity function, $N(\tau)$ denotes the number of events in the subregion $\tau \subset T$ of NHPP. The number of random events follows Poisson distribution where $\lambda_\tau = \int_\tau \lambda(t)dt$. According to [1], at first we need to transform the GP prior on Poisson intensities, which indeed is to use transformation of GP to form a prior distribution and then generate random events from the intensity function drawn from the GP prior. We first randomly drawing events $\{\hat{t}_j\}_{j=1}^J$ from a HPP, then define an upper bound intensity λ^* of a HPP and randomly draw the number of events J in region τ from Poisson distribution with parameters τ, then randomly and uniformly distribute the events $\{\hat{t}_j\}_{j=1}^J$ in region τ. Given the events $\{\hat{t}_j\}_{j=1}^J$, we could sample the intensity function value $\{g(\hat{t}_j)\}_{j=1}^J$ of $\{\hat{t}_j\}_{j=1}^J$ from the GP prior. Since we have already obtained value of intensity function, then we used thinning method to sample observations, initialize $t = 0$, find a constant rate function $\lambda_u(t) = \lambda_u$, let $\lambda(t)$ be the intensity function of the entire process; T_i refers to the $i - th$ event time point and it is independently deleted with a probability $1 - \lambda(t)/\lambda_u(t)$; then the remained points form a NHPP with intensity function $\lambda(t)$.

Clustering NHPP. We generated two kinds of process for synthetic data experiment, one is homogeneous Poisson process (HPP) and another one is NHPP with dynamic intensities. For homogeneous Poisson process, we generated 500 sequences with 20 different intensities. Since each process has an exact intensity, so processes with the same intensity should be in the same cluster, then we got different accurate rate for different hyperparameters showing in Table 1(a). We chose the window decay function that we mentioned in Sect. 3.1 as our f and we initialized $\alpha = 0.005$, which we found worked well. Then we generated NHPP with dynamic intensities, which is also 500 sequences with 20 different intensities. Since for each sequence, the intensity is dynamical, the DTW distance measure can have a good performance in looking for the nearest neighbour that can let our model well performed for NHPP clustering. Accurate result shows in Table 1(b).

Table 1. Accurate clustering rate for HPP and NHPP

	$a = 1$	$a = 5$	$a = 10$	$a = 15$		$a = 1$	$a = 5$	$a = 10$	$a = 15$
Accurate rate	86%	77%	49%	15%	Accurate rate	87%	72%	51%	8%

(a) HPP   (b) NHPP

As we have discussed before, the window decay function only considers customers that are at most distance a from the current customer. When a is too large, the result of window decay function $f(d)$ will be 1 for most customers which leads to a result that most of customers will be clustered into a same cluster. So normally the setting of parameter a could influence final result significantly. However, for sparse observation processes, a can be set a little larger in order to achieve a more accurate clustering outcome.

We used three methods as baseline: the first one is the DP mixture of Beta distribution on CRP; the other two methods are traditional clustering methods which are divisive hierarchical clustering and k-means respectively. For DP mixture of Beta distribution based CRP model, we use Beta DP mixture model to estimate the intensity of each failure process, then clustering with CRP. For k-means and hierarchical we selected median performance among the whole possible condition settings. We discussed model performance by comparing in-cluter-distance and between-cluster-distance between our DTW-ddCRP model with baseline measure showing in Fig. 1.

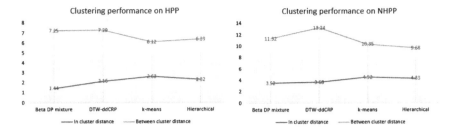

Fig. 1. Model performance comparing with other measures

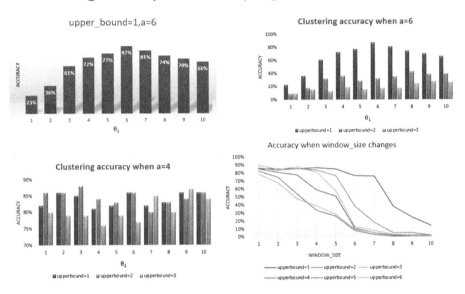

Fig. 2. Clustering accuracy with different hyper-parameters

Hyper-parameter Discussion. We tested all the influence from hyper-parameters in our model, after hundreds of experiments, we found out that several hyper-parameters have great influence on our model performance and others do not, so here we mainly discuss those have great impacts.

In Fig. 2, *upperbound* is a parameter that controls the intensity of each NHPP, the higher of *upperbound* the higher of point density in NHPP. We found that when *upperbound* is too high it may cause a fact that even two NHPP have different intensity function may have too many points which leads to a very low DTW distance, in others words they shows a similar structure information though they do not have same intensity function. Another important parameter is θ_1, which is a parameter that influence the structure of intensity function of NHPP. When θ_1 increases, structure of intensity function changes from volatile to smooth, according to which we found both too low and too high of θ_1 would leads to a bad performance when the other parameters remain the same. Another

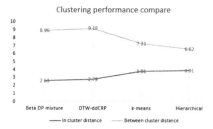

Fig. 3. Model performance comparing with baseline measures

important parameter is the size a of window decay function, an appropriate value can lead us to a perfect clustering result. Generally speaking, when our data set is sparse we need a high value of window size a.

4.2 Real World Data

We use water main failure data as real world data for empirical study. In order to expound water main failure problem, we first need to introduce water main failure data itself. We selected water main failure data that records all the failure events happened from the beginning of 2001 to the end of 2016, which includes over 80 thousand failure events. For each water main, failure event had happened more than once in the sixteen years. We set one month as a time interval, for one water main if failure event happened, log 1 for the certain cell and 0 for those cells that no failure event happened, then for each water main there is a point process which is a NHPP. What we did is to cluster the water mains by clustering these NHPP, after which we can get a general intensity for each water main that can be used to predict probable time the next failure event happens. Then our water main failure problem became NHPP clustering problem, which we have introduced in the introduction section. The original dataset collected 80315 failure events from 2001 to 2016, transform into point process, there came out with 2450 point processes. We found that for some water main, failure process is very sparse, as a result there DTW distance came out to be very small that can not be used to accurately analyze water mains' pattern so we removed those failure processes that the total number of failure events was lower than 10, then we got 593 failure processes.

Model performance comparing on real data is similar with on synthetic data, for DP mixture of Beta distribution based CRP model, we use Beta DP mixture model to estimate the intensity of each failure process then clustering with CRP, and for k-means and hierarchical we use median value. We compared the mean value of in-cluter-distance and between-cluster-distance between our DTW-ddCRP model with baseline measure showing in Fig. 3.

From our experiments we found out that our proposed DTW-ddCRP model has similar performance with the Beta DP mixture model and other two traditional clustering methods. However, our is much more efficiency, especially when the number of dataset is larger and process itself is longer, and we do not need to give any cluster number or clustering restriction as k-means and hierarchical do.

5   Conclusions

In this paper, we proposed a DTW-ddCRP model that can discover the latent intensity pattern of water mains' failure events and realize clustering of the water mains. The proposed model has a distance dependent Bayesian nonparametric prior over NHPP, and DTW similarity measure to reflect relationship between customer to customer, while the assignment is governed by a ddCRP clustering measure. With such construction, the water mains with similar burst pattern can be clustered together with a much higher efficiency. Besides, we do not need to preset the number of clusters for water mains, which is difficult in unsupervised learning, especially for real world data. Instead, our proposed model can automatically generate the cluster number from the provided data.

The empirical study shows expecting outcome, suggesting that our model can well discover the latent intensity pattern of water mains' failure burst process and the obtained result can be use to make accurate prediction in the certain domain, indicating those water mains that needs to be checked and reduce the burst risk.

For the future work, speed improving methods for the distance learning part [16] can be add to improve on clustering efficiency. Meanwhile we will test how to using Bayesian clustering method for continuous sequences, maybe the soft-DTW [5] measure can be added to implement this idea.

References

1. Adams, R.P., Murray, I., MacKay, D.J.: Tractable nonparametric Bayesian inference in poisson processes with gaussian process intensities. In: Proceedings of the 26th Annual International Conference on Machine Learning, pp. 9–16. ACM (2009)
2. Aghabozorgi, S., Shirkhorshidi, A.S., Wah, T.Y.: Time-series clustering-a decade review. Inform. Syst. **53**, 16–38 (2015)
3. Blei, D.M., Frazier, P.I.: Distance dependent chinese restaurant processes. J. Mach. Learn. Res. **12**(Aug), 2461–2488 (2011)
4. Blei, D.M., Griffiths, T.L., Jordan, M.I.: The nested chinese restaurant process and bayesian nonparametric inference of topic hierarchies. J. ACM (JACM) **57**(2), 7 (2010)
5. Cuturi, M., Blondel, M.: Soft-DTW: a differentiable loss function for time-series. In: Proceedings of the 34th International Conference on Machine Learning, vol. 70, pp. 894–903. JMLR.org (2017)
6. Geler, Z., Kurbalija, V., Radovanović, M., Ivanović, M.: Impact of the Sakoe-Chiba band on the DTW time series distance measure for kNN classification. In: Buchmann, R., Kifor, C.V., Yu, J. (eds.) KSEM 2014. LNCS (LNAI), vol. 8793, pp. 105–114. Springer, Cham (2014). https://doi.org/10.1007/978-3-319-12096-6_10
7. Griffiths, T.L., Jordan, M.I., Tenenbaum, J.B., Blei, D.M.: Hierarchical topic models and the nested Chinese restaurant process. In: Advances in Neural Information Processing Systems, pp. 17–24 (2004)

8. Han, J., Pei, J., Kamber, M.: Data Mining: Concepts and Techniques. Elsevier, Amsterdam (2011)
9. Hardiman, S.J., Bercot, N., Bouchaud, J.P.: Critical reflexivity in financial markets: a hawkes process analysis. Eur. Phys. J. B **86**(10), 442 (2013)
10. Hrycej, T.: Gibbs sampling in bayesian networks. Artif. Intell. **46**(3), 351–363 (1990)
11. Kottas, A.: Dirichlet process mixtures of beta distributions, with applications to density and intensity estimation. In: Workshop on Learning with Nonparametric Bayesian Methods, 23rd International Conference on Machine Learning (ICML) (2006)
12. Liao, T.W.: Clustering of time series data–a survey. Pattern Recogn. **38**(11), 1857–1874 (2005)
13. Mueen, A., Keogh, E.: Extracting optimal performance from dynamic time warping. In: Proceedings of the 22nd ACM SIGKDD International Conference on Knowledge Discovery and Data Mining, pp. 2129–2130. ACM (2016)
14. Niekum, S.: A brief introduction to Bayesian nonparametric methods for clustering and time series analysis. Technical report CMU-RI-TR-15-02, Robotics Institute, Carnegie Mellon University (2015)
15. Petitjean, F., Forestier, G., Webb, G.I., Nicholson, A.E., Chen, Y., Keogh, E.: Faster and more accurate classification of time series by exploiting a novel dynamic time warping averaging algorithm. Knowl. Inf. Syst. **47**(1), 1–26 (2016)
16. Rakthanmanon, T., et al.: Searching and mining trillions of time series subsequences under dynamic time warping. In: Proceedings of the 18th ACM SIGKDD International Conference on Knowledge Discovery and Data Mining, pp. 262–270. ACM (2012)
17. Robert, C., Casella, G.: Monte Carlo Statistical Methods. Springer, Heidelberg (2013)
18. Wolff, R.W.: Poisson arrivals see time averages. Oper. Res. **30**(2), 223–231 (1982)
19. Zhang, B., Zhang, L., Guo, T., Wang, Y., Chen, F.: Simultaneous urban region function discovery and popularity estimation via an infinite urbanization process model. In: Proceedings of the 24th ACM SIGKDD International Conference on Knowledge Discovery and Data Mining, pp. 2692–2700. ACM (2018)

Conditionally Decorrelated Multi-Target Regression

Orhan Yazar[1,2(✉)], Haytham Elghazel[1], Mohand-Said Hacid[1],
and Nathalie Castin[2]

[1] Université Lyon 1, LIRIS, UMR 5205, 69622 Villeurbanne, France
{orhan.yazar,haytham.elghazel,mohand-said.hacid}@liris.cnrs.fr
[2] PANZANI Group, 37 bis rue Saint Romain, 696008 Lyon, France
{oyazar,ncastin}@panzani.fr

Abstract. Multi-target regression (MTR) has attracted an increasing amount of attention in recent years. The main challenge in multi-target regression is to create predictive models for problems with multiple continuous targets by considering the inter-target correlation which can greatly influence the predictive performance. There is another thing that most of existing methods omit, the impact of inputs in target correlations (*conditional target correlation*). In this paper, a novel MTR framework, termed as Conditionally Decorrelated Multi-Target Regression (CDMTR) is proposed. CDMTR learns from the MTR data following three elementary steps: *clustering analysis, conditional target decorrelation* and *multi-target regression models induction*. Experimental results on various benchmark MTR data sets approved that the proposed method enjoys significant advantages compared to other state-of-the art MTR methods.

Keywords: Multi-target regression · Conditional target correlation

1 Introduction

Multi-target regression MTR, also known as multivariate or multi-output regression, studies the problem where each data sample is associated with a set of continuous targets. From a computational perspective, multi-target regression is a challenging task that consists of creating predictive models for problems with multiple continuous target outputs by modeling inter-target correlations and input-output relationships [2]. MTR emerges in several modern applications including ecological modeling to predict multiple target variables interpreting the condition of the remnant indigenous vegetation [8], simultaneous prediction of various biophysical parameters (chlorophyll content, leaf area index and fractional vegetation cover) from remote sensing images [4], prediction of blood-drug in medicine [6]. The issue of learning from multi-target data has attracted significant attention from many researchers and a considerable number of approaches have been proposed. The statistical approaches are considered as

© Springer Nature Switzerland AG 2019
T. Gedeon et al. (Eds.): ICONIP 2019, LNCS 11954, pp. 445–457, 2019.
https://doi.org/10.1007/978-3-030-36711-4_37

the first attempt to deal with simultaneously predicting multiple real-valued targets. MTR was first studied in Statistics under the term multivariate regression especially with three well-known methods including the Reduced Rank Regression (RRR) [7] and the two-block PLS [17].

Recently, MTR has received increased attention by Machine Learning researchers inspired by a closely related task called multi-label classification [5]. Similarly to MTR, MLC is also a specific supervised learning task where each instance can be associated with multiple target, yet binary, simultaneously. Due to the tight connection between both tasks, a considerable number of approaches have been proposed on drawing parallels between multi-label classification and multi-target regression. These MTR works can be summarized into two categories: (a) *algorithm adaptation methods* and (b) *problem transformation methods*. Algorithm adaptation methods adapt a specific single-output method (such as decision trees and support vector machines) to directly handle multi-target data sets [9,16]. Problem transformation methods, on the other hand, transform the multi-target regression task into a series of m single learning problems, one for each target. This category includes the traditional one-versus-all or single-target (ST) approach [2], also known as Binary Relevance in the MLC literature, in which the target variables are predicted independently and the potential inter-correlation between them is ignored. In order to improve prediction performances, additional approaches in this category try to model the target relationships by building models that treat other targets as additional input variables (meta-inputs) [19].

The main difficulty in multi-target regression is to assess the inter-target correlation which can greatly influence the final result. There is another thing that most of existing methods omit, the impact of inputs in target correlations (*i.e.* conditional target correlation). With this motivation in mind, a different MTR framework, termed as Conditionally Decorrelated Multi-Target Regression (CDMTR) will be introduced. CDMTR learns from the MTR data following three elementary steps: *clustering analysis, conditional target decorrelation* and *multi-target regression models induction*. In the first step, CDMTR looks for a partition into k disjoint clusters of the training data using a clustering technique on the input space. Clustering aims to investigate the underlying properties of training data for decomposing the original MTR problem into several MTR subproblems. The goal is to effectively capture correlations in the input-feature space to facilitate the subsequent discrimination process. In the following steps, CDMTR performs k MTR local models as follows: it firstly conducts a principal component analysis of the target space for deriving linear combinations of the targets. Subsequently, the transformed targets (*i.e.*, the principal components) are used in a simple single-target regression method that does not have to care about conditional target dependencies, knowing that the transformed targets are uncorrelated in each clustering partition $(1, \ldots, k)$.

Extensive experiments are conducted to evaluate the performance of CDMTR over 12 benchmark data sets. Our results approved that the proposed method enjoys significant advantages compared to other state-of-the art MTR methods.

The rest of the paper is organized as follows: Sect. 2 briefly reviews recent studies on Multi-target regression techniques. Section 3 presents the details of proposed CDMTR approach. Section 4 reports the results of our comparative studies on 12 real-world data sets. We raise several issues for future work in Sect. 5 and conclude with a summary of our contribution.

2   Related Work

Multi-target regression methods aims to create predictive models for problems with multiple continuous targets by considering not only the relationships between features and targets but also the relationships between targets variables [2]. Let X and Y be two random vectors where X consists of d input variables $X_1, \ldots, X_d$ and Y consists of m target variables $Y_1, \ldots, Y_m$. More formally, given a set $\mathcal{D} = [X, Y] = \{(x^1, y^1), \ldots, (x^n, y^n)\}$ of n training instances (x^i, y^i) such as, $x^i = \{x_1^i, \ldots, x_d^i\} \in \mathbb{R}^d$ is a feature vector and $y^i = \{y_1^i, \ldots, y_m^i\} \in \mathbb{R}^m$ indicates its affected targets, the objective in multi-target regression task is to find a function $h : \mathbb{R}^d \longmapsto \mathbb{R}^m$ that assigns to each input vector x^i an output vector of m continuous values $\hat{y}^i = h(x^i)$ [2,10]. The aim of model h is to better approximate the true target vector y^i with $\hat{y}^i$.

$$h : \mathbb{R}^d \longmapsto \mathbb{R}^m$$

$$x^i = \{x_1^i, \ldots, x_d^i\} \longmapsto \hat{y}^i = \{\hat{y}_1^i, \ldots, \hat{y}_m^i\}$$

The sparse literature on multi-label classification (MLC) [5], a closely related task to MTR, has recently inspired many researchers in the machine learning community. The proposed approaches can be divided into two different groups: (i) *algorithm adaptation methods*, and (ii) *problem transformation methods*. The algorithm adaptation methods extend traditional regressors to handle multi-target concepts directly. In this context, Predictive Clustering Trees (PCTs) [9] are adaptation of decision trees capable of MTR. PCT considers the decision tree as a hierarchy of clusters where multi-target data is partitioned. The induction process in PCT is a top-down generation of clusters. It uses the sum of the variances throughout all targets to identify the best separation at each node which lead the tree to predict multiple targets at once. Kocev *et al.* [12] presented a Random Forest based multi-target regression model named Random Forest Predictive Clustering Tree (RFPCT). The RFPCT approach is developed on the top of the PCT algorithm. In RFPCT, each tree makes multi-target regressions, and then predictions are combined by averaging the values for each target. In [18], a Multi-layer Multi-target Regression (MMR) approach was proposed to simultaneously modeling intrinsic inter-target correlations and complex input-output relationships in a general framework. MMR accomplishes a multi layer learning architecture composed of the input, hidden and output (target) layers.

The problem transformation methods aim to transform a multi-target regression task into more single-target regression problems. The MTR task can be reduced to the conventional binary regression problem. This approach is referred to as *single-target* (ST) approach in the literature [2]. In ST, m models are learned; each specialized in one target independently from the others. ST is thus criticised for not considering correlations among the targets. To overcome this problem, additional approaches in this category try to model the target relationships by building models that treat other targets as additional input variables (meta-inputs). In this context, the Regressor Chain (RC) method is proposed in [19] based on the idea of chaining single-target models. RC involves m regressors linked along a chain (given by a random permutation of the set of target variables) where each regressor deals with the single target regression problem associated with target y_j. The feature space of each link in the chain is augmented with the values of previous targets in the chain. As RC is sensitive to the selected chain order, Ensemble of Regressor Chains (ERC) was also proposed in [19] by combining several chaining. The algorithm uses L regressor chains $\{RC_1, RC_2, \ldots, RC_L\}$; where in each RC_k a random chain is performed using a random sequence of targets. For the multi-target regression of a new instance, the decisions of all regressor chains are gathered and combined. This method has been very successful in the MTR domain and provided inspiration for many subsequent works [10,11]. Also derived from the MLC paradigm, Tsoumakas *et al.* [15] presented an ensemble method which firstly constructs new target variables by random linear combinations of original outputs. Next, a *single-target* algorithm is applied to predict the new targets, and finally, the original targets are recovered by inverting the random linear transformation.

3   CDMTR

In this section, we discuss our Conditionally Decorrelated Multi-Target Regression method (termed CDMTR as a shorthand).

Given a set of n multi-target training examples $\mathcal{D} = \{(x^i, y^i) | 1 \leq i \leq n\}$, where $x^i \in X$ is a d dimensional feature vector and $y^i \in Y$ is the set of m continuous targets associated with x^i. Then, CDMTR learns from $\mathcal{D}$ by taking three elementary steps: *clustering analysis, conditional target decorrelation* and *multi-target regression models induction*.

In the first step, CDMTR aims to investigate the underlying properties of the data in X to generate a new representative feature that captures the specific characteristics of the input space. This new feature is able to effectively consider correlations in the input-feature space to facilitate the subsequent conditional target decorrelation process. To achieve this, CDMTR employs clustering techniques which have been widely used as standalone tools to gain insights into the properties of data. In other words, clustering will summarize data by reducing the information on the input space of d features to an information about k groups of similar training instances (*c.f.* Eq. 1). The popular k-means algorithm is adopted here due to its effectiveness and simplicity. The silhouette score [13] index was used to choose the optimal number of clusters for k-means.

$$X = \begin{bmatrix} x_1^1 & x_2^1 & \cdots & x_d^1 \\ x_1^2 & x_2^2 & \cdots & x_d^2 \\ \vdots & \vdots & \ddots & \vdots \\ x_1^n & x_2^n & \cdots & x_d^n \end{bmatrix} \longrightarrow C = \begin{bmatrix} c^1 \\ c^2 \\ \vdots \\ c^n \end{bmatrix} \tag{1}$$

In the second step, CDMTR conducts, in each given cluster, a principal component analysis (PCA) of the target space for deriving linear combinations of the targets. Indeed, our approach aims to capture conditional target correlations by taking feature vectors into account based on the clustering solution. The objective of PCA is to diagonalize the covariance matrices of different clusters simultaneously. The obtained PCA principal components are related to the clusters and then may differ from one cluster to another. The targets become cluster conditionally uncorrelated, which will benefit the subsequent multi-target regression models induction task. Note that we do not claim that the use of PCA in the above process is the best possible practice for target transformation. Actually, the target transformation can be implemented in alternative ways, such as kernel PCA [1]. Nevertheless, the simple use of PCA in CDMTR suffices to yield competitive performance as shown in Sect. 4.

In the third step, CDMTR decomposes the original MTR problem into several MTR subproblems. It aims to induce a family of k multi-target regression models $\{h_1, h_2, \ldots, h_k\}$ with k training data $\mathcal{D}'_c = [X_c, Y'_c]$ ($c \in \{1, \ldots, k\}$) where X_c consists of the d input variables for training instances that belong to cluster c and Y'_c consists of their m corresponding transformed target variables (*i.e.*, the new orthogonal principal components) in c. Specifically, in each cluster c ($c \in \{1, \ldots, k\}$), the transformed targets $Y'_{1,c}, \ldots, Y'_{m,c}$ are used in a simple *single-target* (ST) regression model h_c that assigns to each input vector x^i which belong to c ($c^i = c$) an output vector of m transformed targets $\hat{y}'^i_c = h_c(x^i)$. This model does not have to care about conditional target dependencies, knowing that the transformed targets are uncorrelated in each cluster. Algorithm 1 gives a formal description of the CDMTR training procedure.

Given an unseen example u, the MTR induction process of CDMTR consists to firstly allocate the new instance u to the nearest cluster and apply the relevant *single-target* regression model to obtain predictions. The predicted targets of u are transformed back to the original target space. Algorithm 2 illustrates the detailed prediction step of CDMTR.

It is worth noting that our approach is not a clusterwise-based method. Clusterwise methods aim at finding simultaneously the clusters and the models, by optimizing some criterion instead of finding in two steps first the clusters and after the models, as in CDMTR.

4   Experimental Evaluation

In this section, we investigate the effectiveness of the proposed CDMTR approach and compare its performances against several state-of-art MTR methods.

Algorithm 1. *Training of* CDMTR

Require: $\mathcal{D}_{train} = [X_{train}, Y_{train}]$ a multi-target regression training set of $ntrain$ training instances in which X_{train} consists of d input variables and Y_{train} consists of m target variables, $\mathcal{ST}$ the *single-target* algorithm for MTR

1: Form the partition $C = \{c^1, \dots, c^{ntrain}\}$ of k groups using the k-means clustering on X_{train}, where k is the optimal number of cluster according to the silhouette score.

2: **for** $c = 1 : k$ **do**

3:     $\mathcal{D}_c = [X_c, Y_c] = \{(x_c^1, y_c{}^1), \dots, (x_c^{nc}, y_c{}^{nc})\} \leftarrow \{i \in \mathcal{D}_{train} | c^i = c\}$

4:     Apply PCA on Y_c to create m decorrelated targets Y_c'

5:     $\mathcal{D}_c' = [X_c, Y_c'] \leftarrow \{(x_c^1, y_c'{}^1), \dots, (x_c^{nc}, y_c'{}^{nc})\}$

6:     Train h_c by invoking a single training regressors algorithm on the transformed $\mathcal{D}_c'$, i.e. $h_c \leftarrow \mathcal{ST}(\mathcal{D}_c')$

7: **end for**

8: **return** $\{h_1, h_2, \dots, h_k\}$

Algorithm 2. *Prediction of* CDMTR

Require: u: an unseen example, $\{h_1, h_2, \dots, h_k\}$: a set multi-target regression models, C: a clustering partition

    Allocate u to the nearest cluster c (*i.e.* $c^u = c$) where $c \in \{1, \dots, k\}$

2: Predict the m transformed targets $\hat{y}_c'{}^u$ for u using h_c, the model of cluster c, *i.e.* $\hat{y}_c'{}^u = h_c(u)$

    Perform the inverse transformation related to cluster c to obtain predictions of u for the original targets $\hat{y}_c^u$

4: **return** $\hat{y}_c^u$

4.1 Data Sets and Experimental Setup

To thoroughly evaluate the performance of our approach, a total of twelve real-word multi-target regression data sets given from the Mulan's repository [14] are employed in this paper. The statistics of these data sets are summarized in Table 1.

In the experiments, our approach is compared against several state-of-the-art MTR methods, namely the statistical two-block PLS approach [17], the baseline Single Target regression approach (ST) [2], Random Forest Predictive Clustering Tree (RFPCT) [12], Ensemble of Regressor Chains (ERC) [19] and Regressor Correlation Chain (RCC) [10] that builds a unique chain of targets, capturing the maximum correlation among target outputs. We also compared with Single-target PCA (STPCA) which transforms the multi-target regression task into a series of single regression problems (as ST) behind applying a simple PCA over the target space. In contrast to CDMTR, STPCA does not make use of conditional target correlation.

Following [18,19], we evaluated the performance of the methods using a 5-fold cross validation for RF1/RF2 and 10-fold CV for the rest of the data sets. Specifically, for most data sets (except for RF1/RF2) around 90% of instances randomly chosen from the complete data set were used for the training process

Table 1. Description of the multi-target regression data sets used in the experiments.

Data	Examples	Features	Targets
andro	49	30	6
edm	154	16	2
enb	768	8	2
jura	359	15	3
osales	639	413	12
rf1	9125	64	8
rf2	9125	576	8
scpf	1137	23	3
sf1	323	10	3
sf2	1066	10	3
slump	103	7	3
wq	1060	16	14

(D_{train}), and the remaining 10% were used as a test data set (D_{test}) for measuring the performance of all compared methods. To get reliable statistics over the performance metrics, this process was repeated 5 times. The overall performance measures was computed by averaging over those 50 iterations (25 for RF1/RF2).

The base-line model used in all compared algorithms was Random Forest of 10 regression trees. The ensemble size for ERC is set to 10 as in [10]. The ensemble size of 10 trees was used for RFPCT, and the rest of its parameters were set as recommended in [12]. All the above methods were implemented in the open-source programming environment Python 3.6.0 using scikit learn library.

4.2   Performance Metrics

The generalization performance of a multi-target regression model is evaluated differently from traditional single-target models. Multi-target regression evaluation metrics are more complicated as each instance can be associated with multiple targets simultaneously. The mostly used evaluation measures for assessing multi-output regression models [2,10,19] are:

The Average Relative Root Mean Squared Error: The aRRMSE of a model h generated from a training data set D_{train} is resulting from averaging the relative root mean squared errors (RRMSE) estimated for each target variable on the test data set D_{test}. RRMSE is equal to the Root Mean Squared Error (RMSE) for that target divided by the RMSE of predicting the average value of that target in the training set D_{train}. The aRRMSE is calculated according to Eq. 2 where $\hat{y}_j$ is the predicted values of h on the target variable Y_j, $\bar{Y}_j$ is the mean value of Y_j over the training set D_{train}, n is the number of instances and

Table 2. Average relative root mean square error (aRRMSE) results & algorithm rank.

Data	ST	STPCA	RFPCT	RCC	ERC	CDMTR
andro	0.507	0.504	0.505	0.511	0.448	**0.443**
edm	0.726	0.730	0.725	0.730	0.722	**0.719**
enb	0.113	0.1	0.136	0.128	0.115	**0.094**
jura	0.583	0.589	0.604	**0.582**	0.598	0.584
osales	0.671	0.670	0.758	0.697	**0.642**	0.649
rf1	0.173	0.166	0.135	0.165	0.154	**0.115**
rf2	0.119	0.116	0.140	0.119	0.123	**0.110**
scpf	1.022	0.930	**0.869**	0.899	0.968	0.875
sf1	1.470	1.466	**1.325**	1.339	1.502	1.386
sf2	1.423	1.495	1.420	1.433	1.436	**1.362**
slump	0.656	0.659	0.699	0.658	0.648	**0.634**
wq	0.950	0.949	0.930	0.959	**0.920**	0.949
Ranks	4.125	3.917	3.750	4.083	3.417	1.708

Table 3. Average correlation coefficient (aCC) results & algorithm rank.

Data	ST	STPCA	RFPCT	RCC	ERC	CDMTR
andro	0.775	0.777	0.794	0.772	0.822	**0.829**
edm	0.702	0.702	0.708	0.708	0.708	**0.719**
enb	0.991	0.994	0.989	0.99	0.991	**0.995**
jura	**0.820**	0.813	0.801	0.819	0.807	0.818
osales	0.769	0.773	0.700	0.762	**0.795**	0.790
rf1	0.954	0.951	0.960	0.956	0.957	**0.966**
rf2	0.967	0.968	0.964	0.966	0.966	**0.969**
scpf	0.570	0.578	**0.605**	0.592	0.581	0.598
sf1	0.082	0.084	**0.112**	0.074	0.107	0.102
sf2	0.328	0.325	0.281	0.317	0.324	**0.357**
slump	0.729	0.729	0.709	0.731	0.737	**0.744**
wq	0.359	0.364	0.368	0.352	**0.395**	0.366
Ranks	4.125	3.917	4.000	4.375	2.917	1.667

m is the number of target variables. It is worth noting that the smaller the value of aRRMSE, the better the algorithm performance is.

$$\frac{1}{m}\sum_{j=1}^{m}\sqrt{\frac{\sum_{((x^i,y^i)\in D_{test})}(y_j^i - \hat{y}_j^i)^2}{\sum_{((x^i,y^i)\in D_{test})}(y_j^i - \bar{Y}_j)^2}} \tag{2}$$

The Average Correlation Coefficient: The aCC is obtained by averaging the correlation coefficient between predictions and observed values calculated for each target as follow:

$$\frac{1}{m} \sum_{j=1}^{m} \frac{\sum_{((x^i,y^i)\in D_{test})}(y_j^i - \bar{Y}_j)(\hat{y}_j^i - \bar{\hat{y}}_j)}{\sqrt{\sum_{((x^i,y^i)\in D_{test})}(y_j^i - \bar{Y}_j)^2 \sum_{((x^i,y^i)\in D_{test})}(\hat{y}_j^i - \bar{\hat{y}}_j)^2}} \tag{3}$$

The higher the value of aCC, the better the algorithm performance is.

4.3   Results

Detailed average performances of each compared model over the 12 MTR data sets are reported in Tables 2 and 3. Each table depicts the results for each analyzed multi-target regression metric. The best metric value obtained on each data set is typeset in bold. We note that the two-block PLS approach had the worst results and was found significantly worse than the rest of the algorithm. For simplicity, its results have been excluded in the remaining of this section.

To help summarize the results, we conduct statistical analysis to better assess the obtained results on each metric. Thus, we follow in this study the methodology proposed by [3] for the comparison of several algorithms over multiple data sets. In this study, the non-parametric Friedman test is firstly used to determine if there is a statistically significant difference between the rankings of the compared techniques. The Friedman test reveals here statistically significant differences ($p < 0.05$) for each metric. Next, as recommended by Demsar [3], we perform the Nemenyi post hoc test with average rank diagrams. These diagrams are given on Figs. 1 and 2. The ranks are depicted on the axis, in such a manner that the best ranking algorithms are at the rightmost side of the diagram. The algorithms that do not differ significantly (at $p = 0.05$) are connected with a line. The critical difference (CD) is shown above the graph ($CD = 2.1767$ here).

Regarding the aRRMSE results in Table 2, it is observed that CDMTR performs the best on 7 out of the 12 data sets. The Average rank diagram (*c.f.* Fig. 1) suggests that CDMTR ranks first as well and its performances are statistically superior to the other algorithms, except ERC and RFPCT. It is not statistically better than both methods according to the Nemenyi post hoc test.

The statistical tests we use are conservative and the differences in performance within the best ranked methods are not significant. Following [10], to further support these rank comparisons, the results of the experiments are analyzed using the Wilcoxon signed-rank test. The Wilcoxon test was run for each metric to compute multiple pairwise comparisons among CDMTR and the state-of-the-art methods. The test determines whether significant differences between pairs of algorithms exist. Table 4 shows the p-values for this test on aRRMSE results. According to the Wilcoxon test, shown in Table 4, CDMTR significantly outperforms the other approaches by a noticeable margin (p-value < 0.05).

As far as the aCC is concerned (*c.f.* Table 3), it is also observed that CDMTR performs very well on the same 7 data sets as for aRRMSE. According to the

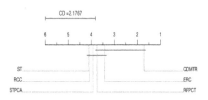

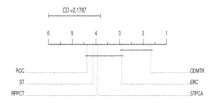

Fig. 1. Average rank diagram of the compared MTR methods on aRRMSE metric.

Fig. 2. Average rank diagram of the compared MTR methods on aCC metric.

Table 4. Wilcoxon signed-rank test p-value for aRRMSE.

CDMTR vs,	Wilcoxon p-value
ST	0.0015
STPCA	0.0010
RFPCT	0.0454
RCC	0.0151
ERC	0.0259

Table 5. Wilcoxon signed-rank test p-value for aCC.

CDMTR vs,	Wilcoxon p-value
ST	0.0015
STPCA	0.0005
RFPCT	0.0317
RCC	0.0010
ERC	0.1035

Table 6. Average runtime results (s) across all data sets.

	ST	STPCA	RFPCT	RCC	ERC	CDMTR
Average runtime	4.32	4.25	1.66	4.33	385.40	5.43

critical difference diagram, shown in Fig. 2, there are 4 out of 5 MTR algorithms beyond that perform significantly worse than our approach. CDMTR is shown to achieve comparable performance to ERC. The Wilcoxon signed-rank test obtained on aCC results (*c.f.* Table 5) does not reveal significant differences at $p = 0.05$ between both algorithms (*i.e.* CDMTR and ERC). These approaches have seemingly similar performances in terms of aCC ($p = 0.1035$).

For a better understanding of the behavior of CDMTR in comparison with the other MTR approaches, we explored in the sequel the conditional target correlation in the MTR data sets. To this end, we adopt Bayesian networks (BNs). BNs are probabilistic models that represent the joint distribution of a set of random variables via a directed acyclic graph (DAG) and its associated conditional probability tables. They lay bare useful information about the target dependencies which is crucial if one is interested in gaining an understanding of the underlying domain. Clearly, the obtained DAG structure allows us to identify the Markov blanket graph for each target node (*i.e.* target variable). Markov blanket contains all variables that shield the node from the rest of the network. This means that the Markov blanket of a target node is the only knowledge

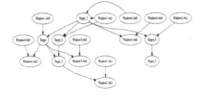

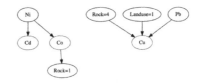

Fig. 3. The joint Markov blanket graph of the multiple targets for Andro data set.

Fig. 4. The joint Markov blanket graph of the multiple targets for Jura data set. Target Cd and Co are conditionally independent given feature Ni. Both targets are also independent to target Cu.

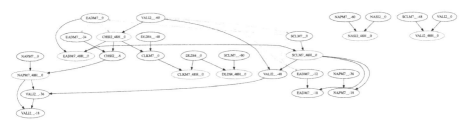

Fig. 5. The joint Markov blanket graph of the multiple targets for RF1 data set.

needed to predict the behavior of that node and its children. Figures 3, 4 and 5 display graphically the joint Markov blanket graph of multiple targets, obtained on Andro, Jura and RF1 data sets, for illustration purposes. The target variables are drawn with a red color. Note that, before running the structural learning of Bayesian networks, we discretize all the variables in four bins.

A graphical inspection of these figures and the results obtained in Tables 2 and 3 reveals that our approach is able to outperform all other approaches especially for data sets in which a strong conditional dependence between targets is observed (*e.g.* Andro and RF1). One can also observe that CDMTR is more appropriate for these data sets compared to the baseline Single Target method treating each target independently (ST) and to the one that omit the impact of inputs when exploring target correlations (STPCA). In the case of data sets (*e.g.* Jura) for which the targets are conditionally independent, CDMTR and the previous approaches seem to have equivalent performances.

Several conclusions may be drawn from these experiments:

- Results suggest that it is more effective to use MTR methods built considering the conditional correlation among targets, rather than ignoring this correlation within the training process, especially for data sets for which the targets are conditionally dependent.
- CDMTR exhibits the highest performances in terms of aRRMSE and aCC measures than the other state-of-the-art approaches. CDMTR significantly

outperforms the other methods except for aCC for which it has seemingly similar performance with ERC.

- Our approach CDMTR does take interactions among targets into account and does not have a significant impact on runtime compared to ERC which had the worst average runtime across all data sets (*c.f.* Table 6).
- We found both *clustering analysis* and *conditional target decorrelation* steps in our approach to be remarkably effective at improving the performance of single target based methods (ST and STPCA) over all the metrics. This effectiveness is more pronounced in the case of data sets in which a strong conditional dependence between targets is observed.

5 Conclusion

This paper proposed a novel method for solving multi-target regression problems. It learns from the MTR data following three elementary steps: *clustering analysis, conditional target decorrelation* and *multi-target regression models induction*. This was done to investigate the effects of exploiting conditional correlations among the target variables during model training. Experiments across benchmark data sets show that our approach achieves highly competitive performance against other state-of-the-art multi-target regression algorithms.

In multi-target regression data where many inter-dependencies between the targets may be present (as for RF1 data set), explicitly modeling all relationships between the targets is intuitively far more reasonable. Using the joint Markov blanket graph to explicitly identify different target powersets and their optimal set of predictors could be a valuable opportunity for future work, that can serve as a powerful learning framework for conditional target correlation analysis geared toward multi-target regression.

References

1. Bakir, G.H., Weston, J., Schölkopf, B.: Learning to find pre-images. In: Advances in Neural Information Processing Systems (NIPS), pp. 449–456 (2003)
2. Borchani, H., Varando, G., Bielza, C., Larrañaga, P.: A survey on multi-output regression. Wiley Interdiscip. Rev. Data Min. Knowl. Discov. **5**(5), 216–233 (2015)
3. Demsar, J.: Statistical comparisons of classifiers over multiple data sets. J. Mach. Learn. Res. **7**, 1–30 (2006)
4. Devis, T., Jochem, V., Luis, A., Fernando, P.C., Gustau, C.V.: Multioutput support vector regression for remote sensing biophysical parameter estimation. Geosci. Remote Sens. Lett. **8**, 804–808 (2011)
5. Gibaja, E., Ventura, S.: A tutorial on multilabel learning. ACM Comput. Surv. **47**(3), 52:1–52:38 (2015)
6. Haiqing, L., Wei, Z., Ying, C., Yumeng, G., Guo-Zheng, L., Xiaoxin, Z.: A novel multi-target regression framework for time-series prediction of drug efficacy. Sci. Rep. **7**, 40652 (2017)
7. Izenman, A.J.: Reduced-rank regression for the multivariate linear model. J. Multivar. Anal. **5**(2), 248–264 (1975)

8. Kocev, D., Dzeroski, S., White, M.D., Newell, G.R., Griffioen, P.A.: Using single- and multi-target regression trees and ensembles to model a compound index of vegetation condition. Ecol. Model. **220**(8), 1159–1168 (2009)
9. Kocev, D., Vens, C., Struyf, J., Dzeroski, S.: Tree ensembles for predicting structured outputs. Pattern Recogn. **46**(3), 817–833 (2013)
10. Melki, G., Cano, A., Kecman, V., Ventura, S.: Multi-target support vector regression via correlation regressor chains. Inf. Sci. **415**, 53–69 (2017)
11. Moyano, J.M., Galindo, E., Ventura, S.: An evolutionary algorithm for optimizing the target ordering in ensemble of regressor chains. In: IEEE Congress on Evolutionary Computation, CEC 2017, Donostia, San Sebastián, Spain, 5–8 June 2017, pp. 2015–2021 (2017)
12. Petković, M., Džeroski, S., Kocev, D.: Feature ranking for multi-target regression with tree ensemble methods. In: Yamamoto, A., Kida, T., Uno, T., Kuboyama, T. (eds.) DS 2017. LNCS (LNAI), vol. 10558, pp. 171–185. Springer, Cham (2017). https://doi.org/10.1007/978-3-319-67786-6_13
13. Rousseeuw, P.: Silhouettes: a graphical aid to the interpretation and validation of cluster analysis. Comput. Appl. Math. **20**, 53–65 (1987)
14. Tsoumakas, G., Xioufis, E.S., Vilcek, J., Vlahavas, I.P.: MULAN: a Java library for multi-label learning. J. Mach. Learn. Res. **12**, 2411–2414 (2011)
15. Tsoumakas, G., Spyromitros-Xioufis, E., Vrekou, A., Vlahavas, I.: Multi-target regression via random linear target combinations. In: Calders, T., Esposito, F., Hüllermeier, E., Meo, R. (eds.) ECML PKDD 2014. LNCS, vol. 8726, pp. 225–240. Springer, Heidelberg (2014). https://doi.org/10.1007/978-3-662-44845-8_15
16. Wei, Z., Xianhui, L., Yi, D., Deming, S.: Multi-output LS-SVR machine in extended feature space. In: IEEE International Conference on Computational Intelligence for Measurement Systems and Applications, pp. 130–134, July 2012
17. Wold, H.: Partial least squares. In: Kotz, S., Johnson, N.L., (eds.), Encyclopedia of Statistical Sciences, vol. 6, pp. 581–591 (1985)
18. Zhen, X., Yu, M., He, X., Li, S.: Multi-target regression via robust low-rank learning. PAMI **40**, 497–504 (2018)
19. Xioufis, E.S., Tsoumakas, G., Groves, W., Vlahavas, I.P.: Multi-target regression via input space expansion: treating targets as inputs. Mach. Learn. **104**(1), 55–98 (2016)

Local Near-Optimal Control for Interconnected Systems with Time-Varying Delays

Qiuye Wu[1], Haowei Lin[1], Bo Zhao[2(✉)], and Derong Liu[1]

[1] School of Automation, Guangdong University of Technology,
Guangzhou 510006, China
{2111704063,2111704048}@mail2.gdut.edu.cn, derong@gdut.edu.cn
[2] School of Systems Science, Beijing Normal University, Beijing 100875, China
zhaobo@bnu.edu.cn

Abstract. In this paper, we develop a novel local near-optimal control (LNOC) for continuous-time (CT) time-varying delayed interconnected systems by observer-critic structure based on adaptive dynamic programming. A boundary function which is approximated by local state observer is presented to substitute the unknown interconnection. Through constructing a novel local value function, the LNOC is obtained by solving the local Hamilton-Jacobi-Bellman equation with the implementation of local critic neural network. By using the Lyapunov's direct method, the proposed LNOC ensures the closed-loop CT time-varying delayed interconnected systems to be asymptotically stable. The effectiveness of the proposed LNOC scheme is illustrated using numerical simulation.

Keywords: Adaptive dynamic programming · Local near-optimal control · Unknown time-varying delays · Observer-critic architecture · Interconnected nonlinear systems

1 Introduction

Decentralized control is an effective method to reduce computational burden and save the communication bandwidth. In the framework of decentralized control, local controllers without data exchange are designed to regulate the interconnected subsystems. These controllers are independent of each other, which implies the lower demand for data storage and the faster response speed for systems.

This work was supported in part by the National Natural Science Foundation of China under Grants 61533017, 61973330, 61603387, 61773075 and U1501251, in part by the Early Career Development Award of SKLMCCS under Grant 20180201, and in part by the State Key Laboratory of Synthetical Automation for Process Industries under Grant 2019-KF-23-03.

T. Gedeon et al. (Eds.): ICONIP 2019, LNCS 11954, pp. 458–468, 2019.
https://doi.org/10.1007/978-3-030-36711-4_38

Optimal design of decentralized control is a significant topic in the control field, particularly in time-varying delayed systems, such as chemical stirred reactors [1], multi-agent systems [2] and communication delay networks [3]. Time-varying delay has been extensively investigated by scholars and engineers [4,5]. However, the analytical solution of the Hamilton-Jacobi-Bellman (HJB) equation is difficult to acquire when the system dynamics cannot be accurately modeled.

Adaptive dynamic programming (ADP) is a powerful tool to acquire the solution of HJB equation based on the neural network (NN) technology [6–9] for both discrete-time (DT) delayed systems [10,11] and continuous-time (CT) delayed systems [12–14]. For DT delayed systems, Zhang *et al.* [11] proposed a model-free ADP-based optimal control scheme for DT multi-delay systems. By using value iteration-based Q-learning algorithm, the measurable input and output data can be utilized to obtain the optimal control. For CT delayed systems, Cui *et al.* [14] established an online off-policy algorithm such that two-stage solution of time-varying HJB equation was obtained without system dynamics. We can observe that considerable efforts have been made on ADP-based methods for the general CT time-delayed nonlinear systems while CT time-varying delayed interconnected systems have been still rarely concerned.

In order to address optimal control problems for aforementioned systems, a novel local near-optimal control (LNOC) scheme is proposed based on ADP. A novel local value function which inserts an adaptive term is constructed such that the developed LNOC can eliminate the effects of time-varying delays in interconnections. With observer-critic architecture, the states of closed-loop CT time-varying delayed interconnected systems are guaranteed to converge to the equilibrium asymptotically rather than ultimately uniformly bounded (UUB) in existing approaches [15]. Furthermore, this paper extends the previous work [15] to obtain LNOC of CT interconnected nonlinear systems subject to time-varying delays instead of general CT nonlinear systems.

2 Problem Formulation and Preliminaries

Consider the following CT affine large-scale nonlinear systems composed of N interconnected subsystems, whose interconnections are both mismatched and state time-varying delayed as

$$\dot{x}_i(t) = f_i(x_i(t)) + g_i(x_i(t))u_i(x_i(t))$$
$$+ h_i(x_1(t - \tau_1(t)), x_2(t - \tau_2(t)), \ldots, x_N(t - \tau_N(t))),$$
$$x_i(t) = \alpha_i(t), \quad t \in [-\tau_{i\max}, 0], \quad i = 1, 2, \ldots, N, \tag{1}$$

where $x = [x_1^\mathsf{T}, x_2^\mathsf{T}, \ldots, x_N^\mathsf{T}]^\mathsf{T} \in \mathbb{R}^n$ is the system state vector, $x_i(t) \in \mathbb{R}^{n_i}$ and $u_i(t) \in \mathbb{R}^{m_i}$ represent the local state vector and local control input vector of the ith subsystem, respectively. $h_i(x_1(t - \tau_1(t)), x_2(t - \tau_2(t)), \ldots, x_N(t - \tau_N(t))) \in \mathbb{R}^{n_i}$ is unknown mismatched interconnection with time-varying delays and $x_j(t - \tau_j(t)) = [x_{j1}(t - \tau_{j1}(t)), \ldots, x_{jk}(t - \tau_{jk}(t)), \ldots, x_{jn_j}(t - \tau_{jn_j}(t))]^\mathsf{T} \in \mathbb{R}^{n_j}$ is time-varying delayed state, $j = 1, 2, \ldots, N$, $\tau_{jk}(t) \in \mathbb{R}$ is unknown bounded time-delay which satisfies $0 < \tau_{jk}(t) \le \tau_{j\max} < \infty$ and $\tau_{j\max} = \max\{\tau_{jk}(t)\}$. $\alpha_i(t) \in$

$\mathcal{C}([-\tau_{i\max}, 0], \mathbb{R}^{n_i})$ is the initial state function, $f_i(\cdot) \in \mathbb{R}^{n_i}$ is the nonlinear drift dynamic, $g_i(\cdot) \in \mathbb{R}^{n_i \times m_i}$ is the input gain function. Assume that the local state vector $x_i = 0$ is the equilibrium of ith interconnected subsystem.

Assumption 1. *For the ith interconnected subsystem (1), $f_i(\cdot)$ and $g_i(\cdot)$ are Lipschiz continuous and differentiable in their augments with $f_i(0) = 0$.*

Assumption 2. *The nonlinear interconnection with time-varying delays is norm-bounded as $\|h_i(x_1(t - \tau_1(t)), x_2(t - \tau_2(t)), \ldots, x_N(t - \tau_N(t)))\| \leq \Sigma_{j=1}^N \varpi_{ij}(x_j(t - \tau_j(t)))$, where $i = 1, 2, \ldots, N$, and $\varpi_{ij}(\cdot)$ is unknown positive norm-bounded smooth functions which satisfies $\varpi_{ij}(0) = 0$.*

For simplicity, denoting $\|\mathcal{Z}_i(x(t))\| = \Sigma_{j=1}^N \varpi_{ij}(x_j(t))$, where the nonlinear term $\mathcal{Z}_i(x) = \mathcal{Z}_i(x_1, x_2, \ldots, x_N) \in \mathbb{R}^{n_i}$ represents the boundary function.

To avoid the common assumptions on satisfying matching conditions [16], reference states are employed to substitute their actual states. Thus, $\mathcal{Z}_i(x)$ can be expressed as

$$\mathcal{Z}_i(x) = \mathcal{Z}_i(x_i, x_{jd}) + \Delta_i(x, x_{jd}), \tag{2}$$

where x_{jd} represents the reference states of other interconnected subsystems, $j \neq i$.

The substitution error $\Delta_i(x, x_{jd})$ satisfies the Lipschitz condition, which implies $\|\Delta_i(x, x_{jd})\|^2 \leq ((N + 1)/2) \sum_{j=1, j \neq i}^n d_{ij}^2 E_j^2$, where $E_j = \|x_j - x_{jd}\|$, d_{ij} is an unknown positive Lipschitz constant.

The objective of this paper is to design a set of LNOC composed of $u_1(x_1)$, $\ldots$, $u_i(x_i)$, $\ldots$, $u_N(x_N)$ such that the stabilization of the closed-loop CT interconnected systems can be guaranteed. In order to find the local control policies $u_i^*(x_i)$, for ith interconnected subsystem (1), the following local value function should be minimized by $u_i^*(x_i)$ as

$$V_i(x_i(0)) = \int_0^\infty \Big(\mathcal{P}_i(x_i(s), x_d(s)) + U_i(x_i(s), u_i(s)) \Big) ds, \tag{3}$$

where $x_d = [x_{1d}^\mathsf{T}, \ldots, x_{id}^\mathsf{T}, \ldots, x_{jd}^\mathsf{T}, \ldots, x_{Nd}^\mathsf{T}]^\mathsf{T}$, $\mathcal{P}_i(x_i, x_d) = \hat{\delta}_i E_i^2 + (3/2) \|\nabla V_i^\mathsf{T}(x_i)\|^2 + (3/2)\|\mathcal{Z}_i(x_i, x_{jd})\|^2$ and $\nabla V_i(x_i) = \partial V_i(x_i)/\partial x_i$. $\mathcal{P}_i(x_i, x_d)$ represents the compensator to eliminate the effects of both time-varying delays and interconnections among subsystems. $U_i(x_i, u_i) = x_i^\mathsf{T} \mathbf{Q}_i x_i + u_i^\mathsf{T} \mathbf{R}_i u_i$ is positive-definite utility function with $U_i(0, 0) = 0$, in which $\mathbf{Q}_i \in \mathbb{R}^{n_i \times n_i}$ and $\mathbf{R}_i \in \mathbb{R}^{m_i \times m_i}$ are positive-definite identity matrices, $\hat{\delta}_i$ denotes the adaptive estimation term which will be introduced later, it can be updated by

$$\dot{\hat{\delta}}_i = \psi_i E_i^2, \tag{4}$$

with the updated rate $\psi_i > 0$.

Then, for the ith interconnected subsystem (1), define the local value function as

$$V_i(x_i(t)) = \int_t^\infty \Big(\mathcal{P}_i(x_i(s), x_d(s)) + U_i(x_i(s), u_i(s)) \Big) ds, \tag{5}$$

and the local nonlinear Lyapunov equation as

$$0 = \nabla V_i^{\mathsf{T}}(x_i)\big(f_i(x_i) + g_i(x_i)u_i(x_i) + \mathcal{Z}_i(x_i, x_{jd})\big) \\ + \mathcal{P}_i(x_i, x_d) + U_i(x_i, u_i), \tag{6}$$

and the local Hamiltonian as

$$H_i(x_i, u_i, \nabla V_i(x_i)) = \nabla V_i^{\mathsf{T}}(x_i)\big(f_i(x_i) + g_i(x_i)u_i(x_i) + \mathcal{Z}_i(x_i, x_{jd})\big) \\ + \mathcal{P}_i(x_i, x_d) + U_i(x_i, u_i),$$

Thus, the local optimal value function and the local HJB equation are given as $V_i^*(x_i) = \min_{u_i} V_i(x_i)$ and $0 = \min_{u_i^*} H_i(x_i, u_i^*, \nabla V_i^*(x_i))$, respectively.

The local optimal control policy u_i^* can be achieved by

$$u_i^*(x_i) = -\frac{1}{2}\mathbf{R}_i^{-1}g_i^{\mathsf{T}}(x_i)\nabla V_i^*(x_i). \tag{7}$$

Generally, the analytical solution of the local HJB equation is very difficult to be obtained. In Sect. 3, the LNOC for the interconnected subsystem (1) is designed in detail.

3 Local Near-Optimal Control Scheme

3.1 NN-Based Identification

In this section, the dynamics of (1) are reconstructed by a local state observer using radial basis function neural network (RBFNN), which is formulated as

$$\dot{\hat{x}}_i = f_i(\hat{x}_i) + g_i(\hat{x}_i)u_i + \hat{\mathcal{Z}}_i(x_i, x_{jd}) + \mathbf{K}_i e_{o,i}, \tag{8}$$

where $e_{o,i} = x_i - \hat{x}_i$ presents the observation error, and $\mathbf{K}_i \in \mathbb{R}^{n_i \times n_i}$ presents the positive-definite observation gain matrix.

The boundary function $\mathcal{Z}_i(x_i, x_{jd})$ can be approximated as $\mathcal{Z}_i(x_i, x_{jd}) = \mathcal{W}_{o,i}^{\mathsf{T}}\sigma_{o,i}(x_i, x_{jd}) + \varepsilon_{o,i}$, where $\mathcal{W}_{o,i} \in \mathbb{R}^{l_{o,i} \times n_i}$ is the ideal weight which is assumed to be norm-bounded as $\|\mathcal{W}_{o,i}\| \leq \mathcal{W}_{oM,i}$ with $\mathcal{W}_{oM,i} \geq 0$ a constant, $l_{o,i}$ represents the number of neurons, $\varepsilon_{o,i} \in \mathbb{R}^{n_i}$ is the approximation error which is assumed to be norm-bounded as $\|\varepsilon_{o,i}\| \leq \varepsilon_{oM,i}$ with $\varepsilon_{oM,i} \geq 0$ a constant. The activation function vector is described as $\sigma_{o,i}(\cdot) = [\sigma_{o,i(1)}(\cdot), \sigma_{o,i(2)}(\cdot), \ldots, \sigma_{o,i(l_{o,i})}(\cdot)]^{\mathsf{T}}$ and

$$\sigma_{o,i(k)}(\cdot) = \exp\left[\frac{-\big((\cdot) - c_k\big)^{\mathsf{T}}\big((\cdot) - c_k\big)}{b_k^2}\right], k = 1, 2, \ldots, l_{o,i}, \tag{9}$$

where c_k and b_k are the center and the width of Gaussian functions $\sigma_{o,i(k)}(\cdot)$, respectively. In practice, the estimated boundary function $\hat{\mathcal{Z}}_i(x_i, x_{jd})$ is represented as $\hat{\mathcal{Z}}_i(x_i, x_{jd}) = \hat{\mathcal{W}}_{o,i}^{\mathsf{T}}\sigma_{o,i}(x_i, x_{jd})$, where $\hat{\mathcal{W}}_{o,i} \in \mathbb{R}^{n_i \times l_{o,i}}$ is the estimated weight matrix. The adaptive update law of $\hat{\mathcal{W}}_{o,i}$ is expressed by

$$\dot{\hat{\mathcal{W}}}_{o,i} = \beta_{o,i}\sigma_{o,i}(x_i, x_{jd})e_{o,i}^{\mathsf{T}}, \tag{10}$$

where $\beta_{o,i} \in \mathbb{R}$ a positive constant. Defining $\tilde{W}_{o,i} = W_{o,i} - \hat{W}_{o,i}$. Combine (1) and (15) with (12), then the dynamics of observation error are formulated by

$$\dot{e}_{o,i} = \left(f_i(x_i) - f_i(\hat{x}_i)\right) + \left(g_i(x_i) - g_i(\hat{x}_i)\right)u_i$$
$$+ h_i(x(t - \tau_i)) - \hat{Z}_i(x_i, x_{jd}) - \mathbf{K}_i e_i, \tag{11}$$

where $h_i(x(t - \tau(t))) = h_i(x_1(t - \tau_1(t)), x_2(t - \tau_2(t)), \ldots, x_N(t - \tau_N(t)))$.

3.2   Local Critic NN Implementation

In light of the universal approximation property of neural network, the local optimal value function $V_i^*(x_i)$ can be reconstructed by $V_i^*(x_i) = W_{c,i}^{*\mathsf{T}} \sigma_{c,i}(x_i) + \varepsilon_{c,i}(x_i)$, where $W_{c,i}^* \in \mathbb{R}^{l_{c,i}}$ stands for the desired weight from the hidden layer to the output layer, $l_{c,i}$ is the number of hidden layer neurons, $\sigma_{c,i}(\cdot) \in \mathbb{R}^{l_{c,i}}$ represents the activation function and $\varepsilon_{c,i}$ represents the approximation error. Then, the partial gradient of $V_i(x_i)$ along corresponding state x_i is expressed as

$$\nabla V_i^*(x_i) = \nabla \sigma_{c,i}^{\mathsf{T}}(x_i) W_{c,i}^* + \nabla \varepsilon_{c,i}^{\mathsf{T}}(x_i), \tag{12}$$

where $\nabla \sigma_{c,i}^{\mathsf{T}}(x_i) = (\partial \sigma_{c,i}(x_i)/\partial x_i)^{\mathsf{T}}$ and $\nabla \varepsilon_{c,i}^{\mathsf{T}}(x_i) = (\partial \varepsilon_{c,i}(x_i)/\partial x_i)^{\mathsf{T}}$.

Under the framework of ADP, the estimation of local critic NN is $\hat{V}_i(x_i) = \hat{W}_{c,i}^{\mathsf{T}} \sigma_{c,i}(x_i)$, where $\hat{W}_{c,i}$ stands for the estimation of $W_{c,i}^*$. Then, the partial gradient of $\hat{V}_i(x_i)$ along corresponding state x_i is

$$\nabla \hat{V}_i(x_i) = \nabla \sigma_{c,i}^{\mathsf{T}}(x_i) \hat{W}_{c,i}. \tag{13}$$

Hence, according to (7), (12) and (13), the LONC can be described by $u_i^*(x_i) = -(1/2)\mathbf{R}_i^{-1} g_i^{\mathsf{T}}(x_i)\left(\nabla \sigma_{c,i}^{\mathsf{T}}(x_i) W_{c,i}^* + \nabla \varepsilon_{c,i}^{\mathsf{T}}(x_i)\right)$, and the estimated one can be expressed as

$$\hat{u}_i(x_i) = -\frac{1}{2}\mathbf{R}_i^{-1} g_i^{\mathsf{T}}(x_i)\left(\nabla \sigma_{c,i}^{\mathsf{T}}(x_i) \hat{W}_{c,i}\right), \tag{14}$$

The Hamiltonian are rewritten as

$$H(x_i, \hat{u}_i, W_{c,i}) = \mathcal{P}_i(x_i, x_d) + U_i(x_i, \hat{u}_i)$$
$$+ W_{c,i}^{\mathsf{T}} \underbrace{\nabla \sigma_{c,i}(x_i)\left(f_i(x_i) + g_i(x_i)\hat{u}_i + \mathcal{Z}(x_i, x_{jd})\right)}_{\vartheta_i} \triangleq e_{\text{cH},i},$$
$$\tag{15}$$

where $e_{\text{cH},i} = -\nabla \varepsilon_{c,i}(x_i)\vartheta_i$, and the approximate Hamiltonian is rewritten as $\hat{H}(x_i, \hat{u}_i, \hat{W}_{c,i}) = \mathcal{P}_i(x_i, x_d) + U_i(x_i, \hat{u}_i) + \hat{W}_{c,i}^{\mathsf{T}}\vartheta_i \triangleq e_{c,i}$. In order to train the local critic NN, the least square method is employed to update $\hat{W}_{c,i}$ by

$$\dot{\hat{W}}_{c,i} = -b_i e_{c,i}\left(\partial e_{c,i}/\partial \hat{W}_{c,i}\right) = -b_i e_{c,i}\vartheta_i, \tag{16}$$

where the learning rate $b_i > 0$.

Define the weight estimation error as $\tilde{W}_{c,i} = W_{c,i}^* - \hat{W}_{c,i}$, the updated law of $\tilde{W}_{c,i}$ can be described by $\dot{\tilde{W}}_{c,i} = -b_i\left(\tilde{W}_{c,i}^{\mathsf{T}}\vartheta_i - e_{\text{cH},i}\right)\vartheta_i$.

3.3   Stability Analysis

Assumption 3. *Denoting $\mathcal{A}_i$ and $\mathcal{B}_i$ as positive constants. Since $f_i(\cdot)$ and $g_i(\cdot)$ are Lipschitz continuous, then $\|f_i(x_i) - f_i(\hat{x}_i)\| \leq \mathcal{A}_i \|e_{o,i}\|$ and $\|g_i(x_i) - g_i(\hat{x}_i)\| \leq \mathcal{B}_i \|e_{o,i}\|$.*

Assumption 4. *$\mathcal{W}_{c,i}$, $\nabla\sigma_{c,i}(x_i)$, $\nabla\varepsilon_{c,i}$ are norm-bounded, i.e., $\|\mathcal{W}_{c,i}\| \leq W_{\mathrm{cM},i}$, $\|\nabla\sigma_{c,i}(x_i)\| \leq \bar{\sigma}_{\mathrm{cM},i}$ and $\|\nabla\varepsilon_{c,i}\| \leq \bar{\varepsilon}_{\mathrm{cM},i}$, and the parameters $W_{\mathrm{cM},i}$, $\bar{\sigma}_{\mathrm{cM},i}$ and $\bar{\varepsilon}_{\mathrm{cM},i}$ are positive constants.*

Theorem 1. *For ith interconnected subsystem (1), the observation error $e_{o,i}$ with the adaptive update law (10) is UUB, and the weight estimation error $\tilde{\mathcal{W}}_{c,i}$ is guaranteed to be UUB as long as $\hat{\mathcal{W}}_{c,i}$ is updated by (16). Furthermore, considering the CT interconnected systems consist of (1), the local state observer (8) and the developed local value function (5) with the adaptive law (4), the LONC $u_1, u_2, \ldots, u_N$ which are obtained by (14) guarantee the closed-loop interconnected systems to be asymptotically stable.*

Proof. For ith interconnected subsystem (1), select the Lyapunov function candidate as $\mathscr{L}_i = (1/2)e_{o,i}^{\mathsf{T}} e_{o,i} + \mathrm{tr}\big((1/2)\tilde{\mathcal{W}}_{o,i}^{\mathsf{T}}\beta_{o,i}^{-1}\tilde{\mathcal{W}}_{o,i}\big) + (1/2)\tilde{\mathcal{W}}_{c,i}^{\mathsf{T}}b_i^{-1}\tilde{\mathcal{W}}_{c,i} + V_i^*(x_i) + (1/2)\tilde{\delta}_i^{\mathsf{T}}\psi_i^{-1}\tilde{\delta}_i$, where $\tilde{\delta}_i = \delta_i - \hat{\delta}_i$ represents the estimation error of δ_i. Thus, the time derivative of $\mathscr{L}_i$ is given by

$$\dot{\mathscr{L}}_i = \underbrace{e_{o,i}^{\mathsf{T}}\dot{e}_{o,i} + \mathrm{tr}\Big(\tilde{\mathcal{W}}_{o,i}^{\mathsf{T}}\beta_{o,i}^{-1}\dot{\tilde{\mathcal{W}}}_{o,i}\Big)}_{\dot{\mathscr{L}}_{o,i}} + \underbrace{\tilde{\mathcal{W}}_{c,i}^{\mathsf{T}}b_i^{-1}\dot{\tilde{\mathcal{W}}}_{c,i}}_{\dot{\mathscr{L}}_{c,i}} + \underbrace{\nabla V_i^*(x_i)\dot{x}_i + \tilde{\delta}_i^{\mathsf{T}}\psi_i^{-1}\dot{\tilde{\delta}}_i}_{\dot{\mathscr{L}}_{\nu,i}}.$$

Let $\|\vartheta_i\| \leq \vartheta_{\mathrm{Max},i}$ with $\vartheta_{\mathrm{Max},i} > 0$ a constant. According to (6), (10), (11) and Assumptions 2 and 3, we have

$$\begin{aligned}
\dot{\mathscr{L}}_{o,i} \leq & -\big(\lambda_{\min}(\mathbf{K}_i) - \mathcal{A}_i - \mathcal{B}_i\|u_i\|\big)\|e_{o,i}\|^2 + \|e_{o,i}^{\mathsf{T}}\|\|\mathcal{Z}(x(t))\| \\
& + \mathrm{tr}\Big(\tilde{\mathcal{W}}_{o,i}^{\mathsf{T}}\sigma_{o,i}(x_i, x_{jd})e_{o,i}^{\mathsf{T}}\Big) - \mathrm{tr}\Big(\tilde{\mathcal{W}}_{o,i}^{\mathsf{T}}\beta_{o,i}^{-1}\dot{\hat{\mathcal{W}}}_{o,i}\Big) \\
& - \|e_{o,i}^{\mathsf{T}}\|\|\mathcal{W}_{o,i}\sigma_{o,i}(x_i, x_{jd})\| + \|e_{o,i}^{\mathsf{T}}\|\underbrace{\left(\sum_{j=1}^{N}\varpi_{ij}(x_i(t - \tau_j(t))) - \sum_{j=1}^{N}\varpi_{ij}(x_i(t))\right)}_{\Xi_i} \\
\leq & -\big(\lambda_{\min}(\mathbf{K}_i) - \mathcal{A}_i - \mathcal{B}_i\|u_i\|\big)\|e_{o,i}\|^2 \\
& + \|e_{o,i}\|\big(\|\mathcal{W}_{o,i}\sigma_{o,i}(x)\| - \|\mathcal{W}_{o,i}\sigma_{o,i}(x_i, x_{jd})\| + \varepsilon_{\mathrm{oM},i} + \Xi_i\big).
\end{aligned}$$

Since Gaussian function (9) is norm-bounded, the nonlinear term $(\|\mathcal{W}_{o,i}\sigma_{o,i}(x)\| - \|\mathcal{W}_{o,i}\sigma_{o,i}(x_i, x_{jd})\|)$ is norm-bounded, i.e., $(\|\mathcal{W}_{o,i}\sigma_{o,i}(x)\| - \|\mathcal{W}_{o,i}\sigma_{o,i}(x_i, x_{jd})\|) \leq \Gamma_i$ with $\Gamma_i > 0$ a constant. Based on Assumption 2, denoting $\|\Xi_i\| < \Xi_{\mathrm{M},i}$ with $\Xi_{\mathrm{M},i}$ a positive constant. Hence, one can conclude that $\dot{\mathscr{L}}_{o,i} < 0$ if

$$\|e_{o,i}\| > \frac{\Gamma_{\mathrm{M},i}}{\lambda_{\min}(\mathbf{K}_i) - \mathcal{D}_i} \quad \text{and} \quad \lambda_{\min}(\mathbf{K}_i) > \mathcal{D}_i, \tag{17}$$

hold, where $\Gamma_{M,i} = \Gamma_i + \varepsilon_{oM,i} + \Xi_{M,i}$ and $\mathcal{D}_i = \mathcal{A}_i + \mathcal{B}_i\|u_i\|$. Next, we will discuss $\left(\dot{\mathscr{L}}_{c,i} + \dot{\mathscr{L}}_{\nu,i}\right)$. In [16,17], the related proof $\dot{\mathscr{L}}_{c,i} \leq (1/2)\left(e_{cH,i}^2 - \|\tilde{\mathcal{W}}_{c,i}^\mathsf{T}\vartheta_i\|^2\right)$ was provided. According to Assumption 4, substituting (15) into $\dot{\mathscr{L}}_{\nu,i}$ and applying Cauchy-Schwartz inequality, one has

$$
\begin{aligned}
\dot{\mathscr{L}}_{\nu,i} \leq &- \mathcal{P}_i(x_i, x_d) - U_i(x_i, \hat{u}_i) + \|\nabla V_i^{*\mathsf{T}}(x_i)\| \left(\|\mathcal{Z}(x)\| + \|\mathcal{Z}(x_i, x_{jd})\|\right) \\
&+ e_{cH,i} - \tilde{\delta}_i E_i^2 + \left(W_{cM,i}\bar{\sigma}_{cM,i} + \bar{\varepsilon}_{cM,i}\right)\Xi_{M,i} + \frac{1}{2}\bar{\varepsilon}_{cM,i}^2 + \frac{1}{2}\|\mathcal{Z}(x_i, x_{jd})\|^2 \\
\leq &- U_i(x_i, \hat{u}_i) + \frac{N+1}{4}\sum_{j=1,j\neq i}^{n} d_{ij}^2 E_j^2 - \hat{\delta}_i E_i^2 - \tilde{\delta}_i E_i^2 \\
&+ e_{cH,i} + \left(W_{cM,i}\bar{\sigma}_{cM,i} + \bar{\varepsilon}_{cM,i}\right)\Xi_{M,i} + \frac{1}{2}\bar{\varepsilon}_{cM,i}^2,
\end{aligned}
$$

Thus, the Lyapunov function candidate of the closed-loop interconnected systems is selected as $\mathscr{L} = \sum_{i=1}^{N}\mathscr{L}_i$. Then, the time derivative of $\mathscr{L}$ is expressed as

$$
\begin{aligned}
\dot{\mathscr{L}} = &\sum_{i=1}^{N}\left(\dot{\mathscr{L}}_{o,i} + \dot{\mathscr{L}}_{c,i} + \dot{\mathscr{L}}_{\nu,i}\right) \\
\leq &\sum_{i=1}^{N}\left(\delta_i E_i^2 - \hat{\delta}_i E_i^2 - \tilde{\delta}_i E_i^2 - U_i(x_i, \hat{u}_i) - \frac{1}{2}\|\tilde{\mathcal{W}}_{c,i}^\mathsf{T}\vartheta_i\|^2\right) \\
&+ \sum_{i=1}^{N}\left(\left(W_{cM,i}\bar{\sigma}_{cM,i} + \bar{\varepsilon}_{cM,i}\right)\Xi_{M,i} + \frac{1}{2}e_{cH,i}^2 + e_{cH,i} + \frac{1}{2}\bar{\varepsilon}_{cM,i}^2\right),
\end{aligned}
$$

where $\delta_i = \left(N(N+1)/4\right)\cdot\max\{d_{ij}^2\}$. Denote $\Theta_i = \left(W_{cM,i}\bar{\sigma}_{cM,i} + \bar{\varepsilon}_{cM,i}\right)\Xi_{M,i} + (1/2)e_{cH,i}^2 + e_{cH,i} + (1/2)\bar{\varepsilon}_{cM,i}^2$, we have

$$
\dot{\mathscr{L}} \leq \sum_{i=1}^{N}\left(- x_i^\mathsf{T}\mathbf{Q}_i x_i + \Theta_i - \frac{1}{2}\lambda_{\min}(\vartheta_i^\mathsf{T}\vartheta_i)\|\tilde{\mathcal{W}}_{c,i}\|^2\right).
$$

Thus, we can observe that $\dot{\mathscr{L}} \leq 0$ if

$$
\|\tilde{\mathcal{W}}_{c,i}\| > (\sqrt{2\Theta_i}/\lambda_{\min}(\vartheta_i^\mathsf{T}\vartheta_i)),
$$

and (17) hold, where $\lambda_{\min}(\vartheta_i^\mathsf{T}\vartheta_i)$ denotes the minimum eigenvalue of $\vartheta_i^\mathsf{T}\vartheta_i$. Therefore, according to the Lyapunov's direct method, we can conclude that the closed-loop form of CT time-varying delayed interconnected systems are asymptotically stable, which ends the proof.

4   Simulation Study

Consider the CT time-varying delayed interconnected nonlinear systems consist of a third-order subsystem and a second-order subsystem as

$$
\dot{x}_1(t) = \begin{bmatrix} -x_{1,1}(t) + x_{1,2}(t) \\ 0.1x_{1,1}(t) - x_{1,2}(t) - x_{1,3}^2(t)\cos(x_{1,1}(t)) \\ x_{1,1}(t)x_{1,2}(t) - \sin(x_{1,3}(t)) \end{bmatrix} + \begin{bmatrix} 0 \\ 1 \\ 0 \end{bmatrix} u_1
$$

$$
+ \begin{bmatrix} 0 \\ 0.7x_{2,1}(t - \tau_2(t)) + \sin\big(x_{1,1}(t - \tau_1(t))x_{2,1}(t - \tau_2(t))\big) \\ 0 \end{bmatrix},
$$

$$
\dot{x}_2(t) = \begin{bmatrix} -0.58x_{2,1}(t) + x_{2,2}(t) \\ 0.7x_{2,2}(t)\cos(x_{2,1}(t)) \end{bmatrix} + \begin{bmatrix} 0 \\ 1 + 0.5x_{2,2}(t) \end{bmatrix} u_2
$$

$$
+ \begin{bmatrix} 0 \\ 1.1x_{2,1}(t - \tau_2(t)) + 0.9\sin\big(x_{1,1}(t - \tau_1(t))\big) \end{bmatrix}, \tag{18}
$$

where $x_1 = [x_{1,1}, x_{1,2}, x_{1,3}]^\mathsf{T}$ and $x_2 = [x_{2,1}, x_{2,2}]^\mathsf{T}$. Refer to [5], after minor modifications, the unknown time-varying delays are set as $\tau_1(t) = 4 + \cos(1.4t)$ sec, $\tau_2(t) = 3 + \sin(0.6t)$ sec.

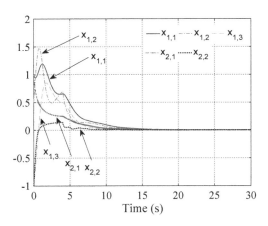

Fig. 1. The state trajectories.

The structures of two RBFNNs are chosen as 3–7–3 and 2–7–2, respectively. Noticing the computational complexity of (18), we construct two local critic NNs by $\hat{V}_1(x_1) = \hat{W}_{1,1}x_{1,1}^3 + \hat{W}_{1,2}x_{1,1}^2x_{1,2} + \hat{W}_{1,3}x_{1,2}^3 + \hat{W}_{1,4}x_{1,2}^2x_{1,3} + \hat{W}_{1,5}x_{1,3}^3 + \hat{W}_{1,6}x_{1,1}x_{1,3}^2 + \hat{W}_{1,7}x_{1,1}x_{1,2}x_{1,3}$ and $\hat{V}_2(x_2) = \hat{W}_{2,1}x_{2,1}^2 + \hat{W}_{2,2}x_{2,1}x_{2,2} + \hat{W}_{2,3}x_{2,2}^2$.

The initial state vectors are chosen as $x_1(t_1) = [1, -1, 0.5]^\mathsf{T}$ and $x_2(t_2) = [1, -1]^\mathsf{T}$, $t_1 \in [-\max\{\tau_1(t_1)\}, 0]$, $t_2 \in [-\max\{\tau_2(t_2)\}, 0]$. The initial estimated

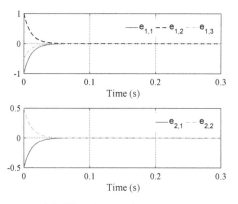

(a) The observation errors.

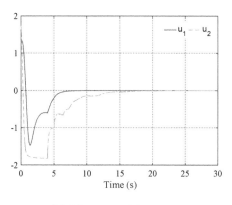

(b) The control inputs.

Fig. 2. The performance of the local state observers and the local near-optimal controllers.

state vectors for local state observers (8) are chosen as $\hat{x}_1(0) = [1, -1, 0.5]^T$ and $\hat{x}_2(0) = [1.5, -1.5]^T$, the reference state vectors of interconnected subsystems are set as $x_{1d}(t) = [0, 0, 0]^T$ and $x_{2d}(t) = [0, 0]^T$, respectively. $\mathbf{Q}_i = \mathbf{I}_3$ and $\mathbf{R}_i = 0.3\mathbf{I}$, where $\mathbf{I}_\kappa$ denotes the identity matrix with κ dimensions, the local observer gains are $\mathbf{K}_1 = 10\mathbf{I}_3$ and $\mathbf{K}_2 = 10\mathbf{I}_2$, the weight learning rates of RBFNNs are $\beta_{o,1} = \beta_{o,2} = 10$, the critic weight learning rate $b_i = 0.03$ and the updated rate $\psi_i = 0.001$, respectively.

After a sufficient learning stage, the weight vectors of two local critic NNs converge to $\mathcal{W}^*_{c,1} = [0.1592, 0.0158, -0.0087, 0.2827, 0.1008, 0.0600, 0.2035]^T$ and $\mathcal{W}^*_{c,2} = [-0.0444, 1.2296, 1.3070]^T$, respectively. Then, Fig. 1 describes that the state trajectories asymptotically converge to the equilibrium. The observation error curves, shown in Fig. 2(a), converge to a small region of zero by using the local state observer. It illustrates that the online identification is successful.

The control curves are presented in Fig. 2(b), which indicates the adaptive regulation process of local near-optimal controllers for (1). Therefore, the closed-loop systems consist of (1) are guaranteed to be asymptotically stable.

5 Conclusion

This paper focuses on investigating a LONC method to address the stabilization problem of CT interconnected nonlinear systems with time-varying delay. The unknown boundary function is successfully identified by the local state observer. By implementing local critic NN, the LONC can be acquired by solving the local HJB equation. By the Lyapunov stability theorem, the proof of the asymptotic stability for the closed-loop systems is provided in detail. Simulation results verify the effectiveness of the proposed LONC scheme.

References

1. Liu, X., Jutan, A., Rohani, S.: Almost disturbance decoupling of MIMO nonlinear systems and application to chemical processes. Automatica **40**(3), 465–471 (2004)
2. Zhang, H., Park, J.-H., Yue, D., Xie, X.: Finite-horizon optimal consensus control for unknown multiagent state-delay systems. IEEE Trans. Cybern. (2018). https://doi.org/10.1109/TCYB.2018.2856510
3. Qi, Y., Cao, Z., Li, X.: Decentralized event-triggered H_∞ control for switched systems with network communication delay. J. Franklin Inst. **356**(3), 1424–1445 (2019)
4. Chen, B., Liu, X., Liu, K., Lin, C.: Adaptive control for nonlinear MIMO time-delay systems based on fuzzy approximation. Inf. Sci. **222**, 576–592 (2013)
5. Yoo, S.-J., Park, J.-B.: Decentralized adaptive output-feedback control for a class of nonlinear large-scale systems with unknown time-varying delayed interactions. Inf. Sci. **186**(1), 222–238 (2012)
6. Liu, D., Wei, Q., Wang, D., Yang, X., Li, H.: Adaptive Dynamic Programming with Applications in Optimal Control. Springer, Cham (2017). https://doi.org/10.1007/978-3-319-50815-3
7. Liu, D., Xu, Y., Wei, Q., Liu, X.: Residential energy scheduling for variable weather solar energy based on adaptive dynamic programming. IEEE/CAA J. Autom. Sin. **5**(1), 36–46 (2018)
8. Wei, Q., Liu, D., Liu, Y., Song, R.: Optimal constrained self-learning battery sequential management in microgrid via adaptive dynamic programming. IEEE/CAA J. Autom. Sin. **4**(2), 168–176 (2017)
9. Jiang, H., Zhang, H.: Iterative ADP learning algorithms for discrete-time multi-player games. Artif. Intell. Rev. **50**(1), 75–91 (2018)
10. Gao, W., Jiang, Z.-P.: Adaptive optimal output regulation of time-delay systems via measurement feedback. IEEE Trans. Neural Netw. Learn. Syst. **30**(3), 938–945 (2019)
11. Zhang, J., Zhang, H., Luo, Y., Feng, T.: Model-free optimal control design for a class of linear discrete-time systems with multiple delays using adaptive dynamic programming. Neurocomputing **135**, 163–170 (2014)

12. Shi, J., Yue, D., Xie, X.: Adaptive optimal tracking control for nonlinear continuous-time systems with time delay using value iteration algorithm. Neurocomputing (2019). https://doi.org/10.1016/j.neucom.2018.07.098
13. Zhu, Y., Zhao, D.: Comprehensive comparison of online ADP algorithms for continuous-time optimal control. Artif. Intell. Rev. **49**(4), 531–547 (2018)
14. Cui, X., Zhang, H., Luo, Y., Jiang, H.: Finite-horizon optimal control of unknown nonlinear time-delay systems. Neurocomputing **238**, 277–285 (2017)
15. Esfandiari, K., Abdollahi, F., Talebi, H.-A.: Adaptive near-optimal neuro controller for continuous-time nonaffine nonlinear systems with constrained input. Neural Netw. **93**, 195–204 (2017)
16. Zhao, B., Wang, D., Shi, G., Liu, D., Li, Y.: Decentralized control for large-scale nonlinear systems with unknown mismatched interconnections via policy iteration. IEEE Trans. Syst. Man Cybern. Syst. **48**(10), 1725–1735 (2018)
17. Zhao, B., Liu, D.: Event-triggered decentralized tracking control of modular reconfigurable robots through adaptive dynamic programming. IEEE Trans. Ind. Electron. (2019). https://doi.org/10.1109/TIE.2019.2914571

Neural Network Applications

Transferring Tree Ensembles to Neural Networks

Chapman Siu[✉]

Faculty of Engineering and Information Technology, University of Technology,
Sydney, NSW 2007, Australia
chapman.siu@student.uts.edu.au

Abstract. Gradient Boosting Decision Tree (GBDT) is a popular machine learning algorithms with implementations such as LightGBM and in popular machine learning toolkits like Scikit-Learn. Many implementations can only produce trees in an offline manner and in a greedy manner. We explore ways to convert existing GBDT implementations to known neural network architectures with minimal performance loss in order to allow decision splits to be updated in an online manner and provide extensions to allow splits points to be altered as a neural architecture search problem. We provide learning bounds for our neural network and demonstrate that our non-greedy approach has comparable performance to state-of-the-art offline, greedy tree boosting models.

1 Introduction

Gradient boosting decision tree (GBDT) [4] is a widely-used machine learning algorithm, and has achieved state of the art performance in many machine learning tasks. With the recent rise of Deep Learning architectures which open the possibility of allowing all parameters to be updated simultaneously with gradient descent rather than splitting procedures, furthermore it promises to be scalable with mini-batch based learning and GPU acceleration with little effort.

In this paper, we present an neural network architecture which we call Tree-Grad, based on Deep Neural Decision Forests [9] which enables boosted decision trees to be trained in an online manner; both in the nature of updating decision split values and the choice of split candidates. We demonstrate that TreeGrad achieves learning bounds previously described by [3] and demonstrate the efficacy of TreeGrad approach by presenting competitive benchmarks to leading GBDT implementations.

1.1 Related Work

Deep Neural Decision Forests [9] demonstrates how neural decision tree forests can replace a fully connected layer using stochastic and differential decision trees which assume the node split structure fixed and the node split is learned.

TreeGrad is an extension of Deep Neural Decision Forests, which treats the node split structure to be a neural network architecture search problem

© Springer Nature Switzerland AG 2019
T. Gedeon et al. (Eds.): ICONIP 2019, LNCS 11954, pp. 471–480, 2019.
https://doi.org/10.1007/978-3-030-36711-4_39

in the manner described by [16]; whilst enforcing neural network compression approaches to render our decision trees to be more interpretable through creating *axis-parallel* splits.

2   Preliminaries

In this section we cover the background of *neural decision tree* algorithms and *ensemble learning*. We also explore the conditions for the class of feedforward neural networks for AdaNet generalization bounds which is used in our analysis.

2.1   Neural Decision Tree

Decision trees can be reframed as a neural network through construction of three layers; the decision node layer, routing layer and prediction (decision tree leaf) layer [9]. The decision node layer for node n is defined to be $d_n(x; \Theta) = \sigma(f_n(x; \Theta))$, where σ is the softmax function which defines the probability of routing the instance x to *binary* nodes under node n, which are typically framed as routing to the left or right subtree of node n. The routing layer is defined to be the probability that each node is used to route an instance to a particular leaf ℓ. If we define μ_ℓ to be the probability of reaching leaf ℓ then it can be written as $\mu_\ell ll(x|\Theta) = \prod_{n \in \mathcal{N}_\ell} d_{n_+}(x; \Theta) d_{n_-}(x; \theta)$, where $\mathcal{N}_\ell$ represents the set of nodes part of the route for leaf ℓ and d_{n_+}, d_{n_-} indicate the probability of moving to the positive route and negative route of node n respectively. The last layer is a dense connected layer from the respective routing layer which leads to the prediction of the neural decision tree as constructed in [9]. We will use this representation as the basis for our analysis of generalization bounds and experiments.

2.2   Ensemble Learning

Boosting is an ensemble learning approach which combines weak learners into a strong learner. There are many variations to boosting. The goal of boosting is to combine weaker learners into a strong learner. There are many variations to boosting. In gradient boosting, the optimal combination of linear weak learners is chosen through training against pseudo-residuals of the chosen loss function [4] [12], which is used as the basis for many ensemble tree model implementations [7,15].

Stacked ensembles is a another ensemble learning approach which is closely related to boosting. Stacking models are an ensemble model in the form $\hat{y} = \sum_k v_k M_k$, for set of real weights v_k, for all k representing the universe of candidate models [2,18]. It has been shown to asymptotically approach Bayesian model averaging and can also be used as a neural architecture search problem for neural network decision tree algorithms [16].

2.3   AdaNet Generalization Bounds

AdaNet Generalization Bounds for feedforward neural networks defined to be a multi-layer architecture where units in each layer are only connected to those in the layer below has been provided by [3]. It requires the weights of each layer to be bounded by l_p-norm, with $p \geq 1$, and all activation functions between each layer to be coordinate-wise and 1-Lipschitz activation functions. This yields the following generalization error bounds provided by Lemma 2 from [3]:

Corollary 1 *(From Lemma 2 [3]). Let $\mathcal{D}$ be distribution over $\mathcal{X} \times \mathcal{Y}$ and S be a sample of m examples chosen independently at a random according to $\mathcal{D}$. With probability at least $1 - \delta$, for $\theta > 0$, the strong decision tree classifier $F(x)$ satisfies that*

$$R(f) \leq \hat{R}_{S,\rho}(f) + \frac{4}{\rho} \sum_{k=1}^{l} |w_k|_1 \mathcal{R}_m(\tilde{\mathcal{H}}_k) + \frac{2}{\rho} \sqrt{\frac{\log l}{m}}$$

$$+ C(\rho, l, m, \delta)$$

$$where \; C(\rho, l, m, \delta) = \sqrt{\lceil \frac{4}{\rho^2} \log(\frac{\rho^2 m}{\log l}) \rceil \frac{\log l}{m} + \frac{\log \frac{2}{\delta}}{2m}}$$

As this bound depends only on the logarithmically on the depth for the network l this demonstrates the importance of strong performance in the earlier layers of the feedforward network.

Now that we have a formulation for ResNet and boosting, we explore further properties of ResNet, and how we may evolve and create more novel architectures.

3   Learning Decision Stumps Using Automatic Differentiation

Consider a *binary* classification problem with input and output spaces given by $\mathcal{X}$ and $\mathcal{Y}$, respectively. A *decision tree* is a tree-structured classifier consisting of *decision nodes* and prediction (or leaf) nodes. A *decision stump* is a machine learning model which consists of a single decision (or split) and prediction (or leaf) nodes corresponding to the split, and is used by decision nodes to determine how each sample $x \in \mathcal{X}$ is routed along the tree. A *decision stump* consists of a decision function $d(.; \Theta) : \mathcal{X} \to [0, 1]$, which is parameterized by Θ which is responsible for routing the sample to the subsequent nodes.

In this paper we will consider only decision functions d which are binary. Typically, in decision tree and tree ensemble models the routing is deterministic, in this paper we will approximate deterministic routing through the use of softmax function with temperature parameter τ, which is defined by $\sigma_\tau(x) = \text{softmax}(x/\tau)$. This is in contrast with the approach in "Deep Neural Decision Forest" where the routing functions were considered to be stochastic which considers the use of softmax instead of usage of temperature annealed softmax to approximate the deterministic routing function [9].

3.1   Decision Stumps

In many implementations of decision trees, the decision node is determined using *axis-parallel* split; whereby the split is determined based on a comparison with a single value [13]. In this paper we are interested both *axis-parallel* and *oblique* splits for the decision function. More specifically, we're interested in the creation of *axis-parallel* from an *oblique* split.

To create an oblique split, we assume that the decision function is a linear classifier function, i.e. $d(x; \Theta) = \sigma(w^\top x + b)$, where Θ is parameterized by the linear coefficients w and the intercept b and $\sigma(x)$ belongs to the class of logistic functions, which include sigmoid and softmax variants. In a similar way an axis-parallel split is create through a linear function $d(x; \Theta) = \sigma(w^\top x + b)$, with the additional constraint that the ℓ_0 norm (defined as $\|w\|_0 = \sum_{j=1}^{|w|} \mathbb{1}(w_j \neq 0)$, where $\mathbb{1}$ is the indicator function) of w is 1, i.e. $\|w\|_0 = 1$.

Learning Decision Stumps as a Model Selection Problem. If we interpret the decision function to be a model selection process, then model selection approaches can be used to determine the ideal model, and hence axis-parallel split for the decision function. One approach is to use a *stacking* model, which has been shown to asymptotically approach Bayesian model averaging and can also be used as a neural network architecture search problem for neural network decision tree algorithms [16]. We then formulate stacking every potential axis-parallel split as follows:

$$y = \sigma\left(\sum_k v_k w^{(k)} x + b\right)$$

$$= \sigma(v_1 w_1^{(1)} x_1 + \dots + v_k w_k^{(1)} x_k + b)$$

From this formulation, we can either choose the best model and create an axis-parallel split, or leave the stacking model which will result in an oblique split. This demonstrates the ability for our algorithm to convert oblique splits to axis-parallel splits for our decision stumps which is also automatically differentiable, which can allow non-greedy decision trees to be created. In the scenario that the best model is preferred, approaches like straight-through Gumbel-Softmax [6, 11] can be applied: for the forward pass, we sample a one-hot vector using Gumbel-Max trick, while for the backward pass, we use Gumbel-Softmax to compute the gradient. This approach is analogous to neural network compression algorithms which aim to aggressively prune parameters at a particular threshold; whereby the threshold chosen is to ensure that each decision boundary contains only one single parameter with all other parameters set to 0.

4   Decision Trees

Extending decision nodes to decision trees has been discussed by [9]. We denote the output of node n to be $d_n(x; \Theta)$, which is then routed along a pre-determined path to the subsequent nodes. When the sample reaches the leaf node ℓ, the tree prediction will be given by a learned value of the leaf node. As the routings are probabilistic in nature, the leaf predictions can be averaged by the probability of reaching the leaf, as done in [9], or through the usage of the Gumbel straight through trick [6].

To provide an explicit form for routing within a decision tree, we observe that routes in a decision tree are fixed and pre-determined. We introduce a routing matrix Q which is a binary matrix which describes the relationship between the nodes and the leaves. If there are n nodes and ℓ leaves, then $Q \in \{0,1\}^{(\ell \times 2n)}$, where the rows of Q represents the presence of each binary decision of the n nodes for the corresponding leaf ℓ.

We define the matrix containing the routing probability of all nodes to be $D(x;\Theta)$. We construct this so that for each node $j = 1,\ldots,n$, we concatenate each decision stump route probability $D(x;\Theta) = [d_{0_+}(x;\Theta_0) \oplus \ldots d_{n_+}(x;\Theta_n) \oplus d_{0_-}(x;\Theta_0) \oplus \cdots \oplus d_{n_-}(x;\Theta_n)]$, where $\oplus$ is the matrix concatenation operation, and d_{i_+}, d_{i_-} indicate the probability of moving to the positive route and negative route of node i respectively. We can now combine matrix Q and $D(x;\Theta)$ to express μ_ℓ as follows:

$$\mu_\ell(x|\theta) = \prod (D(x;\Theta) \odot Q_\ell + (1 - Q_\ell))$$
$$= \exp\left(Q_\ell^\top \log(D(x;\Theta))\right)$$

where Q_ℓ represents the binary vector for leaf ℓ. This is interpreted as the *product pooling* the nodes used to route to a particular leaf ℓ. Accordingly, the final prediction for sample x from the tree T with decision nodes parameterized by Θ is given by

$$\mathbb{P}_T(y|x,\Theta,\pi) = \text{softmax}(\pi^\top \mu(x|\Theta,Q))$$

where π represents the parameters denoting the leaf node values, and $\mu_\ell(x|\Theta,Q)$ is the routing function which provides the probability that the sample x will reach leaf ℓ, i.e. $\sum_\ell \mu_\ell(x|\Theta) = 1$ for all $x \in \mathcal{X}$. The matrix Q is the routing matrix which describes which node is used for each leaf in the tree.

4.1 Decision Trees as a Neural Network

To demonstrate decision tree formulation based on "Deep Neural Decision Forests" and in our extension belongs to this family of neural network models defined by [3]; which require the weights of each layer to be bounded by l_p-norm, with $p \geq 1$, and all activation functions between each layer to be coordinate-wise and 1-Lipschitz activation functions. The size of these layers are based on a pre-determined number of nodes n with a corresponding number of leaves $\ell = n + 1$. Let the input space be $\mathcal{X}$ and for any $x \in \mathcal{X}$, let $h_0 \in \mathbb{R}^k$ denote the corresponding feature vector.

The first layer is decision node layer. This is defined by trainable parameters $\Theta = \{W, b\}$, with $W \in \mathbb{R}^{k \times n}$ and $b \in \mathbb{R}^n$. Define $\tilde{W} = [W \oplus -W]$ and $\tilde{b} = [b \oplus -b]$,

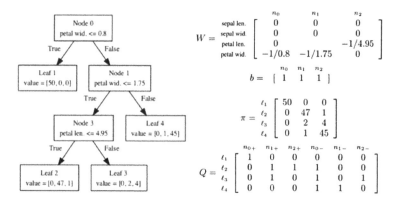

Fig. 1. Left: iris decision tree by scikit learn, right: corresponding parameters for our neural network. If our input $x = (1, 1, 1, 1)$, and we use $\tau = 0.1$ for our temperature annealed softmax as our activation function on our node layer, then the corresponding output for $G(x; \Theta) = (0.08, 0.99, 1, 0.92, 0.01, 0.)$, $\mu(x|\Theta, Q) = (0.08, 0.91, 0, 0.01)$, and predictions $\hat{y} = \pi^\top \mu(.) = (3.79, 42.85, 1.47)$, which would correctly output class 2 in line with the decision tree shown above. Changing the temperature annealed softmax function to a deterministic routing will yield precisely the same result as the Scikit-Learn decision tree.

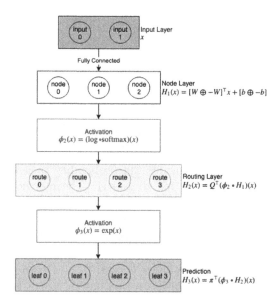

Fig. 2. Decision tree as a three layer neural network. The neural network has two trainable layers: the decision tree nodes, and the leaf nodes.

which represent the positive and negative routes of each node. Then the output of the first layer is $H_1(x) = \tilde{W}^\top x + \tilde{b}$. This is interpreted as the linear decision boundary which dictates how each node is to be routed.

The next is the probability routing layer, which are all untrainable, and are a predetermined binary matrix $Q \in \mathbb{R}^{2n \times (n+1)}$. This matrix is constructed to define an explicit form for routing within a decision tree. We observe that routes in a decision tree are fixed and pre-determined. We introduce a routing matrix Q which is a binary matrix which describes the relationship between the nodes and the leaves. If there are n nodes and ℓ leaves, then $Q \in \{0,1\}^{(\ell \times 2n)}$, where the rows of Q represents the presence of each binary decision of the n nodes for the corresponding leaf ℓ. We define the activation function to be $\phi_2(x) = (\log \circ \operatorname{softmax})(x)$. Then the output of the second layer is $H_2(x) = Q^\top (\phi_2 \circ H_1)(x)$. As $\log(x)$ is 1-Lipschitz bounded function in the domain $(0,1)$ and the range of softmax $\in (0,1)$, then by extension, $\phi_2(x)$ is a 1-Lipschitz bounded function for $x \in \mathbb{R}$. As Q is a binary matrix, then the output of $H_2(x)$ must also be in the range $(-\infty, 0)$.

The final output layer is the leaf layer, this is a fully connected layer to the previous layer, which is defined by parameter $\pi \in \mathbb{R}^{n+1}$, which represents the number of leaves. The activation function is defined to be $\phi_3(x) = \exp(x)$. The output of the last layer is defined to be $H_3(x) = \pi^\top (\phi_3 \circ H_2(x))$. Since $H_2(x)$ has range $(-\infty, 0)$, then $\phi_3(x)$ is a 1-Lipschitz bounded function as $\exp(x)$ is 1-Lipschitz bounded in the domain $(-\infty, 0)$. As each activation function is 1-Lipschitz functions, then our decision tree neural network belongs to the same family of artificial neural networks defined by [3], and thus our decision trees have the corresponding generalisation error bounds related to AdaNet as shown in Corollary 1.

The formulation of these equations and their parameters is shown in Fig. 1 which demonstrates how a decision tree trained in Python Scikit-Learn can have its parameters be converted to a neural decision tree, and Fig. 2 demonstrates the formulation of the three layer network which constructs this decision tree.

4.2 Discussion

Our implementation of decision trees is straightforward and can be implemented using auto-differentiation frameworks with as few as ten lines of code. Our approach has been implemented using Autograd as a starting point and in theory can be moved to a GPU enabled framework.

Methods to seamless move between oblique splits and axis-parallel splits would be to introduce Gumbel-trick to the model. One could choose to keep the parameters in the model, rather than taking them out. The inability to grow or prune nodes is a deficiency in our implementation compared with off-the-shelf decision tree models which ca easily do this readily. Growing or pruning decision trees would be an architectural selection problem and not necessarily a problem related to the training of weights.

The natural extension to building decision trees is boosting decision trees. To that end, AdaNet algorithm [3] can be used combine and boost multiple decision trees; this approach frames the adding of trees to the ensemble to be a neural architecture solution. As AdaNet algorithm leads to a linear span of the base neural network, it does indeed allow direct comparison with offline boosting techniques used in LightGBM or Scikit-Learn.

5   Experiments

We perform experiments on a combination of benchmark classification datasets from the UCI repository to compare our non-greedy decision tree ensemble using neural networks (TreeGrad) against other popular implementations in Light-GBM (LGM) [7] and Scikit-Learn Gradient Boosted Trees (GBT) [15].

The datasets used come from the UCI repository and are listed as follows:

– Adult [8]
– Covertype [1]
– DNA
– Glass Identification
– Mandelon [5]
– Soybean [17]
– Yeast [14]

Our TreeGrad is based on a two stage process. First, constructing a tree where the decision boundaries are oblique boundaries. Next, sparsifying the neural network with axis-parallel boundaries and fine tuning the decision tree. We consider the usage of ℓ_0 regularizer combined with ℓ_1 regularizer in a manner described by [10]. We found sparsifying neural networks preemptively using the ℓ_0 regularizer enabled minimal loss in performance after neural networks were compressed to produce *axis-parallel* splits.

All trees were grown with the same hyperparameters with maximum number of leaves being set to 32. The base architecture chosen for TreeGrad algorithm was determined by LightGBM, where the results shown in Tables 1 and 2 are when all weights are re-initialise to random values. For our boosted trees, we use an ensemble of 100 trees for all datasets and boosted tree implementations.

Table 1. Kendall's Tau of TreeGrad and LGM and GBT feature importance (split metric). Larger values mean 'more similar'.

	Decision tree		Boosted trees (100 trees)	
	LGM	GBT	LGM	GBT
Adult	−0.10	−0.33	0.48	0.47
Covtype	0.22	0.33	0.45	0.44
Dna	0.12	0.13	−0.06	0.28
Glass	0.34	0.07	0.17	0.11
Mandelon	0.54	0.59	0.05	0.07
Soybean	0.08	0.21	0.05	0.05
Yeast	0.47	−0.28	0.47	0.6

When comparing the diversity in features which are selected, we notice that greedy methods, being LGM and GBT generally select similar kinds of features.

Table 2. Accuracy Performance of TreeGrad against LGM and GBT (test dataset). Larger values means better performance.

Dataset	Decision tree			Boosted trees (100 trees)		
	TreeGrad	LGM	GBT	TreeGrad	LGM	GBT
Adult	**0.797**	0.765	0.759	0.860	0.873	**0.874**
Covtype	0.644	**0.731**	0.703	0.832	**0.835**	0.826
Dna	0.850	0.541	**0.891**	**0.950**	0.949	0.946
Glass	**0.688**	0.422	0.594	0.766	**0.813**	0.719
Mandelon	**0.789**	0.752	0.766	**0.882**	0.881	0.866
Soybean	0.662	0.583	**0.892**	**0.936**	**0.936**	0.917
Yeast	**0.553**	0.364	0.517	**0.591**	0.573	0.542
Number of wins	4	1	2	4	3	1
Mean reciprocal rank	**0.762**	0.452	0.619	**0.762**	0.714	0.429

However, in some instances, our non-greedy approach selectes different kinds of features which can be observed in the **adult** data set when considering a single decision tree as shown in Table 1. When we consider the boosting approaches, as there are more trees which are build, and hence more split candidates, the level of agreement changes in distribution. What is interesting is the three datasets with the lowest amount of agreement (DNA, mandelon, soybean) with our Tree-Grad approach actually performs the best against the test dataset as shown in Table 2 which suggests that our TreeGrad algorithm has managed to find some relationships which greedy approaches may have missed.

We also compare the comparison of all three approaches against the test datasets as shown in Table 2. Overall the best performing model is our approach (TreeGrad). TreeGrad's performance is a demonstration that non-greedy approaches can fall back to representations similar to greedy approaches which is competitive with existing greedy algorithms, or discover representations which can not be recovered by greedy approaches. We observe that for boosting approaches LGM has very similar performance compared with TreeGrad, whereas GBT performance begins to fall off compared with its strong performance when considering the single decision tree.

6 Conclusion

We have demonstrated approaches to unify boosted tree models and neural networks, allowing tree models to be transferred to neural network structures. We have provided an approach to rebuild trees in a non-greedy manner and decision splits in the scenario were weights are reset and provided learning bounds for this approach. This approach is demonstrated to be competitive and even an improvement over current greedy tree ensemble algorithms like LightGBM, and empirically better than popular frameworks like Scikit-learn.

There are several avenues for future work. We want to extend this approach to allow decision trees to induced in an online manner; we want to extend the layers within a decision tree to include the ability to use conventional CNN to create new architectures over richer sources of data which decision trees are not usually trained against.

References

1. Blackard, J.A., Dean, D.J.: Comparative accuracies of artificial neural networks and discriminant analysis in predicting forest cover types from cartographic variables. Comput. Electron. Agric. **24**, 131–151 (2000)
2. Breiman, L.: Bagging predictors. Mach. Learn. **24**(421), 123–140 (1996)
3. Cortes, C., Gonzalvo, X., Kuznetsov, V., Mohri, M., Yang, S.: AdaNet: adaptive structural learning of artificial neural networks. In: Precup, D., Teh, Y.W. (eds.) International Conference on Machine Learning. vol. 70, pp. 874–883 (2017)
4. Friedman, J.H.: Greedy function approximation: a gradient boosting machine. Ann. Stat. **29**(5), 1189–1232 (2001)
5. Guyon, I., Gunn, S., Ben-Hur, A., Dror, G.: Result analysis of the nips 2003 feature selection challenge. In: Advances in Neural Information Processing Systems, pp. 545–552 (2005)
6. Jang, E., Gu, S., Poole, B.: Categorical reparameterization with gumbel-softmax. In: International Conference on Learning Representations (2018)
7. Ke, G., et al.: LightGBM: a highly efficient gradient boosting decision tree. In: Advances in Neural Information Processing Systems, pp. 3146–3154 (2017)
8. Kohavi, R.: Scaling up the accuracy of naive-bayes classifiers: a decision-tree hybrid. In: Proceedings of the Second International Conference on Knowledge Discovery and Data Mining, pp. 202–207. AAAI Press (1996)
9. Kontschieder, P., Fiterau, M., Criminisi, A., Bulò, S.R.: Deep neural decision forests. In: International Joint Conference on Artificial Intelligence, pp. 4190–4194 (2016)
10. Louizos, C., Welling, M., Kingma, D.P.: Learning sparse neural networks through L0 regularization. In: International Conference on Learning Representations (2018)
11. Maddison, C.J., Mnih, A., Teh, Y.W.: The concrete distribution: a continuous relaxation of discrete random variables. In: International Conference on Learning Representations (2018)
12. Mason, L., Baxter, J., Bartlett, P.L., Frean, M.R.: Boosting algorithms as gradient descent. In: Advances in Neural Information Processing Systems, pp. 512–518 (2000)
13. Murthy, S.K., Kasif, S., Salzberg, S.: A system for induction of oblique decision trees. J. Artif. Intell. Res. **2**, 1–32 (1994)
14. Nakai, K., Kanehisa, M.: A knowledge base for predicting protein localization sites in eukaryotic cells. Genomics **14**(4), 897–911 (1992)
15. Pedregosa, F., et al.: Scikit-learn: machine learning in Python. J. Mach. Learn. Res. **12**, 2825–2830 (2011)
16. Siu, C.: Automatic induction of neural network decision tree algorithms. In: Arai, K., Bhatia, R., Kapoor, S. (eds.) CompCom 2019. AISC, vol. 997, pp. 697–704. Springer, Cham (2019). https://doi.org/10.1007/978-3-030-22871-2_48
17. Tan, M., Eshelman, L.: Using weighted networks to represent classification knowledge in noisy domains. In: Machine Learning Proceedings 1988, pp. 121–134. Elsevier (1988)
18. Wolpert, D.H.: Stacked generalization. Neural Netw. **5**(2), 241–259 (1992)

Neuro-inspired System with Crossbar Array of Amorphous Metal-Oxide-Semiconductor Thin-Film Devices as Self-plastic Synapse Units

Letter Recognition of Five Alphabets

Mutsumi Kimura[1,2,3]([⊠]), Kenta Umeda[4], Keisuke Ikushima[1],
Toshimasa Hori[1], Ryo Tanaka[1], Tokiyoshi Matsuda[3],
Tomoya Kameda[5], and Yasuhiko Nakashima[2]

[1] Department of Electronics and Informatics, Ryukoku University, Seta,
Otsu 520-2194, Japan
mutsu@rins.ryukoku.ac.jp,
{t17m009, t130185, t18m013}@mail.ryukoku.ac.jp
[2] Graduate School of Science and Technology,
Nara Institute of Science and Technology, Takayama, Ikoma 630-0192, Japan
nakashim@is.naist.jp
[3] High-Tech Research Center, Innovative Materials and Processing Research
Center, Seta, Otsu 520-2194, Japan
toki@rins.ryukoku.ac.jp
[4] Graduate School of Materials Science, Nara Institute of Science and
Technology, Takayama, Ikoma 630-0192, Japan
umeda.kenta.ua9@ms.naist.jp
[5] Graduate School of Information Science, Nara Institute of Science and
Technology, Takayama, Ikoma 630-0192, Japan
kameda.tomoya.kg0@is.naist.jp

Abstract. Artificial intelligences are essential concept and indispensable in future smart societies, while neural networks are typical representative schemes that imitate human brains and mimic biological functions. However, the conventional neural networks are composed of lengthy software that is executed by high-spec computing hardware, the computer size is enormous, and power dissipation is huge. On the other hand, neuro-inspired systems are practical solutions consisting only of customized hardware, and the hardware size and power dissipation can be saved. Therefore, we have been studying neuro-inspired systems with amorphous metal-oxide-semiconductor (AOS) thin-film devices as synapse units and suggesting revised Hebbian learning that is automatically and locally conducted without additional control circuits. Here, the conductance degradation can be employed as self-plastic weight of synapse units. As a result, it is promising that the neuro-inspired systems become three-dimensional integrated systems, the hardware size can be very compact, the power dissipation can be very low, and all functions of biological brains are obtained. In this study, we have been developing neuro-inspired systems with crossbar array of AOS thin-film devices as self-plastic synapse units. First, the crossbar array is produced, and it is discovered that the electric current continuously decreases along the application time. Next, the neuro-inspired system

© Springer Nature Switzerland AG 2019
T. Gedeon et al. (Eds.): ICONIP 2019, LNCS 11954, pp. 481–491, 2019.
https://doi.org/10.1007/978-3-030-36711-4_40

is really constructed by a field-programmable-gate-array LSI and crossbar array, and it is validated that a function of letter recognition is acquired after learning operation. In particular, we succeed in the letter recognition of five alphabets in this paper, whereas we succeeded in that of three alphabets in the previous paper, which is theoretically discussed, namely, the theoretical maximum performance seems to be achieved. Once the fundamental operations are validated, further progressed functions will be achieved by greatening the device and circuit scales.

Keywords: Neuro-inspired system · Crossbar array · Amorphous Metal-Oxide-Semiconductor (AOS) · Thin-film device · Self-plastic synapse units · Letter recognition · Artificial intelligence · Neural network · Revised Hebbian learning

1 Introduction

Artificial intelligences (AIs) [1, 2] are essential concept and indispensable technologies in future smart societies for various applications, for example, information retrieval and provision, language translation and caption composition, expert system, letter and image recognition, autonomous driving, artificial brain, and so on. Neural networks [3, 4] are typical representative schemes of AIs that imitate human brains and mimic biological functions. However, the conventional neural networks are composed of complicated and lengthy software that is executed by high-spec Neumann-type computer, which is not customized for neural networks, the computer size is incredibly enormous, and the power dissipation is unbelievably huge. For example, one of the most illustrious cognitive systems [5] has the size of ten refrigerators and power dissipation of approximately 100 kW. On the other hand, what are called neuro-inspired systems or neuro-morphic systems [6, 7] are practical solutions consisting only of customized hardware and devices, the hardware size and power dissipation can be saved. However, a current neuro-inspired system [8] is a kind of hybrid systems, that is, multiple neuron units are virtually realized by time sharing of a single neuron unit, analogue memories are emulated by multi-bit digital memories, learning function is not included in itself, and so on, and therefore the above-written issues are resolved only in part. A lot of effort are being made to resolve these issues [9].

Therefore, we have been studying neuro-inspired systems specially with amorphous metal-oxide semiconductor (AOS) thin-film devices as synapse units [10, 11]. Although some other devices are proposed for neuro-inspired systems [12], it should be highlighted that the AOS devices [13] have possible potential that they can be stacked by printing fabrication with low expense [14]. Additionally, we have been suggesting revised Hebbian learning [15, 16] that is automatically and locally conducted without additional control circuits. Here, the conductance degradation of the AOS thin-film devices can be purposely employed as self-plastic weight of synapse units. As a result, it should be also highlighted that the neuro-inspired systems become three-dimensional integrated systems [17] in the future, the hardware size can be remarkably compact, and the power consumption can be excellently low. Although some prior papers were published on crossbar arrays of synapse units [18–21], AOS thin-film devices are employed specially in this study. Although some other learning rules, namely, spike timing dependent plasticity (STDP), are taken for neuro-inspired systems [22], the above-written learning rule is one of the expected rules. Furthermore, because biological brains are materially actualized by the neuro-inspired systems, it is also promising that all natural functions are also actualized, namely, distributed parallel computing, self-training, self-organization, damage robustness, fault tolerance, and so on.

In this study, we have been developing neuro-inspired systems with crossbar array of AOS thin-film devices as self-plastic synapse units. Here, amorphous Ga-Sn-O (α-GTO) thin-film devices are employed as the AOS thin-film devices. The α-GTO thin-film device is an expected device using α-GTO semiconductor that is lately published by the authors [23–26]. First, a crossbar array of AOS thin-film devices will be produced, and it will be discovered that the electric current continuously decreases along the application time. Next, a neuro-inspired system will be really constructed by a field-programmable-gate-array (FPGA) LSI and crossbar array of AOS thin-film devices, and it will be validated that a function for letter recognition is acquired after learning operation. In particular, we will succeed in the letter recognition of five alphabets in this paper, whereas we succeeded in that of three alphabets in the previous paper [27], which is theoretically discussed, namely, the theoretical maximum performance seems to be achieved. Once the fundamental operations are validated, further useful and progressed functions will be achieved by greatening the device and circuit scales in the future according to the academic history of neural networks verified by software prior to hardware [4, 28]. In contrast to our previous paper in ICONIP 2018, where double-layer AOS thin-film devices and the same system architecture of the neuro-inspired system are proposed, which was gotten later [29], it is important in some meaning that AOS thin-film devices has a simple structure and we succeed in the letter recognition of five alphabets in this paper. Whereas the hardware size, power dissipation, and processing speed delay can be saved by the multiple-layer AOS thin-film devices in the previous paper, the simple structure in this paper can be produced with low expense.

2   Amorphous Metal-Oxide Semiconductor Thin-Film Device

A device structure of the crossbar array of the AOS thin-film devices is shown in Fig. 1. The crossbar array of the AOS thin-film devices is produced as follows. First, a quartz glass substrate is used, where the substrate thickness is 1 mm and substrate size is 3×3 cm. Next, a Ti thin film is deposited for bottom electrodes by vacuum evaporation through a metal mask, where the film thickness is 50 nm, pattern line and space widths are both 150 and 150 µm, and number of lines is 80. After that, an α-GTO thin film is deposited for active layers by radio-frequency (RF) magnetron sputtering with a ceramic target of Ga:Sn = 1:3 and sputtering gas of Ar:O_2 = 20:1, where the film thickness is 70 nm. Next, another Ti thin film is once more deposited for top electrodes by the same process of the vacuum evaporation as those for the bottom electrodes, where the film thickness, pattern line and space widths, and number of lines are also the same. The top and bottom electrodes are vertically crossed each other. Sequentially, they are baked by thermal annealing at 350 °C for 1 h. Finally, the crossbar array of the AOS thin-film devices is completed, where the AOS thin-films are sandwiched between both 80 top and 80 bottom electrodes, and 80 × 80 = 6400 AOS thin-film devices are produced in the crossbar array.

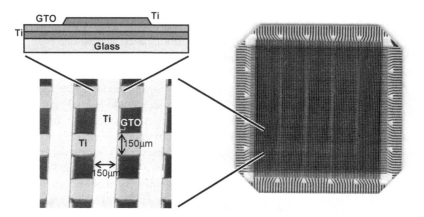

Fig. 1. Device structure of the crossbar array of the AOS thin-film devices. A cross-section schematic, microscope photograph, and substrate overview are shown.

Conductance degradation of the crossbar array of the AOS thin-film devices is shown in Fig. 2. The conductance degradation is measured as follows. First, the application voltage is continuously applied between the top and bottom electrodes, where the application voltage is 3.3 V. Next, the electric current is continuously measured through the AOS thin-film device. It is discovered that the electric current continuously decreases along the application time, which appears by the above-written suitable process condition.

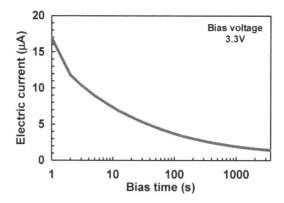

Fig. 2. Conductance degradation of the crossbar array of the AOS thin-film devices. A change of the electric current along the application time is shown.

Deterioration mechanism of the crossbar array of the AOS thin-film devices is shown in Fig. 3. It is supposed that the conductance degradation occurs because the defect sites are formed in the AOS thin films [30]. Free electrons are accelerated by electric field and crash into the crystal lattices in the AOS thin films, and defect sites are formed in the AOS thin films. Some electrons are captured in the defect sites, free electrons decreases, the movements are scattered by Coulomb force, and the conductance degradation occurs. With the revised Hebbian learning, the conductance degradation of the AOS thin-film devices can be purposely employed as self-plastic weight of synapse unit.

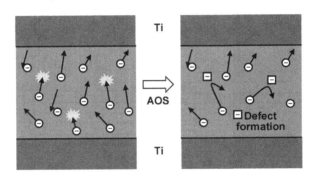

Fig. 3. Degradation mechanism of the crossbar array of the AOS thin-film devices. The conductance degradation is caused by the defect formation.

3   Neuro-inspired System

A system architecture of the neuro-inspired system is shown in Fig. 4. A Hopfield neural network is really constructed by combining 80 neuron units and 80 × 80 = 6400 synapse units. The Hopfield neural network is a neural network whose output signals of all neuron units are transferred to input signals of all neuron units through synapse units. Here, the Hopfield neural network is really constructed by neuron units made in an FPGA LSI and synapse units made by the crossbar array of the AOS thin-film devices. The neuron units made in the FPGA LSI are simple buffer circuits that provide a sigmoid-like function. First, during learning operation, a signal pattern is inputted to the neuron units, and the same signal pattern is outputted and applied to the top electrodes of the crossbar array of the AOS thin-film devices and simultaneously bottom electrodes through the switching units. Next, during recognizing operation, a signal pattern is inputted, the same signal pattern is applied to the bottom electrode of the crossbar array of the AOS thin-film devices, the top electrode is floating, and the signal pattern is soon released. Some analog signals are transmitted from the top electrodes of the crossbar array of the AOS thin-film devices and inputted to the neuron units, and some signal pattern is outputted after dynamic working of the neuro-inspired system.

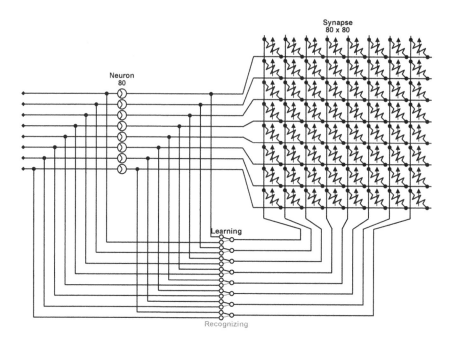

Fig. 4. A system architecture of the neuro-inspired system. A Hopfield neural network is really constructed by combining 80 neuron units and $80 \times 80 = 6400$ synapse units. Neuron units are made in an FPGA LSI, synapse units are made by the crossbar array of the AOS thin-film devices, and they are connected with the switching units. During learning operation, a signal pattern is applied to the top and simultaneously bottom electrodes of the crossbar array of the AOS thin-film devices. During recognizing operation, a signal pattern is applied to the bottom electrode and soon released. Some analog signals are transmitted from the top electrodes and fed back. Some signal pattern is outputted after dynamic working.

Pixel pattern mapping of the neuro-inspired system is shown in Fig. 5. During learning operation, where the voltage difference is incurred between the top and bottom electrodes and the electric current is flowed through the AOS thin-film device, the conductance degradation occurs. The pattern generation of the conductance degradation corresponds to the learning operation. A two-dimensional pixel pattern of 9×9 is transformed to a one-dimensional signal pattern of 80 to utilize the neuro-inspired system for letter recognition. Moreover, because our deposition machine is not prepared very well, some top or bottom electrodes, whose signal pattern is transmitted, are injured. Therefore, majority-rule handling is introduced. Here, one pixel is assigned to nine signals and a state that the pixel is in on-state corresponds to a state that more than five signals are in on-state. The majority-rule handling is not only a compensation method in the neuro-inspired system when some signals are injured but also a representing method in biological eyes because all neurons do not work very well and some image information processing is done on the retinal surface [31].

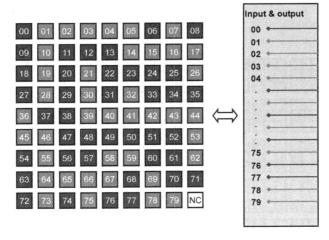

Fig. 5. Pixel pattern mapping of the neuro-inspired system. A two-dimensional pixel pattern is transformed to a one-dimensional signal pattern.

4 Letter Recognition

Experimental results of letter recognition are shown in Fig. 6. First, during learning operation, five alphabets of "**C**", "**L**", "**T**", "**V**", and "**X**" are trained. These five alphabets are all alphabets that can be distinguished by this nine pixel number. Initially, a pixel pattern of "**C**" is transformed to a signal pattern, and the signal pattern is inputted to the neuron units for 1 s. The same signal pattern is outputted and applied to the top electrodes of the crossbar array of the AOS thin-film devices and simultaneously bottom electrodes, and the conductance degradation occurs. Successively, signal patterns of "**L**", "**T**", "**V**", and "**X**" are inputted by turns. Then these operations are repeated several hundred times. Next, during recognizing operation, five alphabets of "**C**", "**L**", "**T**", "**V**", and "**X**" are reproduced. Initially, a one-pixel flipped pattern of "**C**", that is, a slightly distorted pixel pattern, is transformed to a signal pattern with the majority-rule handling, that is, five signals are set to on-state where the pixel is in on-state and vice versa, and the signal pattern is inputted. The same signal pattern is applied to the bottom electrodes of the crossbar array of the AOS thin-film devices, the top electrode is floating, and the signal pattern is soon released. Subsequently, some revised signal pattern is outputted from the neuron units and transformed to some revised pixel pattern with the majority-rule handling, that is, the pixel is set to on-state where more than five signals are in on-state and vice versa. Then these operations are repeated for different distorted pixel patterns. Successively, slightly distorted signal patterns of "**L**", "**T**", "**V**", and "**X**" are inputted, and some signal patterns are outputted. Although the application voltage of 3.3 V is applied during both the learning and recognizing operations, because the learning operation is kept for 1 s and repeated several hundred times, whereas the recognizing operation is kept less than 0.1 s and not repeated, the conductance degradation is negligible during the recognizing operation. Finally, it is validated that the revised pixel pattern is the same as the pixel pattern of

"C", "L", "T", "V", and "X". Because simple pattern matching is usable once the pixel patterns are reproduce, it is validated that a function of letter recognition is acquired.

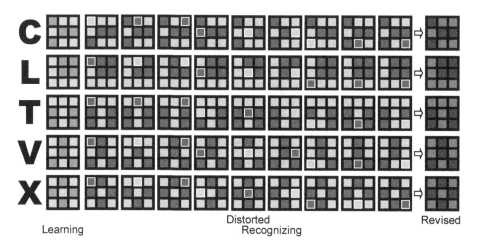

Learning   Distorted   Revised

Recognizing

Fig. 6. Experimental results of letter recognition. Pixel patterns during learning operation, slightly distorted pixel patterns inputted during recognizing operation, and revised pixel patterns outputted during recognizing operation are shown. The one-pixel flipped patterns are indicated by white squares.

In particular, we succeed in the letter recognition of five alphabets in this paper. Based on the basic theory [32], the capacity of the Hopfield associative memory is described in the following equation:

$$m = n/4 \log n, \tag{1}$$

where n is the number of neuron units and m is the maximum number of letters that can be learned in the Hopfield neural network. Here, although this Hopfield neural network is not a simple Hopfield neural network, by substituting $n = 80$, $m = 4.56$ is gotten. This indicates that the theoretical maximum performance seems to be achieved.

5   Conclusion

We have been studying neuro-inspired systems with AOS thin-film devices as synapse units and suggesting revised Hebbian learning that is automatically and locally conducted without additional control circuits. Here, the conductance degradation can be employed as self-plastic weight of synapse units. As a result, it is promising that the neuro-inspired systems become three-dimensional integrated systems, the hardware size can be very compact, the power dissipation can be very low, and all functions of biological brains are obtained. In this study, we have been developing neuro-inspired systems with crossbar array of AOS thin-film devices as self-plastic synapse units.

First, crossbar array was produced, and it was discovered that the electric current continuously decreases along the application time. Next, a neuro-inspired system was really constructed by an FPGA LSI and crossbar array, and it was validated that a function of letter recognition is acquired after learning operation. In particular, we succeeded in the letter recognition of five alphabets in this paper, whereas we had succeeded in that of three alphabets in the previous paper, which was theoretically discussed, namely, the theoretical maximum performance seemed to be achieved. Once the fundamental operations are validated, further progressed functions will be achieved by greatening the device and circuit scales.

In this study, although the AOS thin-film devices are not miniaturized and stacked, it should be noted that the recognizing operation is completed only by several operation steps, which leads to the future high-speed and low-power computing. Moreover, it should be also noted that the neuro-inspired systems and AOS thin-film devices are adaptive and scalable. If it is assumed that the volume of the AOS thin-film device is $1 \ \mu m^3$, which is feasible by current semiconductor technologies, and they are freely stacked, which will be feasible by means of further efforts, the volume of the neuro-inspired system can be less than $0.2 \ \ell$ for synapse units of 200 trillion, which is the same number as those in a human brain. Moreover, if it is assumed that the power dissipation of the AOS thin-film device is 10^{-13} W, which has been attained in the newest devices, the power dissipation of the neuro-inspired system can be roughly 20 W. The volume of $0.2 \ \ell$ is 1/10 of that of a human brain, and the power dissipation of 20 W is the same as that of a human brain. In any case, it is promising that the hardware size can be remarkably compact and power dissipation can be excellently low.

Acknowledgments. This work is partially supported by KAKENHI (C) 16K06733, KAKENHI (C) 19K11876, Yazaki Memorial Foundation for Science and Technology, Support Center for Advanced Telecommunications Technology Research, Research Grants in the Natural Sciences from the Mitsubishi Foundation, Telecommunications Advancement Foundation, collaborative research with ROHM Semiconductor, collaborative research with KOA Corporation, Laboratory for Materials and Structures in Tokyo Institute of Technology, and Research Institute of Electrical Communication in Tohoku University.

References

1. McCarthy, J., Minsky, M.L., Rochester, N., Shannon, C.E.: A proposal for the dartmouth summer research project on artificial intelligence. In: Dartmouth Conference (1956)
2. Russell, S., Norvig, P.: Artificial Intelligence: A Modern Approach. Pearson Education, Prentice Hall (2009)
3. McCulloch, W.S., Pitts, W.: A logical calculus of the ideas immanent in nervous activity. Bull. Math. Biophys. **5**, 115–133 (1943)
4. Wasserman, P.D.: Neural Computing: Theory and Practice. Coriolis Group, Scottsdale (1989)
5. Ferrucci, D., et al.: Building Watson: an overview of the DeepQA project. AI Mag. **31**, 59–79 (2010)

6. Lande, T.S.: Neuromorphic Systems Engineering, Neural Networks in Silicon. Springer, Boston (2013)
7. Suri, M.: Advances in Neuromorphic Hardware Exploiting Emerging Nanoscale Devices. Springer, New Delhi (2017). https://doi.org/10.1007/978-81-322-3703-7
8. Merolla, P.A., et al.: A million spiking-neuron integrated circuit with a scalable communication network and interface. Science **345**, 668–673 (2014)
9. Neckar, A., et al.: Braindrop: a mixed-signal neuromorphic architecture with a dynamical systems-based programming model. Proc. IEEE **107**, 144–164 (2019)
10. Kimura, M., Koga, Y., Nakanishi, H., Matsuda, T., Kameda, T., Nakashima, Y.: In-Ga-Zn-O thin-film devices as synapse elements in a neural network. IEEE J. Electron Devices Soc. **6**, 100–105 (2017)
11. Kameda, T., Kimura, M., Nakashima, Y.: Neuromorphic hardware using simplified elements and thin-film semiconductor devices as synapse elements - simulation of hopfield and cellular neural network. In: Liu, D., Xie, S., Li, Y., Zhao, D., El-Alfy, E.S. (eds.) ICONIP 2017. LNCS, vol. 10639, pp. 769–776. Springer, Heidelberg (2017). https://doi.org/10.1007/978-3-319-70136-3_81
12. Prezioso, M., Merrikh-Bayat, F., Hoskins, B.D., Adam, G.C., Likharev, K.K., Strukov, D.B.: Training and operation of an integrated neuromorphic network based on metal-oxide memristors. Nature **521**, 61–64 (2015)
13. Nomura, K., Ohta, H., Takagi, A., Kamiya, T., Hirano, M., Hosono, H.: Room-temperature fabrication of transparent flexible thin-film transistors using amorphous oxide semiconductors. Nature **432**, 488–492 (2004)
14. Kim, S.J., Yoon, S., Kim, H.J.: Review of solution-processed oxide thin-film transistors. Jpn. J. Appl. Phys. **53**, 02BA02 (2014)
15. Kimura, M., Morita, R., Sugisaki, S., Matsuda, T., Kameda, T., Nakashima, Y.: Cellular neural network formed by simplified processing elements composed of thin-film transistors. Neurocomputing **248**, 112–119 (2017)
16. Kimura, M., Nakamura, N., Yokoyama, T., Matsuda, T., Kameda, T., Nakashima, Y.: Simplification of processing elements in cellular neural networks. In: Hirose, A., Ozawa, S., Doya, K., Ikeda, K., Lee, M., Liu, D. (eds.) ICONIP 2016. LNCS, vol. 9948, pp. 309–317. Springer, Cham (2016). https://doi.org/10.1007/978-3-319-46672-9_35
17. Nomura, K., et al.: Three-dimensionally stacked flexible integrated circuit: amorphous oxide/polymer hybrid complementary inverter using n-type a-In-Ga-Zn-O and p-type poly-(9,9-dioctylfluorene-co-bithiophene) thin-film transistors. Appl. Phys. Lett. **96**, 263509 (2010)
18. Chen, Y., et al.: Nanoscale molecular-switch crossbar circuits. Nanotechnology **14**, 462–468 (2003)
19. Jo, S.H., Chang, T., Ebong, I., Bhadviya, B.B., Mazumder, P., Lu, W.: Nanoscale memristor device as synapse in neuromorphic systems. Nano Lett. **10**, 1297–1301 (2010)
20. Alibart, F., Zamanidoost, E., Strukov, D.B.: Pattern classification by memristive crossbar circuits using ex situ and in situ training. Nat. Commun. **4**, 2072 (2013)
21. Hu, M., et al.: Dot-product engine for neuromorphic computing: programming 1T1M crossbar to accelerate matrix-vector multiplication. In: The 53rd Annual Design Automation Conference (DAC 2016) (2016)
22. Serrano-Gotarredona, T.,. Masquelier, T, Prodromakis, T., Indiveri, G., Linares-Barranco, B.: STDP and STDP variations with memristors for spiking neuromorphic learning systems. Front. Neurosci. **7**, Article 2 (2013)
23. Matsuda, T., Umeda, K., Kato, Y., Nishimoto, D., Furuta, M., Kimura, M.: Rare-metal-free high-performance Ga-Sn-O thin film transistor. Sci. Rep. **7**, 44326 (2017)

24. Matsuda, T., Uenuma, M., Kimura, M.: Thermoelectric effects of amorphous Ga–Sn–O thin film. Jpn. J. Appl. Phys. **56**, 070309 (2017)
25. Okamoto, R., Fukushima, H., Kimura, M., Matsuda, T.: Characteristic evaluation of Ga-Sn-O films deposited using mist chemical vapor deposition. In: The 2017 International Meeting for Future of Electron Devices, Kansai (IMFEDK 2017), pp. 74–75 (2017)
26. Sugisaki, S., et al.: Memristive characteristic of an amorphous Ga-Sn-O thin-film device. Sci. Rep. **9**, 2757 (2019)
27. Kimura, M., et al.: Neuromorphic system with crosspoint-type amorphous Ga-Sn-O thin-film devices as self-plastic synapse elements. ECS Trans. **90**, 157–166 (2019)
28. Dayhoff, J.E.: Neural Network Architectures: An Introduction. Van Nostrand Reinhold, New York (1989)
29. Kimura, M., et al.: Hopfield neural network with double-layer amorphous metal-oxide semiconductor thin-film devices as crosspoint-type synapse elements and working confirmation of letter recognition. In: Cheng, L., Leung, A.C.S., Ozawa, S. (eds.) ICONIP 2018. LNCS, vol. 11307, pp. 637–646. Springer, Cham (2018). https://doi.org/10.1007/978-3-030-04239-4_57
30. Kimura, M., Imai, S.: Degradation evaluation of α-IGZO TFTs for application to AM-OLEDs. IEEE Electron Device Lett. **31**, 963–965 (2010)
31. Vision Society of Japan: Visual Information Processing Handbook. Asakura Publishing, Tokyo (2017)
32. McEliece, R., Posner, E., Rodemich, E., Venkatesh, S.: The capacity of the hopfield associative memory. IEEE Trans. Inform. Theory **33**, 461–482 (1987)

Barrier Function Based Consensus of High-Order Nonlinear Multi-agent Systems with State Constraints

Junjie Fu[1($\boxtimes$)], Guanghui Wen[1], Yuezu Lv[1], and Tingwen Huang[2]

[1] Jiangsu Provincial Key Laboratory of Networked Collective Intelligence,
School of Mathematics, Southeast University, Nanjing 211189, China
fujunjie89@gmail.com, wenguanghui@gmail.com, yzlv@seu.edu.cn
[2] Texas A&M University at Qatar, Doha, Qatar
tingwen.huang@qatar.tamu.edu

Abstract. Consensus control of a class of high-order nonlinear multi-agent systems subject to multiple state constraints and input saturation is studied in this work. Barrier functions are employed to design a distributed controller which achieves consensus without violating the state constraints and input saturation provided that some feasibility conditions on the initial states and controller parameters are satisfied. The feasibility conditions can be checked off-line. Backstepping method and Lyapunov analysis are employed to study the convergence properties of the designed controller.

Keywords: Multi-agent system · Nonlinear systems · State constraints · Input saturation · Consensus · Barrier function

1 Introduction

The technological developments in communication, control and computing have enabled a network of systems to cooperatively solve complex tasks. Examples include multi-robot search and rescue, coverage, sensing, etc. Distributed control is needed when central computing becomes infeasible due to the large scale of the network and distributed consensus control plays a central role in various control tasks of multi-agent systems [12,19]. Extensive results have been obtained on this problem focusing on different agent dynamics and communication topology [2,17].

Regarding practical implementation of consensus controllers, physical constraints of the agent dynamics have to be taken into consideration. Input saturation is one ubiquitous constraint. For agents with simple dynamics such as

This work is supported by the Natural Science Foundation of Jiangsu Province under Grant BK20170695, the National Natural Science Foundation of China under Grants 61703094, the National Priority Research Project NPRP 9 166-1-031 from Qatar National Research Fund.

© Springer Nature Switzerland AG 2019
T. Gedeon et al. (Eds.): ICONIP 2019, LNCS 11954, pp. 492–503, 2019.
https://doi.org/10.1007/978-3-030-36711-4_41

low and high-order integrators, globally bounded nonlinear consensus controllers have been designed to achieve global consensus of the agents [13,21]. In [1], consensus strategies accounting for actuator saturations and the lack of velocity measurements were proposed for a group of agents with double-integrator dynamics based on auxiliary systems. In [16], input saturated global coordinated tracking problem was investigated for multi-agent systems with respectively neutrally stable dynamics and double integrator dynamics subject to detail-balanced directed graphs. Finite-time consensus controllers were proposed for input saturated second-order multi-agent systems in [9]. A nonlinear multi-hop relay based distributed controller was proposed in [28] to achieve global consensus tracking for asymptotically null controllable with bounded control (ANCBC) linear multi-agent systems under detail-balanced digraphs. Bounded observe-based control strategies were proposed in [8] to ensure finite-time coordinated tracking for both low- and high-order uncertain integrator multi-agent systems under general directed communication graphs.

Apart from these results on global coordinated tracking, semi-global coordination of ANCBC linear multi-agent systems under input saturation has been investigated in [22,27] using low-gain control approach. Specifically, semi-global consensus of ANCBC linear multi-agent systems with input saturation using relative output feedback was investigated in [5]. The low-gain control based distributed controllers usually suffer from slow convergence rate due to the limitation on the controller gains. Low-and-high gain control approaches were employed in [25] to achieve global consensus tracking for ANCBC linear multi-agent systems with input saturation under directed switching graphs. Model predictive control have also been employed to handle input saturation. In [6,11], distributed model predictive control (MPC) strategies to achieve consensus of linear and nonlinear multi-agent systems have been proposed. Formation control problems have been studied in [4]. There are also works which analyzed the convergence region when linear consensus controllers are subject to input saturation [3,23].

In many cases, the agents not only have input constraints but also state constraints. For example, for the coordination of multiple unmanned autonomous vehicles, the velocities of the vehicles are usually required to be bounded as well due to the safety concern of the agents or the surrounding working environment. In the attitude alignment control of satellites, the attitudes of the satellites may be required to avoid certain directions for the safety of the sensors. In these cases, it is important to design controllers taking both state and input constraints into account. Several works have appeared recently on this problem. In [14], a distributed velocity-constrained consensus problem is studied for discrete-time second-order multi-agent systems, where each agent's velocity is constrained to lie in a nonconvex set. In [15], the previous results are generalized to the case where both the velocity and control input are constrained in nonconvex sets. In [10], the problem of consensus for double-integrator dynamics with velocity constraints and a constant group reference velocity is addressed with the neighboring topology described by an undirected interaction graph that is connected. In [7], distributed control of second-order multi-agent systems was studied in presence of both velocity and input constraints with general directed communication graphs. Problems of dynamic formation control, leader-following consensus and sampled-data leader-following control were investigated, respectively. The state and input constrained consensus problem is also related to the distributed optimization with constraints [18,20] where the agents' dynamics usually restricted to first-order or second-order systems.

It can be seen that most of the existing results on input and state constrained consensus of multi-agent systems have only concerned agents with simple dynamics such as first-order or second-order integrator systems. The model predictive controller approach have the potential to be applied to complex agent dynamics, but the theoretical analysis is usually difficult and the computation cost may be too large for real time implementation. In this work, we consider a barrier function based method to handle consensus subject to both state and input constraints. The contributions include the following. Firstly, input and state constrained consensus of a class of high-order nonlinear multi-agent systems is studied. Secondly, the communication graphs are allowed to be generally directed graphs. Finally, backstepping design is combined with barrier function method to achieve consensus subject to both input and state constraints.

The rest of the paper is organized as follows. In Sect. 2, some preliminaries and the problem formulation are given. In Sect. 3, distributed consensus controller subject to both input and state constraints is proposed and the convergence of the controller is analyzed. Finally, concluding remarks are presented in Sect. 4.

Notations. I_N denotes the identity matrix with dimension N. 0 is a vector or matrix with all the elements equal to 0. $\mathbf{1}_N \in \mathbb{R}^N$ is a vector with each element equal to 1. For a vector $x = [x_1, \ldots, x_n]^T$, $\bar{x}_j = [x_2, \ldots, x_j]^T$ where $2 \leq j \leq n$. $\mathrm{diag}\{x_1, \ldots, x_n\}$ is a diagonal matrix with the diagonal elements $x_1, \ldots, x_n$. $\mathrm{sgn}(x) = [\mathrm{sgn}(x_1), \ldots, \mathrm{sgn}(x_n)]^T$ is the signum function. $\mathrm{span}\{x\}$ is the linear vector space spanned by x. A positive vector $x = [x_1, \ldots, x_n]^T > 0$ if $x_i > 0, i = 1, 2, \ldots, n$.

2   Preliminaries and Problem Formulation

2.1   Graph Theory

For a multi-agent system, the interaction relation among the agents can be represented by graphs. A directed graph $\mathcal{G} = (\mathcal{V}(\mathcal{G}), \mathcal{E}(\mathcal{G}))$ is composed of a finite set of vertices $\mathcal{V}(\mathcal{G}) = \{e_1, \ldots, e_N\}$ and a finite set of edges $\mathcal{E}(\mathcal{G}) \subset \{(e_i, e_j) : e_i, e_j \in \mathcal{V}(\mathcal{G})\}$. An edge (e_i, e_j) represents the information flow from agent i to agent j. A path in $\mathcal{G}$ from e_{i_1} to e_{i_k} is a sequence of distinct vertices $\{e_{i_1}, \ldots, e_{i_k}\}$ where $(e_{i_j}, e_{i_{j+1}}) \in \mathcal{E}(\mathcal{G})$ for $j = 1, \ldots, k-1$. e_i is reachable from e_j if there exists a path from e_i to e_j. Graph $\mathcal{G}$ is said to be strongly connected if there exists a path between any pair of distinct vertices and contains a spanning tree if there exists a vertex called the root which is reachable from any other vertex in the graph. The weighted adjacency matrix $A(\mathcal{G}) = [a_{ij}] \in \mathbb{R}^{N \times N}$ is defined as $a_{ii} = 0$ and

$a_{ij} > 0$ if and only if $(e_j, e_i) \in \mathcal{E}(\mathcal{G})$. The set of neighbors of node e_i is denoted by $\mathcal{N}_i = \{j : (e_j, e_i) \in \mathcal{E}(\mathcal{G})\}$. The degree of e_i is defined as $\deg(e_i) = d_i = \sum_{j \neq i} a_{ij}$. Then the degree matrix of $\mathcal{G}$ is $D(\mathcal{G}) = \mathrm{diag}\{d_1, \ldots, d_N\}$ and the Laplacian matrix is defined as $L = D(\mathcal{G}) - A(\mathcal{G})$.

Lemma 1 ([26]). *For a strongly connected directed graph $\mathcal{G}$, all of the nonzero eigenvalues of L have positive real parts and zero is a simple eigenvalue of L. Let $p = [p_1, \ldots, p_N]^T > 0$ be a left eigenvector of L, i.e., $L^T p = 0$. Define*

$$P = \mathrm{diag}\{p_1, \ldots, p_N\}, \quad Q = (PL + L^T P)/2. \tag{1}$$

Then, $P > 0$ and $Q \geq 0$. Furthermore, the zero space of Q is $\mathrm{span}\{1_N\}$.

Lemma 2 ([24]). *For any positive constants k_{di}, let $\mathcal{Z} = \{z \in \mathbb{R}^n : |z_i| < k_{di}, i = 1, \ldots, n\}$ and $\mathcal{N} = \mathbb{R}^l \times \mathcal{Z} \subset \mathbb{R}^{l+n}$ be open sets. Consider the system*

$$\dot{\eta} = h(\eta)$$

where $\eta = [w^T, z^T]^T \in \mathcal{N}$ is the state, and the function $h : \mathcal{N} \to \mathbb{R}^{l+n}$ is locally Lipschitz in η on $\mathcal{N}$. Let $\mathcal{Z}_i = \{z_i \in \mathbb{R} : |z_i| < k_{di}\}$. Suppose that there exist positive definite functions $U : \mathbb{R}^l \to \mathbb{R}_+$ and $V_i : \mathcal{Z}_i \to \mathbb{R}_+$, both of which are also continuously differentiable on $\mathbb{R}^l$ and $\mathcal{Z}_i$, respectively, such that

$$V_i(z_i) \to \infty \quad as \quad z_i \to \pm k_{di}.$$

Let $V(\eta) = \sum_{i=1}^n V_i(z_i) + U(w)$ and $z(0) \in \mathcal{Z}$. If the inequality

$$\dot{V} = \frac{\partial V}{\partial \eta} h \leq 0$$

holds in the set $z \in \mathcal{Z}$, then $z(t) \in \mathcal{Z}$, $\forall t \in [0, \infty)$.

2.2   Problem Formulation

Consider a multi-agent system described by the dynamics

$$\begin{aligned}
\dot{x}_{i1} &= x_{i2}, \\
\dot{x}_{i2} &= x_{i3}, \\
&\vdots \\
\dot{x}_{in} &= f_i(x_i) + g_i(x_i)u_i
\end{aligned} \tag{2}$$

where $i = 1, \ldots, N$, $x_i = [x_{i1}, x_{i2}, \ldots, x_{in}]^T \in \mathbb{R}^n$ is the state of agent i, $u_i \in \mathbb{R}$ is the control input, $f_i(x_i) : \mathbb{R}^n \to \mathbb{R}$ and $g_i(x_i) : \mathbb{R}^n \to \mathbb{R}$ are known nonlinear functions.

The communication relation among the agents is assumed to satisfy the following assumption:

Assumption 1. *The communication graph $\mathcal{G}$ of the multi-agent system (2) is directed and strongly connected.*

The objective is to reach consensus, that is, $x_i(t) - x_j(t) \to 0$ as $t \to \infty$ while all the states of the agents and control inputs satisfy given constraints. We consider the following state constraints and input saturation constraint: x_{ij} is required to remain in the set $|x_{ij}(t)| \le k_{cj}$, $\forall t > 0$ where k_{cj} is a positive constant, for all $j = 2, \ldots, n$ and $|u_i| \le k_u$, $i = 1, 2, \ldots, N$.

Remark 1. *Since the first state component x_{i1} of the agents usually represent position-like variables, we do not consider bounded constraints on them. However, simple modifications can be made on the following developed controllers such that state constraints on all components can be handled.*

Assumption 2. *The functions $f_i(x_i)$, $i = 1, 2, \ldots, N$ are known and there exists a positive constant $\bar{f}$ such that $|f_i(x_i)| \le \bar{f}$ for $|x_{ij}| < k_{cj}$, $j = 2, \ldots, n$. The functions $g_i(x_i)$, $i = 1, 2, \ldots, N$ are known and there exists a positive constant $\bar{g}$ such that $0 < \bar{g} \le g_i(x_i)$ for $|x_{ij}| < k_{cj}$, $j = 2, \ldots, n$.*

3   Constrained Consensus with State and Input Constraints

3.1   Controller Design

A backstepping controller design procedure will be employed to achieve consensus subject to both input and state constraints. For agent i, denote $z_{i2} = x_{i2} - \alpha_{i1}$ with

$$\alpha_{i1} = -k_1 \arctan \left[\sum\nolimits_{j=1}^{N} a_{ij}(x_{i1} - x_{j1}) \right]$$

where $k_1 > 0$ is a design parameter. Let $\xi_i = \sum_{j=1}^{N} a_{ij}(x_{i1} - x_{j1})$ and consider

$$V_{i1} = k_1' \int_0^{\xi_i(t)} p_i \arctan(s) ds$$

where p_i are given in Lemma 1. We have

$$\dot{V}_{i1} = k_1' p_i \arctan(\xi_i) \left[\sum\nolimits_{j=1}^{N} a_{ij}(x_{i2} - x_{j2}) \right]$$
$$= k_1' p_i \arctan(\xi_i) \left[\sum\nolimits_{j=1}^{N} a_{ij}(z_{i2} - z_{j2}) + \sum\nolimits_{j=1}^{N} a_{ij}(\alpha_{i1} - \alpha_{j1}) \right].$$

For step 2, note that $\dot{z}_{i2} = x_{i3} - \dot{\alpha}_{i1}$. Denote $z_{i3} = x_{i3} - \alpha_{i2}$ and consider

$$V_{i2} = V_{i1} + \frac{1}{2} \log \frac{k_{b2}^2}{k_{b2}^2 - z_{i2}^2}$$

where k_{b2} is a design parameter. It is easy to see that V_{i2} is positive definite and continuously differentiable in the set $|z_{i2}| < k_{b2}$. Then

$$\dot{V}_{i2} = \dot{V}_{i1} + \frac{z_{i2}}{k_{b2}^2 - z_{i2}^2}(z_{i3} + \alpha_{i2} - \dot{\alpha}_{i1}).$$

Let $\alpha_{i2} = \dot\alpha_{i1} - \left(k_{b2}^2 - z_{i2}^2\right) k_2 z_{i2}$ and it follows

$$\dot V_{i2} = \dot V_{i1} - k_2 z_{i2}^2 + \frac{z_{i2} z_{i3}}{k_{b2}^2 - z_{i2}^2}.$$

For step 3, note that, $\dot z_{i3} = x_{i4} - \dot\alpha_{i2}$. Denote $z_{i4} = x_{i4} - \alpha_{i3}$ and consider

$$V_{i3} = V_{i2} + \frac{1}{2} \log \frac{k_{b3}^2}{k_{b3}^2 - z_{i3}^2}$$

where k_{b3} is a design parameter. Then

$$\dot V_{i3} = \dot V_{i2} + \frac{z_{i3}}{k_{b3}^2 - z_{i3}^2} \left(z_{i4} + \alpha_{i3} - \dot\alpha_{i2}\right).$$

Let $\alpha_{i3} = \dot\alpha_{i2} - \left(k_{b3}^2 - z_{i3}^2\right) k_3 z_{i3} - \frac{k_{b3}^2 - z_{i3}^2}{k_{b2}^2 - z_{i2}^2} z_{i2}$ and we have

$$\dot V_{i3} = \dot V_{i1} - k_2 z_{i2}^2 - k_3 z_{i3}^2 + \frac{z_{i3} z_{i4}}{k_{b3}^2 - z_{i3}^2}.$$

Similarly, for step l, $3 < l \le n-1$, we have $\dot z_{il} = x_{i(l+1)} - \dot\alpha_{i(l-1)}$. Denote $z_{i(l+1)} = x_{i(l+1)} - \alpha_{il}$ and consider

$$V_{il} = V_{i(l-1)} + \frac{1}{2} \log \frac{k_{bl}^2}{k_{bl}^2 - z_{il}^2}$$

where k_{bl} is a design parameter. Then

$$\dot V_{il} = \dot V_{i(l-1)} + \frac{z_{il}}{k_{bl}^2 - z_{il}^2} \left(z_{i(l+1)} + \alpha_{il} - \dot\alpha_{i(l-1)}\right).$$

Let $\alpha_{il} = \dot\alpha_{i(l-1)} - \left(k_{bl}^2 - z_{il}^2\right) k_l z_{il} - \frac{k_{bl}^2 - z_{il}^2}{k_{b(l-1)}^2 - z_{i(l-1)}^2} z_{i(l-1)}$ and we have

$$\dot V_{il} = \dot V_{i1} - k_2 z_{i2}^2 - \cdots - k_l z_{il}^2 + \frac{z_{il} z_{i(l+1)}}{k_{bl}^2 - z_{il}^2}.$$

Finally, for step n, we have $\dot z_{in} = f_i(x_i) + g_i(x_i) u_i - \dot\alpha_{i(n-1)}$. Consider

$$V_i = V_{i(n-1)} + \frac{1}{2} \log \frac{k_{bn}^2}{k_{bn}^2 - z_{in}^2}$$

where k_{bn} is a design parameter. Then

$$\dot V_i = \dot V_{i(n-1)} + \frac{z_{in}}{k_{bn}^2 - z_{in}^2} \left(f_i(x_i) + g_i(x_i) u_i - \dot\alpha_{i(n-1)}\right).$$

Let

$$u_i = \frac{1}{g_i(x_i)} \Bigg[- f_i(x_i) + \dot\alpha_{i(n-1)} - \left(k_{bn}^2 - z_{in}^2\right) k_n z_{in}$$

$$- \frac{k_{bn}^2 - z_{in}^2}{k_{b(n-1)}^2 - z_{i(n-1)}^2} z_{i(n-1)} \Bigg] \tag{3}$$

and it follows

$$\dot{V}_i = \dot{V}_{i1} - k_2 z_{i2}^2 - \cdots - k_n z_{in}^2.$$

For the closed-loop system:

$$\dot{x}_{i1} = z_{i2} + \alpha_{i1},$$
$$\dot{z}_{i2} = z_{i3} - (k_{b2}^2 - z_{i2}^2)k_2 z_{i2},$$
$$\dot{z}_{i3} = z_{i4} - (k_{b3}^2 - z_{i3}^2)k_3 z_{i3} - \frac{(k_{b3}^2 - z_{i3}^2)}{(k_{b2}^2 - z_{i2}^2)} z_{i2},$$
$$\vdots$$
$$\dot{z}_{in} = -(k_{bn}^2 - z_{in}^2)k_n z_{in} - \frac{(k_{bn}^2 - z_{in}^2)}{(k_{b(n-1)}^2 - z_{i(n-1)}^2)} z_{i(n-1)},$$

where $i = 1, 2, \ldots, N$, we consider the Lyapunov function $V = \sum_{i=1}^{N} V_i$. Let $\xi = [\xi_1, \ldots, \xi_N]^T$, $z_j = [z_{1j}, \ldots, z_{Nj}]^T$, $j = 1, \ldots, n$, it holds

$$\dot{V} = \sum_{i=1}^{N} \dot{V}_{i1} - k_2 z_2^T z_2 - \cdots k_n z_n^T z_n$$
$$= k_1' \arctan^T(\xi) PL z_2 - k_1' k_1 \arctan^T(\xi) PL \arctan(\xi)$$
$$\quad - k_2 z_2^T z_2 - \cdots k_n z_n^T z_n$$
$$= k_1' \arctan^T(\xi) PL z_2 - k_1' k_1 \arctan^T(\xi) Q \arctan(\xi)$$
$$\quad - k_2 z_2^T z_2 - \cdots k_n z_n^T z_n.$$

Let $\eta = \arctan(\xi)/\|\arctan(\xi)\|$ and consider the bounded closed set $\mathcal{S} = \{\eta \in \mathbb{R}^N : \eta^T \eta = 1\}$. We show that for any $\eta \in \mathcal{S}$, it holds $\eta^T Q \eta \neq 0$. Suppose this is not true, then there exists a vector $\eta \in \mathcal{S}$ such that $\eta^T Q \eta = 0$. From Lemma 1 we have that $\eta = c \mathbf{1}_N$ where c is some nonzero constant. Then we have $\xi = \bar{c} \mathbf{1}_N$ for a nonzero $\bar{c}$. Then it follows that $p^T \xi = \bar{c} p^T \mathbf{1}_N \neq 0$ which leads to a contradiction. Considering that $\eta^T Q \eta$ is continuous with respect to η, we have that $\lambda(Q) = \min_{\eta \in \mathcal{S}} \eta^T Q \eta$ exists and is larger than zero. Therefore, we have $\arctan^T(\xi) Q \arctan(\xi) \geq \lambda(Q)\|\arctan(\xi)\|^2$. It follows that

$$\dot{V} \leq k_1' \lambda_{\max}(PL) \|\arctan(\xi)\| \|z_2\| - k_1' k_1 \lambda(Q)\|\arctan(\xi)\|^2$$
$$\quad - k_2\|z_2\|^2 - \cdots k_n\|z_n\|^2$$
$$\leq - [k_1' k_1 \lambda(Q) - k_1' \varepsilon \lambda_{\max}(PL)] \|\arctan(\xi)\|^2 \qquad (4)$$
$$\quad - \left[k_2 - \frac{k_1'}{4\varepsilon} \lambda_{\max}(PL)\right] \|z_2\|^2 - \cdots k_n\|z_n\|^2.$$

Under the condition

$$k_1 > \frac{\varepsilon \lambda_{\max}(PL)}{\lambda(Q)}$$
$$k_2 > \frac{k_1'}{4\varepsilon}\lambda_{\max}(PL), k_3 > 0, \ldots, k_n > 0$$

we have $\dot{V} \leq 0$. Consider the closed-loop system with the state $[\xi^T, z_2^T, \ldots, z_n^T]^T$. It follows from (4) and Lemma 2 that $z_j(t) \in \mathcal{Z}_j$ where $j = 2, \ldots, n$ and

$$\mathcal{Z}_j = \{\hat{z} \in R^N : |\hat{z}_i| < k_{bj}, i = 1, \ldots, N\}$$

provided that $z_j(0) \in \mathcal{Z}_j$.

Denote the set

$$\Omega_0 = \{x \in \mathbb{R}^{Nn} : a_j \leq x_{ij} \leq b_j, i = 1, \ldots, N, j = 2, \ldots, n\} \tag{5}$$

where $x = [x_1^T(0), x_2^T, \ldots, x_N^T]^T \in \mathbb{R}^{Nn}$ and let

$$Z_{ij} = \max_{x \in \Omega_0} |z_{ij}(\bar{x}_{ij}, \bar{x}_{kj})|, k \in \mathcal{N}_i, i = 1, \ldots, N, j = 2, \ldots, n. \tag{6}$$

Let

$$D_{zj} = k_{bj} \sqrt{1 - e^{-2\left(\sum_{i=1}^{N} V_{i1}(0)\right)} \prod_{l=1}^{N} \prod_{m=2}^{n} \frac{k_{bm}^2 - Z_{lm}^2}{k_{bm}^2}}$$

and define

$$A_{ij} = \max_{(\bar{x}_{ij}, \bar{z}_{ij}, \bar{x}_{kj}, \bar{z}_{kj}) \in \Omega_{ij}} |\alpha_{ij}(\bar{x}_{ij}, \bar{z}_{ij}, \bar{x}_{kj}, \bar{z}_{kj})|$$

$i = 1, \ldots, N, j = 2, \ldots, n,$

$$B_i = \max_{(\bar{x}_{in}, \bar{z}_{in}, \bar{x}_{kn}, \bar{z}_{kn}) \in \Omega_{in}} |u_i(f_i, g_i, \bar{x}_{in}, \bar{z}_{in}, \bar{x}_{kn}, \bar{z}_{kn})|$$

where

$$\Omega_{ij} = \{\bar{x}_{ij} \in R^{j-1}, \bar{z}_{ij} \in R^{j-1}, \bar{x}_{kj} \in R^{j-1}, \bar{z}_{kj} \in R^{j-1} :$$
$$|x_{ip}| \leq D_{zp} + A_{i(p-1)}, |x_{kp}| \leq D_{zp} + A_{k(p-1)},$$
$$|z_{ip}| \leq D_{zp}, |z_{kp}| \leq D_{zp}, p = 2, \ldots, j, k \in N_i\}$$

with $A_{i1} = \frac{k_1 \pi}{2}$.

Theorem 1. *Given the constraints* $\{k_{c2}, \ldots, k_{cn}, k_u\}$. *Suppose that the initial state* $x(0) \in \Omega_0$ *where* $b_j < k_{cj}$ *and* $a_j > -k_{cj}$. *If there exist positive constants* $\rho = [\bar{a}_n, \bar{b}_n, k_1, \bar{k}_n, \bar{k}_{bn}]$ *that satisfy*

$$k_1 > \frac{\varepsilon \lambda_{\max}(PL)}{\lambda(Q)} \tag{7}$$

$$k_2 > \frac{1}{4\varepsilon} \lambda_{\max}(PL), \tag{8}$$

$$k_3 > 0, \ldots, k_n > 0 \tag{9}$$

$$k_{bj} > Z_{ij}(\rho), i = 1, \ldots, N, j = 2, \ldots, n \tag{10}$$

$$k_{cj} > A_{i(j-1)} + k_{bj}, i = 1, \ldots, N, j = 2, \ldots, n \tag{11}$$

$$k_u > B_i, i = 1, \ldots, N \tag{12}$$

Then

– *all the states* $z_j, j = 2, \ldots, n$ *remain in the set*

$$\Omega_{z_j} = \{\hat{z} \in R^N : |\hat{z}_i| \leq D_{zj}\}.$$

– *all state constraints and input constraints of the agents are never violated.*
– *consensus of the agents is achieved.*

Proof.

- From $x(0) \in \Omega_0$, (5), (6) and (10), it holds $z_j(0) \in \mathcal{Z}_j$. It follows from (4) and Lemma 2 that $z_j(t) \in \mathcal{Z}_j$ where $j = 2, \ldots, n$ and

$$\mathcal{Z}_j = \{\hat{z} \in R^N : |\hat{z}_i| < k_{bj}, i = 1, \ldots, N\}.$$

Then, we have $\dot{V} \leq 0$ which leads to

$$V(t) \leq V(0) = \sum_{i=1}^N V_{i1}(0) + \sum_{i=1}^N \sum_{j=2}^n \frac{1}{2} \log \frac{k_{bj}^2}{k_{bj}^2 - z_{ij}^2(0)}$$
$$\leq \sum_{i=1}^N V_{i1}(0) + \sum_{i=1}^N \sum_{j=2}^n \frac{1}{2} \log \frac{k_{bj}^2}{k_{bj}^2 - Z_{ij}^2}.$$

Therefore

$$\frac{k_{bj}^2}{k_{bj}^2 - z_{ij}^2(t)} \leq e^{2\left(\sum_{i=1}^N V_{i1}(0)\right)} \prod_{i=1}^N \prod_{j=2}^n \frac{k_{bj}^2}{k_{bj}^2 - Z_{ij}^2}$$

which leads to that all the states z_j, $j = 2, \ldots, n$ remain in the set

$$\Omega_{z_j} = \{\hat{z} \in R^N : |\hat{z}_i| \leq D_{zj}\}.$$

- Noting that $x_{i2} = z_{i2} + \alpha_{i1}$ and $|z_{i2}| \leq D_{z2} < k_{b2}$, $|\alpha_{i1}| \leq A_{i1}$, it follows from (11) that $|x_{i2}| < k_{c2}$. To show $|x_{i3}(t)| < k_{c3}$, we first verify that there exists A_{i2} such that $|\alpha_{i2}| \leq A_{i2}, \forall t \geq 0$. Since $|x_{i2}| < D_{z2} + A_{i1}$, $|x_{k2}| < D_{z2} + A_{k1}$, $|z_{i2}| \leq D_{z2}$, $|z_{k2}| \leq D_{z2}$ where $k \in \mathcal{N}_i$, it follows that $(x_{i2}, x_{k2}, z_{i2}, z_{k2}) \in \Omega_{i2}$. Therefore, the stabilizing function α_{i2} is bounded since it is a continuous function. As a result, A_{i2} exists. Then, from $x_{i3} = z_{i3} + \alpha_{i2}$ and $|z_{i3}| \leq D_{z3} < k_{b3}$, $\alpha_{i2} \leq A_{i2}$ and (11) it follows that $|x_{i3}| < k_{c3}$. We can iteratively show that $|x_{i(j+1)}(t)| < k_{c(j+1)}$, $j = 3, \ldots, n$. Since $|x_{ij}| \leq D_{zj} + A_{ij}$, $|x_{kj}| \leq D_{zj} + A_{kj}$, $|z_{ij}| \leq D_{zj}$, $|z_{kj}| \leq D_{zj}$, it is clear that $(\bar{x}_{ij}, \bar{x}_{kj}, \bar{z}_{ij}, \bar{z}_{kj}) \in \Omega_{ij}$ and therefore, the stabilizing function α_{ij} is bounded since it is a continuous function. As a result, A_{ij} exists. Then, from $|z_{i(j+1)}| \leq D_{z(j+1)} < k_{b(j+1)}$ and $\alpha_{ij} \leq A_{ij}$ and (11), it follows that $|x_{i(j+1)}(t)| < k_{c(j+1)}$. Finally, since $(\bar{x}_{in}, \bar{x}_{kn}, \bar{z}_{in}, \bar{z}_{kn}) \in \Omega_{in}$ and (12) it follows that $|u_i| \leq k_u$. Therefore, all the state constraints and input saturation constraints are not violated.
- From (4) and the Lasalle's invariance principle, it follows that $\xi \to 0$, $z_j \to 0$, $j = 2, \ldots, n$. By definition of ξ, it follows that consensus of x_{i1}, $i = 1, \ldots, N$ is achieved and $x_{ij} \to 0, i = 1, \ldots, N, j = 2, \ldots, n$. Therefore, it follows that $x_i(t) - x_j(t) \to 0$ as $t \to \infty$ which means consensus of the agents is achieved.

3.2   Controller Parameter Design

Theorem 1 gives a sufficient condition on the initial states of the agents and the controller parameters to ensure consensus without violating the state and input constraints. If the conditions (7)–(12) are satisfied, then with the same set of controller parameters, from all the initial state in the region Ω_0, consensus is achieved while satisfying the constraints. On the one hand, we want to enlarge the feasible region to be applicable for wider initial states. But note that, increasing the initial condition region also increases the bounds A_{ij} and Z_{ij}, making it more difficult to satisfy the constraints. On the other hand, we also want larger controller gains k_i, $i = 1, \ldots, n$ which leads to faster convergence from (4). But increasing k_i also increases A_{ij} and Z_{ij}. Therefore, a nonlinear constrained optimization problem can be formulated which reflects a tradeoff between enlarging initial condition and increasing convergence speed. We solve the following optimization problem with parameter $\rho = [\bar{a}_n, \bar{b}_n, k_1, \bar{k}_n, \bar{k}_{bn}]$

$$\max \quad F(\rho) = \sum_{i=2}^{n} (b_i - a_i) + \sigma \sum_{i=1}^{n} k_i \tag{13}$$

subject to

$$k_1 > \frac{\varepsilon \lambda_{\max}(PL)}{\lambda}, k_2 > \frac{k_1'}{4\varepsilon} \lambda_{\max}(PL), k_j > 0, j = 3, \ldots, n \tag{14}$$

$$-k_{cj} < a_j < b_j < k_{cj}, j = 2, \ldots, n \tag{15}$$

$$k_{bj} > Z_{ij}(\rho), i = 1, \ldots, N, j = 2, \ldots, n \tag{16}$$

$$k_{cj} > A_{i(j-1)} + k_{bj}, i = 1, \ldots, N, j = 2, \ldots, n \tag{17}$$

$$k_u > B_i, i = 1, \ldots, N \tag{18}$$

where $\varepsilon > 0$ is a positive parameter, $\sigma > 0$ is a positive weighting variable.

Next we show that the optimization problem is always feasible. Note that when $a_2, b_2 \to 0$ and $k_1 \to 0$, it holds $Z_{i2} \to 0$. By choosing ε and k_1' sufficiently small, we have $k_1 \to 0$, $k_2 \to 0$. Then from the definition of α_{i2}, we obtain $\alpha_{i2} \to 0$. By choosing $a_3, b_3 \to 0$, from $z_{i3} = x_{i3} - \alpha_{i2}$ we obtain $Z_{i3} \to 0$. Similarly, by letting $a_j, b_j \to 0$ and $k_1, k_2, \ldots, k_n \to 0$, we have $Z_{ij} \to 0$. Therefore, for any set of $k_{bj} > 0$, there exists ρ which satisfies (16). Furthermore, for sufficiently small k_{bj}, from the definition of A_{ij} and B_i, we have $A_{ij} \to 0, B_i \to 0$ as $k_{bj} \to 0$. Therefore, there exist $k_{bj}, a_j, b_j, k_1', k_j$ which satisfy (14)–(18). Thus, we can solve the optimization problem offline to determine the initial region and a set of controller parameters such that with $x(0) \in \Omega_0$ and control input (3), consensus can be achieved while all the state constraints and input saturation are satisfied.

4   Conclusion

In this work, we studied the state and input constrained consensus problem for a class of high-order nonlinear multi-agent systems. Specifically, all the states apart from the position like state are required to stay in a given bounded interval and the control input also satisfies a saturation bound. A barrier-function based controller design strategy is proposed to solve this problem and a controller is designed through the backstepping method. Sufficient conditions on the initial states and controller parameters are obtained to guarantee constrained consensus. An optimization problem is formulated to determine the feasible region and controller parameters. Further work include considering connectivity maintenance and collision avoidance between the agents in the multi-robot applications.

References

1. Abdessameud, A., Tayebi, A.: On consensus algorithms for double-integrator dynamics without velocity measurement and with input constraints. Syst. Control Lett. **59**(12), 812–821 (2010)
2. Cao, Y., Yu, W., Ren, W., Chen, G.: An overview of recent progress in the study of distributed multi-agent coordination. IEEE Trans. Ind. Inform. **9**(1), 427–438 (2013)
3. Deng, C., Yang, G.H.: Consensus of linear multiagent systems with actuator saturation and external disturbances. IEEE Trans. Circuits Syst. II Express Briefs **64**(3), 284–288 (2017)
4. Dunbar, W.B., Murray, R.M.: Distributed receding horizon control for multi-vehicle formation stabilization. Automatica **42**(4), 549–558 (2006)
5. Fan, M.C., Zhang, H.T., Lin, Z.: Distributed semi-global consensus with relative output feedback and input saturation under directed switching networks. IEEE Trans. Circuits Syst. II: Express Briefs **62**(8), 796–800 (2015)
6. Ferrari-Trecate, G., Galbusera, L., Marciandi, M.P.E., Scattolini, R.: Model predictive control schemes for consensus in multi-agent systems with single-and double-integrator dynamics. IEEE Trans. Autom. Control **54**(11), 2560–2572 (2009)
7. Fu, J., Wen, G., Yu, W., Huang, T., Yu, X.: Consensus of second-order multi-agent systems with both velocity and input constraints. IEEE Trans. Industr. Electron. (2018). https://doi.org/10.1109/TIE.2018.2879292
8. Fu, J., Wang, J.: Observer-based finite-time coordinated tracking for high-order integrator systems with matched uncertainties under directed communication graphs. In: 11th IEEE International Conference on Control & Automation (ICCA). pp. 880–885. IEEE (2014)
9. Fu, J., Wang, Q., Wang, J.: Robust finite-time consensus tracking for second-order multi-agent systems with input saturation under general directed communication graphs. Int. J. Control (2017). https://doi.org/10.1080/00207179.2017.1411609
10. Jesus, T.A., Pimenta, L.C., Tôrres, L.A., Mendes, E.M.: Consensus for double-integrator dynamics with velocity constraints. Int. J. Control Autom. Syst. **12**(5), 930–938 (2014)
11. Li, H., Shi, Y.: Robust distributed model predictive control of constrained continuous-time nonlinear systems: a robustness constraint approach. IEEE Trans. Autom. Control **59**(6), 1673–1678 (2014)
12. Li, M., Wang, D.: 2-D stochastic configuration networks for image data analytics. IEEE Trans. Cybern. (2019). https://doi.org/10.1109/TCYB.2019.2925883
13. Li, Y., Xiang, J., Wei, W.: Consensus problems for linear time-invariant multi-agent systems with saturation constraints. IET Control Theory Appl. **5**(6), 823–829 (2011)
14. Lin, P., Ren, W., Gao, H.: Distributed velocity-constrained consensus of discrete-time multi-agent systems with nonconvex constraints, switching topologies, and delays. IEEE Trans. Autom. Control **62**(11), 5788–5794 (2017)
15. Lin, P., Ren, W., Yang, C., Gui, W.: Distributed consensus of second-order multi-agent systems with nonconvex velocity and control input constraints. IEEE Trans. Autom. Control **63**(4), 1171–1176 (2018)
16. Meng, Z., Zhao, Z., Lin, Z.: On global leader-following consensus of identical linear dynamic systems subject to actuator saturation. Systems Control Lett. **62**(2), 132–142 (2013)

17. Murray, R.M.: Recent research in cooperative control of multivehicle systems. J. Dyn. Syst. Meas. Contr. **129**(5), 571 (2007)
18. Nedic, A., Ozdaglar, A., Parrilo, P.A.: Constrained consensus and optimization in multi-agent networks. IEEE Trans. Autom. Control **55**(4), 922–938 (2010)
19. Olfati-Saber, R.: Flocking for multi-agent dynamic systems: algorithms and theory. IEEE Trans. Autom. Control **51**(3), 401–420 (2006)
20. Qiu, Z., Liu, S., Xie, L.: Distributed constrained optimal consensus of multi-agent systems. Automatica **68**, 209–215 (2016)
21. Ren, W.: On consensus algorithms for double-integrator dynamics. IEEE Trans. Autom. Control **53**(6), 1503–1509 (2008)
22. Su, H., Chen, M.Z.Q., Lam, J., Lin, Z.: Semi-global leader-following consensus of linear multi-agent systems with input saturation via low gain feedback. IEEE Trans. Circuits Syst. I Regul. Pap. **60**(7), 1881–1889 (2013)
23. Takaba, K.: Local synchronization of linear multi-agent systems subject to input saturation. SICE J. Control Meas. Syst. Integr. **8**(5), 334–340 (2015)
24. Tee, K.P., Ge, S.S., Tay, E.H.: Barrier Lyapunov functions for the control of output-constrained nonlinear systems. Automatica **45**(4), 918–927 (2009)
25. Wang, B., Wang, J., Zhang, B., Li, X.: Global cooperative control framework for multiagent systems subject to actuator saturation with industrial applications. IEEE Trans. Syst. Man Cybern. Syst. **47**(7), 1–14 (2016)
26. Zhang, H., Li, Z., Qu, Z., Lewis, F.L.: On constructing Lyapunov functions for multi-agent systems. Automatica **58**, 39–42 (2015). https://doi.org/10.1016/j.automatica.2015.05.006
27. Zhao, Z., Lin, Z.: Semi-global leader-following consensus of multiple linear systems with position and rate limited actuators. Int. J. Robust Nonlinear Control **25**(13), 2083–2100 (2015)
28. Zhao, Z., Lin, Z.: Global leader-following consensus of a group of general linear systems using bounded controls. Automatica **68**, 294–304 (2016)

Transformer-DW: A Transformer Network with Dynamic and Weighted Head

Ruxin Tan, Jiahui Sun, Bo Su$^{(\boxtimes)}$, and Gongshen Liu$^{(\boxtimes)}$

School of Electronic Information and Electrical Engineering,
Shanghai Jiao Tong University, Shanghai, China
{tanruxin,sjh_717,subo,lgshen}@sjtu.edu.cn

Abstract. State-of-the-art results on computer vision often use the CNN model where the number of channels is variant with the depth of CNN layer. The weighted channel has been proposed recently and further improves the performance of CNN. In NLP field, the Transformer structure with multi-head attention is the preferred model to solve many problems. However, Transformer cannot explicitly distinguish the information from different layers and different heads. Inspired by the use of channels in CNN model, we propose a novel model, Transformer-DW, with the dynamic and weighted head mechanism. The dynamic head allows the number of heads to increase adaptively with the depth of network layer thus explicitly modelling differences between layers. The Weighted head assigns a separate value to each head so that each head contributes differently to the task. We apply Transformer-DW to the two different tasks, machine translation and dialogue generation. Various experiments show that Transformer-DW outperforms Transformer and other baselines.

Keywords: Transformer · Dynamic head · Weighted head

1 Introduction

Recently, CNN (Convolutional neural network) has been widely used in computer vision filed. Various CNN-based models have been proposed to apply in some specific area, such as ResNet [1] for image classification, Faster RCNN for image detection [2] and FCN [3] for semantic segmentation. All these CNN-based models follow a paradigm, that is, the number of channels in each CNN layer is increased as the layer deepens. Instead of considering the different channels in the same layer equally, SENet [4] assigns a separate random weight to each channel. Therefore, within the same layer, some channels have a larger weight while others have a smaller weight after step by step training, and it significantly improves the model performance. Zeiler et al. [5] reveal that the channel in an image is a feature graph in some sense and is the detection of one feature, the

© Springer Nature Switzerland AG 2019
T. Gedeon et al. (Eds.): ICONIP 2019, LNCS 11954, pp. 504–515, 2019.
https://doi.org/10.1007/978-3-030-36711-4_42

strength of value in the channel is the response to the strength of the current feature. However, in NLP (Natural Language Processing) field, there is no similar concept corresponding to the channel in CNN.

Transformer is proposed by Vaswani et al. [6]. With a novel module called multi-head attention, it has achieved great performance especially in machine translation. Based on that, Google proposes universal Transformer [7] to control the depth of model layers dynamically. Shaw et al. [8] replace the position embedding with their relative position embedding to improve efficiency. Inspire by the residual connection, Bapna et al. [9] add extra connections between all encoders and the decoders in Transformer. Dai et al. [10] propose Transformer-XL to learn dependency beyond a fixed length without disrupting temporal coherence. However, all these variants do not observe the relationship between heads and consider each head equally. Additionally, the number of heads in Transformer is a constant number during the whole training procedure, which cannot explicitly distinguish the information from different layers.

Inspired by the application of channels in CNN, we propose Transformer-DW, a Transformer with dynamic and weighted head. Specifically, in Transformer-DW, the number of heads is no longer constant and it will increase with the depth of encoder. The degree of increase will vary with different complexity of the task. Additionally, each head within a multi-head attention layer will be assigned a different weight thus each single head will play a different role in a task. All the ways we did are based on the consideration that the head in Transformer is similar to the channel in CNN, i.e., each head can obtain a sentence representation in a certain subspace. Weighted head allows our model to explicitly capture the difference between heads. Dynamic head enables our model to better learn a representation from shallow to high-level spaces.

We have applied the proposed model to two different tasks to verify the performance. The results show that Transformer-DW outperforms other baselines in both machine translation task and dialogue generation task.

The key contributions of this paper can be summarized as follows:

(1) A novel model Transformer-DW is proposed. With dynamic and weighted head, our model can better capture the information within each head.
(2) We establish a connection between CNN and Transformer. Our experiments indicate that the effect of the head in Transformer is similar to the channel in CNN.
(3) The proposed model outperforms other baselines in multiple tasks.

2   Related Work

CNN is a commonly used network in computer vision. LeCun et al. [11] propose LeNet to solve document recognition problems. The number of channels in LeNet increases from 20 to 50. Further, AlexNet [12] is proposed with a deeper network and a larger channel to be applied in ImageNet classification. He et al. [1] propose ResNet and further improve the accuracy of image classification, the number of channels in the last layer increases to 512. Obviously, the number of channels

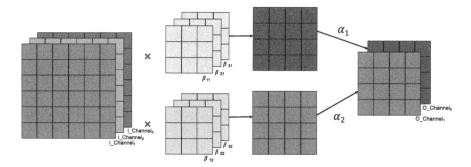

Fig. 1. The schema of the CNN calculation. In this schema, the input $I \in \mathbb{R}^{6\times6\times3}$ consists of 3 channels with each channel height 6 and width 6. First, the three channels will multiply by two different filters with each filter $\beta \in \mathbb{R}^{3\times3\times3}$. Then, two separate output channel will be assigned with a scalar $\alpha \in \mathbb{R}$. Finally, the two output channel will be sent as an input of the next CNN layer.

grows synchronously with the number of network layers and is consistent with the complexity of a task. Based on that, SENet [4] believes that different channels should contribute differently to the task and assigns a weight to each channel.

Transformer has surpassed RNN in many NLP fields. In Transformer, there is an important module, called multi-head attention layer. Specifically, a single head attention layer will calculate sentence embeddings and then obtain a new representation of the sentence. Multi-head means it will repeat this process multiple times. Therefore, after multi-head attention layer, multiple representations will be obtained and then they are simply concatenated together to form a new representation. Many variants have been proposed in recent years, Ahmed et al. [13] assign different weights on each head to apply in machine translation but it focuses on the efficiency of model and still uses the constant head. Zhang et al. [14] propose an average attention network to speed up the decoding rate.

2.1   The Channel of CNN

A channel in an image is a feature map in some sense. The strength of a value in a channel is the response to the strength of the current feature. Specifically, after a convolution layer, the output $O\_Channel \in \mathbb{R}^{H\times W\times M}$ consists of M channels. $\forall j \in \{1, ..., M\}$, $O\_Channel_j \in \mathbb{R}^{H\times W}$ is a matrix with height H and width W. The convolution procedure can be described as:

$$O\_Channel_j = \sum_{i=1}^{N} I\_Channel_i \times \beta_{ij} \tag{1}$$

$$O\_Channel = Concat(O\_Channel_1, ..., O\_Channel_M) \tag{2}$$

Where we assume that the number of input channels is N. $I\_Channel_i \in \mathbb{R}^{H\times W}$ is the $O\_Channel_i$ of the previous convolution layer. $\beta_{ij} \in \mathbb{R}^{H'\times W'}$ is the learning parameter in filter kernels. Nearly all CNN models follow this paradigm and thus consider each channel equally.

SENet [4] has observed the interdependencies between channels. To extract more information in channels, they explicitly recalibrate filter responses in two steps, squeeze and excitation. After that, each channel will be assigned a scalar $\alpha \in \mathbb{R}$:

$$O\_Channel_j = \sum_{i=1}^{N} \alpha_j I\_Channel_i \times \beta_{ij} \tag{3}$$

The above process is shown in Fig. 1.

Additionally, it is accepted by almost all researchers that the number of channels will be set larger with layer deepening. In ResNet [1], as the network layer grows, the number of channels are set to 64, 128, 256, and 512, respectively.

2.2 The Head of Transformer

Transformer is an encoder-decoder framework which consists of two important part, multi-head attention and feed-forward layers. Transformer can be trained in parallel since no RNN is used and it outperforms RNN in many NLP fields.

For multi-head attention, it can be regarded as the multiple repetitions of single-head attention. How the single-head attention works and how to repeat are described as follows.

In single-head attention, it is essentially an original attention, i.e., the similarity value between the query vector and the key vector will be assigned to the corresponding value vector:

$$Attention(Q, K, V) = softmax \left(\frac{QK^T}{\sqrt{d_k}} \right) V \tag{4}$$

Where $\sqrt{d_k}$ can be regarded as a scaling factor and Q, K, V are query, key, value vector respectively. Base on that, $\forall i \in \{1, ..., M\}$, the $head_i$ can be calculated by:

$$head_i = Attention \left(QW_i^Q, KW_i^K, VW_i^V \right) \tag{5}$$

Where $W_i^Q \in \mathbb{R}^{d_{model} \times d_k}$, $W_i^K \in \mathbb{R}^{d_{model} \times d_k}$, $W_i^V \in \mathbb{R}^{d_{model} \times d_v}$ are the learning parameters which map Q, K, V to another dimension. M is the number of head which is a constant number.

The repetition process is much easy and can be given by:

$$MultiHead(Q, K, V) = Concat(head_1, \ldots, head_M)W^O \tag{6}$$

$W^O \in \mathbb{R}^{Md_v \times d_{model}}$ is the projection matrix. In Transformer, we usually set $d_k = d_v = d_{model}/M$.

Comparing Eqs. 5 and 6 with Eqs. 1 and 2, we can observe that there are many similarities. First, the matrix β_{ij} in Eq. 1 is replaced by the Eq. 5, that is,

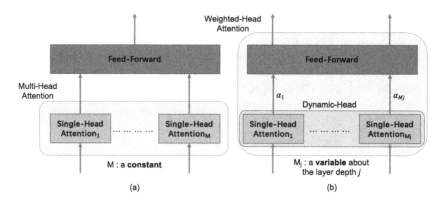

Fig. 2. (a) Multi-head attention of the original Transformer and (b) our Transformer-DW with *dynamic* and *weighted* head.

attention mechanism. In this way, each head calculated by Eq. 5 can be regarded as an $O\_Channel_j$. Finally, all the $head_i$ are concatenated together as we did for all $O\_Channel_j$ in Eq. 2 except that another matrix W^O is used to do an extra projection.

Nearly all Transformer variants follow the Eqs. 4, 5 and 6. It should be noticed that the operation *Concat* in Eq. 6 cannot distinguish the different effect of each head on different tasks as it believes that each head contributes equally to the task.

Inspired by the weight value α_j assigned on each channel in Eq. 3, we propose the weighted head mechanism on the condition that the impact of the channel in CNN is consistent with the head in Transformer.

Another module in Transformer is feed-forward layer which is essentially a multi-layer perceptron and is used to post-process the results after the attention mechanism. With the ReLU activation, It can be defined as:

$$FFN(x) = max(0, xW_1 + b_1)W_2 + b_2 \tag{7}$$

Where W_1, W_2, b_1, b_2 are the learning parameters and x can be regarded as the attention result. For the sake of brevity, we refer the reader to Vaswani et al. [6] for more details.

The other fact we can transfer from the channel of CNN to the head of Transformer is the number of channels is increased as the CNN layer deepens. Since the head in the original Transformer is still constant during training, we propose the dynamic head mechanism so that the head can be varied with the number of Transformer layers. The details about the dynamic head and weighted head will be discussed in the next section.

3   Transformer-DW

Our Transformer-DW is also a variant based on the original Transformer model. As our model name indicates, there are two significant differences that are all

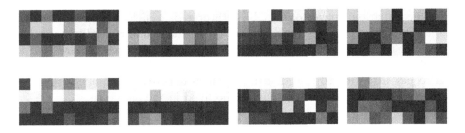

Fig. 3. Multi-head attention distribution heatmaps. For each of the eight graphs, the vertical axis is the input sentence *should be viburnum <eos>*, the horizontal axis is the output sentence of decoder *emperor went down Jiangnan just to see it <eos>*.

about the design of the *head* in Transformer. Figure 2 is the comparison between the original Transformer and Transformer-DW.

Additionally, we have a visual analysis of the multi-head attention in the original Transformer. Figure 3 is an example of the dialogue generation task. For each of the eight graphs, the vertical axis is the input sentence *should be viburnum <eos>*, the horizontal axis is the output sentence of decoder *emperor went down Jiangnan just to see it <eos>*. The eight subgraphs represent eight different heads in this sentence-pair attention matrix. It can be clearly observed that even for the same word in a sentence, there is a great difference in the distribution of attention among the eight subgraphs. It indicates that each head plays a different role in a task and we should explicitly capture the difference. Therefore, this can also prove the rationality and necessity of the mechanism we proposed to some extent.

3.1   Weighted Head

One difference is that Transformer-DW will adaptively recalibrate head-wise feature responses by explicitly modeling interdependencies between heads, that is, we will focus the relationship between heads by assigning weights on each head separately.

Instead of using the Eq. 6 to combine each head, we modify it as:

$$\overline{head_i} = head_i W^{O_i} \times \alpha_i \tag{8}$$

The $\alpha_i \in \mathbb{R}^+$ is the weight value distributed to each head and can be learned during training. $W_i^O \in \mathbb{R}^{d_v \times d_{model}}$ is learned parameter. The method we take is mostly from the Eq. 3, here each $head_i$ corresponds the $O\_Channel_j$ in Eq. 1. α_j in Eq. 3 is naturally replaced by α_i in Eq. 8.

Then the $\overline{head_i}$ will be concatenated together and sent to the feed-forward layer:

$$WeightedHeadAttention(Q, K, V) = FFN(Concat(\overline{head_1}, ..., \overline{head_M})) \tag{9}$$

Further, we require the $\sum \alpha_i = 1$ due to the consideration of model convergence.

In the equation above, α_i can be interpreted as a learned concatenation weight. Therefore, α_i scales the contribution per head and is used to sum them in a weight fashion. In addition, if $\alpha_i = 1$ for all i, we recover the equation for the multi-head attention Eq. 6.

Also pay attention to the M in Eq. 9 which denotes the number of head, it is still a constant number which will be modified in the next part.

3.2 Dynamic Head

Another knowledge we transfer from CNN to Transformer is the head of Transformer will be dynamic, i.e., the number of head is set by H which is the function about the depth of layers. The idea is simple but the key issue is how to accurately determine function H.

After a series of experiments and comparing with the channel of CNN (see experiments section for more details), we give the function H as follow:

$$H(j) = M_j = min(2^j, T) \tag{10}$$

$j \in \mathbb{Z}^+$ is the depth of layers[1] and we assume that the bottom layer depth is 1 so that the number of head is increased from 2. M_j is the number of head in jth layer. Here $T \in \mathbb{Z}^+$ is a hyperparameter that denotes the complexity of a task. The simplest way to measure the complexity of a task is the amount of dataset the model will handle. Intuitively, the more datasets we process, the greater value of T will be selected. We will give a detailed comparison about the effect of the different selection T.

Our preliminary experiments suggest that using dynamic head only in encoder is better. To maintain the property of auto-regressive in sequential encoding, masked attention in the original Transformer is kept unchanged.

4 Experiments

In this section, various experiments will be given to show that Transformer-DW is able to surpass the original Transformer. We conduct our experiments mainly on two tasks.

4.1 Machine Translation

Machine translation is not only the most classic problem in NLP but the first field where the original Transformer was used. Therefore, it is selected as the first task to verify the performance of Transformer-DW. For comparison, we implement Seq2seq [15] and the original Transformer model to compare with Transformer-DW. They help us to analyze the improvement contributed by each part of Transformer-DW.

---

[1] The number of encoder layer and decoder layer of Transformer are both 6, so in this paper, we only consider $1 \leq j \leq 6$.

Table 1. BLEU scores comparison on machine translation task

Size of dataset (K)	Seq2seq	Transformer	+Dynamic head[a]	+Weighted head (Transformer-DW)
5	0.9570	1.2707	1.3862	**2.0117**
50	2.7012	4.0850	4.1877	**4.4335**
200	8.9950	15.1493	16.4290	**16.5072**
2000	9.7631	14.0794	15.4771	**15.8222**
10000	7.2588	14.7497	15.7649	**15.9011**

[a] "+" denotes adding the module one by one.

Table 2. The number of heads per layer.

Size of dataset (K)	T	The number of heads per layer
5	2	$2 \rightarrow 2 \rightarrow 2 \rightarrow 2 \rightarrow 2 \rightarrow 2$
50	4	$2 \rightarrow 4 \rightarrow 4 \rightarrow 4 \rightarrow 4 \rightarrow 4$
200	8	$2 \rightarrow 4 \rightarrow 8 \rightarrow 8 \rightarrow 8 \rightarrow 8$
2000	16	$2 \rightarrow 4 \rightarrow 8 \rightarrow 16 \rightarrow 16 \rightarrow 16$
10000	16	$2 \rightarrow 4 \rightarrow 8 \rightarrow 16 \rightarrow 16 \rightarrow 16$

Training Setup. The dataset we use is the AI Challenger 2018[2] Chinese-to-English corpus which contains 12,893,955 pairs. We randomly selected 5,000, 50,000, 200,000, 2,000,000 and 10,000,000 training corpus from the whole, and thus we constructed five tasks of different complexity for intuitive comparison. Further, we take the principle of *training set:test set* = 10:1 to obtain test sets from the remaining. For the four different complexity task, we set the proper vocabulary size to make sure the vocabulary could cover more than 95% words in training set respectively. All words that do not appear in vocabulary are replaced by *UNK*.

For our Transformer-DW, the word embedding size and hidden model size are set as 512, 2048, respectively. Adam [16] is used for optimization. All models are trained on a single GeForce GTX 1080 Ti GPU and implemented by the open source framework THUMT [17].

Results and Analysis. Table 1 shows the BLEU scores comparison between the two baseline models and Transformer-DW. We can observe that Transformer-DW outperforms the baselines in all five datasets of different sizes. Specifically, When the dataset is 5,000, Transformer-DW shows impressive performance with increasing from 0.9570 to 2.0117. For the other four datasets, Transformer-DW surpasses the original Transformer by 8.5%, 8.9%, 12.4%, 7.8% respectively. The BLEU score is relatively low when datasets are 50,000 and 5,000 as the size is not enough for the model to match the dataset distribution.

---

[2] https://challenger.ai/.

Table 3. The effect of different T when the dataset is $2,000K$

T	Transformer	+Dynamic head	+Weighted head (Transformer-DW)
2	14.0794	14.2512	14.4902
4		14.8745	15.1458
8		15.3723	15.4898
16		**15.4771**	**15.8222**
32		14.3399	15.3835
64		14.2821	14.5900

In order to prove the dynamic head is indeed helpful, we conduct extra experiments that are shown in the fourth column of Table 1. Only adding the dynamic head to the baseline also brings improvement on model performance with 9.1%, 2.5%, 8.4%, 9.9%, 6.8% respectively.

Table 2 gives the details about the different selection T, that is, the number of heads per layer corresponding to the different dataset size when Transformer-DW achieves the scores in Table 1. Once the hyperparameter T is determined, the number of heads per layer can be calculated from Eq. 10. We should notice the maximum number of heads on each dataset is totally different. The smallest dataset 5,000 is 2 while the largest dataset 10,000,000 has a maximum head of 16. It corresponds that more complex task would need more channels or heads.

Further, We study deeper on the effect of different T when the dataset is $2,000K$ and the BLEU scores are shown in Table 3. When the T is selected as 16, our Transformer-DW could achieve the best result. We observe that different T has an impact on the final result. Compared with the best result, the worst result is dropped by 8.4%. It indicates that we should carefully select the value of T and take advantage of Eq. 10 when facing different tasks. Additionally, the results show that only increasing the value of T cannot obtain the corresponding gains as the relationship between the T and $BLEU$ is not a linear function.

4.2 Dialogue Generation

The other task selected is the dialogue generation. Recently, using generative models to solve the dialogue problems has achieved impressive performance. But unlike the machine translation which exists a one-to-one correspondence between parallel language pairs, in dialogue generation, there is often some interdependency between adjacent languages [18]. Therefore, dialogue generation is considered as a more challenging task where the original Transformer has not been used widely. For thorough comparison, besides the basic Transformer model, we implement four extra strong baselines (1) Seq2seq [19]; (2) HRED [20]; (3) VHRED [21]; (4) HRAN [22]. They help us to verify the two mechanisms proposed in Sect. 3 can improve performance.

Table 4. BLEU scores comparison on dialogue generation task

Method	BLEU scores
Seq2seq	0.6935
HRED	0.2215
VHRED	0.1616
HRAN	0.4529
Transformer	0.6537
Transformer-DW	**0.9410**[b]

[b]The score is achieved when T is 32

Table 5. The effect of different T on dialogue generation task

T	BLEU scores
2	0.8542
4	0.9239
8	0.9375
16	0.9131
32	**0.9410**
64	0.9102

Training Setup. Douban dataset [22] is used for evaluation. During the preprocessing period, we ensure the length of each sentence is no more than 50 words. After that, there are 274,786 training data, 1,682 valid data, 13,796 test data. The vocabulary size is set 4,000, covering 98.70% words. The evaluation metric is still a problem in dialogue generation but not the issue of interest in this paper, following Tian et al. [23], we still choose BLEU score as the metric. The setting of parameters on Transformer-DW is same as in machine translation task, and the four baseline models are subject to the settings in the original paper.

Results and Analysis. Table 4 illustrates that Transformer-DW outperforms both the original Transformer and other baseline models on dialogue generation task. It is interesting that the original Transformer performs worse even than Seq2seq, which is totally opposite on machine translation. With the dynamic and weighted head, Transformer-DW is able to achieve the best result with improving by 43.95%. It reveals that the Transformer variant such as Transformer-DW is also effective on dialogue generation task.

Another thing that should be noticed is the selected value of T. Although the Douban dataset size is approximately equal to $200K$, the dialogue generation task is usually considered as a more complex and challenging task than machine translation. Therefore, the final value of T here is larger than the value 8 on

Table 6. Model ablation results

Model	BLEU scores
Transformer-DW	**0.9410**
No Dynamic Head	0.8798
No Weighted Head	0.7247

machine translation task, that is, 32. It again proves that the hyperparameter T can measure the complexity of our task to some extent.

Table 5 is the result about the impact of different T on dialogue generation task. It is generally consistent with the result of machine translation task. Note that in dialogue generation, a larger T would usually be selected when the size of dataset is generally equal to the size in machine translation as the fact that dialogue generation is more complex and challenging than machine translation.

To have an insight of the effectiveness of each component in Transformer-DW, Ablation study is conducted on Douban dataset by removing weighted head or dynamic head. *No Dynamic Head* denotes removing dynamic head and *No Weighted Head* denotes removing weighted head from Transformer-DW. Table 6 shows the result. Comparing with the BLEU score 0.9410 of Transformer-DW, removing dynamic head and weighted head will drop by 6.5%, 22.9%, respectively. It indicates that each head mechanism is helpful.

5   Conclusions

In this paper, we propose a novel structure named Transformer-DW with dynamic and weighted head. Dynamic head means the number of heads will vary with the depth of layer. Weighted head means each head will play a different role on different tasks as each head has its own weight value. Additionally, we apply the model to two different tasks, machine translation and dialogue generation. Both tasks show that Transformer-DW outperforms other baselines. Model ablation results show that both ways are important to the proposed model.

Acknowledgment. This research work has been funded by the National Natural Science Foundation of China (Grant No. 61772337, U1736207), and the National Key Research and Development Program of China No. 2016QY03D0604 and 2018YFC0830703.

References

1. He, K., Zhang, X., Ren, S., Sun, J.: Deep residual learning for image recognition. In: CVPR, pp. 770–778 (2016)
2. Ren, S., He, K., Girshick, R., Sun, J.: Faster R-CNN: towards real-time object detection with region proposal networks. In: NIPS, pp. 91–99 (2015)

3. Long, J., Shelhamer, E., Darrell, T.: Fully convolutional networks for semantic segmentation. In: CVPR, pp. 3431–3440 (2015)
4. Hu, J., Shen, L., Sun, G.: Squeeze-and-excitation networks. In: CVPR, pp. 7132–7141 (2018)
5. Zeiler, M.D., Fergus, R.: Visualizing and understanding convolutional networks. In: Fleet, D., Pajdla, T., Schiele, B., Tuytelaars, T. (eds.) ECCV 2014. LNCS, vol. 8689, pp. 818–833. Springer, Cham (2014). https://doi.org/10.1007/978-3-319-10590-1_53
6. Vaswani, A., et al.: Attention is all you need. In: NIPS, pp. 6000–6010. Curran Associates Inc. (2017)
7. Dehghani, M., Gouws, S., Vinyals, O., Uszkoreit, J., Kaiser, Ł.: Universal transformers (2018). arXiv preprint arXiv:1807.03819
8. Shaw, P., Uszkoreit, J., Vaswani, A.: Self-attention with relative position representations. In: NAACL, vol. 2, pp. 464–468 (2018)
9. Bapna, A., Chen, M., Firat, O., Cao, Y., Wu, Y.: Training deeper neural machine translation models with transparent attention. In: EMNLP, pp. 3028–3033 (2018)
10. Dai, Z., et al.: Transformer-XL: attentive language models beyond a fixed-length context (2019). arXiv preprint arXiv:1901.02860
11. LeCun, Y., Bottou, L., Bengio, Y., Haffner, P., et al.: Gradient-based learning applied to document recognition. Proc. IEEE **86**(11), 2278–2324 (1998)
12. Krizhevsky, A., Sutskever, I., Hinton, G.E.: ImageNet classification with deep convolutional neural networks. In: NIPS, pp. 1097–1105 (2012)
13. Ahmed, K., Keskar, N.S., Socher, R.: Weighted transformer network for machine translation (2017). arXiv preprint arXiv:1711.02132
14. Zhang, B., Xiong, D., Su, J.: Accelerating neural transformer via an average attention network (2018). arXiv preprint arXiv:1805.00631
15. Britz, D., Goldie, A., Luong, M.-T., Le, Q.: Massive exploration of neural machine translation architectures. In: EMNLP, pp. 1442–1451 (2017)
16. Kingma, D.P., Ba, J.: Adam: a method for stochastic optimization (2014). arXiv preprint arXiv:1412.6980
17. Zhang, J., et al.: THUMT: an open source toolkit for neural machine translation (2017). arXiv preprint arXiv:1706.06415
18. Sordoni, A., et al.: A neural network approach to context-sensitive generation of conversational responses. In: NAACL, pp. 196–205 (2015)
19. Shang, L., Lu, Z., Li, H.: Neural responding machine for short-text conversation. In: ACL (Volume 1: Long Papers), pp. 1577–1586 (2015)
20. Serban, I.V., Sordoni, A., Bengio, Y., Courville, A.C., Pineau, J.: Building end-to-end dialogue systems using generative hierarchical neural network models. In: AAAI, vol. 16, pp. 3776–3784 (2016)
21. Serban, I.V., et al.: A hierarchical latent variable encoder-decoder model for generating dialogues. In: AAAI, pp. 3295–3301 (2017)
22. Xing, C., Wu, Y., Wu, W., Huang, Y., Zhou, M.: Hierarchical recurrent attention network for response generation. In: AAAI (2018)
23. Tian, Z., Yan, R., Mou, L., Song, Y., Feng, Y., Zhao, D.: How to make context more useful? An empirical study on context-aware neural conversational models. In: ACL (Volume 2: Short Papers), pp. 231–236 (2017)

Motion-Based Occlusion-Aware Pixel Graph Network for Video Object Segmentation

Saptakatha Adak$^{(\boxtimes)}$ and Sukhendu Das

Visualization and Perception Lab, IIT Madras, Chennai 600036, India
sapta@cse.iitm.ac.in, sdas@iitm.ac.in
http://www.cse.iitm.ac.in/~vplab

Abstract. This paper proposes a dual-channel based Graph Convolutional Network (GCN) for the Video Object Segmentation (VOS) task. The main contribution lies in formulating two pixel graphs based on the raw RGB and optical flow features. Both spatial and temporal features are learned independently, making the network robust to various challenging scenarios in real-world videos. Additionally, a motion orientation-based aggregator scheme efficiently captures long-range dependencies among objects. This not only deals with the complex issue of modelling velocity differences among multiple objects moving in various directions, but also adapts to change of appearance of objects due to pose and scale deformations. Also, an occlusion-aware attention mechanism has been employed to facilitate accurate segmentation under scenarios where multiple objects have temporal discontinuity in their appearance due to occlusion. Performance analysis on DAVIS-2016 and DAVIS-2017 datasets show the effectiveness of our proposed method in foreground segmentation of objects in videos over the existing state-of-the-art techniques. Control experiments using CamVid dataset show the generalising capability of the model for scene segmentation.

Keywords: Video Object Segmentation (VOS) · Graph Convolutional Networks (GCN) · Aggregation mechanisms · Adversarial training

1 Introduction

Video Object Segmentation (VOS) has been a challenging and important problem in the field of Computer Vision and Machine Learning in recent past due to its profound applications in domains like medical imaging, robotics, video editing, video prediction, action recognition etc. In this paper, we deal with the problem of segmenting multiple objects of interest over a sequence of RGB video frames in a semi-supervised setting by providing the ground truth annotation for the initial frame. Although there has been an enormous progress in semantic segmentation using Convolutional Neural Networks (CNNs) [5,20,24], VOS has always remained challenging because of objects moving in and out of frame,

© Springer Nature Switzerland AG 2019
T. Gedeon et al. (Eds.): ICONIP 2019, LNCS 11954, pp. 516–527, 2019.
https://doi.org/10.1007/978-3-030-36711-4_43

lack of any concrete association among objects due to occlusions, shape and appearance deformation, motion blur and background clutter.

A number of methods have been proposed in the recent past based on object matching, mask propagation and object detection to deal with these challenges. In matching-based approaches, the appearance information of the objects of interest is extracted from the given first frame segmentation mask as ground-truth, to propagate the segmentation in the subsequent frames. In [4,22] CNNs are used as the parent network for training on still images followed by fine-tuning of the same with initial annotated mask of video leading to one-shot learning. Tracking of various object parts was proposed in [7] to tackle the challenges like occlusions and deformations.

Temporal coherency across frames was exploited in [2] by embedding the mask propagation in the space-time based MRF model inference. [29] utilized a Siamese framework to incorporate instance detection within mask propagation to segment the target without relying on online fine-tuning for a given video. In addition, Conditional Batch Normalization (CBN) proposed by [30] does not require online learning to extract spatio-temporal features.

VOS based on object proposals use detection algorithms prior to the segmentation module. In [21], supervised targets over video frames detected by Mask R-CNN [13] were cropped to provide as input to the DeeplabV3+ [6] module. Majority of the detection-based methods choose a single proposal in a greedy manner. Although they produce good quality segmentation for long video clips, they fail in cases where multiple objects move with dissimilar speeds in different directions. The main reason behind this is the inability of the networks to explicitly model the spatio-temporal inter-pixel relationships independently.

This paper proposes a dual-channel pixel Graph Convolutional Network (Pixel-GCN) to learn the inter-pixel spatio-temporal relationships in a video, based on RGB image and optical flow features. Incorporation of a direction oriented motion-based aggregator scheme assists the network to model not only the relative velocities between objects moving in different directions with dissimilar speeds, but also the changes in appearance due to pose and scale transformations. A novel occlusion-aware aggregation scheme has been implemented to deal with objects undergoing partial or full occlusions, and situations involving re-appearance of objects in the video. The consolidated spatio-temporal features obtained from combination of the graph reasoned image and flow features lead to significant improvement of performance on VOS datasets viz. DAVIS-2016 and DAVIS-2017, in comparison with existing state-of-the-art methods. We also performed controlled experiments on semantic segmentation of traffic scenes in videos using CamVid Dataset [3] to showcase the ability of our proposed model in complex scenarios.

2   Overview and Formulation of Pixel-GCN

The proposed video object segmentation framework is exhibited in Fig. 1. Given a sequence of M consecutive RGB frames as input, the generator ($\mathbb{G}$) produces

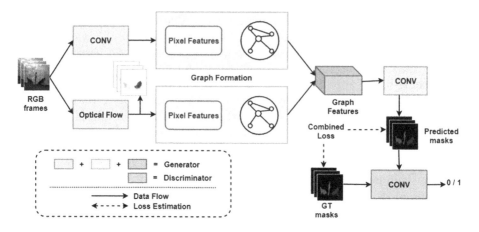

Fig. 1. Proposed Pixel-GCN framework for Video Object Segmentation.

segmentation masks of objects of interest. The dimension of the generated segmentation masks being $W \times H \times 1$, while that of the input RGB frames are $W \times H \times 3$. The generator consists of 2 channels to produce RGB and optical flow based features respectively. The RGB channel is composed of an instance based segmentation module, Mask R-CNN [13] with ResNet-101 [14] backbone. RGB image features from $C4$ module (last convolutional layer of the 4th stage) of ResNet-101 [14] are extracted to produce an intermediate feature map of dimension $W \times H \times D$, where D is the number of features. Likewise, optical flow based feature maps of the same dimensions are generated from the other channel formed using FlowNet 2.0 [15]. To facilitate the graph formation, feature maps of M consecutive frames are combined together to elevate the features from $W \times H \times D$ to $M \times W \times H \times D$ dimension.

The RGB image and optical flow based 3D feature maps are used to construct the image feature based pixel graph ($\mathcal{G}_{rgb}$) and optical flow feature based pixel graph ($\mathcal{G}_{opt}$) respectively. The input as well as the output of each of the individual graphs are same and they are concatenated to form the combined graph based feature map. These synthesized spatio-temporal features are then passed through the rest of the modules of Mask R-CNN [13] to produce the segmentation masks of the objects. Since the end-to-end framework is trained adversarially, the discriminator ($\mathbb{D}$) differentiates the generated masks from the ground truth.

Graph Formulation. Given a video clip, the pixel graphs $\mathcal{G}_{rgb}$ & $\mathcal{G}_{opt}$ are formed using the internal $3D$ feature maps extracted from the ResNet-101 [14] backbone model of the segmentation module and optical flow vector generation network respectively. Throughout the paper, the two graphs ($\mathcal{G}_{rgb}$ & $\mathcal{G}_{opt}$) have been generalized as $\mathcal{G}_{pix}$ for ease of discussion, unless mentioned otherwise.

Using $M \times W \times H \times D$ dimensional intermediate feature map, an undirected graph $\mathcal{G}_{pix}(V, E)$ is formed, where V/E is the set of nodes/edges. As the motivation behind the graph based framework is to model the content as well as motion pattern by learning the inter-pixel relationships in the scene across space-time, $1 \times D$ feature vectors are extracted for the node corresponding to a particular spatio-temporal pixel location of the 3D feature map.

We assume slow and smooth motion patterns across time i.e., the videos do not involve sudden viewpoint changes or significant amount of jitter. However, implementation of the proposed aggregations along with the pixel graph ($\mathcal{G}_{pix}$) formation not only enables the model to recover itself from such challenges, but also aid to resolve situations like occlusion, shape deformation and re-appearance of objects in the video.

3   Proposed Aggregation Mechanisms

The commonly used aggregation function of a GCN [17] is:

$$v_i' = \sigma\Big(\phi(v_i) + \sum_{j \in \mathcal{N}_{v_i}} S_{ij} W \phi(v_j)\Big) \tag{1}$$

where, $\phi(v_i)$ denotes the input feature vector corresponding to node v_i, $\mathcal{N}_{v_i}$ is the set of its neighbouring nodes and θ, the learned parameters of the graph, while v_i' is the output vector. σ is a non-linear activation function (such as ReLU), W denotes the learnable transformation weights and S_{ij} represents the adjacency function. The neighbouring nodes yield varying impact in modelling a particular node feature, depending on the relationships shared by different objects or even various parts of a single deformable object. Incorporation of features from the unrelated nodes during estimation often leads to sub-optimal outcomes from the model. To overcome this limitation, the Pixel-GCN is extended by two novel aggregator schemes: **(i) motion-based aggregation**, and **(ii) occlusion-aware aggregation**. The proposed mechanisms are discussed below.

3.1   Motion Based Aggregation ($\mathcal{A}_{motion}$)

Learning motion patterns from short clips is a challenging task when multiple objects are moving with different velocities in various directions. We propose a motion based direction oriented aggregation to aid the segmentation network for modelling the intricate motion patterns. To estimate this, the Pixel-GCN is modified to use directional weights $\gamma_i \in [0, 1]$ for assigning relative significance on each of the neighbouring nodes. Based on the respective location from the reference node in the feature space, the neighbouring nodes are divided into 4 spatial quadrants (NW, NE, SE & SW). Direction oriented motion based categorization is incorporated in graph modelling by a set of 4 adaptive weights $\Gamma^i = \{\gamma_1^i, \gamma_2^i, \gamma_3^i, \gamma_4^i\}$ for each node v_i. The S_{ij} values in the standard GCN algorithm (see Eq. 1) is replaced with these learned weights, to obtain a modified aggregation function:

$$v_i' = \sigma\Big(\phi(v_i) + \sum_{k=1}^{4} \gamma_k^i \sum_{j \in \mathcal{N}_{v_i}^k} e^{\phi(v_i) \cdot \phi(v_j)^T} W_1 \phi(v_j)\Big) \tag{2}$$

where, $N_{v_i}^k$ denotes the set of neighbouring nodes corresponding to the reference node v_i in one of the four direction based quadrants and $e^{\phi(v_i)\cdot\phi(v_j)^T}$ computes the similarity between pair of nodes. W_1 is the matrix of learnable weights.

To model the adaptive weights, a convolutional network Ω has been incorporated, which is trained on the node features along with corresponding neighbouring nodes in the four spatial sections, described as

$$\Gamma^i = \{\gamma_k^i | k = [1,4]\} = \Omega(v_i, N_{v_i}^k) \tag{3}$$

where, the symbols bear usual meaning. Though the convolutional network for learning the adaptive weights can be constructed in various ways [1,11,27], we designed a two-layer network with average pooling on nodes within each of the spatial quadrants followed by a max-pooling and ReLU activation with fully connected layer for our proposed framework, defined as:

$$\Gamma^i = \sigma\Big(\phi(v_i) + || \ \lambda_k\big(\underset{j\in N_{v_i}^k}{avg} (FC_\theta(\phi(v_j))) \big) \ ||_k\Big), \quad k = [1,4] \tag{4}$$

where, λ_k is the parameter learned for each direction to find the corresponding soft attention weights. This module computes the similarity of the reference node with its neighbours in all the four directions and sets relative importance on all of them depending on their adaptive weights (Γ^i). Thus, the direction oriented motion based strategy not only aids to capture the relative motion pattern but also the long-range dependencies involved among objects in videos.

The local motion flow of the objects along with their directions and relative velocities is learned more precisely in the space-time domain by extending the entire network to include the temporal dimension. In addition, the inter-pixel similarity based relationship also models the long-range interaction between nearby objects as well as change of appearance of the objects due to shape and scale deformation across space-time. Thus, to implement this, adaptive weights for all the nodes, based on the four spatial quadrants (as proposed earlier), are introduced. Equation 4 of the sub-network in spatio-temporal domain is thus:

$$\Gamma^i = \sigma\Big(\phi(v_i) + || \ \lambda_k\big(\underset{j\in N_{v_i}^{k,t}}{avg} (FC_\theta(\phi(v_j))) \big) \ ||_{k,t}\Big), \quad k = [1,4] \tag{5}$$

where, $N_{v_i}^{k,t}$ is the set of neighbouring nodes corresponding to v_i at time-step t in the spatial section k and $|| \cdot ||_t$ denotes the concatenation across time-steps. Thus, the modified set of weights consisting of several sets of adaptive values per time-step is expressed as:

$$\Gamma^i = \{\{\gamma_{k,t}^i\} \ \forall t \in [T - M + 1, T]\} \tag{6}$$

where, T represents the current time-step.

3.2   Occlusion Aware Aggregation ($\mathcal{A}_{occ}$)

To deal occlusion we propose an occlusion-aware aggregator scheme which aids to segment the objects partially or almost fully obstructed by another object. For

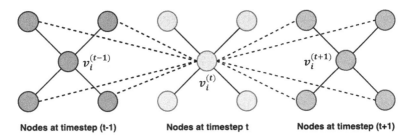

Fig. 2. Pictorial illustration of occlusion-aware aggregation. Dotted lines represent the forward similarity estimation between the neighbouring nodes of $v_i^{(t-1)}$ and node $v_i^{(t)}$, while backward similarity estimation is done between neighbouring nodes of $v_i^{(t+1)}$ and node $v_i^{(t)}$.

simplicity, 3 consecutive frames $\mathcal{I}_{t-1}$, $\mathcal{I}_t$ and $\mathcal{I}_{t+1}$ have been used for estimation. However, it can be extended for videos having more frames.

It is assumed that the unoccluded pixels in the initial frame should be similar to its corresponding pixels in the destination frame. But, this implication does not holds for the occluded pixels which results in three possible events: (i) occluded in the past ($\mathcal{I}_{t-1}$) and visible in the current frame ($\mathcal{I}_t$), (ii) occluded in future ($\mathcal{I}_{t+1}$) and visible in the current frame ($\mathcal{I}_t$), and (iii) occluded across all frames. Thus, to deal with these kind of events a bi-directional computation is done involving forward estimation of similarity between neighbouring nodes of a particular node ($v_i^{(t-1)}$) in the previous frame ($\mathcal{I}_{t-1}$) and the corresponding node ($v_i^{(t)}$) in the current frame ($\mathcal{I}_t$). Whereas, reverse (backward) estimation is done by similarity computation between the node $v_i^{(t)}$ and the neighbouring nodes corresponding to the node $v_i^{(t+1)}$ in the future frame ($\mathcal{I}_{t+1}$) (see Fig. 2). Thus, the occlusion aware aggregator function is defined as:

$$v_i'^{(t)} = \sigma\left(\phi(v_i^{(t)}) + \mathcal{U}_{occ}^t\right) \tag{7}$$

$$\mathcal{U}_{occ}^t = \left(\max\left(0, \delta - |\mathcal{F}(v_i^{(t)}, v_a^{(t-1)}) - \mathcal{F}(v_i^{(t)}, v_b^{(t+1)})|^2\right)\right)W_2\phi(v_i) \tag{8}$$

where, $\mathcal{F}(v_i^{(t)}, v_a^{(t-1)}) = \sum_{a \in \mathcal{N}_{v_i}^{(t-1)}} e^{(v_i^{(t)})\cdot(v_a^{(t-1)})^T}$ refers to the similarity estimation between node v_i at current time-step t and neighbouring nodes v_a of the node v_i at previous time-step ($t-1$). δ is a positive constant and W_2 is the shared transformation weight matrix. Thus, Eqs. 7 and 8 model the consistency between the forward and backward estimation to learn the motion pattern of the objects while penalizing the large disparity in case of occlusion with δ.

The motivation behind the two-way estimation keeping the centre frame as reference is due to the fact that, the motion is often non-linear across space-time and contain sudden variations. Our goal is to estimate the forward similarity from $\mathcal{I}_t$ to $\mathcal{I}_{t+1}$ using the occlusion aware aggregation mechanism by updating the feature vectors of the nodes. It also combines re-identification functionalities with temporal propagation which assists the network to identify missing targets re-appearing in the video after prolonged occlusion despite change in appearances.

4   Training of Pixel-GCN

For implementing the proposed graph based strategy a series of L graph aggregation layers are stacked together. Thus, the overall aggregator function used for reasoning on the graphs, formed by combining Eqs. 2 and 7 is as follows:

$$v_i^{l+1} = \sigma\Big(\phi(v_i^l) + \mathcal{U}_{motion}^l + \| \mathcal{U}_{occ}^{l(t)} \|_t\Big), \quad t = [T - M + 1, T] \qquad (9)$$

where, $\mathcal{U}_{motion}^l = \sum_{k=1}^{4} \gamma_k^i \sum_{j \in \mathcal{N}_{v_i}^{k,l}} e^{\phi(v_i^l) \cdot \phi(v_j^l)^T} W_1 \phi(v_j^l)$ is the motion-based aggregator update, whereas $\| \mathcal{U}_{occ}^l \|_t$ represents the update term of occlusion-aware aggregation function calculated over the frames, $t = [T - M + 1, T]$ (refer Eq. 8). $l = \{0, 1, \cdots, L\}$ are layers of the graph with $l = 0$ and $l = L$ being the input and output layers respectively. v_i^{l+1} denotes the node features at the $(l + 1)^{th}$ graph layer and $v_i^0 = \phi(v_i)$. Thus, the features related to a particular node is updated based on the relations in the graph with neighbouring nodes, and this process of reasoning is propagated in a message passing manner throughout the entire graph. The similarity based graph relations involve learnable parameters which are updated through back-propagation. Finally, the consolidated graph feature is obtained by combining the output features of both the graphs ($\mathcal{G}_{rgb}$ & $\mathcal{G}_{opt}$) from the two channels, as:

$$V_{combined}^L = V_{rgb}^L \oplus V_{opt}^L \qquad (10)$$

where, V_{rgb}^L and V_{opt}^L refers to the features related to the nodes in the final layer L of the respective graphs and $\oplus$ is the concatenation operator.

The combined feature map $V_{combined}^L$ is then passed a series of convolutional and fully-connected modules (refer Fig. 1) to generate the segmentation maps. The entire framework is trained in an adversarial setting [12] by minimizing the overall objective function through back-propagation. The overall loss function is formed using a combination of $\mathcal{L}_1$ loss on the segmentation output, the Gradient Divergence Loss ($\mathcal{L}_{gdl}$) [23] and the standard pixel-wise cross-entropy loss ($\mathcal{L}_{ce}$) components, apart from the general adversarial objective ($\mathcal{L}_{adv}$). The final combined objective is thus:

$$\mathcal{L}_{combined} = \mathcal{L}_{adv} + \mathcal{L}_1(\hat{Y}, Y) + \mathcal{L}_{gdl}(\hat{Y}, Y) + \mathcal{L}_{ce}(\hat{Y}, Y) \qquad (11)$$

where, $\hat{Y}, Y$ are the generated and ground-truth segmentation respectively. $\mathcal{L}_{gdl}$ [23] is used to penalize the model for producing blurry edges.

Assume that there are N nodes in G_{pix}; each having average degree d. Thus, for a GCN with L layers, features from $O(d^L)$ nodes are aggregated to update a single node, whereas computation of each embedding associated with a node takes $O(D^2)$ time due to multiplication with the weight matrix, W; D is number of features. Therefore, average time complexity for each epoch is $O(Nd^L D^2)$.

5   Experiments and Results

Experiments are performed on two real-word Video Object Segmentation (VOS) datasets: (a) DAVIS-2016 [25] and (b) DAVIS-2017 [26], to compare the performance of proposed Pixel-GCN with the recent and state-of-the-art methods. Controlled experiments are performed on CamVid [3] dataset to exhibit the ability of the proposed model in Video Semantic Segmentation (VSS).

Implementation Details. For the task of VOS, the Mask R-CNN [13] network is adopted to the DAVIS [25,26] dataset by using the pre-trained ImageNet [10] weights and then training with COCO [19] dataset, followed by fine-tuning with the training set of DAVIS dataset. Next, the intermediate features of 4 consecutive RGB images, from ResNet-101 backbone of Mask R-CNN model, are used as input to the proposed Pixel-GCN. Updated features from the graph based model, are then passed through the rest of the layers of Mask R-CNN to produce the segmented output. Before validation, Mask R-CNN model is fine-tuned on each video sequence with synthetic in-domain images, generated from first frame of the respective videos using Lucid Dreaming [16]. Finally, consecutive RGB frames are fed to the proposed network to produce segmentation masks of objects present in these frames. Experiments on DAVIS-2016 and DAVIS-2017 are done using the splits of [25] and [26] respectively, while evaluated with respect to Region similarity ($\mathcal{J}$) and Contour accuracy ($\mathcal{F}$). Global metric ($\mathcal{G}$) is the mean of $\mathcal{J}$ and $\mathcal{F}$.

DeeplabV3+ [6] network with Xception65 [8] back-bone is used for semantic segmentation of videos. As the number of segmented ground-truth images are quite less in CamVid [3] dataset, Cityscape [9] pre-trained weights has been deployed followed by fine-tuning on CamVid. The internal features of 4 RGB input images with equal time intervals, obtained from encoder output of DeeplabV3+, having atrous rates of 6, 12 and 18 with output stride of 16 (just before the final 1×1 convolution), is used as input to the graph network while the updated output features are passed through the decoder part of DeeplabV3+ to generate the semantic segmentation masks (for architecture details of Deeplab V3+ refer [6]). During testing, consecutive RGB images are sent to the framework for semantic segmentation of the same. Performance of video semantic segmentation has been evaluated on CamVid [3] road scene dataset using mIoU (mean Intersection-over-Union) metric only. All the experiments have been performed on 2 NVIDIA 1080 GPUs.

Performance Analysis on VOS. Quantitative comparison on DAVIS-2017 validation set given in Table 1 shows that our proposed Pixel-GCN outperforms each of the existing and the state-of-the-art methods in terms of $\mathcal{G}_{mean}$, $\mathcal{J}_{mean}$ and $\mathcal{F}_{mean}$, without using any post-processing module like CRF [18]. Experiments on DAVIS-2016 also proves the superior performance of our model in terms of $\mathcal{J}_{mean}$, but it only falls short in terms of $\mathcal{F}_{mean}$ to PreMVOS [21] where ours is a close second. Previous works exhibit suboptimal performance in situations like rapid motion, occlusion and shape deformation. In our proposed graph network, the directional motion-based aggregation scheme ($\mathcal{A}_{motion}$) aids the

Table 1. Quantitative comparison of the proposed Pixel-GCN with existing state-of-the-art methods on DAVIS-2016 and DAVIS-2017 datasets for VOS. "↑" - higher is better. "*" - w/o proposed aggregation functions ($\mathcal{A}_{motion}$ & $\mathcal{A}_{occ}$) in rows 9 & 10 (Best results in **bold**).

Methods	DAVIS-2017			DAVIS-2016		
	$\mathcal{G}_{mean}$↑	$\mathcal{J}_{mean}$↑	$\mathcal{F}_{mean}$↑	$\mathcal{G}_{mean}$↑	$\mathcal{J}_{mean}$↑	$\mathcal{F}_{mean}$↑
OSMN [30]	54.8	52.5	57.1	73.5	74.0	72.9
FAVOS [7]	58.2	54.6	61.8	81.0	82.4	79.5
OSVOS [4]	60.3	56.6	63.9	80.2	79.8	80.6
OnAVOS [28]	65.4	61.6	69.1	86.6	86.1	84.9
RGMP [29]	66.7	64.8	68.6	81.8	81.5	82.0
OSVOS-S [22]	68.0	64.7	71.3	86.6	85.6	87.5
CINM [2]	70.6	67.2	74.0	84.2	83.4	85.0
PReMVOS [21]	77.8	73.9	81.7	86.8	84.9	**88.6**
vanilla GCN* ($\mathcal{G}_{pix}$, ours)	77.0	73.6	80.5	–	–	–
Pixel-GCN* ($\mathcal{G}_{pix} + \mathcal{G}_{opt}$, ours)	77.6	74.1	81.2	–	–	–
Pixel-GCN-FS (ours)	78.4	74.9	81.8	–	–	–
Pixel-GCN-FF (ours)	**78.9**	**75.6**	**82.2**	**87.3**	**86.5**	88.1

model to generate impressive results over PreMVOS [21] (see results on DAVIS-2017 in Fig. 3). Pixel-GCN not only succeeds in segmenting multiple objects with dissimilar motion patterns, but also remains robust to the appearance change of the objects, while PreMVOS [21] fails in segmenting objects in a few cases. Incorporation of the novel occlusion-aware aggregation function ($\mathcal{A}_{occ}$) has also improved the performance of the proposed model in situations like partial occlusion of objects of interest and also identification of objects or parts re-appearing in the video (refer DAVIS-2016 in Fig. 3).

Apart from these, we have performed ablation study to investigate the individual contribution of each module in our proposed Pixel-GCN (see last 4 rows in Table 1). Using only RGB feature based graph ($\mathcal{G}_{rgb}$) in the vanilla GCN [17] we attain a $\mathcal{J}_{mean}$ of 73.6. Introduction of optical flow feature based graph ($\mathcal{G}_{opt}$) provides the model with more spatio-temporal information to capture the relative motion patterns among objects. We have also experimented with two different models where the first one learns to produce the segmented masks directly, while the other rely on the updated features to be passed through the Mask R-CNN [13] to generate the predicted masks. The former model consists of a series of convolutional layers and a fully-connected layer attached to the graph network along with class-wise cross-entropy loss with adversarial objective for inference purposes. From Table 1 (last 2 rows), it is evident that better results are obtained by processing the updated features than producing the segmentation masks directly. These two models also include the novel aggregation functions ($\mathcal{A}_{motion}$ & $\mathcal{A}_{occ}$) which improve the results of the frameworks by making it robust to complex motions, shape deformation and occlusion in comparison with the vanilla GCN and Pixel-GCN bare-model (without $\mathcal{A}_{motion}$ & $\mathcal{A}_{occ}$) mentioned earlier (see rows 9 & 10 of Table 1).

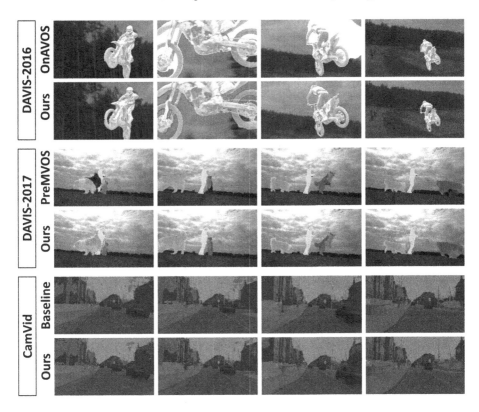

Fig. 3. Qualitative comparison of performance of our Pixel-GCN framework with the existing state-of-the-art methods on DAVIS-2016, DAVIS-2017 and CamVid datasets. The frames are taken at equal intervals of time (Best viewed in colour).

Performance Analysis on VSS. For complete evaluation, our proposed model has been studied on Camvid [3] dataset for semantic segmentation of videos (refer CamVid in Fig. 3). Quantitative comparison of various models along with the full frame and moving objects segmentation baseline in the videos are shown in Table 2. DeeplabV3+ [6] trained in Cityscapes [9] and fine-tuned in CamVid [3] dataset is used as the baseline model keeping the common categories of both the datasets. For evaluation of the proposed models, intermediate features of Xception65 [8] model trained under the same settings are used for graph inference, followed by processing of the output features using decoder network of DeeplabV3+ [6]. From rows 2–6 of Table 2, it is evident that introduction of the aggregation functions ($\mathcal{A}_{motion}$ & $\mathcal{A}_{occ}$) contribute much in the improvement of the performance of the model in comparison with the vanilla or Pixel-GCN bare-model ($\mathcal{G}_{pix} + \mathcal{G}_{opt}$). Also, segmentation using updated features through DeeplabV3+ model produces better results than direct segmentation (see last 2 rows in Table 2).

Table 2. Quantitative comparison of various models on CamVid dataset having features as input for semantic segmentation in videos. "FS": Feature → Segmentation, whereas "FF": Feature → Feature. "∗" - without proposed aggregation functions ($\mathcal{A}_{motion}$ & $\mathcal{A}_{occ}$) in rows 2 & 3 (Best results in **bold**).

Models	IoU (SEG)	IoU-MO (SEG)
Baseline (DeeplabV3+ [6])	62.7	60.3
Vanilla GCN* ($\mathcal{G}_{opt}$)	64.3	61.5
Pixel GCN* ($\mathcal{G}_{pix} + \mathcal{G}_{opt}$)	65.2	63.6
Pixel GCN + $\mathcal{A}_{motion}$	67.5	64.8
Pixel GCN-FS	67.9	65.1
Pixel GCN-FF	**70.1**	**67.8**

6 Conclusion

In this paper, we have introduced a novel approach of segmenting objects in videos using a dual-channel Graph Convolutional Network. The RGB feature based graph provides the contextual information, while the motion patterns are captured through the optical flow based feature graph, by learning the inter-pixel relationship in the space-time domain. In addition, a motion-based aggregator scheme has been proposed to model the non-periodic object movements along with its change in appearance in terms of pose and scale. Use of novel occlusion-aware aggregator aids the network to identify targets under occlusion or re-appearing in the frame. Our model not only shows a superior performance over existing and state-of-the-art methods on real-world VOS datasets viz. DAVIS-2016 and DAVIS-2017, but also produces impressive results on CamVid semantic segmentation dataset.

References

1. Atwood, J., Towsley, D.: Diffusion-convolutional neural networks. In: NIPS (2016)
2. Bao, L., Wu, B., Liu, W.: CNN in MRF: video object segmentation via inference in a CNN-based higher-order spatio-temporal MRF. In: CVPR (2018)
3. Brostow, G.J., Fauqueur, J., Cipolla, R.: Semantic object classes in video: a high-definition ground truth database. Pattern Recogn. Lett. **30**(2), 88–97 (2009)
4. Caelles, S., Maninis, K.K., Pont-Tuset, J., Leal-Taixé, L., Cremers, D., Van Gool, L.: One-shot video object segmentation. In: CVPR (2017)
5. Chen, L.C., Papandreou, G., Kokkinos, I., Murphy, K., Yuille, A.L.: DeepLab: semantic image segmentation with deep convolutional nets, atrous convolution, and fully connected CRFs. TPAMI **40**(4), 834–848 (2017)
6. Chen, L.-C., Zhu, Y., Papandreou, G., Schroff, F., Adam, H.: Encoder-decoder with atrous separable convolution for semantic image segmentation. In: Ferrari, V., Hebert, M., Sminchisescu, C., Weiss, Y. (eds.) ECCV 2018, Part VII. LNCS, vol. 11211, pp. 833–851. Springer, Cham (2018). https://doi.org/10.1007/978-3-030-01234-2_49
7. Cheng, J., Tsai, Y.H., Hung, W.C., Wang, S., Yang, M.H.: Fast and accurate online video object segmentation via tracking parts. In: CVPR (2018)

8. Chollet, F.: Xception: deep learning with depthwise separable convolutions. In: CVPR (2017)
9. Cordts, M., et al.: The cityscapes dataset for semantic urban scene understanding. In: CVPR (2016)
10. Deng, J., Dong, W., Socher, R., Li, L.J., Li, K., Fei-Fei, L.: ImageNet: a large-scale hierarchical image database. In: CVPR (2009)
11. Fout, A., Byrd, J., Shariat, B., Ben-Hur, A.: Protein interface prediction using graph convolutional networks. In: NIPS (2017)
12. Goodfellow, I., et al.: Generative adversarial nets. In: NIPS (2014)
13. He, K., Gkioxari, G., Dollár, P., Girshick, R.: Mask R-CNN. In: ICCV (2017)
14. He, K., Zhang, X., Ren, S., Sun, J.: Deep residual learning for image recognition. In: CVPR (2016)
15. Ilg, E., Mayer, N., Saikia, T., Keuper, M., Dosovitskiy, A., Brox, T.: FlowNet 2.0: evolution of optical flow estimation with deep networks. In: CVPR (2017)
16. Khoreva, A., Benenson, R., Ilg, E., Brox, T., Schiele, B.: Lucid data dreaming for object tracking. In: CVPR Workshops (2017)
17. Kipf, T.N., Welling, M.: Semi-supervised classification with graph convolutional networks. In: ICLR (2016)
18. Krähenbühl, P., Koltun, V.: Efficient inference in fully connected CRFs with Gaussian edge potentials. In: NIPS (2011)
19. Lin, T.-Y., et al.: Microsoft COCO: common objects in context. In: Fleet, D., Pajdla, T., Schiele, B., Tuytelaars, T. (eds.) ECCV 2014, Part V. LNCS, vol. 8693, pp. 740–755. Springer, Cham (2014). https://doi.org/10.1007/978-3-319-10602-1_48
20. Long, J., Shelhamer, E., Darrell, T.: Fully convolutional networks for semantic segmentation. In: CVPR (2015)
21. Luiten, J., Voigtlaender, P., Leibe, B.: PReMVOS: proposal-generation, refinement and merging for video object segmentation. In: Jawahar, C.V., Li, H., Mori, G., Schindler, K. (eds.) ACCV 2018, Part IV. LNCS, vol. 11364, pp. 565–580. Springer, Cham (2019). https://doi.org/10.1007/978-3-030-20870-7_35
22. Maninis, K.K., et al.: Video object segmentation without temporal information. TPAMI **41**(6), 1515–1530 (2018)
23. Mathieu, M., Couprie, C., LeCun, Y.: Deep multi-scale video prediction beyond mean square error. In: ICLR (2016)
24. Peng, C., Zhang, X., Yu, G., Luo, G., Sun, J.: Large kernel matters-improve semantic segmentation by global convolutional network. In: CVPR (2017)
25. Perazzi, F., Pont-Tuset, J., McWilliams, B., Van Gool, L., Gross, M., Sorkine-Hornung, A.: A benchmark dataset and evaluation methodology for video object segmentation. In: CVPR (2016)
26. Pont-Tuset, J., Perazzi, F., Caelles, S., Arbeláez, P., Sorkine-Hornung, A., Van Gool, L.: The 2017 DAVIS challenge on video object segmentation. arXiv:1704.00675 (2017)
27. Schütt, K.T., Arbabzadah, F., Chmiela, S., Müller, K.R., Tkatchenko, A.: Quantum-chemical insights from deep tensor neural networks. Nat. Commun. **8**, 13890 (2017)
28. Voigtlaender, P., Leibe, B.: Online adaptation of convolutional neural networks for video object segmentation. In: BMVC (2017)
29. Wug Oh, S., Lee, J.Y., Sunkavalli, K., Joo Kim, S.: Fast video object segmentation by reference-guided mask propagation. In: CVPR (2018)
30. Yang, L., Wang, Y., Xiong, X., Yang, J., Katsaggelos, A.K.: Efficient video object segmentation via network modulation. In: CVPR (2018)

Modeling Severe Traffic Accidents with Spatial and Temporal Features

Soumya Sourav[1](✉), Devashish Khulbe[2], and Vishal Verma[1]

[1] University of Texas at Dallas, Dallas, TX 75080, USA
{sxs180011,vxv180006}@utdallas.edu
[2] New York University, New York, NY 10003, USA
dk3596@nyu.edu

Abstract. We present an approach to estimate the severity of traffic related accidents in *aggregated* (area-level) and *disaggregated* (point level) data. Exploring spatial features, we measure 'complexity' of road networks using several area level variables. Also using temporal and other situational features from open data for New York City, we use Gradient Boosting models for inference and measuring feature importance along with Gaussian Processes to model spatial dependencies in the data. The results show significant importance of 'complexity' in aggregated model as well as other features in prediction which may be helpful in framing policies and targeting interventions for preventing severe traffic related accidents and injuries.

Keywords: Accident involvement · Road networks characteristics · Spatial modeling

1 Introduction

Traffic related accidents contribute to the deaths of around 1.35 million people and injuries to around 30 million people worldwide. 93% of the world's fatalities on the roads occur in low- and middle-income countries, even though these countries have approximately 60% of the world's vehicles [1]. The above fact is informative regarding the possible link between street conditions and design and fatal accidents. Additionally, road traffic crashes cost most countries 3% of their gross domestic product, indicating that curbing traffic accidents is financially important. With around 60% of the world population predicted to live in cities by 2030, making urban areas safe for pedestrians and vehicles simultaneously is an important area to delve into. Further, assessing the role of multiple location and time factors in prediction can help the concerned authorities in deploying targeted interventions for public safety. With real-time large open data of accidents and information about urban network of streets, we argue that severity of accidents can be estimated using modern Machine Learning (ML) techniques. Recently, ML has proved to be an important tool for predicting traffic accidents

© Springer Nature Switzerland AG 2019
T. Gedeon et al. (Eds.): ICONIP 2019, LNCS 11954, pp. 528–535, 2019.
https://doi.org/10.1007/978-3-030-36711-4_44

and crash severity, with a variety of tools being used for accident risk prediction [2]. In this paper, we present approaches to infer injury-related and fatal accidents for area level and observation level data for New York City. We also introduce a new feature measuring the complexity of area-level street networks. We model the spatial autocorrelation in the data in the area level model which the regular model may not be able to learn. Interpretable techniques like Gradient Boosting are used to measure the feature importance of our variables, the results of which show the impact of several spatial and temporal features [10] in inference.

This work contributes to the current research by introducing some new significant predictors and presenting a way to account for spatial dependencies in accidents data.

1.1 Related Work

Significant amount of literature can be attributed to modeling traffic accident and their severity using diverse set of variables. Features like curvature, road width, urban/rural area and gender of driver area have been shown to be significant in accident modeling [3]. Another work [4] describe models for predicting the expected number of accidents at urban junctions and road links as accurately as possible, explaining 60% of variation for road links. This is indicative of importance of location based features of streets and junctions in accident modeling. An approach [5] models severe accidents for area level predictions using linear model using features like intersection density, vehicle speed and number of households which turned out to be significant. This work also uses Geographic Weighted Regression (GWR) to account for spatial correlation. Deep learning approaches have also been proposed for modeling traffic accidents [9] in the past but we aim to build interpretable models in order to measure importance of features with this paper. Our work aims to further introduce and use new predictors to model and subsequently use non-linear models to predict severe accidents both for area-level and point-level data and also account for possible spatial dependencies for area-level data.

2 Data and Methods

Traffic Accidents. We use open data for New York City maintained by New York City Police Department (NYPD). The data contains entries of motor vehicle related accidents, containing their coordinates, date and time of incident, type of vehicles involved and number of injuries and deaths. For the aggregated model, we aggregate the number of accidents on census tract level for the city. The model is thus a regression problem with the number of severe incidents as a target [8]. For the disaggregated model, the problem is essentially of binary classification type where we aim to classify a traffic accident as severe or non-severe. We define the severity as any incident where number of injuries or deaths are equal to greater than 1. We assign binary values as the target:

$$\begin{cases} 0, & injuries/deaths = 0 \\ 1, & otherwise \end{cases}$$

Considering the data from July 2011 till May 2019, this results in a total of around 1,000,000 non-severe accidents and around 200,000 severe accidents, indicating a problem of imbalance which we address further in this section.

Spatial Autocorrelation. Assuming that our data is not *i.i.d* [11], we measure local spatial autocorrelation for the number of severe accidents y_j for census-tract aggregated level through the *Local Moran's I* statistic calculated as:

$$I_j = (n-1)\frac{y_j - \overline{y}}{\sum_{k=1,k\neq j}^{n} w_{j,k}(y_k - \overline{y})^2} \sum_{k=1,k\neq j}^{n} w_{j,k}(y_k - \overline{y}) \qquad (1)$$

where n is the number of spatial units indexed by i and j; $\overline{y}$ represents the mean of y_j and w represents the spatial weight between the features j and k. The weights for neighbouring and non-neighbouring areas of each census tract j are taken as: $w_{j,k} = 1$ if k is a queen contiguous neighbour of j and $w_{j,k} = 0$ otherwise (Fig. 1).

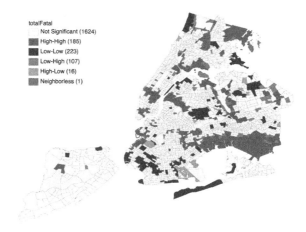

Fig. 1. Local spatial autocorrelation of total severe accidents in New York City (p ≤ 0.05)

Complexity. Introducing a new feature 'complexity' as a proxy for intricacies of street level networks, we define it as a multiple of number of intersections and circuity of a given network. We then measure complexity for our all networks of census tract areas. The circuity is defined as a ratio of network distance to Euclidean distance for a given street network. Considering that the number of intersections has been shown to be correlated to accidents in previous work [5,7], multiplying it with circuity account for further intricacies of the network. Thus, our new feature measures complexity of the networks by accounting for factors like number of turns, intersections and nodes.

Other Variables. Other features we consider are average street width, vehicle types, average number of bike lanes, day of week and time of day of incident, for which only the hour value is taken. Subsequently, the census-tract level aggregated data set results in 2156 observations and the point level (disaggregated) data set contains around 1,200,000 observations.

Table 1. Aggregated (census-tract level) data set

Features (observations)	Mean value	Std. Deviation
Complexity (2156)	30.58	39.34
Avg. Street width in meters (2156)	34.13	5.85
Avg. Bike lanes (2156)	1.47	1.35
Avg. node degree (2156)	3.59	0.83

Data Imbalance. Imbalanced data set is the one which suffers from the problem of classes not being in proportion. This causes a machine learning model to generate fake accuracy reports with the imbalanced data set. With our model, we have tried to evade this problem by the use of SMOTE, since our data is fairly imbalanced with positive class accounting for just about 23% of the total observations [13].

SMOTE (Synthetic Minority Over-Sampling Technique) - It is an oversampling method which can create synthetic samples from minor classes instead of just copying them. The algorithm selects two or more similar instances (using a distance measure) and changing an observation one feature at a time by a random amount within the difference to the neighboring data points. We select SMOTE for over-sampling as it is a relatively simpler method and give good results for data with small number of features [12].

3   Results

3.1   Spatial and Temporal Features

We observe that hour of day of the accident may be important as a predictor, with majority of incidents happening in the evening and night hours. Also, we consider day of week as a predictor, where we observe that weekdays have a slightly greater proportion of accidents as compared to weekends. Also, we decide to model the spatial autocorrelation observed in the data for the *aggregated model* since on observation, there seem to be spatial dependencies in the accidents with some areas having high proportion of incidents.

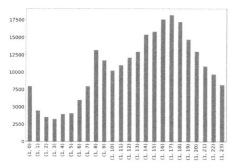

Fig. 2. Hour of day (x-axis) and number of severe accidents (y-axis)

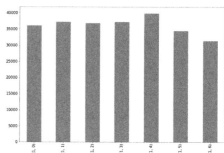

Fig. 3. Day of week (x-axis) and number of severe accidents (y-axis)

3.2 Aggregated Model

For training and testing purposes we implement gradient boosting method with decision trees having depth of 5 as weak learners. The gradient boosting method works on the principle of optimizing the cost function over a function in the space iteratively the function being a weak learner. The gradient of the weak learner is usually in the negative direction. During each iteration, the trees are added to the model to reduce the loss and this is done by parameterizing them. The gradient follows the direction which reduces the residual loss (Figs. 2 and 3).

For the census-tract level model, we estimate the number of severe accidents as a function of spatial features s described in Table 1 as $y = f(s) + \epsilon$, where ϵ is the error term. Further, we model the error ϵ using spatial context $\epsilon = g(x)$, where x are the centroids of the spatial area we are considering. We use Gradient Boosting (GB) model using 20 fold cross validation for the first part and Gaussian Processes with Radial Basis Function (RBF) kernel for modeling the residual error term. Results show that the first step explains around 34% variation (measured by the R^2 value) in the data and further 13% is explained by modeling the residual error term. Looking at the feature importance, complexity turns out to be the most important in prediction followed by average number of nodes, average street width and average number of bike lanes in the census tract (Table 2).

Table 2. Aggregated model

Step	Model used	R^2
$y = f(s) + \epsilon$	Gradient Boosting	0.338
$\epsilon = g(x)$	Gaussian Process	0.132

3.3   Disaggregated Model

For the *disaggregated* data, the goal is to classify each data point as severe or not severe based on the features. The data is thus trained as a binary classification problem with four classifiers with 10-fold cross validation. Oversampling the positive class (severe) points with SMOTE and then training the resulting data with Gradient Boosting results in highest AUC score of 0.72. Along with the temporal features like time, the spatial features are also used which are attributed to the census-tract in which the incident happened (Fig. 4 and Table 3).

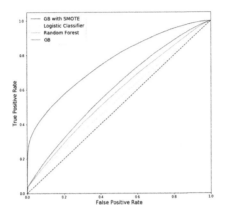

Fig. 4. Receiver operator characteristic (ROC) curve for classification models

Table 3. Disaggregated (point classification) model

Model	AUC
Gradient Boosting with SMOTE	0.729
Gradient Boosting	0.604
Random Forests	0.575
Logistic Regression	0.539

The important features for classification include class of vehicle (specifically whether it was a two-wheeler or truck), complexity of the area and the hour of the incident.

4   Discussion

Feature Importance. The importance of a node in a decision tree is computed as:

$$ni_j = w_j C_j - w_{\text{left}(j)} C_{\text{left}(j)} - w_{\text{right}(j)} C_{\text{right}(j)} \tag{2}$$

where w_j is weighted number of samples in node j, C_j is impurity in this node, and *left(j)* and *right(j)* are its respective children nodes. Then, the feature importances are then averaged over all the trees.

We observe that spatial features which account for complexity like number of intersections, network nodes, circuity along with vehicle type are important features in prediction of severe accidents. Complexity turns out to be the most important predictor in the *aggregated* model while it fairly good in the point level classification too. It is interesting to note that average number of bike lanes is not one of the most important predictors for injury and fatal accident classification, despite one of the research concluding that bike lanes make a route safer [6]. This may be because we took the average number of bike lanes in a neighborhood while making predictions. Maybe a more fine street level feature information on this can change our results, which may be a scope for future work in this work. We also notice that temporal features like day of week and hour of day when incident happened are important information about accidents in general. Most of the accidents take place over the weekdays and during the evening and late-night hours. Though, these temporal features do not contribute much in our predictive model, they are good predictors of vehicle collisions and accidents. The spatial features inform us from a road and street design perspective in a neighborhood while the temporal variables along with information about vehicle in the accidents can be important from a real-time emergency deployment viewpoint.

5   Conclusion

In this work, we presented an approach using Machine Learning techniques to model non-fatal (injury) and fatal (death) traffic accidents in urban environments using spatial and temporal variables. We found the importance of factors like street width, vehicle type, time of day and the new created feature 'complexity' of a street network in prediction of severe accidents both in the area level and point level data. These results indicate and validate that road design is a critical factor in severity of accidents. Additionally, we determined the importance of type of motor vehicles involved that can have an impact on the accident. This information can be critical in implementation of policies regarding construction and design of neighborhood streets, allowance of type of vehicles in an area or can help in effective operation of emergency services.

Future work in this domain can be extended to incorporate other socio-economic features in prediction and determination of most affected demographics in terms of road traffic incidents.

References

1. Road traffic injuries. https://www.who.int/news-room/fact-sheets/detail/road-traffic-injuries

2. Iranitalab, A., Khattak, A.: Comparison of four statistical and machine learning methods for crash severity prediction. Accid. Anal. Prev. **108**, 27–36 (2017). https://doi.org/10.1016/j.aap.2017.08.008. ISSN 0001–4575

3. Abdel-Aty, M.A., Essam Radwan, A.: Modeling traffic accident occurrence and involvement. Accid. Anal. Prev. **32**(5), 633–642 (2000). https://doi.org/10.1016/S0001-4575(99)00094-9. ISSN 0001–4575

4. Greibe, P.: Accident prediction models for urban roads. Accid. Anal. Prev. **35**(2), 273–285 (2003). https://doi.org/10.1016/S0001-4575(02)00005-2. ISSN 0001–4575

5. Hadayeghi, A., Shalaby, A.S., Persaud, B.: Macrolevel accident prediction models for evaluating safety of urban transportation systems. Transp. Res. Rec. **1840**(1), 87–95 (2003). https://doi.org/10.3141/1840-10

6. Harris, M.A., Reynolds, C.C.O., Winters, M., et al.: Comparing the effects of infrastructure on bicycling injury at intersections and non-intersections using a case-crossover design. Inj. Prev. **19**, 303–310 (2013)

7. Persaud, B., Lord, D., Palmisano, J.: Calibration and transferability of accident prediction models for urban intersections. Transp. Res. Rec. **1784**(1), 57–64 (2002). https://doi.org/10.3141/1784-08

8. El-Basyouny, K., Sayed, T.: Comparison of two negative binomial regression techniques in developing accident prediction models. Transp. Res. Rec. **1950**(1), 9–16 (2006). https://doi.org/10.1177/0361198106195000102

9. Abdelwahab, H.T., Abdel-Aty, M.A.: Development of artificial neural network models to predict driver injury severity in traffic accidents at signalized intersections. Transp. Res. Rec. **1746**(1), 6–13 (2001). https://doi.org/10.3141/1746-02

10. Quddus, M.A.: Time series count data models: an empirical application to traffic accidents. Accid. Anal. Prev. **40**(5), 1732–1741 (2008). https://doi.org/10.1016/j.aap.2008.06.011. ISSN 0001–4575

11. Sawalha, Z., Sayed, T.: Traffic accident modeling: some statistical issues. Can. J. Civ. Eng. **33**(9), 1115–1124 (2006). https://doi.org/10.1139/l06-056

12. Chawla, N.V., Bowyer, K.W., Hall, L.O., Kegelmeyer, W.P.: SMOTE: synthetic minority over-sampling technique. J. Artif. Intell. Res. **16**, 321–357 (2002). https://doi.org/10.1613/jair.953

13. Wu, F., Jing, X.-Y., Shan, S., Zuo, W., Yang, J.-Y.: Multiset feature learning for highly imbalanced data classification. In: Thirty-First AAAI Conference on Artificial Intelligence. AAAI Publications (2017)

Sparse Dynamic Binary Neural Networks for Storage and Switching of Binary Periodic Orbits

Shota Anzai, Seitaro Koyama, Shunsuke Aoki, and Toshimichi Saito[(⌧)]

Hosei University, Koganei, Tokyo 184-8584, Japan
`tsaito@hosei.ac.jp`

Abstract. A sparse dynamic binary neural network is characterized by local binary connection and can exhibit various binary periodic orbits. First, we consider a condition of sparse connection parameters that guarantees storage and switching of binary periodic orbits. Second, we give two examples of the network that realize the storage and stitching of two periodic orbits related to insect gaits patterns. Presenting an FPGA-based hardware, typical phenomena are confirmed experimentally.

Keywords: Binary neural networks · Periodic orbits · Stability

1 Introduction

A sparse dynamic binary neural network (SBNN) is an nonlinear dynamical system characterized by local binary connection [1,2]. In the SBNN, each neuron transforms three binary inputs to one binary output via signum activation function [3–5]. A delayed feedback is applied and the SBNN can generate various binary periodic orbits. The SBNN has advantages in precise analysis of the dynamics and FPGA based low power hardware implementation [2–5]. Storage of target binary periodic orbits (TBPOs) and stability analysis of the stored TBPO are important in study of nonlinear dynamics. Real/potential engineering applications include associative memories [6,7], control of switching power converters [8], and central pattern generators in robotics [9,10]. The SBNN is an important study object from both fundamental and application viewpoints.

This paper studies storage and switching of multiple TBPOs in the SBNN. Since general discussion is not easy, we consider two TBPOs related to insect gaits patterns [9]. First, we consider condition for storage and switching of two TBPOs (e.g, TBPO1 and TBPO2) based on two sets of sparse connection parameters (e.g., set1 and set2). In the set1, TBPO1 is stored into the SBNN and all the elements of TBPO2 become initial points falling directly into the TBPO1. In the set2, TBPO2 is stored into the SBNN and all the elements of TBPO1 become initial points falling directly into the TBPO2. Second, after trial-and-errors, we give examples of set1 and set2 that realize storage and switching of two TBPOs corresponding to insect gaits patterns. Presenting an FPGA-based

© Springer Nature Switzerland AG 2019
T. Gedeon et al. (Eds.): ICONIP 2019, LNCS 11954, pp. 536–542, 2019.
https://doi.org/10.1007/978-3-030-36711-4_45

hardware, the storage and switching of the TBPOs are confirmed experimentally. These results will be developed into basic/application studies of sparse dynamic neural networks such as stability analysis of TBPOs for connection parameters and SBNN based central pattern generators for insect gaits.

As novelty of this paper, it should be noted that previous papers discuss neither TBPOs related to insect gaits patterns nor sparse connection parameters for storage and switching of the TBPOs.

2   Sparse Dynamic Binary Neural Networks

The SBNN is characterized by simple sparse connection such that each neuron transforms three binary inputs to one binary output via signum activation function F. The dynamics is described by the difference equation

$$x_i^{t+1} = F\left(w_{ii_a} x_{i_a}^t + w_{ii_b} x_{i_b}^t + w_{ii_c} x_{i_c}^t - T_i\right)$$
$$F(x) = \begin{cases} +1 \text{ if } x \geq 0 \\ -1 \text{ if } x < 0 \end{cases} \quad w_{ij} \in \{-1, +1\}, \ T_i \in \{-4, -2, 0, +2, +4\} \quad (1)$$

where $\boldsymbol{x}^t \equiv (x_1^t, \cdots, x_N^t)^\top$ is an N-dimensional binary state vector at discrete time t and $x_i^t \in \{-1, +1\}$ is the i-th element, $i = 1 \sim N$. The three binary inputs $x_{i_a}^t$, $x_{i_b}^t$, $x_{i_c}^t$ are selected from $\{x_1^t, \cdots, x_N^t\}$ without overlap. Figure 1 illustrates the SBNN for $N = 6$. For convenience, Eq. (1) is abbreviated by

$$x^{t+1} = F(\boldsymbol{W} \boldsymbol{x}^t - \boldsymbol{T}), \ \boldsymbol{W} \equiv \begin{pmatrix} w_{11} & \cdots & w_{1N} \\ \vdots & \ddots & \vdots \\ w_{N1} & \cdots & w_{NN} \end{pmatrix}, \ \boldsymbol{T} \equiv \begin{pmatrix} T_1 \\ \vdots \\ T_N \end{pmatrix}. \quad (2)$$

$\boldsymbol{W}$ and $\boldsymbol{T}$ are referred to as sparse connection matrix and threshold vector, respectively. Given an initial binary vector $\boldsymbol{x}^1$, the SBNN can generate various periodic/transient binary sequences. Since the dynamics is based on Boolean function of 3 inputs, the SBNN is suitable for precise dynamics analysis. Since the local binary connection reduce power consumption as compared with dense connection, the SBNN brings benefits to hardware implementation.

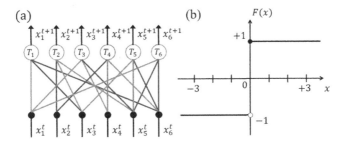

Fig. 1. SBNN for $N = 6$. (a) Network configuration. Red and blue segments denote $w_{ij} = +1$ and $w_{ij} = -1$, respectively. (b) Signum activation function. (Color figure online)

3   Switching of Binary Periodic Orbits

First, we define two target binary periodic orbits (TBPOs):

$$\text{TBPO1 with period } p: (a^1, a^2, \cdots, a^p),\ a^{\tau+1} = F(Wa^\tau - T),\ \tau = 1 \sim p.$$
$$\text{TBPO2 with period } q: (b^1, b^2, \cdots, b^q),\ b^{\tau+1} = F(Wb^\tau - T),\ \tau = 1 \sim q.$$
(3)

where $a^{p+1} \equiv a^1$ and $b^{q+1} \equiv b^1$. Our objective is to set parameters (w_{ij}, T_i) to satisfy the following.

P1: TBPO1 is stored and all the elements in TBPO2 becomes initial points falling directly into the TBPO1. Such an initial point is said to be a direct eventually periodic points (DEPP).

P2: TBPO2 is stored and all the elements in TBPO1 becomes initial points falling directly into the TBPO2.

The P1 and P2 can be realized if the parameters satisfy the following:

$$\text{P1: } \eta^\tau = F(W\xi^\tau - T),\ (\xi^\tau, \eta^\tau) = \begin{cases} (a^\tau, a^{\tau+1}) & \text{for } 1 \le \tau \le p \\ (b^\tau, a^k) & \text{for } p+1 \le \tau \le p+q \end{cases}$$
$$\text{P2: } \eta^\tau = F(W\xi^\tau - T),\ (\xi^\tau, \eta^\tau) = \begin{cases} (a^\tau, b^k) & \text{for } 1 \le \tau \le p \\ (b^\tau, b^{\tau+1}) & \text{for } p+1 \le \tau \le p+q \end{cases}$$
(4)

where a^k is either element of TBPO1 and b^k is either element of TBPO2. For convenience, (ξ^τ, η^τ) is referred to as a teacher signal. If TBPO1 and TBPO satisfy the following, there exists parameters that realize P1 and P2.

$$\begin{cases} L(i) < R(i) \text{ for all } i \\ R(i) = \min_\tau (\sum_{j=1}^N w_{ij} \xi_j^\tau) & \text{for } \tau \text{ such that } \eta_i^\tau = +1 \\ L(i) = \max_\tau (\sum_{j=1}^N w_{ij} \xi_j^\tau) & \text{for } \tau \text{ such that } \eta_i^\tau = -1 \end{cases}$$
(5)

Tables 1 and 2 show two examples of teacher signals for $N = 6$, $p = 2$, and $q = 6$. The TBPO1 and TBPO2 correspond to two insect gaits as shown in Fig. 2(a) and (b) where symbol "+1" means movement and symbol "−1" mean no movement, respectively. Figure 2(c) shows TBPO and DEPP for switching

Table 1. Teacher signal 1: Storage of TBPO1 and switching from TBPO2 to TBPO1

τ	1	2	3	4	5	6	7	8
ξ^τ	a^1	a^2	b^1	b^2	b^3	b^4	b^5	b^6
η^τ	a^2	a^1	a^2	a^1	a^1	a^1	a^1	a^2

Table 2. Teacher signal 2: storage of TBPO2 and switching from TBPO1 to TBPO2

τ	1	2	3	4	5	6	7	8
ξ^τ	a^1	a^2	b^1	b^2	b^3	b^4	b^5	b^6
η^τ	b^1	b^3	b^2	b^3	b^4	b^5	b^6	b^1

of TBPO1 and TBPO2. After trial-and-errors, we have obtained two sets of parameters that realize the objective problems. The teacher signal 1 is realize by

$$W_2 = \begin{pmatrix} 0 & 0 & 0 & -1 & -1 & +1 \\ -1 & 0 & 0 & 0 & +1 & -1 \\ 0 & 0 & 0 & -1 & -1 & +1 \\ -1 & -1 & 0 & 0 & 0 & -1 \\ +1 & 0 & 0 & 0 & -1 & +1 \\ 0 & -1 & 0 & +1 & 0 & -1 \end{pmatrix} \quad T_2 = \begin{pmatrix} 0 \\ 0 \\ 0 \\ 0 \\ 0 \\ 0 \end{pmatrix} \tag{6}$$

The teacher signal 2 is realize by

$$W_6 = \begin{pmatrix} 0 & 0 & 0 & -1 & -1 & +1 \\ -1 & 0 & 0 & 0 & -1 & -1 \\ 0 & 0 & 0 & -1 & +1 & -1 \\ -1 & -1 & 0 & 0 & 0 & -1 \\ +1 & 0 & 0 & 0 & +1 & +1 \\ 0 & +1 & 0 & +1 & 0 & +1 \end{pmatrix} \quad T_6 = \begin{pmatrix} 0 \\ 2 \\ 0 \\ 2 \\ 0 \\ 0 \end{pmatrix} \tag{7}$$

These parameters correspond to network configurations shown in Fig. 2(d). That is, if $W = W_2$ and $T = T_2$ then TBPO1 is stored and TBPO2 becomes DEPP falling directly into TBPO1. If $W = W_6$ and $T = T_6$ then TBPO2 is stored and TBPO1 becomes DEPP falling directly into TBPO2. Switching the two sets of parameters, we can realize switching of the two TBPOs corresponding to two insect gaits.

Using Verilog, we have implemented an FPGA based hardware based on the circuit as shown in Fig. 3. Algorithm 1 shows simplified Verilog code of inverters for negative connection, Algorithm 2 shows code of signum activation functions, and Algorithm 3 shows code of sparse networks. We have performed laboratory experiments with the following tools:

- FPGA board: BASYS3 (Xilinx Artix-7 XC7A35T-ICPG236C)
- Clock frequency: 6 [Hz] [1]
- Measuring instrument: ANALOG DISCOVERY2.
- Multi-instrument software: Waveforms 2015.
- Verilog version: vivado 2018.2 platform (Xilinx).

The switching of TBPO1 and TBPO2 is confirmed experimentally as shown in Fig. 4.

---

[1] The default clock frequency 100 [MHz] is divided for stable measurements.

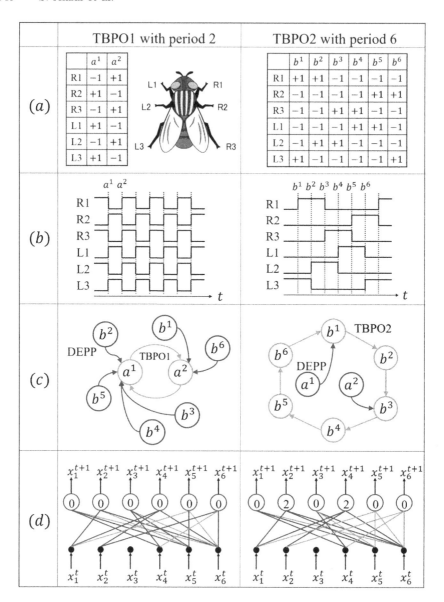

Fig. 2. Storage and switching of TBPO1 and TBPO2 (a) TBPO. (b) Two patterns of insect gaits. (c) TBPO and DEPP. (d) Network configuration.

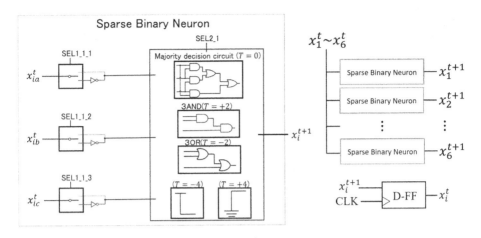

Fig. 3. SBNN circuit design

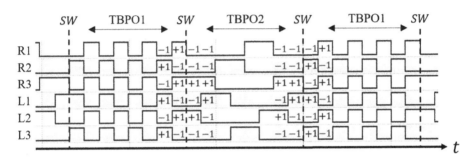

Fig. 4. Measured waveform in an FPGA board

Algorithm 1. inverter

---

module Inverter(input X, input $sel1$, output Y)
case($sel1$)
1 : $Y = X$;
2 : $Y = \neg X$;
endmodule

Algorithm 2. Signum activation function

---

module Signum Activation Function(input a, input b, input c, input $sel2$, output Z)
case($sel2$)
1 : $Z = 1'b0$; $//T = +4$
2 : $Z = a \cap b \cap c$; $//T = +2$
3 : $Z = (a \cap b) \cup (b \cap c) \cup (c \cap a)$; $//T = 0$
4 : $Z = a \cup b \cup c$; $//T = -2$
5 : $Z = 1'b1$; $//T = -4$
endcase
endmodule

Algorithm 3. Binary neuron

module Sparse Binary Neuron(input x_{ia}^t, input x_{ib}^t, input x_{ic}^t, input $sel1$, input $sel2$, output x_i^{t+1})
wire $p1, p2, p3$;

Inverter m1_ 1 $(.X(x_{ia}^t), .sel1(sel1), .Y(p1))$;
Inverter m1_ 2 $(.X(x_{ib}^t), .sel1(sel1), .Y(p2))$;
Inverter m1_ 3 $(.X(x_{ic}^t), .sel1(sel1), .Y(p3))$;

Signum Activation Function m2 $(.a(p1), .b(p2), .c(p3), .sel2(sel2), .Z(x_i^{t+1}))$;
endmodule

4   Conclusions

Storage and switching of TBPOs in SBNN are considered in this paper. First, we have described condition of sparse connection parameters that guarantees storage and switching of two TBPOs. Second. We have given two sets of parameters that realize the storage and switching of two TBPOs related to insect gaits patterns. Presenting an FPGA based hardware, typical phenomena are confirmed experimentally. Future problems include detailed stability analysis of various TBPOs, learning algorithm for storage and switching of various TBPOs, and design of SBNN based central pattern generators.

References

1. Aoki, S., Koyama, S., Saito, T.: Theoretical analysis of dynamic binary neural networks with simple sparse connection. Neurocomputing **341**, 149–155 (2019)
2. Aoki, Shunsuke, Koyama, Seitaro, Saito, Toshimichi: FPGA Based Hardware Implementation of Simple Dynamic Binary Neural Networks. In: Cheng, Long, Leung, Andrew Chi Sing, Ozawa, Seiichi (eds.) ICONIP 2018. LNCS, vol. 11307, pp. 647–655. Springer, Cham (2018). https://doi.org/10.1007/978-3-030-04239-4_58
3. Gray, D.L., Michel, A.N.: A training algorithm for binary feed forward neural networks. IEEE Trans. Neural Netw. **3**(2), 176–194 (1992)
4. M. Courbariaux, M., Bengio, Y., David, J. P.: Binary Connect: training deep neural networks with binary weights during propagations. in NIPS, 3105–3113 (2015)
5. Courbariaux, M., Hubara, I., Soudry, D., El-Yaniv, R., Bengio, Y.: Binarized neural networks: training neural networks with weights and activations constrained to +1 or −1. arXiv:1602.02830 (2016)
6. Araki, K., Saito, T.: An associative memory including time-variant self-feedback. Neural Netw. **7**(8), 1267–1271 (1994)
7. Jiang, X., Gripon, V., Berrou, C., Rabbat, M.: Storing sequences in binary tournament-based neural networks. IEEE Trans. Neural Netw. **27**(5), 913–925 (2016)
8. Vithayathil, J.: Power Electronics. McGraw-Hill (1992)
9. Ramdya, P., Thandiackal, R., Cherney, R., Asselborn, T., Ljspeert, A.J., Floreano, D.: Climbing favours the tripod gait over alternative faster insect gaits. Nat. Commun. **8**, 14494 (2017)
10. Lozano, A., Rodriguez, M., Roberto Barrio, R.: Control strategies of 3-cell central pattern generator via global stimuli. Sci. Rep. **6**, 23622 (2016)

IMDB-Attire: A Novel Dataset for Attire Detection and Localization

Saad Bin Yousuf[1]([⊠]), Hasan Sajid[2], Simon Poon[1],
and Matloob Khushi[1]

[1] School of Computer Science, The University of Sydney, Sydney,
NSW 2006, Australia
saad.yousuf@sydney.edu.au
[2] Department of Robotics and Intelligent Machine Engineering,
National University of Sciences and Technology, Islamabad, Pakistan

Abstract. People's attire, or their way of dressing defines not only their social status and personality but also affects the way people meet and greet them. Attire detection has many useful applications such as clothing preferences in diverse regions of the world could be monitored and quantified. This information is very valuable for fashion designers. Real-time clothing recognition can be useful for security surveillance, where information about an individual's clothes can be used to identify crime suspects. Recently, deep learning algorithms have shown promise in the field of object detection and recognition. These algorithms are data hungry and are only as good as the data they are trained on. In this work, we have focused on three tasks to address this problem. We created a unique dataset of ∼8000 images from IMDBb.com (movie rating website) to address the challenge of real-world application of the algorithm training for attire detection. The dataset contains pictures from movies, making the dataset a good source of images from the wild. We manually labelled 60 different classes of attire. Then we focused on multiclass classification and attire object detection using customized deep learning architectures including YOLO and SSD. We achieved a mean Average Precision (mAP) of 64.14% and an Average Precision (AP) of 91.14% for top 5 classes on YOLO. Available at https://github.com/saadyousuf45/.

Keywords: Attire · Object detection · Classification · SSD · Clothing · YOLO

1 Introduction

Recognizing different types of attire in different environments (wild, street, cluttered, non-lit) is a difficult task and has many applications. Deep learning algorithms recently have shown promise in this aspect, but they require hard manual labor (annotating images manually).

Attire, clothing or apparel is a very important part of our lives. The way we dress delivers a visual message to everyone who sees us. Attire is a source of visual communication to the world. Realtime clothing detection is ongoing research problem and correctly detecting attire in the wild by either segmentation (every pixel is defined as a part of either the attire or not) or bounding boxes is still being researched. In the field of

© Springer Nature Switzerland AG 2019
T. Gedeon et al. (Eds.): ICONIP 2019, LNCS 11954, pp. 543–553, 2019.
https://doi.org/10.1007/978-3-030-36711-4_46

computer science attire or apparel is generally referred to as fashion and the datasets relating to it are described as fashion datasets. Fashion dataset usually do not contain accessories such as watches, earing etc. in them.

Automatic classification using machine learning has in use in every scientific field [1], however, the field of image classification was changed forever in 2012, when in the Olympics of computer vision also known as ImageNet challenge, Alexnet [2] a convolution neural network achieved a significant 10.8% less error rate than the runner-up. Since then, deep learning algorithms [3] have dominated image recognition and localization techniques and outperformed classical image recognition and classification techniques. However, these algorithms are mostly dependent on labelled training data which is in the form of images. This data is used for training and optimizing these algorithms. Many researchers argue that manual annotation is not only labor extensive but also the labelling could become biased to the view of the annotators. However, one cannot downplay the importance of carefully annotated dataset to address a particular problem. When it comes to implementing object detection and classification on attire or any other related problem, many different aspects must be considered. For example, (1) how many labels should we choose to annotate? (2) What type of different images we should use? (3) Quantity and quality of labelled data? Mostly people have used different attributes to classify clothes [4]. When it comes to object detection and classification, previous works pre-define a lot of tags. Datasets frequently don't feature coherent labelling, bounding their scalability. Taken in by the want for magnanimous amounts of inexpensively labelled figures, there are works that search cyberspace for accumulating big imaging data that accompany "free" matching text labelling [5–7]. Nevertheless, this places an advanced problem therein the meta-data tags of these automated labelled images. These are to a lesser extent precise nor uniform once equated with someone's manually marked attributes.

2 Related Work

Generally, clothing detection can be divided into categories such as clothing modelling [8, 9], segmentation [10–12], recognition [13], recommendation systems [14, 15] describing people [16] and classification and retrieval [5, 17–19]. Each category has multiple research problems associated with it. We have decided to focus on the challenge of the real time clothing detection and localization.

Most of the current research in attire detection is directed by online fashion and retail industry [5, 14, 20]. Recommendation systems and fashion aesthetic are usually the target of these works. Datasets used by them are mostly synthetic and are created from web scrapping [20] online retail clothing websites. Most datasets contain only one labelled clothing per image. Researchers have deployed techniques for detecting clothes or retrieving similar clothing. Most researchers have benchmarked the results on their own dataset, however very few people talk about real-time video implementation of their results. We have found that datasets focused on real-world implementations of attire detection are scarce and so we have decided to address this problem.

In the first half of the last two decades many attire related studies have attempted to use different methods to either identify people through clothes [21], or used other techniques to identify fashion and clothing textures [21–24]. One of the earliest works that addressed clothing detection in real-time video was presented by [13]. In this paper the researchers presented a complete system of detecting and segmenting clothes in real-time video. Their main contribution was that they design a system tailored for clothing analysis and segmentation. Evaluation included different clothing representations by combining color [25], bag of word features [26], discrete cosine transform responses and region growing method [24, 27, 28]. They devised a complex clothing segmentation method which includes candidate region, canny edge detection, Voronoi image selection, region merging, region growing and finally background removal. There are many limitations to their work such as for clothing segmentation proper human figure alignment is a prerequisite to feature extraction and classification. They report an average recall of 80% in top eight clothing categories.

Another influential study, Deep Fashion [28, 29] also presents a dataset of around 800 k images. They develop a neural network that jointly trains and predicts landmark (their form of annotations) and attributes. Deep Fashion dataset contains attributes clothing landmarks and cross-pose/cross-domain correspondence of clothing pairs. The dataset contains 50 categories and 1000 attributes, they claim that the landmark detection is better than the bounding box label presented by [29]. However, they have branched into many different aspects of clothing and fashion representation rather than focusing on one. Their neural network outperforms two bounding box datasets [29, 30].

Recently, a new annotated dataset of 120 k images was created to detect important key points in apparel called Fashion Landmarks [31]. Fashion Landmarks are 8 key points that can be used to identify and detect clothing. They selected a large subset of Deep Fashion database [21] to create a new dataset of Fashion landmarks (FLD). They compared detection of fashion landmarks to the detection of human joints to claim that landmark detection is difficult then human joint detection. They also proposed new neural network for landmark estimation. They argued that fashion landmarks simulation can help in recognizing and retrieving clothes. Researchers used a subset of deep fashion dataset of 10000 images and 50 clothing attributes. The bounding boxes were manually annotated. The top 5 recall rates of the 50 attributes for the bounding box is 53%. The top 20 and retrieval accuracy for bounding box is 40%.

Studies simulating clothing have been centered extensively on clothing segmentation versus blank setting [7–10]. Attempts have also been made on shop-clothing image sorting, applying conventional handmade features (e.g. SIFT, HOG) [7, 11–13] to online images and lately deep learning-based characteristics [14–17] have also been used. Turned off by the prices of labelling, consequently a deficiency of big attire attribute annotations by dissimilar sources, cross-domain dressing attribute learning makes up an intriguing job and for the most part not studied [14, 17]. Most datasets are synthetic and mined from online clothing websites. Therefore, mostly images are labelled according to their attributes. Other data sets like DCSA, ACWS, DDAN, DARN [17] don't have any bounding box annotations in them.

Our initial experiments taught us that the number of training images does have an impact on the performances of deep learning algorithms, but a smaller dataset carefully crafted to address a problem has a greater chance of outperforming an algorithm trained on larger datasets (Table 1).

Table 1. Statistics of datasets already present that can be classified as attire related datasets.

Name of dataset	Number of images	Categories + attributes	Localization (manual annotation)
Clothing attribute [17]	1856	26	No
Apparel classification with style [18]	145718	15	No
Matching street clothing [29]	78958	11	Bounding box (Manual Amazon Turks)
Deep domain for Describing people [16]	341958	67	No
Cross Domain with dual Ranking Network [30]	182780	179	No
Deep Fashion [28]	800000	1050	Landmark annotation
Fashion parsing with weak color [32]	2682	36	No
MVC-dataset [20]	161638	264	No

3   Methods

Attire detection and localization is a complex task and very much depend on the annotation and careful labelling of a dataset. In this following section we explain the challenges in this task.

3.1   Relative Complexity of Attire Detection

Attire detection and classification in real time is extremely difficult because of several reasons. Similar attire may look different and different attire may look the same because of orientation of the clothing. In images taken from movies or in real life the camera orientation is different. The camera orientation is different in a selfie then from a regular snap. Then if we look at the lighting conditions, they are different in different environments. Clothes in a photo taken in the same location at noon might look different to the one taken at dusk. Clothes are cluttered in most natural environments. People or objects are covering attire to some extent. Even when humans look at other people from far, they sometime mistake what the person is wearing. One has to account for all of these problems.

3.2   IMDB-Attire Dataset Statistics

To address above challenges we collected ~ 8000 images from IMDB website and manual labelled them for 60 classes. We named the dataset IMDB-attire. Our one of the aims was to develop such a comprehensive dataset of images that would have potential to be utilize for detecting attire from images captured from the wild, such as livestream street cams. Therefore, collection of images from movies have a potential to fulfil this goal. The sizes of the image vary from 22.2 MB to 8 KB. The smallest image dimension was 225×400 pixels whereas the largest image size is 2547×5320 pixels. Of 60 labelled classes, Coat was the most represented (5319) class where median was 271 (Fig. 1).

3.3   Image Annotations

Annotations were saved in standard Pascal VOC Format [33] in *.xml* format [34, 35], using the bounding box annotation method as used by ImageNet challenge [35].

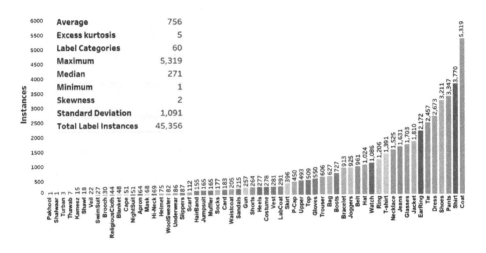

Fig. 1. Bar graph showing statistics of 60 labelled classes in our IMDB-Attire dataset.

4   Object Detector Algorithms

Since convolution neural networks (CNNs) won the ImageNet challenge, a lot of research has been carried out in this field. In the past few years, graph-based methods and Recurrent Neural Networks (RNNs) have achieved these results. In this section we will briefly discuss the two object detectors, that perform well in real time and we have developed networks inspired by both. We discuss their results in the following sections.

4.1   Yolo

YOLO-V3 [36], is the 3rd version of YOLO (You Only Look Once Algorithm) [37]. YOLO-V2 [38] applied a customized architecture darknet-19, an earlier 19-layer network added on with 11 additional layers for object detection. With a 30-layer architecture, YOLO-V2 frequently clambered with miniature object detections. This was blamed upon the release of fine-grained characteristics from the layers when the input was down sampled. To amend this, YOLO-V2 employed an identity mapping, concatenating characteristic mappings of a former layer to get low level features. YOLO-V3 is a good deal better than its former variants because it includes residual blocks, skip connections and up sampling in its architecture. YOLO-V3 is grounded on Darknet, which was a fifty-three layered neural net, all the same YOLO-V3 is 106 layered fully convolution underlying architecture. The detections are established at 3 different scales (down sampled by thirty-two, sixteen and eight) and positions in the network.

4.2 Single Shot Detector (SSD)

Single-shot multi box detector [39] makes up a one-stage object detection algorithm. This implies that, in direct contrast to two-stage models, SSDs don't require an initial step that calls for object proposals. This makes it, broadly, quicker and more effective than two-stage algorithms for example Faster R-CNN [40], though it gives away efficiency in detection of little objects to acquire speed.

5 Experiments

After conducting few experiments 7000 images were selected for training and 500 images for testing. Firstly, the algorithms were trained on training data and then they were tested on the test data of 500 images for validation.

5.1 SSD Training

Keras [41] a high-level wrapper on top of TensorFlow [42] was used to train the SSD network. Training was started with initial weights from the ImageNet competition which is a standard practice while training object detectors. Layers up to convolution layer 4 were frozen during training.

5.2 Input Image Specification for SSD

The dimensions of input image were 512×512 pixels. Number of classes were 60. Custom scales of 0.04, 0.1, 0.26, 0.42, 0.58, 0.74, 0.9 and 1.06 were used. We also used our own aspect ratios. The predictive box sizes were varied with the weight and height of 8, 16, 32, 64, 128, 256 and 512. We performed the standard procedure on all the images of normalizing the coordinates and subtracting the means of all the different image channels in the dataset. While defining our SSD model we used Ridge regularization off 0.0005.

5.3 YOLO Training

YOLO training was performed at the learning rate of 0.00001 with a decay of 0.00005. A batch of around 64 images were subdivided into 32 parts so that it would fit into the GPU memory. We ran around 80,000 iterations for training. To detect small objects YOLO training was performed using RGB image dimensions of 614×614 pixels. A momentum of 0.9, saturation and exposure of 1.5 and Hue of 0.1 for training were chosen. During testing we used dimensions of 416×416 pixels on a video camera.

6   Results

The performance of deep learning algorithms depends on the data they are trained on. When Fig. 1 is compared to Fig. 2, we see over all that the number of instances of coat and pants are more in both the training images and test images. False positive is directly for YOLO are always less than that of SSD. This means that SSD needs far more labels than YOLO to produce the same result (Fig. 2). If the number of instances is below a certain threshold we see that YOLO totally ignores the labels at testing time (Table 2).

6.1   Evaluation Metrics

There are number of evaluation metrics that are used by different researchers to evaluate the accuracy and precision of an object detectors but the most commonly used are mean Average Precision (mAP) and Intersection over Union (IoU). However, we have also documented the precision and recall curves for our labels.

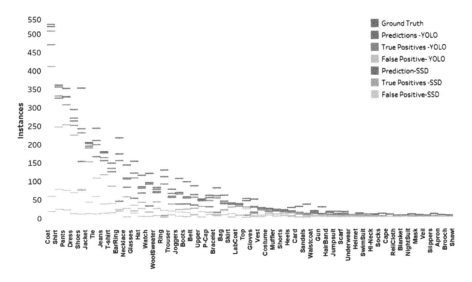

Fig. 2. Comparison of SSD and YOLO inspired algorithms on test data.

Table 2. Comparisons of the two algorithms on the dataset, we report mean average precision overall and the average precision of the top 5 and bottom 5 labels in our dataset.

Algorithm	mAP (over all classes)	Average Precision for top 5 classes	Average Precision for lowest 5 classes	Recall (0.50 thresh)	Precision (0.50 thresh)	F1-Score (0.5 thresh)
Yolo-V3-416	64.14%	91.29%	0.00%	0.68	0.89	0.77
SSD-512	44.76%	89.24%	8.32%	–	–	–

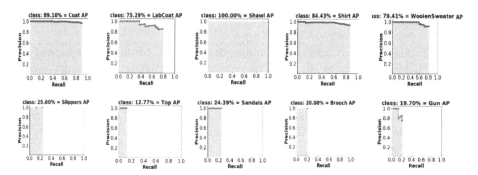

Fig. 3. Graphs showing the recall precision curves of the top 5 and bottom 5 curves (non-zero) for YOLO Inspired algorithm

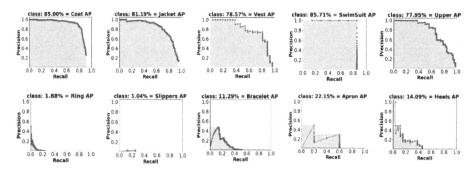

Fig. 4. Graphs showing the recall vs precision curves of the top 5 and bottom 5 curves for SSD inspired algorithm.

YOLO performed better than SSD at test time. The false positives of SSD were way higher than those of YOLO. True predictions of YOLO were also greater than that of SSD. YOLO was also better in detecting small objects, whereas SSD was harder to train than YOLO, because of the constant freezing and unfreezing of layers. Training SSD by unfreezing all the trainable layers was unsuccessful. SSD failed to recognize small objects and that is why its mAP is lower than that of YOLO.

7 Discussions

We have gathered a unique dataset of ∼8000 images from various movies and benchmarked the performance of YOLO and SSD. Benchmarking performance of any dataset is important for the extension of scientific knowledge [43]. We observed that object recognition task is interlinked among difference objects present in an image. For example, in our real time testing we observed that the labels of the objects detected were very much dependent on the surrounding labels and they changed when the surrounding labels changed. Figure 3 shows a comparison between the ground truth

Labels and detections of both of our algorithms. It clearly shows that YOLO is better than SSD. In Table 2, we can see that the average accuracy of both of our algorithms for the top 5 classes is 91.29% and 89.24% respectively, however because of the few instances of some of the other classes the mean average precision overall is 64.14% and 44.76%. One of the major reasons for SSD bad performance was its inability to detect small objects. While YOLO outperformed SSD on every turn, we noticed that some of the labels such as Vest (only 281 instances) and Swimsuit (27) had a very high precision (Fig. 4) in SSD. Data is truly the new gold, the true bench marking of any visual based AI algorithm and its corresponding dataset is the real world. Our excursion in this field has taught us that true test of an Artificial Intelligence (AI) is the real world. Data can be manipulated, and data sets can be designed for problems, and those datasets and algorithms can fail for other scenarios, but true test is real world deployment and that is why we plan to release our dataset and our trained algorithm for the readers to implement at their pleasure to truly test the depth of our work. This dataset is in its development stages, we plan to extend to incorporate age and gender into it. Also, we plan to increase the size of images to 20000 (Fig. 5).

Fig. 5. Some of the different types of images present in the dataset and their bounding box annotations.

References

1. Khushi, M., et al.: Automated classification and characterization of the mitotic spindle following knockdown of a mitosis-related protein. BMC Bioinform. **18**(16), 566 (2017)
2. Krizhevsky, A., Sutskever, I., Hinton, G.E.: ImageNet classification with deep convolutional neural networks. In: Advances in Neural Information Processing Systems (2012)
3. LeCun, Y., Bengio, Y., Hinton, G.: Deep learning. Nature **521**(7553), 436 (2015)
4. Chen, K.-T., Luo, J.: When fashion meets big data: discriminative mining of best selling clothing features. In: Proceedings of the 26th International Conference on World Wide Web Companion. International World Wide Web Conferences Steering Committee (2017)

5. Lao, B., Jagadeesh, K.: Convolutional neural networks for fashion classification and object detection. In: CCCV 2015: Computer Vision, pp. 120–129 (2016)
6. Divvala, S.K., Farhadi, A., Guestrin, C.: Learning everything about anything: webly-supervised visual concept learning. In: Proceedings of the IEEE Conference on Computer Vision and Pattern Recognition (2014)
7. Rohrbach, M., et al.: What helps where–and why? Semantic relatedness for knowledge transfer. In: 2010 IEEE Computer Society Conference on Computer Vision and Pattern Recognition. IEEE (2010)
8. Chen, H., et al.: Composite templates for cloth modeling and sketching. In: 2006 IEEE Computer Society Conference on Computer Vision and Pattern Recognition (CVPR 2006). IEEE (2006)
9. Ng, H.N., Grimsdale, R.L.: Computer graphics techniques for modeling cloth. IEEE Comput. Graph. Appl. **16**(5), 28–41 (1996)
10. Yamaguchi, K., Hadi Kiapour, M., Berg, T.L.: Paper doll parsing: Retrieving similar styles to parse clothing items. In: Proceedings of the IEEE International Conference on Computer Vision (2013)
11. Hasan, B., Hogg, D.C.: Segmentation using deformable spatial priors with application to clothing. In: BMVC (2010)
12. Wang, N., Ai, H.: Who blocks who: simultaneous clothing segmentation for grouping images. In: 2011 International Conference on Computer Vision. IEEE (2011)
13. Yang, M., Yu, K.: Real-time clothing recognition in surveillance videos. In: 2011 18th IEEE International Conference on Image Processing. IEEE (2011)
14. Packer, C., McAuley, J., Ramisa, A.: Visually-aware personalized recommendation using interpretable image representations. arXiv preprint arXiv:1806.09820 (2018)
15. Zhang, X., et al.: Trip outfits advisor: location-oriented clothing recommendation. IEEE Trans. Multimedia **19**(11), 2533–2544 (2017)
16. Chen, Q., et al.: Deep domain adaptation for describing people based on fine-grained clothing attributes. In: Proceedings of the IEEE Conference on Computer Vision and Pattern Recognition (2015)
17. Chen, H., Gallagher, A., Girod, B.: Describing clothing by semantic attributes. In: Fitzgibbon, A., Lazebnik, S., Perona, P., Sato, Y., Schmid, C. (eds.) ECCV 2012. LNCS, vol. 7574, pp. 609–623. Springer, Heidelberg (2012). https://doi.org/10.1007/978-3-642-33712-3_44
18. Bossard, L., Dantone, M., Leistner, C., Wengert, C., Quack, T., Van Gool, L.: Apparel classification with style. In: Lee, K.M., Matsushita, Y., Rehg, J.M., Hu, Z. (eds.) ACCV 2012. LNCS, vol. 7727, pp. 321–335. Springer, Heidelberg (2013). https://doi.org/10.1007/978-3-642-37447-0_25
19. He, Y., Yang, L., Chen, L.: Real-time fashion-guided clothing semantic parsing: a lightweight multi-scale inception neural network and benchmark. In: Workshops at the Thirty-First AAAI Conference on Artificial Intelligence (2017)
20. Liu, K.-H., Chen, T.-Y., Chen, C.-S.: MVC: a dataset for view-invariant clothing retrieval and attribute prediction. In: Proceedings of the 2016 ACM on International Conference on Multimedia Retrieval. ACM (2016)
21. Chao, X., et al.: A framework for robust feature selection for real-time fashion style recommendation. In: Proceedings of the 1st International Workshop on Interactive Multimedia for Consumer Electronics. ACM (2009)
22. Chang, C.-C., Wang, L.-L.: Color texture segmentation for clothing in a computer-aided fashion design system. Image Vis. Comput. **14**(9), 685–702 (1996)
23. Zhang, W., et al.: An intelligent fitting room using multi-camera perception. In: Proceedings of the 13th International Conference on Intelligent User Interfaces. ACM (2008)

24. Freixenet, J., Muñoz, X., Raba, D., Martí, J., Cufí, X.: Yet another survey on image segmentation: region and boundary information integration. In: Heyden, A., Sparr, G., Nielsen, M., Johansen, P. (eds.) ECCV 2002. LNCS, vol. 2352, pp. 408–422. Springer, Heidelberg (2002). https://doi.org/10.1007/3-540-47977-5_27

25. Dalal, N., Triggs, B.: Histograms of oriented gradients for human detection (2005)

26. Yang, J., et al.: Evaluating bag-of-visual-words representations in scene classification. In: Proceedings of the International Workshop on Workshop on Multimedia Information Retrieval. ACM (2007)

27. Adams, R., Bischof, L.: Seeded region growing. IEEE Trans. Pattern Anal. Mach. Intell. **16**(6), 641–647 (1994)

28. Liu, Z., et al.: DeepFashion: Powering robust clothes recognition and retrieval with rich annotations. In: Proceedings of the IEEE Conference on Computer Vision and Pattern Recognition (2016)

29. Hadi Kiapour, M., et al.: Where to buy it: matching street clothing photos in online shops. In: Proceedings of the IEEE International Conference on Computer Vision (2015)

30. Huang, J., et al.: Cross-domain image retrieval with a dual attribute-aware ranking network. In: Proceedings of the IEEE International Conference on Computer Vision (2015)

31. Ge, Y., et al., DeepFashion2: a versatile benchmark for detection, pose estimation, segmentation and re-identification of clothing images. arXiv preprint arXiv:1901.07973 (2019)

32. Liu, S., et al.: Fashion parsing with weak color-category labels. IEEE Trans. Multimedia **16**(1), 253–265 (2014)

33. Everingham, M., et al.: The Pascal visual object classes (VOC) challenge. Int. J. Comput. Vis. **88**(2), 303–338 (2010)

34. Bray, T., et al.: Extensible markup language (XML) 1.0. W3C recommendation, October 2000

35. Deng, J., et al.: ImageNet: a large-scale hierarchical image database. In: 2009 IEEE Conference on Computer Vision and Pattern Recognition. IEEE (2009)

36. Redmon, J., Farhadi, A.: Yolov3: an incremental improvement. arXiv preprint arXiv:1804.02767 (2018)

37. Redmon, J., et al.: You only look once: unified, real-time object detection. In: Proceedings of the IEEE Conference on Computer Vision and Pattern Recognition (2016)

38. Redmon, J., Farhadi, A.: YOLO9000: better, faster, stronger. In: Proceedings of the IEEE Conference on Computer Vision and Pattern Recognition (2017)

39. Liu, W., et al.: SSD: single shot multibox detector. In: Leibe, B., Matas, J., Sebe, N., Welling, M. (eds.) ECCV 2016. LNCS, vol. 9905, pp. 21–37. Springer, Cham (2016). https://doi.org/10.1007/978-3-319-46448-0_2

40. Ren, S., et al.: Faster R-CNN: towards real-time object detection with region proposal networks. In: Advances in Neural Information Processing Systems (2015)

41. Chollet, F.: Keras (2015)

42. Abadi, M., et al.: TensorFlow: a system for large-scale machine learning. In: 12th USENIX Symposium on Operating Systems Design and Implementation (OSDI 2016) (2016)

43. Khushi, M.: Benchmarking database performance for genomic data. J. Cell. Biochem. **116**(6), 877–883 (2015)

From Raw Signals to Human Skills Level in Physical Human-Robot Collaboration for Advanced-Manufacturing Applications

Katleen Blanchet[1,2]([✉]), Selma Kchir[1], Amel Bouzeghoub[2], Olivier Lebec[1], and Patrick Hède[1]

[1] CEA, LIST, 91190 Gif-sur-Yvette, France
{katleen.blanchet,selma.kchir,olivier.lebec,patrick.hede}@cea.fr
[2] Samovar, Télécom SudParis, Institut Polytechnique de Paris,
91120 Palaiseau, France
{katleen.blanchet,amel.bouzeghoub}@telecom-sudparis.eu

Abstract. Providing individualized assistance to a human when she/he is physically interacting with a robot is a challenge that necessarily entails user profiling. The identification of the human profile in advanced-manufacturing is only partially addressed in the literature, through either intrusive, or not fully transparent approaches. As on-the-job training has a negative impact on operators' working conditions, we specifically focus on their skills, and show that they can be observed in a non-intrusive way, through a data-driven approach to extract knowledge from the internal data of the robot. To this end, we have defined useful characteristics derived from raw data, called in this paper Key Skill Indicators (KSI), and have devised a user's skills model based on expert knowledge. Experiments from real cases show promising results, especially that our approach is able to distinguish more finely a skilled human from a novice, and that the latter would benefit from assistance regarding specific skills.

Keywords: Human-robot collaboration · User profiling · Skill level · Expertise · Non-intrusive method · Advanced-Manufacturing

1 Introduction

In manufacturing industry, operators perform repetitive tasks (e.g. assembly) at high frequency, sometimes entailing the carrying of heavy loads. This work has a significant impact on their health (pain, fatigue, illness, musculoskeletal disorders) and increases the risk of accidents and absences. To remedy this, collaborative robots are more and more used in manufacturing tasks to provide operators with a safe assistance and force control. They are primarily intended to augment and complete human capabilities in repetitive and painful tasks. However, human expertise and decision-making are still necessary to the task completion. This research work is carried out in this context of human-robot interaction and we specifically focus on physical Human-Robot Collaboration (pHRC) where the

© Springer Nature Switzerland AG 2019
T. Gedeon et al. (Eds.): ICONIP 2019, LNCS 11954, pp. 554–565, 2019.
https://doi.org/10.1007/978-3-030-36711-4_47

human is interacting in contact with the robot or with objects carried by the robot. As far as we know, human variability is in general not taken into account in the assistance provided by robots. Each operator performs the task at his/her own rhythm, under different specific conditions (more or less sensitive to noise, light) and with a proper control. Moreover, it is established in the literature that certain human factors such as on-the-job training [15] negatively affect the operator's working conditions and thus reduce their performance or, worse, lead to accidents. In addition, the operator's profile encompasses general characteristics, such as age or height, and also features that evolve dynamically as the task progresses, such as intentions, level of skills, and muscle fatigue. As long as the operator does not have a stable performance, the cause of any behaviour change is unclear. In this work, we will therefore focus on the operator's skill level, as we believe that this is the primary source of unsteady behaviour. Due to ethical and time constraints in an industrial setting, the following main challenges arise: How to assess online the skill level of operators in a *non-intrusive* (C1) fashion, i.e. no explicit operator monitoring?; How to provide a full *explainable* profile (C2)?

To our knowledge, few studies in the field of collaborative robotics have developed systems for inferring the user's profile while fulfilling our conditions. Some studies are based on the robot's internal attributes, including their force sensors [6], but only for the purpose of tracking the direction of the force applied by the human. They do not seek to obtain information from the operator profile at a higher semantic level.

As a result, our data-driven contribution is three-fold: (1) A general definition of expertise and a categorization of skill indicators for skill identification, (2) A model that attributes a score to the indicators extracted online from available raw signals of a collaborative robot; and (3) A comprehensive review of the operators skills level as a continuous value from 0 (novice) to 1 (expert), which can then be used to assist them in a personalized way.

The rest of the paper is organized as follows: Sect. 2 details the state of the art on skill level recognition. Our contribution is described in Sect. 3 and implemented in Sect. 4 through an experimental proof of concept. Section 5 concludes with perspectives.

2   Related Work

The user's skills level has been studied in many areas, from adaptive learning [13] to driving assistance [10]. We will focus solely on robotics. Even though user profiling has been the target of various researches in assistive robotics [16], and collaborative robotics [6,8,9,12,14], we found few work dealing specifically with human's skills. They mainly focus on determining human's personality, preferences, fatigue or intention, and rely mostly on external sensors (e.g. gloves, wearable suits, cameras), which is contrary to the non-intrusive criterion (C1). In [11], the authors have modeled user expertise during human-robot interaction through the observation of the user's actions and environment to assign a controller adapted to the skills level of the human. This method focuses on the robot controller adaptation, and does not define any skill indicator explicitly. The users only know that they are being assisted, but does not know why. This can hinder the person's learning because it is difficult to progress if we do not have a clear idea of the target level. In addition, some skills cannot be taught via the robot, but should be delivered as an advice. The authors of [5] focused on a welding task with a robot and highlighted the importance of impedance measurements to discern an expert welder from a novice welder. However, this feature is specific to the task at hand and even if it could be reused for other tasks, more knowledge needs to be added. Papers in medical field and particularly addressing laparoscopic skills [1–3] defined skill indicators and validated them, but their constraints and material are different (teleoperation or laparoscopic instruments). They do not use joint torques of the robot, nor the multiplicity of axes. They also work with simple tasks, with no need to divide them into subtasks, and only binary information (novice/expert or intermediary) are obtained from their indicators, which is not explicit enough to quantify the user skills. As far as we know, the C1 requirement (non-intrusive) is seldom considered. Only proposed a non-intrusive method, which is however not made fully understandable and transparent for the operator, nor general for any collaborative human-robot task (C2 not met).

3   User's Skills Model

In this work, we consider that a *task* is composed of a list of actions accomplished by either a human, a robot, or both, to achieve a goal, i.e. going from an initial state to a desired one. The actions can be atomic or complex, i.e. composed of other actions. In the latter case, we refer to them as subtasks. A *cycle* is a single execution of a task.

3.1   General Approach

Asking operators' online feedback is time-consuming and distracting, thus we need to study their behavior indirectly. Our contributions are then based on the indirect observation of the operator behavior during a given task by collecting the robot's internal raw signals, in particular its joints torque, position, and velocity, and any connected device that changes the robot state. Thus, the data collection method is non-intrusive compared to the existing approaches in the literature, since the operator is not equipped with any monitoring system nor his/her gestures monitored continuously by a camera. Only the efforts applied by the human on the robot and the robot movements generated by this contact are recorded. Any physical contact at any location can be detected, unlike with force sensor methods. Erden et al. [4] have demonstrated that this approach is a viable monitoring alternative in the context of physical human-robot collaboration. Indeed, the robot's response will capture the force exerted by the operator on it with a degree of uncertainty due to contact friction.

When the operator and the collaborative robot perform a task together, the robot's internal data are recorded in the background. Since not all the tasks/subtasks to be performed by the operator require the same skills, we cannot directly analyze the operator's skills over the entire task. Observation windows are therefore created, based on key events (task specific, e.g. pressing a button). This data decomposition is not unique. When a key event is triggered, the skill profile can be generated on the past observation window, through the extraction of features that we call Key Skill Indicators (KSIs) and a skill model which attributes a score to each indicator. This high-level knowledge can allow in the future to provide personalized assistance to the user. In the following, we explain the main steps of our approach.

3.2 Skills and Key Skill Indicators (KSI) Definitions

The operator must learn different skills to master a task. Within pHRC, we have identified 5 key skills (basic skills such as near vision, oral comprehension, dexterity, etc. are assumed to be acquired): the *rapidity*, the *movement* and *effort control*, the *robot/tool* and *task mastery*. We need an intermediary to get this high level information from the low level raw data. We have therefore defined a classification of useful features for each skill, called Key Skill Indicators (KSI) for assessing the operator's level of competence in any physical human-robot collaboration task (see Table 1 for an overview). The choice of the relevant KSI among those proposed is (sub)task specific. When it is not a dimensionless quantity, the units are specified in brackets.

Rapidity characterizes the quickness of human's movement. Time is the first measure that can be used to discriminate a novice, often slower, from a skilled operator, through two KSIs: the *starting time* ζ (s) of the subtask in the task time frame and the *completion time* θ (s), the duration of the subtask. In some cases, it may also be interesting to assess the motion speed (co-manipulation only) through the *maximal velocity* γ (rad/s) and *average velocity* α (rad/s) of the robot for each axis during the subtask performance. An expert will likely manipulate the robot towards the goal faster. In the context of pHRC, the operator exerts a force on the robot. The robot, depending on its mode, can either follow or guide the operator's movement (task of co-manipulation) or holds a given position. In any case, the robot response will reflect the effort applied by the human.

Movement Control (co-manipulation) encompasses the capacity of the operator to move the robot and to correctly coordinate his movements with it (co-manipulation). Since the effort applied by the human on the robot generates a displacement, we do not consider the effort but directly the trajectory. This skill can be identified through the two following KSIs. Note that the time is discretized, and that we consider $T = \frac{\theta}{t_e}$, where t_e is the sampling time, in the remaining of the paper.

- *Path length* λ_p is the robot's trajectory length along each axis a (x, y, z). A novice may choose a less direct path. It is normalized over the distance

Table 1. From low level (raw data) to high level of information (skills) - The list of indicators and data is not exhaustive, we assume that the robot is only equipped with a basic set of sensors.

Skills	Indicators	Raw data
Rapidity	Starting/Completion time	Timer
	Maximal/Average velocity	Joint velocity
Movement control	Path length	Joint position
	Motion smoothness	Joint acceleration
Effort control	Effort length	Joint torques or Actuator currents
	Maximal/Average effort	
Robot/tool mastery	Event(s)	Task-dependant: failure, gripper and button state, etc.
Task mastery	Order	Task dependant: Any useful data
	Repetition	
	Event(s)	Task-dependant: end of task, etc.

travelled to be robust to differences in start and end positions. The path length also involves the *orientation* ω of the end-effector ($\omega = \frac{angle\ travelled}{optimal\ angle}$). X is the Cartesian position.

$$\lambda_p = \frac{1}{|X_a(T) - X_a(1)|} \sum_{k=1}^{T} \sqrt{\sum_a (X_a(k) - X_a(k-1))^2} \tag{1}$$

- *Motion smoothness* σ (s^{-3}) is a measure of a change of acceleration based on the jerk j for each axis [7]. Indeed, a person who is not used to handle the robot may have jerky movements. The value is averaged over distance to account for differences in start and end positions.

$$\sigma_a = \frac{1}{|X_a(T) - X_a(1)|} \sqrt{\frac{1}{2} \sum_{k=1}^{T} j_a(k)^2} \tag{2}$$

Effort Control is the capacity of applying the right effort. In the case of a static robot, the force exerted by the operator on the robot or on an object held by the robot do not induce any movement. It is therefore necessary to evaluate the effort directly through these KSIs:

- *Effort length* λ_e (Nm) is the length of the considered robot joint q torque τ course. An experienced operator is supposed to have an optimal λ_e, acquired gradually by repeating the same movement.

$$\lambda_{e_q} = \sum_{k=1}^{T} |\tau_q(k) - \tau_q(k-1)| \tag{3}$$

– *Maximal effort* ν *(Nm)* and *average effort* μ *(Nm)* are the maximal and average values of the joint torque of the robot respectively. The optimal value of these criteria are task-specific, and can be either high or low, but novices usually do not know how to balance the effort they exert.

Robot/tool mastery is the capacity to use the robot or a tool properly (excluding motion). The associated KSIs are event-based and task-specific (e.g. when a button is pressed, the opening/closing of a gripper, the number of failures of the robot, changes of state/variation of specific data, etc.).

Task mastery is the capacity to remember and carry out the task steps. This skill can be measured through three KSIs: (1) *Repetition* δ, the number of repetitions of each task. A novice will tend to redo a subtask if she or he is unsuccessful the first time; (2) *Order o*, the order of completion of each subtask. A sequence of actions may be more efficient than another; (3) *Event(s)*, as for robot mastery skill, any task-specific event that points toward mastery of the task.

3.3   Level Estimation

A binary value of the operator's skills level is not very meaningful and can not be used to explain to the operator the key success or failure factors of the task achievement, nor to use the information for a future assistance. We have thus devised a method to rate the KSIs as a continuous value between 0 and 1.

Definition 1. *KSI level. Let S_u be the set of users, j the jth cycle of a given task of a user $u \in S_u$, r_i the reference behavior for the ith KSI, $b_{i,j}$ the measured behavior of user u for the ith KSI at cycle j, and $d_{ri}(x) \in [0,1]$ be an appropriate distance minimized when a measured behavior x is close to r_i. The ith KSI level l on a completed task of a given skill can be defined as:*

$$l_i(j) = 1 - d_{r_i}(b_{i,j}) \tag{4}$$

In order to be robust to human error, which is punctual and should have a limited impact on the person's KSI level, and therefore on her/his skill level, we have defined a cumulative average score.

Definition 2. *Cumulative average score. Let m and n be the mth and n^{th} cycles with $m < n$, and $w = n - m$ the observation window size (w should be large enough to be robust to deviations). The cumulative average level c of a KSI i on the nth cycle can be computed as:*

$$c_i(n) = \frac{1}{w} \sum_{j=m}^{n} l_i(j) \tag{5}$$

Definition 3. *Skill level. Let S_i^s be the set of indicators of skill s (of cardinality k), j the jth cycle of a given task carried out by a user $u \in S_u$. The skill level L of u can be defined as:*

$$L(j) = \frac{1}{k} \sum_{i \in S_i^s} c_i(j) \tag{6}$$

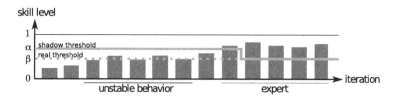

Fig. 1. To avoid repeated changes from novice to expert around β, we have artificially increased the threshold of expertise. We called the artificial threshold α the shadow skilled threshold. First, we have $\beta < \alpha$ and $\beta = \alpha$ when the operator masters the task.

Definition 4. *Skill mastering. Let β be a desired threshold. A user $u \in S_u$ masters a skill s on cycle j iff:*

$$\forall i \in S_i^s, c_i(j) \geq \beta \tag{7}$$

Then, we can derive what makes a user an expert of the task.

Definition 5. *A skilled/expert user. A user $u \in S_u$ is an expert if she/he masters all the skills that are required to perform the task correctly (Eq. (7) is verified for each skill). A user who does not comply to this definition is called a novice.*

We used a complementary asymmetrical Gaussian function for the distance d of Eq. (4). The distance is minimized when the measured behavior $x \in [\mu - \sigma_l, \mu + \sigma_u]$ and null when $x = \mu$, where μ, σ_l and σ_u are respectively the center, the lower and the upper standard deviations of the Gaussian.

$$d_{\mu,\sigma_l,\sigma_u}(x) = \begin{cases} 1 - \exp(-\frac{1}{2}\frac{(x-\mu)^2}{\sigma_l^2}) & \text{if } x \leq \mu \\ 1 - \exp(-\frac{1}{2}\frac{(x-\mu)^2}{\sigma_u^2}) & \text{if } x > \mu \end{cases} \tag{8}$$

The expert behavior on a given indicator cannot be restricted to an exact value, as human behaviour is not repeatable. We have defined an expert interval: any value between β and 1 denotes skilled behaviour (see Eq. (7) and Fig. 1). The lower/upper standard deviation $\sigma_{l/u}$ is then chosen to be computed as:

$$\sigma_{l/u} = \sqrt{-\frac{1}{2\ln\beta}(f_{l/u} - \mu)^2} \tag{9}$$

where $f_{l/u}$ is the desired lower/upper bound of the expert interval.

μ and $f_{l/u}$ can be obtained in two different ways, depending on whether or not data from a skilled operator are available. In the former, the median m, and the first and third quartile q_{25} and q_{25} respectively can be extracted from expert data. Then we can derive the reference behavior coefficients: $\mu = m$, $f_l = q_{25} - z \cdot iQr$, and $f_u = q_{75} + z \cdot iQr$, where iQr is the interquartile range between the third and first quartile and z is a weight representing the confidence in the expert data (the larger z is, the more the expert data is trusted). In the latter, i.e. without available expert data, expert knowledge of the task can be used to define the theoretical reference behaviour (e.g. no failure for the robot mastery skill). The ideal trajectory of human-robot motion can be calculated using a robotic trajectory generation model. Both methods can also be combined.

4   Results

We implemented two scenarios[1] to validate: (1) that it is feasible to discriminate between an expert and a novice through the skill indicators (first experiment), (2) that the skill level is consistent with the participants' experience (second experiment) and (3) that assistance would be beneficial to help participants to progress (both experiments).

4.1   Experimental Setup

Tasks Description. The first experiment was conducted with six volunteers aged from 15 to 25 years old (3 male and 3 female gender). All of them carried out the experiment during 20 cycles (around 30 min). The second one was completed with 9 participants aged from 19 to 32 years old (3 female and 6 male gender). They had around one hour to fill in questionnaires and carry out the task. In both cases, the task under consideration was explained to them with a practical demonstration. No feedback was given to them during the experiment, unless the participants were unable to continue without help. The participants of the first experiment had to fix two objects with screws on a steel bar held by a 3 motorized axis collaborative robot (Syb3 from Isybot[2]) in front of them (see Fig. 2(a)). The task could be divided into two subtasks, one per object (the users had to push a button - triggering event - between the sub-tasks to reorient the bar). At the end of the time period, they had to remove both objects to be able to start again (phase not recorded). The second experiment consisted of moving a 25 kg box from one pile to another using a collaborative robot[3]. This pick and place task was divided into 4 subtasks: *approach*, *pick up*, *move* and *place* the box.

Acquisition Procedure. During the first experiment (Scenario 1), the efforts data of the robot to stay in position while the operator was applying a stress on the bar were recorded each 10 ms on each axis of the robot (see Fig. 2). Since the scenario was new to the participants, we considered that their first 6 cycles were novice cycles and their last 6 were intermediate cycles. Besides, another participant[4] (male, 23 years old) repeated the task for more than 400 cycles (over several days) and was then considered as an expert of the task. We

---

[1] In the Interactive Robotics Laboratory of CEA, LIST premises.
[2] https://www.isybot.com/en/events/syb3/.
[3] Video available: https://youtu.be/sDP0sdgW9J0.
[4] The authors thank Clément Dugué for setting up the experiment.

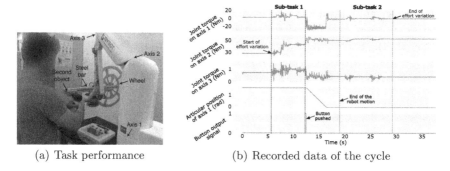

(a) Task performance   (b) Recorded data of the cycle

Fig. 2. Scenario 1: The operator fixes two objects on a steel bar hold by the robot (left). The robot data are recorded and divided in two subtasks (right).

gathered his expert cycles and used only from 5th to 13th cycle each day to avoid acclimation, and fatigue bias. The second experiment (Scenario 2) was carried out by volunteers with different experiences and thus did not all have time to perform the same number of cycles (from 16 to 32). The recorded data are the forces applied on the robot, its state, as well as the one of the effector, and the robot buttons and Human Machine Interface (HMI) state.

Skill Selection. Since the robot in scenario 1 holds an object in front of the user, no perceptible *movement* was detected during the pHRC. Only *rapidity* and *effort control* skills are therefore relevant for this task. On the other hand, in scenario 2, the human and the robot collaborate to move a box together. Since the efforts can be observed through the robot motions, we focus our analysis on the *movement control, robot mastery* and *rapidity* skills.

4.2   Results

Scenario 1. We verified using Mann Whitney U test (null hypothesis: data belong to the same population) that the novice and expert cycles were statistically different for each KSI. The hypothesis was rejected ($p < 0.05$) except for the average effort of axis 2 for the second subtask. The KSIs are therefore useful to distinguish an expert from a novice. On the contrary, according to the Wilcoxon sign-rank test (dependent paired sets since the novice and intermediate belong to the same group), there is no statistical difference between novices and intermediaries for most of the KSIs. This is visually corroborated in the Fig. 3. For instance, it can be noticed on both subtasks for the maximal effort on axis 3 (ν_3) that there is a little difference between the box plots of novice (N) and intermediary (I) operators. The values oscillate between the same range. The slow learning curve can be explained by the muscle fatigue accumulated by the wheel bearing and/or the lack of feedback. According to the maximal and average effort on axis 3 (ν_3 and μ_3) box plots visible on Fig. 3, the second subtask requires much more meticulousness and the expert hardly relied on the robot, whereas a novice had

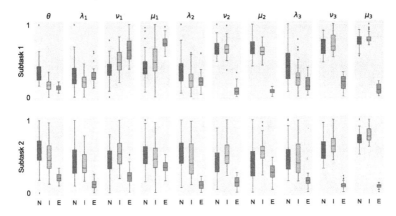

Fig. 3. Box plot of the variability and dispersion of the data for each KSI (colons) for each subtask (rows) and for each level of skills (N - Novice, I - Intermediary, E - Expert). Each box plot contains 36 examples. The central rectangle spans the interquartile range, while the segment inside represents the median. The lines that extend on both sides of the box include the remaining data. The dots show the outliers.

more trouble screwing and pressed harder. This is an interesting result, because unlike our method, even an attentive human supervisor could not easily perceive the effort applied by the operator and advise them accordingly.

Scenario 2. For scenario 2, we went further in the analysis and applied Eq. (6) to the KSIs to obtain the level of the different skills. We used the data of participant 9, familiar with the robot (see Table 2, as expert data). The results are displayed in Fig. 4. In light of Table 2, we can notice in Fig. 4 that the people most accustomed to interacting with robots are those who have finished the experiment (the last row of the bar plot contain data only for participants 6, 4, 8 and 9), and that the one who was not experienced at all (person 3) completed only two cycles of the 8-boxes task. The rapidity skill (based on the completion time and average velocity) score confirms these observations. By focusing on the levels of robot mastery, we can observe that the participants mostly improve over time. This skill is based on the number of impromptu pressing and releasing of buttons and failures recorded, and it appears that they understand why the latter appear by repeating the task multiple times. The movement control skill relies on the path length of the Cartesian positions and the orientation (the motion smoothness was not discriminating enough, the movement was too simple). Since the volunteers were mainly concentrated on the task and control of the robot, most did not seek to optimize their trajectory, which explains the lack of improvement. This highlights the need for help once more. Besides, 5 out of 6 people ('−' and '+' on Table 2) who were not familiar with the robot at the beginning of the experiment reported the need for assistance in their questionnaire.

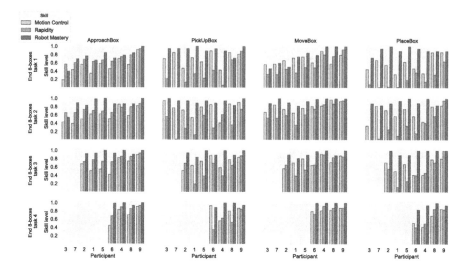

Fig. 4. Skill level of participants for three different skills over the four subtasks (the movement control was removed for pick up and place box since it requires small movements). The term task on the left refers to the transfer of 8 boxes (8 pick and place tasks). The scores were computed at each end of 8-boxes task, with $w = 8$ (Eq. (5)), to keep track of all pick and place tasks. Only four participants were able to accomplish the four 8-boxes tasks during the time allocated.

Table 2. Replies to questions asked in a questionnaire completed before the experiment. The '−' indicates no and the '+' yes (one for once or twice only, two for sometimes, and three for regularly).

Person	3	7, 2, 1, 5	6	4, 8	9
Have you ever manipulated a robotic arm?	−	+	++	+++	+++
Have you ever manipulated the robot used in the experiment?	−	−	+	++	+++

5 Conclusion and Future Work

In this work, we proposed a non-intrusive method to identify the operators' skill profiles based on the skills they need to practise. The explicitness is achieved by defining skill indicators, assessed at each end of task/subtask. We have thus addressed all the challenges raised in the introduction, and we have confirmed the process described in this paper by conducting real experiments.

We are currently working on the application of the skill and its indicators levels to provide the operator with personalized assistance (advice and/or change in robot behaviour). We believe that with our method, humans will be able to increase their skills faster and have more accurate feedback than those given by a human supervisor. We would also like to define and validate more skill indicators to study the coordinated movements of the operator and robot, which are difficult to characterize.

References

1. Chmarra, M.K., Klein, S., de Winter, J.C., Jansen, F.W., Dankelman, J.: Objective classification of residents based on their psychomotor laparoscopic skills. Surg. Endosc. **24**(5), 1031–1039 (2010)
2. Cotin, S., Stylopoulos, N., Ottensmeyer, M., Neumann, P., Rattner, D., Dawson, S.: Metrics for laparoscopic skills trainers: the weakest link!. In: Dohi, T., Kikinis, R. (eds.) MICCAI 2002. LNCS, vol. 2488, pp. 35–43. Springer, Heidelberg (2002). https://doi.org/10.1007/3-540-45786-0_5
3. Enayati, N., Ferrigno, G., De Momi, E.: Skill-based human-robot cooperation in tele-operated path tracking. Auton. Robot. **42**, 1–13 (2018)
4. Erden, M.S., Jonkman, J.A.: Physical human-robot interaction by observing actuator currents. Int. J. Robot. Autom. **27**(3), 233 (2012)
5. Erden, M.S., Billard, A.: End-point impedance measurements at human hand during interactive manual welding with robot. In: 2014 IEEE International Conference on Robotics and Automation (ICRA), pp. 126–133. IEEE (2014)
6. Gribovskaya, E., Kheddar, A., Billard, A.: Motion learning and adaptive impedance for robot control during physical interaction with humans. In: 2011 IEEE International Conference on Robotics and Automation (ICRA), pp. 4326–4332. IEEE (2011)
7. Hogan, N., Flash, T.: Moving gracefully: quantitative theories of motor coordination. Trends Neurosci. **10**(4), 170–174 (1987)
8. Kim, K.S., Sentis, L.: Human body part multicontact recognition and detection methodology. In: 2017 IEEE International Conference on Robotics and Automation (ICRA), pp. 1908–1915. IEEE (2017)
9. Kim, W., Lee, J., Peternel, L., Tsagarakis, N., Ajoudani, A.: Anticipatory robot assistance for the prevention of human static joint overloading in human-robot collaboration. IEEE Robot. Autom. Lett. **3**(1), 68–75 (2018)
10. Martinez, C.M., Heucke, M., Wang, F.Y., Gao, B., Cao, D.: Driving style recognition for intelligent vehicle control and advanced driver assistance: a survey. IEEE Trans. Intell. Transp. Syst. **19**(3), 666–676 (2018)
11. Milliken, L., Hollinger, G.A.: Modeling user expertise for choosing levels of shared autonomy. In: Robotics and Automation (ICRA), pp. 2285–2291. IEEE (2017)
12. Nikolaidis, S., Ramakrishnan, R., Gu, K., Shah, J.: Efficient model learning from joint-action demonstrations for human-robot collaborative tasks. In: Proceedings of the Tenth Annual ACM/IEEE International Conference on Human-Robot Interaction, pp. 189–196. ACM (2015)
13. Normadhi, N.B.A., Shuib, L., Nasir, H.N.M., Bimba, A., Idris, N., Balakrishnan, V.: Identification of personal traits in adaptive learning environment: systematic literature review. Comput. Educ. **130**, 168–190 (2019)
14. Peternel, L., Tsagarakis, N., Caldwell, D., Ajoudani, A.: Adaptation of robot physical behaviour to human fatigue in human-robot co-manipulation. In: 2016 IEEE-RAS 16th International Conference on Humanoid Robots, pp. 489–494 (2016)
15. Mahesa, R.R., Vinodkumar, M., Neethu, V.: Modeling the influence of individual and employment factors on musculoskeletal disorders in fabrication industry. Hum. Factors Ergon. Manuf. Serv. Ind. **27**(2), 116–125 (2017)
16. Rossi, S., Ferland, F., Tapus, A.: User profiling and behavioral adaptation for HRI: a survey. Pattern Recognit. Lett. **99**, 3–12 (2017)

Intelligent Image Retrieval Based on Multi-swarm of Particle Swarm Optimization and Relevance Feedback

Yingying Zhu[1], Yishan Chen[1], Wenlong Han[2], Qiang Huang[1(✉)], and Zhenkun Wen[1]

[1] College of Computer Science and Software Engineering, Shenzhen University, Shenzhen 518060, China
jameshq@szu.edu.cn
[2] Sangfor Technologies Inc., Shenzhen, China

Abstract. In recent years, Convolutional Neural Networks (CNNs) have promoted greatly the development of image retrieval, intelligent image retrieval still faces challenges. An intrinsic challenge in intelligent image retrieval exists the intention gap between the real intention of the users and the representation of users' query, besides the well-known semantic gap. To address these problems, we propose a novel method that incorporates a relevance feedback (RF) method with an evolutionary stochastic algorithm, called multi-swarm of particle swarm optimization (MPSO), as a way to grasp the users' perception of relevance through optimized iterative learning. One main component of our method, MPSO, can effectively prevent the retrieval system from falling into local optimal and dispose of those redundant particles, which can improve the diversity of particles. Moreover, we also present a simple but effective similarity ranking algorithm to increase retrieval speed, which can consider synthetically not only the fitness of each query point in feature space, but also the similarity of the image sequence corresponding to each query point. Extensive experiments on three publicly available datasets demonstrate that our method significantly improves the precision, recall as well as the user experience.

Keywords: Image retrieval · Particle swarm optimization · Relevance feedback · Intention gap

1 Introduction

With the explosive growth of image data on the Internet and intelligent terminals, there is a compelling need for effective image indexing and search. Most content-based image retrieval (CBIR) system allow users to provide an example image as the query according to their intentions. CBIR systems become more intelligent, because the well-known semantic gap between the computational low-level features and high-level semantics [13] has been further narrowed with

© Springer Nature Switzerland AG 2019
T. Gedeon et al. (Eds.): ICONIP 2019, LNCS 11954, pp. 566–578, 2019.
https://doi.org/10.1007/978-3-030-36711-4_48

the repaid advance of CNN technologies [9]. CBIR has still attracted significant attention in both academia and industry [21].

However, besides the well-known semantic gap, the intention gap lies between the representation of users' query/demand and the real intent of the users, which is becoming a major problem restricting the development of image retrieval. The cause of the intention gap is much more difficult to quantify as it is dependent on subjective human interpretation of image retrieval. The intention gap often leads to unsatisfactory search results, even with CNN. As shown in Fig. 1, users may have different intentions for the query image on the left. Some users' intentions are to find the woods with the query and expect the retrieval results like the top two images on the right, while others may want to search a dog and obtain the retrieval images like the bottom two images.

Fig. 1. Different users' intentions for the same image

Users' real search intention is difficult to measure and capture without users' participation and feedback. RF is developed to address this problem, which proved to be a powerful tool to iteratively collect information from the user and transform it into a semantic bias in the retrieval process [18]. Broilo *et al.* [3] embedded the RF process into a stochastic optimization engine (Particle Swarm Optimization, PSO) to provide a better exploration of the search space and avoid the stagnation in local minima. However, there are some critical issues yet unsolved. First, for swarm initialization, the initial position of swarm particles lacks diversity. Selecting the top-ranked images as the initial position is easy to miss the images with lower rank but relevant, while there are some redundant particles in the initial swarm. Second, during the process of matching the optimal solutions with images in the database, there exists the fact that the first-matched image in the second solution may be more relevant than the second-matched image in the best solution, and so on. In this case, the returned retrieval results may miss the more reluctant images. Last, because swarms need to match images in the database many times, leading to consuming much retrieval timing.

To address these problems and enhance the interactive search for complex queries, we propose a novel method that incorporates a RF method with MPSO. In comparison with all the related research as surveyed above, our proposed algorithm achieves the following advantages: (i) the image retrieval problem is formulated as an optimization problem, and MPSO is introduced into RF, which grasp the users' perception of relevance through optimized iterative learning; (ii) our method can not only expand the search scope of particles in the feature space so as to effectively improve the diversity of particles, but also dispose of those redundant particles; and (iii) a novel similarity ranking algorithm has combined the fitness of query points in feature space with the similarity of images in each images sequence corresponding to each query point to improve the retrieval efficiency.

The rest of this paper is organized as follows. Section 2 reviews some related work. The method is described in Sect. 3. Experiments are carried out in Sect. 4.

2   Related Work

We group related work into two dimensions: RF and optimization technologies.

In CBIR systems with RF, a user can mark returned images, which are then fed back into the systems as a new refined query for the next round of retrieval [12]. The process is repeated until user is satisfied with the query result. Generalized CBIR with RF model has different RF strategies such as query re-weighting (QR) [5–7,14] , query point movement (QPM) [14,15] , query expansion (QEX) [12]. More details and methods are shown in [12].

PSO inspired by the behavior of swarms of bees is a population-based stochastic technique that allows solving optimization problems [3]. PSO combines with RF can address some issues of RF techniques which is presented in [3]. A hybrid method has been proposed for image retrieval based on PSO and k-means clustering algorithms [19]. Zhou et al. [22] propose a CBIR approach by using multiple colour channels fusion and PSO. PSO is applied to launch weights fusion and obtain the final retrieval result. And [16] presents a hybrid optimization algorithm which originates from PSO and Support Vector Machine (SVM) to improve the speed and accuracy of image retrieval. [8] tries to embed PSO into its method to find the suitable similarity weighting constants.

There are some methods based on other optimization technologies. [20] describes a CBIR framework based on interactive differential evolution which combines the global and the local retrieval strategy to help users retrieve their preferred images in a user-oriented way. [1] gives a solution for image indexing and similarity ranking by introducing a firefly optimization combined Decision Tree (FF-DT) classifier to reduce the computational complexity in feature extraction. A new non-dominated sorting based on multi-objective whale optimization algorithm is proposed for feature selection in [2].

3   Proposed Method

3.1   Framework

The framework of image retrieval using MPSO and RF is shown in Fig. 2. MPSO-RF includes two iteraive processes: feature re-weighing process and optimization process. Specifically, users select an image as the query and the image retrieval system compares and sorts the similarity between the query and images in the

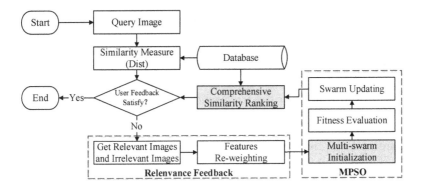

Fig. 2. Flowchart of the proposed method

whole database according to a similarity metric. To this purpose, each image (included the query) is already mapped into a feature vector. We define feature vector of image i as $f_i = [f_i^1, f_i^2, \cdots, f_i^n]$, where n means the dimension of a feature vector and the database has n_{DB} images. All vectors form a matrix $F_{n_{DB}}$. The similarity between the query and image is calculated as a weighted Euclidean distance (see Eq. (1)) computed among feature vector pairs [10]. The weights are all equal to 1 initially.

$$Dist(x, y, w) = \frac{1}{n} \sum_{d=1}^{n} (x^d - y^d)^2 * w^d \qquad (1)$$

Then, the n_{FB} (the number of images retrieved) nearest images are presented to users for feedback. Users label each retrieved image as relevant or irrelevant so that two image subsets are created, which makes it possible to perform feature re-weighting and multi-swarm updating. The optimization process makes the particles of multi-swarm, represented by feature vectors, move towards relevant samples and far away from irrelevant ones in the feature space. As a result, it obtains particles sorted by the fitness.

It is worth noting that the particles are virtual points in feature space, which means they are not represent to any image in the database. They are the optimal solutions obtained by the optimization process and regarded as the query points to search for relevant images in the next step. These query points need to be matched one by one with the features in the database, where every point corresponds to a similar images sequence. Each similar images sequence is a ranking obtained by sorting similarity computed with Eq. (1) (with updated weights) in descending order. The system executes comprehensive similarity to rank the whole database considering fitness and similarity. A new ranking is proposed and the system provides the top n_{FB} images of this ranking for new user feedback. The process is then iterated until convergence.

The whole feature re-weighing process is the same as that in [3], the feature weights are iteratively specified to fit the users' intentions. According to the two subsets of images, the discriminant ratio δ is used to allow the system to understand which features can discriminate relevant and irrelevant images better. The main idea is to calculate the ability of each dimension feature in separating irrelevant images from relevant ones [17]. First, we calculate the value range of each dimension feature in the relevant image set F_r, and then count the number $\phi^d_{N_{F_{ir}}}$ of each dimension feature in the irrelevant image set F_{ir} in the corresponding value range. Then the discriminant ratio δ_d of each dimension can be calculated by Eq. (2), where $N_{F_{ir}}$ is the cardinality of F_{ir}. As shown in Eq. (3), feature weights are updated through the discriminant ratio δ_d and standard deviation $\sigma^d_{F_r}$ of each dimension feature in the relevant image set.

$$\delta_d = 1 - \frac{\phi^d_{N_{F_{ir}}}}{N_{F_{ir}}} \tag{2}$$

$$w_d = \frac{\delta_d}{\sigma^d_{F_r}} \tag{3}$$

In parallel, the optimization process is carried out by constantly updating the multi-swarm, which progressively converges to the image cluster that contains the best solutions found across iterations [3]. We define the particles of the multi-swarm as points in feature space. Each swarm X has m particles. Initially, particles are associated to feature vectors according to RF, as shown in Eq. (4). How to obtain these feature vectors are shown in Sect. 3.2.

$$X = \begin{bmatrix} x_1^1 & x_1^2 & \cdots & x_1^n \\ x_2^1 & x_2^2 & \cdots & x_2^n \\ \vdots & \vdots & \ddots & \vdots \\ x_m^1 & x_m^2 & \cdots & x_m^n \end{bmatrix} = F_m = \begin{bmatrix} f_1^1 & f_1^2 & \cdots & f_1^n \\ f_2^1 & f_2^2 & \cdots & f_2^n \\ \vdots & \vdots & \ddots & \vdots \\ f_m^1 & f_m^2 & \cdots & f_m^n \end{bmatrix} \tag{4}$$

Then, we set each particles to the initial speed vector $v = [v_1, \cdots, v_d, \cdots, v_n]$ using $v_d = \sigma^d_{F_r} * rand()$, where $\sigma^d_{F_r}$ is the standard deviation of the d dimensional features in the relevant image set and $rand()$ can generate a random number between -1 and 1. It indicates the association between the swarm particles and relevant images. The larger $\sigma^d_{F_r}$ is, the bigger the fluctuation of the d dimensional feature is, and the higher speed is given.

After multi-swarm initialization, we define a fitness function to evaluate performance of all particles:

$$f(x_i) = \min_{f_i \in F_r} \{\sum_{d=1}^{n} |\frac{f_i^d - x_i^d}{\Delta f^d}| * w^d\} - \min_{f_i \in F_{ir}} \{\sum_{d=1}^{n} |\frac{f_i^d - x_i^d}{\Delta f^d}| * w^d\} \tag{5}$$

where Δf^d is the d dimensional feature value range. The particles x_i is the point inside feature space so the fitness function indicates the fitness is lower and the position of the particle is better when the particle comes closer to relevant images and is farther from irrelevant images.

Having defined initial position and speed of the particles, we need to set the personal best (pbest) and the global best (gbest) for the optimization process. At the end of the optimization process, each particle holds a pbest $p_i = x_i$ and corresponding pbest fitness is $fit_{p_i} = f(x_i)$. The global best is the best position among each swarm, which means $p_g = \min\{p_1, p_2, \cdots, p_m\}$ and corresponding global best fitness is $fit_{p_g} = f(p_g)$.

When all parameters are set, the particles then can start to search possible relevant images in the feature space. This optimization process is the same as a typical particle swarm optimization algorithm. The speed and position of each particle is updated according to Eqs.(6) and (7):

$$v_i^k = w * v_i^{k-1} + c_1 * r_1 * (p_i^k - x_i^{k-1}) + c_2 * r_2 * (p_g^k - x_i^{k-1}) \tag{6}$$

$$x_i^k = x_i^{k-1} + v_i^k \tag{7}$$

where k means the kth iteration and w is an *inertial weight* parameter; r_1 and r_2 are random numbers between 0 and 1; c_1 and c_2 are two positive constants called acceleration coefficients, aimeing at pulling the particle towards the position related to the cognitive (i.e., pbest p_i^k) or social part (i.e., gbest p_g^k) [3]. And pbest and gbest of the swarm are updated as follows:

$$p_i^k = \{ \begin{array}{ll} x_i^k & if\ f(x_i^k) \leq f(p_i^{k-1}) \\ p_i^{k-1} & if\ f(x_i^k) \geq f(p_i^{k-1}) \end{array} \tag{8}$$

$$p_g = \min\{p_i\} \quad (0 \leq i \leq m) \tag{9}$$

Each time the swarm is updated, and all particles are sorted by the fitness. After that, the particles are the optimal solutions obtained by MPSO and regarded as the query points. MPSO-RF makes use of multi-swarm to expand further the search space and brings the system more relevant results.

3.2 Multi-swarm Initialization

MPSO expands the search space and prevents the retrieval process from falling into the stagnation in local minima, so that the system can increase the diversity of the results. Query points are obtained through MPSO. In order to expand the search space of query points, it is very important to select the initial positions of the multi-swarm. Nevertheless, it will result in the loss of the images that are lower-ranked but relevant by only selecting the feature vectors of the top-ranked images in the retrieval results as the initial position. This is because most of the top-ranked images are similar to each other, so there are some redundant particles in the initialized multi-swarm.

$$D_i = \sum_{k=1}^{N_{F_r}} Dist(f_i, f_k, w) \tag{10}$$

To address this problem, we use the following steps to choose these initial positions:

(i) for the relevant image feature set F_r obtained from RF, the sum D_i of the distance between each feature vector f_i and other feature vectors in F_r is calculated according to Eqs.(1) and (10). When D_i is minimum, its corresponding feature vector has the highest density of F_r, which is denote as point x_1;

(ii) the point x_2 with the greatest distance x_1 in the F_r will be obtained according to Eq.(1);

(iii) according to Eq.(10), x_3 with the maximum sum of distance will also be calculated, and so on. l points will form point set P, as shown in Fig. 3. Generally, $l = 5$;

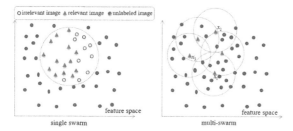

Fig. 3. The different search spaces of single-swarm and multi-swarm

(iv) the points in point set P are regarded as the initial positions of multi-swarm particles. After initialization, the particles are continuously updated in the feature space on the basis of the method described in 3.1. Finally, the particles with lower fitness are selected as query points.

Compared to the single swarm, multiple swarms greatly increase the search space of particles in the feature space, as shown in Fig. 3. Therefore, the search space of query points are greatly expanded. This is equivalent to the second expansion of the original query point: the first time a single query point is expanded to obtain the point set P; the second time multi-swarm based on point set P is used to expand. After these two expansion, the retrieval scope of the system is greatly increased, so that more relevant images can be retrieved.

3.3 Comprehensive Similarity

As above mentioned, the query points sorted by the fitness need to be matched with the images in the database. According to Eq.(1), we can calculate the distance between each query point and feature vectors. Each query point corresponds to a similar images sequence as shown in the left of Fig. 4. The system needs to return a similarity ranking to the users. How to integrate these similar images sequences into a single similarity ranking? [3] obtains the similarity ranking by sorting query points according to the fitness and getting the best-matched images of each query point. However, there is a possibility that the second similar image matched with the first query point (the purple "image" in Fig. 4) is less similar than the green "image" in the second sequence corresponding to the second query point. [3] did not consider how large the fitness gap was between two query points. Therefore, the similar image ranking can not reflect the overall similarity of the images accurately.

Our solution considers not only the fitness of each query point but also the similarity of the image in the similar images sequence corresponding to query point. It is a compositive similarity ranking method called comprehensive similarity, as shown in the following steps.

(i) First, the similarity of the images in each similar image sequence is normalized according to Eq.(11). $S_{sub}^{j}(I_i)$ is the similarity of image I_i in the jth similar image sequence after normalization.

$$S_{sub}^{j}(I_i) = \frac{S_{sub}^{j}(I_i) - min(S_{sub}^{j})}{max(S_{sub}^{j}) - min(S_{sub}^{j})} \tag{11}$$

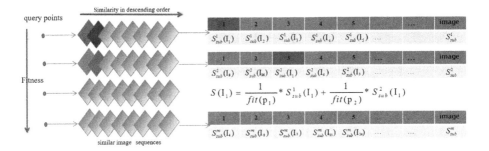

Fig. 4. The calculation process of the comprehensive similarity (Color figure online)

(ii) Considering that query points may be matched with the same image, we obtain the comprehensive similarity of each image by summing the similarity of the same image in the similar image sequences according to Eq.(12). The weight is the fitness of the corresponding query point, m is the number of query points and $S(I_i)$ is the comprehensive similarity of image I_i in all sequences.

$$S(I_i) = \sum_{j=1}^{m} \frac{1}{fit(p_j)} * S_{sub}^{j}(I_i) \tag{12}$$

The calculation process of the comprehensive similarity is shown in Fig. 4, where the orange color indicates that the same image is in different similar image sequences. We can find that the first and second query points have been matched with this image. Summing the similarity of this image in sequence one and sequence two can obtain this image's comprehensive similarity. If the query point itself has better fitness, the comprehensive similarity of the images matched with it is relatively high. At the same time, if several query points are matched with the same image, this image is more likely to be the returned result whose comprehensive similarity is also higher. Compared with the sorting method in [3], our comprehensive similarity ranking method is more comprehensive.

4   Experiment

The dataset we use contains 70 image classes from Caltech-256[1] and Corel-10K[2], 30 image classes from ImageCLEF[3]. Each class has 100 images, so this database has 10000 images totally. Meanwhile, we choose three different features to test our method. The three features are traditional image features (contained 24-dimensional color histogram, 8-dimensional texture feature, 16-dimensional edge histogram), BoW feature (extract SIFT descriptors from image and use Bag-of-Words to get the 100-dimensional feature) and deep features (extracted from VGG16 [11]). Except for Sect. 4.2, the features we used are traditional image features. Considering that MPSO-RF is a random algorithm, our experiments randomly select 20 images from each image class as the queries, and each query is retrieved 5 times and the five retrieval results are averaged.

---

[1] http://www.vision.caltech.edu/Image_Datasets/Caltech256/.
[2] http://www.ci.gxnu.edu.cn/cbir/Dataset.aspx.
[3] https://www.imageclef.org/.

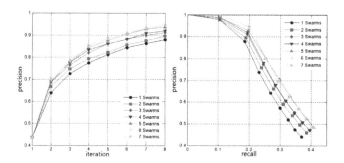

Fig. 5. The influence of the number of swarms on precision and recall

4.1   Parameters Tuning

In this paper, we use MPSO to expand search space of the retrieval system, so the number of swarms has a great impact on the retrieval system. Figure 5 describes the influence of swarm number, in which MPSO-RF is equivalent to PSO-RF [3] when only one swarm is applied. With the increase of swarm number, precision and recall are increasing, which implies the retrieval system is obviously improved. However, when the number exceeds 5, the retrieval performance almost stops improving. The main reason is that the diversity of images is limited in the same image class. The purpose of expanding the search space by MPSO is to cover the diversity of all images within the image class as far as possible. Therefore, when the swarm number exceeds a certain upper limit, the performance improvement almost stops as the number of swarms increases or even reduces the retrieval speed. In general, considering the tradeoff between diversity and speed, the swarm number is set to 5.

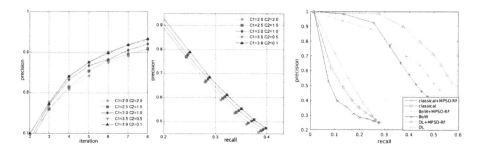

Fig. 6. The influence of the parameters c_1 and c_2

Fig. 7. The performance comparison under different features

Figure 6 illustrates the influence of the individual cognitive coefficient (c_1) and the social cognitive coefficient (c_2) of our method. c_1 and c_2 are important parameters of PSO and PSO-based image retrieval algorithms. c_1 and c_2 are set to $c_1 + c_2 \leq 4$, which has been verified by [4]. When c_1 is larger and c_2 is smaller, the retrieval performance is better. Because c_2 enhances the ability of information sharing among particles, thus preventing the optimization algorithm from falling into local minima, and c_1 enhances the individual search capability of particles so that particles can find more solutions around themselves. Multiple swarms expand the search space and prevent the search process from falling into local minima, and give each particle a larger individual search capability, thus making the retrieval results better. Figure 6 displays that the precision and recall of our method are the best when $c_1 = 3.5$ and $c_2 = 0.5$.

4.2   Proposed Method Under Different Features

This experiment is to verify MPSO-RF can improve the retrieval result under different features; i.e., it is non-sensitive to image features. Three kinds of features are adopted to test the performance of our method. These three features have been mentioned in Sect. 4. Figure 7 illustrates the precision-recall curves of three features with and without MPSO-RF. It is apparent that all features with MPSO-RF perform better than that without MPSO-RF. And the performance of deep features with MPSO-RF is the best, whose precision can reach 98%. The result shows MPSO-RF can improve the retrieval performance significantly.

4.3   Compared to State-of-the-art

This experiment is designed to compare MPSO-RF with other state-of-the-art methods to verify the effectiveness. The selected reference algorithms include: QPM and QPM+AR [12], PSO-RF [3]. Figure 8 is the precision and PR curves of the above four retrieval methods.

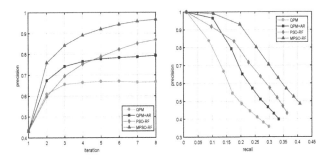

Fig. 8. The performance comparsion on precision and PR-curve of different methods

Compared with PSO-RF, the precision of MPSO-RF increases by nearly 10%. We can also find that the precision of MPSO-RF increases rapidly throughout the process of iteration, while the precision of PSO-RF increases rapidly at first, but hardly increases in the following several iterations. This is due to the lack of diversity of particles in PSO-RF, and the algorithm is prone to fall into local minima after several iterations of the retrieval process. This phenomenon is more obvious when the images even within the same class are diversiform. Our MPSO-RF avoids the stagnation of the retrieval process effectively. Accoring to Fig. 8, we can observe that when the image retrieval algorithms based on RF are deterministic [3], it is easy to fall into stagnation after several iterations (4 in Fig. 8). Even if the retrieval system continues to iterate, the

Table 1. Average run-time for a single iteration(s)

n_{FB}	PSO-RF	MPSO-RF: swarm number					
		1	2	3	4	5	6
10	0.48	0.11	0.23	0.31	0.41	0.53	0.65
20	0.95	0.11	0.23	0.31	0.41	0.53	0.65
30	1.42	0.11	0.23	0.31	0.41	0.53	0.65
40	1.92	0.11	0.23	0.31	0.41	0.53	0.65
50	2.41	0.11	0.23	0.31	0.41	0.53	0.65
60	2.89	0.11	0.23	0.31	0.14	0.53	0.65
70	3.35	0.11	0.23	0.31	0.41	0.53	0.65
80	3.84	0.11	0.23	0.31	0.41	0.53	0.65

improvement of the retrieval performance is limited. The iteration process of PSO-RF and MPSO-RF are based on stochastic particle swarm optimization, which can effectively prevent this situation. Therefore, with the increase of iteration, the precision is increasing. Nevertheless, the query points extended by PSO-RF lack the diversity, so their precision grows not as fast as MPSO-RF.

The PR curves reflect the performance of the retrieval system. The closer the curve is to the upper right corner of the coordinate axis, the better the retrieval performance is. We can observe that MPSO-RF is obviously better than other methods, which proves the feasibility and superiority of our method.

Table 1 compares the retrieval efficiency of PSO-RF and MPSO-RF, where n_{FB} is the number of images retrieved. When the retrieval system needs to return 10 images, PSO-RF takes 0.48 s for each iteration, but our method takes from 0.11 to 0.65 s relying on different the number of swarms. Moreover, as n_{FB} increases, PSO-RF consumes much more time than our method. If eighty images need to be returned, PSO-RF takes 3.84 s, while our method still remains from 0.11 to 0.65 s. Because PSO-RF maps each particle to only one image, so that the retrieval system needs to return many similar images, which cause it to need many query point and need to match with the database many times, which is time-consuming. Our method maps each particle to one similar images sequence and re-ranks them with a comprehensive similarity ranking method, which reduces the number of matching between the particles and the database. Therefore, compared with PSO-RF, the retrieval efficiency of our method has been significantly improved.

5 Conclusion

To narrow the intention gap of image retrieval, a novel method that incorporates relevance feedback (RF) with multi-swarm of particle swarm optimization (MPSO) is presented, which applies feedback to drive a feature re-weighting and optimization. MPSO can help system select the initial position of the multi-swarm particles to improve diversity and reduce computational complexity. In addition, comprehensive similarity we proposed is used to re-rank the images by combining the fitness of each solution and the similarity of each image of corresponding to each solution. Experimental results on three public datasets show the effectiveness of the proposed method.

Acknowledgement. This work was supported by: (i) National Natural Science Foundation of China (Grant No. 61602314); (ii) Natural Science Foundation of Guangdong Province of China (Grant No. 2016A030313043); (iii) Fundamental Research Project in the Science and Technology Plan of Shenzhen (Grant No. JCYJ20160331114551175).

References

1. Anjali, T., Rakesh, N., Akshay, K.M.P.: A novel based decision tree for content based image retrieval: an optimal classification approach. In: 2018 International Conference on Communication and Signal Processing (ICCSP), pp. 0698–0704. April 2018. https://doi.org/10.1109/ICCSP.2018.8524326

2. Aziz, M.A.E., Ewees, A.A., Hassanien, A.E.: Multi-objective whale optimization algorithm for content-based image retrieval. Multimedia Tools Appl. **77**(19), 26135–26172 (2018). https://doi.org/10.1007/s11042-018-5840-9

3. Broilo, M., Rocca, P., De Natale, F.G.B.: Content-based image retrieval by a semi-supervised particle swarm optimization. In: 2008 IEEE 10th Workshop on Multimedia Signal Processing, pp. 666–671, October 2008

4. Clerc, M., Kennedy, J.: The particle swarm - explosion, stability, and convergence in a multidimensional complex space. IEEE Trans. Evol. Comput. **6**(1), 58–73 (2002). https://doi.org/10.1109/4235.985692

5. Djordjevic, D., Izquierdo, E.: An object- and user-driven system for semantic-based image annotation and retrieval. IEEE Trans. Circ. Syst. Video Technol. **17**(3), 313–323 (2007)

6. Grigorova, A., Natale, F.G.B.D., Dagli, C., Huang, T.S.: Content-based image retrieval by feature adaptation and relevance feedback. IEEE Trans. Multimedia **9**(6), 1183–1192 (2007)

7. Kherfi, M.L., Ziou, D.: Image retrieval based on feature weighting and relevance feedback. In: 2004 International Conference on Image Processing, 2004. ICIP 2004. vol. 1, pp. 689–692. Vol. 1 (Oct 2004). https://doi.org/10.1109/ICIP.2004.1418848

8. Liu, P., Guo, J.M., Chamnongthai, K., Prasetyo, H.: Fusion of color histogram and LBP-based features for texture image retrieval and classification. Inf. Sci. **390**, 95–111 (2017)

9. Radenović, F., Tolias, G., Chum, O.: Fine-tuning CNN image retrieval with no human annotation. TPAMI (2018)

10. Rocchio, J.: Relevance feedback in information retrieval. The SMART Retrieval System: Experiments in Automatic Document Processing pp. 313–323 (1971)

11. Simonyan, K., Zisserman, A.: Very Deep Convolutional Networks for Large-Scale Image Recognition (sep 2014), http://arxiv.org/abs/1409.1556

12. Sivakamasundari, G., Seenivasagam, V.: Different relevance feedback techniques in CBIR: a survey and comparative study. In: International Conference on Computing (2012)

13. Smeulders, A.W.M., Worring, M., Santini, S., Gupta, A., Jain, R.: Content-based image retrieval at the end of the early years. IEEE Trans. Pattern Anal. Mach. Intell. **22**(12), 1349–1380 (2000)

14. Su, J.H., Huang, W.J., Yu, P.S., Tseng, V.S.: Efficient relevance feedback for content-based image retrieval by mining user navigation patterns. IEEE Trans. Knowl. Data Eng. **23**(3), 360–372 (2011)

15. Tian, Q., Hong, P., Huang, T.S.: Update relevant image weights for content-based image retrieval using support vector machines. In: 2000 IEEE International Conference on Multimedia and Expo. ICME2000. Proceedings. Latest Advances in the Fast Changing World of Multimedia (Cat. No.00TH8532), vol. 2, pp. 1199–1202 (2000)

16. Wang, X., Luo, G., Qin, K., Chen, A.: A Hybrid PSO and SVM algorithm for content based image retrieval. In: Gervasi, O., Murgante, B., Misra, S., Rocha, A.M.A.C., Torre, C., Taniar, D., Apduhan, B.O., Stankova, E., Wang, S. (eds.) ICCSA 2016. LNCS, vol. 9786, pp. 583–591. Springer, Cham (2016). https://doi.org/10.1007/978-3-319-42085-1_48

17. Wu, Y., Zhang, A.: A feature re-weighting approach for relevance feedback in image retrieval. In: Proceedings. International Conference on Image Processing, vol. 2, p. II (2002). https://doi.org/10.1109/ICIP.2002.1040017

18. Yong, R., Huang, T.S., Ortega, M., Mehrotra, S.: Relevance feedback: a power tool for interactive content-based image retrieval. IEEE Trans. Circ. Syst. Video Technol. 8(5), 644–655 (1998)

19. Younus, Z.S., et al.: Content-based image retrieval using PSO and k-means clustering algorithm. Arabian J. Geosci. 8(8), 6211–6224 (2015)

20. Yu, F., Li, Y., Wei, B., Kuang, L.: Interactive differential evolution for user-oriented image retrieval system. Soft Comput. 20(2), 449–463 (2016)

21. Zheng, L., Yang, Y., Tian, Q.: SIFT Meets CNN: a decade survey of instance retrieval. IEEE Trans. Pattern Anal. Mach. Intell. 40(5), 1224–1244 (2018). https://doi.org/10.1109/TPAMI.2017.2709749

22. Zou, Y., Li, C., Shirahama, K., Jiang, T., Grzegorzek, M.: Environmental microorganism image retrieval using multiple colour channels fusion and particle swarm optimisation. In: 2016 IEEE International Conference on Image Processing (ICIP). pp. 2475–2479. September 2016. https://doi.org/10.1109/ICIP.2016.7532804

Achieving Human–Robot Collaboration with Dynamic Goal Inference by Gradient Descent

Shingo Murata[1,2]([✉]), Wataru Masuda[3], Jiayi Chen[3], Hiroaki Arie[4],
Tetsuya Ogata[5], and Shigeki Sugano[3]

[1] Principles of Informatics Research Division,
National Institute of Informatics, Tokyo, Japan
mrt@nii.ac.jp
[2] Department of Informatics, The Graduate University for Advanced Studies
(SOKENDAI), Tokyo, Japan
[3] Department of Modern Mechanical Engineering, Waseda University, Tokyo, Japan
[4] Future Robotics Organization, Waseda University, Tokyo, Japan
[5] Department of Intermedia Art and Science, Waseda University, Tokyo, Japan

Abstract. Collaboration with a human partner is a challenging task expected of intelligent robots. To realize this, robots need the ability to share a particular goal with a human and dynamically infer whether the goal state is changed by the human. In this paper, we propose a neural network-based computational framework with a gradient-based optimization of the goal state that enables robots to achieve this ability. The proposed framework consists of convolutional variational autoencoders (ConvVAEs) and a recurrent neural network (RNN) with a long short-term memory (LSTM) architecture that learns to map a given goal image for collaboration to visuomotor predictions. More specifically, visual and goal feature states are first extracted by the encoder of the respective ConvVAEs. Visual feature and motor predictions are then generated by the LSTM based on their current state and are conditioned according to the extracted goal feature state. During collaboration after the learning process, the goal feature state is optimized by gradient descent to minimize errors between the predicted and actual visual feature states. This enables the robot to dynamically infer situational (goal) changes of the human partner from visual observations alone. The proposed framework is evaluated by conducting experiments on a human–robot collaboration task involving object assembly. Experimental results demonstrate that a robot equipped with the proposed framework can collaborate with a human partner through dynamic goal inference even when the situation is ambiguous.

Keywords: Human–robot collaboration · Robot learning · Deep learning · Predictive coding · Prediction error minimization

© Springer Nature Switzerland AG 2019
T. Gedeon et al. (Eds.): ICONIP 2019, LNCS 11954, pp. 579–590, 2019.
https://doi.org/10.1007/978-3-030-36711-4_49

1   Introduction

Collaboration with a human partner in everyday situations is a challenging task expected of intelligent robots. Unlike manufacturing robots which need only to repeat the same action sequence, collaborative robots must generate different action sequences in response to their surrounding environment and human partner. When humans perform collaborative tasks such as assembling things or cooking, they usually first share a particular goal with their partner. Based on this shared goal, subtasks for achieving the goal are considered and then each subtask is performed by one or both of the partners sequentially. During task execution, the partner may change the shared goal or realize that achieving the initial goal is inherently difficult due to unforeseen obstacles. In these cases, the partner's changed goal must be inferred, for example, from visual observations such as the present state of the environment and/or the partner. Of course, the use of a more explicit means such as verbal communication is also possible. However, partners do not always state their goal or plan during collaboration if it can be inferred visually. In this study, we consider equipping collaborative robots with the ability to share and infer goals dynamically from visual observations.

Machine-learning-based approaches such as probabilistic modeling [1] and neural network-based modeling [2] have previously been used to realize human–robot collaboration. For example, our previous work demonstrated that a single hierarchical recurrent neural network (RNN) can realize different levels of adaptability for collaboration. However, the goals of the collaboration were shared in the form of a predetermined abstracted vector input to the RNN and the goals were assumed to be static. Tani and others [3,4] have proposed the so-called error regression scheme (ERS) that can dynamically optimize the vector input to suit the environmental situation. This can be viewed as an RNN-based implementation of predictive coding [5] or predictive processing [6]. The vector input is updated by gradient-based optimization to minimize visual prediction errors. Thanks to the integrative learning of visuomotor information, this optimization realizes robots that can adapt to situational changes. Recently, in the field of deep learning, a similar gradient-based optimization has been applied to planning by simulated agents [7,8].

In the present study, we speculate that the approach of using gradient-based optimization can also be applied to the context of human–robot collaboration. We consider a neural network-based computational framework that enables a robot to perform collaborative tasks with a human partner by sharing particular goal information such as an image of the final state of object assembly. Instead of using the predetermined abstracted vector input adopted in the previous work, we consider directly mapping a goal image to visuomotor predictions. More specifically, generated visual predictions are compared with actual images and the prediction errors between them are computed. The initial goal information is modified by gradient descent to minimize errors. This enables the robot to dynamically infer the situational (goal) changes of the human partner from visual observations alone. The proposed framework is validated by conducting experiments on a human–robot collaboration task involving object assembly.

2   Computational Framework

Assume that we can access information about an environmental state, including the human state, as visual image V_t and robot motor state m_t at each time step t, and the final goal state as goal image G. We consider a computational framework that can learn to generate visual image and motor predictions ($\hat{V}_{t+1}$ and $\hat{m}_{t+1}$) based on their current state and the goal image (V_t, m_t, and G). The predicted visual image is utilized to detect situational changes by computing the difference (prediction error) between the prediction and actual observation. The predicted motor state is sent to the robot as a desired state and the robot is controlled based on this prediction.

Due to the high dimensionality of visual and goal images, we consider encoding them into low-dimensional feature states through representation learning with deep autoencoders [9–11] (Fig. 1A) instead of using the original images directly. After representation learning, we perform predictive learning with an RNN [11] (Fig. 1B) by using the time-series data of encoded feature and motor states. After predictive learning, the trained computational framework consisting of the deep autoencoders and RNN is implemented in a robot that performs collaborative tasks with a human partner. During task execution, the robot is expected to adapt to situational changes by gradient-based optimization from the initial goal feature state for dynamic goal inference (Fig. 1C). The details of each scheme are introduced next. The parameter settings for each scheme are introduced in the next section (Sect. 3.3).

2.1   Representation Learning

High-dimensional visual and goal images (V and G) are encoded by learning into low-dimensional visual and goal feature states (v and g) in order to generate reconstructions ($\hat{V}$ and $\hat{G}$) (Fig. 1A). The time indices of visual images, feature states, and reconstructions are omitted because representation learning does not use time dependency. In this study, we use convolutional variational autoencoders (ConvVAEs) consisting of an inference network (encoder) and a generative network (decoder) [12]. The inference network consists of convolution layers followed by full connection layers. The generative network mirrors this architecture and consists of full connection layers followed by transposed convolution (i.e., deconvolution) layers. Two different ConvVAEs (one for visual images V and the other for goal images G) are used as follows:

$$\mu_V, \sigma_V = \mathrm{Enc_V}(V), \qquad \mu_G, \sigma_G = \mathrm{Enc_G}(G), \qquad\qquad (1)$$

$$v = \mu_V + \sigma_V \epsilon, \qquad g = \mu_G + \sigma_G \epsilon, \qquad \epsilon \sim \mathcal{N}(0, I), \quad (2)$$

$$\hat{V} = \mathrm{Dec_V}(v), \qquad \hat{G} = \mathrm{Dec_G}(g). \qquad\qquad (3)$$

Parameters of the ConvVAEs are updated by a gradient-based optimizer, such as gradient descent or Adam [13], to minimize the variational free energy or negative value of evidence lower bound (ELBO) in an offline manner. The variational free

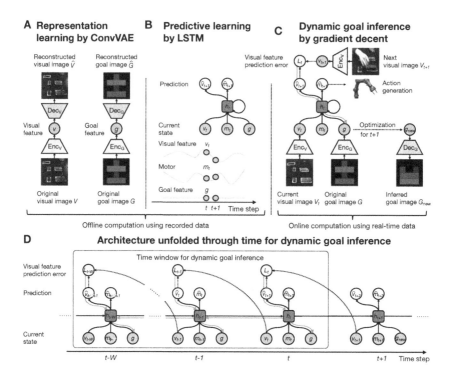

Fig. 1. (A) Representation learning by convolutional variational autoencoders (ConvVAEs). (B) Predictive learning by long short-term memory (LSTM). (C) Dynamic goal inference by gradient descent. (D) Architecture unfolded through time for dynamic goal inference.

energy consists of the reconstruction error (cross entropy) between the original images V or G and the corresponding reconstructions $\hat{V}$ or $\hat{G}$ and the Kullback-Leibler (KL) divergence between the approximate posterior $q(v|V)$ or $q(g|G)$ and unit Gaussian prior $\mathcal{N}(0, I)$. Time-series data of the extracted visual feature states v_t and the extracted goal feature state g are used for predictive learning as explained in the next subsection.

2.2   Predictive Learning

Given the current visual feature state v_t and motor state m_t and conditioned on a particular goal feature state g, an RNN learns to generate visual feature and motor predictions ($\hat{v}_{t+1}$ and $\hat{m}_{t+1}$) (Fig. 1B) as follows:

$$h_t = \text{RNN}(h_{t-1}, v_t, m_t, g), \hat{v}_{t+1} = \tanh(W_{\text{v}} h_t + b_{\text{v}}), \hat{m}_{t+1} = \tanh(W_{\text{m}} h_t + b_{\text{m}}),$$
$$(4)$$

where h_t is a hidden state, W_{v} and W_{m} are weights, and b_{v} and b_{m} are biases. The goal feature state acquired by representation learning can work in a similar manner to a parametric bias (PB) [2,3] that serves as a bifurcation parameter for an RNN from the viewpoint of dynamical systems. Parameters of the RNN are updated by a gradient-based optimizer to minimize the prediction error of each prediction about the visual feature and motor states in an offline manner. In this study, we use a long short-term memory (LSTM) architecture [14] for the RNN.

2.3 Dynamic Goal Inference by Gradient Descent

After training the ConvVAEs and LSTM, the encoders for visual images and goal images are respectively connected to the input for the visual feature state and the input for the goal feature state of the LSTM (Fig. 1C). At each time step, the LSTM generates visual feature and motor predictions ($\hat{v}_{t+1}$ and $\hat{m}_{t+1}$) in an online manner based on their current state and the goal feature state (v_t, m_t, and g). The current visual feature state and the goal feature state are encoded from the current visual image and the goal image (V_t and G), respectively.

For example, when the time step is $t + 1$, the motor state predicted at the previous time step t ($\hat{m}_{t+1}$) is sent to the robot as a target command and the robot is controlled based on this prediction. At the same time, a time window spanning from time step $t - W$ to t is considered (Fig. 1D). The predicted visual feature states $\hat{v}_{t-W+1:t+1}$ within this window are compared with the actual feature states $v_{t-W+1:t+1}$ encoded from the actual visual images $V_{t-W+1:t+1}$ and the sum of visual feature prediction errors $L_{t-W:t}$ are computed:

$$L_{t-W:t} = \sum_{t'=t-W}^{t} \frac{(\hat{v}_{t'+1} - v_{t'+1})^2}{2}. \tag{5}$$

The initial goal feature state $g^{(0)}$ is updated by gradient descent to minimize errors for N times ($g^{(N)}$). This optimization which is referred to as ERS [3,4] enables the robot to realize dynamic goal inference only from visual observations. The newly optimized goal feature state $g_{\text{new}} = g^{(N)}$ at time step $t + 1$ is used to generate predictions for the next time step $t + 2$. In addition, by decoding the optimized goal feature state g_{new}, we can visualize a newly inferred goal image $\hat{G}_{\text{new}}$. This optimization and decoding procedure is described as follows:

$$g^{(n+1)} = g^{(n)} - \alpha \frac{\partial L_{t-W:t}^{(n)}}{\partial g^{(n)}}, \quad \hat{G}_{\text{new}} = \text{Dec}_G(g_{\text{new}}), \tag{6}$$

where $g^{(n)}$ and $L_{t-W:t}^{(n)}$ are the goal feature state and visual feature prediction errors at the nth epoch and α is an optimization step that corresponds to the parameter called learning rate in the learning phases.

3 Experimental Setup

3.1 Task Design

To evaluate our proposed computational framework, we designed a human–robot collaboration task involving object assembly (Fig. 2). Four objects (plastic build-

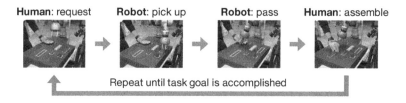

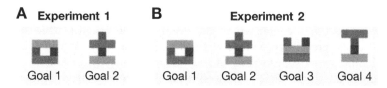

Fig. 2. Human–robot collaboration task involving object assembly.

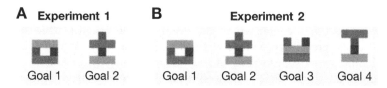

Fig. 3. Multiple goals considered in each experiment. (A) Two different goals in Experiment 1. (B) Four different goals in Experiment 2. (Color figure online)

ing blocks) of different colors are placed in a workspace. The human and robot ("Torobo" developed by Tokyo Robotics) are required to collaboratively assemble these objects by sharing specific goal information represented by the final state of object assembly such as that shown in Fig. 3. The role of the robot in this collaborative task is to pick up the objects and pass them to the human sequentially. The assembly of parts is performed by the human.

The assembly task goal (e.g., Goal 1 in Fig. 3) was initially shared between the human and robot before starting the task. During the task execution, the human first requested an object by reaching out towards the robot, and based on the shared task goal, the robot picked up an object (red block in Fig. 2) and passed it to the human. The human assembled (or placed) the received object in the assembly area. This process was repeated four times until the task goal was accomplished.

In the data recording phase for representation learning and predictive learning, the task goal was shared between the human and robot, and then they performed the collaboration task to accomplish the goal. For simplicity, the robot always picks up the objects starting from what is at the bottom in the goal image; if two are objects on the same level (such as the blue and brown objects in Goals 1 and 3), the object on the right side (blue) is picked up first. For example, in Goal 1, the order of picking up the objects is red, blue, brown, and green.

In the testing phase after the learning processes, the human intentionally changed the task goal from the shared task to a different task in order to evaluate whether the robot could infer the changed goal and adapt to the new situation by using the proposed approach of dynamic goal inference by gradient descent.

We conducted two experiments with different numbers of goals. As shown in Fig. 3A, Experiment 1 considered two goals where one (Goal 1) started from placing the red object and the other (Goal 2) started from placing the green object. In this case, the goal change can easily be identified because there are no ambiguous situations. As shown in Fig. 3B, Experiment 2 considered four goals where two goals (1 and 3) started from placing the red object and the other two (2 and 4) started from placing the green object. In this case, ambiguous situations can occur. For example, consider a situation where the initially shared goal is Goal 2 which starts from placing the green object. If the human suddenly changes the shared goal and picks up the red object first, the modified goal cannot be identified by the robot from this observation alone because Goals 1 and 3 both start from placing the red object and are thus both possible situations. In the experiment, we observed what would happen when the robot was faced with this kind of ambiguous situation.

3.2 Experimental Procedure

Our experiments consisted of three phases: recording training data, training the ConvVAEs and LSTM, and testing the performance of the robot. In the first phase, training data were collected by directly guiding the arm movement of the robot in order to achieve the collaborative task. We set up a camera that captured both the workspace and the human movement. The recorded training data consisted of time-series data of visual images and motor information. The original visual images were resized to 62×62 pixels. The motor information comprised seven joint angle states and the gripper state of the robot arm. In this data recording phase, we recorded six trials of object assembly for each goal. Accordingly, the total number of time-series data items for Experiment 1 with two goals was 12 and that for Experiment 2 with four goals was 24. The length of each time-series data item was 950 time steps.

In the second phase, representation learning was conducted by using the recorded visual images. For learning of the goal images, we synthetically prepared images of size 28×28 pixels as shown in Fig. 3. After the representation learning, predictive learning was performed by using the time-series data of visual feature and motor states, and goal feature states. The time-series data (and goal feature states) were normalized within the range of $[-1, 1]$ because we used $\tanh(\cdot)$ for the prediction generated by the LSTM as shown in Eq. 4.

After representation learning and predictive learning, the trained computational framework was implemented in the robot and the human–robot collaboration task was performed.

3.3 Parameter Settings

In the representation learning, the ConvVAE for visual images consisted of an encoder with two convolution layers followed by two full connection (dense) layers. The decoder mirrored this architecture and consisted of two full connection layers followed by two transpose convolution (i.e., deconvolution) layers. The ConvVAE for goal images consisted of one convolution layer, four full connection layers, and one transpose convolution layer. Table 1 shows the shape of the tensor at each encoder layer in the ConvVAEs. The filter size of the convolution and transposed convolution layers was 3×3 and the stride was 4. We used Adam [13] as the optimizer with a learning rate of 0.001 to update the network parameters consisting of weights and biases. The batch size was 100 and the number of epochs was 100 for learning visual images and 1000 for learning goal images.

Table 1. Shape of the tensor at each encoder layer in the ConvVAEs.

		Visual images	Goal images
Input		$64 \times 64 \times 3$	$28 \times 28 \times 3$
Encoder	Conv1 (softplus)	$16 \times 16 \times 32$	$7 \times 7 \times 16$
	Conv2 (softplus)	$4 \times 4 \times 32$	–
	Dense1 (softplus)	100	100
	Dense2	10 (μ_V), 10 (σ_V: exp)	2 (μ_G), 2 (σ_G: exp)

In predictive learning, we used 100 hidden units for the LSTM. The number of input units was 20, which corresponds to the dimensions of the current state (10-dimensional visual feature state v_t and 8-dimensional motor state m_t) and the 2-dimensional goal feature state g. The number of output units was 18, which corresponds to the dimensions of the predictions (10-dimensional visual feature prediction $\hat{v}_{t+1}$ and 8-dimensional motor prediction $\hat{m}_{t+1}$). We used Adam [13] as the optimizer with a learning rate of 0.001 for updating the network parameters consisting of weights and biases. The batch sizes were 12 for Experiment 1 and 24 for Experiment 2, and each of these corresponds to the total number of training data. The number of epochs was 10000.

In dynamic goal inference, the window length was $W = 30$. We used a gradient descent as the optimizer with an optimization step (learning rate) of $\alpha = 0.2$ to update the goal feature state. The number of epochs was $N = 30$.

4   Results and Discussion

In Experiment 1, after representation learning followed by predictive learning, we first evaluated whether the robot with the proposed computational framework could collaborate with a human partner toward a fixed goal without the dynamic goal inference scheme. The results demonstrated that the robot succeeded in generating adequate action sequences for each goal.

Next we tested whether the robot could adapt to situational changes by using the proposed dynamic goal inference scheme. Figure 4A shows an example of time-series data of the seven-dimensional joint angle states, one-dimensional gripper states, and two-dimensional optimized goal feature states. In this case, although the initially set goal was Goal 2 (the bottom is the green object), the human picked up the red object by himself and placed it in the assembly area. As illustrated in the top panel of the figure, the robot generated the action sequence

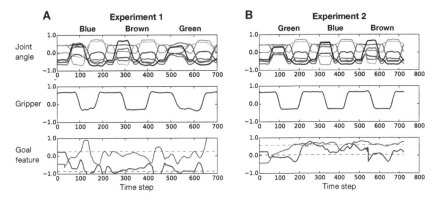

Fig. 4. Time-series data of joint angle and gripper states predicted by the LSTM and goal feature states optimized by gradient descent for dynamic goal inference in (A) Experiment 1 and (B) Experiment 2. (Color figure online)

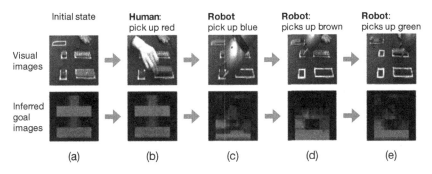

Fig. 5. Visual images and corresponding inferred goal images in Experiment 1. (Color figure online)

of picking up and passing the remaining objects in the order blue, brown, and green, which corresponds to the order for Goal 1. The bottom panel shows that the initial goal feature state was optimized at around time step 30, immediately after the human picked up the red object. The dotted lines show the goal feature state for Goal 1. From this figure, we can understand that the initial goal feature state for Goal 2 was optimized to values close to the feature state for Goal 1 after observing unpredicted situations that produced large visual feature prediction errors. Figure 5 shows the visual images and corresponding inferred goal images decoded from the goal feature states. This shows that the initial goal image in (a) was modified in (c) after the robot observed that the human picked up the red object in (b).

In Experiment 2, we also confirmed the ability of the robot to perform collaboration toward a fixed goal. We then tested whether the robot could adapt to ambiguous situational changes by using the dynamic goal inference scheme described in Sect. 3.1. Figure 4B shows an example of the time-series data of

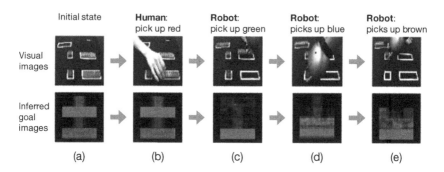

Fig. 6. Visual images and corresponding inferred goal images in Experiment 2. (Color figure online)

an action sequence and optimized goal feature states. Similar to Experiment 1, although the initial goal was Goal 2 (the bottom is the green object), the human picked up the red object by himself and placed it in the assembly area. As illustrated in the top panel of the figure, the robot generated the action sequence of picking up and passing the remaining objects in the order green, blue, and brown, which corresponds to the order for Goal 3. From this figure, we can understand that the initial goal feature state for Goal 2 was optimized at around time step 40 to values close to the feature state for Goal 3 (dotted lines) after the robot observed an unpredicted situation that produced large visual feature prediction errors. Note that our five trials with the same situational changes showed the same dynamic goal inference toward the Goal 3. This may result from the initial randomized parameters including the weights and biases of the LSTM. Figure 6 shows the visual images and corresponding inferred goal images decoded from the goal feature states. The figure shows that the initial goal image in (a) was modified in (c) after the robot observed that the human picked up the red object in (b) in the same manner as in Experiment 1.

The time-series data of the goal feature states in Fig. 4 and the sequences of inferred goal images in Figs. 5 and 6 exhibited some fluctuations even though the robot generated stable action sequences. To understand the relationship between goal feature states and action sequences, we analyzed the goal feature space in Experiment 2. The two-dimensional goal feature space with a range of $[-1, 1]$ was cut into 21×21 segments at intervals of 0.1. The center value of each segment was then set to the LSTM as a constant goal feature state (without optimization) and predictions were generated by closed-loop generation. In this generation method, visual feature and motor predictions ($\hat{v}_{t+1}$ and $\hat{m}_{t+1}$) generated at time step t are utilized as the input to the next time step $t + 1$. The 441 generated action sequences were compared with the reference action sequence for each goal and the distances (errors) between them were computed using dynamic time warping (DTW), which measures similarities between time-series data items. Figure 7 shows the error distribution in the two-dimensional goal feature space for each goal. The initial value and dynamics of the goal feature states in Fig. 4B

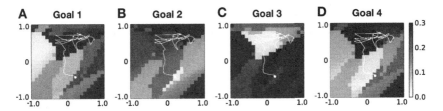

Fig. 7. Error distributions in the goal feature space in Experiment 2 with respect to (A) Goal 1, (B) Goal 2, (C) Goal 3, and (D) Goal 4. Goal feature dynamics and their initial states in Fig. 4B are shown as red trajectories and circles, respectively.

are shown as red circles and trajectories, respectively. From this figure, we can observe that the action sequence to accomplish a particular goal can be generated not by an exact value but instead by values with a range corresponding to each goal. Thanks to this characteristic of the goal feature space, the robot can generate stable actions in spite of fluctuations in the goal features resulting from the gradient-based optimization.

In terms of computational efficiency, we separately trained the ConvVAEs and the LSTM. The unstable change in the inferred goal images decoded from the goal feature states shown in Figs. 5 and 6 is thought to result from this training method. When trained simultaneously, the training of the ConvVAE for goal images is affected by the training of the LSTM and may lead to greater decoding stability. More specifically, the value ranges for reconstructing the goal images using the decoder of the ConvVAE and those for generating the corresponding action sequences with the LSTM can be jointly optimized. However, simultaneous training needs to use backpropagation "through time" (BPTT) not only for the LSTM but also for the ConvVAE, but this requires more computational time than training separately. That is, this can be considered a trade-off problem between computational efficiency and decoding quality.

5   Conclusions

In this study, we proposed a neural network-based computational framework for dynamic goal inference in human–robot collaboration. The proposed framework consisted of two ConvVAEs for representation learning and an LSTM for predictive learning. The ConvVAEs were used to extract visual and goal feature states from visual images and goal images, respectively. Extracted visual and goal feature states were used to train the LSTM to generate visual feature and motor predictions based on their current state and the goal feature state. We conducted experiments on a human–robot collaboration task involving object assembly to evaluate our proposed framework. The experimental results demonstrated that the proposed framework enabled the robot to dynamically infer the human goal state and adapt to situational changes by using gradient descent to minimize visual feature prediction errors. Future work will examine whether collaboration can be realized by a similar process (dynamic inference using gradient descent optimization) when an unlearned goal image is provided and the human acts toward this goal state.

Acknowledgement. This work was supported in part by JST CREST (JPMJCR 15E3), JSPS KAKENHI (JP16H05878), and the Research Institute for Science and Engineering, Waseda University.

References

1. Maeda, G., Ewerton, M., Lioutikov, R., Ben Amor, H., Peters, J., Neumann, G.: Learning interaction for collaborative tasks with probabilistic movement primitives. In: 2014 IEEE-RAS International Conference on Humanoid Robots, vol. 2015, pp. 527–534. IEEE, February 2014
2. Murata, S., Li, Y., Arie, H., Ogata, T., Sugano, S.: Learning to achieve different levels of adaptability for human-robot collaboration utilizing a neuro-dynamical system. IEEE Trans. Cogn. Dev. Syst. **10**(3), 712–725 (2018)
3. Tani, J.: Learning to generate articulated behavior through the bottom-up and the top-down interaction processes. Neural Netw. **16**(1), 11–23 (2003)
4. Murata, S., Yamashita, Y., Arie, H., Ogata, T., Sugano, S., Tani, J.: Learning to perceive the world as probabilistic or deterministic via interaction with others: a neuro-robotics experiment. IEEE Trans. Neural Netw. Learn. Syst. **28**(4), 830–848 (2017)
5. Rao, R.P., Ballard, D.H.: Predictive coding in the visual cortex: a functional interpretation of some extra-classical receptive-field effects. Nat. Neurosci. **2**(1), 79–87 (1999)
6. Clark, A.: Whatever next? predictive brains, situated agents, and the future of cognitive science. Behav. Brain Sci. **36**(3), 181–204 (2013)
7. Hafner, D., et al.: Learning latent dynamics for planning from pixels. In: Chaudhuri, K., Salakhutdinov, R. (eds.) Proceedings of the 36th International Conference on Machine Learning, PMLR, pp. 2555–2565 (2019)
8. Srinivas, A., Jabri, A., Abbeel, P., Levine, S., Finn, C.: Universal planning networks. In Dy, J., Krause, A. (eds.) Proceedings of the 35th International Conference on Machine Learning, PMLR (2018)
9. Hinton, G.E., Salakhutdinov, R.R.: Reducing the dimensionality of data with neural networks. Sci. (New York, N.Y.) **313**(5786), 504–507 (2006)
10. Noda, K., Arie, H., Suga, Y., Ogata, T.: Multimodal integration learning of robot behavior using deep neural networks. Robot. Auton. Syst. **62**(6), 721–736 (2014)
11. Takahashi, K., Ogata, T., Tjandra, H., Yamaguchi, Y., Sugano, S.: Tool-body assimilation model based on body babbling and neurodynamical system. Math. Probl. Eng. **2015**, 1–15 (2015)
12. Kingma, D.P., Welling, M.: Auto-encoding variational Bayes. In: Salakhutdinov, K.C.R. (eds.) Proceedings of the 2nd International Conference on Learning Representations (ICLR), pp. 1–14 (2014)
13. Kingma, D.P., Ba, J.: Adam: a method for stochastic optimization. In: Proceedings of the 3rd International Conference on Learning Representations (ICLR), pp. 1–15 (2015)
14. Hochreiter, S., Schmidhuber, J.: Long short-term memory. Neural Comput. **9**(8), 1735–1780 (1997)

Neuromuscular Activation Based SEMG-Torque Hybrid Modeling and Optimization for Robot Assisted Neurorehabilitation

Weiqun Wang[1,2], Zeng-Guang Hou[1,2,3(✉)], Weiguo Shi[1,2], Xu Liang[1,2], Shixin Ren[1,2], Jiaxing Wang[1,2], and Liang Peng[1]

[1] The State Key Laboratory of Management and Control for Complex Systems, Institute of Automation, Chinese Academy of Sciences, Beijing 100190, China
{weiqun.wang,zengguang.hou,shiweiguo2017,liangxu2013,renshixin2015, wangjiaxing2016,liang.peng}@ia.ac.cn
[2] University of Chinese Academy of Sciences, Beijing 100049, People's Republic of China
[3] The CAS Center for Excellence in Brain Science and Intelligence Technology, Beijing 100190, China

Abstract. Active engagement of human nervous system in the rehabilitation training is of great importance for the neurorehabilitation and motor function recovery of nerve injury patients. To this goal, the human motion intention should be detected and recognized in real time, which can be implemented by modeling the relationships between sEMG signals and the associated joint torques. However, present sEMG-torque modeling methods, including neuromusculoskeletal and black-box modeling methods, have their own deficiencies. Therefore, a hybrid modeling method based on the neuromuscular activations and Gaussian process regression (GPR) algorithm is proposed. Firstly, the preprocessed sEMG signals are converted into neural and muscular activations by the neuromusculoskeletal modeling method. The obtained muscle activations together with the associated joint angles are then transformed into the adjacent joint torques by a GPR algorithm to avoid the complicated modeling process of the muscle contraction dynamics, musculoskeletal geometry, and musculoskeletal dynamics. Moreover, the undetermined parameters of neuromuscular activation and GPR models are calibrated simultaneously based on an optimization algorithm designed in this study. Finally, the performance of the proposed method is demonstrated by validation and comparison experiments. It can be seen from the experiment results that, a high accuracy of torque prediction can be obtained using the proposed hybrid modeling method. Meanwhile, when the difference between the test and calibration trajectories is not very big, the joint torques for the test trajectory can be predicted with a high accuracy as well.

Keywords: Neurorehabilitation · sEMG Modeling · Torque prediction · Parameter optimization · Motion intention recognition

© Springer Nature Switzerland AG 2019
T. Gedeon et al. (Eds.): ICONIP 2019, LNCS 11954, pp. 591–602, 2019.
https://doi.org/10.1007/978-3-030-36711-4_50

1   Motivation

Stroke is one of the leading causes of large number of deaths and disabilities [1]. The damage of sensory-motor nervous system, brought out by stroke, have been producing millions of limb paralyses in the world. It has been proven that, rehabilitation training is effective for recovery of the limb paralyzed patients. Especially, the active type of training, where the voluntary motion intention is involved, is thought to be more efficient [2]. The motion intention of the patients should be detected and recognized in order that the active training can be implemented. However, it is difficult to be carried out by the generally used methods in clinical, where rehabilitation is conducted manually and one-to-one by physiotherapists. The difficulties become extremely hard when the lower limb rehabilitation is considered, for which three physiotherapists are usually needed in the typical training paradigm.

It is widely believed that the difficulties faced by the traditional rehabilitation methods can be addressed to a large extent by rehabilitation robots [3][4]. Rehabilitation tasks can be executed precisely and automatically by robots, such that the physiotherapists can pay more attention to improvement of the therapeutic and training schedules and the rehabilitation technologies. Especially, many advanced rehabilitation methods, of which active rehabilitation training is a typical example, can be carried out by robots. Active type of rehabilitation training have been researched in the field of rehabilitation robots for tens of years [5], where how to detect and recognize human motion intention timely and accurately is still an open question. Physical signals, including joint angles, angular velocities, and joint torques or forces, are relatively stable and suitable for present clinical application, and hence, they have been used in many rehabilitation systems [6,7]. However, limb motion and joint torques or forces are much later than human intentions, and hence, if human motion intention recognition system of the rehabilitation robots is designed based on the physical signals mentioned above, the interaction between human and robots will inevitably become unnatural.

Human intentions come from the brain, go through central and peripheral nervous systems, and reach musculoskeletal system at last. Therefore, they can be detected theoretically at each points of the transmission pathway, such as brain, spinal cord, or muscles, etc. Brain computer interface (BCI), including the invasive and non-invasive types, has been studied in the fields of motion assistance or neurorehabilitation for limb paralyzed patients [8]. Since the electroencephalogram (EEG) signals from the non-invasive BCI are too weak and unstable, most of present non-invasive BCIs can only classify limited number of motion modes [9]. Meanwhile, invasive BCIs are not suitable for the mild to moderate nerve injury patients, which are the major part of the stroke-post paralyzed patients. Compared with EEG signals, surface electromyography (sEMG) signals are relatively robust, and hence, it is supposed that human motion intention can be predicted accurately and stably using sEMG signals.

2   Related Research and Contributions of This Paper

SEMG based recognition of human motion intention has been widely researched in fields of powered prosthetics [10] and rehabilitation robotics [11]. Classification of motion modes and estimation of continuous physical quantities, such as joint angles, angular velocities, and joint torques or forces, are two of the main applications of sEMG in the neurorehabilitation field. Lots of studies on motion mode classification based on sEMG can be found in the literature [12,13], from which it can be seen that present pattern recognition methods can work well for limited motion modes. However, it is different from the natural human motion, which is continuous and compliant. Therefore, prediction of continuous physical quantities that represent human motion intention is thought to be more suitable for clinical application of rehabilitation robots. Due to that human motion can be measured relatively easily than joint torques or muscle forces of human bodies, prediction of human motion qualities based on sEMG have been researched more [14,15]. Whereas, muscle forces or joint torques are related with sEMG more directly [16] and limb motion is just the results of joint torques by human body's dynamics. Hence, if human joint torques can be predicted accurately based on sEMG, the control system with relative fast response performance can be designed, which is helpful for realize the compliant and adaptive human-robot interaction.

The relationships between sEMG and the associated joint torques can be modeled by neuromusculoskeletal modeling methods [16]-[18], which model the whole process from the dynamics of neural activation, muscle activation, and muscle contraction, to muscle skeleton dynamics, or black-box modeling methods like neural networks [14], support vector regression [19], etc. The former has the advantages in interpretability and generalization ability, and the deficiencies in accuracy and modeling complexity. On the other hand, when motion trajectories of human bodies are maintained invariable or the variation range is small during rehabilitation training, which is common for gait training or bicycle pedaling training in clinical lower limb rehabilitation, black-box modeling methods are very efficient due to the high accuracy and modeling concision.

By considering the advantages of neuromusculoskeletal and black-box modeling methods, a hybrid modeling and optimization method is proposed in this sduty. During sEMG-torque modeling, the preprocessed sEMG signals are firstly converted into the neural and muscular activations. The obtained muscle activations are related with the associated multiple joint torques by Gaussian process regression (GPR) methods. Then the undetermined parameters of the hybrid model are calibrated collaboratively by an optimization method designed based on stochastic particle swarm optimization (SPSO) and the conjugate gradient (CG) algorithms. Finally, the performance of the proposed method is demonstrated by the experiments carried out on a lower limb rehabilitation robot (LLRR).

The remainder of this paper is organized as follows: Sect. 2 and 3 describes respectively the sEMG-torque modeling and parameter optimization methods; The experiments and discussion are given in Sect. 4; this paper is concluded in Sect. 5.

3   SEMG-Torque Hybrid Modeling

As analyzed in above section, the neuromusculoskeletal modeling methods outperform the black-box methods in interpretability and generalization ability, while the later have superiority in accuracy and modeling complexity. For the purpose of utilizing above advantages simultaneously, a hybrid modeling method is proposed, where the neural and muscle activation dynamics are modeled using the neuromusculoskeletal modeling method and the relationships between muscle activations and joint torques are modeled by a GPR method. The details of the modeling process are given as follows.

3.1   Neuromuscular Activation Modeling

The sEMG signals are generally preprocessed to eliminate various kinds of noises before modeling. Specifically, sEMG signals are usually high pass filtered to remove direct current effect, notch filtered with a frequency of 50 Hz to prevent the power frequency interference, full wave rectified and lower pass filtered to make their frequencies similar to joint torques. The preprocessed sEMG is then used to derive the neural activation dynamics, which can be described by a discrete equation as follows [16]:

$$u(t) = \alpha e(t - d) + \beta u(t - 1) + \beta u(t - 2), \tag{1}$$

where $u(t)$, $u(t - 1)$, and $u(t - 2)$ represent the muscle activations at time t, $t - 1$, $t - 2$, respectively; $e(t - d)$ is the preprocessed EMG signal by considering the delay time d, which has been reported to range from 10 ms to 100 ms [20]. The exact delay time is difficult to be obtained, therefore, it was often designed by try-and-error method or using empirical values [18]. The following constrains should be satisfied to form a stable equation [16]:

$$\begin{aligned} \beta_1 &= \gamma_1 + \gamma_2, \quad \beta_2 = \gamma_1 \gamma_2, \\ |\gamma_1| &< 1, \quad |\gamma_2| < 1, \\ \alpha - \beta_1 - \beta_2 &= 1, \end{aligned} \tag{2}$$

where γ_1 and γ_2 are undetermined parameters to be optimized together with the delay time d.

By considering simultaneously the research of [21] and normalization of neural activations, the muscle activation dynamics can be given by [17]:

$$a(u) = \frac{e^{AuR^{-1}} - 1}{e^A - 1}, \tag{3}$$

where, $A \in [-3, 0]$, is a nonlinear shape factor defining the curvature of the function, and R is an expected maximum during maximal voluntary contraction (MVC). MVC is difficult to be implemented, and hence, R is usually alternated by the maximal value measured during experiments [15, 18]. In [17], A and R were calibrated by a sequential optimization method, by which however the global optima is difficult to be obtained. Therefore, different from [17], A and R are to be optimized together with other undetermined parameters of the neural activation dynamics and the GPR model.

3.2   Neuromuscular Activations to Joint Torques

It can be seen from the literature that, human joint torques are complicatedly related with muscle activations through muscle contraction dynamics, musculoskeletal geometry, and musculoskeletal dynamics [16], which is difficult to be modeling exactly. Therefore, the relationships between the muscle activations and joint torques are modeled using the GPR method to avoid the complicated process of neuromusculoskeletal modeling.

Let the number of muscles in consideration is N, the input vector of the model can be given by:

$$\mathbf{a} = (a_1, a_2, \ldots, a_N), \tag{4}$$

where $a_1, a_2, \ldots, a_N$ are muscle activations of the 1st, 2nd,...,Nth muscles, which are functions of the associated neural activations given by (3). The mean function and the covariance function for the GPR model are determined by:

$$m(\boldsymbol{a}) = 0, \tag{5}$$

$$k(\boldsymbol{a}, \boldsymbol{a}') = \nu_1 exp(\frac{-\Delta a \Lambda \Delta a^T}{2}) + \nu_2 \delta_{i,j}, \tag{6}$$

where Δa is defined by $\boldsymbol{a} - \boldsymbol{a}'$, and the elements of the diagonal matrix Λ are $\lambda_1, \ldots, \lambda_N$. $\delta_{i,j}$ is the Kronecker delta function. The joint torques to be estimated, $\boldsymbol{\tau}_e$, can be calculated based on the training samples and the test sample $\boldsymbol{a}^*$, as follows:

$$\tau_{e,i}^* = \boldsymbol{k}_*^T \boldsymbol{K}^{-1} \boldsymbol{\tau}_{tr}. \tag{7}$$

where $\tau_{e,i}^*$ represents the element of $\boldsymbol{\tau}_e$ to be estimated; $\boldsymbol{K}$ is a matrix whose elements $k_{i,j}$ is the value of a covariance function $k(\boldsymbol{a}_i, \boldsymbol{a}_j)$; $\boldsymbol{\tau}_{tr}$ is the output vector of the training set; $\boldsymbol{k}_*$ is given by:

$$\boldsymbol{k}_* = [k(\boldsymbol{a}^*, \boldsymbol{a}_1), \ldots, k(\boldsymbol{a}^*, \boldsymbol{a}_N)]. \tag{8}$$

It can be seen that, to estimate joint torques based on muscle activations using the designed GPR model, $\lambda_1, \ldots, \lambda_n$, ν_1, and ν_2 should be determined, which are to be implemented based on an optimization method given in the following text.

It should be noted that, when the undetermined parameters are calibrated, the training data set are to be designed dynamically using the data before the data point to be predicted. It is supposed that the sEMG-torque model designed in this way can be adaptive to variation of the muscle condition.

4   Optimization Based Parameter Calibration

4.1   Formulation of the Optimization Problem

The undetermined parameters of neuromuscular activation dynamics and activation-torque models are calibrated simultaneously based on an optimization method in this study. The optimization problem can be defined as follows.

Design vector

$$\mathbf{X} = (d, \gamma_1, \gamma_2, A_1, \ldots, A_N, R_1, \ldots, R_N, \lambda_1, \ldots, \lambda_N, \nu_1, \nu_2), \tag{9}$$

Objective function to be minimized

$$F(\mathbf{X}) = \sqrt{\sum_{k=1}^{K} (\tau_{e,i,k} - \tau_{m,i,k})^2} \tag{10}$$

where $\tau_{e,i,k}$ and $\tau_{m,i,k}$ are estimated and measured torques of the kth point, and K is the total number of calculation point. $\tau_{e,i,k}$ can be obtained by (7). $\tau_{m,i,k}$ can be obtained by using the inverse dynamic model of the human robot coupling system [7].

Constraints to be satisfied

$$d \in [10, 100],$$
$$\gamma_1, \gamma_2 \in [-1, 1],$$
$$A_n \in [-3, 0],$$
$$R_n \in [u_{max,n}, 2u_{max,n}], \tag{11}$$
$$\lambda_n \in [\lambda_{min,n}, \lambda_{max,n}],$$
$$\nu_1, \nu_1, \in [\nu_{min}, \nu_{max}],$$
$$n = 1, \ldots, N.$$

where $u_{max,n}$ is the maximum of measured sEMG signals from the nth muscle.

4.2   SPSO-CG Algorithm for Searching the Optimal Parameters

It can be seen that, the optimization problem for calibrating the undetermined parameters of this paper is strongly nonlinear. An SPSO-CG algorithm is designed to search the optimal solution in this study, where the SPSO algorithm is used to generate the initial position, and the CG algorithm is then to implemented many cycles to find an optimal position corresponding to the initial position for each particle. Therefore, the global convergence can be maintained by global implement of the SPSO algorithm, and meanwhile, fast convergence speed can be obtained by local implement of the CG algorithm.

The designed SPSO-CG algorithm can be given as follows:

1) The particle swarm is initialized in the given ranges; The particle optimal position is set to the initial position and a global optima is selected from the swarm.

2) The CG algorithm is used to search the optimal position for each particle, and hence, the best position can be found for each particle.
3) If the obtained best position of a particle is better than the global optima, the global optima will be replaced by the particle's best position and the particle's position is to be regenerated.
4) After updating positions of all particles, the algorithm is to stop when the stopping condition is reached, or it will go to 2).

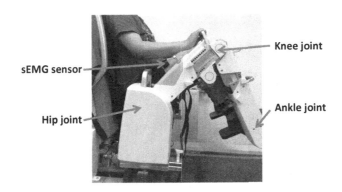

Fig. 1. The LLRR developed at the Institute of Automation, Chinese Academy of Sciences.

5   Experiments and Discussion

5.1   Experiment Platform and Data Acquisition

An LLRR was used as the experiment platform in this study, which was developed by out research group at the Institute of Automation, Chinese Academy of Sciences. As Fig. 1 shows, the robot has two leg mechanisms, each of which consists of three joints, namely hip, knee, and ankle joints, and two links, including thigh and crus links corresponding to thigh and crus of human leg. During rehabilitation training, human legs are bound to the leg mechanisms.

Torque and position sensors are installed at the hip and knee joints of the leg mechanisms, from which the joint torques and angles of the robot can be measured. The voluntary torques of human joints can be calculated by the method of [7].

A set of wireless sEMG system (Delsys, TrignoTM) was used to acquire the sEMG signals. The hip and knee joints, and six muscles, including rectus femoris (RF), vastus lateralis (VL), vastus medialis (VM), biceps femoris (BF), semitendinosus (ST), and semimem-branosus (SM), of human leg were considered to design the sEMG-torque model by the proposed hybrid modeling method. The distribution of the sEMG sensors are given in Fig. 2. The muscles were selected by considering easy measurement and relatively big contribution to hip and knee joint torques.

Experiments were conducted, based on the LLRR and measured data, to demonstrate the feasibility of the proposed method. Firstly, the human-robot dynamics were modeled and identified by an identification experiment, based on which human voluntary joint torques can be estimated by the methods of [7]. Then, two circular trajectories with different radiuses were implemented to calibrate the undetermined parameters and to validate the model performance, respectively. Moreover, two comparison experiments were carried out to show the performance of the proposed method.

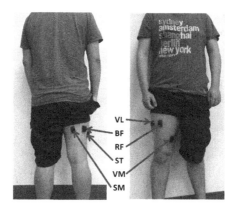

Fig. 2. The distribution of sEMG sensors.

5.2   Optimization Based Parameter Calibration

The hip and knee joint trajectories for calibration and validation are given in Fig. 3. In the calibration and validation experiments, the associated joint trajectories were implemented by the LLRR, during which the subject was required to impose voluntary forces arbitrarily, and meanwhile, the joint angles and torques, and sEMG signals of six muscles were recorded simultaneously. The voluntary torques of human joints can be obtained by the method of [7]. The sEMG signals were firstly high pass filtered with a cut-off frequency of 5 HZ, notch-filtered with a frequency of 50 HZ, full wave rectified, and lower-pass filtered with a cut-off frequency of 100 HZ.

Then the preprocessed sEMG signals and joint torques and the measured joint angles were used to calibrate the undetermined parameters using the SPSO-CG algorithm. The parameters of the SPSO-CG algorithm are given by:

- Maximal number of continuous stopping, n_{stop}: 5;
- Stopping condition: the difference between the maximal and minimal fitness of the particles of the swarm is smaller than 0.3, or the fitness defined by (10) is smaller than 0.001, or n_{stop} is reached;
- Population: 100;
- λ_{min} and ν_{min}: −20.
- λ_{max} and ν_{max}: 20.

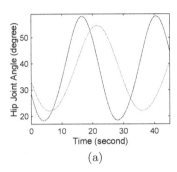 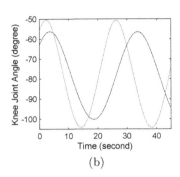

(a)   (b)

Fig. 3. The trajectories of (a) hip and (b) knee joints, for parameter calibration and validation, where the red and blue lines represent the calibration and validation trajectories, respectively. (Color figure online)

Table 1. The optimized parameters for one subject, where $r = 1.0 \times 10^{-5}$.

	$d(ms)$	γ_1	γ_2	A_1	R_1	A_2	R_2	A_3	R_3	A_4	R_4	A_5
hip	60.57	−0.71	−0.52	−0.76	3.87r	−2.18	15.80r	−2.14	3.45r	−0.037	4.31r	−1.48
knee	41.69	−0.26	−0.06	−2.23	2.99r	−1.01	13.90r	−2.94	4.68r	−2.0	4.42r	−0.81
R_5	A_6	R_6	λ_1	λ_2	λ_3	λ_4	λ_5	λ_6	λ_7	λ_8	ν_1	ν_2
9.78r	−2.36	45.40r	−6.88	−6.15	10.68	−19.42	16.65	15.69	4.09	0.49	19.85	−19.01
15.30r	−2.16	26.30r	−5.49	1.42	18.85	−8.79	−9.48	−4.47	−11.31	15.49	18.43	−18.95

Part of the optimized parameters are given in Tabel 1. The root-mean-square values of the estimation errors (RMSEs) defined by (10), for the calibration trajectories, are 1.18×10^{-15} Nm and 5.95×10^{-15} Nm, respectively for the hip and knee joints. It means that the relationships between the sEMG signals and joint torques can be exactly fitted by the designed model.

5.3 Comparison Experiments and Discussion

The comparison experiment was implemented between the designed hybrid model and an sEMG-Torque model designed using BP neural network (BPNN), which is commonly used in sEMG modeling [14]. The data measured from the validation trajectory was used in the comparison experiment.

The measured and estimated joint torques for the designed hybrid model are given in Fig. 4, and the RMSEs for hip and knee joints are respectively 0.49 Nm and 0.43 Nm. Since the validation and calibration trajectories are different from each other, it can be seen from the validation experiment that a satisfied generalization performance can be obtained by proposed hybrid modeling method.

The inputs of the BPNN model are six channels of sEMG signals after preprocessing, which are same as that for the hybrid model. The reconstructed and measured joint torques for the calibration trajectories which are also same as that for the hybrid model, are given in Fig. 5. The RMSEs of the reconstructed torques of hip and knee joints are respectively 3.54 Nm and 1.67 Nm, which is much larger than that for the hybrid model. Moreover, the RMSEs of the estimated torques for the validation trajectories, are 12.14 Nm and 8.21 Nm respectively for the hip and knee joints, which is too large for rehabilitation application.

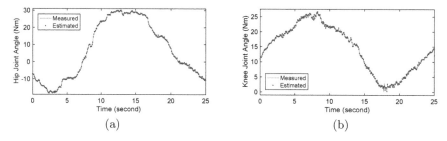

Fig. 4. The measured and estimated torques for the (a) hip and (b) knee joints based on the hybrid model using the data measured from the validation trajectories.

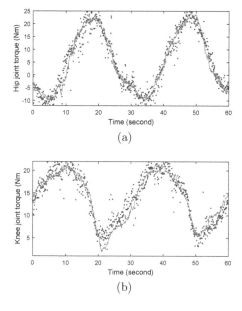

Fig. 5. The measured and estimated torques for the (a) hip and (b) knee joints based on BPNN model using the data measured from the calibration trajectories.

6   Conclusion

A hybrid modeling method is proposed to describe the relationships between the sEMG signals and the associated joint torques, where the neural and muscle activations are modeled by the neuromusculoskeletal modeling method, and the obtained muscle activations are related with the associated joint torques by a GPR method. Meanwhile, an SPSO-CG method is designed to calibrate the undetermined parameters of the hybrid model. It is supposed that, the advantages of neuromusculoskeletal modeling methods and the black-box methods can be utilized simultaneously by the propose hybrid modeling method and the optimization based parameter calibration method. The performance of the proposed method are demonstrated by comprehensive experiments. In the future, the real time peformance of the proposed method is to be further researched and paralyzed patients will also be included to test the clinical feasibility.

Acknowledgments. This research is supported by National Key R&D Program of China (Grant 2017YFB1302303), National Natural Science Foundation of China (Grant 91848110), and Beijing Natural Science Foundation (Grants 3171001 and L172050).

References

1. Corbyn, Z.: Stroke: a growing global burden. Nature, Outlook, 510(7506, pp. S2–S3, 06/26/print 2014
2. Lotze, M., Braun, C., Birbaumer, N., Anders, S., Cohen, L.G.: Motor learning elicited by voluntary drive. Brain **126**, 866–872 (2003)
3. Young, A.J., Ferris, D.P.: State of the art and future directions for lower limb robotic exoskeletons. IEEE Trans. Neural Syst. Rehabil. Eng. **25**(2), 171–182 (2017)
4. Maciejasz, P., Eschweiler, J., Gerlach-Hahn, K., Jansen-Troy, A., Leonhardt, S.: A survey on robotic devices for upper limb rehabilitation. J. NeuroEng. Rehabil. **11**(3), 29 (2014)
5. Krebs, H.I.: Rehabilitation robotics an academic engineer perspective. In: Proceedings of the 2011 Annual International Conference of the IEEE Engineering in Medicine and Biology Society, Boston, MA, USA, pp. 6709–6713 (2011)
6. Zanotto, D., Stegall, P., Agrawal, S.K.: Adaptive assist-as-needed controller to improve gait symmetry in robot-assisted gait training. In: The Proceedings of 2014 IEEE International Conference on Robotics and Automation (ICRA), Hong Kong, China, pp. 724–729 (2014)
7. Wang, W., Hou, Z., Cheng, L., et al.: Towards patients' motion intention recognition: dynamics modeling and identification of iLeg - a lower limb rehabilitation robot under motion constraints. IEEE Trans. Syst. Man Cybern. Syst. **46**(7), 980–992 (2016)
8. Foley, K.E.: Ideas in movement: the next wave of brain-computer interfaces. Nat. Med. **22**(1), 1–5 (2016)
9. Soekadar, S.R., et al.: Hybrid EEG/EOG-based brain/neural hand exoskeleton restores fully independent daily living activities after quadriplegia. Science Robotics, **1**(1) (2016)

10. Yang, D., Jiang, L., Huang, Q., Liu, R., Liu, H.: Experimental study of an EMG-controlled 5-DOF anthropomorphic prosthetic hand for motion restoration. J. Intell. Robot. Syst. **76**(3), 427–441 (2014)

11. Tsukahara, A., Hasegawa, Y., Eguchi, K., Sankai, Y.: Restoration of gait for spinal cord injury patients using hal with intention estimator for preferable swing speed. IEEE Trans. Neural Syst. Rehabil. Eng. **23**(2), 308–318 (2015)

12. Duan, F., Dai, L., Chang, W., Chen, Z., Zhu, C., Li, W.: sEMG-based identification of hand motion commands using wavelet neural network combined with discrete wavelet transform. IEEE Trans. Ind. Electron. **63**(3), 1923–1934 (2016)

13. Jarrassé, N., et al.: Classification of phantom finger, hand, wrist, and elbow voluntary gestures in transhumeral amputees with sEMG. IEEE Trans. Neural Syst. Rehabil. Eng. **25**(1), 71–80 (2017)

14. Zhang, F., et al.: sEMG-based continuous estimation of joint angles of human legs by using BP neural network. Neurocomputing **78**(1), 139–148 (2012)

15. Han, J., Ding, Q., Xiong, A., Zhao, X.: A state-space EMG model for the estimation of continuous joint movements. IEEE Trans. Ind. Electron. **62**(7), 4267–4275 (2015)

16. Buchanan, T.S., Lloyd, D.G., Manal, K., Besier, T.F.: Neuromusculoskeletal modeling: estimation of muscle forces and joint moments and movements from measurements of neural command. J. Appl. Biomech. **20**(4), 367–395 (2004)

17. Fleischer, C., Hommel, G.: A human-exoskeleton interface utilizing electromyography. IEEE Trans. Robot. **24**(4), 872–882 (2008)

18. Ao, D., Song, R., Gao, J.: Movement performance of human-robot cooperation control based on EMG-driven hill-type and proportional models for an ankle power-assist exoskeleton robot. IEEE Trans. Neural Syst. Rehabil. Eng. **25**(8), 1125–1134 (2017)

19. Meng, W., Ding, B., Zhou, Z., Liu, Q., Ai, Q.: An EMG-based force prediction and control approach for robot-assisted lower limb rehabilitation. In: Proceedings of the 2014 IEEE International Conference on Systems, Man and Cybernetics, pp. 2198–2203 (2014)

20. Corcos, D.M., Gottlieb, G.L., Latash, M.L., Almeida, G.L., Agarwal, G.C.: Electromechanical delay: an experimental artifact. J. Electromyogr. Kinesiol. **2**(2), 59–68 (1992)

21. Lloyd, D.G., Besier, T.F.: An EMG-driven musculoskeletal model for estimation of the human knee joint moments across varied tasks. J. Biomech. **36**, 765–776 (2003)

Secure Outsourcing of Lattice Basis Reduction

Jiayang Liu[1] and Jingguo Bi[1,2]

[1] Tsinghua University, Beijing 100084, China
ljy_gattuso@163.com, bijingguo-001@163.com
[2] Beijing Research Institute of Telemetry, Beijing 100094, China

Abstract. In the recent twenty years, lattice basis reduction algorithm, such as the celebrated LLL (A.K. Lenstra-H.W. Lenstra Jr.-L. Lovász) algorithm plays an important role in the public-key schemes design and cryptanalysis. To assess the security of the public-key cryptosystems by lattice reduction algorithms, the most time-consuming part is running the lattice reduction algorithm on the corresponding lattice with high dimension or big coefficients. In this paper, we investigate secure outsourcing for lattice basis reduction for the first time. We propose a lattice basis reduction scheme such that the clients can outsource their main computation workloads to the untrusted cloud servers. We employ rounding technique and unimodular transformation matrix for privacy protection before sending the target lattice basis to the cloud. The results returned from the cloud need to be decrypted and verified to satisfy reduction conditions. The experimental results indicate that our scheme is correct, efficient and feasible.

Keywords: Cloud computing · Outsource-secure · Lattice basis reduction · LLL algorithm · QR-factorization

1 Introduction

Cloud computing provides a shared pool of computation resources such as computational power and storage capacity. The enterprises and individuals, whose research involves mathematics, finance, statistics or computer science, are faced with massive computing needs nowadays. By the way of cloud computing, it can be economical for them to avoid large capital outlays in hardware/software deployment and maintenance. The resource-constrained devices or clients can utilize the unlimited resources in a pay-per-use manner by outsourcing their computation workloads to cloud servers. With all the advantages of high computing power, cheap cost of services, high performance, scalability, accessibility as well as availability, cloud computing has become a hot trend. However, the

Partially supported by National Natural Science Foundation of China Grants No. 61502269, The National Key Research and Development Program of China No. 2017YFA0303903 and Zhejiang Province Key R&D Project No. 2017C01062.

© Springer Nature Switzerland AG 2019
T. Gedeon et al. (Eds.): ICONIP 2019, LNCS 11954, pp. 603–615, 2019.
https://doi.org/10.1007/978-3-030-36711-4_51

process of cloud computing may bring new security concerns. For commercial interests, the cloud has the motivation to save its computing resources or gather more effective information. The outsourced data and the output may be at risk without encryption for an untrusted cloud. Channel security is also a great concern without complete protocol specifications because the cloud itself can not secure individual data subjectively and objectively.

Fully homomorphic encryption [1,2] could be a kind of potential tools for outsourcing by providing both additive and multiplicative homomorphisms. Almost all of the security concerns can be eliminated because addition and multiplication operations are allowed over the ciphertexts while preserving decrypt ability. After a series of improvements [3,4], the unpractical problems, such as an expensive pre-processing phase, the expensive encryptions/decryptions, the extra operations on expanded ciphertexts and key storage, are still not solved eventually. Facing with a broad range of requirements for cloud computing, designing outsource-secure schemes for specific computing problems can be regarded as an alternate way. Because of the particularity of cryptography, the design of outsourcing algorithms need better assurance for security. Many practical outsource-secure schemes have been proposed for modular exponentiation [5–7], matrix multiplication [8,9], matrix determinant computation [10], solving large-scale systems of linear equations [11] and matrix inverse computation [12]. Some other schemes were designed for QR-factorization, linear programming, nonlinear programming and other else computation workloads, but they all need further security analysis. The proposed schemes all tried to satisfy the requirements of correctness, security, robust cheating resistance and high-efficiency. It is convenient to evaluate the correctness and efficiency while the security of schemes is lack of uniform criteria besides brute-force attack.

Lattices, a kind of classical objects in number theory, are widely used in mathematics, cryptanalysis and cryptographic design. A lattice $\mathcal{L}$ is a discrete subgroup of $\mathbb{R}^m$. Lattice basis reduction is one of the important hard problems utilized in public-key cryptography to get a 'better' basis and a set of short basis vectors. LLL algorithm (Lenstra, Lenstra Jr. and Lovász [13]) is a famous polynomial algorithm to find a short vector in a given lattice. However, the running time of the algorithm is quite long on the lattices with high dimension, high rank or extra-large coefficients in the lattice basis matrices. The high frequency of LLL algorithm in public-key cryptography shows that designing outsource-secure scheme for LLL algorithm is meaningful.

In this paper, we investigate secure outsourcing for lattice basis reduction algorithm for the first time. We propose a secure outsourcing scheme of lattice basis reduction algorithm, especially for LLL algorithm, and keep the lattice and the original lattice basis secret. We should consider the mathematical structure and characteristics of lattice. Bi et al. [14] presented significant speedups over Coppersmith's algorithm using rounding technique for lattice basis matrices. Saruchi et al. [15] extended the algorithm of Bi et al. [14] to all of the Euclidean lattices and proposed an efficient reduction algorithm when the lattice is itself a small deformation of an LLL-reduced basis. In our outsourcing scheme, the main techniques to construct an encrypted matrix contain rounding, unimodular transformation matrix and QR-factorization. The clients can outsource the part of LLL-reduction to cloud servers and complete the remaining operations locally e.g. matrix multiplication and verification. In this paper, the correctness, high-efficiency of this scheme and the resistance to general attacks is proved. The experimental results validate the efficiency and effectiveness of our scheme.

The main contributions of our paper are summarized as follows:

– We investigate secure outsourcing for lattice basis reduction algorithm while keeping the lattice secret for the first time.
– We design a scheme to securely outsource LLL-reduction for the general lattices and analyse its correctness, verifiability, security and efficiency.
– We compare the experimental performance of our scheme with the algorithm without outsourcing.

Our paper is organized as follows. Section 2 shows some backgrounds about model of outsource-secure schemes, lattices and lattice basis reduction algorithms. In Sect. 3, we present the outsource-secure LLL-reduction scheme. In Sect. 4, we provide the analyses of correctness, verifiability, efficiency and security for our scheme. Finally, we draw our conclusions in Sect. 5.

2   Preliminary

2.1   Security Model

The system of outsourcing consists of a client and the cloud. A resource-constrained client with limited computational power and storage space needs to outsource its expensive computation task to a cloud server. The cloud server has abundant resources and the ability to supply the cloud service. However, it is shared and not fully trusted by the client. There exist two security models: the semi-honest model, which was introduced separately by Goldreich et al. [16] in 1987 and Golle et al. [17] in 2001; the malicious cloud model, which was introduced separately by Hohenberger, Lysyanskaya [5] in 2005 and Canetti et al. [18] in 2011. The cloud may be not only lazy and curious, but also dishonest. Furthermore, the communication channel between the client and the server is insecure under both security models. In this case, the verifiability and security of outsourcing computation scheme are equally important.

The cloud should faithfully follow the protocol specification in the semi-honest cloud model. We have to make sure that it is infeasible for the cloud to derive any key information from the outsourced task. On the other hand, the cloud can arbitrarily deviate from the protocol specification in the malicious cloud model. Therefore, an outsourcing protocol must be able to handle result verification simultaneously besides basic demands such as correctness and security. Our protocol should be designed to withstand a malicious cloud.

Gennaro et al. [19] presented a framework of securely outsourcing computation to protect input and output privacy. Chen et al. [11] summarized the framework and used it to design a practical outsource-secure algorithm for large-scale systems of linear equations. The scheme consists of key generation algorithm, problem generation algorithm, cloud computation, verification algorithm and solving algorithm. We utilize this framework and rename each part intuitively as Fig. 1.

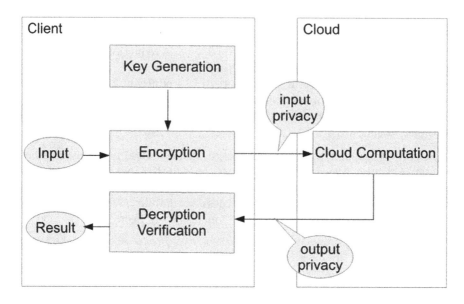

Fig. 1. Secure outsourcing computation scheme

Our outsourcing scheme must have the ability to handle the worst situation that the cloud server is assumed to be lazy, curious and dishonest. According to the previous outsource-secure schemes [9,10], we identify the following goals that our scheme should satisfy to ensure secure and practical outsourcing:

- Correctness: If both the cloud server and the client faithfully follow the protocol specification, the original computation problem can be completed by the cloud and the correct output can be decrypted and verified successfully by the client.
- Security: The protocol can protect the privacy of the client's data. The cloud cannot get sensitive knowledge of the client's input data and the correct result is also hidden from the cloud. These two aspects are respectively noted as input privacy and output privacy.
- Efficiency: The local computation done by client should be substantially less than the original computation without outsourcing. The computation burden on the cloud server should be as close as possible to the existing practical algorithms without outsourcing.
- Robust cheating resistance: No false result from an untrusted cloud server can pass the verification with a non-negligible probability.

2.2   Lattice

Let $\mathbb{R}^m$ be the m-dimensional Euclidean space. A lattice $\mathcal{L}$ is a discrete subgroup of $\mathbb{R}^m$: there exist $n(\le m)$ linearly independent vectors $\mathbf{b}_1, \ldots, \mathbf{b}_n \in \mathbb{R}^m$ s.t. $\mathcal{L}$ is the set $\mathcal{L}(\mathbf{b}_1, \ldots, \mathbf{b}_n)$ of all integral linear combinations of $\mathbf{b}_i$,

$$\mathcal{L}(\mathbf{b}_1, \ldots, \mathbf{b}_n) = \left\{ \sum_{i=1}^n x_i \mathbf{b}_i : x_i \in \mathbb{Z} \right\}.$$

The matrix $\mathbf{B} = (\mathbf{b}_1, \ldots, \mathbf{b}_n)$ is called a *basis* of $\mathcal{L}$ and n is the *rank* (or *dimension*) of $\mathcal{L}$. The (co-)volume of $\mathcal{L}$ is $\mathrm{vol}(\mathcal{L}) = \sqrt{\det(\mathbf{B}^T \mathbf{B})}$ for any basis $\mathbf{B}$ of $\mathcal{L}$, where $\mathbf{B}^T$ denotes $\mathbf{B}$'s transpose. If $\mathbf{B}$ is square, then $\mathrm{vol}(\mathcal{L}) = |\det \mathbf{B}|$, and if $\mathbf{B}$ is further triangular, then $\mathrm{vol}(\mathcal{L})$ is simply the product of the diagonal entries of $\mathbf{B}$ in absolute value. The volume is an important invariant for a certain lattice.

Definition 1 (Successive minima). *Given a lattice $\mathcal{L}$ with rank n, the i-th minima $\lambda_i(\mathcal{L})$ is the radius of the smallest sphere centered in the origin containing i linearly independent lattice vectors, i.e., $\lambda_i(\mathcal{L}) = \inf\{r : \dim(\mathrm{span}(\mathcal{L} \cap B_n(r))) \ge i\}$, where $B_n(r)$ represents the n-dimension ball centered at the origin with radius r.*

To find a short vector in a given lattice, the first polynomial algorithm is the celebrated LLL algorithm [13]: given a basis $(\mathbf{b}_1, \ldots, \mathbf{b}_n)$ of an integer lattice $L \subseteq \mathbb{Z}^m$, LLL algorithm outputs a non-zero $\mathbf{v} \in L$ s.t. $\|\mathbf{v}\| \le 2^{\frac{n-1}{2}} \lambda_1$ in time $O(n^5 m b^3)$ (resp. $n^3 m b \widetilde{O}(n) \widetilde{O}(b)$) without (resp. with) fast integer arithmetic, where $b = \max\limits_{1 \le i \le n} \log \|\mathbf{b}_i\|$. The vector $\mathbf{v}$ is actually the first vector of the basis outputted by the algorithm and the new basis is shorter and 'better' overall.

Proposition 1. *Let $(\mathbf{b}_1, \ldots, \mathbf{b}_n)$ be an LLL-reduced basis of a lattice $\mathcal{L}$. Then:*

1. *$\mathrm{vol}(\mathcal{L}) \le \prod_{i=1}^n \|\mathbf{b}_i\| \le 2^{\frac{n(n-1)}{4}} \mathrm{vol}(\mathcal{L})$.*
2. *$\|\mathbf{b}_1\| \le 2^{\frac{n-1}{4}} (\mathrm{vol}(\mathcal{L}))^{\frac{1}{n}}$.*
3. *$\forall 1 \le i \le n, \|\mathbf{b}_i\| \le 2^{\frac{n-1}{2}} \lambda_i(\mathcal{L})$.*

Let $\mathbf{B} \in \mathbb{R}^{m \times n}$ be full column rank. There exists a unique pair $(\mathbf{Q}, \mathbf{R})$ such that $\mathbf{B} = \mathbf{Q} \cdot \mathbf{R}, \mathbf{Q} \in \mathbb{R}^{m \times n}, \mathbf{R} \in \mathbb{R}^{n \times n}$, the columns of $\mathbf{Q}$ are orthonormal and the matrix $\mathbf{R}$ is upper-triangular with positive diagonal coefficients. The matrices $\mathbf{Q}$ and $\mathbf{R}$ are respectively called the Q-factor and R-factor of B. The quantity $\mathrm{cond}(\mathbf{R}) = \||\mathbf{R}| \cdot |\mathbf{R}^{-1}|\|$, where $|\mathbf{R}| = (|r_{i,j}|)$.

Chang et al. [20] studied and summarized the properties of LLL-reduction under QR-factorization systematically.

Definition 2. ([20] Valid LLL-parameters). *Let $\varXi = (\delta, \eta, \theta)$ with $\eta \in [\frac{1}{2}, 1)$, $\theta \in [0, 1]$ and $\delta \in (\eta^2, 1]$. Let $\mathbf{B} \in \mathbb{R}^{m \times n}$ be nonsingular with QR-factorization $\mathbf{B} = \mathbf{QR}$. The matrix $\mathbf{B}$ is $\varXi$-LLL-reduced if:*

1. *for all $i < j$, we have $|r_{i,j}| \le \eta r_{i,i} + \theta r_{j,j}$ ($\mathbf{B}$ is said size-reduced).*

2. *for all i, we have $\delta r_{i,i}^2 \le r_{i,i+1}^2 + r_{i+1,i+1}^2$ (**B** is said to satisfy Lovász' conditions).*

Particularly, $\eta = \frac{1}{2}, \theta = 0, \delta = \frac{3}{4}$ is equivalent to the classical conditions of LLL-reduction.

3   Outsourcing Scheme for Lattice Basis Reduction

Here we present an outsourcing scheme for lattice basis reduction. We cite the result of Saruchi et al. [15] to establish our scheme. For a basis **B** of the target lattice, we construct a perturbation matrix $\Delta\mathbf{B}$ with the same dimension. We can control the distance between **B** and $\mathbf{B} + \Delta\mathbf{B}$ by limiting the bit lengths of the elements in $\Delta\mathbf{B}$. Aftering reducing $\mathbf{B} + \Delta\mathbf{B}$ with LLL algorithm, we can directly get a LLL-reduced basis of **B**. Thus, we can outsource the part of LLL-reduction of lattices to cloud servers. The main techniques during the encryption process are rounding off the least significant bits and multiplying unimodular transformation matrix to confuse the elements of the lattice basis matrix.

Our scheme is given as follows:

Key Generation:

1. Get the original matrix $\mathbf{B} \in \mathbb{R}^{m \times n}$ with full column rank.
2. Select a unimodular matrix $\mathbf{D} \in \mathbb{Z}^{n \times n}$ randomly. Compute the matrix $\tilde{\mathbf{B}} = \mathbf{BD}$.
3. Choose valid LLL-parameters $\varXi > \varXi_w$. Compute the constants c and β of Theorem 1.
4. Set $\chi \ge \mathrm{cond}(\mathbf{R})$, where $\mathbf{R}$ is the R-factor of $\tilde{\mathbf{B}}$. Set $p = \lceil \log(4cm^7\beta^n\chi^2) \rceil$.
5. For each $i \le n$, find $e_i \in \mathbb{Z}$ such that $\frac{|2^{e_i} - \|\tilde{\mathbf{b}}_i\| |}{\|\tilde{\mathbf{b}}_i\|} \le \frac{3}{4}$. Set $\mathbf{E}_{\tilde{\mathbf{B}}} = 2^{-p}\mathrm{diag}_i(2^{e_i})$ and $\mathbf{M}_{\tilde{\mathbf{B}}} = \lfloor \tilde{\mathbf{B}} \cdot \mathbf{E}_{\tilde{\mathbf{B}}}^{-1} \rfloor$.
6. Secret key: $\mathbf{B}, \mathbf{D}$.

Encryption:

1. Compute the matrix of the new basis $\bar{\mathbf{B}} = \mathbf{M}_{\tilde{\mathbf{B}}} \mathbf{E}_{\tilde{\mathbf{B}}}$.

Cloud Computation:

1. Compute $\mathbf{U}$ such that $\bar{\mathbf{B}}\mathbf{U}$ is $\varXi$-LLL-reduced.

Decryption and Verification:

1. Check whether $\mathbf{U}$ is unimodular or not.
2. Output $\tilde{\mathbf{B}}\mathbf{U}$.
3. Check whether $\tilde{\mathbf{B}}\mathbf{U}$ is a $\varXi_w$-LLL-reduced basis of the lattice $\mathcal{L}(\mathbf{B})$.

4   Analysis

4.1   Correctness and Verifiability Guarantee

The correctness of our scheme is guaranteed by Theorem 1 [15]. Saruchi et al. gave a sufficient condition on the closeness between $\bar{\mathbf{B}} = \mathbf{B} + \varDelta\mathbf{B}$ and $\mathbf{B}$ so that an LLL-reducing transformation $\mathbf{U}$ for $\bar{\mathbf{B}}$ remained valid for $\mathbf{B}$. The main technique is rounding off the least significant bits. The parameters c and $\varXi = (\delta, \eta, \theta)$ and $\varXi_w = (\delta_w, \eta_w, \theta_w)$ in key generation algorithm are chosen according to the follow lemma.

Lemma 1 [20]. *Let* $\eta \in [\frac{1}{2}, 1), \theta \geq 0, \delta \in (\eta^2, 1], \alpha = \frac{\theta\eta + \sqrt{(1+\theta^2)\delta - \eta^2}}{\delta - \eta^2}$ *and* $\mathbf{B} \in \mathbb{R}^{m \times n}$ *be a* (δ, η, θ)-*LLL-reduced basis matrix of* $\mathcal{L}$. *Let* $\varDelta\mathbf{B} \in \mathbb{R}^{m \times n}$ *be a perturbation matrix satisfying*

$$|\varDelta\mathbf{B}| \leq \varepsilon\mathbf{C}|\mathbf{B}|,$$

where $\forall i, j, c_{i,j} = 1, \varepsilon > 0$ *is a small scalar.* ε *satisfies that*

$$\varepsilon' := c_4(1 + \eta + \theta)^n \alpha^n \varepsilon < 1,$$

with c_4 *in Corollary 5.7* [20]. *Then* $\mathbf{B} + \varDelta\mathbf{B}$ *is* $(\delta', \eta', \theta')$-*LLL-reduced with*

$$\delta' = \frac{\delta(1 - \varepsilon')^2}{(1 + \varepsilon')^2(1 + 2\varepsilon'(\eta\alpha + \theta))}, \eta' = \frac{\eta}{1 - \varepsilon'}, \theta' = \frac{\theta + \varepsilon'}{1 - \varepsilon'}.$$

We can find that $(\delta', \eta', \theta')$ in Lemma 1 is 'weaker' than (δ, η, θ), because $\delta' < \delta, \eta' > \eta, \theta' > \theta$. For lattice basis reduction, getting a $(\delta', \eta', \theta')$-LLL-reduced basis is acceptable. The purpose of lattice basis reduction, especially LLL algorithm, is to compute a shorter basis as a whole or get a short vector. A tiny increase of approximation factor would not affect the purposes of application in cryptography, such as pre-processing for other algorithms and searching for short vectors in lattices. Now the following lemma and theorem can prove that $\bar{\mathbf{B}}$ is close enough to $\tilde{\mathbf{B}}$ after encryption. Then $\tilde{\mathbf{B}}\mathbf{U}$ remains to be $\varXi_w$-LLL-reduced when $\bar{\mathbf{B}}\mathbf{U}$ is $\varXi$-LLL-reduced.

Theorem 1 [15]. *For any valid sets of LLL-parameters* $\varXi_w < \varXi (\delta_w < \delta, \eta_w > \eta, \theta_w > \theta)$, *there exists* $c > 0$ *(that may be made explicit) such that the following holds. Let* $\mathbf{B} \in \mathbb{R}^{m \times n}$ *full column rank,* $\mathbf{R}$ *its R-factor, and* $\varDelta\mathbf{B}$ *satisfying* $\max_i \frac{\|\varDelta\mathbf{b}_i\|}{\|\mathbf{b}_i\|} \leq \frac{1}{cm^6\beta^n \mathrm{cond}^2(\mathbf{R})}$ *with* $\beta = (1 + \eta + \theta)\alpha^2$ *and* $\alpha = \frac{\eta\theta + \sqrt{(1+\theta^2)\delta - \eta^2}}{\delta - \eta^2}$. *Then if* $\mathbf{U}$ *is such that* $(\mathbf{B} + \varDelta\mathbf{B})\mathbf{U}$ *is* $\varXi$-*LLL-reduced, then* $\mathbf{B}\mathbf{U}$ *is* $\varXi_w$-*LLL-reduced.*

After we have ensured the correctness of our scheme, we must guarantee the verifiability. To verify the result from the cloud server, we first check whether $\mathbf{U}$ is unimodular. If not, the decryption results $\tilde{\mathbf{B}}\mathbf{U}$ must be not a basis of the lattice $\mathcal{L}(\mathbf{B})$. The client checks whether $\tilde{\mathbf{B}}\mathbf{U}$ is a $\varXi_w$-LLL-reduced basis to make sure that the result is correct. We consider the sufficient conditions of LLL-reduced basis:

$$|\mu_{i,j}| \le \frac{1}{2}, 1 \le j < i \le n; \tag{1}$$

$$\frac{3}{4}\|\mathbf{b}_i^*\|^2 \le \|\mathbf{b}_{i+1}^* + \mu_{i+1,i}\mathbf{b}_i^*\|^2, 1 \le i < n. \tag{2}$$

The computation of verification is $O(n^2 m \log \mathbf{B})$, where $\log \mathbf{B} = \max\limits_{1 \le i \le n} \log \|\mathbf{b}_i\|$, for Gram-Schmidt orthogonalization. If we select $\mathbf{B} \in \mathbb{R}^{m \times n}$, we may take $\log \mathbf{B} = \max\limits_{1 \le i \le n} \log \|\mathbf{b}_i\| +$ (the number of significant digits after the decimal point).

To reduce this part of computation, we can compute the QR-factorization of $\bar{\mathbf{B}}\mathbf{U}$ on the cloud and send Q-factor, R-factor and $\mathbf{U}$ to the client. We can verify the correctness of $\mathbf{U}$ directly by Definition 2 and $\bar{\mathbf{B}}\mathbf{U} = \mathbf{Q} \cdot \mathbf{R}$. This method can decrease the computation workloads on the client side, but the cloud efficiency of our scheme must be reduced due to the additional calculation for QR-factorization. We decide to abandon this method when verifying the result in our scheme.

4.2 Security Analysis

The proposed scheme can protect input privacy if the cloud cannot recover the original matrix $\mathbf{B}$ from the encrypted matrix $\bar{\mathbf{B}}$. $\mathbf{B}$ is encrypted by rounding which is the same technique as the last section. We multiply $\mathbf{B}$ by a unimodular matrix $\mathbf{D}$ to construct $\tilde{\mathbf{B}}$ and hide the most significant bits of $\mathbf{B}$. This process don't change the basis of the lattice $\mathcal{L}(\mathbf{B})$ and it is harder to recover $\mathbf{B}$ from $\bar{\mathbf{B}}$. The encryption of $\tilde{\mathbf{B}}$ is based on the following equation:

$$\mathbf{M}_{\tilde{\mathbf{B}}} = \lfloor \tilde{\mathbf{B}} \cdot \mathbf{E}_{\tilde{\mathbf{B}}}^{-1} \rfloor, \text{where} \mathbf{E}_{\tilde{\mathbf{B}}} = 2^{-p}\text{diag}_i(2^{e_i}), \tag{3}$$

$$\bar{\mathbf{B}} = \mathbf{M}_{\tilde{\mathbf{B}}}\mathbf{E}_{\tilde{\mathbf{B}}}. \tag{4}$$

Without the rounding parameter e_i, p and the intermediate matrix $\mathbf{D}$, it is believed that $\mathbf{B}$ can not be recovered by trivial means. The computational complexity of a brute-force attack is at least $O(mn2^r)$, where r is the bit length of $\bar{\mathbf{B}}$ hid by rounding. $\bar{\mathbf{B}}$ is a basis of a completely different lattice from $\tilde{\mathbf{B}}$ and the most significant bits of the matrix elements can be hidden after multiplying by a perturbation matrix $\mathbf{D}$. If the randomness of $\mathbf{D}$ is strong enough, we can not recover $\mathbf{B}$ directly even $\mathbf{B}$ may have some special structures.

The proposed scheme can protect output privacy if the cloud cannot recover the $\varXi_w$-LLL-reduced basis $\tilde{\mathbf{B}}\mathbf{U}$ from the $\varXi$-LLL-reduced basis $\bar{\mathbf{B}}\mathbf{U}$. Without the private matrix $\mathbf{B}, \mathbf{D}$, there is no direct method to compute $\tilde{\mathbf{B}}\mathbf{U}$. The matrix $\mathbf{U}$ is only an unimodular transformation matrix, so no superfluous information can be obtained from $\mathbf{U}$. The hard problem is reduced to recovering $\mathbf{B}$ from $\bar{\mathbf{B}}$. The security of this problem has been analysed in the part of input privacy.

The original matrix $\mathbf{B}$ and its Ξ_w-LLL-reduced basis $\mathbf{BDU}$ are kept from revealing. Our scheme is feasible and has sufficient security since input privacy and output privacy is protected.

4.3   Efficiency Analysis

Now we consider the efficiency of the proposed scheme. For the cloud, its only computation overhead is generated by running LLL algorithm. The computational complexity of the original LLL algorithm is $O(n^5 m \log^3 \bar{\mathbf{B}})$, where $\log \bar{\mathbf{B}} = \max_{1 \leq i \leq n} \log \|\bar{\mathbf{b}}_i\|$. On the other hand, the main part of the computational complexity on the client side is Gram-Schmidt orthogonalization and matrix multiplication. The computational complexity of conventional matrix multiplication algorithm is $O(n^2 m)$. The computational complexity of key generation and decryption is upper bounded by matrix multiplication algorithm. The local computational complexity is upper bounded by $O(n^2 m \log \mathbf{B})$, which is mainly the computation of verification. Particularly, $\mathbf{B} \in \mathbb{R}^{m \times n}$, it means that we should take $\log \mathbf{B} = \max_{1 \leq i \leq n} \log \|\mathbf{b}_i\| +$ (the number of significant digits after the decimal point). That means $\log \mathbf{B}$ may be much larger than $\log \bar{\mathbf{B}}$ because the elements of $\bar{\mathbf{B}}$ are integers after rounding. However, the local computational complexity $O(n^2 m \log \mathbf{B})$ is substantially less than the computation of LLL algorithm $O(n^5 m \log^3 \bar{\mathbf{B}})$ overall. Then the efficiency of our scheme has been proved.

Now we assess the practical efficiency of the outsourcing scheme with experiments. Firstly, we construct the original matrix $\mathbf{B} \in \mathbb{Z}^{m \times n}$ randomly, where each entry of the matrix are sampled independently and uniformly in $[-2^{10}, 2^{10}]$. To simplify the computational scale, we take the bit length as $\log \mathbf{B} = 10$. In practice, the bit length can be extremely large. Meanwhile, we take $\mathbf{D}$ as upper triangular sparse 0–1 matrix, where the diagonal elements are –1 or 1. Experiment results are presented in Table 1.

In our experiments, we use Shoups NTL library and use Inter(R) Xeon(R) CPU E5620@2.40 GHz with 4 cores in the whole process both on the client side and the cloud side. We list the computation time on client side and cloud side separately in Table 1. In our tables, the time "without outsourcing" refers to the time for the client to run LLL algorithm locally without outsourcing. The time "Cloud" refers to the time for the cloud to compute the outsourced task which mainly includes LLL-reduction algorithm. The time "Client" refers to the time for the cloud to generate the secret key, encrypt the original lattice, decrypt and verify the returned results. It is the sum of time cost for key generation algorithm, encryption algorithm, decryption and verification algorithm. The asymmetric speedup (AS), which is defined as $time_{\text{original}}/time_{\text{client}}$, exhibits the client efficiency gained by outsourcing and represents the savings of the computing resources for the clients. The cloud efficiency (CE), which is defined as $time_{\text{cloud}}/time_{\text{original}}$, represents the overall computation cost on cloud introduced by solving encrypted lattice reduction problem. It is desirable that the value $time_{\text{cloud}}/time_{\text{original}}$ is close to 1. In most cases, the values are a little bigger than 1 because the schemes need some extra operations to keep security.

Table 1. Experiment results for Lattice basis reduction

$m \times n$	Without outsourcing (sec)	Cloud (sec)	Client (sec)	AS	CE
1000×1000	72.4	72.8	20.6	3.5	1.006
1200×1000	77.1	77.4	23.1	3.3	1.003
1500×1500	255.2	254.7	71.4	3.6	0.998
1800×1500	200.6	200.3	83.8	2.4	0.999
2000×2000	480.4	482.2	189.4	2.5	1.004
2400×2000	283.2	283.3	226.5	1.25	1.000

The asymmetric speedup of this scheme is remarkable, while it is not as high as we wish because of the process of verification. The cloud efficiency is almost equal to 1 because $\mathbf{B}, \bar{\mathbf{B}}$ have the same lattice dimension and bit length. The experimental data confirms that secure-outsource scheme for LLL-reduction in cloud computing is economically feasible.

Secondly, we consider the existing models such as the Ajtai-type bases [21] to construct a random lattice basis. The construction that each element of the matrix are sampled independently and uniformly may not be considered random in a mathematical sense. A relatively complete summary for random lattices and random bases was presented by Nguyen and Stehlé [22]. These kinds of random bases can be utilized to clarify the practical behavior of LLL algorithm. In our experiments, we use the knapsack-type bases as the columns of the $(n+1) \times n$ matrices:

$$\begin{pmatrix} A_1 & A_2 & \dots & A_n \\ 1 & 0 & \dots & 0 \\ 0 & 1 & \dots & 0 \\ \vdots & \vdots & \ddots & \vdots \\ 0 & 0 & \dots & 1 \end{pmatrix},$$

where $A_i, 1 \leq i \leq n$ are sampled independently and uniformly in $[-2^{10}, 2^{10}]$. That is, the bit length is $\log \mathbf{B} = 10$. $\mathbf{D}$ is selected as a product of a upper triangular sparse 0–1 matrix and a lower triangular sparse 0–1 matrix, where the diagonal elements are -1 or 1. Experiment results are presented in Table 2.

In this case, the extra cost $((time_{\mathrm{cloud}} + time_{\mathrm{client}})/time_{\mathrm{original}} - 1)$ is obviously greater than the above experimental data. We can confirm that for some bases with specific structure such as the knapsack-type bases, our outsourcing scheme may be uneconomical. This situation is due to the demand of protecting input privacy, while we have to increase the bit lengths of the entries of $\tilde{\mathbf{B}}$. Thus, the running time of LLL algorithm on $\tilde{\mathbf{B}}$ should be increased to a certain extent.

Table 2. Experiment results for Knapsack-type basis

n	Without outsourcing (sec)	Cloud (sec)	Client (sec)	AS	CE
1000	58.3	147.3	19.7	3.0	2.5
1500	196.4	797.6	71.8	2.7	4.1
2000	439.0	2447.3	209.5	2.1	5.6
2500	843.8	5880.6	404.0	2.1	7.0

5 Conclusion

In this paper, we present an outsource-secure scheme for lattice basis reduction for the first time. It is proved that the proposed scheme can meet the design requirements of correctness, robust cheating resistance, high-efficiency and security. The main part of computation workloads, LLL-reduction algorithm, can be outsourced to cloud servers. The clients only need to complete Gram-Schmidt orthogonalization and matrix multiplication locally. Comparing the local workloads, the cloud workloads and the computation cost without outsourcing, our scheme is economical and practical. This outsource-secure scheme can shed light in designing other secure outsourcing schemes related to lattice theory and creating the cloud services of large-scale scientific computation for massive potential clients. Until fully homomorphic encryption or other encryption cryptosystems are universal and practical for cloud computing, designing outsource-secure schemes for specific computing problems separately is useful and necessary in cryptography and computer science.

References

1. Gentry, C.: A fully homomorphic encryption scheme. Ph.D. thesis, Stanford University (2009)
2. Gentry, C.: Fully homomorphic encryption using ideal lattices. In: Proceedings of the 41st Annual ACM Symposium on Theory of Computing, STOC 2009, Bethesda, MD, USA, 31 May–2 June 2009, pp. 169–178 (2009)
3. Gentry, C., Sahai, A., Waters, B.: Homomorphic encryption from learning with errors: conceptually-simpler, asymptotically-faster, attribute-based. In: Canetti, R., Garay, J.A. (eds.) CRYPTO 2013. LNCS, vol. 8042, pp. 75–92. Springer, Heidelberg (2013). https://doi.org/10.1007/978-3-642-40041-4_5
4. Ducas, L., Micciancio, D.: FHEW: bootstrapping homomorphic encryption in less than a second. In: Oswald, E., Fischlin, M. (eds.) EUROCRYPT 2015. LNCS, vol. 9056, pp. 617–640. Springer, Heidelberg (2015). https://doi.org/10.1007/978-3-662-46800-5_24
5. Hohenberger, S., Lysyanskaya, A.: How to securely outsource cryptographic computations. In: Kilian, J. (ed.) TCC 2005. LNCS, vol. 3378, pp. 264–282. Springer, Heidelberg (2005). https://doi.org/10.1007/978-3-540-30576-7_15
6. Chen, X., Li, J., Ma, J., Tang, Q., Lou, W.: New algorithms for secure outsourcing of modular exponentiations. IEEE Trans. Parallel Distrib. Syst. **25**(9), 2386–2396 (2014)

7. Zhou, K., Afifi, M.H., Ren, J.: Expsos: secure and verifiable outsourcing of exponentiation operations for mobile cloud computing. IEEE Trans. Inf. Forensics Secur. **12**(11), 2518–2531 (2017)

8. Atallah, M.J., Frikken, K.B.: Securely outsourcing linear algebra computations. In: Proceedings of the 5th ACM Symposium on Information, Computer and Communications Security, ASIACCS 2010, Beijing, China, 13–16 April 2010, pp. 48–59 (2010)

9. Lei, X., Liao, X., Huang, T., Heriniaina, F.: Achieving security, robust cheating resistance, and high-efficiency for outsourcing large matrix multiplication computation to a malicious cloud. Inf. Sci. **280**, 205–217 (2014)

10. Lei, X., Liao, X., Huang, T., Li, H.: Cloud computing service: the case of large matrix determinant computation. IEEE Trans. Serv. Comput. **8**(5), 688–700 (2015)

11. Chen, X., Huang, X., Li, J., Ma, J., Lou, W., Wong, D.S.: New algorithms for secure outsourcing of large-scale systems of linear equations. IEEE Trans. Inf. Forensics Secur. **10**(1), 69–78 (2015)

12. Hu, C., Alhothaily, A., Alrawais, A., Cheng, X., Sturtivant, C., Liu, H.: A secure and verifiable outsourcing scheme for matrix inverse computation. In: 2017 IEEE Conference on Computer Communications, INFOCOM 2017, Atlanta, GA, USA, 1–4 May 2017, pp. 1–9 (2017)

13. Lenstra, A.K., Lenstra Jr., H.W., Lovász, L.: Factoring polynomials with rational coefficients. Math. Ann. **261**(4), 515–534 (1982)

14. Bi, J., Coron, J.-S., Faugère, J.-C., Nguyen, P.Q., Renault, G., Zeitoun, R.: Rounding and chaining LLL: finding faster small roots of univariate polynomial congruences. In: Krawczyk, H. (ed.) PKC 2014. LNCS, vol. 8383, pp. 185–202. Springer, Heidelberg (2014). https://doi.org/10.1007/978-3-642-54631-0_11

15. Saruchi, Morel, I., Stehlé, D., Villard, G.: LLL reducing with the most significant bits. In: International Symposium on Symbolic and Algebraic Computation, ISSAC 2014, Kobe, Japan, 23–25 July 2014, pp. 367–374 (2014)

16. Goldreich, O., Micali, S., Wigderson, A.: How to play any mental game or A completeness theorem for protocols with honest majority. In: Proceedings of the 19th Annual ACM Symposium on Theory of Computing, New York, NY, USA, pp. 218–229 (1987)

17. Golle, P., Mironov, I.: Uncheatable distributed computations. In: Naccache, D. (ed.) CT-RSA 2001. LNCS, vol. 2020, pp. 425–440. Springer, Heidelberg (2001). https://doi.org/10.1007/3-540-45353-9_31

18. Canetti, R., Riva, B., Rothblum, G.N.: Practical delegation of computation using multiple servers. In: Proceedings of the 18th ACM Conference on Computer and Communications Security, CCS 2011, Chicago, Illinois, USA, 17–21 October 2011, pp. 445–454 (2011)

19. Gennaro, R., Gentry, C., Parno, B.: Non-interactive verifiable computing: outsourcing computation to untrusted workers. In: Rabin, T. (ed.) CRYPTO 2010. LNCS, vol. 6223, pp. 465–482. Springer, Heidelberg (2010). https://doi.org/10.1007/978-3-642-14623-7_25

20. Chang, X.-W., Stehlé, D., Villard, G.: Perturbation analysis of the QR factor R in the context of LLL lattice basis reduction. Math. Comput. **81**(279), 1487–1511 (2012)

21. Ajtai, M.: The worst-case behavior of Schnorr's algorithm approximating the short-est nonzero vector in a lattice. In: Proceedings of the 35th Annual ACM Symposium on Theory of Computing, San Diego, CA, USA, 9–11 June 2003, pp. 396–406 (2003)
22. Nguyen, P.Q., Stehlé, D.: LLL on the average. In: Hess, F., Pauli, S., Pohst, M. (eds.) ANTS 2006. LNCS, vol. 4076, pp. 238–256. Springer, Heidelberg (2006). https://doi.org/10.1007/11792086_18

Social Network Computing

DARIM: Dynamic Approach for Rumor Influence Minimization in Online Social Networks

Adil Imad Eddine Hosni[1,2], Kan Li[1(✉)], and Sadique Ahmad[1,3]

[1] School of Computer Science and Technology, Beijing Institute of Technology,
Beijing 100081, China
{hosni.adil.emp,likan}@bit.edu.cn, ahmad01.shah@gmail.com
[2] Ecole Militaire Polytechnique, 16046 Bordj El-Bahri, Algiers, Algeria
[3] Faculty of Engineering Sciences and Technology, Iqra University Karachi,
Karachi, Pakistan

Abstract. This paper investigates the problem of rumor influence minimization in online social networks (OSNs). Over the years, researchers have proposed strategies to diminish the influence of rumor mainly divided into two well-known methods, namely the anti-rumor campaign strategy and the blocking nodes strategy. Although these strategies have proven to be efficient in different scenarios, their gaps remain in other situations. Therefore, we introduce in this work the dynamic approach for rumor influence minimization (DARIM) that aims to overcome these shortcomings and exploit their advantage. The objective is to find a compromise between the blocking nodes and anti-rumor campaign strategies that minimize the most the influence of a rumor. Accordingly, we present a solution formulated from the perspective of a network inference problem by exploiting the survival theory. Thus, we introduce a greedy algorithm based on the likelihood principle. Since the problem is NP-hard, we prove the objective function is submodular and monotone and provide an approximation within $(1 - 1/e)$ of the optimal solution. Experiments performed in real multiplex and single OSNs provide evidence about the performance of the proposed algorithm compared the work of literature.

Keywords: Rumor propagation · Anti-rumor campaign strategy · Blocking nodes strategy · Rumor influence minimization

1 Introduction

The last decay has witnessed a tremendous increase in the popularity of online social networks (OSNs) such as Facebook, Twitter, or Instagram. These OSNs have contributed massively to global connectivity by bringing people closer together in a small world. However, as every coin have two sides, the adverse effect of OSNs couldn't be avoided, which has to lead the spread of rumors or fake news. The spread rumors in OSNs have a hazardous effect, in which it

© Springer Nature Switzerland AG 2019
T. Gedeon et al. (Eds.): ICONIP 2019, LNCS 11954, pp. 619–630, 2019.
https://doi.org/10.1007/978-3-030-36711-4_52

can change public opinion [14], weakened public trust in governments [9], and create political conflicts [3]. For instance, rumors about vaccines have bolstered the influence of the anti-vaccine movement, contributing to a measles epidemic[1]. Thus, the spread of rumors in OSNs is a significant threat to society and should be halted.

In this fight against the propagation of rumors in OSNs, lot of research have proposed strategy, methods, and algorithms to minimize the influence of these kinds of statements. Works [8,10,12] investigated the blocking nodes or link strategies to limit the spread of undesirable information. However, several researchers have raised concerns about the blocking of users which could impact the users experience in OSNs negatively [10], or it may be considered as a violation of the freedom of expression. Further researches have proposed to initiate a truth campaign that fights the false campaign (rumor) [2,5,6]. The drawbacks of these strategies have been recognized in the late-stages detection of rumors where the efficiency of these methods is reduced [5].

Against these drawbacks, this paper aims to overcome the lacks of the proposed method and exploit their advantage. Therefore, we introduce the dynamic approach for rumor influence minimization (DARIM). The objective is to select K_b node to the blocking nodes strategy and K_t nodes for the truth campaign strategy that minimize the influence of the rumor. Accordingly, a solution has been presented by exploiting both strategies, from the perspective of a network inference problem by using the survival theory. Thus, we introduce a greedy algorithm based on the likelihood principle that guarantees an approximation within 63% of the optimal solution. Systematically, experiments are conducted to illustrate the performer the DARIM in real multiplex, and single OSNs compared the work of literature.

2   Related Work

The problem of rumor propagation in OSNs problem has attracted the interest of researchers. Devising a strategy to minimize the influence of these types of information is one of the significant steps in the fight against these rumors. Recently, there has been a growing interest in problem rumor of influence minimization (RIM) which has been studied on the widely-used information diffusion models: the Independent Cascade (IC) and the Linear Threshold (LT) models [7]. Nevertheless, several works have pointed out the lacks of the LT and the IC modes to reproduce a realistic trend of a rumor propagation. To bridge the gap, works have proposed novel rumor propagation models such as the energy model [4] and the HISBmodel [5]. Considering the topology structure of the networks, human behaviors, or social interactions, many works have proposed strategies to diminish the influence of rumors. Some researchers [10,12] have investigated the blocking nodes or link strategies to limit the spread of undesirable information. However, several concerns have been raised against these strategies, for instance: (1) blocking nodes could impact the user's experience in OSNs negatively [10].

---

[1] https://www.cdc.gov/measles/cases-outbreaks.html.

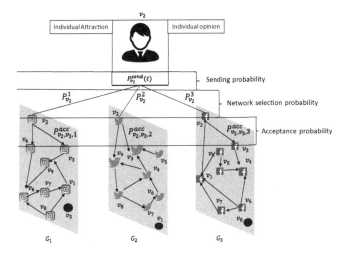

Fig. 1. HISBmodel rumors transmission rules in a multiplex of three (3) OSNs $G^3 = \{G_1 = (V_1, E_1),\ G_2 = (V_2, E_2), G_3 = (V_3, E_3)\}$. The rumor transmission rule is evaluated in three steps: rumor sending probability, network selecting probability, and rumor acceptance probability.

(2) It may be considered as a violation of the freedom of expression. Further researches have proposed to initiate a truth campaign that fights the false campaign (rumor) [2,5,6]. The drawbacks of these strategies are recognized when rumors are detected in late-stages, which reduce the efficiency of these methods [5]. Thus, against these drawbacks, devising method that overcome these shortcomings it mandatory improve the fight against the spread of rumor in OSNs.

3 Problem Formulation

3.1 Online Social Network Definition

Generally, an OSN is represented by a directed or undirected graph $G = (V, E)$, where the set of nodes V represents the users and the set of edges E can be seen as relationships among individuals. However, with the diversity of OSNs, individuals join several networks and forming a multiplex structure of OSNs. A multiplex OSNs with k networks is defined in literature [6] as a set $G^k = \{G_1 = (V_1, E_1),\ G_2 = (V_2, E_2), ..., G_k = (V_k, E_k)\}$, where $G_i = (V_i, E_i)$ is a directed graph representing an OSN. Without loss of generality, networks of the multiplex have a same number of nodes; thus, if a node $v \in G_i$ does not belong to G_j we add this node to G_j as an isolated node as shown in Fig. 1 in black color. Then for each node, inter-layer edges are added to connect its adjacent copies across all the multiplex networks. Finally, we consider the set of all users of the multiplex OSNs as $V = \bigcup\limits_{i=1}^{k} V_i$ where $|V|$=N.

3.2 Rumor Propagation Model

In literature, the rumor diffusion mechanism is seen similar to the spread of epidemics [1], where several models have been proposed to describe this phenomenon. In this work, we have selected the HISBmodel [5] as a rumor diffusion model. Our choice can be justified for these reasons: (1) The HISBmodel considers the individual and social behaviors in the propagation process of rumors, unlike models in the literature. (2) The model allows conducting several RIM strategy without any updates in the model. Thus, the propagation process of the HISBmodel is presented in this part.

Given an multiplex OSN $G^k = \{G_1 = (V_1, E_1),\ G_2 = (V_2, E_2), ..., G_k = (V_k, E_k)\}$ and set of individuals' characteristics C, $\forall c \in C$, $c = (\omega, \beta, \delta)$, where β represents the individual background knowledge factor, ω is the forgetting and remembering factor and δ is the hesitating factor [5]. The rumor spread in a multiplex OSNs in discrete time steps in the form of cascade from one node to another. Initially, a set of individuals are infected with different opinion assigned to each node u randomly. Each infected node u behave toward a rumor differently according it characteristics defined by [5] as follows

$$A_u(t) = A_{int} e^{-\beta_u t} |\sin(\omega_u t + \delta_u)|. \tag{1}$$

Each time step t, an infected node u at time $t-1$ will have a single chance at time t to infect one of its neighbors v with probability $p^i_{u,v}(t)$ in a layer i of the multiplex. The rumor transmission rule is evaluated in three steps: rumor sending probability, network selecting probability, and rumor acceptance probability (see Fig. 1) as follows

$$p^i_{u,v}(t) = p^{send}_u(t) \cdot p^i_u \cdot p^{acc}_{v,u,i}. \tag{2}$$

where

$$p^{send}_u(t) = e^{-\beta_u t} |\sin(\omega_u t + \delta_u)|, \quad p^i_u = \frac{d^i_{in}(u)}{\sum_{j=1}^k d^j_{in}(u)}, \quad p^{acc}_{v,u,i} = \frac{1}{1 + \dfrac{d^i_{in}(v)}{d^i_{in}(u)}} \cdot P, \tag{3}$$

where P is a probability parameter set in the propagation process, and $d^i_{in}(u)$ refers to the in-degree of the node u in the ith layer of ith. First, the sending probability estimates the chances that a user sends a rumor to his neighbors which is defined as $A(t)/A_{int}$. Then, the network selection probability estimates the chances of the node u to send a rumor in the ith layer of the multiplex. Finally, The acceptance probability evaluates the chances that an individual to accept a rumor from his neighbor. The opinion of an infected node v is updated each time a rumor is accepted. In this work, we present a simplified individual opinion by considering that individual either support or refute the rumor. Accordingly, we introduce the subjective judgment $\alpha \in [0, 1]$ factor which reflects the ability of an individual to judge the veracity of a rumor. Therefore, an individual with high values of α will tend to refute the rumor; however, when the judgment factor is low, an individual is more likely to accept the rumor and support it. Moreover, work in [11] has pointed out the effect of herd behavior on the propagation of rumors where it causes people to follow others blindly and adopt their opinions. However, when individuals receive the same information more than one time, it may not affect them as much as the first time, due to the information redundancy. Upon the above analysis, we introduce $\rho \in [0,1]$ the decision factor which evaluates the chance of an individual to change its opinion defined as follows

$$\rho = \frac{\dfrac{\sum AccepteNegativeOpinion}{\sum AcceptedRumors} + \alpha}{2}. \tag{4}$$

Consequently, ρ represents the probability that an individual refute the rumor. Finally, the spreading process ends when rumor popularity fades $R(t) \simeq 0$ defined as follows.

$$R(t) = \sum_{i=1}^{n} R_i(t) \quad \text{where} \quad R_i(t) = \sum_{v \in V} A_v(t) \cdot d_{in}^i(v). \tag{5}$$

3.3   Survival Theory for Rumor Influence Minimization

The survival theory is a mathematical tool widely exploited in the domain of epidemics which estimates the likelihood of the occurrence of an event after observation time. In this paper, the survival theory is used to estimate the likelihood of the infection of an individual by the rumor. Then, the survival function is written as follows

$$S(t) = Pr(T > t) = 1 - F(t), \quad \text{where} \quad f(t) = \frac{dF(t)}{dt} = -S'(t). \tag{6}$$

where T is a random variable representing the infection of an individual by the rumor; t is a specified constant. The survival function represents the probability that individuals survive to the infection of a rumor after the observation deadline t. Given that $F(t)$ is the cumulative distribution function and $f(t)$ is the density function. Another characterization of the distribution of T is given by the hazard rate of an infection of an individual by a rumor, defined as

$$h(t) = \lim_{dt \to 0} \frac{Pr\{t \leqslant T < t + dt | T \geqslant t\}}{dt} = -\frac{S'(t)}{S(t)}, \quad \text{where} \quad S(t) = e^{-\int_0^t h(\tau)d\tau}. \tag{7}$$

In the rest of the paper, this theory will be exploited to analyze the likelihood of nodes getting infected by a rumor.

3.4   Problem Formulation

Studies have proposed strategies to fight against the propagation of these rumors which we can mainly categorize them in the blocking nodes strategies [10,12,13], and the truth campaign strategies [2,5,6]. On the one hand, the blocking nodes strategy has proven to be efficient, but it has raised several concerns in the application in the real worlds OSNs. First, in [10] have stated if the blocking period exceeds a certain threshold, the satisfaction of an individual toward an OSN is reduced. Moreover, the blocking nodes or contents in OSNs is considered in many countries as a violation of the freedom of expression[2]. Additionally, it requires a higher number of nodes blocked than the truth campaign strategy to achieve similar results. However, this strategy shows to have a faster impact on reducing the influence of rumors. On the other hand, truth campaign strategy has raised fewer concerns, but it has been recognized by [5] it low efficiency when the rumor is detected in a late-stage. Moreover, this strategy is more concern in reducing the influence of rumors rather than the propagation, which has relativity slower effect as compared to blocking nodes [5].

Against these drawbacks, We propose in this work an approach that aims to find a compromise between the two strategies. The objective is to select K_b node to be blocked and K_t nodes for the truth campaign strategy that minimize the most the influence of the rumor. Thus, we formulate the problem as follows: given a multiplex OSN $G^k = \{G_1 = (V, E_1), G_2 = (V, E_2), ..., G_k = (V, E_k)\}$, positive constant K that represent our budget, t_{det} detection time of a rumor. Given that $\sigma_b(K_b)$ estimate the likelihood of nodes getting infected after blocking K_b number of nodes; and given that $\sigma_t(t_{K_t})$ estimate the likelihood of nodes getting infected after K_t number of nodes have been selected to lunch a truth campaign. The goal is to find a K_b and K_t the number of nodes selected for both strategies that minimize the most the influence of the rumor.

$$\min[\sigma_b(K_b) + \sigma_t(K_t)]. \tag{8}$$

4   Proposed Solution

In the following, a brief introduction for both strategies will be introduced. Then, we propose DARIM algorithm as a solution for our problem.

4.1   Blocking Node Strategy

This strategy aims to block a certain number of nodes in an OSN so as to limit the propagation of rumors. Thus, given an multiplex OSNs $G^k = \{G_1 = (V_1, E_1), G_2 = (V_2, E_2), ..., G_k = (V_k, E_k)\}$, an constrain K_b and detection time of a rumor T_{det}, the objective function is to block K_b nodes so as to minimize the propagation of a rumor. This strategy selects the nodes that are most likely to be

---

[2] https://bit.ly/2PZ4JFb.

infected by the rumor and support it. Thus, the hazard rate of a node v getting infected and will support rumor at time t is presented

$$h_v(t) = \sum_{i=0}^{k} \sum_{u \in \mathbb{N}^v} p_{u,v}^i(t) \cdot (1 - \rho_v).$$

(9)

Combining equations Eqs. 6, 7, and 9 the cumulative distribution function is shown as follows:

$$F_v(t) = 1 - e^{-(1-\rho_v) \sum_{i=0}^{k} \sum_{u \in \mathbb{N}^v} \int_0^t p_{u,v}^i(\tau)d\tau} = 1 - \prod_{t_i > t: i=0}^{k} \prod_{u \in \mathbb{N}^v} e^{-(1-\rho_v) \int_0^t p_{u,v}^i(\tau)d\tau}.$$

(10)

Then, the likelihood function of node v getting infected at time t, given as follows

$$f_v(t) = \sum_{i=0}^{k} \sum_{u \in \mathbb{N}^v} (1 - \rho_v) p_{u,v}^i(t) \cdot \prod_{i=0}^{k} \prod_{w \in \mathbb{N}^v} e^{-(1-\rho_v) \int_0^t p_{u,w}^i(\tau)d\tau}.$$

(11)

From Eq. 11, we can generalize the likelihood of nodes getting infected

$$f_V(t) = \prod_{v:A_v(t)=0} \sum_{i=0}^{k} \sum_{u \in \mathbb{N}^v} (1 - \rho_v) p_{u,v}^i(t) \prod_{i=0}^{k} \prod_{w \in \mathbb{N}^v} e^{-(1-\rho_v) \int_0^t p_{w,v}^i(\tau)d\tau}.$$

(12)

Thus, given function f, we define σ_b which estimates likelihood the nodes getting infected after K_b nodes have been blocked. The main objective is formulated s follows

$$\min[\sigma_b(K_b)].$$

(13)

4.2 Truth Campaign Strategy

This approach aims to launch an anti-rumor campaign to minimize the influence of a rumor. After a rumor is detected at time T_{det}, the population is divided into two sets $V = V_- \cup V_+$ where V_+ is the set of individual supporting the rumor, and V_- is the set of individual refuting the rumor. The objective is to select K_t nodes form V_+ to launch the truth campaign to minimize the influence of individuals. Thus, the hazard rate of the nodes getting infected by a node u and refute a rumor is as follow.

$$r_u(t) = \sum_{i=1}^{k} \sum_{v \in \mathbb{N}_i^u} p_{u,v}^i(t)\rho_v = p_u^{send}(t) \sum_{i=1}^{k} \sum_{v \in \mathbb{N}_i^u} p_v^i p_{u,v}^{acc}\rho_v.$$

(14)

By substituting $r(t)$ into Eq. 7 and combining equations Eqs. 6 and 7 yields the cumulative distribution function

$$G_v(t) = 1 - e^{-\int_0^t p_u^{send}(\tau) \sum_{i=1}^{k} \sum_{v \in \mathbb{N}_i^u} \rho_v p_u^i p_{u,v}^{acc} d\tau} = 1 - \prod_{i=1}^{k} \prod_{v \in \mathbb{N}^u} e^{-\rho_v p_u^i p_{u,v}^{acc} \int_0^t p_v^{send}(\tau)d\tau}.$$

(15)

Then, the likelihood function of nodes getting infected by v is given as follow

$$g_u(t) = \frac{dG_u(t)}{dt} = \sum_{i=1}^{k} \sum_{v \in \mathbb{N}^u} p_u^i p_{u,v}^{acc} p_u^{send}(t) \rho_v \prod_{i=1}^{n} \prod_{w \in \mathbb{N}^u} e^{-\rho_v p_u^i p_{u,w}^{acc} \int_0^t p_u^{send}(\tau) d\tau}.$$
(16)

From Eq. 16, we could generalize the likelihood function of the nodes getting infected given as follows

$$g_V(t) = \prod_{u \in V: A_u(t) > 0} \sum_{i=1}^{k} \sum_{v \in \mathbb{N}^u} p_u^i p_{u,v}^{acc} p_u^{send}(t) \rho_v \prod_{i=1}^{n} \prod_{w \in \mathbb{N}^u} e^{-\rho_v p_u^i p_{u,w}^{acc} \int_0^t p_u^{send}(\tau) d\tau}.$$
(17)

Therefor, given function g we define σ_t which estimates the nodes getting infected after K_t nodes have lunched a anti-rumor campaign where the main objective is formulated s follows

$$\min[\sigma_t(K_t)].$$
(18)

4.3 Proposed Algorithm

The RIM problem has been proved by different work that is an NP-hard problem, then since RIM problem on a single network is a particular case of a multiplex; hence, this last problem is NP-hard as well. Thus, we need to prove that the proposed algorithm guarantees an approximation ratio from the optimal solution. The submodularity of the functions $\sigma_t(.)$ and $\sigma_b(.)$ present an excellent way to obtain an approximation within a factor of $(1 - 1/e)$. We say a function $\sigma(.)$ is submodular if it satisfies the following condition

$$\sigma(A) + \sigma(B) \geqslant \sigma(A \cup B) + \sigma(A \cap B),$$
(19)

where $A, B \subset I$, $A \subseteq B$ and $v \notin B$. In another word, σ is submodular if it has the diminishing marginal return property. Therefore, given a multiplex OSNs $G^k = \{G_1 = (V_1, E_1), G_2 = (V_2, E_2), ..., G_k = (V_k, E_k)\}$, we prove that the function g and f are submodular which provides proof of the submodularity of $\sigma_t(.)$ and $\sigma_b(.)$. Using the following lemmas we prove the submodularity.

Lemma 1. $\forall A, B \subset V, A \subset B \Longleftrightarrow g_{A \cup B}(t) = g_B(t)$ and $f_{A \cup B}(t) = f_B(t)$.

Proof. We have $\forall A, B \subset V$, and Since $\forall v \in A \Rightarrow v \in B$

$$g_{A \cup B}(t) = \prod_{v \in A \cup B: A_v(t) > 0} g_v(t) = \prod_{v \in B: A_v(t) > 0} g_v(t) = g_B(t),$$
(20)

Along this way

$$f_{A \cup B}(t) = \prod_{v \in A \cup B: A_v(t) = 0} f_v(t) = \prod_{v \in B: A_v(t) = 0} f_v(t) = f_B(t).$$
(21)

Lemma 2. $\forall A, B \subset V, A \subset B \Longleftrightarrow g_{A \cap B}(t) = g_A(t)$ and $f_{A \cap B}(t) = f_A(t)$.

Proof. We have $\forall A, B \subset V$, and given that $A \subset B \Longleftrightarrow A \cap B = A$

$$g_{A \cap B}(t) = \prod_{v \in A \cap B : A_v(t) > 0} g_v(t) = \prod_{v \in A : A_v(t) > 0} g_v(t) = g_A(t), \qquad (22)$$

similarly

$$f_{A \cap B}(t) = \prod_{v \in A \cap B : A_v(t) = 0} f_v(t) = \prod_{v \in A : A_v(t) = 0} f_v(t) = f_A(t). \qquad (23)$$

Lemma 3. *The functions f and g are monotone.*

Proof. We have $\forall A, B, C \subseteq V$ and $A \subseteq B$ and $B \subseteq C$ then

$$g_B(t) = \prod_{v \in B : A_v(t) > 0} g_v(t) = \prod_{v \in A : A_v(t) > 0} g_v(t) + X = g_A(t) + X. \qquad (24)$$

Similarly we can obtain

$$g_C(t) = \prod_{v \in B : A_v(t) > 0} g_v(t) + X' = g_B(t) + X' = g_A(t) + X + X', \qquad (25)$$

where X ans X' are constants number. Therefore, we can claim $g_A(t) \leqslant g_B(t) \leqslant g_C(t)$ which provide prove that g is monotone. Similarly we can prove that f is monotone as well.

Theorem 1. *The influence function of the proposed solution is submodular and monotone.*

Proof. The proof of this theorem can be obtained from the submodularity and monotonicity of the objective functions $\sigma_t(.)$ and $\sigma_b(.)$. According to Lemmas 1 and 2, we can claim that Eq. (19) holds for $\sigma_t(.)$ and $\sigma_b(.)$. Moreover, considering Lemma 3 allows to stat that $\sigma_t(.)$ and $\sigma_b(.)$ are monotone functions. Accordingly, we can prove that $\sigma_t(.)$ and $\sigma_b(.)$ are submodular functions. Finally, since, the class of submodular functions is closed under a non-negative linear combination, we can claim that the objective function of the proposed solution is submodular and monotone.

According to the previous analysis, we introduce a greedy algorithm named DARIM algorithm, which guarantees an approximation ratio from the optimal solution within the factor of $(1 - 1/e)$.

5   Experiments

In this section, experiments have been conducted to highlight the performance of the proposed solution. The employed datasets are detailed in Table 1. The algorithms presented for comparison are as follows: (1) **Random Blocking node**

Algorithm 1. DARIM algorithm

Input: $G^k = \{G_1 = (V_1, E_1), ..., G_k = (V_k, E_k)\}$, V_-, V_+,K and t_{det}.
$N_b = \{\}$ // Set of blocking nodes
$N_t = \{\}$ // Set of nodes lunching truth campaign
for $i \leftarrow 1 : K$ **do**

$\quad u = \underset{v \in V_+}{\arg\max} \left[g_{V_- \cup \{v\}}(t_{det}) - g_{V_-}(t_{det}) \right];$

$\quad w = \underset{v \in V}{\arg\max} \left[f_{V \cup \{v\}}(t_{det}) - f_V(t_{det}) \right];$

$\quad$ **if** $g_u(t_{det}) \geq f_w(t_{det})$ **then**
$\quad\quad$ $N_t = N_t \cup \{u\};$

$\quad$ **else**
$\quad\quad$ $N_b = N_b \cup \{w\};$

Output: N_t, N_b

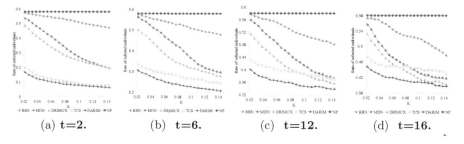

(a) t=2.   (b) t=6.   (c) t=12.   (d) t=16.

Fig. 2. The impact of the rumor influence minimization algorithms on the propagation process in single OSN for different values of t_{det}.

Algorithm (RBA). (2) **Max degree blocking node Algorithm** (MDN). (3) **Blocking node Greedy Algorithm** (Drimux) of [10]. (4) **Truth campaign strategy** (TCS) proposed by [5]. (5) **DARIM** the proposed algorithm. We set the human factors according to [5], and select randomly $0.2\%N$ nodes as initial spreaders of a rumor. For these experiments, we illustrate the impact of K as well as the detection time of the rumor, where each simulation is repeated 1000 times to avoid randomness. The results of the experiments are shown in Figs. 2 and 3 illustrating the impact of the presented algorithm on the propagation of a rumor for a given detection time of a rumor t_{det} and by varying the rate of K in single and multiplex OSNs.

The results show a significant reduction of the impact of a rumor by all the algorithms in the early-stage detection of the rumor as compared to the late-stage detection. Similarly, a significant decrease in the impact of the rumor is seen for higher values of K. Moreover, it is seen in Figs. 2 and 3 that the blocking nodes strategies present better results when K is higher. However, It is shown that the proposed algorithm performs the best among all the presented algorithms in all the presented scenarios. Deeply analyzing the results, it is seen that the TCS and DARIM obtains a good results in the early stage detection

Table 1. Data sets description.

#	#Layer	OSN names	Type	#Nodes	#Edge	$\langle k \rangle$
1	1	Twitter	Directed	4,546	280,846	39.53
2	3	FaceBook	Undirected	663	1,185	1.78
		Twitter	Directed	5,540	62,841	11.52
		Youtube	Undirected	5,702	84,647	14.84

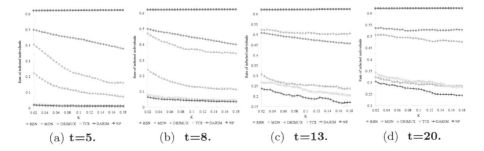

(a) t=5.   (b) t=8.   (c) t=13.   (d) t=20.

Fig. 3. The impact of the rumor influence minimization algorithms on the propagation process in multiplex OSNs for different values of t_{det}.

of the rumor as compared to blocking nodes strategies even in the case when K is low (see Figs. 2(a), (b), 3(a) and (b)). Additionally, blocking nodes strategies and DARIM present better performance than TCS when the rumor is detected in the late-stage and K is relatively higher (see Figs. 2(c), (d),3(c) and (d)). Presumably, when the rumor is detected at a relatively late-stage, it would have already infected a large portion of the nodes in the entire network and individuals will already lose interest about the rumor. Among all, the DARIM presents the best results in the late-stages and early-stage detection, when K is high and low, and in a single and multiplex OSNs. The evidence from these results confirms the outstanding performance of DARIM in reducing the effect of rumors in OSNs by exploiting the advantage of the truth campaign and blocking nodes strategies.

6   Conclusions

This paper investigates rumor influence minimization problem in online social networks (OSNs). Considering the drawbacks of the truth campaign and blocking nodes strategies in minimizing the influence of rumors, we introduce the dynamic approach for rumor influence minimization, which aims to overcome their shortcoming and exploit their advantage. The objective is to select K_b node to the blocking nodes strategy and K_t nodes for the truth campaign strategy that minimize the influence of the rumor. Accordingly, we present a solution formulated from the perspective of a network inference problem by exploiting the survival theory. Thus, we introduce a greedy algorithm based on the likelihood principle that guarantees an approximation within $(1-1/e)$ of the optimal solution. Experiments performed in real multiplex and single OSNs provide evidence about the performance of the proposed algorithm compared the work of literature.

Acknowledgment. This research was supported by National Key R & D Program of China (No. 2016YFB0801100), Beijing Natural Science Foundation (No. 4172054, L181010), and National Basic Research Program of China (No. 2013CB329605).

References

1. Daley, D., Kendall, D.: Epidemics and rumours. Nature **204**, 4963 (1964). https://doi.org/10.1038/2041118a0
2. Fan, L., Lu, Z., Wu, W., Bhavani, T., Ma, H., Bi, Y.: Least cost rumor blocking in social networks. In: IEEE 33rd International Conference on Distributed Computing Systems (2013). https://doi.org/10.1109/ICDCS.2013.34
3. Garrett, R.K.: Troubling consequences of online political rumoring. Hum. Commun. Res. **37**(2), 255–274 (2011)
4. Han, S., Zhuang, F., He, Q., Shi, Z., Ao, X.: Energy model for rumor propagation on social networks. Phys. A Stat. Mech. its Appl. **394**, 99–109 (2014). https://doi.org/10.1016/j.physa.2013.10.003
5. Hosni, A.I.E., Li, K., Ahmed, S.: HISBmodel: a rumor diffusion model based on human individual and social behaviors in online social networks. In: Cheng, L., Leung, A.C.S., Ozawa, S. (eds.) ICONIP 2018. LNCS, vol. 11302, pp. 14–27. Springer, Cham (2018). https://doi.org/10.1007/978-3-030-04179-3_2
6. Hosni, A.I.E., Li, K., Ding, C., Ahmed, S.: Least cost rumor influence minimization in multiplex social networks. In: Cheng, L., Leung, A.C.S., Ozawa, S. (eds.) ICONIP 2018. LNCS, vol. 11306, pp. 93–105. Springer, Cham (2018). https://doi.org/10.1007/978-3-030-04224-0_9
7. Kempe, D., Kleinberg, J., Tardos, É.: Maximizing the spread of influence through a social network. In: KDD, p. 137 (2003)
8. Kimura, M., Saito, K., Motoda, H.: Minimizing the spread of contamination by blocking links in a network. In: AAAI, pp. 1175–1180 (2008)
9. Pogue, D.: How to stamp out fake news. Sci. Am. **316**(2), 24–24 (2017)
10. Wang, B., Chen, G., Fu, L., Song, L., Wang, X.: DRIMUX: dynamic rumor influence minimization with user experience in social networks. IEEE Trans. Knowl. Data Eng. **29**(10), 2168–2181 (2017)
11. Wang, J., Wang, Y.Q., Li, M.: Rumor spreading considering the herd mentality mechanism. In: 2017 36th Chinese Control Conference, pp. 1480–1485. IEEE (2017)
12. Yan, R., Li, Y., Wu, W., Li, D., Wang, Y.: Rumor blocking through online link deletion on social networks. ACM Trans. Knowl. Discov. Data **13**(2), 1–26 (2019). https://doi.org/10.1145/3301302
13. Yao, Q., Shi, R., Zhou, C., Wang, P., Guo, L.: Topic-aware social influence minimization. In: Proceedings of the 24th International Conference on World Wide Web - WWW 2015 Companion (1), pp. 139–140 (2015). https://doi.org/10.1145/2740908.2742767
14. Zubiaga, A., Aker, A., Bontcheva, K., Liakata, M., Procter, R.: Detection and resolution of rumours in social media: a survey (2017). https://doi.org/10.1145/3161603. http://arxiv.org/abs/1704.00656

SRRL: Select Reliable Friends for Social Recommendation with Reinforcement Learning

Zhenni Lu[1,2], Min Gao[1,2(✉)], Xinyi Wang[1,2], Junwei Zhang[1,2], Haider Ali[1,2], and Qingyu Xiong[1,2]

[1] School of Big Data and Software Engineering, Chongqing University, Chongqing 400044, China
[2] Key Laboratory of Dependable Service Computing in Cyber Physical Society, Chongqing University, Ministry of Education, Chongqing 400044, China
{jennylu,gaomin,xywang,jw.zhang,xiong03}@cqu.edu.cn,
bscs.f13.17@gmail.com

Abstract. Along with the boom of social media, researchers consider that incorporating social relationships into traditional recommender systems can help alleviate the problems of data sparsity and cold start. However, recent reports show that social recommendation can hardly get the expected effect. The unsatisfying result can be attributed to the fact that users may share different preferences with their friends because of the randomness in the process of building social networks. In consequence, direct use of social relationships may lead to the degradation of recommendation performance, which makes identifying reliable friends for each user critical. In this paper, we propose an end-to-end social recommendation framework based on reinforcement learning to identify reliable social relationships for users. Specifically, our model consists of two parts: (a) an agent which samples users' reliable social relationships and delivers them to the environment. (b) an environment which takes charge of generating recommendations with sampled social relations and returning rewards to the agent to optimize the sampling procedure. With the interactions between the agent and the environment, our model can dynamically identify reliable friends whose preferences are really similar to the current user. Experimental analysis on two real-world datasets demonstrates that our approach outperforms the state-of-the-art social recommendation algorithms.

Keywords: Reinforcement learning · Social recommendation · Reliable friends

1 Introduction

As a technique that can help users find the items they are really interested in, recommender systems have become popular and effective in mitigating information overload problem. However, traditional recommender systems also suffer

© Springer Nature Switzerland AG 2019
T. Gedeon et al. (Eds.): ICONIP 2019, LNCS 11954, pp. 631–642, 2019.
https://doi.org/10.1007/978-3-030-36711-4_53

from two major challenges: data sparsity and cold start. In order to alleviate the above-mentioned two problems, researchers attempted to incorporate auxiliary information to infer users' preferences. A promising way is to use the information in social networks as social relations become more accessible with the promotion of social platforms. Based on the intuition that people often show affinities to items that their friends like, many social recommendation models combine users' ratings and social relationships to model users' preferences [2,5,10,20,21]. Despite the fact that these methods have shown effectiveness in some cases, through in-depth research, it has been found that there exist some drawbacks in those models which use users' social relationship directly. In fact, users may have totally different tastes with their friends as the process of building online contact networks involves too much randomness, thus indiscriminately using all social relationships to infer users' preferences may introduce noise into recommender systems.

There exists some previous work which focused on extracting useful relationships from social networks [3,4,17,19]. However, most of them are subject to the precondition that all the social relationships used are informative, and they only model the strength of social relationships and adjust impacts of social relationships on users based on the strength in a static view. Unlike these models, we believe that not all of the social relations are helpful, thus introduce a procedure of extracting friends who can truly reflect preferences of users. In this paper, we propose a novel approach which can dynamically identify users' reliable social relationships. More specifically, our model consists of two parts: (1) an agent that is responsible for generating a probability distribution with regard to the current user's social relationships and sampling reliable friends according to the probability distribution; (2) an environment that takes charge of evaluating the quality of these friends and inferring users' preferences based on the sampled friends. The challenge we face is that the process of sampling users' social relationship is discrete so that our model cannot be directly optimized by gradient descent. An effective way to solve this problem is to use policy gradient based reinforcement learning. By applying the strategy of policy gradient, we manage to bypass the non-differential problem and use the reward to bridge the agent and the environment. Particularly, as the reward is real-time, our model can adaptively sample the friends that can boost the recommendation performance according to the feedback, and optimize its parameters in a dynamic view.

To sum up, the main contributions of this paper are as follows:

(1) We incorporate the notion of reliable friends who really share similar tastes with users into probabilistic matrix factorization for social recommendation.
(2) We propose a novel approach which uses policy gradient based reinforcement learning to perform end-to-end training. Through dynamic interactions between the agent which samples reliable friends and the environment which is responsible for assessing these friends, our model can find friends for users that can best reflect their preferences.

(3) We conduct experiments on two real-world datasets and the experimental results show that our proposed method significantly outperforms the existing methods.

2   Related Work

2.1   Social Recommendation

Social relationships tend to have strong effects on human behaviors [14], which stimulates the study of social recommendation. Among these work, SocialMF [8] considers the propagation characteristics of trust, assuming that users' feature vectors are close to their friends'. RSTE [6] is based on the idea of integration which believes that a user's feature vector should be determined by his/her own preference and friends' preferences. SoRec [7] treats social network as a relationship adjacency matrix, and co-factorizes rating matrix and trust matrix. In SoReg [11], social network information is used to design social regularization terms to constrain the objective function of matrix factorization. TrustMF [2] and TrustSVD [5] also integrate the factorization of rating matrix and trust matrix, but they believe that the trust and trusted relationships of users are both indispensable for modeling users' preferences. Unlike these models, TBPR [19] introduces the concept of strong and weak social ties into the probability matrix factorization, while PTPMF [17] assumes that different users have different preferences for strong and weak social ties.

2.2   Reinforcement Learning

Reinforcement learning can be divided into value-based approaches and policy-based approaches [1]. The value-based reinforcement learning calculates the value of each action according to the current state, and then take actions based on the value greedily (e.g., Q-learning [15]). Policy-based reinforcement learning directly outputs actions or the probabilities of actions based on the state (e.g., Policy Gradient). In this paper, we adopt policy gradient based reinforcement learning method [18]. Some work applies reinforcement learning to recommender systems, such as IRGAN [16] which uses GAN and reinforcement learning to generate discrete indices of items relevant to a given user. Unlike them, in this paper we focus on identifying users' reliable friends based on reinforcement learning.

3   Method

In this section, we first outline our model which focuses on dynamically identifying reliable friends for users. Next, we use reinforcement learning terminology to introduce how the agent and the environment work.

3.1   Dynamic Assessment of Social Relationships

So far few studies focus on how to dynamically evaluate the quality of social relations. In practice, the psychological activities of humans are complex and changeable. Naturally, when a person consults a friend, he may agree with the friend's suggestion at first, but he may be affected by other factors, such as the advice of other friends, which change his acceptance of the friend's suggestion. In other words, the effects of social relationships on users are changeable. Analogizing this phenomenon to the training of the social recommendation model, similarly, the proximity between users and their friends may change under the influences of multiple parameters. Some reliable relationships in the early stages of model training may become less reliable or even have a negative impact in the later training process. Therefore, we need an adaptive evaluation mechanism to dynamically assess users' social relationships and eventually find the most reliable friends for users.

The process of dynamically identifying a user's reliable friends is accomplished through interactions between the agent and the environment. Specifically, the agent first generates a probability distribution over the user's friends, and then samples a fixed number (i.e., K) of friends for the user according to the probability distribution. These sampled friends are then delivered to the environment as reliable friends of the user. The environment is a social recommendation model that is responsible for injecting social influence (i.e., identified reliable friends) into traditional matrix factorization model and evaluating these sampled reliable friends. The assessment results are returned to the agent, and the generated reliable friends are updated based on the returned results.

3.2   SRRL: Reinforcement Learning for Social Recommendation

The reinforcement learning framework named SRRL proposed in this paper can dynamically identify users' reliable friends through the interactions between the agent and the environment. Figure 1 illustrates our framework SRRL.

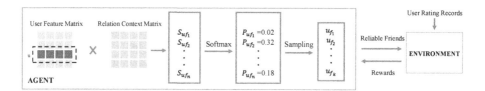

Fig. 1. An overview of the proposed SRRL framework. The agent outputs a probability distribution over the current user's friends. The environment utilizes these sampled friends and the current user's rating records to infer his/her preference, and then outputs rewards to help update the agent in order to optimize the distribution of reliable friends.

The Agent. In our model, the action of the agent is to sample a certain number of reliable friends for each user. More specifically, the agent is implemented as a softmax function that outputs probability distribution over users' friends based on the calculated social relationship strength between users and their friends. The distribution can be formally defined as:

$$P_A\left(f_k|u\right) = \frac{\exp\left(S_A\left(u, f_k\right)\right)}{\sum_f \exp\left(S_A(u, f)\right)} \tag{1}$$

where $P_A\left(f_k|u\right)$ indicates the agent's probability distribution of sampling the friend f_k for user u, and $S_A\left(u, f_k\right)$ indicates a scoring function that reflects the strength of the social relationship between user u and his/her friend f_k. It can be seen from the formula that a friend who has a strong social relationship with user u is more likely to be sampled as a reliable friend of him/her. In collaborative filtering, a commonly adopted model is matrix factorization. Following matrix factorization of the trust matrix, we define scoring function $S_A\left(u, f_k\right)$ as follows, which reflects the intimacy of user u and his/her friend f_k.

$$S_A\left(u, f_k\right) = X_u^T C_{f_k} \tag{2}$$

where X_u and C_{f_k} are the truster-specific feature vector and the trustee-specific feature vector respectively, defined in the d-dimensional space. X_u and C_{f_k} characterize the behaviors of trusting others and being trusted by others, respectively. Finally, we sample a fixed number of friends as reliable friends for each user according to the generated probability distribution and then deliver these friends to the environment.

The Environment. In this paper, we adopt a classic social recommendation model SocialMF [8] for rating prediction task to construct the environment. SocialMF introduces the mechanism of trust propagation, which has been proved to be an important phenomenon in social recommendation. Nevertheless, trust propagation mechanism based on unreliable social relationships can also lead to inferior recommendation performance. Traditional SocialMF assumes the feature vector of each user is dependent on the feature vectors of all his/her friends. In our work, we make each user's feature vector only depend on the feature vectors of his/her reliable friends. In reality, the part of the environment is not fixed, which means that our model is generic and can be re-designed for different tasks. To stay focused, we leave it for future study. In addition, we further consider user/item biases in the traditional SocialMF model, because a large part of the observed rating data is independent of the user's preference for items and only depends on the user's or items' own characteristics, and user/item biases are responsible for modeling these characteristics [9]. Consequently, the loss function of the environment is defined as follows:

$$
\begin{aligned}
L_E = &\sum_{u,i} I_{u,i}^R \left(R_{u,i} - \mu - b_u - b_i - X_u^T Y_i\right)^2 \\
&+ \lambda_T \sum_u \left(X_u - \sum_{k \in F_u} S_{u,k} X_k\right)^2 + \lambda\left(\|X\|^2 + \|Y\|^2 + b_u^2 + b_i^2\right)
\end{aligned} \tag{3}
$$

where N is the number of users and M is the number of items. $R \in \mathbb{R}^{M \times N}$ is a user-item rating matrix. $I_{u,i}^R$ is an indicator function that equals to 1 if u has rated i or equals to 0 otherwise. X_u and Y_i represent K-dimensional user-specific and item-specific latent feature vectors of users u and item i, respectively. $X \in \mathbb{R}^{N \times K}$ is the latent user feature matrix and $Y \in \mathbb{R}^{M \times K}$ is the latent item feature matrix. μ is the average of all ratings. b_u and b_i indicate the biases of user u and item i. $S \in \mathbb{R}^{N \times N}$ is a user-user trust matrix, and $S_{i,k} = 1$ indicates the existence of a social relation from user i to user k, otherwise it equals to 0. We further normalize each row of the trust matrix S so that $\sum_v S_{u,v} = 1$. F_u denotes reliable friends sampled for user u by the agent. λ_T is a parameter which balances the effects of rating preference and social relation and λ controls model complexity.

Given the loss function of the environment, the loss function that the agent needs to maximize is as follows:

$$L_A = \mathbb{E} \left[\frac{\exp \left(1/\left| X_u^T Y_i - X_{f_k}^T Y_i \right| \right)}{\sum_f \exp \left(1/\left| X_u^T Y_i - X_f^T Y_i \right| \right)} \right], f_k \in F_u, i \in I_u, f_k \sim P_A \left(f_k | u \right) \quad (4)$$

The objective of agent is to produce such reliable friends whose scores of the items rated by the current user are close to the ratings of the current user. For the sake of simplicity, we make:

$$\left[\frac{\exp \left(1/\left| X_u^T Y_i - X_{f_k}^T Y_i \right| \right)}{\sum_f \exp \left(1/\left| X_u^T Y_i - X_f^T Y_i \right| \right)} \right] = softmax \left(1/\left| X_u^T Y_i - X_{f_k}^T Y_i \right| \right) \quad (5)$$

Since the sampling of users' friends is discrete, it cannot be directly optimized through the gradient-based methods. A common way is to utilize policy gradient based reinforcement learning approach [13] whose gradient is derived as follows:

$$\nabla_A J^A (u) = \nabla_A \mathbb{E}_{f \sim P_A(f|u)} \sum_{i \in I_u} softmax \left(1/\left| X_u^T Y_i - X_f^T Y_i \right| \right)$$

$$= \sum_{f_n} \nabla_A P_A \left(f_n | u \right) \sum_{i \in I_u} softmax \left(1/\left| X_u^T Y_i - X_{f_n}^T Y_i \right| \right)$$

$$= \sum_{f_n} P_A \left(f_n | u \right) \nabla_A \log P_A \left(f_n | u \right) \sum_{i \in I_u} softmax \left(1/\left| X_u^T Y_i - X_{f_n}^T Y_i \right| \right)$$

$$= \mathbb{E}_{f \sim P_A(f|u)} \left[\nabla_A \log P_A(f|u) \sum_{i \in I_u} softmax \left(1/\left| X_u^T Y_i - X_f^T Y_i \right| \right) \right]$$

$$\simeq \frac{1}{K} \sum_{k=1}^{K} \nabla_A \log P_A \left(f_k | u \right) \sum_{i \in I_u} softmax \left(1/\left| X_u^T Y_i - X_{f_k}^T Y_i \right| \right)$$

$$(6)$$

We perform a sampling approximation that samples K friends as reliable friends for each user in the final step, which is illustrated in Fig. 1. With the terminology of reinforcement learning, the term $\sum_{i \in I_u}$ softmax $\left(1/|X_u^T Y_i - X_{f_n}^T Y_i|\right)$ acts as the reward for policy $P_A(f_k|u)$ taking an action f_k in the environment [16]. To reduce the variance during the reinforcement learning process, we subtracts a baseline from the reward. For simplicity, we assign a constant value to the baseline, which is the average reward of all friends.

The overall logic of our proposed SRRL is summarized in Algorithm 1. The agent first passes the sampled friends as reliable friends of the user to the environment. Then the environment returns higher rewards for friends who share truly similar preferences with the user. By updating the agent based on these rewards, the agent will increase the probabilities of which truly reliable friends will be sampled. With the interactions between the agent and the environment, our model can eventually identify reliable friends for each user that can help predict the user's preference and generate high-quality social recommendation.

Algorithm 1. Select Reliable Friends for Social Recommendation with Reinforcement Learning

---

Input: Agent $P_A(f|u)$; environment SocialMF; training dataset S
1: Initialize $P_A(f|u)$ with random truster-specific feature vectors and trustee-specific feature vectors, initialise SocialMF with random user-specific feature vectors and item-specific feature vectors.
2: Pre-train $P_A(f|u)$, SocialMF using S and entire social network.
3: **repeat**
4:     **for** g-steps **do**
5:         $P_A(f|u)$ generates K reliable friends for each user u
6:         Update agent parameters via policy gradient Eq. (6)
7:     **end for**
8:     **for** d-steps **do**
9:         Use current $P_A(f|u)$ to generate reliable friends as social regularization
10:         Train environment SocialMF by Eq. (3)
11:     **end for**
12: **until** SRRL converges

---

4   Experiments and Results

We evaluate our proposed approach around the following questions:

(1) How does SRRL perform compared to other existing methods?
(2) Whether our method is suitable for users with different trust degrees?
(3) Do different settings of model parameters affect the recommendation performance?

4.1 Experimental Settings

Datesets. Two datasets used in our experiments are Epinions and Ciao. The statistics of datasets are presented in Table 1. For the datasets, we filter out users with less than 5 social relationships. We use a 5-fold cross-validation for learning and testing and then report average performance.

Table 1. Dataset statistics

Datasets	#Users	#Items	#Ratings	#Relations
Epinions	40,163	139,738	664,823	487,182
Ciao	7,375	105,114	284,086	111,781

Evaluate Metrics. The evaluation metrics used in our experiments are mean absolute error (MAE) and root mean square error (RMSE), which are defined as follows:

$$\text{MAE} = \frac{\sum_{i,j} \left| R_{ij} - \hat{R}_{ij} \right|}{N} \tag{7}$$

$$\text{RMSE} = \sqrt{\frac{\sum_{i,j} \left(R_{ij} - \hat{R}_{ij} \right)^2}{N}} . \tag{8}$$

where R_{ij} is the true rating and $\widehat{R}_{ij}$ is the predicted rating. N is the number of ratings. Lower MAE and RMSE indicate that the more accurate the predicted ratings are.

Comparison Methods. To evaluate the performance of SRRL, we compare it with baselines: PMF [12], SoReg [11], SoRec [7], RSTE [6], SocialMF [8], TrustMF [2], and CUNEMF [22]. Among them, PMF is a classic personalized non-social probabilistic matrix factorization model. SoReg and SocialMF introduce social regularization terms to constrain the matrix factorization objective function. SoRec and TrustMF co-factorize rating matrix and trust matrix. RSTE combines the basic matrix factorization approach and a social-network-based approach linearly. CUNEMF calculates similarities between users based on user vectors learned by skip-gram model and then treats the most similar K users as reliable friends of each user.

4.2 Comparison with Other Models (RQ1)

Table 2 shows the performances of our method and all comparison methods over two datasets on the metrics MAE and RMSE. For each comparison method, we also show the improvement of our method on MAE and RMSE, respectively. Among all comparison methods, only PMF is a non-social collaborative filtering model without consideration of social relationships. All the remaining methods are social recommendation models. We can observe from Table 2 that the performance of PMF is the worst among all comparison methods, which confirms the hypothesis proposed in the social recommendation literature that social information can improve the performance of recommender systems. Second, we can observe that our method outperforms all comparison methods on both datasets, showing that instead of using all social relationships indiscriminately, really reliable social relationships can make social information play a greater role in recommender systems. Moreover, it can be seen that CUNEMF which selects a certain number of similar users as reliable friends of each user performs best among all the comparison methods. The performance advantage of CUNEMF further illustrates that identifying friends who really have similar preferences with users in social recommendation can improve recommendation performance.

Table 2. Experimental results on Epinions and Ciao

Datesets	Metrics	PMF	SoReg	SoRec	SocialMF	RSTE	TrustMF	CUNEMF	SRRL
Epinions	MAE	0.87393	0.87505	0.86267	0.86724	0.86174	0.84974	0.84904	**0.79770**
	Imporve	8.7%	8.9%	7.5%	8.0%	7.4%	6.1%	6.0%	-
	RMSE	1.16337	1.15008	1.14068	1.15665	1.14659	1.11852	1.11263	**1.05370**
	Imporve	9.4%	8.4%	7.6%	8.9%	8.1%	5.8%	5.3%	-
Ciao	MAE	0.76719	0.75359	0.75512	0.75770	0.76282	0.75592	0.75250	**0.72980**
	Imporve	4.9%	3.2%	3.4%	3.7%	4.3%	3.5%	3.0%	-
	RMSE	1.03067	1.00961	1.01055	1.02822	1.02082	1.01861	1.00162	**0.97224**
	Imporve	5.7%	3.7%	3.8%	5.4%	4.8%	4.6%	2.9%	-

4.3   Comparison in Trust Degrees (RQ2)

We conduct another experiment to evaluate the performance of our method SRRL with regard to users with different trust degrees (i.e, the number of users' friends). According to trust degrees, we divide users of each dataset into five groups: 1–5, 6–10, 11–20, 20–100, >100, and then calculate prediction error for each group, respectively. The results are shown in Fig. 2. It can be seen that our method SRRL shows the best performance over all user groups with different trust degrees, especially for the group with 21–100 trust relations in Ciao dataset and the group with no more than 6 trust relations in Epinions dataset. This indicates that whether users' social relation data is sparse or dense, finding reliable social relationships for users is necessary.

4.4   Parameter Effect Analysis (RQ3)

Our SRRL method has two hyper-parameters K and λ to control the number of sampled reliable friends and the strength of social regularization term, respec-

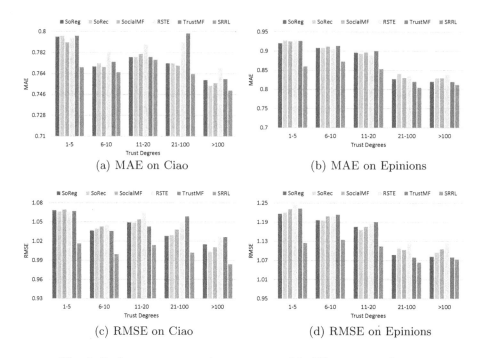

(a) MAE on Ciao

(b) MAE on Epinions

(c) RMSE on Ciao

(d) RMSE on Epinions

Fig. 2. Performance comparison on users with different trust degrees

tively. Here we show the impact of two hyper-parameters on the recommendation performance.

First, we fix λ and change K in the range of [5, 50]. We can observe from Fig. 3 that our model SRRL performs best when K is set to 5 on Ciao dataset and 10 on Epinions dataset. When K is too large (e.g., larger than 30), SRRL behaves similarly to SocialMF which makes use of all social relationships of users. The performance degradation of SRRL further illustrates that only a few reliable friends have a positive impact on inferring user preferences, and thus it is necessary to select reliable friends for users.

Second, we fix K and vary λ from 0.1 to 10. Figure 4 shows the results. It can be seen that for two datasets, the recommendation performance achieves best when λ is set to 3. When λ is smaller than 1, SRRL behaves similarly to the non-social model PMF, which shows the importance of social information for improving recommendation performance. When λ is larger than 5, further increasing λ leads to a model in which having feature vectors too close to those of reliable friends. Therefore, we suggest that λ should be set to 3.

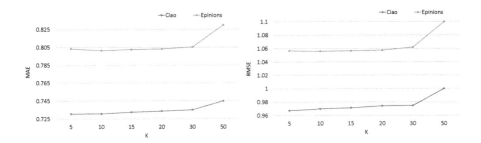

Fig. 3. Performance with respect to different values of K

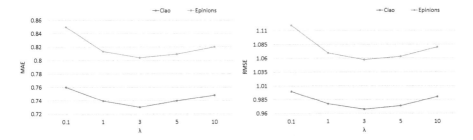

Fig. 4. Performance with respect to different values of λ

5   Conclusion

Due to the noise in social relationships, the performance of social recommendation is limited. One of the main reasons is that not all friends share similar preferences with user, and preference similarities between a user and his/her friends are not immutable. To mitigate the problem, in this paper we propose a social recommendation model named SRRL, which dynamically identifies reliable friends for users based on reinforcement learning. The experimental results on two datasets show the effectiveness of SRRL, which performs better than other models which directly use all social relationships of users. This phenomenon indicates that users' reliable friends can really improve recommendation performance. Besides, compared to CUNEMF model which selects top-k similar users as reliable friends for each user, SRRL also performs better, which illustrates the advantage of assessing social relationships dynamically. In this paper, we only select reliable friends among explicit friends. In the future, we will consider mining useful implicit social relationships for social recommendation.

Acknowledgements. This research is supported by graduate research and innovation foundation of Chongqing, China (Grant No. CYS19052), the Fundamental Research Funds for the Central Universities (No. 2019CDXYRJ0011), the National Key Research and Development Program of China (No. 2018YFF0214706), Chongqing Research Program of Basic Research and Frontier Technology (No. cstc2017jcyjBX0025) and Science and Technology Major Special Project of Guangxi (GKAA17129002).

References

1. Barto, A.G., Sutton, R.S.: Reinforcement learning: an introduction. IEEE Trans. Neural Netw. **9**(5), 1054–1054 (1998)
2. Bo, Y., Yu, L., Liu, J., Li, W.: Social collaborative filtering by trust. In: IJCAI, pp. 2747–2753 (2013)
3. Deng, S., Huang, L., Xu, G., Wu, X., Wu, Z.: On deep learning for trust-aware recommendations in social networks. IEEE Trans. Neural Netw. Learn. Syst. **28**(5), 1164–1177 (2017)
4. Gulati, A., Eirinaki, M.: With a little help from my friends (and their friends): influence neighborhoods for social recommendations. In: WWW, pp. 2778–2784 (2019)
5. Guo, G., Zhang, J., Yorke-Smith, N.: TrustSVD: collaborative filtering with both the explicit and implicit influence of user trust and of item ratings. In: AAAI, pp. 123–129 (2015)
6. Hao, M., King, I., Lyu, M.R.: Learning to recommend with social trust ensemble. In: SIGIR, pp. 203–210 (2009)
7. Hao, M., Yang, H., Lyu, M.R., King, I.: SoRec: social recommendation using probabilistic matrix factorization. In: CIKM, pp. 931–940 (2008)
8. Jamali, M., Ester, M.: A matrix factorization technique with trust propagation for recommendation in social networks. In: RecSys, pp. 135–142 (2010)
9. Koren, Y.: Factorization meets the neighborhood: a multifaceted collaborative filtering model. In: SIGKDD, pp. 426–434 (2008)
10. Liu, C.Y., Zhou, C., Wu, J., Hu, Y., Guo, L.: Social recommendation with an essential preference space. In: AAAI, pp. 346–353 (2018)
11. Ma, H., Zhou, D., Liu, C., Lyu, M.R., King, I.: Recommender systems with social regularization. In: WSDM, pp. 287–296 (2011)
12. Salakhutdinov, R., Mnih, A.: Probabilistic matrix factorization. In: NIPS, pp. 1257–1264 (2007)
13. Sutton, R.S., McAllester, D.A., Singh, S.P., Mansour, Y.: Policy gradient methods for reinforcement learning with function approximation. In: NIPS, pp. 1057–1063 (1999)
14. Tardos, E., Kempe, D., Kleinberg, J.: Maximizing the spread of influence in a social network. In: SIGKDD, pp. 137–137 (2003)
15. Volodymyr, M., et al.: Human-level control through deep reinforcement learning. Nature **518**(7540), 529 (2015)
16. Wang, J., et al.: IRGAN: a minimax game for unifying generative and discriminative information retrieval models. In: SIGIR, pp. 515–524 (2017)
17. Wang, X., Hoi, S.C.H., Ester, M., Bu, J., Chen, C.: Learning personalized preference of strong and weak ties for social recommendation. In: WWW, pp. 1601–1610 (2017)
18. Williams, R.J.: Simple statistical gradient-following algorithms for connectionist reinforcement learning. Mach. Learn. **8**(3–4), 229–256 (1992)
19. Xin, W., Wei, L., Ester, M., Wang, C., Chen, C.: Social recommendation with strong and weak ties. In: CIKM, pp. 5–14 (2016)
20. Yu, J., Gao, M., Li, J., Yin, H., Liu, H.: Adaptive implicit friends identification over heterogeneous network for social recommendation. In: CIKM, pp. 357–366 (2018)
21. Yu, J., Gao, M., Yin, H., Li, J., Gao, C., Wang, Q.: Generating reliable friends via adversarial training to improve social recommendation. CoRR. arXiv:1909.03529 (2019)
22. Zhang, C., Lu, Y., Yan, W., Shah, C., Zhang, X.: Collaborative user network embedding for social recommender systems. In: SIAM, pp. 381–389 (2017)

Aspect-Level Sentiment Classification with Dependency Rules and Dual Attention

Yunkai Yang, Tieyun Qian[✉], and Zhuang Chen

School of Computer Science, Wuhan University, Wuhan, Hubei, China
{brucecser,qty,zhchen18}@whu.edu.cn

Abstract. Aspect-level sentiment classification aims to predict the sentiment polarity towards the given aspects of sentences. Neural network models with attention mechanism have achieved great success in this area. However, existing methods fail to capture enough aspect information. Besides, it is hard for simple attention mechanism to model complex interaction between aspects and contexts. In this paper, we propose a **Seg**ment **M**odel with **D**ual **A**ttention (SegM-DA) to tackle these problems. We combine deep learning models with traditional methods by defining dependency rules to extract auxiliary words, which helps to enrich aspect information. In addition, in order to model structural relation between aspects and contexts, we introduce dependent attention mechanism. Coupled with standard attention mechanism, we establish the dual attention mechanism, which models the interaction from both word- and structure- dependency. We perform aspect-level sentiment classification experiments on two real datasets. The results show that our model can achieve the state-of-the-art performance.

Keywords: Aspect-level sentiment classification · Dependency rule · Dual attention mechanism

1 Introduction

Aspect-level sentiment classification aims to predict the sentiment polarity towards the given aspects of sentences. For example, in the sentence *"The food is delicious but the service is bad"*, the consumer mentions two aspects "food" and "service", and expresses positive and negative sentiment on food and service, respectively. Compared to the document-level or sentence-level sentiment classification, the main challenge of aspect-level task is to model the interaction between aspects and sentences. Especially when there is more than one aspect in a sentence, it is desired to obtain target-dependent final representation to predict the corresponding polarity.

Traditional methods consider this task as a combination of feature engineering and text classification, and most earlier works focus on the former. After that, machine learning algorithms are applied to train a classifier. In recent

© Springer Nature Switzerland AG 2019
T. Gedeon et al. (Eds.): ICONIP 2019, LNCS 11954, pp. 643–655, 2019.
https://doi.org/10.1007/978-3-030-36711-4_54

years, neural network models have made great improvements in many NLP tasks. Some researchers have designed effective neural networks to automatically generate useful low dimensional representations from targets and contexts [2, 17, 19]. However, when modeling aspect information, researchers merely consider aspect phrases that act as an entity without conveying any sentiment. It may cause the insufficient representation of aspect information. Besides, Recurrent Neural Networks (RNNs) with attention mechanism is the most commonly-used technique for this task. For example, the models in [7, 16, 19] employ attention mechanism to measure the semantic relatedness between each context word and the target, then use the induced attention scores to aggregate contextual features for prediction. In these works, the attention weight plays an important part. But it bases on words similarity between aspects and contexts. In other words, it models the word level interaction and ignores the structural relatedness, which is an intrinsic drawback of the standard attention mechanism.

Based on the above observations, we propose a new architecture, named SegM-DA (**Seg**ment **M**odel with **D**ual **A**ttention), to solve the issues above. Firstly, we consider to employ traditional methods to enrich aspect information explicitly, which is hard for deep learning models, especially when the labeled dataset is insufficient. We define dependency rules to extract auxiliary words that show dependent relation with aspect. These words, coupled with aspect words, are applied to our model together to segment and serve as a supplement to aspect information. Because we do not pay much attention to the quality of auxiliary words, our rule extraction procedure is not labor intensive. The reason why we neglect the quality at this stage is that we introduce deep learning model to select the high-quality words later. Similar rule-based methods mainly exist in aspect extraction procedure [8, 10, 12]. However, existing rule-based methods usually need feature extraction and extra sentiment knowledge, which are different from our rules obviously. Secondly, apart from standard attention mechanism, following the idea of [3], we introduce the dependent attention mechanism to model the structural relations. Therefore, we design a dual attention framework, which can achieve enough interaction between aspects and contexts from both word and structure dependency.

2   Related Work

Under supervised learning conditions, aspect-level sentiment classification is typically considered as a classification problem. In earlier approaches, Some rule-based methods like [8, 10, 12] are proposed in aspect extraction procedure, and then algorithms like Naive Bayes and Support Vector Machine (SVM) are applied to classification. They usually rely on manually designed features. Multiple sentiment lexicons are built for this purpose [13, 14].

Neural network methods have made significant improvement on this task in recent years. [15] builds two long-short term memory (LSTM) to learn the two word sequences divided by aspect words respectively to obtain target-dependent representations. [2] introduces recursive neural network to model sentence information from the view of structure. With the success of attention mechanism in computer vision and machine translation, there are some related attempts in this task. [19] employs the average vector of aspect phrases to interact with context by means of attention mechanism. [7] makes further efforts to employ attention from contexts to aspect phrases before the process like [19]. The interactive attentive process helps obtain more accurate representation. In addition, complex attention interaction is introduced. For example, [16] applies deep memory network to store context words, at the same time, multiple hops attention process are conducted between aspect and the memory, and the attention results are aggregated linearly. Unlike [1,16] achieves non-linear combination by means of gated recurrent unit (GRU). [20] also uses memory network, but introduces another auxiliary memory to model the information of aspect category, which solves the problem of long-tailed distribution of aspect words.

Several segment models have been introduced in this field. Apart from [5,15] applies attention mechanism to the context in each segment divided by the aspect, and then aggregates the results by gate mechanism. With the same segmentation mechanism, [6] introduces multi-layer perception (MLP) to segment memory units to obtain related weights. [18] applies a pseudo segment by considering it as a 0–1 annotation task. In order to get segment whose label is 1, the authors employ a conditional random field (CRF) layer to obtain the probability of label-1. Those values act as weights of each word. In [4], although there is no direct segment operation, the authors select convolutional neural network (CNN) to learn opinion-expressed segment information.

It is worth mentioning that our model is similar to [5] in that we both adopt sentence segment. Our model is novel in proposing a new segmentation mechanism which divides sentences by both the aspect and auxiliary words. In contrast, the segment is performed only by the aspect in [5]. Moreover, as for the interaction between segment information and contexts, we employ dual attention mechanism to better capture the effects of dependency attention in addition to the standard one. Finally, we combine the results by simple concatenation instead of complicated gate operation. We compare our model with that in [5] in experiments and the results demonstrate the effectiveness of our model.

3   Our SegM-DA Model

In this section, we introduce our **SegM-DA** model. **SegM-DA** is proposed to capture the interaction between aspects and contexts using both word- and structure- dependency. We first describe how to extract auxiliary information for aspects and explain how to assist our main task with those information. We then illustrate the architecture of SegM-DA. Lastly, we present the objective function.

3.1   Auxiliary Information Extraction

Rules Definition. According to linguistic knowledge, the parts of speech (POS) that may express emotions are *adjective* (*adj*), *negation* (*neg*), *verb* (*v*), *adverb* (*adv*) and *noun* (*n*). Though some of *noun* words may express sentiment, we selectively ignore them because they may introduce much noise. Therefore, we consider aspects as the seed and define six rules to extract the auxiliary *adj*, *neg*, *v* and *adv* words based on linguistics. We illustrate these rules with accompanied examples, where aspects are enclosed in [], and extracted auxiliary words are underlined.

1. If the aspect is modified by an *adj* word, we extract the *adj*.
   Eg. It is a <u>nice</u> [movie]. ⇒ <u>nice</u>
2. If the aspect acts as the complement of an *adj* word, we extract the *adj*.
   Eg. render the [browser] <u>useless</u>. ⇒ <u>useless</u>
3. If the aspect is followed by a clause (the child of the aspect is a *verb*), we extract the *verb* of this clause.
   Eg. I also got the added bonus of a [30" HD Monitor], which really <u>helps</u> to extend my screen and keep my eyes fresh. ⇒ <u>helps</u>
4. If the aspect depends on a *verb* (the parent of the aspect is a *verb*), we judge whether the word is the ROOT.
   - If the *verb* is the ROOT and it is not a copula, we directly extract the *verb*.
     Eg. I <u>love</u> the [lit up keys] and screen. ⇒ <u>love</u>
   - If the *verb* is the ROOT and it is also a copula, we search related *adj* in the sentence and extract it if found.
     Eg. But the [mountain lion] is just too <u>slow</u>. ⇒ <u>slow</u>
   - If the *verb* is not the ROOT and acts as complement, we extract the *verb* and *adj* along parent nodes.
     Eg. Everything is so <u>easy</u> to finish [setup] or configure. ⇒ <u>easy</u>
     Eg. I <u>hate</u> to taste the [sandwich] again. ⇒ <u>hate</u>
   - If the *verb* is not the ROOT and the dependent relation is an affiliation which indicates that the aspect is in a clause, we extract the *verb* and *adj* from its main clause.
     Eg. The most <u>annoying</u> thing, though, is the fact that the [servers] <u>seem</u> to be trained to drive revenue. ⇒ <u>annoying</u>, <u>seem</u>
5. Once a *verb* is extracted, we simultaneously extract *neg* and *adv* related with the *verb*.
6. Rules 1–5 assume that aspects are *noun*, since other parts for being aspects are rare (usually caused by dataset errors and syntactic errors). For those probably illegal aspects, we just extract related *adj* limited in two dependent distances.

   In practice, we first use spaCy[1], a parsing tool, to obtain the dependency tree of each sentence. We then extract auxiliary words following the order of six rules. Since these rules consider the priority of the probability of emotion expression, each POS of the word will be extracted only once, and the latter results are not allowed to cover the words extracted from previous rules. According to extraction statistics, we extract at least one auxiliary word from 82.1% and 85.0% of sentences in two datasets.

---

[1] https://spacy.io/.

Leveraging Auxiliary Information. We use extracted auxiliary words to assist our main task in two parts: (1) Auxiliary words and aspects act as the indicators to collaboratively divide the whole sentence into several semantic segments. (2) Auxiliary words serve as the regularizer to guide the training procedure. The latter part will be illustrated later. We now focus on the segmentation of the sentence using auxiliary words and aspects.

We take the sentence "The [fish] is <u>fresh</u> but the [variety of fish] is nothing out of <u>ordinary</u>." as an example. As for the aspect [fish], the sentence is divided into three segments: "The fish", "fish is fresh", and "fresh but the variety of fish is nothing out of ordinary". While for the aspect [variety of fish], we can get two segments: "The fish is fresh but the variety of fish" and "variety of fish is nothing out of ordinary". Apparently, for the same sentence, different aspects may have different auxiliary words. We can further obtain different segments which could help our model to find useful and related information for aspects.

3.2   Model Architecture

An Overview. The architecture of our **SegM-DA** model is given in Fig. 1. The entire sentence context and all segments generated using aspects and auxiliary words are imported into the model. For clarity, we only present two segments.

Our model mainly consists of three layers: (1) word embedding layer, (2) hidden layer and (3) dual attention layer. With initial word embeddings as the input, the first two layers generate contextual hidden representations of context and segments using bidirectional long-short term memory (Bi-LSTM). This procedure is a fundamental operation in LSTM-based methods. Furthermore, the dual attention mechanism is employed in the third layer to model the interaction between segments and context using both word level and structural dependency. Finally, the average vector of context and results of each segmental interaction are concatenated as the final representation. Since the dual attention layer is the core module, we will describe it in detail later.

Dual Attention Layer. Our goal is to obtain the target-dependent feature representations. After the procedure of hidden layer, we have got hidden vectors h^i for both the words in context and each segment. These segments can be viewed as structural segments, which express information accurately without many noisy words left. In order to acquire complete semantic meanings from these segments, we use the context to interact with all these segments. Unlike most of existing works, we employ dual attention mechanism consisting of standard and dependent attention to model the complicated interaction.

Standard Attention. It is the word-level interaction used to capture the similar words between segments and context. We take one segment as an example to describe the process. The weight α_i of word c_i in context is calculated as below:

$$\alpha_i = \frac{exp(\gamma(h_c^i, s_{avg}))}{\sum_{j=1}^n exp(\gamma(h_c^j, s_{avg}))},$$

(1)

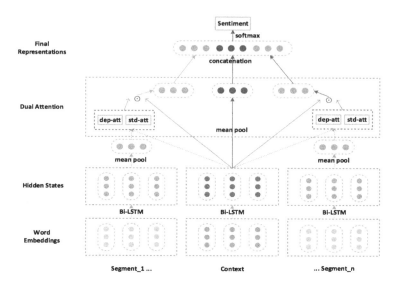

Fig. 1. SegM-DA overview

where γ is a score function to compute the importance of h_c^i in the context, s_{avg} is the average vector of hidden vectors in the segement. The score function γ is defined as follows:

$$\gamma(h_c^i, s_{avg}) = tanh(h_c^i \cdot W_s \cdot s_{avg}^T + b_s) \tag{2}$$

Dependent Attention. Standard attention mechanism treats every word equally before calculation. But intuitively, not all words are equally important for determining the polarity of an aspect. From the perspective of sentence structure, words that have short distance along dependency path to the aspect are more important and should be assigned higher weight and vice versa. Such a mechanism filters out useless words which are non-emotional but likely close to the aspect in sequential distance, and helps to learn a better feature representation. Besides, inspired by [3], we assign weights explicitly with regard to the dependent distance. The details are described as follows:

$$dep\_att_i = \begin{cases} \frac{1}{2^{l_i-1}}, & if \ l_i \in [1, ws] \\ 0, & otherwise \end{cases}, \tag{3}$$

where ws is the window size of dependent attention. The words out of the window will not be considered. According to results above, we obtain the final weight β_i of each context word using dot product:

$$\beta_i = \alpha_i \cdot dep\_att_i \tag{4}$$

Then, for the ith segment s_i, we obtain a particular aggregated representation c_{s_i} for context words:

$$c_{s_i} = \sum_{i=1}^{n} \beta_i h_c^i \tag{5}$$

After the interaction with all segments, we get the final target-dependent feature representation:

$$c_{final} = [c_{avg}, c_{s_1}, c_{s_2}, \ldots, c_{s_m}], \tag{6}$$

where m is the number of segments, c_{avg} is the average vector of context words which represents the overall semantic meaning. Finally, we can get the probability distribution $\mathbf{y} \in \mathbb{R}^C$ for judging the sentiment polarities as *positive, negative* or *neutral:*.

$$\mathbf{y} = softmax(W_z \cdot c_{final} + b_z), \tag{7}$$

where C is the dimension of label, and W_z and b_z are weight matrix and bias term for *softmax* layer, respectively.

3.3   Objective Function

Classification Loss. Once obtaining target-dependent final representations, we train our model by minimizing the cross entropy between the predicted and real probability distributions. The loss function is written as:

$$J(\theta) = -\sum_{i=1}^{C} y_i log(\widehat{y_i}) \tag{8}$$

where y_i is the predicted sentiment and $\widehat{y_i}$ is the ground truth label, θ is the collection of trainable parameters.

Regularizer. Considering that the extracted auxiliary words may express sentiment directly, we use an additional regularizer to guide the learning procedure by encouraging larger attention weights for these words:

$$U(\theta) = -\sum_{i \in I} \beta_i / N_I, \tag{9}$$

where I is the collection of index of auxiliary words, N_I is the number of auxiliary words. Therefore, the final loss function is written as:

$$L(\theta) = J(\theta) + \lambda U(\theta), \tag{10}$$

where λ controls the importance of the regularizer.

4   Experiments

4.1   Experiment Setup

Dataset. We conduct experiments on SemEval 2014 task 4 [11] to validate the effectiveness of our model. The dataset consists of reviews from laptop and restaurant fields. The reviews are labeled with three sentiment polarities: *positive, neutral, negative*, and aspect terms are listed explicitly. Table 1 shows the training and test instance numbers in each category.

Table 1. Statistics of SemEval 2014 dataset.

Dataset	Split	Total	Positive	Negative	Neutral
Laptops	Train	2328	994	870	464
	Test	638	341	128	169
Restaurants	Train	3608	2164	807	637
	Test	1120	728	196	196

Evaluation Metric. The aspect-level sentiment classification is a single-label and multi-class task. Hence we adopt *Accuracy, Precision, Recall* as the metrics. Besides, we also adopt the macro-averaged F-1 score to provide a thorough and overall evaluation.

Hyperparameters Setting. In our experiments, we use 300-dimension word vectors pre-trained by GloVe [9] and the words out-of-vocabulary are initialized by sampling from the uniform distribution U(-0.1, 0.1). All weight matrices are initialized from distribution U(-0.1, 0.1) too. The value of λ controlling the importance of the regularizer is set to 0.1–0.2, and ws controlling the window size of dependency path is 5. We train the model with Stochastic Gradient Descent-optimization algorithm and set the learning rate to 0.001.

4.2 Baselines

We compare our model with the following baseline methods on each dataset.

– **Attention-based methods:** AE-LSTM [19], ATAE-LSTM [19] and IAN [7]. Simple attention mechanism is applied in them to model the interaction between aspects and contexts.
– **Memory-based methods:** MemNet [16], RAM [1] and DAuM [20]. They employ memory network to accomplish multiple attentive interactions.
– **Segment-based methods:** TD-LSTM [15], BiLSTM-ATT-G [5], Cabasc [6], SA-LSTM-P [18] and TNet [4]. They consider the thinking of segment and devote to capture important spans of opinion expression.

We use the official training/testing split to ensure the consistency with baseline methods. With *accuracy* as training metric, we stop training when the best accuracy is not updated for ten consecutive epochs, and report the *accuracy* and *macro-f1* on test set. The results are shown in Table 2.

4.3 Result Analysis

As shown in Table 2, our SegM-DA model overall outperforms all baselines on both datasets. Note that Macro-F1 is the dominant metric in unbalanced classification tasks. Obviously, segment-based methods achieve overall better performances than the other two categories. This superiority demonstrates that

Table 2. Comparison with the baselines.

Method	Laptops				Restaurants			
	Accuracy	Precision	Recall	Macro-F1	Accuracy	Precision	Recall	Macro-F1
AE-LSTM	0.689	0.671	0.613	0.625	0.766	0.698	0.632	0.643
ATAE-LSTM	0.687	0.670	0.612	0.625	0.772	0.708	0.640	0.650
IAN	0.721	0.676	0.667	0.667	0.786	0.720	0.641	0.652
MemNet	0.722	0.708	0.650	0.668	0.801	0.721	0.657	0.678
RAM	0.745	0.697	0.708	0.699	0.800	0.718	0.682	0.689
DAuM	0.745	**0.730**	0.692	0.702	0.817	0.747	0.702	0.715
TD-LSTM	0.681	0.669	0.612	0.623	0.756	0.692	0.631	0.642
BiLSTM-ATT-G	0.744	0.705	0.693	0.699	0.804	0.732	0.685	0.708
Cabasc	0.751	0.723	0.710	0.704	0.809	0.742	0.690	0.695
SA-LSTM-P	0.751	0.710	0.716	0.708	0.811	0.740	0.723	0.730
TNet	**0.760**	0.712	0.718	0.715	0.810	**0.762**	0.680	0.709
SegM-DA	0.757	0.717	**0.721**	**0.717**	**0.819**	0.757	**0.727**	**0.740**

segment-based methods could distill useful information for sentiment classification by incorporating word similarity features with structure dependency features.

There are two reasons why SegM-DA outperforms other segment-based methods: (1) The segmentation mechanism in SegM-DA is more delicate by taking the dependency path into account. (2) The dual attention mechanism in SegM-DA better emphasizes the truly relevant words and de-emphasizes other nonemotional noise.

Apart from SegM-DA, TNet and SA-LSTM-P achieve better results than others among segment-based methods. This is because their model could automatically learn to recognize dominant segments while TD-LSTM, BiLSTM-ATT-G and Cabasc fix the segmentation. Memory-based methods achieve suboptimal performances because they adopt memory network to enhance the interaction between aspects and contexts. Among them, DAuM performs better than others since it considers high-level semantic meanings for aspect words. Simple attention-based methods get the worst results due to the deficiencies of word-level interaction and representation ability, while IAN get relatively better results owing to the bidirectional attention mechanism.

4.4   Effects of Auxiliary Information and Dependent Attention

In order to validate the impacts of our two main components: auxiliary information and dependent attention mechanism. We conduct a set of comparative experiments. We derive several variants from our standard model:

SegM-Att: It is the fundamental version consisting of segment and standard attention components.

SegM-DA w/o dep-att: It is a variant of our model which excludes the dependent attention component.

SegM-DA w/o aux norm: It is a variant of our model which excludes the auxiliary component.

The results are shown in Table 3.

Table 3. Comparison with two variants.

Method	Laptops		Restaurants	
	Accuracy	Macro-F1	Accuracy	Macro-F1
SegM-Att	0.735	0.685	0.802	0.695
SegM-DA w/o dep-att	0.743	0.696	0.805	0.700
SegM-DA w/o aux norm	0.752	0.710	0.815	0.722
SegM-DA	**0.757**	**0.717**	**0.819**	**0.740**

It is clear from Table 3 that the model combining both of the two components consistently outperforms the models with only one component. Although the contribution of dependent attention mechanism is more prominent, taking both components into account can obtain the best results.

4.5   Effects of Segmentation Mechanism

As for segment-based models, our method differs from other methods in that we design the specific segmentation mechanism. Instead of dividing context into left and right parts of the aspect term(s), we segment it based on both the auxiliary words and aspect word(s). This experiment is conducted to validate the effectiveness of our segmentation mechanism. With the same attention mechanism, we compare methods based on our proposed segmentation mechanism with the commonly-used two-segment methods. The comparative methods are listed as follows:

BiSeg-Att: It is a traditional left-right model with the standard attention mechanism.

SegM-Att: It is a variant of our model after removing the dependent attention mechanism.

BiSeg-DA: It is a traditional left-right model with our proposed dual attention mechanism.

Table 4. Evaluation on segmentation mechanism.

Method	Laptops		Restaurants	
	Accuracy	Macro-F1	Accuracy	Macro-F1
BiSeg-Att	0.737	0.690	0.802	0.688
SegM-Att	**0.743**	**0.696**	**0.805**	**0.700**
BiSeg-DA	0.746	0.700	0.813	0.732
SegM-DA	**0.757**	**0.717**	**0.819**	**0.740**

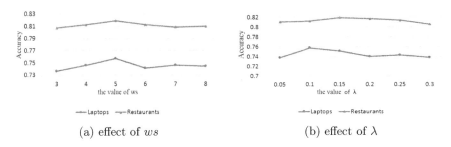

Fig. 2. Effects of hyperparameters

The results shown in Table 4 demonstrate the effectiveness of our proposed segmentation mechanism. Due to the more accurate division, models with our proposed segmentation mechanism consistently outperform those with commonly-used segmentation methods. Apparently, our mechanism can learn more effective representations and further obtain better predictions.

4.6 Effects of Hyperparameters

There are two main hyperparameters in SegM-DA: ws and λ, denoting the window size in dependency path and the importance of regularizer respectively. First, we fix λ to 0.1 and vary ws from 3 to 8 to evaluate the effect of ws. After that, with ws fixed to 5, we vary λ from 0.05 to 0.3 to evaluate its effect. The results are shown in Fig. 2.

From Fig. 2(a), we can see that the curves have an upward trend when $ws <$ 5, and become downward when $ws > 5$. When ws is small, SegM-DA would roughly filter out useful information in the dependency path, and thus gets worse performance. But when ws increases over the threshold 5, more nonemotional noises would be introduced and then hurt the performance. From Fig. 2(b), the key observation is that a relatively small λ could guide the training procedure, i.e. 0.1 and 0.15 for laptop and restaurant datasets respectively. When exceeding those thresholds, the attention learning would be excessively constrained, and the performance of SegM-DA will decrease.

5 Conclusion

In this paper, we present a novel SegM-DA model for aspect-level sentiment classification by combining deep learning models with traditional rule-based methods. We propose six rules to extract auxiliary information for aspects, and utilize them for both segmentation and regularization. Due to the differential segmentations for different aspects, we get more meaningful information than just considering the context words. Besides, we propose an effective dual attention mechanism to learn interactions between the context words and all segments. By taking the dependency path into account, we are able to filter out noisy words even if they are close to the aspect in sequential distance. Experiments on two SemEval datasets demonstrate that SegM-DA overall outperforms all the state-of-the-art baselines.

Acknowledgment. The work described in this paper has been supported in part by the NSFC project (61572376).

References

1. Chen, P., Sun, Z., Bing, L., Yang, W.: Recurrent attention network on memory for aspect sentiment analysis. In: EMNLP, pp. 452–461 (2017)
2. Dong, L., Wei, F., Tan, C., Tang, D., Zhou, M., Xu, K.: Adaptive recursive neural network for target-dependent Twitter sentiment classification. In: ACL (volume 2: Short papers), vol. 2, pp. 49–54 (2014)
3. He, R., Lee, W.S., Ng, H.T., Dahlmeier, D.: Effective attention modeling for aspect-level sentiment classification. In: COLING, pp. 1121–1131 (2018)
4. Li, X., Bing, L., Lam, W., Shi, B.: Transformation networks for target-oriented sentiment classification. arXiv preprint arXiv:1805.01086 (2018)
5. Liu, J., Zhang, Y.: Attention modeling for targeted sentiment. In: EACL, vol. 2, Short Papers, pp. 572–577 (2017)
6. Liu, Q., Zhang, H., Zeng, Y., Huang, Z., Wu, Z.: Content attention model for aspect based sentiment analysis. In: WWW, pp. 1023–1032. International World Wide Web Conferences Steering Committee (2018)
7. Ma, D., Li, S., Zhang, X., Wang, H.: Interactive attention networks for aspect-level sentiment classification. arXiv preprint arXiv:1709.00893 (2017)
8. Nandan, N., Dahlmeier, D., Vij, A., Malhotra, N.: SAP-RI: a constrained and supervised approach for aspect-based sentiment analysis. In: Proceedings of the 8th International Workshop on Semantic Evaluation (SemEval 2014), pp. 517–521 (2014)
9. Pennington, J., Socher, R., Manning, C.: Glove: global vectors for word representation. In: EMNLP, pp. 1532–1543 (2014)
10. Piryani, R., Gupta, V., Singh, V.K., Ghose, U.: A linguistic rule-based approach for aspect-level sentiment analysis of movie reviews. In: Bhatia, S., Mishra, K., Tiwari, S., Singh, V. (eds.) Advances in Computer and Computational Sciences. AISC, vol. 553, pp. 201–209. Springer, Singapore (2017). https://doi.org/10.1007/978-981-10-3770-2_19
11. Pontiki, M., Galanis, D., Pavlopoulos, J., Papageorgiou, H., Androutsopoulos, I., Manandhar, S.: SemEval-2014 task 4: aspect based sentiment analysis. In: SemEval 2014, pp. 27–35. ACL, Aug 2014
12. Poria, S., Ofek, N., Gelbukh, A., Hussain, A., Rokach, L.: Dependency tree-based rules for concept-level aspect-based sentiment analysis. In: Presutti, V., et al. (eds.) SemWebEval 2014. CCIS, vol. 475, pp. 41–47. Springer, Cham (2014). https://doi.org/10.1007/978-3-319-12024-9_5
13. Qiu, G., Liu, B., Bu, J., Chen, C.: Expanding domain sentiment lexicon through double propagation. In: IJCAI (2009)
14. Taboada, M., Brooke, J., Tofiloski, M., Voll, K., Stede, M.: Lexicon-based methods for sentiment analysis. Comput. Linguist. **37**(2), 267–307 (2011)
15. Tang, D., Qin, B., Feng, X., Liu, T.: Effective LSTMs for target-dependent sentiment classification. arXiv preprint arXiv:1512.01100 (2015)

16. Tang, D., Qin, B., Liu, T.: Aspect level sentiment classification with deep memory network. arXiv preprint arXiv:1605.08900 (2016)
17. Vo, D.T., Zhang, Y.: Target-dependent twitter sentiment classification with rich automatic features. In: IJCAI (2015)
18. Wang, B., Lu, W.: Learning latent opinions for aspect-level sentiment classification. In: AAAI (2018)
19. Wang, Y., Huang, M., Zhao, L., et al.: Attention-based LSTM for aspect-level sentiment classification. In: EMNLP, pp. 606–615 (2016)
20. Zhu, P., Qian, T.: Enhanced aspect level sentiment classification with auxiliary memory. In: COLING, pp. 1077–1087 (2018)

Aligning Users Across Social Networks by Joint User and Label Consistence Representation

Xiang Li[1,2,3], Yijun Su[2,3], Neng Gao[1,3], Wei Tang[1,2,3], Ji Xiang[3(✉)], and Yuewu Wang[1,2,3]

[1] State Key Laboratory of Information Security,
Institute of Information Engineering, CAS, Beijing, China
[2] School of Cyber Security, University of Chinese Academy of Sciences,
Beijing, China
[3] Institute of Information Engineering, Chinese Academy of Sciences, Beijing, China
{lixiang9015,suyijun,gaoneng,tangwei,xiangji,wangyuewu}@iie.ac.cn

Abstract. Aligning users belonging to the same person in different social networks has attracted much attention. Recently, embedding methods have been proposed to represent users from different social networks into vector spaces with same dimension. To handle the challenge of *vector space diversity*, existing methods usually make vectors of known aligned users closer/consistent and overlap different vector spaces. However, compared to large amount of users in each social network, the consistence constraint on aligned users is not enough to reduce the diversity. Besides, missing edges/labels may provide incorrect information and affect the effect of the overlap between learned vector spaces. Therefore, we propose the OURLACER method, i.e, jOint UseR and LAbel ConsistencE Representation, to jointly represent each user and label under the consistence constraints of know aligned users and shared labels. Specifically, OURLACER utilizes collective matrix factorization to complete missing edges and labels for each user, which can provide sufficient information to distinguish each user. Moreover, OURLACER adds the consistence constraint on shared labels in different social networks. Because each user has own labels, label consistence can restrict each user and greatly reduce the diversity between learned vector spaces. Extensive experiments conducted on real-world datasets demonstrate that our method significantly outperforms other state-of-the-art methods.

1 Introduction

With the rapid development of Internet, social networks (e.g., Facebook, Twitter and YouTube) have played important roles in our daily life. Nowadays, people are accustomed to surfing on multiple social networks at the same time. According

© Springer Nature Switzerland AG 2019
T. Gedeon et al. (Eds.): ICONIP 2019, LNCS 11954, pp. 656–668, 2019.
https://doi.org/10.1007/978-3-030-36711-4_55

to the statistical data from Pew Research Center report[1], more than half of the users tend to read news from multiple social media sites.

Nevertheless, existing social networks are provided by different companies and isolated from one another, which hinders the positive experience for users across different social networks. User Identity Linkage is to align users belonging to the same person in different social networks and has attracted much attention. Benefited from aligned users, we can complete and integrate users' information for sequent applications such as cross-network recommendation [5,14,22,23], link prediction [1,27,28] and topic analysis [7].

Recently, several embedding methods have been proposed to solve the problem of user identity linkage [9,11,12,18,19,30–32] by mapping users from each social network into a vector space with same dimension. Then, to give correct prediction, these methods overlap different vector spaces by making the vector representations of known aligned users closer or totally same (also called consistence constraint). Similarly, when we don't know any aligned users in advance, making the vector distributions similar can also make effect [8]. In conclusion, reducing **vector space diversity** can produce better vector spaces and overlap probable aligned users in different social networks.

However, existing embedding methods handling the challenge of vector space diversity still have following problems: (1) Missing edges and labels may mislead the process of learning good vector space for each social network, which makes space diversity hard to be reduced. (2) Consistence constraint on known aligned users may not come into effect. For example, two learned vector spaces may only overlap known aligned users while other users are all non-overlapped and the space diversity is still large.

In this paper, to address above problems in the challenge of vector space diversity, we propose the OURLACER method, i.e, j**O**int **U**se**R** and **LA**bel Consistenc**E** **R**epresentation, to jointly represent each user and label under the consistence constraints of know aligned users and shared labels. Specifically, OURLACER learns a good vector space for each social network with missing edges and labels completed by collective matrix factorization. Besides, to reduce the diversity between vector spaces, OURLACER not only utilizes the consistence constraint between known aligned users but also adds the consistence constraint between shared labels in different social networks. Because each user has unique labels, label consistence constraint can restrict each user and reduce the space diversity greatly.

The rest of this paper is organized as follows: We review related work in Sect. 2. Section 3 presents proposed OURLACER approach in detail and optimization algorithm is proposed in Sect. 4. Experimental evaluation and comparison are shown in Sect. 5. At last, Sect. 6 concludes the paper with a brief discussion.

---

[1] http://www.pewresearch.org/fact-tank/2017/11/02/more-americans-are-turning-to-multiple-social-media-sites-for-news/.

2   Related Work

In this section, we review the main lines of works on user identity linkage. Firstly, we briefly introduce traditional methods. Then, we discuss the progress of embedding methods.

Traditional methods have paid much attention to extract useful features and compute reasonable similarity. The first work on UIL problem utilizes usernames [24]. More specifically, they study the behavior patterns during selecting usernames and construct totally more than four hundreds features [25, 26]. Moreover, spatio-temporal information has been specially studied for extracting useful features [2, 3]. For content information, topic distribution has been demonstrated the effect [13]. Furthermore, based on pairwise similarity of artificial features, a new discrimination model has been proposed to promote the performance by viewing user identity linkage as a classification problem [10].

Considering the cost of artificial features, embedding methods have attracted much attention and made great progress. Different embedding methods have been proposed for different types of information. For network information, PALE preserves neighbor links in users' representations and learns the linear/non-linear mapping among known aligned users [11]. IONE models the followee/follower relationship and learn multiple representations for each user [9]. DeepLink introduces the deep neural network based on the learned users' representations by random walk [32]. Besides network information, label information has also been studied. MAH constructs hypergraph by labels for capturing high-order relation [19]. Based on MAH, UMAH emphasizes the effect of shared labels among different social networks and automatically learns the weights of different types of labels [31]. Besides, MASTER utilizes matrix factorization to factorize precomputed similarity matrices into users' representations with kernel tricks [18]. MEgo2Vec views user identity linkage as a classification problem and capture user's attributes and ego network in the user's representation [30]. However, above embedding methods haven't thought over the effect of missing edges and labels when learning users' representations, which can be solved by proposed OURLACER method.

When learning the vector space for each social network, an inevitable challenge is how to reduce the diversity between vector spaces, which means probable aligned users are closer. Existing embedding methods mainly utilize the consistence constraint based on known aligned users [9, 11, 18, 19, 30–32]. Moreover, ULink modifies consistence constraint by making aligned users closer than non-aligned users [12]. However, compared the large amount of users in each social network, the consistence constraint based on limited known aligned users is not enough to reduce the space diversity. In this paper, the proposed OURLACER considers the emergence of same labels in different social networks and adds the consistence constraint based on these shared labels to restrict each user.

3 Proposed Method

In this section, we firstly introduce the basic notations. Then, we present the way of completing missing edges and labels. Finally, we show the two types of consistence constraint and give the final optimization objective.

We use $G_i = (A_i, L_i)$ to represent i-th social network. $A_i \in R^{n_i \times n_i}$ is the adjacency matrix, where 1 represents two users is connected. Different from previous methods, we use 0 to represent missing edge rather than no connection. Besides, $L_i \in R^{n_i \times d_i}$ refers to the label matrix, where each row means the labels of one user. Similarly, we use 0 to represent missing label. n_i means the total number of users in G_i. The final dimension of user representation is m.

3.1 Collective Matrix Factorization

In real life, users in social networks usually own a fraction of labels and links, which means some real labels/links are missing in the social networks. Hence, the vector space learned by existing embedding methods cannot capture full and useful information in fact. To learn a good vector space, we should take into account the missing labels and edges.

As demonstrated in the work of network embedding [16], some classical methods, such as DeepWalk [15], LINE [21], PTE [20] and node2vec [4], can be unified into the matrix factorization framework with closed forms. Therefore, we also apply matrix factorization to learn the final vector representations. Noting that we own not only the adjacency matrix but also the label matrix. Then, we factorize these two matrices jointly. For the i-th social network, we can express the problem as

$$\min_{U_i, V_i} \frac{1}{2}||A_i - U_i U_i^T||_F^2 + \frac{1}{2}||L_i - U_i V_i^T||_F^2 + \frac{\alpha}{2}(||U_i||_F^2 + ||V_i||_F^2), \quad (1)$$

where $U_i \in R^{n_i \times m}$ represents users' vector representations and $V_i \in R^{d_i \times m}$ represents labels' vector representations. α is to control the complexity of U_i and V_i. $|| \cdot ||_F$ stands for Frobenius norm.

Though objective (1) can learn a vector space preserving enough network information and label information, we still cannot complete the missing edges and labels because objective (1) tend to recover original edges in A_i and original labels in L_i exactly. As a result, 0 in A_i is seen as no edge rather than missing edges. Therefore, analogous to transfer learning based collaborative filtering, we use collective matrix factorization [17] to complete missing edges and labels and learn a good vector space for social network G_i by following optimization problem

$$\min_{U_i, V_i} \frac{1}{2}||I_i^A \odot (A_i - U_i U_i^T)||_F^2 + \frac{1}{2}||I_i^L \odot (L_i - U_i V_i^T)||_F^2 + \frac{\alpha}{2}(||U_i||_F^2 + ||V_i||_F^2), \quad (2)$$

where $\odot$ is the Hadamard (element-wise) product and I_i^A is an indicator matrix. $I_i^A(p, q) = 1$ if $A_i(p, q)$ is observed, and otherwise $I_i^A(p, q) = 0$. Similarly,

$I_i^L(p,q) = 1$ if $L_i(p,q)$ is observed, and otherwise $I_i^L(p,q) = 0$. Noting that the normal value in A_i and L_i should be equal to 0 or 1. We change the value from discrete value into the continuous value in $[0,1]$. Hence, we add new constraints on U_i and V_i and the optimization problem can be written as

$$\min_{U_i,V_i} \frac{1}{2}||I_i^A \odot (A_i - U_iU_i^T)||_F^2 + \frac{1}{2}||I_i^L \odot (L_i - U_iV_i^T)||_F^2$$
$$+ \frac{\alpha}{2}(||U_i||_F^2 + ||V_i||_F^2) \tag{3}$$
$$s.t. 0 \le U_i \le 1, 0 \le V_i \le 1.$$

By above optimization problem, we can learn a good vector space for each social network with missing edges and labels completed.

3.2   Consistence Constraint

When learning the good vector space for each social network, we should make the diversity between different vector spaces as small as possible. In this paper, we apply the user consistence constraint widely used in traditional methods and propose a new label consistence constraint, which can restrict each user effectively.

User Consistence Constraint. In real life, we often know some aligned users in different social networks. A direct intuition is to make the representation of same user in different social network closer or totally same. Then, by preserving the network information, different vector spaces can be overlapped. Formally, we get following optimization problem

$$\min_{U_1,U_2} ||T_1U_1 - T_2U_2||_F^2, \tag{4}$$

where $T_i \in R^{a \times n_i}$ is the indicator matrix. $T_i(p,q) = 1$ if the q-th user belongs to the p-th real person. a is the number of known aligned users and all know aligned users are re-numbered from 1 to a.

However, though preserving the network information, we only can restrict neighbors connected to known aligned users and users far away may suffer from the error propagation. Therefore, we should seek to other consistence constraint to bind each user.

Label Consistence Constraint. To restrict each user, we should add constraint on the information owned by each user. Naturally, each user owns unique labels and label consistence constraint is reasonable. Formally, the label consistence constraint can be formulated as

$$\min_{V_1,V_2} ||M_1V_1 - M_2V_2||_F^2, \tag{5}$$

where $M_i \in R^{l \times d_i}$ is the indicator matrix. $M_i(p,q) = 1$ if the q-th label is the p-th shared label. l is the number of shared labels and all shared labels are re-numbered from 1 to l.

Finally, with above two types of consistence constraint, we can get the final optimization problem

$$\min_{U_i, V_i} \sum_i \frac{1}{2}||I_i^A \odot (A_i - U_i U_i^T)||_F^2 + \frac{1}{2}||I_i^L \odot (L_i - U_i V_i^T)||_F^2$$

$$+ \frac{\alpha}{2}(||U_i||_F^2 + ||V_i||_F^2) + \frac{\beta}{2}(||T_1 U_1 - T_2 U_2||_F^2 + ||M_1 V_1 - M_2 V_2||_F^2) \quad (6)$$

$$s.t. 0 \leq U_i \leq 1, 0 \leq V_i \leq 1,$$

where β is a penalty term to control the importance of consistence constraints.

4   Optimization

In this section, we present the optimization algorithm to solve (6). It is hard to get the optimal solution due to the nonconvexity of optimization objective (6). Therefore, we utilize stochastic gradient method with multiplicative updating rules to ensure the nonnegativity of U_i and V_i. Besides, we use an alternative way to update U_1, U_2, V_1, V_2. The whole algorithm is shown in Algorithm 1.

Optimize U_1, U_2: The partial derivatives of objective (6) $w.r.t. U_1, U_2$ are

$$\frac{\partial L}{\partial U_1} = I_1^A \odot (U_1 U_1^T - A_1)U_1 + I_1^L \odot (U_1 V_1^T - L_1)V_1 + \alpha U_1$$

$$+ \beta T_1^T (T_1 U_1 - T_2 U_2)$$

$$\frac{\partial L}{\partial U_2} = I_2^A \odot (U_2 U_2^T - A_2)U_2 + I_2^L \odot (U_2 V_2^T - L_2)V_2 + \alpha U_2 \quad (7)$$

$$+ \beta T_2^T (T_2 U_2 - T_1 U_1).$$

Using the Karush-Kuhn-Tucker (KKT) complementarity conditions, we can obtain the following updating rules:

$$U_1 = U_1 \odot \sqrt{\frac{(I_1^A \odot A_1)U_1 + (I_1^L \odot L_1)V_1 + \beta T_1^T T_2 U_2}{(I_1^A \odot U_1 U_1^T)U_1 + (I_1^L \odot U_1 V_1^T)V_1 + \alpha U_1 + \beta T_1^T T_1 U_1}} \quad (8)$$

$$U_2 = U_2 \odot \sqrt{\frac{(I_2^A \odot A_2)U_2 + (I_2^L \odot L_2)V_2 + \beta T_2^T T_1 U_1}{(I_2^A \odot U_2 U_2^T)U_2 + (I_2^L \odot U_2 V_2^T)V_2 + \alpha U_2 + \beta T_2^T T_2 U_2}}. \quad (9)$$

Optimize V_1, V_2: The partial derivatives of objective (6) $w.r.t. V_1, V_2$ are

$$\frac{\partial L}{\partial V_1} = (U_1^T I_1^L \odot (U_1 V_1^T - L_1))^T + \alpha V_1 + \beta M_1^T (M_1 V_1 - M_2 V_2)$$

$$\frac{\partial L}{\partial V_2} = (U_2^T I_2^L \odot (U_2 V_2^T - L_2))^T + \alpha V_2 + \beta M_2^T (M_2 V_2 - M_1 V_1). \quad (10)$$

Similar to U_1, U_2, we update V_1, V_2 by

$$V_1 = V_1 \odot \sqrt{\frac{((I_1^L)^T \odot L_1^T)U_1 + \beta M_1^T M_2 V_2}{((I_1^L)^T \odot V_1 U_1^T)U_1 + \alpha V_1 + \beta M_1^T M_1 V_1}} \tag{11}$$

$$V_2 = V_2 \odot \sqrt{\frac{((I_2^L)^T \odot L_2^T)U_2 + \beta M_2^T M_1 V_1}{((I_2^L)^T \odot V_2 U_2^T)U_2 + \alpha V_2 + \beta M_2^T M_2 V_2}}. \tag{12}$$

Algorithm 1. Joint User and Label Consistence Representation (OURLACER)

Input: $G_1 = (A_1, L_1), G_2 = (A_2, L_2)$, a known aligned users, l shared labels, parameters α, β, maximal number of iterations *maxiter*
Output: U_1, U_2 and V_1, V_2
1: Initialize U_1, U_2, V_1, V_2 with $(0, 1)$ uniform distribution
2: **for** t=1:*maxiter* **do**
3:     Update U_1 by (8)
4:     Update U_2 by (9)
5:     Update V_1 by (11)
6:     Update V_2 by (12)
7:     **if** objective (6) converge **then** break

Considering the value of U_i and V_i cannot exceed 1, we utilize the projection technique [6, 29] to project elements greater than 1 in U_i and V_i to 1 after each update process.

5   Experiment Study

In this section, we evaluate the performance compared to state-of-the-art methods. The main compared methods used in experiments include:

- Global Method (GM) [26]: By constructing spectral embedding for each user, this algorithm learns a linear transformation between known aligned users and this method can be seen as a basic version of PALE [11].
- MAH [19]: By constructing hypergraphs by labels and edges, each user owns a vector representation while known aligned users in different social networks own totally same vector representation.
- UMAH [31]: Based on MAH, this method considers the effect of shared labels and automatically learns the weights of different types of shared labels.
- OURLACER: Our proposed OURLACER method can learn the vector representation for each user and label with user and label consistence contraint.

Datasets. We use two real-world datasets to evaluate the performance: (1) Twitter *vs.* BlogCatalog: This dataset is provided by [31] and contains 2710 aligned users in both networks. For each user, this dataset has friendship, username and location information. For location information, 6.38% users do not reveal their location information in both networks and 31.03% only publish location information in one network. In the remaining users (62.59%), only 14.39% users input exactly the same location information in the two networks. (2) DBLP 2015 *vs.* 2016: We use "Yoshua Bengio" as the center node, and then crawl the co-authors that can be reached from the center node with no more than two hops. This process was repeated for authors published papers in 2015 and 2016 independently. Then, we can get two co-author networks. Besides, the conferences/journals published at least once in one year are used as the labels of users in that year. Finally, we have 2845 users in 2015, 3234 users in 2016 and 2169 aligned users between two networks. For label information, user in 2015 and 2016 respectively owns 882 and 1005 unique labels. Except unique labels, the number of shared labels is 945.

Performance Metric. To evaluate the performance of comparison methods, *Accuracy* and *Hit Precision@k* are used to evaluate the exact prediction and top-k prediction [31]. Specially, *Hit Precision@k* allocates different weights for different rank k:
$$h(x) = \frac{k - (hit(x) - 1)}{k},$$
where $hit(x)$ is the position of correct linked user in the returned top-k users. Then, *Hit Precision@k* can be computed on N test users by $\frac{\sum_i^N h(x_i)}{N}$. During experiments, we set $k = 5$.

Experiment Setups. Compared methods except MAH have provided their source codes. For MAH, we implement it by matlab according to original paper and the implement of UMAH. We use same training ratio and test setting in UMAH. Noting that we only use the friendship among 2710 users in dataset Twitter-BlogCatalog. Considering existing study on the effect of dimension, we set the dimension of user representation to a big value such as 500. We denote r_o as the ratio of known aligned users among all aligned users. When setting the parameter of our method, we set β to a bigger value such as 10 to make loss of consistence constraint as small as possible. For parameter α, we set it to a same value for both two datasets. For parameters of other compared methods, we set them to reasonable values according to original papers. Because spectral embedding in GM can only capture structure information, we concat normalized label information with spectral embedding to form new user representation.

Overall Prediction Performance. We evaluate the overall prediction performance for compared methods. The ratio of known aligned users is 30%. As shown in Table 1, OURLACER always behaves better than other methods. Compared

Table 1. Overall prediction performance on two datasets with $r_o = 30\%$

Metric	Method	Twitter-BlogCatalog	DBLP 2015–2016
Accuracy	GM	3.54	2.93
	MAH	9.39	5.40
	UMAH	47.27	6.45
	OURLACER	**52.63**	**11.59**
Hit Precision@5	GM	6.72	5.40
	MAH	17.40	12.06
	UMAH	52.13	11.55
	OURLACER	**55.88**	**19.61**

to GM, other methods utilizing label information carefully show better performance, which demonstrate the potential good effect of labels. Furthermore, by comparing MAH and UMAH, we can find modeling the shared labels in two networks simultaneously is better than modeling labels separately. Finally, OURLACER is still much better than UMAH, which means the great effects of filling missing labels/edges and label consistence constraint.

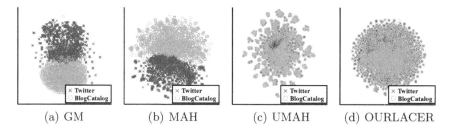

(a) GM   (b) MAH   (c) UMAH   (d) OURLACER

Fig. 1. Visualization of user representations learned by different methods. We plot the overlap results on dataset Twitter-BlogCatalog with $r_o = 30\%$.

Visualization of User Representations. To vividly understand the effect of different methods, we visualize the learned user representations of dataset Twitter-BlogCatalog as shown in Fig. 1. Noting that we only use the representations of testing users. From Fig. 1(a) and (b), we can find the diversity between learned two vector spaces are very big. Besides, Fig. 1(c) and (d) demonstrates that the diversity between two vector spaces can be reduced greatly by carefully modeling label information. Furthermore, Fig. 1(c) shows UMAH tends to learn clustered representations, which means it can restrict users with coarse-grained. By contrary, Fig. 1(d) shows proposed OURLACER can learn the representations more uniformly, which means it can approximately restrict each user by proposed label consistence constraint. From Table 2, the gap between UMAH and

Table 2. Prediction performance by different consistence constraints

Metric	Constraint	Twitter-BlogCatalog	DBLP 2015–2016
Accuracy	user	11.51	8.66
	label	45.89	3.71
	user+label	**52.63**	**11.59**
Hit Precision@5	user	17.40	15.07
	label	47.93	6.73
	user+label	**55.88**	**19.61**

OURLACER on Hit Precision@5 is smaller than it on Accuracy, which demonstrates UMAH learns clustered vector space while OURLACER learns uniform vector space.

Effect of User and Label Consistence Constraint. Besides overall prediction performance, we also study the effect of user consistence constraint and label consistence constraint. The ratio of known aligned users is also set to 30% and the ratios of shared labels are 100% for Twitter-BlogCatalog and 33.37% for DBLP 2015–2016. As shown in Table 2, only one consistence constraint is always worse than two consistence constraints. Hence, our proposed label consistence constrain can make great effect. When the ratio of shared labels increases, the performance of only using label consistence constraint rises greatly. Specifically, the performance of only using label consistence constraint is much higher than only using user consistence contraint for Twitter-BlogCatalog while much smaller for DBLP 2015–2016, which means the effect of proposed label consistence constraint can be enhanced with the increasement of shared labels.

6 Conclusion

Vector space diversity is a great challenge for existing methods. Traditional methods try to learn a vector space for each social network while ignore the effect of missing edges/labels and label consistence among different social networks. Therefore, we propose the jOint UseR and LAbel ConsistencE Representation (OURLACER) method to learn a good space for each social network and greatly reduce the diversity between different vector spaces. Specially, OURLACER learns the vector space by using collective matrix factorization to complete the missing edges and labels. Besides, we propose the label consistence constraint to restrict each user and reduce the vector space diversity. Experiment results demonstrate the effectiveness of OURLACER. Future directions include the consideration of automatically learning the different importances of network information and label information.

Acknowledgments. This work is supported by the National Key Research and Development Program of China, and National Natural Science Foundation of China (No. U163620068).

References

1. Cao, X., Chen, H., Wang, X., Zhang, W., Yu, Y.: Neural link prediction over aligned networks. In: Proceedings of the 32th AAAI Conference on Artificial Intelligence, pp. 249–256 (2018)
2. Chen, W., Yin, H., Wang, W., Zhao, L., Hua, W., Zhou, X.: Exploiting spatio-temporal user behaviors for user linkage. In: Proceedings of the 26th ACM on Conference on Information and Knowledge Management, pp. 517–526 (2017)
3. Chen, W., Yin, H., Wang, W., Zhao, L., Zhou, X.: Effective and efficient user account linkage across location based social networks. In: Proceedings of the 34th IEEE International Conference on Data Engineering, pp. 1085–1096 (2018)
4. Grover, A., Leskovec, J.: node2vec: scalable feature learning for networks. In: Proceedings of the 22nd ACM SIGKDD International Conference on Knowledge Discovery and Data Mining, pp. 855–864 (2016)
5. Hu, G., Zhang, Y., Yang, Q.: CoNet: collaborative cross networks for cross-domain recommendation. In: Proceedings of the 27th ACM International Conference on Information and Knowledge Management, pp. 667–676 (2018)
6. Koutra, D., Tong, H., Lubensky, D.: Big-Align: fast bipartite graph alignment. In: Proceedings of the 13th IEEE International Conference on Data Mining, pp. 389–398 (2013)
7. Lee, R.K.W., Hoang, T.A., Lim, E.P.: On analyzing user topic-specific platform preferences across multiple social media sites. In: Proceedings of the 26th International Conference on World Wide Web, pp. 1351–1359 (2017)
8. Li, C., et al.: Distribution distance minimization for unsupervised user identity linkage. In: Proceedings of the 27th ACM International Conference on Information and Knowledge Management, pp. 447–456 (2018)
9. Liu, L., Cheung, W.K., Li, X., Liao, L.: Aligning users across social networks using network embedding. In: Proceedings of the 25th International Joint Conference on Artificial Intelligence, pp. 1774–1780 (2016)
10. Liu, S., Wang, S., Zhu, F., Zhang, J., Krishnan, R.: HYDRA: large-scale social identity linkage via heterogeneous behavior modeling. In: Proceedings of the 37th ACM SIGMOD International Conference on Management of Data, pp. 51–62 (2014)
11. Man, T., Shen, H., Liu, S., Jin, X., Cheng, X.: Predict anchor links across social networks via an embedding approach. In: Proceedings of the 25th International Joint Conference on Artificial Intelligence, pp. 1823–1829 (2016)
12. Mu, X., Zhu, F., Lim, E.P., Xiao, J., Wang, J., Zhou, Z.H.: User identity linkage by latent user space modelling. In: Proceedings of the 22nd ACM SIGKDD International Conference on Knowledge Discovery and Data Mining, pp. 1775–1784 (2016)
13. Nie, Y., Jia, Y., Li, S., Zhu, X., Li, A., Zhou, B.: Identifying users across social networks based on dynamic core interests. Neurocomputing **210**, 107–115 (2016)
14. Perera, D., Zimmermann, R.: LSTM networks for online cross-network recommendations. In: Proceedings of the 27th International Joint Conference on Artificial Intelligence, pp. 3825–3833 (2018)

15. Perozzi, B., Al-Rfou, R., Skiena, S.: DeepWalk: online learning of social representations. In: Proceedings of the 20th ACM SIGKDD International Conference on Knowledge Discovery and Data Mining, pp. 701–710 (2014)
16. Qiu, J., Dong, Y., Ma, H., Li, J., Wang, K., Tang, J.: Network embedding as matrix factorization: Unifying DeepWalk, LINE, PTE, and node2vec. In: Proceedings of the 11th ACM International Conference on Web Search and Data Mining, pp. 459–467 (2018)
17. Singh, A.P., Gordon, G.J.: Relational learning via collective matrix factorization. In: Proceedings of the 14th ACM SIGKDD International Conference on Knowledge Discovery and Data Mining, pp. 650–658 (2008)
18. Su, S., Sun, L., Zhang, Z., Li, G., Qu, J.: MASTER: across multiple social networks, integrate attribute and structure embedding for reconciliation. In: Proceedings of the 27th International Joint Conference on Artificial Intelligence, pp. 3863–3869 (2018)
19. Tan, S., Guan, Z., Cai, D., Qin, X., Bu, J., Chen, C.: Mapping users across networks by manifold alignment on hypergraph. In: Proceedings of the 28th AAAI Conference on Artificial Intelligence (2014)
20. Tang, J., Qu, M., Mei, Q.: PTE: predictive text embedding through large-scale heterogeneous text networks. In: Proceedings of the 21th ACM SIGKDD International Conference on Knowledge Discovery and Data Mining, pp. 1165–1174 (2015)
21. Tang, J., Qu, M., Wang, M., Zhang, M., Yan, J., Mei, Q.: LINE: large-scale information network embedding. In: Proceedings of the 24th International Conference on World Wide Web, pp. 1067–1077 (2015)
22. Yan, M., Sang, J., Xu, C.: Mining cross-network association for youtube video promotion. In: Proceedings of the 22nd ACM International Conference on Multimedia, pp. 557–566 (2014)
23. Yan, M., Sang, J., Xu, C., Hossain, M.S.: A unified video recommendation by cross-network user modeling. ACM Trans. Multimed. Comput. Commun. Appl. **12**, 53:1–53:24 (2016)
24. Zafarani, R., Liu, H.: Connecting corresponding identities across communities. In: Proceedings of the 3rd International AAAI Conference on Weblogs and Social Media (2009)
25. Zafarani, R., Liu, H.: Connecting users across social media sites: a behavioral-modeling approach. In: Proceedings of the 19th ACM SIGKDD International Conference on Knowledge Discovery and Data Mining, pp. 41–49 (2013)
26. Zafarani, R., Tang, L., Liu, H.: User identification across social media. ACM Trans. Knowl. Discov. Data **10**(2), 16:1–16:30 (2015)
27. Zhang, J., Chen, J., Zhi, S., Chang, Y., Yu, P.S., Han, J.: Link prediction across aligned networks with sparse and low rank matrix estimation. In: Proceedings of the 33rd IEEE International Conference on Data Engineering, pp. 971–982 (2017)
28. Zhang, J., Kong, X., Yu, P.S.: Predicting social links for new users across aligned heterogeneous social networks. In: Proceedings of the 13th IEEE International Conference on Data Mining, pp. 1289–1294 (2013)
29. Zhang, J., Yu, P.S.: Multiple anonymized social networks alignment. In: Proceedings of the 15th IEEE International Conference on Data Mining, pp. 599–608 (2015)
30. Zhang, J., et al.: MEgo2Vec: embedding matched ego networks for user alignment across social networks. In: Proceedings of the 27th ACM International Conference on Information and Knowledge Management, pp. 327–336 (2018)

31. Zhao, W., et al.: Learning to map social network users by unified manifold alignment on hypergraph. IEEE Trans. Neural Netw. Learn. Syst. **29**, 5834–5846 (2018)
32. Zhou, F., Liu, L., Zhang, K., Trajcevski, G., Wu, J., Zhong, T.: DeepLink: a deep learning approach for user identity linkage. In: Proceedings of the 37th IEEE Conference on Computer Communications, pp. 1313–1321 (2018)

Opinion Knowledge Injection Network for Aspect Extraction

Shaolei Zhang[1]([✉]), Gang Lu[2], and Kai Shuang[3]

[1] School of Computer Science, Beijing University of Posts and Telecommunications, Beijing, China
zhangshaolei@bupt.edu.cn
[2] Intelligent Networks and Devices Research Institute, China Telecom Corporation Limited, Guangzhou, China
[3] State Key Laboratory of Networking and Switching Technology, Beijing University of Posts and Telecommunications, Beijing, China

Abstract. Aspect term extraction (ATE) is to extract explicit aspect expressions from online reviews. This paper focused on the supervised extraction of aspect term. Previous models for ATE either ignored the opinion information or improperly utilized the opinion information with a high-coupling method. We proposed a model to perform ATE with the assistance of opinion knowledge, called opinion knowledge injection network. Specifically, the proposed model distills the opinion knowledge through the attention mechanism and joins it into each word to assist aspect extraction. The proposed model achieved surprisingly good results, improving 1.34% and 1.23% than the best results before respectively on the laptop and restaurant datasets, and reached state-of-the-art.

Keywords: Aspect extraction · Opinion knowledge · Unidirectional injection · Attention mechanism

1 Introduction

The aspect-based sentiment analysis (ABSA) task is to identify opinions expressed towards specific entities or attributes of entities [1]. The first step of the ABSA is the aspect term extraction (ATE), which is the key to sentiment analysis. The goal of ATE is to find the phrase that is evaluated in the sentence. For example, in the sentence "The food is simply unforgettable!", "*food*" should be chosen as the aspect term because it is commented with "*unforgettable*".

Aspect term extraction has been performed with supervised approaches [2–4,8] and unsupervised approaches [5–7,9,10]. This paper focuses on supervised approaches which usually perform better than unsupervised approaches.

S. Zhang–This work was supported in part by the National key research and development program of China(2016QY01W0200). Research Innovation Fund for College Students of Beijing University of Posts and Telecommunications. National Key Research and Development Program of China (2017YFB1400603).

T. Gedeon et al. (Eds.): ICONIP 2019, LNCS 11954, pp. 669–681, 2019.
https://doi.org/10.1007/978-3-030-36711-4_56

In supervised aspect extraction, many of the early models only focus on the modeling of the aspect term, ignoring the contribution of the opinion word. According to the definition of the task, if a word/phrase is treated as an aspect term, it should be commented on by some opinion words which indicate the emotional polarity of it. The neglect of the opinion word will result in the word which was not commented in the sentence being incorrectly treated as the aspect term. Take the sentence "The service is fantastic at this fun place." as an example, where "*service*" and "*place*" are aspect terms. Without the assistant of opinion words, the previous models are difficult to extract "*place*" as an aspect term, but as an adverbial more likely.

The opinion word has been exploited in a few models, such as RNCRF [11], CMLA [12], and MIN [16]. Although these methods achieve better performance than the previous models, there are still two shortcomings. (1) These previous models that utilize the opinion word either rely on dependency phase tree [11] or have a high-coupling network architecture [12,16]. Depending on dependency parsing will cause errors in informal comments, and high-coupling network cause that the inaccurate prediction will interfere with each other and amplify. (2) Most previous models are based on RNN and LSTM, and the models that perform both aspect extraction and opinion extraction often require two or more LSTMs and even interact between each layer. This will result in a lower speed, which needs to be considered when the model is actually deployed.

To solve the first problem, making more rational use of opinion information, we proposed a model called Opinion Knowledge Injection Network (OKIN). For each word, OKIN distills the opinion knowledge of it from the whole sentence and injects the opinion knowledge into the representation of the word. To be more reasonable in the representation of opinion knowledge, OKIN computes the relevance between the aspect word and opinion words as association score, and then the opinion knowledge is weighted aggregated by opinion word according to the association score. To avoid the noise being continuously amplified during the coupling of aspect and opinion extraction, we adopt a unidirectional injection method, which only appears on the last layer of the network. Unidirectional injection guarantees that there is only information flow from opinion extraction to aspect extraction without reverse. Unidirectional injection effectively aggregates opinion knowledge into each word while avoiding the inaccurate aspect extraction to generate noise on the opinion extraction and preventing two tasks from interfering with each other. Take the sentence "The service is fantastic at this fun place." as an example as well, where the opinion terms are "*fantastic*" and "*fun*". Previously highly coupled models were prone to errors in dealing with "*place*", but still used "*place*" to associate with opinion words layer by layer, making the "*place*" and "*fun*" both difficult to be predicted accurately. OKIN computes the association score, where "*fantastic*" → "*service*" and "*fun*" → "*place*" will get a higher score. Then, the opinion knowledge of "*fun*" will be aggregated into "*place*" unidirectionally. This approach ensures that the opinion extraction is as accurate as possible and then uses it to assist aspect extraction. Thus, it is much easier to extract the "*place*" as an aspect accurately. To solve the second problem, improving the speed of processing, our model uses CNN instead of LSTM. CNN has been proved is effective to ATE [13]. OKIN uses two CNNs to extract the aspect and the opinion individually and only perform unidirectional injection on the last layer of the network, which is parallelizable.

In summary, our contribution is four-fold: (1) To the best of our knowledge, we are the first to use double CNNs to extract aspect and opinion simultaneously. (2) We proposed unidirectional injection, a more reasonable low-coupling method, to control the spread of noise when utilizing the opinion word in ATE. (3) We provided an acceleration method for aspect and opinion extraction with CNN. (4) We conducted an experiment on two datasets to verify that our model achieves state-of-the-art for aspect term extraction.

2   Related Work

Reference [5] put forward aspect level sentiment analysis in which aspect term extraction is an important task. In recent research, aspect term extraction has been abstracted into sequence labeling tasks.

Aspect term extraction is mainly divided into unsupervised and supervised approaches. The unsupervised approach includes methods such as topic modeling [15,20], syntactic rules-based extraction [8,15], frequent pattern mining [5,14], word alignment [21] and label propagation [22].

The earliest supervised approach was using Conditional Random Fields (CRF) [17]. Recently, more methods are using neural network for aspect term extraction., e.g., using LSTM [18],using CNN [19] and attention mechanism [12,16]. Further, the opinion word is gradually paid more attention to the aspect term extraction. Some models [11,12,16] directly performed aspect term and opinion term co-extraction through dependency parsing or high-coupling network. RNCRF [11] is a novel joint model that integrates recursive neural networks and conditional random fields. For RNCRF, it tends to suffer from parsing errors since the structure of the recursive network hinges on the dependency parse tree. When applied to informal comments, it is easier to make mistakes. CMLA [12] consists of coupled attentions to exploit the correlations between aspect and opinion terms through tensor operators. Similarly, MIN [16] employs three LSTMs, using memory interactions and Sentimental sentence constraints for the aspect and opinion co-extraction. For CMLA and MIN, when coupling the extraction of aspect and opinion on each layer, noise and error are continuously amplified layer by layer. In addition, most of the previous models for aspect extraction were based on RNN and LSTM, until [13] proposed a CNN-based model and proved to be effective.

Existing methods used highly-coupled LSTM-based models, resulting in bad interference between aspect and opinion extraction, and slow processing speed. Therefore, we proposed OKIN with double CNNs and unidirectional injection, reducing the degree of coupling to avoid bad interference and using two parallel CNNs to speed up the processing.

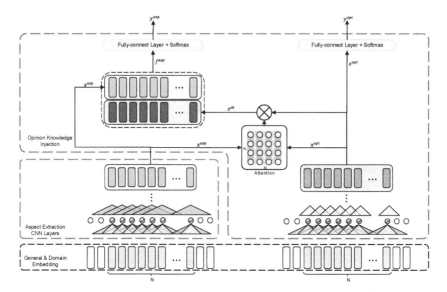

Fig. 1. Proposed model architecture. Gray rectangles, red rectangles, and blue rectangles represent a vector in the embedding layer, the aspect extraction CNN layers, and the opinion extraction CNN layers, respectively. The white rectangles represent zero vector padded. The triangles represent the 1D-CNN filters. (Color figure online)

3   Model

To reduce the coupling degree of the model, OKIN uses two independent CNNs to extract the aspect and opinion feature respectively, and then, connects the two parts together by unidirectional injection. Unidirectional injection limits the direction of possible noise propagation. OKIN first ensures that opinion knowledge is accurate and then use it to assist in aspect extraction. In addition, two independent CNNs can be processed in parallel, which improves processing speed compared to LSTM-based models. The proposed model is depicted in Fig. 1.

Assume the input is a sequence of word indexes $x = \{x_1, \cdots, x_i, \cdots, x_n\}$. The output of the model is $y = \{y_1, \cdots, y_i, \cdots, y_n\}$, $y_i \in \{B, I, O\}$, where 'B' represents the starting position of the aspect term, 'I' represents the subsequent position of the aspect term, and 'O' representing the position that is not the aspect term.

3.1   Embedding Layers

The embedding module of our model also uses double embedding [13]. Let $\omega^{general} \in \mathbb{R}^{d_1 \times |V_1|}$ and $\omega^{domain} \in \mathbb{R}^{d_2 \times |V_2|}$ be the embedding matrix of general embedding and domain embedding, where d_1 and d_2 are the dimension of word vectors and $|V_1|$ and $|V_2|$ are the vocabulary size.

Through matrix $\omega^{general}$ and ω^{domain}, the embedding layer transforms the input x into a list of vectors $x^{general} = \{x_1, \cdots, x_i, \cdots, x_n\}$, where $x_i \in \mathbb{R}^{d_1}$, and $x^{domain} = \{x_1, \cdots, x_j, \cdots, x_n\}$, where $x_j \in \mathbb{R}^{d_2}$. Then we concatenate two embeddings:

$$x^0 = \left[x^{general} : x^{domain} \right], \tag{1}$$

and input x^0 into aspect extraction CNN layers and opinion knowledge injection module.

3.2   Aspect Extraction CNN Layers

Aspect extraction CNN layers contain many 1D-convolution filters and each filter has a fixed kernel size $k = 2c+1$ and step size $s = 1$. We perform convolution on c words before and after the center word $[i - c, i + c]$. For the case of less than c, we pad the zero vector to make up. For the rth convolution filter in l^{th} CNN layer, it performs the following convolution operation and ReLU activation:

$$x_i^{(l+1,r)} = ReLu \left(\left(\sum_{j=-c}^{c} \omega_j^r \times x_{i+j}^{(l)} \right) + b^r \right), \tag{2}$$

where $\omega \in \mathbb{R}^{k \times d_2 \times d_1}$, $b \in \mathbb{R}^{d_2 \times 1}$ are the 1D-convolution parameters. d_1 and d_2 are the number of input channels (word vector dimension) and output channels.

Aspect Extraction CNN layers contain l_{asp} layers. The output of Aspect Extraction CNN layers is $x^{asp} = \{x_1, \cdots, x_i, \cdots, x_n\}$, where $x_i \in \mathbb{R}^{d_{asp} \times 1}$ and d_{asp} is the number of output channel of aspect extraction CNN layers.

3.3   Opinion Knowledge Injection

This module firstly uses CNN layers to extract the opinion feature, similar to the aspect extraction CNN layers. However, the difference is the number of layers and the kernel size of 1D-convolution. Opinion Extraction CNN layers contain l_{opi} layers. The output of Aspect extraction CNN layers is $x^{opi} = \{x_1, \cdots, x_i, \cdots, x_n\}$, where $x_i \in \mathbb{R}^{d_{opi} \times 1}$ and d_{opi} is the number of output channel of opinion extraction CNN layers.

In order to reasonably incorporate the opinion knowledge into each word, OKIN employs the co-attention mechanism between the output of the aspect extraction CNN layers x^{asp} and opinion extraction CNN layers x^{opi}. We apply co-attention as follows:

$$S = ReLU \left((x^{asp})^T \omega x^{opi} \right), \tag{3}$$

Where $\omega \in \mathbb{R}^{d_{asp} \times d_{opi}}$ is the parameter being trained and $S \in \mathbb{R}^{n \times n}$ is the correlation matrix. $S_{i,j}$ represents the association score of the ith word as aspect word and the jth word as opinion word. Then, we perform $softmax$ on each row of the correlation matrix S to obtain the attention weight between the current aspect word and each opinion word:

$$W = softmax\left(S, dim = 1\right), \tag{4}$$

where $\sum_{j=1}^{n} W_{i,j} = 1, 1 \leq i \leq n$. The opinion knowledge of the current aspect word X_i is obtained by weighting all the partial opinion according to the correlation matrix W:

$$x_i^{ok} = \sum_{j=1}^{n} W_{i,j} \times x_j^{opi}, \tag{5}$$

where $x_i^{ok} \in \mathbb{R}^{d_{opi} \times 1}$, $1 \leq i \leq n$, is the opinion knowledge of x_i. Finally, we connect the aspect feature x^{asp} with its opinion knowledge x^{ok} to get the vector containing both the the aspect information and sentimental information,

$$f^{asp} = \left[x^{asp} : x^{ok}\right]. \tag{6}$$

3.4   Loss Function

Since aspect extraction is the main part and opinion extraction is the auxiliary part, we proposed a new loss function $\jmath$, which consists of two parts. The first part is computed by the aspect word with opinion knowledge f^{asp}, and the second part is only computed by the opinion information x^{opi}.

For both f^{asp} and x^{opi}, we applied a fully-connected layer and a $softmax$ to calculate the label distribution probability for each word. Dimension of the output of two fully-connected layers $|\nu| = 3$.

$$P\left(y^{asp} \mid f^{asp}\right) = softmax\left(\omega^{asp} f^{asp} + b^{asp}\right), \tag{7}$$

$$P\left(y^{opi} \mid x^{opi}\right) = softmax\left(\omega^{opi} x^{opi} + b^{opi}\right), \tag{8}$$

where ω^{asp}, b^{asp}, ω^{opi} and b^{opi} are parameters of fully-connected layer.

During the training process, for both aspect extraction and opinion extraction, we use the token-level cross-entropy error between the predicted distribution $P\left(y_i^{\tau} \mid x_i\right)$, $\tau \in \{asp, opi\}$, and the gold distribution $P\left(y_i^{\tau, g} \mid x_i\right)$ as the loss function:

$$L_{\tau} = -\sum_{i=1}^{N} P\left(y_i^{\tau,g} \mid x_i\right) \odot log\left[P\left(y_i^{\tau} \mid x_i\right)\right], \tag{9}$$

Then, the proposed loss functions of both tasks are combined to form the training objective of the entire model:

$$\jmath = L_{asp} + \alpha L_{opi}, \tag{10}$$

Where α is the hyperparameter we set.

4 Experience

To evaluate the proposed model for aspect extraction, we compared OKIN with the previous model in terms of both aspect and opinion extraction and conducted two sets of containment experiments. In addition, we visualized the attention mechanism and made some case studies on the proposed model and the baseline. All the experimental results prove that OKIN is effective for ATE.

4.1 Datasets

The statistics of two benchmark datasets from SemEval challenges [6] was shown in "Table 1". The first dataset is from the laptop domain on subtask 1 of SemEval-2014 Task 4. The second dataset is from the restaurant domain on subtask 1 of SemEval-2016 Task 5. The aspect terms and opinion terms of these two datasets were labeled as spans of characters.

Table 1. Statistics of datasets. S., A., O. represent sentence, aspect, and opinion.

		#S.	#A.	#O.	#S. w/ A.	#S. w/ O.
SemEval-14	TRAIN	3045	2358	4979	1484	2499
Laptop	TEST	800	654	1229	422	652
SemEval-16	TRAIN	2000	1743	2758	1233	1590
Restaurant	TEST	676	622	874	420	522

4.2 Comparison Models

We compare our model with the following four parts: simple original models, models that use the opinion word to assist the aspect extraction, CNN-based models, and the variations of OKIN.

- **CRF:** Conditional Random Fields with basic feature templates.
- **LSTM:** Vanilla bi-directional LSTM with pre-trained word embeddings.
- **IHS RD** [3], **DLIREC** [23], **NLANGP** [24]: The winning systems in the ATE subtask in SemEval ABSA challenge.
- **WDEmb** [9]: Enhanced CRF with word embeddings, dependency path embeddings and linear context embeddings.
- **RNCRF** [11]: A model that integrates recursive neural networks and conditional random fields.
- **CMLA** [12]: A network with coupled multilayer attentions, which propose coupled attentions to exploit the correlations among input tokens.
- **MIN** [16]: A model that jointly handles the extraction tasks of aspects and opinions via memory interactions and Sentimental sentence constraint.

- **DECNN** [13]: A CNN-based aspect extraction model with a double embeddings mechanism without extra supervision.
- **OKIN w/o** L_{opi}: OKIN removes the loss of opinion extraction and does not perform any supervised learning on opinion extraction, which only trains the model with the loss of aspect extraction.
- **OKIN w/o ATT:** OKIN removes the co-attention mechanism and directly stitches the output of the opinion extraction CNN layers to the output of the aspect extraction CNN layers.

4.3   Experiment Setting

We use NLTK to tokenize each sentence into a sequence of words and do not make special treatments for punctuation marks that are different from words. To ensure the fairness of the comparison, our Embedding layers and aspect extraction CNN layers are the same as DECNN [13]. The opinion extraction CNN contains four layers. The first layer ($l = 1$) is the same as the first layer in aspect extraction CNN layers. The next four layers ($l = 2, 3, 4, 5$) each contain a convolution filter ($kernelsize : 3; step : 1; padding : 1$).

We divided 150 samples from the training set as the validation set. The hyperparameter α in loss function is set to 0.7. We apply dropout after each embedding layer and CNN layer, and dropout is set to 0.6. Due to the instability of CNN training, the learning rate was set to 0.0001.

Table 2. Experimental results of aspect extraction(F1 score, %). The first ten results are copied from their papers, '-' indicates the results were not available in their papers.

Model	Laptop	Restaurant
CRF	72.77	66.96
LSTM	75.71	70.35
IHS_RD	74.55	-
DLIREC	73.78	-
NLANGP	-	72.34
WDEmb	75.16	-
RNCRF	78.42	-
CMLA	77.80	-
MIN	77.58	73.44
DECNN	81.59	74.37
OKIN w/o L_{opi}	82.11	74.17
OKIN w/o ATT	81.16	73.58
OKIN	**82.93**	**75.60**

4.4   Results and Analysis

"Table 2" shows that OKIN exceeds all previous models and achieves the best F1 values on the restaurant and laptop dataset. Compared with the winning systems of SemEval ABSA, our model has an absolute advantage of 8.38% and 3.26% on the Laptop and Restaurant datasets, respectively.

Compared to RNCRF, OKIN does not rely on dependency parsing, but the score on the Laptop dataset does exceed 4.51%. OKIN could predict more accurately when dealing with unofficial comments or comments with confusing sentence structures, which perform better than RNCRF. CMLA and MIN emphasize the interaction between aspect and opinion with high-coupling. OKIN proposes unidirectional injection to control the spread of noise, so that OKIN works better than MIN and CMLA on both datasets. To verify the effect of opinion extraction, we evaluated the accuracy of opinion extraction on RNCRF, CMLA and OKIN. As shown in "Table 3", OKIN largely outperforms the RNCRF and CMLA in the accuracy of opinion extraction. This is the effect of using unidirectional injection, we do not allow any aspect information to interfere with the training of the opinion, and directly output the result of the opinion extraction CNN layers to the fully-connected layer and the softmax.

Table 3. Experimental results of opinion extraction(F1 score, %).

Model	Laptop	Restaurant
RNCRF	79.44	-
CMLA	80.17	-
OKIN	**90.56**	**83.22**

One important baseline is DECNN, which is the first model using CNN on the ATE. Our model has an accuracy of 1.34% and 1.23% higher than the DECNN on the datasets of Laptop and Restaurant, which proves that the injection of opinion knowledge can effectively assist in aspect extraction.

In addition, we conducted two sets of ablation study. When we remove the L_{opi} or attention mechanism, the effect is significantly reduced, even lower than the baseline. This shows that the addition of opinion extraction leads to the complexity of the model, which will bring noise. If the proposed model does not use opinion information reasonably, it will achieve the opposite effect, which proves the necessity of L_{opi} and attention mechanisms in the proposed model.

4.5   Attention Visualization and Case Study

As shown in Fig. 2, we visualize the association score in two difficult example sentences.

The first sentence is "The service is fantastic at this fun place.". From Fig. 2(a), we can see that when the aspect word is *"service"* (the second row),

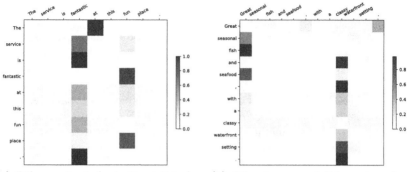

(a) "The service is fantastic at this fun place."

(b) "Great seasonal fish and seafood, with a classy waterfront setting."

Fig. 2. Visualization of the attention. The vertical and horizontal axis represent the word as aspect and opinion, respectively. The deeper the color is, the higher the attention score is, the more the word's opinion knowledge will be injected into the aspect. (Color figure online)

"*fantastic*" is most concerned, followed by "*fun*". Similarly, when the aspect word is "*service*" (the eighth row), "*fun*" is most concerned. It proves that the attention mechanism can effectively associate the aspect word with the opinion word. Almost all words pay more attention to the opinion word. However, the aspect word focuses on the opinion word more closely to one-hot, while other non-aspect word's attention is more dispersed. Therefore, it is more beneficial for the aspect to get more opinion knowledge.

The second sentence is "Great seasonal fish and seafood, with a classy waterfront setting.". The aspect terms for this sentence are "*seasonal fish*" and "*seafood*", which are connected by "*and*". For aspect extraction, if "*A*" is an aspect and when "*A and B*" appears, "*B*" should also be extracted as an aspect. One shortage of DECNN [13] is that it can't predict correctly when requiring the semantics of the conjunction word, while OKIN can avoid this error with the help of opinion words. For example, when "*A and B*" appears, and the opinion word "*C*" exists in the sentence to comment "*A and B*". OKIN can extract comment relationship "*C*" → "*A*" and "*C*" → "*B*" through attention, and inject knowledge of "*C*" into "*A*" and "*B*", thus it is more easier to obtain "*A*" and "*B*" both as aspect term. As shown in Fig. 2(b), we can see that the "*seasonal*" (the second row) and the "*fish*" (the third row) pay more attention to "*great*", and the "*seafood*" (the fifth row) also pays attention to "*great*". So "*seasonal fish*" and "*seafood*" are both correctly identified as aspect terms. By using the transitivity of the comment relationship on conjunctions, our model subtly addresses the errors caused by conjunctions.

As mentioned before, DECNN [13] is the baseline of our model. OKIN introduces opinion knowledge injection to assist aspect extraction and achieve better results. To show that, we pick a few example reviews from the test datasets

Table 4. Prediction comparison between our model and DECNN. The red label is the aspect term, and the blue label is the opinion term.

Input sentences	Output of DECNN	Output of OKIN
1. Seattle's BEST Winelist	*Seattle, Winelist*	*Winelist*
2. DONOT GO!	*DONOT*	*None*
3. Great seasonal fish and seafood, with a classy waterfront setting	*Fish, waterfront setting*	*Seasonal fish, seafood, waterfront setting*
4. I had to buy a wireless mouse to go with it, as I am old school and hate the pad, but knew that before I bought it, now it works great, need to get adjusted to the key board, as I am used to a bigger one and pounding	*Wireless mouse, pad, key board*	*Wireless mouse, pad, works, key board*

as presented in "Table 4". The first two examples illustrate that OKIN avoids no-commented words being identified as aspect terms, and the latter two examples illustrate that OKIN can extract difficult-to-recognize aspect terms with the help of opinion extraction. OKIN also has a good performance in short sentence (i.e., the first and the second), long sentence (i.e., the forth), the sentence with many aspect terms (i.e., the third and the forth), and sentence containing conjunctions (i.e., the third). All these examples prove that OKIN can handle all kinds of online reviews and achieve good results.

5   Conclusion

We considered the weaknesses of complex networks on ATE and provided an effective way to reduce the coupling degree of network and speed up the processing. For models that handle multitasks, we provided a unidirectional injection method that effectively limits the propagation of noise. Finally, we proposed an opinion knowledge injection network for aspect term extraction, which exceeds all existing models.

References

1. Liu, K., Xu, L., Zhao, J.: Opinion target extraction using word-based translation model. In: EMNLP-CoNLL 2012, pp. 1346–1356 (2012)
2. Jakob, N., Gurevych, I.: Extracting opinion targets in a single- and cross-domain setting with conditional random fields. In: EMNLP 2010, pp. 1035–1045 (2010)
3. Chernyshevich, M.: IHS R&D Belarus: crossdomain extraction of product features using CRF. In: Proceedings of the 8th International Workshop on Semantic Evaluation (SemEval 2014), pp. 309–313 (2014)
4. Shu, L., Xu, H., Liu, B.: Lifelong learning CRF for supervised aspect extraction. In: Proceedings of the 55th Annual Meeting of the Association for Computational Linguistics (Volume 2: Short Papers), vol. 2, pp. 148–154 (2017)
5. Minqing, H., Liu, B.: Mining and summarizing customer reviews. In: KDD 2004, pp. 168–177 (2004)
6. Pontiki, M., Galanis, D., Pavlopoulos, J., Papageorgiou, H., Androutsopoulos, I., Manandhar, S.: Semeval-2014 task 4: aspect based sentiment analysis. In: Proceedings of the 8th International Workshop on Semantic Evaluation (SemEval 2014), pp. 27–35 (2014)
7. Zhang, Z., Singh, M.: Limbic: author-based sentiment aspect modeling regularized with word embeddings and discourse relations. In: EMNLP 2018, pp. 3412–3422 (2018)
8. Huang, M., Rao, Y., Liu, Y., Xie, H., Wang, F.L.: Siamese network-based supervised topic modeling. In: EMNLP 2018, vol. 37, no. 1, pp. 4652–4662 (2018)
9. Yin, Y., Wei, F., Dong, L., Xu, K., Zhang, M., Zhou, M.: Unsupervised word and dependency path embeddings for aspect term extraction (2016). arXiv preprint arXiv:1605.07843
10. He, R., Lee, W.S., Ng, H.T., Dahlmeier, D.: An unsupervised neural attention model for aspect extraction. In: Proceedings of the 55th Annual Meeting of the Association for Computational Linguistics (Volume 1: Long Papers), vol. 1, pp. 388–397 (2017)
11. Wang, W., Pan, S.J., Dahlmeier, D., Xiao, X.: Recursive neural conditional random fields for aspect-based sentiment analysis (2016). arXiv preprint arXiv:1603.06679
12. Wang, W., Pan, S.J., Dahlmeier, D., Xiao. X.: Coupled multi-layer attentions for co-extraction of aspect and opinion terms. In: AAAI, pp. 3316–3322 (2017)
13. Xu, H.. Liu, B., Shu, L., Yu, P.S.: Double embeddings and CNN-based sequence labeling for aspect extraction. In: Proceedings of the 56th Annual Meeting of the Association for Computational Linguistics (Volume 2: Short Papers), pp. 592–598 (2018)
14. Popescu, A.-M., Etzioni, O.: Extracting product features and opinions from reviews. In: HLT-EMNLP, vol. 05, pp. 339–346 (2005)
15. Giannakopoulos, A., Musat, C., Hossmann, A., Baeriswyl, M.: Unsupervised aspect term extraction with B-LSTM & CRF using automatically labelled datasets. In: Proceedings of the 8th Workshop on Computational Approaches to Subjectivity, Sentiment and Social Media Analysis, pp. 180–188 (2017)
16. Li, X., Lam, W.: Deep multi-task learning for aspect term extraction with memory interaction. In: EMNLP, vol. 17, pp. 2886–2892 (2017)
17. Lafferty, J., McCallum, A., Pereira, F.C.: Conditional random fields: probabilistic models for segmenting and labeling sequence data. In: ICML 2001, pp. 282–289 (2001)

18. Liu, P., Joty, S., Meng, H.: Finegrained opinion mining with recurrent neural networks and word embeddings. In: EMNLP 2015, pp. 1433–1443 (2015)
19. Poria, S., Cambria, E., Gelbukh, A.: Aspect extraction for opinion mining with a deep convolutional neural network. In: Knowledge-Based Systems, pp. 42–49 (2016)
20. Moghaddam, S., Ester, M.: ILDA: interdependent LDA model for learning latent aspects and their ratings from online product reviews. In: SIGIR, vol. 11, pp. 665–674 (2011)
21. Liu, K., Liheng, X., Liu, Y., Zhao, J.: Opinion target extraction using partially-supervised word alignment model. In: IJCAI, vol. 13, pp. 2134–2140 (2013)
22. Zhou, X., Wan, X., Xiao, J.: Collective opinion target extraction in Chinese microblogs. In: EMNLP, vol. 13, pp. 1840–1850 (2013)
23. Toh, Z., Wang, W.: DLIREC: aspect term extraction and term polarity classification system. In: Proceedings of the 8th International Workshop on Semantic Evaluation (SemEval-2014), pp. 235–240 (2014)
24. Toh, Z., Su, J.: NLANGP at semeval-2016 task 5: improving aspect based sentiment analysis using neural network features. In: Proceedings of the 10th International Workshop on Semantic Evaluation (SemEval-2016), pp. 282–288 (2016)

A Deep Matrix Factorization Method with Missing Not at Random Data for Social Recommendation

Weiye Wang, Ben Yang, Wanting Zhao, and Jinkui Xie[✉]

School of Computer Science and Technology, East China Normal University,
Shanghai 200062, China
ellan@stu.ecnu.edu.cn, isyangben@outlook.com, WantingZhao1995@gmail.com,
jkxie@cs.ecnu.edu.cn

Abstract. With the rapid development of online social networks, a mass of data mining techniques for integrating social relations into ordinary recommendation algorithms have emerged. Despite the extensive studies, social recommendation methods always assume that the data is missing at random (MAR), which is in the rare instance. What's more, no existing work has taken into account both explicit ratings and non-preference implicit feedback when it comes to social recommendation. To tackle these challenges, in this paper, we propose a novel framework, *deep social matrix factorization with missing not at random data* (DSMF-MNAR). Firstly, on the premise that the data is not missing at random, we extend the popular Bayesian Personalized Ranking (BPR) model to complete the user-item rating matrix and user-user trust matrix. Secondly, with the two matrices as the input, we extend the Deep Matrix Factorization (DMF) model to incorporate the user-user trust relationship. Finally, we present a new loss function, in which we factor both explicit ratings and implicit feedback. Extensive experiments conducted on three real-world datasets demonstrate that our proposed method provides the best top-N recommendations, illustrating the benefits of the added model complexity.

Keywords: DMF · MNAR · Social recommendation

1 Introduction

With the explosive growth of online social networks, considerable work in social recommendation has emerged. The mainstream method of social recommendation is incorporating the mechanism of trust into the ordinary model. In Ref. [1], Yang et al. propose a personalized social collaborative filtering method,

This work was supported by the National Nature Science Foundation of China under Grant 61773166, the Natural Science Foundation of Shanghai under Grant 17ZR1408200 and the Science and Technology Commission of Shanghai Municipality under Grant 14DZ2260800.

© Springer Nature Switzerland AG 2019
T. Gedeon et al. (Eds.): ICONIP 2019, LNCS 11954, pp. 682–694, 2019.
https://doi.org/10.1007/978-3-030-36711-4_57

which is capable of handling trust propagation among users. In Ref. [2], Zhao et al. propose a social Bayesian Personalized Ranking (BPR) method, using the assumption that social items are ranked higher than non-social items. Based on Granovetter's conclusion that weak ties are the most important reason for new information or innovations to spread over social networks [3], to yield a fine-grained friend partitioning, Wang et al. extend Zhao's model to incorporate the distinctions of strong and weak ties [4].

However, existing social recommendation methods always assume that the rating data and the trust data are both missing at random (MAR). Results of previous research indicate that the MAR assumption is not suitable for the recommendation data, inasmuch as users consume items they like more than those they dislike [5,6]. When the MAR assumption is incorrect, ordinary methods will severely suffer from the biased parameter estimation and prediction [5]. In addition, existing recommendation methods always focus either on explicit ratings [7,8] or on implicit feedback [9,10], but not on both. Modeling only observed ratings is insufficient to make good top-N recommendations [11], vice versa.

In this paper, on the premise that the data is not missing at random, we propose a model of deep social matrix factorization based on both explicit ratings and implicit feedback. In Ref. [12], Xue et al. propose a deep matrix factorization model, considering both explicit ratings and implicit feedback. However, they do not take social relations into consideration. We extend Xue's model to social recommendation. Our model, which we call *deep social matrix factorization with missing not at random data* (DSMF-MNAR), mainly consists of three phases: (1) matrix completion, (2) low-dimensional vector learning, (3) top-N recommendation. Details of all the three phases will be addressed in Sect. 2.

Organization. In Sect. 2, we introduce our DSMF-MNAR model, further formulate the matrix completion function and DSMF framework. In Sect. 3, experiments on three real-world datasets are conducted to assess the effectiveness of the proposed method. We finally conclude our paper in Sect. 4.

2   Modeling

2.1   Preliminaries

Suppose there are M users $\mathcal{U} = \{u_1, ..., u_M\}$, N items $\mathcal{V} = \{v_1, \ldots, v_N\}$. Let $\mathcal{R} \in \mathbb{R}^{M \times N}$ denote the user-item rating matrix, where $\mathcal{R}_{ij}$ is the rating of user i on item j. Let $\mathcal{T} \in \mathbb{T}^{M \times M}$ denote the user-user trust matrix, whose non-empty entry $\mathcal{T}_{ij}$ denotes user i trusts user j.

A matrix factorization model assumes that the user-item rating matrix $\hat{\mathcal{R}}$ can be approximated by a multiplication of d-rank factors,

$$\hat{\mathcal{R}} = U^T V \qquad (1)$$

where $U \in \mathbb{R}^{d \times M}$ and $V \in \mathbb{R}^{d \times N}$. Usually, d is far less than both M and N. When U and V are both obtained by calculation, the predicted rating $\hat{\mathcal{R}}_{ij}$ can be approximated as follows,

$$\hat{\mathcal{R}}_{ij} = U_i^T V_j \qquad (2)$$

where U_i is the latent feature vector of user i, i.e., the i_{th} column of U and V_j is the latent feature vector of item j, i.e., the j_{th} of V.

The case of user-user trust matrix factorization is the same and hence is as follows,

$$\hat{T}_{kh} = Tr_k^T Te_h \qquad (3)$$

where Tr_k is the latent truster feature vector of user k, i.e., the k_{th} column of Tr, which characterizes how user k trusts others. And Te_h is the latent trustee feature vector of user h, i.e., the h_{th} of Te, which characterizes how user h is trusted by others.

As mentioned in Sect. 1, our model mainly consists of three phases. The architecture of the first two phases is illustrated in Fig. 1.

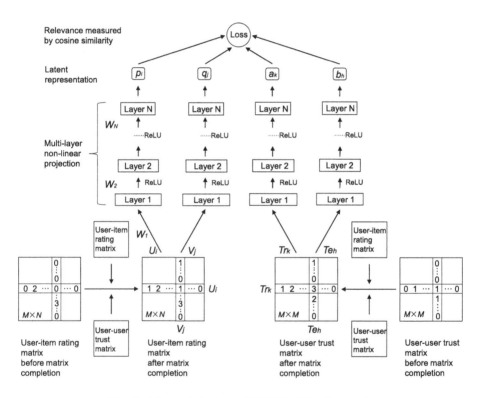

Fig. 1. The architecture of DSMF-MNAR model

The matrix completion phase is in the bottom half of the figure and the low-dimensional vector learning phase is in the top half. As to the top-N recommendation phase, given p_i and q_j, which are the low-dimensional vector representations of U_i and V_j respectively, we can calculate $\hat{\mathcal{R}}_{ij}$ and thus rank all the items for each user.

2.2   Matrix Completion Based on MNAR Assumption

In Ref. [13], Chen et al. conduct an analysis on two well-known social recommendation datasets, Ciao and Epinions, and make three observations as follows: (1) Users tend to consume (rate) the items that they like. (2) Users tend to consume (rate) the items that have been consumed by their friends. (3) The influence of the friends on users' rating values is smaller than their influence on the users' consumption, which is enlightening. We conduct the same experiment on our three real-world datasets, Ciao, Douban and Last.fm, and have replicated Chen's results. Given the three premises, we adopt the method proposed in Ref. [4] and try to complete the user-item rating matrix as much as possible.

For each user, we categorize all the items into four types based on Chen's observation. We let $\mathcal{F}_u = \{u_j \in \mathcal{U}: u \in \mathcal{U} \text{ and } u \text{ trusts } u_j\}$ denote the set of u's friends and $\mathcal{I}_u = \{v \in \mathcal{V}: \text{user } u \text{ has consumed item v}\}$ denote the set of items consumed by user u. The proposed categorization is as follows,

(1) $\mathcal{C}_u^{self}$ $u \in \mathcal{U}$, $\mathcal{C}_u^{self} = \{v \in \mathcal{V}: \exists\, v \in \mathcal{I}_u \text{ s.t. } f \in \mathcal{F}_u \wedge v \notin \mathcal{I}_f\}$ denotes the items only consumed by u itself.
(2) $\mathcal{C}_u^{joint}$ $\mathcal{C}_u^{joint} = \{v \in \mathcal{V} \setminus \mathcal{C}_u^{self}: \exists\, v \in \mathcal{I}_u \text{ s.t. } f \in \mathcal{F}_u \wedge v \in \mathcal{I}_f\}$ denotes the items that have been consumed by both u and at least one of u's friends.
(3) $\mathcal{C}_u^{friend}$ $\mathcal{C}_u^{friend} = \{v \in \mathcal{V} \setminus \mathcal{C}_u^{self}: \exists\, v \notin \mathcal{I}_u \text{ s.t. } f \in \mathcal{F}_u \wedge v \in \mathcal{I}_f\}$ denotes the items only consumed by u's friends.
(4) $\mathcal{C}_u^{none}$ $\mathcal{C}_u^{none} = \{v \in \mathcal{V} \setminus \mathcal{C}_u^{self}: \exists\, v \in \mathcal{V} \text{ s.t. } f \in \mathcal{F}_u,\ v \notin \mathcal{I}_u \wedge v \notin \mathcal{I}_f\}$ denotes the items neither consumed by u nor u's friends.

Mathematically, according to Chen's observation as well, to use the extended model of BPR, we sort the four types above for each user u as below,

$$v_i \succeq v_j,\ if \begin{cases} v_i \in \mathcal{C}_u^{self} \wedge v_j \in \mathcal{C}_u^{joint} & or \\ v_i \in \mathcal{C}_u^{joint} \wedge v_j \in \mathcal{C}_u^{friend} & or \\ v_i \in \mathcal{C}_u^{friend} \wedge v_j \in \mathcal{C}_u^{none} \end{cases} \tag{4}$$

To learn more latent feature vector U_i for each user i and V_j for each user j as much as possible, we define the likelihood function as follows,

$$\mathcal{L} = \prod_{u \in \mathcal{U}} \left(\prod_{v_s \in \mathcal{C}_u^{self}} \prod_{v_j \in \mathcal{C}_u^{joint}} Pr\left[v_s \succeq v_j\right] \right.$$
$$\prod_{v_j \in \mathcal{C}_u^{joint}} \prod_{v_f \in \mathcal{C}_u^{friend}} Pr\left[v_j \succeq v_f\right]$$
$$\left. \prod_{v_f \in \mathcal{C}_u^{friend}} \prod_{v_n \in \mathcal{C}_u^{none}} Pr\left[v_f \succeq v_n\right] \right) \tag{5}$$

where $\Pr\left[v_s \succeq v_j\right]$ denotes the probability that user u prefers item v_s to item v_j, and so on. The past experience indicates that the sigmoid function $\delta(x) = \frac{1}{1+\exp(-x)}$ is convenient for derivative [14], we take $\Pr\left[v_s \succeq v_j\right]$ of user u as an example and thus define the probability as follows,

$$
\begin{aligned}
Pr\left[v_s \succeq v_j\right] &= \delta(\hat{\mathcal{R}}_{us} - \hat{\mathcal{R}}_{uj}) \\
&= \frac{1}{1 + \exp(-(\hat{\mathcal{R}}_{us} - \hat{\mathcal{R}}_{uj}))} \\
&= \frac{1}{1 + \exp(-\langle U_u, V_s \rangle + \langle U_u, V_j \rangle)}
\end{aligned}
\tag{6}
$$

Our final maximization objective is as below,

$$
\begin{aligned}
\mathcal{J} = \ln \mathcal{L} - r \\
= \sum_{u \in \mathcal{U}} \Bigg(\sum_{v_s \in \mathcal{C}_u^{self}} \sum_{v_j \in \mathcal{C}_u^{joint}} \ln \delta(\hat{\mathcal{R}}_{us} - \hat{\mathcal{R}}_{uj}) \\
+ \sum_{v_j \in \mathcal{C}_u^{joint}} \sum_{v_f \in \mathcal{C}_u^{friend}} \ln \delta(\hat{\mathcal{R}}_{uj} - \hat{\mathcal{R}}_{uf}) \\
+ \sum_{v_f \in \mathcal{C}_u^{friend}} \sum_{v_n \in \mathcal{C}_u^{none}} \ln \delta(\hat{\mathcal{R}}_{uf} - \hat{\mathcal{R}}_{un}) \Bigg) \\
- \lambda_u \sum_{u \in \mathcal{U}} \| U_u \|_2^2 - \lambda_v \sum_{v \in \mathcal{V}} \| V_v \|_2^2
\end{aligned}
\tag{7}
$$

where $r = \lambda_u \sum_{u \in \mathcal{U}} \| U_u \|_2^2 + \lambda_v \sum_{v \in \mathcal{V}} \| V_v \|_2^2$ is the added regularization term to avoid overfitting. λ_u and λ_v are both regularization parameters. The whole process for user-item rating matrix completion is shown in Algorithm 1.

With regard to user-user trust matrix completion, we also divide all the users for each user u into four types,

(1) $\mathcal{G}_u^{joint}$ $u \in \mathcal{U}$, $\mathcal{G}_u^{joint} = \{te \in \mathcal{F}_u : \exists\, v \in \mathcal{V} \text{ s.t. } v \in \mathcal{I}_u \wedge v \in \mathcal{I}_{te}\}$ denotes the users who are u's friends and have consumed at least one the same item with u as well.

(2) $\mathcal{G}_u^{friend}$ $\mathcal{G}_u^{friend} = \{te \in \mathcal{F}_u : \exists\, v \in \mathcal{V} \text{ s.t. } (v \notin \mathcal{I}_u \wedge v \in \mathcal{I}_{te}) \vee (v \in \mathcal{I}_u \wedge v \notin \mathcal{I}_{te})\}$ denotes the users that are trusted by user u but have never consumed even one the same item with u

(3) $\mathcal{G}_u^{may}$ $\mathcal{G}_u^{may} = \{te \in \mathcal{U} \setminus \mathcal{F}_u : \exists\, v \in \mathcal{V} \text{ s.t. } v \in \mathcal{I}_{te} \wedge v \in \mathcal{I}_u\}$ denotes the users that have consumed at least one the same item with user u but are not trusted by u

(4) $\mathcal{G}_u^{none}$ $\mathcal{G}_u^{none} = \{te \in \mathcal{U} \setminus \mathcal{F}_u : \exists\, v \in \mathcal{V} \text{ s.t. } (v \notin \mathcal{I}_u \wedge v \in \mathcal{I}_{te}) \vee (v \in \mathcal{I}_u \wedge v \notin \mathcal{I}_{te})\}$ denotes the users that never have any interaction with user u

The computational process of user-user trust matrix completion is the same as user-item rating matrix completion and hence is omitted.

Based on the MNAR assumption, we have completed a part of the missing value in the matrix completion phase and set the scene for low-dimensional vector learning phase.

Algorithm 1. User-item Rating Matrix Completion

Input:
    user-item rating matrix $\mathcal{R} \in \mathbb{R}^{M \times N}$
    user-user trust matrix $\mathcal{T} \in \mathbb{T}^{M \times M}$
Output:
    user-item rating matrix $\hat{\mathcal{R}}$ after matrix completion
1: **for** u from 1 to M **do**
2:    compute $\mathcal{C}_u^{self}$, $\mathcal{C}_u^{joint}$, $\mathcal{C}_u^{friend}$, $\mathcal{C}_u^{none}$
3: **end for**
4: ramdomly initialize U and V
5: **repeat**
6:    **for** u from 1 to M **do**
7:       **for** u from 1 to $\left|\mathcal{C}_u^{joint}\right|$ **do**
8:          $u_s \leftarrow$ a ramdom user from $\mathcal{C}_u^{self}$
9:          $u_j \leftarrow$ a ramdom user from $\mathcal{C}_u^{joint}$
10:         $u_f \leftarrow$ a ramdom user from $\mathcal{C}_u^{friend}$
11:         $u_n \leftarrow$ a ramdom user from $\mathcal{C}_u^{none}$
12:         add u_s, u_j, u_f, u_n to used data used$[u]$// *to mark the items that have been used in the process of sorting items for user u*
13:         add $[u_s, u_j, u_f, u_n]$ to training set
14:       **end for**
15:    **end for**
16:    compute $\mathcal{J}$ using standard gradient descent
17: **until** convergence
18: **for** u from 1 to M **do**
19:    **for** v in used data used$[u]$ **do**
20:       compute $\hat{\mathcal{R}}_{uv}$ with U_u and V_v
21:    **end for**
22: **end for**

2.3 Low-Dimensional Vector Learning with DSMF

In Ref. [12], Xue et al. propose a deep matrix factorization model to map the user and item feature vector into a low-dimensional space, considering both explicit ratings and implicit feedback. However, they do not take social relations into consideration. Thereupon, we extend their model to social recommendation.

As is shown in Fig. 1, in the user-item rating matrix, each user i is represented as a high-dimensional vector U_i and each item j is represented as a high-dimensional vector V_j. Simultaneously, U_i and V_j are i_{th} row and j_{th} column of the user-item rating matrix respectively. In the user-user trust matrix, Tr_k and Te_h have the same expression. In each layer, each input vector will be mapped into a lower dimensional space. We denote the input vector by x, the output vector of layer i $(i \in [1, N])$ by y_i, the i_{th} weight matrix by W_i, the i_{th} bias term by b_i. We get

$$y_i = \begin{cases} W_1 x & \text{if } i = 1 \\ f(W_{i-1} y_{i-1} + b_i) & \text{if } i \in [2, \text{N-1}] \end{cases} \tag{8}$$

where $f()$ is the ReLU function $(f(x) = \max(0, x))$. Generalized to our final low-dimensional vector p_i, q_j, a_k, b_h, we have

$$\begin{aligned} p_i &= f(\ldots f(W_{U2} f(U_i W_{U1}) + b_{U2}) \ldots) \\ q_j &= f(\ldots f(W_{V2} f(V_j W_{V1}) + b_{V2}) \ldots) \\ a_k &= f(\ldots f(W_{Tr2} f(Tr_k W_{Tr1}) + b_{Tr2}) \ldots) \\ b_h &= f(\ldots f(W_{Te2} f(Te_h W_{Te1}) + b_{Te2}) \ldots) \end{aligned} \tag{9}$$

We train all the four neural networks simultaneously and the loss function is as follows,

$$\begin{aligned} \ell = &- \sum_{(i,\,j) \in \mathcal{R}} (\frac{\mathcal{R}_{ij}}{R_{max}} \log \hat{\mathcal{R}}_{ij} + (1 - \frac{\mathcal{R}_{ij}}{R_{max}}) \log (1 - \hat{\mathcal{R}}_{ij})) \\ &- \sum_{(k,\,h) \in \mathcal{T}} (\frac{\mathcal{T}_{kh}}{T_{max}} \log \hat{\mathcal{T}}_{kh} + (1 - \frac{\mathcal{T}_{kh}}{T_{max}}) \log (1 - \hat{\mathcal{T}}_{kh})) \\ &- \alpha \times \sum_{\substack{(i,\,j)\,\in\,\mathcal{R}, \\ (k,\,h)\,\in\,\mathcal{T}, \\ i\,=\,k}} \cos (p_i, tr_k) \end{aligned} \tag{10}$$

where

$$\begin{aligned} \hat{\mathcal{R}}_{ij} &= \cos (p_i, q_j) = \frac{p_i^T q_j}{\|p_i\| \, \|q_j\|} \\ \hat{\mathcal{T}}_{kh} &= \cos (a_k, b_h) = \frac{a_k^T b_h}{\|a_k\| \, \|b_h\|} \end{aligned} \tag{11}$$

and α is the weighting parameter. Inspired by Ref. [1], we add term $\cos (p_i, tr_k)$ to the loss function. The main intuition is that if we see each trustee as an item, for each user, the preference feature vector for trustees should be similar to the preference feature vector for items. After matrix completion, we map all the values in user-item rating matrix $\hat{\mathcal{R}}$ and user-user trust matrix $\hat{\mathcal{T}}$ into an interval $[0, 5]$ respectively by employing the function $f(x) = \frac{5x}{MAX}$. MAX is the maximum of ratings in matrix $\mathcal{R}$ or $\mathcal{T}$, whereupon R_{max} equals to 5 in our work. Because the rating of $\hat{\mathcal{R}}_{ij}$ and $\hat{\mathcal{T}}_{kh}$ may be negative in some iteration, we use

$$\begin{aligned} \hat{\mathcal{R}}_{ij}^{trans} &= \max(\mu, \hat{\mathcal{R}}_{ij}) \\ \hat{\mathcal{T}}_{kh}^{trans} &= \max(\mu, \hat{\mathcal{T}}_{kh}) \end{aligned} \tag{12}$$

to replace $\hat{\mathcal{R}}_{ij}$ and $\hat{\mathcal{T}}_{kh}$ and make sure the ratings greater than zero, where $\mu = 1.0e^{-5}$ is a very small number. We describe the details through pseudo-code in Algorithm 2.

Given model parameters W_U, W_V, W_{Tr}, W_{Te}, we finally compute the low-dimensional vector representation of p_i, q_j, a_k, b_h and thus make the top-N recommendation for each user.

Algorithm 2. Low-dimensional Vector Learning with DSMF

Input:
    training iteration: *Iteration*
    user-item rating matrix $\mathcal{R} \in \mathbb{R}^{M \times N}$ after matrix completion
    user-user trust matrix $\mathcal{T} \in \mathbb{T}^{M \times M}$ after matrix completion
Output:
    $W_{Ui}, i \in [1, N-1]$: weight matrix for user
    $W_{Vj}, j \in [1, N-1]$: weight matrix for item
    $W_{Trk}, k \in [1, N-1]$: weight matrix for truster
    $W_{Teh}, h \in [1, N-1]$: weight matrix for trustee
1: ramdomly initialize W_U, W_V, W_{Tr}, W_{Te}
2: **for** iter from 1 to *Iteration* **do**
3:     compute p_i, q_j, a_k, b_h ← use Equation (9) with U_i, V_j, Tr_k, Te_h
4:     compute $\hat{\mathcal{R}}_{ij}$, $\hat{\mathcal{T}}_{kh}$ ← use Equation (11) with p_i, q_j, a_k, b_h
5:     compute $\hat{\mathcal{R}}_{ij}^{trans}$, $\hat{\mathcal{T}}_{kh}^{trans}$ ← use Equation (12) with $\hat{\mathcal{R}}_{ij}$, $\hat{\mathcal{T}}_{kh}$
6:     compute ℓ ← use Equation (10) with $\hat{\mathcal{R}}_{ij}^{trans}$, $\hat{\mathcal{T}}_{kh}^{trans}$, $\mathcal{R}_{ij}$, $\mathcal{T}_{kh}$
7:     use back propagation to optimize model parameters
8: **end for**

---

3 Experiments

3.1 Description of the Datasets

We use the following three real-world datasets and the statistics of all the three datasets are summerized in Table 1.

- **Ciao.** This dataset contains trust relationships among users as well as their ratings on DVDs. First introduced in Ref. [15], it was crawled from a UK DVD community website. (http://dvd.ciao.co.uk/)
- **Douban.** Extracted from the Chinese Douban movie forum, this dataset contains user-user trust relationships and user-movie ratings [16]. (http://movie.douban.com/)
- **Last.fm.** This dataset contains social networks and music artist listening information from Last.fm online music system, first released in Ref. [17]. (http://www.lastfm.com)

Table 1. Statistics of the three datasets

Statistics	Ciao	Douban	Last.fm
#users	1881	13492	1892
#items	12900	45282	17632
#ratings	33510	2669675	92834
#ties	15155	443753	12717

To tune our DSMF model, we use 80% of each user's rated items as the training set, from which we randomly select 10% as the validation set, and leave the remaining 20% of the data for testing. We record the best parameters according to their performance on the validation set. Afterwards, all the experiments are performed with 5-fold cross validation to find the best parameters. For example, in Algorithm 1, we set $\lambda_u = \lambda_v = 0.01$ after the validation. For each experiment discussed below, we conduct five times and take the mean as the final result.

3.2 Experimental Setup

Methods Compares. We compare our DSMF-MNAR model with the following methods. As our proposed method aims to dig deeper the relationships not only between users and items, but also between users and users, we mainly compare with social recommendation methods.

- **Trust-MF.** Trust-MF is a personalized social collaborative filtering method proposed by Yang et al. [1], which is capable of handing trust propagation among users.
- **TBPR-W.** Proposed by Wang et al. [4], TBPR-W assumes that users prefer their weak ties to strong ties. It is a surprising discovery that people tend to like weak ties in most situations.
- **SPMF-MNAR.** As the state-of-art method based on MNAR, Chen et al. [13] propose a probabilistic generative model of the rating observation process, which mainly focusing on exploiting the social influence on the rating observation process.
- **DMF.** Xue et al. [12] propose a novel matrix factorization model with a neural network architecture, which making full use of both explicit ratings and implicit feedback.

Evaluation Metrics. We adopt four metrics to evaluate the quality of recommendation given by compared methods. They are Mean Absolute Error (MAE), Root Mean Square Error (RMSE), Normalized Discounted Cumulative Gain (NDCG) and Mean Reciprocal Rank (MRR). The definitions of these metrics are as follows,

$$MAE = \frac{\sum_{i,j} |\mathcal{R}_{ij} - \hat{\mathcal{R}}_{ij}|}{N} \qquad RMSE = \sqrt{\frac{\sum_{i,j} (\mathcal{R}_{ij} - \hat{\mathcal{R}}_{ij})^2}{N}} \qquad (13)$$

where $\mathcal{R}_{ij}$ is the rating in the test set, $\hat{\mathcal{R}}_{ij}$ is the predicted rating and N is the number of ratings in the test set.

$$MRR = \frac{1}{M} \sum_{u=1}^{M} \frac{1}{|\mathcal{S}_u|} \sum_{v=1}^{|\mathcal{S}_u|} \frac{1}{rank_u^v} \qquad NDCG = \frac{1}{M} \sum_{u \in \mathcal{U}} \frac{DCG_u}{IDCG_u} \qquad (14)$$

where $\mathcal{S}_u$ denotes the set of items consumed by user u in the testing phase, $rank_u^v$ denotes the rank of item v consumed by user u in descending order and DCG and $IDCG$ are in turn defined as follows,

$$DCG_u = \sum_{v \in \mathcal{S}_u} \frac{1}{\log_2(rank_u^v + 1)} \qquad IDCG_u = \sum_{u=1}^{|\mathcal{S}_u|} \frac{1}{\log_2(u + 1)} \qquad (15)$$

3.3 Results and Analysis

Table 2 demonstrates the performance of all the six recommendation methods on three datasets, measured by four different accuracy metrics. The DSMF is our proposed method without the matrix completion step, which means that it is not based on the MNAR assumption. Generally speaking, our DSMF-MNAR model outperforms all the other methods on every metric.

- **DSMF-MNAR vs Trust-MF vs TBPR-W.** The two baselines are both social recommendation methods, however, they only consider the impact between two directly connected users. Our DSMF-MNAR model learn the latent feature vector from an overall point of view to solve the trouble. Compared to Trust-MF, the advantage is more apparent, whose improvement is 14.67%, 11.96% and 9.74% respectively w.r.t MRR.
- **DSMF-MNAR vs DSMF vs DMF.** DMF is the original model. The results show that incorporating social relations into DMF is able to increase the recommendation satisfaction (DSMF). And considering synthetically the social influence and the MNAR assumption will further improve the effect (DSMF-MNAR).
- **DSMF-MNAR vs SPMF-MNAR.** Both the two methods are social recommendation methods based on MNAR assumption. However, SPMF-MNAR only exploits the directly connected social influence. We compare our method with SPMF-MNAR to further prove that considering both explicit ratings and implicit feedback in social recommendation is very beneficial to recommendation effectiveness.

The other experiment is conducted to investigate the influence of parameter α on the performance of our model. α is a scale parameter, which controls the influence of users' social relations on their consumption. The bigger α is, the much more influence social relations will have on users' consumption. As is shown in Fig. 2, the MAE becomes smaller and smaller from the very beginning and starts to become bigger at the node $\alpha = 1$ on all of the three datasets. Thus, in our experiments, we set $\alpha = 1$ to achieve the best performance.

Table 2. Comparisons of different methods (boldface font denotes the winner in row)

		Trust-MF	TBPR-W	DMF	SPMF-MNAR	DSMF	DSMF-MNAR
Ciao	MAE	0.7745	0.7485	0.7673	0.7523	0.7421	**0.7211**
	Impv	6.89%	3.66%	6.02%	4.15%	2.83%	–
	RMSE	1.1015	1.0889	1.0972	1.1248	1.0874	**1.0191**
	Impv	7.48%	6.41%	7.12%	9.40%	6.28%	–
	NDCG	0.1848	0.1897	0.1857	0.1865	0.1898	**0.1983**
	Impv	7.31%	4.53%	6.79%	6.33%	4.48%	–
	MRR	0.0525	0.0548	0.0540	0.0535	0.0566	**0.0602**
	Impv	14.67%	9.85%	11.48%	12.52%	6.36%	
Last.fm	MAE	0.8173	0.8396	0.8274	0.8132	0.8199	**0.7957**
	Impv	2.64%	5.23%	3.83%	2.15%	2.95%	–
	RMSE	1.0109	1.0098	1.0158	1.0002	1.0097	**0.9879**
	Impv	2.28%	2.17%	2.75%	1.23%	2.16%	–
	NDCG	0.2204	0.2213	0.2253	0.2286	0.2292	**0.2356**
	Impv	6.90%	6.46%	4.57%	3.06%	2.79%	–
	MRR	0.0895	0.0926	0.0952	0.0961	0.0964	**0.1002**
	Impv	11.96%	8.21%	5.25%	4.27%	3.94%	–
Douban	MAE	0.5687	0.5543	0.5621	0.5600	0.5549	**0.5479**
	Impv	3.66%	1.15%	2.53%	2.16%	1.26%	–
	RMSE	0.7552	0.7333	0.7384	0.7313	0.724	**0.7086**
	Impv	6.17%	3.37%	4.04%	3.10%	2.13%	–
	NDCG	0.4426	0.4506	0.4543	0.4517	0.4553	**0.4698**
	Impv	6.15%	4.26%	3.41%	4.01%	3.18%	–
	MRR	0.3428	0.3532	0.3572	0.3565	0.3643	**0.3762**
	Impv	9.74%	6.51%	5.32%	5.53%	3.27%	–

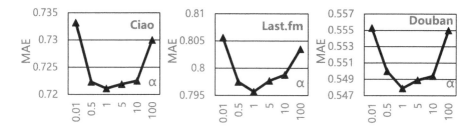

Fig. 2. Impact of parameter α

We also conduct an serious of experiments to investigate our model with different numbers of hidden layers and different numbers of factors on the top layer. For space limitation, we summarise as follows: (1) Our model with 2 layers can get almost the best performance. 3-layers model seems to improve the performance a very little bit but greatly increase the computing time. (2) Conducting experiments on the 2-layer model, we find that the top layer with 64 factors performs the best and leads to overfitting with 128 layers.

4 Conclusion and Furture Work

In this paper, we propose the DSMF-MNAR model to complete the missing data as much as possible and learn the low-dimensional latent vector from an overall point of view. As far as we know, there haven't been other works focusing on both explicit ratings and implicit feedback on the assumption of MNAR in social recommendation. Experiments demonstrate that our model performs the best compared to other mainstream methods. Specially, the advantage is remarkable on Ciao in terms of MRR w.r.t which our model's improvement is 14.67%, 9.85%, 11.48% and 12.52% respectively compared to the four state-of-the-art methods.

For further work, we are interested in integrating the effect of time into our model. At an intuitive level, users' taste on items and friends may change over time. Furturemore, we intend to exploit the process of users' consumption to explore how much social influence it has on each individual user.

References

1. Yang, B., Lei, Y., Liu, D., Liu, J.: Social collaborative filtering by trust. In: Proceedings of the 23rd International Joint Conference on Artificial Intelligence, pp. 2747–2753. AAAI Press (2013)
2. Zhao, T., McAuley, J., King, I.: Leveraging social connections to improve personalized ranking for collaborative filtering. In: ACM International Conference on Information and Knowledge Management, pp. 261–270 (2014)
3. Granovetter, M.S.: The strength of weak ties. Am. J. Social. **78**(6), 1360–1380 (1973)
4. Wang, X., Lu, W., Ester, M., Wang, C., Chen, C.: Social recommendation with strong and weak ties. In: Proceedings of the 25th ACM International Conference on Information and Knowledge Management, pp. 5–14 (2016)
5. Hernandez-Lobato, J.M., Houlsby, N., Ghahramani, Z.: Probabilistic matrix factorization with non-random missing data. In: International Conference on Machine Learning, pp. 1512–1520 (2014)
6. Pradel, B., Usunier, N., Gallinari, P.: Ranking with non-random missing ratings: influence of popularity and positivity on evaluation metrics. In: Proceedings of the 6th ACM Conference on Recommender Systems, pp. 147–154 (2012)
7. Li, S., Kawale, J., Fu, Y.: Deep collaborative filtering via marginalized denoising autoencoder. In: Proceedings of the 24th ACM International Conference on Information and Knowledge Management, pp. 811–820 (2015)
8. Sedhain, S., Menon, A.K., Sanner, S. Xie, L.: Autorec: autoencoders meet collaborative filtering. In: 24th International Conference on World Wide Web, pp. 111–112 (2015)
9. Wu, Y., DuBois, C.: Collaborative denoising auto-encoders for top-n recommender systems. In: Proceedings of the 9th ACM International Conference on Web Search and Data Mining, pp. 153–162 (2016)

10. He, X., Zhang, H., Kan, M., Chua, T.: Fast matrix factorization for online recommendation with implicit feedback. In: Proceedings of the 39th International conference on Research and Development in Information Retrieval, pp. 549–558 (2016)
11. Hu, Y., Koren, Y., Volinsky, C.: Collaborative filtering for implicit feedback datasets. In: 8th IEEE International Conference on Data Mining, pp. 263–272 (2008)
12. Xue, H., Dai, X., Zhang, J., Huang, S., Chen, J.: Deep matrix factorization models for recommender systems. In: 26th International Joint Conference on Artificial Intelligence, pp. 3203–3209 (2017)
13. Chen, J., Wang, C., Ester, M., Shi, Q., Feng, Y., Chen, C.: Social recommendation with missing not at random data. In: Proceedings of the 27th ACM International Conference on Information and Knowledge Management, pp. 29–38 (2018)
14. Rendle, S., Freudenthaler, C., Gantner, Z., Schmidt-Thieme, L.: BPR: Bayesian personalized ranking from implicit feedback. In: 25th International Conference on Uncertainty in Artificial Intelligence, pp. 452–461 (2009)
15. Guo, G., Zhang, J., Yorke-Smith, N.: A novel bayesian similarity measure for recommender systems. In: Proceedings of the 23rd International Joint Conference on Artificial Intelligence, pp. 2619–2625 (2013)
16. https://www.cse.cuhk.edu.hk/irwin.king.new/pub/data/douban
17. Ivan, C., Peter, B., Tsvi, T.: Second workshop on information heterogeneity and fusion in recommender systems. In: Proceedings of the 5th ACM Conference on Recommender Systems, pp. 387–388 (2011)

Pluralistic Ignorance: A Trade-Off Between Group-Conformity and Cognitive Dissonance

Fatima Seeme$^{(\boxtimes)}$ (ID), David Green (ID), and Carlo Kopp (ID)

Monash University, Melbourne, VIC 3800, Australia
fatima.seeme@monash.edu

Abstract. Interactions within groups of people lead to many forms of aberrant social psychology. One is pluralistic ignorance (PI), in which the majority of people in a group express opinions that differ from their real beliefs. PI occurs for various reasons: one is the drive to belong to a group. To understand how PI emerges, this study presents an agent-based model that represents PI as the outcome of the trade-off between agents' group conformity and cognitive dissonance (psychological discomfort). We show that the trade-off can lead to various outcomes, depending on agents' choice, or bias towards one tendency or the other.

Keywords: Pluralistic ignorance · Group conformity · Cognitive dissonance

1 Introduction

Interactions between group members give rise to many socio-psychological phenomena. Notable instances arise in general communities and more recently, in social networks, for instance consensus or polarisation, confirmation bias, groupthink, the "spiral of silence", and pluralistic ignorance [12,13,16,23,25]. Most of these phenomena result primarily from a propensity in individuals to actively seek membership in a group [11]. Conformity with the majority (or the *group-norm*) in a group produces more social benefits, or rewards. Failure to conform may result in lower status, less social acceptance and even being ostracised or expelled [27]. To avoid these unwanted consequences, individuals often express opinions aligned with the *group-norm* despite actually believing otherwise.

Individuals therefore may have a private opinion or belief and an expressed or exposed opinion that is visible to others. When this happens on a large scale, i.e. many individuals express an opinion which is aligned with their subjective perception of group opinion rather than their actual beliefs, the situation is known as *Pluralistic Ignorance* [13]. Pluralistic ignorance (abbreviated here as 'PI') arises in many diverse settings, from college campuses to office environments, in political parties, elections, group meetings, and public health scenarios [10,15,19–22]. It can lead to many well documented problems such as excessive

© Springer Nature Switzerland AG 2019
T. Gedeon et al. (Eds.): ICONIP 2019, LNCS 11954, pp. 695–706, 2019.
https://doi.org/10.1007/978-3-030-36711-4_58

alcohol and drug consumption, risky sexual behaviour amongst students, unethical behaviours, the 'bystander effect' where responsibilities are abandoned in emergencies and other adverse behaviours [1,2,18].

There is a price individuals pay for rejecting their beliefs to gain a social advantage. This price is a psychological discomfort, specifically cognitive dissonance [7]. On a large scale, differences between a population's private and expressed opinions can produce discontent and tension, demonstrably a key causal factor in many instances of political turmoil and social upheaval [14].

This exposes the key behavioural trade-off in individuals playing to maximise their personal benefit: maximising overall benefit demands that cognitive dissonance be minimised, while group conformity is maximised. The central question is whether individuals can effectively balance between the two. In this study we present a model of PI as the interplay between group conformity and cognitive dissonance – discovering how PI emerges from this interplay and how group conformity and cognitive dissonance determine the direction and magnitude of PI in a social group. Our main contributions in this work are:

– A novel model of PI that addresses two conflicting mechanisms - maintenance of group conformity and reduction of cognitive dissonance.
– Exploring how a population is impacted by these mechanisms - can it reach consensus? Is the resulting system stable?
– Considering PI and the underlying social connectivity - can the limited interaction inside a local neighbourhood propagate through a network? Can consensus be achieved? Is it genuine consensus or illusory PI?

In Sect. 2, we discuss how these questions are addressed in the study; Sect. 3 describes the model; Sect. 4 presents the results obtained from simulations; finally, in Sect. 5, we discuss and analyse the results.

2   Approach

Researchers from multiple disciplines have been studying cognitive bias and other socio-psychological phenomena for decades mainly empirically attempting to explain or interpret observed effects from case studies. However, some of the topics in social sciences are inherently difficult to experiment on, also the observer may interfere with measurement or the measured community may play the experimenter (e.g. the Mead controversy [8]). In recent years, researchers have been using social simulation models as a means of overcoming the inherent restrictions and limitations of experimentation with live populations [9,24].

Although previous research on PI consisted mainly of case studies, a few agent based models (ABMs) emerged recently. Some of the models studied PI as an epidemic of unpopular norms by social enforcement [3,28], or as a result of opinion formation under social pressure and peer influence in ABMs [26,29], or as a result of agents' psychological realism under interpersonal influences and conformity [4]. These models discover how the interactions, peer influence and social pressure, shape an individual's expressed opinion, but what if the agents do it spontaneously for their own benefit? In real life, there are many cases where conforming yields a higher payoff and thus individuals spontaneously conform without any apparent pressure.

We have modelled PI as a trade off between group-conformity and cognitive dissonance - one must conform to the group to get a reward from the group, and at the same time keep cognitive dissonance to a minimum to avoid psychological discomfort. This is evident from the literature (PI literature cited above, for example) that individuals may have a privately held opinion which is different from their expressed opinion. Therefore, agents in our model can have two separate opinions: *private opinion* or *actual belief* which is not visible to anyone else, and the publicly *expressed opinion* which is visible to others. Agents can be associated with a group having a *social identity* (SID). Each group has a *norm* or *group opinion*, which is the average of its current members' opinions. There is a reward for conforming to the group, so agents try to maximise their payoff by conforming to the group opinion; at the same time they also try to keep their cognitive dissonance to a minimum by not distorting their expressed opinion too far from their true belief. PI arises when agents express an opinion different from their private opinions. The model is described below.

3   Model Description

There are N agents and k groups that they can be associated with. Each agent i has an expressed opinion x_i, a private opinion y_i, and a social identity (SID) z_i. The agents hold a single opinion at each time which depicts their degree of agreement (analogous to a Likert scale [17]) to a global topic and is represented with positive real numbers. The SIDs are represented with positive integers $\{1, 2, ..., k\}$ in the model.

Agent Interaction: The agents can see the opinions expressed by their neighbours (who they have a connection with), and make a decision based on their observation. Agents cannot estimate the true shared opinion, rather they have a perception of the majority opinion in their immediate neighbourhood.

Opinion Updating: Both synchronous and asynchronous updating mode have been used. In synchronous mode, at time t, all agents update their SID and expressed opinion simultaneously depending on the system state at time $t - 1$; whereas in asynchronous mode, agents update their states at time t sequentially (in random sequence for each iteration).

Organisation: The model looks at both fully connected networks or complete graphs and randomly connected networks. In complete graphs, all agents are connected to every other agent, while in random networks (using an Erdos-Renyi graph [6]), agents are randomly connected to some other agents.

Group Reward: As stated earlier, individuals conforming to the groups enjoy more benefits, this benefit is represented as 'group-reward' G in the model. This reward depends on the degree of conformity - if an agent expresses the group-opinion, it gets the maximum reward, and the reward decreases as the expressed opinion moves further away from the group-opinion.

Consonance Reward: Agents aim to minimise their discomfort by minimising cognitive dissonance, $CD = |x_i - y_i|$. The discomfort increases as CD becomes larger. This is represented as 'consonance reward' or C for the agents. This reward can be considered as mental comfort as opposed to the discomfort one gets from cognitive dissonance.

There are multiple groups in the system, and agents are allowed to switch between groups that yield more benefit for them. Notably the benefit/payoff is a joint outcome of the group-reward and consonance-reward. Thus if an individual is part of a group with a *norm* significantly different from its actual belief, it has to choose x_i carefully that yields a reasonable group-reward without causing too much cognitive dissonance or switch to a different group if that yields better payoff. The Eq. 1 implies that one must consider both rewards to get the best payoff, e.g. total conforming to a group may yield a high group-reward but if the expressed opinion is too far from the private opinion, it decreases the consonance-reward significantly, thus decreasing the overall payoff from that choice. The decision making algorithm is as follows:

- At time t, i has an expressed opinion, private opinion, and an SID (x_i, y_i, z_i). It calculates the current payoff from Eq. 1, using Eqs. 2 and 3:

$$Payoff_i(t) = G_i(t) \times C_i(t) \tag{1}$$

$$G_i(t) = 1 - \frac{|x_i - \bar{X}|}{x_i} \tag{2}$$

$$C_i(t) = 1 - \frac{|x_i - y_i|}{x_i}; \tag{3}$$

Here $\bar{X}$ is the group-opinion or norm, which is the arithmatic mean of its members' opinions.

- It calculates the payoff from switching to a different group at $(t+1)$, for all available groups $(1, 2, .., k)$ using Eqs. 2 and 3 as:

$$Payoff_{group}(t+1) = \{G_1 * C_i(t), G_2 * C_i(t), ..., G_k * C_i(t)\} \tag{4}$$

Also calculate payoff from expressing the mean opinion of z_i, at $(t+1)$, i.e. substituting $x_i = \bar{X}$ in Eq. 1 as:

$$Payoff_{opinion}(t+1) = (1 - \frac{|\bar{X} - \bar{X}|}{\bar{X}}) * (1 - \frac{|\bar{X} - y_i|}{\bar{X}}) \tag{5}$$

Then the agent will compare Eqs. 1, 4, 5 and choose the opinion-SID pair that gives the highest payoff.

4   Simulation and Results

Using the above model, we systematically varied the population, number of opinions and groups, from a fully connected set of agents to an Erdos-Renyi graph, network parameters, synchronous and asynchronous mode of updating, and the key findings are presented in this section. The initial distribution of y, z are uniformly random, and at $t = 1$, all the agents have $x = y$, i.e. there is no discrepancy between their private and expressed opinions initially. The agents then evaluate their payoffs and choose an option giving the highest payoff. Each scenario is iterated over 1000 runs and the ensemble average is plotted for each comparison-metric (showed in Table 1). The y-axis of some of the plots has 'fraction of agents', because they are normalised with N so that different values of N can be compared with each other. PI in the plots represents the number of agents (or as a fraction of the whole population) showing $(x \neq y)$, whereas cognitive dissonance (CD) represents sum of the differences between x and y for all agents, i.e. $\sum_{i \in N} |x_i - y_i|$. Group flux and opinion flux represent, respectively, the fraction of agents switching their groups and opinions at each time step.

Table 1. Parameters & comparison metrics for simulation

Parameters	Range (fully connected)	Range (random network)
N (Population size)	50	$500, 1000, 2500$
k (No. of groups)	$2, 3, 4, 5$	$2, 5, 9$
Updating mode	Synchronous, asynchronous	Asynchronous
PI	Fraction of the whole population showing $(x \neq y)$	
Dissonance	Sum of $(x - y)$ of each agent	
Opinion flux	No. of agents changing expressed opinion at each timestep	
Group flux	No. of agents changing groups at each timestep	

4.1   Fully Connected Agents

This type of interaction is usually limited to a small number of individuals in real life, so the population size is kept small at $N = 50$. Results show that, varying the number of groups affects the fraction of agents in PI: it increases as the number of groups increases in synchronous mode (Fig. 1a), whereas in case of asynchronous updating, almost all agents showed PI (Fig. 1c). Cognitive dissonance is also higher in asynchronous updating (Fig. 1b, d).

We measured the group-flux and opinion-flux, which can be considered as a *measure of stability* - whether the agents are stable in their choice or not. In case of group-flux, asynchronous updating causes the agents to change their groups indefinitely, but synchronous mode stabilises quickly (Fig. 1e). For opinion flux, all agents with all updating modes become stable (zero opinion flux) after some

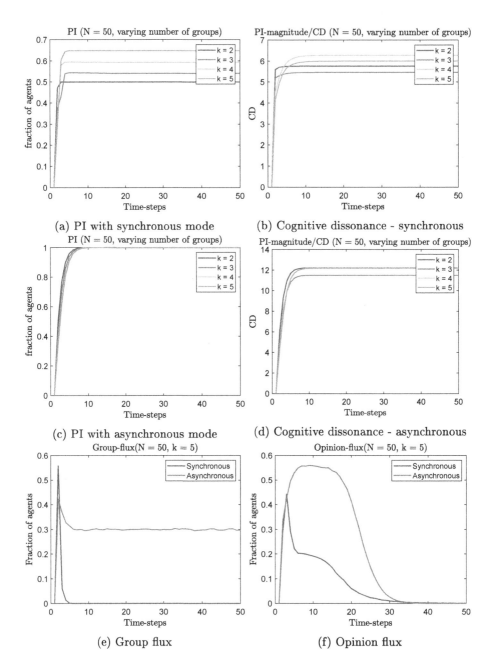

Fig. 1. (a, b, c, d): Fraction of agents with PI and cognitive dissonance (sync vs. async updating), varying number of groups, k; (e, f): Measure of stability: group-flux and opinion flux (sync vs async updating) in a fully connected network.

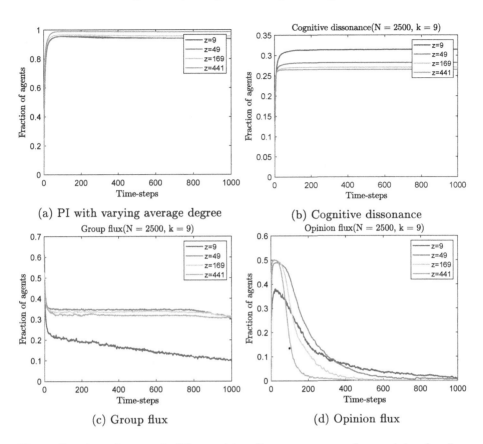

Fig. 2. Fraction of agents in PI, cognitive dissonance, group-flux, opinion-flux in a random network with $N = 2500, k = 9$, varying average degree

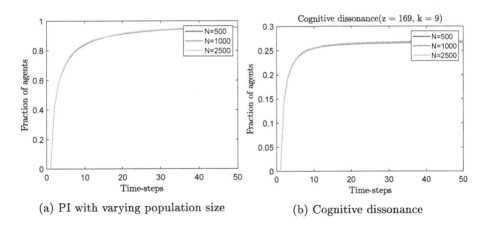

Fig. 3. Fraction of agents in PI and cognitive dissonance (normalised over N) in a random network with average degree, $z = 169, k = 9$, varying population sizes

time (Fig. 1f). The measure of cognitive dissonance can be interpreted as a *measure of unhappiness*, as this causes discomfort in agents. We see that, as the number of agents increases, the dissonance also increases and it is highest for asynchronous updating (Fig. 1d).

4.2   Agents Connected in Random Networks

When agents are connected in a random network, they can see the status of their neighbours only. Thus, the perception of public opinion is limited to agents' local neighbourhoods. We varied size of population, no. of groups and average degree z, which means how many agents on an average are connected to a random agent. The values of z are chosen such that, $z = 9$ represents a network with low density, $z = 49$ means each agent is connected to 49 other agents on an average, which is neither very low or very high in density; $z = 169$ is chosen in line with *Dunbar's number* which says that the maximum number of stable social connections an individual can maintain is around 100–150 [5]. Finally $z = 441$ represents a densely connected network. Each scenario is averaged over 100 iterations.

The network reached consensus, even with $N = 2500, k = 9$, and $z = 441$ (Fig. 5d), which is a very densely connected network with many groups. The agents' tendency to conform to group-norm leads to consensus and PI thereby, i.e. all agents converge to one opinion and thus lead to PI. Varying the number of population with same z, k, yields the same curves as seen in Fig. 3. We can deduce that size of the whole population does not affect the dynamics of PI, it is affected by z, k only. However, the percentage of PI is $\simeq 0.95$ for all populations. Therefore we plotted variation of z for $N = 2500, k = 9$ to see how the average degree effects the system output in terms of flux and cognitive dissonance. We can see in Fig. 2 that dissonance decreases as the network-density increases, i.e. larger z causes slightly lesser dissonance in agents, but more group-flux, that means the agents switch groups more often when their vision is broader with larger neighbourhood size. In terms of opinion, the system is stable as they reached consensus on their expressed opinions.

In the above model, agents must consider both rewards when they make a choice, because if one component is very low, the overall payoff becomes low for them (Eq. 1). This is an expected behaviour from social individuals, to balance group-reward and consonance-reward. However, individuals who value group-reward to such extent that they completely ignore their cognitive dissonance and vice versa will exist. Equation 1 cannot represent these individuals, because if one component is very low, the overall payoff becomes low for them, thus excluding the individuals with extreme choices. Therefore, we also explored an alternative model (Eq. 6), which allows agents the liberty to choose any combination of SID-opinion that gives them the best payoff from their perspective - they can either choose more cognitive dissonance to get better group reward or vice versa. Observations from this alternative model are presented in Fig. 5.

$$P_c(t) = G_i(t) + C_i(t) \tag{6}$$

Varying population N and average degree z did not significantly impact on the results (similar to the base model), hence were omitted for brevity. Therefore, we can deduce that, the number of groups k in the system determines the final output, all else being equal. Figure 5 shows that PI, cognitive dissonance and group flux - all increase significantly as number of groups, k is increased from 2 to 9. Opinions are stable for all scenarios, group-flux is decreasing asymptotically, which is an indication of more stability in the system as fewer agents are switching their group-ids.

Comparing between Figs. 4 and 5, we see similar shapes and values of the plots except for cognitive dissonance which is almost 10 times higher than the base model, all else being equal. Because, as stated above, the alternative model permits instances where cognitive dissonance is not valued as important relative to perceived benefits from group membership and conformity, thus exacts a much smaller individual cost.

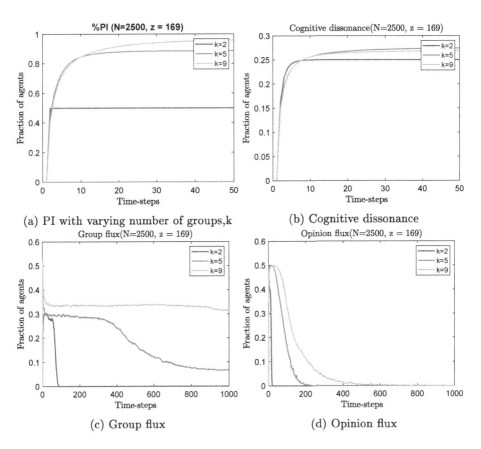

(a) PI with varying number of groups,k

(b) Cognitive dissonance

(c) Group flux

(d) Opinion flux

Fig. 4. Fraction of agents in PI, cognitive dissonance, group-flux, opinion-flux in a random network with average degree, $N = 2500, z = 169$, varying number of groups

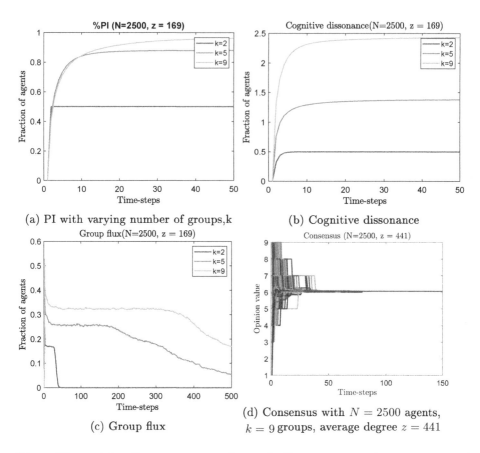

(a) PI with varying number of groups, k

(b) Cognitive dissonance

(c) Group flux

(d) Consensus with $N = 2500$ agents, $k = 9$ groups, average degree $z = 441$

Fig. 5. PI, cognitive dissonance, group-flux with $N = 2500, z = 169$, varying no. of groups, k(alternative model), (d): consensus in both base model and alternative model. Here consensus is plotted against opinion flux in Fig. 4d, because consensus/equilibrium plots show that opinion flux is zero, which happened in both cases

5   Discussion and Conclusions

We have demonstrated a novel model of PI that captures the opposing drives of group conformity against minimising cognitive dissonance. Simulations show that PI depends on the manner of opinion updating, on how shared views are perceived, and upon how many groups the agent may belong to. These mechanisms also impact stability. Notably, the propensity to conform propagates through the network beyond local neighbourhoods, producing a mostly false consensus as beliefs are different. This is interesting as it emulates behaviours seen in some social network contexts, where visibility of the larger network tends to promote PI across the population. Interesting results were found comparing synchronous updates, typical for exposure to broadcast media, against asynchronous updating that is more typical for social media. Convergence to stable but lower PI and cognitive dissonance was much more pronounced in synchronous updating.

Our results show that multi-agent models can provide useful insights about a host of other social phenomena that are closely related to PI. For instance, the payoff model presented here is closely related to the problem of the *iterated prisoner's dilemma*, with non-conformity being akin to defection. PI is also the inverse of *false consensus bias*, in which individuals assume that a group agrees with their opinion. The results also broadly capture a number of other empirically observed effects. A good example are political contests, where both leading candidates are unpopular, and voters choose by balancing their distaste for the respective candidates against their perception of which candidate is seen to be more popular. The model is also able to capture scenarios where the drive to conformity is so strong, that group members may overcome cognitive dissonance, a problem observed in many areas of political discourse, or cult movements.

While the model captures the general behaviours observed in PI scenarios well, further research from empirical observation will be required to establish the mix of behavioural propensities in a population, such as how individuals value the relative payoffs from conformity versus reduced cognitive dissonance. Future research will thus need to address scenarios not explored in our current study, and determine especially sensitivity to varying population behaviours.

References

1. Bjerring, J.C., Hansen, J.U., Pedersen, N.J.L.L.: On the rationality of pluralistic ignorance. Synthese **191**(11), 2445–2470 (2014)
2. Buckley, M.R., Harvey, M.G., Beu, D.S.: The role of pluralistic ignorance in the perception of unethical behavior. J. Bus. Ethics **23**(4), 353–364 (2000)
3. Centola, D., Willer, R., Macy, M.: The emperor's dilemma: a computational model of self-enforcing norms. Am. J. Sociol. **110**(4), 1009–1040 (2005)
4. Duggins, P.: A psychologically-motivated model of opinion change with applications to american politics. J. Artif. Soc. Soc. Simul. **20**(1), 13 (2017). https://doi.org/10.18564/jasss.3316, http://jasss.soc.surrey.ac.uk/20/1/13.html
5. Dunbar, R.I.: Neocortex size as a constraint on group size in primates. J. Hum. Evol. **22**(6), 469–493 (1992)
6. Erdős, P., Rényi, A.: On the evolution of random graphs. Publ. Math. Inst. Hung. Acad. Sci. **5**(1), 17–60 (1960)
7. Festinger, L.: A Theory of Cognitive Dissonance, vol. 2. Stanford University Press, Stanford (1962)
8. Freeman, D.: Margaret Mead and Samoa: The Making and Unmaking of an Anthropological Myth. Harvard University Press, Cambridge (1983)
9. Gilbert, N.: Computational social science: agent-based social simulation. In: Amblard, F., Phan, D. (eds.) Multi-Agent Models and Simulation for Social and Human Sciences. The Bardwell Press, Oxford (2004)
10. Halbesleben, J.R., Wheeler, A.R., Buckley, M.R.: Understanding pluralistic ignorance in organizations: application and theory. J. Manag. Psychol. **22**(1), 65–83 (2007)
11. Hornsey, M.J., Jetten, J.: The individual within the group: balancing the need to belong with the need to be different. Pers. Soc. Psychol. Rev. **8**(3), 248–264 (2004)
12. Janis, I.L., Gilmore, J.B.: The influence of incentive conditions on the success of role playing in modifying attitudes. J. Pers. Soc. Psychol. **1**(1), 17 (1965)

13. Krech, D., Crutchfield, R.S.: Theory and Problems of Social Psychology. McGraw-Hill, New York (1948)
14. Kuran, T.: Sparks and prairie fires: a theory of unanticipated political revolution. Public Choice **61**(1), 41–74 (1989)
15. Kuran, T.: Private Truths, Public Lies: The Social Consequences of Preference Falsification. Harvard University Press, Cambridge (1997)
16. Li, L., Scaglione, A., Swami, A., Zhao, Q.: Consensus, polarization and clustering of opinions in social networks. IEEE J. Sel. Areas Commun. **31**(6), 1072–1083 (2013)
17. Likert, R.: A technique for the measurement of attitudes. Arch. Psychol. **22**(140), 1–55 (1932)
18. Martens, M.P., Page, J.C., Mowry, E.S., Damann, K.M., Taylor, K.K., Cimini, M.D.: Differences between actual and perceived student norms: an examination of alcohol use, drug use, and sexual behavior. J. Am. Coll. Health **54**(5), 295–300 (2006)
19. Miller, D.T., McFarland, C.: Pluralistic ignorance: when similarity is interpreted as dissimilarity. J. Pers. Soc. Psychol. **53**(2), 298 (1987)
20. Miller, D.T., McFarland, C.: When social comparison goes awry: the case of pluralistic ignorance. In: Suls, J., Wills, T.A. (eds.) Social Comparison: Contemporary Theory and Research, pp. 287–313. Lawrence Erlbaum Associates, Inc. (1991)
21. Miller, D.T., Prentice, D.A.: Collective errors and errors about the collective. Pers. Soc. Psychol. Bull. **20**, 541–550 (1994)
22. Perkins, H.W., Meilman, P.W., Leichliter, J.S., Cashin, J.R., Presley, C.A.: Misperceptions of the norms for the frequency of alcohol and other drug use on college campuses. J. Am. Coll. Health **47**(6), 253–258 (1999)
23. Plous, S.: The Psychology of Judgment and Decision Making. Mcgraw-Hill Book Company, New York (1993)
24. Rose, S., Spinks, N., Canhoto, A.I.: Management Research: Applying the Principles. Routledge, Abingdon (2014)
25. Scheufele, D.A.: Opinion climates, spirals of silence and biotechnology: public opinion as a heuristic for scientific decision-making. In: Brossard, D., Shanahan, J., Nesbitt, T.C. (eds.) The Media, the Public and Agricultural Biotechnology, pp. 231–244. CAB International, United Kingdom (2007)
26. Seeme, F.B., Green, D.G.: Pluralistic ignorance: emergence and hypotheses testing in a multi-agent system. In: IEEE International Joint Conference on Neural Networks (IJCNN), pp. 5269–5274 (2016)
27. Sekiguchi, T., Nakamaru, M.: How inconsistency between attitude and behavior persists through cultural transmission. J. Theor. Biol. **271**(1), 124–135 (2011)
28. Wang, S.W., Huang, C.Y., Sun, C.T.: Modeling self-perception agents in an opinion dynamics propagation society. Simulation **90**, 238–248 (2013)
29. Ye, M., Qin, Y., Govaert, A., Anderson, B.D., Cao, M.: An influence network model to study discrepancies in expressed and private opinions. Automatica **107**, 371–381 (2019)

Author Index